# WAYS OF READING

*An Anthology for Writers*

# WAYS OF READING

## An Anthology for Writers

### Fifth Edition

**David Bartholomae**

UNIVERSITY OF PITTSBURGH

**Anthony Petrosky**

UNIVERSITY OF PITTSBURGH

BEDFORD/ST. MARTIN'S

Boston ◆ New York

**For Bedford/St. Martin's**
*Developmental Editor:* John Sullivan
*Production Editor:* Tony Perriello
*Production Supervisor:* Scott Lavelle
*Marketing Manager:* Karen Melton
*Editorial Assistant:* Katie Gilbert
*Production Assistant:* Helaine Denenberg
*Copyeditor:* Lisa A. Wehrle
*Text Design:* Anna George
*Cover Design:* Night & Day Design
*Composition:* Pine Tree Composition, Inc.
*Printing and Binding:* Haddon Craftsmen, Inc.

*President:* Charles H. Christensen
*Editorial Director:* Joan E. Feinberg
*Director of Editing, Design, and Production:* Marcia Cohen
*Managing Editor:* Elizabeth M. Schaaf

Library of Congress Catalog Card Number: 98–87520

Manufactured in the United States of America.
3   2   1   0   9
f   e   d   c

For information, write: Bedford/St. Martin's,
75 Arlington Street, Boston, MA 02116
(617-426-7440)


ISBN: 0–312–17893–X

**ACKNOWLEDGMENTS**


Gloria Anzaldúa, "Entering into the Serpent," and "How to Tame a Wild Tongue." From *Border-lands/La frontera: The New Mestiza,* Copyright © 1987 by Gloria Anzaldúa. Reprinted by permission of Aunt Lute Books.
Paul Auster, "Portrait of an Invisible Man." From *The Invention of Solitude* by Paul Auster. Copyright © Paul Auster, 1982. Reprinted with the permission of Paul Auster. Photos courtesy of Paul Auster and the Carol Mann Agency. Used with permission.
John Berger, "Ways of Seeing." From *Ways of Seeing,* by John Berger. Copyright © 1972 by Penguin Books Ltd. Used by permission of Viking Penguin, a division of Penguin Putnam, Inc. "On Rembrandt's 'Woman in Bed'" and "On Caravaggio's 'The Calling of St. Matthew'" from *And Our Faces, My Heart, Brief as Photos* by John Berger. Copyright © 1984 by John Berger. Reprinted by permission of Pantheon Books, a division of Random House, Inc. Botticelli, *Venus and Mars;* Leonardo da Vinci, "Virgin of the Rocks" and "The Virgin and Child with St. Anne and St. John the Baptist." Alinari/Art Resource, New York. Reproduced by courtesy of the Trustees, The National Gallery, London. Leonardo da Vinci, "Virgin of the Rocks." Reproduced by permission of the Louvre Museum. Pierre Bourdieu and Alain Darbel, from *L'Amour de l'Art.* Reprinted by

*Acknowledgments and copyrights are continued at the back of the book on pages 902–03, which constitute an extension of the copyright page. It is a violation of the law to reproduce these selections by any means whatsoever without the written permission of the copyright holder.*

# Preface

*Ways of Reading* is designed for a course where students are given the opportunity to work on what they read, and to work on it by writing. When we began developing such courses, we realized the problems our students had when asked to write or talk about what they read were not "reading problems," at least not as these are strictly defined. Our students knew how to move from one page to the next. They could read sentences. They had, obviously, been able to carry out many of the versions of reading required for their education—skimming textbooks, cramming for tests, strip-mining books for term papers.

Our students, however, felt powerless in the face of serious writing, in the face of long and complicated texts—the kinds of texts we thought they should find interesting and challenging. We thought (as many teachers have thought) that if we just, finally, gave them something good to read—something rich and meaty—they would change forever their ways of thinking about English. It didn't work, of course. The issue is not only *what* students read, but what they can learn to *do* with what they read. We learned that the problems our students had lay not in the reading material (it was too hard) or in the students (they were poorly prepared) but in the classroom—in the ways we and they imagined what it meant to work on an essay.

There is no better place to work on reading than in a writing course, and this book is intended to provide occasions for readers to write. You will find a number of distinctive features in *Ways of Reading*. For one thing, it contains selections you don't usually see in a college reader: long, powerful, mysterious pieces like John Berger's "Ways of Seeing," Susan Griffin's "Our Secret," Adrienne Rich's "When We Dead Awaken: Writing as Re-Vision," Clifford Geertz's "Deep Play: Notes on the Balinese Cockfight," Mary Louise Pratt's "Arts of the Contact Zone," John Edgar Wideman's "Our Time," W. J. T. Mitchell's "The Photographic Essay: Four Case Studies," and Michel Foucault's "Panopticism." These are the sorts of readings we talk about when we talk with our colleagues. We have learned that we can talk about them with our students as well.

When we chose the essays, we were looking for "readable" texts—that is, texts that leave some work for a reader to do. We wanted selections that invite students to be active, critical readers, that present powerful readings of common experience, that open up the familiar world and make it puzzling, rich, and problematic. We wanted to choose selections that invite students to be active readers and to take responsibility for their acts of interpretation. So we avoided the short set-pieces you find in so many anthologies. In a sense, those short selections misrepresent the act of reading. They can be read in a single sitting; they make arguments that can be easily paraphrased; they solve all the problems they raise; they wrap up Life and put it into a box; and so they turn reading into an act of appreciation, where the most that seems to be required is a nod of the head. And they suggest that a writer's job is to do just that, to write a piece that is similarly tight and neat and self-contained. We wanted to avoid pieces that were so plainly written or tightly bound that there was little for students to do but "get the point."

We learned that if our students had reading problems when faced with long and complex texts, the problems lay in the way they imagined a reader—the role a reader plays, what a reader does, why a reader reads (if not simply to satisfy the requirements of a course). When, for example, our students were puzzled by what they read, they took this as a sign of failure. ("It doesn't make any sense," they would say, as though the sense were supposed to be waiting on the page, ready for them the first time they read through.) And our students were haunted by the thought that they couldn't remember everything they had read (as though one could store all of Geertz's "Deep Play" in memory); or if they did remember bits and pieces, they felt that the fragmented text they possessed was evidence that they could not do what they were supposed to do. Our students were confronting the experience of reading, in other words, but they were taking the problems of reading—problems all readers face—and concluding that there was nothing for them to do but give up.

As expert readers, we have all learned what to do with a complex text. We know that we can go back to a text; we don't have to remember it—in fact, we've learned to mark up a text to ease that re-entry. We know that a reader is a person who puts together fragments. Those coherent readings we construct begin with confusion and puzzlement, and we construct those readings by writing and rewriting—by working on a text.

These are the lessons our students need to learn, and this is why a course in reading is also a course in writing. Our students need to learn that there is something they can do once they have first read through a complicated text; successful reading is not just a matter of "getting" an essay the first time. In a very real sense, you can't begin to feel the power a reader has until you realize the problems, until you realize that no one "gets" Geertz or Rich or Griffin or Wideman all at once. You work on what you read, and then what you have at the end is something that is yours, something you made. And this is what the teaching apparatus in *Ways of Reading* is designed to do. In a sense, it says to students, "OK, let's get to work on these essays; let's see what you can make of them."

This, then, is the second distinctive feature you will find in *Ways of Reading:* reading and writing assignments designed to give students access to the essays. After each selection, for example, you will find "Questions for a Second Reading." We wanted to acknowledge that rereading is a natural way of carrying out the work of a reader, just as rewriting is a natural way of completing the work of a writer. It is not something done out of despair or as a punishment for not getting things right the first time. The questions we have written highlight what we see as central textual or interpretive problems. Geertz, for example, divides his essay into seven sections, each written in a different style. By going back through the essay with this in mind and by asking what Geertz is doing in each case (what his method is and what it enables him to accomplish), a student is in a position to see the essay as the enactment of a method and not just as a long argument with its point hidden away at the end. These questions might serve as preparations for class discussion or ways of directing students' work in journals. Whatever the case, they both honor and direct the work of rereading.

Each selection is also followed by two sets of writing assignments, "Assignments for Writing" and "Making Connections." The first set directs students back into the work they have just read. While the assignments vary, there are some basic principles behind them. They ask students to work on the essay by focusing on difficult or problematic moments in the text; they ask students to work on the author's examples, extending and testing his or her methods of analysis; or they ask students to apply the method of the essay (its way of seeing and understanding the world) to settings or experiences of their own. Students are asked, for example, to give a "Geertzian" reading to scenes from their own immediate culture (the behavior of people at a shopping mall, characteristic styles of dress) and they are asked to imagine that they are working alongside Geertz and making his project their own. Or they are asked to consider the key examples in Rich's "When We Dead Awaken" (poems from various points in her career) to see how as writers they might use the key terms of her argument ("structures of oppression," "renaming") in representing their own experience. The last assignments—"Making Connections"—invite students to read one essay in the context of another, to see, for example, if Pratt's account of the "literate arts of the contact zone" can be used to frame a reading of Gloria Anzaldúa's prose, Harriet Jacobs's narrative, or Paulo Freire's account of education. In a sense, then, the essays are offered as models, but not as "prose models" in the strictest sense. What they model is a way of seeing or reading the world, of both imagining problems and imagining methods to make those problems available to a writer.

At the end of the book, we have included several longer assignment sequences and a goodly number of shorter sequences. In some cases these incorporate single assignments from earlier in the book; in most cases they involve students in projects that extend anywhere from two to three weeks for the shorter sequences to an entire semester's worth of work for the longer ones. Almost all the sequences include several of the essays in the anthology and require a series of separate drafts and revisions. In academic life, readers seldom read single essays in isolation, as though one were "finished" with Geertz after a week or two. Rather, they read with a purpose—with a project in mind or a problem to solve. The assignment sequences are designed to give students a feel for the rhythm and texture of an extended academic project. They offer, that is, one more way of reading and writing. Because these sequences lead students through intellectual projects proceeding from one week to the next, they enable them to develop authority as specialists, to feel the difference between being an expert and being a "common" reader on a single subject. And, with the luxury of time available for self-reflection, students can look back on what they have done, not only to revise what they know, but also to take stock and comment on the value and direction of their work.

Because of their diversity, it is difficult to summarize the assignment sequences. Perhaps the best way to see what we have done is to turn to the back of the book and look at them. They are meant to frame a project for students but to leave open possibilities for new directions. You should feel free to add or drop readings, to mix sequences, and to revise the assignments to fit your course and your schedule.

You will also notice that there are few "glosses" appended to the essays. We have not added many editors' notes to define difficult words or to identify names or allusions to other authors or artists. We've omitted them because their presence suggests something we feel is false about reading. They suggest that good readers know all the words or pick up all the allusions or recognize every name that is mentioned. This is not true. Good readers do what they can and try their best to fill in the blanks; they ignore seemingly unimportant references and look up the important ones. There is no reason for students to feel they lack the knowledge necessary to complete a reading of these texts. We have translated foreign phrases and glossed some technical terms, but we have kept the selections as clean and open as possible.

We have been asked on several occasions whether the readings aren't finally just too hard for students. The answer is no. Students will have to work on the selections, but that is the point of the course and the reason, as we said before, why a reading course is also a course in writing. College students want to believe that they can strike out on their own, make their mark, do something they have never done before. They want to *be* experts, not just hear from them. This is the great pleasure, as well as the great challenge, of undergraduate instruction. It is not hard to convince students they ought to be able to speak alongside of (or even speak back to) Clifford Geertz, Adrienne Rich, or W. E. B. Du Bois. And, if a teacher is patient and forgiving—willing, that is, to let a student work out a reading of Percy, willing to keep from saying, "No, that's not it" and filling the silence with the "right" reading—then students can, with care and assistance, learn to speak for themselves. It takes a certain kind of classroom, to be sure. A teacher who teaches this book will have to be comfortable turning the essays over to the students, even with the knowledge that they will not do immediately on their own what a professional could do—at least not completely, or with the same grace and authority.

In our own teaching, we have learned that we do not have to be experts on every figure or every area of inquiry represented in this book. And, frankly, that has come as a great relief. We can have intelligent, responsible conversations about Geertz's "Deep Play" without being experts on Geertz or on anthropology or ethnography. We needed to prepare ourselves to engage and direct students as readers, but we did not have to prepare ourselves to lecture on Foucault or Rich, or poststructuralism, documentary studies, or American feminism. The classes we have been teaching, and they have been some of the most exciting we have ever taught, have been classes where students—together and with their instructors—work on what these essays might mean.

So here we are, imagining students working shoulder to shoulder with Geertz and Rich and Foucault, even talking back to them as the occasion arises. There is a wonderful Emersonian bravado in all this. But such is the case with strong and active readers. If we allow students to work on powerful texts, they will want to share the power. This is the heady fun of academic life, the real pleasure of thinking, reading, and writing. There is no reason to keep it secret from our students.

**Note to the Fifth Edition.**   The fifth edition of *Ways of Reading* contains seven new selections: essays by Paul Auster, Susan Bordo, Robert Coles, W. E. B. Du Bois, W. J. T. Mitchell, and Carolyn Kay Steedman. We've brought back Ralph Waldo Emerson's "The American Scholar," which appeared in the first two editions, and we've added more John Berger.

Our principle of selection remains the same—we were looking for "readable" texts, pieces that instructors and students would find challenging and compelling, pieces that offer powerful readings of ordinary experience, pieces worth extended work.

We revised the assignment sequences, some to incorporate the new selections, others because, after teaching them again, we thought about them differently. The sequences that were most radically changed are: "The Arts of the Contact Zone," "Reading Culture," and "Writing History." There are five new assignment sequences, all of them reflecting the ways we taught the new selections over the last two years. We have continued to include sequences focusing on autobiographical writing and the personal essay. While there have always been assignments in *Ways of Reading* that ask students to use their experience as subject matter, the new assignments look critically and historically at the genre and insist that reading and thinking can *also* be represented as part of one's "personal" experience. There is a new sequence on documentary projects. It was important, we felt, to extend the study of images from advertising and painting to those in a work like *Let Us Now Praise Famous Men*. We have added a sequence on close reading. This draws on work we have been doing over the last few years as we have tried to find ways of teaching students how and why to think about sentences. We have added a new assignment sequence to contextualize Emerson's "The American Scholar." It includes a long section of Edward T. Channings's "Lectures Read to the Seniors in Harvard College." And we have continued to focus attention on prose models that challenge conventional forms and idioms, that complicate the usual ways of thinking about and representing knowledge and experience. There are several assignment sequences that ask students to write as though they too could participate in such revisionary projects.

We continue to offer a number of shorter "minisequences." The shortest of these might engage a class for two to three weeks, the longest for a month or two. We wrote these minisequences at the request of instructors who wanted more flexibility and a wider range of projects to offer their students.

We've also updated and included new *Resources for Teaching* WAYS OF READING, a long interview with our colleague Jean Carr on having students work with archival materials, and a new essay by a graduate student on problems specific to teaching the materials in *Ways of Reading*. These essays offer advice on how to work with the book. They stand as examples of the kinds of papers graduate students might write when they use *Ways of Reading* in conjunction with a teaching seminar. They stand best, however, as examples of graduate students speaking frankly to other graduate students about teaching and about this book.

With our colleagues, we have taught most of the selections in this book, including the new ones. Several of us worked together to prepare the assignment sequences; most of these, too, have been tested in class. As we have traveled around giving talks, we've met many people who have used *Ways of Reading*. We have been delighted to hear them talk about how it has served their teaching, and we have learned much from their advice and example. It is an unusual and exciting experience to see our course turned into a text, to see our work read, critiqued, revised, and expanded. We have many people to thank. The list that follows can't begin to name all those to whom we owe a debt. And it can't begin to express our gratitude.

**Acknowledgments.**   We owe much to the friendship and wisdom of the people with whom we have worked at Pitt, particularly Jonathan Arac, Ellen Bishop, Jean Ferguson Carr, Steve Carr, Nick Coles, Joe Harris, Paul Kameen, Margaret Marshall, Mariolina Salvatori, and Jim Seitz; Donna Dunbar-Odom, Bianca Falbo, Angie Farkas, Gwen Gorzelsky, Jean Grace, Linda Huff, Julia Sawyer, Steve Sutherland, Kathleen Welsch, Matt Willen, and the graduate students who participated in the 1996 teaching seminar. Ellen Bishop did a fine job drafting headnotes. John Champagne made wonderful suggestions at every stage of the project and gave a close and careful reading to drafts of the manuscript. He is a terrific teacher and a great reader.

And we owe much to colleagues at other schools who have followed our work with interest and offered their support and criticism.

We were also fortunate to have a number of outstanding reviewers on the project. We would first like to thank those who did in-depth reviews of the fourth edition: Carolyn Allen, University of Washington; Patricia Bizzell, College of the Holy Cross; Jean Ferguson Carr, University of Pittsburgh; Pamelyn Dane, Lane Community College; Steve Dilks, University of Missouri–Kansas City; Mary V. Dougherty, Rutgers University; Judith Goleman, University of Massachusetts–Boston; Alfred E. Guy, Jr., New York University; Ken Paul Novak, United States Air Force Academy; Robert S. Newman, State University of New York at Buffalo; Matthew Parfitt, Boston University; Anthony Petruzzi, University of Nebraska at Kearney; Thomas Recchio, University of Connecticut; and Bill Siverly, Portland Community College. And we would like to thank those who reviewed the new selections: Carolyn Allen, University of Washington; Kathryn Flannery, Indiana University; Alfred E. Guy, Jr., New York University; Sandra Howland, University of Massachusetts–Boston; Kathleen Kelly, Northeastern University; Bob Lyman, California State University, Sacramento; and Dawn Skorczewski, Harvard University. We would also like to thank the reviewers who commented extensively on drafts of the manuscript: Rebecca Brittenham, Rutgers University; and Kathleen Kelly, Northeastern University.

We would also like to thank those who responded to our questionnaire: Cora Agatucci, Central Oregon Community College; Christopher T. Andrews, University of Connecticut; Nora Bacon, University of Nebraska at Omaha; Bette-B Bauer, College of St. Mary; Kathleen Blumenthal, College of Charleston; Rebecca Brittenham, Rutgers University; Denise M. Castaldo, Drew University; Brian Cliff, Emory University; Paula Cohen,

Drexel University; Sam Cohen, Baruch College–CUNY; Mary Connerty,
Penn State University, The Behrend College; Joanne Cordón, University of
Connecticut; Tom Curley, Southwest College; Barbara Cutter, Rutgers
University; Chuck Denny, Dull Knife Memorial College; William Eggers,
University of Connecticut; Judith Hawkins, California State University at
San Bernadino; Katherine Henry, Rutgers University; Kim Hochmeister
San Antonio College; Maureen M. Hourigan, Kent State University; Ann-
Marie Kent, University of Massachusetts–Boston; Robert E. McDonough,
Cuyahoga Cummunity College; Gerri McNenny, University of Houston–
Downtown; Jennifer Militello, Daniel Webster College; Mark James Mor-
reale, Marist College; Susan Mueller, University of Missouri–St. Louis;
James S. Murphy, Emory University; Lamar L. Nisly, Bluffton College;
Helon H. Raines, Armstrong Atlantic State University; Susan Reese, Port-
land State University; Mara Reisman, University of Connecticut; Cynthia
Scheinberg, Mills College; Milissa Suekort, Santa Rosa Junior College;
Susan L. Walsh, University of Massachusetts–Boston; Krista Walter, Cali-
fornia State University–Northridge; Heidemarie Z. Weidner, Tennessee
Technological University; Chandra Wells, University of Connecticut;
Whitney Womack, Purdue University; and Elizabeth Zaranek, Penn State
University, The Behrend College.

Chuck Christensen of Bedford/St. Martin's remains the best in the
business. Joan Feinberg helped to shape this project from its very beginning. She is a fine and thoughtful friend as well as a fine and thoughtful
editor. John Sullivan joined the group for the Fifth Edition. He had taught
from an earlier edition of *Ways of Reading* and had, for us, a wonderful
sense of the book's approach to reading, writing, and teaching. John was
organized, resourceful, generous, quick to offer suggestions and to take on
extra work. He soon became as much a collaborator as an editor. His care
and dedication held everything together at times when we were falling
apart. It was a real pleasure to work with him. Susan Doheny handled
permissions. Katherine Gilbert and Jeannine Thibodeau helped locate
books, readings and, later, material for the headnotes. Tony Perriello
guided the manuscript through production. Lisa Wehrle was an excellent
copyeditor, sensitive to the quirks of our prose and attentive to design and
detail.

And, finally, we are grateful to Joyce and Ellen, and to Jesse, Dan,
Kate, Matthew, and Ben, for their love and support.

# Contents

# WAYS OF READING

*An Anthology for Writers*

# Introduction:
# Ways of Reading

### *Making a Mark*

*R*EADING involves a fair measure of push and shove. You make your mark on a book and it makes its mark on you. Reading is not simply a matter of hanging back and waiting for a piece, or its author, to tell you what the writing has to say. In fact, one of the difficult things about reading is that the pages before you will begin to speak only when the authors are silent and you begin to speak in their place, sometimes for them—doing their work, continuing their projects—and sometimes for yourself, following your own agenda.

This is an unusual way to talk about reading, we know. We have not mentioned finding information or locating an author's purpose or identifying main ideas, useful though these skills are, because the purpose of our book is to offer you occasions to imagine other ways of reading. We think of reading as a social interaction—sometimes peaceful and polite, sometimes not so peaceful and polite.

We'd like you to imagine that when you read the works we've collected here, somebody is saying something to you, and we'd like you to imagine that you are in a position to speak back, to say something of your own in turn. In other words, we are not presenting our book as a miniature library (a place to find information) and we do not think of you, the reader, as a term-paper writer (a person looking for information to write down on three-by-five cards).

When you read, you hear an author's voice as you move along; you believe a person with something to say is talking to you. You pay attention, even when you don't completely understand what is being said, trusting that it will all make sense in the end, relating what the author says to what you already know or expect to hear or learn. Even if you don't quite grasp everything you are reading at every moment (and you won't), and even if you don't remember everything you've read (no reader does—at least not in long, complex pieces), you begin to see the outlines of the author's project, the patterns and rhythms of that particular way of seeing and interpreting the world.

When you stop to talk or write about what you've read, the author is silent; you take over—it is your turn to write, to begin to respond to what the author said. At that point this author and his or her text become something you construct out of what you remember or what you notice as you go back through the text a second time, working from passages or examples but filtering them through your own predisposition to see or read in particular ways.

In "The Achievement of Desire," one of the essays in this book, Richard Rodriguez tells the story of his education, of how he was drawn to imitate his teachers because of his desire to think and speak like them. His is not a simple story of hard work and success, however. In a sense, Rodriguez's education gave him what he wanted—status, knowledge, a way of understanding himself and his position in the world. At the same time, his education made it difficult to talk to his parents, to share their point of view; and to a degree, he felt himself becoming consumed by the powerful ways of seeing and understanding represented by his reading and his education. The essay can be seen as Rodriguez's attempt to weigh what he had gained against what he had lost.

If ten of us read his essay, each would begin with the same words on the page, but when we discuss the chapter (or write about it), each will retell and interpret Rodriguez's story differently; we will emphasize different sections—some, for instance, might want to discuss the strange way Rodriguez learned to read, others might be taken by his difficult and changing relations to his teachers, and still others might want to think about Rodriguez's remarks about his mother and father.

Each of us will come to his or her own sense of what is significant, of what the point is, and the odds are good that what each of us makes of the essay will vary from one to another. Each of us will understand Rodriguez's story in his or her own way, even though we read the same piece. At the same time, if we are working with Rodriguez's essay (and not putting it aside or ignoring its peculiar way of thinking about education), we will be working within a framework he has established, one that makes education stand, metaphorically, for a complicated interplay between permanence and change, imitation and freedom, loss and achievement.

In "The Achievement of Desire," Rodriguez tells of reading a book by Richard Hoggart, *The Uses of Literacy*. He was captivated by a section of this book in which Hoggart defines a particular kind of student, the "scholarship boy." Here is what Rodriguez says:

> Then one day, leafing through Richard Hoggart's *The Uses of Literacy*, I found, in his description of the scholarship boy, my-self. For the first time I realized that there were other students like me, and so I was able to frame the meaning of my academic success, its consequent price—the loss.

For Rodriguez, this phrase, "scholarship boy," became the focus of Hoggart's book. Other people, to be sure, would read that book and take different phrases or sections as the key to what Hoggart has to say. Some might argue that Rodriguez misread the book, that it is really about something else, about British culture, for example, or about the class system in England. The power and value of Rodriguez's reading, however, are represented by what he was able to *do* with what he read, and what he was able to do was not record information or summarize main ideas but, as he says, "frame the meaning of my academic success." Hoggart provided a frame, a way for Rodriguez to think and talk about his own history as a student. As he goes on in his essay, Rodriguez not only uses this frame to talk about his experience, but he resists it, argues with it. He casts his experience in Hoggart's terms but then makes those terms work for him by seeing both what they can and what they cannot do. This combination of reading, thinking, and writing is what we mean by *strong reading*, a way of reading we like to encourage in our students.

When we have taught "The Achievement of Desire" to our students, it has been almost impossible for them not to see themselves in Rodriguez's description of the scholarship boy (and this was true of students who were not minority students and not literally on scholarships). They, too, have found a way of framing (even inventing) their own lives as students—students whose histories involve both success and loss. When we have asked our students to write about this essay, however, some students have argued, and quite convincingly, that Rodriguez had either to abandon his family and culture or to remain ignorant. Other students have argued equally convincingly that Rodriguez's anguish was destructive and self-serving, that he was trapped into seeing his situation in terms that he might have replaced with others. He did not necessarily have to turn his back on his family. Some have contended that Rodriguez's problems with his family had nothing to do with what he says about education, that he himself shows how imitation need not blindly lead a person away from his culture, and these student essays, too, have been convincing.

Reading, in other words, can be the occasion for you to put things together, to notice this idea or theme rather than that one, to follow a writer's announced or secret ends while simultaneously following your own. When this happens, when you forge a reading of a story or an essay, you make your mark on it, casting it in your terms. But the story makes its mark on you as well, teaching you not only about a subject (Rodriguez's struggles with his teachers and his parents, for example) but about a way of seeing and understanding a subject. The text provides the opportunity for you to see through someone else's powerful language, to imagine your own familiar settings through the images, metaphors, and ideas of others. Rodriguez's essay, in other words, can make its mark on readers, but they, too, if they are strong, active readers, can make theirs on it.

Readers learn to put things together by writing. It is not something you can do, at least not to any degree, while you are reading. It requires that you work on what you have read, and that work best takes shape when you sit down to write. We will have more to say about this kind of thinking in a later section of the introduction, but for now let us say that writing gives you a way of going to work on the text you have read. To write about a story or essay, you go back to what you have read to find phrases or passages that define what for you are the key moments, that help you interpret sections that seem difficult or troublesome or mysterious. If you are writing an essay of your own, the work that you are doing gives a purpose and a structure to that rereading.

Writing also, however, gives you a way of going back to work on the text of your own reading. It allows you to be self-critical. You can revise not just to make your essay neat or tight or tidy but to see what kind of reader you have been, to examine the pattern and consequences in the choices you have made. Revision, in other words, gives you the chance to work on your essay, but it also gives you an opportunity to work on your reading—to qualify or extend or question your interpretation of, say, "The Achievement of Desire."

We can describe this process of "re-vision," or re-seeing, fairly simply. You should not expect to read "The Achievement of Desire" once and completely understand the essay or know what you want to say. You will work out what you have to say while you write. And once you have constructed a reading—once you have completed a draft of your essay, in other words—you can step back, see what you have done, and go back to work on it. Through this activity—writing and rewriting—we have seen our students become strong, active, and critical readers.

Not everything a reader reads is worth that kind of effort. The pieces we have chosen for this book all provide, we feel, powerful ways of seeing (or framing) our common experience. The selections cannot be quickly summarized. They are striking, surprising, sometimes troubling in how they challenge common ways of seeing the world. Some of them (we're thinking of pieces by Michel Foucault, Clifford Geertz, Adrienne Rich, and Virginia Woolf) have captured and altered the way our culture sees and understands daily experience. The essays have changed the ways people think and write. In fact, every selection in the book is one that has given us, our students, and colleagues that dramatic experience, almost like a discovery, when we suddenly saw things as we had never seen them before and, as a consequence, we had to work hard to understand what had happened and how our thinking had changed.

If we recall, for example, the first time we read Susan Griffin's "Our Secret" or John Edgar Wideman's "Our Time," we know that they have radically shaped our thinking. We carry these essays with us in our minds, mulling over them, working through them, hearing Griffin and Wideman in sentences we write or sentences we read; we introduce the essays in classes we teach whenever we can; we are surprised, reading them for the third or fourth time, to find things we didn't see before. It's not that we failed to "get" these essays the first time around. In fact, we're not sure we have captured them yet, at least not in any final sense, and we disagree in basic ways about what Griffin and Wideman are saying or about how these essays might best be used. Essays like these are not the sort that you can "get" like a loaf of bread at the store. We're each convinced that the essays are ours in that we know best what's going on in them, and yet we have also become theirs, creatures of these essays, because of the ways they have come to dominate our seeing, talking, reading, and writing. This captivity is something we welcome, yet it is also something we resist.

Our experience with these texts is a remarkable one and certainly hard to provide for others, but the challenges and surprises are reasons we read—we hope to be taken and changed in just these ways. Or, to be more accurate, it is why we read outside the daily requirements to keep up with the news or conduct our business. And it is why we bring reading into our writing courses.

## *Ways of Reading*

Before explaining how we organized this book, we would like to say more about the purpose and place of the kind of strong, aggressive, labor-intensive reading we've been referring to.

Readers face many kinds of experiences, and certain texts are written with specific situations in mind and invite specific ways of reading. Some texts, for instance, serve very practical purposes—they give directions or information. Others, like the short descriptive essays often used in English textbooks and anthologies, celebrate common ways of seeing and thinking and ask primarily to be admired. These texts seem self-contained; they announce their own meanings with little effort and ask little from the reader, making it clear how they want to be read and what they have to say. They ask only for a nod of the head or for the reader to take notes and give a sigh of admiration ("yes, that was very well said"). They are clear and direct. It is as though the authors could anticipate all the questions their essays might raise and solve all the problems a reader might imagine. There is not much work for a reader to do, in other words, except, perhaps, to take notes and, in the case of textbooks, to work step-by-step, trying to re-member as much as possible.

This is how assigned readings are often presented in university class-rooms. Introductory textbooks (in biology or business, for instance) are good examples of books that ask little of readers outside of note-taking and memorization. In these texts the writers are experts and your job, as novice, is to digest what they have to say. And, appropriately, the task set before you is to summarize—so you can speak again what the author said, so you can better remember what you read. Essay tests are an example of the writing tasks that often follow this kind of reading. You might, for in-stance, study the human nervous system through textbook readings and lectures and then be asked to write a summary of what you know from both sources. Or a teacher might ask you during a class discussion to para-phrase a paragraph from a textbook describing chemical cell communica-tion to see if you understand what you've read.

Another typical classroom form of reading is reading for main ideas. With this kind of reading you are expected to figure out what most people (or most people within a certain specialized group of readers) would take as the main idea of a selection. There are good reasons to read for main ideas. For one, it is a way to learn how to imagine and anticipate the val-ues and habits of a particular group—test-makers or, if you're studying business, Keynesian economists, perhaps. If you are studying business, to continue this example, you must learn to notice what Keynesian econo-mists notice—for instance, when they analyze the problems of growing government debt—to share key terms, to know the theoretical positions they take, and to adopt for yourself their common examples and interpre-tations, their jargon, and their established findings.

There is certainly nothing wrong with reading for information or read-ing to learn what experts have to say about their fields of inquiry. These are not, however, the only ways to read, although they are the ones most often taught. Perhaps because we think of ourselves as writing teachers, we are concerned with presenting other ways of reading in the college and university curriculum.

A danger arises in assuming that reading is only a search for informa-tion or main ideas. There are ways of thinking through problems and working with written texts which are essential to academic life, but which are not represented by summary and paraphrase or by note-taking and essay exams.

Student readers, for example, can take responsibility for determining the meaning of the text. They can work as though they were doing some-thing other than finding ideas already there on the page and they can be guided by their own impressions or questions as they read. We are not, now, talking about finding hidden meanings. If such things as hidden meanings can be said to exist, they are hidden by readers' habits and prej-udices (by readers' assumptions that what they read should tell them what they already know), or by readers' timidity and passivity (by their unwillingness to take the responsibility to speak their minds and say what they notice).

Reading to locate meaning in the text places a premium on memory, yet a strong reader is not necessarily a person with a good memory. This point may seem minor, but we have seen too many students haunted because they could not remember everything they read or retain a complete essay in their minds. A reader could set herself the task of remembering as much as she could from Walker Percy's "The Loss of the Creature," an essay filled with stories about tourists at the Grand Canyon and students in a biology class, but a reader could also do other things with that essay; a reader might figure out, for example, how both students and tourists might be said to have a common problem seeing what they want to see. Students who read Percy's essay as a memory test end up worrying about bits and pieces (bits and pieces they could go back and find if they had to) and turn their attention away from the more pressing problem of how to make sense of a difficult and often ambiguous essay.

A reader who needs to have access to something in the essay can use simple memory aids. A reader can go back and scan, for one thing, to find passages or examples that might be worth reconsidering. Or a reader can construct a personal index, making marks in the margin or underlining passages that seem interesting or mysterious or difficult. A mark is a way of saying, "This is something I might want to work on later." If you mark the selections in this book as you read them, you will give yourself a working record of what, at the first moment of reading, you felt might be worth a second reading.

If Percy's essay presents problems for a reader, they are problems of a different order from summary and recall. The essay is not the sort that tells you what it says. You would have difficulty finding one sentence that sums up or announces, in a loud and clear voice, what Percy is talking about. At the point you think Percy is about to summarize, he turns to one more example that complicates the picture, as though what he is discussing defies his attempts to sum things up. Percy is talking about tourists and students, about such things as individual "sovereignty" and our media culture's "symbolic packages," but if he has a point to make, it cannot be stated in a sentence or two.

In fact, Percy's essay is challenging reading in part because it does not have a single, easily identifiable main idea. A reader could infer that it has several points to make, none of which can be said easily and some of which, perhaps, are contradictory. To search for information, or to ignore the rough edges in search of a single, paraphrasable idea, is to divert attention from the task at hand, which is not to remember what Percy says but to speak about the essay and what it means to you, the reader. In this sense, the Percy essay is not the sum of its individual parts; it is, more accurately, what its readers make of it.

A reader could go to an expert on Percy to solve the problem of what to make of the essay—perhaps to a teacher, perhaps to a book in the library. And if the reader pays attention, he could remember what the expert said or she could put down notes on paper. But in doing either, the reader only rehearses what he or she has been told, abandoning the responsibility to make the essay meaningful. There are ways of reading, in other words, in which Percy's essay "The Loss of the Creature" is not what it means to the experts but what it means to you as a reader willing to take the chance to construct a reading. You can be the authority on Percy; you don't have to turn to others. The meaning of the essay, then, is something you develop as you go along, something for which you must take final responsibility. The meaning is forged from reading the essay, to be sure, but it is determined by what you do with the essay, by the connections you can make and your explanation of why those connections are important, and by your account of what Percy might mean when he talks about "symbolic packages" or a "loss of sovereignty" (phrases Percy uses as key terms in the essay). This version of Percy's essay will finally be yours; it will not be exactly what Percy said. (Only his words in the order he wrote them would say exactly what he said.) You will choose the path to take through his essay and support it as you can with arguments, explanations, examples, and commentary.

If an essay or story is not the sum of its parts but something you as a reader create by putting together those parts that seem to matter personally, then the way to begin, once you have read a selection in this collection, is by reviewing what you recall, by going back to those places that stick in your memory—or, perhaps, to those sections you marked with checks or notes in the margins. You begin by seeing what you can make of these memories and notes. You should realize that with essays as long and complex as those we've included in this book, you will never feel, after a single reading, as though you have command of everything you read. This is not a problem. After four or five readings (should you give any single essay that much attention), you may still feel that there are parts you missed or don't understand. This sense of incompleteness is part of the experience of reading, at least the experience of reading serious work. And it is part of the experience of a strong reader. No reader could retain one of these essays in her mind, no matter how proficient her memory or how experienced she might be. No reader, at least no reader we would trust, would admit that he understood everything that Michel Foucault or Adrienne Rich or Ralph Waldo Emerson had to say. What strong readers know is that they have to begin, and they have to begin regardless of their doubts or hesitations. What you have after your first reading of an essay is a starting place, and you begin with your marked passages or examples or notes, with questions to answer, or with problems to solve. Strong readings, in other words, put a premium on individual acts of attention and composition.

## *Strong Readers, Strong Texts*

We chose pieces for this book that invite strong readings. Our selections require more attention (or a different form of attention) than a written summary, a reduction to gist, or a recitation of main ideas. They are not "easy" reading. The challenges they present, however, do not make them inaccessible to college students. The essays are not specialized studies; they have interested, pleased, or piqued general and specialist audiences alike. To say that they are challenging is to say, then, that they leave some work for a reader to do. They are designed to teach a reader new ways to read (or to step outside habitual ways of reading), and they anticipate readers willing to take the time to learn. These readers need not be experts on the subject matter. Perhaps the most difficult problem for students is to believe that this is true.

You do not need experts to explain these stories and essays, although you could probably go to the library and find an expert guide to most of the selections we've included. Let's take, for example, Adrienne Rich's "When We Dead Awaken: Writing as Re-Vision." This essay looks at the history of women's writing (and at Rich's development as a poet). It argues that women have been trapped within a patriarchal culture—speaking in men's voices and telling stories prepared by men—and, as a consequence, according to Rich, "We need to know the writing of the past, and know it differently than we have ever known it; not to pass on a tradition but to break its hold over us."

You could go to the library to find out how Rich is regarded by experts, by literary critics or feminist scholars, for example; you could learn how her work fits into an established body of work on women's writing and the representation of women in modern culture. You could see what others have said about the writers she cites: Virginia Woolf, Jane Austen, and Elizabeth Bishop. You could see how others have read and made use of Rich's essay. You could see how others have interpreted the poems she includes as part of her argument. You could look for standard definitions of key terms like "patriarchy" or "formalism."

Though it is often important to seek out other texts and to know what other people are saying or have said, it is often necessary and even desirable to begin on your own. Rich can also be read outside any official system of interpretation. She is talking, after all, about our daily experience. And when she addresses the reader, she addresses a person—not a term-paper writer. When she says, "We need to know the writing of the past, and know it differently than we have ever known it," she means us and what we know and how we know what we know. (Actually the "we" of her essay refers most accurately to women readers, leading men to feel the kind of exclusion women must feel when the reader is always "he." But it is us, the men who are in the act of reading this essay, who feel and respond to this pressure.)

The question, then, is not what Rich's words might mean to a literary critic, or generally to those who study contemporary American culture. The question is what you, the reader, can make of those words given your own experience, your goals, and the work you do with what she has written. In this sense, "When We Dead Awaken" is not what it means to others (those who have already decided what it means) but what it means to you, and this meaning is something you compose when you write about the essay; it is your account of what Rich says and how what she says might be said to make sense.

A teacher, poet, and critic we admire, I. A. Richards, once said, "Read as though it made sense and perhaps it will." To take command of complex material like the selections in this book, you need not subordinate yourself to experts; you can assume the authority to provide such a reading on your own. This means you must allow yourself a certain tentativeness and recognize your limits. You should not assume that it is your job to solve the problems between men and women. You can speak with authority while still acknowledging that complex issues *are* complex.

There is a paradox here. On the one hand, the essays are rich, magnificent, too big for anyone to completely grasp all at once, and before them, as before inspiring spectacles, it seems appropriate to stand humbly, admiringly. And yet, on the other hand, a reader must speak with authority.

In "The American Scholar," Ralph Waldo Emerson says, "Meek young men grow up in libraries, believing it their duty to accept the views, which Cicero, which Locke, which Bacon, have given, forgetful that Cicero, Locke, and Bacon were only young men in libraries when they wrote these books." What Emerson offers here is not a fact but an attitude. There is creative reading, he says, as well as creative writing. It is up to you to treat authors as your equals, as people who will allow you to speak too. At the same time, you must respect the difficulty and complexity of their texts and of the issues and questions they examine. Little is to be gained, in other words, by turning Rich's essay into a message that would fit on a poster in a dorm room: "Be Yourself" or "Stand on Your Own Two Feet."

## Reading with and against the Grain

Reading, then, requires a difficult mix of authority and humility. On the one hand, a reader takes charge of a text; on the other, a reader gives generous attention to someone else's (a writer's) key terms and methods, commits his time to her examples, tries to think in her language, imagines that this strange work is important, compelling, at least for the moment.

Most of the questions in *Ways of Reading* will have you moving back and forth in these two modes, reading with and against the grain of a text, reproducing an author's methods, questioning his or her direction and authority. With the essay "When We Dead Awaken," for example, we have asked students to give a more complete and detailed reading of Rich's poems (the poems included in the essay) than she does, to put her terms to work, to extend her essay by extending the discussion of her examples. We have asked students to give themselves over to her essay—recognizing that this is not necessarily an easy thing to do. Or, again in Rich's name, we have asked students to tell a story of their own experience, a story similar to the one she tells, one that can be used as an example of the ways a person is positioned by a dominant culture. Here we are saying, in effect, read your world in Rich's terms. Notice what she would notice. Ask the questions she would ask. Try out her conclusions.

To read generously, to work inside someone else's system, to see your world in someone else's terms—we call this "reading with the grain." It is a way of working *with* a writer's ideas, in conjunction with someone else's text. As a way of reading, it can take different forms. In the reading and writing assignments that follow the selections in this book, you will sometimes be asked to summarize and paraphrase, to put others' ideas into your terms, to provide your account of what they are saying. This is a way of getting a tentative or provisional hold on a text, its examples and ideas; it allows you a place to begin to work. And sometimes you will be asked to extend a writer's project—to add your examples to someone else's argument, to read your experience through the frame of another's text, to try out the key terms and interpretive schemes in another writer's work. In the assignments that follow the Rich essay, for example, students are asked both to reproduce her argument and to extend her terms to examples from their own experience.

We have also asked students to read against the grain, to read critically, to turn back, for example, *against* Rich's project, to ask questions they believe might come as a surprise, to look for the limits of her vision, to provide alternate readings of her examples, to find examples that challenge her argument, to engage her, in other words, in dialogue. How might her poems be read to counter what she wants to say about them? If her essay argues for a new language for women, how is this language represented in the final poem or the final paragraphs, when the poem seems unreadable and the final paragraph sounds familiarly like the usual political rhetoric? If Rich is arguing for a collective movement, a "we" represented by the "we" of her essay, who is included and who excluded by the terms and strategies of her writing? To what degree might you say that this is a conscious or necessary strategy?

Many of the essays in this book provide examples of writers working against the grain of common sense or everyday language. This is true of John Berger, for example, who redefines the "art museum" against the way it is usually understood. It is true of John Edgar Wideman, who reads against his own text while he writes it—asking questions that disturb the story as it emerges on the page. It is true of Harriet Jacobs, Paul Auster, and Virginia Woolf, whose writings show the signs of their efforts to work against the grain of the standard essay, habitual ways of representing what it means to know something, to be somebody, to speak before others.

This, we've found, is the most difficult work for students to do, this work against the grain. For good reasons and bad, students typically define their skill by reproducing rather than questioning or revising the work of their teachers (or the work of those their teachers ask them to read). It is important to read generously and carefully and to learn to submit to projects that others have begun. But it is also important to know what you are doing—to understand where this work comes from, whose interests it serves, how and where it is kept together by will rather than desire, and what it might have to do with you. To fail to ask the fundamental questions—Where am I in this? How can I make my mark? Whose interests are represented? What can I learn by reading with or against the grain?—to fail to ask these questions is to mistake skill for understanding, and it is to misunderstand the goals of a liberal education. All of the essays in this book, we would argue, ask to be read, not simply reproduced; they ask to be read and to be read with a difference. Our goal is to make that difference possible.

## Reading and Writing: The Questions and Assignments

Strong readers, we've said, remake what they have read to serve their own ends, putting things together, figuring out how ideas and examples relate, explaining as best they can material that is difficult or problematic, translating phrases like Richard Rodriguez's "scholarship boy" into their own terms. At these moments, it is hard to distinguish the act of reading from the act of writing. In fact, the connection between reading and writing can be seen as almost a literal one, since the best way you can show your reading of a rich and dense essay like "The Achievement of Desire" is by writing down your thoughts, placing one idea against another, commenting on what you've done, taking examples into account, looking back at where you began, perhaps changing your mind, and moving on.

Readers, however, seldom read a single essay in isolation, as though their only job were to arrive at some sense of what an essay has to say. Although we couldn't begin to provide examples of all the various uses of reading in academic life, it is often the case that readings provide information and direction for investigative projects, whether they are philosophical or scientific in nature. The reading and writing assignments that follow each selection in this book are designed to point you in certain directions, to give you ideas and projects to work with, and to challenge you to see one writer's ideas through another's.

Strong readers often read critically, weighing, for example, an author's claims and interpretations against evidence—evidence provided by the author in the text, evidence drawn from other sources, or the evidence that is assumed to be part of a reader's own knowledge and experience. Critical reading can produce results as far-reaching as a biochemist publicly challenging the findings and interpretations in an article on cancer research in the *New England Journal of Medicine* or as quiet as a student offering a personal interpretation of a story in class discussion.

You will find that the questions we have included in our reading and writing assignments often direct you to test what you think an author is saying by measuring it against your own experience. Paulo Freire, for example, in "The 'Banking' Concept of Education" talks about the experience of the student, and one way for you to develop or test your reading of his essay is to place what he says in the context of your own experience, searching for examples that are similar to his and examples that differ from his. If the writers in this book are urging you to give strong readings of your common experience, you have access to what they say because they are talking not only to you but about you. Freire has a method that he employs when he talks about the classroom—one that compares "banking" education with "problem-posing" education. You can try out his method and his terms on examples of your own, continuing his argument as though you were working with him on a common project. Or you can test his argument as though you want to see not only where and how it will work but where and how it will not.

You will also find questions that ask you to extend the argument of the essay by looking in detail at some of the essay's own examples. John Berger, for example, gives a detailed analysis of two paintings by Frans Hals in "Ways of Seeing." Other paintings in the essay he refers to only briefly. One way of working on his essay is to look at the other examples, trying to do with them what he has done for you earlier.

Readers, as we have said, seldom read an essay in isolation, as though, having once worked out a reading of Virginia Woolf's "A Room of One's Own," they could go on to something else, something unrelated. It is unusual for anyone, at least in an academic setting, to read in so random a fashion. Readers read most often because they have a project in hand—a question they are working on or a problem they are trying to solve. For example, if as a result of reading Woolf's essay you become interested in the difference between women's writing and men's writing, and you begin to notice things you would not have noticed before, then you can read other essays in the book through this frame. If you have a project in mind, that project will help determine how you read these other essays. Sections of an essay that might otherwise seem unimportant suddenly become important—Gloria Anzaldúa's unusual prose style, Rich's references to Woolf, the moments when Harriet Jacobs addresses the "women of the North." Woolf may enable you to read Jacobs's narrative differently. Jacobs may spur you to rethink Woolf.

In a sense, then, you do have the chance to become an expert reader, a reader with a project in hand, one who has already done some reading, who has watched others at work, and who has begun to develop a method of analysis and a set of key terms. You might read Jacobs's narrative "Incidents in the Life of a Slave Girl," for example, in the context of Mary Louise Pratt's discussion of "autoethnography," or you might read the selections by Gloria Anzaldúa, W. E. B. Du Bois, Ralph Ellison, and John Edgar Wideman as offering differing accounts of racism in America. Imagining yourself operating alongside some of the major figures in contemporary thought can be great fun and heady work—particularly when you have the occasion to speak back to them.

In every case, then, the material we provide to direct your work on the essay, story, or poem will have you constructing a reading, but then doing something with what you have read—using the selection as a frame through which you can understand (through which you can "read") your own experience, the examples of others, or the ideas and methods of other writers.

You may find that you have to alter your sense of who a writer is and what a writer does as you work on your own writing. Writers are often told that they need to begin with a clear sense of what they want to do and what they want to say. The writing assignments we've written, we believe, give you a sense of what you want (or need) to do. We define a problem for you to work on, and the problem will frame the task for you. You will have to decide where you will go in the texts you have read to find materials to work with, the primary materials that will give you a place to begin as you work on your essay. It would be best, however, if you did not feel that you need to have a clear sense of what you want to say before you begin. You may begin to develop a sense of what you want to say while you are writing—as you begin, for example, to examine how and why Anzaldúa's prose could be said to be difficult to read, and what that difficulty might enable you to say about what Anzaldúa expects of a reader. It may also be the case, however, that the subjects you will be writing about are too big for you to assume that you need to have all the answers or that it is up to you to have the final word or to solve the problems once and for all. When you work on your essays, you should cast yourself in the role of one who is exploring a question, examining what might be said, and speculating on possible rather than certain conclusions. If you consider your responses to be provisional, examples of what might be said by a bright and serious student at this point in time, you will be in a position to learn more, as will those who read what you write. Think of yourself, then, as a writer intent on opening a subject up rather than closing one down.

Let us turn briefly now to the three categories of reading and writing assignments you will find in the book.

## Questions for a Second Reading

Immediately following each selection are questions designed to guide your second reading. You may, as we've said, prefer to follow your own instincts as you search for the materials to build your understanding of the essay or story. These questions are meant to assist that process or develop those instincts. Most of the essays and stories in the book are longer and more difficult than those you may be accustomed to reading. They are difficult enough that any reader would have to reread them and work to understand them; these questions are meant to suggest ways of beginning that work.

The second reading questions characteristically ask you to consider the relations between ideas and examples in what you have read or to test specific statements in the essays against your own experience (so that you can get a sense of the author's habit of mind, his or her way of thinking about subjects that are available to you, too). Some turn your attention to what we take to be key terms or concepts, asking you to define these terms by observing how the writer uses them throughout the essay.

These are the questions that seemed "natural" to us; they reflect our habitual way of reading and, we believe, the general habits of mind of the academic community. These questions have no simple answers; you will not find a correct answer hidden somewhere in the selection. In short, they are not the sorts of questions asked on SAT or ACT exams. They are real questions, questions that ask about the basic methods of an essay or about the issues the essay raises. They pose problems for interpretation or indicate sections where, to our minds, there is some interesting work for a reader to do. They are meant to reveal possible ways of reading the text, not to indicate that there is only one correct way, and that we have it.

You may find it useful to take notes as you read through each selection a second time, perhaps in a journal you can keep as a sourcebook for more formal written work.

## Assignments for Writing

This book actually offers three different kinds of writing assignments: assignments that ask you to write about a single essay or story, assignments that ask you to read one selection through the frame of another, and longer sequences of assignments that define a project within which three or four of the selections serve as primary sources. All of these assignments serve a dual purpose. Like the second reading questions, they suggest a way for you to reconsider the stories or essays; they give you access from a different perspective. The assignments also encourage you to be a strong reader and actively interpret what you have read. In one way or another, they all invite you to use a story or an essay as a way of framing experience, as a source of terms and methods to enable you to interpret something else—some other text, events and objects around you, or your own memories and experience. The assignment sequences can be found at the end of the book. The others (titled "Assignments for Writing" and "Making Connections") come immediately after each selection.

"Assignments for Writing" ask you to write about a single selection. Although some of these assignments call for you to paraphrase or reconstruct difficult passages, most ask you to interpret what you have read with a specific purpose in mind. The work you are to do is generally of two sorts. For most of the essays, one question asks you to interpret a moment from your own experience through the frame of the essay. This, you will remember, is the use that Rodriguez made of Richard Hoggart's *The Uses of Literacy.*

Other assignments, however, ask you to turn an essay back on itself or to extend the conclusions of the essay by reconsidering the examples the writer has used to make his or her case. Adrienne Rich's essay "When We Dead Awaken: Writing as Re-Vision" is built around a series of poems she wrote at various stages in her career. She says that the development represented by these poems reflects her growing understanding of the problems women in a patriarchal society have in finding a language for their own experience. She presents the poems as examples but offers little detailed discussion of them. One of the assignments, then, asks you to describe the key differences in these poems. It next asks you to comment on the development of her work and to compare your account of that development with hers.

In her essay, Rich also says that writing is "renaming." This is an interesting and, one senses, a potentially powerful term. For it to be useful, however, a reader must put it to work, to see what results when you accept the challenge of the essay and think about writing as renaming. Another assignment, then, asks you to apply this term to one of her poems and to discuss the poem as an act of renaming. The purpose of this assignment is not primarily to develop your skill as a reader of poems but to develop your sense of the method and key terms of Rich's argument.

A note on the writing assignments: When we talk with teachers and students using *Ways of Reading,* we are often asked about the wording of these assignments. The assignments are long. The wording is often unusual, unexpected. The assignments contain many questions, not simply one. The directions seem indirect, confusing. "Why?" we're asked. "How should we work with these?" When we write assignments, our goal is to point students toward a project, to provide a frame for their reading, a motive for writing, a way of asking certain kinds of questions. In that sense, the assignments should not be read as a set of directions to be followed literally. In fact, they are written to resist that reading, to forestall a writer's desire to simplify, to be efficient, to settle for the first clear line toward the finish. We want to provide a context to suggest how readers and writers might take time, be thoughtful. And we want the projects students work on to become their own. We hope to provoke varied responses, to leave the final decisions to the students. So the assignments try to be open and suggestive rather than narrow and direct. We ask lots of questions, but students don't need to answer them all (or any of them) once they begin to write. Our questions are meant to suggest ways of questioning, starting points. "What do you want?" Our own students ask this question. We want writers to make the most they can of what they read, including our questions and assignments.

## Making Connections

The connections questions will have you work with two or more readings at a time. These are not so much questions that ask you to compare or contrast the essays or stories as they are directions on how you might use one text as the context for interpreting another. Mary Louise Pratt, for example, in "Arts of the Contact Zone" looks at the work of a South American native, an Inca named Guaman Poma, writing in the seventeenth century to King Philip III of Spain. His work, she argues, can be read as a moment of contact, one in which different cultures and positions of power come together in a single text—in which a conquered person responds to the ways he is represented in the mind and the language of the conqueror. Pratt's reading of Guaman Poma's letter to King Philip, and the terms she uses to describe the way she reads it, provides a powerful context for a reader looking at essays by other writers, like Harriet Jacobs or Gloria Anzaldúa, for whom the "normal" or "standard" language of American culture is difficult, troubling, unsatisfactory, or incomplete. There are, then, assignments that ask you both to extend and to test Pratt's reading through your reading of alternative texts. In another assignment, you are asked to consider different ways of writing "history," writing about the past, by looking at the work of two very different writers: John Edgar Wideman, a fiction writer who turns his hand to "real life" when he writes about his brother and his family, and Patricia Nelson Limerick, a professional historian who writes not only about the American West but also about the writing of the American West, about how the American West has been written into popular culture and the popular imagination.

The purpose of all these assignments is to demonstrate how the work of one author can be used as a frame for reading and interpreting the work of another. This can be exciting work, and it demonstrates a basic principle of liberal arts education: students should be given the opportunity to adopt different points of view, including those of scholars and writers who have helped to shape modern thought. These kinds of assignments give you the chance, even as a novice, to try your hand at the work of professionals.

## The Assignment Sequences

The assignment sequences are more broad-ranging versions of the making connections assignments; in the sequences, several reading and writing assignments are linked and directed toward a single goal. They allow you to work on projects that require more time and incorporate more readings than would be possible in a single assignment. And they encourage you to develop your own point of view in concert with those of the professionals who wrote the essays and stories you are reading.

The assignments in a sequence build on one another, each relying on the ones before. A sequence will usually make use of three or four reading selections. The first is used to introduce an area of study or inquiry as well as to establish a frame of reference, a way of thinking about the subject. In the sequence titled "The Aims of Education," you begin with an essay by Paulo Freire. Freire, a Marxist educator, takes a standard account of education (in which students are said to be "given" knowledge by a teacher) and, as he says, "problematizes" that account, opens it up to question, by arguing that such classrooms only reproduce the powerlessness students will face in the larger society. The goal of the sequence is to provide a point for you to work from, one that you can open up to question. Subsequent assignments ask you to develop examples from your own schooling as you work through other accounts of education in, for example, Adrienne Rich's "When We Dead Awaken," Mary Louise Pratt's "Arts of the Contact Zone," or Susan Griffin's "Our Secret."

The sequences allow you to participate in an extended academic project, one in which you take a position, revise it, look at a new example, hear what someone else has to say, revise it again, and see what conclusions you can draw about your subject. These projects always take time—they go through stages and revisions as a writer develops a command over his or her material, pushing against habitual ways of thinking, learning to examine an issue from different angles, rejecting quick conclusions, seeing the power of understanding that comes from repeated effort, and feeling the pleasure writers take when they find their own place in the context of others whose work they admire. This is the closest approximation we can give you of the rhythm and texture of academic life, and we offer our book as an introduction to its characteristic ways of reading, thinking, and writing.

# The Readings

# GLORIA
# ANZALDÚA

*G LORIA ANZALDÚA grew up in southwest Texas, the physical and cul-
tural borderland between the United States and Mexico, an area she has
called "una herida abierta," an open wound, "where the Third World grates
against the first and bleeds." Defining herself as lesbian, feminist, Chicana—a
representative of the new mestiza—she has dramatically revised the usual narrative of American autobiography. "I am a border woman," she says. "I grew up between two cultures, the Mexican (with a heavy Indian influence) and the Anglo
(as a member of a colonized people in our own territory). I have been straddling
that tejas-Mexican border, and others, all my life." Cultural, physical, spiritual,
sexual, linguistic—the borderlands defined by Anzaldúa extend beyond geography. "In fact," she says, "the Borderlands are present where two or more cultures
edge each other, where people of different races occupy the same territory, where
under, lower, middle, and upper classes touch, where the space between two individuals shrinks with intimacy." In a sense, her writing argues against the concept
of an "authentic," unified, homogeneous culture, the pure "Mexican experience,"
a nostalgia that underlies much of the current interest in "ethnic" literature.*

*In the following selections, which represent two chapters from her book Bor-
derlands/La frontera: The New Mestiza (1987), Anzaldúa mixes genres, moving between poetry and prose, weaving stories with sections that resemble the work
of a cultural or political theorist. She tells us a story about her childhood, her*

**21**

*culture, and her people that is at once both myth and history. Her prose, too, is mixed, shifting among Anglo-American English, Castilian Spanish, Tex-Mex, Northern Mexican dialect, and Nahuatl (Aztec), speaking to us in the particular mix that represents her linguistic heritage:* "Presently this infant language, this bastard language, Chicano Spanish, is not approved by any society. But we Chicanos no longer feel that we need to beg entrance, that we need always to make the first overture—to translate to Anglos, Mexicans, and Latinos, apology blurting out of our mouths with every step. Today we ask to be met halfway. This book is our invitation to you." *The book is an invitation, but not always an easy one. The chapters that follow make a variety of demands on the reader. The shifting styles, genres, and languages can be confusing or disturbing, but this is part of the effect of Anzaldúa's prose, part of the experience you are invited to share.*

*In a chapter from the book that is not included here, Anzaldúa gives this account of her writing:*

> *In looking at this book that I'm almost finished writing, I see a mosaic pattern (Aztec-like) emerging, a weaving pattern, thin here, thick there. I see a preoccupation with the deep structure, the underlying structure, with the gesso underpainting that is red earth, black earth. . . . This almost finished product seems an assemblage, a montage, a beaded work with several leitmotifs and with a central core, now appearing, now disappearing in a crazy dance. The whole thing has had a mind of its own, escaping me and insisting on putting together the pieces of its own puzzle with minimal direction from my will.*

*Beyond her prose, she sees the competing values of more traditionally organized narratives,* "art typical of Western European cultures, [which] attempts to manage the energies of its own internal system. . . . It is dedicated to the validation of itself. Its task is to move humans by means of achieving mastery in content, technique, feeling. Western art is always whole and always 'in power.'"

*Anzaldúa's prose puts you, as a reader, on the borderland; in a way, it re-creates the position of the* mestiza. *As you read, you will need to meet this prose halfway, generously, learning to read a text that announces its difference.*

*In addition to* Borderlands/La frontera, *Anzaldúa has edited* Haciendo Caras: Making Face/Making Soul *(1990) and coedited an anthology,* This Bridge Called My Back: Writings by Radical Women of Color *(1983). She has recently published a book for children,* Prietita and the Ghost Woman *(1996), which retells traditional Mexican folktales from a feminist perspective.*

# Entering into the Serpent

*Sueño con serpientes, con serpientes del mar,*
*Con cierto mar, ay de serpientes sueño yo.*
*Largas, transparentes, en sus barrigas llevan*
*Lo que puedan arebatarle al amor.*

*Oh, oh, oh, la mató y aparese una mayor.*
*Oh, con mucho más infierno en digestión.*

I dream of serpents, serpents of the sea,
A certain sea, oh, of serpents I dream.
Long, transparent, in their bellies they carry
All that they can snatch away from love.
Oh, oh, oh, I kill one and a larger one appears.
Oh, with more hellfire burning inside!

— SILVIO RODRÍGUES,
*"Sueño con serpientes"*[1]

In the predawn orange haze, the sleepy crowing of roosters atop the trees. *No vayas al escusado en lo oscuro.* Don't go to the outhouse at night, Prieta, my mother would say. *No se te vaya a meter algo pour allá.* A snake will crawl into your *nalgas,*[2] make you pregnant. They seek warmth in the cold. *Dicen que las culebras* like to suck *chiches,*[3] can draw milk out of you.

*En el escusado* in the half-light spiders hang like gliders. Under my bare buttocks and the rough planks the deep yawning tugs at me. I can see my legs fly up to my face as my body falls through the round hole into the sheen of swarming maggots below. Avoiding the snakes under the porch I walk back into the kitchen, step on a big black one slithering across the floor.

### *Ella tiene su tono*[4]

Once we were chopping cotton in the fields of Jesus Maria Ranch. All around us the woods. *Quelite*[5] towered above me, choking the stubby cotton that had outlived the deer's teeth.

I swung *el ázadón*[6] hard. *El quelite* barely shook, showered nettles on my arms and face. When I heard the rattle the world froze.

I barely felt its fangs. Boot got all the *veneno.*[7] My mother came shrieking, swinging her hoe high, cutting the earth, the writhing body.

I stood still, the sun beat down. Afterwards I smelled where fear had been: back of neck, under arms, between my legs, I felt its heat slide down my body. I swallowed the rock it had hardened into.

When Mama had gone down the row and was out of sight, I took out my pocketknife. I made an X over each prick. My body followed the blood, fell onto the soft ground. I put my mouth over the red and sucked and spit between the rows of cotton.

I picked up the pieces, placed them end on end. *Culebra de cascabel.*[8] I counted the rattlers: twelve. It would shed no more. I buried the pieces between the rows of cotton.

That night I watched the window sill, watched the moon dry the blood on the tail, dreamed rattler fangs filled my mouth, scales covered my body. In the morning I saw through snake eyes, felt snake blood course through my body. The serpent, *mi tono*, my animal counterpart. I was immune to its venom. Forever immune.

Snakes, *víboras:* since that day I've sought and shunned them. Always when they cross my path, fear and elation flood my body. I know things older than Freud, older than gender. She—that's how I think of *la Víbora*, Snake Woman. Like the ancient Olmecs, I know Earth is a coiled Serpent. Forty years it's taken me to enter into the Serpent, to acknowledge that I have a body, that I am a body and to assimilate the animal body, the animal soul.

## *Coatlalopeuh*, She Who Has Dominion over Serpents

*Mi mamagrande Ramona toda su vida mantuvo un altar pequeño en la esquina del comedor. Siempre tenía las velas prendidas. Allí hacía promesas a la Virgen de Guadalupe.* My family, like most Chicanos, did not practice Roman Catholicism but a folk Catholicism with many pagan elements. *La Virgen de Guadalupe*'s Indian name is *Coatlalopeuh*. She is the central deity connecting us to our Indian ancestry.

*Coatlalopeuh* is descended from, or is an aspect of, earlier Mesoamerican fertility and Earth goddesses. The earliest is *Coatlicue*, or "Serpent Skirt." She had a human skull or serpent for a head, a necklace of human hearts, a skirt of twisted serpents, and taloned feet. As creator goddess, she was mother of the celestial deities, and of *Huitzilopochtli* and his sister, *Coyolxauhqui*, She with Golden Bells, Goddess of the Moon, who was decapitated by her brother. Another aspect of *Coatlicue* is *Tonantsi*.[9] The Totonacs, tired of the Aztec human sacrifices to the male god, *Huitzilopochtli*, renewed their reverence for *Tonantsi* who preferred the sacrifice of birds and small animals.[10]

The male-dominated Azteca-Mexica culture drove the powerful female deities underground by giving them monstrous attributes and by substituting male deities in their place, thus splitting the female Self and the female deities. They divided her who had been complete, who possessed both upper (light) and underworld (dark) aspects. *Coatlicue*, the Serpent goddess, and her more sinister aspects, *Tlazolteotl* and *Cihuacoatl*, were "darkened" and disempowered much in the same manner as the Indian *Kali*.

*Tonantsi*—split from her dark guises, *Coatlicue*, *Tlazolteotl*, and *Cihuacoatl*—became the good mother. The Nahuas, through ritual and prayer, sought to oblige *Tonantsi* to ensure their health and the growth of their crops. It was she who gave *México* the cactus plant to provide her people with milk and pulque. It was she who defended her children against the wrath of the Christian God by challenging God, her son, to produce mother's milk (as she had done) to prove that his benevolence equalled his disciplinary harshness.[11]

After the Conquest, the Spaniards and their Church continued to split *Tonantsi/Guadalupe*. They desexed *Guadalupe*, taking *Coatlalopeuh*, the serpent/sexuality, out of her. They completed the split begun by the Nahuas by making *la Virgen de Guadalupe/Virgen María* into chaste virgins and *Tlazolteotl/Coatlicue/la Chingada* into *putas*; into the Beauties and the Beasts. They went even further; they made all Indian deities and religious practices the work of the devil.

Thus *Tonantsi* became *Guadalupe*, the chaste protective mother, the defender of the Mexican people.

> *El nueve de diciembre del año 1531*
> *a las cuatro de la madrugada*
> *un pobre indio que se llamaba Juan Diego*
> *iba cruzando el cerro de Tepeyác*
> *cuando oyó un cantó de pájaro.*
> *Alzó al cabeza vío que en la cima del cerro*
> *estaba cubierta con una brillante nube blanca.*
> *Parada en frente del sol*
> *sobre una luna creciente*
> *sostenida por un ángel*
> *estaba una azteca*
> *vestida en ropa de india.*
> *Nuestra Señora María de Coatlalopeuh*
> *se le apareció.*
> *"Juan Diegito, El-que-habla-como-un-águila,"*
> *la Virgen le dijo en el lenguaje azteca.*
> *"Para hacer mi altar este cerro eligo.*
> *Dile a tu gente que yo soy la madre de Dios,*
> *a los indios yo les ayudaré.*
> *Estó se lo contó a Juan Zumarraga*
> *pero el obispo no le creyo.*
> *Juan Diego volvió, lleño su tilma*[12]
> *con rosas de castilla*
> *creciendo milagrosamiente en la nieve.*
> *Se las llevó al obispo,*
> *y cuando abrío su tilma*
> *el retrato de la Virgen*
> *ahí estaba pintado.*

*Guadalupe* appeared on December 9, 1531, on the spot where the Aztec goddess, *Tonantsi* ("Our Lady Mother"), had been worshiped by the Nahuas and where a temple to her had stood. Speaking Nahua, she told Juan Diego, a poor Indian crossing Tepeyac Hill, whose Indian name was *Cuautlaohuac* and who belonged to the *mazehual* class, the humblest within the Chichimeca tribe, that her name was *María Coatlalopeuh*. *Coatl* is the Nahuatl word for serpent. *Lopeuh* means "the one who has dominion over serpents." I interpret this as "the one who is at one with the beasts." Some spell her name *Coatlaxopeuh* (pronounced *"Cuatlashupe"* in Nahuatl) and say that *"xopeuh"* means "crushed or stepped on with disdain." Some say it means "she who crushed the serpent," with the serpent as the symbol of the indigenous religion, meaning that her religion was to take the place of the Aztec religion.[13] Because *Coatlalopeuh* was homophonous to the Spanish *Guadalupe*, the Spanish identified her with the dark Virgin, *Guadalupe*, patroness of West Central Spain.[14]

From that meeting, Juan Diego walked away with the image of *la Virgen* painted on his cloak. Soon after, Mexico ceased to belong to Spain, and *la Virgen de Guadalupe* began to eclipse all the other male and female religious figures in Mexico, Central America, and parts of the U.S. Southwest. *"Desde entonces para el mexicano ser Guadalupano es algo esencial/*Since then for the Mexican, to be a *Guadalupano* is something essential."[15]

> Mi Virgen Morena          My brown virgin
> Mi Virgen Ranchera       my country virgin
> Eres nuestra Reina        you are our queen
> México es tu tierra        Mexico is your land
> Y tú su bandera.          and you its flag.
> – "La Virgen Ranchera"[16]

In 1660 the Roman Catholic Church named her Mother of God, considering her synonymous with *la Virgen María;* she became *la Santa Patrona de los mexicanos.* The role of defender (or patron) has traditionally been assigned to male gods. During the Mexican Revolution, Emiliano Zapata and Miguel Hidalgo used her image to move *el pueblo mexicano* toward freedom. During the 1965 grape strike in Delano, California, and in subsequent Chicano farmworkers' marches in Texas and other parts of the Southwest, her image on banners heralded and united the farmworkers. *Pachucos* (zoot suiters) tattoo her image on their bodies. Today, in Texas and Mexico she is more venerated than Jesus or God the Father. In the Lower Rio Grande Valley of south Texas it is *la Virgen de San Juan de los Lagos* (an aspect of *Guadalupe*) that is worshiped by thousands every day at her shrine in San Juan. In Texas she is considered the patron saint of Chicanos. *Cuando Carito, mi hermanito,* was missing in action and, later, wounded in Viet Nam, *mi mamá* got on her knees *y le prometío a Ella que si su hijito volvía vivo* she would crawl on her knees and light novenas in her honor.

Today, *la Virgen de Guadalupe* is the single most potent religious, political, and cultural image of the Chicano/*mexicano.* She, like my race, is a synthesis of the old world and the new, of the religion and culture of the two races in our psyche, the conquerors and the conquered. She is the symbol of the *mestizo* true to his or her Indian values. *La cultura chicana* identifies with the mother (Indian) rather than with the father (Spanish). Our faith is rooted in indigenous attributes, images, symbols, magic, and myth. Because *Guadalupe* took upon herself the psychological and physical devastation of the conquered and oppressed *indio*, she is our spiritual, political, and psychological symbol. As a symbol of hope and faith, she sustains and insures our survival. The Indian, despite extreme despair, suffering, and near genocide, has survived. To Mexicans on both sides of the border, *Guadalupe* is the symbol of our rebellion against the rich, upper and middle class; against their subjugation of the poor and the *indio*.

*Guadalupe* unites people of different races, religions, languages: Chicano protestants, American Indians, and whites. *"Nuestra abogada siempre serás/*Our *mediatrix* you will always be." She mediates between the Spanish and the Indian cultures (or three cultures as in the case of *mexicanos* of African or other ancestry) and between Chicanos and the white world. She mediates between humans and the divine, between this reality and the reality of spirit entities. *La Virgen de Guadalupe* is the symbol of ethnic identity and of the tolerance for ambiguity that Chicanos-*mexicanos*, people of mixed race, people who have Indian blood, people who cross cultures, by necessity possess.

*La gente Chicana tiene tres madres.* All three are mediators: *Guadalupe*, the virgin mother who has not abandoned us, *la Chingada (Malinche)*, the raped mother whom we have abandoned, and *la Llorona*, the mother who seeks her lost children and is a combination of the other two.

Ambiguity surrounds the symbols of these three "Our Mothers." *Guadalupe* has been used by the Church to mete out institutionalized oppression: to placate the Indians and *mexicanos* and Chicanos. In part, the true identity of all three has been subverted—*Guadalupe* to make us docile and enduring, *la Chingada* to make us ashamed of our Indian side, and *la Llorona* to make us long-suffering people. This obscuring has encouraged the *virgen/puta* (whore) dichotomy.

Yet we have not all embraced this dichotomy. In the U.S. Southwest, Mexico, Central and South America the *indio* and the *mestizo* continue to worship the old spirit entities (including *Guadalupe*) and their supernatural power, under the guise of Christian saints.[17]

> Las invoco diosas mías, ustedes las indias
> sumergidas en mi carne que son mis sombras.
> Ustedes que persisten mudas en sus cuevas.
> Ustedes Señoras que ahora, como yo,
>                  están en desgracia.

### For Waging War Is My Cosmic Duty: The Loss of the Balanced Oppositions and the Change to Male Dominance

Therefore I decided to leave
The country [Aztlán],
Therefore I have come as one charged with a special duty,
Because I have been given arrows and shields,
For waging war is my duty,

And on my expeditions I
Shall see all the lands,
I shall wait for the people and meet them
In all four quarters and I shall give them
Food to eat and drinks to quench their thirst,
For here I shall unite all the different peoples!
                                    – HUITZILOPOCHTLI
                        speaking to the Azteca-Mexica[18]


Before the Aztecs became a militaristic, bureaucratic state where male
predatory warfare and conquest were based on patrilineal nobility, the
principle of balanced opposition between the sexes existed.[19] The people
worshiped the Lord and Lady of Duality, *Ometecuhtli* and *Omecihuatl*. Before the change to male dominance, *Coatlicue*, Lady of the Serpent Skirt,
contained and balanced the dualities of male and female, light and dark,
life and death.

The changes that led to the loss of the balanced oppositions began
when the Azteca, one of the twenty Toltec tribes, made the last pilgrimage
from a place called Aztlán. The migration south began about the year A.D.
820. Three hundred years later the advance guard arrived near Tula, the
capital of the declining Toltec empire. By the eleventh century, they had
joined with the Chichimec tribe of Mexitin (afterwards called Mexica) into
one religious and administrative organization within Aztlán, the Aztec
territory. The Mexitin, with their tribal god *Tetzauhteotl Huitzilopochtli*
(Magnificent Humming Bird on the Left), gained control of the religious
system.[20] (In some stories *Huitzilopochtli* killed his sister, the moon goddess *Malinalxoch*, who used her supernatural power over animals to control the tribe rather than wage war.)

*Huitzilopochtli* assigned the Azteca-Mexica the task of keeping the
human race (the present cosmic age called the Fifth Sun, *El Quinto Sol*)
alive. They were to guarantee the harmonious preservation of the human
race by unifying all the people on earth into one social, religious, and administrative organ. The Aztec people considered themselves in charge of
regulating all earthly matters.[21] Their instrument: controlled or regulated
war to gain and exercise power.

After 100 years in the central plateau, the Azteca-Mexica went to Chapultepec, where they settled in 1248 (the present site of the park on the
outskirts of Mexico City). There, in 1345, the Aztec-Mexica chose the site
of their capital, Tenochtitlan.[22] By 1428, they dominated the Central Mexican lake area.

The Aztec ruler, *Itzcoatl*, destroyed all the painted documents (books
called codices) and rewrote a mythology that validated the wars of conquest and thus continued the shift from a tribe based on clans to one based
on classes. From 1429 to 1440, the Aztecs emerged as a militaristic state
that preyed on neighboring tribes for tribute and captives.[23] The "wars of

flowers" were encounters between local armies with a fixed number of warriors, operating within the Aztec World, and, according to set rules, fighting ritual battles at fixed times and on predetermined battlefields. The religious purpose of these wars was to procure prisoners of war who could be sacrificed to the deities of the capturing party. For if one "fed" the gods, the human race would be saved from total extinction. The social purpose was to enable males of noble families and warriors of low descent to win honor, fame, and administrative offices, and to prevent social and cultural decadence of the elite. The Aztec people were free to have their own religious faith, provided it did not conflict too much with the three fundamental principles of state ideology: to fulfill the special duty set forth by *Huitzilopochtli* of unifying all peoples, to participate in the wars of flowers, and to bring ritual offerings and do penance for the purpose of preventing decadence.[24]

Matrilineal descent characterized the Toltecs and perhaps early Aztec society. Women possessed property, and were curers as well as priestesses. According to the codices, women in former times had the supreme power in Tula, and in the beginning of the Aztec dynasty, the royal blood ran through the female line. A council of elders of the Calpul headed by a supreme leader, or *tlactlo,* called the father and mother of the people, governed the tribe. The supreme leader's vice-emperor occupied the position of "Snake Woman" or *Cihuacoatl,* a goddess.[25] Although the high posts were occupied by men, the terms referred to females, evidence of the exalted role of women before the Aztec nation became centralized. The final break with the democratic Calpul came when the four Aztec lords of royal lineage picked the king's successor from his siblings or male descendants.[26]

*La Llorona's* wailing in the night for her lost children has an echoing note in the wailing or mourning rites performed by women as they bid their sons, brothers, and husbands good-bye before they left to go to the "flowery wars." Wailing is the Indian, Mexican, and Chicana woman's feeble protest when she has no other recourse. These collective wailing rites may have been a sign of resistance in a society which glorified the warrior and war and for whom the women of the conquered tribes were booty.[27]

In defiance of the Aztec rulers, the *macehuales* (the common people) continued to worship fertility, nourishment, and agricultural female deities, those of crops and rain. They venerated *Chalchiuhtlicue* (goddess of sweet or inland water), *Chicomecoatl* (goddess of food), and *Huixtocihuatl* (goddess of salt).

Nevertheless, it took less than three centuries for Aztec society to change from the balanced duality of their earlier times and from the egalitarian traditions of a wandering tribe to those of a predatory state. The nobility kept the tribute, the commoner got nothing, resulting in a class split. The conquered tribes hated the Aztecs because of the rape of their women

and the heavy taxes levied on them. The *Tlaxcalans* were the Aztec's bitter
enemies and it was they who helped the Spanish defeat the Aztec rulers,
who were by this time so unpopular with their own common people that
they could not even mobilize the populace to defend the city. Thus the
Aztec nation fell not because *Malinali (la Chingada)* interpreted for and
slept with Cortés, but because the ruling elite had subverted the solidarity
between men and women and between noble and commoner.[28]

### Sueño con serpientes

**Coatl.** In pre-Columbian America the most notable symbol was the
serpent. The Olmecs associated womanhood with the Serpent's mouth
which was guarded by rows of dangerous teeth, a sort of *vagina dentate*.
They considered it the most sacred place on earth, a place of refuge, the
creative womb from which all things were born and to which all things returned. Snake people had holes, entrances to the body of the Earth Serpent; they followed the Serpent's way, identified with the Serpent deity,
with the mouth, both the eater and the eaten. The destiny of humankind is
to be devoured by the Serpent.[29]

> Dead,
> the doctor by the operating table said.
> I passed between the two fangs,
> the flickering tongue.
> Having come through the mouth of the serpent,
> swallowed,
> I found myself suddenly in the dark,
> sliding down a smooth wet surface
> down down into an even darker darkness.
> Having crossed the portal, the raised hinged mouth,
> having entered the serpent's belly,
> now there was no looking back, no going back.
>
> Why do I cast no shadow?
> Are there lights from all sides shining on me?
> Ahead, ahead.
> curled up inside the serpent's coils,
> the damp breath of death on my face.
> I knew at that instant; something must change
> or I'd die.
> *Algo tenía que cambiar.*

After each of my four bouts with death I'd catch glimpses of an other-
world Serpent. Once, in my bedroom, I saw a cobra the size of the room,
her hood expanding over me. When I blinked she was gone. I realized she
was, in my psyche, the mental picture and symbol of the instinctual in its
collective impersonal, prehuman. She, the symbol of the dark sexual
drive, the chthonic (underworld), the feminine, the serpentine movement
of sexuality, of creativity, the basis of all energy and life.

## The Presences

She appeared in white, garbed in white,
standing white, pure white.
— BERNARDINO DE SAHAGÚN[30]

On the gulf where I was raised, *en el Valle del Río Grande* in South Texas—that triangular piece of land wedged between the river *y el golfo* which serves as the Texas-U.S./Mexican border—is a Mexican *pueblito* called Hargill (at one time in the history of this one-grocery-store, two-service-stations town there were thirteen churches and thirteen *cantinas*). Down the road, a little ways from our house, was a deserted church. It was known among the *mexicanos* that if you walked down the road late at night you would see a woman dressed in white floating about, peering out the church window. She would follow those who had done something bad or who were afraid. *Los mexicanos* called her *la Jila*. Some thought she was *la Llorona*. She was, I think, *Cihuacoatl*, Serpent Woman, ancient Aztec goddess of the earth, of war and birth, patron of midwives, and antecedent of *la Llorona*. Covered with chalk, *Cihuacoatl* wears a white dress with a decoration half red and half black. Her hair forms two little horns (which the Aztecs depicted as knives) crossed on her forehead. The lower part of her face is a bare jawbone, signifying death. On her back she carries a cradle, the knife of sacrifice swaddled as if it were her papoose, her child.[31] Like *la Llorona*, *Cihuacoatl* howls and weeps in the night, screams as if demented. She brings mental depression and sorrow. Long before it takes place, she is the first to predict something is to happen.

Back then, I, an unbeliever, scoffed at these Mexican superstitions as I was taught in Anglo school. Now, I wonder if this story and similar ones were the culture's attempts to "protect" members of the family, especially girls, from "wandering." Stories of the devil luring young girls away and having his way with them discouraged us from going out. There's an ancient Indian tradition of burying the umbilical cord of an infant girl under the house so she will never stray from it and her domestic role.

*A mis ancas caen los cueros de culebra,*
*cuatro veces por año los arrastro,*
*me tropiezo y me caigo*
*y cada vez que miro una culebra le pregunto*
*¿Qué traes conmigo?*

Four years ago a red snake crossed my path as I walked through the woods. The direction of its movement, its pace, its colors, the "mood" of the trees and the wind and the snake—they all "spoke" to me, told me things. I look for omens everywhere, everywhere catch glimpses of the patterns and cycles of my life. Stones "speak" to Luisah Teish, a Santera; trees whisper their secrets to Chrystos, a Native American. I remember listening to the voices of the wind as a child and understanding its messages.

*Los espíritus* that ride the back of the south wind. I remember their exhalation blowing in through the slits in the door during those hot Texas afternoons. A gust of wind raising the linoleum under my feet, buffeting the house. Everything trembling.

We're not supposed to remember such otherworldly events. We're supposed to ignore, forget, kill those fleeting images of the soul's presence and of the spirit's presence. We've been taught that the spirit is outside our bodies or above our heads somewhere up in the sky with God. We're supposed to forget that every cell in our bodies, every bone and bird and worm has spirit in it.

Like many Indians and Mexicans, I did not deem my psychic experiences real. I denied their occurrences and let my inner senses atrophy. I allowed white rationality to tell me that the existence of the "other world" was mere pagan superstition. I accepted their reality, the "official" reality of the rational, reasoning mode which is connected with external reality, the upper world, and is considered the most developed consciousness—the consciousness of duality.

The other mode of consciousness facilitates images from the soul and the unconscious through dreams and the imagination. Its work is labeled "fiction," make-believe, wish-fulfillment. White anthropologists claim that Indians have "primitive" and therefore deficient minds, that we cannot think in the higher mode of consciousness—rationality. They are fascinated by what they call the "magical" mind, the "savage" mind, the *participation mystique* of the mind that says the world of the imagination—the world of the soul—and of the spirit is just as real as physical reality.[32] In trying to become "objective," Western culture made "objects" of things and people when it distanced itself from them, thereby losing "touch" with them. This dichotomy is the root of all violence.

Not only was the brain split into two functions but so was reality. Thus people who inhabit both realities are forced to live in the interface between the two, forced to become adept at switching modes. Such is the case with the *india* and the *mestiza.*

Institutionalized religion fears trafficking with the spirit world and stigmatizes it as witchcraft. It has strict taboos against this kind of inner knowledge. It fears what Jung calls the Shadow, the unsavory aspects of ourselves. But even more it fears the suprahuman, the god in ourselves.

"The purpose of any established religion . . . is to glorify, sanction, and bless with a superpersonal meaning all personal and interpersonal activities. This occurs through the 'sacraments,' and indeed through most religious rites."[33] But it sanctions only its own sacraments and rites. Voodoo, Santeria, Shamanism, and other native religions are called cults and their beliefs are called mythologies. In my own life, the Catholic Church fails to give meaning to my daily acts, to my continuing encounters with the "other world." It and other institutionalized religions impoverish all life, beauty, pleasure.

The Catholic and Protestant religions encourage fear and distrust of life and of the body; they encourage a split between the body and the spirit and totally ignore the soul; they encourage us to kill off parts of ourselves. We are taught that the body is an ignorant animal; intelligence dwells only in the head. But the body is smart. It does not discern between external stimuli and stimuli from the imagination. It reacts equally viscerally to events from the imagination as it does to "real" events.

So I grew up in the interface trying not to give countenance to *el mal aigre*,[34] evil nonhuman, noncorporeal entities riding the wind, that could come in through the window, through my nose with my breath. I was not supposed to believe in *susto*, a sudden shock or fall that frightens the soul out of the body. And growing up between such opposing spiritualities how could I reconcile the two, the pagan and the Christian?

No matter to what use my people put the supranatural world, it is evident to me now that the spirit world, whose existence the whites are so adamant in denying, does in fact exist. This very minute I sense the presence of the spirits of my ancestors in my room. And I think *la Jila* is *Cihuacoatl*, Snake Woman; she is *la Llorona*, Daughter of Night, traveling the dark terrains of the unknown searching for the lost parts of herself. I remember *la Jila* following me once, remember her eerie lament. I'd like to think that she was crying for her lost children, *los* Chicanos/*mexicanos*.

## La facultad

*La facultad* is the capacity to see in surface phenomena the meaning of deeper realities, to see the deep structure below the surface. It is an instant "sensing," a quick perception arrived at without conscious reasoning. It is an acute awareness mediated by the part of the psyche that does not speak, that communicates in images and symbols which are the faces of feelings, that is, behind which feelings reside/hide. The one possessing this sensitivity is excruciatingly alive to the world.

Those who are pushed out of the tribe for being different are likely to become more sensitized (when not brutalized into insensitivity). Those who do not feel psychologically or physically safe in the world are more apt to develop this sense. Those who are pounced on the most have it the strongest—the females, the homosexuals of all races, the darkskinned, the outcast, the persecuted, the marginalized, the foreign.

When we're up against the wall, when we have all sorts of oppressions coming at us, we are forced to develop this faculty so that we'll know when the next person is going to slap us or lock us away. We'll sense the rapist when he's five blocks down the street. Pain makes us acutely anxious to avoid more of it, so we hone that radar. It's a kind of survival tactic that people, caught between the worlds, unknowingly cultivate. It is latent in all of us.

I walk into a house and I know whether it is empty or occupied. I feel the lingering charge in the air of a recent fight or lovemaking or depression. I sense the emotions someone near is emitting—whether friendly or threatening. Hate and fear—the more intense the emotion, the greater my reception of it. I feel a tingling on my skin when someone is staring at me or thinking about me. I can tell how others feel by the way they smell, where others are by the air pressure on my skin. I can spot the love or greed or generosity lodged in the tissues of another. Often I sense the direction of and my distance from people or objects—in the dark, or with my eyes closed, without looking. It must be a vestige of a proximity sense, a sixth sense that's lain dormant from long-ago times.

Fear develops the proximity sense aspect of *la facultad*. But there is a deeper sensing that is another aspect of this faculty. It is anything that breaks into one's everyday mode of perception, that causes a break in one's defenses and resistance, anything that takes one from one's habitual grounding, causes the depths to open up, causes a shift in perception. This shift in perception deepens the way we see concrete objects and people; the senses become so acute and piercing that we can see through things, view events in depth, a piercing that reaches the underworld (the realm of the soul). As we plunge vertically, the break, with its accompanying new seeing, makes us pay attention to the soul, and we are thus carried into awareness—an experiencing of soul (Self).

We lose something in this mode of initiation, something is taken from us: our innocence, our unknowing ways, our safe and easy ignorance. There is a prejudice and a fear of the dark, chthonic (underworld), material such as depression, illness, death, and the violations that can bring on this break. Confronting anything that tears the fabric of our everyday mode of consciousness and that thrusts us into a less literal and more psychic sense of reality increases awareness and *la facultad*.

## NOTES

[1] From the song *"Sueño con serpientes"* by Silvio Rodrígues, from the album *Días y flores*. Translated by Barbara Dane with the collaboration of Rina Benmauor and Juan Flores.

[2] *Nalgas:* vagina, buttocks.

[3] *Dicen que las culebras like to suck chiches:* they say snakes like to suck women's teats.

[4] *Ella tiene su tono:* she has supernatural power from her animal soul, the *tono*.

[5] *Quelite:* weed.

[6] *Ázadón:* hoe.

[7] *Veneno:* venom, poison.

[8] *Culebra de cascabel:* rattlesnake.

[9] In some Nahuatl dialects *Tonantsi* is called *Tonatzin*, literally "Our Holy Mother." *"Tonan* was a name given in Nahuatl to several mountains, these being the congelations of the Earth Mother at spots convenient for her worship." The Mexica considered the mountain mass southwest of Chapultepec to be their mother. Burr Cartwright Brundage, *The Fifth Sun: Aztec Gods, Aztec World* (Austin, TX: University of Texas Press, 1979), 154, 242.

[10] Ena Campbell, "The Virgin of Guadalupe and the Female Self-image: A Mexican

Case History," *Mother Worship: Themes and Variations,* James J. Preston, ed. (Chapel Hill, NC: University of North Carolina Press, 1982), 22.

[11] Alan R. Sandstrom, "The Tonantsi Cult of the Eastern Nahuas," *Mother Worship: Themes and Variations,* James J. Preston, ed.

[12] *Una tela tejida con asperas fibras de agave.* It is an oblong cloth that hangs over the back and ties together across the shoulders.

[13] Andres Gonzales Guerrero, Jr., *The Significance of Nuestra Señora de Guadalupe and La Raza Cósmica in the Development of a Chicano Theology of Liberation* (Ann Arbor, MI: University Microfilms International, 1984), 122.

[14] *Algunos dicen que Guadalupe es una palabra derivida del lenguaje arabe que significa "Río Oculto."* Tomie de Paola, *The Lady of Guadalupe* (New York, NY: Holiday House, 1980), 44.

[15] *"Desde el cielo una hermosa mañana,"* from *Propios de la misa de Nuestra Señora de Guadalupe,* Guerrero, 124.

[16] From *"La Virgen Ranchera,"* Guerrero, 127.

[17] *La Virgin María* is often equated with the Aztec *Teleoinam,* the Maya *Ixchel,* the Inca *Mamacocha,* and the Yoruba *Yemayá.*

[18] Geoffrey Parrinder, ed., *World Religions: From Ancient History to the Present* (New York, NY: Facts on File Publications, 1971), 72.

[19] Lévi-Strauss's paradigm which opposes nature to culture and female to male has no such validity in the early history of our Indian forebears. June Nash, "The Aztecs and the Ideology of Male Dominance," *Signs* (Winter, 1978), 349.

[20] Parrinder, 72.

[21] Parrinder, 77.

[22] Nash, 352.

[23] Nash, 350, 355.

[24] Parrinder, 355.

[25] Jacques Soustelle, *The Daily Life of the Aztecs on the Eve of the Spanish Conquest* (New York, NY: Macmillan Publishing Company, 1962). Soustelle and most other historians got their information from the Franciscan father, Bernardino de Sahagún, chief chronicler of Indian religious life.

[26] Nash, 252–253.

[27] Nash, 358.

[28] Nash, 361–362.

[29] Karl W. Luckert, *Olmec Religion: A Key to Middle America and Beyond* (Norman, OK: University of Oklahoma Press, 1976), 68, 69, 87, 109.

[30] Bernardino de Sahagún, *General History of the Things of New Spain* (Florentine Codex), Vol. I Revised, trans. Arthur Anderson and Charles Dibble (Sante Fe, NM: School of American Research, 1950), 11.

[31] The Aztecs muted Snake Woman's patronage of childbirth and vegetation by placing a sacrificial knife in the empty cradle she carried on her back (signifying a child who died in childbirth), thereby making her a devourer of sacrificial victims. Snake Woman had the ability to change herself into a serpent or into a lovely young woman to entice young men, who withered away and died after intercourse with her. She was known as a witch and a shape-shifter. Brundage, 168–171.

[32] Anthropologist Lucien Levy-Bruhl coined the word *participation mystique.* According to Jung, "It denotes a peculiar kind of psychological connection . . . [in which] the subject cannot clearly distinguish himself from the object but is bound to it by a direct relationship which amounts to partial identity." Carl Jung, "Definitions," in *Psychological Types, The Collected Works of C. G. Jung,* Vol. 6 (Princeton, NJ: Princeton University Press, 1953), par. 781.

[33] I have lost the source of this quote. If anyone knows what it is, please let the publisher know. [Author's note]

[34] Some *mexicanos* and Chicanos distinguish between *aire,* air, and *mal aigre,* the evil spirits which reside in the air.

# How to Tame a Wild Tongue

"We're going to have to control your tongue," the dentist says, pulling out all the metal from my mouth. Silver bits plop and tinkle into the basin. My mouth is a motherlode.

The dentist is cleaning out my roots. I get a whiff of the stench when I gasp. "I can't cap that tooth yet, you're still draining," he says.

"We're going to have to do something about your tongue," I hear the anger rising in his voice. My tongue keeps pushing out the wads of cotton, pushing back the drills, the long thin needles. "I've never seen anything as strong or as stubborn," he says. And I think, how do you tame a wild tongue, train it to be quiet, how do you bridle and saddle it? How do you make it lie down?

> Who is to say that robbing a people of
> its language is less violent than war?
> — RAY GWYN SMITH[1]

I remember being caught speaking Spanish at recess—that was good for three licks on the knuckles with a sharp ruler. I remember being sent to the corner of the classroom for "talking back" to the Anglo teacher when all I was trying to do was tell her how to pronounce my name. "If you want to be American, speak 'American.' If you don't like it, go back to Mexico where you belong."

"I want you to speak English. Pa' hallar buen trabajo tienes que saber hablar el inglés bien. Qué vale toda tu educación si todavía hablas inglés con un 'accent,'" my mother would say, mortified that I spoke English like a Mexican. At Pan American University, I and all Chicano students were required to take two speech classes. Their purpose: to get rid of our accents.

Attacks on one's form of expression with the intent to censor are a violation of the First Amendment. El Anglo con cara de inocente nos arrancó la lengua. Wild tongues can't be tamed, they can only be cut out.

## Overcoming the Tradition of Silence

*Ahogadas, escupimos el oscuro.*
*Peleando con nuestra propia sombra*
*el silencio nos sepulta.*

*En boca cerrada no entran moscas.* "Flies don't enter a closed mouth" is a saying I kept hearing when I was a child. *Ser habladora* was to be a gossip and a liar, to talk too much. *Muchachitas bien criadas,* well-bred girls don't answer back. *Es una falta de respeto* to talk back to one's mother or father. I remember one of the sins I'd recite to the priest in the confession box the few times I went to confession: talking back to my mother, *hablar pa' 'tras,*

36

*repelar. Hociocona, repelona, chismosa,* having a big mouth, questioning, carrying tales are all signs of being *mal criada.* In my culture they are all words that are derogatory if applied to women—I've never heard them applied to men.

The first time I heard two women, a Puerto Rican and a Cuban, say the word *"nosotras,"* I was shocked. I had not known the word existed. Chicanas use *nosotros* whether we're male or female. We are robbed of our female being by the masculine plural. Language is a male discourse.

> And our tongues have become
> dry        the wilderness has
> dried out our tongues        and
> we have forgotten speech.
> — IRENA KLEPFISZ[2]

Even our own people, other Spanish speakers *nos quieren poner candados en la boca.* They would hold us back with their bag of *reglas de academia.*

## Oyé como ladra: el lenguaje de la frontera

*Quien tiene boca se equivoca.*
– Mexican saying

*"Pocho,* cultural traitor, you're speaking the oppressor's language by speaking English, you're ruining the Spanish language," I have been accused by various Latinos and Latinas. Chicano Spanish is considered by the purist and by most Latinos deficient, a mutilation of Spanish.

But Chicano Spanish is a border tongue which developed naturally. Change, *evolución, enriquecimiento de palabras nuevas por invención o adopción* have created variants of Chicano Spanish, *un nuevo lenguaje. Un lenguaje que corresponde a un modo de vivir.* Chicano Spanish is not incorrect, it is a living language.

For a people who are neither Spanish nor live in a country in which Spanish is the first language; for a people who live in a country in which English is the reigning tongue but who are not Anglo; for a people who cannot entirely identify with either standard (formal, Castilian) Spanish nor standard English, what recourse is left to them but to create their own language? A language which they can connect their identity to, one capable of communicating the realities and values true to themselves—a language with terms that are neither *español ni inglés,* but both. We speak a patois, a forked tongue, a variation of two languages.

Chicano Spanish sprang out of the Chicanos' need to identify ourselves as a distinct people. We needed a language with which we could communicate with ourselves, a secret language. For some of us, language is a homeland closer than the Southwest—for many Chicanos today live in the Midwest and the East. And because we are a complex, heterogeneous people, we speak many languages. Some of the languages we speak are

1. Standard English
2. Working class and slang English
3. Standard Spanish
4. Standard Mexican Spanish
5. North Mexican Spanish dialect
6. Chicano Spanish (Texas, New Mexico, Arizona, and California have regional variations)
7. Tex-Mex
8. *Pachuco* (called *caló*)

My "home" tongues are the languages I speak with my sister and brothers, with my friends. They are the last five listed, with 6 and 7 being closest to my heart. From school, the media, and job situations, I've picked up standard and working class English. From Mamagrande Locha and from reading Spanish and Mexican literature, I've picked up Standard Spanish and Standard Mexican Spanish. From *los recién llegados*, Mexican immigrants, and *braceros*, I learned the North Mexican dialect. With Mexicans I'll try to speak either Standard Mexican Spanish or the North Mexican dialect. From my parents and Chicanos living in the Valley, I picked up Chicano Texas Spanish, and I speak it with my mom, younger brother (who married a Mexican and who rarely mixes Spanish with English), aunts, and older relatives.

With Chicanas from *Nuevo México* or *Arizona* I will speak Chicano Spanish a little, but often they don't understand what I'm saying. With most California Chicanas I speak entirely in English (unless I forget). When I first moved to San Francisco, I'd rattle off something in Spanish, unintentionally embarrassing them. Often it is only with another Chicana *tejano* that I can talk freely.

Words distorted by English are known as anglicisms or *pochismos*. The *pocho* is an anglicized Mexican or American of Mexican origin who speaks Spanish with an accent characteristic of North Americans and who distorts and reconstructs the language according to the influence of English.[3] Tex-Mex, or Spanglish, comes most naturally to me. I may switch back and forth from English to Spanish in the same sentence or in the same word. With my sister and my brother Nune and with Chicano *tejano* contemporaries I speak in Tex-Mex.

From kids and people my own age I picked up *Pachuco*. *Pachuco* (the language of the zoot suiters) is a language of rebellion, both against Standard Spanish and Standard English. It is a secret language. Adults of the culture and outsiders cannot understand it. It is made up of slang words from both English and Spanish. *Ruca* means girl or woman, *vato* means guy or dude, *chale* means no, *simón* means yes, *churro* is sure, talk is *periquiar, pigionear* means petting, *que gacho* means how nerdy, *ponte águila* means watch out, death is called *la pelona*. Through lack of practice and not having others who can speak it, I've lost most of the *Pachuco* tongue.

## Chicano Spanish

Chicanos, after 250 years of Spanish/Anglo colonization, have developed significant differences in the Spanish we speak. We collapse two adjacent vowels into a single syllable and sometimes shift the stress in certain words such as *maíz/maiz, cohete/cuete*. We leave out certain consonants when they appear between vowels: *lado/lao, mojado/mojao*. Chicanos from South Texas pronounce *f* as *j* as in *jue (fue)*. Chicanos use "archaisms," words that are no longer in the Spanish language, words that have been evolved out. We say *semos, truje, haiga, ansina*, and *naiden*. We retain the "archaic" *j*, as in *jalar*, that derives from an earlier *h* (the French *halar* or the Germanic *halon* which was lost to standard Spanish in the sixteenth century), but which is still found in several regional dialects such as the one spoken in South Texas. (Due to geography, Chicanos from the Valley of South Texas were cut off linguistically from other Spanish speakers. We tend to use words that the Spaniards brought over from Medieval Spain. The majority of the Spanish colonizers in Mexico and the Southwest came from Extremadura—Hernán Cortés was one of them—and Andalucía. Andalucians pronounce *ll* like a *y*, and their *d*'s tend to be absorbed by adjacent vowels: *tirado* becomes *tirao*. They brought *el lenguaje popular, dialectos y regionalismos*.)[4]

Chicanos and other Spanish speakers also shift *ll* to *y* and *z* to *s*.[5] We leave out initial syllables, saying *tar* for *estar, toy* for *estoy, hora* for *ahora* (*cubanos* and *puertorriqueños* also leave out initial letters of some words). We also leave out the final syllable such as *pa* for *para*. The intervocalic *y*, the *ll* as in *tortilla, ella, botella*, gets replaced by *tortia* or *toriya, ea, botea*. We add an additional syllable at the beginning of certain words: *atocar* for *tocar, agastar* for *gastar*. Sometimes we'll say *lavaste las vacijas*, other times *lavates* (substituting the *ates* verb endings for the *aste*).

We use anglicisms, words borrowed from English: *bola* from ball, *carpeta* from carpet, *máchina de lavar* (instead of *lavadora*) from washing machine. Tex-Mex argot, created by adding a Spanish sound at the beginning or end of an English word such as *cookiar* for cook, *watchar* for watch, *parkiar* for park, and *rapiar* for rape, is the result of the pressures on Spanish speakers to adapt to English.

We don't use the word *vosotros/as* or its accompanying verb form. We don't say *claro* (to mean yes), *imagínate*, or *me emociona*, unless we picked up Spanish from Latinas, out of a book, or in a classroom. Other Spanish-speaking groups are going through the same, or similar, development in their Spanish.

## Linguistic Terrorism

*Deslenguadas. Somos los del español deficiente.* We are your linguistic nightmare, your linguistic aberration, your linguistic *mestisaje*, the subject of your *burla*. Because we speak with tongues of fire we are culturally crucified. Racially, culturally, and linguistically *somos huérfanos*—we speak an orphan tongue.

Chicanas who grew up speaking Chicano Spanish have internalized the belief that we speak poor Spanish. It is illegitimate, a bastard language. And because we internalize how our language has been used against us by the dominant culture, we use our language differences against each other.

Chicana feminists often skirt around each other with suspicion and hesitation. For the longest time I couldn't figure it out. Then it dawned on me. To be close to another Chicana is like looking into the mirror. We are afraid of what we'll see there. *Pena.* Shame. Low estimation of self. In childhood we are told that our language is wrong. Repeated attacks on our native tongue diminish our sense of self. The attacks continue throughout our lives.

Chicanas feel uncomfortable talking in Spanish to Latinas, afraid of their censure. Their language was not outlawed in their countries. They had a whole lifetime of being immersed in their native tongue; generations, centuries in which Spanish was a first language, taught in school, heard on radio and TV, and read in the newspaper.

If a person, Chicana or Latina, has a low estimation of my native tongue, she also has a low estimation of me. Often with *mexicanas y latinas* we'll speak English as a neutral language. Even among Chicanas we tend to speak English at parties or conferences. Yet, at the same time, we're afraid the other will think we're *agringadas* because we don't speak Chicano Spanish. We oppress each other trying to out-Chicano each other, vying to be the "real" Chicanas, to speak like Chicanos. There is no one Chicano language just as there is no one Chicano experience. A monolingual Chicana whose first language is English or Spanish is just as much a Chicana as one who speaks several variants of Spanish. A Chicana from Michigan or Chicago or Detroit is just as much a Chicana as one from the Southwest. Chicano Spanish is as diverse linguistically as it is regionally.

By the end of this century, Spanish speakers will comprise the biggest minority group in the United States, a country where students in high schools and colleges are encouraged to take French classes because French is considered more "cultured." But for a language to remain alive it must be used.[6] By the end of this century English, and not Spanish, will be the mother tongue of most Chicanos and Latinos.

So, if you want to really hurt me, talk badly about my language. Ethnic identity is twin skin to linguistic identity—I am my language. Until I can take pride in my language, I cannot take pride in myself. Until I can accept as legitimate Chicano Texas Spanish, Tex-Mex, and all the other languages I speak, I cannot accept the legitimacy of myself. Until I am free to write bilingually and to switch codes without having always to translate, while I still have to speak English or Spanish when I would rather speak Spanglish, and as long as I have to accommodate the English speaker rather than having them accommodate me, my tongue will be illegitimate.

I will no longer be made to feel ashamed of existing. I will have my voice: Indian, Spanish, white. I will have my serpent's tongue—my woman's voice, my sexual voice, my poet's voice. I will overcome the tradition of silence.

> My fingers
> move sly against your palm
> Like women everywhere, we speak in code. . . .
>               — MELANIE KAYE/KANTROWITZ[7]

## "Vistas," corridos, y comida:
## My Native Tongue

In the 1960s, I read my first Chicano novel. It was *City of Night* by John Rechy, a gay Texan, son of a Scottish father and a Mexican mother. For days I walked around in stunned amazement that a Chicano could write and could get published. When I read *I Am Joaquín*[8] I was surprised to see a bilingual book by a Chicano in print. When I saw poetry written in Tex-Mex for the first time, a feeling of pure joy flashed through me. I felt like we really existed as a people. In 1971, when I started teaching High School English to Chicano students, I tried to supplement the required texts with works by Chicanos, only to be reprimanded and forbidden to do so by the principal. He claimed that I was supposed to teach "American" and English literature. At the risk of being fired, I swore my students to secrecy and slipped in Chicano short stories, poems, a play. In graduate school, while working toward a Ph.D., I had to "argue" with one adviser after the other, semester after semester, before I was allowed to make Chicano literature an area of focus.

Even before I read books by Chicanos or Mexicans, it was the Mexican movies I saw at the drive-in—the Thursday night special of $1.00 a carload—that gave me a sense of belonging. *"Vámonos a las vistas,"* my mother would call out and we'd all—grandmother, brothers, sister, and cousins—squeeze into the car. We'd wolf down cheese and bologna white bread sandwiches while watching Pedro Infante in melodramatic tearjerkers like *Nosotros los pobres*, the first "real" Mexican movie (that was not an imitation of European movies). I remember seeing *Cuando los hijos se van* and surmising that all Mexican movies played up the love a mother has for her children and what ungrateful sons and daughters suffer when they are not devoted to their mothers. I remember the singing-type "westerns" of Jorge Negrete and Miquel Aceves Mejía. When watching Mexican movies, I felt a sense of homecoming as well as alienation. People who were to amount to something didn't go to Mexican movies, or *bailes*, or tune their radios to *bolero, rancherita*, and *corrido* music.

The whole time I was growing up, there was *norteño* music sometimes called North Mexican border music, or Tex-Mex music, or Chicano music, or *cantina* (bar) music. I grew up listening to *conjuntos*, three- or four-piece bands made up of folk musicians playing guitar, *bajo sexto*, drums, and button accordion, which Chicanos had borrowed from the German immigrants who had come to Central Texas and Mexico to farm and build breweries. In the Rio Grande Valley, Steven Jordan and Little Joe Hernández were popular, and Flaco Jiménez was the accordion king. The rhythms of Tex-Mex music are those of the polka, also adapted from the Germans, who in turn had borrowed the polka from the Czechs and Bohemians.

I remember the hot, sultry evenings when *corridos*—song of love and death on the Texas-Mexican borderlands—reverberated out of cheap amplifiers from the local *cantinas* and wafted in through my bedroom window.

*Corridos* first became widely used along the South Texas/Mexican border during the early conflict between Chicanos and Anglos. The *corridos* are usually about Mexican heroes who do valiant deeds against the Anglo oppressors. Pancho Villa's song, *"La cucaracha,"* is the most famous one. *Corridos* of John F. Kennedy and his death are still very popular in the Valley. Older Chicanos remember Lydia Mendoza, one of the great border *corrido* singers who was called *la Gloria de Tejas*. Her *"El tango negro,"* sung during the Great Depression, made her a singer of the people. The ever-present *corridos* narrated one hundred years of border history, bringing news of events as well as entertaining. These folk musicians and folk songs are our chief cultural mythmakers, and they made our hard lives seem bearable.

I grew up feeling ambivalent about our music. Country-western and rock-and-roll had more status. In the fifties and sixties, for the slightly educated and *agringado* Chicanos, there existed a sense of shame at being caught listening to our music. Yet I couldn't stop my feet from thumping to the music, could not stop humming the words, nor hide from myself the exhilaration I felt when I heard it.

There are more subtle ways that we internalize identification, especially in the forms of images and emotions. For me food and certain smells are tied to my identity, to my homeland. Woodsmoke curling up to an immense blue sky; woodsmoke perfuming my grandmother's clothes, her skin. The stench of cow manure and the yellow patches on the ground; the crack of a .22 rifle and the reek of cordite. Homemade white cheese sizzling in a pan, melting inside a folded *tortilla*. My sister Hilda's hot, spicy *menudo, chile colorado* making it deep red, pieces of *panza* and hominy floating on top. My brother Carito barbequing *fajitas* in the backyard. Even now and 3,000 miles away, I can see my mother spicing the ground beef, pork, and venison with *chile*. My mouth salivates at the thought of the hot steaming *tamales* I would be eating if I were home.

## Si le preguntas a mi mamá, "¿Qué eres?"

> Identity is the essential core of who
> we are as individuals, the conscious
> experience of the self inside.
> — GERSHEN KAUFMAN[9]

*Nosotros los* Chicanos straddle the borderlands. On one side of us, we are constantly exposed to the Spanish of the Mexicans, on the other side we hear the Anglos' incessant clamoring so that we forget our language. Among ourselves we don't say *nosotros los americanos, o nosotros los españoles, o nosotros los hispanos*. We say *nosotros los mexicanos* (by *mexicanos* we do not mean citizens of Mexico; we do not mean a national identity, but a racial one). We distinguish between *mexicanos del otro lado* and *mexicanos de este lado*. Deep in our hearts we believe that being Mexican has nothing to do with which country one lives in. Being Mexican is a state of soul—not one of mind, not one of citizenship. Neither eagle nor serpent, but both. And like the ocean, neither animal respects borders.

> *Dime con quien andas y te diré quien eres.*
> (Tell me who your friends are and I'll tell you who you are.)
> — Mexican saying

*Si le preguntas a mi mamá, "¿Qué eres?" te dirá, "Soy mexicana."* My brothers and sister say the same. I sometimes will answer *"soy mexicana"* and at others will say *"soy Chicana" o "soy tejana."* But I identified as *"Raza"* before I ever identified as *"mexicana"* or "Chicana."

As a culture, we call ourselves Spanish when referring to ourselves as a linguistic group and when copping out. It is then that we forget our predominant Indian genes. We are 70–80 percent Indian.[10] We call ourselves Hispanic[11] or Spanish-American or Latin American or Latin when linking ourselves to other Spanish-speaking peoples of the Western hemisphere and when copping out. We call ourselves Mexican-American[12] to signify we are neither Mexican nor American, but more the noun "American" than the adjective "Mexican" (and when copping out).

Chicanos and other people of color suffer economically for not acculturating. This voluntary (yet forced) alienation makes for psychological conflict, a kind of dual identity—we don't identify with the Anglo-American cultural values and we don't totally identify with the Mexican cultural values. We are a synergy of two cultures with various degrees of Mexicanness or Angloness. I have so internalized the borderland conflict that sometimes I feel like one cancels out the other and we are zero, nothing, no one. *A veces no soy nada ni nadie. Pero hasta cuando no lo soy, lo soy.*

When not copping out, when we know we are more than nothing, we call ourselves Mexican, referring to race and ancestry; *mestizo* when affirming both our Indian and Spanish (but we hardly ever own our Black) ancestry; Chicano when referring to a politically aware people born and/or raised in the United States; *Raza* when referring to Chicanos; *tejanos* when we are Chicanos from Texas.

Chicanos did not know we were a people until 1965 when Cesar Chavez and the farmworkers united and *I Am Joaquín* was published and *la Raza Unida* party was formed in Texas. With that recognition, we became a distinct people. Something momentous happened to the Chicano soul—we became aware of our reality and acquired a name and a language (Chicano Spanish) that reflected that reality. Now that we had a name, some of the fragmented pieces began to fall together—who we were, what we were, how we had evolved. We began to get glimpses of what we might eventually become.

Yet the struggle of identities continues, the struggle of borders is our reality still. One day the inner struggle will cease and a true integration take place. In the meantime, *tenémos que hacer la lucha. ¿Quién está protegiendo los ranchos de mi gente? ¿Quién está tratando de cerrar la fisura entre la india y el blanco en nuestra sangre? El Chicano, si, el Chicano que anda como un ladrón en su propia casa.*

*Los Chicanos*, how patient we seem, how very patient. There is the quiet of the Indian about us.[13] We know how to survive. When other races have given up their tongue we've kept ours. We know what it is to live under the hammer blow of the dominant *norteamericano* culture. But more than we count the blows, we count the days the weeks the years the centuries the aeons until the white laws and commerce and customs will rot in the deserts they've created, lie bleached. *Humildes* yet proud, *quietos* yet wild, *nosotros los mexicanos-Chicanos* will walk by the crumbling ashes as we go about our business. Stubborn, persevering, impenetrable as stone, yet possessing a malleability that renders us unbreakable, we, the *mestizas* and *mestizos*, will remain.

## NOTES

[1] Ray Gwyn Smith, *Moorland Is Cold Country*, unpublished book.

[2] Irena Klepfisz, "*Di rayze aheym*/The Journey Home," in *The Tribe of Dina: A Jewish Women's Anthology*, Melanie Kaye/Kantrowitz and Irena Klepfisz, eds. (Montpelier, VT: Sinister Wisdom Books, 1986), 49.

[3] R. C. Ortega, *Dialectología Del Barrio*, trans. Hortencia S. Alwan (Los Angeles, CA: R. C. Ortega Publisher & Bookseller, 1977), 132.

[4] Eduardo Hernandéz-Chávez, Andrew D. Cohen, and Anthony F. Beltramo, *El Lenguaje de los Chicanos: Regional and Social Characteristics of Language Used by Mexican Americans* (Arlington, VA: Center for Applied Linguistics, 1975), 39.

[5] Hernandéz-Chávez, xvii.

[6] Irena Klepfisz, "Secular Jewish Identity: Yidishkayt in America," in *The Tribe of Dina*, Kaye/Kantrowitz and Klepfisz, eds., 43.

[7] Melanie Kaye/Kantrowitz, "Sign," in *We Speak in Code: Poems and Other Writings* (Pittsburgh, PA: Motheroot Publications, Inc., 1980), 85.

[8] Rodolfo Gonzales, *I Am Joaquín/Yo Soy Joaquín* (New York, NY: Bantam Books, 1972). It was first published in 1967.

[9] Gershen Kaufman, *Shame: The Power of Caring* (Cambridge, MA: Schenkman Books, Inc., 1980), 68.

[10] John R. Chávez, *The Lost Land: The Chicano Images of the Southwest* (Albuquerque, NM: University of New Mexico Press, 1984), 88–90.

[11] "Hispanic" is derived from *Hispanis* (*España*, a name given to the Iberian Peninsula in ancient times when it was a part of the Roman Empire) and is a term designated by the U.S. government to make it easier to handle us on paper.

[12] The Treaty of Guadalupe Hidalgo created the Mexican-American in 1848.

[13] Anglos, in order to alleviate their guilt for dispossessing the Chicano, stressed the Spanish part of us and perpetrated the myth of the Spanish Southwest. We have accepted the fiction that we are Hispanic, that is Spanish, in order to accommodate ourselves to the dominant culture and its abhorrence of Indians. Chávez, 88–91.

●  ●  ●  ●  ●  ●  ●  ●  ●  ●  ●  ●

## QUESTIONS FOR A SECOND READING

1. The most immediate challenge to many readers of these chapters will be the sections that are written in Spanish. Part of the point of a text that mixes languages is to give non-Spanish-speaking readers the feeling of being lost, excluded, left out. What is a reader to do with this prose? One could learn Spanish and come back to reread, but this is not a quick solution and, according to Anzaldúa, not even a completely satisfactory one, since some of her Spanish is drawn from communities of speakers not represented in textbooks and classes.

   So how do you read this text if you don't read Spanish? Do you ignore the words? sound them out? improvise? Anzaldúa gives translations of some words or phrases, but not all. Which ones does she translate? Why? Reread these chapters with the goal of explaining how you handled Anzaldúa's polyglot style.

2. These chapters are made up of shorter sections written in a variety of styles (some as prose poems, some with endnotes, some as stories). And, while the sections are obviously ordered, the order is not a conventional argumentative one. The text is, as Anzaldúa says elsewhere in her book, "an assemblage, a montage, a beaded work, . . . a crazy dance":

   > In looking at this book that I'm almost finished writing, I see a mosaic pattern (Aztec-like) emerging, a weaving pattern, thin here, thick there. . . . This almost finished product seems an assemblage, a montage, a beaded work with several leitmotifs and with a central core, now appearing, now disappearing in a crazy dance. The whole thing has had a mind of its own, escaping me and insisting on putting together the pieces of its own puzzle with minimal direction from my will. It is a rebellious, willful entity, a precocious girl-child forced to grow up too quickly, rough, unyielding, with pieces of feather sticking out here and there, fur, twigs, clay. My child, but not for much longer. This female being is angry, sad, joyful, is Coatlicue, dove, horse, serpent, cactus. Though it is

a flawed thing—clumsy, complex, groping, blind thing, for me it is alive, infused with spirit. I talk to it; it talks to me.

This is not, in other words, a conventional text; it makes unexpected demands on a reader. As you reread, mark sections you could use to talk about how, through the text, Anzaldúa invents a reader and/or a way of reading. Who is Anzaldúa's ideal reader? What does he or she need to be able to do?

3. Although Anzaldúa's text is not a conventional one, it makes an argument and proposes terms and examples for its readers to negotiate. How might you summarize Anzaldúa's argument in these two chapters? How do the individual chapters mark stages or parts of her argument? How might you explain the connections between the chapters? As you reread this selection, mark those passages where Anzaldúa seems to you to be creating a case or argument. What are its key terms? its key examples? its conclusions?


## ASSIGNMENTS FOR WRITING

1. Anzaldúa has described her text as a kind of crazy dance (see the second "Question for a Second Reading"); it is, she says, a text with a mind of its own, "putting together the pieces of its own puzzle with minimal direction from my will." Hers is a prose full of variety and seeming contradictions; it is a writing that could be said to represent the cultural "crossroads" which is her experience/sensibility.

As an experiment whose goal is the development of an alternate (in Anzaldúa's terms, a mixed or *mestiza*) understanding, write an autobiographical text whose shape and motives could be described in her terms: a mosaic, woven, with numerous overlays; a montage, a beaded work, a crazy dance, drawing on the various ways of thinking, speaking, understanding that might be said to be part of your own mixed cultural position, your own mixed sensibility.

To prepare for this essay, think about the different positions you could be said to occupy, the different voices that are part of your background or present, the competing ways of thinking that make up your points of view. Imagine that your goal is to present your world and your experience to those who are not necessarily prepared to be sympathetic or to understand. And, following Anzaldúa, you should work to construct a mixed text, not a single unified one. This will be hard, since you will be writing what might be called a "forbidden" text, one you have not been prepared to write.

2. In "*La conciencia de la mestiza*/Towards a New Consciousness," the last essaylike chapter in her book (the remaining chapters are made up of poems), Anzaldúa steps forward to define her role as writer and yours as reader. She says, among other things,

> Many women and men of color do not want to have any dealings with white people. . . . Many feel that whites should help their own people rid themselves of race hatred and fear first. I, for one, choose to use some of my energy to serve as mediator. I think we need to allow whites to be our allies. Through our literature, art, *corridos*, and folk-

tales we must share our history with them so when they set up committees to help Big Mountain Navajos or the Chicano farmworkers or *los Nicaragüenses* they won't turn people away because of their racial fears and ignorances. They will come to see that they are not helping us but following our lead.

Individually, but also as a racial entity, we need to voice our needs. We need to say to white society: We need you to accept the fact that Chicanos are different, to acknowledge your rejection and negation of us. We need you to own the fact that you looked upon us as less than human, that you stole our lands, our personhood, our self-respect. We need you to make public restitution: to say that, to compensate for your own sense of defectiveness, you strive for power over us, you erase our history and our experience because it makes you feel guilty—you'd rather forget your brutish acts. To say you've split yourself from minority groups, that you disown us, that your dual consciousness splits off parts of yourself, transferring the "negative" parts onto us. . . . To say that you are afraid of us, that to put distance between us, you wear the mask of contempt. Admit that Mexico is your double, that she exists in the shadow of this country, that we are irrevocably tied to her. Gringo, accept the doppelganger in your psyche. By taking back your collective shadow the intracultural split will heal. And finally, tell us what you need from us.

This is only a part of the text—one of the ways it defines the roles of reader and writer—but it is one that asks to be taken account of, with its insistent list of what a white reader must do and say. (Of course not every reader is white, and not all white readers are the same. What Anzaldúa is defining here is a "white" way of reading.)

Write an essay in which you tell a story of reading, the story of your work with the two chapters of *Borderlands/La Frontera* reprinted here. Think about where you felt at home with the text and where you felt lost, where you knew what you were doing and where you needed help; think about the position (or positions) you have taken as a reader and how it measures up against the ways Anzaldúa has figured you in the text, the ways she has anticipated a response, imagined who you are and how you habitually think and read.

3. In "How to Tame a Wild Tongue" (p. 36), Anzaldúa says, "I will no longer be made to feel ashamed of existing. I will have my voice: Indian, Spanish, white. I will have my serpent's tongue—my woman's voice, my sexual voice, my poet's voice." Anzaldúa speaks almost casually about "having her voice," not a single, "authentic" voice, but one she names in these terms: Indian, Spanish, white; woman, lesbian, poet. What is "voice" as defined by these chapters? Where does it come from? What does it have to do with the act of writing or the writer?

As you reread these chapters, mark those passages that you think best represent Anzaldúa's voices. Using these passages as examples, write an essay in which you discuss how these voices are different—both different from one another and different from a "standard" voice (as a "standard" voice is imagined by Anzaldúa). What do these voices represent? How do they figure in your reading? in her writing?

4. Anzaldúa's writing is difficult to categorize as an essay or a story or a poem; it has all of these within it. The writing may appear to have been just put together, but it is more likely that it was carefully crafted to

represent the various voices Anzaldúa understands to be a part of her. She speaks directly about her voices—her woman's voice, her sexual voice, her poet's voice; her Indian, Spanish, and white voices on page 41 of "How to Tame a Wild Tongue."

Following Anzaldúa, write an argument of your own, one that requires you to use a variety of voices, in which you carefully present the various voices that you feel are a part of you or a part of the argument.

When you have completed this assignment, write a two-page essay in which you explain why the argument you made might be worth a reader's attention.

## MAKING CONNECTIONS

1. In "Arts of the Contact Zone" (p. 582), Mary Louise Pratt talks about the "autoethnographic" text, "a text in which people undertake to describe themselves in ways that engage with representations others have made of them," and about "transculturation," the "processes whereby members of subordinated or marginal groups select and invent from materials transmitted by a dominant or metropolitan culture."

   Write an essay in which you present a reading of these two chapters as an example of an autoethnographic and/or transcultural text. You should imagine that you are writing to someone who is not familiar with either Pratt's argument or Anzaldúa's book. Part of your work, then, is to present Anzaldúa's text to readers who don't have it in front of them. You have the example of Pratt's reading of Guaman Poma's *New Chronicle and Good Government*. And you have her discussion of the "literate arts of the contact zone." Think about how Anzaldúa's text might be similarly read, and about how her text does and doesn't fit Pratt's description. Your goal should be to add an example to Pratt's discussion and to qualify it, to give her discussion a new twist or spin now that you have had a chance to look at an additional example.

2. Both Adrienne Rich in "When We Dead Awaken: Writing as Re-Vision" (p. 603) and Gloria Anzaldúa in these two chapters could be said to be writing about the same issues—writing, identity, gender, history. Both texts contain an argument; both, in their peculiar styles, enact an argument—they demonstrate how and why one might need to revise the usual ways of writing. Identify what you understand to be the key points, the key terms, and the key examples in each selection.

   Beginning with the passages you have identified, write an essay in which you examine the similarities and differences in these two texts. Look particularly for the differences, since they are harder to find and harder to explain. Consider the selections as marking different positions on writing, identity, politics, history. How might you account for these differences (if they represent more than the fact that different people are likely to differ)? How are these differences significant?

# PAUL
# AUSTER

*P*AUL AUSTER *(b. 1947) is one of the country's most surprising and productive
  writers. He is the author of eight novels, including the broadly acclaimed
"New York Trilogy":* City of Glass *(1985),* Ghosts *(1986), and* The Locked
Room *(1986);* In the Country of Last Things *(1987);* Leviathan *(1992) (awarded
the 1993 Prix Medicis Etranger); and* The Music of Chance *(1993) (nominated for
the 1991 PEN/Faulkner Award). He has written two memoirs,* The Invention of
Solitude *(1982) and* Hand to Mouth *(1997); several books of essays, including*
The Art of Hunger *(1992); many translations of French literature and philosophy;
and a collection of poems,* Disappearances *(1988). Auster wrote the screenplay for*
Smoke *(1995) and, with Wayne Wang, codirected the companion movie,* Blue in
the Face *(1995). His new movie, which he wrote and directed, is called* Lulu on the
Bridge *(1998). His work has been translated into twenty-two languages.*

*The selection that follows is the first half of* The Invention of Solitude, *a
work made up of two long essays, "Portrait of an Invisible Man" and "The Book
of Memory." Auster's father is at the center of the first; his son is at the center of
the second. Both are reflections on memory, history, and family.*

*In a 1987 interview Auster said of this book:*

> *I don't think of [*The Invention of Solitude*] as an autobiography so
> much as a meditation about certain questions, using myself as the*

*central character. The book is divided into two sections, which were written separately, with a gap of about a year between the two. The first, "Portrait of an Invisible Man," was written in response to my father's death. He simply dropped dead one day, unexpectedly, after being in perfect health, and the shock of it left me with so many unanswered questions about him that I felt I had no choice but to sit down and try to put something on paper. In the act of trying to write about him, I began to realize how problematical it is to presume to know anything about anyone else. While that piece is filled with specific details, it still seems to me not so much an attempt at biography but an exploration of how one might begin to speak about another person, and whether or not it is even possible.*

*Questions about the possibility of writing are at the center of "Portrait of an Invisible Man." Auster raises them directly at moments when he breaks from writing about his father to writing about writing. And they are at the center of "Portrait" as a work in prose. As you read it, you will see that Auster does not rely on the structure and logic of the usual straightforward narrative to represent his father's life. To do so would be to assume that coming to know a person, in this case his father, is a straightforward business. This narrative circles around, stops and starts; it resists the more conventional desire to achieve closure, to have a last word on the subject. Auster's is an unusual and at times difficult prose; it resists conventional storylines and serves rather as a means to experiment with other ways of thinking and knowing the past.*

# Portrait of an Invisible Man

*In searching out the truth be ready for the unexpected, for it is difficult to find and puzzling when you find it.*

— HERACLITUS

One day there is life. A man, for example, in the best of health, not even old, with no history of illness. Everything is as it was, as it will always be. He goes from one day to the next, minding his own business, dreaming only of the life that lies before him. And then, suddenly, it happens there is death. A man lets out a little sigh, he slumps down in his chair, and it is death. The suddenness of it leaves no room for thought, gives the mind no chance to seek out a word that might comfort it. We are left with nothing but death, the irreducible fact of our own mortality. Death after a long illness we can accept with resignation. Even accidental death we can ascribe to fate. But for a man to die of no apparent cause, for a man to die simply because he is a man, brings us so close to the invisible boundary between life and death that we no longer know which side we are on. Life becomes death, and it is as if this death has owned this life all along. Death without warning. Which is to say: life stops. And it can stop at any moment.

The news of my father's death came to me three weeks ago. It was Sunday morning, and I was in the kitchen preparing breakfast for my small son, Daniel. Upstairs my wife was still in bed, warm under the quilts, luxuriating in a few extra hours of sleep. Winter in the country: a world of silence, wood smoke, whiteness. My mind was filled with thoughts about the piece I had been writing the night before, and I was looking ahead to the afternoon when I would be able to get back to work. Then the phone rang. I knew instantly that there was trouble. No one calls at eight o'clock on a Sunday morning unless it is to give news that cannot wait. And news that cannot wait is always bad news.

I could not muster a single ennobling thought.

Even before we packed our bags and set out on the three hour drive to New Jersey, I knew that I would have to write about my father. I had no plan, had no precise idea of what this meant. I cannot even remember making a decision about it. It was simply there, a certainty, an obligation that began to impose itself on me the moment I was given the news. I thought: my father is gone. If I do not act quickly, his entire life will vanish along with him.

Looking back on it now, even from so short a distance as three weeks, I find this a rather curious reaction. I had always imagined that death would numb me, immobilize me with grief. But now that it had happened, I did not shed any tears, I did not feel as though the world had collapsed around me. In some strange way, I was remarkably prepared to accept this death, in spite of its suddenness. What disturbed me was something else, something unrelated to death or my response to it: the realization that my father had left no traces.

He had no wife, no family that depended on him, no one whose life would be altered by his absence. A brief moment of shock, perhaps, on the part of scattered friends, sobered as much by the thought of capricious death as by the loss of their friend, followed by a short period of mourning, and then nothing. Eventually, it would be as though he had never lived at all.

Even before his death he had been absent, and long ago the people closest to him had learned to accept this absence, to treat it as the fundamental quality of his being. Now that he was gone, it would not be difficult for the world to absorb the fact that he was gone forever. The nature of his life had prepared the world for his death—had been a kind of death by anticipation—and if and when he was remembered, it would be dimly, no more than dimly.

Devoid of passion, either for a thing, a person, or an idea, incapable or unwilling to reveal himself under any circumstances, he had managed to keep himself at a distance from life, to avoid immersion in the quick of things. He ate, he went to work, he had friends, he played tennis, and yet for all that he was not there. In the deepest, most unalterable sense, he was an invisible man. Invisible to others, and most likely invisible to himself as well. If, while he was alive, I kept looking for him, kept trying to find the father who was not there, now that he is dead I still feel as though I must go on looking for him. Death has not changed anything. The only difference is that I have run out of time.

For fifteen years he had lived alone. Doggedly, opaquely, as if immune to the world. He did not seem to be a man occupying space, but rather a block of impenetrable space in the form of a man. The world bounced off him, shattered against him, at times adhered to him—but it never got through. For fifteen years he haunted an enormous house, all by himself, and it was in that house that he died.

For a short while we had lived there as a family—my father, my mother, my sister, and I. After my parents were divorced, everyone dispersed: my mother began a new life, I went off to college, and my sister stayed with my mother until she, too, went off to school. Only my father remained. Because of a clause in the divorce agreement which stipulated that my mother still owned a share of the house and would be given half the proceeds whenever it was sold (which made my father reluctant to sell), or from some secret refusal to change his life (so as not to show the world that the divorce had affected him in a way he could not control), or simply from inertia, an emotional lethargy that prevented him from taking any action, he stayed on, living alone in a house that could have accommodated six or seven people.

It was an impressive place: old, solidly built, in the Tudor style, with leaded windows, a slate roof, and rooms of royal proportions. Buying it had been a big step for my parents, a sign of growing wealth. This was the best neighborhood in town, and although it was not a pleasant place to live (especially for children), its prestige outweighed its deadliness. Given the fact that he wound up spending the rest of his life in that house, it is ironic that my father at first resisted moving there. He complained about the price (a constant theme), and when at last he relented, it was with grudging bad humor. Even so, he paid in cash. All in one go. No mortgage, no monthly payments. It was 1959, and business was going well for him.

Always a man of habit, he would leave for work early in the morning, work hard all day, and then, when he came home (on those days he did not work late), take a short nap before dinner. Sometime during our first week in the new house, before we had properly moved in, he made a curious kind of mistake. Instead of driving home to the new house after work, he went directly to the old one, as he had done for years, parked his car in the driveway, walked into the house through the back door, climbed the stairs, entered the bedroom, lay down on the bed, and went to sleep. He slept for about an hour. Needless to say, when the new mistress of the house returned to find a strange man sleeping in her bed, she was a little surprised. But unlike Goldilocks, my father did not jump up and run away. The confusion was eventually settled, and everyone had a good laugh. Even today, it still makes me laugh. And yet, for all that, I cannot help regarding it as a pathetic story. It is one thing for a man to drive to his old house by mistake, but it is quite another, I think, for him not to notice that anything has changed inside it. Even the most tired or distracted mind has a corner of pure, animal response, and can give the body a sense of where it is. One would have to be nearly unconscious not to see, or at least not to feel, that the house was no longer the same. "Habit," as one of Beckett's characters says, "is a great deadener." And if the mind is unable to respond to the physical evidence, what will it do when confronted with the emotional evidence?

During those last fifteen years he changed almost nothing in the house. He did not add any furniture, he did not remove any furniture. The walls remained the same color, the pots and pans were not replaced, even my mother's dresses were not thrown out—but stored away in an attic closet. The very size of the house absolved him from having to make any decisions about the things it contained. It was not that he was clinging to the past, trying to preserve the house as a museum. On the contrary, he seemed to be unaware of what he was doing. It was negligence that governed him, not memory, and even though he went on living in that house all those years, he lived in it as a stranger might have. As the years went by, he spent less and less time there. He ate nearly all his meals in restaurants, arranged his social calendar so as to be busy every night, and used the house as little more than a place to sleep. Once, several years ago, I happened to mention to him how much money I had earned from my writing and translating during the previous year (a pittance by any standard, but more than I had ever made before), and his amused response was that he spent more than that just on eating out. The point is: his life was not centered around the place where he lived. His house was just one of many stopping places in a restless, unmoored existence, and this lack of center had the effect of turning him into a perpetual outsider, a tourist of his own life. You never had the feeling that he could be located.

Still, the house seems important to me, if only to the extent that it was neglected—symptomatic of a state of mind that, otherwise inaccessible, manifested itself in the concrete images of unconscious behavior. The house became the metaphor of my father's life, the exact and faithful representation of his inner world. For although he kept the house tidy and preserved it more or less as it had been, it underwent a gradual and ineluctable process of disintegration. He was neat, he always put things back in their proper place, but nothing was cared for, nothing was ever cleaned. The furniture, especially in the rooms he rarely visited, was covered with dust, cobwebs, the signs of total neglect; the kitchen stove was so encrusted with charred food that it had become unsalvageable; in the cupboard, sometimes languishing on the shelves for years: bug-infested packages of flour, stale crackers, bags of sugar that had turned into solid blocks, bottles of syrup that could no longer be opened. Whenever he prepared a meal for himself, he would immediately and assiduously do the dishes—but rinse them only, never using soap, so that every cup, every saucer, every plate was coated with a film of dingy grease. Throughout the house: the window shades, which were kept drawn at all times, had become so threadbare that the slightest tug would pull them apart. Leaks sprang and stained the furniture, the furnace never gave off enough heat, the shower did not work. The house became shabby, depressing to walk into. You felt as if you were entering the house of a blind man.

His friends and family, sensing the madness of the way he lived in that house, kept urging him to sell it and move somewhere else. But he always managed to ward them off with a non-committal "I'm happy here," or "The house suits me fine." In the end, however, he did decide to move. At the very end. In the last phone conversation we ever had, ten days before he died, he told me the house had been sold and that the closing was set for February first, about three weeks away. He wanted to know if there was anything in the house I could use, and I agreed to come down for a visit with my wife and Daniel on the first free day that opened up. He died before we had a chance to make it.


There is nothing more terrible, I learned, than having to face the objects of a dead man. Things are inert: they have meaning only in function of the life that makes use of them. When that life ends, the things change, even though they remain the same. They are there and yet not there: tangible ghosts, condemned to survive in a world they no longer belong to. What is one to think, for example, of a closetful of clothes waiting silently to be worn again by a man who will not be coming back to open the door? Or the stray packets of condoms strewn among brimming drawers of underwear and socks? Or an electric razor sitting in the bathroom, still clogged with the whisker dust of the last shave? Or a dozen empty tubes of hair coloring hidden away in a leather travelling case?—suddenly revealing things one has no desire to see, no desire to know. There is a poignancy to it, and also a kind of horror. In themselves, the things mean nothing, like the cooking utensils of some vanished civilization. And yet they say something to us, standing there not as objects but as remnants of thought, of consciousness, emblems of the solitude in which a man comes to make decisions about himself: whether to color his hair, whether to wear this or that shirt, whether to live, whether to die. And the futility of it all once there is death.

Each time I opened a drawer or poked my head into a closet, I felt like an intruder, a burglar ransacking the secret places of a man's mind. I kept expecting my father to walk in, to stare at me in disbelief, and ask me what the hell I thought I was doing. It didn't seem fair that he couldn't protest. I had no right to invade his privacy.

A hastily scrawled telephone number on the back of a business card that read: H. Limeburg—Garbage Cans of All Descriptions. Photographs of my parents' honeymoon in Niagara Falls, 1946: my mother sitting nervously on top of a bull for one of those funny shots that are never funny, and a sudden sense of how unreal the world has always been, even in its prehistory. A drawer full of hammers, nails, and more then twenty screwdrivers. A filing cabinet stuffed with cancelled checks from 1953 and the cards I received for my sixth birthday. And then, buried at the bottom of a drawer in the bathroom: the monogrammed toothbrush that had once belonged to my mother and which had not been touched or looked at for more than fifteen years.

The list is inexhaustible.


It soon became apparent to me that my father had done almost nothing to prepare himself for his departure. The only signs of the impending move I could detect in the whole house were a few cartons of books—trivial books (out of date atlases, a fifty-year-old introduction to electronics, a high school Latin grammar, ancient law books) that he had been planning to give away to charity. Other than that, nothing. No empty boxes waiting to be filled. No pieces of furniture given away or sold. No arrangements made with a moving company. It was as though he had not been able to face it. Rather than empty the house, he had simply willed himself to die. Death was a way out, the only legitimate escape.

There was no escape for me, however. The thing had to be done, and there was no one else to do it. For ten days I went through his things, cleared out the house, got it ready for the new owners. It was a miserable time, but also an oddly humorous time, a time of reckless and absurd decisions: sell it, throw it out, give it away. My wife and I bought a big wooden slide for eighteen-month-old Daniel and set it up in the living room. He thrived on the chaos: rummaging among the things, putting lampshades on his head, flinging plastic poker chips around the house, running through the vast spaces of the gradually emptying rooms. At night my wife and I would lie under monolithic quilts watching trashy movies on television. Until the television, too, was given away. There was trouble with the furnace, and if I forgot to fill it with water, it would shut off. One morning we woke up to find that the temperature in the house had dropped to forty degrees. Twenty times a day the phone rang, and twenty times a day I told someone that my father was dead. I had become a furniture salesman, a moving man, a messenger of bad tidings.

The house began to resemble the set for a trite comedy of manners. Relatives swooped in, asking for this piece of furniture or that piece of dinnerware, trying on my father's suits, overturning boxes, chattering away like geese. Auctioneers came to examine the merchandise ("Nothing upholstered, it's not worth a nickel"), turned up their noses, and walked out. Garbage men clumped in with heavy boots and hauled off mountains of trash. The water man read the water meter, the gas man read the gas meter, the oil men read the oil gauge. (One of them, I forget which, who had been given a lot of trouble by my father over the years, said to me with savage complicity, "I don't like to say this"—meaning he did—"but your father was an obnoxious bastard.") The real estate agent came to buy some furniture for the new owners and wound up taking a mirror for herself. A woman who ran a curio shop bought my mother's old hats. A junkman came with a team of assistants (four black men named Luther, Ulysses, Tommy Pride, and Joe Sapp) and carted away everything from a set of barbels to a broken toaster. By the time it was over, nothing was left. Not even a postcard. Not even a thought.

If there was a single worst moment for me during those days, it came when I walked across the front lawn in the pouring rain to dump an armful of my father's ties into the back of a Good Will Mission truck. There must have been more than a hundred ties, and many of them I remembered from my childhood: the patterns, the colors, the shapes that had been embedded in my earliest consciousness, as clearly as my father's face had been. To see myself throwing them away like so much junk was intolerable to me, and it was then, at the precise instant I tossed them into the truck, that I came closest to tears. More than seeing the coffin itself being lowered into the ground, the act of throwing away these ties seemed to embody for me the idea of burial. I finally understood that my father was dead.

Yesterday one of the neighborhood children came here to play with Daniel. A girl of about three and a half who has recently learned that big people were once children, too, and that even her own mother and father have parents. At one point she picked up the telephone and launched into a pretend conversation, then turned to me and said, "Paul, it's your father. He wants to talk to you." It was gruesome. I thought: there's a ghost at the other end of the line, and he really does want to talk to me. It was a few moments before I could speak. "No," I finally blurted out. "It can't be my father. He wouldn't be calling today. He's somewhere else."

I waited until she had hung up the phone and then walked out of the room.

• • •

In his bedroom closet I had found several hundred photographs—stashed away in faded manila envelopes, affixed to the black pages of warped albums, scattered loosely in drawers. From the way they had been stored I gathered he never looked at them, had even forgotten they were there. One very big album, bound in expensive leather with a gold-stamped title on the cover—This is Our Life: The Austers—was totally blank inside. Someone, probably my mother, had once gone to the trouble of ordering this album, but no one had ever bothered to fill it.

Back home, I pored over these pictures with a fascination bordering on mania. I found them irresistible, precious, the equivalent of holy relics. It seemed that they could tell me things I had never known before, reveal some previously hidden truth, and I studied each one intensely, absorbing the least detail, the most insignificant shadow, until all the images had become a part of me. I wanted nothing to be lost.

Death takes a man's body away from him. In life, a man and his body are synonymous; in death, there is the man and there is his body. We say, "This is the body of X," as if this body, which had once been the man himself, not something that represented him or belonged to him, but the very man called X, were suddenly of no importance. When a man walks into a room and you shake hands with him, you do not feel that you are shaking hands with his hand, or shaking hands with his body, you are shaking hands with *him*. Death changes that. This is the body of X, not this is X. The syntax is entirely different. Now we are talking about two things instead of one, implying that the man continues to exist, but only as an idea, a cluster of images and memories in the minds of other people. As for the body, it is no more than flesh and bones, a heap of pure matter.

Discovering these photographs was important to me because they seemed to reaffirm my father's physical presence in the world, to give me the illusion that he was still there. The fact that many of these pictures were ones I had never seen before, especially the ones of his youth, gave me the odd sensation that I was meeting him for the first time, that a part of him was only just beginning to exist. I had lost my father. But at the same time, I had also found him. As long as I kept these pictures before my eyes, as long as I continued to study them with my complete attention, it was as though he were still alive, even in death. Or if not alive, at least not dead. Or rather, somehow suspended, locked in a universe that had nothing to do with death, in which death could never make an entrance.

Most of these pictures did not tell anything new, but they helped to fill in gaps, confirm impressions, offer proof where none had existed before. A series of snapshots of him as a bachelor, for example, probably taken over a number of years, gives a precise account of certain aspects of his personality that had been submerged during the years of his marriage, a side of him I did not begin to see until after his divorce: my father as prankster, as man about town, as good time Charlie. In picture after picture he is standing with women, usually two or three, all of them affecting comical poses, their arms perhaps around each other, or two of them sitting on his lap, or else a theatrical kiss for the benefit of no one but the person taking the picture. In the background: a mountain, a tennis court, perhaps a swimming pool or a log cabin. These were the pictures brought back from weekend jaunts to various Catskill resorts in the company of his bachelor friends: play tennis, have a good time with the girls. He carried on in this way until he was thirty-four.

It was a life that suited him, and I can see why he went back to it after his marriage broke up. For a man who finds life tolerable only by staying on the surface of himself, it is natural to be satisfied with offering no more than this surface to others. There are few demands to be met, and no commitment is required. Marriage, on the other hand, closes the door. Your existence is confined to a narrow space in which you are constantly forced to reveal yourself—and therefore, constantly obliged to look into yourself, to examine your own depths. When the door is open there is never any problem: you can always escape. You can avoid unwanted confrontations, either with yourself or with another, simply by walking away.

My father's capacity for evasion was almost limitless. Because the domain of the other was unreal to him, his incursions into that domain were made with a part of himself he considered to be equally unreal, another self he had trained as an actor to represent him in the empty comedy of the world-at-large. This surrogate self was essentially a tease, a hyperactive child, a fabricator of tall tales. It could not take anything seriously.

Because nothing mattered, he gave himself the freedom to do anything he wanted (sneaking into tennis clubs, pretending to be a restaurant critic in order to get a free meal), and the charm he exercised to make his conquests was precisely what made these conquests meaningless. With the vanity of a woman he hid the truth about his age, made up stories about his business dealings, talked about himself only obliquely—in the third person, as if about an acquaintance of his ("There's a friend of mine who has this problem; what do you think he should do about it? . . ."). Whenever a situation became too tight for him, whenever he felt pushed to the verge of having to reveal himself, he would wriggle out of it by telling a lie. Eventually, the lie came automatically and was indulged in for its own sake. The principle was to say as little as possible. If people never learned the truth about him, then they couldn't turn around and use it against him later. The lie was a way of buying protection. What people saw when he appeared before them, then, was not really him, but a person he had invented, an artificial creature he could manipulate in order to manipulate others. He himself remained invisible, a puppeteer working the strings of his alter-ego from a dark, solitary place behind the curtain.

For the last ten or twelve years of his life he had one steady lady friend, and this was the woman who went out with him in public, who played the role of official companion. Every now and then there was some vague talk of marriage (at her insistence), and everyone assumed that this was the only woman he had anything to do with. After his death, however, other women began to step forward. This one had loved him, that one had worshipped him, another one was going to marry him. The principal girl friend was shocked to learn about these other women: my father had never breathed a word about them to her. Each one had been fed a different line, and each one thought she had possessed him entirely. As it turned out, none of them knew the slightest thing about him. He had managed to elude them all.

Solitary. But not in the sense of being alone. Not solitary in the way Thoreau was, for example, exiling himself in order to find out where he was; not solitary in the way Jonah was, praying for deliverance in the belly of the whale. Solitary in the sense of retreat. In the sense of not having to see himself, of not having to see himself being seen by anyone else.

Talking to him was a trying experience. Either he would be absent, as he usually was, or he would assault you with a brittle jocularity, which was merely another form of absence. It was like trying to make yourself understood by a senile old man. You talked, and there would be no response, or a response that was inappropriate, showing that he hadn't been following the drift of your words. In recent years, whenever I spoke to him on the phone I would find myself saying more than I normally do, becoming aggressively talkative, chatting away in a futile attempt to hold his attention, to provoke a response. Afterwards, I would invariably feel foolish for having tried so hard.

He did not smoke, he did not drink. No hunger for sensual pleasures, no thirst for intellectual pleasures. Books bored him, and it was the rare movie or play that did not put him to sleep. Even at parties you would see him struggling to keep his eyes open, and more often than not he would succumb, falling asleep in a chair as the conversations swirled around him. A man without appetites. You felt that nothing could ever intrude on him, that he had no need of anything the world had to offer.

At thirty-four, marriage. At fifty-two, divorce. In one sense, it lasted years, but in fact it did not last more than a few days. He was never a married man, never a divorced man, but a life-long bachelor who happened to have had an interlude of marriage. Although he did not shirk his outward duties as a husband (he was faithful, he provided for his wife and children, he shouldered all his responsibilities), it was clear that he was not cut out to play this role. He simply had no talent for it.

My mother was just twenty-one when she married him. His conduct during the brief courtship had been chaste. No daring overtures, none of the aroused male's breathless assaults. Now and then they would hold hands, exchange a polite good-night kiss. Love, in so many words, was never declared by either one of them. By the time the wedding came, they were little more than strangers.

It was not long before my mother realized her mistake. Even before the honeymoon was over (that honeymoon, so fully documented in the photographs I found: the two of them sitting together, for instance, on a rock at the edge of a perfectly still lake, a broad path of sunlight behind them leading to the pine slope in shadow, my father with his arms around my mother, and the two of them looking at each other, smiling timidly, as if the photographer had made them hold the pose an instant too long), even before the honeymoon was over, my mother knew the marriage would not work. She went to her mother in tears and said she wanted to leave him. Somehow, her mother managed to persuade her to go back and give it a chance. And then, before the dust had settled, she found herself pregnant. And suddenly it was too late to do anything.

I think of it sometimes: how I was conceived in that Niagara Falls resort for honeymooners. Not that it matters where it happened. But the thought of what must have been a passionless embrace, a blind, dutiful groping between chilly hotel sheets, has never failed to humble me into an awareness of my own contingency. Niagara Falls. Or the hazard of two bodies joining. And then me, a random homunculus, like some dare-devil in a barrel, shooting over the falls.

A little more than eight months later, on the morning of her twenty-second birthday, my mother woke up and told my father that the baby was coming. Ridiculous, he said, that baby's not due for another three weeks—and promptly went off to work, leaving her without a car.

She waited. Thought maybe he was right. Waited a little more, then called a sister-in-law and asked to be driven to the hospital. My aunt stayed with my mother throughout the day, calling my father every few hours to ask him to come. Later, he would say, I'm busy now, I'll get there when I can.

At a little past midnight I poked my way into the world, ass first, no doubt screaming.

My mother waited for my father to show up, but he did not arrive until the next morning—accompanied by his mother, who wanted to inspect grandchild number seven. A short, nervous visit, and then off again to work.

She cried, of course. After all, she was young, and she had not expected it to mean so little to him. But he could never understand such things. Not in the beginning, and not in the end. It was never possible for him to be where he was. For as long as he lived, he was somewhere else, between here and there. But never really here. And never really there.

Thirty years later, this same little drama was repeated. This time I was there, and I saw it with my own eyes.

After my own son was born I had thought: surely this will please him. Isn't every man pleased to become a grandfather?

I had wanted to see him doting on the baby, for him to offer me proof that he was, after all, capable of demonstrating some feeling—that he did, after all, have feelings in the way other people did. And if he could show affection for his grandson, then wouldn't it be an indirect way of showing affection for me? You do not stop hungering for your father's love, even after you are grown up.

But then, people do not change. All told, my father saw his grandson only three or four times, and at no time was he able to distinguish him from the impersonal mass of babies born into the world everyday. Daniel was just two weeks old when he first laid eyes on him. I can remember the day vividly: a blistering Sunday at the end of June, heat wave weather, the country air gray with moisture. My father pulled up in his car, saw my wife putting the baby into the carriage for a nap, and walked over to say hello. He poked his head into the carriage for a tenth of a second, straightened up and said to her, "A beautiful baby. Good luck with it," and then proceeded to walk on into the house. He might just as well have been talking about some stranger's baby encountered in line at the supermarket. For the rest of his visit that day he did not look at Daniel, and not once, ever, did he ask to hold him.

All this, merely as an example.

Impossible, I realize, to enter another's solitude. If it is true that we can ever come to know another human being, even to a small degree, it is only to the extent that he is willing to make himself known. A man will say: I am cold. Or else he will say nothing, and we will see him shivering. Either way, we will know that he is cold. But what of the man who says nothing and does not shiver? Where all is intractable, where all is hermetic and evasive, one can do no more than observe. But whether one can make sense of what he observes is another matter entirely.

I do not want to presume anything.

He never talked about himself, never seemed to know there was anything he *could* talk about. It was as though his inner life eluded even him.

He could not talk about it, and therefore he passed over it in silence.

If there is nothing, then, but silence, is it not presumptuous of me to speak? And yet: if there had been anything more than silence, would I have felt the need to speak in the first place?

My choices are limited. I can remain silent, or else I can speak of things that cannot be verified. At the very least, I want to put down the facts, to offer them as straightforwardly as possible, and let them say whatever they have to say. But even the facts do not always tell the truth.

He was so implacably neutral on the surface, his behavior was so flatly predictable, that everything he did came as a surprise. One could not believe there was such a man—who lacked feeling, who wanted so little of others. And if there was not such a man, that means there was another man, a man hidden inside the man who was not there, and the trick of it, then, is to find him. On the condition that he is there to be found.

To recognize, right from the start, that the essence of this project is failure.


Earliest memory: his absence. For the first years of my life he would leave for work early in the morning, before I was awake, and come home long after I had been put to bed. I was my mother's boy, and I lived in her orbit. I was a little moon circling her gigantic earth, a mote in the sphere of her gravity, and I controlled the tides, the weather, the forces of feeling. His refrain to her was: Don't fuss so much, you'll spoil him. But my health was not good, and she used this to justify the attention she lavished on me. We spent a lot of time together, she in her loneliness and I in my cramps, waiting patiently in doctors' offices for someone to quell the insurrection that continually raged in my stomach. Even then, I would cling to these doctors in a desperate sort of way, wanting them to hold me. From the very beginning, it seems, I was looking for my father, looking frantically for anyone who resembled him.

Later memories: a craving. My mind always ready to deny the facts at the slightest excuse, I mulishly went on hoping for something that was never given to me—or given to me so rarely and arbitrarily that it seemed to happen outside the range of normal experience, in a place where I would never be able to live for more than a few moments at a time. It was not that I felt he disliked me. It was just that he seemed distracted, unable to look in my direction. And more than anything else, I wanted him to take notice of me.

Anything, even the least thing, was enough. How, for example, when the family once went to a crowded restaurant on a Sunday and we had to wait for our table, my father took me outside, produced a tennis ball (from where?), put a penny on the sidewalk, and proceeded to play a game with me: hit the penny with the tennis ball. I could not have been more than eight or nine years old.

In retrospect, nothing could have been more trivial. And yet the fact that I had been included, that my father had casually asked me to share his boredom with him, nearly crushed me with happiness.

More often, there were disappointments. For a moment he would seem to have changed, to have opened up a little, and then, suddenly, he would not be there anymore. The one time I managed to persuade him to take me to a football game (the Giants versus the Chicago Cardinals, at Yankee Stadium or the Polo Grounds, I forget which), he abruptly stood up from his seat in the middle of the fourth quarter and said, "It's time to go now." He wanted to "beat the crowd" and avoid getting stuck in traffic. Nothing I said could convince him to stay, and so we left, just like that, with the game going full tilt. Unearthly despair as I followed him down the concrete ramps, and then, even worse, in the parking lot, with the noise of the invisible crowd roaring behind me.

You could not trust him to know what you wanted, to anticipate what you might have been feeling. The fact that you had to tell him yourself vitiated the pleasure in advance, disrupted a dreamed-of harmony before a note could be played. And then, even if you did tell him, it was not at all sure that he would understand what you meant.

I remember a day very like today. A drizzling Sunday, lethargy and quiet in the house: the world at half-speed. My father was taking a nap, or had just awoken from one, and somehow I was on the bed with him, the two of us alone in the room. Tell me a story. It must have begun like that. And because he was not doing anything, because he was still drowsing in the languor of the afternoon, he did just what I asked, launching into a story without missing a beat. I remember it all so clearly. It seems as if I have just walked out of that room, with its gray light and tangle of quilts on the bed, as if, simply by closing my eyes, I could walk back into it anytime I want.

He told me of his prospecting days in South America. It was a tale of high adventure, fraught with mortal dangers, hair-raising escapes, and improbable twists of fortune: hacking his way through the jungle with a machete, fighting off bandits with his bare hands, shooting his donkey when it broke its leg. His language was flowery and convoluted, probably an echo of the books he himself had read as a boy. But it was precisely this literary style that enchanted me. Not only was he telling me new things about himself, unveiling to me the world of his distant past, but he was telling it with new and strange words. This language was just as important as the story itself. It belonged to it, and in some sense was indistinguishable from it. Its very strangeness was proof of authenticity.

It did not occur to me to think this might have been a made-up story. For years afterward I went on believing it. Even when I had passed the point when I should have known better, I still felt there might have been some truth to it. It gave me something to hold on to about my father, and I was reluctant to let go. At last I had an explanation for his mysterious evasions, his indifference to me. He was a romantic figure, a man with a dark and exciting past, and his present life was only a kind of stopping place, a way of biding his time until he took off on his next adventure. He was working out his plan, figuring out how to retrieve the gold that lay buried deep in the heart of the Andes.

In the back of my mind: a desire to do something extraordinary, to impress him with an act of heroic proportions. The more aloof he was, the higher the stakes became for me. But if a boy's will is tenacious and idealistic, it is also absurdly practical. I was only ten years old, and there was no child for me to save from a burning building, no sailors to rescue at sea. On the other hand, I was a good baseball player, the star of my Little League team, and although my father had no interest in baseball, I thought that if he saw me play, just once, he would begin to see me in a new light.

Finally he did come. My mother's parents were visiting at the time, and my grandfather, a great baseball fan, showed up with him. It was a special Memorial Day game, and the seats were full. If I was ever going to do something remarkable, this was the moment to do it. I can remember catching sight of them in the wooden bleachers, my father in a white shirt with no tie and my grandfather wearing a white handkerchief on his bald head to protect him from the sun—the whole scene in my mind now drenched in this dazzling white light.

It probably goes without saying that I made a mess of it. I got no hits, lost my poise in the field, could not have been more nervous. Of all the hundreds of games I played during my childhood, this one was the worst.

Afterwards, walking to the car with my father, he told me I had played a nice game. No I hadn't, I said, it was terrible. Well, you did your best, he answered. You can't do well everytime.

It was not that he was trying to encourage me. Nor was he trying to be unkind. Rather, he was saying what one says on such occasions, as if automatically. They were the right words to say, and yet they were delivered without feeling, an exercise in decorum, uttered in the same abstracted tone of voice he would use almost twenty years later when he said, "A beautiful baby. Good luck with it." I could see that his mind was somewhere else.

In itself, this is not important. The important thing is this: I realized that even if I had done all the things I had hoped to do, his reaction would have been exactly the same. Whether I succeeded or failed did not essentially matter to him. I was not defined for him by anything I did, but by what I was, and this meant that his perception of me would never change, that we were fixed in an unmoveable relationship, cut off from each other on opposite sides of a wall. Even more than that, I realized that none of this had anything to do with me. It had only to do with him. Like everything else in his life, he saw me only through the mists of his solitude, as if at several removes from himself. The world was a distant place for him, I think, a place he was never truly able to enter, and out there in the distance, among all the shadows that flitted past him, I was born, became his son, and grew up, as if I were just one more shadow, appearing and disappearing in a half-lit realm of his consciousness.

With his daughter, born when I was three and a half, it was somewhat easier for him. But in the end it was infinitely more difficult.

She was a beautiful child. Uncommonly fragile, with great brown eyes that would collapse into tears at the slightest prompting. She spent much of her time alone, a tiny figure wandering through an imaginary land of elves and fairies, dancing on tiptoe in lace-trimmed ballerina costumes, singing in a voice loud enough to be heard only by herself. She was a miniature Ophelia, already doomed, it would seem, to a life of constant inner struggle. She made few friends, had trouble keeping up in school, and was harassed by self-doubts, even at a very young age, that turned the simplest routines into nightmares of anguish and defeat. There were tantrums, fits of terrible crying, constant upheavals. Nothing ever seemed to go well for very long.

More sensitive to the nuances of the unhappy marriage around us than I was, her insecurity became monumental, crippling. At least once a day she would ask our mother if "she loved daddy." The answer was always the same: Of course I do.

It could not have been a very convincing lie. If it had been, there would not have been any need to ask the question again the next day.

On the other hand, it is difficult to see how the truth would have made things any better.


It was almost as if she gave off a scent of helplessness. One's immediate impulse was to protect her, to buffer her against the assaults of the world. Like everyone else, my father pampered her. The more she seemed to cry out for coddling, the more willing he was to give it to her. Long after she was able to walk, for example, he insisted on carrying her down the stairs. There is no question that he did it out of love, did it gladly because she was his little angel. But underneath this coddling was the implicit message that she would never be able to do anything for herself. She was not a person to him, but an angel, and because she was never compelled to act as an autonomous being, she could never become one.

My mother, however, saw what was happening. When my sister was five years old, she took her to an exploratory consultation with a child psychiatrist, and the doctor recommended that some form of therapy be started. That night, when my mother told my father the results of the meeting, he exploded in a violent rage. No daughter of mine, etc. The idea that his daughter needed psychiatric help was no different from being told she was a leper. He would not accept it. He would not even discuss it.

This is the point I am trying to make. His refusal to look into himself was matched by an equally stubborn refusal to look at the world, to accept even the most incontrovertible evidence it thrust under his nose. Again and again throughout his life he would stare a thing in the face, nod his head, and then turn around and say it was not there. It made conversation with him almost impossible. By the time you had managed to establish a common ground with him, he would take out his shovel and dig it out from under your feet.


Years later, when my sister suffered through a series of debilitating mental breakdowns, my father continued to believe there was nothing wrong with her. It was as though he were biologically unable to recognize her condition.

In one of his books R. D. Laing describes the father of a catatonic girl who on each visit to her in the hospital would grab her by the shoulders and shake her as hard as he could, telling her to "snap out of it." My father did not grab hold of my sister, but his attitude was essentially the same. What she needs, he would say, is to get a job, to clean herself up, to start living in the real world. Of course she did. But that was exactly what she could not do. She's just sensitive, he would say, she needs to overcome her shyness. By domesticating the problem to a quirk of personality, he could go on believing there was nothing wrong. It was not blindness so much as a failure of imagination. At what moment does a house stop being a house? When the roof is taken off? When the windows are removed? When the walls are knocked down? At what moment does it become a pile of rubble? She's just different, he would say, there's nothing wrong with her. And then one day the walls of your house finally collapse. If the door is still standing, however, all you have to do is walk through it, and you are back inside. It's pleasant sleeping out under the stars. Never mind the rain. It can't last very long.


Little by little, as the situation continued to get worse, he had to begin to accept it. But even then, at each stage along the way, his acceptance was unorthodox, taking on eccentric, almost self-nullifying forms. He became convinced, for example, that the one thing that could help her was a crash program in mega-vitamin therapy. This was the chemical approach to mental illness. Although it has never been proven to be an effective cure, this method of treatment has quite a large following. One can see why it would have attracted my father. Instead of having to wrestle with a devastating emotional fact, he could look upon the disease as a physical flaw, something that could be cured in the same way you cure the flu. The disease became an external force, a kind of bug that could be eradicated with an equal and opposite external force. In his eyes my sister was able to remain curiously untouched by all this. She was merely the *site* where the battle would take place, which meant that everything that was happening did not really affect *her*.

He spent several months trying to persuade her to begin this mega-vitamin program—even going so far as to take the pills himself, in order to prove that she would not be poisoned—and when at last she gave in, she did not take the pills for more than a week or two. The vitamins were expensive, but he did not balk at spending the money. On the other hand, he angrily resisted paying for other kinds of treatment. He did not believe that a stranger could possibly care about what happened to her. Psychiatrists were all charlatans, interested only in soaking their patients and driving fancy cars. He refused to pay the bills, which limited her to the shabbiest kind of public care. She was a pauper, with no income of her own, but he sent her almost nothing.

He was more than willing to take things into his own hands, however. Although it could not benefit either one of them, he wanted her to live in his house so that he could be the one responsible for looking after her. At least he could trust his own feelings, and he knew that he cared. But then, when she did come (for a few months, following one of her stays in the hospital), he did not disrupt his normal routine to accommodate her—but continued to spend most of his time out, leaving her to rattle around the enormous house like a ghost.

He was negligent and stubborn. But still, underneath it all, I know he suffered. Sometimes, on the phone, when he and I were discussing my sister, I could hear his voice break ever so slightly, as if he were trying to muffle a sob. Unlike everything else he ever came up against, my sister's illness finally *moved him*—but only to leave him with a feeling of utter helplessness. There is no greater sorrow for a parent than this helplessness. You have to accept it, even if you can't. And the more you accept it, the greater your despair becomes.

His despair became very great.


Wandering through the house today, without purpose, depressed, feeling that I have begun to lose touch with what I am writing, I chanced upon these words from a letter by Van Gogh: "Like everyone else, I feel the need of family and friendship, affection and friendly intercourse. I am not made of stone or iron, like a hydrant or a lamp-post."

Perhaps this is what really counts: to arrive at the core of human feeling, in spite of the evidence.


These tiniest of images: incorrigible, lodged in the mud of memory, neither buried nor wholly retrievable. And yet each one, in itself, a fleeting resurrection, a moment otherwise lost. The way he walked, for example, weirdly balanced, bouncing on the balls of his feet, as if he were about to pitch forward, blindly, into the unknown. Or the way he hunched over the table as he ate, his shoulders tensed, always merely consuming the food, never savoring it. Or else the smells that emanated from the cars he used for work: fumes, leaking oil, exhaust; the clutter of cold metal tools; the constant rattle as the car moved. A memory of the day I went driving with him through downtown Newark, no more than six years old, and he slammed down on the brakes, the jolt of it flinging my head against the dashboard: the sudden swarm of black people around the car to see if I was all right, especially the woman who thrust a vanilla ice cream cone at me through the open window, and my saying "no thank you," very politely, too stunned to know what I really wanted. Or else another day in another car, some years later, when my father spat out the window only to realize that the window had not been lowered, and my boundless, irrational delight at seeing the saliva slither down the glass. And still, as a little boy, how he would sometimes take me with him to Jewish restaurants in neighborhoods I had never seen before, dark places filled with old people, each table graced with a tinted blue seltzer bottle, and how I would grow queasy, leave my food untouched, and content myself with watching him wolf down borscht, pirogen, and boiled meats covered with horse radish. I, who was being brought up as an American boy, who knew less about my ancestors than I did about Hopalong Cassidy's hat. Or how, when I was twelve or thirteen, and wanted desperately to go somewhere with a couple of my friends, I called him at work to get his permission, and he said to me, at a loss, not knowing how to put it, "You're just a bunch of greenhorns," and how, for years afterward, my friends and I (one of them now dead, of a heroin overdose) would repeat those words as a piece of folklore, a nostalgic joke.

The size of his hands. Their callusses.
Eating the skin off the top of hot chocolate.
Tea with lemon.
The pairs of black, horn-rimmed glasses scattered through the house: on kitchen counters, on table tops, at the edge of the bathroom sink— always open, lying there like some strange, unclassified form of animal.
Watching him play tennis.
The way his knees sometimes buckled when he walked.
His face.
His resemblance to Abraham Lincoln, and how people always remarked on it.
His fearlessness with dogs.
His face. And again, his face.
Tropical fish.

Often, he seemed to lose his concentration, to forget where he was, as if he had lost the sense of his own continuity. It made him accident prone: smashed thumbnails from using a hammer, numerous little accidents in the car.

His absent-mindedness as a driver: to the point that it sometimes became frightening. I always thought it would be a car that did him in.

Otherwise, his health was so good that he seemed invulnerable, exempt from the physical ills that strike all the rest of us. As though nothing could ever touch him.

The way he spoke: as if making a great effort to rise up out of his solitude, as if his voice were rusty, had lost the habit of speaking. He always hemmed and hawed a lot, cleared his throat, seemed to sputter in midsentence. You felt, very definitely, that he was uncomfortable.

In the same way, it always amused me as a child to watch him sign his name. He could not simply put the pen against the paper and write. As if unconsciously delaying the moment of truth, he would always make a slight, preliminary flourish, a circular movement an inch or two off the page, like a fly buzzing in the air and zeroing in on its spot, before he could get down to business. It was a modified version of the way Art Carney's Norton used to sign his name on *The Honeymooners.*

He even pronounced his words a little oddly. "Upown," for example, instead of "upon," as if the flourish of his hand had its counterpart in his voice. There was a musical, airy quality to it. Whenever he answered the phone, it was a lilting "hellooo" that greeted you. The effect was not so much funny as endearing. It made him seem slightly daft, as if he were out of phase with the rest of the world—but not by much. Just a degree or two.

Indelible tics.


In those crazy, tensed-up moods he sometimes got into, he would always come out with bizarre opinions, not really taking them seriously, but happy to play devil's advocate in order to keep things lively. Teasing people put him in buoyant spirits, and after a particularly inane remark to someone he would often squeeze that person's leg—in a spot that always tickled. He literally liked to pull your leg.


Again the house.

No matter how negligent his care of it might have seemed from the outside, he believed in his system. Like a mad inventor protecting the secret of his perpetual motion machine, he would suffer no one to tamper with it. Once, when my wife and I were between apartments, we stayed in his house for three or four weeks. Finding the darkness of the house oppressive, we raised all the shades to let in the daylight. When my father returned home from work and saw what we had done, he flew into an uncontrollable rage, far out of proportion to any offense that might have been committed.

Anger of this sort rarely came out of him—only when he felt himself cornered, impinged upon, crushed by the presences of others. Money questions sometimes triggered it off. Or else some minor detail: the shades of his house, a broken plate, a little nothing at all.

Nevertheless, this anger was inside him—I believe constantly. Like the house that was well ordered and yet falling apart from within, the man himself was calm, almost supernatural in his imperturbability, and yet prey to a roiling, unstoppable force of fury within. All his life he strove to avoid a confrontation with this force, nurturing a kind of automatic behavior that would allow him to pass to the side of it. Reliance on fixed routines freed him from the necessity of looking into himself when decisions had to be made; the clichè was always quick to come to his lips ("A beautiful baby. Good luck with it") instead of words he had gone out and looked for. All this tended to flatten him out as a personality. But at the same time, it was also what saved him, the thing that allowed him to live. To the extent that he was able to live.

From a bag of loose pictures: a trick photograph taken in an Atlantic City studio sometime during the Forties. There are several of him sitting around a table, each image shot from a different angle, so that at first you think it must be a group of several different men. Because of the gloom that surrounds them, because of the utter stillness of their poses, it looks as if they have gathered there to conduct a sèance. And then, as you study the picture, you begin to realize that all these men are the same man. The sèance becomes a real sèance, and it is as if he has come there only to invoke himself, to bring himself back from the dead, as if, by multiplying himself, he had inadvertently made himself disappear. There are five of him there, and yet the nature of the trick photography denies the possibility of eye contact among the various selves. Each one is condemned to go on staring into space, as if under the gaze of the others, but seeing nothing, never able to see anything. It is a picture of death, a portrait of an invisible man.

Slowly, I am coming to understand the absurdity of the task I have set for myself. I have a sense of trying to go somewhere, as if I knew what I wanted to say, but the farther I go the more certain I am that the path towards my object does not exist. I have to invent the road with each step,

and this means that I can never be sure of where I am. A feeling of moving around in circles, of perpetual back-tracking, of going off in many directions at once. And even if I do manage to make some progress, I am not at all convinced that it will take me to where I think I am going. Just because you wander in the desert, it does not mean there is a promised land.

When I first started, I thought it would come spontaneously, in a trance-like outpouring. So great was my need to write that I thought the story would be written by itself. But the words have come very slowly so far. Even on the best days I have not been able to write more than a page or two. I seem to be afflicted, cursed by some failure of mind to concentrate on what I am doing. Again and again I have watched my thoughts trail off from the thing in front of me. No sooner have I thought one thing than it evokes another thing, and then another thing, until there is an accumulation of detail so dense that I feel I am going to suffocate. Never before have I been so aware of the rift between thinking and writing. For the past few days, in fact, I have begun to feel that the story I am trying to tell is somehow incompatible with language, that the degree to which it resists language is an exact measure of how closely I have come to saying something important, and that when the moment arrives for me to say the one truly important thing (assuming it exists), I will not be able to say it.

There has been a wound, and I realize now that it is very deep. Instead of healing me as I thought it would, the act of writing has kept this wound open. At times I have even felt the pain of it concentrated in my right hand, as if each time I picked up the pen and pressed it against the page, my hand were being torn apart. Instead of burying my father for me, these words have kept him alive, perhaps more so than ever. I not only see him as he was, but as he is, as he will be, and each day he is there, invading my thoughts, stealing up on me without warning: lying in the coffin underground, his body still intact, his fingernails and hair continuing to grow. A feeling that if I am to understand anything, I must penetrate this image of darkness, that I must enter the absolute darkness of earth.

Kenosha, Wisconsin. 1911 or 1912. Not even he was sure of the date. In the confusion of a large, immigrant family, birth records could not have been considered very important. What matters is that he was the last of five surviving children—a girl and four boys, all born within a span of eight years—and that his mother, a tiny, ferocious woman who could barely speak English, held the family together. She was the matriarch, the absolute dictator, the prime mover who stood at the center of the universe.

His father died in 1919, which meant that except for his earliest childhood he had no father. During my own childhood he told me three different stories about his father's death. In one version, he had been killed in a hunting accident. In another, he had fallen off a ladder. In the third, he had been shot down during the First World War. I knew these contradictions made no sense, but I assumed this meant that not even my father knew the facts. Because he had been so young when it happened—only

seven—I figured that he had never been given the exact story. But then, this made no sense either. One of his brothers surely would have told him.

All my cousins, however, told me that they, too, had been given different explanations by their fathers.

No one ever talked about my grandfather. Until a few years ago, I had never seen a picture of him. It was as though the family had decided to pretend he had never existed.

Among the photographs I found in my father's house last month there was one family portrait from those early days in Kenosha. All the children are there. My father, no more than a year old, is sitting on his mother's lap, and the other four are standing around her in the tall, uncut grass. There are two trees behind them and a large wooden house behind the trees. A whole world seems to emerge from this portrait: a distinct time, a distinct place, an indestructible sense of the past. The first time I looked at the picture, I noticed that it had been torn down the middle and then clumsily mended, leaving one of the trees in the background hanging eerily in mid-air. I assumed the picture had been torn by accident and thought no more about it. The second time I looked at it, however, I studied this tear more closely and discovered things I must have been blind to miss before. I saw a man's fingertips grasping the torso of one of my uncles; I saw, very distinctly, that another of my uncles was not resting his hand on his brother's back, as I had first thought, but against a chair that was not there. And then I realized what was strange about the picture: my grandfather had been cut out of it. The image was distorted because part of it had been eliminated. My grandfather had been sitting in a chair next to his wife with one of his sons standing between his knees—and he was not there. Only his fingertips remained: as if he were trying to crawl back into the picture from some hole deep in time, as if he had been exiled to another dimension.

The whole thing made me shake.


I learned the story of my grandfather's death some time ago. If not for an extraordinary coincidence, it never would have become known.

In 1970 one of my cousins went to Europe on a vacation with her husband. On the plane she found herself sitting next to an old man and, as people often do, they struck up a conversation to pass the time. It turned out that his man lived in Kenosha, Wisconsin. My cousin was amused by the coincidence and remarked that her father had lived there as a boy. Out of curiosity, the man asked her the name of her family. When she told him Auster, he turned pale. Auster? Your grandmother wasn't a crazy little woman with red hair, was she? Yes, that was my grandmother, my cousin answered. A crazy little woman with red hair.

And then he told her the story. It had happened more than fifty years before, and yet he still remembered the important details.

When this man returned home from his vacation, he tracked down the newspaper articles connected with the story, had them photocopied, and sent them to my cousin. This was his cover letter:

June 15, 70

Dear——and——:
It was good to get your letter, and altho it did look like the task might be complicated, I had a stroke of luck.—Fran and I went out to dinner with a Fred Plons and his wife, and it was Fred's father who had bought the apartment bldg on Park Ave from your family.—Mr. Plons is about three years younger than myself, but he claimed that the case (at that time) fascinated him and he remembered quite a few details.—He stated that your grandfather was the first person to be buried in the

Jewish Cemetery here in Kenosha.—(Previous to 1919 the Jewish people had no cemetery in Kenosha, but had their loved
ones buried either in Chicago or Milwaukee.) With this information, I had no trouble locating the plot where your grandfather is buried.—And I was able to pin point the date. The rest is
in the copy I am forwarding to you.—

I only ask that your father should never learn of this knowledge that I am passing on to you—I would not want him to
have any more grief than he already has suffered. . . .

I hope that this will shed some light on your Father's actions over the past years.

Our fondest regards to you both—
Ken & Fran

The newspaper articles are sitting on my desk. Now that the moment
has come to write about them, I am surprised to find myself doing everything I can to put it off. All morning I have procrastinated. I have taken
the trash to the dump. I have played with Daniel in the yard for almost an
hour. I have read the entire newspaper—right down to the line scores of
the spring training baseball games. Even now, as I write about my reluctance to write, I find myself impossibly restless: after every few words I
pop up from my chair, pace the floor, listen to the wind outside as it bangs
the loose gutters against the house. The least thing is able to distract me.

It is not that I am afraid of the truth. I am not even afraid to say it. My
grandmother murdered my grandfather. On January 23, 1919, precisely
sixty years before my father died, his mother shot and killed his father in the
kitchen of their house on Fremont avenue in Kenosha, Wisconsin. The facts
themselves do not disturb me any more than might be expected. The difficult thing is to see them in print—unburied, so to speak, from the realm of
secrets and turned into a public event. There are more than twenty articles,
most of them long, all of them from the *Kenosha Evening News*. Even in this
barely legible state, almost totally obscured by age and the hazards of pho-
tocopying, they still have the ability to shock. I assume they are typical of
the journalism of the time, but that does not make them any less sensational.
They are a mixture of scandal-mongering and sentimentality, heightened
by the fact that the people involved were Jews—and therefore strange, almost by definition—which gives the whole account a leering, condescending tone. And yet, granted the flaws in style, the facts seem to be there. I do
not think they explain everything, but there is no question that they explain
a great deal. A boy cannot live through this kind of thing without being affected by it as a man.

In the margins of these articles, I can just manage to decipher some of
the smaller news stories of that time, events that were relegated to near in-
significance in comparison to the murder. For example: the recovery of

Rosa Luxemburg's body from the Landwehr Canal. For example: the Versailles peace conference. And on, day after day, through the following: the Eugene Debs case; a note on Caruso's first film ("The situations . . . are said to be highly dramatic and filled with stirring heart appeal"); battle reports from the Russian Civil War; the funerals of Karl Liebnecht and thirty-one other Spartacists ("More than fifty thousand persons marched in the procession which was five miles long. Fully twenty percent of these bore wreaths. There was no shouting or cheering"); the ratification of the national prohibition amendment ("William Jennings Bryan—the man who made grape juice famous—was there with a broad smile"); the textile strike in Lawrence, Massachusetts, led by the Wobblies; the death of Emiliano Zapata, "bandit leader in southern Mexico"; Winston Churchill; Bela Kun; Premier Lenine (sic); Woodrow Wilson; Dempsey versus Willard.

I have read through the articles about the murder a dozen times. Still, I find it hard to believe that I did not dream them. They loom up at me with all the force of a trick of the unconscious, distorting reality in the same way dreams do. Because the huge headlines announcing the murder dwarf everything else that happened in the world that day, they give the event the same egocentric importance we give to the things that happen in our private lives. It is almost like the drawing a child makes when he is troubled by some inexpressible fear: the most important thing is always the biggest thing. Perspective is lost in favor of proportion—which is dictated not by the eye but by the demands of the mind.

I read these articles as history. But also as a cave drawing discovered on the inner walls of my own skull.


The headlines on the first day, January 24, cover more than a third of the front page.

### HARRY AUSTER KILLED
### WIFE HELD BY POLICE

Former Prominent Real Estate Operator is Shot to Death in the Kitchen of the Home of His Wife On Thursday Night Following a Family Wrangle Over Money—and a Woman.

### WIFE SAYS HUSBAND WAS A SUICIDE

Dead Man Had Bullet Wound in His Neck and in the Left Hip and Wife Admits That Revolver With Which the Shooting Was Done Was Her Property—Nine-Year-Old Son, Witness of the Tragedy, May Hold Solution to the Mystery.

According to the newspaper, "Auster and his wife had separated some time ago and an action for divorce was pending in the Circuit Court for

Kenosha county. They had had trouble on several occasions over money. They had also quarreled over the fact that Auster [illegible] friendly with a young woman known to the wife as 'Fanny.' It is believed that 'Fanny' figured in the trouble between Auster and his wife immediately preceding the shooting. . . ."

Because my grandmother did not confess until the twenty-eighth, there was some confusion about what really happened. My grandfather (who was thirty-six years old) arrived at the house at six o'clock in the evening with "suits of clothing" for his two oldest sons "while it was stated by witnesses Mrs. Auster was in the bedroom putting Sam, the youngest boy, into bed. Sam [my father] declared that he did not see his mother take a revolver from under the mattress as he was tucked into bed for the night."

It seems that my grandfather had then gone into the kitchen to repair an electric switch and that one of my uncles (the second youngest son) had held a candle for him to see by. "The boy declared that he became panic stricken when he heard the shot and saw a flash of a revolver and fled the room." According to my grandmother, her husband had shot himself. She admitted they had been arguing about money, and "then he said, she continued, 'there is going to be an end for you or me,' and he threatened me. I did not know he had the revolver. I had kept it under the mattress of my bed and he knew it."

Since my grandmother spoke almost no English, I assume that this statement, and all others attributed to her, was invented by the reporter. Whatever it was she said, the police did not believe her. "Mrs. Auster repeated her story to the various police officers without making any decided change in it and she professed great surprise when she was told that she was to be held by the police. With a great deal of tenderness she kissed little Sam good night and then went off to the county jail.

"The two Auster boys were guests of the police department last night sleeping in the squad room and this morning the boys were apparently entirely recovered from any fright they had suffered as a result of the tragedy at their home."

Towards the end of the article, this information is given about my grandfather. "Harry Auster was a native of Austria. He came to this country a number of years ago and had resided in Chicago, in Canada, and in Kenosha. He and his wife, according to the story told the police, later returned to Austria but she rejoined her husband in this country about the time they came to Kenosha. Auster bought a number of homes in the second ward and for some time his operations were on a large scale. He built the big triple flat building on South Park avenue and another one known as the Auster flats on South Exchange street. Six or eight months ago he met with financial reverses. . . .

"Some time ago Mrs. Auster appealed to the police to aid her in watching Mr. Auster as she alleged that he had relations with a young woman

which she believed should be investigated. It was in this way that the police first learned of the woman 'Fanny.' . . .

"Many people had seen and talked with Auster on Thursday afternoon and these people all declared that he appeared to be normal and that
he showed no signs of desiring to take his own life. . . ."

The next day was the coroner's inquest. My uncle, as the only witness
to the incident, was called on to testify. "A sad-eyed little boy, nervously
twirling his stocking cap, wrote the second chapter in the Auster murder
mystery Friday afternoon. . . . His attempts to save the family name were
tragically pathetic. Again and again when asked if his parents were quarrelling he would answer 'They were just talking' until at last, apparently
remembering his oath, he added 'and maybe quarrelling—well just a little
bit.'" The article describes the jurors as "weirdly stirred by the boy's efforts to shield both his father and his mother."

The idea of suicide was clearly not going to wash. In the last paragraph the reporter writes that "developments of a startling nature have
been hinted by officials."

Then came the funeral. It gave the anonymous reporter an opportunity
to emulate some of the choicest diction of Victorian melodrama. By now
the murder was no longer merely a scandal. It had been turned into a stirring entertainment.

### WIDOW TEARLESS AT AUSTER GRAVE

Mrs. Anna Auster Under Guard Attends Funeral of
Husband, Harry Auster, Sunday.

"Dry-eyed and without the least sign of emotion or grief, Mrs. Harry
Auster, who is held here in connection with the mysterious death of her
husband, Harry Auster, attended Sunday morning, under guard, the funeral services of the man, in connection with whose death she is being
held.

"Neither at the Crossin Chapel, where she looked for the first time
since Thursday night upon the dead face of her husband nor at the burial
ground did she show the least sign of weakening. The only intimation
which she gave of breaking under the terrific strain of the ordeal was
when over the grave, after the obsequies were finished, she asked for a
conference this afternoon with the Rev. M. Hartman, pastor of the B'nai
Zadek Congregation. . . .

"When the rites were completed Mrs. Auster calmly tightened the fox
fur collar more closely about her throat and signified to the police that she
was ready to leave. . . .

"After short ritualistic ceremonies the funeral procession was formed on Wisconsin street. Mrs. Auster asked that she also be allowed to go to the burial ground and the request was granted readily by the police. She seemed very petulant over the fact that no carriage had been provided for her, perhaps remembering that short season of apparent wealth when the Auster limousine was seen in Kenosha. . . .

". . . The ordeal was made exceptionally long because some delay had occurred in the preparation of the grave and while she waited she called Sam, the youngest boy, to her, and tucked his coat collar more closely around his neck. She spoke quietly to him but with this exception she was silent until after the rites were finished. . . .

"A prominent figure at the funeral was Samuel Auster, of Detroit, the brother of Harry Auster. He took as his especial care the younger children and attempted to console them in their grief.

"In speeches and demonstrations Auster appeared very bitter about his brother's death. He showed clearly that he disbelieved the theory of suicide and uttered remarks which savoured of accusations of the widow. . . .

"The Rev. M. Hartman . . . preached an eloquent sermon at the grave. He lamented the fact that the first person to be buried in the new cemetery should be one who had died by violence and who had been killed in his prime. He paid tribute to the enterprise of Harry Auster but deplored his early death.

"The widow appeared to be unmoved by the tributes paid to her dead husband. She indifferently opened her coat to allow the patriarch to cut a gash in her knitted sweater, a token of grief prescribed by the Hebrew faith.

"Officials in Kenosha fail to give up the suspicion that Auster was killed by his wife. . . ."


The paper of the following day, January 26th, carried the news of the confession. After her meeting with the rabbi, she had requested a conference with the chief of police. "When she entered the room she trembled a little and was plainly agitated as the chief provided a chair. 'You know what your little boy told us,' the latter began when he realized that the psychological moment had come. 'You don't want us to think that he's lying to us, do you?' And the mother, whose face has been for days so masked as to reveal nothing of the horror hidden behind it, tore off the camouflage, became suddenly tender, and sobbed out her awful secret. 'He isn't lying to you at all; everything he has said is true. I shot him and I want to make a confession.'"

This was her formal statement: "My name is Anna Auster. I shot Harry Auster at the city of Kenosha, Wisconsin on the 23rd day of January A.D. 1919. I have heard people remark that three shots were fired, but I do not remember how many shots were fired that day. My reason for shooting the said Harry Auster is on account of the fact that he, the said Harry Auster, abused me. I was just like crazy when I shot the said Harry Auster. I never thought of shooting him, the said Harry Auster, until the moment I shot him. I think that this is the gun I shot the said Harry Auster with. I make this statement of my own free will and without being forced to do so."

The reporter continues, "On the table before Mrs. Auster lay the revolver with which her husband was shot to death. As she spoke of it she touched it falteringly and then drew her hand back with a noticeable tremor of horror. Without speaking the chief laid the gun aside and asked Mrs. Auster if there was more she cared to say.

"'That's all for now,' she replied composedly. 'You sign it for me and I'll make my mark.'

"Her orders—for a little moment she was almost regal again—were obeyed, she acknowledged the signature, and asked to be returned to her cell. . . ."

At the arraignment the next day a plea of not guilty was entered by her attorney. "Muffled in a plush coat and a boa of fox fur, Mrs. Auster entered the court room. . . . She smiled at a friend in the crowd as she took her seat before the desk."

By the reporter's own admission, the hearing was "uneventful." But still, he could not resist making this observation: "An incident occurred upon her return to her barred room which furnished a commentary of Mrs. Auster's state of mind.

"A woman, held on a charge of association with a married man, had been brought to the jail for incarceration in an adjoining cell. Upon seeing her, Mrs. Auster asked about the newcomer and learned the particulars in the case.

"'She ought to get ten years,' she said as the iron door clanged pitilessly. 'It was one of her kind that put me here.'"


After some intricate legal discussions concerning bail that were elaborately reported for the next few days, she was set free. "'Have you any notion that this woman will not appear for trial?' the court asked the attorneys. It was attorney Baker who answered: 'Where could a woman with five children like these go? She clings to them and the court can see that they cling to her.'"

For a week the press was quiet. Then, on February 8th, there was a story about "the active support that the cause is being given by some of the papers published in the Jewish language in Chicago. Some of these papers contained columns arguing the case of Mrs. Auster and it is declared that these articles have strongly urged her defense. . . .

"Friday afternoon Mrs. Auster with one of her children sat in the office of her attorney while portions of these articles were read. She sobbed like a child as the interpreter read to the attorney the contents of these papers. . . .

"Attorney Baker declared this morning that the defense of Mrs. Auster
would be one of emotional insanity. . . .

"It is expected that the trial of Mrs. Auster will be one of the most interesting murder trials ever tried in the Circuit Court for Kenosha county
and the human interest story that has been featured in the defense of the
woman up to this time is expected to be largely developed at the trial."

Then nothing for a month. On March 10th the headlines read:

### ANNA AUSTER TRIED SUICIDE

The suicide attempt had taken place in Peterboro, Ontario in 1910—by
taking carbolic acid and then turning on the gas. The attorney brought this
information before the court in order to be granted a delay in the trial so
that he would have enough time to secure affidavits. "Attorney Baker
held that at the same time the woman had endangered the lives of two of
her children and that the story of the attempted suicide was important in
that it would show the mental condition of Mrs. Auster."

March 27th. The trial was set for April 7th. After that, another week of
silence. And then, on April 4th, as if things had been getting just a bit too
dull, a new development.

### AUSTER SHOOTS BROTHER'S WIDOW

"Sam Auster, brother of Harry Auster . . . made an unsuccessful attempt to avenge the death of his brother just after ten o'clock this morning
when he shot at Mrs. Auster. . . . The shooting occurred just outside the
Miller Grocery Store. . . .

"Auster followed Mrs. Auster outside the door and fired once at her.
Mrs. Auster, though she was not struck by the shot, fell to the sidewalk
and Auster returned to the store declaring according to witnesses, 'Well,
I'm glad I done that.' There he calmly awaited arrest. . . .

"At the police station . . . Auster, entirely broken down nervously,
gave his explanation of the shooting.

"'That woman,' he said, 'has killed my four brothers and my mother.
I've tried to help but she won't let me.' Then as he was being led down to
the cell, he sobbed out, 'God's going to take my part though, I know that.'

"At his cell Auster declared that he had tried everything within his
power to help the children of his dead brother. The fact that the court had
refused to appoint him administrator for the estate because they declared
that the widow had some rights in the case had preyed on his mind recently. . . . 'She's no widow,' he commented on that incident this morning.
'She is a murderer and should have no rights. . . .'"

"Auster will not be arraigned immediately in order to make a thorough investigation of the case. The police admit that the death of his brother and subsequent events may have so preyed on his mind that he was not entirely responsible for his deed. Auster expressed several times a hope that he should die too and every precaution is being taken to prevent him from taking his own life. . . ."

The next day's paper had this to add: "Auster spent a rather troublesome night in the city lockup. Several times the officers found him sobbing in the cell and he appeared to be hysterical. . . .

"It was admitted that Mrs. Auster had suffered from a 'bad case of nerves' as a result of the fright which had attended the attack on her life on Friday, but it was declared that she would be able to be in court when the case against her is called for trial on Monday evening."

After three days the state rested its case. Contending that the murder had been premeditated, the district attorney relied heavily on the testimony of a certain Mrs. Mathews, an employee at the Miller Grocery Store, who contended that "Mrs. Auster came to the store three times on the day of the shooting to use the telephone. On one of those occasions, the witness said, Mrs. Auster called up her husband and asked him to come to the house and fix a light. She said that Auster had promised to come at six o'clock."

But even if she invited him to the house, it does not mean that she intended to kill him once he was there.

It makes no difference anyway. Whatever the facts might have been, the defense attorney shrewdly turned everything to his own advantage. His strategy was to offer overwhelming evidence on two fronts: on the one hand, to prove infidelity on the part of my grandfather, and on the other, to demonstrate a history of mental instability on the part of my grandmother—the two of them combining to produce a case of justifiable homicide or homicide "by reason of insanity." Either one would do.

Attorney Baker's opening remarks were calculated to draw every possible ounce of sympathy from the jury. "He told how Mrs. Auster had toiled with her husband to build up the home and happiness which once was theirs in Kenosha after they had passed through years of hardships. . . . 'Then after they had labored together to build up this home,' continued Attorney Baker, 'there came this siren from the city and Anna Auster was cast aside like a rag. Instead of supplying food for his family, her husband kept Fanny Koplan in a flat in Chicago. The money which she had helped to accumulate was being lavished on a more beautiful woman and after such abuse is there any wonder that her mind was shattered and that for the moment she lost control of her senses.'"

The first witness for the defense was Mrs. Elizabeth Grossman, my grandmother's only sister, who lived on a farm near Brunswick, New Jersey. "She made a splendid witness. She told in a simple manner the whole story of the life of Mrs. Auster; of her birth in Austria; of the death of her mother when Mrs. Auster was but six years of age; of the trip with her sister to this country eight years later; of long hours served as a maker of hats and bonnets in New York millinery shops; of how by this work the immigrant girl accumulated a few hundred dollars. She told of the marriage of the woman to Auster just after she reached her twenty-third birthday and of their business ventures; of their failure in a little candy store and their long trip to Lawrence, Kas., where they attempted to start over and where——, the first child was born; of the return to New York and the second failure in business which ended in bankruptcy and the flight of Auster into Canada. She told of Mrs. Auster following Auster to Canada; of the desertion by Auster of the wife and little children and how he had said that he was 'going to make way with himself' [sic] and how he had told the wife that he was taking fifty dollars so that when he was dead it might be found on him and used to give him a decent burial. . . . She said that during their residence in Canada they were known as Mr. and Mrs. Harry Ball. . . .

"A little break in the story which could not be furnished by Mrs. Grossman, was furnished by former Chief Constable Archie Moore and Abraham Low, both of Peterboro county, Canada. These men told of the departure of Auster from Peterboro and the grief of his wife. Auster, they said, left Peterboro July 14, 1909, and the following night Moore found Mrs. Auster in a room of their shabby home suffering from the effects of gas. She and the children lay on a mattress on the floor while the gas was flowing from four open jets. Moore told of the further fact that he had found a vial of carbolic acid in the room and that traces of the acid had been found on the lips of Mrs. Auster. She was taken to a hospital, the witness declared, and was ill for many days. Both of these men declared that in their opinion there was no doubt but that Mrs. Auster showed signs of insanity at the time she attempted her life in Canada."

Further witnesses included the two oldest children, each of whom chronicled the family's domestic troubles. Much was said about Fanny, and also the frequent squabbles at home. "He said that Auster had a habit of throwing dishes and glass ware and that at one time his mother's arm had been so badly cut that it was necessary to call a physician to attend her. He declared that his father used profane and indecent language toward his mother at these times. . . ."

Another witness from Chicago testified that she had frequently seen my grandmother beat her head against the wall in fits of mental anguish. A police officer from Kenosha told how at "one time he had seen Mrs. Auster running wildly down a street. He stated that her hair was 'more or less' dishevelled and added that she acted much like a woman who had lost her mind." A doctor was also called in, and he contended that she had been suffering from "acute mania."

My grandmother's testimony lasted three hours. "Between stifled sobs and recourse to tears, she told the story of her life with Auster up to the time of the 'accident.' . . . Mrs. Auster stood the ordeal of cross questioning very well, and her story was told over three times in almost the same way."

In his summation "Attorney Baker made a strong emotional plea for the release of Mrs. Auster. In a speech lasting nearly an hour and a half he retold in an eloquent manner of the story of Mrs. Auster. . . . Several times Mrs. Auster was moved to tears by the statements of her attorney and women in the audience were sobbing several times as the attorney painted the picture of the struggling immigrant woman seeking to maintain their home."

The judge gave the jury the option of only two verdicts: guilty or innocent of murder. It took them less than two hours to make their decision. As the bulletin of April 12th put it: "At four thirty o'clock this afternoon the jury in the trial of Mrs. Anna Auster returned a verdict finding the defendant not guilty."

April 14th. "'I am happier now than I have been for seventeen years,' said Mrs. Auster Saturday afternoon as she shook hands with each of the jurors following the return of the verdict. 'As long as Harry lived,' she said to one of them, 'I was worried. I never knew real happiness. Now I regret that he had to die by my hand. I am as happy now as I ever expect to be. . . .'

"As Mrs. Auster left the courtroom she was attended by her daughter . . . and the two younger children, who had waited patiently in the courtroom for the return of the verdict which freed their mother. . . .

"At the county jail Sam Auster . . . while he cannot understand it all, says he is willing to abide by the decision of the twelve jurors. . . .

"'Last night when I heard of the verdict,' he said when interviewed on Sunday morning, 'I dropped on the floor. I could not believe that she could go clear free after killing my brother and her husband. It is all too big for me. I don't understand, but I shall let it go now. I tried once to settle it in my way and failed and I can't do anything now but accept what the court has said.'"

The next day he, too, was released. "'I am going back to my work in the factory,' Auster told the District Attorney. 'Just as soon as I get money enough I am going to raise a head stone over the grave of my brother and then I am going to give my energies to the support of the children of one of my brothers who lived in Austria and who fell fighting in the Austrian army.'

"The conference this morning brought out the fact that Sam Auster is the last of the five Auster brothers. Three of the boys fought with the Austrian army in the world war and all of them fell in battle."

In the last paragraph of the last article about the case, the newspaper reports that "Mrs. Auster is now planning to take the children and leave for the east within a few days. . . . It was said that Mrs. Auster decided to take this action on the advice of her attorneys, who told her that she should go to some new home and start life without any one knowing the story of the trial."

It was, I suppose, a happy ending. At least for the newspaper readers of Kenosha, the clever Attorney Baker, and, no doubt, for my grandmother. Nothing further is said, of course, about the fortunes of the Auster family. The public record ends with this announcement of their departure for the east.

Because my father rarely spoke to me about the past, I learned very little about what followed. But from the few things he did mention, I was able to form a fairly good idea of the climate in which the family lived.

For example, they moved constantly. It was not uncommon for my father to attend two, or even three different schools in a single year. Because they had no money, life became a series of escapes from landlords and creditors. In a family that had already closed in on itself, this nomadism walled them off entirely. There were no enduring points of reference: no home, no town, no friends that could be counted on. Only the family itself. It was almost like living in quarantine.

My father was the baby, and for his whole life he continued to look up to his three older brothers. As a boy he was known as Sonny. He suffered from asthma and allergies, did well in school, played end on the football team and ran the 440 for the track team at Central High in Newark. He graduated in the first year of the Depression, went to law school at night for a semester or two, and then dropped out, exactly as his brothers had done before him.

The four brothers stuck together. There was something almost medieval about their loyalty to one another. Although they had their differences, in many ways did not even like one another, I think of them not as four separate individuals but as a clan, a quadruplicate image of solidarity. Three of them—the youngest three—wound up as business partners and lived in the same town, and the fourth, who lived only two towns away, had been set up in business by the other three. There was scarcely a day that my father did not see his brothers. And that means for his entire life: every day for more than sixty years.

They picked up habits from each other, figures of speech, little gestures, intermingling to such a degree that it was impossible to tell which one had been the source of any given attitude or idea. My father's feelings were unbending: he never said a word against any of his brothers. Again, it was the other defined not by what he did but by what he was. If one of the brothers happened to slight him or do something objectionable, my father would nevertheless refuse to pass judgment. He's my brother, he would say, as if that explained everything. Brotherhood was the first principle, the unassailable postulate, the one and only article of faith. Like belief in God, to question it was heresy.

As the youngest, my father was the most loyal of the four and also the one least respected by the others. He worked the hardest, was the most generous to his nephews and nieces, and yet these things were never fully recognized, much less appreciated. My mother recalls that on the day of her wedding, at the party following the ceremony, one of the brothers actually propositioned her. Whether he would have carried through with the escapade is another matter. But the mere fact of teasing her like that gives a rough idea of how he felt about my father. You do not do that sort of thing on a man's wedding day, even if he is your brother.

At the center of the clan was my grandmother, a Jewish Mammy Yokum, a mother to end all mothers. Fierce, refractory, the boss. It was common loyalty to her that kept the brothers so close. Even as grown men, with wives and children of their own, they would faithfully go to her house every Friday night for dinner—without their families. This was the relationship that mattered, and it took precedence over everything else. There must have been something slightly comical about it: four big men, each one over six feet, waiting on a little old woman, more than a foot shorter than they were.

One of the few times they came with their wives, a neighbor happened to walk in and was surprised to find such a large gathering. Is this your family, Mrs. Auster? he asked. Yes, she answered, with great smiles of pride. This is—. This is—. This is—. And this is Sam. The neighbor was a little taken aback. And these lovely ladies, he asked. Who are they? Oh, she answered with a casual wave of the hand. That's—'s. That's—'s. That's—'s. And that's Sam's.

The picture painted of her in the Kenosha newspaper was by no means inaccurate. She lived for her children. (Attorney Baker: Where could a woman with five children like these go? She clings to them and the court can see that they cling to her.) At the same time, she was a tyrant, given to screaming and hysterical fits. When she was angry, she would beat her sons over the head with a broom. She demanded allegiance, and she got it.

Once, when my father had saved the huge sum of ten or twenty dollars from his newspaper route to buy himself a new bicycle, his mother walked into the room, cracked open his piggy bank, and took the money from him without so much as an apology. She needed the money to pay some bills, and my father had no recourse, no way to air his grievance. When he told me this story his object was not to show how his mother wronged him, but to demonstrate how the good of the family was always more important than the good of any of its members. He might have been unhappy, but he did not complain.

This was rule by caprice. For a child, it meant that the sky could fall on top of him at any moment, that he could never be sure of anything. Therefore, he learned never to trust anyone. Not even himself. Someone would always come along to prove that what he thought was wrong, that it did not count for anything. He learned never to want anything too much.

My father lived with his mother until he was older than I am now. He was the last one to go off on his own, the one who had been left behind to take care of her. It would be wrong to say, however, that he was a mother's boy. He was too independent, had been too fully indoctrinated into the ways of manhood by his brothers. He was good to her, was dutiful and considerate, but not without a certain distance, even humor. After he was married, she called him often, haranguing him about this and that. My father would put the receiver down on the table, walk to the other end of the room and busy himself with some chore for a few minutes, then return to the phone, pick it up, say something innocuous to let her know he was there (uh-huh, uh-huh, mmmmmm, that's right), and then wander off again, back and forth, until she had talked herself out.

The comical side of this obtuseness. And sometimes it served him very well.

I remember a tiny, shriveled creature sitting in the front parlor of a two-family house in the Weequahic section of Newark reading the *Jewish Daily Forward*. Although I knew I would have to do it whenever I saw her, it made me cringe to kiss her. Her face was so wrinkled, her skin so inhumanly soft. Worse than that was her smell—a smell I was much later able to identify as that of camphor, which she must have put in her bureau drawers and which, over the years, had seeped into the fabric of her clothes. This odor was inseparable in my mind from the idea of "grandma."

As far as I can remember, she took virtually no interest in me. The one time she gave me a present, it was a second- or third-hand children's book, a biography of Benjamin Franklin. I remember reading it all the way through and can even recall some of the episodes. Franklin's future wife, for example, laughing at him the first time she saw him—walking through the streets of Philadelphia with an enormous loaf of bread under his arm. The book had a blue cover and was illustrated with silhouettes. I must have been seven or eight at the time.

After my father died, I discovered a trunk that had once belonged to his mother in the cellar of his house. It was locked, and I decided to force it open with a hammer and screwdriver, thinking it might contain some buried secret, some long lost treasure. As the hasp fell down and I raised the lid, there it was, all over again—that smell, wafting up towards me, immediate, palpable, as if it had been my grandmother herself. I felt as though I had just opened her coffin.

There was nothing of interest in it: a set of carving knives, a heap of imitation jewelry. Also a hard plastic dress-up pocketbook, a kind of octagonal box with a handle on it. I gave the thing to Daniel, and he immediately started using it as a portable garage for his fleet of little trucks and cars.

My father worked hard all his life. At nine he had his first job. At eighteen he had a radio repair business with one of his brothers. Except for a brief moment when he was hired as an assistant in Thomas Edison's laboratory (only to have the job taken away from him the next day because Edison learned he was a Jew), my father never worked for anyone but himself. He was a very demanding boss, far more exacting than any stranger could have been.

The radio shop eventually led to a small appliance store, which in turn led to a large furniture store. From there he began to dabble in real estate (buying, for example, a house for his mother to live in), until this gradually displaced the store as the focus of his attention and became a business in its own right. The partnership with two of his brothers carried over from one thing to the next.

Up early every morning, home late at night, and in between, work, nothing but work. Work was the name of the country he lived in, and he was one of its greatest patriots. That is not to say, however, that work was pleasure for him. He worked hard because he wanted to earn as much money as possible. Work was a means to an end—a means to money. But the end was not something that could bring him pleasure either. As the young Marx wrote: "If *money* is the bond binding me to *human life,* binding society to me, binding me and nature and man, is not money the bond of all *bonds*? Can it not dissolve and bind all ties? Is it not, therefore, the universal *agent of separation*?"

He dreamed all his life of becoming a millionaire, of being the richest man in the world. It was not so much the money itself he wanted, but what it represented: not merely success in the eyes of the world, but a way of making himself untouchable. Having money means more than being able to buy things: it means that the world need never affect you. Money in the sense of protection, then, not pleasure. Having been without money as a child, and therefore vulnerable to the whims of the world, the idea of wealth became synonymous for him with the idea of escape: from harm, from suffering, from being a victim. He was not trying to buy happiness, but simply an absence of unhappiness. Money was the panacea, the objectification of his deepest, most inexpressible desires as a human being. He did not want to spend it, he wanted to have it, to know that it was there. Money not as an elixir, then, but as an antidote: the small vial of medicine you carry in your pocket when you go out into the jungle—just in case you are bitten by a poisonous snake.


At times, his reluctance to spend money was so great it almost resembled a disease. It never came to such a point that he would deny himself what he needed (for his needs were minimal), but more subtly, each time he had to buy something, he would opt for the cheapest solution. This was bargain shopping as a way of life.

Implicit in this attitude was a kind of perceptual primitivism. All distinctions were eliminated, everything was reduced to its least common denominator. Meat was meat, shoes were shoes, a pen was a pen. It did not

matter that you could choose between chuck and porterhouse, that there
were throwaway ball points for thirty-nine cents and fifty dollar fountain
pens that would last for twenty years. The truly fine object was almost to
be abhorred: it meant that you would have to pay an extravagant price,
and that made it morally unsound. On a more general level, this translated itself into a permanent state of sensory deprivation: by closing his
eyes to so much, he denied himself intimate contact with the shapes and
textures of the world, cut himself off from the possibility of experiencing
aesthetic pleasure. The world he looked out on was a practical place. Each
thing in it had a value and a price, and the idea was to get the things you
needed at a price that was as close to the value as possible. Each thing was
understood only in terms of its function, judged only by how much it cost,
never as an intrinsic object with its own special properties. In some way, I
imagine it must have made the world seem a dull place to him. Uniform,
colorless, without depth. If you see the world only in terms of money, you
are finally not seeing the world at all.


     As a child, there were times when I became positively embarrassed for
him in public. Haggling with shopkeepers, furious over a high price, arguing as if his very manhood were at stake. A distinct memory of how
everything would wither up inside me, of wanting to be anywhere in the
world except where I was. A particular incident of going with him to buy
a baseball glove stands out. Everyday for two weeks I had visited the store
after school to admire the one I wanted. Then, when my father took me to
the store one evening to buy it, he so exploded at the salesman I was
afraid he was going to tear him to pieces. Frightened, sick at heart, I told
him not to bother, that I didn't want the glove after all. As we were leaving the store, he offered to buy me an ice cream cone. That glove was no
good anyway, he said. I'll buy you a better one some other time.
     Better, of course, meant worse.


     Tirades about leaving too many lights on in the house. He always
made a point of buying bulbs with low wattage.


     His excuse for never taking us to the movies: "Why go out and spend a
fortune when it will be on television in a year or two?"


     The occasional family meal in a restaurant: we always had to order the
least expensive things on the menu. It became a kind of ritual. Yes, he
would say, nodding his head, that's a good choice.
     Years later, when my wife and I were living in New York, he would
sometimes take us out to dinner. The script was always precisely the

same: the moment after we had put the last forkful of food into our mouths, he would ask, "Are you ready to go?" Impossible even to consider dessert.

His utter discomfort in his own skin. His inability to sit still, to make small talk, to "relax."

It made you nervous to be with him. You felt he was always on the verge of leaving.

He loved clever little tricks, prided himself on his ability to outsmart the world at its own game. A niggardliness in the most trivial aspects of life, as ridiculous as it was depressing. With his cars, he would always disconnect the odometers, falsifying the mileage in order to guarantee himself a better trade-in price. In his house, he would always do his own repair work instead of hiring a professional. Because he had a gift for machines and knew how things worked, he would take bizarre short cuts, using whatever materials were at hand to rig up Rube Goldberg solutions to mechanical and electrical problems—rather than spending the money to do it right.

Permanent solutions never interested him. He went on patching and patching, a little piece here, a little piece there, never allowing his boat to sink, but never giving it a chance to float either.

The way he dressed: as if twenty years behind the times. Cheap synthetic suits from the racks of discount stores; unboxed pairs of shoes from the bins of bargain basements. Beyond giving proof of his miserliness, this disregard of fashion reinforced the image of him as a man not quite in the world. The clothes he wore seemed to be an expression of solitude, a concrete way of affirming his absence. Even though he was well off, able to afford anything he wanted, he looked like a poor man, a hayseed who had just stepped off the farm.

In the last years of his life, this changed a little bit. Becoming a bachelor again had probably given him a jolt: he realized that he would have to make himself presentable if he wanted to have any kind of social life. It was not that he went out and bought expensive clothes, but at least the tone of his wardrobe changed: the dull browns and grays were abandoned for brighter colors; the outmoded style gave way to a flashier, more dapper image. Checkered pants, white shoes, yellow turtlenecks, boots with big buckles. But in spite of these efforts, he never looked quite at home in these costumes. They were not an integral part of his personality. It made you think of a little boy who had been dressed up by his parents.

Given his curious relationship to money (his desire for wealth, his inability to spend), it was somehow appropriate that he made his living among the poor. Compared to them, he was a man of enormous riches. And yet, by spending his days among people who had next to nothing, he could keep before his eyes a vision of the thing he most feared in the world: to be without money. It put things in perspective for him. He did not consider himself stingy—but sensible, a man who knew the value of a dollar. He had to be vigilant. It was the only thing that stood between him and the nightmare of poverty.

When the business was at its peak, he and his brothers owned nearly a hundred buildings. Their terrain was the grim industrial region of northern New Jersey—Jersey City, Newark—and nearly all their tenants were black. One says "slumlord," but in this case it would not have been an accurate or fair description. Nor was he in any way an absentee landlord. He was *there,* and he put in hours that would have driven even the most conscientious employee to go out on strike.

The job was a permanent juggling act. There was the buying and selling of buildings, the buying and repairing of fixtures, the managing of several teams of repair men, the renting of apartments, the supervision of the superintendents, listening to tenant complaints, dealing with the visits of building inspectors, constant involvement with the water and electric companies, not to speak of frequent visits to court—both as plaintiff and defendant—to sue for back rent, to answer to violations. Everything was always happening at once, a perpetual assault from a dozen directions at the same time, and only a man who took things in his stride could have handled it. On any given day it was impossible to do everything that had to be done. You did not go home because you were finished, but simply because it was late and you had run out of time. The next day all the problems would be waiting for you—and several new ones as well. It never stopped. In fifteen years he took only two vacations.

He was soft-hearted with the tenants—granting them delays in paying their rent, giving clothes to their children, helping them to find work—and they trusted him. Old men, afraid of being robbed, would give him their most valuable possessions to store in his office safe. Of all the brothers, he was the one people went to with their troubles. No one called him Mr. Auster. He was always Mr. Sam.

While cleaning out the house after his death, I came across this letter at the bottom of a kitchen drawer. Of all the things I found, I am happiest to have retrieved this. It somehow balances the ledger, provides me with living proof whenever my mind begins to stray too far from the facts. The letter is addressed to "Mr. Sam," and the handwriting is nearly illegible.

April 19, 1976

Dear Sam,

I know you are so surprised to hear from me. first of all maybe I better introduce my self to you. I'm Mrs. Nash. I'm Albert Groover Sister in law—Mrs. Groover and Albert that lived at 285 pine Street in Jersey City so long and Mrs. Banks thats my Sister too. Any way. if you can remember.

You made arrangement to get the apartment for my children and I at 327 Johnston Ave right around the Corner from Mr. & Mrs. Groover my Sister.

Anyway I move away left of owing a $40. rent. this was the year of 1964 but I didn't for get I owed this earnest debt. So now here is your money. thanks for being so very nice to the children and I at that time. this is how much I appreciated what you done for us. I hope you can recall back to the time. So you was never forgotten by me.

About 3 weeks ago I called the office but weren't in at that time. may the Good Lord ever to Bless you. I hardly comes to Jersey City if so I would stop by see you.

No matter now I am happy to pay this debt. All for now.
Sincerely
Mrs. JB. Nash

As a boy, I would occasionally go the rounds with him as he collected rent. I was too young to understand what I was seeing, but I remember the impression it made on me, as if, precisely because I did not understand, the raw perceptions of these experiences went directly into me, where they remain today, as immediate as a splinter in the thumb.

The wooden buildings with their dark, inhospitable hallways. And behind each door, a horde of children playing in a bare apartment; a mother, always sullen, overworked, tired, bent over an ironing board. Most vivid is the smell, as if poverty were more than a lack of money, but a physical sensation, a stench that invaded your head and made it impossible to think. Every time I walked into a building with my father, I would hold my breath, not daring to breathe, as if that smell were going to hurt me. Everyone was always happy to meet Mr. Sam's son. I was given innumerable smiles and pats on the head.

Once, when I was a bit older, I can remember driving with him down a street in Jersey City and seeing a boy wearing a T-shirt I had outgrown several months before. It was a very distinctive shirt, with a peculiar combination of yellow and blue stripes, and there was no question that this was the one that had been mine. Unaccountably, I was overcome with a feeling of shame.

Older still, at thirteen, fourteen, fifteen, I would sometimes go in with him to earn money working with the carpenters, painters, and repair men. Once, on an excruciatingly hot day in the middle of summer, I was given the job of helping one of the men tar a roof. The man's name was Joe Levine (a black man who had changed his name to Levine out of gratitude to an old Jewish grocer who had helped him in his youth), and he was my father's most trusted and reliable handyman. We hauled several fifty gallon barrels of tar up to the roof and got to work spreading the stuff over the surface with brooms. The sunlight beating down on that flat black roof was brutal, and after half an hour or so I became extremely dizzy, slipped on a patch of wet tar, fell, and somehow knocked over one of the open barrels, which then spilled tar all over me.

When I got back to the office a few minutes later, my father was greatly amused. I realized that the situation was amusing, but I was too embarrassed to want to joke about it. To my father's credit, he did not get angry at me or make fun of me. He laughed, but in a way that made me laugh too. Then he dropped what he had been doing, took me to the Woolworth's across the street, and bought me some new clothes. It had suddenly become possible for me to feel close to him.


As the years went by, the business started to decline. The business it-self was not at fault, but rather the nature of the business: at that particular time, in that particular place, it was no longer possible to survive. The cities were falling apart, and no one seemed to care. What had once been a more or less fulfilling activity for my father now became simple drudgery. In the last years of his life he hated going to work.

Vandalism became such a severe problem that doing any kind of re-pairs became a demoralizing gesture. No sooner was plumbing installed in a building than the pipes would be ripped out by thieves. Windows were constantly being broken, doors smashed, hallways gutted, fires started. At the same time, it was impossible to sell out. No one wanted the buildings. The only way to get rid of them was to abandon them and let the cities take over. Tremendous amounts of money were lost in this way, an entire life's work. In the end, at the time of my father's death, there were only six or seven buildings left. The whole empire had disin-tegrated.

The last time I was in Jersey City (at least ten years ago) the place had the look of a disaster area, as if it had been pillaged by Huns. Gray, deso-late streets; garbage piled everywhere; derelicts shuffling aimlessly up and down. My father's office had been robbed so many times that by now there was nothing left in it but some gray metal desks, a few chairs, and three or four telephones. Not even a typewriter, not one touch of color. It was not really a work place anymore, but a room in hell. I sat down and looked out at the bank across the street. No one came out, no one went in. The only living things were two stray dogs humping on the steps.

How he managed to pick himself up and go in there everyday is be-yond my understanding. Force of habit, or else sheer stubbornness. Not only was it depressing, it was dangerous. He was mugged several times, and once was kicked in the head so viciously by an attacker that his hear-ing was permanently damaged. For the last four or five years of his life there was a faint and constant ringing in his head, a humming that never went away, not even while he was asleep. The doctors said there was nothing that could be done about it.

In the end, he never went out into the street without carrying a monkey wrench in his right hand. He was over sixty-five years old, and he did not want to take any more chances.

Two sentences that suddenly come to mind this morning as I am showing Daniel how to make scrambled eggs.

"'And now I want to know,' the woman says, with terrible force, 'I want to know whether it is possible to find another father like him anywhere in the world.'" (Isaac Babel)

"Children have always a tendency either to depreciate or to exalt their parents, and to a good son his father is always the best of fathers, quite apart from any objective reason there may be for admiring him." (Proust)

I realize now that I must have been a bad son. Or if not precisely bad, then at least a disappointment, a source of confusion and sadness. It made no sense to him that he had produced a poet for a son. Nor could he understand why a young man with two degrees from Columbia University should take a job after graduation as an ordinary seaman on an oil tanker in the Gulf of Mexico, and then, without rhyme or reason, take off for Paris and spend four years there leading a hand to mouth existence.

His most common description of me was that I had "my head in the clouds," or else that I "did not have my feet on the ground." Either way, I must not have seemed very substantial to him, as if I were somehow a vapor or a person not wholly of this world. In his eyes, you became part of the world by working. By definition, work was something that brought in money. If it did not bring in money, it was not work. Writing, therefore, was not work, especially the writing of poetry. At best it was a hobby, a pleasant way to pass the time in between the things that really mattered. My father thought that I was squandering my gifts, refusing to grow up.

Nevertheless, some kind of bond remained between us. We were not close, but stayed in touch. A phone call every month or so, perhaps three or four visits a year. Each time a book of my poetry was published I would dutifully send it to him, and he would always call to thank me. Whenever I wrote an article for a magazine, I would set aside a copy and make sure I gave it to him the next time I saw him. *The New York Review of Books* meant nothing to him, but the pieces in *Commentary* impressed him. I think he felt that if the Jews were publishing me, then perhaps there was something to it.

Once, while I was still living in Paris, he wrote to tell me he had gone to the public library to read some of my poems that had appeared in a recent issue of *Poetry*. I imagined him in a large, deserted room, early in the morning before going to work: sitting at one of those long tables with his overcoat still on, hunched over words that must have been incomprehensible to him.

I have tried to keep this image in mind, along with all the others that will not leave it.


The rampant, totally mystifying force of contradiction. I understand now that each fact is nullified by the next fact, that each thought engenders an equal and opposite thought. Impossible to say anything without reservation: he was good, or he was bad; he was this, or he was that. All of them are true. At times I have the feeling that I am writing about three or four different men, each one distinct, each one a contradiction of all the others. Fragments. Or the anecdote as a form of knowledge.

Yes.


The occasional flash of generosity. At those rare times when the world was not a threat to him, his motive for living seemed to be kindness. "May the good Lord ever to Bless you."

Friends called him whenever they were in trouble. A car stuck somewhere in the middle of the night, and my father would drag himself out of bed and come to the rescue. In certain ways it was easy for others to take advantage of him. He refused to complain about anything.

A patience that bordered on the superhuman. He was the only person I have ever known who could teach someone to drive without getting angry or crumpling in a fit of nerves. You could be careening straight towards a lamp post, and still he would not get excited.

Impenetrable. And because of that, at times almost serene.


Starting when he was still a young man, he always took a special interest in his oldest nephew—the only child of his only sister. My aunt had an unhappy life, punctuated by a series of difficult marriages, and her son bore the brunt of it: shipped off to military schools, never really given a home. Motivated, I think, by nothing more than kindness and a sense of duty, my father took the boy under his wing. He nursed him along with constant encouragement, taught him how to get along in the world. Later, he helped him in business, and whenever a problem came up, he was always ready to listen and give advice. Even after my cousin married and had his own family, my father continued to take an active interest, putting them up in his house at one point for more than a year, religiously giving presents to his four grand-nephews and grand-nieces on their birthdays, and often going to visit them for dinner.

This cousin was more shaken by my father's death than any of my other relatives. At the family gathering after the funeral he came up to me three or four times and said, "I ran into him by accident just the other day. We were supposed to have dinner together Friday night."

The words he used were exactly the same each time. As if he no longer knew what he was saying.

I felt that we had somehow reversed roles, that he was the grieving son and I was the sympathetic nephew. I wanted to put my arm around his shoulder and tell him what a good man his father had been. After all, he was the real son, he was the son I could never bring myself to be.

For the past two weeks, these lines from Maurice Blanchot echoing in my head: "One thing must be understood: I have said nothing extraordinary or even surprising. What is extraordinary begins at the moment I stop. But I am no longer able to speak of it."

To begin with death. To work my way back into life, and then, finally, to return to death.

Or else: the vanity of trying to say anything about anyone.

In 1972 he came to visit me in Paris. It was the one time he ever travelled to Europe.

I was living that year in a minuscule sixth floor maid's room barely large enough for a bed, a table, a chair, and a sink. The windows and little balcony stared into the face of one of the stone angels that jutted from St. Germain Auxerrois: the Louvre to my left, Les Halles off to my right, and Montmartre in the far distance ahead. I had a great fondness for that room, and many of the poems that later appeared in my first book were written there.

My father was not planning to stay for any length of time, hardly even what you would call a vacation: four days in London, three days in Paris, and then home again. But I was pleased at the thought of seeing him and prepared myself to show him a good time.

Two things happened, however, that made this impossible. I became very ill with the flu; and I had to leave for Mexico the day after his arrival to work on a ghostwriting project.

I waited for him all morning in the lobby of the tourist hotel where he had booked reservations, sweating away with a high fever, almost delirious with weakness. When he did not show up at the appointed time, I stayed on for another hour or two, but finally gave in and went back to my room where I collapsed into bed.

Late in the afternoon he came and knocked on my door, waking me from a deep sleep. The encounter was straight out of Dostoyevsky: bourgeois father comes to visit son in a foreign city and finds the struggling poet alone in a garret, wasting away with fever. He was shocked by what he saw, outraged that anyone could live in such a room, and it galvanized him into action: he made me put on my coat, dragged me off to a neighborhood clinic, and then bought the pills that were prescribed for me. Afterwards, he refused to allow me to spend the night in my room. I was in no condition to argue, so I agreed to stay in his hotel.

The next day I was no better. But there were things to be done, and I picked myself up and did them. In the morning I took my father along with me to the vast Avenue Henri Martin apartment of the movie producer who was sending me to Mexico. For the past year I had been working on and off for this man, doing what amounted to odd jobs—translations, script synopses—things that were only marginally connected to the movies, which anyway did not interest me. Each project was more idiotic than the last, but the pay was good, and I needed the money. Now he wanted me to help his Mexican wife with a book she had been contracted to write for an English publisher: Quetzalcoatl and the mysteries of the plumed serpent. This seemed to be pushing it a bit, and I had already turned him down several times. But each time I said no, his offer had gone up, until now I was being paid so much money that I could no longer turn away. I would only be gone for a month, and I was being paid in cash—in advance.

This was the transaction my father witnessed. For once, I could see that he was impressed. Not only had I led him into this luxurious setting and introduced him to a man who did business in the millions, but now this man was calmly handing me a stack of hundred dollar bills across the table and telling me to have a pleasant trip. It was the money, of course, that made the difference, the fact that my father had seen it with his own eyes. I felt it as a triumph, as if I had somehow been vindicated. For the first time he had been forced to realize that I could take care of myself on my own terms.

He became very protective, indulgent of my weakened condition. Helped me deposit the money in the bank, all smiles and jokes. Then got us a cab and rode all the way to the airport with me. A big handshake at the end. Good luck, son. Knock 'em dead.

You bet.

Nothing now for several days . . .

In spite of the excuses I have made for myself, I understand what is happening. The closer I come to the end of what I am able to say, the more reluctant I am to say anything. I want to postpone the moment of ending, and in this way delude myself into thinking that I have only just begun, that the better part of my story still lies ahead. No matter how useless these words might seem to be, they have nevertheless stood between me and a silence that continues to terrify me. When I step into this silence, it will mean that my father has vanished forever.

The dingy green carpet in the funeral home. And the director, unctuous, professional, suffering from eczema and swollen ankles, going down a checklist of expenses as if I were about to buy a suite of bedroom furniture on credit. He handed me an envelope that contained the ring my father had been wearing when he died. Idly fingering the ring as the conversation droned on, I noticed that the underside of the stone was smeared with the residue of some soapy lubricant. A few moments passed before I made the connection, and then it became absurdly obvious: the lotion had been used to remove the ring from his finger. I tried to imagine the person whose job it was to do such things. I did not feel horror so much as fascination. I remember thinking to myself: I have entered the world of facts, the realm of brute particulars. The ring was gold, with a black setting that bore the insignia of the Masonic brotherhood. My father had not been an active member for over twenty years.

The funeral director kept telling me how he had known my father "in the old days," implying an intimacy and friendship I was sure had never existed. As I gave him the information to be passed on to the newspapers for the obituary, he anticipated my remarks with incorrect facts, rushing ahead of me in order to prove how well acquainted he had been with my father. Each time this happened, I stopped and corrected him. The next day, when the obituary appeared in the paper, many of these incorrect facts were printed.

Three days before he died, my father had bought a new car. He had driven it once, maybe twice, and when I returned to his house after the funeral, I saw it sitting in the garage, already defunct, like some huge, stillborn creature. Later that same day I went off to the garage for a moment to be by myself. I sat down behind the wheel of his car, inhaling the strange factory newness of it. The odometer read sixty-seven miles. That also happened to have been my father's age: sixty-seven years. The brevity of it sickened me. As if that were the distance between life and death. A tiny trip, hardly longer than a drive to the next town.

Worst regret: that I was not given a chance to see him after he died. Ignorantly, I had assumed the coffin would be open during the funeral service, and then, when it wasn't, it was too late to do anything about it.

Never to have seen him dead deprives me of an anguish I would have welcomed. It is not that his death has been made any less real, but now, each time I want to see it, each time I want to touch its reality, I must engage in an act of imagination. There is nothing to remember. Nothing but a kind of emptiness.

When the grave was uncovered to receive the coffin, I noticed a thick orange root thrusting into the hole. It had a strangely calming effect on me. For a brief moment the bare fact of death could no longer be hidden behind the words and gestures of ceremony. Here it was: unmediated, unadorned, impossible to turn my eyes away from. My father was being lowered into the ground, and in time, as the coffin gradually disintegrated, his body would help to feed the same root I had seen. More than anything that had been said or done that day, this made sense to me.

. . .

The rabbi who conducted the funeral service was the same man who had presided over my Bar Mitzvah nineteen years earlier. The last time I had seen him he was a youngish, clean-shaven man. Now he was old, with a full gray beard. He had not known my father, in fact knew nothing about him, and half an hour before the service was to begin I sat down with him and told him what to say in the eulogy. He made notes on little scraps of paper. When it came time for him to deliver the speech, he spoke with great feeling. The subject was a man he had never known, and yet he made it sound as though he were speaking from the heart. Behind me, I could hear women sobbing. He was following what I had told him almost word for word.

It occurs to me that I began writing this story a long time ago, long before my father died.


Night after night, lying awake in bed, my eyes open in the darkness. The impossibility of sleep, the impossibility of not thinking about how he died. I find myself sweating between the sheets, trying to imagine what it feels like to suffer a heart attack. Adrenalin pumps through me, my head pounds, and my whole body seems to contract into a small area behind my chest. A need to experience the same panic, the same mortal pain.

And then, at night, there are the dreams, nearly every night. In one of them, which woke me up just hours ago, I learned from the teenage daughter of my father's lady friend that she, the daughter, had been made pregnant by my father. Because she was so young, it was agreed that my wife and I would raise the child after it was born. The baby was going to be a boy. Everyone knew this in advance.

It is equally true, perhaps, that once this story has ended, it will go on telling itself, even after the words have been used up.


The old gentleman at the funeral was my great uncle, Sam Auster, now almost ninety years old. Tall, hairless, a high-pitched, rasping voice. Not a word about the events of 1919, and I did not have the heart to ask him. I took care of Sam when he was a little boy, he said. But that was all.

When asked if he wanted anything to drink, he requested a glass of hot water. Lemon? No thank you, just hot water.


Again Blanchot: "But I am no longer able to speak of it."


From the house: a document from St. Clair County in the State of Alabama duly announcing my parents' divorce. The signature at the bottom: Ann W. Love.


From the house: a watch, a few sweaters, a jacket, an alarm clock, six tennis rackets, and an old rusted Buick that barely runs. A set of dishes, a coffee table, three or four lamps. A barroom statue of Johnnie Walker for Daniel. The blank photograph album, This Is Our Life: The Austers.

At first I thought it would be a comfort to hold on to these things, that they would remind me of my father and make me think of him as I went about my life. But objects, it seems, are no more than objects. I am used to them now, I have begun to think of them as my own. I read time by his watch, I wear his sweaters, I drive around in his car. But all this is no more than an illusion of intimacy. I have already appropriated these things. My father has vanished from them, has become invisible again. And sooner or later they will break down, fall apart, and have to the thrown away. I doubt that it will even seem to matter.


"... here it holds good that only he who works gets the bread, only he who was in anguish finds repose, only he who descends into the underworld rescues the beloved, only he who draws the knife gets Isaac.... He who will not work must take note of what is written about the maidens of Israel, for he gives birth to the wind, but he who is willing to work gives birth to his own father." (Kierkegaard)


Past two in the morning. An overflowing ashtray, an empty coffee cup, and the cold of early spring. An image of Daniel now, as he lies upstairs in his crib asleep. To end with this.

To wonder what he will make of these pages when he is old enough to read them.

And the image of his sweet and ferocious little body, as he lies upstairs in his crib asleep. To end with this.


• • • • • • • • • • • •


QUESTIONS FOR A SECOND READING

1. In a sense, Auster covers familiar landscape with "Portrait of an Invisible Man." He writes, as he says, to keep "trying to find the father who was not there." And "now that he is dead," Auster goes on, "I still feel as though I must go on looking for him. Death has not changed anything. The only difference is that I have run out of time." So—with this piece of writing as your example—what does it mean for a writer to search through, seek out, investigate both family and the past?

   As you reread, mark passages or sections that will allow you to think more closely about Auster's way of approaching this project, "finding the father who was not there," even to approach Auster critically (that is, by stepping outside of his point of view, his set of values, or his train of

thought). How does Auster represent himself as both writer and son?
What does he use to represent the father? What is readily available? What
does he seek out or discover? What is missing? How does he conduct his
search? What alternative roles might he play?

2.  In an interview Auster said, "I don't think of [*The Invention of Solitude*] as
    an autobiography so much as a meditation about certain questions, using
    myself as the central character." As you reread, keep this statement in
    mind. What would you identify as the "questions" at the center of this
    meditation? Where and how does Auster define himself as a "character"?
    What role does this character play as you process the information he gives
    you about his father?

3.  The most distinctive formal feature in "Portrait of an Invisible Man" is the
    line breaks (the white space or gaps between sections). Auster uses both
    paragraph breaks and line breaks to punctuate or organize his prose. As
    you reread, see if you can find the pattern or logic to this. If you were
    going to write a set of rules for determining when to mark paragraph
    boundaries and when to mark section boundaries, what rules can you di-
    vine from Auster?

4.  At one point Auster utters what might be taken as a Writer's Lament:

    > No sooner have I thought one thing than it evokes another thing, and
    > then another thing, until there is an accumulation of detail so dense
    > that I feel I am going to suffocate. (p. 71)

    And one paragraph earlier he says,

    > Slowly, I am coming to understand the absurdity of the task I have set
    > for myself. I have a sense of trying to go somewhere, as if I knew what I
    > wanted to say, but the farther I go the more certain I am that the path
    > towards my object does not exist. I have to invent the road with each
    > step, and this means that I can never be sure of where I am. (p. 70)

    Auster invites you to think about his problems as a writer's problems, not
    simply as family problems or ethical problems or psychological problems.
    If Auster is an expert writing about his work, what lessons does he offer?
    What can a student writer learn from what he says and what he does?
    What can *you* learn?

        As you reread, look for the points where Auster speaks directly about
    his work as a writer. How does he invent a "road" along or into a project
    like this one? What might you call an "invention"? Mark sections you
    could use in a discussion of what Auster says about writing. Also mark
    passages you could use as distinctive examples of this writer's work *as* a
    writer, examples of his craft, art, or invention.

## ASSIGNMENTS FOR WRITING

1.  By writing "Portrait of an Invisible Man," Auster memorializes his father.
    As you follow the accounts of the father, you learn also about the other
    major character in this text, the son. The Paul Auster in the text is also a
    literary invention, a character. And yet the writing is neither sentimental
    nor celebratory; it is surprisingly unsympathetic. Neither father nor son

plays the roles we expect them to play. The text does not offer the usual narrative of reconciliation; the writer does not take ready positions of admiration or tribute. The writing does not represent or evoke emotional response. One might call it "calculated," although Auster keeps saying that he has no (or can find no) plan. The prose refuses to turn to cliché and it refuses to come to any clear conclusion. (What is the point of the account of the murder, for example?)

For most readers, Auster's portrait is difficult, even troubling. It is useful to begin with the assumption that Auster causes this trouble on purpose. And, having done it, he brings it to publication. He obviously thinks that what he has done was worth doing, worth doing not only for himself (and perhaps for his father), but also for all of us (as we think, perhaps, about fathers or families, memories or the past). As you read back through this piece, what *was* Auster doing? And why? How might you explain or justify this piece of writing?

Write an essay, perhaps cast as a review, in which you explain what it is you think Auster is doing in this piece and why someone might read it with interest. (You can think of a review as an account of the selection for those who have not yet read it.) Don't feel that you have to be positive in your assessment; if you are negative, however, you do need to take the work seriously and not simply dismiss it as, for instance, unpleasant or mean-spirited or self-aggrandizing.

2. Auster stops at several points in his essay to write about writing and the problems he is having with this project. At one point, he says he is reluctant to continue; at another he says that he is going "in circles" or "backtracking" or "going off in many directions at once." He has, he says, examples but no conclusions. "No sooner have I thought one thing than it evokes another thing, and then another thing, until there is an accumulation of detail so dense that I feel I am going to suffocate." "Just because you wander in the desert," he says, "it does not mean there is a promised land."

Locate two or three moments in the text where Auster writes in interesting ways about writing and the problems he is trying to solve. What are those problems? How are they writing problems? How does he solve or attempt to solve them? Is his prose satisfactory to you as his reader? Is there something here for you as a writer? a writing lesson, perhaps? an exercise? technique?

3. Reread "Portrait of an Invisible Man" with an eye toward those features that make Auster's prose distinctive, unusual, experimental. (There are, for example, the line breaks, marking off sections (or fragments), the use of photos and other documentary material, including newspapers and passages from his reading, and the mix of narrative, report, and reflection.) As you reread, think of these features in relation to what he says about his project, about the problems of writing about a person and about the past.

Once you have studied this piece of writing *as* a piece of writing, write an Auster-like piece of your own, one that has the design, ambitions, and rhythms of "Portrait." You might be tempted to shape your project around a subject similar to his and write family history. This would be fine, but don't feel that you have to. Write about something you find interesting and compelling, where there are examples (materials) you won't (or can't) easily explain. This assignment does not, in other words, ask you to begin with an idea or an outline or to know what you are going to say; it is not an exercise in topic sentence, example, and conclusion; it does not ask for an essay with the structure of thesis and proofs.

4. At one point in the text Auster says:

> The rampant, totally mystifying force of contradiction. I understand now that each fact is nullified by the next fact, that each thought engenders an equal and opposite thought. Impossible to say anything without reservation: he was good, or he was bad; he was this, or he was that. All of them are true. At times I have the feeling that I am writing about three or four different men, each one distinct, each one a contradiction of all the others. Fragments. Or the anecdote as a form of knowledge.
>    Yes. (p. 94)

What might it mean to claim the anecdote as a form of knowledge? Write an essay in which you take "Portrait of an Invisible Man" as an experiment in thinking through anecdotes and fragments. Auster uses familiar metaphors for human understanding—wandering, entering the darkness. He makes lists, gathers materials, interprets, moves toward closure (or some sense of an ending). He worries that "when the moment arrives for me to say the one truly important thing (assuming it exists), I will not be able to say it." Yet he does write into and past those moments, and it could be said that he'd been building arguments, coming to understand many things, among them, of course, would be his father, himself, his family, their past, but also memory, thinking, writing, history.

Write an essay in which you discuss the forms of knowledge represented in Auster's essay. Discuss and document the forms of knowledge, where they lead, what they can (and can't) do, and what, with them, one has in the end.

### MAKING CONNECTIONS

1. Both John Edgar Wideman, in "Our Time (p. 707)," and Auster, in "Portrait of an Invisible Man," write texts that could be said to be meditations on writing, in particular on the problems of writing family history. Wideman writes about his brother Robby. Auster writes about his father. For both, however, the writing becomes the occasion to think about the dangers of memory, the limits of record, the difficulties of representing people and the past.

Write an essay in which you both explain and explore the projects represented by the two pieces of writing. What do they do? How do they do what they do? (You should assume that you are presenting this information to someone who has not seen these selections. You will need, then, to choose and present your examples carefully.) In thinking about these authors' different styles and different investments in writing, look for differences, not just similarities. What, for each, is to be gained (or what is at stake) in these projects?

2. At first glance, Auster's text and Susan Griffin's "Our Secret" (p. 404) are strikingly similar. In both the page is broken into sections. Both begin with examples and resist conclusions. The order of presentation is difficult, unconventional, circuitous. These are, however, also strikingly different projects. Griffin, after all, is writing about the Second World War, Auster about his family. Griffin was trained as a historian, Auster as a poet and novelist.

   Write an essay in which you look comparatively at these two texts. What are their characteristic methods of gathering materials, of thinking them through, and of presenting them to readers? What demands do they make of their readers? How do they teach you to read or to read differently? How, for each writer, would you characterize the writer's methods and intentions? And, finally, what can a student learn about writing (or about being a writer) by studying these pieces? What is at stake by following one or both of these examples? What is to be gained?

# JOHN BERGER

*J*OHN BERGER *(b. 1926), like few other art critics, elicits strong and contra-dictory reactions to his writing. He has been called (sometimes in the same re-view) "preposterous" as well as "stimulating," "pompous" yet "exciting." He has been accused of falling prey to "ideological excesses" and of being a victim of his own "lack of objectivity," but he has been praised for his "scrupulous" and "co-gent" observations on art and culture. He is one of Europe's most influential Marxist critics, yet his work has been heralded and damned by leftists and conser-vatives alike. Although Berger's work speaks powerfully, its tone is quiet, thoughtful, measured. According to the poet and critic Peter Schjeldahl, "The most mysterious element in Mr. Berger's criticism has always been the personal-ity of the critic himself, a man of strenuous conviction so loath to bully that even his most provocative arguments sit feather-light on the mind."*

*The first selection is Chapter 1 from* Ways of Seeing, *a book which began as a series on BBC television. In fact, the show was a forerunner of those encyclopedic television series later popular on public television stations in the United States:* Civilization, The Ascent of Man, Cosmos. *Berger's show was less glittery and ambitious, but in its way it was more serious in its claims to be educational. As you watched the screen, you saw a series of images (like those in the following text). These were sometimes presented with commentary, but sometimes in silence, so that you constantly saw one image in the context of another—for example, classic* presentations of women in oil paintings interspersed with images of women from contemporary art, advertising, movies, and "men's magazines." The goal of the exercise, according to Berger, was to "start a process of questioning," to focus his viewer's attention not on a single painting in isolation but on "ways of seeing" in general, on the ways we have learned to look at and understand the images that surround us, and on the culture that teaches us to see things as we do. The method of Ways of Seeing, *a book of art history, was used by Berger in another book,* A Seventh Man, *to document the situation of the migrant worker in Europe.*

*After the chapter from* Ways of Seeing, *we have added two brief passages from a beautiful, slight, and quite compelling book by Berger,* And Our Faces, My Heart, Brief as Photos. *This book is both a meditation on time and space and a long love letter (if you can imagine such a combination!). At several points in the book, Berger turns his (and his reader's) attention to paintings. We have included two instances, his descriptions of Rembrandt's* Woman in Bed *and Caravaggio's* The Calling of St. Matthew *(and we have included reproductions of the paintings). We offer these as supplements to* Ways of Seeing, *as additional examples of how a writer turns images into words and brings the present to the past.*

*Berger has written poems, novels, essays, and film scripts, including* The Success and Failure of Picasso *(1965),* A Fortunate Man *(1967),* G. *(1971), and* About Looking *(1980). He lived and worked in England for years, but he currently lives in Quincy, a small peasant village in Haute-Savoie, France, where he has, for the past few years, been writing a trilogy of books on peasant life, titled* Into Their Labours. *The first book in the series,* Pig Earth *(1979), is a collection of essays, poems, and stories set in Haute-Savoie. The second,* Once in Europa *(1987), consists of five peasant tales that take love as their subject. The third and final book in the trilogy,* Lilac and Flag: An Old Wives' Tale of the City, *published in 1990, is a novel about the migration of peasants to the city. His most recent book,* Photocopies, *is a collection of short stories published in 1996.*

# *Ways of Seeing*

Seeing comes before words. The child looks and recognizes before it can speak.

But there is also another sense in which seeing comes before words. It is seeing which establishes our place in the surrounding world; we explain that world with words, but words can never undo the fact that we are surrounded by it. The relation between what we see and what we know is never settled. Each evening we *see* the sun set. We *know* that the earth is turning away from it. Yet the knowledge, the explanation, never quite fits the sight. The Surrealist painter Magritte commented on this always-present gap between words and seeing in a painting called *The Key of Dreams.*

*The Key of Dreams* by Magritte 1898–1967

The way we see things is affected by what we know or what we be-lieve. In the Middle Ages when men believed in the physical existence of Hell the sight of fire must have meant something different from what it means today. Nevertheless their idea of Hell owed a lot to the sight of fire consuming and the ashes remaining—as well as to their experience of the pain of burns.

When in love, the sight of the beloved has a completeness which no words and no embrace can match: a completeness which only the act of making love can temporarily accommodate.

Yet this seeing which comes before words, and can never be quite cov-ered by them, is not a question of mechanically reacting to stimuli. (It can only be thought of in this way if one isolates the small part of the process which concerns the eye's retina.) We only see what we look at. To look is an act of choice. As a result of this act, what we see is brought within our reach—though not necessarily within arm's reach. To touch something is to situate oneself in relation to it. (Close your eyes, move round the room and notice how the faculty of touch is like a static, limited form of sight.) We never look at just one thing; we are always looking at the relation be-tween things and ourselves. Our vision is continually active, continually moving, continually holding things in a circle around itself, constituting what is present to us as we are.

Soon after we can see, we are aware that we can also be seen. The eye of the other combines with our own eye to make it fully credible that we are part of the visible world.

If we accept that we can see that hill over there, we propose that from that hill we can be seen. The reciprocal nature of vision is more fundamental than that of spoken dialogue. And often dialogue is an attempt to verbalize this—an attempt to explain how, either metaphorically or literally, "you see things," and an attempt to discover how "he sees things."

In the sense in which we use the word in this book, all images are manmade [see above]. An image is a sight which has been recreated or reproduced. It is an appearance, or a set of appearances, which has been detached from the place and time in which it first made its appearance and preserved—for a few moments or a few centuries. Every image embodies a way of seeing. Even a photograph. For photographs are not, as is often assumed, a mechanical record. Every time we look at a photograph, we are aware, however slightly, of the photographer selecting that sight from an infinity of other possible sights. This is true even in the most casual family snapshot. The photographer's way of seeing is reflected in his choice of subject. The painter's way of seeing is reconstituted by the marks he makes on the canvas or paper. Yet, although every image embodies a way of seeing, our perception or appreciation of an image depends also upon our own way of seeing. (It may be, for example, that Sheila is one figure among twenty; but for our own reasons she is the one we have eyes for.)

Images were first made to conjure up the appearance of something that was absent. Gradually it became evident that an image could outlast what it represented; it then showed how something or somebody had once looked—and thus by implication how the subject had once been seen by other people. Later still the specific vision of the image-maker was also recognized as part of the record. An image became a record of how X had seen Y. This was the result of an increasing consciousness of individuality, accompanying an increasing awareness of history. It would be rash to try to date this last development precisely. But certainly in Europe such consciousness has existed since the beginning of the Renaissance.

No other kind of relic or text from the past can offer such a direct testimony about the world which surrounded other people at other times. In this respect images are more precise and richer than literature. To say this is not to deny the expressive or imaginative quality of art, treating it as mere documentary evidence; the more imaginative the work, the more profoundly it allows us to share the artist's experience of the visible.

Yet when an image is presented as a work of art, the way people look at it is affected by a whole series of learnt assumptions about art. Assumptions concerning:

> Beauty
> Truth
> Genius
> Civilization
> Form
> Status
> Taste, etc.

Many of these assumptions no longer accord with the world as it is. (The world-as-it-is is more than pure objective fact, it includes consciousness.) Out of true with the present, these assumptions obscure the past. They mystify rather than clarify. The past is never there waiting to be discovered, to be recognized for exactly what it is. History always constitutes the relation between a present and its past. Consequently fear of the present leads to mystification of the past. The past is not for living in; it is a well of conclusions from which we draw in order to act. Cultural mystification of the past entails a double loss. Works of art are made unnecessarily remote. And the past offers us fewer conclusions to complete in action.

When we "see" a landscape, we situate ourselves in it. If we "saw" the art of the past, we would situate ourselves in history. When we are prevented from seeing it, we are being deprived of the history which belongs to us. Who benefits from this deprivation? In the end, the art of the past is being mystified because a privileged minority is striving to invent a history which can retrospectively justify the role of the ruling classes, and such a justification can no longer make sense in modern terms. And so, inevitably, it mystifies.

Let us consider a typical example of such mystification. A two-volume study was recently published on Frans Hals.[1] It is the authoritative work to date on this painter. As a book of specialized art history it is no better and no worse than the average.

*Regents of the Old Men's Alms House* by Hals 1580–1666

*Regentesses of the Old Men's Alms House* by Hals 1580–1666

The last two great paintings by Frans Hals [above] portray the Governors and the Governesses of an Alms House for old paupers in the Dutch seventeenth-century city of Haarlem. They were officially commissioned portraits. Hals, an old man of over eighty, was destitute. Most of his life he had been in debt. During the winter of 1664, the year he began painting these pictures, he obtained three loads of peat on public charity, otherwise he would have frozen to death. Those who now sat for him were administrators of such public charity.

The author records these facts and then explicitly says that it would be incorrect to read into the paintings any criticism of the sitters. There is no evidence, he says, that Hals painted them in a spirit of bitterness. The author considers them, however, remarkable works of art and explains why. Here he writes of the Regentesses:

> Each woman speaks to us of the human condition with equal importance. Each woman stands out with equal clarity against the *enormous* dark surface, yet they are linked by a firm rhythmical arrangement and the subdued diagonal pattern formed by their heads and hands. Subtle modulations of the *deep,* glowing blacks contribute to the *harmonious fusion* of the whole and form an *unforgettable contrast* with the *powerful* whites and vivid flesh tones where the detached strokes reach *a peak of breadth and strength.* [Berger's italics]

The compositional unity of a painting contributes fundamentally to the power of its image. It is reasonable to consider a painting's composition. But here the composition is written about as though it were in itself the emotional charge of the painting. Terms like *harmonious fusion, unforgettable contrast,* reaching *a peak of breadth and strength* transfer the emotion provoked by the image from the plane of lived experience, to that of disinterested "art appreciation." All conflict disappears. One is left with the unchanging "human condition," and the painting considered as a marvellously made object.

Very little is known about Hals or the Regents who commissioned him. It is not possible to produce circumstantial evidence to establish what their relations were. But there is the evidence of the paintings themselves: the evidence of a group of men and a group of women as seen by another man, the painter. Study this evidence and judge for yourself.

The art historian fears such direct judgement:

> As in so many other pictures by Hals, the penetrating charac-
> terizations almost seduce us into believing that we know the
> personality traits and even the habits of the men and women
> portrayed.

What is this "seduction" he writes of? It is nothing less than the paintings working upon us. They work upon us because we accept the way
Hals saw his sitters. We do not accept this innocently. We accept it in so
far as it corresponds to our own observation of people, gestures, faces, institutions. This is possible because we still live in a society of comparable
social relations and moral values. And it is precisely this which gives
the paintings their psychological and social urgency. It is this—not the
painter's skill as a "seducer"—which convinces us that we *can* know the
people portrayed.

The author continues:

> In the case of some critics the seduction has been a total suc-
> cess. It has, for example, been asserted that the Regent in the
> tipped slouch hat, which hardly covers any of his long, lank
> hair, and whose curiously set eyes do not focus, was shown in
> a drunken state. [below]

This, he suggests, is a libel. He argues that it was a fashion at that time
to wear hats on the side of the head. He cites medical opinion to prove
that the Regent's expression could well be the result of a facial paralysis.
He insists that the painting would have been unacceptable to the Regents

if one of them had been portrayed drunk. One might go on discussing each of these points for pages. (Men in seventeenth-century Holland wore their hats on the side of their heads in order to be thought of as adventurous and pleasure-loving. Heavy drinking was an approved practice. Etcetera.) But such a discussion would take us even farther away from the only confrontation which matters and which the author is determined to evade.

In this confrontation the Regents and Regentesses stare at Hals, a destitute old painter who has lost his reputation and lives off public charity; he examines them through the eyes of a pauper who must nevertheless try to be objective; i.e., must try to surmount the way he sees as a pauper. This is the drama of these paintings. A drama of an "unforgettable contrast."

Mystification has little to do with the vocabulary used. Mystification is the process of explaining away what might otherwise be evident. Hals was the first portraitist to paint the new characters and expressions created by capitalism. He did in pictorial terms what Balzac did two centuries later in literature. Yet the author of the authoritative work on these paintings sums up the artist's achievement by referring to

> Hals's unwavering commitment to his personal vision, which enriches our consciousness of our fellow men and heightens our awe for the ever-increasing power of the mighty impulses that enabled him to give us a close view of life's vital forces.

That is mystification.

In order to avoid mystifying the past (which can equally well suffer pseudo-Marxist mystification) let us now examine the particular relation which now exists, so far as pictorial images are concerned, between the present and the past. If we can see the present clearly enough, we shall ask the right questions of the past.

Today we see the art of the past as nobody saw it before. We actually perceive it in a different way.

This difference can be illustrated in terms of what was thought of as perspective. The convention of perspective, which is unique to European art and which was first established in the early Renaissance, centres everything on the eye of the beholder. It is like a beam from a lighthouse—only instead of light travelling outwards, appearances travel in. The conventions called those appearances *reality*. Perspective makes the single eye the centre of the visible world. Everything converges on to the eye as to the vanishing point of infinity. The visible world is arranged for the spectator as the universe was once thought to be arranged for God.

According to the convention of perspective there is no visual reciprocity. There is no need for God to situate himself in relation to others: he is himself the situation. The inherent contradiction in perspective was that it structured all images of reality to address a single spectator who, unlike God, could only be in one place at a time.

After the invention of the camera this contradiction gradually became apparent.

> I'm an eye. A mechanical eye. I, the machine, show you a world the way only I can see it. I free myself for today and forever from human immobility. I'm in constant movement. I approach and pull away from objects. I creep under them. I move alongside a running horse's mouth. I fall and rise with the falling and rising bodies. This is I, the machine, manoeuvring in the chaotic movements, recording one movement after another in the most complex combinations.
>
> Freed from the boundaries of time and space, I coordinate any and all points of the universe, wherever I want them to be. My way leads towards the creation of a fresh perception of the world. Thus I explain in a new way the world unknown to you.[2]

The camera isolated momentary appearances and in so doing destroyed the idea that images were timeless. Or, to put it another way, the camera showed that the notion of time passing was inseparable from the experience of the visual (except in paintings). What you saw depended upon

Still from *Man with a Movie Camera* by Vertov [1895–1954]

where you were when. What you saw was relative to your position in time and space. It was no longer possible to imagine everything converging on the human eye as on the vanishing point of infinity.

This is not to say that before the invention of the camera men believed that everyone could see everything. But perspective organized the visual field as though that were indeed the ideal. Every drawing or painting that used perspective proposed to the spectator that he was the unique centre of the world. The camera—and more particularly the movie camera—demonstrated that there was no centre.

The invention of the camera changed the way men saw. The visible came to mean something different to them. This was immediately reflected in painting.

For the Impressionists the visible no longer presented itself to man in order to be seen. On the contrary, the visible, in continual flux, became fugitive. For the Cubists the visible was no longer what confronted the single eye, but the totality of possible views taken from points all round the object (or person) being depicted [below].

The invention of the camera also changed the way in which men saw paintings painted long before the camera was invented. Originally paintings were an integral part of the building for which they were designed. Sometimes in an early Renaissance church or chapel one has the feeling that the images on the wall are records of the building's interior life, that together they make up the building's memory—so much are they part of the particularity of the building [p. 115].

The uniqueness of every painting was once part of the uniqueness of the place where it resided. Sometimes the painting was transportable. But it could never be seen in two places at the same time. When the camera re-

*Still Life with Wicker Chair* by Picasso 1881–1973

Church of St. Francis at Assisi

produces a painting, it destroys the uniqueness of its image. As a result its meaning changes. Or, more exactly, its meaning multiplies and fragments into many meanings.

This is vividly illustrated by what happens when a painting is shown on a television screen. The painting enters each viewer's house. There it is surrounded by his wallpaper, his furniture, his mementos. It enters the atmosphere of his family. It becomes their talking point. It lends its meaning to their meaning. At the same time it enters a million other houses and, in each of them, is seen in a different context. Because of the camera, the

painting now travels to the spectator rather than the spectator to the painting. In its travels, its meaning is diversified.

One might argue that all reproductions more or less distort, and that therefore the original painting is still in a sense unique. Here [below] is a reproduction of the *Virgin of the Rocks* by Leonardo da Vinci.

Having seen this reproduction, one can go to the National Gallery to look at the original and there discover what the reproduction lacks. Alternatively one can forget about the quality of the reproduction and simply be reminded, when one sees the original, that it is a famous painting of which somewhere one has already seen a reproduction. But in either case the uniqueness of the original now lies in it being *the original of a reproduction*. It is no longer what its image shows that strikes one as unique; its first meaning is no longer to be found in what it says, but in what it is.

This new status of the original work is the perfectly rational consequence of the new means of reproduction. But it is at this point that a process of mystification again enters. The meaning of the original work no longer lies in what it uniquely says but in what it uniquely is. How is its unique existence evaluated and defined in our present culture? It is defined as an object whose value depends upon its rarity. This market is affirmed and gauged by the price it fetches on the market. But because

*Virgin of the Rocks* by Leonardo da Vinci 1452–1519. Reproduced by courtesy of the Trustees, The National Gallery, London

it is nevertheless "a work of art"—and art is thought to be greater than commerce—its market price is said to be a reflection of its spiritual value. Yet the spiritual value of an object, as distinct from a message or an example, can only be explained in terms of magic or religion. And since in modern society neither of these is a living force, the art object, the "work of art," is enveloped in an atmosphere of entirely bogus religiosity. Works of art are discussed and presented as though they were holy relics: relics which are first and foremost evidence of their own survival. The past in which they originated is studied in order to prove their survival genuine. They are declared art when their line of descent can be certified.

Before the *Virgin of the Rocks* the visitor to the National Gallery would be encouraged by nearly everything he might have heard and read about the painting to feel something like this: "I am in front of it. I can see it. This painting by Leonardo is unlike any other in the world. The National Gallery has the real one. If I look at this painting hard enough, I should

National Gallery

*Virgin of the Rocks* by Leonardo da Vinci 1452–1519.
Louvre Museum

somehow be able to feel its authenticity. The *Virgin of the Rocks* by Leonardo da Vinci: it is authentic and therefore it is beautiful."

To dismiss such feelings as naive would be quite wrong. They accord perfectly with the sophisticated culture of art experts for whom the National Gallery catalogue is written. The entry on the *Virgin of the Rocks* is one of the longest entries. It consists of fourteen closely printed pages. They do not deal with the meaning of the image. They deal with who commissioned the painting, legal squabbles, who owned it, its likely date, the families of its owners. Behind this information lie years of research. The aim of the research is to prove beyond any shadow of doubt that the painting is a genuine Leonardo. The secondary aim is to prove that an almost identical painting in the Louvre is a replica of the National Gallery version.

French art historians try to prove the opposite [see p. 117].

The National Gallery sells more reproductions of Leonardo's cartoon of *The Virgin and Child with St. Anne and St. John the Baptist* [below] than any other picture in their collection. A few years ago it was known only to scholars. It became famous because an American wanted to buy it for two and a half million pounds.

Now it hangs in a room by itself. The room is like a chapel. The drawing is behind bullet-proof perspex. It has acquired a new kind of impressiveness. Not because of what it shows—not because of the meaning of its image. It has become impressive, mysterious, because of its market value.

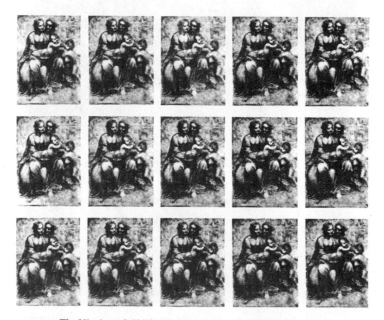

*The Virgin and Child with St. Anne and St. John the Baptist*
by Leonardo da Vinci 1452–1519. Reproduced by courtesy of the
Trustees, The National Gallery, London

• • •

The bogus religiosity which now surrounds original works of art, and which is ultimately dependent upon their market value, has become the substitute for what paintings lost when the camera made them reproducible. Its function is nostalgic. It is the final empty claim for the continuing values of an oligarchic, undemocratic culture. If the image is no longer unique and exclusive, the art object, the thing, must be made mysteriously so.

The majority of the population do not visit art museums. The following table shows how closely an interest in art is related to privileged education.

National proportion of art museum visitors according to level of education:
Percentage of each educational category who visit art museums

| | Greece | Poland | France | Holland | | Greece | Poland | France | Holland |
|---|---|---|---|---|---|---|---|---|---|
| With no educational qualification | 0.02 | 0.12 | 0.15 | — | Only secondary education | 10.5 | 10.4 | 10 | 20 |
| Only primary education | 0.30 | 1.50 | 0.45 | 0.50 | Further and higher education | 11.5 | 11.7 | 12.5 | 17.3 |

Source: Pierre Bourdieu and Alain Darbel, *L'Amour de l'art*, Editions de Minuit, Paris 1969, Appendix 5, table 4

The majority take it as axiomatic that the museums are full of holy relics which refer to a mystery which excludes them: the mystery of unaccountable wealth. Or, to put this another way, they believe that original masterpieces belong to the preserve (both materially and spiritually) of the rich. Another table indicates what the idea of an art gallery suggests to each social class.

Of the places listed below which does a museum remind you of most?

| | Manual workers | Skilled and white collar workers | Professional and upper managerial |
|---|---|---|---|
| | % | % | % |
| Church | 66 | 45 | 30.5 |
| Library | 9 | 34 | 28 |
| Lecture hall | — | 4 | 4.5 |
| Department store or entrance hall in public building | — | 7 | 2 |
| Church and library | 9 | 2 | 4.5 |
| Church and lecture hall | 4 | 2 | — |
| Library and lecture hall | — | — | 2 |
| None of these | 4 | 2 | 19.5 |
| No reply | 8 | 4 | 9 |
| | 100 (n = 53) | 100 (n = 98) | 100 (n = 99) |

Source: as above, Appendix 4, table 8

In the age of pictorial reproduction the meaning of paintings is no longer attached to them; their meaning becomes transmittable: that is to say it becomes information of a sort, and, like all information, it is either put to use or ignored; information carries no special authority within itself. When a painting is put to use, its meaning is either modified or totally changed. One should be quite clear about what this involves. It is not a question of reproduction failing to reproduce certain aspects of an image faithfully; it is a question of reproduction making it possible, even inevitable, that an image will be used for many different purposes and that the reproduced image, unlike an original work, can lend itself to them all.

*Venus and Mars* by Botticelli 1445–1510. Reproduced by courtesy of the Trustees, The National Gallery, London

Let us examine some of the ways in which the reproduced image lends itself to such usage.

Reproduction isolates a detail of a painting from the whole. The detail is transformed. An allegorical figure becomes a portrait of a girl [see bottom, p. 120].

When a painting is reproduced by a film camera it inevitably becomes material for the film-maker's argument.

A film which reproduces images of a painting leads the spectator, through the painting, to the film-maker's own conclusions. The painting lends authority to the film-maker. This is because a film unfolds in time and a painting does not. In a film the way one image follows another, their succession, constructs an argument which becomes irreversible. In a painting all its elements are there to be seen simultaneously. The spectator may need time to examine each element of the painting but whenever he reaches a conclusion, the simultaneity of the whole painting is there to reverse or qualify his conclusion. The painting maintains its own authority [below]. Paintings are often reproduced with words around them [see top, p. 122].

*Procession to Calvary* by Breughel 1525–1569

This is a landscape of a cornfield with birds flying out of it. Look at it for a moment [below]. Then turn the page [p. 123].

It is hard to define exactly how the words have changed the image but undoubtedly they have. The image now illustrates the sentence.

In this essay each image reproduced has become part of an argument which has little or nothing to do with the painting's original independent meaning. The words have quoted the paintings to confirm their own verbal authority. . . .

*Wheatfield with Crows* by Van Gogh 1853–1890

*This is the last picture that Van Gogh painted before he killed himself.*

Reproduced paintings, like all information, have to hold their own against all the other information being continually transmitted [below].

Consequently a reproduction, as well as making its own references to the image of its original, becomes itself the reference point for other images. The meaning of an image is changed according to what one sees immediately beside it or what comes immediately after it. Such authority as it retains, is distributed over the whole context in which it appears [see p. 124].

Because works of art are reproducible, they can, theoretically, be used by anybody. Yet mostly—in art books, magazines, films, or within gilt frames in living-rooms—reproductions are still used to bolster the illusion that nothing has changed, that art, with its unique undiminished authority, justifies most other forms of authority, that art makes inequality seem

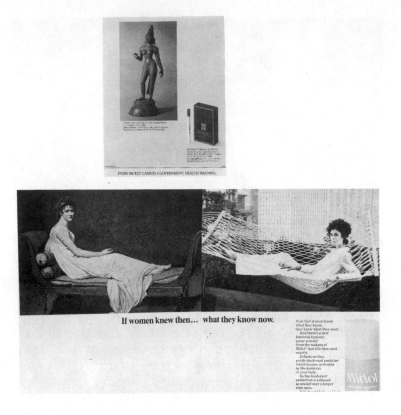

noble and hierarchies seem thrilling. For example, the whole concept of the National Cultural Heritage exploits the authority of art to glorify the present social system and its priorities.

The means of reproduction are used politically and commercially to disguise or deny what their existence makes possible. But sometimes individuals use them differently [p. 125].

Adults and children sometimes have boards in their bedrooms or living-rooms on which they pin pieces of paper: letters, snapshots, reproductions of paintings, newspaper cuttings, original drawings, postcards. On each board all the images belong to the same language and all are more or less equal within it, because they have been chosen in a highly personal way to match and express the experience of the room's inhabitant. Logically, these boards should replace museums.

What are we saying by that? Let us first be sure about what we are not saying.

We are not saying that there is nothing left to experience before original works of art except a sense of awe because they have survived. The way original works of art are usually approached—through museum catalogues, guides, hired cassettes, etc.—is not the only way they might be approached. When the art of the past ceases to be viewed nostalgically, the

works will cease to be holy relics—although they will never re-become what they were before the age of reproduction. We are not saying original works of art are now useless.

Original paintings are silent and still in a sense that information never is. Even a reproduction hung on a wall is not comparable in this respect for in the original the silence and stillness permeate the actual material, the paint, in which one follows the traces of the painter's immediate gestures. This has the effect of closing the distance in time between the painting of the picture and one's own act of looking at it. In this special sense all paintings are contemporary. Hence the immediacy of their testimony. Their historical moment is literally there before our eyes. Cézanne made a similar observation from the painter's point of view. "A minute in the world's life passes! To paint it in its reality, and forget everything for that! To become that minute, to be the sensitive plate . . . give the image of what we see, forgetting everything that has appeared before our time . . ." What we make of that painted moment when it is before our eyes depends upon what we expect of art, and that in turn depends today upon how we have already experienced the meaning of paintings through reproductions.

Nor are we saying that all art can be understood spontaneously. We are not claiming that to cut out a magazine reproduction of an archaic Greek head, because it is reminiscent of some personal experience, and to pin it to a board beside other disparate images, is to come to terms with the full meaning of that head.

The idea of innocence faces two ways. By refusing to enter a conspiracy, one remains innocent of that conspiracy. But to remain innocent may also be to remain ignorant. The issue is not between innocence and knowledge (or between the natural and the cultural) but between a total approach to art which attempts to relate it to every aspect of experience and the esoteric approach of a few specialized experts who are the clerks of the nostalgia of a ruling class in decline. (In decline, not before the proletariat, but before the new power of the corporation and the state.) The real question is: to whom does the meaning of the art of the past properly belong? to those who can apply it to their own lives, or to a cultural hierarchy of relic specialists?

The visual arts have always existed within a certain preserve; originally this preserve was magical or sacred. But it was also physical: it was the place, the cave, the building, in which, or for which, the work was made. The experience of art, which at first was the experience of ritual, was set apart from the rest of life—precisely in order to be able to exercise power over it. Later the preserve of art became a social one. It entered the culture of the ruling class, whilst physically it was set apart and isolated in their palaces and houses. During all this history the authority of art was inseparable from the particular authority of the preserve.

What the modern means of reproduction have done is to destroy the authority of art and to remove it—or, rather, to remove its images which they reproduce—from any preserve. For the first time ever, images of art have become ephemeral, ubiquitous, insubstantial, available, valueless, free. They surround us in the same way as a language surrounds us. They

*Woman Pouring Milk* by Vermeer 1632–1675

have entered the mainstream of life over which they no longer, in themselves, have power.

Yet very few people are aware of what has happened because the means of reproduction are used nearly all the time to promote the illusion that nothing has changed except that the masses, thanks to reproductions, can now begin to appreciate art as the cultured minority once did. Understandably, the masses remain uninterested and sceptical.

If the new language of images were used differently, it would, through its use, confer a new kind of power. Within it we could begin to define our experiences more precisely in areas where words are inadequate. (Seeing comes before words.) Not only personal experience, but also the essential historical experience of our relation to the past: that is to say the experience of seeking to give meaning to our lives, of trying to understand the history of which we can become the active agents.

The art of the past no longer exists as it once did. Its authority is lost. In its place there is a language of images. What matters now is who uses that language for what purpose. This touches upon questions of copyright for reproduction, the ownership of art presses and publishers, the total policy of public art galleries and museums. As usually presented, these are narrow professional matters. One of the aims of this essay has been to show that what is really at stake is much larger. A people or a class which is cut off from its own past is far less free to choose and to act as a people or class than one that has been able to situate itself in history. This is why—and this is the only reason why—the entire art of the past has now become a political issue.

*Many of the ideas in the preceding essay have been taken from another, written over forty years ago by the German critic and philosopher Walter Benjamin.*

*His essay was entitled* The Work of Art in the Age of Mechanical Reproduction. *This essay is available in English in a collection called* Illuminations *(Cape, London, 1970).*

NOTES
---
[1] Seymour Slive, *Frans Hals* (Phaidon, London).

[2] This quotation is from an article written in 1923 by Dziga Vertov, the revolutionary Soviet film director.

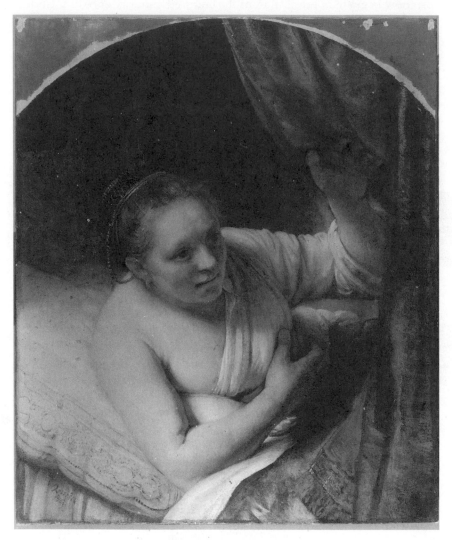

*Woman in Bed* by Rembrandt

# On Rembrandt's *Woman in Bed*

It is strange how art historians sometimes pay so much attention, when trying to date certain paintings, to "style," inventories, bills, auction lists, and so little to the painted evidence concerning the model's age. It is as if they do not trust the painter on this point. For example, when they try to date and arrange in chronological order Rembrandt's paintings of Hendrickje Stoffels. No painter was a greater expert about the process of aging, and no painter has left us a more intimate record of the great love of his life. Whatever the documentary conjectures may allow, the paintings make it clear that the love between Hendrickje and the painter lasted for about twenty years, until her death, six years before his.

She was ten or twelve years younger than he. When she died she was, on the evidence of the paintings, at the very least forty-five, and when he first painted her she could certainly not have been older than twenty-seven. Their daughter, Cornelia, was baptized in 1654. This means that Hendrickje gave birth to their child when she was in her mid-thirties.

The *Woman in Bed* (from Edinburgh) was painted, by my reckoning, a little before or a little after the birth of Cornelia. The historians suggest that it may be a fragment taken from a larger work representing the wedding night of Sarah and Tobias. A biblical subject for Rembrandt was always contemporary. If it is a fragment, it is certain that Rembrandt finished it, and bequeathed it finally to the spectator, as his most intimate painting of the woman he loved.

There are other paintings of Hendrickje. Before the *Bathsheba* in the Louvre, or the *Woman Bathing* in the National Gallery (London), I am wordless. Not because their genius inhibits me, but because the experience from which they derive and which they express—desire experiencing itself as something as old as the known world, tenderness experiencing itself as the end of the world, the eyes' endless rediscovery, as if for the first time, of their love of a familiar body—all this comes before and goes beyond words. No other paintings lead so deftly and powerfully to silence. Yet, in both, Hendrickje is absorbed in her own actions. In the painter's vision of her there is the greatest intimacy, but there is no mutual intimacy between them. They are paintings which speak of his love, not of hers.

In the painting of the *Woman in Bed* there is a complicity between the woman and the painter. This complicity includes both reticence and abandon, day and night. The curtain of the bed, which Hendrickje lifts up with her hand, marks the threshold between daytime and nighttime.

In two years, by daylight, Van Rijn will be declared bankrupt. Ten years before, by daylight, Hendrickje came to work in Van Rijn's house as a nurse for his baby son. In the light of Dutch seventeenth-century accountability and Calvinism, the housekeeper and the painter have distinct and separate responsibilities. Hence their reticence.

At night, they leave their century.

> A necklace hangs loose across her breasts,
> And between them lingers—
>         yet is it a lingering
>         and not an incessant arrival?—
>         the perfume of forever.
>         A perfume as old as sleep,
>         as familiar to the living as to the dead.

Leaning forward from her pillows, she lifts up the curtain with the back of her hand, for its palm, its face, is already welcoming, already making a gesture which is preparatory to the act of touching his head.

She has not yet slept. Her gaze follows him as he approaches. In her face the two of them are reunited. Impossible now to separate the two images: his image of her in bed, as he remembers her: her image of him as she sees him approaching their bed. It is nighttime.

*The Calling of St. Matthew* by Caravaggio

# On Caravaggio's *The Calling*
## *of St. Matthew*

One night in bed you asked me who was my favorite painter. I hesitated, searching for the least knowing, most truthful answer. Caravaggio. My own reply surprised me. There are nobler painters and painters of greater breadth of vision. There are painters I admire more and who are more admirable. But there is none, so it seems—for the answer came unpremeditated—to whom I feel closer.

The few canvases from my own incomparably modest life as a painter, which I would like to see again, are those I painted in the late 1940s of the streets of Livorno. This city was then war-scarred and poor, and it was there that I first began to learn something about the ingenuity of the dispossessed. It was there too that I discovered that I wanted as little as possible to do in this world with those who wield power. This has turned out to be a lifelong aversion.

The complicity I feel with Caravaggio began, I think, during that time in Livorno. He was the first painter of life as experienced by the popolaccio, the people of the backstreets, les sans-culottes, the lumpenproletariat, the lower orders, those of the lower depths, the underworld. There is no word in any traditional European language which does not either denigrate or patronize the urban poor it is naming. That is power.

Following Caravaggio up to the present day, other painters—Brower, Ostade, Hogarth, Goya, Géricault, Guttuso—have painted pictures of the same social milieu. But all of them—however great—were genre pictures, painted in order to show others how the less fortunate or the more dangerous lived. With Caravaggio, however, it was not a question of presenting scenes but of seeing itself. He does not depict the underworld for others: his vision is one that he shares with it.

In art-historical books Caravaggio is listed as one of the great innovating masters of chiaroscuro and a forerunner of the light and shade later used by Rembrandt and others. His vision can of course be considered art-historically as a step in the evolution of European art. Within such a perspective *a* Caravaggio was almost inevitable, as a link between the high art of the Counter Reformation and the domestic art of the emerging Dutch bourgeoisie, the form of this link being that of a new kind of space, defined by darkness as well as by light. (For Rome and for Amsterdam damnation had become an everyday affair.)

For the Caravaggio who actually existed—for the boy called Michelangelo born in a village near Bergamo, not far from where my friends, the Italian woodcutters, come—light and shade, as he imagined and saw them, had a deeply personal meaning, inextricably entwined with his desires and his instinct for survival. And it is by this, not by any art-historical logic, that his art is linked with the underworld.

His chiaroscuro allowed him to banish daylight. Shadows, he felt, offered shelter as can four walls and a roof. Whatever and wherever he painted he really painted interiors. Sometimes—for *The Flight into Egypt* or one of his beloved John the Baptists—he was obliged to include a landscape in the background. But these landscapes are like rugs or drapes hung up on a line across an inner courtyard. He only felt at home—no, that he felt nowhere—he only felt relatively at ease *inside.*

His darkness smells of candles, overripe melons, damp washing waiting to be hung out the next day: it is the darkness of stairwells, gambling corners, cheap lodgings, sudden encounters. And the promise is not in what will flare against it, but in the darkness itself. The shelter it offers is only relative, for the chiaroscuro reveals violence, suffering, longing, mortality, but at least it reveals them intimately. What has been banished, along with the daylight, are distance and solitude—and both these are feared by the underworld.

Those who live precariously and are habitually crowded together develop a phobia about open spaces which transforms their frustrating lack of space and privacy into something reassuring. He shared those fears.

*The Calling of St. Matthew* depicts five men sitting round their usual table, telling stories, gossiping, boasting of what one day they will do, counting money. The room is dimly lit. Suddenly the door is flung open. The two figures who enter are still part of the violent noise and light of the invasion. (Berenson wrote that Christ, who is one of the figures, comes in like a police inspector to make an arrest.)

Two of Matthew's colleagues refuse to look up, the other two younger ones stare at the strangers with a mixture of curiosity and condescension. Why is he proposing something so mad? Who's protecting him, the thin one who does all the talking? And Matthew, the tax-collector with a shifty conscience which has made him more unreasonable than most of his colleagues, points at himself and asks: Is it really I who must go? Is it really I who must follow you?

How many thousands of decisions to leave have resembled Christ's hand here! The hand is held out towards the one who has to decide, yet it is ungraspable because so fluid. It orders the way, yet offers no direct support. Matthew will get up and follow the thin stranger from the room, down the narrow streets, out of the district. He will write his gospel, he will travel to Ethiopa and the South Caspian and Persia. Probably he will be murdered.

And behind the drama of this moment of decision in the room at the top of the stairs, there is a window, giving onto the outside world. Traditionally in painting, windows were treated either as sources of light or as frames framing nature or framing an exemplary event outside. Not so this window. No light enters by it. The window is opaque. We see nothing. Mercifully we see nothing because what is outside is bound to be threatening. It is a window through which only the worst news can come.

. . . . . . . . . . . .

## QUESTIONS FOR A SECOND READING

1. Berger says, "The past is never there waiting to be discovered, to be recognized for exactly what it is. History always constitutes the relation between a present and its past" (p. 108). And he says, "If we 'saw' the art of
   the past, we would situate ourselves in history. When we are prevented
   from seeing it, we are being deprived of the history which belongs to us"
   (p. 108). As you reread this essay, pay particular attention to Berger's uses
   of the word "history." What does it stand for? What does it have to do
   with looking at pictures? How might you define the term if your definition were based on its use in this essay?

   You might take Berger's discussion of the Hals paintings as a case in
   point. What is the relation Berger establishes between the past and the
   present? If he has not "discovered" the past or recognized it for exactly
   what it is, what has Berger done in writing about these paintings? What
   might it mean to say that he has "situated" us in history or has returned
   a history that belongs to us? And in what way might this be said to be a
   political act?

2. Berger argues forcefully that the account of the Hals painting offered by
   the unnamed art historian is a case of "mystification." How would you
   characterize Berger's account of that same painting? Would you say that
   he sees what is "really" there? If so, why wasn't it self-evident? Why does
   it take an expert to see "clearly"? As you read back over the essay, look
   for passages you could use to characterize the way Berger looks at images
   or paintings. If, as he says, "The way we see things is affected by what we
   know or what we believe," what does he know and what does he believe?

## ASSIGNMENTS FOR WRITING

1.     We are not saying that there is nothing left to experience before original works of art except a sense of awe because they have survived. The
   way original works of art are usually approached—through museum
   catalogues, guides, hired cassettes, etc.—is not the only way they might
   be approached. When the art of the past ceases to be viewed nostalgically, the works will cease to be holy relics—although they will never
   re-become what they were before the age of reproduction. We are not
   saying original works of art are now useless. (p. 124)

   Berger argues that there are barriers to vision, problems in the ways we
   see or don't see original works of art, problems that can be located in and
   overcome by strategies of approach.

   For Berger, what we lose if we fail to see properly is history: "If we
   'saw' the art of the past, we would situate ourselves in history. When we
   are prevented from seeing it, we are being deprived of the history which
   belongs to us." It is not hard to figure out who, according to Berger,

prevents us from seeing the art of the past. He says it is the ruling class. It *is* difficult, however, to figure out what he believes gets in the way and what all this has to do with history.

For this assignment, write an essay explaining what, as you read Berger, it is that gets in the way when we look at paintings, and what it is that we might do to overcome the barriers to vision (and to history). You should imagine that you are writing for someone interested in art, perhaps preparing to go to a museum, but someone who has not read Berger's essay. You will, that is, need to be careful in summary and paraphrase.

2. Berger says that the real question is this: "To whom does the meaning of the art of the past properly belong?" Let's say, in Berger's spirit, that it belongs to you. Look again at the painting by Vermeer, *Woman Pouring Milk,* that is included in "Ways of Seeing" (p. 126). Berger includes the painting but without much discussion, as though he were, in fact, leaving it for you. Write an essay that shows others how they might best understand that painting. You should offer this lesson in the spirit of John Berger. Imagine that you are doing this work for him, perhaps as his apprentice.

3.    Original paintings are silent and still in a sense that information never is. Even a reproduction hung on a wall is not comparable in this respect for in the original the silence and stillness permeate the actual material, the paint, in which one follows the traces of the painter's immediate gestures. This has the effect of closing the distance in time between the painting of the picture and one's own act of looking at it. . . . What we make of that painted moment when it is before our eyes depends upon what we expect of art, and that in turn depends today upon how we have already experienced the meaning of paintings through reproductions. (p. 125)

While Berger describes original paintings as silent in this passage, it is clear that these paintings begin to speak if one approaches them properly, if one learns to ask "the right questions of the past." Berger demonstrates one route of approach, for example, in his reading of the Hals paintings, where he asks questions about the people and objects and their relationships to the painter and the viewer. What the paintings might be made to say, however, depends on the viewer's expectations, his or her sense of the questions that seem appropriate or possible. Berger argues that, because of the way art is currently displayed, discussed, and reproduced, the viewer expects only to be mystified.

For this paper, imagine that you are working against the silence and mystification Berger describes. Go to a museum—or, if that is not possible, to a large-format book of reproductions in the library (or, if that is not possible, to the reproductions in this essay)—and select a painting that seems silent and still, yet invites conversation. Your job is to figure out what sorts of questions to ask, to interrogate the painting, to get it to speak, to engage with the past in some form of dialogue. Write an essay in which you record this process and what you have learned from it. Somewhere in your paper, perhaps at the end, turn back to Berger's essay and speak to it about how this process has or hasn't confirmed what you take to be Berger's expectations.

Note: If possible, include with your essay a reproduction of the painting you select. (Check the postcards at the museum gift shop.) In any event, you want to make sure that you describe the painting in sufficient detail for your readers to follow what you say.

4.  In "Ways of Seeing" Berger says

> If the new language of images were used differently, it would, through its use, confer a new kind of power. Within it we could begin to define our experiences more precisely in areas where words are inadequate. . . . Not only personal experience, but also the essential historical experience of our relation to the past: that is to say the experience of seeking to give meaning to our lives, of trying to understand the history of which we can become the active agents. (p. 127)

As a writer, Berger is someone who uses images (including some of the great paintings of the Western tradition) "to define [experience] more precisely in areas where words are inadequate." In a wonderful book, *And our faces, my heart, brief as photos,* a book that is both a meditation on time and space and a long love letter, Berger writes about paintings in order to say what he wants to say to his lover. We have included two examples, descriptions of Rembrandt's *Woman in Bed* and Caravaggio's *The Calling of St. Matthew.*

Read these as examples, as lessons in how and why to look at, to value, to think with, to write about paintings. Then use one or both as a way of thinking about the concluding section of "Ways of Seeing" (pp. 125–127). You can assume that your readers have read Berger's essay but have difficulty grasping what he is saying in that final section, particularly since it is a section that seems to call for action, asking the reader to do something. Of what use might Berger's example be in trying to understand what we might do with and because of paintings?

## MAKING CONNECTIONS

1.  Walker Percy, in "The Loss of the Creature" (p. 565), like Berger in "Ways of Seeing," talks about the problems people have seeing things. "How can the sightseer recover the Grand Canyon?" Percy asks. "He can recover it in any number of ways, all sharing in common the strategem of avoiding the approved confrontation of the tour and the Park Service." There is a way in which Berger also tells a story about tourists—tourists going to a museum to see paintings, to buy postcards, gallery guides, reprints, and T-shirts featuring the image of the Mona Lisa. "The way original works of art are usually approached—through museum catalogues, guides, hired cassettes, etc.—is not the only way they might be approached. When the art of the past ceases to be viewed nostalgically, the works will cease to be holy relics—although they will never re-become what they were before the age of reproduction" (p. 124).

Write an essay in which you describe possible "approaches" to a painting in a museum, approaches that could provide for a better understanding or a more complete "recovery" of that painting than would be possible to a casual viewer, to someone who just wandered in, for example, with no strategy in mind. You should think of your essay as providing real advice to a real person. (You might, if you can, work with a particular painting in a particular museum.) What should that person do? How should that person prepare? What would the consequences be?

At least one of your approaches should reflect Percy's best advice to a viewer who wanted to develop a successful strategy, and at least one should represent the best you feel Berger would have to offer. When you've finished explaining these approaches, go on in your essay to examine the differences between those you associate with Percy and those you associate with Berger. What are the key differences? And what do they say about the different ways these two thinkers approach the problem of why we do or do not see that which lies before us?

2.  Both John Berger in "Ways of Seeing" and Michel Foucault in "Panopticism" (p. 314) discuss what Foucault calls "power relations." Berger claims that "the entire art of the past has now become a political issue," and he makes a case for the evolution of a "new language of images" that could "confer a new kind of power" if people were to understand history in art. Foucault argues that the Panopticon signals an "inspired" change in power relations. "It is," he says, "an important mechanism, for it automatizes and disindividualizes power. Power has its principle not so much in a person as in a certain concerted distribution of bodies, surfaces, lights, gazes; in an arrangement whose internal mechanisms produce the relation in which individuals are caught up" (p. 321).

    Both Berger and Foucault create arguments about power and its methods and goals. As you read through their essays, mark passages you might use to explain how each author thinks about power—where it comes from, who has it, how it works, where you look for it, how you know it when you see it, what it does, where it goes. You should reread the essays as a pair, as part of a single project in which you are seeking to explain theories of power.

    Write an essay in which you present and explain "Ways of Seeing" and "Panopticism" as examples of Berger's and Foucault's theories of power and vision. Both Berger and Foucault are arguing against usual understandings of power and knowledge and history. In this sense, their projects are similar. You should be sure, however, to look for differences as well as similarities.

3.  Clifford Geertz, in "Deep Play: Notes on the Balinese Cockfight" (p. 364), argues that the cockfights are a "Balinese reading of Balinese experience; a story they tell themselves about themselves." They are not, then, just cockfights. Or, as Geertz says, the cockfights can be seen as texts "saying something of something." Berger's essay, "Ways of Seeing," offers a view of our culture and, in particular, of the way our culture reproduces and uses images from the past. They are placed in museums, on bulletin boards, on T-shirts, and in advertisements. They are described by experts in certain predictable tones or phrases. It is interesting to look at our use of those images as a story we tell ourselves about ourselves, as a practice that says something about something else.

    Geertz's analysis of the cockfight demonstrates this way of seeing and interpreting a feature of a culture. Write an essay in which you use Geertz's methods to interpret the examples that Berger provides of the ways our culture reproduces and uses images from the past. If these practices say something about something else, what do they say, and about what do they say it? What story might we be telling ourselves about ourselves?

Note: For this assignment, you should avoid rushing to the conclusion Berger draws—that the story told here is a story about the ruling class and its conspiracy against the proletariat. You should see, that is, what other interpretation you can provide. You may, if you choose, return to Berger's conclusions in your paper, but only after you have worked on some of your own.

# SUSAN BORDO

*USAN BORDO (b. 1947) is the Otis A. Singletary Chair of Humanities at the University of Kentucky. Bordo is a philosopher, and while her work touches on figures and subjects traditional to the study of philosophy (René Descartes, for example), she brings her training to the study of culture, including popular culture and its representations of the body. She is a philosopher, that is, who writes not only about Plato but also about Madonna and O.J.*

*In* Unbearable Weight: Feminism, Western Culture, and the Body *(1993), the source for the selection that follows, Bordo looks at the complicated cultural forces that have produced our ways of understanding and valuing a woman's body. These powerful forces have shaped not only attitudes and lives but, through dieting, training, and cosmetic surgery, the physical body itself.* Unbearable Weight *was nominated for the 1993 Pulitzer Prize; it won the Association for Women in Psychology's Distinguished Publication Award and was named by the* New York Times *as one of the "Notable Books of 1993." Bordo is also the author of* The Flight to Objectivity: Essays on Cartesianism and Culture *(1987) and* Twilight Zones: The Hidden Life of Cultural Images from Plato to O.J. *(1997); she is coeditor (with Alison Jaggar) of* Gender/Body/ Knowledge: Feminist Reconstruction of Being and Knowing *(1989).*

*In "Hunger as Ideology" Bordo looks closely at ideas and images, both past and present, to trace the representation of the female body in relation to what is of-*

*fered as "true" or "real," "natural" or "normal." She is particularly interested in the culture's assumptions about gender identity, about the differences attributed to men and women in the stories we tell ourselves and the ways we picture our attitudes toward food, eating, cooking, body size, and shape. She provides a powerful example of what it means to read closely, to read images as well as words, and to write that close reading into an extended argument. Bordo's writing is witty, committed, and engaging. It brings the concerns of a philosopher to the materials of everyday life.*

# Hunger as Ideology

### The Woman Who Doesn't Eat Much

In a television commercial, two little French girls are shown dressing up in the feathery finery of their mother's clothes. They are exquisite little girls, flawless and innocent, and the scene emphasizes both their youth and the natural sense of style often associated with French women. (The ad is done in French, with subtitles.) One of the girls, spying a picture of the other girl's mother, exclaims breathlessly, "Your mother, she is so slim, so beautiful! Does she eat?" The daughter, giggling, replies: "Silly, just not so much," and displays her mother's helper, a bottle of FibreThin. "Aren't you jealous?" the friend asks. Dimpling, shy yet self-possessed, deeply knowing, the daughter answers, "Not if I know her secrets."

Admittedly, women are continually bombarded with advertisements and commercials for weight-loss products and programs, but this commercial makes many of us particularly angry. On the most obvious level, the commercial affronts with its suggestion that young girls begin early in learning to control their weight, and with its romantic mystification of diet pills as part of the obscure, eternal arsenal of feminine arts to be passed from generation to generation. This romanticization, as often is the case in American commercials, trades on our continuing infatuation with (what we imagine to be) the civility, tradition, and savoir-faire of "Europe" (seen as the stylish antithesis to our own American clumsiness, aggressiveness, crudeness). The little girls are fresh and demure, in a way that is undefinably but absolutely recognizably "European"—as defined, that is, within the visual vocabulary of popular American culture. And FibreThin, in this commercial, is nothing so crass and "medical" and pragmatic (read: American) as a diet pill, but a mysterious, prized (and, it is implied, age-old) "secret," known only to those with both history and taste.

But we expect such hype from contemporary advertisements. Far more unnerving is the psychological acuity of the ad's focus, not on the size and shape of bodies, but on a certain *subjectivity*, represented by the absent but central figure of the mother, the woman who eats, only "not so much." We never see her picture; we are left to imagine her ideal beauty and slenderness. But what she looks like is not important, in any case; what is important is the fact that she has achieved what we might call a "cool" (that is, casual) relation to food. She is not starving herself (an obsession, indicating the continuing power of food), but neither is she desperately and shamefully binging in some private corner. Eating has become, for her, no big deal. In its evocation of the lovely French mother who doesn't eat much, the commercial's metaphor of European "difference" reveals itself as a means of representing that enviable and truly foreign "other": the woman for whom food is merely ordinary, who can take it or leave it.

Another version, this time embodied by a sleek, fashionable African American woman, playfully promotes Virginia Slims Menthol [Fig. 1, p. 141]. This ad, which appeared in *Essence* magazine, is one of a series specifically targeted at the African American female consumer. In contrast to the Virginia Slims series concurrently appearing in *Cosmo* and *People*, a series which continues to associate the product with historically expanded opportunities for women ("You've come a long way, baby" remains the motif and slogan), Virginia Slims pitches to the *Essence* reader by mocking solemnity and self-importance *after* the realization of those opportunities: "Why climb the ladder if you're not going to enjoy the view?" "Big girls don't cry. They go shopping." And, in the variant depicted in Figure 1: "Decisions are easy. When I get to a fork in the road, I eat."

Arguably, the general subtext meant to be evoked by these ads is the failure of the dominant, white culture (those who *don't* "enjoy the view") to relax and take pleasure in success. The upwardly mobile black consumer, it is suggested, will do it with more panache, with more cool—and of course with a cool, Virginia Slims Menthol in hand. In this particular ad, the speaker scorns obsessiveness, not only over professional or interpersonal decision-making, but over food as well. Implicitly contrasting herself to those who worry and fret, she presents herself as utterly "easy" in her relationship with food. Unlike the FibreThin mother, she eats anytime she wants. But *like* the FibreThin mother (and this is the key similarity for my purposes), she has achieved a state beyond craving. Undominated by unsatisfied, internal need, she eats not only freely but without deep desire and without apparent consequence. It's "easy," she says. Presumably, without those forks in the road she might forget about food entirely.

The Virginia Slims woman is a fantasy figure, her cool attitude toward food as remote from the lives of most contemporary African American women as from any others. True, if we survey cultural attitudes toward women's appetites and body size, we find great variety—a variety shaped by ethnic, national, historical, class, and other factors. My eighty-year-old father, the child of immigrants, asks at the end of every meal if I "got enough to eat"; he considers me skinny unless I am plump by my own standards. His attitude reflects not only memories of economic struggle

Figure [1]

and a heritage of Jewish-Russian preference for zaftig women, but the lingering, well into this century, of a once more general Anglo-Saxon cultural appreciation for the buxom woman. In the mid-nineteenth century, hotels and bars were adorned with Bouguereau-inspired paintings of voluptuous female nudes; Lillian Russell, the most photographed woman in America in 1890, was known and admired for her hearty appetite, ample body (over two hundred pounds at the height of her popularity), and "challenging, fleshly arresting" beauty.[1] Even as such fleshly challenges became less widely appreciated in the twentieth century, men of Greek, Italian, Eastern European, and African descent, influenced by their own distinctive cultural heritages, were still likely to find female voluptuousness appealing. And even in the late 1960s and early 1970s, as Twiggy and Jean Shrimpton began to set a new norm for ultra-slenderness, lesbian cultures in the United States continued to be accepting—even celebrating—of fleshy, space-claiming female bodies.

Even more examples could be produced, of course, if we cast our glance more widely over the globe and back through history. Many cultures, clearly, have revered expansiveness in women's bodies and appetites. Some still do. But in the 1980s and 1990s an increasingly universal equation of slenderness with beauty and success has rendered the competing claims of cultural diversity ever feebler. Men who were teenagers from the mid-seventies on, whatever their ethnic roots or economic class, are likely to view long, slim legs, a flat stomach, and a firm rear end as essentials of female beauty. Unmuscled heft is no longer as acceptable as it once was in lesbian communities. Even Miss Soviet Union has become lean and tight, and the robust, earthy actresses who used to star in Russian films have been replaced by slender, Westernized types.

Arguably, a case could once be made for a contrast between (middle-class, heterosexual) white women's obsessive relations with food and a more accepting attitude toward women's appetites within African American communities. But in the nineties, features on diet, exercise, and body-image problems have grown increasingly prominent in magazines aimed at African American readers, reflecting the cultural reality that for most women today—whatever their racial or ethnic identity, and increasingly across class and sexual-orientation differences as well—free and easy relations with food are at best a relic of the past. (More frequently in *Essence* than in *Cosmo*, there may be a focus on health problems associated with overweight among African Americans, in addition to the glamorization of slenderness.) Almost all of us who can afford to be eating well are dieting—and hungry—almost all of the time.

It is thus Dexatrim, not Virginia Slims, that constructs the more realistic representation of women's subjective relations with food. In Dexatrim's commercial that shows a woman, her appetite-suppressant worn off, hurtling across the room, drawn like a living magnet to the breathing, menacing refrigerator, hunger is represented as an insistent, powerful force with a life of its own. This construction reflects the physiological reality of dieting, a state the body is unable to distinguish from starvation.[2] And it reflects its psychological reality as well; for dieters, who live in a state of constant denial, food is a perpetually beckoning presence, its power growing ever greater as the sanctions against gratification become more stringent. A slender body may be attainable through hard work, but a "cool" relation to food, the true "secret" of the beautiful "other" in the FibreThin commercial, is a tantalizing reminder of what lies beyond the reach of the inadequate and hungry self. (Of course, as the ads suggest, a psychocultural transformation remains possible, through FibreThin and Virginia Slims.)

## *Psyching out the Female Consumer*

Sometimes, when I am analyzing and interpreting advertisements and commercials in class, students accuse me of a kind of paranoia about the significance of these representations as carriers and reproducers of culture. After all, they insist, these are just images, not "real life"; any fool knows that advertisers manipulate reality in the service of selling their products. I agree that on some level we "know" this. However, were it a meaningful or *usable* knowledge, it is unlikely that we would be witnessing the current spread of diet and exercise mania across racial and ethnic groups, or the explosion of technologies aimed at bodily "correction" and "enhancement."

Jean Baudrillard offers a more accurate description of our cultural estimation of the relation and relative importance of image and "reality." In *Simulations*, he recalls the Borges fable in which the cartographers of a mighty empire draw up a map so detailed that it ends up exactly covering the territory of the empire, a map which then frays and disintegrates as a symbol of the coming decline of the empire it perfectly represents. Today, Baudrillard suggests, the fable might be inverted: it is no longer the territory that provides the model for the map, but the map that defines the territory; and it is the *territory* "whose shreds are slowly rotting across the map." Thinking further, however, he declares even the inverted fable to be "useless." For what it still assumes is precisely that which is being lost today—namely, the distinction between the territory and its map, between reality and appearance. Today, all that we experience as meaningful are appearances.[3]

Thus, we all "know" that Cher and virtually every other female star over the age of twenty-five is the plastic product of numerous cosmetic surgeries on face and body. But, in the era of the "hyperreal" (as Baudrillard calls it), such "knowledge" is as faded and frayed as the old map in the Borges tale, unable to cast a shadow of doubt over the dazzling, compelling, authoritative images themselves. Like the knowledge of our own mortality when we are young and healthy, the knowledge that Cher's physical appearance is fabricated is an empty abstraction; it simply does not compute. It is the created image that has the hold on our most vibrant, immediate sense of what *is*, of what matters, of what we must pursue for ourselves.

In *constructing* the images, of course, continual use is made of knowledge (or at least what is imagined to be knowledge) of consumers' lives. Indeed, a careful reading of contemporary advertisements reveals continual and astute manipulation of problems that psychology and the popular media have targeted as characteristic dilemmas of the "contemporary woman," who is beset by conflicting role demands and pressures on her time. "Control"—a word that rarely used to appear in commercial contexts—has become a common trope in advertisements for products as disparate as mascara ("Perfect Pen Eyeliner. Puts *you* in control. And isn't that nice for a change?") and cat-box deodorant ("Control. I strive for it. My cat achieves it"). *"Soft felt tip gives you absolute control of your line"* [Fig. 2, p. 145]. It is virtually impossible to glance casually at this ad without reading "line" as "life"—which is, of course, the subliminal coding such ads intend. "Mastery" also frequently figures in ads for cosmetics and hair products: "Master your curls with new Adaptable Perm." The rhetoric of these ads is interestingly contrasted to the rhetoric of mastery and control directed at male consumers. Here, the message is almost always one of mastery and control over *others* rather than the self: "Now it's easier than ever to achieve a position of power in Manhattan" (an ad for a Manhattan health club), or "Don't just serve. Rule" (an ad for Speedo tennis shoes).

Advertisers are aware, too, of more specific *ways* in which women's lives are out of control, including our well-documented food disorders; they frequently incorporate the theme of food obsession into their pitch. The Sugar Free Jell-O Pudding campaign exemplifies a typical commercial strategy for exploiting women's eating problems while obscuring their dark realities. (The advertisers themselves would put this differently, of course.) In the "tip of my tongue" ad [Fig. 3, p. 146], the obsessive mental state of the compulsive eater is depicted fairly accurately, guaranteeing recognition from people with that problem: "If I'm not eating dessert, I'm talking about it. If I'm not talking about it, I'm eating it. And I'm always thinking about it . . . It's just always on my mind."

These thoughts, however, belong to a slender, confident, and—most important—decidedly not depressed individual, whose upbeat, open, and accepting attitude toward her constant hunger is far from that of most women who eat compulsively. "The inside of a binge," Geneen Roth writes, "is deep and dark. At the core . . . is deprivation, scarcity, a feeling that you can never get enough."[4] A student described her hunger as "a black hole that I had to fill up." In the Sugar Free Jell-O ad, by contrast, the mental state depicted is most like that of a growing teenage boy; to be continually hungry is represented as a normal, if somewhat humorous and occasionally annoying, state with no disastrous physical or emotional consequences.

The use of a male figure is one strategy, in contemporary ads, for representing compulsive eating as "natural" and even lovable. Men are *supposed* to have hearty, even voracious, appetites. It is a mark of the manly to eat spontaneously and expansively, and manliness is a frequent commercial code for amply portioned products: "Manwich," "Hungry Man Dinners," "Manhandlers." Even when men advertise diet products (as they more frequently do, now that physical perfection is increasingly being demanded of men as well as women), they brag about their appetites, as in the Tommy Lasorda commercials for Slim-Fast, which feature three burly football players (their masculinity beyond reproach) declaring that if Slim-Fast can satisfy *their* appetites, it can satisfy anyone's. The displacement of the female by a male figure (displacement when the targeted consumer is in fact a woman) thus dispels thoughts of addiction, danger, unhappiness,

Figure [2]

Figure [3]

and replaces them with a construction of compulsive eating (or thinking about food) as benign indulgence of a "natural" inclination. Consider the ad shown in Figure 4 [p. 147], depicting a male figure diving with abandon into the "tempered-to-full-flavor-consistency" joys of Häagen-Dazs deep chocolate.

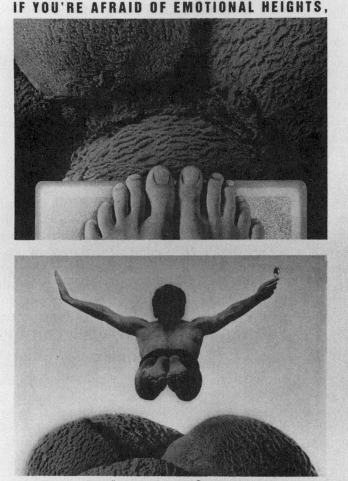

Figure [4]

Emotional heights, intensity, love, and thrills: it is women who habitually seek such experiences from food and who are most likely to be overwhelmed by their relationship to food, to find it dangerous and frightening (especially rich, fattening, soothing food like ice cream). The marketers of Häagen-Dazs know this; they are aware of the well-publicized prevalence of compulsive eating and binge behaviors among women. Indeed, this ad exploits, with artful precision, exactly the sorts of associations that are likely to resonate with a person for whom eating is invested with deep emotional meaning. Why, then, a male diver? In part, as I have been arguing, the displacement is necessary to insure that the grim actualities of women's eating problems remain obscured; the point, after all, is to sell ice cream, not to remind people of how dangerous food actually *is* for women. Too, the advertisers may reckon that women might enjoy seeing a man depicted in swooning surrender to ice cream, as a metaphor for the emotional surrender that so many women crave from their husbands and lovers.

## Food, Sexuality, and Desire

I would argue, however, that more than a purely profit-maximizing, ideologically neutral, Madison Avenue mentality is at work in these ads. They must also be considered as gender ideology—that is, as specifically (consciously or unconsciously) servicing the cultural reproduction of gender difference and gender inequality, quite independent of (although at times coinciding with) marketing concerns. As gender ideology, the ads I have been discussing are not distinctively contemporary but continue a well-worn representational tradition, arguably inaugurated in the Victorian era, in which the depiction of women eating, particularly in sensuous surrender to rich, exciting food, is taboo.[5]

In exploring this dimension, we might begin by attempting to imagine an advertisement depicting a young, attractive woman indulging as freely, as salaciously as the man in the Post cereal ad shown in Figure 5 [p. 149]. Such an image would violate deeply sedimented expectations, would be experienced by many as disgusting and transgressive. When women are positively depicted as sensuously voracious about food (almost never in commercials, and only very rarely in movies and novels), their hunger for food is employed solely as a metaphor for their sexual appetite. In the eating scenes in *Tom Jones* and *Flashdance*, for example, the heroines' unrestrained delight in eating operates as sexual foreplay, a way of prefiguring the abandon that will shortly be expressed in bed. Women are permitted to lust for food itself only when they are pregnant or when it is clear they have been near starvation—as, for example, in *McCabe and Mrs. Miller*, in the scene in which Mrs. Miller, played by Julie Christie, wolfs down half a dozen eggs and a bowl of beef stew before the amazed eyes of McCabe. Significantly, the scene serves to establish Mrs. Miller's "manliness"; a woman who eats like this is to be taken seriously, is not to be trifled with, the movie suggests.

The metaphorical situation is virtually inverted in the representation of male eaters. Although voracious eating may occasionally code male sexual appetite (as in *Tom Jones*), we frequently also find *sexual* appetite operating as a metaphor for eating pleasure. In commercials that feature male eaters, the men are shown in a state of wild, sensual transport over

Figure [5]

heavily frosted, rich, gooey desserts. Their total lack of control is portrayed as appropriate, even adorable; the language of the background jingle is unashamedly aroused, sexual, and desiring.

> I'm thinking about you the whole day through [crooned to a Pillsbury cake]. I've got a passion for you.

> You're my one and only, my creamy deluxe [Betty Crocker frosting].

> You butter me up, I can't resist, you leave me breathless [Betty Crocker frosting].

> Your brownies give me fever. Your cake gives me chills [assorted Betty Crocker mixes].

> I'm a fool for your chocolate. I'm wild, crazy, out of control [assorted Betty Crocker mixes].

> I've got it bad, and I should know, 'cause I crave it from my head right down to my potato [for Pillsbury Potatoes Au Gratin].

> Can't help myself. It's Duncan Hines [assorted cake mixes] and nobody else.

In these commercials food is constructed as a sexual object of desire, and eating is legitimated as much more than a purely nutritive activity. Rather, food is *supposed* to supply sensual delight and succor—not as metaphorically standing for something else, but as an erotic experience in itself. Women are permitted such gratification from food only in measured doses. In another ad from the Diet Jell-O series, eating is metaphorically sexualized: "I'm a girl who just can't say no. I insist on dessert," admits the innocently dressed but flirtatiously posed model [Fig. 6, p. 151]. But at the same time that eating is mildly sexualized in this ad, it is also contained. She is permitted to "feel good about saying 'Yes'"—but ever so demurely, and to a harmless low-calorie product. Transgression beyond such limits is floridly sexualized, as an act of "cheating" [Fig. 7, p. 152]. Women may be encouraged (like the man on the Häagen-Dazs high board) to "dive in"—not, however, into a dangerous pool of Häagen-Dazs Deep Chocolate, but for a "refreshing dip" into Weight Watchers linguini [Fig. 8, p. 153]. Targeted at the working woman ("Just what you need to revive yourself from the workday routine"), this ad also exploits the aquatic metaphor to conjure up images of female independence and liberation ("Isn't it just like us to make waves?").

All of this may seem peculiarly contemporary, revolving as it does around the mass marketing of diet products. But in fact the same metaphorical universe, as well as the same practical prohibitions against female indulgence (for, of course, these ads are not only selling products but teaching appropriate behavior) were characteristic of Victorian gender ideology. Victorians did not have *Cosmo* and television, of course. But they did have conduct manuals, which warned elite women of the dangers of

Figure [6]

You'll think
you're cheating
But you know you're not...
It's Wonder® Light bread.
Should you tell?
    Should you tell your
friend that each full-size slice
of great tasting Wonder
Light is only 40 calories?
    You can't just let her
suffer through carrot sticks
and rice cakes... Can you?

The lighter slice
of America.

Figure [7]

indulgent and over-stimulating eating and advised how to consume in a
feminine way (as little as possible and with the utmost precaution against
unseemly show of desire). *Godey's Lady's Book* warned that it was vulgar
for women to load their plates; young girls were admonished to "be frugal
and plain in your tastes."[6] Detailed lexicons offered comparisons of the
erotic and cooling effects of various foods, often with specific prescriptions for each sex.[7] Sexual metaphors permeate descriptions of potential
transgression:

> Every luxurious table is a scene of temptation, which it requires
> fixed principles and an enlightened mind to withstand. . . .
> Nothing can be more seducing to the appetite than this ar-
> rangement of the viands which compose a feast; as the stomach
> is filled, and the natural desire for food subsides, the palate is
> tickled by more delicate and relishing dishes until it is betrayed
> into excess.[8]

Today, the same metaphors of temptation and fall appear frequently in
advertisements for diet products [see Fig. 9, p. 154]. And in the Victorian
era, as today, the forbiddenness of rich food often resulted in private
binge behavior, described in *The Bazaar Book of Decorum* (1870) as the "secret luncheon," at which "many of the most abstemious at the open dinner
are the most voracious . . . swallowing cream tarts by the dozen, and
caramels and chocolate drops by the pound's weight."[9]

    The emergence of such rigid and highly moralized restrictions on fe-
male appetite and eating are, arguably, part of what Bram Dijkstra has interpreted as a nineteenth-century "cultural ideological counter-offensive"

Figure [8]

Figure [9]

against the "new woman" and her challenge to prevailing gender arrangements and their constraints on women.[10] Mythological, artistic, polemical,
and scientific discourses from many cultures and eras certainly suggest
the symbolic potency of female hunger as a cultural metaphor for unleashed female power and desire, from the blood-craving Kali (who in one
representation is shown eating her own entrails) to the *Malleus Maleficarum*
("For the sake of fulfilling the mouth of the womb, [witches] consort even
with the devil") to Hall and Oates's contemporary rock lyrics: "Oh, oh,
here she comes, watch out boys, she'll chew you up."[11]

    In *Tom Jones* and *Flashdance,* the trope of female hunger as female sexu-
ality is embodied in attractive female characters; more frequently, however, female hunger as sexuality is represented by Western culture in
misogynist images permeated with terror and loathing rather than affec-

tion or admiration. In the figure of the man-eater the metaphor of the devouring woman reveals its deep psychological underpinnings. Eating is not really a metaphor for the sexual act; rather, the sexual act, when initiated and desired by a woman, is imagined as itself an act of eating, of incorporation and destruction of the object of desire. Thus, women's sexual appetites must be curtailed and controlled, because they threaten to deplete and consume the body and soul of the male. Such imagery, as Dijkstra has demonstrated, flourishes in the West in the art of the late nineteenth century. Arguably, the same cultural backlash (if not in the same form) operates today—for example, in the ascendancy of popular films that punish female sexuality and independence by rape and dismemberment (as in numerous slasher films), loss of family and children *(The Good Mother)*, madness and death *(Fatal Attraction, Presumed Innocent)*, and public humiliation and disgrace *(Dangerous Liaisons)*.

Of course, Victorian prohibitions against women eating were not *only* about the ideology of gender. Or, perhaps better put, the ideology of gender contained other dimensions as well. The construction of "femininity" had not only a significant moral and sexual aspect (femininity as sexual passivity, timidity, purity, innocence) but a class dimension. In the reigning body symbolism of the day, a frail frame and lack of appetite signified not only spiritual transcendence of the desires of the flesh but *social* transcendence of the laboring, striving "economic" body. Then, as today, to be aristocratically cool and unconcerned with the mere facts of material survival was highly fashionable. The hungering bourgeois wished to appear, like the aristocrat, above the material desires that in fact ruled his life. The closest he could come was to possess a wife whose ethereal body became a sort of fashion statement of *his* aristocratic tastes. If he could not be or marry an aristocrat, he could have a wife who looked like one, a wife whose non-robust beauty and delicate appetite signified her lack of participation in the taxing "public sphere."[12]

## *Men Eat and Women Prepare*

The metaphorical dualities at work here, whatever their class meanings, presuppose an idealized (and rarely actualized) gendered division of labor in which men strive, compete, and exert themselves in the public sphere while women are cocooned in the domestic arena (which is romanticized and mystified as a place of peace and leisure, and hence connotes transcendence of the laboring, bourgeois body). In the necessity to make such a division of labor appear natural we find another powerful ideological underpinning (perhaps the most important in the context of industrialized society) for the cultural containment of female appetite: the notion that women are most gratified by feeding and nourishing *others*, not themselves. As a literal activity, of course, women fed others long before the "home" came to be identified as women's special place; Caroline Bynum argues that there is reason to believe that food preparation was already a stereotypically female activity in the European Middle Ages.[13] But it was in the industrial era, with its idealization of the domestic arena as a place of nurture and comfort for men and children, that feeding others acquired the extended emotional meaning it has today.

In "An Ode to Mothers" columnist Bud Poloquin defines *Moms* as "those folks who, upon seeing there are only four pieces of pie for five people, promptly announce they never did care for the stuff."[14] Denial of self and the feeding of others are hopelessly enmeshed in this construction of the ideal mother, as they are in the nineteenth-century version of the ideal wife as "she who stands . . . famished before her husband, while he devours, stretched at ease, the produce of her exertions; waits his tardy permission without a word or a look of impatience, and feeds, with the humblest gratitude, and the shortest intermission of labor, on the scraps and offals which he disdains."[15] None of this self-sacrifice, however, is felt as such by the "paragon of womanhood" (as Charles Butler calls her), for it is here, in the care and feeding of others, that woman experiences the one form of desire that is appropriately hers: as Elias Canetti so succinctly puts it, "Her passion is to give food."[16]

Over a decade ago, John Berger trenchantly encapsulated the standard formula he saw as regulating the representation of gender difference, both throughout the history of art and in contemporary advertising: "Men act, and women appear."[17] Today, that opposition no longer seems to hold quite as rigidly as it once did (women are indeed objectified more than ever, but, in this image-dominated culture, men increasingly are too). But if this duality no longer strictly applies, the resilience of others is all the more instructive. Let me replace Berger's formulation with another, apparently more enduring one: "Men eat, and women prepare." At least in the sphere of popular representations, this division of labor is as prescriptive in 1991 as in 1891. Despite the increasing participation of women of all ages and classes in the "public" sphere, her "private" role of nurturer remains ideologically intact.

To be sure, we have inherited some of these representations from a former era—for example, the plump, generous Mammys and Grandmas who symbolically have prepared so many products: Aunt Jemima, Mrs. Smith, Mrs. Paul, Grandma Brown. But our cultural penchant for nostalgia does not get us off the hook here. At the start of the 1990s (and this seems to be even more striking now than five years ago), popular representations almost never depict a man *preparing* food as an everyday activity, routinely performed in the unpaid service of others. Occasionally, men *are* shown serving food—in the role of butler or waiter. They may be depicted roasting various items around a campfire, barbecuing meat, preparing a salad for a special company dinner, or making *instant* coffee (usually in a getaway cabin or vacation boat). But all of these are nonroutine, and their exceptional nature is frequently underscored in the ad. In one commercial, a man fixes instant coffee to serve to his wife in bed on her birthday. "How tough can it be?" he asks. "She makes breakfast every morning." In another ad, a man is shown preparing pancakes for his son's breakfast [Fig.

Figure [10]

10, above]. "My pancakes deserve the rich maple flavor of Log Cabin Syrup," reads the bold type, suggesting ("my pancakes") male proprietorship and ease in the kitchen. The visual image of the father lovingly serving the son undoubtedly destabilizes cultural stereotypes (racial as well as gendered). But in the smaller print below the image we are told that this is

a "special moment" with his son. Immediately the destabilizing image re-
configures into a familiar one: like Dad's secret recipe for barbecue sauce,
this father's pancakes make their appearance only on special occasions. Or
perhaps it is the very fact that Dad is doing the cooking that *makes* this a
significant, intimate occasion for sharing. (Imagine a woman instead of a
man in the ad; would "special moment" not then seem odd?)

Continually, in representations that depict men preparing food, there
will be a conspicuously absent wife or mother (for instance, in the hospital
having a baby) who, it is implied, is *normally* responsible for the daily
labor of food preparation and service. Even when men or boys are used to
advertise convenience foods, the product has usually been left for them
with expert instructions added by Mom. In the Jell-O Heritage [Fig. 11,
p. 159], this absent maternal figure (whether mother or grandmother is not
clear) appears in the small insert to the upper right of the larger image,
which depicts a young man away at college, well supplied with Jell-O
pudding snacks. Significantly (although somewhat absurdly), she is associated with the provision of a "strong foundation" by virtue of the fact
that *she* prepares instant pudding from a mix rather than merely opening
up an already prepared pudding snack. Jell-O, of course, could not present nostalgic images of Grandma preparing *real* "scratch" pudding, since
it does not want to evoke longing for a time when women did not depend
on its products. But in terms of the oppositions exploited in this ad, instant
pudding works just as well; compared to flipping the lid off a pudding
snack, preparing instant pudding *is* a laborious task. It thus belongs to
women's world. Men are almost *never* shown lavishing time on cooking.
*Real* coffee is always prepared by women, as are all the cakes and
casseroles that require more than a moment to put together. When men *are*
shown cooking an elaborate meal, it is always *with* one or two other yuppie men, converting the activity from an act of everyday service into a festive, "Big Chill" occasion. But even these representations are rare. In all
the many dinner parties that Hope and Michael hosted on "Thirtysome-
thing," no man has ever appeared in the kitchen except to sneak a bit of
the meal being prepared by Hope, Nancy, and Melissa.

## Food and Love

At the beginning of the 1992 U.S. presidential campaign, Hillary Clinton, badgered by reporters' endless questions concerning her pursuit of a
professional career, shot back defensively and sarcastically: "Well, I suppose I could have stayed home and baked cookies and had teas ..."
Media audiences never got to hear the end of her remark (or the questioning that preceded it); the "cookies and teas" sound-bite became *the* gender-
transgression of the campaign, replayed over and over, and presented by
opponents as evidence of Hillary's rabid feminism and disdain for traditional maternal values. Rightly protesting this interpretation, Hillary Clinton tried to prove her true womanhood by producing her favorite recipe

Figure [11]

for oatmeal chocolate chip cookies. Barbara Bush, apparently feeling that a gauntlet had been thrown down, responded in kind with a richer, less fibre-conscious recipe of her own. Newspapers across the country asked readers to prepare both and vote on which First Lady had the better cookie.

That the cookie itself should have become the symbol and center of the national debate about Hillary Clinton's adequacy as wife and mother is not surprising. Food is equated with maternal and wifely love throughout our culture. In nearly all commercials that feature men eating—such as the cake commercials whose sexualized rhetoric was quoted earlier—there is a woman in the background (either visible or implied) who has *prepared* the food. (The "Betty Crocker, You Sweet Talker" series has two women: the possessor of the clearly feminine hands offering the cakes, and Betty Crocker herself, to whom all the passionate croonings—"I'm a fool for your chocolate. I'm wild, crazy, out of control"—are addressed.) Most significantly, *always,* the woman in the background speaks the language of love and care through the offering of food: "Nothin' says lovin' like something from the oven"; "Give me that great taste of love"; "Nothing says 'Cookie, I love you' like Nestle's Toll House Cookies Do." In these commercials, male eating is inextricably tied to female offerings of love. This is not represented, however, as female self-abnegation. Rather, it is suggested that women receive *their* gratification through nourishing others, either in the old-fashioned way (taste and emotional pleasure) or in the health-conscious mode:

*Her voice, heard off:* He's like a little boy—normally serious, *then* he eats English muffins with butter [shot of man's face transported with childlike delight] and *I* get to enjoy watching him. A little butter brings a lot of joy.

> *He:* What are you doing?
> *She:* I'm listening to your heart.
> *He:* What does it say?
> *She:* It says that it's glad that you've started jogging, and that you're eating healthier. It's happy that I'm giving us new Promise margarine. Eating foods low in cholesterol is good for you and your heart.
> *He:* Know what else is good for me?
> *She:* What?
> *He:* You.
> *She beams, snuggling deeper into man's chest.*

My analysis, I want to emphasize, is not meant to disparage caring for the physical and emotional well-being of others, "maternal" work that has been scandalously socially undervalued even as it has been idealized and sanctified. Nor am I counterposing to the argument of these ads the construction that women are simply oppressed by such roles. This would be untrue to the personal experiences of many women, including myself. I remember the pride and pleasure that radiated from my mother, who was anxious and unhappy in most other areas of her life, when her famous stuffed cabbage was devoured enthusiastically and in voluminous quantities by my father, my sisters, and me. As a little girl, I loved watching her roll each piece, enclosing just the right amount of filling, skillfully avoiding tearing the tender cabbage leaves as she folded them around the meat. I never felt so safe and secure as at those moments. She was visibly pleased when I asked her to teach me exactly how to make the dish and thrilled when I even went so far as to write the quantities and instructions down as she tried to formulate them into an official recipe (until then, it had been passed through demonstration from mother to daughter, and my mother considered that in writing it down I was conferring a higher status on it). Those periods in my life when I have found myself too busy writing, teaching, and traveling to find the time and energy to prepare special meals for people that I love have been periods when a deep aspect of my self has felt deprived, depressed.

Nor would I want my critique to be interpreted as effacing the collective, historical experiences of those groups, forced into servitude for the families of others, who have been systematically deprived of the freedom *to* care for their own families. Bell hooks points out, for example, that black women's creation of "home- place," of fragile and hard-won "spaces of care and nurturance" for the healing of deep wounds made by racism, sexism, and poverty, was less a matter of obedience to a tyrannical gender-norm than the construction of a "site of cultural resistance."[18] With this in mind, it is clear that the Jell-O Heritage ad discussed earlier is more complex than my interpretation has thus far allowed. Part of an extensive General Foods series aimed at the African American consumer and promoting America's historically black colleges, the ad's association of the maternal figure with "strong foundations" runs far deeper than a nostalgic evocation of Mom's traditional cooking. In this ad, the maternal figure is linked with a black "heritage," with the preservation and communication of culture.

However, at the same time that hooks urges that contemporary black culture should honor the black woman's history of service to her family and her community, she also cautions against the ideological construction of such service as woman's natural role. (Despite the pleasure I take in cooking, in relationships where it has been expected of me I have resented it deeply.) It is this construction that is reinforced in the representations I have been examining, through their failure to depict males as "naturally" fulfilling that role, and—more perniciously—through their failure to depict females as appropriate *recipients* of such care. Only occasionally are little girls represented as being *fed;* more often, they (but never little boys) are shown learning how to feed others [Fig. 12, below]. In this way, caring

Figure [12]

is representationally "reproduced" as a quintessentially and exclusively female activity. It is significant and disquieting that the General Foods series does not include any ads that portray female students discovering their black heritage (or learning how to rely on convenience foods!) at college. It is possible that the ad series is very deliberate here, exploiting contemporary notions that the "crisis in black manhood" is the fault of black women and identifying its products with an imagined world in which opportunities for black men go hand in hand with "natural," prefeminist gender relations. Black men will find their way to college, it is suggested, so long as women remain in the background, encouraging and supporting rather than competing and undermining.

The ubiquitous configuration of woman-food-man, with food expressing the woman's love for the man and at the same time satisfying woman's desire to bestow love, establishes male hunger as thoroughly socially integrated into the network of heterosexual family and love relations. Men can eat *and* be loved; indeed, a central mode by which they receive love is through food from women. For women, by contrast (who are almost never shown being fed by others), eating—in the form of private, *self*-feeding—is represented as a *substitute* for human love. Weight Watchers transparently offers itself as such in its "Who says you can't live on love?" ad [Fig. 13, p. 163]. In other ads, it offers its low-cal spaghetti sauce as "A Friend." Diet Coke, emphasizing the sexual, insists that "sometimes the best relationships are purely fizzical." Miracle Whip Light offers itself as "a light that turns you on."

Notice that in these ads there is no partner, visible or implied, offering the food and thus operating as the true bestower of "love." In many ads— virtually a genre, in fact—the absence of the partner is explicitly thematized, a central aspect of the narrative of the ad. One commercial features a woman in bed, on the phone, refusing date after date in favor of an evening alone with her ice-cream bon bons: "Your Highness? Not tonight!" "The inauguration? Another year!" In another, a woman admits to spending a lot of time alone with her "latest obsession," a chocolate drink, because it gives her "the same feeling as being in love" and "satisfies her innermost cravings anytime [she] wants." She pleads with us, the viewers, not to tell Michael, her boyfriend.

These commercials hit a painful nerve for women. The bon bon commercial may seem merely silly, but the chocolate drink ad begins to evoke, darkly and disturbingly, the psychological and material realities of women's food problems. The talk of "obsession" and "innermost cravings," the furtiveness, the secrecy, the use of food to satisfy emotional needs, all suggest central elements of binge behavior. Frusen Glädjé supplies another piece and gives an important lie to the other, more upbeat commercials [Fig. 14, p. 164]: "He never called. So, Ben and I went out for a walk to pick up a pint of Frusen Glädjé. Ben's better looking anyway." Frusen Glädjé: "It feels so good." Here, as in the Häagen-Dazs ad discussed earlier, the sensuousness of the ice-cream experience is

Figure [13]

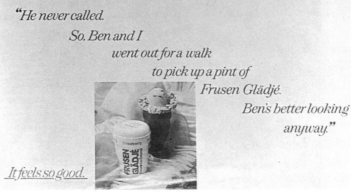

Figure [14]

emphasized; unlike the Häagen-Dazs ad, however, Frusen Glädjé offers solace from emotional depths rather than the thrill of emotional heights. This is, indeed, the prevailing gender reality. For women, the emotional comfort of self-feeding is rarely turned to in a state of pleasure and independence, but in despair, emptiness, loneliness, and desperation. Food is, as one woman put it, "the only thing that will take care of *me*."[19]

## *Food as Transgression*

An extremely interesting fact about male bulimics: they rarely binge alone. They tend to binge at mealtime and in public places, whereas women almost always eat minimally at meals and gorge later, in private.[20] Even in our disorders (or perhaps especially in our disorders) we follow the gender rules. In the commercials I have been discussing, female eating is virtually always represented as private, secretive, illicit. The woman has stolen away from the world of husband, family, friends to a secret corner where she and the food can be alone. A "Do Not Disturb" sign hangs on the door to the room where the woman sits munching on her "purple passion," New York Deli Potato Chips. A husband returns home to discover that in his absence his wife, sitting on the floor, has eaten all the Frusen Glädjé; her voice is mildly defiant, although soft—"I ate all the Frusen Glädjé"—but her face is sheepish and her glance averted. Men sing openly of their wild cravings for Betty Crocker cakes; women's cravings are a dirty, shameful secret, to be indulged in only when no one is looking.

More often than not, however, women are not even permitted, even in private, indulgences so extravagant in scope as the full satisfaction of their hungers. Most commonly, women are used to advertise, *not* ice cream and potato chips (foods whose intake is very difficult to contain and control), but individually wrapped pieces of tiny, bite-size candies: Andes candies, Hershey's kisses, Mon Cheri bon bons. Instead of the mounds of cake and oozing frosting typical of commercials featuring male eaters, women are confined to a "tiny scoop" of flavor, a "tiny piece" of chocolate. As in the Weight Watchers linguini advertisement ("Dive in"), the rhetoric of indulgence is invoked, only to be contained by the product itself: "Indulge a little," urges Andes Candies. "Satisfy your urge to splurge in five delicious bite-size ways." The littleness of the candy and the amount of taste that is packed within its tiny boundaries are frequently emphasized: "Each bite-size piece packs a wallop of milk chocolate crunch." Instead of the emphasis on undifferentiated feelings of sensuous delight that we see in commercials showing men, the pitch aimed at women stresses the exquisite pleasure to be had from a sensually focused and limited experience. The message to women is explicit: "Indulge a *little*." (And only out of sight; even these minuscule bon bons are eaten privately, in isolation, behind closed doors.)

If one genre of commercials hints at the dark secrets of binge behavior—the refusal of female desire to remain circumscribed and repressed; the frustrations of "feeding" others and never being fed yourself—the "bite-size" candy genre represents female hunger as successfully contained within the bounds of appropriate feminine behavior. It is significant, surely, that in all these commercials the woman is found "indulging" only after a day spent serving others. In these commercials, it is permissible for women to feed the self (if such dainty nibbling merits this description) only after first feeding others:

> For my angel, I sewed for days. Now I deserve a little praise.
> I thank me very much with Andes Candies.

> Chances are you spent the day doing things for others. Don't
> you deserve something for yourself? Try a Mon Cheri. [The
> woman is in the bathtub; in the background, dimly heard are
> the voices of the day gone by: "Honey, did you pick up my dry
> cleaning?" "Mrs. Jones, will you type this letter?" "Mommy,
> we want to go to the park!" She sinks down into the tub, un-
> wrapping the candy, in exquisite anticipation.]

These commercials, no less than the Victorian conduct manuals, offer a virtual blueprint for disordered relations to food and hunger. The representation of unrestrained appetite as inappropriate for women, the depiction of female eating as a private, transgressive act, make restriction and denial of hunger central features of the construction of femininity and set up the compensatory binge as a virtual inevitability. Such restrictions on appetite, moreover, are not merely about food intake. Rather, the social control of female hunger operates as a practical "discipline" (to use Foucault's term) that trains female bodies in the knowledge of their limits and possibilities. Denying oneself food becomes the central micro-practice in the education of feminine self-restraint and containment of impulse.

Victorian women were told that it was vulgar to load their plates; in 1990, women students of mine complain of the tortures of the cafeteria— the embarrassment of eating ice cream in front of the male students, the pressure to take just a salad or, better yet, refuse food altogether. Later at night, when they are alone, they confront the deprived and empty feeling left in the wake of such a regimen. As in the commercials, the self-reward and solace is food. The problem, however, after a day of restraint is the requirement for any further containment of the now ravenous self. Unlike the women in the Andes candy commercials, few women who have spent the day submerging their desires, either for the sake of their families or to project the appropriately attractive lack of appetite to a cafeteria full of adolescent boys, really feel rewarded by a bite-size piece of candy, no matter how much chocolate "wallop" it packs. In private, shamefully and furtively, we binge.

## Destabilizing Images?

When, in my classes, we discuss contemporary representations, I encourage my students to bring in examples that appear to violate traditional gender-dualities and the ideological messages contained in them. Frequently, my students view our examination of these "subversive" representations as an investigation and determination of whether or not "progress" has been made. My students want very much to believe that progress is being made, and so do I. But "progress" is not an adequate description of the cultural status of the counter-examples they bring me. Rather, they almost always display a complicated and bewitching tangle of new possibilities and old patterns of representation. They reflect the instabilities that trouble the continued reproduction of the old dualities and ideologies, but they do not show clearly just where we are going.

A television commercial for Hormel microwaveable Kid's Kitchen Meals, for example, opens with two young girls trying to fix a bicycle. A little boy, watching them, offers to help, claiming that "I can fix anything. My dad lets me fix his car. My mom lets me fix dinner." When the girls are skeptical ("Yeah? Well, prove it!"), he fixes a Hormel's Kid's Kitchen Meal for them. Utterly impressed with his culinary skill and on the basis of this ready to trust his mechanical aptitude, they ask, "You know how to fix a bike?" "What? Yeah, I do!" he eagerly replies. Now, is this ad "progressive" or "regressive"? The little girls cannot fix their own bike, a highly traditional, "feminine" limitation. Yet they do not behave in helpless or coquettish ways in the commercial. Far from it. They speak in rough voices and challenging words to the boy, who is physically smaller (and, it appears, younger) than they; "Give me a break!" they mutter scornfully when he claims he can "fix anything." Despite their mechanical inability, they do not act deferential, and in a curious way this neutralizes the gendered meanings of the activities depicted. Not being able to fix a bike is something that could happen to anyone, they seem to believe. And so we may begin to see it this way too.

Then, too, there is the unusual representation of the male cooking for and serving the females. True, it only required a touch of the microwave panel. But this is, after all, only a little boy. One message this commercial may be delivering is that males can engage in traditionally "feminine" activities without threat to their manhood. Cooking for a woman does not mean that she won't respect you in the morning. She will still recognize your authority to fix her bike (indeed, she may become further convinced of it precisely by your mastery of "her" domain). The expansion of possibilities for boys thus extracts from girls the price of continued ineptitude in certain areas (or at least the show of it) and dependence on males. Yet, in an era in which most working women find themselves with two full-time jobs—their second shift beginning at five o'clock, when they return from work to meet their husband's expectations of dinner, a clean and comfortable home, a sympathetic ear—the message that cooking and serving others is not "sissy," though it may be problematic and nonprogressive in many ways, is perhaps the single most *practically* beneficial (to women) message we can convey to little boys.

In its provision of ambiguous and destabilizing imagery, the influx of women into the professional arena has had a significant effect on the representation of gender. Seeking to appeal to a population that wishes to be regarded (at least while on the job) as equal in power and ability to the men with whom they work, advertisers have tried to establish gender symmetry in those representations that depict or evoke the lives of professional couples. Minute Rice thus has two versions of its "I wonder what 'Minute' is cookin' up for dinner tonight?" commercial. In one, father and children come home from work and school to find mother "cookin' up" an elaborate chicken stir-fry to serve over Minute Rice. In the other, a working woman returns to find her male partner "cookin' up" the dinner. The configuration is indeed destabilizing, if only because it makes us aware of how very rare it is to see. But, significantly, there are no children in this commercial, as there are in the more traditional version; the absence of children codes the fact that this is a yuppie couple, the group to which this version is designed to appeal.

And now Häagen-Dazs, the original yuppie ice cream, has designed an ad series for this market [Fig. 15, below, and Fig. 16, p.169]. These ads

Figure [15]

Figure [16]

perfectly illustrate the unstable location of contemporary gender advertisements: they attempt to satisfy representational conventions that still
have a deep psychic grip on Western culture, while at the same time registering every new rhythm of the social heartbeat. "Enter the State of
Häagen-Dazs"—a clear invocation of the public world rather than the domestic domain. The man and woman are dressed virtually identically
(making small allowances for gender-tailoring) in equally no-nonsense,
dark business suits, styled for power. Their hair-styles are equivalent,
brushed back from the face, clipped short but not punky. They have similar expressions: slightly playful, caught in the act but certainly not feeling
guilty. They appear to be indulging in their ice-cream break in the middle
of a workday; this sets up both the fetching representational incongruity
of the ad and its realism. Ice cream has always been represented as relaxation food, to be *indulged* in; it belongs to a different universe than the
work ethic, performance principle, or spirit of competition. To eat it in a
business suit is like having "quickie" sex in the office, irregular and
naughty. Yet everyone knows that people *do* eat ice cream on their breaks
and during their lunch hours. The ad thus appears both realistic and *representationally* odd; we realize that we are seeing images we have not seen
before *except* in real life. And, of course, in real life, women *do* eat Häagen-
Dazs, as much as, if not more than, men.

And yet, intruding into this world of gender equality and eating realism that is designed to appeal to the sensibilities of "progressive" young
men and women is the inescapable disparity in how much and how the
man and woman are eating. He: an entire pint of vanilla fudge, with sufficient abandon to topple the carton, and greedy enough to suck the spoon.
She: a restrained Eve-bite (already taken; no licks or sucks in process
here), out of a single brittle bar (aestheticized as "artfully" nutty, in contrast to his bold, unaccessorized "Vanilla Fudge." Whether unconsciously
reproduced or deliberately crafted to appeal to the psychic contradictions
and ambivalence of its intended audience, the disparity comes from the
recesses of our most sedimented, unquestioned notions about gender.

NOTES

This essay grew out of a shorter piece, "How Television Teaches Women to Hate
Their Hungers," in *Mirror Images* (Newsletter of Anorexia Bulimia Support, Syracuse,
N.Y.) 4, no. 1 (1986): 8–9. An earlier version was delivered at the 1990 meetings of the
New York State Sociological Association, and some of the analysis has been presented in
various talks at Le Moyne and other colleges and community organizations. I owe
thanks to all my students who supplied examples.

[1] Journalist Beatrice Fairfax, quoted in Lois Banner, *American Beauty* (Chicago: University of Chicago Press, 1984), p. 136.

[2] "Starvation Stages in Weight-loss Patients Similar to Famine Victims," *International
Obesity Newsletter* 3 (April 1989).

[3] Jean Baudrillard, *Simulations* (New York: Semiotext(e), 1983), pp. 1–3; quotation is
on p. 2.

[4] Geneen Roth, *Feeding the Hungry Heart* (New York: New American Library, 1982),
p. 15.

[5] See Helena Mitchie, *The Flesh Made Word* (New York: Oxford University Press, 1987), for an extremely interesting discussion of this taboo in Victorian literature.

[6] Quoted from *Godey's* by Joan Jacobs Brumberg, *Fasting Girls* (Cambridge: Harvard University Press, 1988), p. 179.

[7] Mitchie, *The Flesh Made Word*, p. 15. Not surprisingly, red meat came under especial suspicion as a source of erotic inflammation. As was typical for the era, such anxieties were rigorously scientized: for example, in terms of the heat-producing capacities of red meat and its effects on the development of the sexual organs and menstrual flow. But, clearly, an irresistible associational overdetermination—meat as the beast, the raw, the primitive, the masculine—was the true inflammatory agent here. These associations survive today, put to commercial use by the American Beef Association, whose television ads feature James Garner and Cybil Shepard promoting "Beef: Real Food for Real People." Here the nineteenth-century link between meat aversion, delicacy, and refinement is exploited, this time in favor of the meat-eater, whose down-to-earth gutsiness is implicitly contrasted to the prissiness of the weak-blooded vegetarian.

[8] Mrs. H. O. Ward, *The Young Lady's Friend* (Philadelphia: Porter and Coates, 1880), p. 162, quoted in Mitchie, *The Flesh Made Word*, pp. 16–17.

[9] Quoted in Mitchie, *The Flesh Made Word*, p. 193.

[10] Bram Dijkstra, *Idols of Perversity* (New York: Oxford University Press, 1986), pp. 30–31.

[11] *Malleus Malificarum* quoted in Brian Easlea, *Witch-Hunting, Magic, and the New Philosophy* (Atlantic Highlands, N.J.: Humanities Press, 1980), p. 8; Hall and Oates, "Man-Eater."

[12] Women were thus warned that "gluttonous habits of life" would degrade their physical appearance and ruin their marriageability. "Gross eaters" could develop thick skin, broken blood vessels on the nose, cracked lips, and an unattractively "superanimal" facial expression (Brumberg, *Fasting Girls*, p. 179). Of course, the degree to which actual women were able to enact any part of these idealized and idolized constructions was highly variable (as it always is); but *all* women, of all classes and races, felt their effects as the normalizing measuring rods against which their own adequacy was judged (and, usually, found wanting).

[13] Caroline Walker Bynum, *Holy Feast and Holy Fast: The Religious Significance of Food to Medieval Women* (Berkeley: University of California Press, 1987), p. 191.

[14] *Syracuse Herald-American*, May 8, 1988, p. D1.

[15] Charles Butler, *The American Lady*, quoted in Dijkstra, *Idols of Perversity*, p. 18. Margery Spring Rice noted this same pattern of self-sacrifice among British working-class housewives in the 1930s. Faced with the task of feeding a family on an inadequate budget and cooking in cramped conditions, the housewife, according to Rice, often "takes one comparatively easy way out by eating much less than any other member of her family." She gives a multitude of examples from social workers' records, including "'Her food is quite insufficient owing to the claims of the family'"; "'She is . . . a good mother spending most of the housekeeping money on suitable food for the children and often goes without proper food for herself'"; "'Mrs. A . . . gives her family of eight children an excellent diet . . . but cannot eat herself as she is so exhausted by the time she has prepared the family meals'"; and, interestingly, "'the children look well fed and one cannot help believing that Mrs. F. is starving herself unnecessarily'" (*Working-Class Wives: Their Health and Conditions* [London: Virago, 1989; orig. pub. 1939], pp. 157, 160, 162, 167).

[16] Elias Canetti, *Crowds and Power* (New York: Viking, 1962), p. 221.

[17] John Berger, *Ways of Seeing* (London: Penguin, 1977).

[18] bell hooks, *Yearning* (Boston: South End Press, 1990), p. 42.

[19] Marcia Millman, *Such a Pretty Face: Being Fat in America* (New York: Norton, 1980), p. 106.

[20] John Schneider and W. Stewart Agras, "Bulimia in Males: A Matched Comparison with Females," *International Journal of Eating Disorders* 6, no. 2 (March 1987): 235–42.

.   .   .   .   .   .   .   .   .   .   .   .   .

## QUESTIONS FOR A SECOND READING

1. Bordo's essay is designed to allow its readers to raise questions about food and advertising and the ways ads could be said to promote the "re-production of gender difference and gender inequality." And yet, in the same breath, she says "I would argue, however, that more than a purely profit-maximizing . . . Madison Avenue mentality is at work in these ads" (p. 148). If there is more at work here than a company's desire to make money, what is it? As Bordo invites you to think about this, whose inter-ests are served in these ads? As you reread this selection, mark those mo-ments in the text where you see Bordo identifying the cultural pressures that could be said to be at play in these advertisements. What are they? How might they be related? And who, or what, might they benefit?

2. Bordo brings a special training to the materials of popular culture. Among signs of this training in her prose are those terms and sources that are dif-ficult or unfamiliar, particular to philosophy or to cultural studies. As you reread, underline or make a list of the key terms that seem to mark her ex-pertise (to mark the difference between what she can say and what you can say). And mark those figures, like Berger or Baudrillard, who help her to say what she wants to say. Be prepared to identify those terms and ref-erences that mark the work of an expert. From their use and context in Bordo's essay, how might you explain or translate these passages for oth-ers? What could you add if you researched them in the library?

3. Bordo examines advertisements of different sorts—some sell food, for ex-ample, while others sell body images or psychological states—and she compares ads directed toward women with those designed for men. As you reread, make note of how she defines and establishes the differences in the ads designed for (or attractive to) men and those designed for (or attractive to) women. In what materials you have at hand (magazines, TV programs or ads, CD covers), find five or six images, images that *you* find powerful and attractive, images you can place alongside those provided by Bordo. How might they be "read" in her terms? Where and how might her terms be made to seem misguided, limited, or inadequate?

## ASSIGNMENTS FOR WRITING

1. "Hunger as Ideology" begins with a section titled "The Woman Who Doesn't Eat Much" and ends with one titled "Destabilizing Images?" The opening section features several advertisements offering women "free and easy relations with food." The closing one features ads that Bordo suggests disrupt or destabilize the ideology or "commonsense" attitudes and values that we take for granted in our understanding of women, eat-ing, and the body—that which "comes from the recesses of our most sedi-mented, unquestioned notions about gender." Between these two sec-

tions, she covers a range of subjects: "Food, Sexuality, and Desire," "Food and Love," "Food as Transgression."

For this assignment, write an essay in which you present and explain Bordo's argument. You should imagine that you are writing for someone who is interested in these issues but who has not read this particular essay. You will need, then, to be careful, fair, and detailed in your presentation. What are the significant examples for Bordo? How does she read them? And, finally, how does she pull these examples together? What does she conclude?

You should also, however, establish your perspective on the questions and materials at the center of "Hunger as Ideology." The purpose of the summary, in other words, is to establish a position you can attribute to "Bordo." You should do this strategically, in order that you can also establish a position in conversation with what she says. You can frame this other position or point of view in your name (as what, on reflection, *you* think) or in the name of a group you feel you can represent (people of your generation, your gender, your background, your set of commitments, identifications, and practice).

2. Bordo extends an invitation to her students "to bring in examples that appear to violate traditional gender-dualities and the ideological messages contained in them." These, she said, will "display a complicated and bewitching tangle of new possibilities and old patterns of representation" (p. 166).

Write an essay in which you take up Bordo's invitation. On your own or with a group collect a set of advertisements (or images from other sources) that represent food and eating, women and men. Find examples and counterexamples to what she takes to be the traditional gender-dualities and the ideological messages contained in them. In order to present your project to others, write descriptions of the ads, as Bordo does, so that your readers will be able to "read" them (to see them and understand them) as you do. You'll need to place your examples in relation to Bordo's argument about the "old dualities and ideologies" and to what she says about images that "stabilize" and "destabilize." You will need, in other words, to put her terms to work on your examples. Make your goal not only to reproduce Bordo's project but to extend it, to refine it, to put it to the test.

3. Reread Bordo's essay and pay close attention to how she presents and reads her examples. What are the kinds of questions she routinely asks? And, as you look across her examples, think about the principles of selection and arrangement. What methods do you see in her work? What principles or assumptions? What defines her particular expertise?

You might also do this work as a work of criticism. You might think about what Bordo *doesn't* see in the ads she studies. What does she miss? and why? You might think about the questions she doesn't ask of the ads she studies. You might think about the ads she fails (or refuses) to include as part of her project. What is missing? What is unsaid or unnoticed?

Write an essay in which you choose two of Bordo's examples and use them to represent your study of her work. What does she do, as a writer and scholar, with her materials? What are her conclusions? What have you learned about her methods? How do you explain the kind of work represented by "Hunger as Ideology"? Assume that your audience is familiar with the essay but perhaps has not studied it as closely as you have and, as a consequence, could not understand it the way you do.


### MAKING CONNECTIONS

1. In "Hunger as Ideology," Bordo refers to John Berger and his work in *Ways of Seeing*. Both Berger and Bordo are concerned with how we see and read images; both are concerned to correct the ways images are used and read; both trace the ways images serve the interests of money and power; both are writing to get the attention of the public and teach readers how and why they should pay a different kind of attention to the images around them.

   For this assignment, use Bordo's work in "Hunger as Ideology" to reconsider Berger's "Ways of Seeing" (p. 105). Write an essay in which you consider the two essays as examples of an ongoing project. Berger's essay precedes Bordo's by about a quarter of a century. If you look closely at one or two of their examples, and if you look at the larger concerns in their arguments, are they saying the same thing? doing the same work? If so, why? Why is such work still necessary? If not, how do their projects differ? And how might you account for those differences?

2. Robert Coles in "The Tradition: Fact and Fiction" (p. 176) is concerned with the representation of the female body—with what those images mean and what purposes they serve (or might serve). (See, in particular, his discussion of Dorothea Lange's photographs of the "migrant mother" [pp. 185–188] and his discussion of Walker Evans's photos of the tenant's daughter picking cotton [pp. 198–204]. Coles's descriptions are close and careful. They draw, however, on a very different vocabulary than those provided by Bordo.

   Write an essay in which you compare the methods and concerns of Bordo and Coles. You should think about how their projects differ; consider the ways they choose and present images, what they notice, and how they describe and analyze what they notice. Both are concerned with the social context of images. What does Coles offer in describing the larger forces at work in producing the meanings of images? What does he offer in place of Bordo's "ideology"?

# ROBERT
# COLES

*E*arly in his career as a psychologist, Robert Coles spent seven years following
migrant workers north from Florida to gather material for the second volume—Migrants, Sharecroppers, Mountaineers—of his remarkable, Pulitzer
Prize–winning series of books, Children of Crisis. *He learned about the workers'
lives, he said, by visiting "certain homes week after week until it [had] come to
pass that I [had] known certain families for many years." The sacrifice, patience,
compassion, and discipline required for his massive documentary projects—the
eight volumes of the* Children of Crisis *series and, later,* The Inner Lives of
Children—*transform the usual business of research into something magnificent.*

*Coles's project began when he was stationed at Keesler Air Force Base in Biloxi,
Mississippi. He was, he says, a "rather smug and all too self-satisfied child psychiatrist, just out of medical training." He was in the South at the beginning of the civil
rights movement, and the scenes he witnessed, the experience, for example, of black
children taunted and threatened as they walked into newly desegregated schools, led
him to abandon his plans to return to New England to remain instead in the South
to find out how children responded to crisis. He began with standard psychiatric
questions, such as "How did these children respond to stress?," but soon realized,
he said, "that I was meeting families whose assumptions, hopes, fears, and expectations were quite definitely strange to me. I realized, too, how arbitrarily I was fitting
the lives of various individuals into my psychiatric categories—a useful practice*

*under certain circumstances, but now, for me, a distinct hindrance. I was unwittingly setting severe, maybe crippling, limits on what I would allow myself to see, try to comprehend." He learned, through the children, to abandon his carefully rehearsed questions and to talk and listen. The stories he learned to tell are remarkable and moving and have an authority few writers achieve.*

*Born in 1929, Coles graduated from Harvard University in 1950, earned an M.D. degree from Columbia University in 1954, and began his career as a child psychiatrist. He is currently the James Agee Professor of Social Ethics at Harvard University and a founding member of the Center of Documentary Studies at Duke University. An essayist, poet, and scholar, Coles has published over fifty books, including* Women of Crisis *(1978), co-authored with his wife, Jane Hallowell Coles,* The Call of Stories: Teaching and the Moral Imagination *(1989),* Harvard Diary *(1990), and* The Call of Service: A Witness to Idealism *(1994). Coles is also the coeditor of the documentary magazine* DoubleTake.

*The essay that follows is a chapter from Coles's recent book,* Doing Documentary Work *(1997). Coles first presented it in 1996 in a series of lectures given at the New York Public Library. The chapter draws on the last twenty years of his teaching, including courses in the "literary-documentary tradition" at Harvard and at the Center for Documentary Studies at Duke. When Coles refers to "documentary work" he is referring to any attempt to engage, represent, and understand the lives of others. His reference, then, extends to journalists, poets, novelists, and filmmakers; to sociologists, anthropologists, and historians; to physicians, psychologists, and social workers; to anyone who is charged to know deeply and to speak and act for others. There is an urgency in Coles's work, a sense of mission and service, that is rare in academia and in contemporary intellectual life. You can feel this urgency in his conclusion to "The Tradition: Fact and Fiction":*

> *And so it goes, then—doing documentary work is a journey, and is a little more, too, a passage across boundaries (disciplines, occupational constraints, definitions, conventions all too influentially closed for traffic), a passage that can become a quest, even a pilgrimage, a movement toward the sacred truth enshrined not only on tablets of stone, but in the living hearts of those others whom we can hear, see, and get to understand. Thereby, we hope to be confirmed in our own humanity— the creature on this earth whose very nature it is to make just that kind of connection with others during the brief stay we are permitted here.*

# The Tradition: Fact and Fiction

The heart of the matter for someone doing documentary work is the pursuit of what James Agee called "human actuality"—rendering and representing for others what has been witnessed, heard, overheard, or sensed. Fact is "the quality of being actual," hence Agee's concern with actuality. All documentation, however, is put together by a particular mind whose capacities, interests, values, conjectures, suppositions and presuppositions, whose memories, and, not least, whose talents will come to bear directly or indirectly on what is, finally presented to the world in the form of words, pictures, or even music or artifacts of one kind or another. In shaping an article or a book, the writer can add factors and variables in two directions: social and cultural and historical on the one hand, individual or idiosyncratic on the other. As Agee reminds us in his long "country letter," his aria: "All that each person is, and experiences, and shall ever experience, in body and in mind, all these things are differing expressions of himself and of one root, and are identical: and not one of these things nor one of these persons is ever quite to be duplicated, nor replaced, nor has it ever quite had precedent: but each is a new and incommunicably tender life, wounded in every breath, and almost as hardly killed as easily wounded: sustaining, for a while, without defense, the enormous assaults of the universe."

Such an emphasis on human particularity would include the ups and downs of a life, even events (both internal and external) in that life that would seem to have nothing to do with the objectivity of, say, the world of central Alabama, but everything to do with the world of the writer or the photographer who will notice, ignore, take seriously, or find irrelevant Alabama's various moments, happenings, acts and deeds and comments, scenes. Events are filtered through a person's awareness, itself not uninfluenced by a history of private experience, by all sorts of aspirations, frustrations, and yearnings, by those elusive, significant "moods" as they can affect and even sway what we deem of interest or importance, not to mention how we assemble what we have learned into something to present to others—to editors, museum curators first of all, whose personal attitudes, not to mention the nature of their jobs or the values and desires of *their* bosses, all help shape their editorial or curatorial judgment. The web of one kind of human complexity (that of life in Hale County, Alabama) connects with, is influenced by, the web of another kind of human complexity (Agee and Evans and all that informs not only their lives but those of their magazine and book editors).

So often in our discussion of documentary work my students echo Agee, emphasize the "actuality" of the work—its responsibility to fact. They commonly pose for themselves the familiar alternative of fiction, as though we were dealing in clear-cut opposites: if not the true as against the false, at least the real as against the imaginary. But such opposites or alternatives don't quite do justice either conceptually or pragmatically to the aspect of "human actuality" that has to do with the vocational life of writers, photographers, folklorists, musicologists, and filmmakers, those who are trying to engage with people's words, their music, gestures, movements, and overall appearance and then let others know what they have learned. No one going anywhere, on a journalistic trip, on a documentary assignment, for social-science research, or to soak up the atmosphere of a place to aid in the writing of a story or a novel, will claim to be able to see and hear everything, or even claim to be able to notice all that truly matters. Who we are, to some variable extent, determines what we notice and, at another level of intellectual activity, what we regard as worthy of notice, what we find significant. Nor will technology help us all that decisively. I can arrive in America's Alabama or England's Yorkshire, I can find my way to a South Seas island or to central Africa, I can go visit a nearby suburban mall with the best tape recorder in the world, with cameras that take superb pictures, and even with a clear idea of what I am to do, and still I face the matter of looking *and* overlooking, paying instant heed *and* letting something slip by; and I face the matter of sorting out what I *have* noticed, of arranging it for emphasis—the matter, really, of *composition,* be it verbal or visual, the matter of re-presenting; and here that all-important word *narrative* enters. Stories heard or seen now have to turn into stories put together with some guiding intelligence and discrimination: I must select *what* ought to be present; decide on the *tone* of that presentation, its *atmosphere* or *mood.* These words can be as elusive as they are compelling to an essay, an exhibition of pictures, or a film.

Even if the strict limits of oral history are never suspended (*only* the taped interviews with informants are used in a given article or book, or any comments from the practitioner of oral history are confined to an introduction or to explanatory footnotes) there still remains that challenge of selection, with its implications for the narrative: which portions of which tapes are to be used, and with what assertive or clarifying or instructional agenda in mind (in the hope, for instance, of what popular or academic nod of comprehension or applause). How does one organize one's "material," with what topics in mind, what broader themes? How does one deal with the mix of factuality and emotionality that any taped interview presents, never mind a stock of them, and how does one arrange and unfold the events, the incidents: a story's pace, its plot, its coherence, its character development and portrayal, its suggestiveness, its degree of inwardness, its degree of connection to external action, and, all in all, its dramatic power, not to mention its moral authority?

The above words and phrases are summoned all the time by writers and teachers of fiction. Fictional devices, that is, inform the construction of nonfiction, and of course, fiction, conversely, draws upon the actual, the "real-life." A novelist uses his or her lived experience and the observations he or she has made and is making in the course of living a life as elements of a writing life. I remember William Carlos Williams pausing, after a home visit, to write down not only medical notes but a writer's notes: words heard; a revealing moment remembered; the appearance of a room on a particular day, or of a face brimming with surprise or happiness, a head lowered in dismay, a look of anticipation or alarm or dread, fear on a child's face, those details of life, of language, of appearance, of occurrence for which novelists are known, but which the rest of us also crave or require, as readers, of course, but also in our working lives: we all survive and prevail through a mastery of certain details, or fail by letting them slip through our fingers.

A novelist has to have those details at constant hand. He or she has had occasion in so-called real life to become aware of them but now has to fit this personal learning into a story, a narrative that requires both imagination and an idea of what will reach and touch readers persuasively. Nonfiction involves the same process, though we have to be careful of how we use words such as *experience, observation,* and, certainly, *imagination* when discussing nonfiction. A documentarian's report will be strengthened by what has been witnessed, but will be fueled, surely, by what those observations come to mean in his or her head: we absorb sights and sounds, and they become *our* experience, unique to us, in that we, their recipients, are unique. What we offer others in the way of our documentary reports, then, is *our* mix of what we have observed and experienced, as we have assembled it, that assembly having to do, again, with our imaginative capability, our gifts as writers, as editors, as storytellers, as artists. Oscar Lewis and Studs Terkel, working with taped interviews, pages and pages of transcripts, put all of that together in such a way that makes us readers marvel, not only at what we're told but at how it gets told,—and, before that, at how it was elicited from the various individuals these two met and from anyone who worked with them (Lewis trained a team of colleagues to help him out). Others of us might have met the same people but obtained from them different stories, maybe fewer in number or less interesting, less revealing.

I remember well what one of my psychoanalytic supervisors, Elizabeth Zetzel, who was a rather solidly conventional physician with a mind George Eliot would have called "theoretic," told me as she contemplated my protocols (my daily notes of what I had heard from a particular patient). Psychoanalysis, she said, is not only the uncovering of psychological material; it is two people doing so. Therefore, anyone's analysis, undertaken with a particular analyst, is only one of a possible series of hypothetical analyses, depending on who *else* might be the analyst, and what might be looked at and concluded on the basis of that other person's presence as the analyst, rather than the one now being consulted. I had been zealously on the prowl for certain memories that would, frankly, confirm my clinical notion of what had happened earlier in a certain patient's life, and to what effect. Dr. Zetzel had realized (I would later realize) that this was not only *an* inquiry, or the "correct" inquiry, but *my* inquiry—that someone else might have had other clinical interests, other kinds of memories to pursue, other clinical destinations in mind and, very important, would no doubt have engaged with this patient in a different way. (Nietzsche's aphorism holds here: "It takes two to make a truth.")

Moreover, what I make of what I hear from any patient has to do with what I've learned, and with what I have brought from my life to what has been taught me. Psychoanalysis, then, is a person's continuing narrative, however "meandering" rather than formally structured, as it is prompted by and shaped by his or her life, of course, but also as it responds to a particular listener or observer who has his or her own narrative interests and capacities and intentions (his or her observations, experiences, and, as with artists, talent and imagination—ways of sensing and of phrasing what is sensed, skill at putting him- or herself in another's shoes). A profession also has its narrative as well as its intellectual and emotional demands, and it, too, affects a particular practitioner, here a psychoanalyst, in influential ways: an agreed-upon language; an agreed-upon story called a diagnosis or a clinical interpretation or summary, namely, how we (are trained to) tell ourselves what we're hearing before we get around to letting our patients know what we think. Put differently, we develop, as psychiatric or psychoanalytic listeners, a professional narrative, which is offered in response to the narratives we hear in that unusual room where matters of utter intimacy and privacy become a shared documentary experience limited to two people. Others may be brought into the "act," however, since patients talk to people they know, and so do we, in our professional lives (at meetings) and in our writing lives: we share case histories with our colleagues and stories with readers, and surely we tailor our stories to elicit readers' interest—a tradition that goes back to Freud's first books and accounts for those of the many who have followed throughout this profession's now hundred-year history.

All of the above is as intricate and knotty, but also as evident and ordinary, as what happens every day when any two people talk to each other. The words and the pictorial sense vary on both sides, depending upon who the people are; and if one or both of the two talks to a third or a fourth person, that "report" will also vary depending on the person then doing the listening. We have words for the gross distortions of this process: rumor, gossip. We are less likely to account for the almost infinite possible variations on an encounter that constitute a human exchange, or a human response to the non-human world of the landscape or the multi-human world of a social scene. Naturally, a novelist does go one significant step further—reserves the right to use his or her imagination more freely than a documentarian, and to call upon the imaginary as a matter of course: personal fantasies, made-up voices given to made-up characters with made-up names, and scenes described out of the mind's visual reveries, even as its verbal ones supply words. All of the above has to be done with judgment as well as provocative ingenuity and boldness. The imaginary life, like the real one, requires a teller's thoughtfulness, canniness, sensitivity, and talent for dealing with language, or with the visual. What emerges, if it is done successfully, is a kind of truth, sometimes (as in Tolstoy, George Eliot, Dickens; we each make our choices from among these storytellers) an enveloping and unforgettable wisdom that strikes the reader as realer than real, a truth that penetrates deep within one, that leaps beyond verisimilitude or incisive portrayal, appealing and recognizable characterization, and lands on a terrain where the cognitive, the emotional, the reflective, and the moral live side-by-side. "I make up stories all day," I hear a wonderfully able novelist say at a seminar on "documentary studies." "Some people would say I tell lies—my 'business' is to write them down and sell them, with the help of a publisher." We all demur, but he rejects what he hears as an evasive politeness on our part. "All right," he provokes us further, "I do a good job, so I get published, and you like what you read. But there are talented storytellers out there, let's call them that, who spend their lives telling stories, persuading people to get wrapped up in them, just like they talk of getting wrapped up in a good novel . . . and they are telling what you and I would call lies, a string of them, or falsehoods, or *un*truths. Some of them do enough of it that they become known chiefly, essentially, for what they tell *as*—they are 'con artists.' Am I a version of such a person, a successful, socially sanctioned, 'sublimated' version? Is that a useful way of thinking about stories and novels—cleverly or entertainingly put together lies?"

This writer, this novelist who was also a teacher and an effective conversationalist, was forcefully putting a big subject before us. He had, after a fashion, constructed a small story about the matter of storytelling in which he highlighted the matter of fiction as something made up—though often quite full of facts, observations, accurately recalled happenings, and also made up, potentially, of truth, even the highest kind of truth, as many of us would insist. Others in the seminar, of course, spoke of journalism and social science, their claims to another kind of truth, one that pertains to an observed world unconnected to an imagined one; though, again, the journalist's, the photographer's, the social scientist's imagination can all the time influence how a news story or a research project is done, what is obtained in the way of information, remarks, photographs, and how all of that is relayed to others.

I tried, in that seminar, to make sense of my own work, to figure out its nature, and so did we all: this was the purpose of the seminar. During the early 1960s, as I mentioned earlier, I was trying hard to learn how Southern schoolchildren, both black and white, were managing under the stresses of court-ordered desegregation in the South, and how civil rights activists were dealing with their special, often dangerous, even fatally dangerous lives of constant protest. I was doing psychiatric research and beginning to write up my findings for presentation to professional audiences and journals. By then, I'd also been interviewed by newspaper reporters, because I was immersed in a serious educational, social, and racial crisis. I was privileged (I only gradually realized) to be watching a moment of history. Soon I was not only taking what I heard from children, teachers, parents, and young activists and fitting it all into a language, a way of thinking, a theoretical or conceptual apparatus of sorts (lists of defense mechanisms, signs of various symptoms, evidence of successful adaptation); I was developing a general thesis on what makes for collapse in children under duress and what makes for "resiliency." I had developed a list of "variables," aspects of a life that tended to make a child worthy of being described as such by me: a resilient child. Eventually, with enough knowledge of enough children, I had in mind a broader claim, a more ambitious one, a statement on *"the* resilient child."

I was also seeing, in some newspapers, quotations correctly attributed to me that weren't always my words, and that seemed a bit foreign to me because they had been hurriedly scribbled as I talked. Even my exactly transcribed words, *taped* words, sometimes seemed strange to me, because they appeared out of context; they were deprived of the explanatory remarks, the narrative sequence, that had preceded and followed them. My wife would say, "You said *that?"* I would say yes, and then the refrain: "but the reporter used what I said for his purposes"—and I wasn't necessarily being critical. I had tried to explain something, had tried to speak with some qualifications or even with skepticism, second thoughts, or outright misgivings about my own thoughts, themselves being constantly modified by interviews, by conversations with colleagues, by *consideration* of this or that matter, the reflective aspect of what gets called experience.

The reporters, needless to say, had their own purposes to consider, their own experiences; they had gradually accumulated manners of hearing and remembering, of listening to tapes, based on notions of what they were meant to do professionally. I was meant to move from hearing children talk about what was on their minds to thinking about the *projections* these children summoned, the *denials* or *reaction-formations* to which they resorted; a journalist is used to hearing me, and soon enough, asking me pointed questions that aim for an opinion, an explanation, stated as plainly and unequivocally as possible. *Why* is this child doing so well, given the pressures she has to endure? Why is *that* child not doing so well? What is your explanation for the difference? If my explanation was too long-winded, evasive, abstract, or, finally, unconvincing, the reporter pressed, rephrased, got me to reconsider, to say things differently—until what I said helped him or her understand the subject at hand (and would presumably help his or her editor and readers, who inhabit his or her mind, understand). Sometimes I was not only surprised by the printed result, as my wife was, but grateful. Those reporters pushed me to think (and to put things) in ways not familiar to me, and when I remembered what I said, seeing it presented in the context of a story, a part of the reporter's own take on the subject, I found myself learning something, regarding matters with a different emphasis or point of view, responding, it can be said, to the "truth" of that particular interview. All interviews, one hopes, become jointly conducted!

The harder I struggled to make sense of my work, never mind make sense of what others might make of it, the more confused I became: what was I doing, what was I learning, what was I trying to say? I was a child psychiatrist and was learning to be a psychoanalyst, but I wasn't working with patients in an office or a clinic; I was visiting children and their parents in their homes, talking with teachers in schools, and, through SNCC [Student Nonviolent Coordinating Committee], doing things regarded by cities and states of the South as illegal, a challenge both to laws and to long-standing customs. On the one hand, I had to answer to a certain kind of psychiatric voice in me: why *are* you doing all this? On the other hand, I had to answer to the collective voices of civil rights workers: why are you concentrating your energies on *us,* when there's a "sick" society out there; for example, look at your own profession, the utterly segregated universities, medical schools, residency training programs, psychoanalytic institutes—why don't you study all that! Then, I had to contend with my great teacher Dr. W. C. Williams, to whom (1961, 1962) I'd sent some drafts of my psychiatric reports. "For God's sake," he told me once, "try to find a cure for that passive voice you use, for the third person, for all that technical language—it's a syndrome!" My apologies and chagrin and self-pity only elicited this: "Take your readers in hand, take them where you've been, tell them what you've seen, give them some stories you've heard. Most of all, write for *them,* the ordinary folks out there, not for yourself and your buddies in the profession of psychiatry." I can still recall my sense of futility and inadequacy as I thought about those admonishing remarks. I had always known that Dr. Williams could be irritable with people he knew and wanted to help (I'd seen him be so with patients), but now I felt critically judged, and unable to do anything in keeping with the advice given me—lest I lose my last link with my medical and psychiatric and psychoanalytic life: my capacity to write articles that would earn me (not to mention the work I was doing) a hearing, some acceptance.

What Dr. Williams urged, my wife, a high-school teacher of English and history, also urged. She began listening to the tapes we'd collected (she and I worked together, full-time, until our sons were born in 1964, 1966, and 1970). She marked up certain moments in the transcripts which she found interesting, pulled them together, and wrote from memory some descriptions of the scenes in which those comments were made: times, places, details such as the weather, the casual talk exchanged, the food so generously served us, the neighborhood excursions we took—to churches, to markets, a world explored with the help of embattled people who knew that if we were really to understand them, we had to go beyond those clinical questions that I wanted so much to ask them. In time Jane had assembled "moments," she called them, for me to read: a mix of descriptive writing and edited versions of interviews, with suggestions for what she called "personal reflection" on my part. "You'll have some old-fashioned essays," she wrote. "Nothing to be afraid of!"

Plenty to be afraid of, I thought. It took me a couple of years to overcome that apprehension and worry. I was taught and rallied and reassured by Jane, badgered by Dr. Williams, until he died (March 4, 1963), challenged by some of the friends I'd made in SNCC, who kept telling me I should "tell their stories," not try to "shrink" them, and encouraged by Margaret Long, a novelist who worked for the Southern Regional Council, an interracial group long devoted to standing up in many ways to segregation. In 1963 the Council published my first nonprofessional piece (as I

thought of it back then) on the work I was doing: "Separate But Equal
Lives." The very title signified a break for me, a departure from the heavy-
weight jargon I'd learned to use as an expression of professional arrival.
With this new kind of writing, I began to think differently about the very
nature of the work I was doing. The point now was not only to analyze
what children said, or the drawings they made, but to learn about their
*lives*, in the hope of being able to describe them as knowingly and clearly
as possible to anyone who cares to read of them rather than to my colleagues in child psychiatry.

In 1970, well along in such writing, I heard this from one of my old supervisors at the Children's Hospital in Boston, George Gardner: "You're
doing documentary work, documentary child psychiatry, I suppose you
could call it." I was pleased, though also worried—haunted by the judgmental self, its appearance often a measure of careerist anxiety. When I
told my wife what Dr. Gardner had said, she laughed and said, "When Dr.
Gardner settles for 'documentary work' alone, you'll be there!" But where
is her "there"? We never discussed that question at the time. I was almost
afraid to think about what she had in mind, even as I know in retrospect
what she was suggesting—that I try to respond more broadly (less clini-
cally) to these children, give them their due as individuals, as human beings, rather than patients. After all, they weren't "sick," or coming to me
in a hospital or a clinical setting for "help"; they were "out there," living
their lives, and I had come to them in an effort to learn how they "got
along." Those two words increasingly became my methodological description of intent, my rationale of sorts: to try to ascertain as best I could
the character of particular lives, the way they are lived, the assumptions
held, the hopes embraced, the fears and worries borne—in Flannery
O'Connor's felicitous phrase, the particular "habit of being" that informs
*this* person's existence, *that* one's. To render such lives requires that one
take a stand with respect to them—that of the observer, first and foremost,
so that they can be apprehended, but that of the *distanced* observer, the editor, the critic (not of them, but of them as the subject of a story). What of
their lives to offer others, and in what manner of delivery? As I asked that
question I could hear one of Dr. Williams's refrains: "the language, the
language!" Williams was forever trying to do justice both to what he
heard from others, and to what he heard in his own head: the narrative
side of documentary work, the exposition of a particular effort at
exploration.

Documentary work, then, ultimately becomes, for most of us, documentary writing, documentary photographs, a film, a taped series of folk
songs, a collection of children's drawings and paintings: reports of what
was encountered for the ears and eyes of others. Here we weed and
choose from so very much accumulated. Here we connect ourselves critically with those we have come to know—we arrange and direct their
debut on the stage, and we encourage and discourage by selecting some
segments and eliminating others. Moreover, to repeat, some of us add our

own two cents (or more); we work what others have become to *us* into *our* narrative—the titles we give to photographs, the introductions we write for exhibitions, the statements we make with films. Even if our work is presented as only about *them,* we have been at work for weeks, for months, discarding and thereby concentrating what we retain: its significance mightily enhanced because so much else has been taken away.

It is not unfair, therefore, for an Oscar Lewis or a Studs Terkel or a Fred Wiseman to be known as the one who is "responsible" for what are supposedly documentary reports about all those others who were interviewed or filmed. Those others, in a certain way, have become "creations" of Lewis, Terkel, Wiseman—even if we have no explanatory comments from any of them about what they have done, and how, and with what purpose in mind. The stories such documentarians tell us are, in a way, the surviving remnants of so very much that has been left aside. We who cut, weave, edit, splice, crop, sequence, interpolate, interject, connect, pan, come up with our captions and comments, have our say (whenever and wherever and however) have thereby linked our lives to those we have attempted to document, creating a joint presentation for an audience that may or may not have been asked to consider all that has gone into what they are reading, hearing, or viewing.

I remember, a wonderfully enlightening afternoon spent with labor economist Paul Taylor in 1972, while I was working on a biographical study of Dorothea Lange. Jane and I sat in Taylor's spacious, comfortable Berkeley home, the one he and Dorothea Lange occupied together until her death of cancer in 1965. He took me, step by step, through their work together, the work that culminated in *American Exodus* (1939). We examined many of Lange's photographs, some of them prints that were never published or shown. We were looking at an artist's sensibility, as it informed the selections she had made—which picture really worked, really got across what the photographer intended for us to contemplate.

I studied her iconic "migrant mother," a picture known throughout the world, a visual rallying ground of sorts for those who want to be reminded and remind others of jeopardy's pensive life [Fig. 1, p. 186]. There she sits, her right hand touching her lower right cheek, the lady of Nipoma, caught gazing, in March of 1936, one of her children to her left, one to her right, head turned away from us, disinclined to look at the camera and, through it, the legions of viewers with whom it connects. The three figures seem so close, so "tight," it would be said in the South, yet each seems lost to the others: the children lost in the private world they secure by hiding their eyes, the mother lost in a look that is seemingly directed at no one and everyone, a look that is inward and yet that engages with us who look at her, and maybe with her, or through her, at the kind of life she has been living. But only minutes before Lange took that famous picture, she had taken others. At furthest remove [Fig. 2, p. 187] we are shown the same mother and her children in the makeshift tent that is their home; two others, a bit closer, show her with another child who has

Figure [1]

just been suckling at her breast and now has settled into a sleep. In one picture [Fig. 3, p. 188] the mother is alone with that child; in the next, [Fig. 4, p. 189] another of her children has come to her side, its face on her left shoulder. I return to the picture Lange has selected: now the older children are alongside their mother, but her appearance commands our attention—her hair lightly combed, her strong nose and broad forehead and

Figure [2]

wide mouth giving her face authority, her informally layered plainclothes, her worker's arms and fingers telling us that this is someone who every day has to take life on with no conviction of success around any corner.

Dorothea Lange has, in a sense, removed that woman from the very world she is meant, as a Farm Security Administration (FSA) photographer, to document. The tent is gone, and the land on which it is pitched, and the utensils. The children, in a way, are gone, their backs turned to us, their backs a sort of screen upon which we may project our sense of what is happening to them, what they feel. But one child's head is slightly lowered, and the other has covered her face with her right arm—and so a feeling of their sadness, become the viewer's sadness, has surely seized so many of us who have stared and stared at that woman, who is herself staring, and maybe, as in a Rodin sculpture, doing some serious thinking: struggling for a vision, dealing with an apprehension, experiencing a premonition or a nightmarish moment of foreboding. We are told by Lange that she is a "migrant mother," because otherwise she could be quite another kind of working (or nonworking) mother, yet she has been at least somewhat separated from sociological clues, and so she becomes psychologically more available to us, kin to us. A photographer has edited and cropped her work in order to make it more accessible to her anticipated

Figure [3]

viewers. As a documentarian, Lange snapped away with her camera, came back with a series of pictures that narrate a kind of white migrant life in the mid-1930s—and then, looking for one picture that would make the particular universal, that would bring us within a person's world rather than keep us out (as pitying onlookers), she decided upon a photograph that allows us to move from well-meant compassion to a sense of respect, even awe: we see a stoic dignity, a thoughtfulness whose compelling survival under such circumstances is itself something to ponder, something to find arresting, even miraculous.

Another well-known Lange picture that Paul Taylor and I studied was "Ditched, Stalled, and Stranded," taken in California's San Joaquin Valley in 1935. Taylor first showed me the uncropped version of that picture [Fig. 5, p. 190], with a man seated at the steering wheel of a car, his wife beside him. He has a wool cap on, of a kind today more commonly worn in Europe than here. He has a long face with a sturdy nose, and with wide eyes he stares past his wife (the right car door open) toward the viewer. The woman's right hand is in the pocket of her coat, which has a fur collar, and she is looking at an angle to the viewer. She has a round face, and seems to be of ample size. A bit of her dress and her right leg appear beyond the bottom limit of the coat. My dad, politically conservative, had

Figure [4]

seen that version of the picture years ago, and had pointed out to me
that he was not impressed by Lange's title: here, after all, in the middle
of the 1930s, at the height of the Great Depression, a worldwide phenomenon, were a couple who seemed well-clothed, well-fed—and who
had a car. Did I realize, he wondered, how few people in the entire
world, even in America, could be so described at that time? An automobile and a fur-collared coat to him meant something other than being
"ditched, stalled, and stranded."

Figure [5]

Lange chose to crop that photograph for presentation in various exhibitions and books [Fig. 6, p. 191]. She removed the woman, save a touch of
her coat (the cloth part), so the driver looks directly at us. Like the migrant
mother, his gaze connects with our gaze, and we wonder who this man is,
and where he wants to go, or is headed, and why he is described by the
photographer as so thoroughly at an impasse. The photographer, in turn,
tries to provide an answer. The man's left hand holds lightly onto the
steering mechanism just below the wheel, and he seems almost an extension of that wheel, the two of them, along with the title given them, a
metaphor for a troubled nation gone badly awry: whither his direction,
and will he even be able to get going again, to arrive where he would like
to be? Once more, Lange turns a photograph into a melancholy statement
that embraces more than the population of a California agricultural re-

Figure [6]

gion. She does so by cropping (editing) her work, by denying us the possibility of a married couple in which one spouse seems reasonably con-
tented, by reducing a scene to a driver who is readily seen as forlorn, and
also as deeply introspective, eager for us, his fellow citizens, to return the
intensity of his (moral) introspection.

I remember Paul Taylor gazing intently at the migrant mother and the
man who was "ditched, stalled, and stranded"—a return on his part to a
1930s world, but also a moment's opportunity to reflect upon an entire

documentary tradition, in which *American Exodus* figures importantly. No question, Paul and Jane reminded me, social observers and journalists have been journeying into poor neighborhoods, rural and urban, for generations, and in so doing have connected their written reports to a visual effort of one kind or another. Henry Mayhew's sensitively rendered *London Labour and the London Poor*, which describes nineteenth-century London, was accompanied by the drawings of Cruikshank, the well-known English illustrator—an inquiry that included a pictorial response. When George Orwell's *The Road to Wigan Pier* was first published in 1937, its text was supplemented by photographs, poorly reproduced, their maker unacknowledged—yet surely some who read Orwell's provocative and suggestive text were grateful for a glimpse of the world this great essayist had visited.

By the 1930s, under the auspices of the Farm Security Administration, and especially Roy Stryker, who had a keen sense of the relationship between politics and public awareness, a number of photographers were roaming the American land eager to catch sight of, and then, through their cameras, catch hold of a country struggling mightily with the consequences of the Great Depression—in the words of President Franklin Delano Roosevelt (1937) "one-third of a nation ill-housed, ill-clad, ill-nourished." So it is that Russell Lee and Ben Shahn and Arthur Rothstein and Walker Evans and Marion Post Wolcott, and, not least, Dorothea Lange became part of a significant photographic and cultural moment—the camera as an instrument of social awareness, of political ferment.

Though some photographers place great store by the titles they attach to their pictures, or write comments that help locate the viewer, help give him or her a sense of where the scene is or even provide a bit of context (how the person taking the picture happened to be at a particular place at a particular time), most photographers are content to let their work stand on its own, a silent confrontation of us all-too-wordy folk, for whom language (in the form of abstractions and recitations) can sometimes become an obstacle rather than a pathway to the lived truth of various lives. But Dorothea Lange's work in the 1930s, quite able, of course, to stand on its own, became part of something quite unique and important; and that connection (her photographs and the statements of some of the men and women whose pictures she took, joined to text written by Paul Taylor) would become a major achievement in the annals of fieldwork, of social-science research, of public information as rendered by a photographer and an academic (who in this case happened to be husband and wife).

It is possible to take much for granted as one goes through the pages of the 1939 edition of *American Exodus* (it was re-issued in 1969 with a foreword by Paul Taylor). The pictures are still powerful, even haunting, and some of them have become absorbed in an American iconography of sorts—the one titled "U.S. 54 in Southern New Mexico," for instance, or the one taken in the Texas Panhandle in 1938 that shows a woman in profile, her right hand raised to her brow, her left to her neck: a portrait of perplexity, if not desperation. That woman is quoted as saying "If you die, you're dead—that's all," and we, over half a century later, are apt to forget that in the 1930s there was no solid tradition of interviewing the subjects of a photographic study, linking what someone has to say to her or his evident circumstances as rendered by the camera. Again and again Dorothea Lange asked questions, wrote down what she heard (or overheard). Her sharp ears were a match for her shrewd and attentive eyes, and she knew to let both those aspects of her humanity connect with the people she had tried to understand.

Meanwhile, her husband was daring to do an original kind of explorative social science. As he accompanied her, he learned about the individuals, the locales she was photographing: how much workers got paid for picking crops, how much they paid for living in a migratory labor camp, and, more broadly, what had happened in the history of American agriculture from the earliest years of this century to the late 1930s. This was a study, after all, of a nation's fast-changing relationship to its land, of a major shift both in land usage and population: from the old South and the Plains states to California and Arizona, and from small farms or relatively genteel plantations to so-called factory-farms that now utterly dominate our grain and food (and animal) production. A combination of the economic collapse of the 1930s and the disastrous drought of that same time dislodged hundreds of thousands of Americans, some of whom sought jobs in cities, but many of whom embarked on the great trek westward, the last of the major migrations in that direction. For Paul Taylor, such an economic disaster was also a human one, and he knew how to do justice to both aspects of what was truly a crisis for humble small-farm owners or sharecroppers or tenant farmers or field hands. Taylor wanted to let his fellow citizens know the broader social and economic and historical facts and trends that had culminated in the 1930s "exodus"; Lange wanted us to see both the world being left and the world being sought, and to attend the words of the participants in a tragedy (for some) and an opportunity (for others).

Although these two observers and researchers concentrated on the largely white families that departed the plains because a once enormously fertile expanse had become scorched earth, we are also asked to remember the Delta of the South, parts of Mississippi and Louisiana and Arkansas, and, by implication, the especially burdensome life of blacks, whose situation in the 1930s, even for progressives, was of far less concern than it would become a generation later, in the 1960s. The New Deal, it must be remembered, was very much sustained, politically, by the (white) powers-that-be of the South, and black folk, then, as now, on the very bottom of the ladder, were not even voters. Nevertheless, Lange and Taylor paid them heed, and did so prophetically—took us with them to the cities, to Memphis, to show us another exodus, that of millions of such people from the old rural South to its urban centers, or, more commonly, to those up North.

Also prophetically, these two original-minded social surveyors were at pains to attend what we today call the environment—what happens to the land, the water, that human beings can so cavalierly, so insistently take for granted. In picture after picture, we see not only human erosion—people becoming worn and vulnerable—but the erosion of the American land: farmland devastated by the bad luck of a serious drought, but also by years and years of use that become abuse. It was as if the prodigal land had been deemed beyond injury or misfortune. But suddenly the parched land said no to a people, to a nation, and suddenly the roads that covered that land bore an unprecedented kind of traffic: human travail on the move.

But Lange and Taylor go further, give us more to think about than the tragedy of the dust bowl become a major event in a nation already reeling from the collapse of its entire (manufacturing, banking) economy. Some of the pictures of California (the promised land!) tell us that new misfortunes, even catastrophes would soon enough follow what had taken place in Oklahoma and Texas and Kansas and Nebraska and the Dakotas. The lush Imperial Valley, where thousands came in hope of using their hands, their harvesting savvy, to pick crops and make a living, was already in the 1930s becoming a scene of litter, a place where the land had to bear a different kind of assault than that of a succession of plantings that aren't rotated, aren't planned in advance with consideration of what the earth needs as well as what it can enable. The debris, the junk that covers some of the California terrain was no doubt shown to us by Lange so that we could see how disorganized and bewildered and impoverished these would-be agricultural workers had become, see their down-and-out, even homeless lives: the bare earth all they had in the way of a place to settle, to be as families, at least for awhile. Yet today we know how common such sights are across the nation—how those who live under far more comfortable, even affluent circumstances have their own ways of destroying one or another landscape, defacing fields, hills, and valleys that might otherwise be attractive to the eye, an aspect of nature untarnished.

These pictures remind us, yet again, that tragedies have a way of becoming contagious, that one of them can set in motion another, that the temptation to solve a problem quickly (let those people cross the country fast, and find much-needed work fast) can sometimes be costly indeed. There is something ever so desolate about the California of Lange's pictures—even though that state welcomed the people who flocked to it by providing jobs, and the hope that goes with work. Environmental problems to this day plague parts of the western states, problems that have to do with the way both land and water are used. Half a century ago, Lange and Taylor more than hinted at those problems, just as when they followed some of the South's black tenant farmers into the ghettos of a major city, Memphis, they gave us a peek at the urban crisis we would be having in a decade or two.

Also prophetic and important was the manner in which this project was done: informally, unpretentiously, inexpensively, with clear, lucid language and strong, direct, compelling photographs its instruments. For some of us, who still aim to learn from people out there in that so-called field, this particular piece of research stands out as a milestone: it offers us a guiding sense of what was (and presumably still is) possible—direct observation by people interested in learning firsthand from other people, without the mediation of statistics, theory, and endless elaborations of so-called methodology. Here were a man and a woman, a husband and a wife, who drove across our nation with paper, pen, and camera; who had no computers or questionnaires or "coding devices," no tape recorders, or movie cameras, no army of research assistants "trained" to obtain "data." Here were two individuals who would scorn that all-too-commonly upheld tenet of today's social-science research, the claim to be "value-free." They were, rather, a man and a woman of unashamed moral passion, of vigorous and proudly upheld subjectivity, anxious not to quantify or submit what they saw to conceptual assertion but to notice, to see and hear, and in so doing, to feel, then render so that others, too, would know in their hearts as well as their heads what it was that happened at a moment in American history, at a place on the American subcontinent. Here in Lange's photos, finally, the camera came into its own as a means of social and even economic and historical reflection. These pictures, in their powerfully unfolding drama, in their manner of arrangement and presentation and sequencing, in their narrative cogency and fluency, tell us so very much, offer us a gripping sense of where a social tragedy took place and how it shaped the lives of its victims. This is documentary study at its revelatory best—pictures and words joined together in a kind of nurturing interdependence that illustrates the old aphorism that the whole is greater than the sum of its parts.

*American Exodus* was not only a wonderfully sensitive, compellingly engaging documentary study; it challenged others to follow suit, to do their share in taking the measure, for good and bad, of our nation's twentieth-century fate. Dorothea Lange was an energetic ambitious photographer, but she also was a moral pilgrim of sorts, ever ready to give us a record of human experience that truly matters: our day-to-day struggles as members of a family, of a neighborhood, of a nation to make do, to take on life as best we can, no matter the obstacles we face. And so with Paul Taylor, a social scientist who dared pay a pastoral regard to his ordinary fellow citizens, even as he mobilized a broader kind of inquiry into the forces at work on them and on their nation. We can do no better these days than to look at their book, over half a century after it appeared, not only as an aspect of the past (a remarkable social record, an instance of careful collaborative inquiry), but as a summons to what might be done in the years ahead, what very much needs to be done: a humane and literate kind of social inquiry.

Speaking of such inquiry, Paul Taylor was quick to mention *Let Us Now Praise Famous Men* to Jane and me. He reminded us of Walker Evans's genius for careful, sometimes provocative cropping and editing of particular photographs—his ability to sequence his prints, look at their narrative momentum, and choose particular ones for presentation: the exactly memorable, summoning, kindling moments. Taylor made reference to Evans's

photograph in *Let Us Now Praise Famous Men* that introduces one of the
tenant farmers, a young man in overalls, his head slightly tilted to his
right, his eyes (set in an unshaven face topped by curly hair) confronting
the viewer head-on with an almost eerie combination of strength and
pride on the one hand, and an unavoidable vulnerability on the other, as
so many of us have felt (Fig. 7). That picture, now on the cover of the latest
(1988) paperback edition of the book, signals to us the very point of the

Figure [7]

title, of the entire text as Agee conceived it: an ode to those hitherto unacknowledged, a salute to this man and others like him, this man whose fame has awaited a moral awakening of the kind this book hopes to inspire in us, just as the writer and photographer themselves were stirred from a certain slumber by all they witnessed during that Alabama time of theirs.

In the picture of this "famous man," as with certain of Lange's pictures, the viewer is given no room to wander, to be distracted. This is eye-to-eye engagement, a contrast to other possibilities available to Evans of the same man sitting at the same time in the same position. That farmer's daughter was actually sitting in a chair beside her father; one negative gives us a full-length portrait of him and her both, with the door and part of the side of their house and a portion of the porch also visible [Fig. 8, below]. But Evans is struggling for an interiority, that of his subject and that of his subject's future viewer/visitor: let us not only praise this man, lift him to the ranks of the famous, but consider what might be going on within him, and let us, through the motions of our moral imagination, enter his life, try to understand it, and return with that understanding to our own, which is thereby altered. This is a tall order for a single picture, but then Evans and Agee were ambitious, as evidenced by their constant

Figure [8]

citation of the inadequacy of their project (vividly restless dreamers fear-
ing the cold light of a morning).

Taylor also wanted us to look at a sequence of Evans's photographs of
a tenant's daughter, bonneted, at work picking cotton. We who know the
book remember her slouched, bent over the crops [Fig. 9, p. 199]. We don't
see her face, don't really see any of *her*; she *is* her clothes, as if they were
perched on an invisible person who is beyond our human approximations, who is of no apparent age or race. She is huddled over the fertile,
flowering land to the point where she seems part of it, only barely above
it, a lone assertion of our species and, too, a reminder of our incontestable
dependence on the surrounding, the enveloping world of plants and
shrubs. Yet, other negatives taken of that same scene at that same time reveal the girl standing upright [Fig. 10, p. 200], looking in profile at the surrounding terrain [Fig. 11, p. 201], or hunched over a part of it that hasn't
the abundance of crops that we see in the picture Evans chose to show
us [Fig. 12, p. 202]. There is one photograph, taken from above [Fig. 13,
p. 203], that shows only the girl's straw hat, immersed in the foliage—an
"arty" picture, an "interesting" one, a pretty image. With the circularity of
straw (another crop!) imposed, so to speak, on the cotton field, the girl becomes a mere bearer of that hat (only a hump of her is evident).

Evans resists the aesthetic temptations of that last picture and of others
in the series; he picks and chooses his way through a narrative sequence
that might be titled in various ways: Alabama child labor; a young har-
vester; a girl at work picking cotton; or, drawing on Rupert Vance's
wonderfully literate 1930s work at the University of North Carolina, an
instance of a white child's connection to the "cotton culture." A photographer is carving out his own declaration based on his own survey research.
He wants us, finally, to face facelessness, to see a child who isn't looking
at us or at the nearby terrain (despite the fact that he had pictures of the
girl doing both), but whose eyes were watching a row of plants, and
whose body, whose very being, seems scarcely above them, tied to them,
merging with them.

There is, to be sure, an appealing beauty to the picture Evans selected
from this sequence for the book: a graceful curve to the body, an elegance,
a consequence of a learned, relaxed capability to pick and pick, as I saw in
a migrant worker I once knew, who tried to teach me how to harvest cel-
ery. As I watched him look carefully, then make this cut, then the next one
with his knife—swiftly, adroitly, with seeming ease and authority and ex-
actitude—I caught myself thinking of his dignity, his full knowledge of a
particular scene, while at the same time I worried that I was being a romantic: I was struggling with my own obvious lack of skill by ennobling
his hard, tough, ill-paid labor (as, arguably, Orwell did when he went
down into those mines in 1936). And so, perhaps, with this picture of
Evans: we attempt to contemplate people's strenuous exertions even as we
try to rescue them, at least partially, from those exertions. A miner can
have his nobility, or be seen in a noble light by an observer, and that

Figure [9]

Figure [10]

Figure [11]

Figure [12]

Figure [13]

migrant can exact from his terribly burdened life moments of great, knowing competence, and this girl whom Evans noticed so painstakingly can
also have her times of agility, balance, suppleness, the mystery of a lithe,
enshrouded form as it "works on a row." Or are we to think of her only as
an example of exploited child labor? When, that is, does our empathy and
compassion ironically rob those whom we want so hard to understand of
their loveliness, however tough the circumstances of their life? (I recognize the serious dangers, here, of an aesthetic that becomes a moral escape, a shameful avoidance of a grim actuality, a viewer's flight of willful
blindness—hence, I think, Evans's refusal to let us dote on that hat, with
its "interesting" setting.)

Walker Evans, in his own way, addressed the broader question of documentary expression in a lecture at Yale on March 11, 1964. He was sixty-
one then; he had spent a lifetime traveling with his camera, planning and
then executing various photographic expeditions. At Yale he said this:
"My thought is that the term 'documentary' is inexact, vague, and even
grammatically weak, as used to describe a style in photography which
happens to be my style. Further, that what I believe is really good in the
so-called documentary approach in photography is the addition of lyricism. Further, that the lyric is usually produced unconsciously and even
unintentionally and accidentally by the cameraman—and with certain exceptions. Further, that when the photographer presses for the heightened
documentary, he more often than not misses it. . . . The real thing that I'm
talking about has purity and a certain severity, rigor, simplicity, directness, clarity, and it is without artistic pretension in a self-conscious sense
of the word. That's the base of it."

So much there to applaud, especially the descriptive words "inexact"
and "vague" and "grammatically weak": the difficulty we have in doing
justice to the range and variation of writing and photography and film
that a given tradition embraces. The word "documentary" is indeed difficult to pin down; is intended, really, as mentioned earlier, to fill a large
space abutted on all sides by more precise and established and powerful
traditions: that of journalism or reportage, those of certain academic disciplines (sociology and anthropology in particular), and of late, a well-
organized, structured approach to folklore and filmmaking (as opposed to
an "unconscious" or "unintentional" or "accidental" approach)—university departments of "film studies" and "folklore studies." Evans's three
adjectives are themselves meant to be scattershot, if not "inexact" and
"vague"—a means of indicating a style, a manner of approach, or, in his
friend Agee's phrase, "a way of seeing," and also a way of doing: the one
who attempts documentary work as the willing, even eager beneficiary of
luck and chance, the contingent that in a second can open the doors of a
craftsman's imaginative life. Academics have their well-defined, carefully
established, and ever so highly sanctioned (and supported) routines, procedures, requirements, "methodologies," their set language. Journalists
are tied to the news closely or loosely. Nonfiction writing deals with the

consideration of ideas and concepts, with ruminations and reflections of importance to a particular writer and his or her readers. Certain photographs follow suit, address *their* ideas and concepts: light, forms, the spatial arrangements of objects—lines, say, rather than lives. In contrast, even the word *documentarian* (never mind the nature of the work done) may be imprecise, hard to pin down, at times misleading—in fact, no "documents" need be gathered in the name of authenticity, in the name of moving from a suspect (to some) "oral history" to a history of affidavits and wills and letters, the older the better. But that is the way it goes—and there are advantages: no deadline of tomorrow for the morning edition, or three or four days for the Sunday one; no doctoral committee to drive one crazy with nit-picking scrutiny of a language already sanitized and watered-down and submitted to the test of departmental politics, a phenomenon that is surely a twentieth-century manifestation of original sin.

Instead, as Evans suggested, the doer of documentary work is out there in this world of five billion people, free (at least by the nature of his or her chosen manner of approach to people, places, events) to buckle down, to try to find a congenial, even inspiring take on things. Evans celebrates a lyricism, and defines aspects of it nicely: a directness and a lack of pretentiousness, a cleanness of presentation that he dares call severe and pure. It is a lyricism, be it noted, that proved worthy (in its expression by Evans) of companionship with Hart Crane's *The Bridge,* a lyricism that in general bridges the observer, the observed, and the third party, as it were, who is the second observer—a lyricism, Dr. Williams would insist, of "things," a broad rubric for him that included human beings, and a rubric meant to exclude only the rarefied, the insistently abstract. The document in mind (mind you) can for a while be hungrily, ecstatically abstract—the dreaming, the planning, the thinking out of a project—but down the line, somehow, in some way, we have to get to "the thing itself."

Here is Evans being ambitiously abstract, as well as impressively industrious, aspiring, enterprising: "Projects: New York Society in the 1930s. 1. national groups 2. types of the time (b. and wh.) 3. children in streets 4. chalk drawings 5. air views of the city 6. subway 7. ship reporter (this project get police cards)." He continues, "the art audience at galleries, people at bars, set of movie ticket takers, set of newsstand dealers, set of shop windows, the props of upper class set, public schools faces and life." Those notes were, appropriately enough, scribbled on the reverse side of a Bank of Manhattan blank check in New York City during 1934–35. Another series of notes: "the trades, the backyards of N.Y., Harlem, bartenders, interiors of all sorts—to be filed and classified." A letter to Roy Stryker of the FSA in 1934: "Still photography, of general sociological nature." The point was to dream, to wander from topic to topic, and then, finally, to find the specific place and time, so that the eyes were free to follow the reasons of heart and mind both: a lyrical sociology; a journalism of the muse; a dramatic storytelling adventure that attends a scene in order to capture its evident life, probe its secrets, and turn it over as whole and complicated and concrete and elusive as it is has been found to those of us who care to be interested.

In a handsomely generous and affecting tribute to his colleague, his friend, his soulmate, James Agee, written in 1960 for a fresh edition of *Let Us Now Praise Famous Men,* Evans describes James Agee in 1936 as one who "worked in what looked like a rush and a rage." He also refers, in that vein, to Agee's "resolute, private rebellion." I do not think Evans himself was immune to this virus—an utter impatience with, even outrage at a sometimes stuffy and often callous world. As I read Evans or Agee I think of a motley assortment of others who fit in to this odd, cranky crowd— Studs Terkel and Oscar Lewis and George Orwell and Dorothea Lange and Paul Taylor, to name again some whom I've been calling in witness. Once, as I tried to get down to the specifics, a documentary mind preparing for a task, I remembered Evans's comments on what he hoped to do on, of all places, New York City's subways:

> The choice of the subway as locale for these pictures was arrived at not simply because of any particular atmosphere or background having to do with the subway in itself—but because that is where the people of the city range themselves at all hours under the most constant conditions for the work in mind. The work does not care to be "Life in the Subway" and obviously does not "cover" that subject.
>
> These people are everybody. These pictures have been selected and arranged, of course, but the total result of the lineup has claim to some kind of chance-average.
>
> The gallery page is a lottery, that is, the selection that falls there is determined by no *parti pris* such as, say, "I hate women," or "women are dressed foolishly," or "————." It *is* an arrangement, of course, as is the rest of the book, but the forces determining it have to do not only with such considerations as page composition, tone of picture, inferential interest of picture or face in itself.
>
> Speculations from such a page of sixteen women's faces and hats remains then an open matter, the loose privilege of the reader, and whoever chooses to decide from it that people are wonderful or that what America needs is a political revolution is at liberty to do so.

There he is, difficult and ungovernable for others, for his viewers and readers even, prepared to make substantial, maybe overwhelming demands on them. He'll have no truck with the most inviting and, alas, the most banal of titles for his work, even though one suspects that the abstraction "Life in the Subway" crossed his mind more than once as he thought about what he intended to do, its rationale, never mind its locale. He distances himself from all that is implied by the verb "cover," lest he be charged with the sin of inclusiveness, let alone that of a devouring topicality—as in a report or story that "covers" an issue by covering it with all sorts of facts, figures, opinions. Phrases like "chance-average" and "loose privilege" tell of the writer's venerable experience with both our language and this century's toll on our values. Who in the world today will settle for such informality, such a casual and relaxed attitude toward what is (or is not) an *average,* or a *privilege?* "Chance" and "loose" bespeak sipping whiskey in an armchair, with one of the big bands, Tommy Dorsey, maybe, playing "Whispering": a time before computer printouts arrived, or cocksure polls that have a plus or minus accuracy of—God knows what number. As for his concluding challenge (to himself, to all of us), it is one that laughs at ideology, that announces a sensibility contemptuous of singular interpretations, and that gives all of us splendid leeway to do as we damn please in what is volunteered unashamedly as an earnest, persistent, highly personal "visit" with some folks traveling underground.

There is evident discomfort in Evans's message, meant for himself above all; it never appeared in the foreword to the book showing his subway pictures. He wanted to define himself and his pictures so that they were not considered photojournalism, or part of yet another attempt to survey people or expose some (detrimental, damaging) aspect of their life. He was *there,* looking at men and women and children on their hurried way someplace. As the trains roared and sped, he presumably tried to catch hold of himself and others—literally as well as figuratively, a still moment in a quickly shifting scene of entrances and exits, a passing parade of technological and human activity. "I was pretty sure then, yes. I was sure that I was working in the documentary style. Yes, and I was doing social history, broadly speaking"—a cautious embrace at a point in a life's spectrum. But Evans would always qualify, circle around a purported professional location for himself, rather than hone in, dig in, *declare* without reservation. Here he is in a splendidly qualified and edifying further approach: "When you say 'documentary,' you have to have a sophisticated ear to receive that word. It should be documentary style, because documentary is police photography of a scene and a murder . . . that's a real document. You see, art is really useless, and a document has use. And therefore, art is never a document, but it can adopt that style. I do it. I'm called a documentary photographer. But that presupposes a quite subtle knowledge of this distinction."

A struggle there—to grasp, to adopt a style while reserving the artist's right of freedom to roam and select as he wishes. Others (in no way is this matter hierarchical) have their important and necessary obligations (the police photographer and, by extension, a host of people who work for or have joined a variety of institutions: newspapers, magazines, schools, universities). Evans's documentarian draws, in spirit, upon the earthy practicality of a police photographer, and also on the social and political indifference of an artist who, at a certain moment, has to be rid of all ideologies, even those he otherwise finds attractive, lest he become someone's parrot. The "style" he mentions here and elsewhere is nothing superficial; it refers to the connection an artist wants to have with, again, "human actuality," be it that of a police station, a subway, Alabama tenant farmers, Havana's 1930s street life—wherever it is that a Walker Evans imagines himself being, or ends up visiting. The rock-bottom issue is not only one's stated attitude toward "art" in general, but one's sense of oneself.

Once in a discussion at Dartmouth College in the 1970s, Evans took offense at questioners who wanted to know the mechanical details of his work, the kind of camera he used, and, beyond that, the way he developed and printed his photographs. He pointed out that what mattered to him was his intelligence, his taste, and his struggle for what such words imply and convey. Other photographers might have been eager to reply to such inquiries, men and women who are vitally interested in the technological possibilities of the machines they own and use, and who can get from them certain "effects": light or shadows amplified; appearances given new shape; the distortions, the "play" available to skilled men and women who, like Evans, are trying to be artists, photographic artists, but not artists and photographers in the "documentary style" or tradition, for which reality, however shaped and edited and narrated, has in some way to be an initial given. Hence the apprehension, the sorting of that reality in what Evans acknowledged to be a sociological manner, and hence his constantly moving presence in accordance with the demands of such a reality rather than those of a technological artistry, which certainly doesn't need central Alabama or the New York City subway for its expression, an artistry that can even confine itself to one room where the light arrives, moves about, and departs, all the while touching, in various ways, objects, human or inanimate.

William Carlos Williams was among Evans's admirers; he followed his work closely, wrote about it. He struggled, as Evans did, to be almost austere at times in his dispassionate insistence upon seeing many sides to whatever scene he was exploring—even as his big and generous heart could not help but press upon him as he sat at the typewriter, hence his gruff, tough moments followed by his fiery, exclamatory ones. In *Paterson* he struggled in that respect, struggled for a stance: the detached spectator, the informed but reserved onlooker as against the spy, the voyeur (and Evans, along with Agee, uses such imagery to indicate that side of himself: someone who has a lot at stake in what he's trying to do). Like Evans, Williams tried to come to grips with that word *documentary,* and made no bones about his belief that location and time mattered enormously: where one chose to stay and for how long, but also (he kept saying so in dozens of places and ways) the "language—and how it is used," by which he more broadly meant the relation of the watcher to the watched, of the one listening to those who fill his ears with words.

Williams was forever exploring in his mind the nature of a writer's, a photographer's, a filmmaker's dealings with those being called to what he once suggestively described as a "tentative alliance," one that might "fall apart at any minute." I asked for an explanation of that imagery (aware that in 1953, the Second World War and all the horror that preceded it, the pacts and agreements, the duplicities and betrayals, were still very much on his mind), and he was not loath to give it a try:

When you're a doctor seeing a patient you're there by permission: the two of you have an agreement (or if it's a kid, the parents have signed you up, and the kid knows it). You can poke around; no other person in the world can poke around like that. You look and you listen and you poke some more, then you talk to yourself, you remember what you know and you compare notes with what you've seen in other patients (this silent talking, this recalling), and then you've made up your mind, so you start talking. Now, you're telling someone something, rather than asking; you're giving advice—orders, really. But the whole thing [the relationship] is based on that agreement: you can explore this body of mine, and you can ask me any damn thing you want, because that's who you are, a doctor, and that's who I am, a patient.

Now, when I'm walking down the street there [in Paterson, where many of his patients lived] I'm trying to do another kind of "examination"—I'm still poking around, but I'm not doing it under the same terms. I'm hoping people will give me some access—talk with me and help me figure out what's going on around here [we were in Paterson]. I'm trying to look and listen, just as I do with the sick kids I see and their parents. I'm sizing up a place, a whole city, you could say: what is OK, what's working fine, and what's no good, and what "stinks out loud." A guy I know, I'll be standing there in the drugstore with him, and he's telling me "This positively stinks out loud," and I want to hear more. I'm excited, hearing him sound like he's Jeremiah's direct-line descendent. He can't do much more than sign his name. He has trouble reading the newspaper. He has to work to figure out those headlines. It's the radio that tells him everything. He hunkers down with it. He calls it his "friend" sometimes; [and] once I heard him call it his "source." Source of what, I wanted to know. "Everything," that's how specific he could get! "What, for instance?" I asked, and he said, "The Guiding Light," and "Vic and Sade" [two soap operas], and then he said "the local news," he keeps up with it, and if he had another life, he'd like to be a "radio guy," he called it—he meant an announcer, the one who gives people the news. Then, he said: "Only I'd like to go see what's happening out there, and I'd know the people, I'd really know them, before I'd say anything about them. If you talk about people on radio, you should know them, otherwise it's not fair!"

I couldn't get him, what he said, out of my mind for a while. Days later, I'd think of him. It's not so easy to know people! I guess he'd find that out; he's ready to go try, in another life, if he could have it. But when I try to get him going more, about his own life, there's only so far he'll walk with me—and why should he? If you start thinking of yourself as a doctor examining a city, a diagnostician walking the streets, looking for people who can talk to you openly enough, so you can figure out what the illnesses are, the social illnesses, and what's "healthy" about it all—then you've got to *work* to get people to "sign up," to give you the trust you need for them to level with you, really level. Otherwise, you've got formality; you've got off-the-top-of-my-head stuff; you've got a quickie news story on that guy's radio, or the headline he struggles to make out. I feel like saying to him: save your energy, forget the damn headline and keep listening to that radio, if you can find something good on it, a big "if."

I've long felt that such "top-of-the head" ruminations, testy and splenetic, sometimes plaintive (if only it could be easier to learn what Williams so much wanted to learn about the "local pride" that was Paterson!) are themselves texts on documentary work for us to contemplate. Williams was anxious to connect his own thoughts to those of others, to let so-called ordinary people become his teachers, just as his patients all the time taught him. His profound distrust of all aestheticism ("The rest now run out after the rabbits") was prompted by his intuition that solipsistic art was not a suitable haven. He simply wasn't able to be indifferent to social reality in the ways that some of his poet friends found quite congenial. He knew the difficulties of apprehending that social reality, and, too, of finding the right words, the rhythms, the beat that would make his music somehow worthy of the music his ears picked up in Paterson: street music, tenement tunes, soul music and jazz and polkas and the tango and country music. He was always talking about the "American vein," which he tried to tap throughout his writing life—and to do so, he didn't only sit in his study and muse (though he wasn't at all averse to that kind of exploration). "Good luck to those who can keep their distance from the howl, the yell of things," he once said. Later, I'd wonder whether, by chewing out those writing colleagues every once in a while, he wasn't trying to exorcise his envy. But in the end he was who he was, and he more than settled for that existential fact. He built up, he wrote a *Paterson* that whispered and shouted, in good faith, stories of the chaste and bawdy Paterson, his witness to that city and its engagement with generations of needy seekers of all sorts: the words of honor spoken; the covenants abandoned; the people sold down the river; the victories won and lost; the folks who earned good dough, got a leg up; the folks who fell by the wayside. He gave us a chronicle, of course, but also a call to arms—and for him, the war was a struggle, against substantial odds, for a consciousness that isn't blunted and warped by the thousands of deceptions everywhere around. His version of Evans's "documentary style" was a vernacular not showily summoned out of a craving for distinction, but earned in the daily and various rounds of his several working lives (the doctor, the social observer, the historian and chronicler of the nearby, the poet and novelist and essayist, the painter even) whose simultaneity was a constant source of amazement to any of us lucky enough to catch sight of it all.

A precise definition is probably the last thing Walker Evans or William Carlos Williams would suggest for us today who want to consider, yet again, the nature of documentary work. Those two large spirits were unruly enough to scoff at the fantasy of control that informs a pretentiousness which won't allow for indefiniteness—that last word, for the documentarian, a necessity: the arm and leg room of exploration that has to take place, once one heeds the call, the refrain of "outside/outside myself/there is a world to explore," and the further instrumental refrain of "no ideas but in things." The one time I got Dr. Williams to consider the specific subject of "documentary research" or "documentary fieldwork," he laughed, and echoed Evans's wary refusal to get pinned down. He was more curt and gruff than, I suspect, Evans had ever desired to be, and so he dismissed the word documentary, in a way, by asking a rhetorical question, mimicking those who love to give themselves names, the more the better: "Would you want me to tell folks out there that I'm a documentary poet—and are you doing some documentary child psychiatry, now that you're visiting homes of people who haven't got the slightest interest in taking their kids to a clinic, and they don't need to?" He then laughed, to break the tension partially created by his remark, but also initiated by my floundering perplexity, and offered this, in a more gentle mode: "Lots of streets to walk, lots of ways to walk them"—a brief whistle, meant to signal the virtue of an elusive melody as about the best he could do.

To take Dr. Williams's hint, to remember the words of an Apocrypha rescued for our American century's time by James Agee and Walker Evans, let us praise the many "famous people" we can get to meet as we pursue a "documentary style," rather than keep trying to spell out authoritatively various essential characteristics; let the doing be a big part of the defining. Let us, that is, recount and depict, and thereby embody what we're aiming to do and, yes, to be. Let us think of those observers of their fellow human beings who have tried to hug hard what they also know can suddenly escape them, to their apprehending peril. Dr. Williams: "I'll be standing at the store counter talking to that loud-mouthed pest who is trying to con me into buying something stupid that I'll never need, and I should be enjoying the fun of hearing him out—what a *line!*—but instead I demolish him in my mind with *ideas*, ethnic and sociological and psychological, and pretty soon it's no fun for me, or for him either. I've forgotten him; he's disappeared under the withering fire of my clever thinking. I've left him for another ball game!"

To be less exhortative, more declarative, they are of many "sorts and conditions," documentarians (if that is what they want to be called—and we oughtn't be surprised if lots of people decline, say no to that word, maybe any word, any combination of words: "not the letter, but the spirit"). I think of writers or photographers or filmmakers, of musicologists who spend their time enraptured up Appalachian hollows or in

Mississippi's Delta, of folklorists (Zora Neale Hurston was one) crazy for wonderfully wild stories told in odd and loony ways. I think of documentary work that is investigative or reportorial; that is muckraking; that is appreciative or fault-finding; that is pastoral or contemplative; that is prophetic or admonitory; that reaches for humor and irony, or is glad to be strictly deadpan and factually exuberant; that knows exactly where it is going and aims to take the rest of us along, or wants only to make an impression—with each of us defining its nature or intent. In a way, Orwell, in *Wigan Pier*, showed us the range of possibilities as he documented the life of the Brookers (and blasted them sky-high) and documented the life of certain miners (and put them on a tall pedestal), and, in between, wondered about the rest of us, himself and his buddies included: wondered about the way a study of others comes home to roost. In a way, as well, Williams was being more enlightening and helpful than a young listener of his comprehended when he jokingly referred to the documentary side of his prowling, roaming New Jersey patrol, and when he posed for me a consideration of how a clinician ought to think of the documentary work he is trying to do—home and school visits in which he talks with children who are of interest not because they have medical "problems," but because they are part of one or another larger (social or racial or national or economic) "problem." Journalists cover those children in their way; a documentarian will need to put in more time, and have a perspective at once broader and more detailed, one that is, maybe, a follow-up to the first, difficult, sometimes brave (and costly) forays of journalists.

How well, in that regard, I recall conversations with Ralph McGill of the Atlanta *Constitution* during the early years of the civil-rights struggle (1961–63). He had no small interest in the fate of the nine black students who initiated (high school) desegregation in Georgia's capital city during the autumn of 1961, even as my wife, Jane, and I were getting to know those black youths and their white classmates (Atlanta had managed to prevent the kind of riots that had plagued other Southern cities, such as Little Rock and New Orleans). The three of us would meet and talk, and from him, through his great storytelling generosity, Jane and I learned so very much. Often we discussed what Mr. McGill referred to as "the limits of journalism." He would remind us that "news" is the "commodity" his reporters go everywhere to pursue, their words worked into the "product" that gets sold on the streets and delivered to stores and homes. But those reporters (and photojournalists) are also great documentary teachers and scholars: they know so very well how to go meet people, talk with them, take pictures of them, right away take their measure, decide when and how to go further, look for others to question. They know how to make those utterly necessary first steps (find contacts, use them) that the rest of us can be slow in realizing will make all the difference in whether a particular project will unfold. They know, many of them, and they know well, how to pose the toughest, most demanding and scrutinizing questions, at times utterly necessary questions, and ones that naïfs such as I have certainly shirked entertaining, let alone asking. "How did you learn to do your work?" students ask me all the time. I reply: from the great reporters I was lucky to meet and observe, from Pat Watters of the Atlanta *Journal*, from Claude Sitton, the Southern corespondent of the *New York Times*, from the ubiquitous and sometimes riotous Maggie Long, who edited the *New South*, but called herself "an old newspaper hand," and from Dorothy Day, who edited the *Catholic Worker* when I first met her, but who had worked on journalistic assignments for newspapers for years (in the 1920s) before she turned her life so radically around upon her conversion to Catholicism, and who, as she often reminded us, was the daughter of a newspaperman and the sister of two of them.

Yet, as Mr. McGill sadly had to aver: "At a certain point we have to stop"—meaning that a documentary inquiry ends, in favor of the requirements of another documentary initiative. It is then, he explained, that "the magazine boys take over"—his way of referring to the greater amount of space magazines allow, but also, of course, to the more leisurely way of exercising Evans's "documentary style." We never got into specifics, but because of his comparison, I began to think of the essays I read in various magazines (including those published by newspapers) in a different way: began to see the relative degree to which the author turns to people other than himself or herself as fellow bearers of a story's burden, and the degree, as well, to which such people are allowed (encouraged) to teach us by giving of themselves. Today, I think of Truman Capote's *In Cold Blood*, of Ian Frazier's pieces, short and long, of Alec Wilkinson's efforts with migrants in Florida, of his remarkable *A Violent Act*; and I remember *The New Yorker* of William Shawn as very much, at times, given to a "documentary style." Among photographers we can go back to Matthew Brady and the devastation of war that he made a lasting part of our knowledge, if we care to remember; to Lewis Hine and those children through whose condition he aroused our moral sensibility (again, if we care to take notice); to, of course, the FSA men and women; and today, Wendy Ewald, with her many brilliantly ingenious, spiritual explorations of childhood, aided by the children to whom she gives cameras, and whose photographs and words she shares with us. Photographers Alex Harris and Eugene Richards and Susan Meiselas and Gilles Peress and Danny Lyon and Robert Frank and Thomas Roma and Helen Levitt and Lee Friedlander; filmmakers Robert Flaherty and Pare Lorentz and Fred Wiseman and Robert Young and Michael Roemer and Ken Burns and Buddy Squires—all of these men and women are deservedly famous in the way Agee and Evans meant to signify for their Alabama teachers, known to the world as tenant farmers: humble by various criteria, but learned in ways any documentary tradition worth its name would aim to detail, to corroborate.

At a certain point in his research on Gandhi's life, Erik H. Erikson became dissatisfied. He had read many books and had spent a long time talking with a variety of scholars, historians, and political scientists, not to mention his psychoanalytic colleagues. He had obtained access to various library collections; he had attended a number of conferences; he had reviewed, courtesy of microfilm, journalistic accounts of Gandhi's various deeds and evaluations of the significance of his life. Nevertheless, this would-be biographer felt himself at an impasse. Why? I had no answer, despite the fact that I was teaching in his course then, helping him run a seminar, and trying to write about him, even as he was "struggling" with Gandhi (the phrase he often used)—almost as if the two were personally at odds, I sometimes thought.

We are sitting in Erikson's Widener study and I am interested, at the moment, in his work on Luther (my favorite of all his writings). He doesn't want to talk about that; he wants to talk about Gandhi's moral virtues, and, just as important, his flaws, if not vices: "I don't know whether I can proceed without in some way having it out with him [Gandhi]—how he fasted so honorably, risked his life for a just and merciful and fair political settlement, how he developed a decent and civilized manner of protest [nonviolence], and yet how he behaved as a husband and a father." Eventually, Erikson would write his well-known "letter," a breakthrough moment both in *Gandhi's Truth* and in psychoanalytic and historical thinking generally: a direct confrontation, a "having it out" with the spirit (the psychological "remains") of a figure who has left the living yet will endure through the ages. I listen, nod, try to steer us back to the fifteenth century, to *Luther's* contradictions—it is, after all, *my* interview that are we are conducting! Few of my attempted subtleties miss my teacher's notice. Why am I now so interested in *Luther*? Well, Erik, why are *you* now so interested in Gandhi? That is the "line" of our reasoning together: mutual irritation expressed through a reductionist assault, by implication, on one another's motives, all under the dubious protection our shared profession provides. Finally, Erikson tells me, in annoyance at someone *else*, what he'd recently heard said by a distinguished cultural critic (and political philosopher)—that his *Young Man Luther* was a "marvelous novel"! I am taken aback; I keep silent; I worry about what my face wants to do, smile; I worry about what my voice wants to say (that such words are a high compliment), for I feel sure he wouldn't agree. He can sense, though, that I don't share his apparent chagrin. He puts this to me: "What do *you* think?" Lord, *that* question, the endlessly recurrent one of the late-twentieth-century, psychoanalyzed American *haute bourgeoisie!* I gulp. I feel my lips holding on tight to one another. I feel the inquiring openness of those wide blue eyes of this almost awesome figure. I find myself glancing at that shock of white hair flowing backward. I plunge: "Erik, it's a high compliment." I pause. I know I need to amplify, but I'm not prepared to, I'm afraid to. I settle for two more words, "the highest." He stares back at me. His face is immobile. I plead silently for the descent of compassionate understanding upon both of us. Continued silence; seconds become hours. I'm ready to speak, though I don't really know what I'll say—a dangerous situation, people like Erikson and me have long known: random conversational thoughts are a grist for an all-too-familiar (these days) mill, a gradual presentation by the unconscious of various unsettling thoughts.

But suddenly, amid a still persisting silence, the great one's face yields a broad smile. I immediately return it without having any prior thought that I should or would. He ribs me: "I know why you said that." I then pour out my explanation: that "novel" is not a pejorative word, certainly. I then make a statement about the revelatory nature of stories, not unlike the one I have tried to write here and elsewhere. I remind him that no one can know for *sure* what "young man Luther" thought and felt; that his story has to do with speculations, with informed guesses as well as facts, all told persuasively if not convincingly; that imagination is at work in such an effort; and that sometimes, in those "gray areas" or moments, the imagination appeals to or invokes the imaginary—a Luther who becomes more in a writer's mind than he can possibly be with respect to anyone's records, recollections, or reports. I tell him about a question I once heard William Shawn ask of an about-to-be *New Yorker* writer: how would you like us to present this piece? What did Shawn mean? As a factual piece, a profile, or a short story? But, the writer said, it's about someone who was real, who lived! Yes, it certainly is, the distinguished, knowing editor acknowledges, but he could imagine it being presented, with a few narrative changes, as a *story*, with that "someone" as a character in it. Erikson now goes beyond smiles; he laughs heartily and tells me that I seem to be "enjoying all this," and he goes further: "Now, you see why I want to go to India and interview those people who knew Gandhi and worked with him! You see why I want you to show me how you use your tape recorder!"

He stops; it is my turn to laugh. I tell him he'll become a "field worker." He gets irritated, and justifiably so; he reminds me of his expeditions to Indian reservations (the Sioux, the Yurok) in the 1930s and 1940s, trips I well know to have been brave and resourceful (and, yes, imaginative) actions, given the prevailing psychoanalytic orthodoxy then settling in on his generation in the United States. I apologize. He tells me he isn't asking that of me; he wants us, rather, to discuss the nature of those trips, of his forthcoming "visit" to the Indian subcontinent. I call them, cautiously (following his lead), "field trips." He wonders about the adjectival addition of "anthropological." I demur. I say that these days any conversation with a child or adult on one of our Indian reservations gets connected to the discipline of anthropology—an outcome that needs its own kind of historical inquiry, because conversations by Erikson or anyone else (who isn't an anthropologist) in this country ought not be so reflexively regarded. We sit quietly thinking—one of the joys, always, with him: a capacity, a willingness to put aside mere chatter, to endure those lulls which, after all, sometimes fall for a good reason. Finally, he smiles, asks me this: "What would your friend Agee call those 'trips'—or the one I'm going on?"

I have been teaching Agee in my weekly section of Erikson's course, and I have introduced the professor to some of the more compelling passages of *Let Us Now Praise Famous Men*. I smile; we banter. I observe that I don't know what Agee would say, because he's so hard to pin down on such matters, even in connection with his own Alabama trip, but Erikson asks me to surmise. I reply that whatever Agee would say, it would be long, constantly modified, and perhaps hard to fathom without a good deal of effort. Erikson laughs, and tells me that I need to learn to "speak on behalf of Agee," whom I admire and whose values and work and thoughts interest me. No way, I say.

Now I feel him headed toward his own research, toward our earlier discussion, and we get there with the help of his jesting self-criticism, meant also to put more bluntly on the record a perception of mine, maybe even a felt criticism of mine with respect to his work: "You don't seem to want to do with Agee what I may do with Gandhi, and did with Luther: try to figure out what was more or less likely to have happened in someone's life, and then say it—with the knowledge on your part, and [on that of] your readers, that we're not talking about letters or diaries or conversations recalled by someone, but that it's someone today doing the best he can with what *is* available." I think and think, let his words sink in. I take a stab: I say yes, maybe so. But then I try to embrace what I've hitherto kept at arm's length. I use the word *documentary*, and say that in the 1930s that word had a common usage among certain photographers and filmmakers, including Agee's friend Walker Evans. Perhaps, I suggest, Agee, were he to be "sent back" here by his Maker, might oblige us with that word— might allow Erikson's search for a firsthand *documentary* exposure to Indians here, and now Indians abroad, in the hope that what he saw and heard and then described would, in sum, be informative.

He likes the word *documentary*. I've seen him savor English words before, he who spoke German as his native language for over two decades, and who learned to speak such excellent English and write a beautifully flowing, even graceful and spirited English prose. He looks the word up in his much-used Oxford dictionary. I tell him that a dictionary "doesn't always help." Quickly he replies, "What does?" I'm slow in replying: "A word can gradually emerge in its meaning—can fill a gap." "What gap?" We're on to an extended discussion now, one that anticipates by a long three decades these lectures, this book. We speak, especially, about "seeing for oneself," as he keeps putting it—the importance of "making a record that you the writer can believe, before you ask someone else to believe it." I remember that way of saying it, will keep going back to those words, will regard them as helpful, as greatly "clarifying" (a word Erik loved to use): the documentary tradition as a continually developing "record" that is made in so many ways, with different voices and visions, intents and concerns, and with each contributor, finally, needing to meet a personal test, the hurdle of *you*, the would-be narrator, trying to ascertain what you truly believe *is*, though needing to do so with an awareness of the confines of your particular capability—that is, of your warts and wants, your various limits, and, too, the limits imposed upon you by the world around you, the time allotted you (and the historical time fate has given you) for your life to unfold.

When Erikson returned from that voyage to India, he was full of new energy, excited by what he'd been told, what he'd witnessed. He loved being back in his Widener study, but as often happens to us when we have gone on a long and important and memorable journey, he was finding it hard to "settle down." He was full of memories of what he'd experienced; he was trying to do justice to those memories; and he was recounting them, fitting them into a narrative, one the rest of us would soon read; he was speaking of his "colleagues," now not professors in a big-shot university, but rather hitherto (for him) nameless, faceless fellow human beings who would soon become (for us readers) developed characters with something to put on "record." He was, indeed, doing documentary work. And so it goes, then—doing documentary work is a journey, and is a little more, too, a passage across boundaries (disciplines, occupational constraints, definitions, conventions all too influentially closed for traffic), a passage that can become a quest, even a pilgrimage, a movement toward the sacred truth enshrined not only on tablets of stone, but in the living hearts of those others whom we can hear, see, and get to understand. Thereby, we hope to be confirmed in our own humanity—the creature on this earth whose very nature it is to make just that kind of connection with others during the brief stay we are permitted here.

• • • • • • • • • • •

## QUESTIONS FOR A SECOND READING

1. Early in his essay, Coles refers to his students' discussions of documentary work. His students, he says, "emphasize the 'actuality' of the work—its responsibility to fact." They think of documentaries as "the familiar alternative of fiction, as though we were dealing in clear-cut opposites: if not the true as against the false, at least the real as against the imaginary" (p. 177). Coles says that such opposites don't "do justice" to what writers, photographers, and other documentary artists do when they work with "people's words, their music, gestures, movements, and overall appearance" to represent to others what they have seen, heard, and learned.

   So—what *is* the nature of documentary work? What *are* the issues, subtle rather than clear-cut, at the center of Coles's thinking? The essay could be said to be organized in five sections, each thinking through a different example: In the first, Coles talks about his own life and work, the second discusses the work of Dorothea Lange, the third the work of Walker Evans and James Agee, the fourth tells a story about the physician-poet William Carlos Williams, and the fifth a story about psychologist Erik Erikson. As you reread, stop at the end of each section to write notes on what you think it is "about." What is Coles saying about documentary work? What are the issues? When you get to the end, stop to write briefly on the progression of the essay. What is its train of thought? its beginning, middle, and end?

2. Coles offers three interesting examples of artists cropping or choosing photographic images of working class life (the couple in the car, the father and daughter on the porch, the girl picking cotton). Go back to those images and the discussions around them. Be sure that you can represent the argument Coles is making about Lange or Evans and the choices they made in producing or selecting a final image. Then take time to think about alternative arguments. (Coles provides one example in his father's response to "Ditched, Stalled, and Stranded.") How might you argue for one of the discarded images? or against the close-up view? You should think that the choices made by these artists are at least potentially controversial. What are the issues? What is at stake?

3. Coles says that "in shaping an article or a book, the writer can add factors and variables in two directions: social and cultural and historical on the one hand, individual or idiosyncratic on the other" (p. 177). As you reread, see where and how this distinction is stated or implied in Coles's discussions of the various artists or projects he treats in the essay. What examples does he provide of work that is social/cultural/historical and what examples does he provide of work that is individual/idiosyncratic? And where does Coles stand on these two directions? Which does he prefer or promote? And on what grounds?

4. Coles's essay assumes some knowledge of Dorothea Lange, Walker Evans, and James Agee. One way to work on the essay, then, would be to go to the library to get a copy of Lange's *American Exodus* or Agee's *Let Us Now Praise Famous Men*. You could also look for other works by or on these figures. One strategy for rereading would be to reread Coles once you have a better understanding of the materials he works with. This allows you a better sense of *his* agenda and point of view, the shaping force of his imagination.

### ASSIGNMENTS FOR WRITING

1. One of the striking things about Coles's essay is the way it expands the range of what might be considered "documentary work." There is nothing unusual in thinking about Lange, Evans, and Agee; it is striking, however, to think about them in relation to Coles's work as a child psychiatrist and to think then, about William Carlos Williams and Erik Erikson. This essay brings together a range of materials in order to think about a common issue. What is the issue? How does Coles think about it by using and arranging these materials? Where does he come out at the end?

   Write an essay in which you represent this aspect of Coles's work as a writer in "The Tradition: Fact and Fiction." You will need to chart and summarize what he says. You will also need to think about how he does what he does. You could imagine that you are writing a review or writing a piece for a writing textbook or guidebook, one that wants to use Coles's essay as an example of how essays and essayists do their work.

2. It is possible to take Coles's essay as an invitation to do documentary work. The works he cites represent long-term projects and great commitments of time, energy, and spirit. One of the pleasures of being a student, however, is that you have the authority to try things out provisionally, tentatively, and on a smaller scale.

   This assignment has two parts. For the first part, create a written documentary in which you represent some aspect of another person or, to use the language of the essay, in which you are in pursuit of a moment of "human actuality." The text you create can include photographs, interviews, observation—whatever is available. The point is for you to feel what it is like to be responsible, as a writer, for representing someone else, his or her thoughts, words, and actions. To those who do it for a living, this is a deep and deeply fraught responsibility.

   Once you have completed your documentary (and perhaps once it has been read and evaluated by others), write a separate essay in which you use your work as a way of thinking back on and responding to Coles. Where and how, for example, did you serve as a "filter"? Where and how did you shape that material? What decisions did you have to make concerning foreground and background, the individual and idiosyncratic, or the social, cultural, and historical? What work would you need to do if you were to go back to this project and do an even better job with it? You could imagine this as a letter to Coles, a review of his book, or as a plan for future work of your own, perhaps the work of revising the documentary you have begun.

3. This assignment draws on the project outlined in the second of the "Questions for a Second Reading." Coles offers three examples of artists cropping or choosing photographic images of working class life (the couple in the car, the father and daughter on the porch, the girl picking cotton). These are relatively brief discussions, however, and these discussions do not engage with alternative points of view.

   Write an essay in which you begin with Coles's account of the images, summarizing what he says for someone who has not read the essay or who read it a while ago and won't take time to pick it up again. You will need to represent the photographs, their history, and the points that Coles is making. Then, you will need to engage and extend the discussion. Coles, for example, seems to take for granted that the decisions the artists made were good decisions. Were they? What is at stake in choosing one photograph over another or in cropping the image to remove context and to focus in on the individual face? What was at stake for Coles?

   And where and how might you enter this discussion? There should, in other words, be sections of your essay where you are speaking for Coles (and for Evans and Lange); there should also, however, be extended sections where you speak, thinking about the examples and engaging the issues raised by others.

4. "The Tradition: Fact and Fiction" is a chapter in Coles's book *Doing Documentary Work* (1997). The final chapter in the book presents materials from

courses he and his colleagues have taught at Duke University's Center for
Documentary Studies. Here is a brief selection of books and films used in
their courses (his book has a full account):

James Agee, *Let Us Now Praise Famous Men* (1941)
Sherwood Anderson, *Home Town* (1940)
John Berger, *A Seventh Man: Migrant Workers in Europe* (1975)
Debbie Fleming Caffery, *Carry Me Home* (1990)
Bruce Chatwin, *In Patagonia* (1977)
Anton Chekhov, *The Island: A Journey to Sakhalin* (1895)
W. E. B. Du Bois, *The Philadelphia Negro* (1899)
George Eliot, *Scenes of Clerical Life* (1857)
Martin Espada, *City of Coughing and Dead Radiators* (1993)
Robert Flaherty, *Nanook of the North* (film) (1922)
Lee Freidlander, *The Jazz People of New Orleans* (1992)
Zora Neale Hurston, *Dust Tracks on a Road* (1942)
Dorothea Lange, *American Exodus* (1941)
Oscar Lewis, *The Children of Sanchez* (1961)
Henry Mayhew, *London Labour and the London Poor* (1851)
George Orwell, *The Road to Wigan Pier* (1958)
Studs Terkel, *Working* (1975)
William Carlos Williams, *Paterson* (1946)
Frederick Wiseman, *Titicut Follies* (film) (1967); *High School*
  (film) (1968); *Blind* (film) (1986); *Deaf* (film) (1986)

Choose one of these to use as the basis for an essay in which you
apply Coles's notion that any account of the "real," any documentary, is
filtered through an individual's imagination and point of view, and his
sense that documentaries either favor the long view (with emphasis on
social, cultural, and historical contexts) or the short view (with emphasis
on the individual or the idiosyncratic). What is the evidence of the filtering process in the work you have studied? What are the consequences?
Where and how might you use the work you have done to add to or to
speak back to what Coles has to say in "The Tradition: Fact and Fiction"?


MAKING CONNECTIONS

1. In "Hunger as Ideology" (p. 139), Susan Bordo examines representations
   of the female body in contemporary culture. In his discussion of Dorothea
   Lange's photographs of the migrant mother [pp. 185–188] and in his discussion of Walker Evans's photos of the tenant's daughter picking cotton
   [pp. 198–204], Coles is also concerned with the representation of the female body—with what those images mean and the purposes they serve
   (or might serve). Coles's descriptions are close and careful. They draw,
   however, on a very different vocabulary than those provided by Bordo.
      Write an essay in which you compare the methods and concerns of
   Bordo and Coles. You should think about how their projects differ; consider the ways they choose and present images, what they notice, and
   how they describe and analyze what they notice. Both are concerned with

the social context of images. What does Coles offer in describing the larger forces at work in producing the meanings of images? What does he offer in place of Bordo's "ideology"?

2. In "Empire of Innocence" (p. 502), Patricia Limerick writes about the "moral complexity" of Western history, a complexity represented by the difficulty in speaking for the "human actuality" of lives lived in a different time and place. The historian does a form of "documentary work," different, however, from the examples of work at the center of Coles's essay. (Limerick was also involved, in fact, in a project using photographs: *Sweet Medicine: Sites of Indian Massacres, Battlefields, and Treaties* (1995), photographs by Drex Brooks.)

   Reread "Empire of Innocence" and "The Tradition: Fact and Fiction" as a set, as part of a single project investigating the problems of documentary work. Write an essay in which you discuss the issues and problems as represented by each. While it is possible to chart the similarities in the two essays, also focus on the differences. Limerick and Coles have different training and occupy different places in the academy; they serve the culture differently as writers and scholars. How are those differences evident in these brief samples of their work?

# W. E. B.
# DU BOIS

WILLIAM EDWARD BURGHARDT DU BOIS (1868–1963) was the most significant African American intellectual of the first half of the twentieth century. He stands among the most widely read and admired and the most prolific and influential writers of our nation. He was a historian and sociologist, a journalist and political activist, a novelist and playwright. He was the founder and editor of The Crisis, the journal of the National Association for the Advancement of Colored People (NAACP), and the author of over two dozen books. He wrote on virtually every aspect of American political, social, and economic life.

In a tribute on the anniversary of Du Bois's one hundredth birthday, Martin Luther King, Jr. said:

> Dr. Du Bois was a man possessed of priceless dedication to his people. The vast accumulation of achievement and public recognition were not for him pathways to personal affluence and a diffusion of identity. Whatever else he was, with his multitude of careers and professional titles, he was first and always a Black man. He used his richness of talent as a trust for his people. He saw that Negroes were robbed of so many things decisive to their existence that the theft of their history seemed only a small part of their losses. But Dr. Du Bois knew that to

*lose one's history is to lose one's self-understanding and with it the roots for pride. This drove him to become a historian of Negro life, and the combination of his unique zeal and intellect rescued for all of us a heritage whose loss would have profoundly impoverished us.*

W. E. B. Du Bois *was born in Massachusetts. His mother was a domestic servant; his relatives on his mother's side owned and worked a small farm. As a child he attended predominantly white schools and churches. It was here, he wrote, that he first felt the peculiar experience of being "a problem" by being black. At school, in the face of a moment of discrimination, "it dawned upon me with a certain suddenness that I was different from others; or like, mayhap, in heart and life and longing, but shut out from their world by a vast veil." The immediate effect on the young Du Bois was a deep determination to succeed: "by reading law, by healing the sick, by telling the wonderful tales that swam in my head,—some way." He grew up, however, with the peculiar sensation of "double-consciousness, this sense of always looking at one's self through the eyes of others, of measuring one's soul by the tape of a world that looks on in amused contempt and pity. One ever feels his two-ness,—an American, a Negro; two souls, two thoughts, two unreconciled strivings; two warring ideals in one dark body, whose dogged strength alone keeps it from being torn asunder."*

*In 1885 he left the North to attend Fisk University in Nashville, Tennessee. It was here that he first became immersed in the life and culture of black Americans. For two summers, he taught school in a small black community near Alexandria, Tennessee, and began a life-long interest in African American folk songs and spirituals. From Fisk, Du Bois went to Harvard University, then to the University of Berlin. He received his Ph.D. in history from Harvard in 1895, the first black American to receive a Harvard Ph.D. In 1896, Du Bois published his dissertation,* The Suppression of the African Slave-Trade to the United States.

*Du Bois's first teaching position was at Wilberforce University in Ohio, and his next book was a sociological study of the African American community in Philadelphia,* The Philadelphia Negro *(1899). By this time Du Bois had begun to write as a journalist and essayist in magazines such as the* Atlantic Monthly, The Dial, The New World, *the* Annals of the American Academy of Political and Social Science, *and* World's Work, *speaking for the experience of black Americans and speaking against racial violence and segregation. All this was in preparation for his masterwork,* The Souls of Black Folk *(1903).* The Souls of Black Folk *is a mixture of reverie and history, prophecy and autobiography. It is an eloquent and unconventional work of writing designed to introduce both black and white readers to the distinctive history and heritage of black America, its culture, religion, values, and forms of expression.*

*Perhaps the best way to introduce the project of the book and the selections that follow, Chapters 4, 5, and 6 of* The Souls of Black Folk, *is to reproduce a section of Du Bois's introduction, called "The Forethought." In it he describes the outline and intent of his book and introduces the metaphor of the "Veil," a figure of speech that comes to represent the forces of mind, politics, and economy that* divide black from white Americans. He ends with a reference to the "Sorrow Songs," his term for the spirituals created and sung by African American slaves:

> Herein lie buried many things which if read with patience may show the strange meaning of being black here in the dawning of the Twentieth Century. This meaning is not without interest to you, Gentle Reader; for the problem of the Twentieth Century is the problem of the color-line.
>
> I pray you, then, receive my little book in all charity, studying my words with me, forgiving mistake and foible for sake of the faith and passion that is in me, and seeking the grain of truth hidden there.
>
> I have sought to sketch, in vague, uncertain outline, the spiritual world in which ten thousand Americans live and strive. First, in two chapters I have tried to show what Emancipation meant to them, and what was its aftermath. In a third chapter I have pointed out the slow rise of personal leadership, and criticised candidly the leader who bears the chief burden of his race today [Booker T. Washington]. Then, in two other chapters I have sketched in swift outline the two worlds within and without the Veil, and thus have come to the central problem of training men for life. Venturing now into deeper detail, I have in two chapters studied the struggles of the massed millions of the black peasantry, and in another have sought to make clear the present relations of the sons of master and man.
>
> Leaving, then, the world of the white man, I have stepped within the Veil, raising it that you may view faintly its deeper recesses,—the meaning of its religion, the passion of its human sorrow, and the struggle of its greater souls. . . .
>
> Before each chapter, as now printed, stands a bar from the Sorrow Songs,—some echo of haunting melody from the only American music which welled up from black souls in the dark past. And, finally, need I add that I who speak here am bone of the bone and flesh of the flesh of them that live within the Veil?

# Of the Meaning of Progress

Willst Du Deine Macht verkünden,
Wähle sie die frei von Sünden,
Steh'n in Deinem ew'gen Haus!
Deine Geister sende aus!
Die Unsterblichen, die Reinen,
Die nicht fühlen, die nicht weinen!
Nicht die zarte Jungfrau wähle,
Nicht der Hirtin weiche Seele!

— SCHILLER

Once upon a time I taught school in the hills of Tennessee, where the broad dark vale of the Mississippi begins to roll and crumple to greet the Alleghanies. I was a Fisk student then, and all Fisk men thought that Tennessee—beyond the Veil—was theirs alone, and in vacation time they sallied forth in lusty bands to meet the county school-commissioners. Young and happy, I too went, and I shall not soon forget that summer, seventeen years ago.

First, there was a Teachers' Institute at the county-seat; and there distinguished guests of the superintendent taught the teachers fractions and spelling and other mysteries,—white teachers in the morning, Negroes at night. A picnic now and then, and a supper, and the rough world was softened by laughter and song. I remember how—But I wander.

There came a day when all the teachers left the Institute and began the hunt for schools. I learn from hearsay (for my mother was mortally afraid of fire-arms) that the hunting of ducks and bears and men is wonderfully interesting, but I am sure that the man who has never hunted a country school has something to learn of the pleasures of the chase. I see now the white, hot roads lazily rise and fall and wind before me under the burning July sun; I feel the deep weariness of heart and limb as ten, eight, six miles stretch relentlessly ahead; I feel my heart sink heavily as I hear again and again, "Got a teacher? Yes." So I walked on and on—horses were too expensive until I had wandered beyond railways, beyond stage lines, to a land of "varmints" and rattlesnakes, where the coming of a stranger was an event, and men lived and died in the shadow of one blue hill.

Sprinkled over hill and dale lay cabins and farmhouses, shut out from the world by the forests and the rolling hills toward the east. There I found at last a little school. Josie told me of it; she was a thin, homely girl of twenty, with a dark-brown face and thick, hard hair. I had crossed the stream at Watertown, and rested under the great willows; then I had gone to the little cabin in the lot where Josie was resting on her way to town. The gaunt farmer made me welcome, and Josie, hearing my errand, told me anxiously that they wanted a school over the hill; that but once since the war had a teacher been there; that she herself longed to learn,—and thus she ran on, talking fast and loud, with much earnestness and energy.

Next morning I crossed the tall round hill, lingered to look at the blue and yellow mountains stretching toward the Carolinas, then plunged into the wood, and came out at Josie's home. It was a dull frame cottage with four rooms, perched just below the brow of the hill, amid peach-trees. The father was a quiet, simple soul, calmly ignorant, with no touch of vulgarity. The mother was different,—strong, bustling, and energetic, with a quick, restless tongue, and an ambition to live "like folks." There was a crowd of children. Two boys had gone away. There remained two growing girls; a shy midget of eight; John, tall, awkward, and eighteen; Jim, younger, quicker, and better looking; and two babies of indefinite age. Then there was Josie herself. She seemed to be the centre of the family: always busy at service, or at home, or berry-picking; a little nervous and inclined to scold, like her mother, yet faithful, too, like her father. She had about her a certain fineness, the shadow of an unconscious moral heroism that would willingly give all of life to make life broader, deeper, and fuller for her and hers. I saw much of this family afterwards, and grew to love them for their honest efforts to be decent and comfortable, and for their knowledge of their own ignorance. There was with them no affectation. The mother would scold the father for being so "easy"; Josie would roundly berate the boys for carelessness; and all knew that it was a hard thing to dig a living out of a rocky sidehill.

I secured the school. I remember the day I rode horseback out to the commissioner's house with a pleasant young white fellow who wanted the white school. The road ran down the bed of a stream; the sun laughed and the water jingled, and we rode on. "Come in," said the commissioner,—"come in. Have a seat. Yes, that certificate will do. Stay to dinner. What do you want a month?" "Oh," thought I, "this is lucky"; but even then fell the awful shadow of the Veil, for they ate first, then I—alone.

The schoolhouse was a log hut, where Colonel Wheeler used to shelter his corn. It sat in a lot behind a rail fence and thorn bushes, near the sweetest of springs. There was an entrance where a door once was, and within, a massive rickety fireplace; great chinks between the logs served as windows. Furniture was scarce. A pale blackboard crouched in the corner. My desk was made of three boards, reinforced at critical points, and my chair, borrowed from the landlady, had to be returned every night. Seats for the children—these puzzled me much. I was haunted by a New England vision of neat little desks and chairs, but, alas! the reality was rough plank benches without backs, and at times without legs. They had the one virtue of making naps dangerous,—possibly fatal, for the floor was not to be trusted.

It was a hot morning late in July when the school opened. I trembled when I heard the patter of little feet down the dusty road, and saw the growing row of dark solemn faces and bright eager eyes facing me. First came Josie and her brothers and sisters. The longing to know, to be a student in the great school at Nashville, hovered like a star above this child-woman amid her work and worry, and she studied doggedly. There were the Dowells from their farm over toward Alexandria,—Fanny, with her smooth black face and wondering eyes; Martha, brown and dull; the pretty girl-wife of a brother, and the younger brood.

There were the Burkes,—two brown and yellow lads, and a tiny haughty-eyed girl. Fat Reuben's little chubby girl came, with golden face and old-gold hair, faithful and solemn. 'Thenie was on hand early,—a jolly, ugly, good-hearted girl, who slyly dipped snuff and looked after her little bow-legged brother. When her mother could spare her, 'Tildy came,—a midnight beauty, with starry eyes and tapering limbs; and her brother, correspondingly homely. And then the big boys,—the hulking Lawrences; the lazy Neills, unfathered sons of mother and daughter; Hickman, with a stoop in his shoulders; and the rest.

There they sat, nearly thirty of them, on the rough benches, their faces shading from a pale cream to a deep brown, the little feet bare and swinging, the eyes full of expectation, with here and there a twinkle of mischief, and the hands grasping Webster's blue-back spelling-book. I loved my school, and the fine faith the children had in the wisdom of their teacher was truly marvellous. We read and spelled together, wrote a little, picked flowers, sang, and listened to stories of the world beyond the hill. At times the school would dwindle away, and I would start out. I would visit Mun Eddings, who lived in two very dirty rooms, and ask why little Lugene, whose flaming face seemed ever ablaze with the dark-red hair uncombed, was absent all last week, or why I missed so often the inimitable rags of Mack and Ed. Then the father, who worked Colonel Wheeler's farm on shares, would tell me how the crops needed the boys; and the thin, slovenly mother, whose face was pretty when washed, assured me that Lugene must mind the baby. "But we'll start them again next week." When the Lawrences stopped, I knew that the doubts of the old folks about book-learning had conquered again, and so, toiling up the hill, and getting as far into the cabin as possible, I put Cicero "pro Archia Poeta" into the simplest English with local applications, and usually convinced them—for a week or so.

On Friday nights I often went home with some of the children,—sometimes to Doc Burke's farm. He was a great, loud, thin Black, ever working, and trying to buy the seventy-five acres of hill and dale where he lived; but people said that he would surely fail, and the "white folks would get it all." His wife was a magnificent Amazon, with saffron face and shining hair, uncorseted and barefooted, and the children were strong and beautiful. They lived in a one-and-a-half-room cabin in the hollow of the farm, near the spring. The front room was full of great fat white beds, scrupulously neat; and there were bad chromos on the walls, and a tired centre-table. In the tiny back kitchen I was often invited to "take out and help" myself to fried chicken and wheat biscuit, "meat" and corn pone, string-beans and berries. At first I used to be a little alarmed at the approach of bedtime in the one lone bedroom, but embarrassment was very deftly avoided. First, all the children nodded and slept, and were stowed away in one great pile of goose feathers; next, the mother and the father discreetly slipped away to the kitchen while I went to bed; then, blowing out the dim light, they retired in the dark. In the morning all were up and away before I thought of awaking. Across the road, where fat Reuben lived, they all went outdoors while the teacher retired, because they did not boast the luxury of a kitchen.

I liked to stay with the Dowells, for they had four rooms and plenty of good country fare. Uncle Bird had a small, rough farm, all woods and hills, miles from the big road; but he was full of tales,—he preached now and then,—and with his children, berries, horses, and wheat he was happy and prosperous. Often, to keep the peace, I must go where life was less lovely; for instance, 'Tildy's mother was incorrigibly dirty, Reuben's larder was limited seriously, and herds of untamed insects wandered over the Eddingses' beds. Best of all I loved to go to Josie's, and sit on the porch, eating peaches, while the mother bustled and talked: how Josie had bought the sewing-machine; how Josie worked at service in winter, but that four dollars a month was "mighty little" wages; how Josie longed to go away to school, but that it "looked like" they never could get far enough ahead to let her; how the crops failed and the well was yet unfinished; and, finally, how "mean" some of the white folks were.

For two summers I lived in this little world; it was dull and humdrum. The girls looked at the hill in wistful longing, and the boys fretted and haunted Alexandria. Alexandria was "town,"—a straggling, lazy village of houses, churches, and shops, and an aristocracy of Toms, Dicks, and Captains. Cuddled on the hill to the north was the village of the colored folks, who lived in three- or four-room unpainted cottages, some neat and homelike, and some dirty. The dwellings were scattered rather aimlessly, but they centred about the twin temples of the hamlet, the Methodist, and the Hard-Shell Baptist churches. These, in turn, leaned gingerly on a sad-colored schoolhouse. Hither my little world wended its crooked way on Sunday to meet other worlds, and gossip, and wonder, and make the weekly sacrifice with frenzied priest at the altar of the "old-time religion." Then the soft melody and mighty cadences of Negro song fluttered and thundered.

I have called my tiny community a world, and so its isolation made it; and yet there was among us but a half-awakened common consciousness, sprung from common joy and grief, at burial, birth, or wedding; from a common hardship in poverty, poor land, and low wages; and, above all, from the sight of the Veil that hung between us and Opportunity. All this caused us to think some thoughts together; but these, when ripe for speech, were spoken in various languages. Those whose eyes twenty-five and more years before had seen "the glory of the coming of the Lord," saw in every present hindrance or help a dark fatalism bound to bring all things right in His own good time. The mass of those to whom slavery was a dim recollection of childhood found the world a puzzling thing: it asked little of them, and they answered with little, and yet it ridiculed their offering. Such a paradox they could not understand, and therefore sank into listless indifference, or shiftlessness, or reckless bravado. There were, however, some—such as Josie, Jim, and Ben—to whom War, Hell, and Slavery were but childhood tales, whose young appetites had been whetted to an edge by school and story and half-awakened thought. Ill could they be content, born without and beyond the World. And their weak wings beat against their barriers,—barriers of caste, of youth, of life; at last, in dangerous moments, against everything that opposed even a whim.

The ten years that follow youth, the years when first the realization comes that life is leading somewhere,—these were the years that passed after I left my little school. When they were past, I came by chance once more to the walls of Fisk University, to the halls of the chapel of melody. As I lingered there in the joy and pain of meeting old school-friends, there swept over me a sudden longing to pass again beyond the blue hill, and to see the homes and the school of other days, and to learn how life had gone with my school-children; and I went.

Josie was dead, and the gray-haired mother said simply, "We've had a heap of trouble since you've been away." I had feared for Jim. With a cultured parentage and a social caste to uphold him, he might have made a venturesome merchant or a West Point cadet. But here he was, angry with life and reckless; and when Farmer Durham charged him with stealing wheat, the old man had to ride fast to escape the stones which the furious fool hurled after him. They told Jim to run away; but he would not run, and the constable came that afternoon. It grieved Josie, and great awkward John walked nine miles every day to see his little brother through the bars of Lebanon jail. At last the two came back together in the dark night. The mother cooked supper, and Josie emptied her purse, and the boys stole away. Josie grew thin and silent, yet worked the more. The hill became steep for the quiet old father, and with the boys away there was little to do in the valley. Josie helped them to sell the old farm, and they moved nearer town. Brother Dennis, the carpenter, built a new house with six rooms; Josie toiled a year in Nashville, and brought back ninety dollars to furnish the house and change it to a home.

When the spring came, and the birds twittered, and the stream ran proud and full, little sister Lizzie, bold and thoughtless, flushed with the passion of youth, bestowed herself on the tempter, and brought home a nameless child. Josie shivered and worked on, with the vision of school-days all fled, with a face wan and tired,—worked until, on a summer's day, some one married another; then Josie crept to her mother like a hurt child, and slept—and sleeps.

I paused to scent the breeze as I entered the valley. The Lawrences have gone,—father and son forever,—and the other son lazily digs in the earth to live. A new young widow rents out their cabin to fat Reuben. Reuben is a Baptist preacher now, but I fear as lazy as ever, though his cabin has three rooms; and little Ella has grown into a bouncing woman, and is ploughing corn on the hot hillside. There are babies a-plenty, and one half-witted girl. Across the valley is a house I did not know before, and there I found, rocking one baby and expecting another, one of my schoolgirls, a daughter of Uncle Bird Dowell. She looked somewhat worried with her new duties, but soon bristled into pride over her neat cabin and the tale of her thrifty husband, the horse and cow, and the farm they were planning to buy.

My log schoolhouse was gone. In its place stood Progress; and Progress, I understand, is necessarily ugly. The crazy foundation stones still marked the former site of my poor little cabin, and not far away, on six weary boulders, perched a jaunty board house, perhaps twenty by thirty feet, with three windows and a door that locked. Some of the window-glass was broken, and part of an old iron stove lay mournfully under the house. I peeped through the window half reverently, and found things that were more familiar. The blackboard had grown by about two feet, and the seats were still without backs. The county owns the lot now, I hear, and every year there is a session of school. As I sat by the spring and looked on the Old and the New I felt glad, very glad, and yet—

After two long drinks I started on. There was the great double log-house on the corner. I remembered the broken, blighted family that used to live there. The strong, hard face of the mother, with its wilderness of hair, rose before me. She had driven her husband away, and while I taught school a strange man lived there, big and jovial, and people talked. I felt sure that Ben and 'Tildy would come to naught from such a home. But this is an odd world; for Ben is a busy farmer in Smith County, "doing well, too," they say, and he had cared for little 'Tildy until last spring, when a lover married her. A hard life the lad had led, toiling for meat, and laughed at because he was homely and crooked. There was Sam Carlon, an impudent old skinflint, who had definite notions about "niggers," and hired Ben a summer and would not pay him. Then the hungry boy gathered his sacks together, and in broad daylight went into Carlon's corn; and when the hard-fisted farmer set upon him, the angry boy flew at him like a beast. Doc Burke saved a murder and a lynching that day.

The story reminded me again of the Burkes, and an impatience seized me to know who won in the battle, Doc or the seventy-five acres. For it is a hard thing to make a farm out of nothing, even in fifteen years. So I hurried on, thinking of the Burkes. They used to have a certain magnificent barbarism about them that I liked. They were never vulgar, never immoral, but rather rough and primitive, with an unconventionality that spent itself in loud guffaws, slaps on the back, and naps in the corner. I hurried by the cottage of the misborn Neill boys. It was empty, and they were grown into fat, lazy farm-hands. I saw the home of the Hickmans, but Albert, with his stooping shoulders, had passed from the world. Then I came to the Burkes' gate and peered through; the inclosure looked rough and untrimmed, and yet there were the same fences around the old farm save to the left, where lay twenty-five other acres. And lo! the cabin in the hollow had climbed the hill and swollen to a half-finished six-room cottage.

The Burkes held a hundred acres, but they were still in debt. Indeed, the gaunt father who toiled night and day would scarcely be happy out of debt, being so used to it. Some day he must stop, for his massive frame is showing decline. The mother wore shoes, but the lion-like physique of other days was broken. The children had grown up. Rob, the image of his father, was loud and rough with laughter. Birdie, my school baby of six, had grown to a picture of maiden beau, tall and tawny. "Edgar is gone," said the mother, with head half bowed,—"gone to work in Nashville; he and his father couldn't agree."

Little Doc, the boy born since the time of my school, took me horse-back down the creek next morning toward Farmer Dowell's. The road and the stream were battling for mastery, and the stream had the better of it. We splashed and waded, and the merry boy, perched behind me, chattered and laughed. He showed me where Simon Thompson had bought a bit of ground and a home; but his daughter Lana, a plump, brown, slow girl, was not there. She had married a man and a farm twenty miles away. We wound on down the stream till we came to a gate that I did not recognize, but the boy insisted that it was "Uncle Bird's." The farm was fat with the growing crop. In that little valley was a strange stillness as I rode up; for death and marriage had stolen youth and left age and childhood there. We sat and talked that night after the chores were done. Uncle Bird was grayer, and his eyes did not see so well, but he was still jovial. We talked of the acres bought,—one hundred and twenty-five,—of the new guest-chamber added, of Martha's marrying. Then we talked of death: Fanny and Fred were gone; a shadow hung over the other daughter, and when it lifted she was to go to Nashville to school. At last we spoke of the neighbors, and as night fell, Uncle Bird told me how, on a night like that, 'Thenie came wandering back to her home over yonder, to escape the blows of her husband. And next morning she died in the home that her little bow-legged brother, working and saving, had bought for their widowed mother.

My journey was done, and behind me lay hill and dale, and Life and Death. How shall man measure Progress there where the dark-faced Josie lies? How many heartfuls of sorrow shall balance a bushel of wheat? How hard a thing is life to the lowly, and yet how human and real! And all this life and love and strife and failure,—is it the twilight of nightfall or the flush of some faint-dawning day?

Thus sadly musing, I rode to Nashville in the Jim Crow car.

# Of the Wings of Atalanta

O black boy of Atlanta!
  But half was spoken;
The slave's chains and the master's
  Alike are broken;
The one curse of the races
  Held both in tether;
They are rising—all are rising—
  The black and white together.
                    —WHITTIER

South of the North, yet north of the South, lies the City of a Hundred Hills, peering out from the shadows of the past into the promise of the future. I have seen her in the morning, when the first flush of day had half-roused her; she lay gray and still on the crimson soil of Georgia; then the blue smoke began to curl from her chimneys, the tinkle of bell and scream of whistle broke the silence, the rattle and roar of busy life slowly gathered and swelled, until the seething whirl of the city seemed a strange thing in a sleepy land.

Once, they say, even Atlanta slept dull and drowsy at the foot-hills of the Alleghanies, until the iron baptism of war awakened her with its sullen waters, aroused and maddened her, and left her listening to the sea. And the sea cried to the hills and the hills answered the sea, till the city rose like a widow and cast away her weeds, and toiled for her daily bread; toiled steadily, toiled cunningly,—perhaps with some bitterness, with a touch of *réclame*,—and yet with real earnestness, and real sweat.

It is a hard thing to live haunted by the ghost of an untrue dream; to see the wide vision of empire fade into real ashes and dirt; to feel the pang of the conquered, and yet know that with all the Bad that fell on one black day, something was vanquished that deserved to live, something killed that in justice had not dared to die; to know that with the Right that triumphed, triumphed something of Wrong, something sordid and mean, something less than the broadest and best. All this is bitter hard; and many a man and city and people have found in it excuse for sulking, and brooding, and listless waiting.

Such are not men of the sturdier make; they of Atlanta turned resolutely toward the future; and that future held aloft vistas of purple and gold:—Atlanta, Queen of the cotton kingdom; Atlanta, Gateway to the Land of the Sun; Atlanta, the new Lachesis, spinner of web and woof for the world. So the city crowned her hundred hills with factories, and stored her shops with cunning handiwork, and stretched long iron ways to greet the busy Mercury in his coming. And the Nation talked of her striving.

Perhaps Atlanta was not christened for the winged maiden of dull Bœotia; you know the tale,—how swarthy Atalanta, tall and wild, would marry only him who out-raced her; and how the wily Hippomenes laid three apples of gold in the way. She fled like a shadow, paused, startled over the first apple, but even as he stretched his hand, fled again; hovered over the second, then, slipping from his hot grasp, flew over river, vale, and hill; but as she lingered over the third, his arms fell round her, and looking on each other, the blazing passion of their love profaned the sanctuary of Love, and they were cursed. If Atlanta be not named for Atalanta, she ought to have been.

Atalanta is not the first or the last maiden whom greed of gold has led to defile the temple of Love; and not maids alone, but men in the race of life, sink from the high and generous ideals of youth to the gambler's code of the Bourse; and in all our Nation's striving is not the Gospel of Work befouled by the Gospel of Pay? So common is this that one-half think it normal; so unquestioned, that we almost fear to question if the end of racing is not gold, if the aim of man is not rightly to be rich. And if this is the fault of America, how dire a danger lies before a new land and a new city, lest Atlanta, stooping for mere gold, shall find that gold accursed!

It was no maiden's idle whim that started this hard racing; a fearful wilderness lay about the feet of that city after the War,—feudalism, poverty, the rise of the Third Estate, serfdom, the re-birth of Law and Order, and above and between all, the Veil of Race. How heavy a journey for weary feet! what wings must Atalanta have to flit over all this hollow and hill, through sour wood and sullen water, and by the red waste of sun-baked clay! How fleet must Atalanta be if she will not be tempted by gold to profane the Sanctuary!

The Sanctuary of our fathers has, to be sure, few Gods,—some sneer, "all too few." There is the thrifty Mercury of New England, Pluto of the North, and Ceres of the West; and there, too, is the half-forgotten Apollo of the South, under whose ægis the maiden ran,—and as she ran she forgot him, even as there in Bœotia Venus was forgot. She forgot the old ideal of the Southern gentleman,—that new-world heir of the grace and courtliness of patrician, knight, and noble; forgot his honor with his foibles, his kindliness with his carelessness, and stooped to apples of gold,—to men busier and sharper, thriftier and more unscrupulous. Golden apples are beautiful—I remember the lawless days of boyhood, when orchards in crimson and gold tempted me over fence and field—and, too, the merchant who has dethroned the planter is no despicable *parvenu.* Work and wealth are the mighty levers to lift this old new land; thrift and toil and saving are the highways to new hopes and new possibilities; and yet the warning is needed lest the wily Hippomenes tempt Atalanta to thinking that golden apples are the goal of racing, and not mere incidents by the way.

Atlanta must not lead the South to dream of material prosperity as the touchstone of all success; already the fatal might of this idea is beginning to spread; it is replacing the finer type of Southerner with vulgar money-getters; it is burying the sweeter beauties of Southern life beneath pretence and ostentation. For every social ill the panacea of Wealth has been urged,—wealth to overthrow the remains of the slave feudalism; wealth to raise the "cracker" Third Estate; wealth to employ the black serfs, and the prospect of wealth to keep them working; wealth as the end and aim of politics, and as the legal tender for law and order; and, finally, instead of Truth, Beauty, and Goodness, wealth as the ideal of the Public School.

Not only is this true in the world which Atlanta typifies, but it is threatening to be true of a world beneath and beyond that world,—the Black World beyond the Veil. To-day it makes little difference to Atlanta, to the South, what the Negro thinks or dreams or wills. In the soul-life of the land he is to-day, and naturally will long remain, unthought of, half forgotten; and yet when he does come to think and will and do for himself,—and let no man dream that day will never come,—then the part he plays will not be one of sudden learning, but words and thoughts he has been taught to lisp in his race-childhood. To-day the ferment of his striving toward self-realization is to the strife of the white world like a wheel within a wheel: beyond the Veil are smaller but like problems of ideals, of leaders and the led, of serfdom, of poverty, of order and subordination, and, through all, the Veil of Race. Few know of these problems, few who know notice them; and yet there they are, awaiting student, artist, and seer,—a field for somebody sometime to discover. Hither has the temptation of Hippomenes penetrated; already in this smaller world, which now indirectly and anon directly must influence the larger for good or ill, the habit is forming of interpreting the world in dollars. The old leaders of Negro opinion, in the little groups where there is a Negro social consciousness, are being replaced by new; neither the black preacher nor the black teacher leads as he did two decades ago. Into their places are pushing the farmers and gardeners, the well-paid porters and artisans, the businessmen,—all those with property and money. And with all this change, so curiously parallel to that of the Other-world, goes too the same inevitable change in ideals. The South laments to-day the slow, steady disappearance of a certain type of Negro,—the faithful, courteous slave of other days, with his incorruptible honesty and dignified humility. He is passing away just as surely as the old type of Southern gentleman is passing, and from not dissimilar causes,—the sudden transformation of a fair far-off ideal of Freedom into the hard reality of bread-winning and the consequent deification of Bread.

In the Black World, the Preacher and Teacher embodied once the ideals of this people,—the strife for another and a juster world, the vague dream of righteousness, the mystery of knowing; but to-day the danger is that these ideals, with their simple beauty and weird inspiration, will suddenly sink to a question of cash and a lust for gold. Here stands this black young Atalanta, girding herself for the race that must be run; and if her eyes be still toward the hills and sky as in the days of old, then we may look for noble running; but what if some ruthless or wily or even thoughtless Hippomenes lay golden apples before her? What if the Negro people be wooed from a strife for righteousness, from a love of knowing, to regard dollars as the be-all and end-all of life? What if to the Mammonism of America be added the rising Mammonism of the re-born South, and the Mammonism of this South be reinforced by the budding Mammonism of its half-awakened black millions? Whither, then, is the new-world quest of Goodness and Beauty and Truth gone glimmering? Must this, and that fair flower of Freedom which, despite the jeers of latter-day striplings, sprung from our fathers' blood, must that too degenerate into a dusty quest of gold,—into lawless lust with Hippomenes?

• • •

The hundred hills of Atlanta are not all crowned with factories. On one, toward the west, the setting sun throws three buildings in bold relief against the sky. The beauty of the group lies in its simple unity:—a broad lawn of green rising from the red street with mingled roses and peaches; north and south, two plain and stately halls; and in the midst, half hidden in ivy, a larger building, boldly graceful, sparingly decorated, and with one low spire. It is a restful group,—one never looks for more; it is all here, all intelligible. There I live, and there I hear from day to day the low hum of restful life. In winter's twilight, when the red sun glows, I can see the dark figures pass between the halls to the music of the night-bell. In the morning, when the sun is golden, the clang of the day-bell brings the hurry and laughter of three hundred young hearts from hall and street, and from the busy city below,—children all dark and heavy-haired,—to join their clear young voices in the music of the morning sacrifice. In a half-dozen class-rooms they gather then,—here to follow the love-song of Dido, here to listen to the tale of Troy divine; there to wander among the stars, there to wander among men and nations,—and elsewhere other well-worn ways of knowing this queer world. Nothing new, no time-saving devices,—simply old time-glorified methods of delving for Truth, and searching out the hidden beauties of life, and learning the good of living. The riddle of existence is the college curriculum that was laid before the Pharaohs, that was taught in the groves by Plato, that formed the *trivium* and *quadrivium,* and is to-day laid before the freedmen's sons by Atlanta University. And this course of study will not change; its methods will grow more deft and effectual, its content richer by toil of scholar and sight of seer; but the true college will ever have one goal,—not to earn meat, but to know the end and aim of that life which meat nourishes.

The vision of life that rises before these dark eyes has in it nothing mean or selfish. Not at Oxford or at Leipsic, not at Yale or Columbia, is there an air of higher resolve or more unfettered striving; the determination to realize for men, both black and white, the broadest possibilities of life, to seek the better and the best, to spread with their own hands the Gospel of Sacrifice,—all this is the burden of their talk and dream. Here, amid a wide desert of caste and proscription, amid the heart-hurting slights and jars and vagaries of a deep race-dislike, lies this green oasis, where hot anger cools, and the bitterness of disappointment is sweetened by the springs and breezes of Parnassus; and here men may lie and listen, and learn of a future fuller than the past, and hear the voice of Time:

"Entbehren sollst du, sollst entbehren."

They made their mistakes, those who planted Fisk and Howard and Atlanta before the smoke of battle had lifted; they made their mistakes, but those mistakes were not the things at which we lately laughed somewhat uproariously. They were right when they sought to found a new educational system upon the University: where, forsooth, shall we ground knowledge save on the broadest and deepest knowledge? The roots of the tree, rather than the leaves, are the sources of its life; and from the dawn of history, from Academus to Cambridge, the culture of the University has been the broad foundation-stone on which is built the kindergarten's A B C.

But these builders did make a mistake in minimizing the gravity of the problem before them; in thinking it a matter of years and decades; in therefore building quickly and laying their foundation carelessly, and lowering the standard of knowing, until they had scattered haphazard through the South some dozen poorly equipped high schools and mis-called them universities. They forgot, too, just as their successors are for-getting, the rule of inequality:—that of the million black youth, some were fitted to know and some to dig; that some had the talent and capacity of university men, and some the talent and capacity of blacksmiths; and that true training meant neither that all should be college men nor all artisans, but that the one should be made a missionary of culture to an untaught people, and the other a free workman among serfs. And to seek to make the blacksmith a scholar is almost as silly as the more modern scheme of making the scholar a blacksmith; almost, but not quite.

The function of the university is not simply to teach breadwinning, or to furnish teachers for the public schools, or to be a centre of polite society; it is, above all, to be the organ of that fine adjustment between real life and the growing knowledge of life, an adjustment which forms the secret of civilization. Such an institution the South of to-day sorely needs. She has religion, earnest, bigoted:—religion that on both sides the Veil often omits the sixth, seventh, and eighth commandments, but substitutes a dozen supplementary ones. She has, as Atlanta shows, growing thrift and love of toil; but she lacks that broad knowledge of what the world knows and knew of human living and doing, which she may apply to the thousand problems of real life to-day confronting her. The need of the South is knowledge and culture,—not in dainty limited quantity, as before the war, but in broad busy abundance in the world of work; and until she has this, not all the Apples of Hesperides, be they golden and bejewelled, can save her from the curse of the Bœotian lovers.

The Wings of Atalanta are the coming universities of the South. They alone can bear the maiden past the temptation of golden fruit. They will not guide her flying feet away from the cotton and gold; for—ah, thought-ful Hippomenes!—do not the apples lie in the very Way of Life? But they will guide her over and beyond them, and leave her kneeling in the Sanc-tuary of Truth and Freedom and broad Humanity, virgin and undefiled. Sadly did the Old South err in human education, despising the education of the masses, and niggardly in the support of colleges. Her ancient uni-versity foundations dwindled and withered under the foul breath of slavery; and even since the war they have fought a failing fight for life in the tainted air of social unrest and commercial selfishness, stunted by the death of criticism, and starving for lack of broadly cultured men. And if this is the white South's need and danger, how much heavier the danger and need of the freedmen's sons! how pressing here the need of broad ideals and true culture, the conservation of soul from sordid aims and petty passions! Let us build the Southern university—William and Mary, Trinity, Georgia, Texas, Tulane, Vanderbilt, and the others—fit to live; let us build, too, the Negro universities:—Fisk, whose foundation was ever broad; Howard, at the heart of the Nation; Atlanta at Atlanta, whose ideal of scholarship has been held above the temptation of numbers. Why not here, and perhaps elsewhere, plant deeply and for all time centres of learning and living, colleges that yearly would send into the life of the South a few white men and a few black men of broad culture, catholic tolerance, and trained ability, joining their hands to other hands, and giving to this squabble of the Races a decent and dignified peace?

Patience, Humility, Manners, and Taste, common schools and kindergartens, industrial and technical schools, literature and tolerance,—all these spring from knowledge and culture, the children of the university. So must men and nations build, not otherwise, not upside down.

Teach workers to work,—a wise saying; wise when applied to German boys and American girls; wiser when said of Negro boys, for they have less knowledge of working and none to teach them. Teach thinkers to think,—a needed knowledge in a day of loose and careless logic; and they whose lot is gravest must have the carefulest training to think aright. If these things are so, how foolish to ask what is the best education for one or seven or sixty million souls! shall we teach them trades, or train them in liberal arts? Neither and both: teach the workers to work and the thinkers to think; make carpenters of carpenters, and philosophers of philosophers, and fops of fools. Nor can we pause here. We are training not isolated men but a living group of men,—nay, a group within a group. And the final product of our training must be neither a psychologist nor a brickmason, but a man. And to make men, we must have ideals, broad, pure, and inspiring ends of living,—not sordid money-getting, not apples of gold. The worker must work for the glory of his handiwork, not simply for pay; the thinker must think for truth, not for fame. And all this is gained only by human strife and longing; by ceaseless training and education; by founding Right on righteousness and Truth on the unhampered search for Truth; by founding the common school on the university, and the industrial school on the common school; and weaving thus a system, not a distortion, and bringing a birth, not an abortion.

When night falls on the City of a Hundred Hills, a wind gathers itself from the seas and comes murmuring westward. And at its bidding, the smoke of the drowsy factories sweeps down upon the mighty city and covers it like a pall, while yonder at the University the stars twinkle above Stone Hall. And they say that yon gray mist is the tunic of Atalanta pausing over her golden apples. Fly, my maiden, fly, for yonder comes Hippomenes!

# Of the Training of Black Men

Why, if the Soul can fling the Dust aside,
And naked on the Air of Heaven ride,
    Were 't not a Shame—were 't not a Shame for him
In this clay carcase crippled to abide?
                                    —OMAR KHAYYÁM (FITZGERALD)

From the shimmering swirl of waters where many, many thoughts ago the slave-ship first saw the square tower of Jamestown, have flowed down to our day three streams of thinking: one swollen from the larger world here and overseas, saying, the multiplying of human wants in culture-lands calls for the world-wide coöperation of men in satisfying them. Hence arises a new human unity, pulling the ends of earth nearer, and all men, black, yellow, and white. The larger humanity strives to feel in this contact of living Nations and sleeping hordes a thrill of new life in the world, crying, "If the contact of Life and Sleep be Death, shame on such Life." To be sure, behind this thought lurks the afterthought of force and dominion,—the making of brown men to delve when the temptation of beads and red calico cloys.

The second thought streaming from the death-ship and the curving river is the thought of the older South,—the sincere and passionate belief that somewhere between men and cattle, God created a *tertium quid*, and called it a Negro,—a clownish, simple creature, at times even lovable within its limitations, but straitly foreordained to walk within the Veil. To be sure, behind the thought lurks the afterthought,—some of them with favoring chance might become men, but in sheer self-defence we dare not let them, and we build about them walls so high, and hang between them and the light a veil so thick, that they shall not even think of breaking through.

And last of all there trickles down that third and darker thought,—the thought of the things themselves, the confused, half-conscious mutter of men who are black and whitened, crying "Liberty, Freedom, Opportunity—vouchsafe to us, O boastful World, the chance of living men!" To be sure, behind the thought lurks the afterthought,—suppose, after all, the World is right and we are less than men? Suppose this mad impulse within is all wrong, some mock mirage from the untrue?

So here we stand among thoughts of human unity, even through conquest and slavery; the inferiority of black men, even if forced by fraud; a shriek in the night for the freedom of men who themselves are not yet sure of their right to demand it. This is the tangle of thought and afterthought wherein we are called to solve the problem of training men for life.

Behind all its curiousness, so attractive alike to sage and *dilettante*, lie its dim dangers, throwing across us shadows at once grotesque and awful. Plain it is to us that what the world seeks through desert and wild we have within our threshold,—a stalwart laboring force, suited to the semi-tropics; if, deaf to the voice of the Zeitgeist, we refuse to use and develop these men, we risk poverty and loss. If, on the other hand, seized by the brutal afterthought, we debauch the race thus caught in our talons, selfishly sucking their blood and brains in the future as in the past, what shall save us from national decadence? Only that saner selfishness, which Education teaches men, can find the rights of all in the whirl of work.

Again, we may decry the color-prejudice of the South, yet it remains a heavy fact. Such curious kinks of the human mind exist and must be reckoned with soberly. They cannot be laughed away, nor always successfully stormed at, nor easily abolished by act of legislature. And yet they must not be encouraged by being let alone. They must be recognized as facts, but unpleasant facts; things that stand in the way of civilization and religion and common decency. They can be met in but one way,—by the breadth and broadening of human reason, by catholicity of taste and culture. And so, too, the native ambition and aspiration of men, even though they be black, backward, and ungraceful, must not lightly be dealt with. To stimulate wildly weak and untrained minds is to play with mighty fires; to flout their striving idly is to welcome a harvest of brutish crime and shameless lethargy in our very laps. The guiding of thought and the deft coordination of deed is at once the path of honor and humanity.

And so, in this great question of reconciling three vast and partially contradictory streams of thought, the one panacea of Education leaps to the lips of all:—such human training as will best use the labor of all men without enslaving or brutalizing; such training as will give us poise to encourage the prejudices that bulwark society, and to stamp out those that in sheer barbarity deafen us to the wail of prisoned souls within the Veil, and the mounting fury of shackled men.

But when we have vaguely said that Education will set this tangle straight, what have we uttered but a truism? Training for life teaches living; but what training for the profitable living together of black men and white? A hundred and fifty years ago our task would have seemed easier. Then Dr. Johnson blandly assured us that education was needful solely for the embellishments of life, and was useless for ordinary vermin. To-day we have climbed to heights where we would open at least the outer courts of knowledge to all, display its treasures to many, and select the few to whom its mystery of Truth is revealed, not wholly by birth or the accidents of the stock market, but at least in part according to deftness and aim, talent and character. This programme, however, we are sorely puzzled in carrying out through that part of the land where the blight of slavery fell hardest, and where we are dealing with two backward peoples. To make here in human education that ever necessary combination of the permanent and the contingent—of the ideal and the practical in workable equilibrium—has been there, as it ever must be in every age and place, a matter of infinite experiment and frequent mistakes.

In rough approximation we may point out four varying decades of work in Southern education since the Civil War. From the close of the war until 1876, was the period of uncertain groping and temporary relief. There were army schools, mission schools, and schools of the Freedman's Bureau in chaotic disarrangement seeking system and coöperation. Then followed ten years of constructive definite effort toward the building of complete school systems in the South. Normal schools and colleges were founded for the freedmen, and teachers trained there to man the public schools. There was the inevitable tendency of war to underestimate the prejudices of the master and the ignorance of the slave, and all seemed clear sailing out of the wreckage of the storm. Meantime, starting in this decade yet especially developing from 1885 to 1895, began the industrial revolution of the South. The land saw glimpses of a new destiny and the stirring of new ideals. The educational system striving to complete itself saw new obstacles and a field of work ever broader and deeper. The Negro colleges, hurriedly founded, were inadequately equipped, illogically distributed, and of varying efficiency and grade; the normal and high schools were doing little more than common-school work, and the common schools were training but a third of the children who ought to be in them, and training these too often poorly. At the same time the white South, by reason of its sudden conversion from the slavery ideal, by so much the more became set and strengthened in its racial prejudice, and crystallized it into harsh law and harsher custom; while the marvellous pushing forward of the poor white daily threatened to take even bread and butter from the mouths of the heavily handicapped sons of the freedmen. In the midst, then, of the larger problem of Negro education sprang up the more practical question of work, the inevitable economic quandary that faces a people in the transition from slavery to freedom, and especially those who make that change amid hate and prejudice, lawlessness and ruthless competition.

The industrial school springing to notice in this decade, but coming to full recognition in the decade beginning with 1895, was the proffered answer to this combined educational and economic crisis, and an answer of singular wisdom and timeliness. From the very first in nearly all the schools some attention had been given to training in handiwork, but now was this training first raised to a dignity that brought it in direct touch with the South's magnificent industrial development, and given an emphasis which reminded black folk that before the Temple of Knowledge swing the Gates of Toil.

Yet after all they are but gates, and when turning our eyes from the temporary and the contingent in the Negro problem to the broader question of the permanent uplifting and civilization of black men in America, we have a right to inquire, as this enthusiasm for material advancement mounts to its height, if after all the industrial school is the final and sufficient answer in the training of the Negro race; and to ask gently, but in all sincerity, the ever-recurring query of the ages, Is not life more than meat, and the body more than raiment? And men ask this to-day all the more eagerly because of sinister signs in recent educational movements. The tendency is here, born of slavery and quickened to renewed life by the crazy imperialism of the day, to regard human beings as among the material resources of a land to be trained with an eye single to future dividends. Race-prejudices, which keep brown and black men in their "places," we are coming to regard as useful allies with such a theory, no matter how much they may dull the ambition and sicken the hearts of struggling human beings. And above all, we daily hear that an education that encourages aspiration, that sets the loftiest of ideals and seeks as an end culture and character rather than breadwinning, is the privilege of white men and the danger and delusion of black.

Especially has criticism been directed against the former educational efforts to aid the Negro. In the four periods I have mentioned, we find first, boundless, planless enthusiasm and sacrifice; then the preparation of teachers for a vast public-school system; then the launching and expansion of that school system amid increasing difficulties; and finally the training of workmen for the new and growing industries. This development has been sharply ridiculed as a logical anomaly and flat reversal of nature. Soothly we have been told that first industrial and manual training should have taught the Negro to work, then simple schools should have taught him to read and write, and finally, after years, high and normal schools could have completed the system, as intelligence and wealth demanded.

That a system logically so complete was historically impossible, it needs but a little thought to prove. Progress in human affairs is more often a pull than a push, surging forward of the exceptional man, and the lifting of his duller brethren slowly and painfully to his vantage-ground. Thus it was no accident that gave birth to universities centuries before the common schools, that made fair Harvard the first flower of our wilderness. So in the South: the mass of the freedmen at the end of the war lacked the intelligence so necessary to modern workingmen. They must first have the common school to teach them to read, write, and cipher; and they must have higher schools to teach teachers for the common schools. The white teachers who flocked South went to establish such a common-school system. Few held the idea of founding colleges; most of them at first would have laughed at the idea. But they faced, as all men since them have faced, that central paradox of the South,—the social separation of the races. At that time it was the sudden volcanic rupture of nearly all relations between black and white, in work and government and family life. Since then a new adjustment of relations in economic and political affairs has grown up,—an adjustment subtle and difficult to grasp, yet singularly ingenious, which leaves still that frightful chasm at the color-line across which men pass at their peril. Thus, then and now, there stand in the South two separate worlds; and separate not simply in the higher realms of social intercourse, but also in church and school, on railway and street-car, in hotels and theatres, in streets and city sections, in books and newspapers, in asylums and jails, in hospitals and graveyards. There is still enough of contact for large economic and group coöperation, but the separation is so thorough and deep that it absolutely precludes for the present between the races anything like that sympathetic and effective group-training and leadership of the one by the other, such as the American Negro and all backward peoples must have for effectual progress.

This the missionaries of '68 soon saw; and if effective industrial and trade schools were impracticable before the establishment of a common-school system, just as certainly no adequate common schools could be founded until there were teachers to teach them. Southern whites would not teach them; Northern whites in sufficient numbers could not be had. If the Negro was to learn, he must teach himself, and the most effective help that could be given him was the establishment of schools to train Negro teachers. This conclusion was slowly but surely reached by every student of the situation until simultaneously, in widely separated regions, without consultation or systematic plan, there arose a series of institutions designed to furnish teachers for the untaught. Above the sneers of critics at the obvious defects of this procedure must ever stand its one crushing rejoinder: in a single generation they put thirty thousand black teachers in the South; they wiped out the illiteracy of the majority of the black people of the land, and they made Tuskegee possible.

Such higher training-schools tended naturally to deepen broader development: at first they were common and grammar schools, then some became high schools. And finally, by 1900, some thirty-four had one year or more of studies of college grade. This development was reached with different degrees of speed in different institutions: Hampton is still a high school, while Fisk University started her college in 1871, and Spelman Seminary about 1896. In all cases the aim was identical,—to maintain the standards of the lower training by giving teachers and leaders the best practicable training; and above all, to furnish the black world with adequate standards of human culture and lofty ideals of life. It was not enough that the teachers of teachers should be trained in technical normal methods; they must also, so far as possible, be broad-minded, cultured men and women, to scatter civilization among a people whose ignorance was not simply of letters, but of life itself.

It can thus be seen that the work of education in the South began with higher institutions of training, which threw off as their foliage common schools, and later industrial schools, and at the same time strove to shoot their roots ever deeper toward college and university training. That this was an inevitable and necessary development, sooner or later, goes without saying; but there has been, and still is, a question in many minds if the natural growth was not forced, and if the higher training was not either overdone or done with cheap and unsound methods. Among white Southerners this feeling is widespread and positive. A prominent Southern journal voiced this in a recent editorial.

> The experiment that has been made to give the colored students classical training has not been satisfactory. Even though many were able to pursue the course, most of them did so in a parrot-like way, learning what was taught, but not seeming to appropriate the truth and import of their instruction, and graduating without sensible aim or valuable occupation for their future. The whole scheme has proved a waste of time, efforts, and the money of the state.

While most fair-minded men would recognize this as extreme and overdrawn, still without doubt many are asking, Are there a sufficient number of Negroes ready for college training to warrant the undertaking? Are not too many students prematurely forced into this work? Does it not have the effect of dissatisfying the young Negro with his environment? And do these graduates succeed in real life? Such natural questions cannot be evaded, nor on the other hand must a Nation naturally skeptical as to Negro ability assume an unfavorable answer without careful inquiry and patient openness to conviction. We must not forget that most Americans answer all queries regarding the Negro *a priori,* and that the least that human courtesy can do is to listen to evidence.

The advocates of the higher education of the Negro would be the last to deny the incompleteness and glaring defects of the present system: too many institutions have attempted to do college work, the work in some cases has not been thoroughly done, and quantity rather than quality has sometimes been sought. But all this can be said of higher education throughout the land; it is the almost inevitable incident of educational growth, and leaves the deeper question of the legitimate demand for the higher training of Negroes untouched. And this latter question can be settled in but one way, —by a first-hand study of the facts. If we leave out of view all institutions which have not actually graduated students from a course higher than that of a New England high school, even though they be called colleges; if then we take the thirty-four remaining institutions, we may clear up many misapprehensions by asking searchingly, What kind of institutions are they? what do they teach? and what sort of men do they graduate?

And first we may say that this type of college, including Atlanta, Fisk, and Howard, Wilberforce and Lincoln, Biddle, Shaw, and the rest, is peculiar, almost unique. Through the shining trees that whisper before me as I write, I catch glimpses of a boulder of New England granite, covering a grave, which graduates of Atlanta University have placed there, with this inscription:

> IN GRATEFUL MEMORY OF THEIR
> FORMER TEACHER AND FRIEND
> AND OF THE UNSELFISH LIFE HE
> LIVED, AND THE NOBLE WORK HE
> WROUGHT; THAT THEY, THEIR
> CHILDREN, AND THEIR CHIL-
> DREN'S CHILDREN MIGHT BE
> BLESSED.

This was the gift of New England to the freed Negro: not alms, but a friend; not cash, but character. It was not and is not money these seething millions want, but love and sympathy, the pulse of hearts beating with red blood;—a gift which to-day only their own kindred and race can bring to the masses, but which once saintly souls brought to their favored children in the crusade of the sixties, that finest thing in American history, and one of the few things untainted by sordid greed and cheap vainglory. The teachers in these institutions came not to keep the Negroes in their place, but to raise them out of the defilement of the places where slavery had wallowed them. The colleges they founded were social settlements; homes where the best of the sons of the freedmen came in close and sympathetic touch with the best traditions of New England. They lived and ate together, studied and worked, hoped and harkened in the dawning light. In actual formal content their curriculum was doubtless old-fashioned, but in educational power it was supreme, for it was the contact of living souls.

From such schools about two thousand Negroes have gone forth with the bachelor's degree. The number in itself is enough to put at rest the argument that too large a proportion of Negroes are receiving higher training. If the ratio to population of all Negro students throughout the land, in both college and secondary training, be counted, Commissioner Harris assures us "it must be increased to five times its present average" to equal the average of the land.

Fifty years ago the ability of Negro students in any appreciable numbers to master a modern college course would have been difficult to prove. To-day it is proved by the fact that four hundred Negroes, many of whom have been reported as brilliant students, have received the bachelor's degree from Harvard, Yale, Oberlin, and seventy other leading colleges. Here we have, then, nearly twenty-five hundred Negro graduates, of whom the crucial query must be made, How far did their training fit them for life? It is of course extremely difficult to collect satisfactory data on such a point,—difficult to reach the men, to get trustworthy testimony, and to gauge that testimony by any generally acceptable criterion of success. In 1900, the Conference at Atlanta University undertook to study these graduates, and published the results. First they sought to know what these graduates were doing, and succeeded in getting answers from nearly two-thirds of the living. The direct testimony was in almost all cases corroborated by the reports of the colleges where they graduated, so that in the main the reports were worthy of credence. Fifty-three per cent of these graduates were teachers,—presidents of institutions, heads of normal schools, principals of city school-systems, and the like. Seventeen per cent were clergymen; another seventeen per cent were in the professions, chiefly as physicians. Over six per cent were merchants, farmers, and artisans, and four per cent were in the government civil-service. Granting even that a considerable proportion of the third unheard from are unsuccessful, this is a record of usefulness. Personally I know many hundreds of these graduates, and have corresponded with more than a thousand; through others I have followed carefully the life-work of scores; I have taught some of them and some of the pupils whom they have taught, lived in homes which they have builded, and looked at life through their eyes. Comparing them as a class with my fellow students in New England and in Europe, I cannot hesitate in saying that nowhere have I met men and women with a broader spirit of helpfulness, with deeper devotion to their life-work, or with more consecrated determination to succeed in the face of bitter difficulties than among Negro college-bred men. They have, to be sure, their proportion of ne'er-do-weels, their pedants and lettered fools, but they have a surprisingly small proportion of them; they have not that culture of manner which we instinctively associate with university men, forgetting that in reality it is the heritage from cultured homes, and that no people a generation removed from slavery can escape a certain unpleasant rawness and *gaucherie*, despite the best of training.

With all their larger vision and deeper sensibility, these men have usually been conservative, careful leaders. They have seldom been agitators, have withstood the temptation to head the mob, and have worked steadily and faithfully in a thousand communities in the South. As teachers, they have given the South a commendable system of city schools and large numbers of private normal-schools and academies. Colored college-bred men have worked side by side with white college graduates at Hampton; almost from the beginning the backbone of Tuskegee's teaching force has been formed of graduates from Fisk and Atlanta. And to-day the institute is filled with college graduates, from the energetic wife of the principal down to the teacher of agriculture, including nearly half of the executive council and a majority of the heads of departments. In the professions, college men are slowly but surely leavening the Negro church, are healing and preventing the devastations of disease, and beginning to furnish legal protection for the liberty and property of the toiling masses. All this is needful work. Who would do it if Negroes did not? How could Negroes do it if they were not trained carefully for it? If white people need colleges to furnish teachers, ministers, lawyers, and doctors, do black people need nothing of the sort?

If it is true that there are an appreciable number of Negro youth in the land capable by character and talent to receive that higher training, the end of which is culture, and if the two and a half thousand who have had something of this training in the past have in the main proved themselves useful to their race and generation, the question then comes, What place in the future development of the South ought the Negro college and college-bred man to occupy? That the present social separation and acute race-sensitiveness must eventually yield to the influences of culture, as the South grows civilized, is clear. But such transformation calls for singular wisdom and patience. If, while the healing of this vast sore is progressing, the races are to live for many years side by side, united in economic effort, obeying a common government, sensitive to mutual thought and feeling, yet subtly and silently separate in many matters of deeper human inti-macy,—if this unusual and dangerous development is to progress amid peace and order, mutual respect and growing intelligence, it will call for social surgery at once the delicatest and nicest in modern history. It will demand broad-minded, upright men, both white and black, and in its final accomplishment American civilization will triumph. So far as white men are concerned, this fact is to-day being recognized in the South, and a happy renaissance of university education seems imminent. But the very voices that cry hail to this good work are, strange to relate, largely silent or antagonistic to the higher education of the Negro.

Strange to relate! for this is certain, no secure civilization can be built in the South with the Negro as an ignorant, turbulent proletariat. Suppose we seek to remedy this by making them laborers and nothing more: they are not fools, they have tasted of the Tree of Life, and they will not cease to think, will not cease attempting to read the riddle of the world. By taking away their best equipped teachers and leaders, by slamming the door of opportunity in the faces of their bolder and brighter minds, will you make them satisfied with their lot? or will you not rather transfer their leading from the hands of men taught to think to the hands of untrained dema-gogues? We ought not to forget that despite the pressure of poverty, and despite the active discouragement and even ridicule of friends, the de-mand for higher training steadily increases among Negro youth: there were, in the years from 1875 to 1880, 22 Negro graduates from Northern colleges; from 1885 to 1890 there were 43, and from 1895 to 1900, nearly 100 graduates. From Southern Negro colleges there were, in the same three periods, 143, 413, and over 500 graduates. Here, then, is the plain thirst for training; by refusing to give this Talented Tenth the key to knowledge, can any sane man imagine that they will lightly lay aside their yearning and contentedly become hewers of wood and drawers of water?

No. The dangerously clear logic of the Negro's position will more and more loudly assert itself in that day when increasing wealth and more in-tricate social organization preclude the South from being, as it so largely is, simply an armed camp for intimidating black folk. Such waste of energy cannot be spared if the South is to catch up with civilization. And as the black third of the land grows in thrift and skill, unless skilfully guided in its larger philosophy, it must more and more brood over the red past and the creeping, crooked present, until it grasps a gospel of revolt and revenge and throws its new-found energies athwart the current of advance. Even to-day the masses of the Negroes see all too clearly the anomalies of their position and the moral crookedness of yours. You may marshal strong indictments against them, but their counter-cries, lacking though they be in formal logic, have burning truths within them which you may not wholly ignore, O Southern Gentlemen! If you deplore their presence here, they ask, Who brought us? When you cry, Deliver us from the vision of intermarriage, they answer that legal marriage is infinitely better than systematic concubinage and prostitution. And if in just fury you accuse their vagabonds of violating women, they also in fury quite as just may reply: The wrong which your gentlemen have done against helpless black women in defiance of your own laws is written on the foreheads of two millions of mulattoes, and written in ineffaceable blood. And finally, when you fasten crime upon this race as its peculiar trait, they answer that slavery was the arch-crime, and lynching and lawlessness its twin abortion; that color and race are not crimes, and yet they it is which in this land receives most unceasing condemnation, North, East, South, and West.

I will not say such arguments are wholly justified,—I will not insist that there is no other side to the shield; but I do say that of the nine millions of Negroes in this nation, there is scarcely one out of the cradle to whom these arguments do not daily present themselves in the guise of terrible truth. I insist that the question of the future is how best to keep these millions from brooding over the wrongs of the past and the difficulties of the present, so that all energies may be bent toward a cheerful striving and co-operation with their white neighbors toward a larger, juster, and fuller future. That one wise method of doing this lies in the closer knitting of the Negro to the great industrial possibilities of the South is a great truth. And this the common schools and the manual training and trade schools are working to accomplish. But these alone are not enough. The foundations of knowledge in this race, as in others, must be sunk deep in the college and university if we would build a solid, permanent structure. Internal problems of social advance must inevitably come,—problems of work and wages, of families and homes, of morals and the true valuing of the things of life; and all these and other inevitable problems of civilization the Negro must meet and solve largely for himself, by reason of his isolation; and can there be any possible solution other than by study and thought and an appeal to the rich experience of the past? Is there not, with such a group and in such a crisis, infinitely more danger to be apprehended from half-trained minds and shallow thinking than from over-education and over-refinement? Surely we have wit enough to found a Negro college so manned and equipped as to steer successfully between the *dilettante* and the fool. We shall hardly induce black men to believe that if their stomachs be full, it matters little about their brains. They already dimly perceive that the paths of peace winding between honest toil and dignified manhood call for the guidance of skilled thinkers, the loving, reverent comradeship between the black lowly and the black men emancipated by training and culture.

The function of the Negro college, then, is clear: it must maintain the standards of popular education, it must seek the social regeneration of the Negro, and it must help in the solution of problems of race contact and cooperation. And finally, beyond all this, it must develop men. Above our modern socialism, and out of the worship of the mass, must persist and evolve that higher individualism which the centres of culture protect; there must come a loftier respect for the sovereign human soul that seeks to know itself and the world about it; that seeks a freedom for expansion and self-development; that will love and hate and labor in its own way, untrammeled alike by old and new. Such souls aforetime have inspired and guided worlds, and if we be not wholly bewitched by our Rhine-gold, they shall again. Herein the longing of black men must have respect: the rich and bitter depth of their experience, the unknown treasures of their inner life, the strange rendings of nature they have seen, may give the world new points of view and make their loving, living, and doing precious to all human hearts. And to themselves in these the days that try their souls, the chance to soar in the dim blue air above the smoke is to their finer spirits boon and guerdon for what they lose on earth by being black.

I sit with Shakespeare and he winces not. Across the color line I move arm in arm with Balzac and Dumas, where smiling men and welcoming women glide in gilded halls. From out the caves of evening that swing between the strong-limbed earth and the tracery of the stars, I summon Aristotle and Aurelius and what soul I will, and they come all graciously with no scorn nor condescension. So, wed with Truth, I dwell above the Veil. Is this the life you grudge us, O knightly America? Is this the life you long to change into the dull red hideousness of Georgia? Are you so afraid lest peering from this high Pisgah, between Philistine and Amalekite, we sight the Promised Land?

•   •   •   •   •   •   •   •   •   •   •   •

## QUESTIONS FOR A SECOND READING

1. Throughout these three chapters from *The Souls of Black Folk*, Du Bois's writing is rich in figurative language and rich in allusion, in references to a history of writing, reading, and thinking. Du Bois's prose is not straightforward and simple. It is carefully worked and highly elaborated. As you reread, choose three or four passages from each chapter where the lan-

guage calls attention to itself, passages that show evidence of a writer trying to *do* something unusual or out of the ordinary, creating certain effects
or presenting certain challenges.

Review these passages carefully and be prepared to talk about what
Du Bois is doing and why he is doing it. What can a writer learn from Du
Bois's example?

For the purposes of this exercise, assume that Du Bois is doing something other than decorating his sentences or making the writing "pretty."
Assume that he is trying to think things through and that this writing is a
necessary part of that thinking. Or assume that he is trying to make certain demands on himself, his subject matter, and his reader, and this language is evidence of these demands. Or assume that he is trying to establish an identity for himself, as a writer; what is that identity? Or assume
that he is trying to teach a reader how to read; what is this way of
reading?

What, then, is Du Bois doing in the sentences you have chosen? How
does the language change from chapter to chapter? Where is it the same?
What are the risks or liabilities of this way of writing?

2. As you reread these three chapters, read them as parts of a single argument about the "work of education in the South." How do these three
   chapters speak back and forth to each other? How do they fit together?
   What is Du Bois's argument in each chapter? How does one lead to or revise the other?

3. As you reread these chapters, think about the context for Du Bois's argument; do this by reading closely and looking to see when and how he represents his audience, particularly those readers he feels he will have to
   work the hardest to convince. Where, in each chapter, do you see Du Bois
   working hardest on these readers? What ideas is Du Bois working
   against? Where and how do questions of race come to play?

### ASSIGNMENTS FOR WRITING

1. In "The Forethought," the introduction to *The Souls of Black Folk*, Du Bois
   writes

   > Herein lie buried many things which if read with patience may show
   > the strange meaning of being black here in the dawning of the Twen-
   > tieth Century. This meaning is not without interest to you, Gentle
   > Reader; for the problem of the Twentieth Century is the problem of the
   > color-line.

   This can be read as a sign of Du Bois's concern that his book will be misread and misunderstood. In "The Forethought" he makes one more attempt to prepare a reader for his book and the project it represents. What
   might it mean to read this book with "patience"? Who is his "gentle
   reader" (and is that phrase offered with faith or with irony)? How might
   the chapters you have read be used to think about "the strange meaning
   of being black here in the dawning of the Twentieth Century"?

   Choose *one* of the three chapters and write an essay that addresses
   these questions, or that uses the chapter to think about Du Bois's project

as it is articulated in his introduction. Below are some questions to direct
your work with whichever chapter you choose.

   **"Of the Meaning of Progress":** As a sociologist and a historian, Du
Bois presented his readers, black as well as white, with detailed accounts
of areas of black experience that would otherwise have remained invisible, unrepresented, and unknown. It is worth recalling that the book
which preceded *The Souls of Black Folk, The Philadelphia Negro,* was a study
commissioned by the University of Pennsylvania and based upon interview, observation, and questionnaire. And from 1897 on, Du Bois was
planning, proposing, and supervising a series of sociological studies of
black American life. "Of the Meaning of Progress" can be read as a report
on black life in a rural community. How is the report organized? What
does it choose to see or to ignore? How does Du Bois establish his relationship to the scenes and people described? How does he represent his
relationship to his audience?

   **"Of the Wings of Atalanta" or "Of the Training of Black Men":** Both
of these are arguments concerning the history and direction of higher education in the South. Both essays argue (if indirectly) that to understand
the "meaning of being black," one must understand ideas as those ideas
belong to and have bearing on the position of African Americans in the
South. As you work with one of these chapters, see what textual evidence
you can find to help establish the context for Du Bois's argument. Who is
he arguing with and on what terms? Where do you see Du Bois working
hardest on these readers? What ideas is Du Bois working against? What
strategies does he use? How and where does he work to teach a reader to
both understand and to be convinced? Where and how do questions of
race come to play?

2. In "The Forethought," the introduction to *The Souls of Black Folk,* Du Bois
   writes

   > Herein lie buried many things which if read with patience may show
   > the strange meaning of being black here in the dawning of the Twen-
   > tieth Century. This meaning is not without interest to you, Gentle
   > Reader; for the problem of the Twentieth Century is the problem of the
   > color-line.

   While we have chosen only three of the 14 chapters in *The Souls of Black
   Folk,* we chose these three because they seem to ask to be read together.
   How and why might they *now* require "patience" of their readers? How
   might they be read, together, as an attempt to lead a reader to an understanding of the "strange meaning of being black . . . in the dawning of the
   Twentieth Century"? What do they say about the problem of the color-
   line? What do they have to say to the Twenty-First Century?

   Write an essay that looks at these three chapters in light of the project
   and the concerns outlined by Du Bois in "The Forethought." You should
   imagine that your reader is interested in knowing something about Du
   Bois and, through his writing, about the experience of African Americans
   almost 100 years ago. You should think of yourself as a historian, using
   this text (not only what it says but *how* it says what it says) as your primary document. And, as you help someone to think through these chapters, you should ask: How might this writing be interesting and useful to
   us now, 100 years later? Where and how are Du Bois's concerns, for ex-

ample represented in the curriculum of your university? If you look at the structures of education today, what might one say, following Du Bois, about the problems of the color-line?

3. Throughout these three chapters, Du Bois's writing is rich in figurative language and rich in allusion, in references to a history of writing, reading, and thinking. Du Bois's prose is not straightforward and simple. It is carefully worked and highly elaborated. It serves his project—to represent and understand the "strange experience of being black," and to do so for readers who are not necessarily prepared to understand.

   Write an essay on the style of these three chapters from *The Souls of Black Folk.* You will need to choose a workable set of examples—passages from each chapter where the language calls attention to itself, passages that show evidence of a writer trying to *do* something unusual or out of the ordinary, passages that create certain effects or present certain challenges.

   You could, if you chose, write only about a single chapter. Since the style varies across the chapters, if you choose to write about all three you should take time to think about differences between the chapters—thinking about both how and why they differ.

   You should imagine that you are writing for readers who have read *The Souls of Black Folk,* but who won't have the text in front of them. You will need to introduce and present these passages. And you will need to be prepared to talk about what Du Bois is doing and why he is doing it.

   For the purposes of this exercise, you should assume that Du Bois is doing something other than decorating his sentences or making the writing "pretty." Assume that he is trying to think things through and this writing is a necessary part of that thinking. Or assume that he is trying to make certain demands on himself, his subject matter, and his reader, and this language is evidence of these demands. Or assume that he is trying to establish an identity for himself, as a writer; what is that identity? Or, assume that he is trying to teach a reader how to read; what is this way of reading?

   What, then, is Du Bois doing in the sentences you have chosen? What might a writer learn from his example?

4. There is an interesting and characteristic sentence toward the end of the chapter "Of the Training of Black Men," one that nicely illustrates a difficulty Du Bois has in writing women into his account of education. He says that when he compares "Negro students" in the South

   > with my fellow students in New England and in Europe, I cannot hesitate in saying that nowhere have I met men and women with a broader spirit of helpfulness, with deeper devotion to their life-work, or with more consecrated determination to succeed in the face of bitter difficulties than among Negro college-bred men.

The "men and women" at the opening of the sentence become "college-bred men" by its close. Go back and reread these three chapters looking carefully to see how and where women are represented. Where are Du Bois's sympathies? What does he take for granted? What does he struggle to acknowledge? (It might also be useful to do some research for this assignment—to find out, for example, about the educational opportunities available to women and, in particular, to black women at the turn of the century; or to read other pieces by Du Bois on the status of women. For the latter, the collection of essays and articles in The Library of America Edition, *W. E. B. Du Bois: Writings,* is particularly useful.)

Write an essay in which you represent and discuss the ways Du Bois figures women into his account of the issues confronting the education of black Americans in the South at the turn of the century. Where and how are they present? Where and how are they absent? And how would you account for their position in these texts?

As a word of caution: it should be clear that it is not enough to claim that Du Bois is sexist and/or a product of his time. It serves no good purpose to reduce Du Bois to a stick figure (and it would be wrong); texts are all in one way or another products of their times and a student would have to do a considerable amount of work to be able to speak responsibly about what Americans thought or said in 1903. Your work here is to locate in Du Bois's writings passages that will allow you to think about his efforts to write about gender, race, and education.

## MAKING CONNECTIONS

1. In each of the three sections of "The American Scholar" by Ralph Waldo Emerson (p. 294), Emerson charts out influences on the mind and spirit of the scholar. In section I, for example, he says, "the first in time and the first in importance of the influences upon the mind is that of nature. . . . The scholar must needs stand wistful and admiring before this great spectacle." "The next great influence into the spirit of the scholar," he says in section II, "is the mind of the Past,—in whatever form, whether of literature, of art, of institutions, that mind is inscribed." And in the third section Emerson argues against the image of the scholar as "a recluse, a valetudinarian,—as unfit for any handiwork or public labor" in favor of the scholar as a "man of action" in the world.

   W. E. B. Du Bois, in these three chapters from *The Souls of Black Folk,* also lays out a program for the creation of the American scholar, although he is writing about a different set of students than the privileged white elite who attended Harvard University in 1837. Compared to Emerson, Du Bois is more concerned with institutions and political programs, with the social structures necessary for young black men and women to receive a university education a little more than a half century after Emerson's Phi Beta Kappa oration.

   Write an essay in which you take the structure of Emerson's essay and respond to each of its sections from Du Bois's perspective. You can, if you choose, write in Du Bois's voice and style. Whether you do this or not, be sure to engage and to bring to bear his terms and examples. What, in other words, do you imagine Du Bois would have to say to Emerson? How might you locate Du Bois's vision of education and the scholarly life within or against Emerson's?

2. Du Bois writes to reform American education. There are other writers in *Ways of Reading* who write as reformers, although with different starting points, different concerns, and different agendas: Paulo Freire, "The

'Banking' Concept of Education" (p. 348); Mary Louise Pratt, "Arts of the Contact Zone" (p. 582); and Adrienne Rich, "When We Dead Awaken: Writing as Re-Vision" (p. 603).

Write an essay in which you put one of these essays into conversation with the three chapters from *The Souls of Black Folk*. Where and how do they speak to the same issues? Where and how do they differ in their arguments and in their approach? How are they different as pieces of writing—different in style and in intent? You will need to carefully represent the positions of each. You will need to think about differences, as well as similarities. And you should think about how and why the differences might be attributed to history, to race, or to gender.

3. Both Harriet Jacobs's *Incidents in the Life of a Slave Girl* (p. 459) and Du Bois's *The Souls of Black Folk* begin with a preface that appeals to the reader, registering a particular concern that the legitimacy and the authority of the author be established. Both stand as powerful examples of texts by African American writers, at least in part, to a white audience who, at its best and most sympathetic, might be unprepared to understand what follows. As you read both selections, pay particular attention to how and where Jacobs and Du Bois address their readers, both directly (speaking to the reader by name) and indirectly (anticipating a reader's misgivings or failures to understand).

   Write an essay in which you use these two examples to think about style and address, about writers and their audiences, as black Americans wrote to white Americans in 1861 and 1903.

# RALPH
# ELLISON

"*A* N EXTRAVAGANCE OF LAUGHTER" *was written toward the end of Ralph Ellison's career, when he was seventy-one, for the collection of essays titled* Going to the Territory. *It tells the story of an event in the 1930s, when Ellison visited New York, met Richard Wright and other African American artists and intellectuals, and first began to imagine his career as a writer. Ellison grew up in Oklahoma City, where his parents had migrated in hopes of a greater freedom than they could find in the Deep South. "Going to the territory"—that is, going to the Indian territories, including those in Oklahoma—was a phrase used earlier by escaped slaves to describe the hope for a greater freedom. While the conditions of black life were different in the West, Oklahoma City was racially segregated. Ellison's father died there when he was three. He lived with his mother and brother in relative poverty, but always with the belief that he could overcome the limits imposed by economic insecurity and racial prejudice. (His father had named him after Ralph Waldo Emerson; Ellison would later argue for the importance of Emersonian self-determination and self-reliance, sometimes in ways that made him suspect among black and Left intellectuals, who felt that he was ignoring the determining factors of poverty, racism, and oppression.)*

*As a child growing up in Oklahoma City, Ellison fell in love with African American music, particularly jazz. He played the trumpet, taught himself Louis*

*Armstrong solos, and traded yard work for private lessons from the conductor of the Oklahoma City Orchestra. Ellison went to Tuskegee as a music major. His dream was to write a symphony that would bring the blues into classical form. It is at this point that Ellison made his first trip to New York. He was looking to make money to support his education and he was hoping to meet Richard Wright. He later returned and, with Richard Wright's aid, began to work with the Federal Writers Project. In 1952 he published* Invisible Man, *one of the most widely read and most influential novels of the twentieth century. It won the National Book Award and was immediately a best-seller.*

*For the rest of his career, Ellison was much in the public eye. In the 1960s and 1970s, he was often represented as an "Uncle Tom," as too enamored of white European culture and values, as too uncommitted to black causes to serve an emerging and militant African American counterculture. He was also criticized for not joining Martin Luther King, Jr.'s opposition to the Vietnam War and for not stepping forward as a spokesman for the civil rights movement.*

*In a famous exchange in the early 1960s, one that captured the attention of readers both inside and outside the academy, literary critic Irving Howe criticized the optimism of* Invisible Man *and accused Ellison (and James Baldwin) of abandoning the harsh truths of American racism portrayed in Richard Wright's* Native Son. *Howe wrote of Ellison's novel,*

> *Nor is one easily persuaded by the hero's discovery that "my world had become one of infinite possibilities," by his refusal to be the "invisible man" whose body is manipulated by various social groups. Though the unqualified assertion of self-liberation was a favorite strategy among American literary people in the fifties, it is also vapid and insubstantial. It violates the reality of social life, the interplay between external conditions and personal will. . . . The unfortunate fact remains that to define one's individuality is to stumble upon social barriers which stand in the way, all too much in the way, of "infinite possibilities."*

*Here is part of Ellison's response to Howe:*

> *Evidently Howe feels that unrelieved suffering is the only "real" Negro experience, and that the true Negro writer must be ferocious.*
>
> *But there is also an American Negro tradition which teaches one to deflect racial provocation and to master and contain pain. It is a tradition which abhors as obscene any trading on one's own anguish for gain or sympathy; which springs not from a desire to deny the harshness of existence but from a will to deal with it as men at their best have always done. It takes fortitude to be a man and no less to be an artist. Perhaps it takes even more if the black man would be an artist. If so, there are no exemptions. It would seem to me, therefore, that the question of how the "sociology of his existence" presses upon a Negro writer's work depends upon how much of his life the individual writer is able to transform into art. What moves a writer to eloquence is less meaningful than what he makes of it. How much, by the way, do we know of Sophocles' wounds?*

> *One unfamiliar with what Howe stands for would get the impression that when he looks at a Negro he sees not a human being but an abstract embodiment of living hell.*

*In his book* Heroism and the Black Intellectual: Ralph Ellison, Politics, and Afro-American Intellectual Life *(1994), Jerry Watts makes the point that Ellison was not arguing against political involvement. Ellison, rather, was arguing that art is a form of political engagement. In his essays, Ellison looks at jazz, at the blues, at novels and poems, at the African American church, and in "An Extravagance of Laughter," at jokes and stories as forms of artistic production.*

*"An Extravagance of Laughter" thus stands as the writer's way of thinking back to a moment in a theater in New York. Since it was written at the end of Ellison's career, it can also be read as a way of thinking back over a lifetime as a public figure, not only living out but standing for key moments in our country's history and its racial politics. In his* Los Angeles Times *review of* Going to the Territory, *David Bradley said,*

> *These essays never fail to be elegantly written, beautifully composed, and intellectually sophisticated. The personality that emerges from the pages is witty, literate, endearingly modest, delightfully puckish. So much so that, while one cannot completely forgive Ellison for not writing that novel we've all been waiting for, one does start to wonder if we have not been waiting for the wrong thing.*

*Ellison himself offers "An Extravagance of Laughter" as an "autobiographical investigation." It ranges wide in its thinking, well beyond the episode in a Broadway theater, and offers a wonderful example of how writing can serve as an instrument of inquiry. As an essay, it moves by indirection; it takes its time; its movements are both surprising and subtle—in fact, the structure might be described in relation to Ellison's passion for jazz. The writer begins by stating a theme, improvises, follows this thread and then that, and then returns to the theme at the end. In his 1986* New York Times *review, John Edgar Wideman says, "What captures the reader . . . are the subtle jazz-like changes Mr. Ellison rings against the steady backbeat of his abiding concerns as an artist and critic." In an essay published in 1945, Ellison offered this definition of the blues: "As a form, the blues is an autobiographical chronicle of personal catastrophe expressed lyrically." And the attraction of the blues, he said,*

> *lies in this, that they at once express both the agony of life and the possibility of conquering it through sheer toughness of spirit. They fall short of tragedy only in that they provide no solution, offer no scapegoat but the self.*

*Ralph Ellison (1914–1994) published three books. The novel,* Invisible Man *(1952), and two collections of essays,* Shadow and Act *(1964) and* Going to the

Territory (1986). *When he died in 1994, he was still at work on his second novel. Ellison taught at Bard College, at the University of Chicago, and in 1970 was named the Albert Schweitzer Professor of the Humanities at New York University, where he taught until his retirement.*

# An Extravagance of Laughter

In December 1983 the good news that Erskine Caldwell had reached his eightieth birthday reminded me that although I have had the pleasure of seeing him on and off for some twenty years, I have never been able to offer him an apology for an offense of which I was guilty back in the 1930s. Perhaps I failed because my offense took the form of laughter—or, to be more precise, of a particular quality and an *extravagance* of laughter; which, since it came at the expense of Caldwell's most famous work of comedy, may explain both my confusion and my reluctance. And since the work in question was *designed* and intended to evoke laughter, any account of why I should term my particular laughter "offensive" will require a bit of autobiographical exploration which may well enable me both to understand my failure to apologize and to clarify the role which that troublesome moment of laughter was to play in my emotional and intellectual development.

Charles Baudelaire observed that "the wise man never laughs but that he trembles." Therefore, for the moment let it suffice to say that being both far from wise and totally unaware of Baudelaire's warning, I not only laughed extravagantly but trembled even *as* I laughed; and thus I found myself utterly unprepared for the Caldwell-inspired wisdom which erupted from that incongruous juxtaposition of mirth and quaking. This is no excuse, however, because Aesop and Uncle Remus have taught us that comedy is a disguised form of philosophical instruction; and especially when it allows us to glimpse the animal instincts operating beneath the surface of our civilized affectations. For by allowing us to laugh at that which is normally *un*laughable, comedy provides an otherwise unavailable clarification of vision that calms that clammy trembling which ensues whenever we pierce the veil of conventions that guard us from the basic absurdity of the human condition. During such moments the world of appearances is turned upside down, and in my case Caldwell's comedy plunged me quite unexpectedly into the deepest levels of a most American realm of the absurd while providing me with the magical wings with which to ascend back to a world which, for all his having knocked it quite out of kilter, I then found more rational. Caldwell had no way of knowing what I was experiencing, but even though I caused unforeseen trouble, he was a wise and skillful guide, and thus it is that I offer him both my apologies and, for reasons to be made clear a bit later, my heartfelt thanks.

It all began in 1936, a few weeks after my arrival in New York, when I was lucky enough to be invited by an old hero and new-found friend, Langston Hughes, to be his guest at what would be my introduction to Broadway theater. I was so delighted and grateful for the invitation that I failed to ask my host the title of the play, and it was not until we arrived at the theater that I learned that it would be Jack Kirkland's dramatization of Erskine Caldwell's famous novel *Tobacco Road*. No less successful than in its original form, the play was well on its way to a record-breaking seven-year run in the theater, and that alone was enough to increase my expectations. And so much so that I failed to note the irony of circumstance that would have as my introduction to New York theater a play with a Southern setting and characters that were based upon a type and class of whites whom I had spent the last three years trying to avoid. Had I been more alert, it might have occurred to me that somehow a group of white Alabama farm folk had learned of my presence in New York, thrown together a theatrical troupe, and flown north to haunt me. But being dazzled by the lights, the theatrical atmosphere, the babble of the playgoing crowd, it didn't. And yet that irony arose precisely from the mixture of motives—practical, educational, and romantic—that had brought me to the North in the first place.

Among these was my desire to enjoy a summer free of the South and its problems while meeting the challenge of being on my own for the first time in a great Northern city. Fresh out of Alabama, with my junior year at Tuskegee Institute behind me, I was also in New York seeking funds with which to complete my final year as a music major—a goal at which I was having less success than I had hoped. However, there had been compensations. For between working in the Harlem YMCA cafeteria as a substitute for vacationing waiters and countermen and searching for a more profitable job, I had used my free time exploring the city's many cultural possibilities, making new acquaintances, and enjoying the many forms of social freedom that were unavailable to me in Alabama. The very idea of being in New York was dreamlike, for like many young Negroes of the time, I thought of it as the freest of American cities and considered Harlem as the site and symbol of Afro-American progress and hope. Indeed, I was both young and bookish enough to think of Manhattan as my substitute for Paris and of Harlem as a place of Left Bank excitement. So now that I was there in its glamorous scene, I meant to make the most of its opportunities.

Yes, but I had discovered, much to my chagrin, that while I was physically out of the South, I was restrained—sometimes consciously, sometimes not—by certain internalized thou-shalt-nots that had structured my public conduct in Alabama. It was as though I had come to the Eden of American culture and found myself indecisive as to which of its fruits were free for my picking. Thus, for all my bright expectations, my explorations had taken on certain aspects of an unanticipated and amorphous rite of initiation in which the celebrant—if indeed one existed—remained mute and beyond my range of ear and vision. Therefore, I found myself forced to act as my own guide and instructor, and had to enact, touch-and-go, the archetypical American role of pioneer in what was our most sophisticated and densely populated city. And in the process I found myself being compelled, as it were, to improvise a makeshift map of the city's racially determined do's-and-don'ts and impose it upon the objective scene by dealing consciously with such complications of character and custom as might materialize in the course of my explorations.

I missed, in brief, a sense of certainty which the South imposed in the forms of signs and symbols that marked the dividing lines of racial segregation. This was an embarrassing discovery, so given what I assumed would be the shortness of my visit, I tried to deal with it and remained quite eager to take the risks necessary to achieve New York's promises. After certain disappointments, however, I had been going about it in the manner of one learning to walk again upon a recently mended leg that still felt strange without the protective restraint of a plaster cast now left happily behind. So there were moments when I reminded myself of the hero of the old Negro folktale who, after arriving mistakenly in heaven and being issued a pair of wings, was surprised to learn that there were certain earthlike restrictions which required people of his complexion to fly with one wing strapped to their sides. But, while surprised, the new arrival came to the philosophical conclusion that even in heaven, that place of unearthly perfection, there had to be rules and regulations. And since rules were usually intended to make one think, no less than to provide guidance, he decided to forgo complaint and get on with the task of mastering the challenge of one-wing flying. As a result, he soon became so proficient at the art that by the time he was cast out of heaven for violating its traffic regulations, he could declare (and so truthfully that not even Saint Peter could say him nay) that he was the most skillful one-winged flyer ever to have been grounded by heavenly decision.

So, following the example of my legendary ancestor, I determined to master my own equivalent of one-winged flying in such a manner as to do the least violence to myself or to such arcane rules of New York's racial arrangements as I might encounter. Which meant that I would have to mask myself and confront its mysteries with a combination of uncertainty and daring. Thus it was that by the time I stumbled onto *Tobacco Road,* I had been nibbling steadily at the "Big Apple"—which even in those days was the Harlemite's fond name for the city—and in the process had discovered more than an ambiguous worm or two. Nevertheless, it should be remembered that worms teach small earthly truths even as serpents teach theology.

Beyond the borders of Harlem's brier patch—which seemed familiar because of my racial and cultural identification with the majority of its people and the lingering spell that had been cast nationwide by the music, dance, and literature of the so-called Harlem Renaissance—I viewed New Yorkers through the overlay of my Alabama experience. Contrasting the whites I encountered with those I had observed in the South, I weighed class against class and compared Southern styles with their Northern counterparts. I listened to diction and noted dress, and searched for attitudes in inflections, carriage, and manners. And in pursuing this aspect of my extracurricular education, I explored the landscape.

I crossed Manhattan back and forth from river to river and up, down, and around again, from Spuyten Duyvil Creek to the Battery, looking and listening and gadding about; rode streetcar and el, subway and bus; took a hint from Edna Millay and spent an evening riding back and forth on the Staten Island Ferry. For given my Oklahoma-Alabama perspective, even New York's forms of transportation were unexpected sources of education. From the elevated trains I saw my first penthouses with green trees growing atop tall buildings, caught remote glimpses of homes, businesses, and factories while moving above the teeming streets, and felt a sense of quiet tranquility despite the bang and clatter. Yes, but the subways were something else again.

In fact, the subways were utterly confusing to my Southern-bred idea of good manners, and especially the absence of a certain gallantry that men were expected to extend toward women. Subway cars appeared to be underground arenas in which Northern social equality took the form of an endless shoving match in which the usual rules of etiquette were turned upside down—or so I concluded after watching a five-o'clock foot race in a crowded car.

The contest was between a huge white woman who carried an armful of bundles, and a small Negro man who lugged a large suitcase. At the time I was standing against the track-side door, and when the train stopped at a downtown station I saw the two come charging through the opening doors like race horses leaving the starting gate at Belmont. And as they spied and dashed for the single empty seat, the outcome appeared up for grabs, but it was the woman, thanks to a bustling, more ruthless stride (and more subway know-how) who won—though but by a hip and a hair. For just as they reached the seat she swung a well-padded hip and knocked the man off stride, thus causing him to lose his balance as she turned, slipped beneath his reeling body, and plopped into the seat. It was a maneuver which produced a startling effect—at least on me.

For as she banged into the seat it caused the man to spin and land smack-dab into her lap—in which massive and heaving center of gravity he froze, stared into her face nose-tip to nose, and then performed a springlike leap to his feet as from a red-hot stove. It was but the briefest conjunction, and then, as he reached down and fumbled for his suitcase, the woman began adjusting her bundles, and with an elegant toss of her head she looked up into his face with the most ladylike and triumphant of smiles.

I had no idea of what to expect next, but to her sign of good sports-womanship the man let out with an exasperated "Hell, you can have it, I don't want it!" A response which evoked a phrase from an old forgotten ditty to which my startled mind added the unstated line—"Sleeping in the bed with your hand right on it"—and shook me with visions of the train screeching to a stop and a race riot beginning . . .

But not at all. For while the defeated man pushed his way to another part of the car the crowd of passengers simply looked on and laughed. The interracial aspects of the incident with its evocation of the naughty lyric left me shaken, but I was learning something of the truth of what Henry James meant by the arduousness of being an American. And that went double for a Tuskegee student who was trying to adjust to the New York under-ground. I never knew what to expect, because there appeared to be no agreed-upon rules of conduct. Indeed, in the subways the operating slogan appeared to be "Every Man and Woman for Themselves." Or perhaps it was "Hurray for Me and Phoo-phoo on You!" But *whatever* its operating principle, whenever I rode the subway trains something I had never seen before seemed fated to happen.

As during a trip in another crowded car when I found myself standing beside a Negro man who stood just in front of a seat that was about to be vacated—when suddenly from on his other side a woman decided to chal-lenge him for its possession. This time, however, it was the man who won. For in a flash the man folded his arms, dropped into the posture of a Cos-sack dancer, and was in the seat before the woman could make her move. Then, as she grabbed a handhold and glared down into his face, he re-stored something of my sense of reality by saying, "Madam, all you had to do was risk the slight possibility that I just *might* be a gentleman. Because if you had, I would have been *compelled* to step aside."

And then, opening a copy of *The Wall Street Journal*, he proceeded to read.

But for all their noise and tension, it was not the subways that most in-trigued me. For although a pleasant way to explore the city, my rides in New York buses soon aroused questions about matters that I had hoped to leave behind. And yet the very fact that I encountered little on Northern buses that was distressing allowed me to face up to a problem which had puzzled me down South: the relationship between Southern buses and racial status. In the South you occupied the back of the bus, and nowhere *but* the back, or so help you God. So being in the North and encouraged by my anonymity, I experimented by riding all *over* New York buses, exclud-ing only the driver's seat—front end, back end, right side, left side, sitting or standing as the route and flow of passengers demanded. *And,* since those were the glorious days of double-deckers, both enclosed and open, I even rode *top* side.

Thus having convinced myself that no questions of racial status would be raised by where I chose to ride, I asked myself whether a seat at the back of the bus wasn't actually more desirable than one at the front. For not only did it provide more leg room, it offered a more inclusive perspective on both the interior and exterior scenes. I found the answer obvious and quite amusing, but then, as though to raise to consciousness more serious questions that I had too long ignored, the buses forced a more troubling contradiction upon my attention. Now that I was no longer forced by law and compelled by custom to ride at the back and to surrender my seat to any white who demanded it, what was more desirable—the possibility of exercising what was routinely accepted in the North as an abstract, highly symbolic (even trivial) form of democratic freedom, or the creature comfort which was to be had by occupying a spot from which more of the passing scene could be observed? And in my own personal terms, what was more important—my own individual comfort, or the exercise of the democratic right to be squeezed and jostled by strangers? The highly questionable privilege of being touched by anonymous whites—not to mention reds, browns, blacks, and yellows—or the minor pleasure afforded by having a maximum of breathing space? Such questions were akin to that of whether you lived in a Negro neighborhood because you were forced to do so, or because you preferred living among those of your own background. Which was easy to answer, because having experienced life in mixed neighborhoods as a child, I preferred to live where people spoke my own version of the American language, and where misreadings of tone or gesture were less likely to ignite lethal conflict. Segregation laws aside, this was a matter of personal choice, for even though class and cultural differences existed among Negroes, it was far easier to deal with hostilities arising between yourself and your own people than with, say, Jeeter Lester or, more realistically, Lester Maddox. And that even though I would have found it far better to be Lestered by Jeeter than mattock-handled by Maddox, that most improbable governor of a state that I had often visited!

But my interrogation by the New York scene (for that is what it had become) was not to stop there, for once my mind got rolling on buses, it was difficult to stop and get off. So I became preoccupied with defining the difference between Northern and Southern buses. Of the two, New York buses were simpler, if only for being earthbound. They were merely a form of transportation, an inflated version of a taxicab or passenger car which one took to get from one locality to another. And as far as one's destination and motives were concerned they were neutral. But this was far from true of Southern buses. For when compared with its New York counterparts, even the most dilapidated of Southern buses seemed (from my New York perspective) to be a haunted form of transportation.

A Southern bus was a contraption contrived by laying the South's social pyramid on its side, knocking out a few strategic holes, and rendering it vehicular through the addition of engine, windows, and wheels. Thus converted, with the sharp apex of the pyramid blunted and equipped with fare box and steering gear, and its sprawling base curtailed severely and narrowly aligned (and arrayed with jim-crow signs), a ride in such a vehicle became, at least for Negroes, as unpredictable as a trip in a spaceship doomed to be caught in the time warp of history—that man-made "fourth dimension" which ever confounds our American grasp of "real," or *actual,* time or duration.

For blacks and whites alike, Southern buses were places of hallucination, but especially for Negroes. Because once inside, their journey ended even before the engine fired and the wheels got rolling. Then, as with a "painted ship upon a painted ocean," the engine chugged, the tires scuffed, and the scenery outside flashed and flickered, but they themselves remained, like Zeno's arrow, ever in the same old place. Thus the motorized mobility of the social pyramid did little to advance the Negroes' effort toward equality. Because although they were allowed to enter the section that had been—in its vertical configuration—its top, any semblance of upward mobility ended at the fare box—from whence, once their fares were deposited, they were sent, forthwith, straight to the rear, or horizontalized bottom. And along the way almost *anything* could happen, from push to shove, assaults on hats, heads, or aching corns, to unprovoked tongue-lashings from the driver or from any white passenger, drunk or sober, who took exception to their looks, attitude, or mere existence. Nor did the perils of this haunted, gauntletlike passage end at the back of the bus. For often it was so crowded that there was little breathing space, and since the segregated passengers were culturally as "Southern" as the whites, the newcomer might well encounter a few contentious Negroes who would join in the assault—if only because he appeared uneasy in his command of the life-preserving "cool" which protected not only the individual Negro but each member of the group in his defenseless, nonindividualized status. In brief, all were faceless nobodies caught up in an endless trip to nowhere—or so it seemed to me in my Northern sanctuary.

For even as the phantomized bus went lurching and fuming along its treadmill of a trajectory, the struggle within scuffled and raged in fitful retrograde. Thus, as it moved without moving, those trapped inside played out their roles like figures in dreams—with one group ever forcing the other to the backmost part, and the other ever watching and waiting as they bowed to force and clung to sanity. And indeed the time would come when such bus en-scened pantomime would erupt in a sound and fury of action that would engulf the South and change American society. And most surprising and yet most fittingly, it would begin when a single tired Negro woman refused to go on with what had now become an unbearable farce. Then would come fire and gunshot, cattle prods and attack dogs, but the enchantment would end, and at last the haunted bus would shift gears and move on to the road of reality and toward the future. . . .

But of this I had no way of knowing at the time. I only knew that

Southern bus rides had the power to haunt and confuse my New York passage. Moreover, they were raising the even more troublesome question of to what extent had I failed to grasp a certain degree of freedom that had always existed in my group's state of unfreedom? Of what had I neglected to avail myself through fear or lack of interest while sitting silently behind jim-crow signs? For after all, a broad freedom of expression within restrictions could be heard in jazz and seen in sports, and that freedom was made movingly manifest in religious worship. There was an Afro-American dimension in Southern culture, and the lives of many black Southerners possessed a certain verve and self-possessed fullness— so to what extent had I overlooked similar opportunities for self-discovery while accepting a definition of possibility laid down by those who would deny me freedom?

Thus, while I enjoyed my summer, such New York-provoked questions made for a certain unease which I tried to ignore. Nevertheless, they made me aware that whatever its true shape turned out to be, Northern freedom could be grasped only by my running the risk of the unknown and by acting in the face of uncertainty. Which meant that I would have to keep moving into racially uncharted areas. Otherwise I would remain physically in Harlem and psychologically in Alabama—neither of which was acceptable. Harlem was "Harlem," a dream place of glamour and excitement—what with its music, its dance, its style. But it was all of this because it was a part of (and apart *from*) the larger city. Harlem, I came to feel, was the shining transcendence of a national negative, and it took its fullest meaning from that which it was not, and without which I would have regarded it as less interesting than, say, Kansas City, Missouri—or South Side Chicago. Harlem, whose ironic inhabitants described it a thousand times a day as being "nowhere," took much of its meaning from the larger metropolis; so I could only achieve the fullest measure of its attractions by experiencing that which it was not. Which meant, in the broadest sense, that I would have to use Harlem as a base and standard of measurement from which to pursue, in all its plenitude, that which was denied me in the South. In brief, if I were to grasp American freedom, I was compelled to continue my explorations of downtown Manhattan.

Yes, but as I say, my explorations of the city were rendered uncertain by the ongoing conflict between the past and the present as they existed within me: between the dream in my head and the murky, seek-and-find-it shiftings of the New York scene; between the confounding complexity of America's racial arrangements as they coincided and differed according to the customs, laws, and values fostered by both North and South. I still clung to the Southern Negro's conception of New York as the freest of American cities, but although now far removed from the geographical region where old-time things are defiantly not forgotten, I was learning that even here, where memories of the past were deliberately repressed, if not forgotten, the past itself continued to shape perceptions and attitudes.

And it appeared that for some New Yorkers, I *myself* constituted a living symbol of that complexity of American experience which they had never known, and a disquieting reminder of their involvement in certain unsavory aspects of America's social reality that they preferred to ignore.

And yet, given my persistent questing, how could they? For I, who was an unwilling and not always conscious embodiment of that historical complexity, and a symbol of the Civil War's sacrificial bloodshed, kept showing up in areas of culture where few of my people were to be seen. Thus, in my dark singularity I often appeared to be perceived more as a symbol than as an individual, more as a threatening sign (a dark cloud no larger than a human hand, but somehow threatening) than as a disinterested seeker after culture. This made for problems because I had no way of anticipating the response to my presence.

Prior to stumbling onto *Tobacco Road*—at which I shall presently arrive—I had already encountered some of the complexity evoked by my probings. As the guest of a white female friend who reported musical events for a magazine, I had occupied a seat in the orchestra section of Carnegie Hall without inciting protest. But shortly thereafter I had been denied admission to a West Side cinema house that featured European movies. Then I had learned that while one midtown restaurant would make you welcome, in another (located in Greenwich Village, Harlem's twin symbol of Manhattan's freedom), the waiters would go through the polite motions of seating you but then fill your food with salt. And to make certain that you got the message, they would enact a rite of exorcism in which the glasses and crockery, now considered hopelessly contaminated by your touch, were enfolded in the tablecloth and smithereened in the fireplace.

Or again, upon arriving at a Central Park West apartment building to deliver a music manuscript for the Tuskegee composer William L. Dawson, you encountered a doorman with a European accent who was so rude that you were tempted to break his nose. Fortunately, you didn't, for after you refused to use the servant's elevator he rang up the tenant into whose hands alone you were instructed to make the delivery, Jacques Gordon of the Gordon String Quartet, who hurried down and invited you up to his apartment. Where, to your surprise and delight, he talked with you without condescension about his recordings, questioned you sympathetically about your musical background, and encouraged you in your ambitions to become a composer. So if you weren't always welcome to break bread in public places, an interest in the arts *could* break down social distance and allow for communication that was uninhibited by questions of race— or so it seemed.

As on a Madison Avenue bus when an enthusiastic, bright-eyed little old Jewish lady, fresh from an art exhibition with color catalogue in hand, would engage you in conversation and describe knowingly the styles and intentions of French painters of whom you'd never heard.

"Then you must go to galleries," she insisted.

"Stir yourself and go to museums," she demanded.

"This is one of the world's great centers of art, so learn about them! Why are you waiting? Enough already!" she exhorted.

And eventually, God bless her, I did.

But then, on another bus ride, a beautifully groomed and expensively dressed woman would become offended when you retrieved and attempted to return the section of a newspaper that she had dropped when preparing to depart, apparently mistaking what was intended as an act of politeness for a reprimand from a social inferior. So it appeared that in New York one had to choose the time, place, and person even when exercising one's Southern good manners.

On the other hand, it soon became clear that one could learn the subtleties of New York's racial manners only by being vulnerable and undiscriminating oneself; an attitude which the vast anonymity of the great metropolis encouraged. Here the claustrophobic provincialism which marked, say, Montgomery, Alabama, of that period, was absent, but one had to be on guard because reminders of the South could spring up from behind the most unlikely of façades.

Shopping for a work of T. S. Eliot's in a 59th Street bookstore, I struck up a conversation with a young City College student who turned out to share my literary interests, and in recounting an incident of minor embarrassment having to do with my misinterpretation of a poetic trope, I used the old cliché "And was my face red"—whereupon, between the utterance and the reality, the idea I intended to convey and my stereotype phrase, there fell the shadow of things I sought to forget.

"What do you mean by 'red,'" he said, impaling me upon the points of his smirking stare, "what you *really* mean is 'ashes of roses'!"

And suddenly I was slapped into a conscious awareness of certain details of his presence that my eyes had registered but to which, in the context of our exchange, my brain had attached no special significance. Intent upon sharing his ideas of Eliot, I had seen only that which I wished to see, but now, out of the eyes of my past I saw that our differences of background and religion were imprinted upon his face no less indelibly than mine upon my own. And in my Southern-trained ear the echo of his trace of accent became amplified, the slight kink in his hair sprang into focus, and his nose evoked superimposed images of the Holy Land and Cyrano.

I didn't like it, but there it was—I had been hit in midflight; and so, brought down to earth, I joined in his laughter. But while he laughed in bright major chords I responded darkly in minor-sevenths and flatted-fifths, and I doubted that he was attuned to the deeper source of our inharmonic harmony. For how could he know that when a child in Oklahoma, I had played with members of his far-flung tribe and thus learned in friendly games of mutual insult the hoary formulae with which to make him squirm. But why bother? Out of some obscure need a stranger had chosen to define to his own advantage that which was at best a fleeting relationship. Perhaps because I had left an opening that was irresistible. Or perhaps he saw my interest in poetry as an invasion of his special turf, which had to be repelled with a reminder of my racial status. For what right had *I* to be interested in Eliot, even though the great poet had written of himself as having been "a small boy with a nigger drawl"?

Or was he implying that I was trying verbally to pass for white? But if so, wasn't that to confuse words with reality and a metaphor with the thing or condition it named? And didn't he realize that there might be as much of irony in one of his background embracing Eliot as he seemed to find in my doing so? And how take poetry seriously if he himself would limit the range of metaphor, that indispensable linguistic device for making unities of diversities?

That chance encounter left me a bit disenchanted, but also consciously aware of certain vague assumptions which I held concerning racial relations that I'd find in the North. I had hoped that in New York there would exist generally a type of understanding which obtained in the South between certain individual whites and Negroes. This was a type of Southern honor that did little to alter the general system of inequity, but it allowed individual whites to make exceptions in exerting the usual gestures of white supremacy. Such individuals refused to use racial epithets and tried, within the limitations of the system, to treat Negroes fairly. This was a saving grace and a balm to the aches and pains of the South's endless racial contention.

Thus I had assumed that in the North there would exist a general understanding between outsiders of whatever color or background, and that all would observe a truce or convention through which they would shun insults that focused on race, religion, or physical appearance; entities that were inherited and about which all were powerless to modify or change. (At that time I was unaware that there were whites who passed themselves off as being of other backgrounds.) And yet I realized that except for those rare Southern examples, there was no firm base for my expectations. For I knew that from the days of the minstrel shows to the musicals and movies then current, many non-Negro outsiders had reaped fame and fortune by assuming the stereotyped mask of blackness. I knew also that our forms of popular culture, from movies to comic strips, were a source of a national mythology in which Negroes were the chief scapegoats, and that the function of that mythology was to allow whites a more secure place (if only symbolically) in American society. Only years later would I learn that during periods of intense social unrest, even sensitive intellectuals who had themselves been victims of discrimination would find it irresistible to use their well-deserved elevation to the upper levels of their professions as platforms from which, in the name of the most abstract—and fashionable—of philosophical ideas, to reduce Negroes to stereotypes that were no less reductive and demeaning than those employed by the most ignorant and bigoted of white Southerners. Fortunately, that knowledge was still in the future, and so, doing unto another as I would have had him do unto me, I dismissed my chance acquaintance as an insecure individual, and not the representative of a group or general attitude. But he did serve as a warning that if I wished to communicate with New Yorkers, I must watch my metaphors, for here one man's cliché was another man's facile opportunity for victimage.

So I was learning that exploring New York was a journey without a map, Baedeker or Henry James, and that how one was received by the natives depended more upon how one presented oneself than upon any iron-clad rule of exclusion. Here the portals to many places of interest were guarded by hired help, and if you approached with uncertain mien, you were likely to be turned away by anyone from doormen to waiters to ticket agents. However, if you acted as though you were in fact a New Yorker exercising a routine freedom, chances were that you'd be accepted. Which is to say that in many instances I found that my air and attitude could offset the inescapable fact of my color. For it seemed that in the hustle and bustle of the most theatrical of American cities, one was accepted on the basis of what one *appeared* to be. This involved risks to one's self-esteem, not to mention the discipline demanded by a constant state of wariness.

But W. B. Yeats had reminded us that "there is a relation between personal discipline and the theatrical sense [and that] if we cannot imagine ourselves as different from what we are and assume the second self, we cannot impose a discipline upon ourselves, though we may accept one from others." And he advised us that "active virtue, as distinct from the passive acceptance of a current code, is the wearing of a mask."

At the time I was unaware of Yeats's observation, but if I had been so fortunate, I would have applied it to my own situation by changing his "we" to "an Afro-American," his "what we are" to "what many whites assume an American Negro to be," and his "current code" to "prevailing racial attitudes." But with his contention that the assertion of a second self is to assume a mask, and that to do so is "the condition of an arduous full life," I would have agreed wholeheartedly. For in effect, I was attempting to act out a self-elected role and to improvise into being a "second self" that I strongly felt but vaguely visualized. And although I was finding life far from full, I was certainly finding it arduous.

For in Yeats's sense, "masking" is more than the adoption of a disguise. Rather, it is a playing upon possibility, a strategy through which the individual projects a self-elected identity and makes of himself a "work of art." And in my case it was a means of discovering the dimensions and cost of Northern freedom. In his critical biography *Yeats: The Man & the Masks*, Richard Ellman notes that the great Irish poet was writing of himself, but his theory applies, nevertheless, to the problematic nature of American identity. For while all human societies are "dramatic"—at least to the extent that, as Kenneth Burke points out, the members of all societies "enact roles . . . change roles . . . participate . . . [and] develop modes of social appeal"—the semi-open structure of American society, with its many opportunities for individual self-transformation, intensifies the dramatic element by increasing the possibilities for both cooperation and conflict. It is a swiftly changing society in which traditional values are ever under attack, even as they are exploited by individuals and group alike. And with its up-ward—yes, and *downward*—mobility and its great geographical space, masking (which includes speech, and costume as well as pose and posture) serves the individual as a means for projecting that aspect of his social self which seems useful in a given situation.

Such a state of affairs encourages hope and confidence in those who are not assigned and restricted to predesignated roles in the hierarchal drama of American society. Melville has great fun with the comic aspects of this situation in *The Confidence Man.* To an extent, and for an endless variety of motives—benign or malignant, competitive or cooperative, creative and/or destructive—the "American" is a self-confident man or woman who is engaged in projecting a second self and dealing with the second selves of others. The American creed of democratic equality en-courages the belief in a second chance that is to be achieved by being born again—and not simply in the afterlife, but here and now, on earth. Change your name and increase your chances. Create by an act of immaculate self-conception an autobiography like that which transformed James Gatz into "Jay Gatsby." Alter the shape of your nose, tint of skin, or texture of hair. Change your sexual identity by dress or by surgery. "Get thee to boutique and barbershop and *Unisex* thyself," the ads exhort us—for anything is possible in pursuit of the second self. It sounds fantastic, but the second self's hope for a second chance has now been extended even beyond the limits of physical death, thanks to the ability of medical science to trans-plant hearts, lungs, and kidneys. Are you dissatisfied with your inherited self? Your social status? Then have a change of heart and associate with those of a different kidney!

> College boy, thy courage muster,
> Shave off that Fuzzy
> Cookie duster—
> Use Burma Shave!

So, to enjoy the wonders of New York, I assumed a mask which I con-ceived as that of a "New Yorker," and decided to leave it to those whites who might object to seek out the questioning Tuskegeian who was hidden behind the mask. But a famous poet had invited me to see *Tobacco Road*, and suddenly, there in the darkness of a Broadway theater, I was snatched back to rural Alabama, and before I realized what was happening, I had blown my cover.

Nor was it that the likes of Jeeter Lester and his family were new to me. As a Tuskegee student I had often seen them in Macon County, Al-abama; but in that setting their capacity for racial violence would have been far more overwhelming than their comical wrong-headedness. In-deed, in look, gesture, and deed they had crowded me so continuously that I had been tempted to armor myself against their threat by denying them *their* humanity as they sought to deny me mine. And so in my mind I assigned them to a limbo beneath the threshold of basic humanity.

Which was one of the Southern Negroes' strategies for dealing with poor whites, and an attitude given expression in the child's jingle:

> My name is Ran,
> I work in the sand, but
> I'd rather be a *nigger*
> Than a poor white man . . .

But while such boasting brags—and there were others (*These white folks think they so fine/But their raggedy drawers/Stink just like mine* is another)—provided a release of steam, they were not only childish but ultimately frustrating. For if such sentiments were addressed directly, their intended targets could prove dangerous. Thus the necessity for keeping one's negative opinions of whites within one's own group became a life-preserving discipline. One countered racial provocation by cloaking one's feelings in that psychologically inadequate equivalent of a plaster cast—or bullet-proof vest—known as "cool." I had read Hemingway's definition, but for Negroes, "grace under pressure" was far less a gauge of courage than of good common sense. The provocative words of whites were intended to goad one *beyond* words and into the area of physical violence. But while sticks and stones broke bones, mere words could be dismissed by considering their source and keeping a cool eye on the odds arrayed against one. So when racial epithets flew, we reminded ourselves that our mission was not that of proving our courage to any mouthy white who sought to provoke us, but to stay alive and pursue our education. Coolness helped to keep our values warm, and racial hostility stoked our fires of inspiration. But even for students protected by a famous campus, this was an arduous discipline, and one which obviated any superstitious overevaluation of whiteness. Nevertheless, I tried, as I say, to avoid the class of whites from which Erskine Caldwell drew the characters of *Tobacco Road*.

For during the summer of 1933, while hoboing to Tuskegee, I had been hustled off a freight train by railroad detectives in the rail yards of Decatur, Alabama. This was at a time when the town and the surrounding countrysides were undergoing a siege of lynch-fever stirred up by the famous trial in which the Scottsboro boys were charged with the rape of two white girls on a freight train. I escaped unharmed, but the incident returned to mind whenever I went traveling. Therefore, I gave Jeeter Lester types a wide berth but found it impossible to avoid them entirely—because many were law-enforcement officers who served on the highway patrols with a violent zeal like that which Negro slave narratives ascribed to the "paterollers" who had guarded the roads during slavery. (As I say, Southern buses were haunted, and so, in a sense, were Southern roads and highways.) And that was especially true of a section of the route between Tuskegee and Columbus, Georgia. I traveled it frequently, both as a member of a jazz orchestra and when on pleasure trips to Columbus. And it was on such travels that I was apt to relive my Decatur experience.

By a fateful circumstance of geography the forty-mile route passed through Phenix City, Alabama, then a brawling speed-trap of a town through which it was impossible to drive either slow enough or fast enough to satisfy the demands of its traffic policemen. No one, black or white, escaped their scrutiny, but since Tuskegee students were regarded as on their way to becoming "uppity educated nigras," we were especially vulnerable. The police lay in wait for us, clocked our speed by a standard known only to themselves, and used any excuse to delay and harass us. Usually they limited themselves to fines and verbal abuse, but I was told that the year before I arrived the police had committed an act that had caused great indignation on campus and become the inspiration of much bull-session yarn-spinning.

On that occasion, I was told, two Phenix City policemen had stopped a carload of Tuskegee students and learned during the course of routine questioning that one of the group, a very black-skinned young man, bore the surname of "Whyte"—and then, as one of my informants said, "It was shame on him!"

For when Whyte uttered his name the cops stared, exchanged looks of mock disbelief, and became red-faced with manic inspiration.

"Damn, boy," one of them said, "y'all been drinking?"

"No, sir," Whyte said.

"Well now, I don't know about that," the cop said, "'cause you sho sound drunk to *me.*"

"No, sir," Whyte said. "Because I don't drink."

"You sho?"

"Yes, sir!"

So then the cop turns to his buddy and says, "What you think, Lonzo? Is he drunk, or am I mistaken?"

"Well now, if you want my opinion," the other cop said, "he's either drunk or something very serious is wrong with him. Yes, suh, something *seerious* is wrong with this boy."

"And why is that, Lonzo," the first cop said.

"'Cause it stands to reason that there's no way in the *world* for a nigra as black as that to pretend that his name is 'White.' Not unless he's blind-staggers drunk or else plum out of his nappy-headed cotton-pickin' mind!"

"That's *my* exact opinion," the first cop said. "But anyway, lets us give 'im another chance. So now once agin, boy—what is your last name?"

"Officer, it's Whyte," Whyte said. "That's the truth and I'll swear to it."

So that's when the other cop, ol' Lonzo, *he* takes over. He frowns at Whyte and shakes his head like he's dealing with a *very* sad case. And naturally, he's a big potbellied mother who chews Brown Mule tobacco.

"Damn, boy," he says (in what proved to be a long-range prediction of

then unimaginable things to come), "if we let you git away with a damn
lie like that, next thing we know that ol' Ramblin' Wreck over at Georgia
Tech'll have a goddamn nigra *engineer!* Now, you think about that and
let's have that name agin!"

"But, Officer," Whyte said, "Whyte's the only last name I have."

And then, gentlemen, my informant, a sergeant in the ROTC and student of veterinary medicine, said, "the battle was *on!*" He then described
how with simulated indignation the policemen forced Whyte to pronounce his name again and again while insisting that they simply couldn't
believe that such a gross misnaming was possible—especially in the
South—and gave a detailed account of the policemen's reactions.

"Man," he said, "they went after Whyte like he had insulted their
mammas! And when he still wouldn't deny his name, they came down on
him like he was responsible for all the fuckup [meaning the genetic un-
tidiness and confusion of black and white nomenclature] of Southern
history!"

"So, then, man," another informant broke in, "those crackers got so
damn disgusted with ol' Whyte that every time he said his name, the ignorant bastards tried to dot where they thought an 'i' should have been by
pounding his head with their blackjacks. They did everything but shoot
that cat!"

"That's right, cousin," someone else said, "they made him whisper his
name and they made him shout it. They made him write it down on a pad
and then they made him spell it out—and I mean out *loud!* And when he
spelled it with a 'y' instead of an 'i' they swore he was lying and trying to
be smart, and really went up side his head!"

"Yeah, man," my original informant said, "and when Whyte still
wouldn't change his statement, they made him give the names of his
mother and father, his granddaddys and grandmammas on both sides
and their origins in slavery, present whereabouts, police records, and occupations—"

"That's right, cousin, and since ol' Whyte came from a very, *very* large
family and the cops were putting all that pressure on him, the poor cat
sounded like a country preacher scatting out the 'begats' from the Book of
Genesis—Damn!"

And then it was back to Whyte's offensive surname, and the head-
whipping sounded, in the words of another informant—a music major
and notorious prevaricator—"like somebody beating out the *Anvil Chorus*
on a coconut!"

"Yeah, cousin, but what really made the bastards mad was that ol'
Whyte wouldn't let some crackers beat him out of his name!"

"Oh, yes, and you have to give it to him. That Whyte was a damn
good man!"

Finally, tired of the hazing and defeated in their effort to make Whyte
deny his heritage, the cops knocked him senseless and ordered his friends
to place him in the car and get out of town. . . .

Although obviously exaggerated in the telling, it was a nasty incident. However, my point is not its violence, but the contradiction between its ineffectiveness as intimidation while serving as a theme for a tall-tale improvisation. Thus was violence transcended with cruel but homeopathic laughter, and racial cruelty transformed by a traditional form of folk art. It did nothing to change the Phenix City police, and probably wouldn't have even if they heard the recitation. They continued to make life so uncertain that each time we reached Columbus and returned safely to Tuskegee, it was as though we'd passed through fire and emerged, like the mythical phoenix bird (after which, presumably, the town was named), from the flames. Still we continued to risk the danger, for such was our eagerness for the social life of Columbus—the pleasure of parties, dances, and picnics in the company of pretty girls—that we continued to run the gauntlet.

But it didn't cancel out the unpleasantness or humiliation. Thus, back on campus we were compelled to buffer the pain and negate the humiliation by making grotesque comedy out of the extremes to which whites would go to keep us in what they considered to be our "place." Once safe at Tuskegee, we'd become fairly hysterical as we recounted our adventures and laughed as much at ourselves as at the cops. We mocked their modes of speech and styles of intimidation, and teased one another as we parodied our various modes of feigning fear when telling them who we were and where we were headed. It was a wild, he-man, schoolboy silliness but the only way we knew for dealing with the inescapable conjunction of laughter and pain. My problem was that I couldn't completely dismiss such experiences with laughter. I brooded and tried to make sense of it beyond that provided by our ancestral wisdom. That a head with a few knots on it was preferable to a heart with bullets through it was obviously true. And if the philosopher's observation that absolute power corrupts absolutely was also true, then an absolute power based on mere whiteness made for a deification of madness. Depending on the circumstance, whiteness might well be a sign of evil, of a "motiveless malignancy" which was to be avoided as strange dogs in rabid weather.

But you were surrounded by whiteness, and it was far from secure in its power. It thrived on violence and sought endlessly for victims, and in its hunger to enforce racial discrimination, it was most indiscriminating as to its victims. It didn't care whether its victims were guilty or innocent, for guilt lay not in individual acts of wrong-doing but in non-whiteness, in Negroness. Whiteness was a form of manifest destiny which designated Negroes as its territory and challenge. Whiteness struck at signs, at coloration, hair texture, and speech idiom, and thus denied you individuality. How then avoid it, when history and geography brought it ever in juxtaposition with blackness? How escape it when it asserted itself in law, in the layout of towns, the inflections of voices, the nuances of manners, the quality of mercy, justice, and charity? When it raged at interracial sex, but then violated its own values in the manner of Senator Bilbo (the name means "shackle"), who was said to find sexual satisfaction only with

Negro prostitutes? How escape it when it violated its own most sacred principles, both in spirit and in law, while converting the principles of democracy by which we sought to live into their opposites?

Considered soberly and without the consolation of laughter, it was mad, surreal, and further complicated by the fact that not all whites abhorred Negroes. The evil expressed itself most virulently in the mass and appeared to be regional, a condition of place, of climate, since most whites who supported the school were Northerners who appeared for a few days in spring and then departed. And since not even all white Southerners were hostile, you had ever to make fine distinctions between individuals just as you had to distinguish between the scenes and circumstances in which you encountered them. Your safety demanded a careful attention as to detail and mood of social scene, because you had to avoid even friendly whites when they were in the company of their fellows. Because it was in crowds that the hate, fear, and blood-madness took over. And when it did it could transform otherwise friendly whites into mindless members of mobs. Most of all, you must avoid them when women of their group were present. For when a Negro male came into view, the homeliest white woman became a goddess, a cult figure deified in the mystique of whiteness, a being from whom a shout or cry or expression of hand or eye could unleash a rage for human sacrifice. And when the ignorant, torch-bearing armies assembled by night, black men burned in the fire of white men's passions.

If all of this seems long ago and far away, it is worth remembering that the past, as William Faulkner warned, is never past. Nor are its social and political consequences guaranteed to be limited to a single geographical area. The past emerges no less in the themes and techniques of art than in the contentions of politics, and since art (and especially the art of the Depression period) is apt to be influenced by politics, it is necessary at this point to take a backward glance at my Tuskegee student's perception, admittedly immature and subjective, of Southern society as it influenced my reaction to *Tobacco Road*.

In the South of that day the bottom rung of the social ladder was reserved for that class of whites who were looked down upon as "poor white trash," and the area immediately beneath them and below the threshold of upward social mobility was assigned to Negroes, whether educated or ignorant, prosperous or poor. But although they were barely below the poor whites in economic status (and were sometimes better off), it was the Negroes who were designated the South's untouchable caste. As such they were perceived as barely controllable creatures of untamed instincts and a group against whom all whites were obligated to join in the effort required for keeping them within their assigned place. This mindless but widely held perception was given doctrinal credibility through oppressive laws and an endless rhetorical reiteration of anti-Negro stereotypes. Negroes were seen as ignorant, cowardly, thieving, lying, hypocritical and superstitious in their religious beliefs and practices, morally loose, drunken, filthy of personal habit, sexually animalistic, rude, crude, and disgusting in their public conduct, and aesthetically just plain unpleasant. And if a few were not, it was due to the presence of "white" blood, a violation of the Southern racial code which rendered mixed-bloods especially dangerous and repugnant.

In brief, Negroes were considered guilty of all the seven deadly sins except the sin of pride, and were seen as a sometimes comic but nevertheless threatening negative to the whites' idealized image of themselves. Most Negroes were characterized—in the jargon of sociology—by a "high visibility" of pigmentation which made the group easily distinguishable from other citizens and therefore easy to keep in line and politically powerless. That powerlessness was justified and reinforced by the stereotypes, which denied blacks individuality and allowed any Negro to be interchangeable with any other. Thus, as far as many whites were concerned, not only were blacks faceless, but that facelessness made the idea of mistaken identity meaningless, and the democratic assumption that Negro citizens should share the individual's recognized responsibility for the welfare of society was regarded as subversive.

In this denial of personality (sponsored by both law and custom) anti-Negro stereotypes served as an efficient and easily manipulated instrument of governance. Moreover, they prepared Negroes for the role of sacrificial scapegoat in the ritual drama of Southern society, and helped bind the poor whites to the middle and upper classes with whom they shared ethnic identity. Being uncomfortably close to the Negroes in economic status, the poor whites clung to the stereotypes as to a life raft in turbulent waters, and politicians were able to use their fear and antipathy toward blacks as a sure-fire source of power. Because not only were the stability of social order and the health of business seen as depending upon white dominance, but the sanctity of the *moral* order as well. For whether denied or admitted, in this area religion was in the service of politics.

Thus, by pitting the interests of the poor whites against those of the Negroes, Southern congressmen countered the South's Civil War defeat by using its carefully nurtured racial conflict as a means for amassing great political power in Washington. Being representatives of what were, in effect, one-party states, enabled them to advance to the chairmanship of powerful governmental committees, and through the political horse-trading which keeps the national government functioning, that power was used to foil the progress of Negroes in areas far from the geopolitical center of white supremacy. Here, however, it should be noted that Negroes owe much of their progress since the Second World War to presidents who were of Southern background and heritage. People change, but as Faulkner has pointed out, "was" is never "was," it is "now," and in the South a concern with preserving the "wasness" of slavocracy was an obsession which found facile expression in word and in deed. Their memories of the War Between the States, of Reconstruction, and the difficult times that followed the Hayes-Tilden Compromise had long been mythologized both as a means for keeping Negroes powerless and for ensuring the loyalty of poor whites in keeping them so. Thus it is ironic that even though the condition of blacks became a national standard by which many whites, both North and South, measured their social advancement, Negroes themselves remained at the bottom of society and the most anti-Negro of whites remained with them. It was Booker T. Washington who had warned that it is impossible to keep another man in a ditch without remaining with him, but unfortunately, that advice came from a powerful Southern leader who was also an ex-slave.

More and more, through depression and war, America lived up to its claim of being the land of opportunity whose rewards were available to the individual through the assertion of a second self; but for many poor and unambitious Southern whites the challenge of such an assertion was far less inviting than clinging to the conviction that they by the mere fact of race, color, and tradition alone were superior to the black masses below them. And yet, in their own way, they were proud idealists to whom the South's racial arrangement was sacred beyond most benefits made possible by social change. Therefore, they continued to wrestle with the stereotype of Negro inferiority much as Brer Rabbit kept clinging to Tar Baby's stickiness. And they were so eager to maintain their grip on the status quo and to ignore its costs and contradictions that they willingly used anything, including physical violence, to do so. For in rationalizing their condition, they required victims, real or symbolic, and in the daily rituals which gave support to their cherished myth of white supremacy, anti-Negro stereotypes and epithets served as symbolic substitutes for that primitive blood-rite of human sacrifice to which they resorted in times of racial tension—but which, for a complexity of reasons, political, economic, and humane, were rejected by their more responsible leaders. So it was fortunate, both for Afro-Americans and for the nation as a whole, that the Southern rituals of race were usually confined to the realm of the symbolic. Anti-Negro stereotypes were the currency through which the myth of white supremacy was kept alive, while the awe-inspiring enactment of the myth took the form of a rite in which a human victim was sacrificed. It then became a ritual drama that was usually enacted in a preselected scene (such as a clearing in the woods or in the courthouse square) in an atmosphere of high excitement and led by a masked celebrant dressed in a garish costume who manipulated the numinous objects (lynch ropes, the American flag, shotgun, gasoline, and whiskey jugs) associated with the rite as he inspired and instructed the actors in their gory task. This was the anthropological meaning of lynching, a blood-rite that ended in the death of a scapegoat whose obliteration was seen as necessary to the restoration of social order. Thus it served to affirm white goals and was enacted to terrorize Negroes.

Normally, the individual dies his own death, but because lynch mobs are driven by a passionate need to destroy the distinction between the actual and the symbolic, its victim is forced to undergo death for all his group. Nor is he sacrificed to ensure its fertility or save its soul, but to fill its members with an unreasoning fear of whiteness.

For the lynch mob, blackness is a sign of satanic evil given human form. It is the dark consubstantial shadow which symbolizes all that its opponents reject in social change and in democracy. And thus it does not matter if its sacrificial victim be guilty or innocent, because the lynch mob's object is to propitiate its insatiable god of whiteness, that myth-figure worshipped as the true source of all things bright and beautiful, by destroying the human attributes of its god's antagonist which they perceive as the power of blackness. In action, racial discrimination is as nondiscriminating as a car bomb detonated in a crowded public square—because both car bomb and lynch rope are savagely efficient ways of destroying distinctions between the members of a hated group while rendering quite meaningless any moral questioning that might arise regarding the method used. For the ultimate goal of lynchers is that of achieving ritual purification through destroying the lynchers' identification with the basic *humanity* of their victims. Hence their deafness to cries of pain, their stoniness before the sight and stench of burning flesh, their exhilarated and grotesque self-righteousness. And hence our horror at the idea of supposedly civilized men destroying—and in the name of their ideal conception of the human—an aspect of their own humanity. Yes, but for the group thus victimized, such sacrifices are the source of emotions that move far beyond the tragic conception of pity and terror and down into the abysmal levels of conflict and folly from which arise our famous American humor. Brother, the blackness of *Afro-American* "black humor" is not black, it is tragically human and finds its source and object in the notion of "whiteness". . .

But let me not overstate beyond the point necessary for conveying an idea of my state of mind prior to my unanticipated stumble onto *Tobacco Road*. The threat, real or imagined, of being the subject of such victimization was offset by that hopeful attitude that is typical of youth and necessary for dealing with life everywhere. So while racial danger was always with me, I lived with it as with threats of natural disaster or acts of God. And just as Henry James felt it prudent to warn Americans against a "superstitious evaluation of Europe," Negro folklore with its array of survival strategies warned me against an overevaluation of white pretensions. And despite their dominance and low opinion of Negro intelligence, whites suspected the presence of profound reservations even when Negroes were far less assertive than they are today. This made for a constant struggle over the nature of reality, in which each group probed and sparred as they tried to determine the other's true motives and opinions. A poignant instance of such struggle appears in Faulkner's *The Sound and the Fury* when Quentin Compson gives Deacon, a raffish Negro mythomaniac who does odd jobs around Harvard, an important letter to be delivered to Quentin's roommate the following afternoon. But when Deacon notes that the envelope is sealed, he suspects that he is being sent on a fool's errand such as whites delighted in sending Negroes down South. This causes him to drop his Northern mask for that of an old inarticulate "darkey," a pose which reminds Quentin of a Negro retainer whom he'd known as a child. Deacon then asks if a joke is being played on him; which Quentin denies. But then, appealing for that flattering reassurance that Southern whites were accustomed to exacting from Negroes, he asks Deacon if any South-erner had ever played a joke on him. Deacon's reply, as was often true of such exchanges, is ambiguous.

"You're right," he says, "they're fine folks. But you can't live with them."

Then, looking through Deacon into his own hopeless despair, Quentin asks, "Did you ever try?"

But the answer is not forthcoming. For in a flash the transplanted black Southerner had retired behind one of the many trickster's masks which his second self had assumed upon coming north and agrees briskly to deliver the letter. Ironically, however, there *is* a fool's errand involved, but it isn't Deacon's. For the letter conveys Quentin's intention to drown himself. Thus Deacon, who has rejected the role assigned him by his native South, ends up playing not the traditional black fool but, all unknowingly, the death-messenger for a pathetic Southern aristocrat who is driven to self-destruction by the same prideful confusion of values from which, as Southerners, both suffered. Having tried to live in the South, both had come north dragging the past behind them; but while Deacon used his Southern craftiness to play upon life's possibilities, the past-haunted Quentin destroyed himself because he was unable to reconcile the mythi-cal South he loved with that which had sent Deacon packing.

As Deacon said, many white Southerners were "fine folks," and that was the problem. Whites both hostile and friendly were part of my college scene, and thus a good part of my extracurricular education consisted in learning to live with them while retaining my self-esteem. Negro folklore taught the preservation of one's humanity by masking one's motives and emotions, just as it prepared one to be unsurprised at anything that whites might do, because a concern with race could negate all human bonds, in-cluding those of shared blood and experience.

So I tried to observe such ancestral wisdom as I awaited the day when I could leave the South. The catch here was that even the roads that led *away* from the South were also haunted; a circumstance which I should have learned, but did not, from numerous lyrics that were sung to the blues. And so, full of great expectations, I went north. And where unedu-cated Deacon assumed the mask of a former Harvard divinity student, I took on that of a sophisticated New Yorker.

In *Tobacco Road*, Erskine Caldwell appears to have taken a carefully screened assemblage of anti-Negro stereotypes and turned them against the very class in which they found their most fervent proponents—and what he did with them was most outrageous. Indeed, he turned things around in such a manner that it was as though Whyte, the Tuskegee victim of the Phenix City hazing, had read Mark Twain, George Washington Harris, Rabelais, Groucho Marx, and Voltaire, learned to write, and then, passing for "white" in order to achieve a more intimate knowledge of his characters, had proceeded to embody the most outrageous stereotypes in the Jeeter Lester family, in-laws, and friends. (Caldwell, I hasten to add, is a Georgia-born Anglo-Saxon.)

Nevertheless, Caldwell presents Jeeter Lester as an ignorant, impoverished, Depression-ruined poor white who urges Ellie May, his sixteen-year-old younger daughter, to seduce her older sister's husband so that he, Lester, may steal the equally impoverished young man's only food, a bag of turnips. The father of other mature children who now live in the city, he is a slothful farmer whose run-down farm is in such neglect that even the rats have abandoned the corncrib, and a criminally negligent son whose aged mother must forage for food in the woods, where, by the play's end, she dies alone and neglected. And yet Caldwell keeps Jeeter within the range of the human by having him be so utterly himself. He makes him a poor-white version of the "great sinner" on the order of Dostoevsky's elder Karamazov, and with a similar vitality and willfulness. He is a lecher who has fathered children by his neighbor's wife, and has incestuous inclinations toward one of his married daughters. But it is his stubborn refusal to bow before the economic and ecological developments that have rendered his type of farming no longer possible which gives the play its movement. Jeeter is a symbol of human willfulness reduced to its illogical essence.

Ada, Mrs. Lester, is an ineffectual wife and mother who has no control over either her husband or their children. Half starved and worn-out from childbearing, she exerts what physical and moral strength she has in trying to save Pearl, her pride and joy through a casual affair with a stranger, from the decay of Tobacco Road.

Pearl, whom Jeeter married off at the age of twelve, is the wife of Lov, a struggling young workman with whom she refuses either to sleep or talk—a situation utterly baffling for Lov, and annoying to Jeeter because it has become a subject for local Negro laughter.

Ellie May, the younger daughter, is harelipped, and so helplessly frustrated sexually that Jeeter tries to persuade Lov to exchange her for Pearl and take her away from Tobacco Road before, as he says, the Negroes get her. But if in Ellie May the Lester sex drive has gotten quite out of hand, in her brother Dude it is unawakened.

Dude, the adolescent son (who opens the play with a mindless bouncing of a ball against the house), is sadistic, disdainful of parental authority, and utterly disrespectful of life and death. And if Jeeter is a comic embodiment of selfish wrong-headedness, Dude (who takes more than his share

of Jeeter's stolen turnips by physical force), is the embodiment of his father's character gone to violence. He is also the agent of his mother's
death.

In brief, the Lester family is as seedy as the house in which they live.
They have plunged through the fragile floor of civilized humanity, and
even the religion which had once given a semblance of order to their lives
had become as superstitious as that which the stereotypes attribute to
Negroes.

That superstition is exploited by Sister Bessie Rice, a dowdy itinerant
preacher of no known denomination who sees sin in even the most innocent of human actions and uses prayer as a magical incantation through
which to manipulate her listener's residue of religious belief to her own
advantage. She is a confidence woman who promises for small contributions to cure all ills through the magic of prayer.

Homely and gregarious in manner, Sister Bessie is a widow in search of
a mate, both as husband and as a preaching partner with whom she can be
more efficient in spreading her version of religion. Her unlikely choice toward this goal is teen-age Dude. But while Jeeter is quite agreeable to such a
union of April and December, Dude is uninterested. Until, that is, Sister
Bessie promises to use the money left by her deceased husband to purchase
a new automobile. This does the trick. With Dude in tow, Sister Bessie buys
first a marriage license and then the car; whereupon they speed back to the
Lester farm. There Sister Bessie loses no time in performing her own marriage ceremony. And this accomplished, she rushes Dude to their wedding
chamber—outside of which Jeeter stands on a chair in an effort to watch her
initiate Dude into the sexual mysteries of wedlock.

As it turns out, however, Dude is less interested in connubial pleasure
than in driving the new car—which, blowing its horn idiotically and
speeding, he does, so recklessly that he runs into a loaded wagon and
wrecks the car. Later he backs the car over his mother and kills her. Thus,
not even the wedding of modern technology with sex and religion can restore Tobacco Road to a state of fertility. The sex instinct remained out of
control, religious values corrupted, the laws guiding the relations between
parents and children destroyed, and the words and rituals that once imposed religious and political ideals upon human conduct were used to justify greed, incest, sloth, and theft. In brief, the economic Depression, abet-
ted by Jeeter's sloth and wrong-headedness, has deprived the family not
only of its livelihood but denuded them of civilized humanity. Ultimately
it was Ada's efforts to save Pearl from further humiliation and Jeeter's
dogged will to survive the imbalance of nature and the bank's foreclosure
on his farm that redeemed the family from a total fall into bestiality.

And yet, Caldwell's handling of such material does not produce a response of disgust and hopelessness in the audience. Instead it is swept by
a wave of cathartic laughter which leaves it optimistic. Perhaps, as it has
been noted in Cleanth Brooks, R. W. B. Lewis, and Robert Penn Warren's
*American Literature: The Makers and the Making,* the Lesters' "lack of any

burden of guilt and their ability to dispense with most of the contrivances of civilization gave a sense of release to a great many people."

I would add that during the Depression days of the play's great success, there was such great need for relief, both economic and spiritual, that the grotesque nature of its comedy was fully justified. Perhaps its viewers laughed, and then in retrospect grasped the interplay of social and economic forces upon which the play is focused, and trembled. Which, given Caldwell's anger over the despoilation of the South, must have been his intention.

According to Kenneth Burke, "Comedy should enable us to be observers of ourselves while acting. Its ultimate end would not be passiveness but maximum consciousness. [It should allow] one to 'transcend' himself by noting his own foibles . . . [and should] provide a rationale for locating the irrational and the non-rational."

To follow the action of a comedy is to react through its actors, and to identify either with them or with the values with which they struggle. For as David Daziel Duncan has written, "the difference between symbolic and social drama is the difference between imaginary and real obstacles, but to produce effects on audiences, symbolic drama must reflect the real obstacles of social drama. Conflict must be resolved in the symbolic realm by the expression of attitudes which make conformity possible. All such expression, like prayer, is an exhortation to the self and to others. It is a preparation for social action, an investment of the self with confidence and strength." Duncan is speaking of the drama of everyday life in which all successful stage plays are rooted, and when we consider the popularity of *Tobacco Road*, it suggests that during the Great Depression it was most successful in providing its viewers with a rationale for locating the irrational both in themselves and in their society.

The greater the stress within society the stronger the comic antidote required. And in this instance the stress imposed by the extreme dislocations of American society was so strong and chaotic that it called for a comedy of the grotesque. Jeeter Lester, the poor white as fool, was made to act the clown in order to save his audience's sanity. Here it is instructive to use the Southern Negroes' handling of stress for comparison. For since such stress was an enforced norm of their lives, Negroes struggled with the role assigned them for the same ends that Shakespeare juxtaposed the Fool with Lear—which was to maintain a measure of common sense before the extreme assertions of Lear's kingly pride. In the Lear-like drama of white supremacy Negroes were designated both clowns and fools, but they "fooled" by way of maintaining their own sense of rational order, no matter how they were perceived by whites. For it was far better to be looked down upon as "niggers" than to lose themselves in a world rendered surreal through an excess of racial pride. Their challenge was to endure while imposing their claims upon America's conscience and consciousness, just as they had imposed their style upon its culture. Forced to be wary observers, they recognized that American life is of a whole, and that what happens to blacks will accrue eventually, one way or another, to the nation as a whole. This is their dark-visioned version of the broader "American Joke." Like Faulkner, Caldwell appears to have recognized its existence, for in responding to the imbalance which was shaking American social hierarchy from its apex to its base, he placed the yokelike anti-Negro stereotypes upon the necks of whites, and thus his audience reacted with a shock of recognition. Caldwell was answering a deeply felt need, and it is interesting that it was during the period of *Tobacco Road*'s record-breaking run that the Museum of Modern Art's presentation of its famous exhibit of Dadaist art was widely successful.

For me the shock of Caldwell's art began when Ellie May and Lov were swept up by a forbidden sexual attraction so strong that, uttering sounds of animal passion, they went floundering and skittering back-to-back across the stage in the startling action which father Jeeter, that randy Adam in an Eden gone to weed, named "horsing." For when the two went into their bizarre choreography of sexual "frustrabation" I was reduced to such helpless laughter that I distracted the entire balcony and embarrassed both myself and my host. It was a terrible moment, for before I could regain control, more attention was being directed toward me than at the action unfolding on the stage.

Then it was as though I had been stripped naked, kicked out of a low-flying plane onto an Alabama road, and ordered to laugh for my life. I laughed and laughed, bending and straightening in a virtual uncontrollable cloud-and-dam-burst of laughter, a self-immolation of laughter over which I had no control. And yet I was hypersensitive to what was happening around me, a fact which left me all the more embarrassed.

Seeing an expression of shocked disbelief on the face of my host, I imagined him saying, "Damn, if I'd known this would be his reaction I would have picked a theater with laughing-barrels!"

And suddenly, in addition to my soul-wracking agony of embarrassment, I was being devastated by an old in-group joke which played upon the themes of racial conflict, social freedom, and the blackness of Negro laughter; a joke whose setting was some small Southern town in which Negro freedom of expression was so restricted that its public square was marked by a series of huge whitewashed barrels labeled FOR COLORED, and into which any Negro who felt a laugh coming on was forced—*pro bono publico*—to thrust his boisterous head.

The joke was used by Tuskegee students, who considered themselves more sophisticated to kid freshmen from small Southern towns, but although I had heard it many times, it now flashed in my mind with implications that had hitherto escaped me. And as it played a counterpoint between my agony of laughter and the action taking place on the stage set of *Tobacco Road* below, it was as though Erskine Caldwell had snared me as an offstage instrument for extending the range of his outrageous plotting—and I mean with a cacophony of minor thirds and flatted-fifths voiced fortissimo by braying gut-bucket brasses!

For now, in my hypersubjective state, viewers around me in the balcony were no longer following the action unfolding on the stage; they were getting to their feet to gawk at me. It was as though I had plunged into a nightmare in which my personality was split in twain, with the lucid side looking on in wonder while the manic side convulsed my body as though a drunken accordionist was using it to belt out the "Beer Barrel Polka." And while I wheezed and choked with laughter, my disgusted lucid self dramatized its cool detachment by noting that things were getting so out of control that Northern white folk in balcony and loge were now catching fire and beginning to howl and cheer the disgraceful loss of self-control being exhibited by a young Negro who had become deranged by the shock wave of comedy set in motion by a troupe of professional actors who were doing nothing more extraordinary than portraying the outrageous antics of a group of Southern whites who were totally imaginary; a young man who was so gross as to demonstrate his social unacceptability by violating a whole *encyclopedia* of codes that regulated proper conduct no less in the theater than in society at large.

In my distorted consciousness the theater was rapidly becoming the scene of a virtual orgy of disgraceful conduct, with everyone getting into the scene-stealing action. And so much so, that now the lucid side of me noted with despair that Jeeter Lester (played by Will Geer) and the other Lesters were now shading their eyes and peering open-mouthed toward the balcony—as if to say "What the hell's happening? Who's upstaging the stage and turning *Tobacco Road* upside down?" Or perhaps, in shock and dismay, they too were thinking of laughing-barrels.

For in the joke the barrels were considered a civic necessity and had been improvised as a means of protecting the sensibilities of whites from a peculiar form of insanity suffered exclusively by Negroes, who in light of their social status and past condition of servitude were regarded as having absolutely *nothing* in their daily experience which could possibly inspire *rational* laughter. And yet Negroes continued—much as one side of me was doing—to laugh.

They laughed even when overcome by mirth while negotiating the public square, an area graced by its proud military statue, its Civil War cannon and pyramid of cannon balls, which was especially off-limits to all forms of Negro profanation. Thus, since any but the most inaudible Negro laughter was forbidden in public, Negroes who were wise—or at least fast on their feet—took off *posthaste* for a laughing-barrel. (Just as I, in my predicament, would gladly have done.) For despite their eccentric risibility, the local Negroes bowed to public pressure and cooperated—at least to the extent that they were physically able.

But now as I continued to roar at the weird play-without-a-play in which part of me was involved, my sober self marked the fact that the entire audience was being torn in twain. Most of the audience was white, but now many who occupied seats down in the orchestra section were beginning to protest the unscheduled disruption taking place above them.

Leaping to their feet, they were shaking their fists at those in the balcony, and they in turn were shouting their disdain for those so lacking in an appreciation for the impromptu broadening of the expected comedy. And as they raged at one another in what was rapidly becoming a Grangerford-Shepherdson feud of expletives, I recalled a similar conflict which took place in the laughing-barrel town and cracked up again.

For there, too, certain citizens had assumed their democratic right of dissent to oppose the barrels as an *ipso jure* form of reverse discrimination. Why not, they argued, force Negroes to control themselves at their *own* expense, as did everyone else. An argument which fell on deaf ears, because it ignored the self-evident fact that Negro self-control was the very *last* thing in the world that they really wanted—whether in this or in any other area of Negro lives. Therefore, these passionate quodlibetarians and their objections to quotas were ignored because the great majority of the citizenry regarded their unique form of public accommodation as bestowing a dual blessing upon their town. And to an extent, that blessing included the Negroes. For not only did the laughing-barrels save many a black a sore behind (and the understaffed police force, energy sorely needed in other areas), they performed the far more important function of providing whites a means of saving face before the confounding, persistent, and embarrassing mystery of black laughter.

Unfortunately, it was generally agreed that the barrels were by no means an *elegant* solution of what whites regarded as a most grievous and inelegant problem. For after all, having to observe the posture of a Negro stuck halfway into a laughing-barrel (or rising and falling helplessly in a theater balcony) was far from an aesthetic experience. Nor was that all, for often when seen laughing with their heads stuck in a barrel and standing, as it were, upside down upon the turbulent air, Negroes appeared to be taken over by a form of schizophrenia which left them even more psychically frazzled than whites regarded them as being by nature.

But while the phenomenon was widely discussed, not even the wisest of whites could come up with a satisfactory explanation. All they knew was that when such an incident occurred, instead of sobering up, as any white man in a similar situation would have done, a Negro might well take off and laugh all the harder (as I in my barrelless state was doing). For it appeared that in addition to reacting to whatever ignorant, harebrained notion had set him off in the first place, the Negro was apt to double up with a second gale of laughter—and that triggered, apparently, by his own mental image of himself laughing at himself laughing upside down. It was, all whites agreed, another of the many Negro mysteries with which it was their lot to contend; and *whatever* its true cause, it was most disturbing to a white observer.

And especially on Market Day, a time when the public square teemed with whites and blacks seeking in their separate-but-equal fashions to combine business with pleasure while taking advantage of the square's holiday atmosphere. For on Market Days, thanks to the great influx of Negroes, the uproar from laughing-barrels could become so loud and raucous that it not only disturbed the serenity of the entire square, but shook up the whites' fierce faith in the stability of their most cherished traditions. For on such occasions the uproar from the laughing-barrels could become so contagious and irresistible that any whites who were so unfortunate as to be caught near the explosions of laughter would find themselves compelled to join in—and this included even such important figures as the mayor, lawyer, cotton broker, Baptist minister, and brewers of prime "white-lightning" whiskey. It was an appalling state of affairs, for despite their sternest resistance, even such distinguished whites literally cracked up and roared! And although it was recognized that it sprang from the *unnatural* and corrupting blackness of Negro laughter, it was a fact of Southern life, and thus it was that from time to time even the most dignified and tradition-bound whites found themselves joining in. (As, much to the discomfort of my somber balcony-trapped self, the whites around me were doing.)

Nor did it help that many of the town's whites suspected that when a Negro had his head thrust into a laughing-barrel he became endowed with a strange form of extrasensory perception—or second sight—which allowed him to respond, and uproariously, to their unwilling participation. For it was clear that given a black laugher's own uncouth uproar, he could not possibly *hear* its infectious damage to them. And when such reversals occurred the whites assumed that in some mysterious fashion the Negro involved was not only laughing at *himself* laughing, but was also laughing at *them* laughing at his laughing against their own most determined wills. And if such was the truth, it suggested that somehow a Negro (and this meant *any* Negro) could become with a single hoot-and-cackle both the source and master of an outrageous and untenable situation. So it was viewed as a most aggravating problem, and, indeed, the most vicious of vicious circles ever to be imposed upon the long-suffering South by the white man's burden.

For since it was an undisputed fact that whites and blacks were of different species, it followed that they could by no means be expected to laugh at the same things. Therefore, when whites found themselves joining in with the coarse merriment issuing from the laughing-barrels, they suffered the double embarrassment of laughing against their own God-given nature while being unsure of exactly why, or at what, specifically, they were laughing. Which meant that somehow the Negro in the barrel had them *over* a barrel.

This, then, was the crux of the town's dilemma: efforts to control Negro laughter with laughing-barrels was as futile as attaining Christian grace by returning to the womb, because a Negro laughing in a laughing-barrel simply turned the world upside down and inside out. And in so doing, he *in*-verted (and thus *sub*-verted) tradition and thus the preordained and cherished scheme of Southern racial relationships was blasted asunder. Therefore, it was feared that if such unhappy instances of interracial laughter occurred with any frequency, it would create a crisis in which social order would be fatally undermined by something as unpolitical as a bunch of Negroes with their laughing heads stuck into the interiors of a batch of old whitewashed whiskey barrels.

The outrageous absurdity of this state of affairs was as vexing to the town as that in which I found myself as the old joke banged and shuddered through my memory. For despite the fact that the whites had done everything they could think of to control the blackness of Negro laughter, the Negroes continued to laugh. And the disapproval of the general public notwithstanding, they were even *bursting* barrels all over the public square, and thus adding to the high cost of maintaining public order. *And* since this was (in more ways than one!) at white expense, the whites were faced with a Hobson's choice between getting rid of the Negroes and suffering the economic loss of their labor, or living with the commotion in the laughing-barrels. (Yes, but they had at least a ghost of a choice, while by now it was as though I had been taken over by embattled Siamese twins who couldn't agree for disagreeing, and neither of whom could exit the scene, thanks to the detachment of one and the mirth-wracked state of the other.)

In the town, however, great argument raged on both sides of the question. All agreed that the laughing-barrels were an economic burden, but the proponents of the "Barrel Act," as it was known, justified their position with philosophical arguments to the effect that while it was true that the unique public facilities were costly, they served not only as a form of noise-pollution control, but the higher—and more spiritual—purpose of making it unnecessary for white folks to suffer the indignity of having to observe the confounding and degrading spectacle of a bunch of uncultivated Negroes knocking themselves out with a form of laughter that had no apparent motivation or discernible target . . .

What a terrible time and place to be ambushed by such an irreverent joke! By now my eyes were so full of tears that I could no longer see Hughes or anyone else, but at least the moisture had the effect of calming me down. Then, as the unruly world of *Tobacco Road* finally returned, my divided selves were made one again by a sense of catharsis. Yes, but at the expense of undergoing what a humiliating, body-wracking conflict of emotions! Embarrassment, self-anger, ethnic scorn, and at last a feeling of comic relief. And all because Erskine Caldwell compelled me to laugh at his symbolic, and therefore nonthreatening, Southern whites, and thus he shocked me into recognizing certain absurd aspects of our common humanity. Kenneth Burke would probably have said that I had been hit with a "perspective by incongruity," leading to a reversal of expectations in which the juxtaposition of past and present, comic Southland and quasi-illusory New York, had set up vibrations that routed my self-composure. It was as though I had plunged through the wacky mirrors of a fun house, to discover on the other side a weird distortion of perspective which made for a painful but redeeming rectification of vision. And in a flash, time was telescoped and the imaginary assumed the lineaments of past experiences through which Jeeter Lester's comic essence became a recognizable property of characters and events that I had known in the past.

Because, thanks to Governor "Alfalfa Bill" Murray's Jeeter Lesterish appeal to the bias of Oklahoma's farm vote, hadn't I seen the state capitol's grounds a-wave with grain "as high as an elephant's eye" (which proved to be a foreshadowing of events which led, years later, to the adoption of Rodgers and Hammerstein's "Oklahoma" as the state's official song)? And a bit later, hadn't I seen those same graciously landscaped grounds splattered with far more oil rigs than there were holes dug by Ty Ty in his futile search for gold in Caldwell's *God's Little Acre?* I had indeed, and the main difference was that the oil rigs produced oil; otherwise, Alfalfa Bill might have stepped out of a Caldwell novel. Thus I now recognized that there was much more of Jeeter Lester's outrageousness in my past than I had ever imagined, and quite a bit of it showed up on my side of the color line.

There were uneducated men whose attitudes and bearing ripped through the usual stereotypes like a Brahma bull goring the paper image displayed on Bull Durham Tobacco Company billboards. Their violence was usually directed against their own kind, but they were known to go after whites as well, and were no more respectful of what most people considered civilized conduct than Jeeter Lester. I had known the type in Oklahoma and admired a few for insisting upon being themselves. Often they were of vernacular folk culture but with active minds and were absolutely unrestrained in attacking any subject that caught their attention. Once while working as a barbershop shoeshine boy I had heard such a group engage in a long discussion of Mr. John D. Rockefeller Senior's relations with the women whom they assumed it natural for such a powerful man to have. They took it for granted that he had no less than a "stable full" and speculated as to how much he paid for their favors, and concluded that he rewarded them with trunks full of brand-new dimes.

Then they discussed the brands of brandy and whiskey which they assumed Mr. Rockefeller drank, and argued over the designs and costs of the silk underwear worn by his favorite fancy women, and then almost came to blows when estimating the number of "yard chillun" he had scattered around the country and abroad.

Poor old John D., he didn't know it, but they put him through the windmill of their fantasies with gusto. And what's more, he emerged enhanced in their sight as an even more exceptional man among such exceptional men as themselves—thanks to their having endowed him with a sexual potency and an utter disregard for genteel conduct that would have blown that gentleman's mind.

Before they were done they had the founder of Standard Oil shooting pool, playing strip poker, and engaging in a barbecue-eating contest with J. P. Morgan and Henry Ford—from which, naturally, he emerged the winner. Only when they put him through a Charleston contest with "Tickle-toes from Tulsa," a famous Negro dancer, did he fall below their exacting standards. Nevertheless he remained the mighty Rockefeller, though so magnified that he was far more "John Henry" than John David- son. And in working him over, they created such an uproar of laughter that the owner had to ask them to leave the barbershop. But by that time, both to my bewilderment and to my delight, they had touched one of the most powerful men of the nation with the tarbrush of their comic imagina- tions, Afro-Americanized him, and claimed him as one of their very own.

It was amazing how consistently they sought (like Jeeter Lester) to make the world conform to the narrow compass of their own hopes and dreams. And there were still others who in pursuing their self-reliant wrong-headedness had given me a glimpse of the "tragic."

For had not I seen a good part of my community, including teen-age boys, reduced to despair over the terrible death of a self-taught genius of an automobile mechanic, who after burning his fingers while working with the electrical system of a Model T Ford had cut out the offending flesh with his pocketknife—an act of ignorant pride which resulted in his death by lockjaw? In those days any boy who could lay hands on a coil from a Model T and the hand-cranked magneto from a discontinued tele- phone would rig it as a device for shocking his unsuspecting friends, but now to our dismay, death was revealed to be lurking within our rare elec- trical toys.

But even closer to my immediate experience, wasn't Ellie May's and Lov's "horsing" all over the stage of *Tobacco Road* embarrassingly sym- bolic of my own frustration as a healthy young man whose sexual outlet was limited (for the most part) to "belly-rubbing" with girls met casually at public dances? It was and it wasn't, depending upon my willingness to make or withhold a human identification. Actually, I had no choice but to identify, for Caldwell's art had seen to that.

Thus, for all its intentional outrageousness, the comedy of *Tobacco Road* was deeply rooted in the crazy-quilt life I knew. And Caldwell had me both coming and going, black side, white side, and straight down my improvised American middle. On one side of my mind I had thought of my life as being of a whole, segregated but in many ways superior to that of the Lesters. On the other side, I thought of the Lester type as being, in the Negro folk phrase, "a heap of whiteness gone to waste" and therefore a gross caricature of anything that was viable in the idea of white supe- riority. But now Caldwell had highlighted the warp and woof of my own ragtag American pattern. And so, laughing hysterically, I felt like the fat man whom I'd seen slip and fall on the icy sidewalk and who lay there laughing while passers-by looked on in bewilderment—until he got to his feet still laughing and punched the one man who had joined in his laughter square in the mouth. In my case, however, there was no one to punch, because I embodied both fat man and the passer-by who was so rash as to ignore Baudelaire's warning. Therefore I laughed and I trembled, and gained thereby a certain wisdom.

I couldn't have put it into words at the time, but by forcing me to see the comedy in Jeeter Lester's condition and allowing me to react to it in an interracial situation without the threat of physical violence, Caldwell told me something important about who I was. And by easing the conflict that I was having with my Southern experience (yes, and with my South-Southwestern identity), helped initiate me into becoming, if not a "New Yorker," at least a more tolerant American. I suppose such preposterous comedy is an indispensable agency for dealing with American experience precisely because it allows for redeeming perspectives on our rampant incongruities. Given my background and yearnings, there was no question but that I needed such redemption, and for that I am eternally grateful to Erskine Caldwell—Southerner, American humorist, and mighty destroyer of laughing-barrels.

.  .  .  .  .  .  .  .  .  .  .  .

### QUESTIONS FOR A SECOND READING

1. From the opening pages, Ellison works with a theory of laughter, one represented early in the text through references to Baudelaire, Aesop, and Uncle Remus. The terms of this discussion appear again and again as points of reference for Ellison when he is talking about humor or the uses of humor or when he is telling stories of jokes and reversals. As you work back through the text, be prepared to write out a quick paraphrase of the argument available to Ellison through these and later references to the "idea" of laughter—to what it is that laughter could be said to represent. And look to see how, as Ellison works with them, these ideas can be used (or altered) to think about African American experience especially in the long (and strange) section on the "laughing-barrels."

2. In the middle of the essay, Ellison cites W. B. Yeats, the Irish poet, on "masks" in a passage that concludes with the (perhaps surprising) assertion that "active virtue . . . is the wearing of a mask." And then, to make Yeats's words work for him, Ellison has to imagine a revision of the passage, adapting it as a concept that can be used to think about African American experience. As you reread, let the opening of the essay lead you to that passage. Then, when you get there, take a moment to work out the Ellison revision of Yeats: What does it say once the substitutions are made? And, from that, how do you read the rest of the essay? What is Ellison saying about "active virtue"? And to whom is he speaking?

3. "An Extravagance of Laughter" is an essay that works by indirection. It takes a long time and several turns to get from the opening reference to *Tobacco Road* to the story of what happened at the performance. And even then, the conclusions, if there are any, are difficult and subtle. This is how Ellison, the writer, works; this is how readers work (or learn to work) as they give themselves over to the text. As you reread, think about how you would describe and chart this essay as a project or as a piece of work. What are its stages and strategies? What is its design? What are its characteristic

methods? Ellison refers to the essay as an "autobiographical exploration." From your perspective, what is this genre? If you had to write such an exploration (or help others to write one), what instructions could you provide?

ASSIGNMENTS FOR WRITING

1. It is interesting that Ellison feels the need to apologize to Erskine Caldwell and not Langston Hughes. Caldwell was not present in the theater; Hughes was present and thereby implicated in the scene in a way that Caldwell was not. He had reason to be embarrassed by his young friend, newly arrived from the South.

   One way of thinking about this is to assume that Hughes needed no explanation. As an African American, there are things he would know and understand that Caldwell, who was white, would not. In this sense, the essay is very much an attempt to explain to a white audience the particular experience of an African American. If you think about the essay this way, Ellison's concluding comment, "Caldwell told me something important about who I was," refers to how the play, and his response, allowed Ellison to understand who he was in relation to America's complicated regional and racial geography, where it is important not only to think about race, but to think about race in relation to Oklahoma, Alabama, and New York. So what *does* Ellison come to understand? Why was this situation hard to understand, and why is it hard to explain? That is, why doesn't Ellison just say what he has to say on the first page and be done with it?

   Ellison refers to "An Extravagance of Laughter" as an autobiographical exploration, a way of thinking things through. So what are his conclusions? Write an essay in which you explain what it is that Ellison represents as the end of that exploration. What is the end? Where does he arrive? How does he get there? How does he represent the difficulty of exploring and explaining his "emotional and intellectual" development? You should assume that your readers know something about Ralph Ellison but that they have never read this piece.

2. For most readers, one of the strangest and most difficult moments in the essay comes toward the end, when Ellison introduces the "old in-group joke" of the laughing-barrels and then uses them as a point of reference in thinking about humor, about the South, and about the relations between blacks and whites.

   What can you make of this section of "An Extravagance of Laughter"? Write an essay, one directed at other readers of this piece, ideally your colleagues in this class, showing how you read this section of the essay, explaining what you can make of the text. What is Ellison doing? What is he getting at? What does this section have to do with the rest of the essay—that is, how does the rest of the essay prepare you to read the example of the laughing-barrels? Or how does the example of the laughing-barrels prepare you to read (or to reflect on) the rest of the essay?

3. Ellison refers to "An Extravagance of Laughter" as an "autobiographical exploration." An earlier assignment asks students to think about this in

relation to content—what does Ellison learn? You could also use the phrase "autobiographical exploration" to name a *way* of writing, a method, one that combines autobiography with a desire to analyze and to explore (to think about experience, not just recount it) and, at least in Ellison's case, to think broadly about ideas and issues (about W. B. Yeats and masks, about humor, about race relations in the North and South in the 1930s).

As you prepare to write this assignment, read through the essay again to think about it as a way of doing one's work, as a project, as a way of writing. What are its key features? What is its shape or design? How does Ellison the writer do what he does? And you might ask: What would it take to learn to write like this? How is this writing related to the writing taught in school? Where and how might it serve you as a student? (The third "Question for a Second Reading" is designed to prompt this kind of reflection.)

Once you have developed a sense of Ellison's method, write an autobiographical exploration of your own, one that has the rhythm and the moves, the shape and the design of "An Extravagance of Laughter." As far as subject matter is concerned, consider Ellison's text an invitation to you to write about race or difference or region or travel or difficult moments, but don't feel compelled to follow his lead. You can write about anything you want. The key is to follow the essay as an example of a *way* of writing—moving slowly, turning this way and that, combining stories and reflection, working outside of a rigid structure of thesis and proof.


### MAKING CONNECTIONS

1. One of the obvious questions that a reader might ask of Ellison's essay "An Extravagance of Laughter" has to do with his methods of writing, thinking, and working. What, one might ask, are his characteristic ways of gathering materials, of thinking them through, of presenting them to readers? As you work through Ellison's essay, think about the writing as an example of method and intention. You also might ask yourself, for instance, questions about the kinds of readers his work requires: What does he assume of his readers? How does he teach his readers to read?

    The same questions can be asked of Susan Griffin's essay "Our Secret" (p. 404) (or of the selections by Gloria Anzaldúa, p. 22, or of the excerpt from Virginia Woolf's "A Room of One's Own," p. 750). What, you might ask, are her characteristic ways of gathering materials, of thinking them through, and of presenting them to a reader? How would you describe her method? What are its key features? What would you say she is doing, for example, in the first two paragraphs? What happens next? What is an "autobiographical exploration" as it is represented in this text? And what does she assume of her readers? Who *is* the audience and how does she teach her readers to read?

    Write an essay in which you use the selections by Ellison and Griffin (or those by Anzaldúa or Woolf) to talk about writers, their methods, and the writerly project of "autobiographical explorations." Be sure to work closely with examples from each reading. Be sure to look for differences as well as similarities. And see, in your essay, if you can move beyond your discussion of their examples to think more generally about the problems of writing. About oneself? You might ask, what is it that adults work on when they work on their writing? What is it that younger writers need to learn? What might a writer learn from these two examples? Where and how might the lessons learned serve in the academy or outside?

2. Both Ellison, in "An Extravagance of Laughter," and John Edgar Wideman, in "Our Time" (p. 707), write about the experience of growing up, and of growing up black in the United States. Wideman and Ellison are major figures in American cultural life. And the selections you are reading were written at about the same time, in the mideighties (Wideman's in 1984, Ellison's in 1985). They write about different moments in American history, however, and they speak from different generations of experience. Wideman was not yet alive when Ellison met Langston Hughes in New York and attended the performance of *Tobacco Road.*

Write an essay in which you discuss the differences in the experience *and* the point of view of each writer. How were their lives different? How do they see things differently? What differences are there in their points of reference—in the way they imagine the difficulties in doing what they do as writers and in the resources they draw on to do their work?

# RALPH WALDO EMERSON

*R*ALPH WALDO EMERSON (1803–1882) is probably one of the most famous, most eloquent, and least read figures in American literature. He was
a poet, a preacher, a visionary, and an itinerant lecturer; he left behind a remarkable series of essays, lectures, notebooks, and journals; and yet he is best known
for his influence on those who followed him: Melville, Thoreau, Whitman, Dickinson, Frost, Hart Crane, and Wallace Stevens.

Textbooks most often introduce Emerson as the central figure in American
transcendentalism. He does not, however, have to be read as a representative
philosopher; to do so, in fact, violates his own feisty individualism and his struggle
to stay free of schools of thought and the pressure of received opinion. He can be read
for the pleasure of his unusual style of speaking and thinking and for the force of his
immediate argument. The essay that follows, "The American Scholar," is about education, including university education, and it says some rather surprising things,
including the following about the use of books (like the one you are reading right
now): "Books are for the scholar's idle times," and "Meek young men grow up in libraries, believing it their duty to accept the views, which Cicero, which Locke, which
Bacon, have given, forgetful that Cicero, Locke, and Bacon were only young men in
libraries when they wrote these books." It is a shame to think that the only way to
read Emerson is as an example of what people once thought (and, in fact, it is wrong
to think that in the nineteenth century most people thought or said such things). It

*is possible, alternatively, to read Emerson as a person with something to say to American scholars at today's colleges and universities.*

*"The American Scholar" was presented as a lecture to the Harvard chapter of Phi Beta Kappa on August 31, 1837. It has been called "the most influential address ever made before an American college audience," and America's "intellectual Declaration of Independence." It was also called "misty, dreamy, and unintelligible." Emerson's prose is not orderly, straightforward, or systematic. It does not easily or quickly connect one thing to another but puts the responsibility in the hands of the reader—in your hands—which, according to one of the essay's arguments, is exactly where it belongs.*

# The American Scholar

An Oration
Delivered Before the Phi Beta Kappa Society,
at Cambridge, August 31, 1837

MR. PRESIDENT, AND GENTLEMEN,

I greet you on the re-commencement of our literary year. Our anniversary is one of hope, and, perhaps, not enough of labor. We do not meet for games of strength or skill, for the recitation of histories, tragedies and odes, like the ancient Greeks; for parliaments of love and poesy, like the Troubadours; not for the advancement of science, like our contemporaries in the British and European capitals. Thus far, our holiday has been simply a friendly sign of the survival of the love of letters amongst a people too busy to give to letters any more. As such, it is precious as the sign of an indestructible instinct. Perhaps the time is already come, when it ought to be, and will be something else; when the sluggard intellect of this continent will look from under its iron lids and fill the postponed expectation of the world with something better than the exertions of mechanical skill. Our day of dependence, our long apprenticeship to the learning of other lands, draws to a close. The millions that around us are rushing into life, cannot always be fed on the sere remains of foreign harvests. Events, actions arise, that must be sung, that will sing themselves. Who can doubt that poetry will revive and lead in a new age, as the star in the constellation Harp which now flames in our zenith, astronomers announce, shall one day be the pole-star for a thousand years?

In the light of this hope, I accept the topic which not only usage, but the nature of our association, seem to prescribe to this day—the American Scholar. Year by year, we come up hither to read one more chapter of his biography. Let us inquire what light new days and events have thrown on his chapter, his duties, and his hopes.

It is one of those fables, which out of an unknown antiquity, convey an unlooked-for wisdom, that the gods, in the beginning, divided Man into men, that he might be more helpful to himself; just as the hand was divided into fingers, the better to answer its end.

The old fable covers a doctrine ever new and sublime; that there is One Man,—present to all particular men only partially, or through one faculty; and that you must take the whole society to find the whole man. Man is not a farmer, or a professor, or an engineer, but he is all. Man is priest, and scholar, and statesman, and producer, and soldier. In the *divided* or social state, these functions are parcelled out to individuals, each of whom aims to do his stint of the joint work, whilst each other performs his. The fable implies that the individual, to possess himself, must sometimes return from his own labor to embrace all the other laborers. But unfortunately, this original unit, this fountain of power, has been so distributed to multitudes, has been so minutely subdivided and peddled out, that it is spilled into drops, and cannot be gathered. The state of society is one in which the members have suffered amputation from the trunk, and strut about so many walking monsters,—a good finger, a neck, a stomach, an elbow, but never a man.

Man is thus metamorphosed into a thing, into many things. The planter, who is Man sent out into the field to gather food, is seldom cheered by any idea of the true dignity of his ministry. He sees his bushel and his cart, and nothing beyond, and sinks into the farmer, instead of Man on the farm. The tradesman scarcely ever gives an ideal worth to his work, but is ridden by the routine of his craft, and the soul is subject to dollars. The priest becomes a form; the attorney, a statute-book; the mechanic, a machine; the sailor, a rope of a ship.

In this distribution of functions, the scholar is the delegated intellect. In the right state, he is, *Man Thinking*. In the degenerate state, when the victim of society, he tends to become a mere thinker, or, still worse, the parrot of other men's thinking.

In this view of him, as Man Thinking, the whole theory of his office is contained. Him nature solicits, with all her placid, all her monitory pictures. Him the past instructs. Him the future invites. Is not, indeed, every man a student, and do not all things exist for the student's behoof? And, finally, is not the true scholar the only true master? But, as the old oracle said, "All things have two handles. Beware of the wrong one." In life, too often, the scholar errs with mankind and forfeits his privilege. Let us see him in his school, and consider him in reference to the main influences he receives.

## I

The first in time and the first in importance of the influences upon the mind is that of nature. Every day, the sun; and, after sunset, night and her stars. Ever the winds blow; ever the grass grows. Every day, men and women, conversing, beholding and beholden. The scholar must needs stand wistful and admiring before this great spectacle. He must settle its value in his mind. What is nature to him? There is never a beginning, there is never an end to the inexplicable continuity of this web of God, but always circular power returning into itself. Therein it resembles his own spirit, whose beginning, whose ending he never can find—so entire, so boundless. Far, too, as her splendors shine, system on system shooting like rays, upward, downward, without centre, without circumference,—in the mass and in the particle nature hastens to render account of herself to the mind. Classification begins. To the young mind, every thing is individual, stands by itself. By and by, it finds how to join two things, and see in them one nature; then three, then three thousand; and so, tyrannized over by its own unifying instinct, it goes on trying things together, diminishing anomalies, discovering roots running under ground, whereby contrary and remote things cohere, and flower out from one stem. It presently learns, that, since the dawn of history, there has been a constant accumulation and classifying of facts. But what is classification but the perceiving that these objects are not chaotic, and are not foreign, but have a law which is also a law of the human mind? The astronomer discovers that geometry, a pure abstraction of the human mind, is the measure of planetary motion. The chemist finds proportions and intelligible method throughout matter: and science is nothing but the finding of analogy, identity in the most remote parts. The ambitious soul sits down before each refractory fact; one after another, reduces all strange constitutions, all new powers, to their class and their law, and goes on forever to animate the last fibre of organization, the outskirts of nature, by insight.

Thus to him, to this school-boy under the bending dome of day, is suggested, that he and it proceed from one root; one is leaf and one is flower; relation, sympathy, stirring in every vein. And what is that Root? Is not that the soul of his soul?—A thought too bold—a dream too wild. Yet when this spiritual light shall have revealed the law of more earthly natures,—when he has learned to worship the soul, and to see that the natural philosophy that now is, is only the first gropings of its gigantic hand, he shall look forward to an ever expanding knowledge as to a becoming creator. He shall see that nature is the opposite of the soul, answering to it part for part. One is seal, and one is print. Its beauty is the beauty of his own mind. Its laws are the laws of his own mind. Nature then becomes to him the measure of his attainments. So much of nature as he is ignorant of, so much of his own mind does he not yet possess. And, in fine, the ancient precept, "Know thyself," and the modern precept, "Study nature," becomes at last one maxim.

## II

The next great influence into the spirit of the scholar, is, the mind of the Past,—in whatever form, whether of literature, of art, of institutions, that mind is inscribed. Books are the best type of the influence of the past, and perhaps we shall get at the truth—learn the amount of the influence more conveniently—by considering their value alone.

The theory of books is noble. The scholar of the first age received into him the world around; brooded thereon; gave it the new arrangement of his own mind, and uttered it again. It came into him—life; it went out from him—truth. It came to him—short-lived actions; it went out from him—immortal thoughts. It came to him—business; it went from him—poetry. It was—dead fact; now, it is quick thought. It can stand, and it can go. It now endures, it now flies, it now inspires. Precisely in proportion to the depth of mind from which it issued, so high does it soar, so long does it sing.

Or, I might say, it depends on how far the process had gone, of transmuting life into truth. In proportion to the completeness of the distillation, so will the purity and imperishableness of the product be. But none is quite perfect. As no air-pump can by any means make a perfect vacuum, so neither can any artist entirely exclude the conventional, the local, the perishable from his book, or write a book of pure thought that shall be as efficient, in all respects, to a remote posterity, as to contemporaries, or rather to the second age. Each age, it is found, must write its own books; or rather, each generation for the next succeeding. The books of an older period will not fit this.

Yet hence arises a grave mischief. The sacredness which attaches to the act of creation,—the act of thought,—is instantly transferred to the record. The poet chanting, was felt to be a divine man. Henceforth the chant is divine also. The writer was a just and wise spirit. Henceforward it is settled, the book is perfect; as love of the hero corrupts into worship of his statue. Instantly, the book becomes noxious. The guide is a tyrant. We sought a brother, and lo, a governor. The sluggish and perverted mind of the multitude, always slow to open to the incursions of Reason, having once so opened, having once received this book, stands upon it, and makes an outcry, if it is disparaged. Colleges are built on it. Books are written on it by thinkers, not by Man Thinking; by men of talent, that is, who start wrong, who set out from accepted dogmas, not from their own sight of principles. Meek young men grow up in libraries, believing it their duty to accept the views which Cicero, which Locke, which Bacon have given, forgetful that Cicero, Locke and Bacon were only young men in libraries when they wrote these books.

Hence, instead of Man Thinking, we have the bookworm. Hence, the book-learned class, who value books, as such; not as related to nature and the human constitution, but as making a sort of Third Estate with the world and the soul. Hence, the restorers of readings, the emendators, the bibliomaniacs of all degrees.

This is bad; this is worse than it seems. Books are the best of things, well used; abused, among the worst. What is the right use? What is the one end which all means go to effect? They are for nothing but to inspire. I had better never see a book than to be warped by its attraction clean out of my own orbit, and made a satellite instead of a system. The one thing in the world of value, is, the active soul,—the soul, free, sovereign, active. This every man is entitled to; this every man contains within him, although in almost all men, obstructed, and as yet unborn. The soul active sees absolute truth; and utters truth, or creates. In this action, it is genius; not the privilege of here and there a favorite, but the sound estate of every man. In its essence, it is progressive. The book, the college, the school of art, the institution of any kind, stop with some past utterance of genius. This is good, say they,—let us hold by this. They pin me down. They look backward and not forward. But genius always looks forward. The eyes of man are set in his forehead, not in his hindhead. Man hopes. Genius creates. To create,—to create,—is the proof of a divine presence. Whatever talents may be, if the man create not, the pure efflux of the Deity is not his:—cinders and smoke, there may be, but not yet flame. There are creative manners, there are creative actions, and creative words; manners, actions, words, that is, indicative of no custom or authority, but springing spontaneous from the mind's own sense of good and fair.

On the other part, instead of being its own seer, let it receive always from another mind its truth, though it were in torrents of light, without periods of solitude, inquest and self-recovery, and a fatal disservice is done. Genius is always sufficiently the enemy of genius by over-influence. The literature of every nation bear me witness. The English dramatic poets have Shakspearized now for two hundred years.

Undoubtedly there is a right way of reading,—so it be sternly subordinated. Man Thinking must not be subdued by his instruments. Books are for the scholar's idle times. When he can read God directly, the hour is too precious to be wasted in other men's transcripts of their readings. But when the intervals of darkness come, as come they must,—when the soul seeth not, when the sun is hid, and the stars withdraw their shining,—we repair to the lamps which were kindled by their ray to guide our steps to the East again, where the dawn is. We hear that we may speak. The Arabian proverb says, "A fig tree looking on a fig tree, becometh fruitful."

It is remarkable, the character of the pleasure we derive from the best books. They impress us ever with the conviction that one nature wrote and the same reads. We read the verses of one of the great English poets, of Chaucer, or Marvell, of Dryden, with the most modern joy,—with a pleasure, I mean, which is in great part caused by the abstraction of all *time* from their verses. There is some awe mixed with the joy of our surprise, when this poet, who lived in some past world, two or three hundred years ago, says that which lies close to my own soul, that which I also had well-nigh thought and said. But for the evidence thence afforded to the philosophical doctrine of the identity of all minds, we should suppose some preestablished harmony, some foresight of souls that were to be, and some preparation of stores for their future wants, like the fact observed in insects, who lay up food before death for the young grub they shall never see.

I would not be hurried by any love of system, by any exaggeration of instincts, to underrate the Book. We all know, that as the human body can be nourished on any food, though it were boiled grass and the broth of shoes, so the human mind can be fed by any knowledge. And great and heroic men have existed, who had almost no other information than by the printed page. I only would say, that it needs a strong head to bear that diet. One must be an inventor to read well. As the proverb says, "He that would bring home the wealth of the Indies, must carry out the wealth of the Indies." There is then creative reading, as well as creative writing. When the mind is braced by labor and invention, the page of whatever book we read becomes luminous with manifold allusion. Every sentence is doubly significant, and the sense of our author is as broad as the world. We then see, what is always true, that as the seer's hour of vision is short and rare among heavy days and months, so is its record, perchance, the least part of his volume. The discerning will read in his Plato or Shakspeare, only that least part,—only the authentic utterances of the oracle,—and all the rest he rejects, were it never so many times Plato's and Shakspeare's.

Of course, there is a portion of reading quite indispensable to a wise man. History and exact science he must learn by laborious reading. Colleges, in like manner, have their indispensable office,—to teach elements. But they can only highly serve us, when they aim not to drill, but to create; when they gather from far every ray of various genius to their hospitable halls, and, by the concentrated fires, set the hearts of their youth on flame. Thought and knowledge are natures in which apparatus and pretension avail nothing. Gowns, and pecuniary foundations, though of towns of gold, can never countervail the least sentence or syllable of wit. Forget this, and our American colleges will recede in their public importance whilst they grow richer every year.

### III

There goes in the world a notion that the scholar should be a recluse, a valetudinarian,—as unfit for any handiwork or public labor, as a penknife for an axe. The so-called "practical men" sneer at speculative men, as if, because they speculate or *see*, they could do nothing. I have heard it said that the clergy,—who are always more universally than any other class, the scholars of their day,—are addressed as women: that the rough, spontaneous conversation of men they do not hear, but only a mincing and diluted speech. They are often virtually disfranchised; and, indeed, there are advocates for their celibacy. As far as this is true of the studious classes, it is not just and wise. Action is with the scholar subordinate, but it is essential. Without it, he is not yet man. Without it, thought can never ripen into truth. Whilst the world hangs before the eye as a cloud of beauty, we cannot even see its beauty. Inaction is cowardice, but there can be no scholar without the heroic mind. The preamble of thought, the transition through which it passes from the unconscious to the conscious, is action. Only so much do I know, as I have lived. Instantly we know whose words are loaded with life, and whose not.

The world,—this shadow of the soul, or *other me,* lies wide around. Its attractions are the keys which unlock my thoughts and make me acquainted with myself. I run eagerly into the resounding tumult. I grasp the hands of those next to me, and take my place in the ring to suffer and to work, taught by an instinct that so shall the dumb abyss be vocal with speech. I pierce its order; I dissipate its fear; I dispose of it within the circuit of my expanding life. So much only of life as I know by experience, so much of wilderness have I vanquished and planted, or so far have I extended my being, my dominion. I do not see how any man can afford, for the sake of his nerves and his nap, to spare any action in which he can partake. It is pearls and rubies to his discourse. Drudgery, calamity, exasperation, want, are instructors in eloquence and wisdom. The true scholar grudges every opportunity of action past by, as a loss of power.

It is the raw material out of which the intellect moulds her splendid products. A strange process too, this, by which experience is converted into thought, as a mulberry leaf is converted into satin. The manufacture goes forward at all hours.

The actions and events of our childhood and youth are now matters of calmest observation. They lie like fair pictures in the air. Not so with our recent actions,—with the business which we now have in hand. On this we are quite unable to speculate. Our affections as yet circulate through it. We no more feel or know it, than we feel the feet, or the hand, or the brain of our body. The new deed is yet a part of life,—remains for a time immersed in our unconscious life. In some contemplative hour, it detaches itself from the life like a ripe fruit, to become a thought of the mind. Instantly, it is raised, transfigured; the corruptible has put on incorruption. Always now it is an object of beauty, however base its origin and neighborhood. Observe, too, the impossibility of antedating this act. In its grub state, it cannot fly, it cannot shine,—it is a dull grub. But suddenly, without observation, the selfsame thing unfurls beautiful wings, and is an angel of wisdom. So is there no fact, no event, in our private history, which shall not, sooner or later, lose its adhesive inert form, and astonish us by soaring from our body into the empyrean. Cradle and infancy, school and playground, the fear of boys, and dogs, and ferules, the love of little maids and berries, and many another fact that once filled the whole sky, are gone already; friend and relative, profession and party, town and country, nation and world, must also soar and sing.

Of course, he who has put forth his total strength in fit actions, has the richest return of wisdom. I will not shut myself out of this globe of action and transplant an oak into a flower pot, there to hunger and pine; nor trust the revenue of some single faculty, and exhaust one vein of thought, much like those Savoyards, who, getting their livelihood by carving shepherds, shepherdesses, and smoking Dutchmen, for all Europe, went out one day to the mountain to find stock, and discovered that they had whittled up the last of their pine trees. Authors we have in numbers, who have written out their vein, and who, moved by a commendable prudence, sail for Greece or Palestine, follow the trapper into the prairie, or ramble round Algiers to replenish their merchantable stock.

If it were only for a vocabulary the scholar would be covetous of action. Life is our dictionary. Years are well spent in country labors; in town—in the insight into trades and manufactures; in frank intercourse with many men and women; in science; in art; to the one end of mastering in all their facts a language, by which to illustrate and embody our perceptions. I learn immediately from any speaker how much he has already lived, through the poverty or the splendor of his speech. Life lies behind us as the quarry from whence we get tiles and copestones for the masonry of to-day. This is the way to learn grammar. Colleges and books only copy the language which the field and the work-yard made.

But the final value of action, like that of books, and better than books, is, that it is a resource. That great principle of Undulation in nature, that shows itself in the inspiring and expiring of the breath; in desire and satiety; in the ebb and flow of the sea, in day and night, in heat and cold, and as yet more deeply ingrained in every atom and every fluid, is known to us under the name of Polarity,—these "fits of easy transmission and reflection," as Newton called them, are the law of nature because they are the law of spirit.

The mind now thinks; now acts; and each fit reproduces the other. When the artist has exhausted his materials, when the fancy no longer paints, when thoughts are no longer apprehended, and books are a weariness,—he has always the resource to *live.* Character is higher than intellect. Thinking is the function. Living is the functionary. The stream retreats to its source. A great soul will be strong to live, as well as strong to think. Does he lack organ or medium to impart his truths? He can still fall back on this elemental force of living them. This is a total act. Thinking is a partial act. Let the grandeur of justice shine in his affairs. Let the beauty of affection cheer his lowly roof. Those "far from fame" who dwell and act with him, will feel the force of his constitution in the doings and passages of the day better than it can be measured by any public and designed display. Time shall teach him that the scholar loses no hour which the man lives. Herein he unfolds the sacred germ of his instinct, screened from influence. What is lost in seemliness is gained in strength. Not out of those on whom systems of education have exhausted their culture, comes the helpful giant to destroy the old or to build the new, but out of unhandselled savage nature, out of terrible Druids and Berserkirs, come at last Alfred and Shakspeare.

I hear therefore with joy whatever is beginning to be said of the dignity and necessity of labor to every citizen. There is virtue yet in the hoe and the spade, for learned as well as for unlearned hands. And labor is every where welcome; always we are invited to work; only be this limitation observed, that a man shall not for the sake of wider activity sacrifice any opinion to the popular judgments and modes of action.

I have now spoken of the education of the scholar by nature, by books, and by action. It remains to say somewhat of his duties.

They are such as become Man Thinking. They may all be comprised in self-trust. The office of the scholar is to cheer, to raise, and to guide men by showing them facts amidst appearance. He plies the slow, unhonored, and unpaid task of observation. Flamsteed and Herschel, in their glazed observatories, may catalogue the stars with the praise of all men, and, the results being splendid and useful, honor is sure. But he, in his private observatory, cataloguing obscure and nebulous stars of the human mind, which as yet no man has thought of as such,—watching days and months, sometimes, for a few facts; correcting still his old records;—must relinquish display and immediate fame. In the long period of his preparation, he must betray often an ignorance and shiftlessness in popular arts, incurring the disdain of the able who shoulder him aside. Long he must stammer in his speech; often forego the living for the dead. Worse yet, he must accept—how often! poverty and solitude. For the ease and pleasure of treading the old road, accepting the fashions, the education, the religion of society, he takes the cross of making his own, and, of course, the self-accusation, the faint heart, the frequent uncertainty and loss of time which are the nettles and tangling vines in the way of the self-relying and self-directed; and the state of virtual hostility in which he seems to stand to society, and especially to educated society. For all this loss and scorn, what offset? He is to find consolation in exercising the highest functions of human nature. He is one who raises himself from private considerations, and breathes and lives on public and illustrious thoughts. He is the world's eye. He is the world's heart. He is to resist the vulgar prosperity that retrogrades ever to barbarism, by preserving and communicating heroic sentiments, noble biographies, melodious verse, and the conclusions of history. Whatsoever oracles the human heart in all emergencies, in all solemn hours has uttered as its commentary on the world of actions,—these he shall receive and impart. And whatsoever new verdict Reason from her inviolable seat pronounces on the passing men and events of to-day,—this he shall hear and promulgate.

These being his functions, it becomes him to feel all confidence in himself, and to defer never to the popular cry. He and he only knows the world. The world of any moment is the merest appearance. Some great decorum, some fetish of a government, some ephemeral trade, or war, or man, is cried up by half mankind and cried down by the other half, as if all depended on this particular up or down. The odds are that the whole question is not worth the poorest thought which the scholar has lost in listening to the controversy. Let him not quit his belief that a popgun is a popgun, though the ancient and honorable of the earth affirm it to be the crack of doom. In silence, in steadiness, in severe abstraction, let him hold by himself; add observation to observation, patient of neglect, patient of reproach; and bide his own time,—happy enough if he can satisfy himself alone that this day he has seen something truly. Success treads on every right step. For the instinct is sure that prompts him to tell his brother what he thinks. He then learns that in going down into the secrets of his own mind, he has descended into the secrets of all minds. He learns that he who has mastered any law in his private thoughts, is master to that extent of all men whose language he speaks, and of all into whose language his own can be translated. The poet in utter solitude remembering his spontaneous thoughts and recording them, is found to have recorded that which men in crowded cities find true for them also. The orator distrusts at first the fitness of his frank confessions,—his want of knowledge of the persons he addresses,—until he finds that he is the complement of his hearers;—that they drink his words because he fulfils for them their own nature; the deeper he dives into his privatest secretest presentiment,—to his wonder he finds, this is the most acceptable, most public, and universally true. The people delight in it; the better part of every man feels. This is my music; this is myself.

In self-trust, all the virtues are comprehended. Free should the scholar be,—free and brave. Free even to the definition of freedom, "without any hindrance that does not arise out of his own constitution." Brave; for fear is a thing which a scholar by his very function puts behind him. Fear always springs from ignorance. It is a shame to him if his tranquility, amid dangerous times, arises from the presumption that like children and women, his is a protected class; or if he seek a temporary peace by the diversion of his thoughts from politics or vexed questions, hiding his head like an ostrich in the flowering bushes, peeping into microscopes, and turning rhymes, as a boy whistles to keep his courage up. So is the danger a danger still: so is the fear worse. Manlike let him turn and face it. Let him look into its eye and search its nature, inspect its origin,—see the whelping of this lion,—which lies no great way back; he will then find in himself a perfect comprehension of its nature and extent; he will have made his hands meet on the other side, and can henceforth defy it, and pass on superior. The world is his who can see through its pretension. What deafness, what stone-blind custom, what overgrown error you behold, is there only by sufferance,—by your sufferance. See it to be a lie, and you have already dealt it its mortal blow.

Yes, we are the cowed,—we the trustless. It is a mischievous notion that we are come late into nature; that the world was finished a long time ago. As the world was plastic and fluid in the hands of God, so it is ever to so much of his attributes as we bring to it. To ignorance and sin, it is flint. They adapt themselves to it as they may; but in proportion as a man has anything in him divine, the firmament flows before him, and takes his signet and form. Not he is great who can alter matter, but he who can alter my state of mind. They are the kings of the world who give the color of their present thought to all nature and all art, and persuade men by the cheerful serenity of their carrying the matter, that this thing which they do, is the apple which the ages have desired to pluck, now at last ripe, and inviting nations to the harvest. The great man makes the great thing. Wherever Macdonald sits, there is the head of the table. Linnæus makes botany the most alluring of studies and wins it from the farmer and the herb-woman. Davy, chemistry: and Cuvier, fossils. The day is always his, who works in it with serenity and great aims. The unstable estimates of men crowd to him whose mind is filled with a truth, as the heaped waves of the Atlantic follow the moon.

For this self-trust, the reason is deeper than can be fathomed,—darker than can be enlightened. I might not carry with me the feeling of my audience in stating my own belief. But I have already shown the ground of my hope, in adverting to the doctrine that man is one. I believe man has been wronged: he has wronged himself. He has almost lost the light that can lead him back to his prerogatives. Men are become of no account. Men in history, men in the world of to-day are bugs, are spawn, and are called "the mass" and "the herd." In a century, in a millennium, one or two men; that is to say—one or two approximations to the right state of every man. All the rest behold in the hero or the poet their own green and crude being—ripened; yes, and are content to be less, so *that* may attain to its full stature. What a testimony—full of grandeur, full of pity, is borne to the demands of his own nature, by the poor clansman, the poor partisan, who rejoices in the glory of his chief. The poor and the low find some amends to their immense moral capacity, for their acquiescence in a political and social inferiority. They are content to be brushed like flies from the path of a great person, so that justice shall be done by him to that common nature which it is the dearest desire of all to see enlarged and glorified. They sun themselves in the great man's light, and feel it to be their own element. They cast the dignity of man from their downtrod selves upon the shoulders of a hero, and will perish to add one drop of blood to make that great heart beat, those giant sinews combat and conquer. He lives for us, and we live in him.

Men such as they are, very naturally seek money or power; and power because it is as good as money,—the "spoils," so called, "of office." And why not? for they aspire to the highest, and this, in their sleep-walking, they dream is highest. Wake them, and they shall quit the false good and leap to the true, and leave governments to clerks and desks. This revolution is to be wrought by the gradual domestication of the idea of Culture. The main enterprise of the world for splendor, for extent, is the upbuilding of a man. Here are the materials strown along the ground. The private life of one man shall be a more illustrious monarchy,—more formidable to its enemy, more sweet and serene in its influence to its friend, than any kingdom in history. For a man, rightly viewed, comprehendeth the particular natures of all men. Each philosopher, each bard, each actor, has only done for me, as by a delegate, what one day I can do for myself. The books which once we valued more than the apple of the eye, we have quite exhausted. What is that but saying that we have come up with the point of view which the universal mind took through the eyes of that one scribe; we have been that man, and have passed on. First, one; then, another; we drain all cisterns, and waxing greater by all these supplies, we crave a better and more abundant food. The man has never lived that can feed us ever. The human mind cannot be enshrined in a person who shall set a barrier on any one side to this unbounded, unboundable empire. It is one central fire which flaming now out of the lips of Etna, lightens the capes of Sicily; and now out of the throat of Vesuvius, illuminates the towers and vineyards of Naples. It is one light which beams out of a thousand stars. It is one soul which animates all men.

But I have dwelt perhaps tediously upon this abstraction of the Scholar. I ought not to delay longer to add what I have to say, of nearer reference to the time and to this country.

Historically, there is thought to be a difference in the ideas which predominate over successive epochs, and there are data for marking the genius of the Classic, of the Romantic, and now of the Reflective or Philosophical age. With the views I have intimated of the oneness or the identity of the mind through all individuals, I do not much dwell on these differences. In fact, I believe each individual passes through all three. The boy is a Greek; the youth, romantic; the adult, reflective. I deny not, however, that a revolution in the leading idea may be distinctly enough traced.

Our age is bewailed as the age of Introversion. Must that needs be evil? We, it seems, are critical. We are embarrassed with second thoughts. We cannot enjoy any thing for hankering to know whereof the pleasure consists. We are lined with eyes. We see with our feet. The time is infected with Hamlet's unhappiness,—

"Sicklied o'er with the pale cast of thought."

Is it so bad then? Sight is the last thing to be pitied. Would we be blind? Do we fear lest we should outsee nature and God, and drink truth dry? I look upon the discontent of the literary class as a mere announcement of the fact that they find themselves not in the state of mind of their fathers, and regret the coming state as untried; as a boy dreads the water before he has learned that he can swim. If there is any period one would desire to be born in,—is it not the age of Revolution; when the old and the new stand side by side, and admit of being compared; when the energies of all men are searched by fear and by hope; when the historic glories of the old, can be compensated by the rich possibilities of the new era? This time, like all times, is a very good one, if we but know what to do with it.

I read with joy some of the auspicious signs of the coming days as they glimmer already through poetry and art, through philosophy and science, through church and state.

One of these signs is the fact that the same movement which effected the elevation of what was called the lowest class in the state, assumed in litera- ture a very marked and as benign an aspect. Instead of the sublime and beautiful, the near, the low, the common, was explored and poetized. That which had been negligently trodden under foot by those who were harness- ing and provisioning themselves for long journeys into far countries, is sud- denly found to be richer than all foreign parts. The literature of the poor, the feelings of the child, the philosophy of the street, the meaning of household life, are the topics of the time. It is a great stride. It is a sign—is it not? of new vigor, when the extremities are made active, when currents of warm life run into the hands and the feet. I ask not for the great, the remote, the romantic; what is doing in Italy or Arabia; what is Greek art, or Provencal Minstrelsy; I embrace the common, I explore and sit at the feet of the familiar, the low. Give me insight into to-day, and you may have the antique and future worlds. What would we really know the meaning of? The meal in the firkin; the milk in the pan; the ballad in the street; the news of the boat; the glance of the eye; the form and the gait of the body;—show me the ultimate reason of these matters;—show me the sublime presence of the highest spiritual cause lurking, as always it does lurk, in these suburbs and extremities of na- ture; let me see every trifle bristling with the polarity that ranges it instantly on an eternal law; and the shop, the plough, the leger, referred to the like cause by which light undulates and poets sing;—and the world lies no longer a dull miscellany and lumber room, but has form and order; there is no trifle; there is no puzzle; but one design unites and animates the farthest pinnacle and the lowest trench.

This idea has inspired the genius of Goldsmith, Burns, Cowper, and, in a newer time, of Goethe, Wordsworth, and Carlyle. This idea they have differently followed and with various success. In contrast with their writ- ing, the style of Pope, of Johnson, of Gibbon, looks cold and pedantic. This writing is blood-warm. Man is surprised to find that things near are not less beautiful and wondrous than things remote. The near explains the far. The drop is a small ocean. A man is related to all nature. This perception of the worth of the vulgar, is fruitful in discoveries. Goethe, in this very thing the most modern of the moderns, has shown us, as none ever did, the genius of the ancients.

There is one man of genius who has done much for this philosophy of life, whose literary value has never yet been rightly estimated;—I mean Emanuel Swedenborg. The most imaginative of men, yet writing with the precision of a mathematician, he endeavored to engraft a purely philo- sophical Ethics on the popular Christianity of his time. Such an attempt, of course, must have difficulty which no genius could surmount. But he saw and showed the connexion between nature and the affections of the soul. He pierced the emblematic or spiritual character of the visible, audible, tangible world. Especially did his shade-loving muse hover over and in- terpret the lower parts of nature; he showed the mysterious bond that allies moral evil to the foul material forms, and has given in epical parables a theory of insanity, of beasts, of unclean and fearful things.

Another sign of our times, also marked by an analogous political movement is, the new importance given to the single person. Every thing that tends to insulate the individual,—to surround him with barriers of natural respect, so that each man shall feel the world is his, and man shall treat with man as a sovereign state with a sovereign state;—tends to true union as well as greatness. "I learned," said the melancholy Pestalozzi, "that no man in God's wide earth is either willing or able to help any other man." Help must come from the bosom alone. The scholar is that man who must take up into himself all the ability of the time, all the contributions of the past, all the hopes of the future. He must be an university of knowledges. If there be one lesson more than another which should pierce his ear, it is, The world is nothing, the man is all; in yourself is the law of all nature, and you know not yet how a globule of sap ascends; in yourself lumbers the whole of Reason; it is for you to know all, it is for you to dare all. Mr. President and Gentlemen, this confidence in the unsearched might of man, belongs by all motives, by all prophecy, by all preparation, to the American Scholar. We have listened too long to the courtly muses of Europe. The spirit of the American freeman is already suspected to be timid, imitative, tame. Public and private avarice make the air we breathe thick and fat. The scholar is decent, indolent, complaisant. See already the tragic consequence. The mind of this country taught to aim at low objects, eats upon itself. There is no work for any but the decorous and the complaisant. Young men of the fairest promise, who begin life upon our shores, inflated by the mountain winds, shined upon by all the stars of God, find the earth below not in unison with these,—but are hindered from action by the disgust which the principles on which business is managed inspire, and turn drudges, or die of disgust,—some of them suicides. What is the remedy? They did not yet see, and thousands of young men as hopeful now crowding to the barriers for the career, do not yet see, that if the single man plant himself indomitably on his instincts, and there abide, the huge world will come round to him. Patience—patience;—with the shades of all the good and great for company; and for solace, the perspective of your own infinite life; and for work, the study and the communication of principles, the making those instincts prevalent, the conversion of the world. Is it not the chief disgrace in the world, not to be an unit;—not to be reckoned one character;—not to yield that peculiar fruit which each man was created to bear, but to be reckoned in the gross, in the hundred, or the thousand, of the party, the section, to which we belong; and our opinion predicted geographically, as the north, or the south. Not so, brothers and friends,—please God, ours shall not be so. We will walk on our own feet; we will work with our own hands; we will speak our own minds. The study of letters shall be no longer a name for pity, for doubt, and for sensual indulgence. The dread of man and the love of man shall be a wall of defence and a wreath of joy around all. A nation of men will for the first time exist, because each believes himself inspired by the Divine Soul which also inspires all men.

•  •  •  •  •  •  •  •  •  •  •  •  •  •

## QUESTIONS FOR A SECOND READING

1. Emerson's prose is difficult to read and the difficulty is not simply the difficulty of long sentences or big words. Emerson's writing is difficult because it is unusual. His sentences and paragraphs don't do what we are trained to think sentences and paragraphs are supposed to do. As readers, we are not trained to read him.

    As you reread, see if you can derive a "theory" to account for Emerson's prose. What are his characteristic sentences? How are they constructed? How are they voiced? How would you outline or describe a characteristic paragraph? If you take a section, say the section he marks as section II, how is it organized? How does he get from paragraph to paragraph and from beginning to end? And how is this system different from the system you were taught in school—as both a reader and a writer? (As an exercise, you might want to try to write an Emersonian paragraph.)

2. At the end of his essay, Emerson says "If the single man plant himself indomitably on his instincts, and there abide, the huge world will come round to him." As you reread this essay, what do you come to understand about "instinct," as Emerson refers to it? Could you say, for example, that Emerson is arguing that every student should be free to do what he or she wants? If so, what role would teachers or writers play in a person's education? If not, what should a student do other than take notes, read carefully, and follow the rules?

3. The scholar in this essay is both a person who learns and a person who teaches. (The latter is described most fully in the section on the scholar's duties.) How does Emerson describe the best possible relationship between a scholar and his or her teachers? How does he describe the best possible relationship between the scholar and those he or she would teach? In what ways, if at all, would the scholar change as he or she moved from the role of student into the role of teacher?

4. In section I of the essay, Emerson charts the growth of a young person's mind and at the end concludes that, if all goes well, "Know Thyself" and "Study Nature" become "at last one maxim." What does he mean by this? It sounds lofty and pious, but if you take your own case or the case of a child you know well, how might you use section I to comment on current practices in American education? What would be your most useful and powerful examples?

5. In section II of the essay, Emerson talks about the relationship between the scholar and the "mind of the past" and, in particular, about the proper

and improper uses of books. Books, he says, "are the best of things, well used; abused, among the worst." What do you suppose Emerson would say is the best use of this essay? As you read through the essay, what kind of reader does Emerson invite you to be? What would you have to do—specifically and at specific places—to be an "Emersonian" reader of Emerson?

### ASSIGNMENTS FOR WRITING

1. Emerson says that in the three numbered sections of his essay he has "spoken of the education of the scholar by nature, by books and by action." Let's say that you wanted to take Emerson as a guide and imagine an appropriate "Emersonian" curriculum or institution. Write an essay (cast, perhaps, as a position paper or an article for an alumni magazine) that uses "The American Scholar" to comment specifically on the curriculum at your own school. (It might be useful to go to your college catalogue, or whatever documents your school has prepared to explain its curriculum, to see what they have to say about the role of nature, books, and action in a person's education.)

2. Let's imagine Emerson himself as a teacher who wants to have his students read "The American Scholar" (perhaps along with some other selections from this anthology). What kind of assignment might he give? What, that is, would he ask you to *do* with the readings? What would he do as your teacher? Write an essay that considers both how, in practice, a modern teacher might encourage an Emersonian use of books and why, so far as you are concerned, a modern teacher might want to.

3. There is no question but that Emerson's text is difficult to read, and the difficulty is not simply a matter of big or unusual words. The text just doesn't do what we expect it to do. Some of its elusiveness can be attributed to the time during which it was written—expectations were different then—but this should not keep you from making the most of your own responses as a reader. For one thing, it's not completely true; not everyone in the 1830s wrote like Emerson. For another, it assumes that a nonspecialist cannot or should not read works from the past. One way of imagining your connection to the 1830s is to imagine that your encounter with this text is somehow typical—that you, too, are Emerson's contemporary.

   Take a section of the essay that you find characteristically difficult. (Section II is an interesting one to work with.) Reread it, paying close attention to the experience of reading. Where are you surprised? Where are you confused? How might this be part of a strategy, part of Emerson's design? What is Emerson doing? What is he asking you to do? This should be an exercise in close reading. You want to pay attention to how paragraph leads to paragraph, sentence leads to sentence; to notice the ways examples or statements are offered and taken away.

   Write an essay in which you describe in close detail the story of what it was like to read this section of "The American Scholar." Tell a story of reading, one where you and Emerson are the main characters—complicated characters, not stick figures (the Innocent Child and the Inscrutable

Genius). When you are done, see what connections you can make with Emerson's argument—with what he says is a proper relation between readers and writers. In what ways might his difficulties and yours be said to be unfortunate? In what ways might they be signs of his attempts to get the language (and a reader) to do what he wants them to do?

4. It's obvious that Emerson's essay is addressed to men. A text such as this can be an occasion for a close reading of the ways in which an author creates or imagines gender—and all of the social characteristics associated with it, especially what an author considers to be "natural" to men and women. It's possible to think of an author's claims for something as being "natural," in other words, as a device that both masks and reveals social attributes that could be said to be constructed through culture. The word "natural," or an author's implications that some things are "natural" to men or women, can become, then, a site for a close study of the beliefs and values an author might be assuming about men and women or about manliness and womanliness.

   This assignment has two parts. The first invites you to work with Emerson's "The American Scholar" to study how he figures what is "natural" for men, and, therefore, by implication what might be (or might not be) natural for women. The second part asks you to situate this understanding of Emerson's construction of men and manliness—and his indirect construction of women and womanliness—in a larger context defined by something else he has written.

   For the first part of this assignment, then, pick two or three passages from Emerson's "The American Scholar" where you understand him to be writing about what he takes to be "natural" to men or manliness. Write an essay in which you discuss the assumptions about men and women he reveals in these passages. What, too, do the passages mask or hide about his assumptions about women?

   To complete the second part of this assignment, you will need to go to the library, or to use the Internet, to locate another essay by Emerson that has to do with education and culture, so that you can enlarge your critique of gender in Emerson's writings to include his figuring of what's "natural" to men and women in this additional text. Once you have read and studied this additional text, write a second section to your essay in which you extend your discussion of Emerson. How does your second reading inflect your first one of "The American Scholar"? What else can you say now? Or what do you want to say differently? You'll want to work closely with two or three significant passages from each of the texts you've chosen, but even before you do that, you'll want to choose these texts carefully, so that they allow you to write about how he figures what he sees as "natural" for men and women.

## MAKING CONNECTIONS

1. In each of the three sections of "The American Scholar," Emerson charts out influences on the mind and spirit of the scholar. In section I, for example, he says, "the first in time and the first in importance of the influ-

ences upon the mind is that of nature. . . . The scholar must needs stand wistful and admiring before this great spectacle." "The next great influence into the spirit of the scholar," he says in section II, "is the mind of the Past,—in whatever form, whether of literature, of art, of institutions, that mind is inscribed." And in the third section Emerson argues against the image of the scholar as "a recluse, a valetudinarian,—as unfit for any handiwork or public labor" in favor of the scholar as a "man of action" in the world.

W. E. B. Du Bois, in the three chapters from *The Souls of Black Folk* (pp. 224, 231, 238), also lays out a program for the creation of the American scholar, although he is writing about a different set of students than the privileged white elite who attended Harvard University in 1837. Compared to Emerson, Du Bois is more concerned with institutions and political programs, with the social structures necessary for young black men and women to receive a university education a little more than a half century after Emerson's Phi Beta Kappa oration.

Write an essay in which you take the structure of Emerson's essay and respond to each of its sections from Du Bois's perspective. You can, if you choose, write in Du Bois's voice and style. Whether you do this or not, be sure to engage and to bring to bear his terms and examples. What, in other words, do you imagine Du Bois would have to say to Emerson? How might you locate Du Bois's vision of education and the scholarly life within or against Emerson's?

2. Emerson, in "The American Scholar," seems to be arguing for freedom or for a form of education that allows students to be free. A similar capsule summary could be given of the essays by Paulo Freire, "The 'Banking' Concept of Education" (p. 348); Mary Louise Pratt, "Arts of the Contact Zone" (p. 582); and Adrienne Rich, "When We Dead Awaken: Writing as Re-Vision" (p. 603). If we grant them this common ground or common motive, it is interesting to consider the significant differences in their arguments. Write an essay in which you compare Emerson's essay with one of the other three. What does "freedom" come to mean for each? What does this freedom have to do with knowledge or vocation or method or whatever it is that a student is supposed to gain by an education?

# MICHEL
# FOUCAULT

$M$ICHEL FOUCAULT (1926–1984) stands at the end of the twentieth century as one of the world's leading intellectuals. He was trained as a philosopher, but much of his work, like that presented in Discipline and Punish: The Birth of the Prison (1975), traces the presence of certain ideas across European history. So he could also be thought of as a historian, but a historian whose goal is to revise the usual understanding of history—not as a progressive sequence but as a series of repetitions governed by powerful ideas, terms, and figures. Foucault was also a public intellectual, involved in such prominent issues as prison reform. He wrote frequently for French newspapers and reviews. His death from AIDS was front-page news in Le Monde, the French equivalent of the New York Times. He taught at several French universities and in 1970 was appointed to a professorship at the College de France, the highest position in the French system. He traveled widely, lecturing and visiting at universities throughout the world.

Foucault's work is central to much current work in the humanities and the social sciences. In fact, it is hard to imagine any area of the academy that has not been influenced by his writing. There is a certain irony in all this, since Foucault argued persuasively that we need to give up thinking about knowledge as individually produced; we have to stop thinking the way we do about the "author" or the "genius," about individuality or creativity; we have to stop thinking as though *there were truths that stand beyond the interests of a given moment. It is both dangerous and wrong, he argued, to assume that knowledge is disinterested. Edward Said had this to say of Foucault:*

> *His great critical contribution was to dissolve the anthropological models of identity and subjecthood underlying research in the humanistic and social sciences. Instead of seeing everything in culture and society as ultimately emanating from either a sort of unchanging Cartesian ego or a heroic solitary artist, Foucault proposed the much juster notion that all work, like social life itself, is collective. The principal task therefore is to circumvent or break down the ideological biases that prevent us from saying that what enables a doctor to practice medicine or a historian to write history is not mainly a set of individual gifts, but an ability to follow rules that are taken for granted as an unconscious a priori by all professionals. More than anyone before him, Foucault specified rules for those rules, and even more impressively, he showed how over long periods of time the rules became epistemological enforcers of what (as well as of how) people thought, lived, and spoke.*

*These rules, these unconscious enforcers, are visible in "discourse"—ways of thinking and speaking and acting that we take for granted as naturally or inevitably there but that are constructed over time and preserved by those who act without question, without stepping outside the discourse and thinking critically. But, says Foucault, there is no place "outside" the discourse, no free, clear space. There is always only another discursive position. A person in thinking, living, and speaking expresses not merely himself or herself but the thoughts and roles and phrases governed by the available ways of thinking and speaking. The key questions to ask, then, according to Foucault, are not Who said this? or Is it original? or Is it true? or Is it authentic? but Who talks this way? or What unspoken rules govern this way of speaking? or Where is this discourse used? Who gets to use it? when? and to what end?*

*The following selection is the third chapter of* Discipline and Punish: The Birth of the Prison *(translated from the French by Alan Sheridan). In this book, Foucault is concerned with the relationships between knowledge and power, arguing that knowledge is not pure and abstract but is implicated in networks of power relations. Or, as he puts it elsewhere, people govern themselves "through the production of truth." This includes the "truths" that determine how we imagine and manage the boundaries between the "normal" and the transgressive, the lawful and the delinquent. In a characteristic move, Foucault reverses our intuitive sense of how things are. He argues, for example, that it is not the case that prisons serve the courts and a system of justice but that the courts are the products, the servants of "the prison," the prison as an idea, as the central figure in a way of thinking about transgression, order, and the body, a way of thinking that is persistent and general, present, for example, through all efforts to produce the normal or "disciplined individual": "in the central position that [the prison] occupies, it is not alone, but linked to a whole series of 'carceral' mechanisms which seem distinct enough—since they are intended to alleviate pain, to cure, to comfort—but which all tend, like the prison, to exercise a power of normalization." Knowledge stands in an antagonistic role in* Discipline and Punish; *it is part of a problem, not a route to a solution.*

*You will find "Panopticism" difficult reading. All readers find Foucault's prose tough going. It helps to realize that it is necessarily difficult. Foucault, remember, is trying to work outside of, or in spite of, the usual ways of thinking and writing. He is trying* not *to reproduce the standard discourse but to point to what it cannot or will not say. He is trying to make gestures beyond what is ordinarily, normally said. So his prose struggles with its own situation. Again, as Edward Said says, "What [Foucault] was interested in . . . was 'the more' that can be discovered lurking in signs and discourses but that is irreducible to language and speech; 'it is this "more,"' he said, 'that we must reveal and describe.' Such a concern appears to be both devious and obscure, yet it accounts for a lot that is specially unsettling in Foucault's writing. There is no such thing as being at home in his writing, neither for reader nor for writer." While readers find Foucault difficult, he is widely read and widely cited. His books include* The Birth of the Clinic: An Archaeology of Medical Perception *(1963),* The Order of Things: An Archaeology of the Human Sciences *(1966),* The Archaeology of Knowledge *(1969),* Madness and Civilization *(1971), and the three-volume* History of Sexuality *(1976, 1979, 1984).*

# Panopticism

The following, according to an order published at the end of the seventeenth century, were the measures to be taken when the plague appeared in a town.[1]

First, a strict spatial partitioning: the closing of the town and its outlying districts, a prohibition to leave the town on pain of death, the killing of all stray animals; the division of the town into distinct quarters, each governed by an intendant. Each street is placed under the authority of a syndic, who keeps it under surveillance; if he leaves the street, he will be condemned to death. On the appointed day, everyone is ordered to stay indoors: it is forbidden to leave on pain of death. The syndic himself comes to lock the door of each house from the outside; he takes the key with him and hands it over to the intendant of the quarter; the intendant keeps it until the end of the quarantine. Each family will have made its own provisions; but, for bread and wine, small wooden canals are set up between the street and the interior of the houses, thus allowing each person to receive his ration without communicating with the suppliers and other residents; meat, fish, and herbs will be hoisted up into the houses with pulleys and baskets. If it is absolutely necessary to leave the house, it will be done in turn, avoiding any meeting. Only the intendants, syndics, and guards will move about the streets and also, between the infected houses, from one corpse to another, the "crows," who can be left to die: these are "people of little substance who carry the sick, bury the dead, clean, and do many vile and abject offices." It is a segmented, immobile, frozen space. Each individual is fixed in his place. And, if he moves, he does so at the risk of his life, contagion, or punishment.

Inspection functions ceaselessly. The gaze is alert everywhere: "A considerable body of militia, commanded by good officers and men of substance," guards at the gates, at the town hall, and in every quarter to ensure the prompt obedience of the people and the most absolute authority of the magistrates, "as also to observe all disorder, theft and extortion." At each of the town gates there will be an observation post; at the end of each street sentinels. Every day, the intendant visits the quarter in his charge, inquires whether the syndics have carried out their tasks, whether the inhabitants have anything to complain of; they "observe their actions." Every day, too, the syndic goes into the street for which he is responsible; stops before each house: gets all the inhabitants to appear at the windows (those who live overlooking the courtyard will be allocated a window looking onto the street at which no one but they may show themselves); he calls each of them by name; informs himself as to the state of each and every one of them—"in which respect the inhabitants will be compelled to speak the truth under pain of death"; if someone does not appear at the window, the syndic must ask why: "In this way he will find out easily enough whether dead or sick are being concealed." Everyone locked up in his cage, everyone at his window, answering to his name and showing himself when asked—it is the great review of the living and the dead.

This surveillance is based on a system of permanent registration: reports from the syndics to the intendants, from the intendants to the magistrates or mayor. At the beginning of the "lock up," the role of each of the inhabitants present in the town is laid down, one by one; this document bears "the name, age, sex of everyone, notwithstanding his condition": a copy is sent to the intendant of the quarter, another to the office of the town hall, another to enable the syndic to make his daily roll call. Everything that may be observed during the course of the visits—deaths, illnesses, complaints, irregularities—is noted down and transmitted to the intendants and magistrates. The magistrates have complete control over medical treatment; they have appointed a physician in charge; no other practitioner may treat, no apothecary prepare medicine, no confessor visit a sick person without having received from him a written note "to prevent anyone from concealing and dealing with those sick of the contagion, unknown to the magistrates." The registration of the pathological must be constantly centralized. The relation of each individual to his disease and to his death passes through the representatives of power, the registration they make of it, the decisions they take on it.

Five or six days after the beginning of the quarantine, the process of purifying the houses one by one is begun. All the inhabitants are made to leave; in each room "the furniture and goods" are raised from the ground or suspended from the air; perfume is poured around the room; after carefully sealing the windows, doors, and even the keyholes with wax, the perfume is set alight. Finally, the entire house is closed while the perfume is consumed; those who have carried out the work are searched, as they were on entry, "in the presence of the residents of the house, to see that they did not have something on their persons as they left that they did not have on entering." Four hours later, the residents are allowed to reenter their homes.

This enclosed, segmented space, observed at every point, in which the individuals are inserted in a fixed place, in which the slightest movements are supervised, in which all events are recorded, in which an uninterrupted work of writing links the center and periphery, in which power is exercised without division, according to a continuous hierarchical figure, in which each individual is constantly located, examined, and distributed among the living beings, the sick, and the dead—all this constitutes a compact model of the disciplinary mechanism. The plague is met by order; its function is to sort out every possible confusion: that of the disease, which is transmitted when bodies are mixed together; that of the evil, which is increased when fear and death overcome prohibitions. It lays down for each individual his place, his body, his disease, and his death, his well-being, by means of an omnipresent and omniscient power that subdivides itself in a regular, uninterrupted way even to the ultimate determination of the individual, of what characterizes him, of what belongs to him, of what happens to him. Against the plague, which is a mixture, discipline brings into play its power, which is one of analysis. A whole literary fiction of the festival grew up around the plague: suspended laws, lifted prohibitions, the frenzy of passing time, bodies mingling together without respect, individuals unmasked, abandoning their statutory identity and the figure under which they had been recognized, allowing a quite different truth to appear. But there was also a political dream of the plague, which was exactly its reverse: not the collective festival, but strict divisions; not laws transgressed, but the penetration of regulation into even the smallest details of everyday life through the mediation of the complete hierarchy that assured the capillary functioning of power; not masks that were put on and taken off, but the assignment to each individual of his "true" name, his "true" place, his "true" body, his "true" disease. The plague as a form, at once real and imaginary, of disorder had as its medical and political correlative discipline. Behind the disciplinary mechanisms can be read the haunting memory of "contagions," of the plague, of rebellions, crimes, vagabondage, desertions, people who appear and disappear, live and die in disorder.

If it is true that the leper gave rise to rituals of exclusion, which to a certain extent provided the model for and general form of the great Confinement, then the plague gave rise to disciplinary projects. Rather than the massive, binary division between one set of people and another, it called for multiple separations, individualizing distributions, an organization in depth of surveillance and control, an intensification and a ramification of power. The leper was caught up in a practice of rejection, of exile-enclosure; he was left to his doom in a mass among which it was useless to differentiate; those sick of the plague were caught up in a meticulous tactical partitioning in which individual differentiations were the constricting effects of a power that multiplied, articulated, and subdivided itself; the great confinement on the one hand; the correct training on the other. The leper and his separation; the plague and its segmentations. The first is marked; the second analyzed and distributed. The exile of the leper and the arrest of the plague do not bring with them the same political dream. The first is that of a pure community, the second that of a disciplined society. Two ways of exercising power over men, of controling their relations, of separating out their dangerous mixtures. The plague-stricken town, traversed throughout with hierarchy, surveillance, observation, writing; the town immobilized by the functioning of an extensive power that bears in a distinct way over all individual bodies—this is the utopia of the perfectly governed city. The plague (envisaged as a possibility at least) is the trial in the course of which one may define ideally the exercise of disciplinary power. In order to make rights and laws function according to pure theory, the jurists place themselves in imagination in the state of nature; in order to see perfect disciplines functioning, rulers dreamed of the state of plague. Underlying disciplinary projects the image of the plague stands for all forms of confusion and disorder; just as the image of the leper, cut off from all human contact, underlies projects of exclusion.

They are different projects, then, but not incompatible ones. We see them coming slowly together, and it is the peculiarity of the nineteenth century that it applied to the space of exclusion of which the leper was the symbolic inhabitant (beggars, vagabonds, madmen, and the disorderly formed the real population) the technique of power proper to disciplinary partitioning. Treat "lepers" as "plague victims," project the subtle segmentations of discipline onto the confused space of internment, combine it with the methods of analytical distribution proper to power, individualize the excluded, but use procedures of individualization to mark exclusion—this is what was operated regularly by disciplinary power from the beginning of the nineteenth century in the psychiatric asylum, the penitentiary, the reformatory, the approved school, and to some extent, the hospital. Generally speaking, all the authorities exercising individual control function according to a double mode; that of binary division and branding (mad/sane; dangerous/harmless; normal/abnormal); and that of coercive assignment, of differential distribution (who he is; where he must be; how he is to be characterized; how he is to be recognized; how a constant surveillance is to be exercised over him in an individual way, etc.). On the one hand, the lepers are treated as plague victims; the tactics of individualizing disciplines are imposed on the excluded; and, on the other hand, the universality of disciplinary controls makes it possible to brand the "leper" and to bring into play against him the dualistic mechanisms of exclusion. The constant division between the normal and the abnormal, to which every individual is subjected, brings us back to our own time, by applying the binary branding and exile of the leper to quite different objects; the existence of a whole set of techniques and institutions for measuring, supervising, and correcting the abnormal brings into play the disciplinary mechanisms to which the fear of the plague gave rise. All the mechanisms of power which, even today, are disposed around the abnormal individual, to brand him and to alter him, are composed of those two forms from which they distantly derive.

Bentham's *Panopticon* is the architectural figure of this composition. We know the principle on which it was based: at the periphery, an annular building; at the center, a tower; this tower is pierced with wide windows that open onto the inner side of the ring; the peripheric building is divided into cells, each of which extends the whole width of the building; they have two windows, one on the inside, corresponding to the windows of the tower; the other, on the outside, allows the light to cross the cell from one end to the other. All that is needed, then, is to place a supervisor

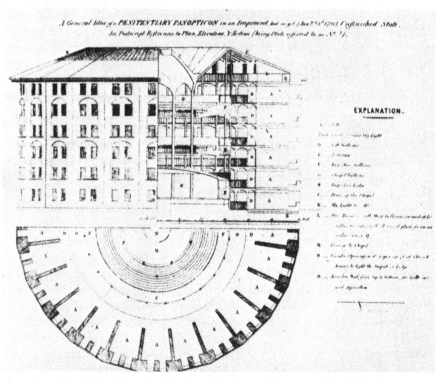

Plan of the Panopticon by J. Bentham (*The Works of Jeremy Bentham,* ed. Bowring, vol. IV, 1843, 172–73)

in a central tower and to shut up in each cell a madman, a patient, a condemned man, a worker, or a schoolboy. By the effect of backlighting, one
can observe from the tower, standing out precisely against the light, the
small captive shadows in the cells of the periphery. They are like so many
cages, so many small theaters, in which each actor is alone, perfectly individualized and constantly visible. The panoptic mechanism arranges spatial unities that make it possible to see constantly and to recognize immediately. In short, it reverses the principle of the dungeon; or rather of its
three functions—to enclose, to deprive of light, and to hide—it preserves
only the first and eliminates the other two. Full lighting and the eye of a
supervisor capture better than darkness, which is ultimately protected.
Visibility is a trap.

To begin with, this made it possible—as a negative effect—to avoid
those compact, swarming, howling masses that were to be found in places
of confinement, those painted by Goya or described by Howard. Each individual, in his place, is securely confined to a cell from which he is seen
from the front by the supervisor; but the side walls prevent him from coming into contact with his companions. He is seen, but he does not see; he is
the object of information, never a subject in communication. The arrangement of his room, opposite the central tower, imposes on him an axial visibility; but the divisions of the ring, those separated cells, imply a lateral invisibility. And this invisibility is a guarantee of order. If the inmates are
convicts, there is no danger of a plot, an attempt at collective escape, the
planning of new crimes for the future, bad reciprocal influences; if they
are patients, there is no danger of contagion; if they are madmen, there is
no risk of their committing violence upon one another; if they are schoolchildren, there is no copying, no noise, no chatter, no waste of time; if they
are workers, there are no disorders, no theft, no coalitions, none of those
distractions that slow down the rate of work, make it less perfect, or cause
accidents. The crowd, a compact mass, a locus of multiple exchanges, individualities merging together, a collective effect, is abolished and replaced
by a collection of separated individualities. From the point of view of the
guardian, it is replaced by a multiplicity that can be numbered and supervised; from the point of view of the inmates, by a sequestered and observed solitude (Bentham 60–64).

Hence the major effect of the Panopticon: to induce in the inmate a
state of conscious and permanent visibility that assures the automatic
functioning of power. So to arrange things that the surveillance is permanent in its effects even if it is discontinuous in its action; that the perfection
of power should tend to render its actual exercise unnecessary; that this
architectural apparatus should be a machine for creating and sustaining a
power relation independent of the person who exercises it; in short, that
the inmates should be caught up in a power situation of which they are
themselves the bearers. To achieve this, it is at once too much and too little
that the prisoner should be constantly observed by an inspector: too little,
for what matters is that he knows himself to be observed; too much,

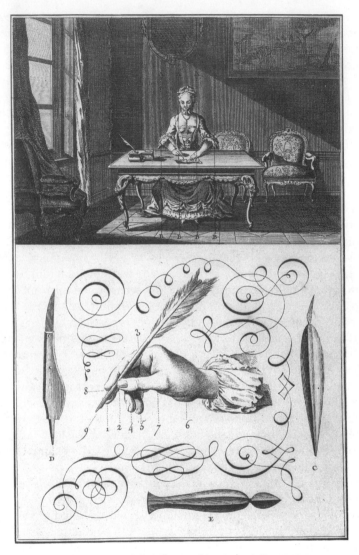

Handwriting model. *Collections historiques de l'I.N.R.D.P.*

because he has no need in fact of being so. In view of this, Bentham laid down the principle that power should be visible and unverifiable. Visible: the inmate will constantly have before his eyes the tall outline of the central tower from which he is spied upon. Unverifiable: the inmate must never know whether he is being looked at at any one moment; but he must be sure that he may always be so. In order to make the presence or absence of the inspector unverifiable, so that the prisoners, in their cells, cannot even see a shadow, Bentham envisaged not only venetian blinds

Interior of the penitentiary at Stateville, United States, twentieth century

on the windows of the central observation hall, but, on the inside, partitions that intersected the hall at right angles and, in order to pass from one quarter to the other, not doors but zigzag openings; for the slightest noise, a gleam of light, a brightness in a half-opened door would betray the presence of the guardian.[2] The Panopticon is a machine for dissociating the see/being seen dyad: in the peripheric ring, one is totally seen, without ever seeing; in the central tower, one sees everything without ever being seen.[3]

It is an important mechanism, for it automatizes and disindividualizes power. Power has its principle not so much in a person as in a certain concerted distribution of bodies, surfaces, lights, gazes; in an arrangement whose internal mechanisms produce the relation in which individuals are caught up. The ceremonies, the rituals, the marks by which the sovereign's surplus power was manifested are useless. There is a machinery that assures dissymmetry, disequilibrium, difference. Consequently, it does not matter who exercises power. Any individual, taken almost at random, can operate the machine: in the absence of the director, his family, his friends, his visitors, even his servants (Bentham 45). Similarly, it does not matter what motive animates him: the curiosity of the indiscreet, the malice of a child, the thirst for knowledge of a philosopher who wishes to visit this museum of human nature, or the perversity of those

Lecture on the evils of alcoholism in the auditorium of Fresnes prison

who take pleasure in spying and punishing. The more numerous those anonymous and temporary observers are, the greater the risk for the inmate of being surprised and the greater his anxious awareness of being observed. The Panopticon is a marvelous machine which, whatever use one may wish to put it to, produces homogeneous effects of power.

A real subjection is born mechanically from a fictitious relation. So it is not necessary to use force to constrain the convict to good behavior, the madman to calm, the worker to work, the schoolboy to application, the patient to the observation of the regulations. Bentham was surprised that panoptic institutions could be so light: there were no more bars, no more chains, no more heavy locks; all that was needed was that the separations should be clear and the openings well arranged. The heaviness of the old "houses of security," with their fortresslike architecture, could be replaced by the simple, economic geometry of a "house of certainty." The efficiency of power, its constraining force have, in a sense, passed over to the other side—to the side of its surface of application. He who is subjected to a field of visibility, and who knows it, assumes responsibility for the constraints of power; he makes them play spontaneously upon himself; he inscribes in himself the power relation in which he simultaneously plays both roles; he becomes the principle of his own subjection. By this very fact, the external power may throw off its physical weight; it tends to the noncorporal; and, the more it approaches this limit, the more constant, profound, and permanent are its effects: it is a perpetual victory that avoids any physical confrontation and which is always decided in advance.

Bentham does not say whether he was inspired, in his project, by Le Vaux's menagerie at Versailles: the first menagerie in which the different elements are not, as they traditionally were, distributed in a park (Loisel 104–7). At the center was an octagonal pavilion which, on the first floor, consisted of only a single room, the king's *salon;* on every side large windows looked out onto seven cages (the eighth side was reserved for the entrance), containing different species of animals. By Bentham's time, this menagerie had disappeared. But one finds in the program of the Panopticon a similar concern with individualizing observation, with characterization and classification, with the analytical arrangement of space. The Panopticon is a royal menagerie; the animal is replaced by man, individual distribution by specific grouping, and the king by the machinery of a furtive power. With this exception, the Panopticon also does the work of a naturalist. It makes it possible to draw up differences: among patients, to observe the symptoms of each individual, without the proximity of beds, the circulation of miasmas, the effects of contagion confusing the clinical tables; among schoolchildren, it makes it possible to observe performances (without there being any imitation or copying), to map aptitudes, to assess characters, to draw up rigorous classifications, and in relation to normal development, to distinguish "laziness and stubbornness" from "incurable imbecility"; among workers, it makes it possible to note the aptitudes of each worker, compare the time he takes to perform a task, and if they are paid by the day, to calculate their wages (Bentham 60–64).

So much for the question of observation. But the Panopticon was also a laboratory; it could be used as a machine to carry out experiments, to alter behavior, to train or correct individuals. To experiment with medicines and monitor their effects. To try out different punishments on prisoners, according to their crimes and character, and to seek the most effective ones. To teach different techniques simultaneously to the workers, to decide which is the best. To try out pedagogical experiments—and in particular to take up once again the well-debated problem of secluded education, by using orphans. One would see what would happen when, in their sixteenth or eighteenth year, they were presented with other boys or girls; one could verify whether, as Helvetius thought, anyone could learn anything; one would follow "the genealogy of every observable idea"; one could bring up different children according to different systems of thought, making certain children believe that two and two do not make four or that the moon is a cheese, then put them together when they are twenty or twenty-five years old; one would then have discussions that would be worth a great deal more than the sermons or lectures on which so much money is spent; one would have at least an opportunity of making discoveries in the domain of metaphysics. The Panopticon is a privileged place for experiments on men, and for analyzing with complete certainty the transformations that may be obtained from them. The Panopticon may even provide an apparatus for supervising its own mechanisms. In this central tower, the director may spy on all the employees that he has under his orders: nurses, doctors, foremen, teachers, warders; he will be able to judge them continuously, alter their behavior, impose upon them the methods he thinks best; and it will even be possible to observe the director himself. An inspector arriving unexpectedly at the center of the Panopticon will be able to judge at a glance, without anything being concealed from him, how the entire establishment is functioning. And, in any case, enclosed as he is in the middle of this architectural mechanism, is not the director's own fate entirely bound up with it? The incompetent physician who has allowed contagion to spread, the incompetent prison governor or workshop manager will be the first victims of an epidemic or a revolt. "'By every tie I could devise,' said the master of the Panopticon, 'my own fate had been bound up by me with theirs'" (Bentham 177). The Panopticon functions as a kind of laboratory of power. Thanks to its mechanisms of observation, it gains in efficiency and in the ability to penetrate into men's behavior; knowledge follows the advances of power, discovering new objects of knowledge over all the surfaces on which power is exercised.

The plague-stricken town, the panoptic establishment—the differences are important. They mark, at a distance of a century and a half, the transformations of the disciplinary program. In the first case, there is an exceptional situation: against an extraordinary evil, power is mobilized; it makes itself everywhere present and visible; it invents new mechanisms; it separates, it immobilizes, it partitions; it constructs for a time what is both a counter-city and the perfect society; it imposes an ideal functioning, but one that is reduced, in the final analysis, like the evil that it combats, to a simple dualism of life and death: that which moves brings death, and one kills that which moves. The Panopticon, on the other hand, must be understood as a generalizable model of functioning; a way of defining power relations in terms of the everyday life of men. No doubt Bentham presents it as a particular institution, closed in upon itself. Utopias, perfectly closed in upon themselves, are common enough. As opposed to the ruined prisons, littered with mechanisms of torture, to be seen in Piranese's engravings, the Panopticon presents a cruel, ingenious cage. The fact that it should have given rise, even in our own time, to so many variations, projected or realized, is evidence of the imaginary intensity that it has possessed for almost two hundred years. But the Panopticon must not be understood as a dream building: it is the diagram of a mechanism of power reduced to its ideal form; its functioning, abstracted from any obstacle, resistance, or friction, must be represented as a pure architectural and optical system: it is in fact a figure of political technology that may and must be detached from any specific use.

It is polyvalent in its applications; it serves to reform prisoners, but also to treat patients, to instruct schoolchildren, to confine the insane, to supervise workers, to put beggars and idlers to work. It is a type of location of bodies in space, of distribution of individuals in relation to one another, of hierarchical organization, of disposition of centers and channels of power, of definition of the instruments and modes of intervention of power, which can be implemented in hospitals, workshops, schools, prisons. Whenever one is dealing with a multiplicity of individuals on whom a task or a particular form of behavior must be imposed, the panoptic schema may be used. It is—necessary modifications apart—applicable "to all establishments whatsoever, in which, within a space not too large to be covered or commanded by buildings, a number of persons are meant to be kept under inspection" (Bentham 40; although Bentham takes the penitentiary house as his prime example, it is because it has many different functions to fulfill—safe custody, confinement, solitude, forced labor, and instruction).

In each of its applications, it makes it possible to perfect the exercise of power. It does this in several ways: because it can reduce the number of those who exercise it, while increasing the number of those on whom it is exercised. Because it is possible to intervene at any moment and because the constant pressure acts even before the offenses, mistakes, or crimes have been committed. Because, in these conditions, its strength is that it never intervenes, it is exercised spontaneously and without noise, it constitutes a mechanism whose effects follow from one another. Because, without any physical instrument other than architecture and geometry, it acts directly on individuals; it gives "power of mind over mind." The panoptic schema makes any apparatus of power more intense: it assures its economy (in material, in personnel, in time); it assures its efficacy by its preventative character, its continuous functioning and its automatic mechanisms. It is a way of obtaining from power "in hitherto unexampled quantity," "a great and new instrument of government . . . ; its great excellence consists in the great strength it is capable of giving to *any* institution it may be thought proper to apply it to" (Bentham 66).

It's a case of "it's easy once you've thought of it" in the political sphere. It can in fact be integrated into any function (education, medical treatment, production, punishment); it can increase the effect of this function, by being linked closely with it; it can constitute a mixed mechanism in which relations of power (and of knowledge) may be precisely adjusted, in the smallest detail, to the processes that are to be supervised; it can establish a direct proportion between "surplus power" and "surplus production." In short, it arranges things in such a way that the exercise of power is not added on from the outside, like a rigid, heavy constraint, to the functions it invests, but is so subtly present in them as to increase their efficiency by itself increasing its own points of contact. The panoptic mechanism is not simply a hinge, a point of exchange between a mechanism of power and a function; it is a way of making power relations function in a function, and of making a function function through these power relations. Bentham's preface to *Panopticon* opens with a list of the benefits to be obtained from his "inspection-house": "*Morals reformed—health preserved—industry invigorated—instruction diffused—public burthens lightened*—Economy seated, as it were, upon a rock—the gordian knot of the Poor-Laws not cut, but untied—all by a simple idea in architecture!" (Bentham 39).

Furthermore, the arrangement of this machine is such that its enclosed nature does not preclude a permanent presence from the outside: we have seen that anyone may come and exercise in the central tower the functions of surveillance, and that, this being the case, he can gain a clear idea of the way in which the surveillance is practiced. In fact, any panoptic institution, even if it is as rigorously closed as a penitentiary, may without difficulty be subjected to such irregular and constant inspections: and not only by the appointed inspectors, but also by the public; any member of society will have the right to come and see with his own eyes how the schools, hospitals, factories, prisons function. There is no risk, therefore, that the increase of power created by the panoptic machine may degenerate into tyranny; the disciplinary mechanism will be democratically controlled, since it will be constantly accessible "to the great tribunal committee of the world."[4] This Panopticon, subtly arranged so that an observer may observe, at a glance, so many different individuals, also enables everyone to come and observe any of the observers. The seeing machine was once a sort of dark room into which individuals spied; it has become a transparent building in which the exercise of power may be supervised by society as a whole.

The panoptic schema, without disappearing as such or losing any of its properties, was destined to spread throughout the social body; its vocation was to become a generalized function. The plague-stricken town provided an exceptional disciplinary model: perfect, but absolutely violent; to the disease that brought death, power opposed its perpetual threat of death; life inside it was reduced to its simplest expression; it was, against the power of death, the meticulous exercise of the right of the sword. The Panopticon, on the other hand, has a role of amplification; although it arranges power, although it is intended to make it more economic and more effective, it does so not for power itself, nor for the immediate salvation of a threatened society: its aim is to strengthen the social forces—to increase production, to develop the economy, spread education, raise the level of public morality; to increase and multiply.

How is power to be strengthened in such a way that, far from impeding progress, far from weighing upon it with its rules and regulations, it actually facilitates such progress? What intensificator of power will be able at the same time to be a multiplicator of production? How will power, by increasing its forces, be able to increase those of society instead of confiscating them or impeding them? The Panopticon's solution to this problem is that the productive increase of power can be assured only if, on the one hand, it can be exercised continuously in the very foundations of society, in the subtlest possible way, and if, on the other hand, it functions outside these sudden, violent, discontinuous forms that are bound up with the exercise of sovereignty. The body of the king, with its strange material and physical presence, with the force that he himself deploys or transmits to some few others, is at the opposite extreme of this new physics of power represented by panopticism; the domain of panopticism is, on the contrary, that whole lower region, that region of irregular bodies, with their details, their multiple movements, their heterogeneous forces, their spatial relations; what are required are mechanisms that analyze distributions, gaps, series, combinations, and which use instruments that render visible, record, differentiate, and compare: a physics of a relational and multiple power, which has its maximum intensity not in the person of the king, but in the bodies that can be individualized by these relations. At the theoretical level, Bentham defines another way of analyzing the social body and the power relations that traverse it; in terms of practice, he defines a procedure of subordination of bodies and forces that must increase the utility of power while practicing the economy of the prince. Panopticism is the general principle of a new "political anatomy" whose object and end are not the relations of sovereignty but the relations of discipline.

The celebrated, transparent, circular cage, with its high tower, powerful and knowing, may have been for Bentham a project of a perfect disciplinary institution; but he also set out to show how one may "unlock" the disciplines and get them to function in a diffused, multiple, polyvalent way throughout the whole social body. These disciplines, which the classical age had elaborated in specific, relatively enclosed places—barracks, schools, workshops—and whose total implementation had been imagined only at the limited and temporary scale of a plague-stricken town, Bentham dreamed of transforming into a network of mechanisms that would be everywhere and always alert, running through society without interruption in space or in time. The panoptic arrangement provides the formula for this generalization. It programs, at the level of an elementary and

easily transferable mechanism, the basic functioning of a society penetrated through and through with disciplinary mechanisms.

There are two images, then, of discipline. At one extreme, the disci-
pline-blockade, the enclosed institution, established on the edges of society, turned inwards towards negative functions: arresting evil, breaking
communications, suspending time. At the other extreme, with panopticism, is the discipline-mechanism: a functional mechanism that must improve the exercise of power by making it lighter, more rapid, more effective, a design of subtle coercion for a society to come. The movement from
one project to the other, from a schema of exceptional discipline to one of
a generalized surveillance, rests on a historical transformation: the gradual extension of the mechanisms of discipline throughout the seventeenth
and eighteenth centuries, their spread throughout the whole social body,
the formation of what might be called in general the disciplinary society.

A whole disciplinary generalization—the Benthamite physics of power
represents an acknowledgment of this—had operated throughout the classical age. The spread of disciplinary institutions, whose network was beginning to cover an ever larger surface and occupying above all a less and
less marginal position, testifies to this: what was an islet, a privileged
place, a circumstantial measure, or a singular model, became a general
formula; the regulations characteristic of the Protestant and pious armies
of William of Orange or of Gustavus Adolphus were transformed into regulations for all the armies of Europe; the model colleges of the Jesuits, or
the schools of Batencour or Demia, following the example set by Sturm,
provided the outlines for the general forms of educational discipline; the
ordering of the naval and military hospitals provided the model for the
entire reorganization of hospitals in the eighteenth century.

But this extension of the disciplinary institutions was no doubt only
the most visible aspect of various, more profound processes.

1. *The functional inversion of the disciplines.* At first, they were expected to
neutralize dangers, to fix useless or disturbed populations, to avoid the inconveniences of over-large assemblies; now they were being asked to play a
positive role, for they were becoming able to do so, to increase the possible
utility of individuals. Military discipline is no longer a mere means of preventing looting, desertion, or failure to obey orders among the troops; it has
become a basic technique to enable the army to exist, not as an assembled
crowd, but as a unity that derives from this very unity an increase in its
forces; discipline increases the skill of each individual, coordinates these
skills, accelerates movements, increases fire power, broadens the fronts of
attack without reducing their vigor, increases the capacity for resistance,
etc. The discipline of the workshop, while remaining a way of enforcing respect for the regulations and authorities, of preventing thefts or losses,
tends to increase aptitudes, speeds, output, and therefore profits; it still exerts a moral influence over behavior, but more and more it treats actions in
terms of their results, introduces bodies into a machinery, forces into an

economy. When, in the seventeenth century, the provincial schools or the Christian elementary schools were founded, the justifications given for them were above all negative: those poor who were unable to bring up their children left them "in ignorance of their obligations: given the difficulties they have in earning a living, and themselves having been badly brought up, they are unable to communicate a sound upbringing that they themselves never had"; this involves three major inconveniences: ignorance of God, idleness (with its consequent drunkenness, impurity, larceny, brigandage), and the formation of those gangs of beggars, always ready to stir up public disorder and "virtually to exhaust the funds of the Hôtel-Dieu" (Demia 60–61). Now, at the beginning of the Revolution, the end laid down for primary education was to be, among other things, to "fortify," to "develop the body," to prepare the child "for a future in some mechanical work," to give him "an observant eye, a sure hand and prompt habits" (Talleyrand's Report to the Constituent Assembly, 10 September 1791, quoted by Léon 106). The disciplines function increasingly as techniques for making useful individuals. Hence their emergence from a marginal position on the confines of society, and detachment from the forms of exclusion or expiation, confinement, or retreat. Hence the slow loosening of their kinship with religious regularities and enclosures. Hence also their rooting in the most important, most central, and most productive sectors of society. They become attached to some of the great essential functions: factory production, the transmission of knowledge, the diffusion of aptitudes and skills, the war-machine. Hence, too, the double tendency one sees developing throughout the eighteenth century to increase the number of disciplinary institutions and to discipline the existing apparatuses.

2. *The swarming of disciplinary mechanisms.* While, on the one hand, the disciplinary establishments increase, their mechanisms have a certain tendency to become "deinstitutionalized," to emerge from the closed fortresses in which they once functioned and to circulate in a "free" state; the massive, compact disciplines are broken down into flexible methods of control, which may be transferred and adapted. Sometimes the closed apparatuses add to their internal and specific function a role of external surveillance, developing around themselves a whole margin of lateral controls. Thus the Christian School must not simply train docile children; it must also make it possible to supervise the parents, to gain information as to their way of life, their resources, their piety, their morals. The school tends to constitute minute social observatories that penetrate even to the adults and exercise regular supervision over them: the bad behavior of the child, or his absence, is a legitimate pretext, according to Demia, for one to go and question the neighbors, especially if there is any reason to believe that the family will not tell the truth; one can then go and question the parents themselves, to find out whether they know their catechism and the prayers, whether they are determined to root out the vices of their children, how many beds there are in the house and what the sleeping arrangements are; the visit may end with the giving of alms, the present of

a religious picture, or the provision of additional beds (Demia 39–40). Similarly, the hospital is increasingly conceived of as a base for the medical observation of the population outside; after the burning down of the Hôtel-Dieu in 1772, there were several demands that the large buildings, so heavy and so disordered, should be replaced by a series of smaller hospitals; their function would be to take in the sick of the quarter, but also to gather information, to be alert to any endemic or epidemic phenomena, to open dispensaries, to give advice to the inhabitants, and to keep the authorities informed of the sanitary state of the region.[5]

One also sees the spread of disciplinary procedures, not in the form of enclosed institutions, but as centers of observation disseminated throughout society. Religious groups and charity organizations had long played this role of "disciplining" the population. From the Counter-Reformation to the philanthropy of the July monarchy, initiatives of this type continued to increase; their aims were religious (conversion and moralization), economic (aid and encouragement to work), or political (the struggle against discontent or agitation). One has only to cite by way of example the regulations for the charity associations in the Paris parishes. The territory to be covered was divided into quarters and cantons and the members of the associations divided themselves up along the same lines. These members had to visit their respective areas regularly. "They will strive to eradicate places of ill-repute, tobacco shops, life-classes, gaming house, public scandals, blasphemy, impiety, and any other disorders that may come to their knowledge." They will also have to make individual visits to the poor; and the information to be obtained is laid down in regulations: the stability of the lodging, knowledge of prayers, attendance at the sacraments, knowledge of a trade, morality (and "whether they have not fallen into poverty through their own fault"); lastly, "one must learn by skillful questioning in what way they behave at home. Whether there is peace between them and their neighbors, whether they are careful to bring up their children in the fear of God . . . , whether they do not have their older children of different sexes sleeping together and with them, whether they do not allow licentiousness and cajolery in their families, especially in their older daughters. If one has any doubts as to whether they are married, one must ask to see their marriage certificate."[6]

3. *The state-control of the mechanisms of the discipline.* In England, it was private religious groups that carried out, for a long time, the functions of social discipline (cf. Radzinovitz 203–14); in France, although a part of this role remained in the hands of parish guilds or charity associations, another—and no doubt the most important part—was very soon taken over by the police apparatus.

The organization of a centralized police had long been regarded, even by contemporaries, as the most direct expression of royal absolutism; the sovereign had wished to have "his own magistrate to whom he might directly entrust his orders, his commissions, intentions, and who was entrusted with the execution of orders and orders under the King's private seal" (a note by Duval, first secretary at the police magistrature, quoted in Funck-Brentano I). In effect, in taking over a number of preexisting functions—the search for criminals, urban surveillance, economic and political supervision—the police magistratures and the magistrature-general that presided over them in Paris transposed them into a single, strict, administrative machine: "All the radiations of force and information that spread from the circumference culminate in the magistrate-general. . . . It is he who operates all the wheels that together produce order and harmony. The effects of his administration cannot be better compared than to the movement of the celestial bodies" (Des Essarts 344, 528).

But, although the police as an institution were certainly organized in the form of a state apparatus, and although this was certainly linked directly to the center of political sovereignty, the type of power that it exercises, the mechanisms it operates, and the elements to which it applies them are specific. It is an apparatus that must be coextensive with the entire social body and not only by the extreme limits that it embraces, but by the minuteness of the details it is concerned with. Police power must bear "over everything": it is not, however, the totality of the state nor of the kingdom as visible and invisible body of the monarch; it is the dust of events, actions, behavior, opinions—"everything that happens";[7] the police are concerned with "those things of every moment," those "unimportant things," of which Catherine II spoke in her Great Instruction (Supplement to the *Instruction for the Drawing Up of a New Code*, 1769, article 535). With the police, one is in the indefinite world of a supervision that seeks ideally to reach the most elementary particle, the most passing phenomenon of the social body: "The ministry of the magistrates and police officers is of the greatest importance; the objects that it embraces are in a sense definite, one may perceive them only by a sufficiently detailed examination" (Delamare, unnumbered preface): the infinitely small of political power.

And, in order to be exercised, this power had to be given the instrument of permanent, exhaustive, omnipresent surveillance, capable of making all visible, as long as it could itself remain invisible. It had to be like a faceless gaze that transformed the whole social body into a field of perception: thousands of eyes posted everywhere, mobile attentions ever on the alert, a long, hierarchized network which, according to Le Maire, comprised for Paris the forty-eight *commissaires*, the twenty *inspecteurs*, then the "observers," who were paid regularly, the *"basses mouches,"* or secret agents, who were paid by the day, then the informers, paid according to the job done, and finally the prostitutes. And this unceasing observation had to be accumulated in a series of reports and registers; throughout the eighteenth century, an immense police text increasingly covered society by means of a complex documentary organization (on the police registers in the eighteenth century, cf. Chassaigne). And, unlike the methods of judicial or administrative writing, what was registered in this way were forms of behavior, attitudes, possibilities, suspicions—a permanent account of individuals' behavior.

Now, it should be noted that, although this police supervision was entirely "in the hands of the king," it did not function in a single direction. It was in fact a double-entry system: it had to correspond, by manipulating the machinery of justice, to the immediate wishes of the king, but it was also capable of responding to solicitations from below; the celebrated *lettres de cachet*, or orders under the king's private seal, which were long the symbol of arbitrary royal rule and which brought detention into disrepute on political grounds, were in fact demanded by families, masters, local notables, neighbors, parish priests; and their function was to punish by confinement a whole infrapenality, that of disorder, agitation, disobedience, bad conduct; those things that Ledoux wanted to exclude from his architecturally perfect city and which he called "offenses of nonsurveillance." In short, the eighteenth-century police added a disciplinary function to its role as the auxiliary of justice in the pursuit of criminals and as an instrument for the political supervision of plots, opposition movements, or revolts. It was a complex function since it linked the absolute power of the monarch to the lowest levels of power disseminated in society; since, between these different, enclosed institutions of discipline (workshops, armies, schools), it extended an intermediary network, acting where they could not intervene, disciplining the nondisciplinary spaces; but it filled in the gaps, linked them together, guaranteed with its armed force an interstitial discipline and a metadiscipline. "By means of a wise police, the sovereign accustoms the people to order and obedience" (Vattel 162).

The organization of the police apparatus in the eighteenth century sanctioned a generalization of the disciplines that became coextensive with the state itself. Although it was linked in the most explicit way with everything in the royal power that exceeded the exercise of regular justice, it is understandable why the police offered such slight resistance to the rearrangement of the judicial power; and why it has not ceased to impose its prerogatives upon it, with ever-increasing weight, right up to the present day; this is no doubt because it is the secular arm of the judiciary; but it is also because, to a far greater degree than the judicial institution, it is identified, by reason of its extent and mechanisms, with a society of the disciplinary type. Yet it would be wrong to believe that the disciplinary functions were confiscated and absorbed once and for all by a state apparatus.

"Discipline" may be identified neither with an institution nor with an apparatus; it is a type of power, a modality for its exercise, comprising a whole set of instruments, techniques, procedures, levels of application, targets; it is a "physics" or an "anatomy" of power, a technology. And it may be taken over either by "specialized" institutions (the penitentiaries or "houses of correction" of the nineteenth century), or by institutions that use it as an essential instrument for a particular end (schools, hospitals), or by preexisting authorities that find in it a means of reinforcing or reorganizing their internal mechanisms of power (one day we should show how intrafamilial relations, essentially in the parents-children cell, have become "disciplined," absorbing since the classical age external schemata, first educational and military, then medical, psychiatric, psychological, which have made the family the privileged locus of emergence for the disciplinary question of the normal and the abnormal), or by apparatuses that have made discipline their principle of internal functioning (the disciplinarization of the administrative apparatus from the Napoleonic period), or finally by state apparatuses whose major, if not exclusive, function is to assure that discipline reigns over society as a whole (the police).

On the whole, therefore, one can speak of the formation of a disciplinary society in this movement that stretches from the enclosed disciplines, a sort of social "quarantine," to an indefinitely generalizable mechanism of "panopticism." Not because the disciplinary modality of power has replaced all the others; but because it has infiltrated the others, sometimes undermining them, but serving as an intermediary between them, linking them together, extending them, and above all making it possible to bring the effects of power to the most minute and distant elements. It assures an infinitesimal distribution of the power relations.

A few years after Bentham, Julius gave this society its birth certificate (Julius 384–86). Speaking of the panoptic principle, he said that there was much more there than architectural ingenuity: it was an event in the "history of the human mind." In appearance, it is merely the solution of a technical problem; but, through it, a whole type of society emerges. Antiquity had been a civilization of spectacle. "To render accessible to a multitude of men the inspection of a small number of objects": this was the problem to which the architecture of temples, theaters, and circuses responded. With spectacle, there was a predominance of public life, the intensity of festivals, sensual proximity. In these rituals in which blood flowed, society found new vigor and formed for a moment a single great body. The modern age poses the opposite problem: "To procure for a small number, or even for a single individual, the instantaneous view of a great multitude." In a society in which the principal elements are no longer the community and public life, but, on the one hand, private individuals and, on the other, the state, relations can be regulated only in a form that is the exact reverse of the spectacle: "It was to the modern age, to the ever-growing influence of the state, to its ever more profound intervention in all the details and all the relations of social life, that was reserved the task of increasing and perfecting its guarantees, by using and directing towards that great aim the building and distribution of buildings intended to observe a great multitude of men at the same time."

Julius saw as a fulfilled historical process that which Bentham had described as a technical program. Our society is one not of spectacle, but of surveillance; under the surface of images, one invests bodies in depth; behind the great abstraction of exchange, there continues the meticulous, concrete training of useful forces; the circuits of communication are the supports of an accumulation and a centralization of knowledge; the play of signs defines the anchorages of power; it is not that the beautiful totality of the individual is amputated, repressed, altered by our social order, it is rather that the individual is carefully fabricated in it, according to a whole technique of forces and bodies. We are much less Greeks than we believe. We are neither in the amphitheater, nor on the stage, but in the panoptic machine, invested by its effects of power, which we bring to ourselves since we are part of its mechanism. The importance, in historical mythology, of the Napoleonic character probably derives from the fact that it is at the point of junction of the monarchical, ritual exercise of sovereignty and the hierarchical, permanent exercise of indefinite discipline. He is the individual who looms over everything with a single gaze which no detail, however minute, can escape: "You may consider that no part of the Empire is without surveillance, no crime, no offense, no contravention that remains unpunished, and that the eye of the genius who can enlighten all embraces the whole of this vast machine, without, however, the slightest detail escaping his attention" (Treilhard 14). At the moment of its full blossoming, the disciplinary society still assumes with the Emperor the old aspect of the power of spectacle. As a monarch who is at one and the same time a usurper of the ancient throne and the organizer of the new state, he combined into a single symbolic, ultimate figure the whole of the long process by which the pomp of sovereignty, the necessarily spectacular manifestations of power, were extinguished one by one in the daily exercise of surveillance, in a panopticism in which the vigilance of intersecting gazes was soon to render useless both the eagle and the sun.

The formation of the disciplinary society is connected with a number of broad historical processes—economic, juridico-political, and lastly, scientific—of which it forms part.

1. Generally speaking, it might be said that the disciplines are techniques for assuring the ordering of human multiplicities. It is true that there is nothing exceptional or even characteristic in this: every system of power is presented with the same problem. But the peculiarity of the disciplines is that they try to define in relation to the multiplicities a tactics of power that fulfills three criteria: firstly, to obtain the exercise of power at the lowest possible cost (economically, by the low expenditure it involves; politically, by its discretion, its low exteriorization, its relative invisibility, the little resistance it arouses); secondly, to bring the effects of this social power to their maximum intensity and to extend them as far as possible, without either failure or interval; thirdly, to link this "economic" growth of power with the output of the apparatuses (educational, military, industrial, or medical) within which it is exercised; in short, to increase both the docility and the utility of all the elements of the system. This triple objective of the disciplines corresponds to a well-known historical conjuncture. One aspect of this conjuncture was the large demographic thrust of the eighteenth century; an increase in the floating population (one of the primary objects of discipline is to fix; it is an antinomadic technique); a change of quantitative scale in the groups to be supervised or manipulated (from the beginning of the seventeenth century to the eve of the French Revolution, the school population had been increasing rapidly, as

had no doubt the hospital population; by the end of the eighteenth century, the peacetime army exceeded 200,000 men). The other aspect of the conjuncture was the growth in the apparatus of production, which was becoming more and more extended and complex; it was also becoming more costly and its profitability had to be increased. The development of the disciplinary methods corresponded to these two processes, or rather, no doubt, to the new need to adjust their correlation. Neither the residual forms of feudal power nor the structures of the administrative monarchy, nor the local mechanisms of supervision, nor the unstable, tangled mass they all formed together could carry out this role: they were hindered from doing so by the irregular and inadequate extension of their network, by their often conflicting functioning, but above all by the "costly" nature of the power that was exercised in them. It was costly in several senses: because directly it cost a great deal to the Treasury; because the system of corrupt offices and farmed-out taxes weighed indirectly, but very heavily, on the population; because the resistance it encountered forced it into a cycle of perpetual reinforcement; because it proceeded essentially by levying (levying on money or products by royal, seigniorial, ecclesiastical taxation; levying on men or time by *corvées* of press-ganging, by locking up or banishing vagabonds). The development of the disciplines marks the appearance of elementary techniques belonging to a quite different economy: mechanisms of power which, instead of proceeding by deduction, are integrated into the productive efficiency of the apparatuses from within, into the growth of this efficiency and into the use of what it produces. For the old principle of "levying-violence," which governed the economy of power, the disciplines substitute the principle of "mildness-production-profit." These are the techniques that make it possible to adjust the multiplicity of men and the multiplication of the apparatuses of production (and this means not only "production" in the strict sense, but also the production of knowledge and skills in the school, the production of health in the hospitals, the production of destructive force in the army).

In this task of adjustment, discipline had to solve a number of problems for which the old economy of power was not sufficiently equipped. It could reduce the inefficiency of mass phenomena: reduce what, in a multiplicity, makes it much less manageable than a unity; reduce what is opposed to the use of each of its elements and of their sum; reduce everything that may counter the advantages of number. That is why discipline fixes; it arrests or regulates movements; it clears up confusion; it dissipates compact groupings of individuals wandering about the country in unpredictable ways; it establishes calculated distributions. It must also master all the forces that are formed from the very constitution of an organized multiplicity; it must neutralize the effects of counterpower that spring from them and which form a resistance to the power that wishes to dominate it: agitations, revolts, spontaneous organizations, coalitions—anything that may establish horizontal conjunctions. Hence the fact that the disciplines use procedures of partitioning and verticality, that they introduce, between the different elements at the same level, as solid separations as possible, that they define compact hierarchical networks, in short, that they oppose to the intrinsic, adverse force of multiplicity the technique of the continuous, individualizing pyramid. They must also increase the particular utility of each element of the multiplicity, but by means that are the most rapid and the least costly, that is to say, by using the multiplicity itself as an instrument of this growth. Hence, in order to extract from bodies the maximum time and force, the use of those overall methods known as timetables, collective training, exercises, total and detailed surveillance. Furthermore, the disciplines must increase the effect of utility proper to the multiplicities, so that each is made more useful than the simple sum of its elements: it is in order to increase the utilizable effects of the multiple that the disciplines define tactics of distribution, reciprocal adjustment of bodies, gestures, and rhythms, differentiation of capacities, reciprocal coordination in relation to apparatuses or tasks. Lastly, the disciplines have to bring into play the power relations, not above but inside the very texture of the multiplicity, as discreetly as possible, as well articulated on the other functions of these multiplicities and also in the least expensive way possible: to this correspond anonymous instruments of power, coextensive with the multiplicity that they regiment, such as hierarchical surveillance, continuous registration, perpetual assessment, and classification. In short, to substitute for a power that is manifested through the brilliance of those who exercise it, a power that insidiously objectifies those on whom it is applied; to form a body of knowledge about these individuals, rather than to deploy the ostentatious signs of sovereignty. In a word, the disciplines are the ensemble of minute technical inventions that made it possible to increase the useful size of multiplicities by decreasing the inconveniences of the power which, in order to make them useful, must control them. A multiplicity, whether in a workshop or a nation, an army or a school, reaches the threshold of a discipline when the relation of the one to the other becomes favorable.

If the economic take-off of the West began with the techniques that made possible the accumulation of capital, it might perhaps be said that the methods for administering the accumulation of men made possible a political take-off in relation to the traditional, ritual, costly, violent forms of power, which soon fell into disuse and were superseded by a subtle, calculated technology of subjection. In fact, the two processes—the accumulation of men and the accumulation of capital—cannot be separated; it would not have been possible to solve the problem of the accumulation of men without the growth of an apparatus of production capable of both sustaining them and using them; conversely, the techniques that made the cumulative multiplicity of men useful accelerated the accumulation of capital. At a less general level, the technological mutations of the apparatus of production, the division of labor and the elaboration of the disciplinary techniques sustained an ensemble of very close relations (cf. Marx, *Capital*, vol. I, chapter XIII and the very interesting analysis in Guerry and

Deleule). Each makes the other possible and necessary; each provides a model for the other. The disciplinary pyramid constituted the small cell of power within which the separation, coordination, and supervision of tasks was imposed and made efficient; and analytical partitioning of time, gestures, and bodily forces constituted an operational schema that could easily be transferred from the groups to be subjected to the mechanisms of production; the massive projection of military methods onto industrial organization was an example of this modeling of the division of labor following the model laid down by the schemata of power. But, on the other hand, the technical analysis of the process of production, its "mechanical" breaking-down, were projected onto the labor force whose task it was to implement it: the constitution of those disciplinary machines in which the individual forces that they bring together are composed into a whole and therefore increased is the effect of this projection. Let us say that discipline is the unitary technique by which the body is reduced as a "political" force at the least cost and maximized as a useful force. The growth of a capitalist economy gave rise to the specific modality of disciplinary power, whose general formulas, techniques of submitting forces and bodies, in short, "political anatomy," could be operated in the most diverse political regimes, apparatuses, or institutions.

2. The panoptic modality of power—at the elementary, technical, merely physical level at which it is situated—is not under the immediate dependence or a direct extension of the great juridico-political structures of a society; it is nonetheless not absolutely independent. Historically, the process by which the bourgeoisie became in the course of the eighteenth century the politically dominant class was masked by the establishment of an explicit, coded, and formally egalitarian juridical framework, made possible by the organization of a parliamentary, representative regime. But the development and generalization of disciplinary mechanisms constituted the other, dark side of these processes. The general juridical form that guaranteed a system of rights that were egalitarian in principle was supported by these tiny, everyday, physical mechanisms, by all those systems of micropower that are essentially nonegalitarian and asymmetrical that we call the disciplines. And although, in a formal way, the representative regime makes it possible, directly or indirectly, with or without relays, for the will of all to form the fundamental authority of sovereignty, the disciplines provide, at the base, a guarantee of the submission of forces and bodies. The real, corporal disciplines constituted the foundation of the formal, juridical liberties. The contract may have been regarded as the ideal foundation of law and political power; panopticism constituted the technique, universally widespread, of coercion. It continued to work in depth on the juridical structures of society, in order to make the effective mechanisms of power function in opposition to the formal framework that it had acquired. The "Enlightenment," which discovered the liberties, also invented the disciplines.

In appearance, the disciplines constitute nothing more than an infralaw. They seem to extend the general forms defined by law to the infinitesimal level of individual lives; or they appear as methods of training that enable individuals to become integrated into these general demands. They seem to constitute the same type of law on a different scale, thereby making it more meticulous and more indulgent. The disciplines should be regarded as a sort of counterlaw. They have the precise role of introducing insuperable asymmetries and excluding reciprocities. First, because discipline creates between individuals a "private" link, which is a relation of constraints entirely different from contractual obligation; the acceptance of a discipline may be underwritten by contract; the way in which it is imposed, the mechanisms it brings into play, the nonreversible subordination of one group of people by another, the "surplus" power that is always fixed on the same side, the inequality of position of the different "partners" in relation to the common regulation, all these distinguish the disciplinary link from the contractual link, and make it possible to distort the contractual link systematically from the moment it has as its content a mechanism of discipline. We know, for example, how many real procedures undermine the legal fiction of the work contract: workshop discipline is not the least important. Moreover, whereas the juridical systems define juridical subjects according to universal norms, the disciplines characterize, classify, specialize; they distribute along a scale, around a norm, hierarchize individuals in relation to one another and, if necessary, disqualify and invalidate. In any case, in the space and during the time in which they exercise their control and bring into play the asymmetries of their power, they effect a suspension of the law that is never total, but is never annulled either. Regular and institutional as it may be, the discipline, in its mechanism, is a "counterlaw." And, although the universal juridicism of modern society seems to fix limits on the exercise of power, its universally widespread panopticism enables it to operate, on the underside of the law, a machinery that is both immense and minute, which supports, reinforces, multiplies the asymmetry of power and undermines the limits that are traced around the law. The minute disciplines, the panopticisms of every day may well be below the level of emergence of the great apparatuses and the great political struggles. But, in the genealogy of modern society, they have been, with the class domination that traverses it, the political counterpart of the juridical norms according to which power was redistributed. Hence, no doubt, the importance that has been given for so long to the small techniques of discipline, to those apparently insignificant tricks that it has invented, and even to those "sciences" that give it a respectable face; hence the fear of abandoning them if one cannot find any substitute; hence the affirmation that they are at the very foundation of society, and an element in its equilibrium, whereas they are a series of mechanisms for unbalancing power relations definitively and everywhere; hence the persistence in regarding them as the humble, but concrete form of every morality, whereas they are a set of physico-political techniques.

To return to the problem of legal punishments, the prison with all the corrective technology at its disposal is to be resituated at the point where the codified power to punish turns into a disciplinary power to observe; at the point where the universal punishments of the law are applied selectively to certain individuals and always the same ones; at the point where the redefinition of the juridical subject by the penalty becomes a useful training of the criminal; at the point where the law is inverted and passes outside itself, and where the counterlaw becomes the effective and institutionalized content of the juridical forms. What generalizes the power to punish, then, is not the universal consciousness of the law in each juridical subject; it is the regular extension, the infinitely minute web of panoptic techniques.

3. Taken one by one, most of these techniques have a long history behind them. But what was new, in the eighteenth century, was that, by being combined and generalized, they attained a level at which the formation of knowledge and the increase of power regularly reinforce one another in a circular process. At this point, the disciplines crossed the "technological" threshold. First the hospital, then the school, then, later, the workshop were not simply "reordered" by the disciplines; they became, thanks to them, apparatuses such that any mechanism of objectification could be used in them as an instrument of subjection, and any growth of power could give rise in them to possible branches of knowledge; it was this link, proper to the technological systems, that made possible within the disciplinary element the formation of clinical medicine, psychiatry, child psychology, educational psychology, the rationalization of labor. It is a double process, then: an epistemological "thaw" through a refinement of power relations; a multiplication of the effects of power through the formation and accumulation of new forms of knowledge.

The extension of the disciplinary methods is inscribed in a broad historical process: the development at about the same time of many other technologies—agronomical, industrial, economic. But it must be recognized that, compared with the mining industries, the emerging chemical industries or methods of national accountancy, compared with the blast furnaces or the steam engine, panopticism has received little attention. It is regarded as not much more than a bizarre little utopia, a perverse dream—rather as though Bentham had been the Fourier of a police society, and the Phalanstery had taken on the form of the Panopticon. And yet this represented the abstract formula of a very real technology, that of individuals. There were many reasons why it received little praise; the most obvious is that the discourses to which it gave rise rarely acquired, except in the academic classifications, the status of sciences; but the real reason is no doubt that the power that it operates and which it augments is a direct, physical power that men exercise upon one another. An inglorious culmination had an origin that could be only grudgingly acknowledged. But it would be unjust to compare the disciplinary techniques with such inventions as the steam engine or Amici's microscope. They are much less; and yet, in a way, they are much more. If a historical equivalent or at least a point of comparison had to be found for them, it would be rather in the "inquisitorial" technique.

The eighteenth century invented the techniques of discipline and the examination, rather as the Middle Ages invented the judicial investigation. But it did so by quite different means. The investigation procedure, an old fiscal and administrative technique, had developed above all with the reorganization of the Church and the increase of the princely states in the twelfth and thirteenth centuries. At this time it permeated to a very large degree the jurisprudence first of the ecclesiastical courts, then of the lay courts. The investigation as an authoritarian search for a truth observed or attested was thus opposed to the old procedures of the oath, the ordeal, the judicial duel, the judgment of God, or even of the transaction between private individuals. The investigation was the sovereign power arrogating to itself the right to establish the truth by a number of regulated techniques. Now, although the investigation has since then been an integral part of Western justice (even up to our own day), one must not forget either its political origin, its link with the birth of the states and of monarchical sovereignty, or its later extension and its role in the formation of knowledge. In fact, the investigation has been the no doubt crude, but fundamental element in the constitution of the empirical sciences; it has been the juridico-political matrix of this experimental knowledge, which, as we know, was very rapidly released at the end of the Middle Ages. It is perhaps true to say that, in Greece, mathematics were born from techniques of measurement; the sciences of nature, in any case, were born, to some extent, at the end of the Middle Ages, from the practices of investigation. The great empirical knowledge that covered the things of the world and transcribed them into the ordering of an indefinite discourse that observes, describes, and establishes the "facts" (at a time when the Western world was beginning the economic and political conquest of this same world) had its operating model no doubt in the Inquisition—that immense invention that our recent mildness has placed in the dark recesses of our memory. But what this politico-juridical, administrative, and criminal, religious and lay, investigation was to the sciences of nature, disciplinary analysis has been to the sciences of man. These sciences, which have so delighted our "humanity" for over a century, have their technical matrix in the petty, malicious minutiae of the disciplines and their investigations. These investigations are perhaps to psychology, psychiatry, pedagogy, criminology, and so many other strange sciences, what the terrible power of investigation was to the calm knowledge of the animals, the plants, or the earth. Another power, another knowledge. On the threshold of the classical age, Bacon, lawyer and statesman, tried to develop a methodology of investigation for the empirical sciences. What Great Observer will produce the methodology of examination for the human sciences? Unless, of course, such a thing is not possible. For, although it is true that, in becoming a technique for the empirical sciences, the investigation has detached itself from the inquisitorial procedure, in which it was historically rooted, the examination has remained extremely close to the disciplinary power that shaped it. It has always been and still is an intrinsic element of the disciplines. Of course it seems to have undergone a speculative purification by integrating itself with such sciences as psychology and psychiatry. And, in effect, its appearance in the form of tests, interviews, interrogations, and consultations is apparently in order to rectify the mechanisms of discipline: educational psychology is supposed to correct the rigors of the school, just as the medical or psychiatric interview is supposed to rectify the effects of the discipline of work. But we must not be misled; these techniques merely refer individuals from one disciplinary authority to another, and they reproduce, in a concentrated or formalized form, the schema of power-knowledge proper to each discipline (on this subject, cf. Tort). The great investigation that gave rise to the sciences of nature has become detached from its politico-juridical model; the examination, on the other hand, is still caught up in disciplinary technology.

In the Middle Ages, the procedure of investigation gradually superseded the old accusatory justice, by a process initiated from above; the disciplinary technique, on the other hand, insidiously and as if from below, has invaded a penal justice that is still, in principle, inquisitorial. All the great movements of extension that characterize modern penality—the problematization of the criminal behind his crime, the concern with a punishment that is a correction, a therapy, a normalization, the division of the act of judgment between various authorities that are supposed to measure, assess, diagnose, cure, transform individuals—all this betrays the penetration of the disciplinary examination into the judicial inquisition.

What is now imposed on penal justice as its point of application, its "useful" object, will no longer be the body of the guilty man set up against the body of the king; nor will it be the juridical subject of an ideal contract; it will be the disciplinary individual. The extreme point of penal justice under the Ancien Régime was the infinite segmentation of the body of the regicide: a manifestation of the strongest power over the body of the greatest criminal, whose total destruction made the crime explode into its truth. The ideal point of penality today would be an indefinite discipline: an interrogation without end, an investigation that would be extended without limit to a meticulous and ever more analytical observation, a judgment that would at the same time be the constitution of a file that was never closed, the calculated leniency of a penalty that would be interlaced with the ruthless curiosity of an examination, a procedure that would be at the same time the permanent measure of a gap in relation to an inaccessible norm and the asymptotic movement that strives to meet in infinity. The public execution was the logical culmination of a procedure governed by the Inquisition. The practice of placing individuals under "observation" is a natural extension of a justice imbued with disciplinary methods and examination procedures. Is it surprising that the cellular prison, with its regular chronologies, forced labor, its authorities of surveillance and registration, its experts in normality, who continue and multiply the functions of the judge, should have become the modern instrument of penalty? Is it surprising that prisons resemble factories, schools, barracks, hospitals, which all resemble prisons?

## NOTES

[1] Archives militaires de Vincennes, A 1,516 91 sc. Pièce. This regulation is broadly similar to a whole series of others that date from the same period and earlier.

[2] In the *Postscript to the Panopticon*, 1791, Bentham adds dark inspection galleries painted in black around the inspector's lodge, each making it possible to observe two stories of cells.

[3] In his first version of the *Panopticon*, Bentham had also imagined an acoustic surveillance, operated by means of pipes leading from the cells to the central tower. In the *Postscript* he abandoned the idea, perhaps because he could not introduce into it the principle of dissymmetry and prevent the prisoners from hearing the inspector as well as the inspector hearing them. Julius tried to develop a system of dissymmetrical listening (Julius 18).

[4] Imagining this continuous flow of visitors entering the central tower by an underground passage and then observing the circular landscape of the Panopticon, was Bentham aware of the Panoramas that Barker was constructing at exactly the same period (the first seems to have dated from 1787) and in which the visitors, occupying the central place, saw unfolding around them a landscape, a city, or a battle. The visitors occupied exactly the place of the sovereign gaze.

[5] In the second half of the eighteenth century, it was often suggested that the army should be used for the surveillance and general partitioning of the population. The army, as yet to undergo discipline in the seventeenth century, was regarded as a force capable of instilling it. Cf., for example, Servan, *Le Soldat citoyen*, 1780.

[6] Arsenal, MS. 2565. Under this number, one also finds regulations for charity associations of the seventeenth and eighteenth centuries.

[7] Le Maire in a memorandum written at the request of Sartine, in answer to sixteen questions posed by Joseph II on the Parisian police. This memorandum was published by Gazier in 1879.

## BIBLIOGRAPHY

Archives militaires de Vincennes, A 1,516 91 sc.
Bentham, J., *Works*, ed. Bowring, IV, 1843.
Chassaigne, M., *La Lieutenance générale de police*, 1906.
Delamare, N., *Traité de police*, 1705.
Demia, C., *Règlement pour les écoles de la ville de Lyon*, 1716.
Des Essarts, T. N., *Dictionnaire universel de police*, 1787.
Funck-Brentano, F., *Catalogue des manuscrits de la bibliothèque de l'Arsenal*, IX.
Guerry, F., and Deleule, D., *Le Corps productif*, 1973.
Julius, N. H., *Leçons sur les prisons*, I, 1831 (Fr. trans.).
Léon, A., *La Révolution française et l'éducation technique*, 1968.
Loisel, G., *Histoire des ménageries*, II, 1912.
Marx, Karl, *Capital*, vol. I, ed. 1970.
Radzinovitz, L., *The English Criminal Law*, II, 1956.
Servan, J., *Le Soldat citoyen*, 1780.
Tort, Michel, *Q.I.*, 1974.
Treilhard, J. B., *Motifs du code d'instruction criminelle*, 1808.
Vattel, E. de, *Le Droit des gens*, 1768.

• • • • • • • • • • • •

## QUESTIONS FOR A SECOND READING

1.  Foucault's text begins with an account of a system enacted in the seventeenth century to control the spread of plague. After describing this system of surveillance, he compares it to the "rituals of exclusion" used to control lepers. He says, "The exile of the leper and the arrest of the plague do not bring with them the same political dream" (p. 317). At many points he sets up similar pairings, all in an attempt to understand the relations of power and knowledge in modern public life.

    As you reread, mark the various points at which Foucault works out the differences between a prior and the current "political dream" of order. What are the techniques or instruments that belong to each? What moments in history are defined by each? How and where are they visible in public life?

2.  Toward the end of the chapter Foucault says, "The extension of the disciplinary methods is inscribed in a broad historical process." Foucault writes a difficult kind of history (at one point he calls it a genealogy), since it does not make use of the usual form of historical narrative—with characters, plots, scenes, and action. As you reread, take notes that will allow you to trace time, place, and sequence (and, if you can, agents and agency) in Foucault's account of the formation of the disciplinary society based on technologies of surveillance. Why do you think he avoids a narrative mode of presentation?

3.  As you reread Foucault's text, bring forward the stages in his presentation (or the development of his argument). Mark those moments that you consider key or central to the working out of his argument concerning the panopticon. What sentences of his would you use to represent key moments in the text? The text at times turns to numbered sections. How, for example, do they function? Describe the beginning, middle, and end of the essay. Describe the skeleton or understructure of the chapter. What are its various stages or steps? How do they relate to each other?

## ASSIGNMENTS FOR WRITING

1.  About three-quarters of the way into this chapter, Foucault says,

    > Our society is one not of spectacle, but of surveillance; under the surface of images, one invests bodies in depth; behind the great abstraction of exchange, there continues the meticulous, concrete training of useful forces; the circuits of communication are the supports of an accumulation and a centralization of knowledge; the play of signs defines the anchorages of power; it is not that the beautiful totality of the individual is amputated, repressed, altered by our social order, it is rather that the individual is carefully fabricated in it, according to a whole technique of forces and bodies. (pp. 333–34)

This prose is eloquent and insists on its importance to our moment and our society; it is also very hard to read or to paraphrase. Who is doing what to whom? How do we think about the individual's being carefully fabricated in the social order?

Take this chapter as a problem to solve. What is it about? What are its key arguments? its examples and conclusions? Write an essay that summarizes "Panopticism." Imagine that you are writing for readers who have read the chapter (although they won't have the pages in front of them). You will need to take time to present and discuss examples from the text. Your job is to help your readers figure out what it says. You get the chance to take the lead and be the teacher. You should feel free to acknowledge that you don't understand certain sections even as you write about them.

So, how do you write about something you don't completely understand? Here's a suggestion. When you have completed your summary, read it over and treat it as a draft. Ask questions like these: What have I left out? What was I tempted to ignore or finesse? Go back to those sections of the chapter that you ignored and bring them into your essay. Revise by adding discussions of some of the very sections you don't understand. You can write about what you think Foucault *might* be saying—you can, that is, be cautious and tentative; you can admit that the text is what it is, hard to read. You don't have to master this text. You do, however, need to see what you can make of it.

2. About a third of the way through his text, Foucault asserts, "The Panopticon is a marvelous machine which, whatever use one may wish to put it to, produces homogeneous effects of power." Write an essay in which you explain the machinery of the panopticon as a mechanism of power. Paraphrase Foucault and, where it seems appropriate, use his words. Present Foucault's account as you understand it. As part of your essay, and in order to explain what he is getting at, turn to two examples—one of his, perhaps, and then one of your own.

3. Perhaps the most surprising thing about Foucault's argument in "Panopticism" is the way it equates prisons with schools, hospitals, and workplaces, sites we are accustomed to imagining as very different from a prison. Foucault argues against our commonly accepted understanding of such things.

At the end of the chapter Foucault asks two questions. These are rhetorical questions, strategically placed at the end. Presumably we are prepared to feel their force and to think of possible answers.

> Is it surprising that the cellular prison, with its regular chronologies, forced labor, its authorities of surveillance and registration, its experts in normality, who continue and multiply the functions of the judge, should have become the modern instrument of penality? Is it surprising that prisons resemble factories, schools, barracks, hospitals, which all resemble prisons? (pp. 341–42)

For this assignment, take the invitation of Foucault's conclusion. No, you want to respond, it is not surprising that "experts in normality, who continue and multiply the functions of the judge, should have become the modern instrument of penality." No, it is not surprising that "prisons resemble factories, schools, barracks, hospitals, which all resemble prisons." Why isn't it surprising? Or, why isn't it surprising if you are thinking along with Foucault?

Write an essay in which you explore one of these possible resemblances. You may, if you choose, cite Foucault. You can certainly pick up some of his key terms or examples and put them into play. You should imagine, however, that it is your turn. With your work on Foucault behind you, you are writing to a general audience about "experts in normality" and the key sites of surveillance and control.

### MAKING CONNECTIONS

1. Both John Berger in "Ways of Seeing" (p. 105) and Foucault in "Panopticism" discuss what Foucault calls "power relations." Berger claims that "the entire art of the past has now become a political issue," and he makes a case for the evolution of a "new language of images" which could "confer a new kind of power" if people were to understand history in art. Foucault argues that the Panopticon signals an "inspired" change in power relations. "It is," he says,

   > an important mechanism, for it automatizes and disindividualizes power. Power has its principle not so much in a person as in a certain concerted distribution of bodies, surfaces, lights, gazes; in an arrangement whose internal mechanisms produce the relation in which individuals are caught up. (p. 321)

   Both Berger and Foucault create arguments about power, its methods and goals. As you read through their essays, mark passages you might use to explain how each author thinks about power—where it comes from, who has it, how it works, where you look for it, how you know when you see it, what it does, where it goes. You should reread the essays as a pair, as part of a single project in which you are looking to explain theories of power.

   Write an essay in which you present and explain "Ways of Seeing" and "Panopticism" as examples of Berger's and Foucault's theories of power. Both Berger and Foucault are arguing against usual understandings of power and knowledge and history. In this sense, their projects are similar. You should be sure, however, to look for differences as well as similarities.

2. Both "The American Scholar" (p. 294) by Ralph Waldo Emerson and "Panopticism" by Foucault present difficulties to their readers. Let's assume that these essays are deliberately difficult, that they are difficult for all readers, not just for college students, and that the difficulty is necessary and strategic, not just an error in judgment or evidence of a writer's failure to be clear.

   Go to each selection and, as you review it, look for sections or examples you could use to define the peculiar difficulties each presents its readers—or to you as its reader. Think about the different demands the two essays make. And think about how you would explain the experience of reading these to someone getting ready to work on them for the first time. What demands do they make of a reader? How do they ask to be read? Why would anyone want to read (or to write) this way? What have you learned about reading by having worked on these texts?

Write an essay in which you use these two selections as examples of the kinds of reading demanded at the university. What makes this material hard to read? How might one value (rather than regret) the work of reading as it is defined in these cases? What advice would you give to students who follow you, who might also be asked to read these selections?

# PAULO
# FREIRE

*P*AULO FREIRE *(pronounce it "Fr-air-ah" unless you can make a Portuguese "r") is one of the most influential radical educators of our world. A native of Recife, Brazil, he spent most of his early career working in poverty-stricken areas of his homeland, developing methods for teaching illiterate adults to read and write and (as he would say) to think critically and, thereby, to take power over their own lives. Because he has created a classroom where teachers and students have equal power and equal dignity, his work has stood as a model for educators around the world. It led also to sixteen years of exile after the military coup in Brazil in 1964. During that time he taught in Europe and in the United States and worked for the Allende government in Chile, training the teachers whose job it would be to bring modern agricultural methods to the peasants.*

*Freire (1921–1997) worked with the adult education programs of UNESCO, the Chilean Institute of Agrarian Reform, and the World Council of Churches. He was professor of educational philosophy at the Catholic University of São Paulo. He is the author of* Education for Critical Consciousness, The Politics of Education, The Pedagogy of the Oppressed, Revised Edition *(from which the following essay is drawn), and* Learning to Question: A Pedagogy of Liberation *(with Antonio Faundez).*

*For Freire, education is not an objective process, if by objective we mean "neutral" or "without bias or prejudice." Because teachers could be said to have something that their students lack, it is impossible to have a "neutral" classroom; and when teachers present a subject to their students they also present a point of view on that subject. The choice, according to Freire, is fairly simple: teachers either work "for the liberation of the people—their humanization—or for their domestication, their domination." The practice of teaching, however, is anything but simple. According to Freire, a teacher's most crucial skill is his or her ability to assist students' struggle to gain control over the conditions of their lives, and this means helping them not only to know but "to know that they know."*

*Freire edited, along with Henry A. Giroux of Miami University in Ohio, a series of books on education and teaching. In* Literacy: Reading the Word and the World, *a book for the series, Freire describes the interrelationship between reading the written word and understanding the world that surrounds us.*

> *My parents introduced me to reading the word at a certain moment in this rich experience of understanding my immediate world. Deciphering the word flowed naturally from reading my particular world; it was not something superimposed on it. I learned to read and write on the grounds of the backyard of my house, in the shade of the mango trees, with words from my world rather than from the wider world of my parents. The earth was my blackboard, the sticks my chalk.*

*For Freire, reading the written word involves understanding a text in its very particular social and historical context. Thus reading always involves "critical perception, interpretation, and rewriting of what is read."*

# The "Banking" Concept of Education

A careful analysis of the teacher-student relationship at any level, inside or outside the school, reveals its fundamentally *narrative* character. This relationship involves a narrating Subject (the teacher) and patient, listening objects (the students). The contents, whether values or empirical dimensions of reality, tend in the process of being narrated to become lifeless and petrified. Education is suffering from narration sickness.

The teacher talks about reality as if it were motionless, static, compartmentalized, and predictable. Or else he expounds on a topic completely alien to the existential experience of the students. His task is to "fill" the students with the contents of his narration—contents which are detached from reality, disconnected from the totality that engendered them and could give them significance. Words are emptied of their concreteness and become a hollow, alienated, and alienating verbosity.

The outstanding characteristic of this narrative education, then, is the sonority of words, not their transforming power. "Four times four is sixteen; the capital of Pará is Belém." The student records, memorizes, and repeats these phrases without perceiving what four times four really means, or realizing the true significance of "capital" in the affirmation "the capital of Pará is Belém," that is, what Belém means for Pará and what Pará means for Brazil.

Narration (with the teacher as narrator) leads the students to memorize mechanically the narrated content. Worse yet, it turns them into "containers," into "receptacles" to be "filled" by the teacher. The more completely she fills the receptacles, the better a teacher she is. The more meekly the receptacles permit themselves to be filled, the better students they are.

Education thus becomes an act of depositing, in which the students are the depositories and the teacher is the depositor. Instead of communicating, the teacher issues communiqués and makes deposits which the students patiently receive, memorize, and repeat. This is the "banking" concept of education, in which the scope of action allowed to the students extends only as far as receiving, filing, and storing the deposits. They do, it is true, have the opportunity to become collectors or cataloguers of the things they store. But in the last analysis, it is the people themselves who are filed away through the lack of creativity, transformation, and knowledge in this (at best) misguided system. For apart from inquiry, apart from the praxis, individuals cannot be truly human. Knowledge emerges only through invention and re-invention, through the restless, impatient, continuing, hopeful inquiry human beings pursue in the world, with the world, and with each other.

In the banking concept of education, knowledge is a gift bestowed by those who consider themselves knowledgeable upon those whom they consider to know nothing. Projecting an absolute ignorance onto others, a characteristic of the ideology of oppression, negates education and knowledge as processes of inquiry. The teacher presents himself to his students as their necessary opposite; by considering their ignorance absolute, he justifies his own existence. The students, alienated like the slave in the Hegelian dialectic, accept their ignorance as justifying the teacher's existence—but, unlike the slave, they never discover that they educate the teacher.

The *raison d'être* of libertarian education, on the other hand, lies in its drive towards reconciliation. Education must begin with the solution of the teacher-student contradiction, by reconciling the poles of the contradiction so that both are simultaneously teachers *and* students.

This solution is not (nor can it be) found in the banking concept. On the contrary, banking education maintains and even stimulates the contradiction through the following attitudes and practices, which mirror oppressive society as a whole:

a. the teacher teaches and the students are taught;
b. the teacher knows everything and the students know nothing;

c.  the teacher thinks and the students are thought about;

d.  the teacher talks and the students listen—meekly;

e.  the teacher disciplines and the students are disciplined;

f.  the teacher chooses and enforces his choice, and the students comply;

g.  the teacher acts and the students have the illusion of acting through the action of the teacher;

h.  the teacher chooses the program content, and the students (who were not consulted) adapt to it;

i.  the teacher confuses the authority of knowledge with his or her own professional authority, which she and he sets in opposition to the freedom of the students;

j.  the teacher is the Subject of the learning process, while the pupils are mere objects.

It is not surprising that the banking concept of education regards men as adaptable, manageable beings. The more students work at storing the deposits entrusted to them, the less they develop the critical consciousness which would result from their intervention in the world as transformers of that world. The more completely they accept the passive role imposed on them, the more they tend simply to adapt to the world as it is and to the fragmented view of reality deposited in them.

The capability of banking education to minimize or annul the students' creative power and to stimulate their credulity serves the interests of the oppressors, who care neither to have the world revealed nor to see it transformed. The oppressors use their "humanitarianism" to preserve a profitable situation. Thus they react almost instinctively against any experiment in education which stimulates the critical faculties and is not content with a partial view of reality but always seeks out the ties which link one point to another and one problem to another.

Indeed, the interests of the oppressors lie in "changing the consciousness of the oppressed, not the situation which oppresses them";[1] for the more the oppressed can be led to adapt to that situation, the more easily they can be dominated. To achieve this end, the oppressors use the banking concept of education in conjunction with a paternalistic social action apparatus, within which the oppressed receive the euphemistic title of "welfare recipients." They are treated as individual cases, as marginal persons who deviate from the general configuration of a "good, organized, and just" society. The oppressed are regarded as the pathology of the healthy society, which must therefore adjust these "incompetent and lazy" folk to its own patterns by changing their mentality. These marginals need to be "integrated," "incorporated" into the healthy society that they have "forsaken."

The truth is, however, that the oppressed are not "marginals," are not people living "outside" society. They have always been "inside"—inside the structure which made them "beings for others." The solution is not to "integrate" them into the structure of oppression, but to transform that structure so that they can become "beings for themselves." Such transformation, of course, would undermine the oppressors' purposes; hence their utilization of the banking concept of education to avoid the threat of student *conscientização.*°

The banking approach to adult education, for example, will never propose to students that they critically consider reality. It will deal instead with such vital questions as whether Roger gave green grass to the goat, and insist upon the importance of learning that, on the contrary, *R*oger gave green grass to the *r*abbit. The "humanism" of the banking approach masks the effort to turn women and men into automatons—the very negation of their ontological vocation to be more fully human.

Those who use the banking approach, knowingly or unknowingly (for there are innumerable well-intentioned bank-clerk teachers who do not realize that they are serving only to dehumanize), fail to perceive that the deposits themselves contain contradictions about reality. But, sooner or later, these contradictions may lead formerly passive students to turn against their domestication and the attempt to domesticate reality. They may discover through existential experience that their present way of life is irreconcilable with their vocation to become fully human. They may perceive through their relations with reality that reality is really a *process,* undergoing constant transformation. If men and women are searchers and their ontological vocation is humanization, sooner or later they may perceive the contradiction in which banking education seeks to maintain them, and then engage themselves in the struggle for their liberation.

But the humanist, revolutionary educator cannot wait for this possibility to materialize. From the outset, her efforts must coincide with those of the students to engage in critical thinking and the quest for mutual humanization. His efforts must be imbued with a profound trust in people and their creative power. To achieve this, they must be partners of the students in their relations with them.

The banking concept does not admit to such partnership—and necessarily so. To resolve the teacher-student contradiction, to exchange the role of depositor, prescriber, domesticator, for the role of student among students would be to undermine the power of oppression and serve the cause of liberation.

Implicit in the banking concept is the assumption of a dichotomy between human beings and the world: a person is merely *in* the world, not *with* the world or with others; the individual is spectator, not re-creator. In this view, the person is not a conscious being *(corpo consciente);* he or she is rather the possessor of *a* consciousness: an empty "mind" passively open to the reception of deposits of reality from the world outside. For example,

---

**conscientização**　According to Freire's translator, "The term *conscientização* refers to learning to perceive social, political, and economic contradictions, and to take action against the oppressive elements of reality."

my desk, my books, my coffee cup, all the objects before me—as bits of the world which surrounds me—would be "inside" me, exactly as I am inside my study right now. This view makes no distinction between being accessible to consciousness and entering consciousness. The distinction, however, is essential: the objects which surround me are simply accessible to my consciousness, not located within it. I am aware of them, but they are not inside me.

It follows logically from the banking notion of consciousness that the educator's role is to regulate the way the world "enters into" the students. The teacher's task is to organize a process which already occurs spontaneously, to "fill" the students by making deposits of information which he or she considers to constitute true knowledge.[2] And since people "receive" the world as passive entities, education should make them more passive still, and adapt them to the world. The educated individual is the adapted person, because she or he is better "fit" for the world. Translated into practice, this concept is well suited to the purposes of the oppressors, whose tranquility rests on how well people fit the world the oppressors have created, and how little they question it.

The more completely the majority adapt to the purposes which the dominant minority prescribe for them (thereby depriving them of the right to their own purposes), the more easily the minority can continue to prescribe. The theory and practice of banking education serve this end quite efficiently. Verbalistic lessons, reading requirements,[3] the methods for evaluating "knowledge," the distance between the teacher and the taught, the criteria for promotion: everything in this ready-to-wear approach serves to obviate thinking.

The bank-clerk educator does not realize that there is no true security in his hypertrophied role, that one must seek to live *with* others in solidarity. One cannot impose oneself, nor even merely co-exist with one's students. Solidarity requires true communication, and the concept by which such an educator is guided fears and proscribes communication.

Yet only through communication can human life hold meaning. The teacher's thinking is authenticated only by the authenticity of the students' thinking. The teacher cannot think for her students, nor can she impose her thought on them. Authentic thinking, thinking that is concerned about *reality*, does not take place in ivory tower isolation, but only in communication. If it is true that thought has meaning only when generated by action upon the world, the subordination of students to teachers becomes impossible.

Because banking education begins with a false understanding of men and women as objects, it cannot promote the development of what Fromm calls "biophily," but instead produces its opposite: "necrophily."

> While life is characterized by growth in a structured, functional manner, the necrophilous person loves all that does not grow, all that is mechanical. The necrophilous person is driven by the desire to transform the organic into the inorganic, to approach

life mechanically, as if all living persons were things. . . . Memory, rather than experience; having, rather than being, is what counts. The necrophilous person can relate to an object—a flower or a person—only if he possesses it; hence a threat to his possession is a threat to himself; if he loses possession he loses contact with the world. . . . He loves control, and in the act of controlling he kills life.[4]

Oppression—overwhelming control—is necrophilic; it is nourished by love of death, not life. The banking concept of education, which serves the interests of oppression, is also necrophilic. Based on a mechanistic, static, naturalistic, spatialized view of consciousness, it transforms students into receiving objects. It attempts to control thinking and action, leads women and men to adjust to the world, and inhibits their creative power.

When their efforts to act responsibly are frustrated, when they find themselves unable to use their faculties, people suffer. "This suffering due to impotence is rooted in the very fact that the human equilibrium has been disturbed."[5] But the inability to act which causes people's anguish also causes them to reject their impotence, by attempting

. . . to restore [their] capacity to act. But can [they], and how? One way is to submit to and identify with a person or group having power. By this symbolic participation in another person's life, [men have] the illusion of acting, when in reality [they] only submit to and become part of those who act.[6]

Populist manifestations perhaps best exemplify this type of behavior by the oppressed, who, by identifying with charismatic leaders, come to feel that they themselves are active and effective. The rebellion they express as they emerge in the historical process is motivated by that desire to act effectively. The dominant elites consider the remedy to be more domination and repression, carried out in the name of freedom, order, and social peace (that is, the peace of the elites). Thus they can condemn—logically, from their point of view—"the violence of a strike by workers and [can] call upon the state in the same breath to use violence in putting down the strike."[7]

Education as the exercise of domination stimulates the credulity of students, with the ideological intent (often not perceived by educators) of indoctrinating them to adapt to the world of oppression. This accusation is not made in the naïve hope that the dominant elites will thereby simply abandon the practice. Its objective is to call the attention of true humanists to the fact that they cannot use banking educational methods in the pursuit of liberation, for they would only negate that very pursuit. Nor may a revolutionary society inherit these methods from an oppressor society. The revolutionary society which practices banking education is either misguided or mistrusting of people. In either event, it is threatened by the specter of reaction.

Unfortunately, those who espouse the cause of liberation are themselves surrounded and influenced by the climate which generates the banking concept, and often do not perceive its true significance or its de-humanizing power. Paradoxically, then, they utilize this same instrument of alienation in what they consider an effort to liberate. Indeed, some "rev-olutionaries" brand as "innocents," "dreamers," or even "reactionaries" those who would challenge this educational practice. But one does not lib-erate people by alienating them. Authentic liberation—the process of hu-manization—is not another deposit to be made in men. Liberation is a praxis: the action and reflection of men and women upon their world in order to transform it. Those truly committed to the cause of liberation can accept neither the mechanistic concept of consciousness as an empty ves-sel to be filled, nor the use of banking methods of domination (propa-ganda, slogans—deposits) in the name of liberation.

Those truly committed to liberation must reject the banking concept in its entirety, adopting instead a concept of women and men as conscious beings, and consciousness as consciousness intent upon the world. They must abandon the educational goal of deposit-making and replace it with the posing of the problems of human beings in their relations with the world. "Problem-posing" education, responding to the essence of con-sciousness—*intentionality*—rejects communiqués and embodies communi-cations. It epitomizes the special characteristic of consciousness: being *con-scious of*, not only as intent on objects but as turned in upon itself in a Jasperian "split"—consciousness as consciousness *of* consciousness.

Liberating education consists in acts of cognition, not transferrals of in-formation. It is a learning situation in which the cognizable object (far from being the end of the cognitive act) intermediates the cognitive ac-tors—teacher on the one hand and students on the other. Accordingly, the practice of problem-posing education entails at the outset that the teacher-student contradiction be resolved. Dialogical relations—indispensable to the capacity of cognitive actors to cooperate in perceiving the same cog-nizable object—are otherwise impossible.

Indeed, problem-posing education, which breaks with the vertical pat-terns characteristic of banking education, can fulfill its function as the practice of freedom only if it can overcome the above contradiction. Through dialogue, the teacher-of-the-students and the students-of-the-teacher cease to exist and a new term emerges: teacher-student with students-teachers. The teacher is no longer merely the-one-who-teaches, but one who is himself taught in dialogue with the students, who in turn while being taught also teach. They become jointly responsible for a process in which all grow. In this process, arguments based on "author-ity" are no longer valid; in order to function, authority must be *on the side of* freedom, not *against* it. Here, no one teaches another, nor is anyone self-taught. People teach each other, mediated by the world, by the cognizable objects which in banking education are "owned" by the teacher.

The banking concept (with its tendency to dichotomize everything) distinguishes two stages in the action of the educator. During the first, he cognizes a cognizable object while he prepares his lessons in his study or his laboratory; during the second, he expounds to his students about that object. The students are not called upon to know, but to memorize the contents narrated by the teacher. Nor do the students practice any act of cognition, since the object towards which that act should be directed is the property of the teacher rather than a medium evoking the critical reflection of both teacher and students. Hence in the name of the "preservation of culture and knowledge" we have a system which achieves neither true knowledge nor true culture.

The problem-posing method does not dichotomize the activity of the teacher-student: she is not "cognitive" at one point and "narrative" at another. She is always "cognitive," whether preparing a project or engaging in dialogue with the students. He does not regard cognizable objects as his private property, but as the object of reflection by himself and the students. In this way, the problem-posing educator constantly re-forms his reflections in the reflection of the students. The students—no longer docile listeners—are now critical co-investigators in dialogue with the teacher. The teacher presents the material to the students for their consideration, and re-considers her earlier considerations as the students express their own. The role of the problem-posing educator is to create, together with the students, the conditions under which knowledge at the level of the *doxa* is superseded by true knowledge, at the level of the *logos*.

Whereas banking education anesthetizes and inhibits creative power, problem-posing education involves a constant unveiling of reality. The former attempts to maintain the *submersion* of consciousness; the latter strives for the *emergence* of consciousness and *critical intervention* in reality.

Students, as they are increasingly posed with problems relating to themselves in the world and with the world, will feel increasingly challenged and obliged to respond to that challenge. Because they apprehend the challenge as interrelated to other problems within a total context, not as a theoretical question, the resulting comprehension tends to be increasingly critical and thus constantly less alienated. Their response to the challenge evokes new challenges, followed by new understandings; and gradually the students come to regard themselves as committed.

Education as the practice of freedom—as opposed to education as the practice of domination—denies that man is abstract, isolated, independent, and unattached to the world; it also denies that the world exists as a reality apart from people. Authentic reflection considers neither abstract man nor the world without people, but people in their relations with the world. In these relations consciousness and world are simultaneous: consciousness neither precedes the world nor follows it.

> La conscience et le monde sont dormés d'un même coup: extérieur par essence à la conscience, le monde est, par essence relatif à elle.[8]

In one of our culture circles in Chile, the group was discussing (based on a codification) the anthropological concept of culture. In the midst of the discussion, a peasant who by banking standards was completely ignorant said: "Now I see that without man there is no world." When the educator responded: "Let's say, for the sake of argument, that all the men on earth were to die, but that the earth itself remained, together with trees, birds, animals, rivers, seas, the stars . . . wouldn't all this be a world?" "Oh no," the peasant replied emphatically. "There would be no one to say: 'This is a world.'"

The peasant wished to express the idea that there would be lacking the consciousness of the world which necessarily implies the world of consciousness. *I* cannot exist without a *non-I*. In turn, the *not-I* depends on that existence. The world which brings consciousness into existence becomes the world *of* that consciousness. Hence, the previously cited affirmation of Sartre: *"La conscience et le monde sont dormés d'un même coup."*

As women and men, simultaneously reflecting on themselves and on the world, increase the scope of their perception, they begin to direct their observations towards previously inconspicuous phenomena:

> In perception properly so-called, as an explicit awareness [*Gewahren*], I am turned towards the object, to the paper, for instance. I apprehend it as being this here and now. The apprehension is a singling out, every object having a background in experience. Around and about the paper lie books, pencils, inkwell, and so forth, and these in a certain sense are also "perceived," perceptually there, in the "field of intuition"; but whilst I was turned towards the paper there was no turning in their direction, nor any apprehending of them, not even in a secondary sense. They appeared and yet were not singled out, were not posited on their own account. Every perception of a thing has such a zone of background intuitions or background awareness, if "intuiting" already includes the state of being turned towards, and this also is a "conscious experience," or more briefly a "consciousness of" all indeed that in point of fact lies in the co-perceived objective background.[9]

That which had existed objectively but had not been perceived in its deeper implications (if indeed it was perceived at all) begins to "stand out," assuming the character of a problem and therefore of challenge. Thus, men and women begin to single out elements from their "background awarenesses" and to reflect upon them. These elements are now objects of their consideration, and, as such, objects of their action and cognition.

In problem-posing education, people develop their power to perceive critically *the way they exist* in the world *with which* and *in which* they find themselves; they come to see the world not as a static reality, but as a reality in process, in transformation. Although the dialectical relations of women and men with the world exist independently of how these relations are perceived (or whether or not they are perceived at all), it is also true that the form of action they adopt is to a large extent a function of how they perceive themselves in the world. Hence, the teacher-student and the students-teachers reflect simultaneously on themselves and the world without dichotomizing this reflection from action, and thus establish an authentic form of thought and action.

Once again, the two educational concepts and practices under analysis come into conflict. Banking education (for obvious reasons) attempts, by mythicizing reality, to conceal certain facts which explain the way human beings exist in the world; problem-posing education sets itself the task of demythologizing. Banking education resists dialogue; problem-posing education regards dialogue as indispensable to the act of cognition which unveils reality. Banking education treats students as objects of assistance; problem-posing education makes them critical thinkers. Banking education inhibits creativity and domesticates (although it cannot completely destroy) the *intentionality* of consciousness by isolating consciousness from the world, thereby denying people their ontological and historical vocation of becoming more fully human. Problem-posing education bases itself on creativity and stimulates true reflection and action upon reality; thereby responding to the vocation of persons as beings who are authentic only when engaged in inquiry and creative transformation. In sum: banking theory and practice, as immobilizing and fixating forces, fail to acknowledge men and women as historical beings; problem-posing theory and practice take the people's historicity as their starting point.

Problem-posing education affirms men and women as beings in the process of *becoming*—as unfinished, uncompleted beings in and with a likewise unfinished reality. Indeed, in contrast to other animals who are unfinished, but not historical, people know themselves to be unfinished; they are aware of their incompletion. In this incompletion and this awareness lie the very roots of education as an exclusively human manifestation. The unfinished character of human beings and the transformational character of reality necessitate that education be an ongoing activity.

Education is thus constantly remade in the praxis. In order to *be*, it must *become*. Its "duration" (in the Bergsonian meaning of the word) is found in the interplay of the opposites *permanence* and *change*. The banking method emphasizes permanence and becomes reactionary; problem-posing education—which accepts neither a "well-behaved" present nor a predetermined future—roots itself in the dynamic present and becomes revolutionary.

Problem-posing education is revolutionary futurity. Hence, it is prophetic (and, as such, hopeful). Hence, it corresponds to the historical nature of humankind. Hence, it affirms women and men as beings who transcend themselves, who move forward and look ahead, for whom immobility represents a fatal threat, for whom looking at the past must only be a means of understanding more clearly what and who they are so that they can more wisely build the future. Hence, it identifies with the movement which engages people as beings aware of their incompletion—an historical movement which has its point of departure, its Subjects and its objective.

The point of departure of the movement lies in the people themselves. But since people do not exist apart from the world, apart from reality, the movement must begin with the human-world relationship. Accordingly, the point of departure must always be with men and women in the "here and now," which constitutes the situation within which they are submerged, from which they emerge, and in which they intervene. Only by starting from this situation—which determines their perception of it—can they begin to move. To do this authentically they must perceive their state not as fated and unalterable, but merely as limiting—and therefore challenging.

Whereas the banking method directly or indirectly reinforces men's fatalistic perception of their situation, the problem-posing method presents this very situation to them as a problem. As the situation becomes the object of their cognition, the naïve or magical perception which produced their fatalism gives way to perception which is able to perceive itself even as it perceives reality, and can thus be critically objective about that reality.

A deepened consciousness of their situation leads people to apprehend that situation as an historical reality susceptible of transformation. Resignation gives way to the drive for transformation and inquiry, over which men feel themselves to be in control. If people, as historical beings necessarily engaged with other people in a movement of inquiry, did not control that movement, it would be (and is) a violation of their humanity. Any situation in which some individuals prevent others from engaging in the process of inquiry is one of violence. The means used are not important; to alienate human beings from their own decision-making is to change them into objects.

This movement of inquiry must be directed towards humanization—the people's historical vocation. The pursuit of full humanity, however, cannot be carried out in isolation or individualism, but only in fellowship and solidarity; therefore it cannot unfold in the antagonistic relations between oppressors and oppressed. No one can be authentically human while he prevents others from being so. Attempting *to be more* human, individualistically, leads to *having more*, egotistically, a form of dehumanization. Not that it is not fundamental *to have* in order *to be* human. Precisely because it *is* necessary, some men's *having* must not be allowed to constitute an obstacle to others' *having*, must not consolidate the power of the former to crush the latter.

Problem-posing education, as a humanist and liberating praxis, posits as fundamental that the people subjected to domination must fight for their emancipation. To that end, it enables teachers and students to become Subjects of the educational process by overcoming authoritarianism and an alienating intellectualism; it also enables people to overcome their false perception of reality. The world—no longer something to be described with deceptive words—becomes the object of that transforming action by men and women which results in their humanization.

Problem-posing education does not and cannot serve the interests of the oppressor. No oppressive order could permit the oppressed to begin to question: Why? While only a revolutionary society can carry out this education in systematic terms, the revolutionary leaders need not take full power before they can employ the method. In the revolutionary process, the leaders cannot utilize the banking method as an interim measure, justified on grounds of expediency, with the intention of *later* behaving in a genuinely revolutionary fashion. They must be revolutionary—that is to say, dialogical—from the outset.

## NOTES

[1] Simone de Beauvoir, *La pensée de droite, aujourd'hui* (Paris); ST, *El pensamiento político de la derecha* (Buenos Aires, 1963), p. 34.

[2] This concept corresponds to what Sartre calls the "digestive" or "nutritive" concept of education, in which knowledge is "fed" by the teacher to the students to "fill them out." See Jean-Paul Sartre, "Une idée fondamentale de la phénomenologie de Husserl: L'intentionalité," *Situations* I (Paris, 1947).

[3] For example, some professors specify in their reading lists that a book should be read from pages 10 to 15—and do this to "help" their students!

[4] Eric Fromm, *The Heart of Man* (New York, 1966), p. 41.

[5] Ibid., p. 31.

[6] Ibid.

[7] Reinhold Niebuhr, *Moral Man and Immoral Society* (New York, 1960), p. 130.

[8] Sartre, op. cit., p. 32. [The passage is obscure but could be read as "Consciousness and the world are given at one and the same time: the exterior world as it enters consciousness is relative to our ways of seeing and understanding that world."—Editors' note]

[9] Edmund Husserl, *Ideas—General Introduction to Pure Phenomenology* (London, 1969), pp. 105–06.

• • • • • • • • • • • •

## QUESTIONS FOR A SECOND READING

1. While Freire speaks powerfully about the politics of the classroom, he provides few examples of actual classroom situations. As you go back through the essay, try to ground (or to test) what he says with examples of your own. What would take place in a "problem-posing" class in English, history, psychology, or math? What is an "authentic form of thought and action"? How might you describe what Freire refers to as "reflection"? What, really, might teachers be expected to learn from their students? What example can you give of a time when you were "conscious of consciousness" and it made a difference to you with your school work?

   You might also look for moments when Freire does provide examples of his own. On pages 351–52, for example, Freire makes the distinction between a student's role as a "spectator" and as "re-creator" by referring to his own relationship to the objects on his desk. How might you explain this distinction? Or, how might you use the example of his books and coffee cup to explain the distinction he makes between "being accessible to consciousness" and "entering consciousness"?

2. Freire uses two terms drawn from Marxist literature: *praxis* and *alienation*. From the way these words are used in the essay, how would you define them? And how might they be applied to the study of education?

3. A writer can be thought of as a teacher and a reader as a student. If you think of Freire as your teacher in this essay, does he enact his own principles? Does he speak to you as though he were making deposits in a bank? Or is there a way in which the essay allows for dialogue? Look for sections in the essay you could use to talk about the role Freire casts you in as a reader.

## ASSIGNMENTS FOR WRITING

1. Surely all of us, anyone who has made it through twelve years of formal education, can think of a class, or an occasion outside of class, to serve as a quick example of what Freire calls the "banking" concept of education, where students were turned into "containers" to be "filled" by their teachers. If Freire is to be useful to you, however, he must do more than enable you to call up quick examples. He should allow you to say more than that a teacher once treated you like a container or that a teacher once gave you your freedom.

Write an essay that focuses on a rich and illustrative incident from your own educational experience and read it (that is, interpret it) as Freire would. You will need to provide careful detail: things that were said and done, perhaps the exact wording of an assignment, a textbook, or a teacher's comments. And you will need to turn to the language of Freire's argument, to take key phrases and passages and see how they might be used to investigate your case.

To do this you will need to read your account as not simply the story of you and your teacher, since Freire is not writing about individual personalities (an innocent student and a mean teacher, a rude teacher, or a thoughtless teacher) but about the roles we are cast in, whether we choose to be or not, by our culture and its institutions. The key question, then, is not who you were or who your teacher was but what roles you played and how those roles can lead you to better understand the larger narrative or drama of Education (an organized attempt to "regulate the way the world 'enters into' the students," p. 352).

Freire would not want you to work passively or mechanically, however, as though you were following orders. He would want you to make your own mark on the work he has begun. Use your example, in other words, as a way of testing and examining what Freire says, *particularly those passages that you find difficult or obscure.*

2. Problem-posing education, according to Freire, "sets itself the task of de-mythologizing"; it "stimulates true reflection and action"; it allows students to be "engaged in inquiry and creative transformation." These are grand and powerful phrases, and it is interesting to consider what they might mean if applied to the work of a course in reading and writing.

   If the object for study were Freire's essay, "The 'Banking' Concept of Education," what would Freire (or a teacher determined to adapt his practices) ask students to *do* with the essay? What writing assignment might he set for his students? Prepare that assignment, or a set of questions or guidelines or instructions (or whatever) that Freire might prepare for his class.

   Once you've prepared the writing assignment, write the essay that you think would best fulfill it. And, once you've completed the essay, go on, finally, to write the teacher's comments on it—to write what you think Freire, or a teacher following his example, might write on a piece of student work.

## MAKING CONNECTIONS

1. Freire says,

   > Students, as they are increasingly posed with problems relating to themselves in the world and with the world, will feel increasingly challenged and obliged to respond to that challenge. Because they apprehend the challenge as interrelated to other problems within a total context, not as a theoretical question, the resulting comprehension tends to be increasingly critical and thus constantly less alienated. (p. 355)

   Students learn to respond, Freire says, through dialogue with their teachers. Freire could be said to serve as your first teacher here. He has raised the issue for you and given you some language you can use to frame questions and to imagine the possibilities of response.

   Using one of the essays in this book as a starting point, pose a problem that challenges you and makes you feel obliged to respond, a problem that, in Freire's terms, relates to you "in the world and with the world." This is a chance for you, in other words, to pose a Freirean question and then to write a Freirean essay, all as an exercise in the practice of freedom.

   When you are done, you might reread what you have written to see how it resembles or differs from what you are used to writing. What are the indications that you are working with greater freedom? If you find evidence of alienation or "domination," to what would you attribute it and what, then, might you do to overcome it?

2. Freire writes about the distribution of power and authority in the classroom and argues that education too often alienates individuals from their own historical situation. Richard Rodriguez, in "The Achievement of Desire" (p. 621), writes about his education as a process of difficult but necessary alienation from his home, his childhood, and his family. And he

writes about power—about the power that he gained and lost as he became increasingly successful as a student.

But Freire and Rodriguez write about education as a central event in
the shaping of an adult life. It is interesting to imagine what they might
have to say to each other. Write a dialogue between the two in which they
discuss what Rodriguez has written in "The Achievement of Desire."
What would they say to each other? What questions would they ask?
How would they respond to each other in the give-and-take of conversation?

Note: This should be a dialogue, not a debate. Your speakers are trying to learn something about each other and about education. They are
not trying to win points or convince a jury.

# CLIFFORD
# GEERTZ

*C* LIFFORD GEERTZ *was born in San Francisco in 1926. After two years in the U.S. Navy Reserve, he earned a B.A. from Antioch College and a Ph.D. from Harvard. A Fellow of the National Academy of Science, the American Academy of Arts and Sciences, and the American Philosophical Society, Geertz has been a professor in the department of social science of the Institute for Advanced Study in Princeton, New Jersey, since 1970. He has written several books (mostly anthropological studies of Third World cultures) and published two collections of essays,* Interpretation of Cultures *(1977) and* Local Knowledge *(1985). Interpretation of Cultures, from which the following essay is drawn, became a classic and won for Geertz the rare distinction of being an academic whose scholarly work is eagerly read by people outside his academic discipline, even outside the academic community altogether. His book* Works and Lives: The Anthropologist as Author *(1989) won the National Book Critics Circle Award for Criticism. Geertz's most recent work,* After the Fact: Two Countries, Four Decades, One Anthropologist, *is a collection of essays from his 1995 Jerusalem-Harvard lectures.*

*"Deep Play" was first presented at a Paris conference organized by Geertz, the literary critic Paul de Man, and the American Academy of Arts and Sciences. The purpose of the conference was to bring together scholars from various academic departments (in the humanities, the social sciences, and the natural*

sciences) to see if they could find a way of talking to each other and, in doing so, find a common ground to their work. The conference planners believed that there was a common ground, that all of these scholars were bound together by their participation in what they called "systematic study of meaningful forms." This is a grand phrase, but Geertz's essay clearly demonstrates what work of this sort requires of an anthropologist. The essay begins with a story, an anecdote, and the story Geertz tells is as open to your interpretation as it is to anyone's else's. What follow, however, are Geertz's attempts to interpret the story he has told, first this way and then that. As you watch him work—finding patterns, making comparisons, drawing on the theories of experts, proposing theories of his own—you are offered a demonstration of how he finds meaningful forms and then sets out to study them systematically.

"Deep Play," in fact, was sent out as a model for all prospective conference participants, since it was a paper that showed not only what its author knew about his subject (cockfights in Bali) but what he knew about the methods and procedures that gave him access to his subject. It is a witty and sometimes dazzling essay with a wonderful story to tell—a story of both a Balinese cockfight and an anthropologist trying to write about and understand people whose culture seems, at first, so very different from his own.

# Deep Play: Notes on the Balinese Cockfight

## The Raid

Early in April of 1958, my wife and I arrived, malarial and diffident, in a Balinese village we intended, as anthropologists, to study. A small place, about five hundred people, and relatively remote, it was its own world. We were intruders, professional ones, and the villagers dealt with us as Balinese seem always to deal with people not part of their life who yet press themselves upon them: as though we were not there. For them, and to a degree for ourselves, we were nonpersons, specters, invisible men.

We moved into an extended family compound (that had been arranged before through the provincial government) belonging to one of the four major factions in village life. But except for our landlord and the village chief, whose cousin and brother-in-law he was, everyone ignored us in a way only a Balinese can do. As we wandered around, uncertain, wistful, eager to please, people seemed to look right through us with a gaze focused several yards behind us on some more actual stone or tree. Almost nobody greeted us; but nobody scowled or said anything unpleasant to us either, which would have been almost as satisfactory. If we ventured to approach someone (something one is powerfully inhibited from doing in such an atmosphere), he moved, negligently but definitively, away. If, seated or leaning against a wall, we had him trapped, he said nothing at all, or mumbled what for the Balinese is the ultimate non-word—"yes." The indifference, of course, was studied; the villagers were watching every move we made and they had an enormous amount of quite accurate information about who we were and what we were going to be doing. But they acted as if we simply did not exist, which, in fact, as this behavior was designed to inform us, we did not, or anyway not yet.

This is, as I say, general in Bali. Everywhere else I have been in Indonesia, and more latterly in Morocco, when I have gone into a new village people have poured out from all sides to take a very close look at me, and, often, an all-too-probing feel as well. In Balinese villages, at least those away from the tourist circuit, nothing happens at all. People go on pounding, chatting, making offerings, staring into space, carrying baskets about while one drifts around feeling vaguely disembodied. And the same thing is true on the individual level. When you first meet a Balinese, he seems virtually not to relate to you at all; he is, in the term Gregory Bateson and Margaret Mead made famous, "away."[1] Then—in a day, a week, a month (with some people the magic moment never comes)—he decides, for reasons I have never been quite able to fathom, that you *are* real, and then he becomes a warm, gay, sensitive, sympathetic, though, being Balinese, always precisely controlled person. You have crossed, somehow, some moral or metaphysical shadow line. Though you are not exactly taken as a Balinese (one has to be born to that), you are at least regarded as a human being rather than a cloud or a gust of wind. The whole complexion of your relationship dramatically changes to, in the majority of cases, a gentle, almost affectionate one—a low-keyed, rather playful, rather mannered, rather bemused geniality.

My wife and I were still very much in the gust of wind stage, a most frustrating, and even, as you soon begin to doubt whether you are really real after all, unnerving one, when, ten days or so after our arrival, a large cockfight was held in the public square to raise money for a new school.

Now, a few special occasions aside, cockfights are illegal in Bali under the Republic (as, for not altogether unrelated reasons, they were under the Dutch), largely as a result of the pretensions to puritanism radical nationalism tends to bring with it. The elite, which is not itself so very puritan, worries about the poor, ignorant peasant gambling all his money away, about what foreigners will think, about the waste of time better devoted to building up the country. It sees cockfighting as "primitive," "backward," "unprogressive," and generally unbecoming an ambitious nation. And, as with those other embarrassments—opium smoking, begging, or uncovered breasts—it seeks, rather unsystematically, to put a stop to it.

Of course, like drinking during prohibition or, today, smoking marihuana, cockfights, being a part of "The Balinese Way of Life," nonetheless go on happening, and with extraordinary frequency. And, like prohibition or marihuana, from time to time the police (who, in 1958 at least, were almost all not Balinese but Javanese) feel called upon to make a raid, confiscate the cocks and spurs, fine a few people, and even now and then expose some of them in the tropical sun for a day as object lessons which never, somehow, get learned, even though occasionally, quite occasionally, the object dies.

As a result, the fights are usually held in a secluded corner of a village in semisecrecy, a fact which tends to slow the action a little—not very much, but the Balinese do not care to have it slowed at all. In this case, however, perhaps because they were raising money for a school that the government was unable to give them, perhaps because raids had been few recently, perhaps, as I gathered from subsequent discussion, there was a notion that the necessary bribes had been paid, they thought they could take a chance on the central square and draw a larger and more enthusiastic crowd without attracting the attention of the law.

They were wrong. In the midst of the third match, with hundreds of people, including, still transparent, myself and my wife, fused into a single body around the ring, a superorganism in the literal sense, a truck full of policemen armed with machine guns roared up. Amid great screeching cries of "pulisi! pulisi!" from the crowd, the policemen jumped out, and, springing into the center of the ring, began to swing their guns around like gangsters in a motion picture, though not going so far as actually to fire them. The superorganism came instantly apart as its components scattered in all directions. People raced down the road, disappeared head first over walls, scrambled under platforms, folded themselves behind wicker screens, scuttled up coconut trees. Cocks armed with steel spurs sharp enough to  cut off a finger or run a hole through a foot were running wildly around. Everything was dust and panic.

On the established anthropological principle, When in Rome, my wife and I decided, only slightly less instantaneously than everyone else, that the thing to do was run too. We ran down the main village street, northward, away from where we were living, for we were on that side of the ring. About halfway down another fugitive ducked suddenly into a compound—his own, it turned out—and we, seeing nothing ahead of us but rice fields, open country, and a very high volcano, followed him. As the three of us came tumbling into the courtyard, his wife, who had apparently been through this sort of thing before, whipped out a table, a tablecloth, three chairs, and three cups of tea, and we all, without any explicit communication whatsoever, sat down, commenced to sip tea, and sought to compose ourselves.

A few moments later, one of the policemen marched importantly into the yard, looking for the village chief. (The chief had not only been at the fight, he had arranged it. When the truck drove up he ran to the river, stripped off his sarong, and plunged in so he could say, when at length they found him sitting there pouring water over his head, that he had been away bathing when the whole affair had occurred and was ignorant of it. They did not believe him and fined him three hundred rupiah, which the village raised collectively.) Seeing my wife and I, "White Men," there in the yard, the policeman performed a classic double take. When he found his voice again he asked, approximately, what in the devil did we think we were doing there. Our host of five minutes leaped instantly to our defense, producing an impassioned description of who and what we were, so detailed and so accurate that it was my turn, having barely communicated with a living human being save my landlord and the village chief for more than a week, to be astonished. We had a perfect right to be there, he said, looking the Javanese upstart in the eye. We were American professors; the government had cleared us; we were there to study culture; we were going to write a book to tell Americans about Bali. And we had all been there drinking tea and talking about cultural matters all afternoon and did not know anything about any cockfight. Moreover, we had not seen the village chief all day, he must have gone to town. The policeman retreated in rather total disarray. And, after a decent interval, bewildered but relieved to have survived and stayed out of jail, so did we.

The next morning the village was a completely different world for us. Not only were we no longer invisible, we were suddenly the center of all attention, the object of a great outpouring of warmth, interest, and, most especially, amusement. Everyone in the village knew we had fled like everyone else. They asked us about it again and again (I must have told the story, small detail by small detail, fifty times by the end of the day), gently, affectionately, but quite insistently teasing us: "Why didn't you just stand there and tell the police who you were?" "Why didn't you just say you were only watching and not betting?" "Were you really afraid of those little guns?" As always, kinesthetically minded and, even when fleeing for their lives (or, as happened eight years later, surrendering them), the world's most poised people, they gleefully mimicked, also over and over again, our graceless style of running and what they claimed were our panic-stricken facial expressions. But above all, everyone was extremely pleased and even more surprised that we had not simply "pulled out our papers" (they knew about those too) and asserted our Distinguished Visitor status, but had instead demonstrated our solidarity with what were now our covillagers. (What we had actually demonstrated was our cowardice, but there is fellowship in that too.) Even the Brahmana priest, an old, grave, halfway-to-Heaven type who because of its associations with the underworld would never be involved, even distantly, in a cockfight, and was difficult to approach even to other Balinese, had us called into his courtyard to ask us about what had happened, chuckling happily at the sheer extraordinariness of it all.

In Bali, to be teased is to be accepted. It was the turning point so far as our relationship to the community was concerned, and we were quite literally "in." The whole village opened up to us, probably more than it ever would have otherwise (I might actually never have gotten to that priest, and our accidental host became one of my best informants), and certainly very much faster. Getting caught, or almost caught, in a vice raid is perhaps not a very generalizable recipe for achieving that mysterious necessity of anthropological field work, rapport, but for me it worked very well. It led to a sudden and unusually complete acceptance into a society extremely difficult for outsiders to penetrate. It gave me the kind of immediate, inside-view grasp of an aspect of "peasant mentality" that anthropologists not fortunate enough to flee headlong with their subjects from armed authorities normally do not get. And, perhaps most important of all, for the other things might have come in other ways, it put me very quickly on to a combination emotional explosion, status war, and philosophical drama of central significance to the society whose inner nature I desired to understand. By the time I left I had spent about as much time looking into cockfights as into witchcraft, irrigation, caste, or marriage.

## Of Cocks and Men

Bali, mainly because it is Bali, is a well-studied place. Its mythology, art, ritual, social organization, patterns of child rearing, forms of law, even styles of trance, have all been microscopically examined for traces of that elusive substance Jane Belo called "The Balinese Temper."[2] But, aside from a few passing remarks, the cockfight has barely been noticed, although as a popular obsession of consuming power it is at least as important a revelation of what being a Balinese "is really like" as these more celebrated phenomena.[3] As much of America surfaces in a ball park, on a golf links, at a race track, or around a poker table, much of Bali surfaces in a cock ring. For it is only apparently cocks that are fighting there. Actually, it is men.

To anyone who has been in Bali any length of time, the deep psychological identification of Balinese men with their cocks is unmistakable. The double entendre here is deliberate. It works in exactly the same way in Balinese as it does in English, even to producing the same tired jokes, strained puns, and uninventive obscenities. Bateson and Mead have even suggested that, in line with the Balinese conception of the body as a set of separately animated parts, cocks are viewed as detachable, self-operating penises, ambulant genitals with a life of their own.[4] And while I do not have the kind of unconscious material either to confirm or disconfirm this intriguing notion, the fact that they are masculine symbols *par excellence* is about as indubitable, and to the Balinese about as evident, as the fact that water runs downhill.

The language of everyday moralism is shot through, on the male side of it, with roosterish imagery. *Sabung,* the word for cock (and one which appears in inscriptions as early as A.D. 922), is used metaphorically to mean "hero," "warrior," "champion," "man of parts," "political candidate," "bachelor," "dandy," "lady-killer," or "tough guy." A pompous man whose behavior presumes above his station is compared to a tailless cock who struts about as though he had a large, spectacular one. A desperate man who makes a last, irrational effort to extricate himself from an impossible situation is likened to a dying cock who makes one final lunge at his tormentor to drag him along to a common destruction. A stingy man, who promises much, gives little, and begrudges that is compared to a cock which, held by the tail, leaps at another without in fact engaging him. A marriageable young man still shy with the opposite sex or someone in a new job anxious to make a good impression is called "a fighting cock caged for the first time."[5] Court trials, wars, political contests, inheritance disputes, and street arguments are all compared to cockfights.[6] Even the very island itself is perceived from its shape as a small, proud cock, poised, neck extended, back taut, tail raised, in eternal challenge to large, feckless, shapeless Java.[7]

But the intimacy of men with their cocks is more than metaphorical. Balinese men, or anyway a large majority of Balinese men, spend an enormous amount of time with their favorites, grooming them, feeding them, discussing them, trying them out against one another, or just gazing at them with a mixture of rapt admiration and dreamy self-absorption. Whenever you see a group of Balinese men squatting idly in the council shed or along the road in their hips down, shoulders forward, knees up fashion, half or more of them will have a rooster in his hands, holding it between his thighs, bouncing it gently up and down to strengthen its legs, ruffling its feathers with abstract sensuality, pushing it out against a neighbor's rooster to rouse its spirit, withdrawing it toward his loins to calm it again. Now and then, to get a feel for another bird, a man will fiddle this way with someone else's cock for a while, but usually by moving around to squat in place behind it, rather than just having it passed across to him as though it were merely an animal.

In the houseyard, the high-walled enclosures where the people live, fighting cocks are kept in wicker cages, moved frequently about so as to maintain the optimum balance of sun and shade. They are fed a special diet, which varies somewhat according to individual theories but which is mostly maize, sifted for impurities with far more care than it is when mere humans are going to eat it and offered to the animal kernel by kernel. Red pepper is stuffed down their beaks and up their anuses to give them spirit. They are bathed in the same ceremonial preparation of tepid water, medicinal herbs, flowers, and onions in which infants are bathed, and for a prize cock just about as often. Their combs are cropped, their plumage dressed, their spurs trimmed, their legs massaged, and they are inspected for flaws with the squinted concentration of a diamond merchant. A man who has a passion for cocks, an enthusiast in the literal sense of the term, can spend most of his life with them, and even those, the overwhelming majority, whose passion though intense has not entirely run away with them, can and do spend what seems not only to an outsider, but also to themselves, an inordinate amount of time with them. "I am cock crazy," my landlord, a quite ordinary *afficionado* by Balinese standards, used to moan as he went to move another cage, give another bath, or conduct another feeding. "We're all cock crazy."

The madness has some less visible dimensions, however, because although it is true that cocks are symbolic expressions or magnifications of their owner's self, the narcissistic male ego writ out in Aesopian terms, they are also expressions—and rather more immediate ones—of what the Balinese regard as the direct inversion, aesthetically, morally, and metaphysically, of human status: animality.

The Balinese revulsion against any behavior regarded as animal-like can hardly be overstressed. Babies are not allowed to crawl for that reason. Incest, though hardly approved, is a much less horrifying crime than bestiality. (The appropriate punishment for the second is death by drowning, for the first being forced to live like an animal.)[8] Most demons are represented—in sculpture, dance, ritual, myth—in some real or fantastic animal form. The main puberty rite consists in filing the child's teeth so they will not look like animal fangs. Not only defecation but eating is regarded as a disgusting, almost obscene activity, to be conducted hurriedly and privately, because of its association with animality. Even falling down or any form of clumsiness is considered to be bad for these reasons. Aside from cocks and a few domestic animals—oxen, ducks—of no emotional significance, the Balinese are aversive to animals, and treat their large number of dogs not merely callously but with a phobic cruelty. In identifying with his cock, the Balinese man is identifying not just with his ideal self, or even his penis, but also, and at the same time, with what he most fears, hates, and ambivalence being what it is, is fascinated by—The Powers of Darkness.

The connection of cocks and cockfighting with such Powers, with the animalistic demons that threaten constantly to invade the small, cleared off space in which the Balinese have so carefully built their lives and devour its inhabitants, is quite explicit. A cockfight, any cockfight, is in the first instance a blood sacrifice offered, with the appropriate chants and oblations, to the demons in order to pacify their ravenous, cannibal hunger. No temple festival should be conducted until one is made. (If it is omitted someone will inevitably fall into a trance and command with the voice of an angered spirit that the oversight be immediately corrected.) Collective responses to natural evils—illness, crop failure, volcanic eruptions—almost always involve them. And that famous holiday in Bali, The Day of Silence (*Njepi*), when everyone sits silent and immobile all day long in order to avoid contact with a sudden influx of demons chased momentarily out of hell, is preceded the previous day by large-scale cockfights (in this case legal) in almost every village on the island.

In the cockfight, man and beast, good and evil, ego and id, the creative power of aroused masculinity and the destructive power of loosened animality fuse in a bloody drama of hatred, cruelty, violence, and death. It is little wonder that when, as is the invariable rule, the owner of the winning cock takes the carcass of the loser—often torn limb from limb by its enraged owner—home to eat, he does so with a mixture of social embarrassment, moral satisfaction, aesthetic disgust, and cannibal joy. Or that a man who has lost an important fight is sometimes driven to wreck his family shrines and curse the gods, an act of metaphysical (and social) suicide. Or that in seeking earthly analogues for heaven and hell the Balinese compare the former to the mood of a man whose cock has just won, the latter to that of a man whose cock has just lost.

## The Fight

Cockfights (*tetadjen; sabungan*) are held in a ring about fifty feet square. Usually they begin toward late afternoon and run three or four hours until sunset. About nine or ten separate matches (*sehet*) comprise a program. Each match is precisely like the others in general pattern: there is no main match, no connection between individual matches, no variation in their format, and each is arranged on a completely ad hoc basis. After a fight has ended and the emotional debris is cleaned away—the bets paid, the curses cursed, the carcasses possessed—seven, eight, perhaps even a dozen men slop negligently into the ring with a cock and seek to find there a logical opponent for it. This process, which rarely takes less than ten minutes and often a good deal longer, is conducted in a very subdued, oblique, even dissembling manner. Those not immediately involved give it at best but disguised, sidelong attention; those who, embarrassedly, are, attempt to pretend somehow that the whole thing is not really happening.

A match made, the other hopefuls retire with the same deliberate indifference, and the selected cocks have their spurs (*tadji*) affixed—razorsharp, pointed steel swords, four or five inches long. This is a delicate job which only a small portion of men, a half-dozen or so in most villages, know how to do properly. The man who attaches the spurs also provides them, and if the rooster he assists wins its owner awards him the spur-leg of the victim. The spurs are affixed by winding a long length of string around the foot of the spur and the leg of the cock. For reasons I shall come to presently, it is done somewhat differently from case to case, and is an obsessively deliberate affair. The lore about spurs is extensive—they are sharpened only at eclipses and the dark of the moon, should be kept out of the sight of women, and so forth. And they are handled, both in use and out, with the same curious combination of fussiness and sensuality the Balinese direct toward ritual objects generally.

The spurs affixed, the two cocks are placed by their handlers (who may or may not be their owners) facing one another in the center of the ring.[9] A coconut pierced with a small hole is placed in a pail of water, in which it takes about twenty-one seconds to sink, a period known as a *tjeng* and marked at beginning and end by the beating of a slit gong. During these twenty-one seconds the handlers (*pengangkeb*) are not permitted to touch their roosters. If, as sometimes happens, the animals have not fought during this time, they are picked up, fluffed, pulled, prodded, and otherwise insulted, and put back in the center of the ring and the process begins again. Sometimes they refuse to fight at all, or one keeps running away, in which case they are imprisoned together under a wicker cage, which usually gets them engaged.

Most of the time, in any case, the cocks fly almost immediately at one another in a wing-beating, head-thrusting, leg-kicking explosion of animal fury so pure, so absolute, and in its own way so beautiful, as to be almost abstract, a Platonic concept of hate. Within moments one or the other drives home a solid blow with his spur. The handler whose cock has delivered the blow immediately picks it up so that it will not get a return blow, for if he does not the match is likely to end in a mutually mortal tie as the two birds wildly hack each other to pieces. This is particularly true if, as often happens, the spur sticks in its victim's body, for then the aggressor is at the mercy of his wounded foe.

With the birds again in the hands of their handlers, the coconut is now sunk three times after which the cock which has landed the blow must be set down to show that he is firm, a fact he demonstrates by wandering idly around the ring for a coconut sink. The coconut is then sunk twice more and the fight must recommence.

During this interval, slightly over two minutes, the handler of the wounded cock has been working frantically over it, like a trainer patching a mauled boxer between rounds, to get it in shape for a last, desperate try for victory. He blows in its mouth, putting the whole chicken head in his own mouth and sucking and blowing, fluffs it, stuffs its wounds with various sorts of medicines, and generally tries anything he can think of to arouse the last ounce of spirit which may be hidden somewhere within it. By the time he is forced to put it back down he is usually drenched in chicken blood, but, as in prize fighting, a good handler is worth his weight in gold. Some of them can virtually make the dead walk, at least long enough for the second and final round.

In the climactic battle (if there is one; sometimes the wounded cock simply expires in the handler's hands or immediately as it is placed down again), the cock who landed the first blow usually proceeds to finish off his weakened opponent. But this is far from an inevitable outcome, for if a cock can walk he can fight, and if he can fight, he can kill, and what counts is which cock expires first. If the wounded one can get a stab in and stagger on until the other drops, he is the official winner, even if he himself topples over an instant later.

Surrounding all this melodrama—which the crowd packed tight around the ring follows in near silence, moving their bodies in kinesthetic sympathy with the movement of the animals, cheering their champions on with wordless hand motions, shiftings of the shoulders, turnings of the head, falling back *en masse* as the cock with the murderous spurs careens toward one side of the ring (it is said that spectators sometimes lose eyes and fingers from being too attentive), surging forward again as they glance off toward another—is a vast body of extraordinarily elaborate and precisely detailed rules.

These rules, together with the developed lore of cocks and cockfighting which accompanies them, are written down in palm leaf manuscripts (*lontar; rontal*), passed on from generation to generation as part of the general legal and cultural tradition of the villages. At a fight, the umpire (*saja komong; djuru kembar*)—the man who manages the coconut—is in charge of their application and his authority is absolute. I have never seen an umpire's judgment questioned on any subject, even by the more despondent losers, nor have I ever heard, even in private, a charge of unfairness directed against one, or, for that matter, complaints about umpires in general. Only exceptionally well-trusted, solid, and, given the complexity of the code, knowledgeable citizens perform this job, and in fact men will bring their cocks only to fights presided over by such men. It is also the umpire to whom accusations of cheating, which, though rare in the extreme, occasionally arise, are referred; and it is he who in the not infrequent cases where the cocks expire virtually together decides which (if either, for, though the Balinese do not care for such an outcome, there can be ties) went first. Likened to a judge, a king, a priest, and a policeman, he is all of these, and under his assured direction the animal passion of the fight proceeds within the civic certainty of the law. In the dozens of cockfights I saw in Bali, I never once saw an altercation about rules. Indeed, I never saw an open altercation, other than those between cocks, at all.

This crosswise doubleness of an event which, taken as a fact of nature, is rage untrammeled and, taken as a fact of culture, is form perfected, defines the cockfight as a sociological entity. A cockfight is what, searching for a name for something not vertebrate enough to be called a group and not structureless enough to be called a crowd, Erving Goffman has called a "focused gathering"—a set of persons engrossed in a common flow of activity and relating to one another in terms of that flow.[10] Such gatherings meet and disperse; the participants in them fluctuate; the activity that focuses them is discreet—a particulate process that reoccurs rather than a continuous one that endures. They take their form from the situation that evokes them, the floor on which they are placed, as Goffman puts it; but it is a form, and an articulate one, nonetheless. For the situation, the floor is itself created, in jury deliberations, surgical operations, block meetings, sit-ins, cockfights, by the cultural preoccupations—here, as we shall see, the celebration of status rivalry—which not only specify the focus but, assembling actors and arranging scenery, bring it actually into being.

In classical times (that is to say, prior to the Dutch invasion of 1908), when there were no bureaucrats around to improve popular morality, the staging of a cockfight was an explicitly societal matter. Bringing a cock to an important fight was, for an adult male, a compulsory duty of citizenship; taxation of fights, which were usually held on market day, was a major source of public revenue; patronage of the art was a stated responsibility of princes; and the cock ring, or *wantilan,* stood in the center of the village near those other monuments of Balinese civility—the council house, the origin temple, the marketplace, the signal tower, and the banyan tree. Today, a few special occasions aside, the newer rectitude makes so open a statement of the connection between the excitements of collective life and those of blood sport impossible, but, less directly expressed, the connection itself remains intimate and intact. To expose it, however, it is necessary to turn to the aspect of cockfighting around which all the others pivot, and through which they exercise their force, an aspect I have thus far studiously ignored. I mean, of course, the gambling.

## Odds and Even Money

The Balinese never do anything in a simple way that they can contrive to do in a complicated one, and to this generalization cockfight wagering is no exception.

In the first place, there are two sorts of bets, or *toh*.[11] There is the single axial bet on the center between the principals (*toh ketengah*), and there is the cloud of peripheral ones around the ring between members of the audience (*toh kesasi*). The first is typically large; the second typically small. The first is collective, involving coalitions of bettors clustering around the owner; the second is individual, man to man. The first is a matter of deliberate, very quiet, almost furtive arrangement by the coalition members and the umpire huddled like conspirators in the center of the ring; the second is a matter of impulsive shouting, public offers, and public acceptances by the excited throng around its edges. And most curiously, and as we shall see most revealingly, *where the first is always, without exception, even money, the second, equally without exception, is never such.* What is a fair coin in the center is a biased one on the side.

The center bet is the official one, hedged in again with a webwork of rules, and is made between the two cock owners, with the umpire as overseer and public witness.[12] This bet, which, as I say, is always relatively and sometimes very large, is never raised simply by the owner in whose name it is made, but by him together with four or five, sometimes seven or eight, allies—kin, village mates, neighbors, close friends. He may, if he is not especially well-to-do, not even be the major contributor, though, if only to show that he is not involved in any chicanery, he must be a significant one.

Of the fifty-seven matches for which I have exact and reliable data on the center bet, the range is from fifteen ringgits to five hundred, with a mean at eighty-five and with the distribution being rather noticeably trimodal: small fights (15 ringgits either side of 35) accounting for about 45 percent of the total number; medium ones (20 ringgits either side of 70) for about 25 percent; and large (75 ringgits either side of 175) for about 20 percent, with a few very small and very large ones out at the extremes. In a society where the normal daily wage of a manual laborer—a brickmaker, an ordinary farmworker, a market porter—was about three ringgits a day, and considering the fact that fights were held on the average about every two-and-a-half days in the immediate area I studied, this is clearly serious gambling, even if the bets are pooled rather than individual efforts.

The side bets are, however, something else altogether. Rather than the solemn, legalistic pactmaking of the center, wagering takes place rather in the fashion in which the stock exchange used to work when it was out on the curb. There is a fixed and known odds paradigm which runs in a continuous series from ten-to-nine at the short end to two-to-one at the long: 10-9, 9-8, 8-7, 7-6, 6-5, 5-4, 4-3, 3-2, 2-1. The man who wishes to back the *underdog cock* (leaving aside how favorites, *kebut,* and underdogs, *ngai,* are established for the moment) shouts the short-side number indicating the odds he wants *to be given.* That is, if he shouts *gasal,* "five," he wants the underdog at five-to-four (or, for him, four-to-five); if he shouts "four," he wants it at four-to-three (again, he putting up the "three"), if "nine," at nine-to-eight, and so on. A man backing the favorite, and thus considering giving odds if he can get them short enough, indicates the fact by crying out the color-type of that cock—"brown," "speckled," or whatever.[13]

As odds-takers (backers of the underdog) and odds-givers (backers of the favorite) sweep the crowd with their shouts, they begin to focus in on one another as potential betting pairs, often from far across the ring. The taker tries to shout the giver into longer odds, the giver to shout the taker into shorter ones.[14] The taker, who is the wooer in this situation, will signal how large a bet he wishes to make at the odds he is shouting by holding a number of fingers up in front of his face and vigorously waving them. If the giver, the wooed, replies in kind, the bet is made; if he does not, they unlock gazes and the search goes on.

The side betting, which takes place after the center bet has been made and its size announced, consists then in a rising crescendo of shouts as backers of the underdog offer their propositions to anyone who will accept them, while those who are backing the favorite but do not like the price being offered, shout equally frenetically the color of the cock to show they too are desperate to bet but want shorter odds.

Almost always odds-calling, which tends to be very consensual in that at any one time almost all callers are calling the same thing, starts off toward the long end of the range—five-to-four or four-to-three—and then moves, also consensually, toward the short end with greater or lesser speed and to a greater or lesser degree. Men crying "five" and finding themselves answered only with cries of "brown" start crying "six," either drawing the other callers fairly quickly with them or retiring from the scene as their too-generous offers are snapped up. If the change is made and partners are still scarce, the procedure is repeated in a move to "seven," and so on, only rarely, and in the very largest fights, reaching the ultimate "nine" or "ten" levels. Occasionally, if the cocks are clearly mismatched, there may be no upward movement at all, or even a movement down the scale to four-to-three, three-to-two, very, very rarely two-to-one, a shift which is accompanied by a declining number of bets as a shift upward is accompanied by an increasing number. But the general pattern is for the betting to move a shorter or longer distance up the scale toward the, for sidebets, nonexistent pole of even money, with the overwhelming majority of bets falling in the four-to-three to eight-to-seven range.[15]

As the moment for the release of the cocks by the handlers approaches, the screaming, at least in a match where the center bet is large, reaches almost frenzied proportions as the remaining unfulfilled bettors try desperately to find a last minute partner at a price they can live with. (Where the center bet is small, the opposite tends to occur: betting dies off, trailing into silence, as odds lengthen and people lose interest.) In a large-bet, well-made match—the kind of match the Balinese regard as "real cockfighting"—the mob scene quality, the sense that sheer chaos is about to break loose, with all those waving, shouting, pushing, clambering men is quite strong, an effect which is only heightened by the intense stillness that falls with instant suddenness, rather as if someone had turned off the current, when the slit gong sounds, the cocks are put down, and the battle begins.

When it ends, anywhere from fifteen seconds to five minutes later, *all bets are immediately paid*. There are absolutely no IOU's, at least to a betting opponent. One may, of course, borrow from a friend before offering or accepting a wager, but to offer or accept it you must have the money already in hand and, if you lose, you must pay it on the spot, before the next match begins. This is an iron rule, and as I have never heard of a disputed umpire's decision (though doubtless there must sometimes be some), I have also never heard of a welshed bet, perhaps because in a worked-up cockfight crowd the consequences might be, as they are reported to be sometimes for cheaters, drastic and immediate.

It is, in any case, this formal asymmetry between balanced center bets and unbalanced side ones that poses the critical analytical problem for a theory which sees cockfight wagering as the link connecting the fight to the wider world of Balinese culture. It also suggests the way to go about solving it and demonstrating the link.

The first point that needs to be made in this connection is that the higher the center bet, the more likely the match will in actual fact be an even one. Simple considerations of rationality suggest that. If you are betting fifteen ringgits on a cock, you might be willing to go along with even money even if you feel your animal somewhat the less promising. But if you are betting five hundred you are very, very likely to be loath to do so. Thus, in large-bet fights, which of course involve the better animals, tremendous care is taken to see that the cocks are about as evenly matched as to size, general condition, pugnacity, and so on as is humanly possible. The different ways of adjusting the spurs of the animals are often employed to secure this. If one cock seems stronger, an agreement will be made to position his spur at a slightly less advantageous angle—a kind of handicapping, at which spur affixers are, so it is said, extremely skilled. More care will be taken, too, to employ skillful handlers and to match them exactly as to abilities.

In short, in a large-bet fight the pressure to make the match a genuinely fifty-fifty proposition is enormous, and is consciously felt as such. For medium fights the pressure is somewhat less, and for small ones less yet, though there is always an effort to make things at least approximately equal, for even at fifteen ringgits (five days' work) no one wants to make an even money bet in a clearly unfavorable situation. And, again, what statistics I have tend to bear this out. In my fifty-seven matches, the favorite won thirty-three times overall, the underdog twenty-four, a 1.4 to 1 ratio. But if one splits the figures at sixty ringgits center bets, the ratios turn out to be 1.1 to 1 (twelve favorites, eleven underdogs) for those above this line, and 1.6 to 1 (twenty-one and thirteen) for those below it. Or, if you take the extremes, for very large fights, those with center bets over a hundred ringgits the ratio is 1 to 1 (seven and seven); for very small fights, those under forty ringgits, it is 1.9 to 1 (nineteen and ten).[16]

Now, from this proposition—that the higher the center bet the more exactly a fifty-fifty proposition the cockfight is—two things more or less immediately follow: (1) the higher the center bet, the greater is the pull on the side betting toward the short-odds end of the wagering spectrum and vice versa; (2) the higher the center bet, the greater the volume of side betting and vice versa.

The logic is similar in both cases. The closer the fight is in fact to even money, the less attractive the long end of the odds will appear and, therefore, the shorter it must be if there are to be takers. That this is the case is apparent from mere inspection, from the Balinese's own analysis of the matter, and from what more systematic observations I was able to collect. Given the difficulty of making precise and complete recordings of side betting, this argument is hard to cast in numerical form, but in all my cases the odds-giver, odds-taker consensual point, a quite pronounced minimax saddle where the bulk (at a guess, two-thirds to three-quarters in most cases) of the bets are actually made, was three or four points further along the scale toward the shorter end for the large-center-bet fights than for the small ones, with medium ones generally in between. In detail, the fit is not, of course, exact, but the general pattern is quite consistent: the power of the center bet to pull the side bets toward its own even-money pattern is directly proportional to its size, because its size is directly proportional to the degree to which the cocks are in fact evenly matched. As for the volume question, total wagering is greater in large-center-bet fights because such fights are considered more "interesting" not only in the sense that they are less predictable, but, more crucially, that more is at stake in them—in terms of money, in terms of the quality of the cocks, and consequently, as we shall see, in terms of social prestige.[17]

The paradox of fair coin in the middle, biased coin on the outside is thus a merely apparent one. The two betting systems, though formally incongruent, are not really contradictory to one another, but part of a single larger system in which the center bet is, so to speak, the "center of gravity," drawing, the larger it is the more so, the outside bets toward the short-odds end of the scale. The center bet thus "makes the game," or per-haps better, defines it, signals what, following a notion of Jeremy Ben-tham's, I am going to call its "depth."

The Balinese attempt to create an interesting, if you will, "deep," match by making the center bet as large as possible so that the cocks matched will be as equal and as fine as possible, and the outcome, thus, as unpredictable as possible. They do not always succeed. Nearly half the matches are rela-tively trivial, relatively uninteresting—in my borrowed terminology, "shal-low"—affairs. But that fact no more argues against my interpretation than the fact that most painters, poets, and playwrights are mediocre argues against the view that artistic effort is directed toward profundity and, with a certain frequency, approximates it. The image of artistic technique is in-deed exact: the center bet is a means, a device, for creating "interesting," "deep" matches, *not* the reason, at least not the main reason, *why* they are in-teresting, the source of their fascination, the substance of their depth. The question why such matches are interesting—indeed, for the Balinese, ex-quisitely absorbing—takes us out of the realm of formal concerns into more broadly sociological and social-psychological ones, and to a less purely eco-nomic idea of what "depth" in gaming amounts to.[18]

## *Playing with Fire*

Bentham's concept of "deep play" is found in his *The Theory of Legisla-tion*.[19] By it he means play in which the stakes are so high that it is, from his utilitarian standpoint, irrational for men to engage in it at all. If a man whose fortune is a thousand pounds (or ringgits) wages five hundred of it on an even bet, the marginal utility of the pound he stands to win is clearly less than the marginal disutility of the one he stands to lose. In gen-uine deep play, this is the case for both parties. They are both in over their heads. Having come together in search of pleasure they have entered into a relationship which will bring the participants, considered collectively, net pain rather than net pleasure. Bentham's conclusion was, therefore, that deep play was immoral from the first principles and, a typical step for him, should be prevented legally.

But more interesting than the ethical problem, at least for our concerns here, is that despite the logical force of Bentham's analysis men do engage in such play, both passionately and often, and even in the face of law's re-venge. For Bentham and those who think as he does (nowadays mainly lawyers, economists, and a few psychiatrists), the explanation is, as I have said, that such men are irrational—addicts, fetishists, children, fools, sav-ages, who need only to be protected against themselves. But for the Bali-nese, though naturally they do not formulate it in so many words, the ex-planation lies in the fact that in such play money is less a measure of utility, had or expected, than it is a symbol of moral import, perceived or imposed.

It is, in fact, in shallow games, ones in which smaller amounts of money are involved, that increments and decrements of cash are more nearly synonyms for utility and disutility, in the ordinary, unexpanded sense—for pleasure and pain, happiness and unhappiness. In deep ones, where the amounts of money are great, much more is at stake than material gain: namely esteem, honor, dignity, respect—in a word, though in Bali a profoundly freighted word, status.[20] It is at stake symbolically, for (a few cases of ruined addict gamblers aside) no one's status is actually altered by the outcome of a cockfight; it is only, and that momentarily, affirmed or insulted. But for the Balinese, for whom nothing is more pleasurable than an affront obliquely delivered or more painful than one obliquely received—particularly when mutual acquaintances, undeceived by surfaces, are watching—such appraisive drama is deep indeed.

This, I must stress immediately, is *not* to say that the money does not matter, or that the Balinese is no more concerned about losing five hundred ringgits than fifteen. Such a conclusion would be absurd. It is because money *does,* in this hardly unmaterialistic society, matter and matter very much that the more of it one risks the more of a lot of other things, such as one's pride, one's poise, one's dispassion, one's masculinity, one also risks, again only momentarily but again very publicly as well. In deep cockfights an owner and his collaborators, and, as we shall see, to a lesser but still quite real extent also their backers on the outside, put their money where their status is.

It is in large part *because* the marginal disutility of loss is so great at the higher levels of betting that to engage in such betting is to lay one's public self, allusively and metaphorically, through the medium of one's cock, on the line. And though to a Benthamite this might seem merely to increase the irrationality of the enterprise that much further, to the Balinese what it mainly increases is the meaningfulness of it all. And as (to follow Weber rather than Bentham) the imposition of meaning on life is the major end and primary condition of human existence, that access of significance more than compensates for the economic costs involved.[21] Actually, given the even-money quality of the larger matches, important changes in material fortune among those who regularly participate in them seem virtually nonexistent, because matters more or less even out over the long run. It is, actually, in the smaller, shallow fights, where one finds the handful of more pure, addict-type gamblers involved—those who *are* in it mainly for the money—that "real" changes in social position, largely downward, are affected. Men of this sort, plungers, are highly dispraised by "true cockfighters" as fools who do not understand what the sport is all about, vulgarians who simply miss the point of it all. They are, these addicts, regarded as fair game for the genuine enthusiasts, those who do understand, to take a little money away from, something that is easy enough to do by luring them, through the force of their greed, into irrational bets on mismatched cocks. Most of them do indeed manage to ruin themselves in a remarkably short time, but there always seem to be one or two of them around, pawning their land and selling their clothes in order to bet, at any particular time.[22]

This graduated correlation of "status gambling" with deeper fights and, inversely, "money gambling" with shallower ones is in fact quite general. Bettors themselves form a sociomoral hierarchy in these terms. As noted earlier, at most cockfights there are, around the very edges of the cockfight area, a large number of mindless, sheer-chance type gambling games (roulette, dice throw, coin-spin, pea-under-the-shell) operated by concessionaires. Only women, children, adolescents, and various other sorts of people who do not (or not yet) fight cocks—the extremely poor, the socially despised, the personally idiosyncratic—play at these games, at, of course, penny ante levels. Cockfighting men would be ashamed to go anywhere near them. Slightly above these people in standing are those who, though they do not themselves fight cocks, bet on the smaller matches around the edges. Next, there are those who fight cocks in small, or occasionally medium matches, but have not the status to join in the large ones, though they may bet from time to time on the side in those. And finally, there are those, the really substantial members of the community, the solid citizenry around whom local life revolves, who fight in the larger fights and bet on them around the side. The focusing element in these focused gatherings, these men generally dominate and define the sport as they dominate and define the society. When a Balinese male talks, in that almost venerative way, about "the true cockfighter," the *bebatoh* ("bettor") or *djuru kurung* ("cage keeper"), it is this sort of person, not those who bring the mentality of the pea-and-shell game into the quite different, inappropriate context of the cockfight, the driven gambler (*potét*, a word which has the secondary meaning of thief or reprobate), and the wistful hanger-on, that they mean. For such a man, what is really going on in a match is something rather close to an *affaire d'honneur* (though, with the Balinese talent for practical fantasy, the blood that is spilled is only figuratively human) than to the stupid, mechanical crank of a slot machine.

What makes Balinese cockfighting deep is thus not money in itself, but what, the more of it that is involved the more so, money causes to happen: the migration of the Balinese status hierarchy into the body of the cockfight. Psychologically an Aesopian representation of the ideal/demonic, rather narcissistic, male self, sociologically it is an equally Aesopian representation of the complex fields of tension set up by the controlled, muted, ceremonial, but for all that deeply felt, interaction of those selves in the context of everyday life. The cocks may be surrogates for their owners' personalities, animal mirrors of psychic form, but the cockfight is— or more exactly, deliberately is made to be—a simulation of the social matrix, the involved system of crosscutting, overlapping, highly corporate groups—villages, kingroups, irrigation societies, temple congregations, "castes"—in which its devotees live.[23] And as prestige, the necessity to affirm it, defend it, celebrate it, justify it, and just plain bask in it (but not, given the strongly ascriptive character of Balinese stratification, to seek it), is perhaps the central driving force in the society, so also—ambulant penises, blood sacrifices, and monetary exchanges aside—is it of the cockfight. This apparent amusement and seeming sport is, to take another phrase from Erving Goffman, "a status bloodbath."[24]

The easiest way to make this clear, and at least to some degree to demonstrate it, is to invoke the village whose cockfighting activities I observed the closest—the one in which the raid occurred and from which my statistical data are taken.

As all Balinese villages, this one—Tihingan, in the Klungkung region of southeast Bali—is intricately organized, a labyrinth of alliances and oppositions. But, unlike many, two sorts of corporate groups, which are also status groups, particularly stand out, and we may concentrate on them, in a part-for-whole way, without undue distortion.

First, the village is dominated by four large, patrilineal, partly endogamous descent groups which are constantly vying with one another and form the major factions in the village. Sometimes they group two and two, or rather the two larger ones versus the two smaller ones plus all the unaffiliated people; sometimes they operate independently. There are also subfactions within them, subfactions within the subfactions, and so on to rather fine levels of distinction. And second, there is the village itself, almost entirely endogamous, which is opposed to all the other villages round about in its cockfight circuit (which, as explained, is the market region), but which also forms alliances with certain of these neighbors against certain others in various supravillage political and social contexts. The exact situation is thus, as everywhere in Bali, quite distinctive; but the general pattern of a tiered hierarchy of status rivalries between highly corporate but various based groupings (and, thus, between the members of them) is entirely general.

Consider, then, as support of the general thesis that the cockfight, and especially the deep cockfight, is fundamentally a dramatization of status concerns, the following facts, which to avoid extended ethnographic description I will simply pronounce to be facts—though the concrete evidence—examples, statements, and numbers that could be brought to bear in support of them is both extensive and unmistakable:

1. A man virtually never bets against a cock owned by a member of his own kingroup. Usually he will feel obliged to bet for it, the more so the closer the kin tie and the deeper the fight. If he is certain in his mind that it will not win, he may just not bet at all, particularly if it is only a second cousin's bird or if the fight is a shallow one. But as a rule he will feel he must support it and, in deep games, nearly always does. Thus the great majority of the people calling "five" or "speckled" so demonstratively are expressing their allegiance to their kinsman, not their evaluation of his bird, their understanding of probability theory, or even their hopes of unearned income.

2. This principle is extended logically. If your kingroup is not involved you will support an allied kingroup against an unallied one in the same way, and so on through the very involved networks of alliances which, as I say, make up this, as any other, Balinese village.

3. So, too, for the village as a whole. If an outsider cock is fighting any cock from your village, you will tend to support the local one. If, what is a rare circumstance but occurs every now and then, a cock from outside your cockfight circuit is fighting one inside it you will also tend to support the "home bird."

4. Cocks which come from any distance are almost always favorites, for the theory is the man would not have dared to bring it if it was not a good cock, the more so the further he has come. His followers are, of course, obliged to support him, and when the more grand-scale legal cockfights are held (on holidays, and so on) the people of the village take what they regard to be the best cocks in the village, regardless of ownership, and go off to support them, although they will almost certainly have to give odds on them and to make large bets to show that they are not a cheapskate village. Actually, such "away games," though infrequent, tend to mend the ruptures between village members that the constantly occurring "home games," where village factions are opposed rather than united, exacerbate.

5. Almost all matches are sociologically relevant. You seldom get two outsider cocks fighting, or two cocks with no particular group backing, or with group backing which is mutually unrelated in any clear way. When you do get them, the game is very shallow, betting very slow, and the whole thing very dull, with no one save the immediate principals and an addict gambler or two at all interested.

6. By the same token, you rarely get two cocks from the same group, even more rarely from the same subfaction, and virtually never from the same sub-subfaction (which would be in most cases one extended family) fighting. Similarly, in outside village fights two members of the village will rarely fight against one another, even though, as bitter rivals, they would do so with enthusiasm on their home grounds.

7. On the individual level, people involved in an institutionalized hostility relationship, called *puik*, in which they do not speak or otherwise have anything to do with each other (the causes of this formal breaking of relations are many: wife-capture, inheritance arguments, political differences) will bet very heavily, sometimes almost maniacally, against one another in what is a frank and direct attack on the very masculinity, the ultimate ground of his status, of the opponent.

8. The center bet coalition is, in all but the shallowest games, *always* made up by structural allies—no "outside money" is involved. What is "outside" depends upon the context, of course, but given it, no outside money is mixed in with the main bet; if the principals cannot raise it, it is not made. The center bet, again especially in deeper games, is thus the most direct and open expression of social opposition, which is one

of the reasons why both it and match making are surrounded by such an air of unease, furtiveness, embarrassment, and so on.

9. The rule about borrowing money—that you may borrow *for* a bet but not *in* one—stems (and the Balinese are quite conscious of this) from similar considerations: you are never at the *economic* mercy of your enemy that way. Gambling debts, which can get quite large on a rather short-term basis, are always to friends, never to enemies, structurally speaking.

10. When two cocks are structurally irrelevant or neutral so far as *you* are concerned (though, as mentioned, they almost never are to each other) you do not even ask a relative or a friend whom he is betting on, because if you know how he is betting and he knows you know, and you go the other way, it will lead to strain. This rule is explicit and rigid; fairly elaborate, even rather artificial precautions are taken to avoid breaking it. At the very least you must pretend not to notice what he is doing, and he what you are doing.

11. There is a special word for betting against the grain, which is also the word for "pardon me" (*mpura*). It is considered a bad thing to do, though if the center bet is small it is sometimes all right as long as you do not do it too often. But the larger the bet and the more frequently you do it, the more the "pardon me" tack will lead to social disruption.

12. In fact, the institutionalized hostility relation, *puik,* is often formally initiated (though its causes always lie elsewhere) by such a "pardon me" bet in a deep fight, putting the symbolic fat in the fire. Similarly, the end of such a relationship and resumption of normal social intercourse is often signalized (but, again, not actually brought about) by one or the other of the enemies supporting the other's bird.

13. In sticky, cross-loyalty situations, of which in this extraordinarily complex social system there are of course many, where a man is caught between two more or less equally balanced loyalties, he tends to wander off for a cup of coffee or something to avoid having to bet, a form of behavior reminiscent of that of American voters in similar situations.[25]

14. The people involved in the center bet are, especially in deep fights, virtually always leading members of their group—kinship, village, or whatever. Further, those who bet on the side (including these people) are, as I have already remarked, the more established members of the village—the solid citizens. Cockfighting is for those who are involved in the everyday politics of prestige as well, not for youth, women, subordinates, and so forth.

15. So far as money is concerned, the explicitly expressed attitude toward it is that it is a secondary matter. It is not, as I have said, of no importance; Balinese are no happier to lose several weeks' income than anyone else. But they mainly look on the monetary aspects of the cockfight as self-balancing, a matter of just moving money around, circulating it among

a fairly well-defined group of serious cockfighters. The really important wins and losses are seen mostly in other terms, and the general attitude toward wagering is not any hope of cleaning up, of making a killing (addict gamblers again excepted), but that of the horseplayer's prayer: "O, God, please let me break even." In prestige terms, however, you do not want to break even, but, in a momentary, punctuate sort of way, win utterly. The talk (which goes on all the time) is about fights against such-and-such a cock of So-and-So which your cock demolished, not on how much you won, a fact people, even for large bets, rarely remember for any length of time, though they will remember the day they did in Pan Loh's finest cock for years.

16. You must bet on cocks of your own group aside from mere loyalty considerations, for if you do not people generally will say, "What! Is he too proud for the likes of us? Does he have to go to Java or Den Pasar [the capital town] to bet, he is such an important man?" Thus there is a general pressure to bet not only to show that you are important locally, but that you are not so important that you look down on everyone else as unfit even to be rivals. Similarly, home team people must bet against outside cocks or the outsiders will accuse it—a serious charge—of just collecting entry fees and not really being interested in cockfighting, as well as again being arrogant and insulting.

17. Finally, the Balinese peasants themselves are quite aware of all this and can and, at least to an ethnographer, do state most of it in approximately the same terms as I have. Fighting cocks, almost every Balinese I have ever discussed the subject with has said, is like playing with fire only not getting burned. You activate village and kingroup rivalries and hostilities, but in "play" form, coming dangerously and entrancingly close to the expression of open and direct interpersonal and intergroup aggression (something which, again, almost never happens in the normal course of ordinary life), but not quite, because, after all, it is "only a cockfight."

More observations of this sort could be advanced, but perhaps the general point is, if not made, at least well-delineated, and the whole argument thus far can be usefully summarized in a formal paradigm:

THE MORE A MATCH IS . . .

1. Between near status equals (and/or personal enemies)
2. Between high status individuals

THE DEEPER THE MATCH.

THE DEEPER THE MATCH . . .

1. The closer the identification of cock and man (or: more properly, the deeper the match the more the man will advance his best, most closely-identified-with cock).

2. The finer the cocks involved and the more exactly they will be matched.

3. The greater the emotion that will be involved and the more the general absorption in the match.

4. The higher the individual bets center and outside, the shorter the outside bet odds will tend to be, and the more betting there will be overall.

5. The less an "economic" and the more a "status" view of gaming will be involved, and the "solider" the citizens who will be gaming.[26]

Inverse arguments hold for the shallower the fight, culminating, in a reversed-signs sense, in the coin-spinning and dice-throwing amusements. For deep fights there are no absolute upper limits, though there are of course practical ones, and there are a great many legendlike tales of great Duel-in-the-Sun combats between lords and princes in classical times (for cockfighting has always been as much an elite concern as a popular one), far deeper than anything anyone, even aristocrats, could produce today anywhere in Bali.

Indeed, one of the great culture heroes of Bali is a prince, called after his passion for the sport, "The Cockfighter," who happened to be away at a very deep cockfight with a neighboring prince when the whole of his family—father, brothers, wives, sisters—were assassinated by commoner usurpers. Thus spared, he returned to dispatch the upstarts, regain the throne, reconstitute the Balinese high tradition, and build its most powerful, glorious, and prosperous state. Along with everything else that the Balinese see in fighting cocks—themselves, their social order, abstract hatred, masculinity, demonic power—they also see the archetype of status virtue, the arrogant, resolute, honor-mad player with real fire, the *ksatria* prince.[27]

### Feathers, Blood, Crowds, and Money

"Poetry makes nothing happen," Auden says in his elegy of Yeats, "it survives in the valley of its saying . . . a way of happening, a mouth." The cockfight too, in this colloquial sense, makes nothing happen. Men go on allegorically humiliating one another and being allegorically humiliated by one another, day after day, glorying quietly in the experience if they have triumphed, crushed only slightly more openly by it if they have not. *But no one's status really changes.* You cannot ascend the status ladder by winning cockfights; you cannot, as an individual, really ascend it at all. Nor can you descend it that way.[28] All you can do is enjoy and savor, or suffer and withstand, the concocted sensation of drastic and momentary movement along an aesthetic semblance of that ladder, and kind of behind-the-mirror status jump which has the look of mobility without its actuality.

As any art form—for that, finally, is what we are dealing with—the cockfight renders ordinary, everyday experience comprehensible by presenting it in terms of acts and objects which have had their practical consequences removed and been reduced (or, if you prefer, raised) to the level of sheer appearances, where their meaning can be more powerfully articulated and more exactly perceived. The cockfight is "really real" only to the cocks—it does not kill anyone, castrate anyone, reduce anyone to animal status, alter the hierarchical relations among people, nor refashion the hierarchy; it does not even redistribute income in any significant way. What it does is what, for other peoples with other temperaments and other conventions, *Lear* and *Crime and Punishment* do; it catches up these themes—death, masculinity, rage, pride, loss, beneficence, chance—and, ordering them into an encompassing structure, presents them in such a way as to throw into relief a particular view of their essential nature. It puts a construction on them, makes them, to those historically positioned to appreciate the construction, meaningful—visible, tangible, graspable—"real," in an ideational sense. An image, fiction, a model, a metaphor, the cockfight is a means of expression; its function is neither to assuage social passions nor to heighten them (though, in its play-with-fire way, it does a bit of both), but, in a medium of feathers, blood, crowds, and money, to display them.

The question of how it is that we perceive qualities in things—paintings, books, melodies, plays—that we do not feel we can assert literally to be there has come, in recent years, into the very center of aesthetic theory.[29] Neither the sentiments of the artist, which remain his, nor those of the audience, which remain theirs, can account for the agitation of one painting or the serenity of another. We attribute grandeur, wit, despair, exuberance to strings of sounds; lightness, energy, violence, fluidity to blocks of stone. Novels are said to have strength, buildings eloquence, plays momentum, ballets repose. In this realm of eccentric predicates, to say that the cockfight, in its perfected cases at least, is "disquietful" does not seem at all unnatural, merely, as I have just denied it practical consequence, somewhat puzzling.

The disquietfulness arises, "somehow," out of a conjunction of three attributes of the fight: its immediate dramatic shape; its metaphoric content; and its social context. A cultural figure against a social ground, the fight is at once a convulsive surge of animal hatred, a mock war of symbolical selves, and a formal simulation of status tensions, and its aesthetic power derives from its capacity to force together these diverse realities. The reason it is disquietful is not that it has material effects (it has some, but they are minor); the reason that it is disquietful is that, joining pride to selfhood, selfhood to cocks, and cocks to destruction, it brings to imaginative realization a dimension of Balinese experience normally well-obscured from view. The transfer of a sense of gravity into what is in itself a rather blank and unvarious spectacle, a commotion of beating wings and throbbing legs, is effected by interpreting it as expressive of something unsettling in the way its authors and audience live, or, even more ominously, what they are.

As a dramatic shape, the fight displays a characteristic that does not seem so remarkable until one realizes that it does not have to be there: a radically atomistical structure.[30] Each match is a world unto itself, a particulate burst of form. There is the match making, there is the betting, there is the fight, there is the result—utter triumph and utter defeat—and there is the hurried, embarrassed passing of money. The loser is not consoled. People drift away from him, look through him, leave him to assimilate his momentary descent into nonbeing, reset his face, and return, scarless and intact, to the fray. Nor are winners congratulated, or events rehashed; once a match is ended the crowd's attention turns totally to the next, with no looking back. A shadow of the experience no doubt remains with the principals, perhaps even with some of the witnesses, of a deep fight, as it remains with us when we leave the theater after seeing a powerful play well-performed; but it quite soon fades to become at most a schematic memory—a diffuse glow or an abstract shudder—and usually not even that. Any expressive form lives only in its own present—the one it itself creates. But, here, that present is severed into a string of flashes, some more bright than others, but all of them disconnected, aesthetic quanta. Whatever the cockfight says, it says in spurts.

But, as I have argued lengthily elsewhere, the Balinese live in spurts.[31] Their life, as they arrange it and perceive it, is less a flow, a directional movement out of the past, through the present, toward the future than an on-off pulsation of meaning and vacuity, an arhythmic alternation of short periods when "something" (that is, something significant) is happening and equally short ones where "nothing" (that is, nothing much) is— between what they themselves call "full" and "empty" times, or, in another idiom, "junctures" and "holes." In focusing activity down to a burning-glass dot, the cockfight is merely being Balinese in the same way in which everything from the monadic encounters of everyday life, through the changing pointillism of *gamelan* music, to the visiting-day-of-the-gods temple celebrations are. It is not an imitation of the punctuateness of Balinese social life, nor a depiction of it, nor even an expression of it; it is an example of it, carefully prepared.[32]

If one dimension of the cockfight's structure, its lack of temporal directionality, makes it seem a typical segment of the general social life, however, the other, its flat-out, head-to-head (or spur-to-spur) aggressiveness, makes it seem a contradiction, a reversal, even a subversion of it. In the normal course of things, the Balinese are shy to the point of obsessiveness of open conflict. Oblique, cautious, subdued, controlled, masters of indirection and dissimulation—what they call *alus*, "polished," "smooth"— they rarely face what they can turn away from, rarely resist what they can evade. But here they portray themselves as wild and murderous, manic explosions of instinctual cruelty. A powerful rendering of life as the Balinese most deeply do not want it (to adapt a phrase Frye has used of Gloucester's blinding) is set in the context of a sample of it as they do in fact have it.[33] And, because the context suggests that the rendering, if less than a straightforward description is nonetheless more than an idle fancy, it is here that the disquietfulness—the disquietfulness of the *fight*, not (or, anyway, not necessarily) its patrons, who seem in fact rather thoroughly to enjoy it—emerges. The slaughter in the cock ring is not a depiction of how things literally are among men, but, what is almost worse, of how, from a particular angle, they imaginatively are.[34]

The angle, of course, is stratificatory. What, as we have already seen, the cockfight talks most forcibly about is status relationships, and what it says about them is that they are matters of life and death. That prestige is a profoundly serious business is apparent everywhere one looks in Bali— in the village, the family, the economy, the state. A peculiar fusion of Polynesian title ranks and Hindu castes, the hierarchy of pride is the moral backbone of the society. But only in the cockfight are the sentiments upon which that hierarchy rests revealed in their natural colors. Enveloped elsewhere in a haze of etiquette, a thick cloud of euphemism and ceremony, gesture and allusion, they are here expressed in only the thinnest disguise of an animal mask, a mask which in fact demonstrates them far more effectively than it conceals them. Jealousy is as much a part of Bali as poise, envy as grace, brutality as charm; but without the cockfight the Balinese would have a much less certain understanding of them, which is, presumably, why they value it so highly.

Any expressive form works (when it works) by disarranging semantic contexts in such a way that properties conventionally ascribed to certain things are unconventionally ascribed to others, which are then seen actually to possess them. To call the wind a cripple, as Stevens does, to fix tone and manipulate timbre, as Schoenberg does, or, closer to our case, to picture an art critic as a dissolute bear, as Hogarth does, is to cross conceptual wires; the established conjunctions between objects and their qualities are altered and phenomena—fall weather, melodic shape, or cultural journalism—are clothed in signifiers which normally point to other referents.[35] Similarly, to connect—and connect, and connect—the collision of roosters with the divisiveness of status is to invite a transfer of perceptions from the former to the latter, a transfer which is at once a description and a judgment. (Logically, the transfer could, of course, as well go the other way; but, like most of the rest of us, the Balinese are a great deal more interested in understanding men than they are in understanding cocks.)

What sets the cockfight apart from the ordinary course of life, lifts it from the realm of everyday practical affairs, and surrounds it with an aura of enlarged importance is not, as functionalist sociology would have it, that it reinforces status discriminations (such reinforcement is hardly necessary in a society where every act proclaims them), but that it provides a metasocial commentary upon the whole matter of assorting human beings into fixed hierarchical ranks and then organizing the major part of collective existence around that assortment. Its function, if you want to call it that, is interpretive: it is a Balinese reading of Balinese experience; a story they tell themselves about themselves.

## Saying Something of Something

To put the matter this way is to engage in a bit of metaphorical refocusing of one's own, for it shifts the analysis of cultural forms from an endeavor in general parallel to dissecting an organism, diagnosing a symptom, deciphering a code, or ordering a system—the dominant analogies in contemporary anthropology—to one in general parallel with penetrating a literary text. If one takes the cockfight, or any other collectively sustained symbolic structure, as a means of "saying something of something" (to invoke a famous Aristotelian tag), then one is faced with a problem not in social mechanics but social semantics.[36] For the anthropologist, whose concern is with formulating sociological principles, not with promoting or appreciating cockfights, the question is, what does one learn about such principles from examining culture as an assemblage of texts?

Such an extension of the notion of a text beyond written material, and even beyond verbal, is, though metaphorical, not, of course, all that novel. The *interpretatio naturae* tradition of the Middle Ages, which, culminating in Spinoza, attempted to read nature as Scripture, the Nietzschean effort to treat value systems as glosses on the will to power (or the Marxian one to treat them as glosses on property relations), and the Freudian replacement of the enigmatic text of the manifest dream with the plain one of the latent, all offer precedents, if not equally recommendable ones.[37] But the idea remains theoretically undeveloped; and the more profound corollary, so far as anthropology is concerned, that cultural forms can be treated as texts, as imaginative works built out of social materials, has yet to be systematically exploited.[38]

In the case at hand, to treat the cockfight as a text is to bring out a feature of it (in my opinion, the central feature of it) that treating it as a rite or a pastime, the two most obvious alternatives, would tend to obscure: its use of emotion for cognitive ends. What the cockfight says it says in a vocabulary of sentiment—the thrill of risk, the despair of loss, the pleasure of triumph. Yet what it says is not merely that risk is exciting, loss depressing, or triumph gratifying, banal tautologies of affect, but that it is of these emotions, thus exampled, that society is built and individuals put together. Attending cockfights and participating in them is, for the Balinese, a kind of sentimental education. What he learns there is what his culture's ethos and his private sensibility (or, anyway, certain aspects of them) look like when spelled out externally in a collective text; that the two are near enough alike to be articulated in the symbolics of a single such text; and—the disquieting part—that the text in which this revelation is accomplished consists of a chicken hacking another mindlessly to bits.

Every people, the proverb has it, loves its own form of violence. The cockfight is the Balinese reflection on theirs: on its look, its uses, its force, its fascination. Drawing on almost every level of Balinese experience, it brings together themes—animal savagery, male narcissism, opponent gambling, status rivalry, mass excitement, blood sacrifice—whose main connection is their involvement with rage and the fear of rage, and, binding them into a set of rules which at once contains them and allows them play, builds a symbolic structure in which, over and over again, the reality of their inner affiliation can be intelligibly felt. If, to quote Northrop Frye again, we go to see *Macbeth* to learn what a man feels like after he has gained a kingdom and lost his soul, Balinese go to cockfights to find out what a man, usually composed, aloof, almost obsessively self-absorbed, a kind of moral autocosm, feels like when, attacked, tormented, challenged, insulted, and driven in result to the extremes of fury, he has totally triumphed or been brought totally low. The whole passage, as it takes us back to Aristotle (though to the *Poetics* rather than the *Hermeneutics*), is worth quotation:

> But the poet [as opposed to the historian], Aristotle says, never makes any real statements at all, certainly no particular or specific ones. The poet's job is not to tell you what happened, but what happens: not what did take place, but the kind of thing that always does take place. He gives you the typical, recurring, or what Aristotle calls universal event. You wouldn't go to *Macbeth* to learn about the history of Scotland—you go to it to learn what man feels like after he's gained a kingdom and lost his soul. When you meet such a character as Micawber in Dickens, you don't feel that there must have been a man Dickens knew who was exactly like this: you feel that there's a bit of Micawber in almost everybody you know, including yourself. Our impressions of human life are picked up one by one, and remain for most of us loose and disorganized. But we constantly find things in literature that suddenly coordinate and bring into focus a great many such impressions, and this is part of what Aristotle means by the typical or universal human event.[39]

It is this kind of bringing of assorted experiences of everyday life to focus that the cockfight, set aside from that life as "only a game" and reconnected to it as "more than a game," accomplishes, and so creates what, better than typical or universal, could be called a paradigmatic human event—that is, one that tells us less what happens than the kind of thing that would happen if, as is not the case, life were art and could be as freely shaped by styles of feeling as *Macbeth* and *David Copperfield* are.

Enacted and reenacted, so far without end, the cockfight enables the Balinese, as, read and reread, *Macbeth* enables us, to see a dimension of his own subjectivity. As he watches fight after fight, with the active watching of an owner and a bettor (for cockfighting has no more interest as a pure spectator sport than croquet or dog racing do), he grows familiar with it and what it has to say to him, much as the attentive listener to string quartets or the absorbed viewer of still lifes grows slowly more familiar with them in a way which opens his subjectivity to himself.[40]

Yet, because—in another of those paradoxes, along with painted feelings and unconsequenced acts, which haunt aesthetics—that subjectivity does not properly exist until it is thus organized, art forms generate and regenerate the very subjectivity they pretend only to display. Quartets, still lifes, and cockfights are not merely reflections of a preexisting sensibility analogically represented; they are positive agents in the creation and maintenance of such a sensibility. If we see ourselves as a pack of Micawbers it is from reading too much Dickens (if we see ourselves as unillusioned realists, it is from reading too little); and similarly for Balinese, cocks, and cockfights. It is in such a way, coloring experience with the light they cast it in, rather than through whatever material effects they may have, that the arts play their role, as arts, in social life.[41]

In the cockfight, then, the Balinese forms and discovers his temperament and his society's temper at the same time. Or, more exactly, he forms and discovers a particular face of them. Not only are there a great many other cultural texts providing commentaries on status hierarchy and self-regard in Bali, but there are a great many other critical sectors of Balinese life besides the stratificatory and the agonistic that receive such commentary. The ceremony consecrating a Brahmana priest, a matter of breath control, postural immobility, and vacant concentration upon the depths of being, displays a radically different, but to the Balinese equally real, property of social hierarchy—its reach toward the numinous transcendent. Set not in the matrix of the kinetic emotionality of animals, but in that of the static passionlessness of divine mentality, it expresses tranquillity not disquiet. The mass festivals at the village temples, which mobilize the whole local population in elaborate hostings of visiting gods—songs, dances, compliments, gifts—assert the spiritual unity of village mates against their status inequality and project a mood of amity and trust.[42] The cockfight is not the master key to Balinese life, any more than bullfighting is to Spanish. What it says about that life is not unqualified nor even unchallenged by what other equally eloquent cultural statements say about it. But there is nothing more surprising in this than in the fact that Racine and Molière were contemporaries, or that the same people who arrange chrysanthemums cast swords.[43]

The culture of a people is an ensemble of texts, themselves ensembles, which the anthropologist strains to read over the shoulders of those to whom they properly belong. There are enormous difficulties in such an enterprise, methodological pitfalls to make a Freudian quake, and some moral perplexities as well. Nor is it the only way that symbolic forms can be sociologically handled. Functionalism lives, and so does psychologism. But to regard such forms as "saying something of something," and saying it to somebody, is at least to open up the possibility of an analysis which attends to their substance rather than to reductive formulas professing to account for them.

As in more familiar exercises in close reading, one can start anywhere in a culture's repertoire of forms and end up anywhere else. One can stay, as I have here, within a single, more or less bounded form and circle steadily within it. One can move between forms in search of broader unities or informing contrasts. One can even compare forms from different cultures to define their character in reciprocal relief. But whatever the level at which one operates, and however intricately, the guiding principle is the same: societies, like lives, contain their own interpretations. One has only to learn how to gain access to them.

## REFERENCES

[1]Gregory Bateson and Margaret Mead, *Balinese Character: A Photographic Analysis* (New York: New York Academy of Sciences, 1942), p. 68.

[2]Jane Belo, "The Balinese Temper," in Jane Belo, ed., *Traditional Balinese Culture* (New York: Columbia University Press, 1970; originally published in 1935), pp. 85–110.

[3]The best discussion of cockfighting is again Bateson and Mead's (*Balinese Character*, pp. 24–25, 140), but it, too, is general and abbreviated.

[4]Ibid., pp. 25–26. The cockfight is unusual within Balinese culture in being a single-sex public activity from which the other sex is totally and expressly excluded. Sexual differentiation is culturally extremely played down in Bali and most activities, formal and informal, involve the participation of men and women on equal ground, commonly as linked couples. From religion, to politics, to economics, to kinship, to dress, Bali is a rather "uni-sex" society, a fact both its customs and its symbolism clearly express. Even in contexts where women do not in fact play much of a role—music, painting, certain agricultural activities—their absence, which is only relative in any case, is more a mere matter of fact than socially enforced. To this general pattern, the cockfight, entirely of, by, and for men (women—at least *Balinese* women—do not even watch), is the most striking exception.

[5]Christiaan Hooykass, *The Lay of the Jaya Prana* (London, 1958), p. 39. The lay has a stanza (no. 17) with the reluctant bridegroom use. Jaya Prana, the subject of a Balinese Uriah myth, responds to the lord who has offered him the loveliest of six hundred servant girls: "Godly King, my Lord and Master/I beg you, give me leave to go/such things are not yet in my mind;/like a fighting cock encaged/indeed I am on my mettle/I am alone/as yet the flame has not been fanned."

[6]For these, see V. E. Korn, *Het Adatrecht van Bali,* 2d ed. ('S-Gravenhage: G. Naeff, 1932), index under *toh.*

[7]There is indeed a legend to the effect that the separation of Java and Bali is due to the action of a powerful Javanese religious figure who wished to protect himself against a Balinese culture hero (the ancestor of two Ksatria castes) who was a passionate cockfighting gambler. See Christiaan Hooykass, *Agama Tirtha* (Amsterdam: Noord-Hollandsche, 1964), p. 184.

[8]An incestuous couple is forced to wear pig yokes over their necks and crawl to a pig trough and eat with their mouths there. On this, see Jane Belo, "Customs Pertaining to Twins in Bali," in Belo, ed., *Traditional Balinese Culture*, p. 49; on the abhorrence of animality generally, Bateson and Mead, *Balinese Character*, p. 22.

[9]Except for unimportant, small-bet fights (on the question of fight "importance," see below) spur affixing is usually done by someone other than the owner. Whether the owner handles his own cock or not more or less depends on how skilled he is at it, a consideration whose importance is again relative to the importance of the fight. When spur affixers and cock handlers are someone other than the owner, they are almost always a close relative—a brother or cousin—or a very intimate friend of his. They are thus almost extensions of his personality, as the fact that all three will refer to the cock as "mine," say "I" fought So-and-So, and so on, demonstrates. Also, owner-handler-affixer triads tend to be fairly fixed, though individuals may participate in several and often exchange roles within a given one.

[10] Erving Goffman, *Encounters: Two Studies in the Sociology of Interaction* (Indianapolis: Bobbs-Merrill, 1961), pp. 9–10.

[11] This word, which literally means an indelible stain or mark, as in a birthmark or a vein in a stone, is used as well for a deposit in a court case, for a pawn, for security offered in a loan, for a stand-in for someone else in a legal or ceremonial context, for an earnest advanced in a business deal, for a sign placed in a field to indicate its ownership is in dispute, and for the status of an unfaithful wife from whose lover her husband must gain satisfaction or surrender her to him. See Korn, *Het Adatrecht van Bali*; Theodoor Pigeaud, *Javaans-Nederlands Handwoordenbock* (Groningen: Wolters, 1938); H. H. Juynboll, *Oudjavaansche-Nederlandsche Woordenlijst* (Leiden: Brill, 1923).

[12] The center bet must be advanced in cash by both parties prior to the actual fight. The umpire holds the stakes until the decision is rendered and then awards them to the winner, avoiding, among other things, the intense embarrassment both winner and loser would feel if the latter had to pay off personally following his defeat. About 10 percent of the winner's receipts are subtracted for the umpire's share and that of the fight sponsors.

[13] Actually, the typing of cocks, which is extremely elaborate (I have collected more than twenty classes, certainly not a complete list), is not based on color alone, but on a series of independent, interacting, dimensions, which include, beside color, size, bone thickness, plumage, and temperament. (But *not* pedigree. The Balinese do not breed cocks to any significant extent, nor, so far as I have been able to discover, have they ever done so. The *asil*, or jungle cock, which is the basic fighting strain everywhere the sport is found, is native to southern Asia, and one can buy a good example in the chicken section of almost any Balinese market for anywhere from four or five ringgits up to fifty or more.) The color element is merely the one normally used as the type name, except when the two cocks of different types—as on principle they must be—have the same color, in which case a secondary indication from one of the other dimensions ("large speckled" v. "small speckled," etc.) is added. The types are coordinated with various cosmological ideas which help shape the making of matches, so that, for example, you fight a small, headstrong, speckled brown-on-white cock with flat-lying feathers and thin legs from the east side of the ring on a certain day of the complex Balinese calendar, and a large, cautious, all-black cock with tufted feathers and stubby legs from the north side on another day, and so on. All this is again recorded in palm-leaf manuscripts and endlessly discussed by the Balinese (who do not all have identical systems), and full-scale componential-cum-symbolic analysis of cock classifications would be extremely valuable both as an adjunct to the description of the cockfight and in itself. But my data on the subject, though extensive and varied, do not seem to be complete and systematic enough to attempt such an analysis here. For Balinese cosmological ideas more generally see Belo, ed., *Traditional Balinese Culture*, and J. L. Swellengrebel, ed., *Bali: Studies in Life, Thought, and Ritual* (The Hague: W. van Hoeve, 1960); for calendrical ones, Clifford Geertz, *Person, Time, and Conduct in Bali: An Essay in Cultural Analysis* (New Haven: Southeast Asia Studies, Yale University, 1966), pp. 45–53.

[14] For purposes of ethnographic completeness, it should be noted that it is possible for the man backing the favorite—the odds-giver—to make a bet in which he wins if his cock wins or there is a tie, a slight shortening of the odds (I do not have enough cases to be exact, but ties seem to occur about once every fifteen or twenty matches.) He indicates his wish to do this by shouting *sapih* ("tie") rather than the cock-type, but such bets are in fact infrequent.

[15] The precise dynamics of the movement of the betting is one of the most intriguing, most complicated, and, given the heroic conditions under which it occurs, most difficult to study, aspects of the fight. Motion picture recording plus multiple observers would probably be necessary to deal with it effectively. Even impressionistically—the only approach open to a lone ethnographer caught in the middle of all this—it is clear that certain men lead both in determining the favorite (that is, making the opening cock-type calls which

always initiate the process) and in directing the movement of the odds, these "opinion lead-ers" being the more accomplished cockfighters-cum-solid-citizens to be discussed below. If these men begin to change their calls, others follow; if they begin to make bets, so do others and—though there is always a large number of frustrated bettors crying for shorter or longer odds to the end—the movement more or less ceases. But a detailed understanding of the whole process awaits what, alas, it is not very likely ever to get: a decision theorist armed with precise observations of individual behavior.

[16] Assuming only binominal variability, the departure from a fifty-fifty expectation in the sixty ringgits and below case is 1.38 standard deviations, or (in a one-direction test) an eight in one hundred possibility by chance alone; for the below forty ringgits case it is 1.65 standard deviations, or about five in one hundred. The fact that these de-partures though real are not extreme merely indicates, again, that even in the smaller fights the tendency to match cocks at least reasonably evenly persists. It is a matter of relative relaxation of the pressures toward equalization, not their elimination. The ten-dency for high-bet contests to be coin-flip propositions is, of course, even more striking, and suggests the Balinese know quite well what they are about.

[17] The reduction in wagering in smaller fights (which, of course, feeds on itself; one of the reasons people find small fights uninteresting is that there is less wagering in them, and contrariwise for large ones) takes place in three mutually reinforcing ways. First, there is a simple withdrawal of interest as people wander off to have a cup of cof-fee or chat with a friend. Second, the Balinese do not mathematically reduce odds, but bet directly in terms of stated odds as such. Thus, for a nine-to-eight bet, one man wa-gers nine ringgits, the other eight; for five-to-four, one wagers five, the other four. For any given currency unit, like the ringgit, therefore, 6.3 times as much money is involved in a ten-to-nine bet as in a two-to-one bet, for example, and, as noted, in small fights bet-ting settles toward the longer end. Finally, the bets which are made tend to be one-rather than two-, three-, or in some of the very largest fights, four- or five-finger ones. (The fingers indicate the *multiples* of the stated bet odds at issue, not absolute figures. Two fingers in a six-to-five situation means a man wants to wager ten ringgits on the underdog against twelve, three in an eight-to-seven situation, twenty-one against twenty-four, and so on.)

[18] Besides wagering there are other economic aspects of the cockfight, especially its very close connection with the local market system which, though secondary both to its motivation and to its function, are not without importance. Cockfights are open events to which anyone who wishes may come, sometimes from quite distant areas, but well over 90 percent, probably over 95, are very local affairs, and the locality concerned is de-fined not by the village, nor even by the administrative district, but by the rural market system. Bali has a three-day market week with familiar "solar-system" type rotation. Though the markets themselves have never been very highly developed, small morning affairs in a village square, it is the microregion such rotation rather generally marks out—ten or twenty square miles, seven or eight neighboring villages (which in contem-porary Bali is usually going to mean anywhere from five to ten to eleven thousand people) from which the core of any cockfight audience, indeed virtually all of it, will come. Most of the fights are in fact organized and sponsored by small combines of petty rural merchants under the general premise, very strongly held by them and indeed by all Balinese, that cockfights are good for trade because "they get money out of the house, they make it circulate." Stalls selling various sorts of things as well as assorted sheer-chance gambling games (see below) are set up around the edge of the area so that this even takes on the quality of a small fair. This connection of cockfighting with markets and market sellers is very old, as, among other things, their conjunction in inscriptions (Roelof Goris, *Prasasti Bali*, 2 vols. [Bandung: N. V. Masa Baru, 1954]) indicates. Trade has followed the cock for centuries in rural Bali and the sport has been one of the main agencies of the island's monetization.

[19] The phrase is found in the Hildreth translation, International Library of Psychol-ogy, 1931, note to p. 106; see L. L. Fuller, *The Morality of Law* (New Haven: Yale Univer-sity Press, 1964), pp. 6ff.

[20]Of course, even in Bentham, utility is not normally confined as a concept to monetary losses and gains, and my argument here might be more carefully put in terms of a denial that for the Balinese, as for any people, utility (pleasure, happiness . . .) is merely identifiable with wealth. But such terminological problems are in any case secondary to the essential point: the cockfight is not roulette.

[21]Max Weber, *The Sociology of Religion* (Boston: Beacon Press, 1963). There is nothing specifically Balinese, of course, about deepening significance with money, as Whyte's description of corner boys in a working-class district of Boston demonstrates: "Gambling plays an important role in the lives of Cornerville people. Whatever game the corner boys play, they nearly always bet on the outcome. When there is nothing at stake, the game is not considered a real contest. This does not mean that the financial element is all-important. I have frequently heard men say that the honor of winning was much more important than the money at stake. The corner boys consider playing for money the real test of skill and, unless a man performs well when money is at stake, he is not considered a good competitor." W. F. Whyte, *Street Corner Society*, 2d ed. (Chicago: University of Chicago Press, 1955), p. 140.

[22]The extreme to which this madness is conceived on occasion to go—and the fact that it is considered madness—is demonstrated by the Balinese folktale *I Tuhung Kuning.* A gambler becomes so deranged by his passion that, leaving on a trip, he orders his pregnant wife to take care of the prospective newborn if it is a boy but to feed it as meat to his fighting cocks if it is a girl. The mother gives birth to a girl, but rather than giving the child to the cocks she gives them a large rat and conceals the girl with her own mother. When the husband returns the cocks, crowing a jingle, inform him of the deception and, furious, he sets out to kill the child. A goddess descends from heaven and takes the girl up to the skies with her. The cocks die from the food given them, the owner's sanity is restored, the goddess brings the girl back to the father and reunites him with his wife. The story is given as "Geel Komkommertje" in Jacoba Hooykaas-van Leeuwen Boomkamp, *Sprookjes en Verhalen van Bali* ('S-Gravenhage: Van Hoeve, 1956), pp. 19–25.

[23]For a fuller description of Balinese rural social structure, see Clifford Geertz, "Form and Variation in Balinese Village Structure," *American Anthropologist*, 61 (1959), 94–108; "Tihingan, A Balinese Village," in R. M. Koentjaraningrat, *Villages in Indonesia* (Ithaca: Cornell University Press, 1967), pp. 210–43; and, though it is a bit off the norm as Balinese villages go, V. E. Korn, *De Dorpsrepubliek tnganan Pagringsingan* (Santpoort [Netherlands]: C. A. Mees, 1933).

[24]Goffman, *Encounters*, p. 78.

[25]B. R. Berelson, P. F. Lazersfeld, and W. N. McPhee, *Voting: A Study of Opinion Formation in a Presidential Campaign* (Chicago: University of Chicago Press, 1954).

[26]As this is a formal paradigm, it is intended to display the logical, not the casual, structure of cockfighting. Just which of these considerations leads to which, in what order, and by what mechanisms, is another matter—one I have attempted to shed some light on in the general discussion.

[27]In another of Hooykaas-van Leeuwen Boomkamp's folk tales ("De Gast," *Sprookjes en Verhalen van Bali*, pp. 172–80), a low caste *Sudra*, a generous, pious, and carefree man who is also an accomplished cockfighter, loses, despite his accomplishment, fight after fight until he is not only out of money but down to his last cock. He does not despair, however—"I bet," he says, "upon the Unseen World."

His wife, a good and hard-working woman, knowing how much he enjoys cockfighting, gives him her last "rainy day" money to go and bet. But, filled with misgivings due to his run of ill luck, he leaves his own cock at home and bets merely on the side. He soon loses all but a coin or two and repairs to a food stand for a snack, where he meets a decrepit, odorous, and generally unappetizing older beggar leaning on a staff. The old man asks for food, and the hero spends his last coins to buy him some. The old man then asks to pass the night with the hero, which the hero gladly invites him to do. As there is no food in the house, however, the hero tells his wife to kill the last cock for dinner. When the old man discovers this fact, he tells the hero he has three cocks in his own mountain hut and says the hero may have one of them for fighting. He also asks for the hero's son to accompany him as a servant, and, after the son agrees, this is done.

The old man turns out to be Siva and, thus, to live in a great palace in the sky, though the hero does not know this. In time, the hero decides to visit his son and collect the promised cock. Lifted up into Siva's presence, he is given the choice of three cocks. The first crows: "I have beaten fifteen opponents." The second crows, "I have beaten twenty-five opponents." The third crows, "I have beaten the King." "That one, the third, is my choice," says the hero, and returns with it to earth.

When he arrives at the cockfight, he is asked for an entry fee and replies, "I have no money; I will pay after my cock has won." As he is known never to win, he is let in because the king, who is there fighting, dislikes him and hopes to enslave him when he loses and cannot pay off. In order to insure that this happens, the king matches his finest cock against the hero's. When the cocks are placed down, the hero's flees, and the crowd, led by the arrogant king, hoots in laughter. The hero's cock then flies at the king himself, killing him with a spur stab in the throat. The hero flees. His house is encircled by the king's men. The cock changes into a Garuda, the great mythic bird of Indic legend, and carries the hero and his wife to safety in the heavens.

When the people see this, they make the hero king and his wife queen and they return as such to earth. Later his son, released by Siva, also returns and the hero-king announces his intention to enter a hermitage. ("I will fight no more cockfights. I have bet on the Unseen and won.") He enters the hermitage and his son becomes king.

[28] Addict gamblers are really less declassed (for their status is, as everyone else's, inherited) than merely impoverished and personally disgraced. The most prominent addict gambler in my cockfight circuit was actually a very high caste *satria* who sold off most of his considerable lands to support his habit. Though everyone privately regarded him as a fool and worse (some, more charitable, regarded him as sick), he was publicly treated with the elaborate deference and politeness due his rank. On the independence of personal reputation and public status in Bali, see Geertz, *Person, Time, and Conduct*, pp. 28–35.

[29] For four, somewhat variant treatments, see Susanne Langer, *Feeling and Form* (New York: Scribner's, 1953); Richard Wollheim, *Art and Its Objects* (New York: Harper and Row, 1968); Nelson Goodman, *Languages of Art* (Indianapolis: Bobbs-Merrill, 1968); Maurice Merleau-Ponty, "The Eye and the Mind," in his, *The Primacy of Perception* (Evanston: Northwestern University Press, 1964), pp. 159–90.

[30] British cockfights (the sport was banned there in 1840) indeed seem to have lacked it, and to have generated, therefore, a quite different family of shapes. Most British fights were "mains," in which a preagreed number of cocks were aligned into two teams and fought serially. Score was kept and wagering took place both on the individual matches and on the main as a whole. There were also "battle Royales," both in England and on the Continent, in which a large number of cocks were let loose at once with the one left standing at the end the victor. And in Wales, the so-called "Welsh main" followed an elimination pattern, along the lines of a present-day tennis tournament, winners proceeding to the next round. As a genre, the cockfight has perhaps less compositional flexibility than, say, Latin comedy, but it is not entirely without any. On cockfighting more generally, see Arch Ruport, *The Art of Cockfighting* (New York: Devin-Adair, 1949); G. R. Scott, *History of Cockfighting* (1957); and Lawrence Fitz-Barnard, *Fighting Sports* (London: Odhams Press, 1921).

[31] *Person, Time, and Conduct*, esp. pp. 42ff. I am, however, not the first person to have argued it: see G. Bateson, "Bali, the Value System of a Steady State," and "An Old Temple and a New Myth," in Belo, ed., *Traditional Balinese Culture*, pp. 384–402 and 111–36.

[32] For the necessity of distinguishing among "description," "representation," "exemplification," and "expression" (and the irrelevance of "imitation" to all of them), as modes of symbolic reference, see Goodman, *Languages of Art*, pp. 6–10, 45–91, 225–41.

[33] Northrop Frye, *The Educated Imagination* (Bloomington: University of Indiana Press, 1964), p. 99.

[34] There are two other Balinese values and disvalues which, connected with punctuate temporality on the one hand and unbridled aggressiveness on the other, reinforce the sense that the cockfight is at once continuous with ordinary social life and a direct negation of it: what the Balinese call *ramé*, and what they call *paling. Ramé* means crowded, noisy, and active, and is a highly sought after social state: crowded markets, mass festivals, busy streets are all *ramé*, as of course, is, in the extreme, a cockfight. *Ramé* is what happens in the "full" times (its opposite, *sepi*, "quiet," is what happens in the "empty" ones.) *Paling* is social vertigo, the dizzy, disoriented, lost, turned around feeling one gets when one's place in the coordinates of social space is not clear, and it is a tremendously disfavored, immensely anxiety-producing state. Balinese regard the exact maintenance of spatial orientation ("not to know where north is" is to be crazy), balance, decorum, status relationships, and so forth, as fundamental to ordered life (*krama*) and *paling*, the sort of whirling confusion of position the scrambling cocks exemplify as its profoundest enemy and contradiction. On *ramé*, see Bateson and Mead, *Balinese Character*, pp. 3, 64; on *paling*, ibid., p. 11, and Belo, ed., *Traditional Balinese Culture*, pp. 90ff.

[35] The Stevens reference is to his "The Motive for Metaphor" ("You like it under the trees in autumn,/Because everything is half dead./The wind moves like a cripple among the leaves/And repeats words without meaning"); the Schoenberg reference is to the third of his *Five Orchestral Pieces* (Opus 16), and is borrowed from H. H. Drager, "The Concept of 'Tonal Body,'" in Susanne Langer, ed., *Reflections of Art* (New York: Oxford University Press, 1961), p. 174. On Hogarth, and on this whole problem—there called "multiple matrix matching"—see E. H. Gombrich, "The Use of Art for the Study of Symbols," in James Hogg, ed., *Psychology and the Visual Arts* (Baltimore: Penguin Books, 1969), pp. 149–70. The more usual term for this sort of semantic alchemy is "metaphorical transfer," and good technical discussions of it can be found in M. Black, *Models and Metaphors* (Ithaca: Cornell University Press, 1962), pp. 25ff; Goodman, *Languages of Art*, pp. 44ff; and W. Percy, "Metaphor as Mistake," *Sewanee Review*, 66 (1958), 78–99.

[36] The tag is from the second book of the *Organon, On Interpretation*. For a discussion of it, and for the whole argument for freeing "the notion of text . . . from the notion of scripture or writing," and constructing, thus, a general hermeneutics, see Paul Ricoeur, *Freud and Philosophy* (New Haven: Yale University Press, 1970), pp. 20ff.

[37] Ibid.

[38] Lévi-Strauss's "structuralism" might seem an exception. But it is only an apparent one, for, rather than taking myths, totem rites, marriage rules, or whatever as texts to interpret, Lévi-Strauss takes them as ciphers to solve, which is very much not the same thing. He does not seek to understand symbolic forms in terms of how they function in concrete situations to organize perceptions (meanings, emotions, concepts, attitudes); he seeks to understand them entirely in terms of their internal structure, *indépendent de tout sujet, de tout objet, et de toute contexte*. For my own view of this approach—that is suggestive and indefensible—see Clifford Geertz, "The Cerebral Savage: On the Work of Lévi-Strauss," *Encounter*, 48 (1967), 25–32.

[39] Frye, *The Educated Imagination*, pp. 63–64.

[40] The use of the, to Europeans, "natural" visual idiom for perception—"see," "watches," and so forth—is more than usually misleading here, for the fact that, as mentioned earlier, Balinese follow the progress of the fight as much (perhaps, as fighting cocks are actually rather hard to see except as blurs of motion, more) with their bodies as with their eyes, moving their limbs, heads, and trunks in gestural mimicry of the cocks' maneuvers, means that much of the individual's experience of the fight is kinesthetic rather than visual. If ever there was an example of Kenneth Burke's definition of a symbolic act as "the dancing of an attitude" (*The Philosophy of Literary Form*, rev. ed. [New York: Vintage Books, 1957], p. 9) the cockfight is it. On the enormous role of kinesthetic perception in Balinese life, [see] Bateson and Mead, *Balinese Character*, pp. 84–88; on the active nature of aesthetic perception in general, [see] Goodman, *Languages of Art*, pp. 241–44.

[41] All this coupling of the occidental great with the oriental lowly will doubtless disturb certain sorts of aestheticians as the earlier effort of anthropologists to speak of Christianity and totemism in the same breath disturbed certain sorts of theologians. But as ontological questions are (or should be) bracketed in the sociology of religion, judgmental ones are (or should be) bracketed in the sociology of art. In any case, the attempt to deprovincialize the concept of art is but part of the general anthropological conspiracy to deprovincialize all important social concepts—marriage, religion, law, rationality—and though this is a threat to aesthetic theories which regard certain works of art as beyond the reach of sociological analysis, it is no threat to the conviction, for which Robert Graves claims to have been reprimanded at his Cambridge tripos, that some poems are better than others.

[42] For the consecration ceremony, see V. E. Korn, "The Consecration of the Priest," in Swellengrebel, ed., *Bali*, pp. 131–54; for (somewhat exaggerated) village communion, Roelof Goris, "The Religious Character of the Balinese Village," ibid., pp. 79–100.

[43] That what the cockfight has to say about Bali is not altogether without perception and the disquiet it expresses about the general pattern of Balinese life is not wholly without reason is attested by the fact that in two weeks of December 1965, during the upheavals following the unsuccessful coup in Djakarta, between forty and eighty thousand Balinese (in a population of about two million) were killed, largely by one another—the worst outburst in the country. (John Hughes, *Indonesian Upheaval* [New York: McKay, 1967], pp. 173–83. Hughes's figures are, of course, rather casual estimates, but they are not the most extreme.) This is not to say, of course, that the killings were caused by the cockfight, could have been predicted on the basis of it, or were some sort of enlarged version of it with real people in the place of the cocks—all of which is nonsense. It is merely to say that if one looks at Bali not just through the medium of its dances, its shadowplays, its sculpture, and its girls, but—as the Balinese themselves do—also through the medium of its cockfight, the fact that the massacre occurred seems, if no less appealing, less like a contradiction to the laws of nature. As more than one real Gloucester has discovered, sometimes people actually get life precisely as they most deeply do not want it.

•   •   •   •   •   •   •   •   •   •   •

## QUESTIONS FOR A SECOND READING

1. Geertz says that the cockfight provides a "commentary upon the whole matter of sorting human beings into fixed hierarchical ranks and then organizing the major parts of collective existence around that assortment." The cockfights don't reinforce the patterns of Balinese life; they comment on them. Perhaps the first question to ask as you go back to the essay is "What is that commentary?" What do the cockfights say? And what don't they say?

2. "Deep Play: Notes on the Balinese Cockfight" is divided into seven sections. As you reread the essay, pay attention to the connections between these sections and the differences in the ways they are written. For each, think about what they propose to do (some, for example, tell stories, some use numbers, some have more footnotes than others).

What is the logic or system that makes one section follow another? Do you see the subtitles as seven headings on a topic outline?

If you look at the differences in the style or method of each section, what might they be said to represent? If each is evidence of something Geertz, as an anthropologist, knows how to do, what, in each case, is he doing? What is his expertise? And why, in each case, would it require this particular style of writing? The last two sections are perhaps the most difficult to read and understand. They also make repeated reference to literary texts. Why? What is Geertz doing here?

3. Throughout the essay Geertz is working very hard to *do* something with what he observed in Bali. (There are "enormous difficulties in such an enterprise," he says.) He is also, however, working hard *not* to do some things. (He doesn't want to be a "formalist," for example.) As you read the essay for the second time, look for passages that help you specifically define what it is Geertz wants to do and what it is he wants to be sure not to do.

4. It could be argued that "Deep Play" tells again the story of how white Western men have taken possession of the Third World, here with Geertz performing an act of intellectual colonization. In the opening section, for example, Geertz (as author) quickly turns both his wife and the Balinese people into stock characters, characters in a story designed to make him a hero. And, in the service of this story, he pushes aside the difficult political realities of Bali—the later killing of Balinese by the police is put in parentheses (so as not to disturb the flow of the happy story of how an anthropologist wins his way into the community). The remaining sections turn Balinese culture into numbers and theories, reducing the irreducible detail of people's lives into material for the production of goods (an essay furthering his career). And, one could argue, the piece ends by turning to Shakespeare and Dickens to "explain" the Balinese, completing the displacement of Balinese culture by Western culture.

This, anyway, is how such an argument might be constructed. As you reread the essay, mark passages you could use, as the author, to argue both for and against Geertz and his relationship to this story of colonization. To what extent can one say that Geertz is, finally, one more white man taking possession of the Third World? And to what extent can one argue that Geertz, as a writer, is struggling against this dominant, conventional narrative, working to revise it or to distance himself from it?

ASSIGNMENTS FOR WRITING

1. If this essay were your only evidence, how might you describe the work of an anthropologist? What do anthropologists do and how do they do it? Write an essay in which you look at "Deep Play" section by section, including the references, describing on the basis of each what it is that an anthropologist must be able to do. In each case, you have the chance to watch Geertz at work. (Your essay, then, might well have sections that correspond to Geertz's.) When you have worked through them all, write a

final section that discusses how these various skills or arts fit together to define the expertise of someone like Geertz.

2. Geertz says that "the culture of a people is an ensemble of texts, themselves ensembles, which the anthropologist strains to read over the shoulders of those to whom they properly belong." Anthropologists are expert at "reading" in this way. One of the interesting things about being a student is that you get to (or you have to) act like an expert, even though, properly speaking, you are not. Write an essay in which you prepare a Geertzian "reading" of some part of our culture you know well. Ideally, you should go out and observe the behavior you are studying, examining it and taking notes with your project in mind. You should imagine that you are working in Geertz's spirit, imitating his method and style and carrying out work that he has begun.

3. This is really a variation on the first assignment. This assignment, however, invites you to read against the grain of Geertz's essay. Imagine that someone has made the argument outlined briefly in the fourth "Question for a Second Reading"—that "Deep Play" is just one more version of a familiar story, a story of a white man taking possession of everything that is not already made in his own image. If you were going to respond to this argument—to extend it or to answer it—to what in the essay would you turn for evidence? And what might you say about what you find?

   Write an essay, then, in which you respond to the argument that says "Deep Play" is one more version of the familiar story of a white man taking possession of that which is not his.

### MAKING CONNECTIONS

1. Susan Bordo in "Hunger as Ideology" (p. 139), Jane Tompkins in "Indians" (p. 673), and Susan Griffin in "Our Secret" (p. 404) could all be said to take an "anthropological" view of the people and practices they study. The worlds they describe are familiar (at least compared with Bali), and yet, as writers, they distance themselves from those worlds, make the familiar seem exotic, look at the people involved as "natives" whose behavior they choose to read as a strange and arbitrary text.

   Choose one of these selections—by Bordo, Tompkins, or Griffin—and read it along with Geertz's. Take the position that both authors read cultural patterns and cultural artifacts. Look at the characteristic examples of their ways of reading. What might you say about their methods? Do they look for the same things?

   Write an essay in which you explore and describe the different methods of the two writers. As researchers, what do they notice? What do they do with what they notice? Do they seek the same *kinds* of conclusions? How do they gather their materials, weight them, think them through? How, that is, do they do their work? And what might you conclude about the possibilities and limitations of each writer's project?

2. In "The Loss of the Creature" (p. 565), Walker Percy writes about tourists (actually several different kinds of tourists) and the difficulty they have

seeing what lies before them. Properly speaking, anthropologists are not tourists. There is a scholarly purpose to their travel, and presumably they have learned or developed the strategies necessary to get beyond the pre-formed "symbolic complexes" which would keep them from seeing the place or the people they have traveled to study. Geertz is an expert, in other words, not just any "layman seer of sights."

In his travels to Bali, Geertz seems to get just what he wants. He gets both the authentic experience and a complex understanding of that experience. If you read "Deep Play" from the perspective of Percy's essay, however, it is interesting to ask whether Percy would say that this was the case, and to ask how Percy would characterize the "strategies" that define Geertz's approach to his subject.

Write an essay in which you place Geertz in the context of Percy's tourists—not all of them, but the two or three whose stories seem most interesting when placed alongside Geertz's. The purpose of your essay should be to determine whether or not Geertz has solved the problem Percy defines for the tourist in "The Loss of the Creature."

# SUSAN
# GRIFFIN

*S*USAN GRIFFIN *(b. 1943) is a well-known and respected feminist writer,
poet, essayist, lecturer, teacher, playwright, and filmmaker. She has published more than twenty books, including an Emmy Award–winning play,*
Voices, *with a preface by Adrienne Rich (1975); two books of poetry,* Like the
Iris of an Eye *(1976) and* Unremembered Country *(1987); and four books of
nonfiction that have become key feminist texts,* Women and Nature: The Roaring inside Her *(1978),* Rape: The Power of Consciousness *(1979),* Pornography and Silence: Culture's Revenge against Nature *(1981), and* A Chorus
of Stones: The Private Life of War *(1992). Her most recent book is* The Eros of
Everyday Life *(1996), a collection of essays on women in Western culture.*

*"Our Secret" is a chapter from Susan Griffin's moving and powerful book* A
Chorus of Stones, *winner of the Bay Area Book Reviewers Association Award
and a finalist for the Pulitzer Prize in nonfiction. The book explores the connections between present and past, public life and private life, an individual life and
the lives of others. Griffin writes, for example, "I do not see my life as separate
from history. In my mind my family secrets mingle with the secrets of statesmen
and bombers." In one section of the book she writes of her mother's alcoholism and
her father's response to it. In another she writes of her paternal grandmother, who
was banished from the family for reasons never spoken. Next to these she thinks
about Heinrich Himmler, head of the Nazi secret police, or Hugh Trenchard of the*

*British Royal Air Force, who introduced the saturation bombing of cities and civilians to modern warfare, or Wernher von Braun and the development of rockets and rocketry. "As I held these [figures and scenes] in my mind," she writes, "a certain energy was generated between them. There were two subjects but one theme: denying and bearing witness."*

A Chorus of Stones *combines the skills of a careful researcher working with the documentary records of war, the imaginative powers of a novelist entering the lives and experiences of those long dead, and a poet's attention to language. It is a remarkable piece of writing, producing in its form and style the very experience of surprise and connectedness that Griffin presents as the product of her research. "It's not a historian's history," she once told an interviewer. "What's in it is true, but I think of it as a book that verges on myth and legend, because those are the ways we find the deepest meanings and significance of events."*

*Griffin's history is not a historian's history; her sociology is not a sociologist's; her psychology is not written in conventional forms or registers. She is actively engaged in the key research projects of our time, providing new knowledge and new ways of thinking and seeing, but she works outside the usual forms and boundaries of the academic disciplines. There are other ways of thinking about this, she seems to say. There are other ways to do this work. Her book on rape, for example, ends with a collage of women's voices, excerpts from public documents, and bits and pieces from the academy.*

*"Our Secret" has its own peculiar structure and features—the sections in italics, for example. As a piece of writing, it proceeds with a design that is not concerned to move quickly or efficiently from introduction to conclusion. It is, rather, a kind of collage or collection of stories, sketches, anecdotes, fragments. While the sections in the essay are presented as fragments, the essay is not, however, deeply confusing or disorienting. The pleasure of the text, in fact, is moving from here to there, feeling a thread of connection at one point, being surprised by a new direction at another. The writing is careful, thoughtful, controlled, even if this is not the kind of essay that announces its thesis and then collects examples for support. It takes a different attitude toward examples—and toward the kind of thinking one might bring to bear in gathering them and thinking them through. As Griffin says, "the telling and hearing of a story is not a simple act." It is not simple and, as her writing teaches us, it is not straightforward. As you read this essay, think of it as a lesson in reading, writing, and thinking. Think of it as a lesson in working differently. And you might ask why it is that this kind of writing is seldom taught in school.*

# Our Secret

*The nucleus of the cell derives its name from the Latin* nux, *meaning nut. Like the stone in a cherry, it is found in the center of the cell, and like this stone, keeps its precious kernel in a shell.*

She is across the room from me. I am in a chair facing her. We sit together in the late darkness of a summer night. As she speaks the space between us grows larger. She has entered her past. She is speaking of her childhood. Her father. The war. Did I know her father fought in the Battle of the Bulge? What was it for him, this great and terrible battle? She cannot say. He never spoke of it at home. They knew so little, her mother, her brothers, herself. Outside, the sea has disappeared. One finds the water now only by the city lights that cease to shine at its edges. California. She moved here with her family when her father became the commander of a military base. There were nuclear missiles standing just blocks from where she lived. But her father never spoke about them. Only after many years away from home did she learn what these weapons were.

*The first guided missile is developed in Germany, during World War II. It is known as the* Vergeltungswaffe, *or the Vengeance weapon. Later, it will be called the V-1 rocket.*

She is speaking of another life, another way of living. I give her the name Laura here. She speaks of the time after the war, when the cold war was just beginning. The way we are talking now, Laura tells me, was not possible in her family. I nod in recognition. Certain questions were never answered. She learned what not to ask. She begins to tell me a story. Once when she was six years old she went out with her father on a long trip. It was not even a year since the war ended. They were living in Germany.

They drove for miles and miles. Finally they turned into a small road at the edge of a village and drove through a wide gate in a high wall. The survivors were all gone. But there were other signs of this event beyond and yet still within her comprehension. Shoes in great piles. Bones. Women's hair, clothes, stains, a terrible odor. She began to cry a child's frightened tears and then to scream. She had no words for what she saw. Her father admonished her to be still. Only years later, and in a classroom, did she find out the name of this place and what had happened here.

*The shell surrounding the nucleus is not hard and rigid; it is a porous membrane. These pores allow only some substances to pass through them, mediating the movement of materials in and out of the nucleus.*

• • •

Often I have looked back into my past with a new insight only to find that some old, hardly recollected feeling fits into a larger pattern of meaning. Time can be measured in many ways. We see time as moving forward and hope that by our efforts this motion is toward improvement. When the atomic bomb exploded, many who survived the blast say time stopped with the flash of light and was held suspended until the ash began to descend. Now, in my mind, I can feel myself moving backward in time. I am as if on a train. And the train pushes into history. This history seems to exist somewhere, waiting, a foreign country behind a border and, perhaps, also inside me. From the windows of my train, I can see what those outside do not see. They do not see each other, or the whole landscape through which the track is laid. This is a straight track, but still there are bends to fit the shape of the earth. There are even circles. And returns.

*The missile is guided by a programmed mechanism. There is no electronic device that can be jammed. Once it is fired it cannot stop.*

It is 1945 and a film is released in Germany. This film has been made for other nations to see. On the screen a train pulls into a station. The train is full of children. A man in a uniform greets the children warmly as they step off the train. Then the camera cuts to boys and girls who are swimming. The boys and girls race to see who can reach the other side of the pool first. Then a woman goes to a post office. A man goes to a bank. Men and women sit drinking coffee at a cafe. The film is called *The Führer Presents the Jews with a City*. It has been made at Terezin concentration camp.

*Through the pores of the nuclear membrane a steady stream of ribonucleic acid, RNA, the basic material from which the cell is made, flows out.*

It is wartime and a woman is writing a letter. *Everyone is on the brink of starvation,* she says. In the right-hand corner of the page she has written *Nordhausen, Germany 1944.* She is writing to Hans. *Do you remember,* she asks, the day this war was declared? The beauty of the place. The beauty of the sea. *And I bathed in it that day, for the last time.*

In the same year, someone else is also writing a letter. In the right-hand corner he has put his name followed by a title. *Heinrich Himmler. Reichsführer, SS. Make no mention of the special treatment of the Jews,* he says, use only the words Transportation of the Jews toward the Russian East.

A few months later this man will deliver a speech to a secret meeting of leaders in the district of Posen. *Now you know all about it, and you will keep quiet,* he will tell them. Now we share a secret and *we should take our secret to our graves.*

• • •

*The missile flies from three to four thousand feet above the earth and this makes it difficult to attack from the ground.*

The woman who writes of starvation is a painter in her seventy-seventh year. She has lost one grandchild to this war. And a son to the war before. Both boys were named Peter. Among the drawings she makes which have already become famous: a terrified mother grasps a child, *Death Seizes Children;* an old man curls over the bent body of an old woman, *Parents;* a thin face emerges white from charcoal, *Beggars.*

*A small but critical part of the RNA flowing out of the pores holds most of the knowledge issued by the nucleus. These threads of RNA act as messengers.*

Encountering such images, one is grateful to be spared. But is one ever really free of the fate of others? I was born in 1943, in the midst of this war. And I sense now that my life is still bound up with the lives of those who lived and died in this time. Even with Heinrich Himmler. All the details of his existence, his birth, childhood, adult years, death, still resonate here on earth.

*The V-1 rocket is a winged plane powered by a duct motor with a pulsating flow of fuel.*

It is April 1943, Heinrich Himmler, Reichsführer SS, has gained control of the production of rockets for the Third Reich. The SS Totenkampf stand guard with machine guns trained at the entrance to a long tunnel, two miles deep, fourteen yards wide and ten yards high, sequestered in the Harz Mountains near Nordhausen. Once an old mining shaft, this tunnel serves now as a secret factory for the manufacture of V-1 and V-2 missiles. The guards aim their machine guns at the factory workers who are in-mates of concentration camp Dora.

*Most of the RNA flowing out of the cell is destined for the construction of a substance needed to compensate for the continual wearing away of the cell.*

It is 1925. Heinrich Himmler, who is now twenty-five years old, has been hired as a secretary by the chief of the Nazi Party in Landshut. He sits behind a small desk in a room overcrowded with party records, corre-spondence, and newspaper files. On the wall facing him he can see a por-trait of Adolf Hitler. He hopes one day to meet the Führer. In anticipation of that day, while he believes no one watches, he practices speaking to this portrait.

It is 1922. Heinrich visits friends who have a three-year-old child. Before going to bed this child is allowed to run about naked. And this disturbs Heinrich. He writes in his diary, *One should teach a child a sense of shame.*

It is the summer of 1910. Heinrich begins his first diary. He is ten years old. He has just completed elementary school. His father tells him his childhood is over now. In the fall he will enter Wilhelms Gymnasium. There the grades he earns will determine his prospects for the future. From now on he must learn to take himself seriously.

*Eight out of ten of the guided missiles will land within eight miles of their targets.*

His father Gebhard is a schoolmaster. He knows the requirements. He provides the boy with pen and ink. Gebhard was once a tutor for Prince Heinrich of Wittelsbach. He has named his son Heinrich after this prince. He is grateful that the prince consented to be Heinrich's godparent. Heinrich is to write in his diary every day. Gebhard writes the first entry in his son's diary, to show the boy how it is to be done.

*July 13 Departed at 11:50 and arrive safely on the bus in L. We have a very pretty house. In the afternoon we drink coffee at the coffee house.*

I open the cover of the journal I began to keep just as I started my work on this book. I want to see what is on the first page. *It is here I begin a new life,* I wrote. Suffering many losses at once, I was alone and lonely. Yet suddenly I felt a new responsibility for myself. *The very act of keeping a journal,* I sensed, would help me into this life that would now be my own.

*Inside the nucleus is the nucleolus where the synthesis of RNA takes place. Each nucleolus is filled with a small jungle of fern-like structures all of whose fronds and stalks move and rotate in perfect synchrony.*

It is 1910. The twenty-second of July. Gebhard adds the words *first swim* to his son's brief entry, *thirteenth wedding anniversary of my dear parents.* 1911. Over several entries Heinrich lists each of thirty-seven times he takes a swim, in chronological order. *11:37 A.M. Departed for Lindau.* He does not write of his feelings. *August 8, Walk in the park.* Or dreams. *August 10, Bad weather.*

In the last few years I have been searching, though for what precisely I cannot say. Something still hidden which lies in the direction of Heinrich Himmler's life. I have been to Berlin and Munich on this search, and I have walked over the gravel at Dachau. Now as I sit here I read once again the fragments from Heinrich's boyhood diary that exist in English. I have begun to think of these words as ciphers. Repeat them to myself, hoping to find a door into the mind of this man, even as his character first forms so that I might learn how it is he becomes himself.

The task is not easy. The earliest entries in this diary betray so little. Like the words of a schoolboy commanded to write what the teacher requires of him, they are wooden and stiff. The stamp of his father's character is so heavy on this language that I catch not even a breath of a self here. It is easy to see how this would be true. One simply has to imagine Gebhard standing behind Heinrich and tapping his foot.

His father must have loomed large to him. Did Gebhard lay his hand on Heinrich's shoulder? The weight of that hand would not be comforting. It would be a warning. A reminder. Heinrich must straighten up now and be still. Yet perhaps he turns his head. Maybe there is a sound outside. A bird. Or his brother Gebhard's voice. But from the dark form behind him he hears a name pronounced. This is his name, *Heinrich*. The sound rolls sharply off his father's tongue. He turns his head back. He does not know what to write. He wants to turn to this form and beseech him, but this man who is his father is more silent than stone. And now when Heinrich can feel impatience all around him, he wants to ask, *What should I write?* The edge of his father's voice has gotten sharper. *Why can't you remember?* Just write what happened yesterday. And make sure you get the date right. *Don't you remember?* We took a walk in the park together and we ran into the duchess. Be certain you spell her name correctly. And look here, you must get the title right. That is extremely important. Cross it out. Do it again. *The title.*

The boy is relieved. His mind has not been working. His thoughts were like paralyzed limbs, immobile. Now he is in motion again. He writes the sentences as they are dictated to him. *The park.* He crosses out the name. He writes it again. Spelling it right. *The duchess.* And his father makes one more correction. The boy has not put down the correct time for their walk in the park.

And who is the man standing behind? In a photograph I have before me of the aging Professor and Frau Himmler, as they pose before a wall carefully composed with paintings and family portraits, Frau Himmler adorned with a demure lace collar, both she and the professor smiling kindly from behind steel-rimmed glasses, the professor somewhat rounded with age, in a dark three-piece suit and polka-dot tie, looks so ordinary.

*The missile carries a warhead weighing 1,870 pounds. It has three different fuses to insure detonation.*

Ordinary. What an astonishing array of images hide behind this word. The ordinary is of course never ordinary. I think of it now as a kind of mask, not an animated mask that expresses the essence of an inner truth, but a mask that falls like dead weight over the human face, making flesh a stationary object. One has difficulty penetrating the heavy mask that Gebhard and his family wore, difficulty piercing through to the creatures behind.

It must not have been an easy task to create this mask. One detects the dimensions of the struggle in the advice of German child-rearing experts from this and the last century. *Crush the will,* they write. *Establish dominance. Permit no disobedience. Suppress everything in the child.*

I have seen illustrations from the books of one of these experts, perhaps the most famous of these pedagogues, Dr. Daniel Gottlieb Moritz Schreber. At first glance these pictures recall images of torture. But they are instead pictures of children whose posture or behavior is being corrected. A brace up the spine, a belt tied to a waist and the hair at the back of the neck so the child will be discouraged from slumping, a metal plate at the edge of a desk keeping the child from curling over her work, a child tied to a bed to prevent poor sleeping posture or masturbation. And there are other methods recommended in the text. An enema to be given before bedtime. The child immersed in ice-cold water up to the hips, before sleep.

The nightmare images of the German child-rearing practices that one discovers in this book call to mind the catastrophic events of recent German history. I first encountered this pedagogy in the writing of Alice Miller. At one time a psychoanalyst, she was haunted by the question, *What could make a person conceive the plan of gassing millions of human beings to death?* In her work, she traces the origins of this violence to childhood.

Of course there cannot be one answer to such a monumental riddle, nor does any event in history have a single cause. Rather a field exists, like a field of gravity that is created by the movements of many bodies. Each life is influenced and it in turn becomes an influence. Whatever is a cause is also an effect. Childhood experience is just one element in the determining field.

As a man who made history, Heinrich Himmler shaped many childhoods, including, in the most subtle of ways, my own. And an earlier history, a history of governments, of wars, of social customs, an idea of gender, the history of a religion leading to the idea of original sin, shaped Heinrich Himmler's childhood as certainly as any philosophy of child raising. One can take for instance any formative condition of his private life, the fact that he was a frail child, for example, favored by his mother, who could not meet masculine standards, and show that this circumstance derived its real meaning from a larger social system that gave inordinate significance to masculinity.

Yet to enter history through childhood experience shifts one's perspective not away from history but instead to an earlier time just before history has finally shaped us. Is there a child who existed before the conventional history that we tell of ourselves, one who, though invisible to us, still shapes events, even through this absence? How does our sense of history change when we consider childhood, and perhaps more important, why is it that until now we have chosen to ignore this point of origination, the birthplace and womb of ourselves, in our consideration of public events?

In the silence that reverberates around this question, an image is born in my mind. I can see a child's body, small, curled into itself, knees bent toward the chest, head bending softly into pillows and blankets, in a posture thought unhealthy by Dr. Schreber, hand raised to the face, delicate mouth making a circle around the thumb. There is comfort as well as sadness in this image. It is a kind of a self-portrait, drawn both from memory and from a feeling that is still inside me. As I dwell for a moment with this image I can imagine Heinrich in this posture, silent, curled, fetal, giving comfort to himself.

But now, alongside this earlier image, another is born. It is as if these two images were twins, always traveling in the world of thought together. One does not come to mind without the other. In this second portrait, which is also made of feeling and memory, a child's hands are tied into mittens. And by a string extending from one of the mittens, her hand is tied to the bars of her crib. She is not supposed to be putting her finger in her mouth. And she is crying out in rage while she yanks her hand violently trying to free herself of her bonds.

To most of existence there is an inner and an outer world. Skin, bark, surface of the ocean open to reveal other realities. What is inside shapes and sustains what appears. So it is too with human consciousness. And yet the mind rarely has a simple connection to the inner life. At a certain age we begin to define ourselves, to choose an image of who we are. I am this and not that, we say, attempting thus to erase whatever is within us that does not fit our idea of who we should be. In time we forget our earliest selves and replace that memory with the image we have constructed at the bidding of others.

One can see this process occur in the language of Heinrich's diaries. If in the earliest entries, except for the wooden style of a boy who obeys authority, Heinrich's character is hardly apparent, over time this stilted style becomes his own. As one reads on, one no longer thinks of a boy who is forced to the task, but of a prudish and rigid young man.

In Heinrich's boyhood diaries no one has been able to find any record of rage or of events that inspire such rage. Yet one cannot assume from this evidence that such did not exist. His father would have permitted neither anger nor even the memory of it to enter these pages. That there must be no visible trace of resentment toward the parent was the pedagogy of the age. Dr. Schreber believed that children should learn to be grateful. The pain and humiliation children endure are meant to benefit them. The parent is only trying to save the child's soul.

Now, for different reasons, I too find myself on the track of a child's soul. The dimensions of Heinrich Himmler's life have put me on this track. I am trying to grasp the inner state of his being. For a time the soul ceased to exist in the modern mind. One thought of a human being as a kind of machine, or as a cog in the greater mechanism of society, operating within another machine, the earth, which itself operates within the greater mechanical design of the universe.

When I was in Berlin, I spoke to a rabbi who had, it seemed to me, lost his faith. When I asked him if he still believed in God, he simply shook his head and widened his eyes as if to say, *How is this possible?* He had been telling me about his congregation: older people, many of Polish origin, survivors of the holocaust who were not able to leave Germany after the war because they were too ill to travel. He was poised in this painful place by choice. He had come to lead this congregation only temporarily but, once feeling the condition of his people, decided to stay. Still, despite his answer, and as much as the holocaust made a terrible argument for the death of the spirit, talking in that small study with this man, I could feel from him the light of something surviving.

The religious tradition that shaped Heinrich's childhood argues that the soul is not part of flesh but is instead a prisoner of the body. But suppose the soul is meant to live in and through the body and to know itself in the heart of earthly existence?

Then the soul is an integral part of the child's whole being, and its growth is thus part of the child's growth. It is, for example, like a seed planted underground in the soil, naturally moving toward the light. And it comes into its fullest manifestation thus only when seen, especially when self meeting self returns a gaze.

What then occurs if the soul in its small beginnings is forced to take on a secret life? A boy learns, for instance, to hide his thoughts from his father simply by failing to record them in his journals. He harbors his secrets in fear and guilt, confessing them to no one until in time the voice of his father chastising him becomes his own. A small war is waged in his mind. Daily implosions take place under his skin, by which in increments something in him seems to disappear. Gradually his father's voice subsumes the vitality of all his desires and even his rage, so that now what he wants most passionately is his own obedience, and his rage is aimed at his own failures. As over time his secrets fade from memory, he ceases to tell them, even to himself, so that finally a day arrives when he believes the image he has made of himself in his diaries is true.

The child, Dr. Schreber advised, *should be permeated by the impossibility of locking something in his heart.* The doctor who gave this advice had a son who was hospitalized for disabling schizophrenia. Another of his children committed suicide. But this was not taken as a warning against his approach. His methods of educating children were so much a part of the canon of everyday life in Germany that they were introduced into the state school system.

That this philosophy was taught in school gives me an interior view of the catastrophe to follow. It adds a certain dimension to my image of these events to know that a nation of citizens learned that no part of themselves could be safe from the scrutiny of authority, nothing locked in the heart, and at the same time to discover that the head of the secret police of this nation was the son of a schoolmaster. It was this man, after all, Heinrich Himmler, Reichsführer SS, who was later to say, speaking of the mass arrests of Jews, *Protective custody is an act of care.*

* * *

The polite manner of young Heinrich's diaries reminds me of life in my grandmother's home. Not the grandmother I lost and later found, but the one who, for many years, raised me. She was my mother's mother. The family would assemble in the living room together, sitting with a certain reserve, afraid to soil the surfaces. What was it that by accident might have been made visible?

All our family photographs were posed. We stood together in groups of three or four and squinted into the sun. My grandmother directed us to smile. I have carried one of these photographs with me for years without acknowledging to myself that in it my mother has the look she always had when she drank too much. In another photograph, taken near the time of my parents' divorce, I can see that my father is almost crying, though I could not see this earlier. I must have felt obliged to see only what my grandmother wanted us to see. Tranquil, domestic scenes.

*In the matrix of the mitochondria all the processes of transformation join together in a central vortex.*

We were not comfortable with ourselves as a family. There was a great shared suffering and yet we never wept together, except for my mother, who would alternately weep and then rage when she was drunk. Together, under my grandmother's tutelage, we kept up appearances. Her effort was ceaseless.

When at the age of six I went to live with her, my grandmother worked to reshape me. I learned what she thought was correct grammar. The manners she had studied in books of etiquette were passed on to me, not by casual example but through anxious memorization and drill. Napkin to be lifted by the corner and swept onto the lap. Hand to be clasped firmly but not too firmly.

We were not to the manner born. On one side my great-grandfather was a farmer, and on the other a butcher newly emigrated from Ireland, who still spoke with a brogue. Both great-grandfathers drank too much, the one in public houses, the other more quietly at home. The great-grandfather who farmed was my grandmother's father. He was not wealthy but he aspired to gentility. My grandmother inherited both his aspiration and his failure.

We considered ourselves finer than the neighbors to our left with their chaotic household. But when certain visitors came, we were as if driven by an inward, secret panic that who we really were might be discovered. Inadvertently, by some careless gesture, we might reveal to these visitors who were our betters that we did not belong with them, that we were not real. Though of course we never spoke of this, to anyone, not even ourselves.

Gebhard Himmler's family was newly risen from poverty. Just as in my family, the Himmlers' gentility was a thinly laid surface, maintained no doubt only with great effort. Gebhard's father had come from a family of peasants and small artisans. Such a living etched from the soil, and by one's hands, is tenuous and hard. As is frequently the case with young men born to poverty, Johann became a soldier. And, like many young soldiers, he got himself into trouble more than once for brawling and general mischief. On one occasion he was reproved for what was called *immoral behavior with a low woman.* But nothing of this history survived in his son's version of him. By the time Gebhard was born, Johann was fifty-six years old and had reformed his ways. Having joined the royal police force of Bavaria, over the years he rose to the rank of sergeant. He was a respectable man, with a respectable position.

Perhaps Gebhard never learned of his father's less than respectable past. He was only three years old when Johann died. If he had the slightest notion, he did not breathe a word to his own children. Johann became the icon of the Himmler family, the heroic soldier who single-handedly brought his family from the obscurity of poverty into the warm light of the favored. Yet obscure histories have a way of casting a shadow over the present. Those who are born to propriety have a sense of entitlement, and this affords them some ease as they execute the correct mannerisms of their class. More recent members of the elect are less certain of themselves; around the edges of newly minted refinement one discerns a certain fearfulness, expressed perhaps as uncertainty, or as its opposite, rigidity.

One can sense that rigidity in Gebhard's face as a younger man. In a photograph of the Himmler family, Gebhard, who towers in the background, seems severe. He has the face of one who looks for mistakes. He is vigilant. Heinrich's mother looks very small next to him, almost as if she is cowering. She has that look I have seen many times on my father's face, which one can only describe as ameliorating. Heinrich is very small. He stands closest to the camera, shimmering in a white dress. His face is pretty, even delicate.

I am looking now at the etching called *Poverty,* made in 1897. Near the center, calling my attention, a woman holds her head in her hands. She stares through her hands into the face of a sleeping infant. Though the infant and the sheet and pillow around are filled with light, one recognizes that the child is dying. In a darker corner, two worried figures huddle, a father and another child. Room, mother, father, child exist in lines, a multitude of lines, and each line is filled with a rare intelligence.

Just as the physicist's scrutiny changes the object of perception, so does art transmute experience. One cannot look upon what Käthe Kollwitz has drawn without feeling. The lines around the child are bleak with unreason. Never have I seen so clearly that what we call poverty is simply a raw exposure to the terror and fragility of life. But there is more in this image. There is meaning in the frame. One can feel the artist's eyes. Her gaze is in one place soft, in another intense. Like the light around the infant, her attention interrupts the shadow that falls across the room.

The artist's choice of subject and the way she saw it were both radical departures, not only from certain acceptable assumptions in the world of art, but also from established social ideas because the poor were thought of as less than human. The death of a child to a poor parent was supposed to be a less painful event. In her depiction, the artist told a different story.

Heinrich is entering a new school now, and so his father makes a list of all his future classmates. Beside the name of each child he writes the child's father's name, what this father does for a living, and his social position. Heinrich must be careful, Gebhard tells him, to choose whom he befriends. In his diaries the boy seldom mentions his friends by name. Instead he writes that he played, for instance, with the landlord's child.

There is so much for Heinrich to learn. Gebhard must teach him the right way to bow. The proper forms of greeting. The history of his family; the history of his nation. Its heroes. His grandfather's illustrious military past. There is an order in the world and Heinrich has a place in this order which he must be trained to fill. His life is strictly scheduled. At this hour a walk in the woods so that he can appreciate nature. After that a game of chess to develop his mind. And after that piano, so that he will be cultured.

If a part of himself has vanished, that part of the self that feels and wants, and from which hence a coherent life might be shaped, Heinrich is not at sea yet. He has no time to drift or feel lost. Each moment has been spoken for, every move prescribed. He has only to carry out his father's plans for him.

But everything in his life is not as it should be. He is not popular among his classmates. Should it surprise us to learn that he has a penchant for listening to the secrets of his companions, and that afterward he repeats these secrets to his father, the schoolmaster? There is perhaps a secret he would like to learn and one he would like to tell, but this has long since been forgotten. Whatever he learns now he must tell his father. He must not keep anything from him. He must keep his father's good will at all costs. For, without his father, he does not exist.

And there is another reason Heinrich is not accepted by his classmates. He is frail. As an infant, stricken by influenza, he came close to perishing and his body still retains the mark of that illness. He is not strong. He is not good at the games the other boys play. At school he tries over and over to raise himself on the crossbars, unsuccessfully. He covets the popularity of his stronger, more masculine brother, Gebhard. But he cannot keep up with his brother. One day, when they go out for a simple bicycle ride together, Heinrich falls into the mud and returns with his clothes torn.

It is 1914. A war begins. There are parades. Young men marching in uniform. Tearful ceremonies at the railway station. Songs. Decorations. Heinrich is enthusiastic. The war has given him a sense of purpose in life. Like other boys, he plays at soldiering. He follows the war closely, writing in his diary of the progress of armies, *This time with 40 Army Corps and*

*Russia and France against Germany.* The entries he makes do not seem so listless now; they have a new vigor. As the war continues, a new ambition gradually takes the shape of determination. Is this the way he will finally prove himself? Heinrich wants to be a soldier. And above all he wants a uniform.

It is 1915. In her journal Käthe Kollwitz records a disturbing sight. The night before at the opera she found herself sitting next to a young soldier. He was blinded. He sat *without stirring, his hands on his knees, his head erect.* She could not stop looking at him, and the memory of him, she writes now, *cuts her to the quick.*

It is 1916. As Heinrich comes of age he implores his father to help him find a regiment. He has many heated opinions about the war. But his thoughts are like the thoughts and feelings of many adolescents; what he expresses has no steady line of reason. His opinions are filled with contradictions, and he lacks that awareness of self which can turn ambivalence into an inner dialogue. Yet, beneath this amorphous bravado, there is a pattern. As if he were trying on different attitudes, Heinrich swings from harshness to compassion. In one place he writes, *The Russian prisoners multiply like vermin.* (Should I write here that this is a word he will one day use for Jews?) But later he is sympathetic to the same prisoners because they are so far away from home. Writing once of *the silly old women and petty bourgeois . . . who so dislike war,* in another entry, he remembers the young men he has seen depart on trains and he asks, *How many are alive today?*

Is the direction of any life inevitable? Or are there crossroads, points at which the direction might be changed? I am looking again at the Himmler family. Heinrich's infant face resembles the face of his mother. His face is soft. And his mother? In the photograph she is a fading presence. She occupied the same position as did most women in German families, secondary and obedient to the undisputed power of her husband. She has a slight smile which for some reason reminds me of the smile of a child I saw in a photograph from an album made by the SS. This child's image was captured as she stood on the platform at Auschwitz. In the photograph she emanates a certain frailty. Her smile is a very feminine smile. Asking, or perhaps pleading, *Don't hurt me.*

Is it possible that Heinrich, looking into that child's face, might have seen himself there? What is it in a life that makes one able to see oneself in others? Such affinities do not stop with obvious resemblance. There is a sense in which we all enter the lives of others.

It is 1917, and a boy who will be named Heinz is born to Catholic parents living in Vienna. Heinz's father bears a certain resemblance to Heinrich's father. He is a civil servant and, also like Gebhard, he is pedantic and correct in all he does. Heinrich will never meet this boy. And yet their paths will cross.

Early in the same year as Heinz's birth, Heinrich's father has finally succeeded in getting him into a regiment. As the war continues for one more year, Heinrich comes close to achieving his dream. He will be a soldier. He is sent to officer's training. Yet he is not entirely happy. *The food is bad,* he writes to his mother, *and there is not enough of it. It is cold. There are bedbugs. The room is barren.* Can she send him food? A blanket? Why doesn't she write him more often? Has she forgotten him? They are calling up troops. Suppose he should be called to the front and die?

But something turns in him. Does he sit on the edge of a neat, narrow military bunk bed as he writes in his diary that he does not want to be like a boy who whines to his mother? Now, he writes a different letter: *I am once more a soldier body and soul.* He loves his uniform; the oath he has learned to write; the first inspection he passes. He signs his letters now, *Miles Heinrich.* Soldier Heinrich.

I am looking at another photograph. It is of two boys. They are both in military uniform. Gebhard, Heinrich's older brother, is thicker and taller. Next to him Heinrich is still diminutive. But his face has become harder, and his smile, though faint like his mother's smile, has gained a new quality, harsh and stiff like the little collar he wears.

Most men can remember a time in their lives when they were not so different from girls, and they also remember when that time ended. In ancient Greece a young boy lived with his mother, practicing a feminine life in her household, until the day he was taken from her into the camp of men. From this day forward the life that had been soft and graceful became rigorous and hard, as the older boy was prepared for the life of a soldier.

My grandfather on my mother's side was a contemporary of Heinrich Himmler. He was the youngest boy in the family and an especially pretty child. Like Heinrich and all small boys in this period, he was dressed in a lace gown. His hair was long and curled about his face. Like Heinrich, he was his mother's favorite. She wanted to keep him in his finery. He was so beautiful in it, and he was her last child. My great-grandmother Sarah had a dreamy, artistic nature, and in his early years my grandfather took after her. But all of this made him seem girlish. And his father and older brothers teased him mercilessly. Life improved for him only when he graduated to long pants. With them he lost his dreamy nature too.

The soul is often imagined to be feminine. All those qualities thought of as soulful, a dreaminess or artistic sensibility, are supposed to come more naturally to women. Ephemeral, half seen, half present, nearly ghostly, with only the vaguest relation to the practical world of physical law, the soul appears to us as lost. The hero, with his more masculine virtues, must go in search of her. But there is another, older story of the soul. In this story she is firmly planted on the earth. She is incarnate and visible everywhere. Neither is she faint of heart, nor fading in her resolve. It is she, in fact, who goes bravely in search of desire.

1918. Suddenly the war is over. Germany has lost. Heinrich has failed to win his commission. He has not fought in a single battle. Prince Heinrich, his namesake, has died. The prince will be decorated for heroism, after his death. Heinrich returns home, not an officer or even a soldier any longer. He returns to school, completing his studies at the gymnasium and then the university. But he is adrift. Purposeless. And like the world he belongs to, dissatisfied. Neither man nor boy, he does not know what he wants.

Until now he could rely on a strict regimen provided by his father. Nothing was left uncertain or undefined for long in his father's house. The thoroughness of Gebhard's hold over his family comes alive for me through this procedure: every package, letter or money order to pass through the door was by Gebhard's command to be duly recorded. And I begin to grasp a sense of Gebhard's priorities when I read that Heinrich, on one of his leaves home during the war, assisted his mother in this task. The shadow of his father's habits will stretch out over history. They will fall over an office in Berlin through which the SS, and the entire network of concentration camps, are administered. Every single piece of paper issued with regard to this office will pass over Heinrich's desk, and to each page he will add his own initials. Schedules for trains. Orders for building supplies. Adjustments in salaries. No detail will escape his surmise or fail to be recorded.

But at this moment in his life Heinrich is facing a void. I remember a similar void, when a long and intimate relationship ended. What I felt then was fear. And at times panic. In a journal I kept after this separation, I wrote, *Direct knowledge of the illusory nature of panic. The feeling that I had let everything go out of control.* I could turn in only one direction: inward. Each day I abated my fears for a time by observing myself. But what exists in that direction for Heinrich? He has not been allowed to inhabit that terrain. His inner life has been sealed off both from his father and himself.

*I am not certain what I am working for,* he writes, and then, not able to let this uncertainty remain, he adds, *I work because it is my duty.* He spends long hours in his room, seldom leaving the house at all. He is at sea. Still somewhat the adolescent, unformed, not knowing what face he should put on when going out into the world, in his journal he confesses that he still lacks that *naturally superior kind of manner that he would dearly like to possess.*

Is it any wonder then that he is so eager to rejoin the army? The army gave purpose and order to his life. He wants his uniform again. In his uniform he knows who he is. But his frailty haunts him. Over and over he shows up at recruiting stations throughout Bavaria only to be turned away each time, with the single word, *Untauglich.* Unfit. At night the echo of this word keeps him awake.

When he tries to recover his pride, he suffers another failure of a similar kind. A student of agriculture at the university, now he dreams of becoming a farmer. He believes he can take strength and vitality from the soil. After all his own applications are rejected, his father finds him a position in the countryside. He rides toward his new life on his motorcycle and is pelted by torrents of rain. Though he is cold and hungry, he is also exuberant. He has defeated his own weakness. But after only a few weeks his body fails him again. He returns home ill with typhus and must face the void once more.

*What Germany needs now is a man of iron.* How easy it is to hear the irony of these words Heinrich records in his journal. But at this moment in history, he is hearing another kind of echo. There are so many others who agree with him. The treaty of Versailles is taken as a humiliation. An unforgivable weakness, it is argued, has been allowed to invade the nation.

1920. 1922. 1923. Heinrich is twenty, twenty-two, twenty-three. He is growing up with the century. And he starts to adopt certain opinions popular at this time. As I imagine myself in his frame of mind, facing a void, cast into unknown waters, these opinions appear like rescue ships on the horizon, a promise of *terra firma,* the known.

It is for instance fashionable to argue that the emergence of female equality has drained the nation of its strength. At social gatherings Heinrich likes to discuss the differences between men and women. That twilight area between the certainties of gender, homosexuality, horrifies him. A man should be a man and a woman a woman. Sexually explicit illustrations in a book by Oscar Wilde horrify him. Uncomfortable with the opposite sex, so much so that one of his female friends believes he hates women, he has strong feelings about how men and women ought to relate. *A real man,* he sets down in his diary, *should love a woman as a child who must be admonished perhaps even punished, when she is foolish, though she must also be protected and looked after because she is so weak.*

As I try to enter Heinrich's experience, the feeling I sense behind these words is of immense comfort. I know who I am. My role in life, what I am to feel, what I am to be, has been made clear. I am a man. I am the strong protector. And what's more, I am needed. There is one who is weak. One who is weaker than I am. And I am the one who must protect her.

And yet behind the apparent calm of my present mood, there is an uneasiness. Who is this one that I protect? Does she tell me the truth about herself? I am beginning to suspect that she hides herself from me. There is something secretive in her nature. She is an unknown, even dangerous, territory.

The year is 1924. And Heinrich is still fascinated with secrets. He discovers that his brother's fiancée has committed one or maybe even two indiscretions. At his urging, Gebhard breaks off the engagement. But Heinrich is still not satisfied. He writes a friend who lives near his brother's former fiancée, *Do you know of any other shameful stories?* After this, he hires a private detective to look into her past.

Is it any coincidence that in the same year he writes in his diary that he has met a *great man, genuine and pure?* This man, he notes, may be the new leader Germany is seeking. He finds he shares a certain drift of thought with this man. He is discovering who he is now, partly by affinity and partly by negation. In his picture of himself, a profile begins to emerge cast in light and shadow. He knows now who he is and who he is not. He is not Jewish.

And increasingly he becomes obsessed with who he is not. In this pursuit, his curiosity is fed by best-selling books, posters, films, journals; he is part of a larger social movement, and this no doubt gives him comfort, and one cannot, in studying the landscape of his mind as set against the landscape of the social body, discover where he ends and the milieu of this time begins. He is perhaps like a particle in a wave, a wave which has only the most elusive relationship with the physical world, existing as an afterimage in the mind.

I can imagine him sitting at a small desk in his bedroom, still in his father's home. Is it the same desk where he was required to record some desultory sentences in his diary every day? He is bent over a book. It is evening. The light is on, shining on the pages of the book. Which book among the books he has listed in his journal does he read now? Is it *Das Liebnest* (*The Lovenest*), telling the story of a liaison between a Jewish man and a gentile woman? *Rasse?* Explaining the concept of racial superiority? Or is it *Judas Schuldsbach* (*The Book of Jewish Guilt*). Or *Die Sünde wider das Blut* (*The Sin Against the Blood*).

One can follow somewhat his train of thought here and there where he makes comments on what he reads in his journal. When he reads *Tscheka,* for instance, a history of the secret police in Russia, he says he is disappointed. *Everyone knows,* he writes, that the Jews control the secret police in Russia. But nowhere in the pages of this book does he find a mention of this "fact."

His mind has begun to take a definite shape, even a predictable pattern. Everywhere he casts his eyes he will discover a certain word. Wherever his thoughts wander he brings them back to this word. *Jew. Jude. Jew.* With this word he is on firm ground again. In the sound of the word, a box is closed, a box with all the necessary documents, with all the papers in order.

My grandfather was an anti-Semite. He had a long list of enemies that he liked to recite. Blacks were among them. And Catholics. And the English. He was Protestant and Irish. Because of his drinking he retired early (though we never discussed the cause). In my childhood I often found him sitting alone in the living room that was darkened by closed venetian blinds which kept all our colors from fading. Lonely myself, I would try to speak with him. His repertoire was small. When I was younger he would tell me stories of his childhood, and I loved those stories. He talked about the dog named Blackie that was his then. A ceramic statue of a small black dog resembling him stood near the fireplace. He loved this dog in a way that was almost painful to hear. But he could never enter that intricate world of expressed emotion in which the shadings of one's life as it is felt and experienced become articulated. This way of speaking was left to the women of our family. As I grew older and he could no longer tell me the story of his dog, he would talk to me about politics. It was then that, with a passion he revealed nowhere else, he would recite to me his long list filled with everyone he hated.

I did not like to listen to my grandfather speak this way. His face would get red, and his voice took on a grating tone that seemed to abrade not only the ears but some other slower, calmer velocity within the body of the room. His eyes, no longer looking at me, blazed with a kind of blindness. There was no reaching him at these moments. He was beyond any kind of touch or remembering. Even so, reciting the long list of those he hated, he came temporarily alive. Then, once out of this frame of mind, he lapsed into a kind of fog which we called, in the family, his retirement.

There was another part of my grandfather's mind that also disturbed me. But this passion was veiled. I stood at the borders of it occasionally catching glimpses. He had a stack of magazines by the chair he always occupied. They were devoted to the subject of crime, and the crimes were always grisly, involving photographs of women or girls uncovered in ditches, hacked to pieces or otherwise mutilated. I was never supposed to look in these magazines, but I did. What I saw there could not be reconciled with the other experience I had of my grandfather, fond of me, gentle, almost anachronistically protective.

Heinrich Himmler was also fascinated with crime. Along with books about Jews, he read avidly on the subjects of police work, espionage, torture. Despite his high ideals regarding chastity, he was drawn to torrid, even pornographic fiction, including *Ein Sadist im Priesterrock* (*A Sadist in Priestly Attire*) which he read quickly, noting in his journal that it was a book *about the corruption of women and girls . . . in Paris.*

Entering the odd and often inconsistent maze of his opinions, I feel a certain queasiness. I cannot find a balance point. I search in vain for some center, that place which is in us all, and is perhaps even beyond nationality, or even gender, the felt core of existence, which seems to be at the same time the most real. In Heinrich's morass of thought there are no connecting threads, no integrated whole. I find only the opinions themselves, standing in an odd relation to gravity, as if hastily formed, a rickety, perilous structure.

I am looking at a photograph. It was taken in 1925. Or perhaps 1926. A group of men pose before a doorway in Landshut. Over this doorway is a wreathed swastika. Nearly all the men are in uniform. Some wear shiny black boots. Heinrich is among them. He is the slightest, very thin. Heinrich Himmler. He is near the front. At the far left there is the blurred figure of a man who has been caught in motion as he rushes to join the other men. Of course I know his feeling. The desire to partake, and even to be part of memory.

Photographs are strange creations. They are depictions of a moment that is always passing; after the shutter closes, the subject moves out of the frame and begins to change outwardly or inwardly. One ages. One shifts to a different state of consciousness. Subtle changes can take place in an instant, perhaps one does not even feel them—but they are perceptible to the camera.

The idea we have of reality as a fixed quantity is an illusion. Everything moves. And the process of knowing oneself is in constant motion too, because the self is always changing. Nowhere is this so evident as in the process of art which takes one at once into the self and into *terra incognita,* the land of the unknown. *I am groping in the dark,* the artist Käthe Kollwitz writes in her journal. Here, I imagine she is not so much uttering a cry of despair as making a simple statement. A sense of emptiness always precedes creation.

Now, as I imagine Himmler, dressed in his neat uniform, seated behind his desk at party headquarters, I can feel the void he feared begin to recede. In every way his life has taken on definition. He has a purpose and a schedule. Even the place left by the cessation of his father's lessons has now been filled. He is surrounded by men whose ideas he begins to adopt. From Alfred Rosenberg he learns about the history of Aryan blood, a line Rosenberg traces back to thousands of years before Christ. From Walther Darré he learns that the countryside is a source of Nordic strength. (And that Jews gravitate toward cities.)

Yet I do not find the calmness of a man who has found himself in the descriptions I have encountered of Heinrich Himmler. Rather, he is filled with an anxious ambivalence. If there was once someone in him who felt strongly one way or the other, this one has long ago vanished. In a room filled with other leaders, he seems to fade into the woodwork, his manner obsequious, his effect inconsequential. He cannot make a decision alone. He is known to seek the advice of other men for even the smallest decisions. In the years to come it will be whispered that he is being led by his own assistant, Reinhard Heydrich. He has made only one decision on his own with a consistent resolve. Following Hitler with unwavering loyalty, he is known as *der treuer Heinrich,* true Heinrich. He describes himself as an instrument of the Führer's will.

But still he has something of his own. Something hidden. And this will make him powerful. He is a gatherer of secrets. As he supervises the sale of advertising space for the Nazi newspaper, *Der Völkischer Beobachter,* he instructs the members of his staff to gather information, not only on the party enemies, the socialists and the communists, but on Nazi Party members themselves. In his small office he sits surrounded by voluminous files that are filled with secrets. From this he will build his secret police. By 1925, with an order from Adolf Hitler, the Schutzstaffel, or SS, has become an official institution.

His life is moving now. Yet in this motion one has the feeling not of a flow, as in the flow of water in a cell, nor as the flow of rivers toward an ocean, but of an engine, a locomotive moving at high speed, or even a missile, traveling above the ground. History has an uncanny way of creating its own metaphors. In 1930, months after Himmler is elected to the Reichstag, Wernher von Braun begins his experiments with liquid fuel missiles that will one day soon lead to the development of the V-2 rocket.

The successful journey of a missile depends upon the study of ballistics. Gravitational fields vary at different heights. The relationship of a projectile to the earth's surface will determine its trajectory. The missile may give the illusion of liberation from the earth, or even abandon. Young men dreaming of space often invest the missile with these qualities. Yet, paradoxically, one is more free of the consideration of gravity while traveling the surface of the earth on foot. There is no necessity for mathematical calculation for each step, nor does one need to apply Newton's laws to take a walk. But the missile has in a sense been forced away from its own presence; the wisdom that is part of its own weight has been transgressed. It finds itself thus careening in a space devoid of memory, always on the verge of falling, but not falling and hence like one who is constantly afraid of illusion, gripped by an anxiety that cannot be resolved even by a fate that threatens catastrophe.

The catastrophes which came to pass after Heinrich Himmler's astonishing ascent to power did not occur in his own life, but came to rest in the lives of others, distant from him, and out of the context of his daily world. It is 1931. Heinz, the boy born in Vienna to Catholic parents, has just turned sixteen, and he is beginning to learn something about himself. All around him his school friends are falling in love with girls. But when he searches inside himself, he finds no such feelings. He is pulled in a different direction. He finds that he is still drawn to another boy. He does not yet know, or even guess, that these feelings will one day place him in the territory of a target.

It is 1933. Heinrich Himmler, Reichsführer SS, has become President of the Bavarian police. In this capacity he begins a campaign against *subversive elements*. Opposition journalists, Jewish business owners, Social Democrats, Communists—names culled from a list compiled on index cards by Himmler's deputy, Reinhard Heydrich—are rounded up and arrested. When the prisons become too crowded, Himmler builds temporary camps. Then, on March 22, the Reichsführer opens the first official and permanent concentration camp at Dachau.

It is 1934. Himmler's power and prestige in the Reich are growing. Yet someone stands in his way. Within the hierarchy of the state police forces, Ernst Röhm, Commandant of the SA, stands over him. But Himmler has made an alliance with Hermann Göring, who as President Minister of Prussia controls the Prussian police, known as the Gestapo. Through a telephone-tapping technique Göring has uncovered evidence of a seditious plot planned by Röhm against the Führer, and he brings this evidence to Himmler. The Führer, having his own reasons to proceed against Röhm, a notorious homosexual and a socialist, empowers the SS and the Gestapo to form an execution committee. This committee will assassinate Röhm, along with the other leaders of the SA. And in the same year, Göring transfers control of the Gestapo to the SS.

But something else less easy to conquer stands in the way of his dreams for himself. It is his own body. I can see him now as he struggles. He is on a playing field in Berlin. And he has broken out in a sweat. He has been trying once again to earn the Reich's sports badge, an honor whose requirements he himself established but cannot seem to fulfill. For three years he has exercised and practiced. On one day he will lift the required weights or run the required laps, but at every trial he fails to throw the discus far enough. His attempt is always a few centimeters short.

And once he is Reichsführer, he will set certain other standards for superiority that, no matter how heroic his efforts, he will never be able to meet. A sign of the *Übermensch*, he says, is blondness, but he himself is dark. He says he is careful to weed out any applicant for the SS who shows traces of a mongolian ancestry, but he himself has the narrow eyes he takes as a sign of such a descent. *I have refused to accept any man whose size was below six feet because I know only men of a certain size have the necessary quality of blood,* he declares, standing just five foot seven behind the podium.

It is the same year, and Heinz, who is certain now that he is a homosexual, has decided to end the silence which he feels to be a burden to him. From the earliest years of his childhood he has trusted his mother with all of his secrets. Now he will tell her another secret, the secret of whom he loves. *My dear child,* she tells him, *it is your life and you must live it.*

It is 1936. Though he does not know it, Himmler is moving into the sphere of Heinz's life now. He has organized a special section of the Gestapo to deal with homosexuality and abortion. On October 11, he declares in a public speech, *Germany's forebears knew what to do with homosexuals. They drowned them in bogs.* This was not punishment, he argues, but *the extermination of unnatural existence.*

As I read these words from Himmler's speech, they call to mind an image from a more recent past, an event I nearly witnessed. On my return from Berlin and after my search for my grandmother, I spent a few days in

Maine, close to the city of Bangor. This is a quiet town, not much used to violence. But just days before I arrived a young man had been murdered there. He was a homosexual. He wore an earring in one ear. While he walked home one evening with another man, three boys stopped him on the street. They threw him to the ground and began to kick him. He had trouble catching his breath. He was asthmatic. They picked him up and carried him to a railing of a nearby bridge. He told them he could not swim. Yet still, they threw him over the railing of the bridge into the stream, and he drowned. I saw a picture of him printed in the newspaper. That kind of beauty only very graceful children possess shined through his adult features. It was said that he had come to New England to live with his lover. But the love had failed, and before he died he was piecing his life back together.

When Himmler heard that one of his heroes, Frederick the Great, was a homosexual, he refused to believe his ears. I remember the year when my sister announced to my family that she was a lesbian. I can still recall the chill of fear that went up my spine at the sound of the word "queer." We came of age in the fifties; this was a decade of conformity, awash with mood both public and private, bearing on the life of the body and the body politic. Day after day my grandfather would sit in front of the television set watching as Joseph McCarthy interrogated witnesses about their loyalty to the flag. At the same time, a strict definition of what a woman or a man is had returned to capture the shared imagination. In school I was taught sewing and cooking, and I learned to carry my books in front of my chest to strengthen the muscles which held up my breasts.

I was not happy to hear that my sister was a homosexual. Moved from one member of my family to another, I did not feel secure in the love of others. As the child of divorce I was already different. *Where are your mother and father? Why don't you live with them?* I dreaded these questions. Now my sister, whom I adored and in many ways had patterned myself after, had become an outcast, moved even further out of the circle than I.

It is March 1938. Germany has invaded Austria. Himmler has put on a field-gray uniform for the occasion. Two hand grenades dangle from his Sam Browne belt. Accompanied by a special command unit of twenty-eight men armed with tommy guns and light machine guns, he proceeds to Vienna. Here he will set up Gestapo headquarters in the Hotel Metropole before he returns to Berlin.

It is a Friday, in March of 1939. Heinz, who is twenty-two years old now, and a university student, has received a summons. He is to appear for questioning at the Hotel Metropole. Telling his mother it can't be anything serious, he leaves. He enters a room and stands before a desk. The man behind the desk does not raise his head to nod. He continues to write. When he puts his pen down and looks up at the young man, he tells him,

*You are a queer, homosexual, admit it.* Heinz tries to deny this. But the man behind the desk pulls out a photograph. He sees two faces here he knows. His own face and the face of his lover. He begins to weep.

I have come to believe that every life bears in some way on every other. The motion of cause and effect is like the motion of a wave in water, continuous, within and not without the matrix of being, so that all consequences, whether we know them or not, are intimately embedded in our experience. But the missile, as it hurls toward its target, has lost its context. It has been driven farther than the eye can see. How can one speak of direction any longer? Nothing in the space the missile passes through can seem familiar. In the process of flight, alienated by terror, this motion has become estranged from life, has fallen out of the natural rhythm of events.

I am imagining Himmler as he sits behind his desk in January of 1940. The procedures of introduction into the concentration camps have all been outlined or authorized by Himmler himself. He supervises every detail of these operations. Following his father's penchant for order, he makes many very explicit rules, and requires that reports be filed continually. Train schedules, orders for food supplies, descriptions of punishments all pass over his desk. He sits behind a massive door of carved wood, in his office, paneled in light, unvarnished oak, behind a desk that is normally empty, and clean, except for the bust of Hitler he displays at one end, and a little drummer boy at the other, between which he reads, considers and initials countless pieces of paper.

*One should teach a child a sense of shame.* These words of Himmler's journals come back to me as I imagine Heinz now standing naked in the snow. The weather is below zero. After a while he is taken to a cold shower, and then issued an ill-fitting uniform. Now he is ordered to stand with the other prisoners once more out in the cold while the commandant reads the rules. All the prisoners in these barracks are homosexuals. There are pink triangles sewn to their uniforms. They must sleep with the light on, they are told, and with their hands outside their blankets. This is a rule made especially for homosexual men. Any man caught with his hands under his blankets will be taken outside into the icy night where several bowls of water will be poured over him, and where he will he made to stand for an hour.

Except for the fact that this punishment usually led to death from cold and exposure, this practice reminds me of Dr. Schreber's procedure for curing children of masturbation. Just a few nights ago I woke up with this thought: *Was Dr. Schreber afraid of children?* Or the child he once was? Fear is often just beneath the tyrant's fury, a fear that must grow with the trajectory of his flight from himself. At Dachau I went inside a barrack. It was a standard design, similar in many camps. The plan of the camps too was standard, and resembled, so I was told by a German friend, the camp sites designed for the Hitler Youth. This seemed to me significant, not as a clue in an analysis, but more like a gesture that colors and changes a speaker's words.

It is the summer of 1940. After working for nearly a decade on liquid fuel rockets, Wernher von Braun begins to design a missile that can be used in the war. He is part of a team trying to meet certain military specifications. The missile must be carried through railway tunnels. It must cover a range of 275 kilometers and carry a warhead weighing one metric ton. The engineers have determined that the motor of this rocket, a prototype of the V-2, will need to be fueled by a pump, and now a pump has been made. Von Braun is free to turn his attention to the turbine drive.

When I think of this missile, or of men sleeping in a barrack, hands exposed, lying on top of worn blankets, an image of Himmler's hands comes to me. Those who remember him say that as he conducted a conversation, discussing a plan, for example, or giving a new order, his hands would lie on top of his desk, limp and inert. He did not like to witness the consequences of his commands. His plans were launched toward distant targets and blind to the consequences of flesh.

After a few months, in one of countless orders which mystify him, coming from a nameless source, and with no explanation, but which he must obey, Heinz is transferred from Sachsenhausen to Flossenbürg. The regime at this camp is the same, but here the commandant, unlike Himmler, does not choose to distance himself from the suffering of others. He is instead drawn to it. He will have a man flogged for the slightest infraction of the rules, and then stand to watch as this punishment is inflicted. The man who is flogged is made to call out the number of lashes as he is lashed, creating in him, no doubt, the feeling that he is causing his own pain. As the man's skin bursts open and he cries out in pain, the commandant's eyes grow excited. His face turns red. His hand slips into his trousers, and he begins to handle himself.

Was the commandant in this moment in any way an extension of the Reichsführer, living out a hidden aspect of this man, one who takes pleasure in the pain of others? This explanation must shed some light, except perhaps as it is intended through the category of an inexplicable perversity to put the crimes Himmler committed at a distance from any understanding of ourselves. The Reichsführer's sexuality is so commonplace. He was remarkable only for the extent of his prudery as a young man. Later, like so many men, he has a wife, who dominates him, and a mistress, younger, more docile, adoring, whom he in turn adores. It has been suggested that he takes pleasure in seeing the naked bodies of boys and young men. If he has a sexual fetish it is certainly this, the worship of physical perfection in the male body. And this worship has its sadistic aspects: his efforts to control reproduction, to force SS men to procreate with many women, the kidnapping from occupied countries of children deemed worthy. Under the veneer of his worship, an earlier rage must haunt him. The subject of cruel insults from other boys with hardier bodies, and the torturous methods his father used to raise him, does he not feel rage toward his persecutors, a rage that, in the course of time, enters history? Yet this is an essential part of the picture: he is dulled to rage. So many of his feelings are inaccessible to him. Like the concentration camps he commands, in many ways he remains absent to himself. And in this he is not so different from the civilization that produced him.

Writing this, I have tried to find my own rage. The memory is immediate. I am a child, almost nine years old. I sit on the cold pavement of a winter day in Los Angeles. My grandmother has angered me. There is a terrible injustice. A punishment that has enraged me. As I sit picking blades of grass and arranging them into piles, I am torturing her in my mind. I have tied her up and I am shouting at her. Threatening her. Striking her. I batter her, batter her as if with each blow, each landing of my hand against her flesh, I can force my way into her, I can be inside her, I can grab hold of someone inside her, someone who feels, who feels as I do, who feels the hurt I feel, the wound I feel, who feels pain as I feel pain. I am forcing her to feel what I feel. I am forcing her to know me. And as I strike her, blow after blow, a shudder of weeping is released in me, and I become utterly myself, the weeping in me becoming rage, the rage turning to tears, all the time my heart beating, all the time uttering a soundless, bitter, passionate cry, a cry of vengeance and of love.

Is this what is in the torturer's heart? With each blow of his whip does he want to make the tortured one feel as he himself has felt? The desire to know and be known is strong in all of us. Many years after the day I imagined myself as my grandmother's torturer I came to understand that, just as I had wanted my grandmother to feel what I had felt, she wanted me to feel as she had felt. Not what she felt as a woman, but what she had felt long ago as a child. Her childhood was lost to her, the feelings no longer remembered. One way or another, through punishment, severity, or even ridicule, she could goad me into fury and then tears. I expressed for her all she had held inside for so long.

One day, the commandant at Flossenbürg encounters a victim who will not cry and Heinz is a witness to this meeting. As usual this prisoner must count out the number of blows assigned to him. The beating commences. And the prisoner counts out the numbers. But otherwise he is silent. Except for the numbers, not a cry, not a sound, passes his lips. And this puts the commandant in a rage. He orders the guard to strike harder with the lash; he increases the number of lashes; he orders the prisoner to begin counting from zero again. Finally, the beating shall continue *until the swine starts screaming,* he shouts. And now, when the prisoner's blood is flowing to the ground, he starts to howl. And with this, the commandant's face grows red, and his hands slip into his trousers again.

A connection between violence and sexuality threads its way through many histories. As we sit in the living room together, looking out over the water, Laura's stories move in and out of the world of her family, and of our shared world, its habits, its wars. She is telling me another story about her father, the general. They were living on the missile base. She had been out late baby-sitting. When she returned home the house was dark. She had no key. It was raining hard. She rang. There was no answer. Then she began to pound on the door. Suddenly the door opened. The hallway was dark. She was yanked into this darkness by her father. He was standing naked. Without speaking to her he began to slap her hard across the face, again and again, and did not stop until her mother, appearing in the stairs in a bathrobe, stood between them. *I knew,* she told me, *they had been making love.*

What was the source of his rage? Did it come from childhood, or battle, or both, the battle awakening the panic of an earlier abuse? The training a soldier receives is to wreak his anger on others. Anyone near receives it. I have heard stories of a man waking at night screaming in terror, reaching for a gun hidden under the pillow, and pointing it or even firing at his own family. In a play about Heracles by Euripides, the great warrior, who has just returned from the underworld, thinking that he has vanquished death, is claimed by madness. He believes himself to be in the home of his enemy. But he is in his own home and, finding his own children, mistakes them for the children of his enemy, clubs one to death and then kills the other two with arrows.

But it is not only warriors who wreak vengeance on their own children. Suffering is passed on from parent to child unto many generations. Did I know as a child that my grandmother's unclaimed fury had made its way into my mother's psyche too? With all her will my mother tried not to repeat against her own children the crimes that had battered her. Where my grandmother was tyrannical, my mother was tolerant and gave free reign. Where my grandmother goaded with critical remarks, my mother was encouraging, and even elaborately praising. But, like my grandfather, my mother drank too much. It was a way of life for her. Sooner or later the long nights would come. Every time I returned home, either to live with her or to visit, I prayed she would not drink again, while I braced myself for what I knew to be inevitable. The evening would begin with a few beers at home, followed by an endless tour of several bars. Either I went along and waited in cars, or I waited at home. In the early morning she would return, her eyes wandering like moths in their sockets. We would sit in two chairs opposite each other, as if these were prearranged places, marked out for us on the stage by a powerful but invisible director. She would start by joking with me. She was marvelously witty when she was drunk. All her natural intelligence was released then and allowed to bloom. But this performance was brief. Her humor turned by dark degrees to meanness. What must have daily constricted her, a kind of sea monster, feeding beneath the waters of her consciousness, and strong, would rise up to stop her glee and mine. Then she would strike. If I was not in my chair to receive her words, she would come and get me. What she said was viperous to me, sank like venom into my veins, and burned a path inside me. Even today I can remember very few of the words she used. She said that my laugh was too loud, or ugly. That I was incapable of loving. I am thankful now that, because she was not in her right mind, I knew at least in a part of myself that these accusations were unfounded. Yet they produced a doubt in me, a lingering shadow, the sense that perhaps I deserved whatever suffering befell me, and that shadow lingers.

Even if a feeling has been made secret, even if it has vanished from memory, can it have disappeared altogether? A weapon is lifted with the force of a forgotten memory. The memory has no words, only the insistence of a pain that has turned into fury. A body, tender in its childhood or its nakedness, lies under this weapon. And this body takes up the rage, the pain, the disowned memory with each blow.

1893. *Self-portrait at Table.* An etching and aquatint, the first in a long series of self-portraits that span the artist's life. A single lamp illuminates her face, the upper part of the body and the table where she sits. Everything else is in darkness. At first glance one thinks of loneliness. But after a moment it is solitude one sees. And a single moment in that solitude, as if one note of music, resonant and deep, played uninterrupted, echoing from every surface, coming to full consciousness in this woman, who in this instant looks out to those who will return her gaze with a face that has taken in and is expressing the music in the air about her. Solemnly and with a quiet patience, her hands pause over the etching she makes, a form she is bringing into being, the one she recognizes as herself.

Who are we? The answer is not easy. There are so many strands to the story, and one must trace every strand. I begin to suspect each thread goes out infinitely and touches everything, everyone. I read these words from an ancient gnostic text, words that have been lost to us for a long time: *For I am the first and the last.* Though in another account we have heard the beginning of this speech spoken by Jesus, here these words come to us in the voice of the goddess. *I am the honored one and scorned one,* the older text goes on. *I am the whore and the holy one. I am the wife and the virgin. I am the barren one, and many are her sons.* These words take on a new meaning for me, as I remember them now. *I am the silence that is incomprehensible,* the text reads, and ends, *I am the utterance of my name.*

Were you to trace any life, and study even the minute consequences, the effect, for instance, of a three-minute walk over a patch of grass, of words said casually to a stranger who happens to sit nearby in a public place, the range of that life would extend way beyond the territory we imagine it to inhabit. This is of course less difficult to understand when imagining the boundaries of a life such as Heinrich Himmler had.

After my visit to Dachau, I went to Paris where, in the fourteenth arrondissement, in the Métro station, I met Hélène. She stopped to help me read my map. We found we were going in the same direction, and thus it was on our way there that we began to speak. Something told me she had survived a concentration camp. And she had. She too fell into the circle of Himmler's life and its consequences. Himmler never went to Paris. At the time of the first mass arrests there he was taking a group of high Nazi officials on a tour of Auschwitz. During the tour, by his orders, the prisoners were made to stand at attention for six hours under the hot sun, but that is another story. Under his command, the Gestapo in Paris began to prepare for the mass arrests of Jews.

Paris had fallen to the German armies in July 1940. By September of that year a notice went up in all the neighborhoods. *Avis aux Israélites*, it read. *Notice to Israelites. By the demand of the occupying authorities, Israelites must present themselves, by October 2, without delay, equipped with identification papers, to the office of the Censor, to complete an identity card.* The notice was signed by the mayor and threatened the most severe punishment for the failure to comply. Through this process vital information was recorded about each Jewish family. Names, ages, addresses, occupations, places of work. An index card was made up for each person. And each card was then duplicated and sent to the offices of the Gestapo on Avenue Foch. There, the cards were duplicated several more times so that the names could be filed by several categories, alphabetically by surname, by address, by arrondissement, occupation, and nationality. At this point in history, work that would be done by computer now was painstakingly completed by countless men and women. Their labor continued feverishly almost until the hour of the first mass arrests, the *rafles*, two years later.

One can trace every death to an order signed by Himmler, yet these arrests could never have taken place on such a massive scale without this vast system of information. What did they think, those who were enlisted for this work? They were civilians. French. There were of course Nazi collaborators, among them, those who shared the same philosophy, or who simply obeyed and profited from whoever might be in power. But among the men and women who did this work, my suspicion is, there were many who tried to keep from themselves the knowledge of what they did. Of course, the final purpose of their labors was never revealed to those who prepared the machinery of arrest. If a man allowed his imagination to stray in the direction of this purpose, he could no doubt comfort himself with the argument that he was only handling pieces of paper. He could tell himself that matters were simply being set in order. The men and women who manufacture the trigger mechanisms for nuclear bombs do not tell themselves they are making weapons. They say simply that they are metal forgers.

There are many ways we have of standing outside ourselves in ignorance. Those who have learned as children to become strangers to themselves do not find this a difficult task. Habit has made it natural not to feel. To ignore the consequences of what one does in the world becomes ordinary. And this tendency is encouraged by a social structure that makes fragments of real events. One is never allowed to see the effects of what one does. But this ignorance is not entirely passive. For some, blindness becomes a kind of refuge, a way of life that is chosen, even with stubborn volition, and does not yield easily even to visible evidence.

The arrests were accompanied by an elaborate procedure, needed on some level, no doubt, for practical reasons, but also serving another purpose. They garbed this violence in the cloak of legality. A mind separated from the depths of itself cannot easily tell right from wrong. To this mind, the outward signs of law and order signify righteousness. That Himmler had such a mind was not unique in his generation, nor, I suspect, in ours.

In a museum in Paris I found a mimeographed sheet giving instructions to the Parisian police on how to arrest Jews. They must always carry red pencils, the sheet admonished, because all records regarding the arrests of Jews must be written in red. And the instructions went on to specify that, regarding the arrests of Jews, all records must be made in triplicate. Finally, the sheet of instructions included a way to categorize those Jews arrested. I could not make any sense of the categories. I only knew them to be crucial. That they might determine life and death for a woman, or man, or child. And that in the mind that invented these categories they had to have had some hidden significance, standing, like the crudely shaped characters of a medieval play, for shades of feeling, hidden states of being, secret knowledge.

For the most part, the men who designed the first missiles were not interested in weapons so much as flight. In his account of the early work at Peenemünde laboratories, Wernher von Braun explains that the scientists there had discovered a way to fund their research by making rockets appeal to the military. Colonel Dornberger told the other scientists that they could not hope to continue if all they created were experimental rockets. All Wernher von Braun wanted was to design vehicles that would travel to the moon. In the early fifties, in a book he wrote with two other scientists, he speaks of the reasons for such a flight. Yes, he says, curiosity and adventure play a part. But the primary reason is *to increase man's knowledge of the universe.*

To tell a story, or to hear a story told, is not a simple transmission of information. Something else in the telling is given too, so that, once hearing, what one has heard becomes a part of oneself. Hélène and I went to the museum in Paris together. There, among photographs of the first mass arrests and the concentration camp at Drancy, she told me this story. Reading the notice signed by the mayor, she presented herself immediately at the office of the censor. She waited with others, patiently. But when her turn in line came, the censor looked at her carefully. She was blond and had blue eyes. *Are you really Jewish?* he asked her.

The question of who was and who was not Jewish was pivotal to the Nazi mind and much legal controversy hung in the balance of this debate. For a few years, anyone with three Jewish grandparents was considered Jewish. An ancestor who belonged to the faith, but was not of Jewish blood would be Jewish. One who did not belong to the faith, but was of Jewish blood, was also Jewish. At the heart of this controversy, I hear the whisper of ambivalence, and perhaps the smallest beginning of compassion. For, to this mind, the one who is not Jewish becomes recognizable as like oneself.

*Yes, I am Jewish,* she said. *But your mother,* he asked again. *Can you be certain? Yes,* she said. *Ask her, go home and ask her,* he said, putting his stamp away. *But my mother is dead,* she protested. Then, he said, keeping his stamp in the drawer, *Your father. Your father must not be Jewish. Go home and ask him. I know he is Jewish,* Hélène answered. *There is no doubt that he is Jewish. He has always been Jewish, and I am Jewish too.* Then the man was silent, he shook his head. And, looking past her, said, *Perhaps your father was not really your father. Have you thought of that? Perhaps he was not your father?* She was young. *Of course he's my father. How can you say that? Certainly he is my father,* she insisted. *He is Jewish and so am I.* And she demanded that her papers be stamped.

What was in this man's mind as he questioned her? Did he say to himself, Perhaps here is someone I can save? Did he have what Pierre Sauvage has called *a moment of goodness?* What we know as goodness is not a static quality but arrives through a series of choices, some imperceptible, which are continually presented to us.

It is 1941. And Heinrich Himmler pays a visit to the Russian front. He has been put in charge of organizing the *Einsatzgruppen,* moving groups of men who carry out the killing of civilians and partisans. He watches as a deep pit is dug by the captured men and women. Then, suddenly, a young man catches his eye. He is struck by some quality the man possesses. He takes a liking to him. He has the commandant of the *Einsatzgruppen* bring the young man to him. *Who was your father?* he asks. *Your mother? Your grandparents? Do you have at least one grandparent who was not Jewish?* He is trying to save the young man. But he answers no to all the questions. So Himmler, strictly following the letter of the law, watches as the young man is put to death.

The captured men, women, and children are ordered to remove their clothing then. Naked, they stand before the pit they have dug. Some scream. Some attempt escape. The young men in uniform place their rifles against their shoulders and fire into the naked bodies. They do not fall silently. There are cries. There are open wounds. There are faces blown apart. Stomachs opened up. The dying groan. Weep. Flutter. Open their mouths.

There is no photograph of the particular moment when Heinrich Himmler stares into the face of death. What does he look like? Is he pale? He is stricken, the accounts tell us, and more than he thought he would be. He has imagined something quieter, more efficient, like the even rows of numbers, the alphabetical lists of names he likes to put in his files. Something he might be able to understand and contain. But one cannot contain death so easily.

*Death with Girl in Her Lap.* One of many studies the artist did of death. A girl is drawn, her body dead or almost dead, in that suspended state where the breath is almost gone. There is no movement. No will. The lines the artist has drawn are simple. She has not rendered the natural form of head, arm, buttock, thigh exactly. But all these lines hold the feeling of a body in them. And as my eyes rest on this image, I can feel my own fear of death, and also, the largeness of grief, how grief will not let you remain insulated from your own feelings, or from life itself. It is as if I knew this girl. And death, too, appears to know her, cradling the fragile body with tenderness; she seems to understand the sorrow of dying. Perhaps this figure has taken into herself all the deaths she has witnessed. And in this way, she has become merciful.

Because Himmler finds it so difficult to witness these deaths, the commandant makes an appeal to him. If it is hard for you, he says, think what it must be for these young men who must carry out these executions, day after day. Shaken by what he has seen and heard, Himmler returns to Berlin resolved to ease the pain of these men. He will consult an engineer and set him to work immediately on new designs. Before the year has ended, he presents the *Einsatzgruppen* with a mobile killing truck. Now the young men will not have to witness death day after day. A hose from the exhaust pipe funnels fumes into a chamber built on the bed of a covered truck, which has a red cross painted on its side so its passengers will not be alarmed as they enter it.

To a certain kind of mind, what is hidden away ceases to exist.

Himmler does not like to watch the suffering of his prisoners. In this sense he does not witness the consequences of his own commands. But the mind is like a landscape in which nothing really ever disappears. What seems to have vanished has only transmuted to another form. Not wishing to witness what he has set in motion, still, in a silent part of himself, he must imagine what takes place. So, just as the child is made to live out the unclaimed imagination of the parent, others under Himmler's power were made to bear witness for him. Homosexuals were forced to witness and sometimes take part in the punishment of other homosexuals, Poles of other Poles, Jews of Jews. And as far as possible, the hands of the men of the SS were protected from the touch of death. Other prisoners were required to bury the bodies, or burn them in the ovens.

Hélène was turned in by a Jewish man who was trying, no doubt, to save his own life, and she was put under arrest by another Jewish man, an inmate of the same camp to which she was taken. She was grateful that she herself had not been forced to do harm. But something haunted her. A death that came to stand in place of her own death. As we walked through the streets of Paris she told me this story.

By the time of her arrest she was married and had a young son. Her husband was taken from their apartment during one of the mass arrests that began in July of 1942. Hélène was out at the time with her son. For some time she wandered the streets of Paris. She would sleep at night at the homes of various friends and acquaintances, leaving in the early morning so that she would not arouse suspicion among the neighbors. This was the hardest time, she told me, because there was so little food, even less than she was to have at Drancy. She had no ration card or any way of earning money. Her whole existence was illegal. She had to be as if invisible. She collected scraps from the street. It was on the street that she told me this story, as we walked from the fourth arrondissement to the fifth, crossing the bridge near Notre Dame, making our way toward the Boulevard St. Michel.

Her husband was a citizen of a neutral country and for this reason legally destined for another camp. From this camp he would not be deported. Instead he was taken to the French concentration camp at Drancy. After his arrest, hoping to help him, Hélène managed to take his papers to the Swiss Consulate. But the papers remained there. After her own arrest she was taken with her son to Drancy, where she was reunited with her husband. He told her that her efforts were useless. But still again and again she found ways to smuggle out letters to friends asking them to take her husband's papers from the Swiss Consulate to the camp at Drancy. One of these letters was to save their lives.

After a few months, preparations began to send Hélène and her family to Auschwitz. Along with many other women, she was taken to have her hair cut short, though those consigned to that task decided she should keep her long, blond hair. Still, she was herded along with the others to the train station and packed into the cars. Then, just two hours before the train was scheduled to leave, Hélène, her son, and her husband were pulled from the train. Her husband's papers had been brought by the Swiss consul to the camp. The Commandant, by assuming Hélène shared the same nationality with her husband, had made a fortuitous mistake.

But the train had to have a specific number of passengers before it could leave. In Hélène's place the guards brought a young man. She would never forget his face, she told me, or his name. Later she tried to find out whether he had lived or died but could learn nothing.

• • •

Himmler did not partake in the actual preparations for what he called "the final solution." Nor did he attend the Wannsee Conference where the decision to annihilate millions of human beings was made. He sent his assistant Heydrich. Yet Heydrich, who was there, did not count himself entirely present. He could say that each decision he made was at the bequest of Heinrich Himmler. In this way an odd system of insulation was created. These crimes, these murders of millions, were all carried out in absentia, as if by no one in particular.

This ghostlike quality, the strange absence of a knowing conscience, as if the living creature had abandoned the shell, was spread throughout the entire chain of command. So a French bureaucrat writing a letter in 1942 speaks in detail of the mass arrests that he himself supervised as if he had no other part in these murders except as a kind of spiritless cog in a vast machine whose force compelled him from without. *The German authorities have set aside especially for that purpose enough trains to transport 30,000 Jews,* he writes. *It is therefore necessary that the arrests made should correspond to the capacity of the trains.*

It is August 23, 1943. The first inmates of concentration camp Dora have arrived. Is there some reason why an unusually high percentage of prisoners ordered to work in this camp are homosexuals? They are set to work immediately, working with few tools, often with bare hands, to convert long tunnels carved into the Harz Mountains into a factory for the manufacture of missiles. They work for eighteen hours each day. Six of these hours are set aside for formal procedures, roll calls, official rituals of the camp. For six hours they must try to sleep in the tunnels, on the damp earth, in the same area where the machines, pickaxes, explosions, and drills are making a continually deafening noise, twenty-four hours of every day. They are fed very little. They see the daylight only once a week, at the Sunday roll call. The tunnels themselves are illuminated with faint light bulbs. The production of missiles has been moved here because the factories at Peenemünde were bombed. Because the secret work at Peenemünde had been revealed to the Allies by an informer, after the bombing the Reichsführer SS proposed that the factories should be installed in a concentration camp. Here, he argued, security could be more easily enforced; only the guards had any freedom, and they were subject to the harsh discipline of the SS. The labor itself could be hidden under the soil of the Harz Mountains.

Memory can be like a long, half-lit tunnel, a tunnel where one is likely to encounter phantoms of a self, long concealed, no longer nourished with the force of consciousness, existing in a tortured state between life and death. In his account of his years at Peenemünde, Wernher von Braun never mentions concentration camp Dora. Yet he was seen there more than once by inmates who remembered him. As the designing engineer, he had to supervise many details of production. Conditions at camp Dora

could not have escaped his attention. Dora did not have its own cremato-
rium. And so many men and women died in the course of a day that the
bodies waiting to be picked up by trucks and taken to the ovens of
Buchenwald were piled high next to the entrance to the tunnels.

Perhaps von Braun told himself that what went on in those tunnels
had nothing to do with him. He had not wished for these events, had not
wanted them. The orders came from someone who had power over him.
In the course of this writing I remembered a childhood incident that made
me disown myself in the same way. My best friend, who was my neighbor, had a mean streak and because of this had a kind of power over the
rest of us who played with her. For a year I left my grandmother's house
to live with my mother again. On my return I had been replaced by another little girl, and the two of them excluded me. But finally my chance
arrived. My friend had a quarrel with her new friend and enlisted me in
an act of revenge. Together we cornered her at the back of a yard, pushing
her into the garbage cans, yelling nasty words at her, throwing things at
her.

My friend led the attack, inventing the strategies and the words which
were hurled. With part of myself I knew what it was to be the object of this
kind of assault. But I also knew this was the way to regain my place with
my friend. Later I disowned my acts, as if I had not committed them. Because I was under the sway of my friend's power, I told myself that what I
did was really her doing. And in this way became unreal to myself. It was
as if my voice threatening her, my own anger, and my voice calling
names, had never existed.

I was told this story by a woman who survived the holocaust. The war
had not yet begun. Nor the exiles. Nor the mass arrests. But history was
on the point of these events, tipping over, ready to fall into the relentless
path of consequences. She was then just a child, playing games in the
street. And one day she found herself part of a circle of other children.
They had surrounded a little boy and were calling him names because he
was Jewish. He was her friend. But she thought if she left this circle, or
came to his defense, she herself would lose her standing among the others.
Then, suddenly, in an angry voice her mother called her in from the street.
As soon as the door shut behind her, her mother began to shout, words incomprehensible to her, and slapped her across the face. *Your father*, her
mother finally said, after crying, and in a quieter voice, *was Jewish*. Her father had been dead for three years. Soon after this day her mother too
would die. As the danger grew worse her gentile relatives would not har-
bor her any longer, and she joined the fate of those who tried to live in the
margins, as if invisible, as if mere shadows, terrified of a direct glance, of
recognition, existing at the unsteady boundary of consciousness.

In disowning the effects we have on others, we disown ourselves. My
father watched the suffering of my childhood and did nothing. He was

aware of my mother's alcoholism and the state of her mind when she drank. He knew my grandmother to be tyrannical. We could speak together of these things almost dispassionately, as if both of us were disinterested witnesses to a fascinating social drama. But after a day's visit with him, spent at the park, or riding horses, or at the movies, he would send me back into that world of suffering we had discussed so dispassionately.

His disinterest in my condition was not heartless. It reflected the distance he kept from his own experience. One could sense his suffering but he never expressed it directly. He was absent to a part of himself. He was closer to tears than many men, but he never shed those tears. If I cried he would fall into a frightened silence. And because of this, though I spent a great deal of time with him, he was always in a certain sense an absent father. Unknowingly I responded in kind, for years, feeling a vaguely defined anger that would neither let me love nor hate him.

My father learned his disinterest under the guise of masculinity. Boys don't cry. There are whole disciplines, institutions, rubrics in our culture which serve as categories of denial.

Science is such a category. The torture and death that Heinrich Himmler found disturbing to witness became acceptable to him when it fell under this rubric. He liked to watch the scientific experiments in the concentration camps. And then there is the rubric of military order. I am looking at a photograph. It was taken in 1941 in the Ukraine. The men of an *Einstazgruppen* are assembled in a group pose. In front of them their rifles rest in ceremonial order, composed into tripods. They stand straight and tall. They are clean-shaven and their uniforms are immaculate, in *apple-pie order,* as we would say in America.

It is not surprising that cleanliness in a profession that sheds blood would become a compulsion. Blood would evidence guilt and fear to a mind trying to escape the consequence of its decisions. It is late in the night when Laura tells me one more story. Her father is about to be sent to Europe, where he will fight in the Battle of the Bulge and become a general. For weeks her mother has prepared a party. The guests begin to arrive in formal dress and sparkling uniforms. The white-gloved junior officers stand to open the doors. Her mother, regal in satin and jewels, starts to descend the staircase. Laura sits on the top stair watching, dressed in her pajamas. Then suddenly a pool of blood appears at her mother's feet, her mother falls to the floor, and almost as quickly, without a word uttered, a junior officer sweeps up the stairs, removes her mother into a waiting car, while another one cleans up the blood. No one tells Laura that her mother has had a miscarriage, and the party continues as if no event had taken place, no small or large death, as if no death were about to take place, nor any blood be spilled.

But the nature of the material world frustrates our efforts to remain free of the suffering of others. The mobile killing van that Himmler summoned into being had some defects. Gas from the exhaust pipes leaked into the cabin where the drivers sat and made them ill. When they went to remove the bodies from the van they were covered with blood and excrement, and their faces bore expressions of anguish. Himmler's engineers fixed the leak, increased the flow of gas so the deaths would be quicker, and built in a drain to collect the bodily fluids that are part of death.

There are times when no engineers can contain death. Over this same landscape through which the mobile killing vans traveled, an invisible cloud would one day spread, and from it would descend a toxic substance that would work its way into the soil and the water, the plants and the bodies of animals, and into human cells, not only in this landscape of the Ukraine, but in the fjords of Norway, the fields of Italy and France, and even here, in the far reaches of California, bringing a death that recalled, more than forty years later, those earlier hidden deaths.

You can see pictures of them. Whole families, whole communities. The fabric on their backs almost worn through. Bodies as if ebbing away before your eyes. Poised on an edge. The cold visible around the thin joints of arms and knees. A bed made in a doorway. Moving then, over time, deeper and deeper into the shadows. Off the streets. Into back rooms, and then to the attics or the cellars. Windows blackened. Given less and less to eat. Moving into smaller and smaller spaces. Sequestered away like forbidden thoughts, or secrets.

Could he have seen in these images of those he had forced into hiding and suffering, into agony and death, an image of the outer reaches of his own consciousness? It is only now that I can begin to see he has become part of them. Those whose fate he sealed. Heinrich Himmler. A part of Jewish history. Remembered by those who fell into the net of his unclaimed life. Claimed as a facet of the wound, part of the tissue of the scar. A mark on the body of our minds, both those of us who know this history and those who do not.

For there is a sense in which we are all witnesses. Hunger, desperation, pain, loneliness, these are all visible in the streets about us. The way of life we live, a life we have never really chosen, forces us to walk past what we see. And out at the edge, beyond what we see or hear, we can feel a greater suffering, cries from a present or past starvation, a present or past torture, cries of those we have never met, coming to us in our dreams, and even if these cries do not survive in our waking knowledge, still, they live on in the part of ourselves we have ceased to know.

I think now of the missile again and how it came into being. Scientific inventions do not spring whole like Athena from the head of Zeus from the analytic implications of scientific discoveries. Technological advance takes shape slowly in the womb of society and is influenced and fed by our shared imagination. What we create thus mirrors the recesses of our own minds, and perhaps also hidden capacities. Television mimics the ability to see in the mind's eye. And the rocket? Perhaps the night flight of the soul, that ability celebrated in witches to send our thoughts as if through the air to those distant from us, to send images of ourselves, and even our secret feelings, out into an atmosphere beyond ourselves, to see worlds far flung from and strange to us becomes manifest in a sinister fashion in the missile.

Self-portrait in charcoal. Since the earliest rendering she made of her own image, much time has passed. The viewer here has moved closer. Now the artist's head fills the frame. She is much older in years and her features have taken on that androgyny which she thought necessary to the work of an artist. Her hair is white on the paper where the charcoal has not touched it. She is in profile and facing a definite direction. Her eyes look in that direction. But they do not focus on anyone or anything. The portrait is soft, the charcoal rubbed almost gently over the surface, here light, here dark. Her posture is one not so much of resolution as resignation. The portrait was drawn just after the First World War, the war in which her son Peter died. I have seen these eyes in the faces of those who grieve, eyes that are looking but not focused, seeing perhaps what is no longer visible.

*After the war, German scientists who developed the V-1 and V-2 rocket immigrate to the United States where they continue to work on rocketry. Using the Vengeance weapon as a prototype, they develop the first ICBM missiles.*

On the twenty-third of May 1945, as the war in Europe comes to an end, Heinrich Himmler is taken prisoner by the Allied command. He has removed the military insignia from his clothing, and he wears a patch over one eye. Disguised in this manner, and carrying the identity papers of a man he had condemned to death, he attempts to cross over the border at Bremervörde. No one at the checkpoint suspects him of being the Reichsführer SS. But once under the scrutiny of the guards, all his courage fails him. Like a trembling schoolboy, he blurts out the truth. Now he will be taken to a center for interrogation, stripped of his clothing and searched. He will refuse to wear the uniform of the enemy, so he will be given a blanket to wrap over his underclothing. Taken to a second center for interrogation, he will be forced to remove this blanket and his underclothes. The interrogators, wishing to make certain he has no poison hidden anywhere, no means by which to end his life and hence avoid giving testimony, will surround his naked body. They will ask him to open his mouth. But just as one of them sees a black capsule wedged between his teeth, he will jerk his head away and swallow. All attempts to save his life will fail. He will not survive to tell his own story. His secrets will die with him.

There were many who lived through those years who did not wish to speak of what they saw or did. None of the German rocket engineers bore witness to what they saw at concentration camp Dora. Common rank and file members of the Nazi Party, those without whose efforts or silent support the machinery could not have gone on, fell almost as a mass into silence. In Berlin and Munich I spoke to many men and women, in my generation or younger, who were the children of soldiers, or party members, or SS men, or generals, or simply believers. Their parents would not speak to them of what had happened. The atmosphere in both cities was as if a pall had been placed over memory. And thus the shared mind of this nation has no roots, no continuous link with what keeps life in a pattern of meaning.

Lately I have come to believe that an as yet undiscovered human need and even a property of matter is the desire for revelation. The truth within us has a way of coming out despite all conscious efforts to conceal it. I have heard stories from those in the generation after the war, all speaking of the same struggle to ferret truth from the silence of their parents so that they themselves could begin to live. One born the year the war ended was never told a word about concentration camps, at home or in school. She began to wake in the early morning hours with nightmares which mirrored down to fine and accurate detail the conditions of the camps. Another woman searching casually through some trunks in the attic of her home found a series of pamphlets, virulently and cruelly anti-Semitic, which had been written by her grandfather, a high Nazi official. Still another pieced together the truth of her father's life, a member of the Gestapo, a man she remembered as playful by contrast to her stern mother. He died in the war. Only over time could she put certain pieces together. How he had had a man working under him beaten. And then, how he had beaten her.

Many of those who survived the holocaust could not bear the memories of what happened to them and, trying to bury the past, they too fell into silence. Others continue to speak as they are able. The manner of speech varies. At an artist's retreat in the Santa Cruz Mountains I met a woman who survived Bergen Belsen and Auschwitz. She inscribes the number eight in many of her paintings. And the number two. This is the story she is telling with those numbers. It was raining the night she arrived with her mother, six brothers and sisters at Auschwitz. It fell very hard, she told me. We were walking in the early evening up a hill brown in the California fall. The path was strewn with yellow leaves illuminated by the sun in its descent. They had endured the long trip from Hungary to Poland, without food or water. They were very tired. Now the sky seemed very black but the platform, lit up with stadium lights, was blinding after the darkness of the train. She would never, she told me, forget the shouting. It is as if she still cannot get the sound out of her ears. The Gestapo gave one shrill order after another, in a language she did not yet understand. They were herded in confusion, blows coming down on them randomly from the guards, past a tall man in a cape. This was Dr. Mengele. He made a single gesture toward all her family and continued it toward her but in a different direction. For days, weeks, months after she had learned what their fate had been she kept walking in the direction of their parting and beyond toward the vanishing point of her vision of them.

There were seven from her family who died there that night. The eighth to die was her father. He was sent to a different camp and died on the day of liberation. Only two lived, she and one brother. The story of one life cannot be told separately from the story of other lives. Who are we? The question is not simple. What we call the self is part of a larger matrix of relationship and society. Had we been born to a different family, in a different time, to a different world, we would not be the same. All the lives that surround us are in us.

On the first day that I met Lenke she asked a question that stays with me still. Why do some inflict on others the suffering they have endured? What is it in a life that makes one choose to do this, or not? It is a question I cannot answer. Not even after several years pondering this question in the light of Heinrich Himmler's soul. Two years after my conversation with Lenke, as if there had been a very long pause in our dialogue, I was given a glimpse in the direction of an answer. Leo told me his story; it sounded back over time, offering not so much solution as response.

*The nucleus of every cell in the human body contains the genetic plan for the whole organism.*

We sat together in a large and noisy restaurant, light pouring through the windows, the present clamoring for our attention, even as we moved into the past. Leo was nine years old when the war entered his life. He remembers standing in a crowd, he told me, watching as a partisan was flogged and executed by the Germans. *What do you think I felt?* he asked me, the irony detectable in his voice. What he told me fell into his narration as part of a larger picture. The capture, the roughness, the laceration of flesh, the sight of death, all this excited him.

Violence was not new to him. Through bits and pieces surrounding the central line of his story I came to some idea of what his childhood must have been. His father was a cold man, given to rages over small errors. Leo was beaten often. Such attacks had already forced his older half brother out of the house. It was to this brother that Leo bonded and gave his love.

Leo remembered a party before the war. The room was lively with talk until his older brother arrived. Then a silence fell over everyone. The older men were afraid of this young man, even his father. And to Leo, his brother, with his air of power and command, was a hero. He could scarcely understand the roots of this power, moored in a political system of terror so effective, few even spoke of it. Leo's brother was a young member of Stalin's secret police. Cast into the streets while still a boy, he learned the arts of survival. Eventually he was arrested for assaulting and robbing a man. It was under this circumstance that he offered himself to the NKVD, the forerunner of the KGB, as an interrogator. He learned to torture men and women suspected of treason or of harboring secrets.

He wore high black leather boots and a black leather jacket, which impressed Leo. Leo followed him about, and they would take long walks together, his brother telling him the stories he could tell no one else. How he had tortured a woman. How he had made blood flow from the nipples of her breasts.

Everything he heard from his brother he took into himself. Such love as Leo had for his brother can be a forceful teacher. He did not see his brother often, nor was his intimacy with him great enough to create familiarity. What he had was a continual taste awakening hunger. Never did he know the daily presence of the beloved, or all his imperfections, the real person dwelling behind the mask of the ideal, the shiny and impervious leather. To fill the nearly perpetual absence of his brother he clung to this ideal. An appearance of strength. A certain arrogance in the face of violence, promising an even greater violence. Love always seeks a resting place.

I knew a similar attachment to my sister. Separated when I was six and she was thirteen, the experience of love I knew with her was longing, and over time this bonded me to longing itself. And to the books she brought me to read, the poems she read to me, worlds she pointed me toward.

And the German occupation of the Ukraine? The accident at Chernobyl had taken place just weeks before we met. But long before this event, the same land suffered other wounds. As the Soviet army retreated, they burned crops and killed livestock. Even before the German invasion, the land was charred and black for miles around. Then when the German army came, the executions began. And the deportations. Many were taken away to forced labor camps. Leo was among them.

His father was an agronomist with some knowledge of how to increase crop yields. The whole family was transported to Germany, but at the scientist's camp Leo was transported in another direction. His father watched him go, Leo told me, with no protest, not even the protestation of tears.

What was it like for him in the labor camp to which he was sent? His telling of the past existed in a framework of meaning he had built slowly over the years, and with great pain, forced to this understanding by events that he himself had brought into being, later in his life.

It is a question of passion, he told me. While he was in the camps, he began to worship the uniformed members of the SS and the SA, just as he had loved his brother. Their strength, their ideals, their willingness to do violence, to live for something beyond themselves, the black leather they wore, the way they were clean and polished and tall. He saw those who, like himself, were imprisoned as small and demeaned, caught in the ugliness of survival, lacking any heroism, cowardly, petty. Even now, as he looked back himself with another eye, his disdain for those who suffered persisted in a phantom form, in the timbre of his voice.

The punishment of the guards did not embitter him. In his mind he believed he himself was always justly punished. Once, against the rules, he stole food, honey, while he was working. He did not accept his own hunger as an argument for kindness. He admired the strength with which he was hit. Even the intimacy of the blows gave him a certain pride in himself. Loving the arms that hit him, he could think of this power as his own.

But there were two assaults which he could not forgive. They humiliated him. Now as I write I can see that to him his attackers must have been unworthy of his admiration. He was on a work detail in the neighboring village when a boy his own age slapped him. And later an old woman spat in his face.

This was all he told me of his time of imprisonment. After the liberation, he went into Germany to search for his family. Did he believe that perhaps, even now, something outside of the circle drawn by what he had suffered existed for him? Was there a seed of hope, a wish that made him, thin, weak, on shaking legs, travel the hundreds of miles, sleeping in trains and train stations, to search? He was exhausted, I can imagine, past that edge of weariness in which whatever is real ceases entirely to matter and existence itself is just a gesture, not aimed any longer at outcome, but just a simple expression of what remains and so can seem even brighter. He was making a kind of pilgrimage.

It is in this way, coldness beyond cold, frailty beyond endurance, that sorrow becomes a power. A light begins to shine past the fire of ovens, yet from them, as if stars, or turning leaves, falling and trapped in their fall, nevertheless kept their brilliance, and this brilliance a beacon, like a code, flashes out the precise language of human suffering. Then we know that what we suffer is not going to pass by without meaning.

*Self-portrait, 1923.* The artist's face is drawn of lines left white on the page which seem as if they were carved out of night. We are very close to her. It is only her face we see. Eye to eye, she looks directly at us. But her eyes are unfocused and weary with that kind of tiredness that has accumulated over so much time we think of it as aging. Her mouth, wide and frank, does not resist gravity any longer. This mouth smiles with an extraordinary subtlety. We can almost laugh with this mouth, drawn with lines which, like all the lines on the page, resemble scars, or tears in a fabric.

A story is told as much by silence as by speech. Like the white spaces in an etching, such silences render form. But unlike an etching in which the whole is grasped at once, the silence of a story must be understood over time. Leo described to me what his life was like after he found his parents, but he did not describe the moment, or even the day or week, when he found them. Only now as I write these words does the absence of joy in this reunion begin to speak to me. And in the space of this absence I can feel the kind of cold that can extinguish the most intense of fires.

Leo was soon streetwise. His family was near starvation. He worked the black market. Older men buying his goods would ask him for women, and he began to procure for them. He kept his family alive. His father, he told me, never acknowledged his effort. When they moved to America a few years later and Leo reminded him that his work had fed him, his father exclaimed, in a voice of shock and disparagement, *And what you did!*

*In 1957, the Soviet Union develops the SS-6, a surface-to-surface missile. It is launched with thirty-two engines. Failing as a weapon, this device is used to launch the first satellite into space. In 1961, the Soviet Union develops the SS-7. These missiles carry nuclear warheads. They are launched from hardened silos to protect them from attack.*

In America he was sent to high school. But he did not know how to be an ordinary boy among boys. He became a street fighter. Together with a group of boys among whom he was the toughest, he would look for something to happen. More than once they devised a trap for homosexual men. They would place the prettiest boy among them on a park bench and wait behind the trees and bushes. Usually a man would pull up in his car and go to sit on the bench next to the boy. When this man made any gesture of seduction, or suggested the boy leave with him, the boys would suddenly appear and, surrounding him, beat him and take his money.

I am thinking of these boys as one after another they forced the weight of their bodies into another man's body and tried to hurt him, to bloody him, to defeat him. I know it is possible to be a stranger to one's feelings. For the years after I was separated from my mother, I forgot that I missed her. My feeling was driven so deep, it was imperceptible, so much a part of me, I would not have called it grief. It is said that when boys or young men attack a man they find effeminate or believe to be homosexual they are trying to put at a distance all traces of homosexuality in themselves. But what does this mean? What is the central passion in this issue of manhood, proven or disproven? In my imagination I witness again the scene that Leo described to me. It is a passionate scene, edged by a love the boys feel for each other, and by something more, by a kind of grief, raging because it is buried so deep inside. Do they rage against this man's body because of what has been withheld from them, held back, like the food of intimacy, imprisoned and guarded in the bodies of older men, in the bodies of fathers? Is it this rage that fires the mettle of what we call manhood?

Yet, are we not all affected by this that is withheld in men? Are we not all forged in the same inferno? It was never said directly, but I know my great-grandfather beat my grandfather, and lectured him, drunkenly, humiliating and shaming him. I am told that as adults they quarreled violently over politics. No one in my family can remember the substance of the disagreement, only the red faces, the angry voices. Now, as I look back to imagine my grandfather passionately reciting the list of those he hated, our black neighbors, the Jews, the Communists, I follow the path of his staring eyes and begin to make out a figure. It is my great-grandfather Colvin, receiving even after his death too indifferently the ardent and raging pleas of his son. And hearing that voice again, I hear an echo from my grandfather's daughter, my mother, whose voice when she had been drinking too much had the same quality, as of the anguish of feeling held back for so long it has become monstrous, the furies inside her unleashed against me.

Leo's telling had a slightly bitter edge, a style which felt like the remnant of an older harshness. He kept looking at me as if to protect himself from any sign of shock in my face. Now he was not certain he would tell me the rest of his story. But he did.

Just after he graduated from high school, the Korean War began. He was drafted, and sent directly to Korea. Was he in combat? Leo shook his head. He was assigned to an intelligence unit. He spoke Russian. And he was directed to interrogate Russian prisoners who were captured behind enemy lines. He told me this story. He was given two men to question. With the first man he made every kind of threat. But he carried nothing out. The man was resolutely silent. And Leo learned nothing from him. He left the room with all his secrets. *You can never*, Leo told me later, *let any man get the better of you.* With the second man he was determined not to fail. He would get him to tell whatever he knew. He made the same threats again, and again met silence. Then, suddenly, using his thumb and finger, he put out the man's eye. And as the man was screaming and bleeding, he told him he would die one way or the other. He was going to be shot. But he had the choice now of seeing his executioners or not, of dying in agony or not. And then the man told him his secrets.

*Self-portrait, 1927.* She has drawn herself in charcoal again, and in profile. And she still looks out but now her eyes are focused. She is looking at something visible, distant, but perhaps coming slowly closer. Her mouth still turns down, and this must be a characteristic expression because her face is lined in that direction. The form of her face is drawn with soft strokes, blended into the page, as one life blends into another life, or a body into earth. There is something in the quality of her attention, fine lines sketched over her eyebrow. A deeper black circle under her eye. With a resolute, unhappy awareness, she recognizes what is before her.

*The life plan of the body is encoded in the DNA molecule, a substance that has the ability to hold information and to replicate itself.*

*Self-portrait, 1934.* As I look now I see in her face that whatever it was she saw before has now arrived. She looks directly at us again and we are even closer to her than before. One finger at the edge of the frame pulls against her eyebrow, against lines drawn there earlier, as if to relieve pain. All the lines lead downward, like rain. Her eyes are open but black, at once impenetrable and infinite. There is a weariness here again, the kind from which one never recovers. And grief? It is that grief I have spoken of earlier, no longer apart from the flesh and bone of her face.

After many years of silence, my mother and I were able to speak of what happened between us and in our family. It was healing for us, to hear and speak the truth, and made for a closeness we had not felt before. Both of us knew we were going to speak before we did.

Before a secret is told one can often feel the weight of it in the atmosphere. Leo gazed at me for a long moment. There was more he wanted to tell me and that I wanted to hear. The rest of his story was elsewhere, in the air, in our hands, the traffic on the street, felt. He shook his head again before he began. The war was over, but he had started in a certain direction and now he could not stop. He befriended a young man from the army. This man looked up to him the way he had to his brother. He wanted to teach the younger man what he knew. He had already committed several robberies, and he wanted an accomplice. They went out together, looking for an easy target for the young man to practice on. They found someone who was easy. He was old, and black. Leo showed his friend how to hold his gun, up close to the temple, pointing down. The boy did this. But the old man, terrified, simply ran. As Leo directed him, the younger man held the gun out in front of him to shoot and he pulled the trigger. But the cartridge of the bullet stuck in the chamber. So the man, still alive, kept running. Then, as Leo urged him on, his friend ran after the old man and, jumping on his back, began to hit him on the head with the butt of his pistol. The moment overtook him. Fear, and exhilaration at mastering fear, a deeper rage, all made a fuel for his fury. He hit and hit again and again. He drew blood. Then the man ceased to cry out, ceased to struggle. He lay still. And the younger man kept on hitting, so that the moment of the older man's death was lost in a frenzy of blows. Then finally there was silence. The young man, knowing he had caused a death, stood up shaking and walked away. He was stunned, as if he himself had been beaten. And Leo, who had been calling and shouting to encourage his friend, who had been laughing, he said, so hard he had to hold himself, was silent too. He went to stand by the body of the old man. Blood poured profusely from the wounds on his head. He stared into the face of this dead man. And now in his telling of the story he was crying. He paused. What was it there in that face for him, broken, afraid, shattered, flesh and bone past repair, past any effort, any strength? *I could see,* he told me, *that this man was just like me.*

*In 1963 America develops a new missile, the Titan II. It has a larger range, a larger carrying capacity, a new guidance system, and an improved vehicle for re-entry. These missiles are still being deployed.*

1938. *Self-portrait.* The artist is once again in profile. But now she faces another direction. The bones of her cheeks, mouth, nose, eyes are still all in shadow. Her eyebrows arch in tired anticipation. She has drawn herself with the simplest of strokes. Charcoal blending softly downward, all the strokes moving downward. This is old age. Not a single line drawn for vanity, or for the sake of pretense, protects us from her age. She is facing toward death.

We knew, both Leo and I, that now he was telling me what was most crucial to him. In the telling, some subtle change passed through him. Something unknown was taking shape here, both of us witnesses, both of us part of the event. This that he lived through was what I was seeking to understand. What he saw in the face of the dead man did not leave him. For a long time he was afraid of his own dreams. Every night, the same images returned to him, but images in motion, belonging to a longer narration. He dreamed that he entered a park and began to dig up a grave there. Each night he would plunge his hands in the earth and find the body buried there. But each night the body he found was more and more eroded. This erosion filled him with horror. He could not sleep alone. Every night he would find a different woman to sleep with him. Every night he would drink himself into insensibility. But the images of dreams began to come to him even in his waking hours. And so he began to drink ceaselessly. Finally he could not go on as before. Two months after the death he had witnessed he confessed his part in it.

For many reasons his sentence was light. Both he and his friend were young. They had been soldiers. He knew that, had the man he helped to kill not been black, his sentence would have been longer; or he may himself have been put to death. He said nothing of his years of imprisonment. Except that these years served to quiet the dreams that had haunted him. His wit, his air of toughness, all he had seen make him good at the work he does now with boys who have come into conflict with society, a work which must in some way be intended as restitution.

Yet, as he spoke, I began to see that he believed some part of his soul would never be retrieved. *There is a circle of humanity,* he told me, *and I can feel its warmth. But I am forever outside.*

I made no attempt to soften these words. What he said was true. A silence between us held what had been spoken. Then gradually we began to make small movements. Hands reaching for a key, a cigarette. By a quiet agreement, his story was over, and we were in the present again.

The telling and the hearing of a story is not a simple act. The one who tells must reach down into deeper layers of the self, reviving old feelings, reviewing the past. Whatever is retrieved is reworked into a new form, one that narrates events and gives the listener a path through these events that leads to some fragment of wisdom. The one who hears takes the story in, even to a place not visible or conscious to the mind, yet there. In this inner place a story from another life suffers a subtle change. As it enters the memory of the listener it is augmented by reflection, by other memories, and even the body hearing and responding in the moment of the telling. By such transmissions, consciousness is woven.

Over a year has passed now since I heard Leo's story. In my mind's eye, I see the events of his life as if they were carved out in woodblock prints, like the ones Käthe Kollwitz did. Of all her work, these most resemble Expressionist art. Was it intended that the form be so heavy, as if drawn centuries back into a mute untold history? Her work, and the work of the Expressionist movement, was called degenerate by the Nazis. These images, images of tumultuous inner feelings, or of suffering caused and hidden by social circumstance, were removed from the walls of museums and galleries.

When I was in Munich, a German friend told me that her generation has been deprived of German culture. What existed before the Third Reich was used in Nazi propaganda, and so has become as if dyed with the stain of that history. The artists and writers of the early twentieth century were silenced; they went into exile or perished. The link with the past was broken. Yet, even unremembered, the past never disappears. It exists still and continues under a mantle of silence, invisibly shaping lives.

*The DNA molecule is made of long, fine, paired strands. These strands are helically coiled.*

What is buried in the past of one generation falls to the next to claim. The children of Nazis and survivors alike have inherited a struggle between silence and speech.

The night I met Hélène at a Métro station in Paris I was returning from dinner with a friend. Ten years older than I, Jewish, French, in 1942, the year before my own birth, Natalie's life was put in danger. She was given false papers and shepherded with other children out of Paris through an underground movement. She lived out the duration of war in the countryside in the home of an ambassador who had diplomatic immunity. A woman who has remained one of her closest friends to this day was with her in this hiding place. The night we had dinner Natalie told me a story about her. This friend, she said, grew up determined to shed her past. She made Natalie promise never to reveal who she was or what had happened to her. She changed her name, denied that she was Jewish, and raised her children as gentiles. Then, opening her hands in a characteristic gesture, Natalie smiled at me. The story was to take a gently ironic turn. The past was to return. This summer, she told me, she had held one end of a bridal canopy, what in a Jewish wedding is called a chuppa, at the wedding of her friend's daughter. This girl was marrying the son of an Orthodox rabbi. And her son too, knowing nothing of his mother's past, had gravitated toward Judaism.

*In 1975 the SS-19 missile is deployed in the Soviet Union. It carries several warheads, each with a different target. A computer within it controls and detects deviations from its programmed course.*

One can find traces of every life in each life. There is a story from my own family history that urges its way onto the page here. Sometime in the eighteenth century three brothers migrated from Scotland to the United States. They came from Aberdeen and bore the name Marks, a name common in that city to Jewish families who had immigrated from Germany to escape the pogroms. Jacob Marks, who descended from these brothers, was my great-great-grandfather. The family story was that he was descended from Huguenots. In our family, only my sister and I speak of the possibility that he could have been Jewish. Jacob married Rosa and they gave birth to a daughter whom they named Sarah. She married Thomas Colvin, and their last son was Ernest Marks Colvin, my grandfather, the same grandfather who would recite to me his furious list of those he hated, including Jews.

Who would my grandfather, I wonder now, have been if he had known his own history. Could he then have seen the shape of his life as part of a larger configuration? Wasn't he without this knowledge like the missile, or the neutron torn away from gravity, the matrix that sustains and makes sense of experience?

*In any given cell only a small fraction of the genes are active. Messages to awaken these genes are transmitted by the surrounding cytoplasm, messages from other cells, or from outside substances.*

I cannot say for certain what our family history was. I know only that I did gravitate myself toward what seemed missing or lost in me. In my first years of high school I lived alone with my father. He was often gone, at work or staying with his girlfriend. I adopted the family of a school friend, spending hours with them, baby-sitting their younger children, helping with household tasks, sharing meals, spending an evening speaking of art or politics. Then one evening, as I returned home, I saw a strange man standing near my door. He had come to tell me my father was dead, struck by an automobile while he was crossing the street in the light of dusk. I turned for solace and finally shelter to my adopted family. In the short time we lived together, out of my love for them, I took on their gestures, the manner and rhythm of their thought, ways of cooking, cadences, a sprinkling of Yiddish vocabulary. I became in some ways Jewish.

*In the late seventies the United States develops a circuitry for the Minuteman rocket which allows for a target to be changed in the midst of flight.*

Is there any one of us who can count ourselves outside the circle circumscribed by our common past? Whether or not I was trying to reweave threads severed from my family history, a shared heritage of despair and hope, of destruction and sustenance, was within me. What I received from my adopted family helped me to continue my life. My suffering had been placed, even wordlessly, in a larger stream of suffering, and as if wrapped and held by a culture that had grown up to meet suffering, to retell the tales and place them in a larger context by which all life continues.

*L'chayim.* Life. Held to even at the worst times. The dream of a better world. The schoolbook, tattered, pages flying loose, gripped in the hands of a young student, his coat open at the shoulder and along the front where the fabric was worn. The ghetto of Slonim. 1938. The Passover cup, fashioned secretly by inmates at Terezin, the Passover plate, the menorah, made at the risk of death from purloined materials. Pictures drawn by those who were there. Despair, the attrition of pain, daily cold, hunger somehow entering the mark of pencil or brush. Butterflies painted by children who all later perished. Stitches made across Lenke's drawings, reminding us of the stitches she sustained in one operation after another, after her liberation, when she was stricken with tuberculosis of the spine. The prisoner forced to pick up discarded clothing of those sent to the gas chambers, who said that among this clothing, as he gathered it, he saw *Stars of David like a drift of yellow flowers.*

*As the fertilized egg cell starts to divide, all the daughter cells have identical DNA, but the cells soon cease to look alike, and in a few weeks, a number of different kinds of cells can be recognized in the embryo.*

I am thinking again of a child's body. Curled and small. Innocent. The skin soft like velvet to the touch. Eyes open and staring without reserve or calculation, quite simply, into the eyes of whoever appears in this field of vision. Without secrets. Arms open, ready to receive or give, just in the transpiration of flesh, sharing the sound of the heartbeat, the breath, the warmth of body on body.

*In 1977 the Soviet Union puts the SS-NX-17 and SS N-18 into service. These are ballistic missiles to be launched from submarines. In 1978 the United States perfects the underwater launch system of the Tomahawk missile.*

I could not, in the end, for some blessed reason, turn away from myself. Not at least in this place. The place of desire. I think now of the small lines etching themselves near the eyes of a woman's face I loved. And how, seeing these lines, I wanted to stroke her face. To lean myself, my body, my skin into her. A part of me unravels as I think of this, and I am taken toward longing, and beyond, into another region, past the walls of this house, or all I can see, stretching farther than the horizon where right now sea and sky blend. It is as if my cells are moving in a larger wave, a wave that takes in every history, every story.

*At the end of nine months a multitude of different cells make up the newborn infant's body, including nerve cells, muscle cells, skin cells, retinal cells, liver cells, brain cells, cells of the heart that beats, cells of the mouth that opens, cells of the throat that cries . . .*

When I think of that young man now, who died in the river near the island of my father's birth, died because he loved another man, I like to imagine his body bathed in the pleasure of that love. To believe that the hands that touched this young man's thighs, his buttocks, his penis, the mouth that felt its way over his body, the man who lay himself between his legs, or over, around his body did this lovingly, and that then the young man felt inside his flesh what radiated from his childlike beauty. Part angel. Bathed in a passionate sweetness. Tasting life at its youngest, most original center, the place of reason, where one is whole again as at birth.

*In the last decade the Soviet Union improves its antiballistic missiles to make them maneuverable and capable of hovering in midair. The United States continues to develop and test the MX missile, with advanced inertial guidance, capable of delivering ten prearmed electronically guided warheads, each with maneuverability, possessing the power and accuracy to penetrate hardened silos. And the Soviet Union begins to design a series of smaller one-warhead mobile missiles, the SS-25, to be driven around by truck, and the SS-X-24, to be drawn on railroad tracks. And the United States develops a new warhead for the Trident missile carrying fourteen smaller warheads that can be released in a barrage along a track or a road.*

A train is making its way through Germany. All along its route those who are in the cars can look out and see those who are outside the cars. And those who are outside can see those who are inside. Sometimes words are exchanged. Sometimes there is a plea for water. And sometimes, at the risk of life, water is given. Sometimes names are called out, or curses are spoken, under the breath. And sometimes there is only silence.

Who are those on the inside and where are they going? There are rumors. It is best not to ask. There are potatoes to buy with the last of the rations. There is a pot boiling on the stove. And, at any rate, the train has gone; the people have vanished. You did not know them. You will not see them again. Except perhaps in your dreams. But what do those images mean? Images of strangers. Agony that is not yours. A face that does not belong to you. And so in the daylight you try to erase what you have encountered and to forget those tracks that are laid even as if someplace in your body, even as part of yourself.

· · · · · · · · · · · ·

### QUESTIONS FOR A SECOND READING

1. One of the challenges a reader faces with Griffin's text is knowing what to make of it. It's a long piece, but the reading is not difficult. The sections are short and straightforward. While the essay is made up of fragments, the arrangement is not deeply confusing or disorienting. Still, the piece has no single controlling idea; it does not move from thesis to conclusion.

One way of reading the essay is to see what one can make of it, what it might add up to. In this sense, the work of reading is to find an idea, passage, image, or metaphor—something in the text—and use this to organize the essay.

As you prepare to work back through the text, think about the point of reference you could use to organize your reading. Is the essay "about" Himmler? secrets? fascism? art? Germany? the United Sates? families and child-rearing? gay and lesbian sexuality? Can one of the brief sections be taken as a key to the text? What about the italicized sections—how are they to be used?

You should not assume that one of these is the right way to read. Assume, rather, that one way of working with the text is to organize it around a single point of reference, something you could say that Griffin "put there" for you to notice and to use.

Or you might want to do this in your name rather than Griffin's. That is, you might, as you reread, chart the connections *you* make, connections that you feel belong to you (to your past, your interests, your way of reading), and think about where and how you are drawn into the text (and with what you take to be Griffin's interests and desires). You might want to be prepared to talk about why you sum things up the way you do.

2. Although this is not the kind of prose you would expect to find in a textbook for a history course, and although the project is not what we usually think of as a "research" project, Griffin is a careful researcher. The project is serious and deliberate; it is "about" history, both family history and world history. Griffin knows what she is doing. So what *is* Griffin's project? As you reread, look to those sections where Griffin seems to be speaking to her readers about her work—about how she reads and how she writes, about how she gathers her materials and how she studies them. What is she doing? What is at stake in adopting such methods? How and why might you teach someone to do this work?

### ASSIGNMENTS FOR WRITING

1. Griffin's text gathers together related fragments and works on them, but does so without yoking examples to a single, predetermined argument or thesis. In this sense, it is a kind of antiessay. One of the difficulties readers of this text face is in its retelling. If someone says to you, "Well, what was it about?," the answer is not easy or obvious. The text is so far-reaching, so carefully composed of interrelated stories and reflections, and so suggestive in its implications and in the connections it enables that it is difficult to summarize without violence, without seriously reducing the text.

But, imagine that somebody asks, "Well, what was it about?" Write an essay in which you present your reading of "Our Secret." You want to give your reader a sense of what the text is like (or what it is like to read the text), and you want to make clear that the account you are giving is your reading, your way of working it through. You might, in fact, want to suggest what you leave out or put to the side. (The first "Question for a Second Reading" might help you prepare for this.)

2. At several points in her essay, Griffin argues that we—all of us, especially all of us who read her essay—are part of a complex web of connections. At one point she says,

> Who are we? The question is not simple. What we call the self is part of a larger matrix of relationship and society. Had we been born to a different family, in a different time, to a different world, we would not be the same. All the lives that surround us are in us. (p. 441)

At another point she asks, "Is there any one of us who can count ourselves outside the circle circumscribed by our common past?" (p. 449). She speaks of a "field,"

> like a field of gravity that is created by the movements of many bodies. Each life is influenced and it in turn becomes an influence. Whatever is a cause is also an effect. Childhood experience is just one element in the determining field. (p. 409)

One way of thinking about this concept of the self (and of interrelatedness), at least under Griffin's guidance, is to work on the connections that she implies and asserts. As you reread the selection, look for powerful and surprising juxtapositions, fragments that stand together in interesting and suggestive ways. Think about the arguments represented by the blank space between those sections. (And look for Griffin's written statements about "relatedness.") Look for connections that seem important to the text (and to you) and representative of Griffin's thinking (and yours). Then, write an essay in which you use these examples to think through your understanding of Griffin's claims for this "larger matrix," the "determining field," or our "common past."

3. It is useful to think of Griffin's prose as experimental. She is trying to do something that she can't do in the "usual" essay form. She wants to make a different kind of argument or engage her reader in a different manner. And so she mixes personal and academic writing. She assembles fragments and puts seemingly unrelated material into surprising and suggestive relationships. She breaks the "plane" of the page with italicized intersections. She organizes her material, but not in the usual mode of thesis-example-conclusion. The arrangement is not nearly so linear. At one point, when she seems to be prepared to argue that German child-rearing practices produced the Holocaust, she quickly says:

> Of course there cannot be one answer to such a monumental riddle, nor does any event in history have a single cause. Rather a field exists, like a field of gravity that is created by the movements of many bodies. Each life is influenced and it in turn becomes an influence. Whatever is a cause is also an effect. Childhood experience is just one element in the determining field." (p. 409)

Her prose serves to create a "field," one where many bodies are set in relationship.

It is useful, then, to think about Griffin's prose as the enactment of a method, as a way of doing a certain kind of intellectual work. One way to study this, to feel its effects, is to imitate it, to take it as a model. For this assignment, write a Griffin-like essay, one similar in its methods of organization and argument. You will need to think about the stories you might tell, about the stories and texts you might gather (stories and texts not your own). As you write, you will want to think carefully about arrangement and about commentary (about where, that is, you will speak to your reader *as* the writer of the piece). You should not feel bound to Griffin's subject matter, but you should feel that you are working in her spirit.

### MAKING CONNECTIONS

1.  Is it surprising that prisons resemble factories, schools, barracks, hospitals, which all resemble prisons? (p. 342)

    —MICHEL FOUCAULT
    *Panopticism*

    The child, Dr. Schreber advised, *should be permeated by the impossibility of locking something in his heart.* . . . That this philosophy was taught in school gives me an interior view of the catastrophe to follow. It adds a certain dimension to my image of these events to know that a nation of citizens learned that no part of themselves could be safe from the scrutiny of authority, nothing locked in the heart, and at the same time to discover that the head of the secret police of this nation was the son of a schoolmaster. It was this man, after all, Heinrich Himmler, Reichsführer SS, who was later to say, speaking of the mass arrests of Jews, *Protective custody is an act of care.* (p. 411)

    —SUSAN GRIFFIN
    *Our Secret*

    Both Griffin and Foucault write about the "fabrication" of human life and desire within the operations of history and of specific social institutions—the family, the school, the military, the factory, the hospital. Both are concerned with the relationship between forces that are hidden, secret, and those that are obvious, exposed. Both write with an urgent concern for the history of the present, for the ways our current condition is tied to history, politics, and culture.

    And yet these are very different pieces to read. They are written differently—that is, they differently invite a reader's participation and understanding. They take different examples from history. They offer different accounts of the technologies of order and control. It can even be said that they do their work differently and that they work toward different ends.

    Write an essay in which you use one of the essays to explain and to investigate the other—where you use Griffin as a way of thinking about Foucault or Foucault as a way of thinking about Griffin. "To explain," "to investigate"—perhaps you would prefer to think of this encounter as a dialogue or a conversation, a way of bringing the two texts together. You should imagine that your readers are familiar with both texts, but have not yet thought of the two together. You should imagine that your readers do not have the texts in front of them, that you will need to do the work of presentation and summary.

2. Both Gloria Anzaldúa in the two chapters reprinted here from her book *Borderlands/La Frontera* (p. 22) and Susan Griffin in "Our Secret" write mixed texts, or what might be called "montages." Neither of their pieces proceeds as simply a story or an essay, although both have elements of fiction and nonfiction in them (and, in Anzaldúa's case, poetry). They both can be said to be making arguments and to be telling stories. Anzaldúa, in her chapters, is directly concerned with matters of identity and the ways identity is represented through sexuality, religion, and culture. Griffin is concerned with the "self" as "part of a larger matrix of relationship and society."

   Write an essay in which you present and explain Anzaldúa's and Griffin's key arguments about the relation of identity, history, culture, and society. What terms and examples do they provide? What arguments or concerns? What different positions do they take? And what about their writing styles? How might their concerns be reflected in the ways they write?

3. At one point in her essay, Griffin refers to masks:

   > Ordinary. What an astonishing array of images hide behind this word. The ordinary is of course never ordinary. I think of it now as a kind of mask, not an animated mask that expresses the essence of an inner truth, but a mask that falls like dead weight over the human face, making flesh a stationary object. One has difficulty penetrating the heavy mask that Gebhard [Himmler] and his family wore, difficulty piercing through to the creatures behind. (p. 408)

   Ralph Ellison, in "An Extravagance of Laughter" (p. 257), also speaks about masks, although to a very different end, as he thinks about the relations between black Americans and white Americans in the 1930s. He, too, thinks about how the ordinary was never ordinary and about the difficulty of piercing through to the creatures behind.

   Write an essay in which you bring Ellison's essay—the stories he tells but also his way of understanding those stories—into play with Griffin's essay. If, for example, she were to turn her attention to race relations in this country by weaving Ellison and his example into her work, what might she notice and what might she say? Or, if you would like to work in the other direction, if you take Ellison as a starting point, what can you learn from his way of thinking about, of reviewing and using the past, that you could use to take a position on Griffin and her work, her sense of how and why we might search out and listen to other people's stories?

4. One of the obvious questions that a reader might ask of Griffin's essay, "Our Secret," has to do with her methods of writing, thinking, and working. What, one might ask, are her characteristic ways of gathering materials, of thinking them through, of presenting them to readers? As you work back through her essay, think about the writing as an example of method and intention. You also might ask yourself, for instance, questions about the kinds of readers her work requires. What does she assume about her readers? How does she teach her readers to read?

   The same questions can be asked of Ellison's essay, "An Extravagance of Laughter." What, you might ask, are his characteristic ways of gathering materials, of thinking them through, and of presenting them to a reader? How would you describe his method? What are its key features? What would you say he is doing, for example, in the first two paragraphs? Then what happens? What is an "autobiographical exploration" as it is represented in this text? And what does he assume of his readers? Who *is* the audience and how does he teach his readers to read?

Write an essay in which you use Griffin and Ellison to talk about writers and their methods. Be sure to work closely with examples from each. Be sure to look for differences as well as similarities. And see, in your essay, if you can move beyond your discussion of their examples to think more generally about the problems of writing. You might ask, what is it experienced writers work on when they work on their writing? What is it that writers need to learn? What might a writer learn from these two examples? Where and how might it serve in the academy? outside?

# HARRIET
# JACOBS

*H*ARRIET JACOBS *was born in North Carolina in or around 1815. The selection that follows reproduces the opening chapters of her autobiography,*
Incidents in the Life of a Slave Girl, *and tells the story of her life from childhood to early adulthood, through the birth of her first child. In these chapters Jacobs describes how she came to understand her identity as men's property—as a
slave and as a woman—as that identity was determined by her particular situation (her appearance, her education, the psychology of her owner, the values of her
family) and by the codes governing slavery in the South.*

*In the remaining chapters of her book, Jacobs tells of the birth of a second
child, of her escape from her owner, Dr. Flint, and of seven years spent hiding in a
crawl space under the roof of her grandmother's house. The father of her children,
Mr. Sands, did not, as she thought he might, purchase and free her, although he
eventually did purchase her children and allow them to live with her grandmother. He did not free the children, and they never bore his name.*

*Around 1842 Jacobs fled to New York, where she made contact with her chil-
dren and found work as a nursemaid in the family of Nathaniel P. Willis, a magazine editor who with his wife helped hide Jacobs from southern slaveholders and
eventually purchased Jacobs and her children and gave them their freedom.*

*This is the end of Jacobs's story as it is reported in* Incidents. *Recent research,
however, enables us to tell the story of the production of this autobiography, the*

*text that represents its author's early life. Through her contact with the Willises, Jacobs met both black and white abolitionists and became active in the antislavery movement. She told her story to Amy Post, a feminist and abolitionist, and Post encouraged her to record it, which she did by writing in the evenings between 1853 and 1858. After unsuccessfully seeking publication in England, and with the help of the white abolitionist writer L. Maria Child, who read the manuscript and served as an editor (by rearranging sections and suggesting that certain incidents be expanded into chapters), Jacobs published* Incidents *in Boston in 1861 under the pseudonym "Linda Brent," along with Child's introduction, which is also reproduced here. During the Civil War, Jacobs left the Willises to be a nurse for black troops. She remained active, working with freed slaves for the next thirty years, and died in Washington, D.C., in 1897.*

*For years scholars questioned the authenticity of this autobiography, arguing that it seemed too skillful to have been written by a slave, and that more likely it had been written by white abolitionists as propaganda for their cause. The recent discovery, however, of a cache of letters and the research of Jean Fagan Yellin have established Jacobs's authorship and demonstrated that Child made only minor changes and assisted primarily by helping Jacobs find a publisher and an audience.*

*Still, the issue of authorship remains a complicated one, even if we can be confident that the writing belongs to Jacobs and records her struggles and achievements. The issue of authorship becomes complicated if we think of the dilemma facing Jacobs as a writer, telling a story that defied description to an audience who could never completely understand. There is, finally, a precarious relationship between the story of a slave's life, the story Jacobs had to tell, and the stories available to her and to her readers as models—stories of privileged, white, middle-class life: conventional narratives of family and childhood, love and marriage.*

*Houston Baker, one of our leading scholars of black culture, has described the situation of the slave narrator this way:*

> *But the slave narrator must also accomplish the almost unthinkable (since thought and language are inseparable) task of transmuting an authentic, unwritten self—a self that exists outside the conventional literary discourse structures of a white reading public—into a literary representation. . . . The voice of the unwritten self, once it is subjected to the linguistic codes, literary conventions, and audience expectations of a literate population, is perhaps never again the authentic voice of black American slavery. It is, rather, the voice of a self transformed by an autobiographical act into a sharer in the general public discourse about slavery.*

*The author of* Incidents *could be said to stand outside "the general public discourse," both because she was a slave and because she was a woman. The story she has to tell does not fit easily into the usual stories of courtship and marriage or the dominant attitudes toward sexuality and female "virtue." When you read Jacobs's concerns about her "competence," about her status as a woman or as a writer, concerns that seem strange in the face of this powerful text; when you hear her ad-*

*dressing her readers, sometimes instructing them, sometimes apologizing, trying to bridge the gap between her experience and theirs, you should think not only of the trials she faced as a woman and a mother but also of her work as a writer. Here, too, she is struggling to take possession of her life.*

# Incidents in the Life of a Slave Girl

## Written by Herself

Northerners know nothing at all about Slavery. They think it is perpetual bondage only. They have no conception of the depth of *degradation* involved in that word, SLAVERY; if they had, they would never cease their efforts until so horrible a system was overthrown.

— A WOMAN OF NORTH CAROLINA

Rise up, ye women that are at ease! Hear my voice, ye careless daughters! Give ear unto my speech.

– *Isaiah xxxii.9*

## *Preface by the Author*
### Linda Brent

Reader, be assured this narrative is no fiction. I am aware that some of my adventures may seem incredible; but they are, nevertheless, strictly true. I have not exaggerated the wrongs inflicted by Slavery; on the contrary, my descriptions fall far short of the facts. I have concealed the names of places, and given persons fictitious names. I had no motive for secrecy on my own account, but I deemed it kind and considerate towards others to pursue this course.

I wish I were more competent to the task I have undertaken. But I trust my readers will excuse deficiencies in consideration of circumstances. I was born and reared in Slavery; and I remained in a Slave State twenty-seven years. Since I have been at the North, it has been necessary for me to work diligently for my own support, and the education of my children. This has not left me much leisure to make up for the loss of early opportunities to improve myself; and it has compelled me to write these pages at irregular intervals, whenever I could snatch an hour from household duties.

When I first arrived in Philadelphia, Bishop Paine advised me to publish a sketch of my life, but I told him I was altogether incompetent to such an undertaking. Though I have improved my mind somewhat since that time, I still remain of the same opinion; but I trust my motives will excuse what might otherwise seem presumptuous. I have not written my experiences in order to attract attention to myself; on the contrary, it would have been more pleasant to me to have been silent about my own history. Neither do I care to excite sympathy for my own sufferings. But I do earnestly desire to arouse the women of the North to a realizing sense of the condition of two millions of women at the South, still in bondage, suffering what I suffered, and most of them far worse. I want to add my testimony to that of abler pens to convince the people of the Free States what Slavery really is. Only by experience can any one realize how deep, and dark, and foul is that pit of abominations. May the blessing of God rest on this imperfect effort in behalf of my persecuted people!

## Introduction by the Editor

### L. Maria Child

The author of the following autobiography is personally known to me, and her conversation and manners inspire me with confidence. During the last seventeen years, she has lived the greater part of the time with a distinguished family in New York, and has so deported herself as to be highly esteemed by them. This fact is sufficient, without further credentials of her character. I believe those who know her will not be disposed to doubt her veracity, though some incidents in her story are more romantic than fiction.

At her request, I have revised her manuscript; but such changes as I have made have been mainly for purposes of condensation and orderly arrangement. I have not added any thing to the incidents, or changed the import of her very pertinent remarks. With trifling exceptions, both the ideas and the language are her own. I pruned excrescences a little, but otherwise I had no reason for changing her lively and dramatic way of telling her own story. The names of both persons and places are known to me; but for good reasons I suppress them.

It will naturally excite surprise that a woman reared in Slavery should be able to write so well. But circumstances will explain this. In the first place, nature endowed her with quick perceptions. Secondly, the mistress, with whom she lived till she was twelve years old, was a kind, considerate friend, who taught her to read and spell. Thirdly, she was placed in favorable circumstances after she came to the North; having frequent intercourse with intelligent persons, who felt a friendly interest in her welfare, and were disposed to give her opportunities for self-improvement.

I am well aware that many will accuse me of indecorum for presenting these pages to the public; for the experiences of this intelligent and much-injured woman belong to a class which some call delicate subjects, and others indelicate. This peculiar phase of Slavery has generally been kept veiled; but the public ought to be made acquainted with its monstrous features, and I willingly take the responsibility of presenting them with the veil withdrawn. I do this for the sake of my sisters in bondage, who are suffering wrongs so foul, that our ears are too delicate to listen to them. I do it with the hope of arousing conscientious and reflecting women at the North to a sense of their duty in the exertion of moral influence on the question of Slavery, on all possible occasions. I do it with the hope that every man who reads this narrative will swear solemnly before God that, so far as he has power to prevent it, no fugitive from Slavery shall ever be sent back to suffer in that loathsome den of corruption and cruelty.

## Incidents in the Life of a Slave Girl, Seven Years Concealed

### I
### Childhood

I was born a slave; but I never knew it till six years of happy childhood had passed away. My father was a carpenter, and considered so intelligent and skilful in his trade, that, when buildings out of the common line were to be erected, he was sent for from long distances, to be head workman. On condition of paying his mistress two hundred dollars a year, and supporting himself, he was allowed to work at his trade, and manage his own affairs. His strongest wish was to purchase his children; but, though he several times offered his hard earnings for that purpose, he never succeeded. In complexion my parents were a light shade of brownish yellow, and were termed mulattoes. They lived together in a comfortable home; and, though we were all slaves, I was so fondly shielded that I never dreamed I was a piece of merchandise, trusted to them for safe keeping, and liable to be demanded of them at any moment. I had one brother, William, who was two years younger than myself—a bright, affectionate child. I had also a great treasure in my maternal grandmother, who was a remarkable woman in many respects. She was the daughter of a planter in South Carolina, who, at his death, left her mother and his three children free, with money to go to St. Augustine, where they had relatives. It was during the Revolutionary War; and they were captured on their passage, carried back, and sold to different purchasers. Such was the story my grandmother used to tell me; but I do not remember all the particulars. She was a little girl when she was captured and sold to the keeper of a large hotel. I have often heard her tell how hard she fared during childhood. But as she grew older she evinced so much intelligence, and was so faithful, that her master and mistress could not help seeing it was for their interest to take care of such a valuable piece of property. She became an indispensable personage in the household, officiating in all capacities, from cook and wet nurse to seamstress. She was much praised for her cooking; and her nice crackers became so famous in the neighborhood that many people were desirous of obtaining them. In consequence of numerous requests of this kind, she asked permission of her mistress to bake crackers at night, after all the household work was done; and she obtained leave to do it, provided she would clothe herself and her children from the profits. Upon these terms, after working hard all day for her mistress, she began her midnight bakings, assisted by her two oldest children. The business proved profitable; and each year she laid by a little, which was saved for a fund to purchase her children. Her master died, and the property was divided among his heirs. The widow had her dower in the hotel, which she continued to keep open. My grandmother remained in her service as a slave; but her children were divided among her master's children. As she had five, Benjamin, the youngest one, was sold, in order that each heir might have an equal portion of dollars and cents. There was so little difference in our ages that he seemed more like my brother than my uncle. He was a bright, handsome lad, nearly white; for he inherited the complexion my grandmother had derived from Anglo-Saxon ancestors. Though only ten years old, seven hundred and twenty dollars were paid for him. His sale was a terrible blow to my grandmother; but she was naturally hopeful, and she went to work with renewed energy, trusting in time to be able to purchase some of her children. She had laid up three hundred dollars, which her mistress one day begged as a loan, promising to pay her soon. The reader probably knows that no promise or writing given to a slave is legally binding; for, according to Southern laws, a slave, *being* property, can *hold* no property. When my grandmother lent her hard earnings to her mistress, she trusted solely to her honor. The honor of a slaveholder to a slave!

To this good grandmother I was indebted for many comforts. My brother Willie and I often received portions of the crackers, cakes, and preserves she made to sell; and after we ceased to be children we were indebted to her for many more important services.

Such were the unusually fortunate circumstances of my early childhood. When I was six years old, my mother died; and then, for the first time, I learned, by the talk around me, that I was a slave. My mother's mistress was the daughter of my grandmother's mistress. She was the foster sister of my mother; they were both nourished at my grandmother's breast. In fact, my mother had been weaned at three months old, that the babe of the mistress might obtain sufficient food. They played together as children; and, when they became women, my mother was a most faithful servant to her whiter foster sister. On her death-bed her mistress promised that her children should never suffer for any thing; and during her lifetime she kept her word. They all spoke kindly of my dead mother, who had been a slave merely in name, but in nature was noble and womanly. I grieved for her, and my young mind was troubled with the thought who would now take care of me and my little brother. I was told that my home was now to be with her mistress; and I found it a happy one. No toilsome or disagreeable duties were imposed upon me. My mistress was so kind to me that I was always glad to do her bidding, and proud to labor for her as much as my young years would permit. I would sit by her side for hours, sewing diligently, with a heart as free from care as that of any free-born white child. When she thought I was tired, she would send me out to run and jump; and away I bounded, to gather berries or flowers to decorate her room. Those were happy days—too happy to last. The slave child had no thought for the morrow; but there came that blight, which too surely waits on every human being born to be a chattel.

When I was nearly twelve years old, my kind mistress sickened and died. As I saw the cheek grow paler, and the eye more glassy, how earnestly I prayed in my heart that she might live! I loved her; for she had been almost like a mother to me. My prayers were not answered. She died, and they buried her in the little churchyard, where, day after day, my tears fell upon her grave.

I was sent to spend a week with my grandmother. I was now old enough to begin to think of the future; and again and again I asked myself what they would do with me. I felt sure I should never find another mistress so kind as the one who was gone. She had promised my dying mother that her children should never suffer for any thing; and when I remembered that, and recalled her many proofs of attachment to me, I could not help having some hopes that she had left me free. My friends were almost certain it would be so. They thought she would be sure to do it, on account of my mother's love and faithful service. But, alas! we all know that the memory of a faithful slave does not avail much to save her children from the auction block.

After a brief period of suspense, the will of my mistress was read, and we learned that she had bequeathed me to her sister's daughter, a child of five years old. So vanished our hopes. My mistress had taught me the precepts of God's Word: "Thou shalt love thy neighbor as thyself." "Whatsoever ye would that men should do unto you, do ye even so unto them." But I was her slave, and I suppose she did not recognize me as her neighbor. I would give much to blot out from my memory that one great wrong. As a child, I loved my mistress; and, looking back on the happy days I spent with her, I try to think with less bitterness of this act of injustice. While I was with her, she taught me to read and spell; and for this privilege, which so rarely falls to the lot of a slave, I bless her memory.

She possessed but few slaves; and at her death those were all distributed among her relatives. Five of them were my grandmother's children, and had shared the same milk that nourished her mother's children. Notwithstanding my grandmother's long and faithful service to her owners, not one of her children escaped the auction block. These God-breathing machines are no more, in the sight of their masters, than the cotton they plant, or the horses they tend.

## II
### The New Master and Mistress

Dr. Flint, a physician in the neighborhood, had married the sister of my mistress, and I was now the property of their little daughter. It was not without murmuring that I prepared for my new home; and what added to

my unhappiness, was the fact that my brother William was purchased by
the same family. My father, by his nature, as well as by the habit of trans-
acting business as a skilful mechanic, had more of the feelings of a freeman than is common among slaves. My brother was a spirited boy; and
being brought up under such influences, he early detested the name of
master and mistress. One day, when his father and his mistress both happened to call him at the same time, he hesitated between the two; being
perplexed to know which had the strongest claim upon his obedience. He
finally concluded to go to his mistress. When my father reproved him for
it, he said, "You both called me, and I didn't know which I ought to go to
first."

"You are *my* child," replied our father, "and when I call you, you
should come immediately, if you have to pass through fire and water."

Poor Willie! He was now to learn his first lesson of obedience to a master. Grandmother tried to cheer us with hopeful words, and they found an
echo in the credulous hearts of youth.

When we entered our new home we encountered cold looks, cold
words, and cold treatment. We were glad when the night came. On my
narrow bed I moaned and wept, I felt so desolate and alone.

I had been there nearly a year, when a dear little friend of mine was
buried. I heard her mother sob, as the clods fell on the coffin of her only
child, and I turned away from the grave, feeling thankful that I still had
something left to love. I met my grandmother, who said, "Come with me,
Linda"; and from her tone I knew that something sad had happened. She
led me apart from the people, and then said, "My child, your father is
dead." Dead! How could I believe it? He had died so suddenly I had not
even heard that he was sick. I went home with my grandmother. My heart
rebelled against God, who had taken from me mother, father, mistress,
and friend. The good grandmother tried to comfort me. "Who knows the
ways of God?" said she. "Perhaps they have been kindly taken from the
evil days to come." Years afterwards I often thought of this. She promised
to be a mother to her grandchildren, so far as she might be permitted to do
so; and strengthened by her love, I returned to my master's. I thought I
should be allowed to go to my father's house the next morning; but I was
ordered to go for flowers, that my mistress's house might be decorated for
an evening party. I spent the day gathering flowers and weaving them
into festoons, while the dead body of my father was lying within a mile of
me. What cared my owners for that? he was merely a piece of property.
Moreover, they thought he had spoiled his children, by teaching them to
feel that they were human beings. This was blasphemous doctrine for a
slave to teach; presumptuous in him, and dangerous to the masters.

The next day I followed his remains to a humble grave beside that of
my dear mother. There were those who knew my father's worth, and respected his memory.

My home now seemed more dreary than ever. The laugh of the little
slave-children sounded harsh and cruel. It was selfish to feel so about the

joy of others. My brother moved about with a very grave face. I tried to comfort him, by saying, "Take courage, Willie; brighter days will come by and by."

"You don't know any thing about it, Linda," he replied. "We shall have to stay here all our days; we shall never be free."

I argued that we were growing older and stronger, and that perhaps we might, before long, be allowed to hire our own time, and then we could earn money to buy our freedom. William declared this was much easier to say than to do; moreover, he did not intend to *buy* his freedom. We held daily controversies upon this subject.

Little attention was paid to the slaves' meals in Dr. Flint's house. If they could catch a bit of food while it was going, well and good. I gave myself no trouble on that score, for on my various errands I passed my grandmother's house, where there was always something to spare for me. I was frequently threatened with punishment if I stopped there; and my grandmother, to avoid detaining me, often stood at the gate with something for my breakfast or dinner. I was indebted to *her* for all my comforts, spiritual or temporal. It was *her* labor that supplied my scanty wardrobe. I have a vivid recollection of the linsey-woolsey dress given me every winter by Mrs. Flint. How I hated it! It was one of the badges of slavery.

While my grandmother was thus helping to support me from her hard earnings, the three hundred dollars she had lent her mistress was never repaid. When her mistress died, her son-in-law, Dr. Flint, was appointed executor. When grandmother applied to him for payment, he said the estate was insolvent, and the law prohibited payment. It did not, however, prohibit him from retaining the silver candelabra, which had been purchased with that money. I presume they will be handed down in the family, from generation to generation.

My grandmother's mistress had always promised her that, at her death, she should be free; and it was said that in her will she made good the promise. But when the estate was settled, Dr. Flint told the faithful old servant that, under existing circumstances, it was necessary she should be sold.

On the appointed day, the customary advertisement was posted up, proclaiming that there would be a "public sale of negroes, horses, &c." Dr. Flint called to tell my grandmother that he was unwilling to wound her feelings by putting her up at auction, and that he would prefer to dispose of her at private sale. My grandmother saw through his hypocrisy; she understood very well that he was ashamed of the job. She was a very spirited woman, and if he was base enough to sell her, when her mistress intended she should be free, she was determined the public should know it. She had for a long time supplied many families with crackers and preserves; consequently, "Aunt Marthy," as she was called, was generally known, and every body who knew her respected her intelligence and good character. Her long and faithful service in the family was also well known, and the intention of her mistress to leave her free. When the day of sale came, she took her place among the chattels, and at the first call she sprang upon the auction-block. Many voices called out, "Shame! Shame! Who is going to sell *you*, Marthy? Don't stand there! That is no place for *you*." Without saying a word she quietly awaited her fate. No one bid for her. At last, a feeble voice, said, "Fifty dollars." It came from a maiden lady, seventy years old, the sister of my grandmother's deceased mistress. She had lived forty years under the same roof with my grandmother; she knew how faithfully she had served her owners, and how cruelly she had been defrauded of her rights; and she resolved to protect her. The auctioneer waited for a higher bid; but her wishes were respected; no one bid above her. She could neither read nor write; and when the bill of sale was made out, she signed it with a cross. But what consequence was that, when she had a big heart overflowing with human kindness? She gave the old servant her freedom.

At that time, my grandmother was just fifty years old. Laborious years had passed since then; and now my brother and I were slaves to the man who had defrauded her of her money, and tried to defraud her of her freedom. One of my mother's sisters, called Aunt Nancy, was also a slave in his family. She was a kind, good aunt to me; and supplied the place of both housekeeper and waiting maid to her mistress. She was, in fact, at the beginning and end of every thing.

Mrs. Flint, like many southern women, was totally deficient in energy. She had not strength to superintend her household affairs; but her nerves were so strong, that she could sit in her easy chair and see a woman whipped, till the blood trickled from every stroke of the lash. She was a member of the church; but partaking of the Lord's supper did not seem to put her in a Christian frame of mind. If dinner was not served at the exact time on that particular Sunday, she would station herself in the kitchen, and wait till it was dished, and then spit in all the kettles and pans that had been used for cooking. She did this to prevent the cook and her children from eking out their meagre fare with the remains of the gravy and other scrapings. The slaves could get nothing to eat except what she chose to give them. Provisions were weighed out by the pound and ounce, three times a day. I can assure you she gave them no chance to eat wheat bread from her flour barrel. She knew how many biscuits a quart of flour would make, and exactly what size they ought to be.

Dr. Flint was an epicure. The cook never sent a dinner to his table without fear and trembling; for if there happened to be a dish not to his liking, he would either order her to be whipped, or compel her to eat every mouthful of it in his presence. The poor, hungry creature might not have objected to eating it; but she did object to having her master cram it down her throat till she choked.

They had a pet dog, that was a nuisance in the house. The cook was ordered to make some Indian mush for him. He refused to eat, and when his head was held over it, the froth flowed from his mouth into the basin. He died a few minutes after. When Dr. Flint came in, he said the mush had not been well cooked, and that was the reason the animal would not eat it. He sent for the cook, and compelled her to eat it. He thought that the woman's stomach was stronger than the dog's; but her sufferings afterwards proved that he was mistaken. This poor woman endured many cruelties from her master and mistress; sometimes she was locked up, away from her nursing baby, for a whole day and night.

When I had been in the family a few weeks, one of the plantation slaves was brought to town, by order of his master. It was near night when he arrived, and Dr. Flint ordered him to be taken to the work house, and tied up to the joist, so that his feet would just escape the ground. In that situation he was to wait till the doctor had taken his tea. I shall never forget that night. Never before, in my life, had I heard hundreds of blows fall, in succession, on a human being. His piteous groans, and his "O, pray don't, massa," rang in my ear for months afterwards. There were many conjectures as to the cause of this terrible punishment. Some said master accused him of stealing corn; others said the slave had quarrelled with his wife, in presence of the overseer, and had accused his master of being the father of her child. They were both black, and the child was very fair.

I went into the work house next morning, and saw the cowhide still wet with blood, and the boards all covered with gore. The poor man lived, and continued to quarrel with his wife. A few months afterwards Dr. Flint handed them both over to a slave-trader. The guilty man put their value into his pocket, and had the satisfaction of knowing that they were out of sight and hearing. When the mother was delivered into the trader's hands, she said, "You *promised* to treat me well." To which he replied, "You have let your tongue run too far; damn you!" She had forgotten that it was a crime for a slave to tell who was the father of her child.

From others than the master persecution also comes in such cases. I once saw a young slave girl dying soon after the birth of a child nearly white. In her agony she cried out, "O Lord, come and take me!" Her mistress stood by, and mocked at her like an incarnate fiend. "You suffer, do you?" she exclaimed. "I am glad of it. You deserve it all, and more too."

The girl's mother said, "The baby is dead, thank God; and I hope my poor child will soon be in heaven, too."

"Heaven!" retorted the mistress. "There is no such place for the like of her and her bastard."

The poor mother turned away, sobbing. Her dying daughter called her, feebly, and as she bent over her, I heard her say, "Don't grieve so, mother; God knows all about it; and HE will have mercy upon me."

Her sufferings, afterwards, became so intense, that her mistress felt unable to stay; but when she left the room, the scornful smile was still on her lips. Seven children called her mother. The poor black woman had but the one child, whose eyes she saw closing in death, while she thanked God for taking her away from the greater bitterness of life.

### III
### The Slaves' New Year's Day

Dr. Flint owned a fine residence in town, several farms, and about fifty slaves, besides hiring a number by the year.

Hiring-day at the south takes place on the 1st of January. On the 2d, the slaves are expected to go to their new masters. On a farm, they work until the corn and cotton are laid. They then have two holidays. Some masters give them a good dinner under the trees. This over, they work until Christmas eve. If no heavy charges are meantime brought against them, they are given four or five holidays, whichever the master or overseer may think proper. Then comes New Year's eve; and they gather together their little alls, or more properly speaking, their little nothings, and wait anxiously for the dawning of day. At the appointed hour the grounds are thronged with men, women, and children, waiting, like criminals, to hear their doom pronounced. The slave is sure to know who is the most humane, or cruel master, within forty miles of him.

It is easy to find out, on that day, who clothes and feeds his slaves well; for he is surrounded by a crowd, begging, "Please, massa, hire me this year. I will work *very* hard, massa."

If a slave is unwilling to go with his new master, he is whipped, or locked up in jail, until he consents to go, and promises not to run away during the year. Should he chance to change his mind, thinking it justifiable to violate an extorted promise, woe unto him if he is caught! The whip is used till the blood flows at his feet; and his stiffened limbs are put in chains, to be dragged in the field for days and days!

If he lives until the next year, perhaps the same man will hire him again, without even giving him an opportunity of going to the hiring-ground. After those for hire are disposed of, those for sale are called up.

O, you happy free women, contrast *your* New Year's day with that of the poor bond-woman! With you it is a pleasant season, and the light of the day is blessed. Friendly wishes meet you every where, and gifts are showered upon you. Even hearts that have been estranged from you soften at this season, and lips that have been silent echo back, "I wish you a happy New Year." Children bring their little offerings, and raise their rosy lips for a caress. They are your own, and no hand but that of death can take them from you.

But to the slave mother New Year's day comes laden with peculiar sorrows. She sits on her cold cabin floor, watching the children who may all be torn from her the next morning; and often does she wish that she and they might die before the day dawns. She may be an ignorant creature, degraded by the system that has brutalized her from childhood; but she has a mother's instincts, and is capable of feeling a mother's agonies.

On one of these sale days, I saw a mother lead seven children to the auction-block. She knew that *some* of them would be taken from her; but they took *all*. The children were sold to a slave-trader, and their mother was bought by a man in her own town. Before night her children were all far away. She begged the trader to tell her where he intended to take them; this he refused to do. How *could* he, when he knew he would sell them, one by one, wherever he could command the highest price? I met that mother in the street, and her wild, haggard face lives to-day in my mind. She wrung her hands in anguish, and exclaimed, "Gone! All gone! Why *don't* God kill me?" I had no words wherewith to comfort her. Instances of this kind are of daily, yea, of hourly occurrence.

Slaveholders have a method, peculiar to their institution, of getting rid of *old* slaves, whose lives have been worn out in their service. I knew an old woman, who for seventy years faithfully served her master. She had become almost helpless, from hard labor and disease. Her owners moved to Alabama, and the old black woman was left to be sold to any body who would give twenty dollars for her.

## IV
## The Slave Who Dared to Feel Like a Man

Two years had passed since I entered Dr. Flint's family, and those years had brought much of the knowledge that comes from experience, though they had afforded little opportunity for any other kinds of knowledge.

My grandmother had, as much as possible, been a mother to her orphan grandchildren. By perseverance and unwearied industry, she was now mistress of a snug little home, surrounded with the necessaries of life. She would have been happy could her children have shared them with her. There remained but three children and two grandchildren, all slaves. Most earnestly did she strive to make us feel that it was the will of God: that He had seen fit to place us under such circumstances; and though it seemed hard, we ought to pray for contentment.

It was a beautiful faith, coming from a mother who could not call her children her own. But I, and Benjamin, her youngest boy, condemned it. We reasoned that it was much more the will of God that we should be situated as she was. We longed for a home like hers. There we always found sweet balsam for our troubles. She was so loving, so sympathizing! She always met us with a smile, and listened with patience to all our sorrows. She spoke so hopefully, that unconsciously the clouds gave place to sunshine. There was a grand big oven there, too, that baked bread and nice things for the town, and we knew there was always a choice bit in store for us.

But, alas! even the charms of the old oven failed to reconcile us to our hard lot. Benjamin was now a tall, handsome lad, strongly and gracefully made, and with a spirit too bold and daring for a slave. My brother William, now twelve years old, had the same aversion to the word master that he had when he was an urchin of seven years. I was his confidant. He came to me with all his troubles. I remember one instance in particular. It was on a lovely spring morning, and when I marked the sunlight dancing here and there, its beauty seemed to mock my sadness. For my master, whose restless, craving, vicious nature roved about day and night, seeking whom to devour, had just left me, with stinging, scorching words; words that scathed ear and brain like fire. O, how I despised him! I thought how glad I should be, if some day when he walked the earth, it would open and swallow him up, and disencumber the world of a plague.

When he told me that I was made for his use, made to obey his command in *every* thing; that I was nothing but a slave, whose will must and should surrender to his, never before had my puny arm felt half so strong.

So deeply was I absorbed in painful reflections afterwards, that I neither saw nor heard the entrance of any one, till the voice of William sounded close beside me. "Linda," said he, "what makes you look so sad? I love you. O, Linda, isn't this a bad world? Every body seems so cross and unhappy. I wish I had died when poor father did."

I told him that every body was *not* cross, or unhappy; that those who had pleasant homes, and kind friends, and who were not afraid to love them, were happy. But we, who were slave-children, without father or mother, could not expect to be happy. We must be good; perhaps that would bring us contentment.

"Yes," he said, "I try to be good; but what's the use? They are all the time troubling me." Then he proceeded to relate his afternoon's difficulty with young master Nicholas. It seemed that the brother of master Nicholas had pleased himself with making up stories about William. Master Nicholas said he should be flogged, and he would do it. Whereupon he went to work; but William fought bravely, and the young master, finding he was getting the better of him, undertook to tie his hands behind him. He failed in that likewise. By dint of kicking and fisting, William came out of the skirmish none the worse for a few scratches.

He continued to discourse on his young master's *meanness;* how he whipped the *little* boys, but was a perfect coward when a tussle ensued between him and white boys of his own size. On such occasions he always took to his legs. William had other charges to make against him. One was his rubbing up pennies with quicksilver, and passing them off for quarters of a dollar on an old man who kept a fruit stall. William was often sent to buy fruit, and he earnestly inquired of me what he ought to do under such circumstances. I told him it was certainly wrong to deceive the old man, and that it was his duty to tell him of the impositions practised by his young master. I assured him the old man would not be slow to comprehend the whole, and there the matter would end. William thought it might with the old man, but not with *him.* He said he did not mind the smart of the whip, but he did not like the *idea* of being whipped.

While I advised him to be good and forgiving I was not unconscious of the beam in my own eye. It was the very knowledge of my own shortcomings that urged me to retain, if possible, some sparks of my brother's God-given nature. I had not lived fourteen years in slavery for nothing. I had felt, seen, and heard enough, to read the characters, and question the motives, of those around me. The war of my life had begun; and though one of God's most powerless creatures, I resolved never to be conquered. Alas, for me!

If there was one pure, sunny spot for me, I believed it to be in Benjamin's heart, and in another's, whom I loved with all the ardor of a girl's first love. My owner knew of it, and sought in every way to render me miserable. He did not resort to corporal punishment, but to all the petty, tyrannical ways that human ingenuity could devise.

I remember the first time I was punished. It was in the month of February. My grandmother had taken my old shoes, and replaced them with a new pair. I needed them; for several inches of snow had fallen, and it still continued to fall. When I walked through Mrs. Flint's room, their creaking grated harshly on her refined nerves. She called me to her, and asked what I had about me that made such a horrid noise. I told her it was my new shoes. "Take them off," said she; "and if you put them on again, I'll throw them into the fire."

I took them off, and my stockings also. She then sent me a long distance, on an errand. As I went through the snow, my bare feet tingled. That night I was very hoarse; and I went to bed thinking the next day would find me sick, perhaps dead. What was my grief on waking to find myself quite well!

I had imagined if I died, or was laid up for some time, that my mistress would feel a twinge of remorse that she had so hated "the little imp," as she styled me. It was my ignorance of that mistress that gave rise to such extravagant imaginings.

Dr. Flint occasionally had high prices offered for me; but he always said, "She don't belong to me. She is my daughter's property, and I have no right to sell her." Good, honest man! My young mistress was still a child, and I could look for no protection from her. I loved her, and she returned my affection. I once heard her father allude to her attachment to me; and his wife promptly replied that it proceeded from fear. This put unpleasant doubts into my mind. Did the child feign what she did not feel? or was her mother jealous of the mite of love she bestowed on me? I concluded it must be the latter. I said to myself, "Surely, little children are true."

One afternoon I sat at my sewing, feeling unusual depression of spirits. My mistress had been accusing me of an offence, of which I assured her I was perfectly innocent; but I saw, by the contemptuous curl of her lip, that she believed I was telling a lie.

I wondered for what wise purpose God was leading me through such thorny paths, and whether still darker days were in store for me. As I sat musing thus, the door opened softly, and William came in. "Well, brother," said I, "what is the matter this time?"

"O Linda, Ben and his master have had a dreadful time!" said he.

My first thought was that Benjamin was killed. "Don't be frightened, Linda," said William; "I will tell you all about it."

It appeared that Benjamin's master had sent for him, and he did not immediately obey the summons. When he did, his master was angry, and began to whip him. He resisted. Master and slave fought, and finally the master was thrown. Benjamin had cause to tremble; for he had thrown to the ground his master—one of the richest men in town. I anxiously awaited the result.

That night I stole to my grandmother's house, and Benjamin also stole thither from his master's. My grandmother had gone to spend a day or two with an old friend living in the country.

"I have come," said Benjamin, "to tell you good by. I am going away."

I inquired where.

"To the north," he replied.

I looked at him to see whether he was in earnest. I saw it all in his firm, set mouth. I implored him not to go, but he paid no heed to my words. He said he was no longer a boy, and every day made his yoke more galling. He had raised his hand against his master, and was to be publicly whipped for the offence. I reminded him of the poverty and hardships he must encounter among strangers. I told him he might be caught and brought back; and that was terrible to think of.

He grew vexed, and asked if poverty and hardships with freedom, were not preferable to our treatment in slavery. "Linda," he continued, "we are dogs here; foot-balls, cattle, every thing that's mean. No, I will not stay. Let them bring me back. We don't die but once."

He was right; but it was hard to give him up. "Go," said I, "and break your mother's heart."

I repented of my words ere they were out.

"Linda," said he, speaking as I had not heard him speak that evening, "how *could* you say that? Poor mother! be kind to her, Linda; and you, too, cousin Fanny."

Cousin Fanny was a friend who had lived some years with us.

Farewells were exchanged, and the bright, kind boy, endeared to us by so many acts of love, vanished from our sight.

It is not necessary to state how he made his escape. Suffice it to say, he was on his way to New York when a violent storm overtook the vessel. The captain said he must put into the nearest port. This alarmed Benjamin, who was aware that he would be advertised in every port near his own town. His embarrassment was noticed by the captain. To port they went. There the advertisement met the captain's eye. Benjamin so exactly answered its description, that the captain laid hold on him, and bound him in chains. The storm passed, and they proceeded to New York. Before reaching that port Benjamin managed to get off his chains and throw them overboard. He escaped from the vessel, but was pursued, captured, and carried back to his master.

When my grandmother returned home and found her youngest child had fled, great was her sorrow; but, with characteristic piety, she said, "God's will be done." Each morning, she inquired if any news had been heard from her boy. Yes, news *was* heard. The master was rejoicing over a letter, announcing the capture of his human chattel.

That day seems but as yesterday, so well do I remember it. I saw him led through the streets in chains, to jail. His face was ghastly pale, yet full of determination. He had begged one of the sailors to go to his mother's house and ask her not to meet him. He said the sight of her distress would take from him all self-control. She yearned to see him, and she went; but she screened herself in the crowd, that it might be as her child had said.

We were not allowed to visit him; but we had known the jailer for years, and he was a kind-hearted man. At midnight he opened the jail door for my grandmother and myself to enter, in disguise. When we entered the cell not a sound broke the stillness. "Benjamin, Benjamin!" whispered my grandmother. No answer. "Benjamin!" she again faltered. There was a jingle of chains. The moon had just risen, and cast an uncertain light through the bars of the window. We knelt down and took Benjamin's cold hands in ours. We did not speak. Sobs were heard, and Benjamin's lips were unsealed; for his mother was weeping on his neck. How vividly does memory bring back that sad night! Mother and son talked together. He asked her pardon for the suffering he had caused her. She said she had nothing to forgive; she could not blame his desire for freedom. He told her that when he was captured, he broke away, and was about casting himself into the river, when thoughts of *her* came over him, and he desisted. She asked if he did not also think of God. I fancied I saw his face grow fierce in the moonlight. He answered, "No, I did not think of him. When a man is hunted like a wild beast he forgets there is a God, a heaven. He forgets every thing in his struggle to get beyond the reach of the bloodhounds."

"Don't talk so, Benjamin," said she. "Put your trust in God. Be humble, my child, and your master will forgive you."

"Forgive me for *what*, mother? For not letting him treat me like a dog? No! I will never humble myself to him. I have worked for him for nothing all my life, and I am repaid with stripes and imprisonment. Here I will stay till I die, or till he sells me."

The poor mother shuddered at his words. I think he felt it; for when he next spoke, his voice was calmer. "Don't fret about me, mother. I ain't worth it," said he. "I wish I had some of your goodness. You bear every thing patiently, just as though you thought it was all right. I wish I could."

She told him she had not always been so; once, she was like him; but when sore troubles came upon her, and she had no arm to lean upon, she learned to call on God, and he lightened her burdens. She besought him to do likewise.

We overstaid our time, and were obliged to hurry from the jail.

Benjamin had been imprisoned three weeks, when my grandmother went to intercede for him with his master. He was immovable. He said Benjamin should serve as an example to the rest of his slaves; he should be kept in jail till he was subdued, or be sold if he got but one dollar for him. However, he afterwards relented in some degree. The chains were taken off, and we were allowed to visit him.

As his food was of the coarsest kind, we carried him as often as possible a warm supper, accompanied with some little luxury for the jailer.

Three months elapsed, and there was no prospect of release or of a purchaser. One day he was heard to sing and laugh. This piece of indecorum was told to his master, and the overseer was ordered to re-chain him. He was now confined in an apartment with other prisoners, who were covered with filthy rags. Benjamin was chained near them, and was soon covered with vermin. He worked at his chains till he succeeded in getting out of them. He passed them through the bars of the window, with a request that they should be taken to his master, and he should be informed that he was covered with vermin.

This audacity was punished with heavier chains, and prohibition of our visits.

My grandmother continued to send him fresh changes of clothes. The old ones were burned up. The last night we saw him in jail his mother still begged him to send for his master, and beg his pardon. Neither persuasion nor argument could turn him from his purpose. He calmly answered, "I am waiting his time."

Those chains were mournful to hear.

Another three months passed, and Benjamin left his prison walls. We that loved him waited to bid him a long and last farewell. A slave-trader had bought him. You remember, I told you what price he brought when ten years of age. Now he was more than twenty years old, and sold for three hundred dollars. The master had been blind to his own interest. Long confinement had made his face too pale, his form too thin; moreover, the trader had heard something of his character, and it did not strike him as suitable for a slave. He said he would give any price if the handsome lad was a girl. We thanked God that he was not.

Could you have seen that mother clinging to her child, when they fastened the irons upon his wrists; could you have heard her heart-rending groans, and seen her bloodshot eyes wander wildly from face to face, vainly pleading for mercy; could you have witnessed that scene as I saw it, you would exclaim, *Slavery is damnable!*

Benjamin, her youngest, her pet, was forever gone! She could not realize it. She had had an interview with the trader for the purpose of ascertaining if Benjamin could be purchased. She was told it was impossible, as he had given bonds not to sell him till he was out of the state. He promised that he would not sell him till he reached New Orleans.

With a strong arm and unvaried trust, my grandmother began her work of love. Benjamin must be free. If she succeeded, she knew they would still be separated; but the sacrifice was not too great. Day and night she labored. The trader's price would treble that he gave; but she was not discouraged.

She employed a lawyer to write to a gentleman, whom she knew, in New Orleans. She begged him to interest himself for Benjamin, and he willingly favored her request. When he saw Benjamin, and stated his business, he thanked him; but said he preferred to wait a while before making the trader an offer. He knew he had tried to obtain a high price for him, and had invariably failed. This encouraged him to make another effort for freedom. So one morning, long before day, Benjamin was missing. He was riding over the blue billows, bound for Baltimore.

For once his white face did him a kindly service. They had no suspicion that it belonged to a slave; otherwise, the law would have been followed out to the letter, and the *thing* rendered back to slavery. The brightest skies are often overshadowed by the darkest clouds. Benjamin was taken sick, and compelled to remain in Baltimore three weeks. His strength was slow in returning; and his desire to continue his journey seemed to retard his recovery. How could he get strength without air and exercise? He resolved to venture on a short walk. A by-street was selected, where he thought himself secure of not being met by any one that knew him; but a voice called out, "Halloo, Ben, my boy! what are you doing *here*?"

His first impulse was to run; but his legs trembled so that he could not stir. He turned to confront his antagonist, and behold, there stood his old master's next door neighbor! He thought it was all over with him now; but it proved otherwise. That man was a miracle. He possessed a goodly number of slaves, and yet was not quite deaf to that mystic clock, whose ticking is rarely heard in the slaveholder's breast.

"Ben, you are sick," said he. "Why, you look like a ghost. I guess I gave you something of a start. Never mind, Ben, I am not going to touch you. You had a pretty tough time of it, and you may go on your way rejoicing for all men. But I would advise you to get out of this place plaguy quick, for there are several gentlemen here from our town." He described the nearest and safest route to New York, and added, "I shall be glad to tell your mother I have seen you. Good by, Ben."

Benjamin turned away, filled with gratitude, and surprised that the town he hated contained such a gem—a gem worthy of a purer setting.

This gentleman was a Northerner by birth, and had married a southern lady. On his return, he told my grandmother that he had seen her son, and of the service he had rendered him.

Benjamin reached New York safely, and concluded to stop there until he had gained strength enough to proceed further. It happened that my grandmother's only remaining son had sailed for the same city on business for his mistress. Through God's providence, the brothers met. You may be sure it was a happy meeting. "O Phil," exclaimed Benjamin, "I am here at last." Then he told him how near he came to dying, almost in sight of free land, and how he prayed that he might live to get one breath of free air. He said life was worth something now, and it would be hard to die. In the old jail he had not valued it; once, he was tempted to destroy it; but something, he did not know what, had prevented him; perhaps it was fear. He had heard those who profess to be religious declare there was no heaven for self-murderers; and as his life had been pretty hot here, he did not desire a continuation of the same in another world. "If I die now," he exclaimed, "thank God, I shall die a freeman!"

He begged my uncle Phillip not to return south; but stay and work with him, till they earned enough to buy those at home. His brother told him it would kill their mother if he deserted her in her trouble. She had pledged her house, and with difficulty had raised money to buy him. Would he be bought?

"No, never!" he replied. "Do you suppose, Phil, when I have got so far out of their clutches, I will give them one red cent? No! And do you suppose I would turn mother out of her home in her old age? That I would let her pay all those hard-earned dollars for me, and never to see me? For you know she will stay south as long as her other children are slaves. What a good mother! Tell her to buy *you*, Phil. You have been a comfort to her, and I have been a trouble. And Linda, poor Linda; what'll become of her? Phil, you don't know what a life they lead her. She has told me something about it, and I wish old Flint was dead, or a better man. When I was in jail, he asked her if she didn't want *him* to ask my master to forgive me, and take me home again. She told him, No; that I didn't want to go back. He got mad, and said we were all alike. I never despised my own master half as much as I do that man. There is many a worse slaveholder than my master; but for all that I would not be his slave."

While Benjamin was sick, he had parted with nearly all his clothes to pay necessary expenses. But he did not part with a little pin I fastened in his bosom when we parted. It was the most valuable thing I owned, and I thought none more worthy to wear it. He had it still.

His brother furnished him with clothes, and gave him what money he had.

They parted with moistened eyes; and as Benjamin turned away, he said, "Phil, I part with all my kindred." And so it proved. We never heard from him again.

Uncle Phillip came home; and the first words he uttered when he entered the house were, "Mother, Ben is free! I have seen him in New York." She stood looking at him with a bewildered air. "Mother, don't you believe it?" he said, laying his hand softly upon her shoulder. She raised her hands, and exclaimed, "God be praised! Let us thank him." She dropped on her knees, and poured forth her heart in prayer. Then Phillip must sit down and repeat to her every word Benjamin had said. He told her all; only he forbore to mention how sick and pale her darling looked. Why should he distress her when she could do him no good?

The brave old woman still toiled on, hoping to rescue some of her other children. After a while she succeeded in buying Phillip. She paid eight hundred dollars, and came home with the precious document that secured his freedom. The happy mother and son sat together by the old hearthstone that night, telling how proud they were of each other, and how they would prove to the world that they could take care of themselves, as they had long taken care of others. We all concluded by saying, "He that is *willing* to be a slave, let him be a slave."

## V

## The Trials of Girlhood

During the first years of my service in Dr. Flint's family, I was accustomed to share some indulgences with the children of my mistress. Though this seemed to me no more than right, I was grateful for it, and tried to merit the kindness by the faithful discharge of my duties. But I now entered on my fifteenth year—a sad epoch in the life of a slave girl. My master began to whisper foul words in my ear. Young as I was, I could not remain ignorant of their import. I tried to treat them with indifference or contempt. The master's age, my extreme youth, and the fear that his conduct would be reported to my grandmother, made me bear this treatment for many months. He was a crafty man, and resorted to many means to accomplish his purposes. Sometimes he had stormy, terrific ways, that made his victims tremble; sometimes he assumed a gentleness that he thought must surely subdue. Of the two, I preferred his stormy moods, although they left me trembling. He tried his utmost to corrupt the pure principles my grandmother had instilled. He peopled my young mind with unclean images, such as only a vile monster could think of. I turned from him with disgust and hatred. But he was my master. I was compelled to live under the same roof with him—where I saw a man forty years my senior daily violating the most sacred commandments of nature. He told me I was his property; that I must be subject to his will in all things. My soul revolted against the mean tyranny. But where could I turn for protection? No matter whether the slave girl be as black as ebony or as fair as her mistress. In either case, there is no shadow of law to protect her from insult, from violence, or even from death; all these are inflicted by fiends who bear the shape of men. The mistress, who ought to protect the helpless victim, has no other feelings towards her but those of jealousy and rage. The degradation, the wrongs, the vices, that grow out of slavery, are more than I can describe. They are greater than you would willingly believe. Surely, if you credited one half the truths that are told you concerning the helpless millions suffering in this cruel bondage, you at the north would not help to tighten the yoke. You surely would refuse to do for the master, on your own soil, the mean and cruel work which trained bloodhounds and the lowest class of whites do for him at the south.

Every where the years bring to all enough of sin and sorrow; but in slavery the very dawn of life is darkened by these shadows. Even the little child, who is accustomed to wait on her mistress and her children, will learn, before she is twelve years old, why it is that her mistress hates such and such a one among the slaves. Perhaps the child's own mother is among those hated ones. She listens to violent outbreaks of jealous passion, and cannot help understanding what is the cause. She will become prematurely knowing in evil things. Soon she will learn to tremble when she hears her master's footfall. She will be compelled to realize that she is no longer a child. If God has bestowed beauty upon her, it will prove her greatest curse. That which commands admiration in the white woman only hastens the degradation of the female slave. I know that some are too much brutalized by slavery to feel the humiliation of their position; but many slaves feel it most acutely, and shrink from the memory of it. I cannot tell how much I suffered in the presence of these wrongs, nor how I am still pained by the retrospect. My master met me at every turn, reminding me that I belonged to him, and swearing by heaven and earth that he would compel me to submit to him. If I went out for a breath of fresh air, after a day of unwearied toil, his footsteps dogged me. If I knelt by my mother's grave, his dark shadow fell on me even there. The light heart which nature had given me became heavy with sad forebodings. The other slaves in my master's house noticed the change. Many of them pitied me; but none dared to ask the cause. They had no need to inquire. They knew too well the guilty practices under that roof; and they were aware that to speak of them was an offence that never went unpunished.

I longed for some one to confide in. I would have given the world to have laid my head on my grandmother's faithful bosom, and told her all my troubles. But Dr. Flint swore he would kill me, if I was not as silent as the grave. Then, although my grandmother was all in all to me, I feared her as well as loved her. I had been accustomed to look up to her with a respect bordering upon awe. I was very young, and felt shamefaced about telling her such impure things, especially as I knew her to be very strict on such subjects. Moreover, she was a woman of a high spirit. She was usually very quiet in her demeanor; but if her indignation was once roused, it was not very easily quelled. I had been told that she once chased a white gentleman with a loaded pistol, because he insulted one of her daughters. I dreaded the consequences of a violent outbreak; and both pride and fear kept me silent. But though I did not confide in my grandmother, and even evaded her vigilant watchfulness and inquiry, her presence in the neighborhood was some protection to me. Though she had been a slave, Dr. Flint was afraid of her. He dreaded her scorching rebukes. Moreover, she was known and patronized by many people; and he did not wish to have his villany made public. It was lucky for me that I did not live on a distant plantation, but in a town not so large that the inhabitants were ignorant of each other's affairs. Bad as are the laws and customs in a slaveholding community, the doctor, as a professional man, deemed it prudent to keep up some outward show of decency.

O, what days and nights of fear and sorrow that man caused me! Reader, it is not to awaken sympathy for myself that I am telling you truthfully what I suffered in slavery. I do it to kindle a flame of compassion in your hearts for my sisters who are still in bondage, suffering as I once suffered.

I once saw two beautiful children playing together. One was a fair white child; the other was her slave, and also her sister. When I saw them embracing each other, and heard their joyous laughter, I turned sadly away from the lovely sight. I foresaw the inevitable blight that would fall on the little slave's heart. I knew how soon her laughter would be changed to sighs. The fair child grew up to be a still fairer woman. From childhood to womanhood her pathway was blooming with flowers, and overarched by a sunny sky. Scarcely one day of her life had been clouded when the sun rose on her happy bridal morning.

How had those years dealt with her slave sister, the little playmate of her childhood? She, also, was very beautiful; but the flowers and sunshine of love were not for her. She drank the cup of sin, and shame, and misery, whereof her persecuted race are compelled to drink.

In view of these things, why are ye silent, ye free men and women of the north? Why do your tongues falter in maintenance of the right? Would that I had more ability! But my heart is so full, and my pen is so weak! There are noble men and women who plead for us, striving to help those who cannot help themselves. God bless them! God give them strength and courage to go on! God bless those, every where, who are laboring to advance the cause of humanity!

## VI
### The Jealous Mistress

I would ten thousand times rather that my children should be the half-starved paupers of Ireland than to be the most pampered among the slaves of America. I would rather drudge out my life on a cotton plantation, till the grave opened to give me rest, than to live with an unprincipled master and a jealous mistress. The felon's home in a penitentiary is preferable. He may repent, and turn from the error of his ways, and so find peace; but it is not so with a favorite slave. She is not allowed to have any pride of character. It is deemed a crime in her to wish to be virtuous.

Mrs. Flint possessed the key to her husband's character before I was born. She might have used this knowledge to counsel and to screen the young and the innocent among her slaves; but for them she had no sympathy. They were the objects of her constant suspicion and malevolence. She watched her husband with unceasing vigilance; but he was well practiced in means to evade it. What he could not find opportunity to say in words he manifested in signs. He invented more than were ever thought of in a deaf and dumb asylum. I let them pass, as if I did not understand what he meant; and many were the curses and threats bestowed on me for my stupidity. One day he caught me teaching myself to write. He frowned, as if he was not well pleased; but I suppose he came to the conclusion that such an accomplishment might help to advance his favorite

scheme. Before long, notes were often slipped into my hand. I would return them, saying, "I can't read them, sir." "Can't you?" he replied; "then I
must read them to you." He always finished the reading by asking, "Do
you understand?" Sometimes he would complain of the heat of the tea
room, and order his supper to be placed on a small table in the piazza. He
would seat himself there with a well-satisfied smile, and tell me to stand
by and brush away the flies. He would eat very slowly, pausing between
the mouthfuls. These intervals were employed in describing the happiness
I was so foolishly throwing away, and in threatening me with the penalty
that finally awaited my stubborn disobedience. He boasted much of the
forbearance he had exercised towards me, and reminded me that there
was a limit to his patience. When I succeeded in avoiding opportunities
for him to talk to me at home, I was ordered to come to his office, to do
some errand. When there, I was obliged to stand and listen to such language as he saw fit to address to me. Sometimes I so openly expressed my
contempt for him that he would become violently enraged, and I wondered why he did not strike me. Circumstanced as he was, he probably
thought it was better policy to be forbearing. But the state of things grew
worse and worse daily. In desperation I told him that I must and would
apply to my grandmother for protection. He threatened me with death,
and worse than death, if I made any complaint to her. Strange to say, I did
not despair. I was naturally of a buoyant disposition, and always I had a
hope of somehow getting out of his clutches. Like many a poor, simple
slave before me, I trusted that some threads of joy would yet be woven
into my dark destiny.

I had entered my sixteenth year, and every day it became more apparent that my presence was intolerable to Mrs. Flint. Angry words frequently passed between her and her husband. He had never punished me
himself, and he would not allow any body else to punish me. In that respect, she was never satisfied; but, in her angry moods, no terms were too
vile for her to bestow upon me. Yet I, whom she detested so bitterly, had
far more pity for her than he had, whose duty it was to make her life
happy. I never wronged her, or wished to wrong her; and one word of
kindness from her would have brought me to her feet.

After repeated quarrels between the doctor and his wife, he announced his intention to take his youngest daughter, then four years old,
to sleep in his apartment. It was necessary that a servant should sleep in
the same room, to be on hand if the child stirred. I was selected for that office, and informed for what purpose that arrangement had been made. By
managing to keep within sight of people, as much as possible, during the
day time, I had hitherto succeeded in eluding my master, though a [razor]
was often held to my throat to force me to change this line of policy. At
night I slept by the side of my great aunt, where I felt safe. He was too
prudent to come into her room. She was an old woman, and had been in
the family many years. Moreover, as a married man, and a professional
man, he deemed it necessary to save appearances in some degree. But he

resolved to remove the obstacle in the way of his scheme; and he thought he had planned it so that he should evade suspicion. He was well aware how much I prized my refuge by the side of my old aunt, and he determined to dispossess me of it. The first night the doctor had the little child in his room alone. The next morning, I was ordered to take my station as nurse the following night. A kind Providence interposed in my favor. During the day Mrs. Flint heard of this new arrangement, and a storm followed. I rejoiced to hear it rage.

After a while my mistress sent for me to come to her room. Her first question was, "Did you know you were to sleep in the doctor's room?"

"Yes, ma'am."

"Who told you?"

"My master."

"Will you answer truly all the questions I ask?"

"Yes, ma'am."

"Tell me, then, as you hope to be forgiven, are you innocent of what I have accused you?"

"I am."

She handed me a Bible, and said, "Lay your hand on your heart, kiss this holy book, and swear before God that you tell me the truth."

I took the oath she required, and I did it with a clear conscience.

"You have taken God's holy word to testify your innocence," said she. "If you have deceived me, beware! Now take this stool, sit down, look me directly in the face, and tell me all that has passed between your master and you."

I did as she ordered. As I went on with my account her color changed frequently, she wept, and sometimes groaned. She spoke in tones so sad, that I was touched by her grief. The tears came to my eyes; but I was soon convinced that her emotions arose from anger and wounded pride. She felt that her marriage vows were desecrated, her dignity insulted; but she had no compassion for the poor victim of her husband's perfidy. She pitied herself as a martyr; but she was incapable of feeling for the condition of shame and misery in which her unfortunate, helpless slave was placed.

Yet perhaps she had some touch of feeling for me; for when the conference was ended, she spoke kindly, and promised to protect me. I should have been much comforted by this assurance if I could have had confidence in it; but my experiences in slavery had filled me with distrust. She was not a very refined woman, and had not much control over her passions. I was an object of her jealousy, and, consequently, of her hatred; and I knew I could not expect kindness or confidence from her under the circumstances in which I was placed. I could not blame her. Slaveholders' wives feel as other women would under similar circumstances. The fire of her temper kindled from small sparks, and now the flame became so intense that the doctor was obliged to give up his intended arrangement.

I knew I had ignited the torch, and I expected to suffer for it after-

wards; but I felt too thankful to my mistress for the timely aid she rendered me to care much about that. She now took me to sleep in a room
adjoining her own. There I was an object of her especial care, though not
of her especial comfort, for she spent many a sleepless night to watch
over me. Sometimes I woke up, and found her bending over me. At other
times she whispered in my ear, as though it was her husband who was
speaking to me, and listened to hear what I would answer. If she startled
me, on such occasions, she would glide stealthily away; and the next
morning she would tell me I had been talking in my sleep, and ask who
I was talking to. At last, I began to be fearful for my life. It had been often
threatened; and you can imagine, better than I can describe, what an unpleasant sensation it must produce to wake up in the dead of night and
find a jealous woman bending over you. Terrible as this experience was,
I had fears that it would give place to one more terrible.

My mistress grew weary of her vigils; they did not prove satisfactory.
She changed her tactics. She now tried the trick of accusing my master of
crime, in my presence, and gave my name as the author of the accusation.
To my utter astonishment, he replied, "I don't believe it; but if she did acknowledge it, you tortured her into exposing me." Tortured into exposing
him! Truly, Satan had no difficulty in distinguishing the color of his soul! I
understood his object in making this false representation. It was to show
me that I gained nothing by seeking the protection of my mistress; that the
power was still all in his own hands. I pitied Mrs. Flint. She was a second
wife, many years the junior of her husband; and the hoary-headed miscre-
ant was enough to try the patience of a wiser and better woman. She was
completely foiled, and knew not how to proceed. She would gladly have
had me flogged for my supposed false oath; but, as I have already stated,
the doctor never allowed any one to whip me. The old sinner was politic.
The application of the lash might have led to remarks that would have exposed him in the eyes of his children and grandchildren. How often did I
rejoice that I lived in a town where all the inhabitants knew each other! If
I had been on a remote plantation, or lost among the multitude of a
crowded city, I should not be a living woman at this day.

The secrets of slavery are concealed like those of the Inquisition. My
master was, to my knowledge, the father of eleven slaves. But did the
mothers dare to tell who was the father of their children? Did the other
slaves dare to allude to it, except in whispers among themselves? No, indeed! They knew too well the terrible consequences.

My grandmother could not avoid seeing things which excited her suspicions. She was uneasy about me, and tried various ways to buy me; but
the never-changing answer was always repeated: "Linda does not belong
to *me*. She is my daughter's property, and I have no legal right to sell her."
The conscientious man! He was too scrupulous to *sell* me; but he had no
scruples whatever about committing a much greater wrong against the
helpless young girl placed under his guardianship, as his daughter's property. Sometimes my persecutor would ask me whether I would like to be

sold. I told him I would rather be sold to any body than to lead such a life as I did. On such occasions he would assume the air of a very injured individual, and reproach me for my ingratitude. "Did I not take you into the house, and make you the companion of my own children?" he would say. "Have I ever treated you like a negro? I have never allowed you to be punished, not even to please your mistress. And this is the recompense I get, you ungrateful girl!" I answered that he had reasons of his own for screening me from punishment, and that the course he pursued made my mistress hate me and persecute me. If I wept, he would say, "Poor child! Don't cry! don't cry! I will make peace for you with your mistress. Only let me arrange matters in my own way. Poor, foolish girl! you don't know what is for your own good. I would cherish you. I would make a lady of you. Now go, and think of all I have promised you."

I did think of it.

Reader, I draw no imaginary pictures of southern homes. I am telling you the plain truth. Yet when victims make their escape from this wild beast of Slavery, northerners consent to act the part of bloodhounds, and hunt the poor fugitive back into his den, "full of dead men's bones, and all uncleanness." Nay, more, they are not only willing, but proud, to give their daughters in marriage to slaveholders. The poor girls have romantic notions of a sunny clime, and of the flowering vines that all the year round shade a happy home. To what disappointments are they destined! The young wife soon learns that the husband in whose hands she has placed her happiness pays no regard to his marriage vows. Children of every shade of complexion play with her own fair babies, and too well she knows that they are born unto him of his own household. Jealousy and hatred enter the flowery home, and it is ravaged of its loveliness.

Southern women often marry a man knowing that he is the father of many little slaves. They do not trouble themselves about it. They regard such children as property, as marketable as the pigs on the plantation; and it is seldom that they do not make them aware of this by passing them into the slave-trader's hands as soon as possible, and thus getting them out of their sight. I am glad to say there are some honorable exceptions.

I have myself known two southern wives who exhorted their husbands to free those slaves towards whom they stood in a "parental relation"; and their request was granted. These husbands blushed before the superior nobleness of their wives' natures. Though they had only counselled them to do that which it was their duty to do, it commanded their respect, and rendered their conduct more exemplary. Concealment was at an end, and confidence took the place of distrust.

Though this bad institution deadens the moral sense, even in white women, to a fearful extent, it is not altogether extinct. I have heard southern ladies say of Mr. Such a one, "He not only thinks it no disgrace to be the father of those little niggers, but he is not ashamed to call himself their master. I declare, such things ought not to be tolerated, in any decent society!"

## VII
## The Lover

Why does the slave ever love? Why allow the tendrils of the heart to twine around objects which may at any moment be wrenched away by the hand of violence? When separations come by the hand of death, the pious soul can bow in resignation, and say, "Not my will, but thine be done, O Lord!" But when the ruthless hand of man strikes the blow, regardless of the misery he causes, it is hard to be submissive. I did not reason thus when I was a young girl. Youth will be youth. I loved, and I indulged the hope that the dark clouds around me would turn out a bright lining. I forgot that in the land of my birth the shadows are too dense for light to penetrate. A land

> Where laughter is not mirth; nor thought the mind;
> Nor words a language; nor e'en men mankind.
> Where cries reply to curses, shrieks to blows,
> And each is tortured in his separate hell.

There was in the neighborhood a young colored carpenter; a free-born man. We had been well acquainted in childhood, and frequently met together afterwards. We became mutually attached, and he proposed to marry me. I loved him with all the ardor of a young girl's first love. But when I reflected that I was a slave, and that the laws gave no sanction to the marriage of such, my heart sank within me. My lover wanted to buy me; but I knew that Dr. Flint was too wilful and arbitrary a man to consent to that arrangement. From him, I was sure of experiencing all sorts of opposition, and I had nothing to hope from my mistress. She would have been delighted to have got rid of me, but not in that way. It would have relieved her mind of a burden if she could have seen me sold to some distant state, but if I was married near home I should be just as much in her husband's power as I had previously been,—for the husband of a slave has no power to protect her. Moreover, my mistress, like many others, seemed to think that slaves had no right to any family ties of their own; that they were created merely to wait upon the family of the mistress. I once heard her abuse a young slave girl, who told her that a colored man wanted to make her his wife. "I will have you peeled and pickled, my lady," said she, "if I ever hear you mention that subject again. Do you suppose that I will have you tending *my* children with the children of that nigger?" The girl to whom she said this had a mulatto child, of course not acknowledged by its father. The poor black man who loved her would have been proud to acknowledge his helpless offspring.

Many and anxious were the thoughts I revolved in my mind. I was at a loss what to do. Above all things, I was desirous to spare my lover the insults that had cut so deeply into my own soul. I talked with my grandmother about it, and partly told her my fears. I did not dare to tell her the worst. She had long suspected all was not right, and if I confirmed her suspicions I knew a storm would rise that would prove the overthrow of all my hopes.

This love-dream had been my support through many trials; and I could not bear to run the risk of having it suddenly dissipated. There was a lady in the neighborhood, a particular friend of Dr. Flint's, who often visited the house. I had a great respect for her, and she had always manifested a friendly interest in me. Grandmother thought she would have great influence with the doctor. I went to this lady, and told her my story. I told her I was aware that my lover's being a free-born man would prove a great objection; but he wanted to buy me; and if Dr. Flint would consent to that arrangement, I felt sure he would be willing to pay any reasonable price. She knew that Mrs. Flint disliked me; therefore, I ventured to suggest that perhaps my mistress would approve of my being sold, as that would rid her of me. The lady listened with kindly sympathy, and promised to do her utmost to promote my wishes. She had an interview with the doctor, and I believe she pleaded my cause earnestly; but it was all to no purpose.

How I dreaded my master now! Every minute I expected to be summoned to his presence; but the day passed, and I heard nothing from him. The next morning, a message was brought to me: "Master wants you in his study." I found the door ajar, and I stood a moment gazing at the hateful man who claimed a right to rule me, body and soul. I entered, and tried to appear calm. I did not want him to know how my heart was bleeding. He looked fixedly at me, with an expression which seemed to say, "I have half a mind to kill you on the spot." At last he broke the silence, and that was a relief to both of us.

"So you want to be married, do you?" said he, "and to a free nigger."

"Yes, sir."

"Well, I'll soon convince you whether I am your master, or the nigger fellow you honor so highly. If you *must* have a husband, you may take up with one of my slaves."

What a situation I should be in, as the wife of one of *his* slaves, even if my heart had been interested!

I replied, "Don't you suppose, sir, that a slave can have some preference about marrying? Do you suppose that all men are alike to her?"

"Do you love this nigger?" said he, abruptly.

"Yes, sir."

"How dare you tell me so!" he exclaimed, in great wrath. After a slight pause, he added, "I supposed you thought more of yourself; that you felt above the insults of such puppies."

I replied, "If he is a puppy I am a puppy, for we are both of the negro race. It is right and honorable for us to love each other. The man you call a puppy never insulted me, sir; and he would not love me if he did not believe me to be a virtuous woman."

He sprang upon me like a tiger, and gave me a stunning blow. It was the first time he had ever struck me; and fear did not enable me to control my anger. When I had recovered a little from the effects, I exclaimed, "You have struck me for answering you honestly. How I despise you!"

There was silence for some minutes. Perhaps he was deciding what should be my punishment; or, perhaps, he wanted to give me time to reflect on what I had said, and to whom I had said it. Finally, he asked, "Do you know what you have said?"

"Yes, sir; but your treatment drove me to it."

"Do you know that I have a right to do as I like with you,—that I can kill you, if I please?"

"You have tried to kill me, and I wish you had; but you have no right to do as you like with me."

"Silence!" he exclaimed, in a thundering voice. "By heavens, girl, you forget yourself too far! Are you mad? If you are, I will soon bring you to your senses. Do you think any other master would bear what I have borne from you this morning? Many masters would have killed you on the spot. How would you like to be sent to jail for your insolence?"

"I know I have been disrespectful, sir," I replied; "but you drove me to it; I couldn't help it. As for the jail, there would be more peace for me there than there is here."

"You deserve to go there," said he, "and to be under such treatment, that you would forget the meaning of the word *peace*. It would do you good. It would take some of your high notions out of you. But I am not ready to send you there yet, notwithstanding your ingratitude for all my kindness and forbearance. You have been the plague of my life. I have wanted to make you happy, and I have been repaid with the basest ingratitude; but though you have proved yourself incapable of appreciating my kindness, I will be lenient towards you, Linda. I will give you one more chance to redeem your character. If you behave yourself and do as I require, I will forgive you and treat you as I always have done; but if you disobey me, I will punish you as I would the meanest slave on my plantation. Never let me hear that fellow's name mentioned again. If I ever know of your speaking to him, I will cowhide you both; and if I catch him lurking about my premises, I will shoot him as soon as I would a dog. Do you hear what I say? I'll teach you a lesson about marriage and free niggers! Now go, and let this be the last time I have occasion to speak to you on this subject."

Reader, did you ever hate? I hope not. I never did but once; and I trust I never shall again. Somebody has called it "the atmosphere of hell"; and I believe it is so.

For a fortnight the doctor did not speak to me. He thought to mortify me; to make me feel that I had disgraced myself by receiving the honorable addresses of a respectable colored man, in preference to the base proposals of a white man. But though his lips disdained to address me, his eyes were very loquacious. No animal ever watched its prey more narrowly than he watched me. He knew that I could write, though he had failed to make me read his letters; and he was now troubled lest I should exchange letters with another man. After a while he became weary of silence; and I was sorry for it. One morning, as he passed through the hall, to leave the house, he contrived to thrust a note into my hand. I thought I had better read it, and spare myself the vexation of having him read it to me. It expressed regret for the blow he had given me, and reminded me that I myself was wholly to blame for it. He hoped I had become convinced of the injury I was doing myself by incurring his displeasure. He wrote that he had made up his mind to go to Louisiana; that he should take several slaves with him, and intended I should be one of the number. My mistress would remain where she was; therefore I should have nothing to fear from that quarter. If I merited kindness from him, he assured me that it would be lavishly bestowed. He begged me to think over the matter, and answer the following day.

The next morning I was called to carry a pair of scissors to his room. I laid them on the table, with the letter beside them. He thought it was my answer, and did not call me back. I went as usual to attend my young mistress to and from school. He met me in the street, and ordered me to stop at his office on my way back. When I entered, he showed me his letter, and asked me why I had not answered it. I replied, "I am your daughter's property, and it is in your power to send me, or take me, wherever you please." He said he was very glad to find me so willing to go, and that we should start early in the autumn. He had a large practice in the town, and I rather thought he had made up the story merely to frighten me. However that might be, I was determined that I would never go to Louisiana with him.

Summer passed away, and early in the autumn Dr. Flint's eldest son was sent to Louisiana to examine the country, with a view to emigrating. That news did not disturb me. I knew very well that I should not be sent with *him.* That I had not been taken to the plantation before this time, was owing to the fact that his son was there. He was jealous of his son; and jealousy of the overseer had kept him from punishing me by sending me into the fields to work. Is it strange that I was not proud of these protectors? As for the overseer, he was a man for whom I had less respect than I had for a bloodhound.

Young Mr. Flint did not bring back a favorable report of Louisiana, and I heard no more of that scheme. Soon after this, my lover met me at the corner of the street, and I stopped to speak to him. Looking up, I saw my master watching us from his window. I hurried home, trembling with fear. I was sent for, immediately, to go to his room. He met me with a blow. "When is mistress to be married?" said he, in a sneering tone. A shower of oaths and imprecations followed. How thankful I was that my lover was a free man! that my tyrant had no power to flog him for speaking to me in the street!

Again and again I revolved in my mind how all this would end. There was no hope that the doctor would consent to sell me on any terms. He had an iron will, and was determined to keep me, and to conquer me. My lover was an intelligent and religious man. Even if he could have obtained permission to marry me while I was a slave, the marriage would give him no power to protect me from my master. It would have made him miserable to witness the insults I should have been subjected to. And then, if we had children, I knew they must "follow the condition of the mother." What a terrible blight that would be on the heart of a free, intelligent father! For *his* sake, I felt that I ought not to link his fate with my own unhappy destiny. He was going to Savannah to see about a little property left him by an uncle; and hard as it was to bring my feelings to it, I earnestly entreated him not to come back. I advised him to go to the Free States, where his tongue would not be tied, and where his intelligence would be of more avail to him. He left me, still hoping the day would come when I could be bought. With me the lamp of hope had gone out. The dream of my girlhood was over. I felt lonely and desolate.

Still I was not stripped of all. I still had my good grandmother, and my affectionate brother. When he put his arms round my neck, and looked into my eyes, as if to read there the troubles I dared not tell, I felt that I still had something to love. But even that pleasant emotion was chilled by the reflection that he might be torn from me at any moment, by some sudden freak of my master. If he had known how we loved each other, I think he would have exulted in separating us. We often planned together how we could get to the north. But, as William remarked, such things are easier said than done. My movements were very closely watched, and we had no means of getting any money to defray our expenses. As for grandmother, she was strongly opposed to her children's undertaking any such project. She had not forgotten poor Benjamin's sufferings, and she was afraid that if another child tried to escape, he would have a similar or a worse fate. To me, nothing seemed more dreadful than my present life. I said to myself, "William *must* be free. He shall go to the north, and I will follow him." Many a slave sister has formed the same plans. . . .

## X
## A Perilous Passage in the Slave Girl's Life

After my lover went away, Dr. Flint contrived a new plan. He seemed to have an idea that my fear of my mistress was his greatest obstacle. In the blandest tones, he told me that he was going to build a small house for me, in a secluded place, four miles away from the town. I shuddered; but I was constrained to listen, while he talked of his intention to give me a home of my own, and to make a lady of me. Hitherto, I had escaped my dreaded fate, by being in the midst of people. My grandmother had already had high words with my master about me. She had told him pretty plainly what she thought of his character, and there was considerable gossip in the neighborhood about our affairs, to which the open-mouthed jealousy of Mrs. Flint contributed not a little. When my master said he was going to build a house for me, and that he could do it with little trouble and expense, I was in hopes something would happen to frustrate his scheme; but I soon heard that the house was actually begun. I vowed before my Maker that I would never enter it. I had rather toil on the plantation from dawn till dark; I had rather live and die in jail, than drag on, from day to day, through such a living death. I was determined that the master, whom I so hated and loathed, who had blighted the prospects of my youth, and made my life a desert, should not, after my long struggle with him, succeed at last in trampling his victim under his feet. I would do any thing, every thing, for the sake of defeating him. What *could* I do? I thought and thought, till I became desperate, and made a plunge into the abyss.

And now, reader, I come to a period in my unhappy life, which I would gladly forget if I could. The remembrance fills me with sorrow and shame. It pains me to tell you of it; but I have promised to tell you the truth, and I will do it honestly, let it cost me what it may. I will not try to screen myself behind the plea of compulsion from a master; for it was not so. Neither can I plead ignorance or thoughtlessness. For years, my master had done his utmost to pollute my mind with foul images, and to destroy the pure principles inculcated by my grandmother, and the good mistress of my childhood. The influences of slavery had had the same effect on me that they had on other young girls; they had made me prematurely knowing, concerning the evil ways of the world. I knew what I did, and I did it with deliberate calculation.

But, O, ye happy women, whose purity has been sheltered from childhood, who have been free to choose the objects of your affection, whose homes are protected by law, do not judge the poor desolate slave girl too severely! If slavery had been abolished, I, also, could have married the man of my choice; I could have had a home shielded by the laws; and I should have been spared the painful task of confessing what I am now about to relate; but all my prospects had been blighted by slavery. I wanted to keep myself pure; and, under the most adverse circumstances, I tried hard to preserve my self-respect; but I was struggling alone in the powerful grasp of the demon Slavery; and the monster proved too strong for me. I felt as if I was forsaken by God and man; as if all my efforts must be frustrated; and I became reckless in my despair.

I have told you that Dr. Flint's persecutions and his wife's jealousy had given rise to some gossip in the neighborhood. Among others, it chanced that a white unmarried gentleman had obtained some knowledge of the circumstances in which I was placed. He knew my grandmother, and often spoke to me in the street. He became interested for me, and asked questions about my master, which I answered in part. He expressed a great deal of sympathy, and a wish to aid me. He constantly sought opportunities to see me, and wrote to me frequently. I was a poor slave girl, only fifteen years old.

So much attention from a superior person was, of course, flattering; for human nature is the same in all. I also felt grateful for his sympathy, and encouraged by his kind words. It seemed to me a great thing to have such a friend. By degrees, a more tender feeling crept into my heart. He was an educated and eloquent gentleman; too eloquent, alas, for the poor slave girl who trusted in him. Of course I saw whither all this was tending. I knew the impassable gulf between us; but to be an object of interest to a man who is not married, and who is not her master, is agreeable to the pride and feelings of a slave, if her miserable situation has left her any pride or sentiment. It seems less degrading to give one's self, than to submit to compulsion. There is something akin to freedom in having a lover who has no control over you, except that which he gains by kindness and attachment. A master may treat you as rudely as he pleases, and you dare not speak; moreover, the wrong does not seem so great with an unmarried man, as with one who has a wife to be made unhappy. There may be sophistry in all this; but the condition of a slave confuses all principles of morality, and, in fact, renders the practice of them impossible.

When I found that my master had actually begun to build the lonely cottage, other feelings mixed with those I have described. Revenge, and calculations of interest, were added to flattered vanity and sincere gratitude for kindness. I knew nothing would enrage Dr. Flint so much as to know that I favored another; and it was something to triumph over my tyrant even in that small way. I thought he would revenge himself by selling me, and I was sure my friend, Mr. Sands, would buy me. He was a man of more generosity and feeling than my master, and I thought my freedom could be easily obtained from him. The crisis of my fate now came so near that I was desperate. I shuddered to think of being the mother of children that should be owned by my old tyrant. I knew that as soon as a new fancy took him, his victims were sold far off to get rid of them; especially if they had children. I had seen several women sold, with his babies at the breast. He never allowed his offspring by slaves to remain long in sight of himself and his wife. Of a man who was not my master I could ask to have my children well supported; and in this case, I felt confident I should obtain the boon. I also felt quite sure that they would be made free. With all these thoughts revolving in my mind, and seeing no other way of escaping the doom I so much dreaded, I made a headlong plunge. Pity me, and pardon me, O virtuous reader! You never knew what it is to be a slave; to be entirely unprotected by law or custom; to have the laws reduce you to the condition of a chattel, entirely subject to the will of another. You never exhausted your ingenuity in avoiding the snares, and eluding the power of a hated tyrant; you never shuddered at the sound of his footsteps, and trembled within hearing of his voice. I know I did wrong. No one can feel it more sensibly than I do. The painful and humiliating memory will haunt me to my dying day. Still, in looking back, calmly, on the events of my life, I feel that the slave woman ought not to be judged by the same standard as others.

The months passed on. I had many unhappy hours. I secretly mourned over the sorrow I was bringing on my grandmother, who had so tried to shield me from harm. I knew that I was the greatest comfort of her old age, and that it was a source of pride to her that I had not degraded myself, like most of the slaves. I wanted to confess to her that I was no longer worthy of her love; but I could not utter the dreaded words.

As for Dr. Flint, I had a feeling of satisfaction and triumph in the thought of telling *him.* From time to time he told me of his intended arrangements, and I was silent. At last, he came and told me the cottage was completed, and ordered me to go to it. I told him I would never enter it. He said, "I have heard enough of such talk as that. You shall go, if you are carried by force; and you shall remain there."

I replied, "I will never go there. In a few months I shall be a mother."

He stood and looked at me in dumb amazement, and left the house without a word. I thought I should be happy in my triumph over him. But now that the truth was out, and my relatives would hear of it, I felt wretched. Humble as were their circumstances, they had pride in my good character. Now, how could I look them in the face? My self-respect was gone! I had resolved that I would be virtuous, though I was a slave. I had said, "Let the storm beat! I will brave it till I die." And now, how humiliated I felt!

I went to my grandmother. My lips moved to make confession, but the words stuck in my throat. I sat down in the shade of a tree at her door and began to sew. I think she saw something unusual was the matter with me. The mother of slaves is very watchful. She knows there is no security for her children. After they have entered their teens she lives in daily expectation of trouble. This leads to many questions. If the girl is of a sensitive nature, timidity keeps her from answering truthfully, and this well-meant course has a tendency to drive her from maternal counsels. Presently, in came my mistress, like a mad woman, and accused me concerning her husband. My grandmother, whose suspicions had been previously awakened, believed what she said. She exclaimed, "O Linda! has it come to this? I had rather see you dead than to see you as you now are. You are a disgrace to your dead mother." She tore from my fingers my mother's wedding ring and her silver thimble. "Go away!" she exclaimed, "and never come to my house again." Her reproaches fell so hot and heavy, that they left me no chance to answer. Bitter tears, such as the eyes never shed but once, were my only answer. I rose from my seat, but fell back again, sobbing. She did not speak to me; but the tears were running down her furrowed cheeks, and they scorched me like fire. She had always been so kind to me! *So* kind! How I longed to throw myself at her feet, and tell her all the truth! But she had ordered me to go, and never to come there again. After a few minutes, I mustered strength, and started to obey her. With what feelings did I now close that little gate, which I used to open with such an eager hand in my childhood! It closed upon me with a sound I never heard before.

Where could I go? I was afraid to return to my master's. I walked on recklessly, not caring where I went, or what would become of me. When I had gone four or five miles, fatigue compelled me to stop. I sat down on the stump of an old tree. The stars were shining through the boughs above me. How they mocked me, with their bright, calm light! The hours passed by, and as I sat there alone a chilliness and deadly sickness came over me. I sank on the ground. My mind was full of horrid thoughts. I prayed to die; but the prayer was not answered. At last, with great effort I roused myself, and walked some distance further, to the house of a woman who had been a friend of my mother. When I told her why I was there, she spoke soothingly to me; but I could not be comforted. I thought I could bear my shame if I could only be reconciled to my grandmother. I longed to open my heart to her. I thought if she could know the real state of the case, and all I had been bearing for years, she would perhaps judge me less harshly. My friend advised me to send for her. I did so; but days of agonizing suspense passed before she came. Had she utterly forsaken me? No. She came at last. I knelt before her, and told her the things that had poisoned my life; how long I had been persecuted; that I saw no way of escape; and in an hour of extremity I had become desperate. She listened in silence. I told her I would bear any thing and do any thing, if in time I had hopes of obtaining her forgiveness. I begged of her to pity me, for my dead mother's sake. And she did pity me. She did not say, "I forgive you"; but she looked at me lovingly, with her eyes full of tears. She laid her old hand gently on my head, and murmured, "Poor child! Poor child!"

## XI
## The New Tie to Life

I returned to my good grandmother's house. She had an interview with Mr. Sands. When she asked him why he could not have left her one ewe lamb,—whether there were not plenty of slaves who did not care about character,—he made no answer; but he spoke kind and encouraging words. He promised to care for my child, and to buy me, be the conditions what they might.

I had not seen Dr. Flint for five days. I had never seen him since I made the avowal to him. He talked of the disgrace I had brought on myself; how I had sinned against my master, and mortified my old grandmother. He intimated that if I had accepted his proposals, he, as a physician, could have saved me from exposure. He even condescended to pity me. Could he have offered wormwood more bitter? He, whose persecutions had been the cause of my sin!

"Linda," said he, "though you have been criminal towards me, I feel for you, and I can pardon you if you obey my wishes. Tell me whether the fellow you wanted to marry is the father of your child. If you deceive me, you shall feel the fires of hell."

I did not feel as proud as I had done. My strongest weapon with him was gone. I was lowered in my own estimation, and had resolved to bear his abuse in silence. But when he spoke contemptuously of the lover who had always treated me honorably; when I remembered that but for *him* I might have been a virtuous, free, and happy wife, I lost my patience. "I have sinned against God and myself," I replied; "but not against you."

He clinched his teeth, and muttered, "Curse you!" He came towards me, with ill-suppressed rage, and exclaimed, "You obstinate girl! I could grind your bones to powder! You have thrown yourself away on some worthless rascal. You are weak-minded, and have been easily persuaded by those who don't care a straw for you. The future will settle accounts between us. You are blinded now; but hereafter you will be convinced that your master was your best friend. My lenity towards you is a proof of it. I might have punished you in many ways. I might have had you whipped till you fell dead under the lash. But I wanted you to live; I would have bettered your condition. Others cannot do it. You are my slave. Your mistress, disgusted by your conduct, forbids you to return to the house; therefore I leave you here for the present; but I shall see you often. I will call tomorrow."

He came with frowning brows, that showed a dissatisfied state of mind. After asking about my health, he inquired whether my board was paid, and who visited me. He then went on to say that he had neglected his duty; that as a physician there were certain things that he ought to have explained to me. Then followed talk such as would have made the most shameless blush. He ordered me to stand up before him. I obeyed. "I command you," said he, "to tell me whether the father of your child is white or black." I hesitated. "Answer me this instant!" he exclaimed. I did answer. He sprang upon me like a wolf, and grabbed my arm as if he would have broken it. "Do you love him?" said he, in a hissing tone.

"I am thankful that I do not despise him," I replied.

He raised his hand to strike me; but it fell again. I don't know what arrested the blow. He sat down, with lips tightly compressed. At last he spoke. "I came here," said he, "to make you a friendly proposition; but your ingratitude chafes me beyond endurance. You turn aside all my good intentions towards you. I don't know what it is that keeps me from killing you." Again he rose, as if he had a mind to strike me.

But he resumed. "On one condition I will forgive your insolence and crime. You must henceforth have no communication of any kind with the father of your child. You must not ask any thing from him, or receive any thing from him. I will take care of you and your child. You had better promise this at once, and not wait till you are deserted by him. This is the last act of mercy I shall show towards you."

I said something about being unwilling to have my child supported by a man who had cursed it and me also. He rejoined, that a woman who had sunk to my level had no right to expect any thing else. He asked, for the last time, would I accept his kindness? I answered that I would not.

"Very well," said he; "then take the consequences of your wayward course. Never look to me for help. You are my slave, and shall always be my slave. I will never sell you, that you may depend upon."

Hope died away in my heart as he closed the door after him. I had calculated that in his rage he would sell me to a slave-trader; and I knew the father of my child was on the watch to buy me.

About this time my uncle Phillip was expected to return from a voyage. The day before his departure I had officiated as bridesmaid to a young friend. My heart was then ill at ease, but my smiling countenance did not betray it. Only a year had passed; but what fearful changes it had wrought! My heart had grown gray in misery. Lives that flash in sunshine, and lives that are born in tears, receive their hue from circumstances. None of us know what a year may bring forth.

I felt no joy when they told me my uncle had come. He wanted to see me, though he knew what had happened. I shrank from him at first; but at last consented that he should come to my room. He received me as he always had done. O, how my heart smote me when I felt his tears on my burning cheeks! The words of my grandmother came to my mind,—"Perhaps your mother and father are taken from the evil days to come." My disappointed heart could now praise God that it was so. But why, thought I, did my relatives ever cherish hopes for me? What was there to save me from the usual fate of slave girls? Many more beautiful and more intelligent than I had experienced a similar fate, or a far worse one. How could they hope that I should escape?

My uncle's stay was short, and I was not sorry for it. I was too ill in mind and body to enjoy my friends as I had done. For some weeks I was unable to leave my bed. I could not have any doctor but my master, and I would not have him sent for. At last, alarmed by my increasing illness, they sent for him. I was very weak and nervous; and as soon as he entered the room, I began to scream. They told him my state was very critical. He had no wish to hasten me out of the world, and he withdrew.

When my babe was born, they said it was premature. It weighed only four pounds; but God let it live. I heard the doctor say I could not survive till morning. I had often prayed for death; but now I did not want to die, unless my child could die too. Many weeks passed before I was able to leave my bed. I was a mere wreck of my former self. For a year there was scarcely a day when I was free from chills and fever. My babe also was sickly. His little limbs were often racked with pain. Dr. Flint continued his visits, to look after my health; and he did not fail to remind me that my child was an addition to his stock of slaves.

I felt too feeble to dispute with him, and listened to his remarks in silence. His visits were less frequent; but his busy spirit could not remain quiet. He employed my brother in his office, and he was made the medium of frequent notes and messages to me. William was a bright lad, and of much use to the doctor. He had learned to put up medicines, to leech, cup, and bleed. He had taught himself to read and spell. I was proud of my brother; and the old doctor suspected as much. One day, when I had not seen him for several weeks, I heard his steps approaching the door. I dreaded the encounter, and hid myself. He inquired for me, of course; but I was nowhere to be found. He went to his office, and despatched William with a note. The color mounted to my brother's face when he gave it to me; and he said, "Don't you hate me, Linda, for bringing you these things?" I told him I could not blame him; he was a slave, and obliged to obey his master's will. The note ordered me to come to his office. I went. He demanded to know where I was when he called. I told him I was at home. He flew into a passion, and said he knew better. Then he launched out upon his usual themes,—my crimes against him, and my ingratitude for his forbearance. The laws were laid down to me anew, and I was dismissed. I felt humiliated that my brother should stand by, and listen to such language as would be addressed only to a slave. Poor boy! He was powerless to defend me; but I saw the tears, which he vainly strove to keep back. This manifestation of feeling irritated the doctor. William could do nothing to please him. One morning he did not arrive at the office so early as usual; and that circumstance afforded his master an opportunity to vent his spleen. He was put in jail. The next day my brother sent a trader to the doctor, with a request to be sold. His master was greatly incensed at what he called his insolence. He said he had put him there to reflect upon his bad conduct, and he certainly was not giving any evidence of repentance. For two days he harassed himself to find somebody to do his office work; but every thing went wrong without William. He was released, and ordered to take his old stand, with many threats, if he was not careful about his future behavior.

As the months passed on, my boy improved in health. When he was a year old, they called him beautiful. The little vine was taking deep root in my existence, though its clinging fondness excited a mixture of love and pain. When I was most sorely oppressed I found a solace in his smiles. I loved to watch his infant slumbers; but always there was a dark cloud over my enjoyment. I could never forget that he was a slave. Sometimes I wished that he might die in infancy. God tried me. My darling became very ill. The bright eyes grew dull, and the little feet and hands were so icy cold that I thought death had already touched them. I had prayed for his death, but never so earnestly as I now prayed for his life; and my prayer was heard. Alas, what mockery it is for a slave mother to try to pray back her dying child to life! Death is better than slavery. It was a sad thought that I had no name to give my child. His father caressed him and treated him kindly, whenever he had a chance to see him. He was not unwilling that he should bear his name; but he had no legal claim to it; and if I had bestowed it upon him, my master would have regarded it as a new crime, a new piece of insolence, and would, perhaps, revenge it on the boy. O, the serpent of Slavery has many and poisonous fangs!

•   •   •   •   •   •   •   •   •   •   •   •   •

## QUESTIONS FOR A SECOND READING

1. This text makes it difficult to say what we are prepared to say: that slaves were illiterate, uneducated, simple in their speech and thought. Jacobs's situation was not typical, to be sure, but she challenges the assumptions we bring to our imagination of this country's past and its people. This text has to be read carefully or it becomes familiar, a product of what we think we already know.

   As you reread, mark sentences or phrases or paragraphs you might use to illustrate Jacobs's characteristic style or skill as a writer. And mark those features of the text you might use to identify this text as the work of a woman held in slavery. Where and how is doing this difficult? surprising? a problem?

2. In her preface, Jacobs says that she doesn't care to excite sympathy for her suffering but to "arouse the women of the North to a realizing sense of the condition of two millions of women at the South." As you reread this selection, pay attention to the ways Jacobs addresses (and tries to influence) her readers. Why would she be suspicious of sympathy? What do you suppose she might have meant by "a realizing sense"? What kind of reader does she want? Why does she address women?

   Be sure to mark those sections that address the reader directly, and also those that seem to give evidence of Jacobs as a writer, working on the material, highlighting some incidents and passing over others (why do we get "incidents" and not the full story?), organizing our experience of the text, shaping scenes and sentences, organizing chapters. What is Jacobs doing in this text? What might her work as a writer have to do with her position (as a female slave) in relation to the world of her readers?

3. The emotional and family relations between people are difficult to chart in this selection, partly because they defy easy categorization. Can we, for example, assume that blacks and whites lived separately? that blacks were in bondage and whites were free? that family lines and color lines were distinct markers? that lovers were lovers and enemies were enemies? As you reread, pay close attention to the ways people are organized by family, love, community, and color. See what you can determine about the codes that govern relations in this representation of slave culture. And ask where and how Jacobs places herself in these various networks.

## ASSIGNMENTS FOR WRITING

1. In the preface to her edition of *Incidents in the Life of a Slave Girl,* Jean Fagin Yellin says the following about Jacobs's narrative:

   > Contrasting literary styles express the contradictory thrusts of the story. Presenting herself as a heroic slave mother, Jacobs's narrator includes clear detail, uses straightforward language, and when address-

ing the reader directly, utilizes standard abolitionist rhetoric to lament
the inadequacy of her descriptions and to urge her audience to involve
themselves in antislavery efforts. But she treats her sexual experiences
obliquely, and when addressing the reader concerning her sexual behavior, pleads for forgiveness in the overwrought style of popular fiction. These melodramatic confessions are, however, subsumed within
the text. What finally dominates is a new voice. It is the voice of a
woman who, although she cannot discuss her sexual past without expressing deep conflict, nevertheless addresses this painful personal
subject in order to politicize it, to insist that the forbidden topic of the
sexual abuse of slave women be included in public discussions of the
slavery question. By creating a narrator who presents her private sexual history as a subject of public political concern, Jacobs moves her
book out of the world of conventional nineteenth-century polite discourse. In and through her creation of Linda Brent, who yokes her success story as a heroic slave mother to her confession as a woman who
mourns that she is not a storybook heroine, Jacobs articulates her
struggle to assert her womanhood and projects a new kind of female
hero.

Yellin's account of the "voice" in Jacobs's text gives us a way to foreground the difference between life and narrative, a person (Harriet Jacobs) and a person rendered on the page ("Linda Brent," the "I" of the
narrative), between the experience of slavery and the conventional ways
of telling the story of slavery, between experience and the ways in which
experience is shaped by a writer, readers, and a culture. It is interesting, in
this sense, to read Yellin's account of *Incidents* along with Houston
Baker's more general account of the "voice of the Southern slave" (quoted
at length on p. 458). Baker, you may recall, said: "The voice of the unwritten self, once it is subjected to the linguistic codes, literary conventions,
and audience expectations of a literate population, is perhaps never again
the authentic voice of black American slavery. It is, rather, the voice of a
self transformed by an autobiographical act into a sharer in the general
public discourse about slavery."

Jacobs's situation as a writer could be said to reproduce her position
as a slave, cast as a member of the community but not as a person. Write
an essay in which you examine Jacobs's work as a writer. Consider the
ways she works on her reader (a figure she both imagines and constructs)
and also the ways she works on her material (a set of experiences, a language, and the conventional ways of telling the story of one's life). To do
this, you will need to reread the text as something constructed (see the
second "Question for a Second Reading").

2. We can take these opening chapters of *Incidents in the Life of a Slave Girl* as
   an account of a girl's coming of age, particularly in the sense that coming
   of age is a cultural (and not simply a biological) process. The chapters represent the ways in which Jacobs comes to be positioned as a woman in the
   community, and they represent her understanding of that process (and
   the necessary limits to her understanding, since no person can stand completely outside her culture and what it desires her to believe or to take as
   natural).
       Read back through *Incidents,* paying particular attention to what Ja-
   cobs sees as the imposed structure of slave culture and what she takes as

part of human nature. Remember that there are different ways of reading the codes that govern human relations. What Jacobs takes to be unnatural may well seem natural to Dr. Flint. Jacobs could be said to be reading "against" what Flint, or the Slave Owner as a generic type, would understand as naturally there.

Now read through again, this time reading against Jacobs, to see how her view of relationships could be said to be shaped also by a set of beliefs and interests. Look for a system governing Jacobs's understanding. You might ask, for instance, what system leads her to see Dr. Flint and Mr. Sands as different, since they could also be said to be similar—both slave owners, both after the same thing. How does Jacobs place herself in relation to other slaves? other blacks? Jacobs is light skinned. How does she fit into a system governed by color? Both Mrs. Flint and her grandmother react strongly to Jacobs. What system governs Jacobs's sense of the difference between these two women?

Write an essay in which you try to explain the codes that govern the relations between people in slave culture, at least as that culture is represented in "Incidents."

## MAKING CONNECTIONS

1. Alice Walker's reading of the history of African American women in her essay, "In Search of Our Mothers' Gardens" (p. 694), pays particular attention to the "creative spirit" of these women in the face of oppressive working and living conditions. Of her mother, Walker writes:

> Her face, as she prepares the Art that is her gift, is a legacy of respect she leaves to me, for all that illuminates and cherishes life. She has handed down respect for the possibilities—and the will to grasp them.
> (p. 701)

And to the poet Phillis Wheatley she writes: "It is not so much what you sang, as that you kept alive, in so many of our ancestors, *the notion of song*" (p. 698).

Although Walker does not include Harriet Jacobs in her essay, one could imagine ways in which Jacobs's work as a writer is appropriate to Walker's discussion of African American women's creativity. As you reread Jacobs's selection, note the choices she makes as a writer: her language, her selection of incidents and details, her method of addressing an audience, the ways in which she negotiates a white literary tradition. Where, for instance, do you see her writing purposely negotiating a literary tradition that is not hers? Who does she imagine as her audience? How does she use language differently for different purposes? Why?

How would you say that the writerly choices Jacobs makes and enacts allow her to express a creativity that otherwise would have been stifled? What type of legacy does she create in her narrative to pass on to her descendants? And, as Walker writes in honor of her mother and Wheatley, what might Walker or you write in honor of Jacobs?

Write an essay in which you extend Walker's project by considering where and how Jacobs's work as a writer and artist would complement

Walker's argument for the "creative spirit" of African American women in the face of oppressive conditions.

2. In "When We Dead Awaken: Writing as Re-Vision" (p. 603), Adrienne Rich says, "Re-vision—the act of looking back, of seeing with fresh eyes, of entering an old text from a new critical direction—is for women more than a chapter in cultural history: it is an act of survival. Until we can understand the assumptions in which we are drenched we cannot know ourselves" (p. 604).

    Let's imagine that one of the difficulties we have in reading *Incidents* is that we approach it drenched in assumptions; we look with old eyes (or the wrong eyes). In honor of the challenge Rich sets for a reader—or, for that matter, in honor of Harriet Jacobs and the challenge she sets for a reader—write an essay in which you show what it would mean to revise your reading (or what you take to be most people's reading, the "common" reading) of *Incidents*. You will want to show both how the text would be read from this new critical direction and what effort (or method) would be involved in pushing against the old ways of reading.

3. Here, from "Arts of the Contact Zone" (p. 582), is Mary Louise Pratt on the "autoethnographic" text:

    > Guaman Poma's *New Chronicle* is an instance of what I have proposed to call an *autoethnographic* text, by which I mean a text in which people undertake to describe themselves in ways that engage with representations others have made of them. Thus if ethnographic texts are those in which European metropolitan subjects represent to themselves their others (usually their conquered others), autoethnographic texts are representations that the so-defined others construct *in response to* or in dialogue with those texts. [T]hey involve a selective collaboration with and appropriation of idioms of the metropolis or the conqueror. These are merged or infiltrated to varying degrees with indigenous idioms to create self-representations intended to intervene in metropolitan modes of understanding. . . . Such texts often constitute a marginalized group's point of entry into the dominant circuits of print culture. It is interesting to think, for example, of American slave autobiography in its autoethnographic dimensions, which in some respects distinguish it from Euramerican autobiographical tradition. (pp. 585–86)

    Reread Jacobs's "Incidents in the Life of a Slave Girl" after reading Pratt's essay. Using the example of Pratt's work with the *New Chronicle*, write an essay in which you present a reading of Jacobs's text as an example of an autoethnographic and/or transcultural text. You should imagine that you are working to put Pratt's ideas to the test, but also to see what you can say on your own about *Incidents* as a text, as something written and read.

# PATRICIA NELSON LIMERICK

*P*ATRICIA NELSON LIMERICK (b. 1951) is one of this country's most influential historians. She is certainly one of the most visible, with appearances on national radio, television, and even a profile in People magazine. Limerick is a revisionist historian, revising the usual stories we tell of the American
West (stories of open spaces, cowboys and Indians, the frontier, progress, the
spread of civilization). These stories, she says, have a persistent power over the
American imagination, affecting everything from movies and books to federal land
management and American foreign policy. Generations of Americans, she says in
a characteristically memorable formulation, grew up playing cowboys and Indians, while it was impossible to play master and slave. And the reason, she argues,
is that southern historians did their job well and western historians did not. The
West was not an empty place but a meeting ground. The movement west was not
a simple story of progress but a complicated story of conquest and negotiation.

Limerick did her undergraduate work at the University of California at Santa
Cruz and received her M.A. and Ph.D. from Yale University. She taught at Harvard before moving to her current position as Professor of History at the University of Colorado at Boulder. Her major work is her book The Legacy of Conquest: The Unbroken Past of the American West (1987), from which the
following selection is taken. Her first book was Desert Passages: Encounters
with the American Deserts (1985). She is coeditor of A Society to Match the

Scenery *(1991) and* Trails: Toward a New Western History *(1991). Limerick also wrote the text for* Sweet Medicine: Sites of Indian Massacres, Battle-fields, and Treaties *(photographs by Drex Brooks, 1995). In 1995, she was named a Fellow by the MacArthur Foundation. Her most recent book is* The Real West *(1996).*

*"Empire of Innocence" is the first chapter of* The Legacy of Conquest. *Here, Limerick looks at the problems of historical understanding as writing problems, problems related to the work of any writer attempting to represent others and the past. In this sense, the selection is particularly useful for an undergraduate writing course.*

*As a historian, Limerick is redirecting her profession's attention to the American West and changing the terms that govern their conception of its history. Her ambitions, however, extend beyond the academy. Her work is "popular" in a way that much of the work of academic historians is not, and it is directed at changing the way Americans think—not only about the past but in the present. And, unlike that of many contemporary intellectuals, Limerick's thinking is hopeful, utopian. This is the final paragraph of* The Legacy of Conquest:

> *When Anglo-Americans look across the Mexican border or into an Indian reservation, they are more likely to see stereotypes than recognizable individuals or particular groups; the same distortion of vision no doubt works the other way too. The unitary character known as "the white man" has never existed, nor has "the Indian." Yet the phrases receive constant use, as if they carried necessary meaning. Indians, Hispanics, Asians, Blacks, Anglos, businesspeople, workers, politicians, bureaucrats, natives, and newcomers, we share the same region and its history, but we wait to be introduced. The serious exploration of the historical process that made us neighbors provides that introduction.*

*The "serious exploration of the historical process" for Limerick, as you will see, involves a serious attention to reading and writing. We need to read carefully but also differently; we need, for example, to read not only Anglo-American accounts of Native American history but also Native American accounts of that history, including Native American accounts of the early contacts with European settlers. And we need to write in ways that allow us to represent, rather than erase, experiences and points of view that lie outside the standard narrative. As Limerick says, "One skill essential to the writing of Western American history is a capacity to deal with multiple points of view. It is as if one were a lawyer at a trial designed on the principle of the Mad Hatter's tea party—as soon as one begins to understand and empathize with the plaintiff's case, it is time to move over and empathize with the defendant." Yet it is even more complicated than this, for "seldom are there only two parties or only two points of view." Part of the pleasure of reading Limerick's prose is the opportunity it provides to hear, in brief, a variety of representative anecdotes from the American West, and part of the pleasure is the opportunity it provides to witness her judgment. There is more at work here, in other words, than "empathy." It is interesting to ask what else enables*

*Limerick to do the work she does and to think, through her examples, about what it might mean to "deal" as a reader or writer with multiple points of view.*

# Empire of Innocence

## I

When academic territories were parceled out in the early twentieth century, anthropology got the tellers of tales and history got the keepers of written records. As anthropology and history diverged, human differences that hinged on literacy assumed an undeserved significance. Working with oral, preindustrial, prestate societies, anthropologists acknowledged the power of culture and of a received worldview; they knew that the folk conception of the world was not narrowly tied to proof and evidence. But with the disciplinary boundary overdrawn, it was easy for historians to assume that literacy, the modern state, and the commercial world had produced a different sort of creature entirely—humans less inclined to put myth over reality, more inclined to measure their beliefs by the standard of accuracy and practicality.

When anthropology and history moved closer together, so did their subjects of inquiry. Tribal people or nationalists, tellers of stories or keepers of account books, humans live in a world in which mental reality does not have to submit to narrow tests of accuracy.

To analyze how white Americans thought about the West, it helps to think anthropologically. One lesson of anthropology is the extraordinary power of cultural persistence; with American Indians, for instance, beliefs and values will persist even when the supporting economic and political structures have vanished. What holds for Indians holds as well for white Americans; the values they attached to westward expansion persist, in cheerful defiance of contrary evidence.

Among those persistent values, few have more power than the idea of innocence. The dominant motive for moving West was improvement and opportunity, not injury to others. Few white Americans went West intending to ruin the natives and despoil the continent. Even when they were trespassers, westering Americans were hardly, in their own eyes, criminals; rather, they were pioneers. The ends abundantly justified the means; personal interest in the acquisition of property coincided with national interest in the acquisition of territory, and those interests overlapped in turn with the mission to extend the domain of Christian civilization. Innocence of intention placed the course of events in a bright and positive light; only over time would the shadows compete for our attention.

One might expect John Wesley Hardin, the Texan mass murderer and outlaw, to forswear the role of innocent. But this is an assumption to be made with caution in Western history. Hardin was, after all, of innocent stock, the son of a preacher who named his son John Wesley, after the founder of Methodism. "In prison," a recent editor of Hardin's autobiography notes, "Hardin read the Bible and many books on theology. There he was appointed superintendent of the Sunday schools." If one read Hardin's autobiography with no knowledge of the author's later career, one might mistake the tone for that of a model citizen and pillar of the community. "Our parents taught us from infancy to be honest, truthful, and brave," he said, going on to provide further evidence of his good character: "I always tried to excel in my studies, and generally stood at the head," and if that was not enough, " I was always a very child of nature, and her ways and moods were my study."[1]

To be sure, Hardin fought a lot, but this was consonant with parental instructions that honor and the willingness to defend that honor came in the same package. When he was fifteen, he shot and killed a black man. This was to Hardin's mind not a loss of innocence, but a defense of it. The Negro, he said, had tried to bully him; the year was 1868, and Texas was at the mercy of postwar Reconstruction, bullied by "Yankee soldiers," "carpet-baggers and bureau-agents," blacks, and "renegades"—all of them "inveterate enemies of the South." And so, Hardin said, "unwillingly, I became a fugitive, not from justice be it known, but from the injustice and misrule of the people who had subjugated the South." Hardin did go on to kill twenty or more men, but he appears never to have wavered from his chosen role: the gunfighter as Western injured innocent, with a strong Southern accent.[2]

The idea of the innocent victim retains extraordinary power, and no situation made a stronger symbolic statement of this than that of the white woman murdered by Indians. Here was surely a clear case of victimization, villainy, and betrayed innocence. But few deaths of this kind occurred in American history with such purity; they were instead embedded in the complex dynamics of race relations, in which neither concept—villain or victim—did much to illuminate history.

Narcissa Prentiss Whitman made a very unlikely villain. Deeply moved by the thought of Western Indians living without knowledge of Christianity, Narcissa Prentiss wrote her mission board in 1835, "I now offer myself to the American Board to be employed in their service among the heathen. . . ."[3] In 1836, she left her home in New York to rescue the Indians in Oregon. An unattached female could hardly be a missionary, and before her departure Narcissa Prentiss hastily married another Oregon volunteer, Marcus Whitman. The Whitmans and Henry and Eliza Spalding set off to cross the country. Pioneers on the overland trail, they faced stiff challenges from nature and some from human nature. The fur trappers and traders with whom they traveled resented the delays and sermons that came with missionary companionship. The missionaries themselves presented less than a united front. They had the strong, contentious personalities of self-appointed agents of God. They also had a history;

Henry Spalding had courted Narcissa, and lost. Anyone who thinks of the nineteenth-century West as a land of fresh starts and new beginnings might think of Henry Spalding and Narcissa Whitman and the memories they took with them to Oregon.

Arrived in the Oregon country, the missionaries—like salesmen dividing up markets—divided up tribes and locations. The Whitmans set to work on the Cayuse Indians. Narcissa Whitman's life in Oregon provides little support for the image of life in the West as free, adventurous, and romantic. Most of the time, she labored. She had one child of her own; she adopted many others—mixed-blood children of fur trappers, and orphans from the overland trail. "My health has been so poor," she wrote her sister in 1846, "and my family has increased so rapidly, that it has been impossible. You will be astonished to know that we have eleven children in our family, and not one of them our own by birth, but so it is. Seven orphans were brought to our door in Oct., 1844, whose parents both died on the way to this country. Destitute and friendless, there was no other alternative—we must take them in or they must perish."[4]

Depending on one's point of view, the Whitman mission had a lucky or an unlucky location—along the Oregon Trail, where exhausted travelers arrived desperate for food, rest, and help. Narcissa Whitman's small home served as kitchen, dining hall, dormitory and church building, while she longed for privacy and rest. She often cooked three meals a day for twenty people. For five years, she had no stove and cooked in an open fireplace.

In the midst of crowds, she was lonely, writing nostalgic letters to friends and family in the East who seemed to answer infrequently; she went as long as two years without a letter from home. Separated by distance and sometimes by quarrels, Narcissa and the other missionary wives in Oregon tried for a time to organize a nineteenth-century version of a woman's support group; at a certain hour every day, they would pause in their work, think of each other, and pray for strength to be proper mothers to their children in the wilderness.

Direct tragedy added to loneliness, overwork, and frustration. The Whitmans' only child, two years old, drowned while playing alone near a stream. Providence was testing Narcissa Whitman's faith in every imaginable way.

Then, in November of 1847, after eleven years with the missionaries among them, when the white or mixed-blood mission population had grown to twenty men, ten women, and forty-four children, the Cayuse Indians rose in rebellion and killed fourteen people—including Marcus and Narcissa Whitman.

Was Narcissa Whitman an innocent victim of brutality and ingratitude? What possessed the Cayuses?

One skill essential to the writing of Western American history is a capacity to deal with multiple points of view. It is as if one were a lawyer at a trial designed on the principle of the Mad Hatter's tea party—as soon as one begins to understand and empathize with the plaintiff's case, it is time to move over and empathize with the defendant. Seldom are there only two parties or only two points of view. Taking into account division within groups—intertribal conflict and factions within tribes and, in Oregon, settlers against missionaries, Protestants against Catholics, British Hudson's Bay Company traders against Americans—it is taxing simply to keep track of the points of view.

Why did the Cayuses kill the Whitmans? The chain of events bringing the Whitmans to the Northwest was an odd and arbitrary one. In a recent book, the historian Christopher Miller explains that the Whitman mission was hardly the first crisis to hit the Columbia Plateau and its natives. A "three hundred year cold spell," a "result of the Little Ice Age," had shaken the environment, apparently reducing food sources. Moreover, the effects of European presence in North America began reaching the plateau even before the Europeans themselves arrived. The "conjunction of sickness, with the coming of horses, guns, climatic deterioration, and near constant war" added up to an "eighteenth-century crisis." Punctuated by a disturbing and perplexing ash fall from a volcanic explosion, the changes brought many of the Plateau Indians to the conviction that the world was in trouble. They were thus receptive to a new set of prophecies from religious leaders. A central element of this new worldview came in the reported words of the man known as the Spokan Prophet, words spoken around 1790: "Soon there will come from the rising sun a different kind of man from any you have yet seen, who will bring with them a book and will teach you everything, after that the world will fall to pieces," opening the way to a restored and better world. Groups of Indians therefore began to welcome whites, since learning from these newcomers was to be an essential stage in the route to a new future.[5]

In 1831, a small party of Nez Percé and Flathead Indians journeyed to St. Louis, Missouri. For years, Western historians said that these Indians had heard of Jesuits through contacts with fur traders and had come to ask for their own "Black Robes." That confident claim aside, Christopher Miller has recently written that it is still a "mystery how it all came to pass." Nonetheless, he argues persuasively that the Northwest Indians went to St. Louis pursuing religious fulfillment according to the plateau millennial tradition; it was their unlikely fate to be misunderstood by the equally millennial Christians who heard the story of the visit. A Protestant man named William Walker wrote a letter about the meetings in St. Louis, and the letter was circulated in church newspapers and read at church meetings, leaving the impression that the Indians of Oregon were begging for Christianity.[6]

And so, in this chain of circumstances "so bizarre as to seem providential," in Miller's words, the Cayuses got the Whitmans, who had responded to the furor provoked by the letter. Irritations began to pile up. The Whitmans set out to transform the Cayuses from hunters, fishers, and gatherers to farmers, from heathens to Presbyterians. As the place became a way station for the Oregon Trail, the mission began to look like an agency for the service of white people. This was not, in fact, too far from the founder's view of his organization. "It does not concern me so much what is to become of any particular set of Indians," Marcus Whitman wrote his parents, "as to give them the offer of salvation through the gospel and the opportunity of civilization. . . . I have no doubt our greatest work is to be to aid the white settlement of this country and help to found its religious institutions."[7]

The Cayuses began to suffer from white people's diseases, to which they had no immunity. Finally, in 1847, they were devastated by measles. While the white people at the mission seldom died from measles, the Indians noticed that an infected Cayuse nearly always died. It was an Indian conviction that disease was "the result of either malevolence or spiritual transgression"; either way, the evidence pointed at the missionaries. When the Cayuses finally turned on the Whitmans, they were giving up "the shared prophetic vision" that these newcomers would teach a lesson essential to reshaping the world.[8] The Cayuses were, in other words, acting in and responding to currents of history of which Narcissa Whitman was not a primary determinant.

Descending on the Cayuses, determined to bring light to the "benighted ones" living in "the thick darkness of heathenism," Narcissa Whitman was an intolerant invader. If she was not a villain, neither was she an innocent victim. Her story is melancholy but on the whole predictable, one of many similar stories in Western history that trigger an interventionist's urge. "Watch out, Narcissa," one finds oneself thinking, 140 years too late, "you think you are doing good works, but you are getting yourself—and others—into deep trouble." Given the inability of Cayuses to understand Presbyterians, and the inability of Presbyterians to understand Cayuses, the trouble could only escalate. Narcissa Whitman would not have imagined that there was anything to understand; where the Cayuses had religion, social networks, a thriving trade in horses, and a full culture, Whitman would have seen vacancy or, worse, heathenism.

Narcissa Whitman knew she was volunteering for risk; her willingness to take on those risks is, however, easier to understand because it was based on religion. Irrational faith is its own explanation; one can analyze its components, but the fact remains that extraordinary faith leads to extraordinary action. The mystery is not that Narcissa Whitman risked all for the demands of the deity but that so many others risked all for the demands of the profit motive.

## II

Missionaries may be an extreme case, but the pattern they represent had parallels in other Western occupations. Whether the target resource was gold, farmland, or Indian souls, white Americans went west convinced that their purposes were as commonplace as they were innocent. The pursuit of improved fortunes, the acquisition of property, even the desire for adventure seemed so self-evident that they needed neither explanation nor justification.

If the motives were innocent, episodes of frustration and defeat seemed inexplicable, undeserved, and arbitrary. Squatters defied the boundaries of Indian territory and then were aggrieved to find themselves harassed and attacked by Indians. Similarly, prospectors and miners went where the minerals were, regardless of Indian territorial claims, only to be outraged by threats to their lives and supply lines. Preemptors who traveled ahead of government surveys later complained of insecure land titles. After the Civil War, farmers expanded onto the Great Plains, past the line of semi-aridity, and then felt betrayed when the rains proved inadequate.

Western immigrants understood not just that they were taking risks but also that risks led to rewards. When nature or natives interrupted the progression from risk to reward, the Westerner felt aggrieved. Most telling were the incidents in which a rush of individuals—each pursuing a claim to a limited resource—produced their own collective frustration. In resource rushes, people hoping for exclusive opportunity often arrived to find a crowd already in place, blanketing the region with prior claims, constricting individual opportunity, and producing all the problems of food supply, housing, sanitation, and social order that one would expect in a growing city, but not in a wilderness.

If one pursues a valuable item and finds a crowd already assembled, one's complicity in the situation is obvious. The crowd has, after all, resulted from a number of individual choices very much like one's own. But frustration cuts off reflection on this irony; in resource rushes in which the sum of the participants' activities created the dilemma, each individual could still feel himself the innocent victim of constricting opportunity.

Contrary to all of the West's associations with self-reliance and individual responsibility, misfortune has usually caused white Westerners to cast themselves in the role of the innocent victim. One large group was composed of those who felt injured at the hands of nature. They had trusted nature, and when nature behaved according to its own rules and not theirs, they felt betrayed. The basic plot played itself out with a thousand variations.

Miners resented the wasted effort of excavating sites that had looked promising and proved barren. Cattlemen overgrazed the grasslands and then resented nature's failure to rebound. Farmers on the Southern Plains used mechanized agriculture to break up the land and weaken the ground cover, then unhappily watched the crop of dust they harvested. City dwellers accumulated automobiles, gas stations, and freeways, and then cursed the inversion patterns and enclosing mountains that kept the automobile effluvia before their eyes and noses. Homeowners purchased houses on steep slopes and in precarious canyons, then felt betrayed when the earth's surface continued to do what it has done for millennia: move around from time to time. And, in one of the most widespread and serious versions, people moved to arid and semiarid regions, secure in the faith that water would somehow be made available, then found the prospect of water scarcity both surprising and unfair.

In many ways, the most telling case studies concern plants. When, in the 1850s, white farmers arrived in Island County, Washington, they had a clear sense of their intentions: "to get the land subdued and the wilde nature out of it," as one of them put it. They would uproot the useless native plants and replace them with valuable crops, transforming wilderness to garden. On one count, nature did not cooperate—certain new plants, including corn, tomatoes, and wheat, could not adapt to the local climate and soil. On another count, nature proved all too cooperative. Among the plants introduced by white farmers, weeds frequently did better than crops. "Weeds," Richard White notes, "are an inevitable result of any human attempt to restrict large areas of land to a single plant." Laboring to introduce valued plants, the farmer came up against "his almost total inability to prevent the entry of unwanted invaders." Mixed with crop seeds, exotic plants like the Canadian thistle prospered in the plowed fields prepared for them, and then moved into the pastures cleared by overgrazing. The thistle was of no interest to sheep: "once it had replaced domesticated grasses the land became incapable of supporting livestock."[9]

A similar development took place between the Rockies and the Sierras and Cascades. There, as well, "species foreign to the region, brought accidentally by the settlers, came to occupy these sites to the virtual exclusion of the native colonizers." With the introduction of wheat, "entry via adulterated seed lots of the weeds of wheat . . . was inevitable." One particular species—cheatgrass—took over vast territories, displacing the native bunch grasses and plaguing farmers in their wheatfields. There is no more effective way to feel authentically victimized than to plant a crop and then to see it besieged by weeds. Farmers thus had their own, complicated position as injured innocents, plagued by a pattern in nature that their own actions had created.[10]

Yet another category of injured innocents were those who had believed and acted upon the promises of promoters and boomers. Prospective miners were particularly susceptible to reading reports of the gold strikes, leaping into action, and then cursing the distortions and exaggerations that had misled them into risking so much for so little reward. The pattern was common because resource rushes created a mood of such fevered optimism that trust came easily; people wanted so much to believe that their normal skepticism dropped away.

The authenticity of the sense of victimization was unquestionable. Still, there was never any indication that repeated episodes of victimization would reduce the pool of volunteers. Bedrock factors kept promoters and boomers supplied with believers: there *were* resources in the West, and the reports might be true; furthermore, the physical fact of Western distances meant, first, that decision making would have to rely on a chain of information stretched thin by the expanse of the continent and, second, that the truth of the reports and promises could not be tested without a substantial investment of time and money simply in getting to the site. One might well consume one's nest egg merely in reaching the place of expected reward.

Blaming nature or blaming human beings, those looking for a scapegoat had a third, increasingly popular target: the federal government. Since it was the government's responsibility to control the Indians and, in a number of ways increasing into the twentieth century, to control nature, Westerners found it easy to shift the direction of their resentment. Attacked by Indians or threatened by nature, aggrieved Westerners took to pointing accusingly at the federal government. In effect, Westerners centralized their resentments much more efficiently than the federal government centralized its powers.

Oregon's situation was a classic example of this transition. The earliest settlers were rewarded with Congress's Oregon Donation Act of 1850. Settlers arriving by a certain year were entitled to a generous land grant. This act had the considerable disadvantage of encouraging white settlement without benefit of treaties and land cessions from Oregon Indians. The Donation Act thus invited American settlers to spread into territory that had not been cleared for their occupation. It was an offer that clearly infringed on the rights of the Indians and that caused the government to stretch its powers thin. After the California gold rush, when prospectors spread north into the Oregon interior, a multifront Indian war began. Surely, the white miners and settlers said, it is now the obligation of the federal government to protect us and our property.[11]

At this point, a quirk of historical casting brought an unusual man named General John Wool into the picture. As the head of the Army's Pacific Division, General Wool was charged with cleaning up the mess that Oregon development had created. He was to control the Indians, protect the settlers, and end the wars. Here Wool's unusual character emerged: assessing this situation, he decided—and said bluntly—that the wars were the results of settler intrusion; he went so far as to propose a moratorium on further settlement in the Oregon interior, a proposal that outraged the sensitive settlers. Wool's personality did not make this difference of opinion more amicable. He was, in fact, something of a prig; in pictures, the symmetrical and carefully waxed curls at his temples suggest that he and the Oregon pioneers might have been at odds without the troubles of Indian policy.[12]

Denounced by both the Oregon and the Washington legislatures, Wool's blunt approach did not result in a new direction in Indian affairs. The wars were prosecuted to their conclusions; the Indians, compelled to yield territory. But the Oregon settlers in 1857 knew what they thought of Wool. He was a supposed agent of the federal government, an agent turned inexplicably into a friend of the Indians and an enemy of the Americans.

It was not the first or the last time that white Americans would suspect the federal government and Indians of being in an unholy alliance. To the degree that the federal government fulfilled its treaty and statutory obligations to protect the Indians and their land, it would then appear to be not only soft on Indians but even in active opposition to its own citizens.

One other elemental pattern of their thought allowed Westerners to slide smoothly from blaming Indians to blaming the federal government.

The idea of captivity organized much of Western sentiment. Actual white men, women, and children were at times taken captive by Indians, and narratives of those captivities were, from colonial times on, a popular form of literature. It was an easy transition of thought to move from the idea of humans held in an unjust and resented captivity to the idea of land and natural resources held in Indian captivity—in fact, a kind of monopoly in which very few Indians kept immense resources to themselves, refusing to let the large numbers of willing and eager white Americans make what they could of those resources. Land and natural resources, to the Anglo-American mind, were meant for development; when the Indians held control, the excluded whites took up the familiar role of injured innocents. The West, in the most common figure of speech, had to be "opened"—a metaphor based on the assumption that the virgin West was "closed," locked up, held captive by Indians.

As the federal government took over Indian territory, either as an addition to the public domain or as reservations under the government's guardianship, white Westerners kept the same sense of themselves as frustrated innocents, shut out by monopoly, but they shifted the blame. Released from Indian captivity, many Western resources, it seemed to white Americans, had merely moved into a federal captivity.

In 1979, the Nevada state legislature, without any constitutional authority, passed a law seizing from the federal government 49 million acres from the public domain within the state. This empty but symbolic act was the first scene in the media event known as the Sagebrush Rebellion, in which Western businessmen lamented their victimization at the hands of the federal government and pleaded for the release of the public domain from its federal captivity. Ceded to the states, the land that once belonged to all the people of the United States would at last be at the disposal of those whom the Sagebrush Rebels considered to be the *right* people—namely, themselves.[13]

Like many rebellions, this one foundered with success: the election of Ronald Reagan in 1980 and the appointment of James Watt as secretary of the interior meant that the much-hated federal government was now in the hands of two Sagebrush Rebels. It was not at all clear what the proper rebel response to the situation should be. In any case, the rebel claim to victimization had lost whatever validity it had ever had.

Reciting the catalog of their injuries, sufferings, and deprivations at the hands of federal officials, the rebels at least convinced Western historians of the relevance of their expertise. It was a most familiar song; the Western historian could recognize every note. Decades of expansion left this motif of victimization entrenched in Western thinking. It was second nature to see misfortune as the doings of an outside force, preying on innocence and vulnerability, refusing to play by the rules of fairness. By assigning responsibility elsewhere, one eliminated the need to consider one's own participation in courting misfortune. There was something odd and amusing about the late-twentieth-century businessmen adopting for themselves the role that might have suited Narcissa Whitman—that of the martyred innocents, trying to go about their business in the face of cruel and arbitrary opposition.

Even if the Sagebrush Rebels had to back off for a time, that did not mean idleness for the innocent's role. In 1982, Governor Richard Lamm of Colorado and his coauthor, Michael McCarthy, published a book defending the West—"a vulnerable land"—from the assault of development. "A new Manifest Destiny," they said, "has overtaken America. The economic imperative has forever changed the spiritual refuge that was the West." The notion of a time in Western history when "the economic imperative" had not been a dominant factor was a quaint and wishful thought, but more important, Lamm and McCarthy thought, some Westerners now "refused" to submit to this change. "They—we—are the new Indians," Lamm and McCarthy concluded. "And they—we—will not be herded to the new reservations."[14]

In this breakthrough in the strategy of injured innocence, Lamm and McCarthy chose the most historically qualified innocent victims—the Indians facing invasion, fighting to defend their homelands—and appropriated their identity for the majority whites who had moved to the West for the good life, for open space and freedom of movement, and who were beginning to find their desires frustrated. Reborn as the "new Indians," Lamm's constituency had traveled an extraordinary, circular route. Yesterday's villains were now to be taken as today's victims; they were now the invaded, no longer the invaders. In keeping with this change, the *old* Indians received little attention in the book; as capacious as the category "injured innocent" had proven itself to be, the line had to be drawn somewhere.

Occasionally, continuities in American history almost bowl one over. What does Colorado's utterly twentieth-century governor have in common with the East Coast's colonial elite in the eighteenth century? "Having practically destroyed the aboriginal population and enslaved the Africans," one colonial historian has said, "the white inhabitants of English America began to conceive of themselves as the victims, not the agents, of Old World colonialism." "The victims, not the agents"—the changes and differences are enormous, but for a moment, if one looks from Revolutionary leaders, who held black slaves as well as the conviction that they were themselves enslaved by Great Britain, to Governor Richard Lamm, proclaiming himself and his people to be the new Indians, American history appears to be composed of one, continuous fabric, a fabric in which the figure of the innocent victim is the dominant motif.[15]

## III

Of all the possible candidates, the long-suffering white female pioneer seemed to be the closest thing to an authentic innocent victim. Torn from family and civilization, overworked and lonely, disoriented by an unfamiliar landscape, frontierswomen could seem to be tragic martyrs to their husbands' willful ambitions.

But what relation did these sufferers bear to the actual white women in the West? Did their experiences genuinely support the image? Where in Western history did women fit? By the 1970s, it was commonly recognized that Turner-style history simply left women out. How, then, to address the oversight? Was it the sort of error that one could easily correct—revise the shopping list, retrace one's steps, put the forgotten item in the grocery cart, and then proceed with one's usual routine? Or was the inclusion of women a more consequential process of revision that would make it impossible to resume old habits and routines?

We can best answer the question by considering the Western women apparently at the opposite end of the spectrum from Narcissa Whitman—the women who came West not to uplift men but to cater to their baser needs. The prostitute was as much a creature of Western stereotype as the martyred missionary, and in many ways a more appealing one. But while the colorful dance hall girl held sway in the movies, Western historians either looked discreetly away from this service industry or stayed within the stereotypes of a colorful if naughty subject.

When professional scholars finally took up the subject, their investigations disclosed the grim lives led by the majority of Western prostitutes. With few jobs open to women, prostitution provided a route to income, though it seldom led past subsistence. A few well-rewarded mistresses of rich men and a few madams skilled in a complicated kind of management may have prospered, but most prostitutes did well to keep revenue a fraction ahead of overhead costs—rent, clothing, food, payoffs to law officers. A woman might work independently, renting her own quarters and conducting her own solicitation, or she might try for security (shelter, food, and a degree of protection from violence) by working in a brothel. At the bottom ranks, even those unappealing alternatives disappeared; vagrant women at the farthest margins of society, or Chinese women controlled as virtual slaves, had little choice open to them. Western prostitution was, in other words, a very stratified operation: the adventuress of doubtful morality and the respectable married woman, though in different spheres, were both far removed from the down-and-out cribworker, without even a brothel to call home.

When prostitutes tried to find stability in marriage, they found their partners in an unpromising pool of saloon owners, pimps, and criminals, men who were often violent and who were neither inclined nor able to rescue their spouses from their rough lives. When prostitutes bore children, as they often did, their occupations made child care an extraordinary challenge and the children stood scant chance of rising to reputability. Many daughters of prostitutes followed their mothers into the business. Many factors—the sense of entrapment, the recognition that age was sure to reduce a woman's marketability, financial troubles—drove prostitutes to suicide. "Suicide," the historian Anne Butler has noted, "emerged as the most commonly employed means to retire from prostitution."[16] Excluded from much of society, prostitutes could not even expect to find comradeship with their colleagues; the intrinsic competition of the business put them at odds, and this rivalry, often unleashed by alcohol, led to frequent quarrels and even physical fights.

A study of Western prostitution leaves certain general lessons for Western history at large. First and foremost, one learns that the creature known as "the pioneer woman" is a generic concept imposed on a diverse reality. White, black, Hispanic, Chinese, and Indian women composed the work force of prostitution, scattered across a wide range of incomes. Moreover, anyone inclined to project a sentimentalized hope for women's essential solidarity into the past need only consider the case of Julia Bulette, a prostitute murdered in Virginia City in 1867. John Milleain was convicted of her murder after items stolen from Bulette were found in his possession. But he had murdered a prostitute, and this engaged the sympathy and support of some of the town's respectable ladies. "Respectable women," Marion S. Goldman has reported, "circulated a petition to the governor to commute Milleain's sentence from death to life imprisonment, visited him in jail, and made sure that he drank wine and ate omelettes during the days following his conviction." Just before his execution, Milleain offered his gratitude: "I also thank the ladies of Virginia who came to see me in my cell and brought with them consolation that only they could find for the circumstances."[17]

This curious sympathy pointed to the larger pattern: the elevation of respectable women rested on the downgrading of the disreputable. Fallen women could initiate young men into sexual activity and thus allow respectable young women to avoid the fall. Prostitutes offered men an outlet that enabled wives to hold on to the role of pure creatures set above human biological compulsions. Most of all, prostitution was an unending reminder of the advantages of conventional female domestic roles. The benefits of marriage never appeared more attractive than in contrast to the grim and unprotected struggle for subsistence of the prostitute. Accordingly, few Western communities tried to eliminate prostitution; instead, they tried to regulate and contain it. In towns dependent on mining, cattle, or military posts, with a substantial population of male workers, prostitution was essential to the town's prosperity. The whole exercise of regulating prostitution, beyond the economic benefits, "emphasiz[ed] the respectable community's behavioral boundaries, and heighten[ed] solidarity among respectable women."[18]

Second, the history of prostitutes also serves to break up an apparently purposeful monolith: white society under the compulsions of Manifest Destiny. If women were victims of oppression, who were their oppressors? In a mining town like Nevada City, the prostitute's most frequent patrons were wageworkers, miners who risked their lives daily in hard underground labor. The miners, as Marion Goldman has suggested, were themselves "treated like objects rather than individuals" and were thus conditioned to "think of themselves and others that way."[19] The economic elite of the towns often owned the real estate in which prostitution took place; vice districts were among the more rewarding Western investment opportunities. And the official representatives of the law took their cut of the enterprise in regular payoffs to prevent arbitrary arrests. In the broad sweep of Western history, it may look as if a united social unit called "white people" swept Indians off their lands; that group, as the history of prostitution shows, was not a monolith at all but a complex swirl of people as adept at preying on each other as at preying on Indians.

Third, the history of prostitution restores the participants of Western history to a gritty, recognizably physical reality. Testifying as a witness in a Nevada case in 1878, Belle West was asked to identify her occupation. "I go to bed with men for money," she said.[20] A century later, Belle West's frankness will not let us take refuge in sentimental and nostalgic images of the Western past. Acknowledge the human reality of Western prostitutes, and you have taken a major step toward removing Western history from the domain of myth and symbol and restoring it to actuality. Exclude women from Western history, and unreality sets in. Restore them, and the Western drama gains a fully human cast of characters—males and females whose urges, needs, failings, and conflicts we can recognize and even share.

It appears to be an insult and a disservice to place the murdered Narcissa Whitman and the murdered Julia Bulette in the same chapter. But women who in their own times would have fled each other's company turn out to teach similar historical lessons. It is the odd obligation of the historian to reunite women who would have refused to occupy the same room. Examine the actual experiences of white women in the West, at any level of respectability, and the stereotypes are left in tatters.

Consider Mrs. Amelia Stewart Knight. In 1853, she, her husband, and seven children went overland to Oregon and met the usual hazards—a grueling struggle through the muddy Midwestern prairies, difficult river crossings, dangerous alkali water, failing livestock. Mrs. Knight did occasionally record a bout of poor health, but frailty did not afflict women to the exclusion of men. "Still in camp," she wrote one day early in the journey, "husband and myself being sick. . . ."[21]

Supervising seven children elicited few complaints from Mrs. Knight. One simply has to imagine what some of her terse entries meant in practice: "Sunday, May 1st Still fine weather; wash and scrub all the children." The older children evidently helped out in caring for the younger ones; even with the best management, though, misadventures took place. The youngest child, Chatfield, seemed most ill-fated: "Chat has been sick all day with fever, partly caused by mosquitoe bites. . . . Here Chat fell out of the wagon but did not get hurt much. . . . [And then just five days later] Here Chat had a very narrow escape from being run over. Just as we were all getting ready to start, Chatfield the rascal, came around the forward wheel to get into the wagon and at that moment the cattle started and he fell under the wagon. Somehow he kept from under the wheels and escaped with only a good or I should say, a bad scare. I never was so frightened in my life."[22]

In the days just before they left the trail and headed for the Columbia River, a trying road through forests forced Mrs. Knight and the children to walk. "I was obliged to take care of myself and little ones as best I could," she wrote, and they spent their days "winding around the fallen timber and brush, climbing over logs creeping under fallen timber, sometimes lifting and carrying Chat."[23]

And then, near the end of the journey, Mrs. Knight had her eighth child. She had throughout this trip been in the later stages of pregnancy, and, in that final phase of walking, she had been at full term.

In endurance and stamina, Mrs. Knight was clearly the equal—if not the better—of the Kit Carsons and the Jedediah Smiths. The tone of her diary suggests few complaints and no self-glorification. It seems illogical to feel sorry for her, when she appears not to have felt sorry for herself.

The developing pictures of Western women's history suggest that Mrs. Knight, while perhaps braver than most women (and men), was no anomaly. Far from revealing weak creatures held captive to stronger wills, new studies show female Western settlers as full and vigorous participants in history. A recent close study of homesteading in northeastern Colorado demonstrates that single women took advantage of the spinster's and widow's right to claim land under the Homestead Act. In two counties, claim entries by women were 12 percent of the whole and, later in the process, as high as 18 percent. Many wives, though not entitled to claims of their own, nonetheless acted as genuine partners in the homestead, contributing equal labor and taking part in decisions.[24] While individuals may have conformed to the image of the passive, suffering female pioneer, the majority were too busy for such self-dramatization. Cooking, cleaning, washing, caring for children, planting gardens—any number of activities took priority over brooding.

One measure of independence and freedom in Western male settlers was the capacity to scorn others—to see oneself as being a superior sort of creature, placed above others. On that and many other counts, white women were active self-determiners. Downgrading Indians, Hispanics, Mormons, immoral men, or fallen women, many white women made it clear that the disorientation of migration had not stolen their confident ability to sort and rank humanity from best to worst.

In the record of their words and actions, the women of Western history have made a clear statement that they do not deserve or need special handling by historians. There is no more point in downgrading them as vulnerable victims than in elevating them as saintly civilizers. The same woman could be both inspirational in her loyalty to her family's welfare and disheartening in her hatred of Indians. Those two attributes were not contradictory; they were two sides to the same coin. We cannot emphasize one side at the expense of the other, without fracturing a whole, living person into disconnected abstractions.

Our inability to categorize the murdered Narcissa Whitman, or the murdered Julia Bulette, teaches us a vital lesson about Western history. Prostitutes were not consistently and exclusively sinners, nor were wives and mothers consistently and exclusively saints. Male or female, white Westerners were both sinned against and sinning. One person's reward often meant another person's loss; white opportunity meant Indian dispossession. Real Westerners, contrary to the old divisions between good guys and bad guys, combined the roles of victim and villain.

Acknowledging the moral complexity of Western history does not require us to surrender the mythic power traditionally associated with the region's story. On the contrary, moral complexity provides the base for parables and tales of greater and deeper meaning. Myths resting on tragedy and on unforeseen consequences, the ancient Greeks certainly knew, have far more power than stories of simple triumphs and victories. In movies and novels, as well as in histories, the stories of men and women who both entered and created a moral wilderness have begun to replace the simple contests of savagery and civilization, cowboys and Indians, white hats and black hats. By questioning the Westerner's traditional stance as innocent victim, we do not debunk Western history but enrich it.

NOTES

[1]John Wesley Hardin, *The Life of John Wesley Hardin*, ed. Robert G. McCubbin (Norman: Univ. of Oklahoma Press, 1961), xvii, 6–7.

[2]Ibid., 13, 14.

[3]Clifford Drury, ed., *First White Women over the Rockies*, vol. 1 (Glendale, Calif.: Arthur H. Clark, 1963), 29.

[4]Ibid., 152.

[5]Christopher L. Miller, *Prophetic Worlds: Indians and Whites on the Columbia Plateau* (New Brunswick: Rutgers Univ. Press, 1985), 23, 25, 33, Spokan Prophet quoted on 45.

[6]Ibid., 60.

[7]Ibid., 1; Marcus Whitman quoted in Robert V. Hine and Edwin R. Bingham, eds., *The American Frontier: Readings and Documents* (Boston: Little, Brown, 1972), 162.

[8]Miller, *Prophetic Worlds*, 105, 117.

[9]Richard White, *Land Use, Environment, and Social Change: The Shaping of Island County, Washington* (Seattle: Univ. of Washington Press, 1980), 46, 68, Walter Crockett quoted on 35.

[10]Richard N. Mack, "Invaders at Home on the Range," *Natural History*, February 1984, 43.

[11]Dorothy O. Johansen and C. M. Gates, *Empire of the Columbia: A History of the Pacific Northwest*, 2d ed. (New York: Harper & Row, 1967), 250, 252.

[12]Robert Utley, *Frontiersmen in Blue: The United States Army and the Indian, 1848–1865* (1967; Lincoln: Univ. of Nebraska Press, 1981), 178–200.

[13]"The Angry West vs. the Rest," *Newsweek*, September 17, 1979, 31–40; "West Senses Victory in Sagebrush Rebellion," *U.S. News and World Report*, December 1, 1980, 29, 30.

[14]Richard D. Lamm and Michael McCarthy, *The Angry West: A Vulnerable Land and Its Future* (Boston: Houghton Mifflin, 1982), 4.

[15]Carole Shammas, "English-Born and Creole Elites in Turn-of-the-Century Virginia," in Thad Tate and David Ammerman, eds., *The Chesapeake in the Seventeenth Century: Essays on Anglo-American Society and Politics* (New York: W. W. Norton, 1979), 274.

[16]Anne M. Butler, *Daughters of Joy, Sisters of Mercy: Prostitutes in the American West, 1865–1890* (Urbana: Univ. of Illinois Press, 1985), 68.

[17]Marion S. Goldman, *Gold Diggers and Silver Miners: Prostitution and Social Life on the Comstock Lode* (Ann Arbor: Univ. of Michigan Press, 1981), 144, John Milleain quoted on 144.

[18]Ibid., 137.

[19]Ibid., 158.

[20]Ibid., 108.

[21]Amelia Stewart Knight, "Diary, 1853," in Lillian Schlissel, ed., *Women's Diaries of the Westward Journey* (New York: Schocken Books, 1982), 206.

[22]Ibid., 203, 208, 209, 210.

[23]Ibid., 215.

[24]Katherine Llewellyn Hill Harris, "Women and Families on Northeastern Colorado Homesteads, 1873–1920" (Ph.D. diss., Univ. of Colorado, 1983).

• • • • • • • • • • • •

## QUESTIONS FOR A SECOND READING

1. This selection, the opening chapter of Limerick's book *The Legacy of Conquest*, offers a view of history as both an area of research, and something written, a writer's account of past events. In it, Limerick offers criticism and advice, an account of the problems of constructing a history of the American West. As you reread, look for passages that define the problems and the possible solutions for historians. The question, then, is not what Limerick says about the American West but what she says about reading and writing history.

2. It is possible to read this chapter as addressed to a general public, not simply to professional historians. As you reread, think about how and why Limerick tries to define or constitute her audience. Why might the general reading public, in the 1980s and '90s, read this book? What, specifically, do you find to let you answer this question in Limerick's terms?

## ASSIGNMENTS FOR WRITING

1. One way to work on Limerick's selection is to take the challenge and write history—to write the kind of history, that is, that takes into account the problems she defines: the problems of myth, point of view, fixed ideas. You are not a professional historian, you are probably not using this book in a history course, and you probably don't have the time to produce a carefully researched history, one that covers all the bases, but you can think of this as an exercise in history writing, a minihistory, a place to start. Here are two options:

a. Go to your college library or, perhaps, the local historical society and find two or three first-person accounts of a single place, person, or event in your community. (This does not have to be a history of the American West.) Try to work with original documents. The more varied the accounts, the better. Then, working with these texts as your primary sources, write a history, one that you can offer as a response to Limerick's selection.

b. While you can find materials in a library, you can also work with records that are closer to home. Imagine, for example, that you are going to write a family or neighborhood history. You have your own memories and experiences to work from, but for this to be a history (and not a "personal essay"), you will need to turn to other sources as well: interviews, old photos, newspaper clippings, letters, diaries—whatever you can find. After gathering your materials, write a family or neighborhood history, one that you can offer as a response to Limerick's work.

Choose one of the two projects. When you are done, write a quick one-page memo to Limerick. What can you tell her about the experience of a novice historian that she might find useful or interesting?

2. It is possible to see this selection as addressed to the general public, not just to professional historians. Limerick seems to write for a wide audience; she seems to believe that what she has to say about the West (and about history) has bearing on public issues, on our public imagination. What might a general public find important in Limerick's work? How might it be helpful to the present? What are the points of connection between what she says and, for example, your home or college community? What does she say that might be important to that community?

You could imagine that you stand in a position between Limerick and the community. Drawing on what you have read, or taking these selections as your beginning, write an essay that might be published on the op-ed page of your local (or school) newspaper, or as a review essay for a local magazine. Write a piece that introduces Limerick's work to your community or that places Limerick's project and concerns in the context of a local issue.

## MAKING CONNECTIONS

1. Like Limerick, Paul Auster in "Portrait of an Invisible Man" (p. 50) and Jane Tompkins in "Indians" (p. 673) deal with historical materials, and both, to varying degrees, discuss the problems of reading and writing history. Auster and Tompkins, however, are not historians, at least not in the strict, disciplinary sense of the word. They don't work in history departments; in this sense, their commitments to and understandings of history are, perhaps, a bit different.

Reread these three selections as a set, as part of a single project investigating the problems of writing history and understanding the past. Mark sections you might use as examples. Write an essay in which you discuss these three approaches to history. While it is possible to chart the similarities in these essays, focus on the differences. How is the work of each different from the others? What concerns or methods belong to each? Is it useful to see Auster and Tompkins as different from Limerick in ways that might be traced to their professional preparation?

2. While John Edgar Wideman is not writing a history in "Our Time" (p. 707), at least in the strict sense of the term, he *is* writing history—he is trying to recover and understand the story of his brother Robby, his family, and their neighborhood. He is trying to recover all those factors that might be said to have led to or produced his brother's present situation.

   It is interesting to read "Our Time" and Limerick's chapter as alternate ways of thinking about and writing history. As you reread these selections, mark passages you might use to illustrate the styles, methods, and/or concerns of each writer. You should reread the essays as a pair, as part of a single project investigating the problems of writing about other people and about the past. With Limerick's selection as a point of reference, what do Wideman's methods allow him to do and prevent him from knowing/learning/doing? With Wideman's selection as a point of reference, what about Limerick's methods—what do they allow her to do and prevent her from knowing/learning/doing?

   As a way of thinking about writing and history, write an essay in which you present your examples from each selection and discuss these two approaches to writing about the past.

# W. J. T.
# MITCHELL

*W. J. T. MITCHELL (b. 1941) is Gaylord Donnelley Distinguished Service Professor of English and Art History at the University of Chicago. His books include* Iconology *(1987),* Blake's Composite Art *(1978),* The Language of Images *(1980),* Against Theory *(1985),* Art and the Public Sphere *(1993), and* Landscape and Power *(1994). He is the editor of one of the leading journals in the humanities,* Critical Inquiry, *and has received fellowships from the Guggenheim Foundation, the National Endowment for the Humanities, the Rockefeller Foundation, and the American Philosophical Society. Mitchell's career as a scholar and teacher is distinguished not only by its productivity and wide-reaching influence (his work, for example, is read beyond his discipline and outside the academy) but also for the ways it has brought together subjects usually treated as separate: literature and art, words and pictures, language and vision.*

*The following selection is taken from his 1994 prize-winning book,* Picture Theory. Picture Theory *is a massive, brilliant, and controversial book whose goal is to examine the interaction of words and images, verbal and visual representations, in a variety of media, including literature, painting, advertising, and film. It not only describes these interactions but traces their linkages to issues of knowledge, power, value, and human interest. (The selection included below looks at the hybrid medium of the photographic essay.)*

Picture Theory *brings together the materials and arguments of seminars Mitchell taught at the University of Chicago, seminars with titles like "Image and Text" and "Verbal and Visual Representation." His book is not, he says, so much a textbook as a "pedagogical primer or prompt-book for classroom experiments," experiments that would bring together the study of literature and the study of visual art under the general category of "representation." For Mitchell, this urgently needed form of study should be central to the undergraduate curriculum.*

*Here is Mitchell in the introduction to* Picture Theory:

> *W. E. B. Du Bois said "the problem of the Twentieth Century is the problem of the color-line." As we move into an era in which "color" and "line" (and the identities they designate) have become potently manipulable elements in pervasive technologies of simulation and mass mediation, we may find that the problem of the twenty-first century is the problem of the image. Certainly I would not be the first to suggest that we live in a culture dominated by pictures, visual simulations, stereotypes, illusions, copies, reproductions, imitations, and fantasies. Anxieties about the power of visual culture are not just the province of critical intellectuals. Everyone knows that television is bad for you and that its badness has something to do with the passivity and fixation of the spectator. But then people have always known, at least since Moses denounced the Golden Calf, that images were dangerous, that they can captivate the onlooker and steal the soul. . . . What we need is a critique of visual culture that is alert to the power of images for good and evil and that is capable of discriminating the variety and historical specificity of their uses.*

*Mitchell's work is a contribution to that effort. A key word in* Picture Theory, *one you will find in the chapter below, is "ekphrasis." Ekphrasis was originally used to name a minor literary genre, poems written about paintings; for Mitchell the term stands for the more general topic of "the verbal representation of visual representation" (words standing for images) and the human desire across time to believe that words can make us see or that they can give voice to (articulate, explain) something which is beyond or outside of language. In the chapter that follows, Mitchell considers four "classic" texts of photojournalism to consider what is at stake in representing the world through picture and paragraph, and what is at stake in the arguments over which medium (photography or writing) can best make the claim to represent reality most truly, completely, or powerfully. Rather than choosing a side, Mitchell opens up the debate as a significant and useful contestation. His goal is to provide a practical example of how to think through particular texts, like a book of photojournalism, to larger questions of how we know what we know about the world, how we come to value what we value, and how power operates both through us and on us.*

# The Photographic Essay:
# Four Case Studies

*Three questions:*

1. *What is the relation of photography and language?*
2. *Why does it matter what this relation is?*
3. *How are these questions focused in the medium known as the "photographic essay"?*

*Three answers:*

1. *Photography is and is not a language; language also is and is not a "photography."*
2. *The relation of photography and language is a principal site of struggle for value and power in contemporary representations of reality; it is the place where images and words find and lose their conscience, their aesthetic and ethical identity.*
3. *The photographic essay is the dramatization of these questions in an emergent form of mixed, composite art.*

What follows is an attempt to connect these questions and answers.

## Photography and Language

> The totality of this relationship is perhaps best indicated by saying that appearances constitute a half-language.
>
> —JOHN BERGER,
> *Another Way of Telling*

The relationship of photography and language admits of two basic descriptions, fundamentally antithetical. The first stresses photography's difference from language, characterizing it as a "message without a code," a purely objective transcript of visual reality.[1] The second turns photography into a language, or stresses its absorption by language in actual usage. This latter view is currently in favor with sophisticated commentators on photography. It is getting increasingly hard to find anyone who will defend the view (variously labeled "positivist," "naturalistic," or "superstitious and naive") that photographs have a special causal and structural relationship with the reality that they represent. Perhaps this is due to the dominance of linguistic and semiotic models in the human sciences or to the skepticism, relativism, and conventionalism which dominates the world of advanced literary criticism. Whatever the reason, the dominant view of photography is now the kind articulated by Victor Burgin when he notes that "we rarely see a photograph *in use* which is not accompanied by language" and goes on to claim that the rare exceptions only confirm the domination of photography by language: "even the uncaptioned 'art' photograph," argues Burgin, "is invaded by language in the very moment it is looked at: in memory, in association, snatches of words and images continually intermingle and exchange one for the other."[2] Indeed, Burgin carries his argument well beyond looking at photography to "looking" as such, deriding the "naive idea of purely retinal vision," unaccompanied by language, a view which he associates with "an error of even greater consequence: that ubiquitous belief in 'the visual' as a realm of experience totally separated from, indeed antithetical to, 'the verbal'" (p. 53). Burgin traces "the idea that there are two quite distinct forms of communication, words and images" from the neoplatonic faith in a "divine language of things, richer than the language of words" to Ernst Gombrich's modern defense of the "natural" and "nonconventional" status of the photograph. "Today," concludes Burgin, "such relics are obstructing our view of photography" (p. 70).

What is it that troubles me about this conclusion? It isn't that I disagree with the claim that "language" (in some form) usually enters the experience of viewing photography or of viewing anything else. And it isn't the questioning of a reified distinction between words and images, verbal and visual representation; there seems no doubt that these different media interact with one another at numerous levels in cognition, consciousness, and communication. What troubles me, I suppose, is the confidence of tone, the assurance that we are able "today" to cast off certain "relics" that have mystified us for over two thousand years in favor of, presumably, a clear, unobstructed view of the matter. I'm especially struck by the figure of the "relic" as an obstructive image in contrast to the unobstructed view, since this is precisely the opposition which has (superstitiously) differentiated photography from more traditional forms of imagery and which formerly differentiated perspectival representation from "pre-scientific" modes of pictorial representation. Burgin's conclusions, in other words, are built upon a figurative opposition ("today/yesterday"; "clear view/obstructive relic") he has already dismissed as erroneous in its application to photography and vision. This return of an inconvenient figure suggests, at a minimum, that the relics are not quite so easily disposed of.

I'm also troubled by Burgin's confidence that "our view" can so easily be cleared up. Who is the "we" that has this "view"? It is implicitly divided between those who have overcome their superstitions about photography and those naifs who have not. "Our view" of photography is, in other words, far from homogeneous, but is the site of a struggle between the enlightened and the superstitious, moderns and ancients, perhaps even "moderns" and "postmoderns." Symptoms of this struggle emerge in Burgin's rhetoric when he speaks of the photograph as "invaded by language" (p. 51); what he seems not to consider is that this invasion might well provoke a resistance or that there might be some value

at stake in such a resistance, some real motive for a defence of the non-
linguistic character of the photograph. Burgin seems content to affirm the
"fluidity" (p. 52) of the relation between photography and language and
to treat photography as "a complex of exchanges between the verbal and
the visual" (p. 58).

But why should we suppose this model of free and fluid "exchanges" between photography and language to be true or desirable?
How do we account for the stubbornness of the naive, superstitious
view of photography? What could possibly motivate the persistence in
erroneous beliefs about the radical difference between images and
words and the special status of photography? Are these mistaken beliefs
simply conceptual errors, like mistakes in arithmetic? Or are they more
on the order of ideological beliefs, convictions that resist change by ordinary means of persuasion and demonstration? What if it were the case
that the "relics" which "obstruct" our view of photography also *constitute* that view? What if the only adequate formulation of the relation of
photography and language was a paradox: photography both is and is
not a language?

This, I take it, is what lies at the heart of what Roland Barthes calls "the
photographic paradox," "the co-existence of two messages, the one without a code (the photographic analogue), the other with a code (the 'art,' or
the treatment, or the 'writing,' or the rhetoric of the photograph)."[3]
Barthes works through a number of strategies to clarify and rationalize
this paradox. The most familiar is the division of the photographic "message" into "denotation" and "connotation," the former associated with the
"mythical," nonverbal status of the photograph "in the perfection and
plenitude of its analogy," the latter with the readability and textuality of
the photograph. Barthes sometimes writes as if he believes that this division of the photographic message into "planes" or "levels" may solve the
paradox:

> how, then, can the photograph be at once 'objective' and 'in-
> vested,' natural and cultural? It is through an understanding of
> the mode of imbrication of denoted and connoted messages
> that it may one day be possible to reply to that question. (p. 20)

But his more characteristic gesture is to reject easy answers predicted on a
model of "free exchange" of verbal and visual messages, connoted or denoted "levels": "structurally," he notes, "the paradox is clearly not the collusion of a denoted message and a connoted message . . . it is that the connoted (or coded) message develops on the basis of a message *without a
code*" (p. 19). To put the matter more fully: one connotation always present
in the photograph is that it is a pure denotation; that is simply what it
means to recognize it as a photograph rather than some other sort of
image. Conversely, the denotation of a photograph, what we take it to represent, is never free from what we take it to mean. The simplest snapshot

of a bride and groom at a wedding is an inextricably woven network of denotation and connotation: we cannot divide it into "levels" which distinguish it as a "pure" reference to John and Mary, or a man and a woman, as opposed to its "connotations" of festivity. Connotation goes all the way down to roots of the photograph, to the motives for its production, to the selection of its subject matter, to the choice of angles and lighting. Similarly, "pure denotation" reaches all the way up to the most textually "readable" features of the photograph: the photograph is "read" *as if it were* the trace of an event, a "relic" of an occasion as laden with aura and mystery as the bride's garter or her fading bouquet. The distinction between connotation and denotation does not resolve the paradox of photography; it only allows us to restate it more fully.

Barthes emphasizes this point when he suggests that the "structural paradox" of photography "coincides with an ethical paradox: when one wants to be 'neutral,' 'objective,' one strives to copy reality meticulously, as though the analogical were a factor of resistance against the investment of values" (pp. 19–20). The "value" of photography resides precisely in its freedom from "values," just as, in cognitive terms, its principal connotation or "coded" implication is that it is pure denotation, without a code. The persistence of these paradoxes suggests that the "mode of imbrication" or overlapping between photography and language is best understood, not as a structural matter of "levels" or as a fluid exchange, but (to use Barthes's term) as a site of "resistance." This is not to suggest that resistance is always successful or that "collusion" and "exchange" between photography and language is impossible or automatically undesirable. It is to say that the exchanges which seem to make photography just another language, an adjunct or supplement to language, make no sense without an understanding of the resistance they overcome. What we need to explore now is the nature of this resistance and the values which have motivated it.

## The Photographic Essay

> The immediate instruments are two: the motionless camera and the printed word.
>
> —JAMES AGEE,
> *Let Us Now Praise Famous Men*[4]

The ideal place to study the interaction of photography and language is in that subgenre (or is it a medium within the medium?) of photography known as the "photographic essay." The classic examples of this form (Jacob Riis's *How the Other Half Lives,* Margaret Bourke-White and Erskine Caldwell's *You Have Seen Their Faces*) give us a literal conjunction of photographs and text—usually united by a documentary purpose, often political, journalistic, sometimes scientific (sociology). There is an argument by Eugene Smith that the photographic series or sequence, even without text,

can be regarded as a photo-essay,[5] and there are distinguished examples
of such works (Robert Frank's *The Americans*).[6] I want to concentrate, however, on the kinds of photographic essays which contain strong textual
elements, where the text is most definitely an "invasive" and even domi-
neering element. I also want to focus on the sort of photo-essay whose text
is concerned, not just with the subject matter in common between the two
media, but with the way in which the media address that subject matter.
Early in Jacob Riis's *How the Other Half Lives* he describes an incident in
which his flash powder almost set a tenement on fire. This event is not
represented in the photographs: what we see, instead, are scenes of tenement squalor in which dazed subjects (who have often been roused from
their sleep) are displayed in passive bedazzlement under the harsh illumi-
nation of Riis's flash powder [Figure 1, below]. Riis's textual anecdote reflects on the scene of production of his images, characterizing and criticiz-
ing the photographer's own competence, perhaps even his ethics. We
might say that Riis allows his text to subvert his images, call them into
question. A better argument would be that the text "enables" the images
(and their subjects) to take on a kind of independence and humanity that

[Figure 1]. Jacob Riis, *Lodgers in Bayard St. Tenement . . .* Page spread from *How the Other
Half Lives* (1890). Photo reproduced courtesy of the Museum of the City of New York.

would be unavailable under an economy of straightforward "exchange" between photographer and writer. The photographs may be "evidence" for propositions quite at odds with the official uses that Riis wants to put them: The beholder, in turn, is presented with an uncomfortable question: is the political, epistemological power of these images (their "shock" value) a justification for the violence that accompanies their production? (Riis worked as a journalist in close collaboration with the police; many of these photos were taken during nighttime raids; these are, in a real sense, surveillance photographs; they also had a profound effect on reform efforts in the New York slums.) Riis's joining of an inconvenient, disruptive text foregrounds this dilemma, draws us into it. A resistance arises in the text-photo relation; we move less easily, less quickly from reading to seeing. Admittedly, this resistance is exceptional in Riis, whose general practice is to assume a straightforward exchange of information between text and image. But its emergence even in this relatively homogeneous photo-essay alerts us to its possibility, its effect and motivations.

Another way to state this dilemma is as a tension between the claims of the ethical and the political, the aesthetic and the rhetorical. Photo-essays have been, by and large, the product of progressive, liberal consciences, associated with political reform and leftist causes. But the best of them, I want to suggest, do not treat photography or language simply as instruments in the service of a cause or an institution. Nor are they content to advertise the fine moral or artistic sensitivities of their producers. The problem is to mediate these disparate claims, to make the instrumentality of both writing and photography and their interactions serve the highest interests of "the cause" by subjecting it to criticism while advancing its banner. Agee distinguishes between the "immediate instruments" of the photo-essay, "the still camera and the printed word," and the "governing instrument—which is also one of the centers of the subject—[which] is individual, anti-authoritative human consciousness" (p. xiv). The production of the photo-essay, the actual labor that goes into it, should not be, in Agee's view, simply an instrumental application of media to politics, ideology, or any other subject matter. The "taking" of human subjects by a photographer (or a writer) is a concrete social encounter, often between a damaged, victimized, and powerless individual and a relatively privileged observer, often acting as the "eye of power," the agent of some social, political, or journalistic institution. The "use" of this person as instrumental subject matter in a code of photographic messages is exactly what links the political aim with the ethical, creating exchanges and resistances at the level of value that do not concern the photographer alone, but which reflect back on the writer's (relatively invisible) relation to the subject as well and on the exchanges between writer and photographer.[7]

One last question about the genre: why should it be called the "photographic *essay*"? Why not the photo novel or lyric or narrative or just the "photo text"? There are, of course, examples of all these forms: Wright Morris has used his photographs to illustrate his fiction; Paul Strand and Nancy Newhall link photographs with lyric poems in *Time in New England*; Jan Baetens has analyzed the emergent French genre of the "photographic novel." What warrant is there for thinking of the "photo-essay" as an especially privileged model for the conjunction of photography and language? One reason is simply the dominance of the essay as the textual form that conventionally accompanies photography in magazines and newspapers. But there are, I think, some more fundamental reasons for a decorum that seems to link the photograph with the essay in the way that history painting was linked to the epic or landscape painting to the lyric poem. The first is the presumption of a common referential reality: not "realism" but "reality," nonfictionality, even "scientificity" are the generic connotations that link the essay with the photograph.[8] The second is the intimate fellowship between the informal or personal essay, with its emphasis on a private "point of view," memory, and autobiography, and photography's mythic status as a kind of materialized memory trace imbedded in the context of personal associations and private "perspectives." Third, there is the root sense of the essay as a partial, incomplete "attempt," an effort to get as much of the truth about something into its brief compass as the limits of space and writerly ingenuity will allow. Photographs, similarly, seem necessarily incomplete in their imposition of a frame that can never include everything that was there to be, as we say, "taken." The generic incompleteness of the informal literary essay becomes an especially crucial feature of the photographic essay's relations of image and text. The text of the photo-essay typically discloses a certain reserve or modesty in its claims to "speak for" or interpret the images; like the photograph, it admits its inability to appropriate everything that was there to be taken and tries to let the photographs speak for themselves or "look back" at the viewer.

In the remainder of this essay I want to examine four photo-essays that, in various ways, foreground the dialectic of exchange and resistance between photography and language, the things that make it possible (and sometimes impossible) to "read" the pictures, or to "see" the text illustrated in them. I will limit myself to four main examples: the first, Agee and Evans's *Let Us Now Praise Famous Men*, generally acknowledged as a "classic" (and a modernist) prototype for the genre, will be used mainly to lay out the principles of the form. The other three, exemplifying more recent and perhaps "postmodern" strategies (Roland Barthes's *Camera Lucida*, Malek Alloula's *The Colonial Harem*, and Edward Said and Jean Mohr's *After the Last Sky*), will be analyzed in increasing detail to show the encounter of principles with practice. The basic questions to be addressed with each of these works are the same: what relationship between photography and writing do they articulate? What tropes of differentiation govern the division of labor between photographer and writer, image and text, the viewer and the reader?

## *Spy and Counter-spy:* **Let Us Now Praise Famous Men**

> Who are you who will read these words and study these pho-
> tographs, and through what cause, by what chance and for
> what purpose, and by what right do you qualify to, and what
> will you do about it.
>
> —JAMES AGEE

The central formal requirements of the photographic essay are memo-
rably expressed in James Agee's introduction to *Let Us Now Praise Famous
Men:* "The photographs are not illustrative. They and the text are coequal,
mutually independent, and fully collaborative" (p. xv). These three requirements—equality, independence, and collaboration—are not simply
given by putting any text together with any set of photographs, and they
are not so easily reconcilable. Independence and collaboration, for instance, are values that may work at cross-purposes, and a "co-equality" of
photography and writing is easier to stipulate than it is to achieve or even
to imagine. Agee notes, for instance, that "the impotence of the reader's
eye" (p. xv) will probably lead to an underestimation of Evans's photographs; it is not hard to imagine a deafness or illiteracy underestimating
the text as well—a fate that actually befell *Let Us Now Praise Famous Men*
when it reached the editors of *Fortune* magazine, who had commissioned
it.[9] Agee's generic requirements are not only imperatives for the producers of an art form that seems highly problematic, they are also prescriptions for a highly alert reader/viewer that may not yet exist, that may in
fact have to be created.

It is easy enough to see how *Famous Men* satisfies the requirements of
independence and co-equality. The photographs are completely separate,
not only from Agee's text, but from any of the most minimal textual features that conventionally accompany a photo-essay: no captions, legends,
dates, names, locations, or even numbers are provided to assist a "reading" of the photographs. Even a relatively "pure" photographic essay like
Robert Frank's *The Americans* provides captions telling the subject and the
location. Frank's opening image, for instance, of shadowy figures at the
window of a flag-draped building [Figure 2, p. 530], is accompanied by
the caption "Parade—Hoboken, New Jersey" which immediately gives us
informational location not provided by the photograph and names a subject which it does not represent. Evans allows us no such clues or access
to his photographs. If we have studied Agee's text at some length, we
may surmise that the opening photograph is of Chester Bowles, and we
may think we can identify three different tenant families in Evans's pictures based on their descriptions in Agee's text, but all of these connections must be excavated; none of them are unequivocally given by any
"key" that links text to images. The location of Evans's photos at the front
of the volume is an even more aggressive declaration of photographic independence. In contrast to the standard practices of interweaving photos
with text or placing them in a middle or concluding section where they

[Figure 2]. Robert Frank, *Parade—Hoboken, New Jersey* (1955–1956), from *The Americans* (1958). Copyright © Robert Frank. Courtesy, Pace/MacGill Gallery, New York.

can appear in the context provided by the text, Evans and Agee force us to confront the photographs without context, before we have had a chance to see a preface, table of contents, or even a title page. When we do finally reach the contents, we learn that we are already in "Book Two" and that the photographs are the "Book One," which we have already "read."

The "co-equality" of photos and text is, in one sense, a direct consequence of their independence, each medium being given a "book" of its own, each equally free of admixture with the other—Evans providing photos without text, Agee a text without photos. But equality is further suggested by the feeling that Evans's photos really do constitute, in W. Eugene Smith's phrase, an "essay" in their own right.[10] The sequence of Evans's photos does not tell a story but suggests rather a procession of general "topics" epitomized by specific figures—after the anomalous opening figure [Figure 3, p. 531] whose rumpled sport coat suggests a wealth and class somewhat above those of the tenant farmers, a survey of representative figures: Father [Figure 4, p. 532], Mother [Figure 5, p. 533], Bedroom [Figure 6, p. 534], House [Figure 7, p. 535], and Children (Girl-Boy-Girl) of descending ages [Figures 8, 9, 10, pp. 536–38].[11] It is possible to construct a master-narrative if we insist on one. Agee provides one some eighty pages later if we are alert to it: "a man and a woman are drawn together upon a bed and there is a child and there are children"

[Figure 3]. Walker Evans, photograph from *Let Us Now Praise Famous Men* (1939) by James Agee and Walker Evans. Photograph courtesy of the Library of Congress.

(p. 55). We can even give these figures proper names: George and Annie Mae Gudger, their house, their children. But these text-image "exchanges" are not *given* to us by either the text or the images; if anything, the organization of the volume makes this difficult; it resists the straightforward collaboration of photo and text. And this resistance is not overcome by repeated readings and viewings, as if a secret code linking the photos to the

[Figure 4]. Walker Evans, photograph from *Let Us Now Praise Famous Men* (1939) by
James Agee and Walker Evans. Photograph courtesy of the Library of Congress.

text were there to be deciphered. When all the "proper" names and places
are identified, we are reminded that these are fictional names: the
Gudgers, Rickettses, and Woodses do not exist by those names. We may
feel we "know" them through Evans's images, through Agee's intimate
meditations on their lives, but we never do, and we never will.

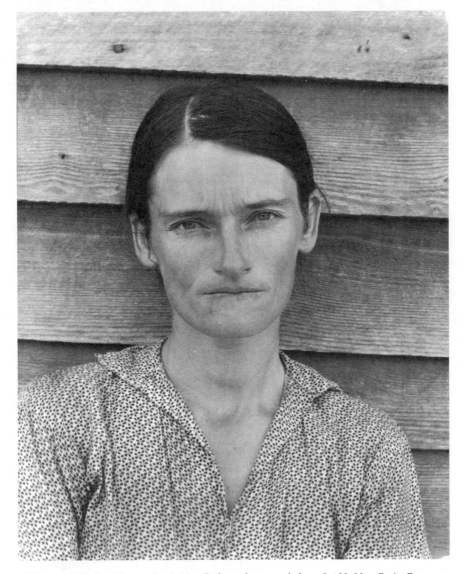

[Figure 5]. Walker Evans, *Annie Mae Gudger*, photograph from *Let Us Now Praise Famous Men* (1939) by James Agee and Walker Evans. © Copyright, Estate of Walker Evans.

What is the meaning of this blockage between photo and text? One answer would be to link it with the aesthetics of a Greenbergian modernism, a search for the "purity" of each medium, uncontaminated by the mixing of pictorial and verbal codes. Evans's photos are like aggressively untitled abstract paintings, bereft of names, reference, and "literary" elements. They force us back onto the formal and material features of the images in

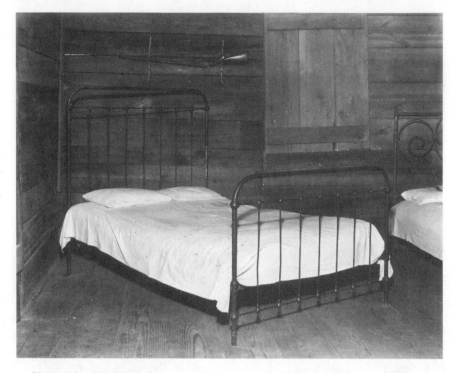

[Figure 6]. Walker Evans, photograph from *Let Us Now Praise Famous Men* (1939) by James Agee and Walker Evans. Photograph courtesy of the Library of Congress.

themselves. The portrait of Annie Mae Gudger [see Figure 5, p. 533], for instance, becomes a purely formal study of flatness and worn, "graven" surfaces: the lines of her face, the weathered grain of the boards, the faded dress, the taut strands of her hair, the gravity of her expression all merge into a visual complex that is hauntingly beautiful and enigmatic. She becomes an "icon," arguably the most famous of all the anonymous men and women captured by Evans's camera, a pure aesthetic object, liberated from contingency and circumstance into a space of pure contemplation, the Mona Lisa of the Depression.

There is something deeply disturbing, even disagreeable, about this (unavoidable) aestheticizing response to what after all is a real person in desperately impoverished circumstances. Why should we have a right to look on this woman and find her fatigue, pain, and anxiety beautiful? What gives us the right to look upon her, as if we were God's spies? These questions are, of course, exactly the sorts of hectoring challenges Agee's text constantly confronts us with; they are also the questions that Evans's photos force on us when he shows us the tenant farmers as beautiful, formal studies filled with mystery, dignity, and presence. We can-

[Figure 7]. Walker Evans, photograph from *Let Us Now Praise Famous Men* (1939) by James Agee and Walker Evans. Photograph courtesy of the Library of Congress.

not feel easy with our aesthetic appreciation of Annie Mae Gudger any more than we can pronounce her true name. Her beauty, like her identity, is held in reserve from us, at a distance: she looks back at us, withholding unreadable secrets. She asks as many questions of us as we of her: "who are you who will read these words and study these photographs?"

The aestheticizing separation of Evans's images from Agee's text is not, then, simply a formal characteristic but an ethical strategy, a way of preventing easy access to the world they represent. I call this an "ethical" strategy because it may well have been counterproductive for any political aims. The collaboration of Erskine Caldwell and Margaret Bourke-White in the representation of tenant farmers provides an instructive comparison. *You Have Seen Their Faces* offers unimpeded exchange between photos and text: Bourke-White's images interweave with Caldwell's essay; each photo is accompanied by a "legend" locating the shot and a "quotation" by the central figure. Consider *Hamilton, Alabama*/"We manage to get along" [Figure 11, p. 539].[12] The photograph restates the legend in its pictorial code, creating with its low-angle viewpoint and wide-angle lens an

[Figure 8]. Walker Evans, photograph from *Let Us Now Praise Famous Men* (1939) by James Agee and Walker Evans. Photograph courtesy of the Library of Congress.

impression of monumentality and strength (note especially how large the figures' hands are made to seem). This sort of rhetorical reinforcement and repetition is by far the more conventional arrangement of the photo-essay, and it may explain the enormous popular success of *You Have Seen Their Faces.*

It also illustrates vividly the kind of rhetorical relation of photo and text that Evans and Agee were resisting. This is not to say that Evans and Agee are "unrhetorical," but that their "collaboration" is governed by a rhetoric of resistance rather than one of exchange and cooperation. Their images and words are "fully collaborative" in the project of subverting what they saw as a false and facile collaboration with governmental and journalistic institutions (the Farm Security Administration, *Fortune* maga-zine).[13] The blockage between photo and text is, in effect, a sabotaging of an effective surveillance and propaganda apparatus, one which creates easily manipulable images and narratives to support political agendas. Agee and Evans may well have agreed with many of the reformist polit-ical aims of Caldwell and Bourke-White and the institutions they repre-sented: where they parted company is on what might be called the "ethics of espionage." Agee repeatedly characterizes himself and Evans as "spies": Agee is "a spy, traveling as a journalist"; Evans "a counter-

[Figure 9]. Walker Evans, photograph from *Let Us Now Praise Famous Men* (1939) by James Agee and Walker Evans. Photograph courtesy of the Library of Congress.

spy, traveling as a photographer" (p. xxii). The "independence" of their collaboration is the strict condition for this spy/counter-spy relation; it is their way of keeping each other honest, playing the role of "conscience" to one another. Evans exemplifies for Agee the ruthless violence of their work and the possibility of doing it with some sort of honor. The visibility

[Figure 10]. Walker Evans, photograph from *Let Us Now Praise Famous Men* (1939) by James Agee and Walker Evans. Photograph courtesy of the Library of Congress.

of the photographic apparatus brings their espionage out into the open, and Agee admires the openness of Evans at work, his willingness to let his human subjects pose themselves, stage their own images in all their dignity and vulnerability, rather than treating them as material for pictorial self-expression. Agee, for his part, is all self-expression, as if the objectivity and restraint of Evans's work had to be countered by the fullest subjectivity and copiousness of confession. This division of labor

[Figure 11]. Margaret Bourke-White, *HAMILTON, ALABAMA. "We manage to get along."*
From *You Have Seen Their Faces*, by Erskine Caldwell and Margaret Bourke-White.
Courtesy of the Estate of Margaret Bourke-White.

is not just an ethics of production affecting the work of the writer and photographer;[14] it is, in a very real sense, an ethics of form imposed on the reader/viewer in the structural division of the photos and text. Our labor as beholders is as divided as that of Agee and Evans, and we find ourselves drawn, as they were, into a vortex of collaboration and resistance.[15]

## Labyrinth and Thread: Camera Lucida

A labyrinthine man never seeks the truth, but only his Ariadne.
—NIETZSCHE
(quoted by Barthes)[16]

The strong, "agonistic" form of the photographic essay tends, as we have seen, to be as concerned with the nature of photography, writing, and the relation of the two, as with its represented subject matter (tenant farming, New York tenements, migrant workers, etc.). But most essays on photography (including this one) are not "photographic essays" in the sense I am giving the term here. Walter Benjamin's "A Short History of Photography" is not a photographic essay for the obvious reason that it is not illustrated. But even if it were, the photos would only be there to illustrate the text; they would not have the independence or co-equality that permits collaboration in a truly composite form.

One of the few "essays on photography" that approaches the status of a photographic essay is Barthes's *Camera Lucida*. The "independence" and "co-equality" of the photographs in Barthes's text is achieved, not by grouping them in a separate "book" where their own syntactical relations may emerge, but by a consistent subversion of the textual strategies that tend to incorporate photographs as "illustrative" or evidentiary examples. We open *Camera Lucida* to a frontispiece [Figure 12, p. 541], a color polaroid by Daniel Boudinet that never receives any commentary in the text. The only words of Barthes that might be applied to it are equivocal or negative ("Polaroid? Fun, but disappointing, except when a great photographer is involved" [p. 9]; "I am not very fond of Color . . . color is a coating applied *later on* to the original truth of the black-and-white photograph . . . an artifice, a cosmetic (like the kind used to paint corpses)" [p. 81]. Are we to suppose, then, that Barthes simply "likes" this photograph and admires Boudinet's art? These criteria are continually subverted in Barthes's text by his seemingly capricious preferences, his refusal to assent to canonized masterpieces and masters: "there are moments when I detest Photographs: what have I to do with Atget's old tree trunks, with Pierre Boucher's nudes, with Germain Krull's double exposures (to cite only the old names)?" (p. 16). The Boudinet polaroid stands independent of Barthes's text: the best "reading" we can get it is perhaps simply as an emblem of the unreadability of photography, its occupation of a site forever prior to and outside Barthes's text. The photo presents an image of a veiled, intimate *boudoir*, simultaneously erotic and funereal, its tantalizingly partial revelation of light gleaming through the cleavage in the curtains like the secret at the center of a labyrinth. Barthes tells us that "it is a mistake to associate Photography . . . with the notion of a dark passage *(camera obscura)*. It is *camera lucida* that we should say" (p. 106). But the darkened chamber of Barthes's frontispiece refuses to illustrate his text. If there is a *camera lucida* in this image it resides beyond the curtains of this scene, or perhaps in the luminous opening at its center, an evocation of the camera's aperture.[17]

[Figure 12]. Daniel Boudinet, *Polaroid, 1979*, in Roland Barthes, *Camera Lucida* (1981).
© 1993 ARS, New York/SPADEM, Paris.

Most of the other photographs in Barthes's text seem, at first glance, purely illustrative, but a closer reading subverts this impression. Barthes's commentaries are doggedly resistant to the rhetoric of the *"studium,"* the "rational intermediary of an ethical or political culture" (p. 26) that allows photographs to be "read" or that would allow a scientific theory of the photograph to emerge. Instead, Barthes emphasizes what he calls the *"punctum,"* the stray, pointed detail that "pricks" or "wounds" him. These details (a necklace, bad teeth, folded arms, dirt streets) are accidental,

uncoded, nameless features that open the photograph metonymically onto
a contingent realm of memory and subjectivity: "it is what I add to the
photograph and *what is nonetheless already there*" (p. 55), what is more often
remembered about a photograph than what is seen in its actual presence.[18]
The effect of this rhetoric is to render Barthes's text almost useless as a
semiological theory of photography, while making it indispensable *to*
such a theory. By insisting on his own personal experiences of photographs, by accepting the naive, primitive "astonishment," "magic," and
"madness" of photography, Barthes makes his own experience the raw
material of experimental data for a theory—a data, however, that is filled
with consciousness of a skepticism about the theories that will be brought
to it.[19]

The photograph that is of most importance to Barthes's text, a "private" picture of his mother taken in a glassed-in conservatory or "Winter
Garden" when she was five years old, is not reproduced. "Something like
the essence of the Photograph," says Barthes, "floated in this particular
picture." If "all the world's photographs formed a Labyrinth, I knew at the
center of this Labyrinth I should find nothing but this sole picture" (p. 73).
But Barthes cannot take us into the center of the labyrinth except blind-
folded, by ekphrasis, leading us with the thread of language. Barthes
"cannot reproduce" the photograph of his mother because it "would be
nothing but an indifferent picture" for anyone else. In its place he inserts a
photograph by Nadar of *The Artist's Mother (or Wife)* [Figure 13, p. 543],
which one "no one knows for certain" (p. 70).[20] This photograph receives
only the most minimal, even banal commentary ("one of the loveliest photographs in the world" [p. 70]) and an equally banal caption which pre-
tends to be quoted from the text, but (characteristically) is misquoted or
constructed especially for this image: "'Who do you think is the world's
greatest photographer?' 'Nadar'" (p. 68). Barthes's substitution of this maternal image for his own mother launches him into a series of increasingly
general associative substitutions: this photograph becomes "*the* Photograph" becomes "*the* Image"; Barthes's mother becomes "The Artist's
Mother" becomes "*the* Mother." The link between "Image" and "Mother"
is then summarized as a universal cultural complex which has been reproduced in the particularity of Barthes's own experience of photography:

> Judaism rejected the image in order to protect itself from the
> risk of worshipping the Mother. . . . Although growing up in a
> religion-without-images where the Mother is not worshipped
> (Protestantism) but doubtless formed culturally by Catholic art,
> when I confronted the Winter Garden photograph I gave my-
> self up to the Image, to the Image-Repertoire. (pp. 74–75)

Barthes is not a photographer; he made none of the photographs in his
book, his only responsibility being to collect and arrange them within his
text. He therefore has no collaborator in the usual sense. His collaborator
is "Photography" itself, exemplified by an apparently miscellaneous collection of images, some private and personal, most the work of recognized

[Figure 13]. Nadar, *The Artist's Mother (or Wife)* (n.d.), in Roland Barthes, *Camera Lucida* (1981). © 1993 ARS, New York/SPADEM, Paris.

masters from Niepce to Stieglitz to Mapplethorpe and Avedon.[21] "All the world's photographs" are treated by Barthes as a labyrinth whose unrepresentable center conceals the Mother, *his* mother. A mother who, like the subjects of all photographs, "is dead and . . . is going to die" (p. 95) unites all the photographs in Barthes's text, endowing them with the independent unity that enables them to look back at us while withholding their secrets. The Nadar portrait, its maternal figure gazing abstractedly out of the photo, mouth discreetly covered by the rose she kisses, is the closest we come to an emblem of this self-possession and reserve.

The relation of the photographs to Barthes's text is, then, that of labyrinth and thread, the "maternal image-repertoire" and the umbilical cord of language. His role as a writer is not to master the photos, but to surrender himself as captivated observer, as naive subject of the idolatrous magic of images. The whole project is an attempt to suspend the appropriate "scientific" and "professional" discourse of photography in order to cultivate photography's resistance to language, allowing the photographs to "speak" their own language—not "its usual blah-blah: 'Technique,' 'Reality,' 'Reportage,' 'Art,' etc." but making "the image speak in silence" (p. 55). Barthes dismisses, therefore, much "sophisticated" commentary on photography, his own included:

> It is the fashion, nowadays, among Photography's commentators (sociologists and semiologists), to seize upon a semantic relativity: no "reality" (great scorn for the "realists" who do not see that the photograph is always coded) . . . the photograph, they say, is not an *analogon* of the world; what it represents is fabricated, because the photographic optic is subject to Albertian perspective (entirely historical) and because the inscription on the picture makes a three-dimensional object into a two-dimensional effigy. (p. 88)

Barthes declares this argument "futile," not just because photographs, like all images, are "analogical" in their coded structure, but because realism must be located in a different place: "the realists do not take the photograph for a 'copy' of reality, but for an emanation of *past reality:* a *magic,* not an art." This lost "magic" of photography, based in its naive realist stage (also its place in modernism), is what Barthes's text attempts to recover and why it must seem to efface itself, "give itself up to" its photographs, even as it weaves them into a labyrinth of theory and desire, science and autobiography.[22]

### *Voyeurism and Exorcism:* The Colonial Harem

> It is as if the postcard photographer had been entrusted with a social mission: *put the collective phantasm into images.* He is the first to benefit from what he accomplishes through the delegation of power. The true voyeurism is that of the colonial society as a whole.
>
> —MALEK ALLOULA

The "magic" of photography can be the occasion of mystification as well as ecstasy, a point that is made by Malek Alloula's photographic essay on French colonial postcards of Algerian women.[23] Alloula dedicates his book to Barthes and adopts his basic vocabulary for the description of photographic magic, but he inverts Barthes's textual strategies in order to confront a body of images that exercised a detestable, pernicious magic over the representation of Algeria:

> What I read on these cards does not leave me indifferent. It demonstrates to me, were that still necessary, the desolate poverty of a gaze that I myself, as an Algerian, must have been the object of at some moment in my personal history. Among us, we believe in the nefarious effects of the evil eye (the evil gaze). We conjure them with our hand spread out like a fan. I close my hand back upon a pen to write *my* exorcism: *this text.* (p. 5)

There is no nostalgia here for a lost "primitive" or "realist" stage; there is no room for the *"punctum"* or ecstatic "wound" Barthes locates in the accidental detail. There is only the massive trauma of the "degrading fantasm" legitimating itself under the sign of photographic "reality." These photographs exclude all the "accidents" Barthes associates with the subversive "white magic" of the image. They stage for the voyeuristic French consumer the fantasy of "Oriental" luxury, lust, and indolence, as the unveiled "booty" before the colonial gaze. The critical text is counter-magic, a contrary incantation, repetitiously intoning its execrations on the filthy European pornographers with their ethnographic alibis.

Alloula's text fulfills the three conditions of the photographic essay in a quite unsuspected manner: his text is obviously independent of the images, that independence a direct result of Algeria's revolutionary independence of the French empire (Barbara Harlow's introduction places the book quite explicitly in the framework of Pontecorvo's film, *The Battle of Algiers*). There is "equality" of text and image in at least two senses. First, the text offers a point-by-point critical refutation of the implicit "argument" of the images. Second, it attempts to realize a contrary visual image or "staring back" into the face of the predatory colonial gaze. Alloula's text presents itself as a kind of substitute for a body of photographs that should have been taken, but never were:

> A reading of the sort that I propose to undertake would be entirely superfluous if there existed photographic traces of the gaze of the colonized upon the colonizer. In their absence, that is, in the absence of a confrontation of opposed gazes, I attempt here . . . to return this immense postcard to its sender. (p. 5)

Finally, there is "collaboration" in the sense that the postcards must be reproduced along with the text and thus forced to collaborate in their own deconstruction, their own "unveiling," much as the *algérienne* were forced to collaborate in the misrepresentation of Algerian women and their images forced to collaborate in a false textualizing—their insertion into a staged fantasy of exotic sexuality and unveiling, the colonial "chit-chat" (full of crude jokes) written on their backs, the colonial seal stamped across their faces, canceling the postage and their independent existence in one stroke.

Alloula's project is clearly beset on every side by contradictory impulses, the most evident being the necessity of reproducing the offending postcards in a book which may look to the casual observer like a coffeetable "collector's item" of exactly the sort he denounces. Occasional "classics" and "masterpieces" emerge, even in a pornographic genre:

> It is on "accomplishments" of this sort that a lucrative business of card collecting has been built and continues to thrive. It is also by means of this type of "accomplishment" that the occultation of meaning is effected, the meaning of the postcard that is of interest to us here. (p. 118)

"Aestheticization," far from being an antidote to the pornographic, is seen as an extension of it, a continuing cover-up of evil under the sign of beauty and rarity. This problem was also confronted by Agee, who dreaded the notion that his collaboration with Evans would be mystified by notions of special expertise or authority, chief among these the authority of the "artist": "the authors," he said, "are trying to deal with it not as journalists, sociologists, politicians, entertainers, humanitarians, priests, or artists, but seriously" (p. xv). "Seriousness" here means something quite antithetical to the notion of a canonical "classic" stamped with "aesthetic merit" and implies a sense of temporary, tactical intervention in an immediate human problem, not a claim on the indefinite future. That is why Agee wanted to print *Let Us Now Praise Famous Men* on newspaper stock. When told that "the pages would crumble to dust in a few years," he said, "that might not be a bad idea" (Stott, p. 264).

Let us add, then, to the generic criteria of the photographic essay a notion of seriousness which is frequently construed in anti-aesthetic terms, as a confrontation with the immediate, the local and limited, with the unbeautiful, the impoverished, the ephemeral, in a form that regards itself as simultaneously *indispensable* and *disposable*. The text of Alloula's *The Colonial Harem* sometimes reads as if it wanted to shred or incinerate the offending postcards it reproduces so well, to disfigure the pornographic beauty of the colonized women. But that would be, like most shreddings of historical documents, only a cover-up that would guarantee historical amnesia and a return of the repressed. Although Alloula can never quite say this, one feels that his essay is not simply a polemic against the French evil, but a tacit confession and purgation. Alloula reproduces the offending images, not just to aggressively "return an immense postcard to its sender," but to repossess and redeem those images, to "exorcise" an ideological spell that captivated mothers, wives, and sisters, as well as the "male society" that "no longer exists" (p. 122) in the colonial gaze. The rescue of women is an overcoming of impotence; the text asserts its manhood by freeing the images from the evil eye.

Barthes found the secret of photography in an image of his prepubescent mother at the center of a labyrinth. His text is the thread that takes us toward that center, a ritual surrender to the maternal image-repertoire. Alloula drives us out of the mystified labyrinth constructed by European representations of Arab women. He avenges the prostitution not only of the Mother, but of Photography itself, seeking to reverse the pornographic process.

What are we left with? Are the images redeemed, and if so, in what terms and for what sort of observer? How do we see, for instance, the final photograph of the book [Figure 14, below], which Alloula only mentions in passing, and whose symmetry approaches abstraction, reminiscent of an art nouveau fantasy? Can an American observer, in particular, see

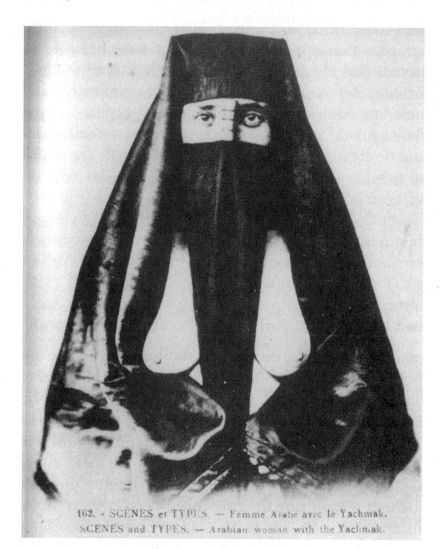

162. - SCENES et TYPES. — Femme Arabe avec le Yachmak.
SCENES and TYPES. — Arabian woman with the Yachmak.

[Figure 14]. *Scenes and Types: Arabian woman with the Yachmak* (n.d.), from *The Colonial Harem* (1986) by Malek Alloula, translated by Myrna and Wlad Godzich (French edition, 1981; English edition, Minneapolis: University of Minnesota Press, 1986).

these photographs as anything more than quaint, archaic pornography, hauntingly beautiful relics of a lost colonial era, "collector's items" for a coffee-table book? I don't have a simple answer to this question, but my first impulse is to register a feeling of *impotence* in the face of these women, whose beauty is now mixed with danger, whose nakedness now becomes a veil that has always excluded me from the labyrinth of their world.[24] I feel exiled from what I want to know, to understand, or (more precisely) what I want to acknowledge and to be acknowledged by. In particular, Alloula's text forces these acknowledgments from me: that I cannot read these photographs; that any narrative I might have brought to them is now shattered; that the labyrinth of photography, of the maternal image-repertoire, defies penetration and colonization by any textual system, including Malek Alloula's. The photographs, so long exchanged, circulated, inscribed, and traded, now assert their independence and equality, looking at us as they collaborate in the undoing of the colonial gaze.

## *Exile and Return:* After the Last Sky

> But I am the exile.
> Seal me with your eyes.
> —MAHMOUD DARWISH

Feelings of exile and impotence in the face of the imperial image are the explicit subject of Edward Said and Jean Mohr's photographic essay on the Palestinians. But instead of the aggressive "return of the repressed" in the form of degraded, pornographic images, *After the Last Sky*[25] projects a new set of images, self-representations of the colonized and dispossessed subjects, representations of their views of the colonizers: "our intention was to show Palestinians through Palestinian eyes without minimizing the extent to which even to themselves they feel different" (p. 6). The text is (as in *Camera Lucida*) a thread leading the writer and his readers back into the labyrinth of otherness and the self-estrangement of exile. Its task is to see that the "photographs are not" seen as "the exhibition of a foreign specimen" (p. 162), without, on the other hand, simply domesticating them. Said's text is not, then, like Alloula's, a scourge to drive Western eyes out the labyrinth. If Alloula treats the collaboration of text and image as a violent, coercive confrontation, Said and Mohr create a dialogical relation of text and image that is collaborative in the classic (that is, modernist) sense articulated by Agee and Evans, a cooperative endeavor by two like-minded and highly talented professionals, writer and photographer.

The results of this "positive" collaboration are anything but straightforward. The independence of text and image is not asserted directly, as in Agee and Evans, by a strict physical separation. Said and Mohr follow something closer to the mode of *Camera Lucida*'s dialectical, intertwined relation of photos and essay, a complex of exchange and resistance.[26]

Writer and photographer both refuse the stereotyped division of labor that would produce a "text with illustrations" or an "album with captions." Said's text oscillates between supplementary relations to the images (commentary, meditations, reflections on photography) and "independent" material (the history of the Palestinians, autobiographical anecdotes, political criticism). Mohr's photographs oscillate between "illustrative" relations (pictures of boys lifting weights, for instance, document the "cult of physical strength" Said describes among Palestinian males) and "independent" statements that receive no direct commentary in the text, or play some kind of ironic counterpoint to it. An example: Said's discussion of his father's lifelong attempt to escape memories and material mementos of Jerusalem is juxtaposed (on the facing page) with an image that conveys just the opposite message and which receives no commentary, only a minimal caption: "the former mayor of Jerusalem and his wife, in exile in Jordan" [Figure 15, p. 550]. Behind them a photographic mural of the Mosque of Omar in Jerusalem occupies the entire wall of their living room. The collaboration of image and text here is not simply one of mutual support. It conveys the anxiety and ambivalence of the exile whose memories and mementos, the tokens of personal and national identity, may "seem . . . like encumbrances" (p. 14). The mural seems to tell us that the former mayor and his wife *cherish* these encumbrances, but their faces do not suggest that this in any way reduces their weight.

The relation of photographs and writing in *After the Last Sky* is consistently governed by the dialectic of *exile* and its overcoming, a double relation of estrangement and re-unification. If, as Said claims, "exile is a series of portraits without names, without context" (p. 12), return is figured in the attachment of names to photographs, contexts to images. But "return" is never quite so simple: sometimes the names are lost, unrecoverable; too often the attachment of text to an image can seem arbitrary, unsatisfactory. Neither pole in the dialectic of exile is univocally coded: estrangement is both imposed from without by historical circumstance and from within by the painfulness of memory, the will to forget and shed the "encumbrance" of Palestinian identity. "Re-unification," similarly, is the utopian object of desire and yet an object of potential aversion in its utopian impracticality. "Homecoming," says Said, "is out of the question. You learn to transform the mechanics of loss into a constantly postponed metaphysics of return" (p. 150). Where does the exile go "after the last sky" has clouded over, after Beirut, Cairo, Amman, the West Bank have failed to provide a home? What attitude do the physically exiled Palestinians take to the "exiles at home," the "present absentees" who live in "The Interior," inside Israel? The ambivalence expressed in these questions is also inscribed in the delicate, intricate, and precarious relations of text and image—the inside and outside, as it were, of this book.

The casual "Outsider," the beholder who takes this simply as an album of photographs, will have no difficulty grasping the major polemical point of the book, which is to counter the usual visual representation of

[Figure 15]. Jean Mohr, *Mayor of Jerusalem*, page spread from *After the Last Sky*, by
Edward W. Said. Copyright © 1986 by Edward W. Said. Reprinted by permission
of Pantheon Books, a division of Random House, Inc.

Palestinians as menacing figures with *kaffiyas* and ski-masks. Anonymous
"terrorists" are displaced by a set of visual facts that everyone knows in theory, but rarely acknowledges in practice—that Palestinians are also women,
children, businessmen, teachers, farmers, poets, shepherds, and auto mechanics. That the representation of Palestinians as ordinary human beings,
"capturable" by ordinary, domestic sorts of snapshots, should be in itself

remarkable is a measure of how extraordinarily limited the normal image of the Palestinian is. There is an acceptable "icon" of the Palestinian, as Said puts it, and the images in *After the Last Sky*—domestic, peaceful, ordinary— do not fit this decorum, as anyone will find who attempts to insert this book among the other photographic texts that adorn the typical coffee-table.

The history of this particular set of photographs suggests that this decorum is not simply natural or empirical but has to be reinforced by the most stringent prohibitions. Jean Mohr was commissioned to take the pictures for an exhibition at the International Conference on the Question of Palestine held by the United Nations in Geneva in 1983. "The official response," as Said notes

> was puzzling. . . . You can hang them up, we were told, but no writing can be displayed with them. No legends, no explanations. A compromise was finally negotiated whereby the name of the country or place (Jordan, Syria, West Bank, Gaza) could be affixed to the much-enlarged photographs, but not one word more. (p. 3)

The precise motives for this bureaucratic "prohibition on writing" never become clear. Said speculates that the various Arab states who participated in the conference (Israel and the United States did not) found the Palestinian cause "useful up to a point—for attacking Israel, for railing against Zionism, imperialism, and the United States," but the notion of considering the Palestinians *as a people* (that is, with a story, a text, an argument) was unacceptable. The prohibition on writing was perhaps a way of keeping these disturbing images from taking on an even more disturbing voice. Context, narrative, historical circumstances, identities, and places were repressed in favor of what might be seen as a parody of the abstract and "modernist" space of visual exhibition: minimal captions, no "legends," pure visual display without reference or representation. Exile is a series of photographs without texts.

*After the Last Sky,* then, is a violation of a double prohibition against a certain kind of image (nonbellicose, nonsublime) and against a writing joined to these images. This might seem an excessively formalistic point. But Said notes that "most literary critics . . . focus on what is said in Palestinian writing . . . [its] sociological and political meaning. But it is the *form* that should be looked at" (p. 38). This "form" is not something distinct from content; it *is* the content in its most material, particular sense, the specific places it carves out as the site of Palestinian existence. As such, it resists the reduction of the Palestinian question to a political issue, insisting on the ethical as well as aesthetic relation of text and image. The collaboration of photographer and writer in *After the Last Sky* cannot be seen, then, simply as corrective to the prohibition which segregates the Palestinian image from the Palestinian text. This collaboration is also embedded in a complex field of heterogeneities that can never quite be accommodated to traditional dialectical forms of aesthetic unity. We don't find a

Coleridgean "multeity in unity" in this book, but something more like a multeity of glimpses of unity, seen as if through a pair of spectacles, one lens of which is shattered. (This image, drawn from one of the most striking photographs in the book, is one I will return to later.)

The two lenses of this book are writing and photography, neither understood abstractly or generically but as constructions of specific histories, places, and displacements. The photographer, a German born in Geneva, naturalized as a Swiss citizen in 1939, has had concrete experience of intra-European exile. The writer is a Palestinian Christian born in Jerusalem, exiled to Lebanon, Egypt, the United States. From one point of view the writer is the insider, the clear, intact lens who can represent through his own experience a focused image of "the Palestinian"; the photographer is the alien, unable to speak the languages of Palestine or Israel, "seeing" only the mute, inarticulate fragments of lives that the camera allows (thus, many of the people in Mohr's photographs are anonymous, unidentified, and photography re-doubles the exile of image from referent). From another point of view, the photographer is the clear, intact lens. His Swiss neutrality allows him what was denied to the writer in the 1980s, the freedom to travel throughout Israel and the West Bank, to go "inside" Palestine and represent it with the transparent accuracy of photography. The writer is the alien, the outsider, estranged from a land he dimly remembers as a child, a land in which he would have been, as an urbane, Christian intellectual, estranged from the rural, local culture of the Palestinian masses. The writer acknowledges that he himself is the "cracked lens," unable to see, quite literally, the native country he longs for except in fragmentary glimpses provided by others.

The divisions of labor we have traced between writer and photographer—spy and counter-spy, thread and labyrinth, voyeur and exorcist—are consistently undermined by the tightly woven collaboration of *After the Last Sky*. But there is one vestige of traditional divisions of labor in the way Said's meditations on gender difference suggest the collaboration of a male text with a body of female images. Like Barthes, Said installs Woman at the center of the photographic matrix. The section of the book called "Interiors" (concerned with Palestinians who live inside Israel, with domestic spaces and the theme of privacy) is mainly devoted to images of women. Said also follows Barthes in finding that the primal scene of the photograph involves his mother. A British customs official rips up her passport, destroying her legal identity and (presumably) her photographic image in the same gesture. Like Alloula, Said is vindicating the disfigured image of his mother; like Barthes, he is trying to re-assemble the fragments of her identity. But he also portrays the women as the real preservers of this identity, associated with "the land" and the idea of home, portrayed as clinging irrationally, stubbornly, to "memories, title deeds, and legal claims" (p. 81). The women are also the keepers of images in the Palestinian interior, the ones who hang up too many pictures too high on the walls, who save the photograph albums and mementos that may encumber the male Palestinian who wants to travel light. (Recall that Said's father "spent his life trying to escape these objects" [p. 14].) Yet Said acknowledges a "crucial absence of women" (p. 77) in the representation of Palestinians. The official icon is one of "automatic manhood," the macho terrorist who may feel himself both goaded and reproached by the "protracted discipline" (p. 79) of women's work.

Like Barthes, Said wants to preserve the feminine mystique of the image, its difference from the male writer's "articulate discourse" (p. 79). Thus, it sometimes seems as if he would prefer to leave the female images unidentified and therefore mysterious. Like Barthes, he does not reproduce an image of his mother, but substitutes an image of an elderly woman, generalized as an emblem—"a face, I thought when I first saw it, of our life at home" (p. 84). But six months later Said is reminded by his sister that this woman [Figure 16, below] is actually a distant relative whom he met in the forties and fifties, a reminder that produces mixed emotions:

> As soon as I recognized Mrs. Farraj, the suggested intimacy of the photograph's surface gave way to an explicitness with few secrets. She is a real person—Palestinian—with a real history at the interior of ours. But I do not know whether the photograph can, or does, say things as they really are. Something has been lost. But the representation is all we have. (p. 84)

[Figure 16]. Jean Mohr, *Amman, 1984. Mrs. Farraj.* In *After the Last Sky,* by Edward W. Said. Copyright © 1986 by Edward W. Said. Reprinted by permission of Pantheon Books, a division of Random House, Inc.

The uncharacteristic awkwardness of Said's writing here is, I think, a tacit acknowledgment of his ambivalence toward the associative complex, Woman/Image/Home, a confession of his complicity in the sentimentalizing of women and of the lost pastoral homeland that fixates the imagination of the Palestinian male.[27] His candor about this ambivalence, his recognition that the photographic image has a life beyond the discursive, political uses he would make of it, allows the photograph to "look back" at him and us and assert the independence we associate with the strong form of the photo-essay. The poetic secrecy and intimacy he had hoped to find in this image is replaced by a prosaic familiarity and openness.

Jean Mohr provides Said with a striking emblem of his own ambivalence in a photograph which comes closer than any other in this book to supplying a portrait of the writer. Once again, the photo is an unidentified portrait, exiled from its referent, an image of an "elderly Palestinian villager" with a broken lens in his glasses [Figure 17, below]. The photograph reminds Said of Rafik Halabi, "a Palestinian-Druze-Israeli" whose book, *The West Bank Story,* is highly critical of Israeli occupation, but "who writes from the viewpoint of a loyal Israeli" who served in the army and "subscribes to Zionism." Said finds Halabi's position impossibly contradictory. Either he is "deluded" or "up to some elaborate rhetorical game" which Said does not understand. Either way, "the result is a book that runs on two completely different tracks" (p. 127). It occurs to Said, of course, that there is

[Figure 17]. Jean Mohr, *Elderly Palestinian Villager. Ramallah, 1984.* In *After the Last Sky,* by Edward W. Said. Copyright © 1986 by Edward W. Said. Reprinted by permission of Pantheon Books, a division of Random House, Inc.

something of himself, and perhaps of his own book, in this image: "Perhaps I am only describing *my* inability to order things coherently, sequentially, logically, and perhaps the difficulties of resolution I have discerned in Halabi's book and in the old man with broken glasses are mine, not theirs" (p. 130). First, the image is a double portrait of the Other as Insider, "a symbol, I said to myself, of some duality in our life that won't go away—refugees and terrorists, victims and victimizers, and so on" (p. 128). Not a bad reading, but Said is unhappy with it, as he is generally with emblematic readings that reduce the photograph to convenient verbal formulas. The man's face is "strong and gentle," the "blotch is on the lens, not in him" (p. 128). He has agreed to be photographed this way, so he can watch the camera and exert some control over his own image.

The resulting visual field (both for the wearer of the glasses and the beholder), Said notes, will always disclose a "small disturbance," a "curiously balanced imbalance" which is "very similar to the textual imbalance in Halabi's book" and, clearly, in Said and Mohr's. The Palestinians, a people without a geographic center and with only the most fragile cultural and historical identity have "no one central image," no "dominant theory," no "coherent discourse"; they are "without a center. Atonal" (p. 129). At moments like this, one glimpses Said's allegiance to the musical aesthetics of modernism, to that combination of pessimism and formalism we associate with Adorno. Said's composite, decentered, shifting, imbalanced collaboration with Mohr is nonetheless a shapely, congruent, and formal creation, a material embodiment of the reality he wants to represent, built out of a refusal to simplify, to sentimentalize or settle for polemic. Both writer and photographer could see themselves in this anonymous portrait, itself in exile from its subject: exile is indeed "a series of portraits without names, without contexts" (p. 12). But if photographs sundered from texts portray exile, photographs *with* text are images of return, sites of reconciliation, accommodation, acknowledgment. The delicate balancing act of a book "on two different tracks" may be a rhetorical game Said does not understand even as he is compelled to play it, but then he remarks that Palestinians sometimes "puzzle even ourselves" (p. 53).

The "central image" of the Palestinians is, for the moment, a double vision of just this sort—secular, rational, yet deeply involved in the emotions of victimage—figures in a rhetoric of paranoia which constructs them as the enemy of the victims of the Holocaust or as mere pawns in geopolitical schemes. Said and Mohr cannot be content, therefore, with a propaganda piece to "pretty up the image" of the Palestinians; they must work as well for an *internally directed* representation and critique, chiding not only the Arab and Israeli and Big Power interests, but the Palestinians themselves, Said included. The Palestinians' failings—their pursuit of inappropriate revolutionary models such as Cuba and Algeria, their impatient, macho romanticism, their failure to organize properly with the "protracted discipline" of women, their lack of a coherent history—are all part

of the picture. The idea of the book, then, is ultimately to help bring the
Palestinians into existence for themselves as much as for others; it is that
most ambitious of books, a nation-making text.

Texts that make nations are, of course, what we call "classics," the
worst fate (according to Agee) that can befall a book. It was a fate that befell *Let Us Now Praise Famous Men* after a period of neglect and misunderstanding. Our understanding of the thirties, particularly the Depression, is
often seen as a product of Evans's and Agee's collaboration, and it helped
to form an image of a nation in poverty, presented with dignity, sympathy, and truth. But Evans and Agee could never hope, as Said and Mohr
do, to address the people they represent, to help bring them into being as
a people. Whether this book fulfills such a hope is a question that will be
settled beyond its pages: "there is no completely coherent discourse adequate to us, and I doubt whether at this point, if someone could fashion
such a discourse, we could be adequate for it" (p. 129). It is at such moments of inadequacy, perhaps, that a mixed, hybrid discourse like that of
the photographic essay emerges as a historical necessity.

Insofar as my own remarks here have been essays toward the definition of a genre or a medium, an attempt to articulate the formal principles
of the photographic essay, they might be seen as a betrayal of the anti-
aesthetic, anticanonical experimentalism of this form. Why attempt to
"classicize" by classifying and formalizing a medium that is so young and
unpredictable? The photographic essay occupies a strange conceptual
space in our understanding of representation, a place where "form" seems
both indispensable and disposable. On the one hand, it seems to participate in what Stanley Cavell has described as the tendency of "modernist
painting" to "break down the concept of genre altogether,"[28] as if the
medium were not given naturally, but had to be re-invented, re-evaluated
in each new instance; this is the tendency I've associated with the mutual
"resistance" of photography and writing, the insistence on the distinctive
character of each medium, the search for a "purity" of approach that is
both aesthetic and ethical. On the other hand, the roots of the photo-essay
in documentary journalism, newspapers, magazines, and the whole ensemble of visual-verbal interactions in mass media connect it to popular
forms of communication that seem quite antithetical to modernism in
their freedom of exchange between image and text and their material
ephemerality. Perhaps this is just a way of placing the photographic essay
at the crossroads between modernism and postmodernism, understanding it as a form in which the resistance to image-text exchange is (in contrast to painting) most crucial precisely because it has the most to overcome.[29] If this crossroads occupies a real place in our cultural history, it is
one we cannot leave unmapped. To take literally the antiformalist rhetoric
of the photographic essay would be to empty it of its specific, historical
materiality as a representational practice and to neglect those labors of
love in which we are enjoined to collaborate.

## NOTES

[1] The phrase "message without a code" is from Roland Barthes's essay, "The Photographic Message," in *Image/Music/Text*, translated by Stephen Heath (New York: Hill and Wang, 1977), p. 19. I am grateful to David Antin and Alan Trachtenberg for their many intelligent suggestions and questions about an earlier version of this essay.

[2] Victor Burgin, "Seeing Sense," in *The End of Art Theory: Criticism and Post-Modernity* (Atlantic Highlands, NJ: Humanities Press, 1986), p. 51; further page references will be cited in the text.

[3] Roland Barthes, "The Photographic Message," in *Image/Music/Text*, p. 19; further page references will be cited in the text.

[4] James Agee and Walker Evans, *Let Us Now Praise Famous Men* (Originally published, 1939; New York: Houghton Mifflin, 1980), p. xiv; further page references will be cited in the text.

[5] See Tom Moran, *The Photo Essay: Paul Fusco and Will McBride*, in the Masters of Contemporary Photography series (Los Angeles, CA: Alskog, Inc., 1974). Eugene Smith's remarks on the genre of the photo-essay were made in conversation with the editors of this book and appear on pages 14–15.

[6] Robert Frank, *The Americans* (1st edition, 1959; rev. and enlarged ed., New York: Grossman Publishers, 1969). Frank's book is not entirely free of text, however. All the photographs are accompanied by brief captions, usually a designation of subject, time, or location, and there is an introduction by Jack Kerouac that emphasizes the implicit verbal coding of Frank's photographs: "What a poem this is, what poems can be written about this book of pictures some day by some young new writer . . ." (p. iii).

[7] For an excellent account of the way writers address the ethical issues of "approach to the subject" made visible by the photographic apparatus in action, see Carol Schloss, *In Visible Light: Photography and the American Writer: 1840–1940* (New York: Oxford University Press, 1987), p. 11.

[8] Recall the classic photo-essays based in scientific discourse such as geological surveys (Timothy O'Sullivan, for instance) and sociological studies (the work of Dorothea Lange and Paul Taylor). The modern discipline of art history is inconceivable without the illustrated slide lecture and the photographic reproduction of images. Any discourse that relies on the accurate mechanical reproduction of visual evidence engages with photography at some point.

[9] For a good account of the reception of Agee and Evans's work, see William Stott, *Documentary Expression and Thirties America* (New York: Oxford University Press, 1973), pp. 261–66.

[10] Eugene Smith argues that photojournalists tend to work within narrative conventions, producing "picture stories": "that's a form of its own, not an essay" (*The Photo Essay*, p. 15).

[11] This "topical" and nonnarrative format persists throughout the sequence of Evans's photos. The photos are divided into three sections, the first concentrating on the Gudgers and Woodses, the second on the Rickettses, and the third on the towns in their neighborhood.

[12] The reader who supposes that these quotations have some documentary authenticity, or even an expressive relation to the photographic subject, should heed Bourke-White's opening note: "the legends under the pictures are intended to express the authors' own conceptions of the sentiments of the individuals portrayed; they do not pretend to reproduce the actual sentiments of these persons." The candor of this admission is somewhat offset by the persistent fiction of the "quotation" throughout the text. This manipulation of verbal material is quite in keeping with Bourke-White's penchant for re-arranging the objects in the sharecroppers' households to conform with her own aesthetic tastes.

[13] Jefferson Hunter's book, *Image and Word: The Interaction of Twentieth Century Photographs and Texts* (Cambridge, MA: Harvard University Press, 1987) notes this

resistance but sees it merely as an "affront" to convention that made *Famous Men* "unsuccessful in 1941" and "uninfluential now" on the practice of photo-text collaboration. Hunter takes the "stylistic consistency" of Bourke-White and Caldwell as a model for the way "collaborative efforts succeed" (p. 79).

[14] For an excellent account of what I'm calling an "ethics of production," see Carol Schloss's chapter on Agee and Evans in her *In Visible Light*.

[15] I use the word "vortex" here to echo Agee's allusions to the Blakean vortex and to the presence of Blake as a presiding genius in *Famous Men*. I do not know how familiar Agee was with Blake's work as a composite artist, but if he knew the illuminated books, he must have been struck by the oft-remarked independence of Blake's engravings from his texts, an independence which is coupled, of course, with the most intimate collaboration. For more on Blakean text-image relations, see my *Blake's Composite Art* (Princeton, NJ: Princeton University Press, 1977), and chapter 4 above.

[16] Roland Barthes, *Camera Lucida* (French original, 1981; New York: Hill and Wang, 1981), p. 73; further page references will be cited in the text.

[17] The *camera lucida,* as Barthes knew, is not properly translated as a "light room" in opposition to a "dark room." It is "the name of that apparatus, anterior to Photography, which permitted drawing an object through a prism, one eye on the model, the other on the paper" (p. 106). The opening in the curtains, as optical aperture, plays precisely this role.

[18] "I may know better a photograph I remember than a photograph I am looking at, as if direct vision oriented its language wrongly, engaging it in an effort of description which will always miss its point of effect, the *punctum*" (p. 53). The opposition between *studium* and *punctum* is coordinated, in Barthes's discussion, with related distinctions between the public and the private, the professional and the amateur. The captions further reinforce what Barthes calls "the two ways of the Photograph," dividing themselves into a scholarly, bibliographic identification of photographer, subject, date, etc. and an italicized quotation registering Barthes's personal response, the *punctum*. This practice of double captioning is, I think, a pervasive convention in photographic essays, often signaled by hyphenation (as in Robert Frank's *The Americans*), or contrasting type-styles (as in *You Have Seen Their Faces*): *Hamilton, Alabama/* "We manage to get along."

[19] Victor Burgin regards the antiscientific rhetoric of *Camera Lucida* with dismay: "The passage in *Camera Lucida* where Barthes lambasts the scientist of the sign (his own other self) has become widely quoted amongst precisely the sorts of critics Barthes opposed" ("Re-reading *Camera Lucida*," in *The End of Art Theory*, p. 91). Burgin's reduction of this to a straightforward political clash ignores the fact that the "sorts of critics" Barthes "opposed" included *himself,* and this opposition is precisely what gives his criticism ethical and political force.

[20] Joel Snyder informs me that these identifications are confused. The photograph was taken by Paul Nadar, the artist's son, and is of his mother, Nadar's wife. Given the use Barthes makes of the photograph, the confusion of father and son, wife and mother, is hardly surprising. The manifest uncertainty of the caption and its misquotation of Barthes's own text suggest that Barthes was deliberately attaching a confused "legend" to this photo.

[21] The twenty-five European and American photos in *Camera Lucida* range from journalism to art photos to personal family photographs and include examples of "old masters" (the "first photograph"—by Niepce; Charles Clifford, "The Alhambra"; G. W. Wilson, "Queen Victoria") from the nineteenth century as well as twentieth-century works. The effort is clearly to suggest "Photography" in its full range without making any effort to be comprehensive or systematic.

[22] This respect for the "naive realism" of photography is also a crucial feature of Agee's text. Agee notes "how much slower white people are to catch on than negroes, who understand the meaning of a camera, a weapon, a stealer of images and souls, a gun, an evil eye" (p. 362).

[23] Malek Alloula, *The Colonial Harem,* translated by Myrna and Wlad Godzich

(French edition, 1981; English edition, Minneapolis: University of Minnesota Press, 1986); further page references will be cited in the text.

[24]This impotence is perhaps nothing more than the familiar liberal guilt of the white male American becoming conscious of complicity in the ethos of imperialism. But it is also a more personal reaction which stems from a not altogether pleasant failure to react "properly" to the pornographic image, a failure which I can't take credit for as a matter of moral uprightness (morality, I suspect, only enters in when the proper reaction is there to be resisted). I had registered this feeling at the first perusal of the photographs in *The Colonial Harem*. Needless to say, a sensation of the uncanny attended my reading of the final paragraph of Alloula's text: "Voyeurism turns into an obsessive neurosis. The great erotic dream, ebbing from the sad faces of the wage earners in the poses, lets appear, in the flotsam perpetuated by the postcard, another figure: that of *impotence*" (p. 122).

[25]Edward Said and Jean Mohr, *After the Last Sky* (London: Pantheon, 1986); further page references will be cited in the text.

[26]Mohr's earlier collaborations with John Berger are clearly an important precedent also. See especially *The Seventh Man* (Originally published, Penguin, 1975; London: Writers and Readers, 1982), a photographic essay on migrant workers in Europe.

[27]"I can see the women everywhere in Palestinian life, and I see how they exist between the syrupy sentimentalism of roles we ascribe to them (mothers, virgins, martyrs) and the annoyance, even dislike that their unassimilated strength provokes in our warily politicized, automatic manhood" (p. 77).

[28]Stanley Cavell, *The World Viewed: Reflections on the Ontology of Film,* enlarged edition (Cambridge, MA: Harvard University Press, 1979), p. 106.

[29]I say "in contrast to painting" because the emancipation of painting from language, or at least the rhetoric of emancipation, has dominated the sophisticated understanding of painting for most of this century. For a fuller version of this argument, see chapter 7. . . .

•   •   •   •   •   •   •   •   •   •   •

## QUESTIONS FOR A SECOND READING

1. Mitchell's essay is very straightforward and helpful in its structure. It opens with three questions and three answers. These are followed by six sections. The first two raise issues and questions related to photography and language and to the medium of the "photographic essay"; the last four present the case studies, the readings of particular texts from the point of view of the issues and questions raised at the opening. With all of this assistance, "The Photographic Essay" is still not easy to read. The arguments are subtle (and in some cases counterintuitive), and they refer constantly to other books and ideas, to a conversation among scholars and artists with a long history and, at times, a specialized vocabulary.

   As you reread, let the structure of the essay organize your work. When you finish the first two sections, stop to summarize and restate the argument. Underline or write down the key terms and questions. Mitchell, for example, alludes to naive and sophisticated responses to photos. What are they? What is Mitchell's position?

   The "case studies" work with books that you may not have seen or read and may not have at hand. And yet they require you to know something about them. Mitchell, in other words, must provide summary, example, and illustration as part of his discussion. After each of the case studies, stop, go back, and be ready to provide an account of the book at the center of each case study. Who wrote it? What is its project? And then be ready to provide an account of Mitchell's discussion. What use is Mitchell making of this book? What point? How does it serve his project?

2. This is an essay written by a scholar, a specialist in literature, art history, critical theory, and cultural studies. The specialized terms he uses are drawn from these fields of study. Sometimes he uses them as though they were familiar; in other cases he locates them in relation to a particular text and author. As you reread, underline or create a list of those terms that seem significant and particular to Mitchell's project, terms like "code," "trope," "dialectical," "figurative," "non-linguistic," "modernism," and "post-modernism." As an exercise, create a glossary of terms for use by other readers of this text. From their use and context, or (as a last resort) from other sources you can find, prepare definitions of these terms. Or, better yet, write summary sentences about "The Photographic Essay" that put these terms to work.

3. At the end of the second section, Mitchell says, "In the remainder of this essay I want to examine four photo-essays that, in various ways, fore-ground the dialectic of exchange and resistance between photography and language, the things that make it possible (and sometimes impos-sible) to 'read' the pictures, or to 'see' the text illustrated in them." As you reread, locate and mark those moments in the four case studies where Mitchell foregrounds "the dialectic of exchange and resistance between photography and language." What are the examples? How do the texts differ? Why, for Mitchell, is this interesting or important?

4. There are four books that serve as central examples to Mitchell's study: *Let Us Now Praise Famous Men,* James Agee and Walker Evans; *Camera Lucida,* Roland Barthes; *The Colonial Harem,* Malek Alloula; and *After the Last Sky,* Edward Said and Jean Mohr. Jacob Riis's *How the Other Half Lives* also provides an important illustration in the second section of the essay. Go to the library to study one of these texts. Find one or two examples you could copy and bring to class to extend or challenge Mitchell's discussion of that text. Be sure you are bringing to class words as well as images.

### ASSIGNMENTS FOR WRITING

1. To introduce the four case studies in "The Photographic Essay," Mitchell says, "I want to examine four photo-essays that, in various ways, fore-ground the dialectic of exchange and resistance between photography and language." For this assignment, work closely with the four case stud-ies to bring forward what remains implied in Mitchell's text, the *differences* in the four cases. What *are* the "various ways" they foreground the dialec-tic of exchange and resistance between photography and language? What position does Mitchell seem to take on the value or achievement of each of the four books? What seems to you to be the significant or interesting dif-

ferences? Mitchell's essay is designed to prepare you to be a reader of the photographic essay. From the examples Mitchell gives, what sorts of books would you be hoping to find?

You should imagine that you are writing for someone who has not read "The Photographic Essay." You will need, then, to be sure to represent and summarize the text. (See the first "Question for a Second Reading.") The point of the summary, however, is to define a position from which you can begin to do your work. And, to repeat what was said above, your work is to bring forward what Mitchell does not foreground—his sense of the differences between the four cases and the implication or value of those differences. And, in relation to what you see in Mitchell, your job is to articulate your own position on the range, importance, and possibility of the genre of the photo-essay.

2.  These four books provide the central examples for Mitchell's study: *Let Us Now Praise Famous Men,* James Agee and Walker Evans; *Camera Lucida,* Roland Barthes; *The Colonial Harem,* Malek Alloula; and *After the Last Sky,* Edward Said and Jean Mohr. Jacob Riis's *How the Other Half Lives* also provides an important illustration in the second section of the essay. Go to the library to study one of these texts. Or, find an example of a "photographic essay" that you could put alongside Mitchell's examples.

    For this assignment, take up Mitchell's project by extending his work in "The Photographic Essay" and considering new or additional examples. You should assume that you are writing for a reader who is familiar with Mitchell's essay (but who does not have the book open on his or her desk). Your work is to put Mitchell to the test—to extend, test, and perhaps challenge or qualify his account of the genre. As with his project, the basic questions are these: What relationship between photography and writing do these examples articulate? What tropes of differentiation govern the division of labor between photography and writer, image and text, the viewer and the reader?

3.  In the introduction to *Picture Theory,* Mitchell says,

    > What we need is a critique of visual culture that is alert to the power of images for good and evil and that is capable of discriminating the variety and historical specificity of their uses.

    One way to think about the "variety and historical specificity" of the use of images is to look at the examples Mitchell provides in this chapter, examples of writers using images as the subjects of their writing, but also the example of his own use and "reading" of those images.

    At times, Mitchell is quick to include us in his ways of reading. In response to the Walker Evans photograph of Annie Mae Gudger, he says:

    > There is something deeply disturbing, even disagreeable, about this (unavoidable) aestheticizing response to what after all is a real person in desperately impoverished circumstances. Why should we have a right to look on this woman and find her fatigue, pain, and anxiety beautiful? (p. 534)

    His readers are written into the "we" of such sentences. At times he highlights the "reading" represented by the writer of the photo-essay, as he does, for example, in his account of Roland Barthes's use of Nadar's *The*

*Artist's Mother (or Wife)*. And at times he singles himself out as an individual case, as, for example, when he says of the postcard image of the "Arabian Woman with the Yachmak":

> Can an American observer, in particular, see these photographs as anything more than quaint, archaic pornography, hauntingly beautiful relics of a lost colonial era, "collector's items" for a coffee-table book? I don't have a simple answer to this question, but my first impulse is to register a feeling of *impotence* in the face of these women, whose beauty is now mixed with danger, whose nakedness now becomes a veil that has always excluded me from the labyrinth of their world. (pp. 547–48)

Write an essay in which you present a close reading of Mitchell's text, looking specifically at the ways it figures (or represents) readers reading. What variety of readings does he chart? Where and how are they historically specific? What lessons are there to be learned from these examples? What does Mitchell seem to be saying about appropriate ways of reading? What about you—what's your position?

## MAKING CONNECTIONS

1. In "Ways of Seeing" (p. 105), John Berger says, "Original paintings are silent and still in a sense that information never is." Both Berger and Mitchell are interested in the use of images, what happens to them when they are packaged, deployed, reproduced, turned into text. For both, the use of images is a sign of the health of the individual and the health of the culture.

   Write an essay in which you use Berger's essay to weigh, evaluate, and understand Mitchell's. You will need, of course, to take time to summarize what Berger says and to establish his position. Once you have established his point of view, turn to Mitchell, particularly the example he provides of someone trying to understand what is at stake when we speak for images. Would Berger see Mitchell, for example, as someone who justifies and practices "mystification"?

   Or, write an essay in which you use Mitchell's essay to weigh, evaluate, and understand Berger, both the Berger of "Ways of Seeing" and the Berger who speaks for Rembrandt's *Woman in Bed* (p. 129) and On Caravaggio's *The Calling of St. Matthew* (p. 131). You will need, of course, to take time to summarize what Mitchell says and to establish his position on the relationship of words and images. And you will need to think (as Mitchell might think) about the difference between photographs and paintings and what is at stake in providing a written account of a painted image. Once you have established his point of view, turn to Berger, particularly the example he provides of someone who places words next to images. Perhaps the questions to ask would be these: What relationship between painting and writing do these examples articulate? What tropes of differentiation govern the division of labor between painter and writer, image and text, the viewer and the reader?

2. Both Robert Coles, in "The Tradition: Fact and Fiction" (p. 176), and Mitchell, in "The Photographic Essay," write about the genre of the

photo-essay and, in particular, about *Let Us Now Praise Famous Men*, the "classic" text by James Agee and Walker Evans. Write an essay in which you elaborate the differences in their approaches to and accounts of this text. You can imagine that you are writing for a reader who has read none of the texts at hand, so you will need to be careful in summary (perhaps reproducing some of the illustrations). What does each notice or choose to notice in the text? How are these decisions related to the larger projects of the two authors? to their underlying commitments and concerns? And, finally, where are you on the differences between the two? Would you align yourself with one or the other writer? From their example, is there a position you would define as your own or as an alternative?

Note: Your work with this project would be greatly enhanced by your reviewing, as well, the full text of *Let Us Now Praise Famous Men*. With the text, you can establish a more complete sense of context, including what both writers miss or leave out. You can think about the agenda or desires that led to their selection of exemplary material.

3. Mitchell is concerned with the ways both words and images take possession of their subjects. And, in his account, there is a political dimension to this. It is a matter of the rich looking at and describing the poor in *Let Us Now Praise Famous Men*, of colonial power and the colonized in *The Colonial Harem* and *After the Last Sky*. (It is harder to name the victims and agents of appropriation in *Camera Lucida*. It would be worth your time to read that section carefully to see what terms Barthes offers.) In Mary Louise Pratt's terms in "Arts of the Contact Zone" (p. 582), both the photos and the texts represent moments of contact between persons of different cultures and unequal status.

Write an essay in which you consider two of the "cases" in "The Photographic Essay" in terms of Pratt's discussion of the contact zone. How would she understand the status and meaning of the words and images used to represent the "other"? How is her understanding different from Mitchell's? Both could be said to be interested in the role of power, the political, and history in the use and formation of texts. Which account seems most useful to you? most useful for what?

# WALKER

# PERCY

W*ALKER PERCY, in his midforties, after a life of relative obscurity and after a career as, he said, a "failed physician," wrote his first novel,* The Movie-goer. *It won the National Book Award for fiction in 1962, and Percy emerged as one of this country's leading novelists. Little in his background would have predicted such a career.*

*After graduating from Columbia University's medical school in 1941, Percy (b. 1916) went to work at Bellevue Hospital in New York City. He soon contracted tuberculosis from performing autopsies on derelicts and was sent to a sanitorium to recover, where, as he said, "I was in bed so much, alone so much, that I had nothing to do but read and think. I began to question everything I had once believed." He returned to medicine briefly but suffered a relapse and during his long recovery began "to make reading a full-time occupation." He left medicine, but not until 1954, almost a decade later, did he publish his first essay, "Symbol as Need."*

*The essays that followed, including "The Loss of the Creature," all dealt with the relationships between language and understanding or belief, and they were all published in obscure academic journals. In the later essays, Percy seemed to turn away from academic forms of argument and to depend more and more on stories or anecdotes from daily life—to write, in fact, as a storyteller and to be wary of abstraction or explanation. Robert Coles has said that it was Percy's failure to find a form that would reach a larger audience that led him to try his hand at a novel. You will notice in the essay that follows that Percy delights in piling example upon example; he never seems to settle down to a topic sentence, or any sentence for that matter that sums everything up and makes the examples superfluous.*

*In addition to* The Moviegoer, *Percy has written five other novels, including* Lancelot *(1977),* Love in the Ruins *(1971), and* The Thanatos Syndrome *(1987). He has published two books of essays,* The Message in the Bottle: How Queer Man Is, How Queer Language Is, and What One Has to Do with the Other *(1975, from which "The Loss of the Creature" is taken), and* Lost in the Cosmos: The Last Self-help Book *(1983). Walker Percy died at his home in Covington, Louisiana, on May 10, 1990, leaving a considerable amount of unpublished work, some of which has been gathered into a posthumous collection,* Signposts in a Strange Land *(1991).* The Correspondence of Shelby Foote and Walker Percy *was published in 1996.*

# The Loss of
# the Creature

## I

Every explorer names his island Formosa, beautiful. To him it is beautiful because, being first, he has access to it and can see it for what it is. But to no one else is it ever as beautiful—except the rare man who manages to recover it, who knows that it has to be recovered.

Garcia López de Cárdenas discovered the Grand Canyon and was 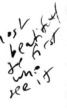 amazed at the sight. It can be imagined: One crosses miles of desert, breaks through the mesquite, and there it is at one's feet. Later the government set the place aside as a national park, hoping to pass along to millions the experience of Cárdenas. Does not one see the same sight from the Bright Angel Lodge that Cárdenas saw?

The assumption is that the Grand Canyon is a remarkably interesting and beautiful place and that if it had a certain value $P$ for Cárdenas, the same value $P$ may be transmitted to any number of sightseers—just as Banting's discovery of insulin can be transmitted to any number of diabetics. A counterinfluence is at work, however, and it would be nearer the truth to say that if the place is seen by a million sightseers, a single sightseer does not receive value $P$ but a millionth part of value $P$.

It is assumed that since the Grand Canyon has the fixed interest value $P$, tours can be organized for any number of people. A man in Boston decides to spend his vacation at the Grand Canyon. He visits his travel bureau, looks at the folder, signs up for a two-week tour. He and his family take the tour, see the Grand Canyon, and return to Boston. May we say that this man has seen the Grand Canyon? Possibly he has. But it is more likely that what he has done is the one sure way not to see the canyon.

Why is it almost impossible to gaze directly at the Grand Canyon under these circumstances and see it for what it is—as one picks up a strange object from one's back yard and gazes directly at it? It is almost impossible because the Grand Canyon, the thing as it is, has been appropriated by the symbolic complex which has already been formed in the sightseer's mind. Seeing the canyon under approved circumstances is seeing the symbolic complex head on. The thing is no longer the thing as it confronted the Spaniard; it is rather that which has already been formulated—by picture postcard, geography book, tourist folders, and the words *Grand Canyon*. As a result of this preformulation, the source of the sightseer's pleasure undergoes a shift. Where the wonder and delight of the Spaniard arose from his penetration of the thing itself, from a progressive discovery of depths, patterns, colors, shadows, etc., now the sightseer measures his satisfaction *by the degree to which the canyon conforms to the preformed complex*. If it does so, if it looks just like the postcard, he is pleased; he might even say, "Why it is every bit as beautiful as a picture postcard!" He feels he has not been cheated. But if it does not conform, if the colors are somber, he will not be able to see it directly; he will only be conscious of the disparity between what it is and what it is supposed to be. He will say later that he was unlucky in not being there at the right time. The highest point, the term of the sightseer's satisfaction, is not the sovereign discovery of the thing before him; it is rather the measuring up of the thing to the criterion of the preformed symbolic complex.

Seeing the canyon is made even more difficult by what the sightseer does when the moment arrives, when sovereign knower confronts the thing to be known. Instead of looking at it, he photographs it. There is no confrontation at all. At the end of forty years of preformulation and with the Grand Canyon yawning at his feet, what does he do? He waives his right of seeing and knowing and records symbols for the next forty years. For him there is no present; there is only the past of what has been formulated and seen and the future of what has been formulated and not seen. The present is surrendered to the past and the future.

The sightseer may be aware that something is wrong. He may simply be bored; or he may be conscious of the difficulty: that the great thing yawning at his feet somehow eludes him. The harder he looks at it, the less he can see. It eludes everybody. The tourist cannot see it; the bellboy at the Bright Angel Lodge cannot see it: for him it is only one side of the space he lives in, like one wall of a room; to the ranger it is a tissue of everyday signs relevant to his own prospects—the blue haze down there means that he will probably get rained on during the donkey ride.

How can the sightseer recover the Grand Canyon? He can recover it in any number of ways, all sharing in common the stratagem of avoiding the approved confrontation of the tour and the Park Service.

It may be recovered by leaving the beaten track. The tourist leaves the tour, camps in the back country. He arises before dawn and approaches the

South Rim through a wild terrain where there are no trails and no railed-in lookout points. In other words, he sees the canyon by avoiding all the facilities for seeing the canyon. If the benevolent Park Service hears about this fellow and thinks he has a good idea and places the following notice in the Bright Angel Lodge: *Consult ranger for information on getting off the beaten track*—the end result will only be the closing of another access to the canyon.

It may be recovered by a dialectical movement which brings one back to the beaten track but at a level above it. For example, after a lifetime of avoiding the beaten track and guided tours, a man may deliberately seek out the most beaten track of all, the most commonplace tour imaginable: he may visit the canyon by a Greyhound tour in the company of a party from Terre Haute—just as a man who has lived in New York all his life may visit the Statue of Liberty. (Such dialectical savorings of the familiar as the familiar are, of course, a favorite stratagem of *The New Yorker* magazine.) The thing is recovered from familiarity by means of an exercise in familiarity. Our complex friend stands behind his fellow tourists at the Bright Angel Lodge and sees the canyon through them and their predicament, their picture taking and busy disregard. In a sense, he exploits his fellow tourists; he stands on their shoulders to see the canyon.

Such a man is far more advanced in the dialectic than the sightseer who is trying to get off the beaten track—getting up at dawn and approaching the canyon through the mesquite. This stratagem is, in fact, for our complex man the weariest, most beaten track of all.

It may be recovered as a consequence of a breakdown of the symbolic machinery by which the experts present the experience to the consumer. A family visits the canyon in the usual way. But shortly after their arrival, the park is closed by an outbreak of typhus in the south. They have the canyon to themselves. What do they mean when they tell the home folks of their good luck: "We had the whole place to ourselves"? How does one see the thing better when the others are absent? Is looking like sucking: the more lookers, the less there is to see? They could hardly answer, but by saying this they testify to a state of affairs which is considerably more complex than the simple statement of the schoolbook about the Spaniard and the millions who followed him. It is a state in which there is a complex distribution of sovereignty, of zoning.

It may be recovered in a time of national disaster. The Bright Angel Lodge is converted into a rest home, a function that has nothing to do with the canyon a few yards away. A wounded man is brought in. He regains consciousness; there outside his window is the canyon.

The most extreme case of access by privilege conferred by disaster is the Huxleyan novel of the adventures of the surviving remnant after the great wars of the twentieth century. An expedition from Australia lands in Southern California and heads east. They stumble across the Bright Angel Lodge, now fallen into ruins. The trails are grown over, the guard rails fallen away, the dime telescope at Battleship Point rusted. But there is the canyon, exposed at last. Exposed by what? By the decay of those facilities which were designed to help the sightseer.

This dialectic of sightseeing cannot be taken into account by planners, for the object of the dialectic is nothing other than the subversion of the efforts of the planners.

The dialectic is not known to objective theorists, psychologists, and the like. Yet it is quite well known in the fantasy-consciousness of the popular arts. The devices by which the museum exhibit, the Grand Canyon, the ordinary thing, is recovered have long since been stumbled upon. A movie shows a man visiting the Grand Canyon. But the movie maker knows something the planner does not know. He knows that one cannot take the sight frontally. The canyon must be approached by the stratagems we have mentioned: the Inside Track, the Familiar Revisited, the Accidental Encounter. Who is the stranger at the Bright Angel Lodge? Is he the ordinary tourist from Terre Haute that he makes himself out to be? He is not. He has another objective in mind, to revenge his wronged brother, counterespionage, etc. By virtue of the fact that he has other fish to fry, he may take a stroll along the rim after supper and then we can see the canyon through him. The movie accomplishes its purpose by concealing it. Overtly the characters (the American family marooned by typhus) and we the onlookers experience pity for the sufferers, and the family experience anxiety for themselves; covertly and in truth they are the happiest of people and we are happy through them, for we have the canyon to ourselves. The movie cashes in on the recovery of sovereignty through disaster. Not only is the canyon now accessible to the remnant: the members of the remnant are now accessible to each other, a whole new ensemble of relations becomes possible—friendship, love, hatred, clandestine sexual adventures. In a movie when a man sits next to a woman on a bus, it is necessary either that the bus break down or that the woman lose her memory. (The question occurs to one: Do you imagine there are sightseers who see sights just as they are supposed to? a family who live in Terre Haute, who decide to take the canyon tour, who go there, see it, enjoy it immensely, and go home content? a family who are entirely innocent of all the barriers, zones, losses of sovereignty I have been talking about? Wouldn't most people be sorry if Battleship Point fell into the canyon, carrying all one's fellow passengers to their death, leaving one alone on the South Rim? I cannot answer this. Perhaps there are such people. Certainly a great many American families would swear they had no such problems, that they came, saw, and went away happy. Yet it is just these families who would be happiest if they had gotten the Inside Track and been among the surviving remnant.)

It is now apparent that as between the many measures which may be taken to overcome the opacity, the boredom, of the direct confrontation of the thing or creature in its citadel of symbolic investiture, some are less authentic than others. That is to say, some stratagems obviously serve other purposes than that of providing access to being—for example, various unconscious motivations which it is not necessary to go into here.

Let us take an example in which the recovery of being is ambiguous, where it may under the same circumstances contain both authentic and unauthentic components. An American couple, we will say, drives down into Mexico. They see the usual sights and have a fair time of it. Yet they are never without the sense of missing something. Although Taxco and Cuernavaca are interesting and picturesque as advertised, they fall short of "it." What do the couple have in mind by "it"? What do they really hope for? What sort of experience could they have in Mexico so that upon their return, they would feel that "it" had happened? We have a clue: Their hope has something to do with their own role as tourists in a foreign country and the way in which they conceive this role. It has something to do with other American tourists. Certainly they feel that they are very far from "it" when, after traveling five thousand miles, they arrive at the plaza in Guanajuato only to find themselves surrounded by a dozen other couples from the Midwest.

Already we may distinguish authentic and unauthentic elements. First, we see the problem the couple faces and we understand their efforts to surmount it. The problem is to find an "unspoiled" place. "Unspoiled" does not mean only that a place is left physically intact; it means also that it is not encrusted by renown and by the familiar (as in Taxco), that it has not been discovered by others. We understand that the couple really want to get at the place and enjoy it. Yet at the same time we wonder if there is not something wrong in their dislike of their compatriots. Does access to the place require the exclusion of others?

Let us see what happens.

The couple decide to drive from Guanajuato to Mexico City. On the way they get lost. After hours on a rocky mountain road, they find themselves in a tiny valley not even marked on the map. There they discover an Indian village. Some sort of religious festival is going on. It is apparently a corn dance in supplication of the rain god.

The couple know at once that this is "it." They are entranced. They spend several days in the village, observing the Indians and being themselves observed with friendly curiosity.

Now may we not say that the sightseers have at last come face to face with an authentic sight, a sight which is charming, quaint, picturesque, unspoiled, and that they see the sight and come away rewarded? Possibly this may occur. Yet it is more likely that what happens is a far cry indeed from an immediate encounter with being, that the experience, while masquerading as such, is in truth a rather desperate impersonation. I use the word *desperate* advisedly to signify an actual loss of hope.

The clue to the spuriousness of their enjoyment of the village and the festival is a certain restiveness in the sightseers themselves. It is given expression by their repeated exclamations that "this is too good to be true," and by their anxiety that it may not prove to be so perfect, and finally by their downright relief at leaving the valley and having the experience in the bag, so to speak—that is, safely embalmed in memory and movie film.

What is the source of their anxiety during the visit? Does it not mean that the couple are looking at the place with a certain standard of performance in mind? Are they like Fabre, who gazed at the world about him with wonder, letting it be what it is; or are they not like the overanxious mother who sees her child as one performing, now doing badly, now doing well? The village is their child and their love for it is an anxious love because they are afraid that at any moment it might fail them.

We have another clue in their subsequent remark to an ethnologist friend. "How we wished you had been there with us! What a perfect goldmine of folkways! Every minute we would say to each other, if only you were here! You must return with us." This surely testifies to a generosity of spirit, a willingness to share their experience with others, not at all like their feelings toward their fellow Iowans on the plaza at Guanajuato!

I am afraid this is not the case at all. It is true that they longed for their ethnologist friend, but it was for an entirely different reason. They wanted him, not to share their experience, but to certify their experience as genuine.

"This is it" and "Now we are really living" do not necessarily refer to the sovereign encounter of the person with the sight that enlivens the mind and gladdens the heart. It means that now at last we are having the acceptable experience. The present experience is always measured by a prototype, the "it" of their dreams. "Now I am really living" means that now I am filling the role of sightseer and the sight is living up to the prototype of sights. This quaint and picturesque village is measured by a Platonic ideal of the Quaint and the Picturesque.

Hence their anxiety during the encounter. For at any minute something could go wrong. A fellow Iowan might emerge from a 'dobe hut; the chief might show them his Sears catalog. (If the failures are "wrong" enough, as these are, they might still be turned to account as rueful conversation pieces. "There we were expecting the chief to bring us a churinga and he shows up with a Sears catalog!") They have snatched victory from disaster, but their experience always runs the danger of failure.

They need the ethnologist to certify their experience as genuine. This is borne out by their behavior when the three of them return for the next corn dance. During the dance, the couple do not watch the goings-on; instead they watch the ethnologist! Their highest hope is that their friend should find the dance interesting. And if he should show signs of true absorption, an interest in the goings-on so powerful that he becomes oblivious of his friends—then their cup is full. "Didn't we tell you?" they say at last. What they want from him is not ethnological explanations; all they want is his approval.

What has taken place is a radical loss of sovereignty over that which is as much theirs as it is the ethnologist's. The fault does not lie with the ethnologist. He has no wish to stake a claim to the village; in fact, he desires the opposite: he will bore his friends to death by telling them about the village and the meaning of the folkways. A degree of sovereignty has been surrendered by the couple. It is the nature of the loss, moreover, that they are not aware of the loss, beyond a certain uneasiness. (Even if they read this and admitted it, it would be very difficult for them to bridge the gap in their confrontation of the world. Their consciousness of the corn dance cannot escape their consciousness of their consciousness, so that with the onset of the first direct enjoyment, their higher consciousness pounces and certifies: "Now you are doing it! Now you are really living!" and, in certifying the experience, sets it at nought.)

Their basic placement in the world is such that they recognize a priority of title of the expert over his particular department of being. The whole horizon of being is staked out by "them," the experts. The highest satisfaction of the sightseer (not merely the tourist but any layman seer of sights) is that his sight should be certified as genuine. The worst of this impoverishment is that there is no sense of impoverishment. The surrender of title is so complete that it never even occurs to one to reassert title. A poor man may envy the rich man, but the sightseer does not envy the expert. When a caste system becomes absolute, envy disappears. Yet the caste of layman-expert is not the fault of the expert. It is due altogether to the eager surrender of sovereignty by the layman so that he may take up the role not of the person but of the consumer.

I do not refer only to the special relation of layman to theorist. I refer to the general situation in which sovereignty is surrendered to a class of privileged knowers, whether these be theorists or artists. A reader may surrender sovereignty over that which has been written about, just as a consumer may surrender sovereignty over a thing which has been theorized about. The consumer is content to receive an experience just as it has been presented to him by theorists and planners. The reader may also be content to judge life by whether it has or has not been formulated by those who know and write about life. A young man goes to France. He too has a fair time of it, sees the sights, enjoys the food. On his last day, in fact as he sits in a restaurant in Le Havre waiting for his boat, something happens. A group of French students in the restaurant get into an impassioned argument over a recent play. A riot takes place. Madame la concierge joins in, swinging her mop at the rioters. Our young American is transported. This is "it." And he had almost left France without seeing "it"!

But the young man's delight is ambiguous. On the one hand, it is a pleasure for him to encounter the same Gallic temperament he had heard about from Puccini and Rolland. But on the other hand, the source of his pleasure testifies to a certain alienation. For the young man is actually barred from a direct encounter with anything French excepting only that which has been set forth, authenticated by Puccini and Rolland—those who know. If he had encountered the restaurant scene without reading Hemingway, without knowing that the performance was so typically, charmingly French, he would not have been delighted. He would only have been anxious at seeing things get so out of hand. The source of his delight is the sanction of those who know.

This loss of sovereignty is not a marginal process, as might appear from my example of estranged sightseers. It is a generalized surrender of the horizon to those experts within whose competence a particular seg-ment of the horizon is thought to lie. Kwakiutls are surrendered to Franz Boas; decaying Southern mansions are surrendered to Faulkner and Tennessee Williams. So that, although it is by no means the intention of the expert to expropriate sovereignty—in fact he would not even know what sovereignty meant in this context—the danger of theory and consumption is a seduction and deprivation of the consumer.

In the New Mexico desert, natives occasionally come across strange-looking artifacts which have fallen from the skies and which are stenciled: *Return to U.S. Experimental Project, Alamogordo. Reward.* The finder returns the object and is rewarded. He knows nothing of the nature of the object he has found and does not care to know. The sole role of the native, the highest role he can play, is that of finder and returner of the mysterious equipment.

The same is true of the laymen's relation to *natural* objects in a modern technical society. No matter what the object or event is, whether it is a star, a swallow, a Kwakiutl, a "psychological phenomenon," the layman who confronts it does not confront it as a sovereign person, as Crusoe confronts a seashell he finds on the beach. The highest role he can conceive himself as playing is to be able to recognize the title of the object, to return it to the appropriate expert and have it certified as a genuine find. He does not even permit himself to see the thing—as Gerard Hopkins could see a rock or a cloud or a field. If anyone asks him why he doesn't look, he may reply that he didn't take that subject in college (or he hasn't read Faulkner).

This loss of sovereignty extends even to oneself. There is the neurotic who asks nothing more of his doctor than that his symptoms should prove interesting. When all else fails, the poor fellow has nothing to offer but his own neurosis. But even this is sufficient if only the doctor will show interest when he says, "Last night I had a curious sort of dream; perhaps it will be significant to one who knows about such things. It seems I was standing in a sort of alley—" (I have nothing else to offer you but my own unhappiness. Please say that it, at least, measures up, that it is a *proper* sort of unhappiness.)

## II

A young Falkland Islander walking along a beach and spying a dead dogfish and going to work on it with his jackknife has, in a fashion wholly unprovided in modern educational theory, a great advantage over the Scarsdale high-school pupil who finds the dogfish on his laboratory desk. Similarly the citizen of Huxley's *Brave New World* who stumbles across a volume of Shakespeare in some vine-grown ruins and squats on a potsherd to read it is in a fairer way of getting at a sonnet than the Harvard sophomore taking English Poetry II.

The educator whose business it is to teach students biology or poetry is unaware of a whole ensemble of relations which exist between the student and the dogfish and between the student and the Shakespeare sonnet. To put it bluntly: A student who has the desire to get at a dogfish or a Shakespeare sonnet may have the greatest difficulty in salvaging the creature itself from the educational package in which it is presented. The great difficulty is that he is not aware that there is a difficulty; surely, he thinks, in such a fine classroom, with such a fine textbook, the sonnet must come across! What's wrong with me?

The sonnet and the dogfish are obscured by two different processes. The sonnet is obscured by the symbolic package which is formulated not by the sonnet itself but by the *media* through which the sonnet is transmitted, the media which the educators believe for some reason to be transparent. The new textbook, the type, the smell of the page, the classroom, the aluminum windows and the winter sky, the personality of Miss Hawkins—these media which are supposed to transmit the sonnet may only succeed in transmitting themselves. It is only the hardiest and cleverest of students who can salvage the sonnet from this many-tissued package. It is only the rarest student who knows that the sonnet must be salvaged from the package. (The educator is well aware that something is wrong, that there is a fatal gap between the student's learning and the student's life: the student reads the poem, appears to understand it, and gives all the answers. But what does he recall if he should happen to read a Shakespeare sonnet twenty years later? Does he recall the poem or does he recall the smell of the page and the smell of Miss Hawkins?)

One might object, pointing out that Huxley's citizen reading his sonnet in the ruins and the Falkland Islander looking at his dogfish on the beach also receive them in a certain package. Yes, but the difference lies in the fundamental placement of the student in the world, a placement which makes it possible to extract the thing from the package. The pupil at Scarsdale High sees himself placed as a consumer receiving an experience-package; but the Falkland Islander exploring his dogfish is a person exercising the sovereign right of a person in his lordship and mastery of creation. He too could use an instructor and a book and a technique, but he would use them as his subordinates, just as he uses his jackknife. The biology student does not use his scalpel as an instrument, he uses it as a magic wand! Since it is a "scientific instrument," it should do "scientific things."

The dogfish is concealed in the same symbolic package as the sonnet. But the dogfish suffers an additional loss. As a consequence of this double deprivation, the Sarah Lawrence student who scores A in zoology is apt to know very little about a dogfish. She is twice removed from the dogfish, once by the symbolic complex by which the dogfish is concealed, once again by the spoliation of the dogfish by theory which renders it invisible. Through no fault of zoology instructors, it is nevertheless a fact that the zoology laboratory at Sarah Lawrence College is one of the few places in the world where it is all but impossible to see a dogfish.

The dogfish, the tree, the seashell, the American Negro, the dream, are rendered invisible by a shift of reality from concrete thing to theory which Whitehead has called the fallacy of misplaced concreteness. It is the mistaking of an idea, a principle, an abstraction, for the real. As a consequence of the shift, the "specimen" is seen as less real than the theory of the specimen. As Kierkegaard said, once a person is seen as a specimen of a race or a species, at that very moment he ceases to be an individual. Then there are no more individuals but only specimens.

To illustrate: A student enters a laboratory which, in the pragmatic view, offers the student the optimum conditions under which an educational experience may be had. In the existential view, however—that view of the student in which he is regarded not as a receptacle of experience but as a knowing being whose peculiar property it is to see himself as being in a certain situation—the modern laboratory could not have been more effectively designed to conceal the dogfish forever.

The student comes to his desk. On it, neatly arranged by his instructor, he finds his laboratory manual, a dissecting board, instruments, and a mimeographed list:

> *Exercise 22: Materials*
> 1 dissecting board
> 1 scalpel
> 1 forceps
> 1 probe
> 1 bottle india ink and syringe
> 1 specimen of *Squalus acanthias*

The clue of the situation in which the student finds himself is to be found in the last item: 1 specimen of *Squalus acanthias.*

The phrase *specimen of* expresses in the most succinct way imaginable the radical character of the loss of being which has occurred under his very nose. To refer to the dogfish, the unique concrete existent before him, as a "specimen of *Squalas acanthias*" reveals by its grammar the spoliation of the dogfish by the theoretical method. This phrase, *specimen of,* example of, instance of, indicates the ontological status of the individual creature in the eyes of the theorist. The dogfish itself is seen as a rather shabby expression of an ideal reality, the species *Squalus acanthias.* The result is the radical devaluation of the individual dogfish. (The *reductio ad absurdum* of Whitehead's shift is Toynbee's employment of it in his historical method. If a gram of NaCl is referred to by the chemist as a "sample of" NaCl, one may think of it as such and not much is missed by the oversight of the act of being of this particular pinch of salt, but when the Jews and the Jewish religion are understood as—in Toynbee's favorite phrase—a "classical example of" such and such a kind of *Voelkerwanderung,* we begin to suspect that something is being left out.)

If we look into the ways in which the student can recover the dogfish (or the sonnet), we will see that they have in common the stratagem of avoiding the educator's direct presentation of the object as a lesson to be learned and restoring access to sonnet and dogfish as beings to be known, reasserting the sovereignty of knower over known.

In truth, the biography of scientists and poets is usually the story of the discovery of the indirect approach, the circumvention of the educator's presentation—the young man who was sent to the *Technikum* and on his way fell into the habit of loitering in book stores and reading poetry; or the young man dutifully attending law school who on the way became curious about the comings and goings of ants. One remembers the scene in *The Heart Is a Lonely Hunter* where the girl hides in the bushes to hear the Capehart in the big house play Beethoven. Perhaps she was the lucky one after all. Think of the unhappy souls inside, who see the record, worry about scratches, and most of all worry about whether they are *getting it,* whether they are bona fide music lovers. What is the best way to hear Beethoven: sitting in a proper silence around the Capehart or eavesdropping from an azalea bush?

However it may come about, we notice two traits of the second situation: (1) an openness of the thing before one—instead of being an exercise to be learned according to an approved mode, it is a garden of delights which beckons to one; (2) a sovereignty of the knower—instead of being a consumer of a prepared experience, I am a sovereign wayfarer, a wanderer in the neighborhood of being who stumbles into the garden.

One can think of two sorts of circumstances through which the thing may be restored to the person. (There is always, of course, the direct recovery: A student may simply be strong enough, brave enough, clever enough to take the dogfish and the sonnet by storm, to wrest control of it from the educators and the educational package.) First by ordeal: The Bomb falls; when the young man recovers consciousness in the shambles of the biology laboratory, there not ten inches from his nose lies the dogfish. Now all at once he can **see** it directly and without let, just as the exile or the prisoner or the sick man sees the sparrow at his window in all its inexhaustibility; just as the commuter who has had a heart attack sees his own hand for the first time. In these cases, the simulacrum of everydayness and of consumption has been destroyed by disaster; in the case of the bomb, literally destroyed. Secondly, by apprenticeship to a great man: one day a great biologist walks into the laboratory; he stops in front of our student's desk; he leans over, picks up the dogfish, and, ignoring instruments and procedure, probes with a broken fingernail into the little carcass. "Now here is a curious business," he says, ignoring also the proper jargon of the speciality. "Look here how this little duct reverses its direction and drops into the pelvis. Now if you would look into a coelacanth, you would see that it—" And all at once the student can see. The technician and the sophomore who loves his textbooks are always offended by the genuine research man because the latter is usually a little vague and always humble before the thing; he doesn't have much use for the equipment or the jargon. Whereas the technician is never vague and never humble before the thing; he holds the thing disposed of by the principle, the formula, the textbook outline; and he thinks a great deal of equipment and jargon.

But since neither of these methods of recovering the dogfish is peda-gogically feasible—perhaps the great man even less so than the Bomb—I wish to propose the following educational technique which should prove equally effective for Harvard and Shreveport High School. I propose that English poetry and biology should be taught as usual, but that at irregular intervals, poetry students should find dogfishes on their desks and biol-ogy students should find Shakespeare sonnets on their dissection boards. I am serious in declaring that a Sarah Lawrence English major who began poking about in a dogfish with a bobby pin would learn more in thirty minutes than a biology major in a whole semester; and that the latter upon reading on her dissecting board

> That time of year Thou may'st in me behold
> When yellow leaves, or none, or few, do hang
> Upon those boughs which shake against the cold—
> Bare ruin'd choirs where late the sweet birds sang

might catch fire at the beauty of it.

The situation of the tourist at the Grand Canyon and the biology stu-dent are special cases of a predicament in which everyone finds himself in a modern technical society—a society, that is, in which there is a division between expert and layman, planner and consumer, in which experts and planners take special measures to teach and edify the consumer. The mea-sures taken are measures appropriate to the consumer: the expert and the planner *know* and *plan*, but the consumer *needs* and *experiences*.

There is a double deprivation. First, the thing is lost through its packaging. The very means by which the thing is presented for con-sumption, the very techniques by which the thing is made available as an item of need-satisfaction, these very means operate to remove the thing from the sovereignty of the knower. A loss of title occurs. The measures which the museum curator takes to present the thing to the public are self-liquidating. The upshot of the curator's efforts are not that everyone can see the exhibit but that no one can see it. The curator protests: why are they so indifferent? Why do they even deface the ex-hibit? Don't they know it is theirs? But it is not theirs. It is his, the cu-rator's. By the most exclusive sort of zoning, the museum exhibit, the park oak tree, is part of an ensemble, a package, which is almost im-penetrable to them. The archaeologist who puts his find in a museum so that everyone can see it accomplishes the reverse of his expectations. The result of his action is that no one can see it now but the archeolo-gist. He would have done better to keep it in his pocket and show it now and then to strangers.

The tourist who carves his initials in a public place, which is theoretically "his" in the first place, has good reasons for doing so, reasons which the exhibitor and planner know nothing about. He does so because in his role of consumer of an experience (a "recreational experience" to satisfy a "recreational need") he knows that he is disinherited. He is deprived of his title over being. He knows very well that he is in a very special sort of zone in which his only rights are the rights of a consumer. He moves like a ghost through schoolroom, city streets, trains, parks, movies. He carves his initials as a last desperate measure to escape his ghostly role of consumer. He is saying in effect: I am not a ghost after all; I am a sovereign person. And he establishes title the only way remaining to him, by staking his claim over one square inch of wood or stone.

Does this mean that we should get rid of museums? No, but it means that the sightseer should be prepared to enter into a struggle to recover a sight from a museum.

The second loss is the spoliation of the thing, the tree, the rock, the swallow, by the layman's misunderstanding of scientific theory. He believes that the thing is *disposed of* by theory, that it stands in the Platonic relation of being a *specimen* of such and such an underlying principle. In the transmission of scientific theory from theorist to layman, the expectation of the theorist is reversed. Instead of the marvels of the universe being made available to the public, the universe is disposed of by theory. The loss of sovereignty takes this form: as a result of the science of botany, trees are not made available to every man. On the contrary. The tree loses its proper density and mystery as a concrete existent and, as merely another *specimen* of a species, becomes itself nugatory.

Does this mean that there is no use taking biology at Harvard and Shreveport High? No, but it means that the student should know what a fight he has on his hands to rescue the specimen from the educational package. The educator is only partly to blame. For there is nothing the educator can do to provide for this need of the student. Everything the educator does only succeeds in becoming, for the student, part of the educational package. The highest role of the educator is the maieutic role of Socrates: to help the student come to himself not as a consumer of experience but as a sovereign individual.

The thing is twice lost to the consumer. First, sovereignty is lost: it is theirs, not his. Second, it is radically devalued by theory. This is a loss which has been brought about by science but through no fault of the scientist and through no fault of scientific theory. The loss has come about as a consequence of the seduction of the layman by science. The layman will be seduced as long as he regards beings as consumer items to be experienced rather than prizes to be won, and as long as he waives his sovereign rights as a person and accepts his role of consumer as the highest estate to which the layman can aspire.

As Mounier said, the person is not something one can study and provide for; he is something one struggles for. But unless he also struggles for himself, unless he knows that there is a struggle, he is going to be just what the planners think he is.

* * * * * * * * * * * *

## QUESTIONS FOR A SECOND READING

1. Percy's essay proceeds by adding example to example, one after another. If all the examples were meant to illustrate the same thing, the same general point or idea, then one would most likely have been enough. The rest would have been redundant. It makes sense, then, to assume that each example gives a different view of what Percy is saying, that each modifies the others, or qualifies them, or adds a piece that was otherwise lacking. It's as though Percy needed one more to get it right or to figure out what was missing along the way. As you read back through the essay, pay particular attention to the *differences* between the examples (between the various tourists going to the Grand Canyon, or between the tourists at the Grand Canyon and the tourists in Mexico). Also note the logic or system that leads from one to the next. What progress of thought is represented by the movement from one example to another, or from tourists to students?

2. The essay is filled with talk about "loss"—the loss of sovereignty, the loss of the creature—but it is resolutely ambiguous about what it is that we have lost. As you work your way back through, note the passages that describe what we are missing and why we should care. Are we to believe, for example, that Cárdenas actually had it (whatever "it" is)—that he had no preconceived notions when he saw the Grand Canyon? Mightn't he have said, "I claim this for my queen" or "There I see the glory of God" or "This wilderness is not fit for man"? To whom, or in the name of what, is this loss that Percy chronicles such a matter of concern? If this is not just Percy's peculiar prejudice, if we are asked to share his concerns, whose interests or what interests are represented here?

3. The essay is made up of stories or anecdotes, all of them fanciful. Percy did not, in other words, turn to first-person accounts of visitors to the Grand Canyon or to statements by actual students or teachers. Why not, do you suppose? What does this choice say about his "method"—about what it can and can't do? As you reread the essay, look for sections you could use to talk about the power and limits of Percy's method.

## ASSIGNMENTS FOR WRITING

1. Percy tells several stories—some of them quite good stories—but it is often hard to know just what he is getting at, just what point it is he is trying to make. If he's making an argument, it's not the sort of argument that is easy to summarize. And if the stories (or anecdotes) are meant to serve

as examples, they are not the sort of examples that lead directly to a single, general conclusion or that serve to clarify a point or support an obvious thesis. In fact, at the very moment when you expect Percy to come forward and pull things together, he offers yet another story, as though another example, rather than any general statement, would get you closer to what he is saying.

There are, at the same time, terms and phrases to suggest that this is an essay with a point to make. Percy talks, for example, about "the loss of sovereignty," "symbolic packages," "consumers of experience," and "dialectic," and it seems that these terms and phrases are meant to name or comment on key scenes, situations, or characters in the examples.

For this assignment, tell a story of your own, one that is suggested by the stories Percy tells—perhaps a story about a time you went looking for something or at something, or about a time when you did or did not find a dogfish in your Shakespeare class. You should imagine that you are carrying out a project that Walker Percy has begun, a project that has you looking back at your own experience through the lens of "The Loss of the Creature," noticing what Percy would notice and following the paths that he would find interesting. Try to bring the terms that Percy uses—like "sovereign," "consumer," "expert," and "dialectic"—to bear on the story you have to tell. Feel free to imitate Percy's style and method in your essay.

2.  Percy charts several routes to the Grand Canyon: you can take the packaged tour, you can get off the beaten track, you can wait for a disaster, you can follow the "dialectical movement which brings one back to the beaten track but at a level above it." This last path (or stratagem), he says, is for the complex traveler.

> Our complex friend stands behind his fellow tourists at the Bright
> Angel Lodge and sees the canyon through them and their predicament,
> their picture taking and busy disregard. In a sense, he exploits his fel-
> low tourists; he stands on their shoulders to see the canyon. (p. 567)

The complex traveler sees the Grand Canyon through the example of the common tourists with "their predicament, their picture taking and busy disregard." He "stands on their shoulders" to see the canyon. This distinction between complex and common approaches is an important one in the essay. It is interesting to imagine how the distinction could be put to work to define ways of reading.

Suppose that you read "The Loss of the Creature" as a common reader. What would you see? What would you identify as key sections of the text? What would you miss? What would you say about what you see?

If you think of yourself, now, as a complex reader, modeled after any of Percy's more complex tourists or students, what would you see? What would you identify as key sections of the text? What would you miss? What would you say about what you see?

For this assignment, write an essay with three sections. You may number them, if you choose. The first section should represent the work of a common reader with "The Loss of the Creature," and the second should represent the work of a complex reader. The third section should look back and comment on the previous two. In particular, you might address these questions: Why might a person prefer one reading over the other? What is to be gained or lost with both?

## MAKING CONNECTIONS

1.  In "The Loss of the Creature," Percy writes about tourists and the difficulty they have seeing that which lies before them. In "Deep Play: Notes on the Balinese Cockfight" (p. 364), Clifford Geertz tells the story of his travels in Bali. Anthropologists, properly speaking, are not tourists. There is a scholarly purpose to their travel and, presumably, they have learned or developed the strategies necessary to get beyond the preformed "symbolic complex" that would keep them from seeing the place or the people they have traveled to study. They are experts, in other words, not common sightseers.

    In his travels to Bali, Geertz seems to get just what he wants. He gets both the authentic experience and a complex understanding of that experience. If you read "Deep Play" from the perspective of Percy's essay, however, it is interesting to ask whether Percy would say that this was the case (whether Percy might say that Geertz has gone as far as one can go after Cárdenas), and it is interesting to ask how Percy would characterize the "strategies" that define Geertz's approach to his subject.

    Write an essay in which you place Geertz in the context of Percy's tourists (not all of them, but two of three whose stories seem most interesting when placed alongside Geertz's). The purpose of your essay is to offer a Percian reading of Geertz's essay—to study his text, that is, in light of the terms and methods Percy has established in "The Loss of the Creature."

2.      But the difference lies in the fundamental placement of the student in the world. . . . (Walker Percy, p. 573)

        What I am about to say to you has taken me more than twenty years to admit: *A primary reason for my success in the classroom was that I couldn't forget that schooling was changing me and separating me from the life I enjoyed before becoming a student.* (Richard Rodriguez, p. 623)

    Both Percy and Richard Rodriguez, in "The Achievement of Desire" (p. 621), write about students and how they are "placed" in the world by teachers and by the way schools characteristically represent knowledge, the novice, and the expert. And both tell stories to make their points, stories of characteristic students in characteristic situations. Write an essay in which you tell a story of your own, one meant to serve as a corrective or a supplement to the stories Percy and Rodriguez tell. You will want both to tell your story and to use it as a way of returning to and commenting on Percy and Rodriguez, and the arguments they make. Your authority can rest on the fact that you are a student and as a consequence have ways of understanding that position that they do not.

# MARY LOUISE
# PRATT

*M*ARY LOUISE PRATT *(b. 1948) grew up in Listowel, Ontario, a small Canadian farm town. She got her B.A. at the University of Toronto and her Ph.D. from Stanford University, where she is now a professor in the departments of comparative literature and Spanish and Portuguese. At Stanford, she was one of the cofounders of the new freshman culture program, a controversial series of required courses that replaced the old Western civilization core courses. The course she is particularly associated with is called "Europe and the Americas"; it brings together European representations of the Americas with indigenous American texts. As you might guess from the essay that follows, the new program at Stanford expands the range of countries, languages, cultures, and texts that are seen as a necessary introduction to the world; it also, however, revises the very idea of culture that many of us take for granted—particularly the idea that culture, at its best, expresses common values in a common language.*

*Pratt is the author of* Toward a Speech Act Theory of Literary Discourse *(1977) and coauthor of* Women, Culture, and Politics in Latin America *(1990), the textbook* Linguistics for Students of Literature *(1980),* Amor Brujo: The Images and Culture of Love in the Andes *(1990), and* Imperial Eyes: Studies in Travel Writing and Transculturation *(1992). The essay that follows was revised to serve as the introduction to* Imperial Eyes, *which is particularly about European travel writing in the eighteenth and nineteenth* centuries, when Europe was "discovering" Africa and the Americas. It argues that travel writing produced "the rest of the world" for European readers. It didn't "report" on Africa or South America; it produced an "Africa" or an "America" for European consumption. Travel writing produced places that could be thought of as barren, empty, undeveloped, inconceivable, needful of European influence and control, ready to serve European industrial, intellectual, and commercial interests. The reports of travelers or, later, scientists and anthropologists are part of a more general process by which the emerging industrial nations took possession of new territory.

The European understanding of Peru, for example, came through European accounts, not from attempts to understand or elicit responses from Andeans, Peruvian natives. When such a response was delivered, when an Andean, Guaman Poma, wrote to King Philip III of Spain, his letter was unreadable. Pratt is interested in just those moments of contact between peoples and cultures. She is interested in how King Philip read (or failed to read) a letter from Peru, but also in how someone like Guaman Poma prepared himself to write to the king of Spain. To fix these moments, she makes use of a phrase she coined, the "contact zone," which, she says,

> I use to refer to the space of colonial encounters, the space in which peoples geographically and historically separated come into contact with each other and establish ongoing relations, usually involving conditions of coercion, radical inequality, and intractable conflict. . . . By using the term "contact," I aim to foreground the interactive, improvisational dimensions of colonial encounters so easily ignored or suppressed by diffusionist accounts of conquest and domination. A "contact" perspective emphasizes how subjects are constituted in and by their relations to each other. It treats the relations among colonizers and colonized, or travelers and "travelees," not in terms of separateness or apartheid, but in terms of copresence, interaction, interlocking understandings and practices.

Like Adrienne Rich's "When We Dead Awaken: Writing as Re-Vision" (and, for that matter, Clifford Geertz's "Deep Play" and Virginia Woolf's "A Room of One's Own"), "Arts of the Contact Zone" was first written as a lecture. It was delivered as a keynote address at the second Modern Language Association Literacy Conference, held in Pittsburgh, Pennsylvania, in 1990.

# Arts of the Contact Zone

Whenever the subject of literacy comes up, what often pops first into my mind is a conversation I overheard eight years ago between my son Sam and his best friend, Willie, aged six and seven, respectively: "Why don't you trade me Many Trails for Carl Yats . . . Yesits . . . Ya-strum-scrum." "That's not how you say it, dummy, it's Carl Yes . . . Yes . . . oh, I don't know." Sam and Willie had just discovered baseball cards. Many Trails was their decoding, with the help of first-grade English phonics, of the name Manny Trillo. The name they were quite rightly stumped on was Carl Yastremski. That was the first time I remembered seeing them put their incipient literacy to their own use, and I was of course thrilled.

Sam and Willie learned a lot about phonics that year by trying to decipher surnames on baseball cards, and a lot about cities, states, heights, weights, places of birth, stages of life. In the years that followed, I watched Sam apply his arithmetic skills to working out batting averages and subtracting retirement years from rookie years; I watched him develop senses of patterning and order by arranging and rearranging his cards for hours on end, and aesthetic judgment by comparing different photos, different series, layouts, and color schemes. American geography and history took shape in his mind through baseball cards. Much of his social life revolved around trading them, and he learned about exchange, fairness, trust, the importance of processes as opposed to results, what it means to get cheated, taken advantage of, even robbed. Baseball cards were the medium of his economic life too. Nowhere better to learn the power and arbitrariness of money, the absolute divorce between use value and exchange value, notions of long- and short-term investment, the possibility of personal values that are independent of market values.

Baseball cards meant baseball card shows, where there was much to be learned about adult worlds as well. And baseball cards opened the door to baseball books, shelves and shelves of encyclopedias, magazines, histories, biographies, novels, books of jokes, anecdotes, cartoons, even poems. Sam learned the history of American racism and the struggle against it through baseball; he saw the Depression and two world wars from behind home plate. He learned the meaning of commodified labor, what it means for one's body and talents to be owned and dispensed by another. He knows something about Japan, Taiwan, Cuba, and Central America and how men and boys do things there. Through the history and experience of baseball stadiums he thought about architecture, light, wind, topography, meteorology, the dynamics of public space. He learned the meaning of expertise, of knowing about something well enough that you can start a conversation with a stranger and feel sure of holding your own. Even with an adult—especially with an adult. Throughout his preadolescent years, baseball history was Sam's luminous point of contact with grown-ups, his lifeline to caring. And, of course, all this time he was also playing baseball, struggling his way through the stages of the local Little League system, lucky enough to be a pretty good player, loving the game and coming to know deeply his strengths and weaknesses.

Literacy began for Sam with the newly pronounceable names on the picture cards and brought him what has been easily the broadest, most varied, most enduring, and most integrated experience of his thirteen-year life. Like many parents, I was delighted to see schooling give Sam the tools with which to find and open all these doors. At the same time I found it unforgivable that schooling itself gave him nothing remotely as meaningful to do, let alone anything that would actually take him beyond the referential, masculinist ethos of baseball and its lore.

However, I was not invited here to speak as a parent, nor as an expert on literacy. I was asked to speak as an MLA [Modern Language Association] member working in the elite academy. In that capacity my contribution is undoubtedly supposed to be abstract, irrelevant, and anchored outside the real world. I wouldn't dream of disappointing anyone. I propose immediately to head back several centuries to a text that has a few points in common with baseball cards and raises thoughts about what Tony Sarmiento, in his comments to the conference, called new visions of literacy. In 1908 a Peruvianist named Richard Pietschmann was exploring in the Danish Royal Archive in Copenhagen and came across a manuscript. It was dated in the city of Cuzco in Peru, in the year 1613, some forty years after the final fall of the Inca empire to the Spanish and signed with an unmistakably Andean indigenous name: Felipe Guaman Poma de Ayala. Written in a mixture of Quechua and ungrammatical, expressive Spanish, the manuscript was a letter addressed by an unknown but apparently literate Andean to King Philip III of Spain. What stunned Pietschmann was that the letter was twelve hundred pages long. There were almost eight hundred pages of written text and four hundred of captioned line drawings. It was titled *The First New Chronicle and Good Government*. No one knew (or knows) how the manuscript got to the library in Copenhagen or how long it had been there. No one, it appeared, had ever bothered to read it or figured out how. Quechua was not thought of as a written language in 1908, nor Andean culture as a literate culture.

Pietschmann prepared a paper on his find, which he presented in London in 1912, a year after the rediscovery of Machu Picchu by Hiram Bingham. Reception, by an international congress of Americanists, was apparently confused. It took twenty-five years for a facsimile edition of the work to appear in Paris. It was not till the late 1970s, as positivist reading habits gave way to interpretive studies and colonial elitisms to postcolonial pluralisms, that Western scholars found ways of reading Guaman Poma's *New Chronicle and Good Government* as the extraordinary intercultural tour de force that it was. The letter got there, only 350 years too late, a miracle and a terrible tragedy.

I propose to say a few more words about this erstwhile unreadable text, in order to lay out some thoughts about writing and literacy in what I like to call the *contact zones*. I use this term to refer to social spaces where cultures meet, clash, and grapple with each other, often in contexts of highly asymmetrical relations of power, such as colonialism, slavery, or their aftermaths as they are lived out in many parts of the world today. Eventually I will use the term to reconsider the models of community that many of us rely on in teaching and theorizing and that are under challenge today. But first a little more about Guaman Poma's giant letter to Philip III.

Insofar as anything is known about him at all, Guaman Poma exemplified the sociocultural complexities produced by conquest and empire. He was an indigenous Andean who claimed noble Inca descent and who had adopted (at least in some sense) Christianity. He may have worked in the Spanish colonial administration as an interpreter, scribe, or assistant to a Spanish tax collector—as a mediator, in short. He says he learned to write from his half brother, a mestizo whose Spanish father had given him access to religious education.

Guaman Poma's letter to the king is written in two languages (Spanish and Quechua) and two parts. The first is called the *Nueva corónica,* "New Chronicle." The title is important. The chronicle of course was the main writing apparatus through which the Spanish presented their American conquests to themselves. It constituted one of the main official discourses. In writing a "new chronicle," Guaman Poma took over the official Spanish genre for his own ends. Those ends were, roughly, to construct a new picture of the world, a picture of a Christian world with Andean rather than European peoples at the center of it—Cuzco, not Jerusalem. In the *New Chronicle* Guaman Poma begins by rewriting the Christian history of the world from Adam and Eve (Fig. 1 [p. 586]), incorporating the Amerindians into it as offspring of one of the sons of Noah. He identifies five ages of Christian history that he links in parallel with the five ages of canonical Andean history—separate but equal trajectories that diverge with Noah and reintersect not with Columbus but with Saint Bartholomew, claimed to have preceded Columbus in the Americas. In a couple of hundred pages, Guaman Poma constructs a veritable encyclopedia of Inca and pre-Inca history, customs, laws, social forms, public offices, and dynastic leaders. The depictions resemble European manners and customs description, but also reproduce the meticulous detail with which knowledge in Inca society was stored on *quipus* and in the oral memories of elders.

Guaman Poma's *New Chronicle* is an instance of what I have proposed to call an *autoethnographic* text, by which I mean a text in which people undertake to describe themselves in ways that engage with representations others have made of them. Thus if ethnographic texts are those in which European metropolitan subjects represent to themselves their others (usually their conquered others), autoethnographic texts are representations that the so-defined others construct *in response to* or in dialogue with those texts. Autoethnographic texts are not, then, what are usually thought of as autochthonous forms of expression or self-representation (as the Andean *quipus* were). Rather they involve a selective collaboration with and appropriation of idioms of the metropolis or the conqueror. These are merged or infiltrated to varying degrees with indigenous idioms to create self-representations intended to intervene in metropolitan modes of understanding. Autoethnographic works are often addressed to both metropolitan audiences and the speaker's own community. Their reception is thus highly indeterminate. Such texts often constitute a marginalized group's point of entry into the dominant circuits of print culture. It is interesting to think, for example, of American slave autobiography in its autoethnographic dimensions, which in some respects distinguish it from Euramerican autobiographical tradition. The concept might help explain why some of the earliest published writing by Chicanas took the form of folkloric manners and customs sketches written in English and published in English-language newspapers or folklore magazines (see Treviño). Autoethnographic representation often involves concrete collaborations between people, as between literate ex-slaves and abolitionist intellectuals, or between Guaman Poma and the Inca elders who were his informants. Often, as in Guaman Poma, it involves more than one language. In recent decades autoethnography, critique, and resistance have reconnected with writing in a contemporary creation of the contact zone, the *testimonio*.

Guaman Poma's *New Chronicle* ends with a revisionist account of the Spanish conquest, which, he argues, should have been a peaceful en-

*Figure 1. Adam and Eve*

counter of equals with the potential for benefiting both, but for the mindless greed of the Spanish. He parodies Spanish history. Following contact
with the Incas, he writes, "In all Castille, there was a great commotion. All
day and at night in their dreams the Spaniards were saying, 'Yndias, yndias, oro, plata, oro, plata del Piru'" ("Indies, Indies, gold, silver, gold, silver from Peru") (Fig. 2 [below]). The Spanish, he writes, brought nothing
of value to share with the Andeans, nothing "but armor and guns con la
codicia de oro, plata oro y plata, yndias, a las Yndias, Piru" ("with the lust
for gold, silver, gold and silver, Indies, the Indies, Peru") (372). I quote
these words as an example of a conquered subject using the conqueror's
language to construct a parodic, oppositional representation of the conqueror's own speech. Guaman Poma mirrors back to the Spanish (in their
language, which is alien to him) an image of themselves that they often
suppress and will therefore surely recognize. Such are the dynamics of
language, writing, and representation in contact zones.

The second half of the epistle continues the critique. It is titled *Buen gobierno y justicia,* "Good Government and Justice," and combines a description

*Figure 2. Conquista. Meeting of Spaniard and Inca. The Inca says in Quechua,
"You eat this gold?" Spaniard replies in Spanish, "We eat this gold."*

of colonial society in the Andean region with a passionate denunciation of Spanish exploitation and abuse. (These, at the time he was writing, were decimating the population of the Andes at a genocidal rate. In fact, the potential loss of the labor force became a main cause for reform of the system.) Guaman Poma's most implacable hostility is invoked by the clergy, followed by the dreaded *corregidores,* or colonial overseers (Fig. 3 [below]). He also praises good works, Christian habits, and just men where he finds them, and offers at length his views as to what constitutes "good government and justice." The Indies, he argues, should be administered through a collaboration of Inca and Spanish elites. The epistle ends with an imaginary question-and-answer session in which, in a reversal of hierarchy, the king is depicted asking Guaman Poma questions about how to reform the empire—a dialogue imagined across the many lines that divide the Andean scribe from the imperial monarch, and in which the subordinated subject single-handedly gives himself authority in the colonizer's language and verbal repertoire. In a way, it worked—this extraordinary text did get written—but in a way it did not, for the letter never reached its addressee.

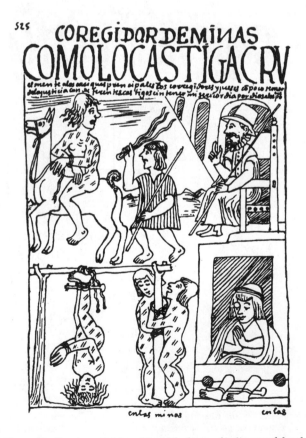

*Figure 3. Corregidor de minas. Catalog of Spanish abuses of indigenous labor force.*

To grasp the import of Guaman Poma's project, one needs to keep in mind that the Incas had no system of writing. Their huge empire is said to be the only known instance of a full-blown bureaucratic state society built and administered without writing. Guaman Poma constructs his text by appropriating and adapting pieces of the representational repertoire of the invaders. He does not simply imitate or reproduce it; he selects and adapts it along Andean lines to express (bilingually, mind you) Andean interests and aspirations. Ethnographers have used the term *transculturation* to describe processes whereby members of subordinated or marginal groups select and invent from materials transmitted by a dominant or metropolitan culture. The term, originally coined by Cuban sociologist Fernando Ortiz in the 1940s, aimed to replace overly reductive concepts of acculturation and assimilation used to characterize culture under conquest. While subordinate peoples do not usually control what emanates from the dominant culture, they do determine to varying extents what gets absorbed into their own and what it gets used for. Transculturation, like autoethnography, is a phenomenon of the contact zone.

As scholars have realized only relatively recently, the transcultural character of Guaman Poma's text is intricately apparent in its visual as well as its written component. The genre of the four hundred line drawings is European—there seems to have been no tradition of representational drawing among the Incas—but in their execution they deploy specifically Andean systems of spatial symbolism that express Andean values and aspirations.[1]

In figure 1, for instance, Adam is depicted on the left-hand side below the sun, while Eve is on the right-hand side below the moon, and slightly lower than Adam. The two are divided by the diagonal of Adam's digging stick. In Andean spatial symbolism, the diagonal descending from the sun marks the basic line of power and authority dividing upper from lower, male from female, dominant from subordinate. In figure 2, the Inca appears in the same position as Adam, with the Spaniard opposite, and the two at the same height. In figure 3, depicting Spanish abuses of power, the symbolic pattern is reversed. The Spaniard is in a high position indicating dominance, but on the "wrong" (right-hand) side. The diagonals of his lance and that of the servant doing the flogging mark out a line of illegitimate, though real, power. The Andean figures continue to occupy the left-hand side of the picture, but clearly as victims. Guaman Poma wrote that the Spanish conquest had produced *"un mundo al reves,"* "a world in reverse."

In sum, Guaman Poma's text is truly a product of the contact zone. If one thinks of cultures, or literatures, as discrete, coherently structured, monolingual edifices, Guaman Poma's text, and indeed any autoethnographic work, appears anomalous or chaotic—as it apparently did to the European scholars Pietschmann spoke to in 1912. If one does not think of cultures this way, then Guaman Poma's text is simply heterogeneous, as the Andean region was itself and remains today. Such a text is heterogeneous on the reception end as well as the production end: it will read very differently to people in different positions in the contact zone. Because it deploys

European and Andean systems of meaning making, the letter necessarily means differently to bilingual Spanish-Quechua speakers and to monolingual speakers in either language; the drawings mean differently to monocultural readers, Spanish or Andean, and to bicultural readers responding to the Andean symbolic structures embodied in European genres.

In the Andes in the early 1600s there existed a literate public with considerable intercultural competence and degrees of bilingualism. Unfortunately, such a community did not exist in the Spanish court with which Guaman Poma was trying to make contact. It is interesting to note that in the same year Guaman Poma sent off his letter, a text by another Peruvian was adopted in official circles in Spain as the canonical Christian mediation between the Spanish conquest and Inca history. It was another huge encyclopedic work, titled the *Royal Commentaries of the Incas*, written, tellingly, by a mestizo, Inca Garcilaso de la Vega. Like the mestizo half brother who taught Guaman Poma to read and write, Inca Garcilaso was the son of an Inca princess and a Spanish official, and had lived in Spain since he was seventeen. Though he too spoke Quechua, his book is written in eloquent, standard Spanish, without illustrations. While Guaman Poma's life's work sat somewhere unread, the *Royal Commentaries* was edited and reedited in Spain and the New World, a mediation that coded the Andean past and present in ways thought unthreatening to colonial hierarchy.[2] The textual hierarchy persists; the *Royal Commentaries* today remains a staple item on Ph.D. reading lists in Spanish, while the *New Chronicle and Good Government*, despite the ready availability of several fine editions, is not. However, though Guaman Poma's text did not reach its destination, the transcultural currents of expression it exemplifies continued to evolve in the Andes, as they still do, less in writing than in storytelling, ritual, song, dance-drama, painting and sculpture, dress, textile art, forms of governance, religious belief, and many other vernacular art forms. All express the effects of long-term contact and intractable, unequal conflict.

Autoethnography, transculturation, critique, collaboration, bilingualism, mediation, parody, denunciation, imaginary dialogue, vernacular expression—these are some of the literate arts of the contact zone. Miscomprehension, incomprehension, dead letters, unread masterpieces, absolute heterogeneity of meaning—these are some of the perils of writing in the contact zone. They all live among us today in the transnationalized metropolis of the United States and are becoming more widely visible, more pressing, and, like Guaman Poma's text, more decipherable to those who once would have ignored them in defense of a stable, centered sense of knowledge and reality.

## Contact and Community

The idea of the contact zone is intended in part to contrast with ideas of community that underlie much of the thinking about language, communication, and culture that gets done in the academy. A couple of years ago, thinking about the linguistic theories I knew, I tried to make sense of a utopian quality that often seemed to characterize social analyses of language by the academy. Languages were seen as living in "speech communities," and these tended to be theorized as discrete, self-defined, coherent entities, held together by a homogeneous competence or grammar shared identically and equally among all the members. This abstract idea of the speech community seemed to reflect, among other things, the utopian way modern nations conceive of themselves as what Benedict Anderson calls "imagined communities."[3] In a book of that title, Anderson observes that with the possible exception of what he calls "primordial villages," human communities exist as *imagined* entities in which people "will never know most of their fellow-members, meet them or even hear of them, yet in the mind of each lives the image of their communion." "Communities are distinguished," he goes on to say, "not by their falsity/genuineness, but by *the style in which they are imagined*" (15; emphasis mine). Anderson proposes three features that characterize the style in which the modern nation is imagined. First, it is imagined as *limited,* by "finite, if elastic, boundaries"; second, it is imagined as *sovereign;* and, third, it is imagined as *fraternal,* "a deep, horizontal comradeship" for which millions of people are prepared "not so much to kill as willingly to die" (15). As the image suggests, the nation-community is embodied metonymically in the finite, sovereign, fraternal figure of the citizen-soldier.

Anderson argues that European bourgeoisies were distinguished by their ability to "achieve solidarity on an essentially imagined basis" (74) on a scale far greater than that of elites of other times and places. Writing and literacy play a central role in this argument. Anderson maintains, as have others, that the main instrument that made bourgeois nation-building projects possible was print capitalism. The commercial circulation of books in the various European vernaculars, he argues, was what first created the invisible networks that would eventually constitute the literate elites and those they ruled as nations. (Estimates are that 180 million books were put into circulation in Europe between the years 1500 and 1600 alone.)

Now obviously this style of imagining of modern nations, as Anderson describes it, is strongly utopian, embodying values like equality, fraternity, liberty, which the societies often profess but systematically fail to realize. The prototype of the modern nation as imagined community was, it seemed to me, mirrored in ways people thought about language and the speech community. Many commentators have pointed out how modern views of language as code and competence assume a unified and homogeneous social world in which language exists as a shared patrimony—as a device, precisely, for imagining community. An image of a universally shared literacy is also part of the picture. The prototypical manifestation of language is generally taken to be the speech of individual adult native speakers face-to-face (as in Saussure's famous diagram) in monolingual, even monodialectal situations—in short, the most homogeneous case linguistically and socially. The same goes for written communication. Now one could certainly imagine a theory that assumed different things— that argued, for instance, that the most revealing speech situation for understanding language was one involving a gathering of people each of whom spoke two languages and understood a third and held only one language in common with any of the others. It depends on what workings of language you want to see or want to see first, on what you choose to define as normative.

In keeping with autonomous, fraternal models of community, analyses of language use commonly assume that principles of cooperation and shared understanding are normally in effect. Descriptions of interactions between people in conversation, classrooms, medical and bureaucratic settings, readily take it for granted that the situation is governed by a single set of rules or norms shared by all participants. The analysis focuses then on how those rules produce or fail to produce an orderly, coherent exchange. Models involving games and moves are often used to describe interactions. Despite whatever conflicts or systematic social differences might be in play, it is assumed that all participants are engaged in the same game and that the game is the same for all players. Often it is. But of course it often is not, as, for example, when speakers are from different classes or cultures, or one party is exercising authority and another is submitting to it or questioning it. Last year one of my children moved to a new elementary school that had more open classrooms and more flexible curricula than the conventional school he started out in. A few days into the term, we asked him what it was like at the new school. "Well," he said, "they're a lot nicer, and they have a lot less rules. But know *why* they're nicer?" "Why?" I asked. "So you'll obey all the rules they don't have," he replied. This is a very coherent analysis with considerable elegance and explanatory power, but probably not the one his teacher would have given.

When linguistic (or literate) interaction is described in terms of orderliness, games, moves, or scripts, usually only legitimate moves are actually named as part of the system, where legitimacy is defined from the point of view of the party in authority—regardless of what other parties might see themselves as doing. Teacher-pupil language, for example, tends to be described almost entirely from the point of view of the teacher and teaching, not from the point of view of pupils and pupiling (the word doesn't even exist, though the thing certainly does). If a classroom is analyzed as a social world unified and homogenized with respect to the teacher, whatever students do other than what the teacher specifies is invisible or anomalous to the analysis. This can be true in practice as well. On several occasions my fourth grader, the one busy obeying all the rules they didn't have, was given writing assignments that took the form of answering a series of questions to build up a paragraph. These questions often asked him to identify with the interests of those in power over him—parents, teachers, doctors, public authorities. He invariably sought ways to resist or subvert these assignments. One assignment, for instance, called for imagining "a helpful invention." The students were asked to write single-sentence responses to the following questions:

> What kind of invention would help you?
> How would it help you?
> Why would you need it?
> What would it look like?
> Would other people be able to use it also?
> What would be an invention to help your teacher?
> What would be an invention to help your parents?

Manuel's reply read as follows:

> A grate adventchin

> Some inventchins are GRATE!!!!!!!!!!! My inventchin would be a shot that would put every thing you learn at school in your brain. It would help me by letting me graduate right now!! I would need it because it would let me play with my friends, go on vacachin and, do fun a lot more. It would look like a regular shot. Ather peaple would use to. This inventchin would help my teacher parents get away from a lot of work. I think a shot like this would be GRATE!

Despite the spelling, the assignment received the usual star to indicate the task had been fulfilled in an acceptable way. No recognition was available, however, of the humor, the attempt to be critical or contestatory, to parody the structures of authority. On that score, Manuel's luck was only slightly better than Guaman Poma's. What is the place of unsolicited oppositional discourse, parody, resistance, critique in the imagined classroom community? Are teachers supposed to feel that their teaching has been most successful when they have eliminated such things and unified the social world, probably in their own image? Who wins when we do that? Who loses?

Such questions may be hypothetical, because in the United States in the 1990s, many teachers find themselves less and less able to do that even if they want to. The composition of the national collectivity is changing and so are the styles, as Anderson put it, in which it is being imagined. In the 1980s in many nation-states, imagined national syntheses that had retained hegemonic force began to dissolve. Internal social groups with histories and lifeways different from the official ones began insisting on those histories and lifeways *as part of their citizenship,* as the very mode of their membership in the national collectivity. In their dialogues with dominant institutions, many groups began asserting a rhetoric of belonging that made demands beyond those of representation and basic rights granted from above. In universities we started to hear, "I don't just want you to let me be here, I want to belong here; this institution should belong to me as much as it does to anyone else." Institutions have responded with, among other things, rhetorics of diversity and multiculturalism whose import at this moment is up for grabs across the ideological spectrum.

These shifts are being lived out by everyone working in education today, and everyone is challenged by them in one way or another. Those of us committed to educational democracy are particularly challenged as that notion finds itself besieged on the public agenda. Many of those who govern us display, openly, their interest in a quiescent, ignorant, manipulable electorate. Even as an ideal, the concept of an enlightened citizenry seems to have disappeared from the national imagination. A couple of years ago the university where I work went through an intense and wrenching debate over a narrowly defined Western-culture requirement that had been instituted there in 1980. It kept boiling down to a debate over the ideas of national patrimony, cultural citizenship, and imagined community. In the end, the requirement was transformed into a much more broadly defined course called Cultures, Ideas, Values.[4] In the context of the change, a new course was designed that centered on the Americas and the multiple cultural histories (including European ones) that have intersected here. As you can imagine, the course attracted a very diverse student body. The classroom functioned not like a homogeneous community or a horizontal alliance but like a contact zone. Every single text we read stood in specific historical relationships to the students in the class, but the range and variety of historical relationships in play were enormous. Everybody had a stake in nearly everything we read, but the range and kind of stakes varied widely.

It was the most exciting teaching we had ever done, and also the hardest. We were struck, for example, at how anomalous the formal lecture became in a contact zone (who can forget Atahuallpa throwing down the Bible because it would not speak to him?). The lecturer's traditional (imagined) task—unifying the world in the class's eyes by means of a monologue that rings equally coherent, revealing, and true for all, forging an ad hoc community, homogeneous with respect to one's own words—this task became not only impossible but anomalous and unimaginable. Instead, one had to work in the knowledge that whatever one said was going to be systematically received in radically heterogeneous ways that we were neither able nor entitled to prescribe.

The very nature of the course put ideas and identities on the line. All the students in the class had the experience, for example, of hearing their culture discussed and objectified in ways that horrified them; all the students saw their roots traced back to legacies of both glory and shame; all the students experienced face-to-face the ignorance and incomprehension, and occasionally the hostility, of others. In the absence of community values and the hope of synthesis, it was easy to forget the positives; the fact, for instance, that kinds of marginalization once taken for granted were gone. Virtually every student was having the experience of seeing the world described with him or her in it. Along with rage, incomprehension, and pain, there were exhilarating moments of wonder and revelation, mutual understanding, and new wisdom—the joys of the contact zone. The sufferings and revelations were, at different moments to be sure, experienced by every student. No one was excluded, and no one was safe.

The fact that no one was safe made all of us involved in the course appreciate the importance of what we came to call "safe houses." We used the term to refer to social and intellectual spaces where groups can constitute themselves as horizontal, homogeneous, sovereign communities with high degrees of trust, shared understandings, temporary protection from legacies of oppression. This is why, as we realized, multicultural curricula should not seek to replace ethnic or women's studies, for example. Where there are legacies of subordination, groups need places for healing and mutual recognition, safe houses in which to construct shared understandings, knowledges, claims on the world that they can then bring into the contact zone.

Meanwhile, our job in the Americas course remains to figure out how to make that crossroads the best site for learning that it can be. We are looking for the pedagogical arts of the contact zone. These will include, we are sure, exercises in storytelling and in identifying with the ideas, interests, histories, and attitudes of others; experiments in transculturation and collaborative work and in the arts of critique, parody, and comparison (including unseemly comparisons between elite and vernacular cultural forms); the redemption of the oral; ways for people to engage with suppressed aspects of history (including their own histories), ways to move *into and out of* rhetorics of authenticity; ground rules for communication across lines of difference and hierarchy that go beyond politeness but maintain mutual respect; a systematic approach to the all-important concept of *cultural mediation*. These arts were in play in every room at the extraordinary Pittsburgh conference on literacy. I learned a lot about them there, and I am thankful.

## WORKS CITED

Adorno, Rolena. *Guaman Poma de Ayala: Writing and Resistance in Colonial Peru.* Austin: U of Texas P, 1986.

Anderson, Benedict. *Imagined Communities: Reflections on the Origins and Spread of Nationalism.* London: Verso, 1984.

Garcilaso de la Vega, El Inca. *Royal Commentaries of the Incas.* 1613. Austin: U of Texas P, 1966.

Guaman Poma de Ayala, Felipe. *El primer nueva corónica y buen gobierno.* Manuscript. Ed. John Murra and Rolena Adorno. Mexico: Siglo XXI, 1980.

Pratt, Mary Louise. "Linguistic Utopias." *The Linguistics of Writing.* Ed. Nigel Fabb et al. Manchester: Manchester UP, 1987. 48–66.

Treviño, Gloria. "Cultural Ambivalence in Early Chicano Prose Fiction." Diss. Stanford U, 1985.

## NOTES

[1] For an introduction in English to these and other aspects of Guaman Poma's work, see Rolena Adorno. Adorno and Mercedes Lopez-Baralt pioneered the study of Andean symbolic systems in Guaman Poma.

[2] It is far from clear that the *Royal Commentaries* was as benign as the Spanish seemed to assume. The book certainly played a role in maintaining the identity and aspirations of indigenous elites in the Andes. In the mid–eighteenth century, a new edition of the *Royal Commentaries* was suppressed by Spanish authorities because its preface included a prophecy by Sir Walter Raleigh that the English would invade Peru and restore the Inca monarchy.

[3] The discussion of community here is summarized from my essay "Linguistic Utopias."

[4] For information about this program and the contents of courses taught in it, write Program in Cultures, Ideas, Values (CIV), Stanford Univ., Stanford, CA 94305.


• • • • • • • • • • • •


## QUESTIONS FOR A SECOND READING

1. Perhaps the most interesting question "Arts of the Contact Zone" raises for its readers is how to put together the pieces: the examples from Pratt's children, the discussion of Guaman Poma and the *New Chronicle and Good Government*, the brief history of European literacy, and the discussion of curriculum reform at Stanford. The terms that run through the sections are, among others, these: "contact," "community," "autoethnography," "transculturation." As you reread, mark those passages you might use to trace the general argument that cuts across these examples.

2. This essay was originally delivered as a lecture. Before you read her essay again, create a set of notes on what you remember as important, relevant, or worthwhile. Imagine yourself as part of her audience. Then reread the essay. Where would you want to interrupt her? What questions could you ask her that might make "Arts of the Contact Zone" more accessible to you?

3. This is an essay about reading and writing and teaching and learning, about the "literate arts" and the "pedagogical arts" of the contact zone. Surely the composition class, the first-year college English class, can be imagined as a contact zone. And it seems in the spirit of Pratt's essay to identify (as a student) with Guaman Poma. As you reread, think about how and where this essay might be said to speak directly to you about your education as a reader and writer in a contact zone.

4. There are some difficult terms in this essay: "autochthonous," "autoethnography," "transculturation." The last two are defined in the text; the first you will have to look up. (We did.) In some ways, the slipperiest of the key words in the essay is "culture." At one point Pratt says,

> If one thinks of cultures, or literatures, as discrete, coherently structured, monolingual edifices, Guaman Poma's text, and indeed any autoethnographic work, appears anomalous or chaotic—as it apparently did to the European scholars Pietschmann spoke to in 1912. If one does not think of cultures this way, then Guaman Poma's text is simply heterogeneous, as the Andean region was itself and remains today. Such a text is heterogeneous on the reception end as well as the production

end: it will read very differently to people in different positions in the contact zone. (p. 589)

If one thinks of cultures as "coherently structured, monolingual edifices," the text appears one way; if one thinks otherwise the text is "simply heterogeneous." What might it mean to make this shift in the way one thinks of culture? Can you do it—that is, can you read the *New Chronicle* from both points of view, make the two points of view work in your own imagining? Can you, for example, think of a group that you participate in as a "community"? Then can you think of it as a "contact zone"? Which one seems "natural" to you? What does Pratt assume to be the dominant point of view now, for *her* readers?

As you reread, not only do you want to get a sense of how to explain these two attitudes toward culture, but you need to practice shifting your point of view from one to the other. Think, from inside the position of each, of the things you would be expected to say about Poma's text, Manuel's invention, and your classroom.

### ASSIGNMENTS FOR WRITING

Here, briefly, are two descriptions of the writing one might find or expect in the "contact zone." They serve as an introduction to the three writing assignments.

> Autoethnography, transculturation, critique, collaboration, bilingualism, mediation, parody, denunciation, imaginary dialogue, vernacular expression—these are some of the literate arts of the contact zone. Miscomprehension, incomprehension, dead letters, unread masterpieces, absolute heterogeneity of meaning—these are some of the perils of writing in the contact zone. They all live among us today in the transnationalized metropolis of the United States and are becoming more widely visible, more pressing, and, like Guaman Poma's text, more decipherable to those who once would have ignored them in defense of a stable, centered sense of knowledge and reality. (p. 590)

> We are looking for the pedagogical arts of the contact zone. These will include, we are sure, exercises in storytelling and in identifying with the ideas, interests, histories, and attitudes of others; experiments in transculturation and collaborative work and in the arts of critique, parody, and comparison (including unseemly comparisons between elite and vernacular cultural forms); the redemption of the oral; ways for people to engage with suppressed aspects of history (including their own histories), ways to move *into and out of* rhetorics of authenticity; ground rules for communication across lines of difference and hierarchy that go beyond politeness but maintain mutual respect; a systematic approach to the all-important concept of *cultural mediation.* (p. 595)

1. One way of working with Pratt's essay, of extending its project, would be to conduct your own local inventory of writing from the contact zone. You might do this on your own or in teams with others from your class. You will want to gather several similar documents, your "archive," before you make your final selection. Think about how to make that choice.

What makes one document stand out as representative? Here are two ways you might organize your search:

a. You could look for historical documents. A local historical society might have documents written by Native Americans ("Indians") to the white settlers. There may be documents written by slaves to masters or to northern whites explaining their experience with slavery. There may be documents by women (like suffragettes) trying to negotiate for public positions and rights. There may be documents from any of a number of racial or ethnic groups—Hispanic, Jewish, Irish, Italian, Polish, Swedish—trying to explain their positions to the mainstream culture. There may, perhaps at union halls, be documents written by workers to owners. Your own sense of the heritage of your area should direct your search.

b. Or you could look for contemporary documents in the print that is around you, things that you might otherwise overlook. Pratt refers to one of the characteristic genres of the Hispanic community, the *"testimonio."* You could look at the writing of any marginalized group, particularly writing intended, at least in part, to represent the experience of outsiders to the dominant culture (or to be in dialogue with that culture or to respond to that culture). These documents, if we follow Pratt's example, would encompass the work of young children or students, including college students.

Once you have completed your inventory, choose a document you would like to work with and present it carefully and in detail (perhaps in even greater detail than Pratt's presentation of the *New Chronicle*). You might imagine that you are presenting this to someone who would not have seen it and would not know how to read it, at least not as an example of the literate arts of the contact zone.

2. Another way of extending the project of Pratt's essay would be to write your own autoethnography. It should not be too hard to locate a setting or context in which you are the "other"—the one who speaks from outside rather than inside the dominant discourse. Pratt says that the position of the outsider is marked not only by differences of language and ways of thinking and speaking but also by differences in power, authority, status. In a sense, she argues, the only way those in power can understand you is in *their* terms. These are terms you will need to use to tell your story, but your goal is to describe your position in ways that "engage with representations others have made of [you]" without giving in or giving up or disappearing in their already formed sense of who you are.

This is an interesting challenge. One of the things that will make the writing difficult is that the autoethnographic or transcultural text calls upon skills not usually valued in American classrooms: bilingualism, parody, denunciation, imaginary dialogue, vernacular expression, storytelling, unseemly comparisons of high and low cultural forms—these are some of the terms Pratt offers. These do not fit easily with the traditional genres of the writing class (essay, term paper, summary, report) or its traditional values (unity, consistency, sincerity, clarity, correctness, decorum).

You will probably need to take this essay (or whatever it should be called) through several drafts. It might be best to begin as Pratt's student, using her description as a preliminary guide. Once you get a sense of your own project, you may find that you have terms or examples to add to her list of the literate arts of the contact zone.

3. Citing Benedict Anderson and what he calls "imagined communities," Pratt argues that our idea of community is "strongly utopian, embodying values like equality, fraternity, liberty, which the societies often profess but systematically fail to realize." Against this utopian vision of community, Pratt argues that we need to develop ways of understanding (even noticing) social and intellectual spaces that are not homogeneous, unified; we need to develop ways of understanding and valuing difference.

Think of a community of which you are a member, a community that is important to you. And think about the utopian terms you are given to name and describe this community. Think, then, about this group in Pratt's terms—as a "contact zone." How would you name and describe this social space? Write an essay in which you present these alternate points of view on a single social group. You will need to present this discussion fully, so that someone who is not part of your group can follow what you say, and you should take time to think about the consequences (for you, for your group) of this shift in point of view, in terms.

### MAKING CONNECTIONS

1. In "The Photographic Essay: Four Case Studies" (p. 522), W. J. T. Mitchell is concerned with the ways both words and images take possession of their subjects. And, in his account, there is a political dimension to this. It is a matter of the rich looking at and describing the poor in *Let Us Now Praise Famous Men*, of colonial power and the colonized in *The Colonial Harem* and *After the Last Sky*. (It is harder to name the victims and agents of appropriation in *Camera Lucida*. It would be worth your time to read that section carefully to see what terms Barthes offers.) In Pratt's terms in "Arts of the Contact Zone," both the photos and the texts represent moments of contact between persons of different cultures and unequal status.

Write an essay in which you consider two of the cases in "The Photographic Essay" in terms of Pratt's discussion of the contact zone. How would she understand the status and meaning of the words and images used to represent the "other"? How is her understanding different from Mitchell's? Both could be said to be interested in the role of power, the political, and history in the use and formation of texts. Which account seems most useful to you? Useful for what?

2. Here, from "Arts of the Contact Zone," is Pratt on the "autoethnographic" text:

> Guaman Poma's *New Chronicle* is an instance of what I have proposed to call an *authoethnographic* text, by which I mean a text in which people undertake to describe themselves in ways that engage with representations others have made of them. Thus if ethnographic texts are those in which European metropolitan subjects represent to them-

selves their others (usually their conquered others), autoethnographic texts are representations that the so-defined others construct *in response* to or in dialogue with those texts. [T]hey involved a selective collaboration with and appropriation of idioms of the metropolis or the conqueror. These are merged or infiltrated to varying degrees with indigenous idioms to create self-representations intended to intervene in metropolitan modes of understanding. . . . Such texts often constitute a marginalized group's point of entry into the dominant circuits of print culture. (pp. 585–86)

The chapters from W. E. B. Du Bois's *The Souls of Black Folk* (p. 224) present an interesting opportunity to think about Pratt's concept of the "autoethnographic text." While the book is written to represent African American life, thought, and culture (the "souls of black folk") to a white, metropolitan audience, Du Bois's relationship to his subject is not a simple one. As a writer writing about southern black culture, he is urban, highly educated, and a northerner by birth. The first of the three chapters, "Of the Meaning of Progress," could be read as ethnography—that is, as a documentary account written by an outsider. In the remaining two chapters, Du Bois writes from the inside, as a black educator representing to others the circumstances and urgencies in the university education of African American men.

Using the example of Pratt's work with the *New Chronicle,* write an essay in which you present a reading of two of Du Bois's chapters ("Of the Meaning of Progress" and one of the others) as examples of the "arts of the contact zone." You should look, in particular, at the differences in style, form, and address in the two chapters.

What do these examples allow you to add to Pratt's discussion of the autoethnographic and/or transcultural text? Where do you see Du Bois working to insure that he can be heard (and read) by white readers? Where do you see him working to preserve his own integrity and the integrity of his subjects—where, that is, do you see him establishing his authority? In what ways is he not simply giving in to the prejudices and expectations of his readers?

# ADRIENNE
# RICH

*A* DRIENNE RICH (b. 1929) once said that whatever she knows, she wants to "know it in [her] own nerves." As a writer, Rich found it necessary to acknowledge her anger at both the oppression of women and her immediate experience of that oppression. She needed to find the "anger that is creative." "Until I could tap into the very rich ocean," she said, "I think that my work was constrained in certain ways. There's this fear of anger in women, which is partly because we've been told it was always destructive, it was always unseemly, and unwomanly, and monstrous."

Rich's poetry combines passion and anger with a "yen for order." She wrote her first book of poems, A Change of World, while an undergraduate at Radcliffe College. The book won the 1951 Yale Younger Poets Award and a generous introduction from W. H. Auden, who was one of the judges. In 1991 she won the Commonwealth Award in Literature and in 1992 the Robert Frost Medal from the Poetry Society of America for a lifetime of achievement in literature. Her other works, which include The Diamond Cutters (1955), Snapshots of a Daughter-in-Law (1963, 1967), Necessities of Life (1966), Leaflets (1969), The Will to Change (1970), and Diving into the Wreck (1973), show an increasing concern for the political and psychological consequences of life in patriarchal society. When offered the National Book Award for Diving into the Wreck, Rich refused it as an individual but accepted it, in a statement written with two other nominees—*Audre Lorde and Alice Walker (whose essay "In Search of Our Mothers' Gardens" appears on p. 694)—in the name of all women:*

> *We . . . together accept this award in the name of all the women whose voices have gone and still go unheard in a patriarchal world, and in the name of those who, like us, have been tolerated as token women in this culture, often at great cost and in great pain. . . . We dedicate this occasion to the struggle for self-determination of all women, of every color, identification, or derived class, . . . the women who will understand what we are doing here and those who will not understand yet; the silent women whose voices have been denied us, the articulate women who have given us the strength to do our work.*

*After graduating from Radcliffe in 1951, Rich married and raised three sons. One of her prose collections,* Of Woman Born: Motherhood as Experience and Institution *(1976), treats her experience as both mother and daughter with eloquence, even as it calls for the destruction of motherhood as an institution. In 1970 Rich left her marriage, and six years later she published a book of poems that explore a lesbian relationship. But the term "lesbian" for Rich referred to "nothing so simple and dismissible as the fact that two women might go to bed together." As she says in "It Is the Lesbian in Us," a speech reprinted in* On Lies, Secrets, and Silence: Selected Prose *(1979), it refers also to "a sense of desiring oneself; above all, of choosing oneself; it was also a primary intensity; between women, an intensity which in the world at large was trivialized, caricatured, or invested with evil. . . . It is the lesbian in us who drives us to feel imaginatively, render in language, grasp, the full connection between woman and woman."*

*Rich has published thirteen books of poetry and four collections of prose. In* Blood, Bread and Poetry: Selected Prose *(1986), she offers a series of commencement speeches, reviews, lectures, and articles on feminism, gay and lesbian rights, racism, anti-Semitism, and the necessity for the artist, university, and state to find a commitment to social justice. Her most recent book of poems is* Dark Fields of the Republic: Poems 1991–1995 *(1995). In 1991, she published* An Atlas of the Difficult World: Poems, 1988–91, *which was awarded the 1992 Los Angeles Times Book Prize for poetry and was a finalist for both the National Book Award and the National Book Critics Circle Award. In 1993 she published* Collected Early Poems: 1950–1970, *and in 1996 she edited* The Best American Poetry 1996. *Rich has taught at Columbia, Brandeis, Cornell, Rutgers, and Stanford universities, Swarthmore College, and the City College of New York. Among her many awards and honors she has held two Guggenheim Fellowships and an Amy Lowell Traveling Fellowship. She has been a member of the department of literature of the American Academy and Institute of Arts and Letters since 1990. She lives in California.*

# When We Dead Awaken:
## Writing as Re-Vision°

*The Modern Language Association is both marketplace and funeral parlor for the professional study of Western literature in North America. Like all gatherings of the professions, it has been and remains a "procession of the sons of educated men" (Virginia Woolf): a congeries of old-boys' networks, academicians rehearsing their numb canons in sessions dedicated to the literature of white males, junior scholars under the lash of "publish or perish" delivering papers in the bizarrely lit drawing-rooms of immense hotels: a ritual competition veering between cynicism and desperation.*

*However, in the interstices of these gentlemanly rites (or, in Mary Daly's words, on the boundaries of this patriarchal space),[1] some feminist scholars, teachers, and graduate students, joined by feminist writers, editors, and publishers, have for a decade been creating more subversive occasions, challenging the sacredness of the gentlemanly canon, sharing the rediscovery of buried works by women, asking women's questions, bringing literary history and criticism back to life in both senses. The Commission of the Status of Women in the Profession was formed in 1969, and held its first public event in 1970. In 1971 the Commission asked Ellen Peck Killoh, Tillie Olsen, Elaine Reuben, and myself, with Elaine Hedges as moderator, to talk on "The Woman Writer in the Twentieth Century." The essay that follows was written for that forum, and later published, along with the other papers from the forum and workshops, in an issue of* College English *edited by Elaine Hedges ("Women Writing and Teaching," vol. 34, no. 1, October 1972). With a few revisions, mainly updating, it was reprinted in* American Poets *in 1976, edited by William Heyen (New York: Bobbs-Merrill, 1976). That later text is the one published here.*

The challenge flung by feminists at the accepted literary canon, at the methods of teaching it, and at the biased and astigmatic view of male "literary scholarship," has not diminished in the decade since the first Women's Forum; it has become broadened and intensified more recently by the challenges of black and lesbian feminists pointing out that feminist literary criticism itself has overlooked or held back from examining the work of black women and lesbians. The dynamic between a political vision and the demand for a fresh vision of literature is clear: without a growing feminist movement, the first inroads of feminist scholarship

---

As Rich explains, this essay—written in 1971—was first published in 1972 and then included in her volume *On Lies, Secrets, and Silence* (1979). At that time she added the introductory note reprinted here, as well as some notes, identified as *"A.R., 1978."* [Editor's note in the Norton edition.]

could not have been made; without the sharpening of a black feminist consciousness, black women's writing would have been left in limbo between misogynist black male critics and white feminists still struggling to unearth a white women's tradition; without an articulate lesbian/feminist movement, lesbian writing would still be lying in that closet where many of us used to sit reading forbidden books "in a bad light."

Much, much more is yet to be done; and university curricula have of course changed very little as a result of all this. What *is* changing is the availability of knowledge, of vital texts, the visible effects on women's lives of seeing, hearing our wordless or negated experience affirmed and pursued further in language.

Ibsen's *When We Dead Awaken* is a play about the use that the male artist and thinker—in the process of creating culture as we know it—has made of women, in his life and in his work; and about a woman's slow struggling awakening to the use to which her life has been put. Bernard Shaw wrote in 1900 of this play:

> [Ibsen] shows us that no degradation ever devised or permitted is as disastrous as this degradation; that through it women can die into luxuries for men and yet can kill them; that men and women are becoming conscious of this; and that what remains to be seen as perhaps the most interesting of all imminent social developments is what will happen "when we dead awaken."[2]

It's exhilarating to be alive in a time of awakening consciousness; it can also be confusing, disorienting, and painful. The awakening of dead or sleeping consciousness has already affected the lives of millions of women, even those who don't know it yet. It is also affecting the lives of men, even those who deny its claims upon them. The argument will go on whether an oppressive economic class system is responsible for the oppressive nature of male/female relations, or whether, in fact, patriarchy—the domination of males—is the original model of oppression on which all others are based. But in the last few years the women's movement has drawn inescapable and illuminating connections between our sexual lives and our political institutions. The sleepwalkers are coming awake, and for the first time this awakening has a collective reality; it is no longer such a lonely thing to open one's eyes.

Re-vision—the act of looking back, of seeing with fresh eyes, of entering an old text from a new critical direction—is for women more than a chapter in cultural history: it is an act of survival. Until we can understand the assumptions in which we are drenched we cannot know ourselves. And this drive to self-knowledge, for women, is more than a search for identity: it is part of our refusal of the self-destructiveness of male-dominated society. A radical critique of literature, feminist in its impulse, would take the work first of all as a clue to how we live, how we have been living, how we have been led to imagine ourselves, how our language has trapped as well as liberated us, how the very act of naming has been till now a male prerogative, and how we can begin to see and name—and therefore live—afresh. A change in the concept of sexual identity is essential if we are not going to see the old political order reassert itself in every new revolution. We need to know the writing of the past, and know it differently than we have ever known it; not to pass on a tradition but to break its hold over us.

For writers, and at this moment for women writers in particular, there is the challenge and promise of a whole new psychic geography to be explored. But there is also a difficult and dangerous walking on the ice, as we try to find language and images for the consciousness we are just coming into, and with little in the past to support us. I want to talk about some aspect of this difficulty and this danger.

Jane Harrison, the great classical anthropologist, wrote in 1914 in a letter to her friend Gilbert Murray:

> By and by, about "Women," it has bothered me often—why do women never want to write poetry about Man as a sex—why is Woman a dream and a terror to man and not the other way around? . . . Is it mere convention and propriety, or something deeper?[3]

I think Jane Harrison's question cuts deep into the myth-making tradition, the romantic tradition; deep into what women and men have been to each other; and deep into the psyche of the woman writer. Thinking about that question, I began thinking of the work of two twentieth-century women poets, Sylvia Plath and Diane Wakoski. It strikes me that in the work of both Man appears as, if not a dream, a fascination and a terror; and that the source of the fascination and the terror is, simply, Man's power—to dominate, tyrannize, choose, or reject the woman. The charisma of Man seems to come purely from his power over her and his control of the world by force, not from anything fertile or life-giving in him. And, in the work of both these poets, it is finally the woman's sense of *herself*—embattled, possessed—that gives the poetry its dynamic charge, its rhythms of struggle, need, will, and female energy. Until recently this female anger and this furious awareness of the Man's power over her were not available materials to the female poet, who tended to write of Love as the source of her suffering, and to view that victimization by Love as an almost inevitable fate. Or, like Marianne Moore and Elizabeth Bishop, she kept sexuality at a measured and chiseled distance in her poems.

One answer to Jane Harrison's question has to be that historically men and women have played very different parts in each others' lives. Where woman has been a luxury for man, and has served as the painter's model and the poet's muse, but also as comforter, nurse, cook, bearer of his seed, secretarial assistant, and copyist of manuscripts, man has played a quite different role for the female artist. Henry James repeats an incident which the writer Prosper Mérimée described, of how, while he was living with George Sand, he once opened his eyes, in the raw winter dawn, to see his companion, in a dressing-gown, on her knees before the domestic hearth, a candle-stick beside her and a red *madras* round her head, making bravely, with her own hands the fire that was to enable her to sit down betimes to urgent pen and paper. The story represents him as having felt that the spectacle chilled his ardor and tried his taste; her appearance was unfortunate, her occupation an inconsequence, and her industry a reproof—the result of all which was a lively irritation and an early rupture.[4]

The specter of this kind of male judgment, along with the misnaming and thwarting of her needs by a culture controlled by males, has created problems for the woman writer: problems of contact with herself, problems of language and style, problems of energy and survival.

In rereading Virginia Woolf's *A Room of One's Own* (1929) for the first time in some years, I was astonished at the sense of effort, of pains taken, of dogged tentativeness, in the tone of that essay. And I recognized that tone. I had heard it often enough, in myself and in other women. It is the tone of a woman almost in touch with her anger, who is determined not to appear angry, who is *willing* herself to be calm, detached, and even charming in a roomful of men where things have been said which are attacks on her very integrity. Virginia Woolf is addressing an audience of women, but she is acutely conscious—as she always was—of being overheard by men: by Morgan and Lytton and Maynard Keynes and for that matter by her father, Leslie Stephen.[5] She drew the language out into an exacerbated thread in her determination to have her own sensibility yet protect it from those masculine presences. Only at rare moments in that essay do you hear the passion in her voice; she was trying to sound as cool as Jane Austen, as Olympian as Shakespeare, because that is the way the men of the culture thought a writer should sound.

No male writer has written primarily or even largely for women, or with the sense of women's criticism as a consideration when he chooses his materials, his theme, his language. But to a lesser or greater extent, every woman writer has written for men even when, like Virginia Woolf, she was supposed to be addressing women. If we have come to the point when this balance might begin to change, when women can stop being haunted, not only by "convention and propriety" but by internalized fears of being and saying themselves, then it is an extraordinary moment for the woman writer—and reader.

I have hesitated to do what I am going to do now, which is to use myself as an illustration. For one thing, it's a lot easier and less dangerous to talk about other women writers. But there is something else. Like Virginia Woolf, I am aware of the women who are not with us here because they are washing the dishes and looking after the children. Nearly fifty years after she spoke, that fact remains largely unchanged. And I am thinking also of women whom she left out of the picture altogether—women who are washing other people's dishes and caring for other people's children, not to mention women who went on the streets last night in order to feed their children. We seem to be special women here, we have liked to think of ourselves as special, and we have known that men would tolerate, even romanticize us as special, as long as our words and actions didn't threaten their privilege of tolerating or rejecting us and our work according to *their* ideas of what a special woman ought to be. An important insight of the radical women's movement has been how divisive and how ultimately destructive is this myth of the special woman, who is also the token woman. Every one of us here in this room has had great luck—we are teachers, writers, academicians; our own gifts could not have been enough, for we all know women whose gifts are buried or aborted. Our struggles can have meaning and our privileges—however precarious under patriarchy—can be justified only if they can help to change the lives of women whose gifts—and whose very being—continue to be thwarted and silenced.

My own luck was being born white and middle-class into a house full of books, with a father who encouraged me to read and write. So for about twenty years I wrote for a particular man, who criticized and praised me and made me feel I was indeed "special." The obverse side of this, of course, was that I tried for a long time to please him, or rather, not to dis-please him. And then of course there were other men—writers, teachers— the Man, who was not a terror or a dream but a literary master and a mas- ter in other ways less easy to acknowledge. And there were all those poems about women, written by men: it seemed to be a given that men wrote poems and women frequently inhabited them. These women were almost always beautiful, but threatened with the loss of beauty, the loss of youth—the fate worse than death. Or, they were beautiful and died young, like Lucy and Lenore. Or, the woman was like Maud Gonne, cruel and disastrously mistaken, and the poem reproached her because she had refused to become a luxury for the poet.

A lot is being said today about the influence that the myths and im- ages of women have on all of us who are products of culture. I think it has been a peculiar confusion to the girl or woman who tries to write because she is peculiarly susceptible to language. She goes to poetry or fiction looking for *her* way of being in the world, since she too has been putting words and images together; she is looking eagerly for guides, maps, possi- bilities; and over and over in the "words' masculine persuasive force" of literature she comes up against something that negates everything she is about: she meets the image of Woman in books written by men. She finds a terror and a dream, she finds a beautiful pale face, she finds La Belle Dame Sans Merci, she finds Juliet or Tess or Salomé, but precisely what she does not find is that absorbed, drudging, puzzled, sometimes inspired creature, herself, who sits at a desk trying to put words together.

So what does she do? What did I do? I read the older women poets with their peculiar keenness and ambivalence: Sappho, Christina Rossetti, Emily Dickinson, Elinor Wylie, Edna Millay, H. D. I discovered that the woman poet most admired at the time (by men) was Marianne Moore, who was maidenly, elegant, intellectual, discreet. But even in reading these women I was looking in them for the same things I had found in the poetry of men, because I wanted women poets to be the equals of men, and to be equal was still confused with sounding the same.

I know that my style was formed first by male poets: by the men I was reading as an undergraduate—Frost, Dylan Thomas, Donne, Auden, MacNeice, Stevens, Yeats. What I chiefly learned from them was craft.[6] But poems are like dreams: in them you put what you don't know you know. Looking back at poems I wrote before I was twenty-one, I'm startled because beneath the conscious craft are glimpses of the split I even then experienced between the girl who wrote poems, who defined herself in writing poems, and the girl who was to define herself by her relationships with men. "Aunt Jennifer's Tigers" (1951), written while I was a student, looks with deliberate detachment at this split.

> Aunt Jennifer's tigers stride across a screen,
> Bright topaz denizens of a world of green.
> They do not fear the men beneath the tree;
> They pace in sleek chivalric certainty.
>
> Aunt Jennifer's fingers fluttering through her wool
> Find even the ivory needle hard to pull.
> The massive weight of Uncle's wedding band
> Sits heavily upon Aunt Jennifer's hand.
>
> When Aunt is dead, her terrified hands will lie
> Still ringed with ordeals she was mastered by.
> The tigers in the panel that she made
> Will go on striding, proud and unafraid.

In writing this poem, composed and apparently cool as it is, I thought I was creating a portrait of an imaginary woman. But this woman suffers from the opposition of her imagination, worked out in tapestry, and her lifestyle, "ringed with ordeals she was mastered by." It was important to me that Aunt Jennifer was a person as distinct from myself as possible—distanced by the formalism of the poem, by its objective, observant tone—even by putting the woman in a different generation.

In those years formalism was part of the strategy—like asbestos gloves, it allowed me to handle materials I couldn't pick up barehanded. A later strategy was to use the persona of a man, as I did in "The Loser" (1958):

> *A man thinks of the woman he once loved:*
> *first, after her wedding, and then nearly a*
> *decade later.*
>
> I
> I kissed you, bride and lost, and went
> home from that bourgeois sacrament,

your cheek still tasting cold upon
my lips that gave you benison
with all the swagger that they knew—
as losers somehow learn to do.

Your wedding made my eyes ache; soon
the world would be worse off for one
more golden apple dropped to ground
without the least protesting sound,
and you would windfall lie, and we
forget your shimmer on the tree.

Beauty is always wasted: if
not Mignon's song sung to the deaf,
at all events to the unmoved.
A face like yours cannot be loved
long or seriously enough.
Almost, we seem to hold it off.

II

Well, you are tougher than I thought.
Now when the wash with ice hangs taut
this morning of St. Valentine,
I see you strip the squeaking line,
your body weighed against the load,
and all my groans can do no good.

Because you still are beautiful,
though squared and stiffened by the pull
of what nine windy years have done.
You have three daughters, lost a son.
I see all your intelligence
flung into that unwearied stance.

My envy is of no avail.
I turn my head and wish him well
who chafed your beauty into use
and lives forever in a house
lit by the friction of your mind.
You stagger in against the wind.

I finished college, published my first book by a fluke, as it seemed to me, and broke off a love affair. I took a job, lived alone, went on writing, fell in love. I was young, full of energy, and the book seemed to mean that others agreed I was a poet. Because I was also determined to prove that as a woman poet I could also have what was then defined as a "full" woman's life, I plunged in my early twenties into marriage and had three children before I was thirty. There was nothing overt in the environment to warn me: these were the fifties, and in reaction to the earlier wave of feminism, middle-class women were making careers of domestic perfection, working to send their husbands through professional schools, then retiring to raise large families. People were moving out to the suburbs, technology was going to be the answer to everything, even sex; the family was in its glory. Life was extremely private; women were isolated from each other by the loyalties of marriage. I have a sense that women didn't talk to each other much in the fifties—not about their secret emptinesses, their frustrations. I went on trying to write; my second book and first child appeared in the same month. But by the time that book came out I was already dissatisfied with those poems, which seemed to me mere exercises for poems I hadn't written. The book was praised, however, for its "gracefulness"; I had a marriage and a child. If there were doubts, if there were periods of null depression or active despairing, these could only mean that I was ungrateful, insatiable, perhaps a monster.

About the time my third child was born, I felt that I had either to consider myself a failed woman and a failed poet, or to try to find some synthesis by which to understand what was happening to me. What frightened me most was the sense of drift, of being pulled along a current which called itself my destiny, but in which I seemed to be losing touch with whoever I had been, with the girl who had experienced her own will and energy almost ecstatically at times, walking around a city or riding a train at night or typing in a student room. In a poem about my grandmother I wrote (of myself): "A young girl, thought sleeping, is certified dead" "Halfway"). I was writing very little, partly from fatigue, that female fatigue of suppressed anger and loss of contact with my own being; partly from the discontinuity of female life with its attention to small chores, errands, work that others constantly undo, small children's constant needs. What I did write was unconvincing to me; my anger and frustration were hard to acknowledge in or out of poems because in fact I cared a great deal about my husband and my children. Trying to look back and understand that time I have tried to analyze the real nature of the conflict. Most, if not all, human lives are full of fantasy—passive day-dreaming which need not be acted on. But to write poetry or fiction, or even to think well, is not to fantasize, or to put fantasies on paper. For a poem to coalesce, for a character or an action to take shape, there has to be an imaginative transformation of reality which is in no way passive. And a certain freedom of the mind is needed—freedom to press on, to enter the currents of your thought like a glider pilot, knowing that your motion can be sustained, that the buoyancy of your attention will not be suddenly snatched away. Moreover, if the imagination is to transcend and transform experience it has to question, to challenge, to conceive of alternatives, perhaps to the very life you are living at that moment. You have to be free to play around with the notion that day might be night, love might be hate; nothing can be too sacred for the imagination to turn into its opposite or to call experimentally by another name. For writing is renaming. Now, to be maternally with small children all day in the old way, to be with a man in the old way of marriage, requires a holding-back, a putting-aside of that imaginative activity, and demands instead a kind of conservatism. I want to make it clear that I am *not* saying that in order to write well, or think

well, it is necessary to become unavailable to others, or to become a devouring ego. This has been the myth of the masculine artist and thinker;
and I do not accept it. But to be a female human being trying to fulfill traditional female functions in a traditional way *is* in direct conflict with the
subversive function of the imagination. The word traditional is important
here. There must be ways, and we will be finding out more and more
about them, in which the energy of creation and the energy of relation can
be united. But in those years I always felt the conflict as a failure of love in
myself. I had thought I was choosing a full life; the life available to most
men, in which sexuality, work, and parenthood could coexist. But I felt, at
twenty-nine, guilt toward the people closest to me, and guilty toward my
own being.

I wanted, then, more than anything, the one thing of which there was
never enough: time to think, time to write. The fifties and early sixties
were years of rapid revelations: the sit-ins and marches in the South, the
Bay of Pigs, the early antiwar movement, raised large questions—questions for which the masculine world of the academy around me seemed to
have expert and fluent answers. But I needed to think for myself—about
pacifism and dissent and violence, about poetry and society, and about
my own relationship to all these things. For about ten years I was reading
in fierce snatches, scribbling in notebooks, writing poetry in fragments; I
was looking desperately for clues, because if there were no clues then I
thought I might be insane. I wrote in a notebook about this time:

> Paralyzed by the sense that there exists a mesh of relation-
> ships—e.g., between my anger at the children, my sensual life,
> pacifism, sex (I mean sex in its broadest significance, not
> merely sexual desire)—an interconnectedness which, if I could
> see it, make it valid, would give me back myself, make it pos-
> sible to function lucidly and passionately. Yet I grope in and
> out among these dark webs.

I think I began at this point to feel that politics was not something "out
there" but something "in here" and of the essence of my condition.

In the late fifties I was able to write, for the first time, directly about experiencing myself as a woman. The poem was jotted in fragments during children's naps, brief hours in a library, or at 3:00 A.M. after rising with a wakeful
child. I despaired of doing any continuous work at this time. Yet I began to
feel that my fragments and scraps had a common consciousness and a common theme, one which I would have been very unwilling to put on paper at
an earlier time because I had been taught that poetry should be "universal,"
which meant, of course, nonfemale. Until then I had tried very much *not* to
identify myself as a female poet. Over two years I wrote a ten-part poem
called "Snapshots of a Daughter-in-Law" (1958–1960), in a longer looser
mode than I'd ever trusted myself with before. It was an extraordinary relief
to write that poem. It strikes me now as too literary, too dependent on allusion; I hadn't found the courage yet to do without authorities, or even to use

the pronoun "I"—the woman in the poem is always "she." One section of it,
No. 2, concerns a woman who thinks she is going mad; she is haunted by
voices telling her to resist and rebel, voices which she can hear but not obey.

> 2.
> Banging the coffee-pot into the sink
> she hears the angels chiding, and looks out
> past the raked gardens to the sloppy sky.
> Only a week since They said: *Have no patience.*
>
> The next time it was: *Be insatiable.*
> Then: *Save yourself; others you cannot save.*
> Sometimes she's let the tapstream scald her arm,
> a match burn to her thumbnail,
>
> or held her hand above the kettle's snout
> right in the woolly steam. They are probably angels,
> since nothing hurts her anymore, except
> each morning's grit blowing into her eyes.

The poem "Orion," written five years later, is a poem of reconnection
with a part of myself I had felt I was losing—the active principle, the energetic imagination, the "half-brother" whom I projected, as I had for many
years, into the constellation Orion. It's no accident that the words "cold
and egotistical" appear in this poem, and are applied to myself.

> Far back when I went zig-zagging
> through tamarack pastures
> you were my genius, you
> my cast-iron Viking, my helmed
> lion-heart king in prison.
> Years later now you're young
>
> my fierce half-brother, staring
> down from that simplified west
> your breast open, your belt dragged down
> by an oldfashioned thing, a sword
> the last bravado you won't give over
> though it weighs you down as you stride
>
> and the stars in it are dim
> and maybe have stopped burning.
> But you burn, and I know it;
> as I throw back my head to take you in
> an old transfusion happens again:
> divine astronomy is nothing to it.
>
> Indoors I bruise and blunder,
> break faith, leave ill enough
> alone, a dead child born in the dark.
> Night cracks up over the chimney,
> pieces of time, frozen geodes
> come showering down in the grate.

> A man reaches behind my eyes
> and finds them empty
> a woman's head turns away
> from my head in the mirror
> children are dying my death
> and eating crumbs of my life.
>
> Pity is not your forte.
> Calmly you ache up there
> pinned aloft in your crow's nest,
> my speechless pirate!
> You take it all for granted
> and when I look you back
>
> it's with a starlike eye
> shooting its cold and egotistical spear
> where it can do least damage.
> Breathe deep! No hurt, no pardon
> out here in the cold with you
> you with your back to the wall.

The choice still seemed to be between "love"—womanly, maternal love, altruistic love—a love defined and ruled by the weight of an entire culture; and egotism—a force directed by men into creation, achievement, ambition, often at the expense of others, but justifiably so. For weren't they men, and wasn't that their destiny as womanly, selfless love was ours? We know now that the alternatives are false ones—that the word "love" is itself in need of re-vision.

There is a companion poem to "Orion," written three years later, in which at last the woman in the poem and the woman writing the poem become the same person. It is called "Planetarium," and it was written after a visit to a real planetarium, where I read an account of the work of Caroline Herschel, the astronomer, who worked with her brother William, but whose name remained obscure, as his did not.

> *Thinking of Caroline Herschel, 1750–1848,*
> *astronomer, sister of William; and others*
>
> A woman in the shape of a monster
> a monster in the shape of a woman
> the skies are full of them
>
> a woman      'in the snow
> among the Clocks and instruments
> or measuring the ground with poles'
>
> in her 98 years to discover
> 8 comets
>
> she whom the moon ruled
> like us
> levitating into the night sky
> riding the polished lenses

Galaxies of women, there
doing penance for impetuousness
ribs chilled
in those spaces        of the mind

An eye,

  'virile, precise and absolutely certain'
from the mad webs of Uranusborg

                    encountering the NOVA

every impulse of light exploding
from the core
as life flies out of us

        Tycho whispering at last
        'Let me not seem to have lived in vain'

What we see, we see
and seeing is changing

the light that shrivels a mountain
and leaves a man alive

Heartbeat of the pulsar
heart sweating through my body

The radio impulse
pouring in from Taurus

        I am bombarded yet        I stand

I have been standing all my life in the
direct path of a battery of signals
the most accurately transmitted most
untranslateable language in the universe
I am a galactic cloud so deep        so invo-
luted that a light wave could take 15
years to travel through me        And has
taken        I am an instrument in the shape
of a woman trying to translate pulsations
into images        for the relief of the body
and the reconstruction of the mind.

In closing I want to tell you about a dream I had last summer. I dreamed
I was asked to read my poetry at a mass women's meeting, but when I
began to read, what came out were the lyrics of a blues song. I share this
dream with you because it seemed to me to say something about the problems and the future of the woman writer, and probably of women in general. The awakening of consciousness is not like the crossing of a frontier—
one step and you are in another country. Much of woman's poetry has been
of the nature of the blues song: a cry of pain, of victimization, or a lyric of seduction.[7] And today, much poetry by women—and prose for that matter—

is charged with anger. I think we need to go through that anger, and we will betray our own reality if we try, as Virginia Woolf was trying, for an objectivity, a detachment, that would make us sound more like Jane Austen or Shakespeare. We know more than Jane Austen or Shakespeare knew: more than Jane Austen because our lives are more complex, more than Shakespeare because we know more about the lives of women—Jane Austen and Virginia Woolf included.

Both the victimization and the anger experienced by women are real, and have real sources, everywhere in the environment, built into society, language, the structures of thought. They will go on being trapped and explored by poets, among others. We can neither deny them, nor will we rest there. A new generation of women poets is already working out of the psychic energy released when women begin to move out towards what the feminist philosopher Mary Daly has described as the "new space" on the boundaries of patriarchy.[8] Women are speaking to and of women in these poems, out of a newly released courage to name, to love each other, to share risk and grief and celebration.

To the eye of a feminist, the work of Western male poets now writing reveals a deep, fatalistic pessimism as to the possibilities of change, whether societal or personal, along with a familiar and threadbare use of women (and nature) as redemptive on the one hand, threatening on the other; and a new tide of phallocentric sadism and overt woman-hating which matches the sexual brutality of recent films. "Political" poetry by men remains stranded amid the struggles for power among male groups; in condemning U.S. imperialism or the Chilean junta the poet can claim to speak for the oppressed while remaining, as male, part of a system of sexual oppression. The enemy is always outside the self, the struggle somewhere else. The mood of isolation, self-pity, and self-imitation that pervades "nonpolitical" poetry suggests that a profound change in masculine consciousness will have to precede any new male poetic—or other—inspiration. The creative energy of patriarchy is fast running out; what remains is its self-generating energy for destruction. As women, we have our work cut out for us.

NOTES

[1] Mary Daly, *Beyond God the Father* (Boston: Beacon, 1973), pp. 40–41.

[2] G. B. Shaw, *The Quintessence of Ibsenism* (New York: Hill & Wang, 1922), p. 139.

[3] J. G. Stewart, *Jane Ellen Harrison: A Portrait from Letters* (London: Merlin, 1959), p. 140.

[4] Henry James, "Notes on Novelists," in *Selected Literary Criticism of Henry James,* Morris Shapira, ed. (London: Heinemann, 1963), pp. 157–58.

[5] *A. R., 1978:* This intuition of mine was corroborated when, early in 1978, I read the correspondence between Woolf and Dame Ethel Smyth (Henry W. and Albert A. Berg Collection, The New York Public Library, Astor, Lenox and Tilden Foundations); in a letter dated June 8, 1933, Woolf speaks of having kept her own personality out of *A Room of One's Own* lest she not be taken seriously: ". . . how personal, so will they say,

rubbing their hands with glee, women always are; *I even hear them as I write.*" (Italics mine.)

[6] *A. R., 1978:* Yet I spent months, at sixteen, memorizing and writing imitations of Millay's sonnets; and in notebooks of that period I find what are obviously attempts to imitate Dickinson's metrics and verbal compression. I knew H. D. only through anthologized lyrics; her epic poetry was not then available to me.

[7] *A. R., 1978:* When I dreamed that dream, was I wholly ignorant of the tradition of Bessie Smith and other women's blues lyrics which transcended victimization to sing of resistance and independence?

[8] Mary Daly, *Beyond God the Father: Towards a Philosophy of Women's Liberation* (Boston: Beacon, 1973).

● ● ● ● ● ● ● ● ● ● ● ●

## QUESTIONS FOR A SECOND READING

1. Rich says, "We need to know the writing of the past, and know it differently than we have ever known it; not to pass on a tradition but to break its hold over us." In what ways does this essay, as an example of a woman writing, both reproduce and revise the genre? As she is writing here, what does Rich *do* with the writing of the past—with the conventions of the essay or the public lecture? As you reread the essay, mark sections that illustrate the ways Rich is either reproducing or revising the conventions of the essay or the public lecture. Where and how does she revise the genre? Where and how does she not? Where does Rich resist tradition? Where does she conform? How might you account for the differences?

2. It is a rare pleasure to hear a poet talk in detail about her work. As you read back through the essay, pay particular attention to what Rich notices in her poems. What *does* she notice? What does she say about what she notices? What does this allow you to say about poems or the making of poems? What does it allow you to say about the responsibilities of a reader?

3. As Rich writes her essay, she refers to a number of literary figures like Morgan, Lytton, and Maynard Keynes, Lucy and Lenore and Maude Gonne, and Plath, Bishop, and Wakoski. Reading through her essay again, make a complete list of the names Rich draws into her discussion. Who are these people? To answer this question you will need to do some library investigation checking such sources as a biographical index, *Who's Who,* and literary texts, or consulting with a reference librarian on how to find such information.

   Once you've identified the names on your list, the next question to consider is how this knowledge influences your reading of Rich. What does each individual represent that merits her or his inclusion? To answer this question you will need to have located and read through at least one text by the individuals—one "primary source," that is—or one text about the individuals—a "secondary source"—you are researching. Why might

Rich have chosen to include particular references at particular moments? What differences do they make in her arguments? in your reading of her arguments?


### ASSIGNMENTS FOR WRITING

1. Rich says,

   > For a poem to coalesce, for a character or an action to take shape, there has to be an imaginative transformation of reality which is in no way passive. . . . Moreover, if the imagination is to transcend and transform experience it has to question, to challenge, to conceive of alternatives, perhaps to the very life you are living at that moment. You have to be free to play around with the notion that day might be night, love might be hate; nothing can be too sacred for the imagination to turn into its opposite or to call experimentally by another name. For writing is re-naming. (p. 610)

   This is powerful language, and it is interesting to imagine how it might work for a person trying to read and understand one of Rich's poems. For this assignment, begin with a close reading of the quotation from Rich: What is your understanding of her term "imaginative transformation"? What does it allow a writer to do? And why might that be important? Then, as a way of testing Rich's term and your reading of it, choose one of the poems Rich includes in the essay and write an essay of your own that considers the poem as an act of "imaginative transformation." What is transformed into what? and to what end? or to what consequence? What can you say about the poem as an act of "renaming"? as a form of political action?

2. In "When We Dead Awaken: Writing as Re-Vision," Rich chooses five of her poems to represent stages in her history as a poet; however, it is a history not charted entirely (or mostly) by conscious decisions on her part as she tells us when she writes: "poems are like dreams: in them you put what you don't know you know." It is through the act of "re-vision"—of entering the old text of her poems from a new critical direction—that patterns in her work as a writer begin to emerge.

   Write an essay in which you explore Rich's term—"re-vision"—by describing what you consider to be a significant pattern of change in Rich's poems. As you do this work, you will want to attend closely to and quote from the language of her poems and what she has to say about them. You might want to consider such questions as: How does her explanation of herself as a poet inform your reading of her poems? What did she put into her poems that she didn't yet know on a conscious level? What does her poetry reveal about the evolution of Rich as a poet? as a woman?

3. > I have hesitated to do what I am going to do now, which is to use myself as an illustration. For one thing, it's a lot easier and less dangerous to talk about other[s]. (p. 606)

   > Until we can understand the assumptions in which we are drenched we cannot know ourselves. (p. 604)

Although Rich tells a story of her own, she does so to provide an illustration of an even larger story—one about what it means to be a woman and a writer. Tell a story of your own about the ways you might be said to have been named or shaped or positioned by an established and powerful culture. Like Rich does (and perhaps with similar hesitation), use your own experience as an illustration, as a way of investigating both your own situation and the situation of people like you. You should imagine that this assignment is a way for you to use (and put to the test) some of Rich's terms, words like "re-vision," "renaming," and "structure." You might also want to consider defining key terms specific to your story (for Rich, for example, a defining term is "patriarchy").

4. Rich says, "We need to know the writing of the past, and know it differently than we have ever known it; not to pass on a tradition but to break its hold over us." That "us" includes you too. Look back over your own writing (perhaps the drafts and revisions you have written for this course), and think back over comments teachers have made, textbooks you've seen; think about what student writers do and what they are told to do, about the secrets students keep and the secrets teachers keep. You can assume, as Rich does, that there are ways of speaking about writing that are part of the culture of schooling and that they are designed to preserve certain ways of writing and thinking and to discourage others.

   One might argue, in other words, that there are traditions here. As you look at the evidence of the "past" in your own work, what are its significant features? What might you name this tradition (or these traditions)? How would you illustrate its hold on your work or the work of students generally? What might you have to do to begin to "know it differently," "to break its hold," or to revise? And, finally, why would someone want (or not want) to break its hold?

## MAKING CONNECTIONS

1. There are striking parallels between Rich's essay and Virginia Woolf's "A Room of One's Own" (p. 750) but also some striking differences. If you think of Rich's essay as a revision of Woolf's—that is, if you imagine that Rich had, for whatever reason, rewriten Woolf's essay for her own time and her own purposes—what would you notice in the differences between the two essays and what might you say about what you notice? Write an essay in which you discuss "When We Dead Awaken" as a demonstration of Rich's efforts to reread and rewrite the writing of the past.

2. Susan Bordo (p. 138), Carolyn Steedman (p. 643), and Gloria Anzaldúa (p. 21) all make strong statements about the situation of women—in relation to the past, to language, politics, and culture. The essays have certain similarities, but it is also interesting to consider their differences and what these differences might be said to represent. Choose one selection to compare with "When We Dead Awaken," read the two together, marking passages you might use in a discussion, and write an essay in which you examine the interesting differences between these essays. Consider the es-

says as different forms or schools of feminist thought, different ways of thinking critically about the situations of women. Assume that there is more to say than "different people have different opinions," or "different people write about different subjects." How else might you account for these differences? their significance?

# RICHARD
# RODRIGUEZ

*R*ICHARD RODRIGUEZ, *the son of Mexican immigrants, was born in San Francisco in 1944. He grew up in Sacramento, where he attended Catholic schools before going on to Stanford University, Columbia University, the Warburg Institute in London, and the University of California at Berkeley, eventually completing a Ph.D. in English Renaissance literature. His essays have been published in* Saturday Review, The American Scholar, Change, *and elsewhere. He now lives in San Francisco and works as a lecturer, educational consultant, and freelance writer. He has published several books:* Days of Obligation: An Argument with My Mexican Father *(1992),* The Ethics of Change *(1992), and* Hunger of Memory *(1981).*

*In* Hunger of Memory, *a book of autobiographical essays that the* Christian Science Monitor *called "beautifully written, wrung from a sore heart," Rodriguez tells the story of his education, paying particular attention to both the meaning of his success as a student and, as he says, "its consequent price—the loss." Rodriguez's loss is represented most powerfully by his increased alienation from his parents and the decrease of intimate exchanges in family life. His parents' primary language was Spanish; his, once he became eager for success in school, was English. But the barrier was not only a language barrier. Rodriguez discovered that the interests he developed at school and through his reading were interests he did not share with those at home—in fact, his desire to speak of them tended to threaten and humiliate his mother and father.*

*This separation, Rodriguez argues, is a necessary part of every person's development, even though not everyone experiences it so dramatically. We must leave home and familiar ways of speaking and understanding in order to participate in public life. On these grounds, Rodriguez has been a strong voice against bilingual education, arguing that classes conducted in Spanish will only reinforce Spanish-speaking students' separateness from mainstream American life. Rodriguez's book caused a great deal of controversy upon publication, particularly in the Hispanic community. As one critic argued, "It is indeed painful that Mr. Rodriguez has come to identify himself so completely with the majority culture that he must propagandize for a system of education which can only produce other deprived and impoverished souls like himself."*

*The selection that follows, Chapter 2 of* Hunger of Memory, *deals with Rodriguez's experiences in school. "If," he says, "because of my schooling I had grown culturally separated from my parents, my education finally had given me ways of speaking and caring about that fact." This essay is a record of how he came to understand the changes in his life. A reviewer writing in the* Atlantic Monthly *concluded that* Hunger of Memory *will survive in our literature "not because of some forgotten public issues that once bisected Richard Rodriguez's life, but because his history of that life has something to say about what it means to be American . . . and what it means to be human."*

# The Achievement of Desire

I stand in the ghetto classroom—"the guest speaker"—attempting to lecture on the mystery of the sounds of our words to rows of diffident students. "Don't you hear it? Listen! The music of our words. *'Sumer is icumen in. . . .'* And songs on the car radio. We need Aretha Franklin's voice to fill plain words with music—her life." In the face of their empty stares, I try to create an enthusiasm. But the girls in the back row turn to watch some boy passing outside. There are flutters of smiles, waves. And someone's mouth elongates heavy, silent words through the barrier of glass. Silent words—the lips straining to shape each voiceless syllable: *"Meet meee late errr."* By the door, the instructor smiles at me, apparently hoping that I will be able to spark some enthusiasm in the class. But only one student seems to be listening. A girl, maybe fourteen. In this gray room her eyes shine with ambition. She keeps nodding and nodding at all that I say; she even takes notes. And each time I ask a question, she jerks up and down in her desk like a marionette, while her hand waves over the bowed heads of her classmates. It is myself (as a boy) I see as she faces me now (a man in my thirties).

The boy who first entered a classroom barely able to speak English, twenty years later concluded his studies in the stately quiet of the reading room in the British Museum. Thus with one sentence I can summarize my academic career. It will be harder to summarize what sort of life connects the boy to the man.

With every award, each graduation from one level of education to the next, people I'd meet would congratulate me. Their refrain [was] always the same: "Your parents must be very proud." Sometimes then they'd ask me how I managed it—my "success." (How?) After a while, I had several quick answers to give in reply. I'd admit, for one thing, that I went to an excellent grammar school. (My earliest teachers, the nuns, made my success their ambition.) And my brother and both my sisters were very good students. (They often brought home the shiny school trophies I came to want.) And my mother and father always encouraged me. (At every graduation they were behind the stunning flash of the camera when I turned to look at the crowd.)

As important as these factors were, however, they account inadequately for my academic advance. Nor do they suggest what an odd success I managed. For although I was a very good student, I was also a very bad student. I was a "scholarship boy," a certain kind of scholarship boy. Always successful, I was always unconfident. Exhilarated by my progress. Sad. I became the prized student—anxious and eager to learn. Too eager, too anxious—an imitative and unoriginal pupil. My brother and two sisters enjoyed the advantages I did, and they grew to be as successful as I, but none of them ever seemed so anxious about their schooling. A second-grade student, I was the one who came home and corrected the "simple" grammatical mistakes of our parents. ("Two negatives make a positive.") Proudly I announced—to my family's startled silence—that a teacher had said I was losing all trace of a Spanish accent. I was oddly annoyed when I was unable to get parental help with a homework assignment. The night my father tried to help me with an arithmetic exercise, he kept reading the instructions, each time more deliberately, until I pried the textbook out of his hands, saying, "I'll try to figure it out some more by myself."

When I reached the third grade, I outgrew such behavior. I became more tactful, careful to keep separate the two very different worlds of my day. But then, with ever-increasing intensity, I devoted myself to my studies. I became bookish, puzzling to all my family. Ambition set me apart. When my brother saw me struggling home with stacks of library books, he would laugh, shouting: "Hey, Four Eyes!" My father opened a closet one day and was startled to find me inside, reading a novel. My mother would find me reading when I was supposed to be asleep or helping around the house or playing outside. In a voice angry or worried or just curious, she'd ask: "What do you see in your books?" It became the family's joke. When I was called and wouldn't reply, someone would say I must be hiding under my bed with a book.

(How did I manage my success?)

What I am about to say to you has taken me more than twenty years to admit: *A primary reason for my success in the classroom was that I couldn't forget that schooling was changing me and separating me from the life I enjoyed before becoming a student.* That simple realization! For years I never spoke to anyone about it. Never mentioned a thing to my family or my teachers or classmates. From a very early age, I understood enough, just enough about my classroom experiences to keep what I knew repressed, hidden beneath layers of embarrassment. Not until my last months as a graduate student, nearly thirty years old, was it possible for me to think much about the reasons for my academic success. Only then. At the end of my schooling, I needed to determine how far I had moved from my past. The adult finally confronted, and now must publicly say, what the child shuddered from knowing and could never admit to himself or to those many faces that smiled at his every success. ("Your parents must be very proud. . . .")

## *I*

At the end, in the British Museum (too distracted to finish my dissertation) for weeks I read, speed-read, books by modern educational theorists, only to find infrequent and slight mention of students like me. (Much more is written about the more typical case, the lower-class student who barely is helped by his schooling.) Then one day, leafing through Richard Hoggart's *The Uses of Literacy*, I found, in his description of the scholarship boy, myself. For the first time I realized that there were other students like me, and so I was able to frame the meaning of my academic success, its consequent price—the loss.

Hoggart's description is distinguished, at least initially, by deep understanding. What he grasps very well is that the scholarship boy must move between environments, his home and the classroom, which are at cultural extremes, opposed. With his family, the boy has the intense pleasure of intimacy, the family's consolation in feeling public alienation. Lavish emotions texture home life. *Then*, at school, the instruction bids him to trust lonely reason primarily. Immediate needs set the pace of his parents' lives. From his mother and father the boy learns to trust spontaneity and nonrational ways of knowing. *Then*, at school, there is mental calm. Teachers emphasize the value of a reflectiveness that opens a space between thinking and immediate action.

Years of schooling must pass before the boy will be able to sketch the cultural differences in his day as abstractly as this. But he senses those differences early. Perhaps as early as the night he brings home an assignment from school and finds the house too noisy for study.

> He has to be more and more alone, if he is going to "get on."
> He will have, probably unconsciously, to oppose the ethos of
> the hearth, the intense gregariousness of the working-class

> family group. Since everything centres upon the living-room,
> there is unlikely to be a room of his own; the bedrooms are cold
> and inhospitable, and to warm them or the front room, if there
> is one, would not only be expensive, but would require an
> imaginative leap—out of the tradition—which most families
> are not capable of making. There is a corner of the living-room
> table. On the other side Mother is ironing, the wireless is on,
> someone is singing a snatch of song or Father says intermit-
> tently whatever comes into his head. The boy has to cut himself
> off mentally, so as to do his homework, as well as he can.[1]

The next day, the lesson is as apparent at school. There are even rows of
desks. Discussion is ordered. The boy must rehearse his thoughts and
raise his hand before speaking out in a loud voice to an audience of classmates. And there is time enough, and silence, to think about ideas (big
ideas) never considered at home by his parents.

Not for the working-class child alone is adjustment to the classroom
difficult. Good schooling requires that any student alter early childhood
habits. But the working-class child is usually least prepared for the
change. And, unlike many middle-class children, he goes home and sees
in his parents a way of life not only different but starkly opposed to that of
the classroom. (He enters the house and hears his parents talking in ways
his teachers discourage.)

Without extraordinary determination and the great assistance of others—at home and at school—there is little chance for success. Typically
most working-class children are barely changed by the classroom. The exception succeeds. The relative few become scholarship students. Of these,
Richard Hoggart estimates, most manage a fairly graceful transition.
Somehow they learn to live in the two very different worlds of their day.
There are some others, however, those Hoggart pejoratively terms "scholarship boys," for whom success comes with special anxiety. Scholarship
boy: good student, troubled son. The child is "moderately endowed," intellectually mediocre, Hoggart supposes—though it may be more pertinent to note the special qualities of temperament in the child. High-strung
child. Brooding. Sensitive. Haunted by the knowledge that one *chooses* to
become a student. (Education is not an inevitable or natural step in growing up.) Here is a child who cannot forget that his academic success distances him from a life he loved, even from his own memory of himself.

Initially, he wavers, balances allegiance. ("The boy is himself [until he
reaches, say, the upper forms] very much of *both* the worlds of home and
school. He is enormously obedient to the dictates of the world of school,
but emotionally still strongly wants to continue as part of the family
circle.") Gradually, necessarily, the balance is lost. The boy needs to spend
more and more time studying, each night enclosing himself in the silence
permitted and required by intense concentration. He takes his first step toward academic success, away from his family.

From the very first days, through the years following, it will be with his parents—the figures of lost authority, the persons toward whom he feels deepest love—that the change will be most powerfully measured. A separation will unravel between them. Advancing in his studies, the boy notices that his mother and father have not changed as much as he. Rather, when he sees them, they often remind him of the person he once was and the life he earlier shared with them. He realizes what some Romantics also know when they praise the working class for the capacity for human closeness, qualities of passion and spontaneity, that the rest of us experience in like measure only in the earliest part of our youth. For the Romantic, this doesn't make working-class life childish. Working-class life challenges precisely because it is an *adult* way of life.

The scholarship boy reaches a different conclusion. He cannot afford to admire his parents. (How could he and still pursue such a contrary life?) He permits himself embarrassment at their lack of education. And to evade nostalgia for the life he has lost, he concentrates on the benefits education will bestow upon him. He becomes especially ambitious. Without the support of old certainties and consolations, almost mechanically, he assumes the procedures and doctrines of the classroom. The kind of allegiance the young student might have given his mother and father only days earlier, he transfers to the teacher, the new figure of authority. "[The scholarship boy] tends to make a father-figure of his form-master," Hoggart observes.

But Hoggart's calm prose only makes me recall the urgency with which I came to idolize my grammar school teachers. I began by imitating their accents, using their diction, trusting their every direction. The very first facts they dispensed, I grasped with awe. Any book they told me to read, I read—then waited for them to tell me which books I enjoyed. Their every casual opinion I came to adopt and to trumpet when I returned home. I stayed after school "to help"—to get my teacher's undivided attention. It was the nun's encouragement that mattered most to me. (She understood exactly what—my parents never seemed to appraise so well—all my achievements entailed.) Memory gently caressed each word of praise bestowed in the classroom so that compliments teachers paid me years ago come quickly to mind even today.

The enthusiasm I felt in second-grade classes I flaunted before both my parents. The docile, obedient student came home a shrill and precocious son who insisted on correcting and teaching his parents with the remark: "My teacher told us. . . ."

I intended to hurt my mother and father. I was still angry at them for having encouraged me toward classroom English. But gradually this anger was exhausted, replaced by guilt as school grew more and more attractive to me. I grew increasingly successful, a talkative student. My hand was raised in the classroom; I yearned to answer any question. At home, life was less noisy than it had been. (I spoke to classmates and teachers more often each day than to family members.) Quiet at home, I sat with my papers for hours each night. I never forgot that schooling had irretrievably changed my family's life. That knowledge, however, did not weaken ambition. Instead, it strengthened resolve. Those times I remembered the loss of my past with regret, I quickly reminded myself of all the things my teachers could give me. (They could make me an educated man.) I tightened my grip on pencil and books. I evaded nostalgia. Tried hard to forget. But one does not forget by trying to forget. One only remembers. I remembered too well that education had changed my family's life. I would not have become a scholarship boy had I not so often remembered.

Once she was sure that her children knew English, my mother would tell us, "You should keep up your Spanish." Voices playfully groaned in response. "¡Pochos!" my mother would tease. I listened silently.

After a while, I grew more calm at home. I developed tact. A fourth-grade student, I was no longer the show-off in front of my parents. I became a conventionally dutiful son, politely affectionate, cheerful enough, even—for reasons beyond choosing—my father's favorite. And much about my family life was easy then, comfortable, happy in the rhythm of our living together: hearing my father getting ready for work; eating the breakfast my mother had made me; looking up from a novel to hear my brother or one of my sisters playing with friends in the backyard; in winter, coming upon the house all lighted up after dark.

But withheld from my mother and father was any mention of what most mattered to me: the extraordinary experience of first-learning. Late afternoon: in the midst of preparing dinner, my mother would come up behind me while I was trying to read. Her head just over mine, her breath warmly scented with food. "What are you reading?" Or, "Tell me all about your new courses." I would barely respond, "Just the usual things, nothing special." (A half smile, then silence. Her head moving back in the silence. Silence! Instead of the flood of intimate sounds that had once flowed smoothly between us, there was this silence.) After dinner, I would rush to a bedroom with papers and books. As often as possible, I resisted parental pleas to "save lights" by coming to the kitchen to work. I kept so much, so often, to myself. Sad. Enthusiastic. Troubled by the excitement of coming upon new ideas. Eager. Fascinated by the promising texture of a brand-new book. I hoarded the pleasures of learning. Alone for hours. Enthralled. Nervous. I rarely looked away from my books—or back on my memories. Nights when relatives visited and the front rooms were warmed by Spanish sounds, I slipped quietly out of the house.

It mattered that education was changing me. It never ceased to matter. My brother and sisters would giggle at our mother's mispronounced words. They'd correct her gently. My mother laughed girlishly one night, trying not to pronounce *sheep* as *ship*. From a distance I listened sullenly. From that distance, pretending not to notice on another occasion, I saw my father looking at the title pages of my library books. That was the scene on my mind when I walked home with a fourth-grade companion and heard him say that his parents read to him every night. (A strange-sounding book—*Winnie the Pooh*.) Immediately, I wanted to know, "What is it like?" My companion, however, thought I wanted to know about the plot of the book. Another day, my mother surprised me by asking for a "nice" book to read. "Something not too hard you think I might like." Carefully I chose one, Willa Cather's *My Ántonia*. But when, several weeks later, I happened to see it next to her bed unread except for the first few pages, I was furious and suddenly wanted to cry. I grabbed up the book and took it back to my room and placed it in its place, alphabetically on my shelf.

"Your parents must be very proud of you." People began to say that to me about the time I was in sixth grade. To answer affirmatively, I'd smile. Shyly I'd smile, never betraying my sense of the irony: I was not proud of my mother and father. I was embarrassed by their lack of education. It was not that I ever thought they were stupid, though stupidly I took for granted their enormous native intelligence. Simply, what mattered to me was that they were not like my teachers.

But, "Why didn't you tell us about the award?" my mother demanded, her frown weakened by pride. At the grammar school ceremony several weeks after, her eyes were brighter than the trophy I'd won. Pushing back the hair from my forehead, she whispered that I had "shown" the *gringos*. A few minutes later, I heard my father speak to my teacher and felt ashamed of his labored, accented words. Then guilty for the shame. I felt such contrary feelings. (There is no simple road-map through the heart of the scholarship boy.) My teacher was so soft-spoken and her words were edged sharp and clean. I admired her until it seemed to me that she spoke too carefully. Sensing that she was condescending to them, I became nervous. Resentful. Protective. I tried to move my parents away. "You both must be very proud of Richard," the nun said. They responded quickly. (They were proud.) "We are proud of all our children." Then this afterthought: "They sure didn't get their brains from us." They all laughed. I smiled.

Tightening the irony into a knot was the knowledge that my parents were always behind me. They made success possible. They evened the path. They sent their children to parochial schools because the nuns "teach better." They paid a tuition they couldn't afford. They spoke English to us.

For their children my parents wanted chances they never had—an easier way. It saddened my mother to learn that some relatives forced their children to start working right after high school. To *her* children she would say, "Get all the education you can." In schooling she recognized the key to job advancement. And with the remark she remembered her past.

As a girl new to America my mother had been awarded a high school diploma by teachers too careless or busy to notice that she hardly spoke English. On her own, she determined to learn how to type. That skill got her jobs typing envelopes in letter shops, and it encouraged in her an optimism about the possibility of advancement. (Each morning when her sisters put on uniforms, she chose a bright-colored dress.) The years of young womanhood passed, and her typing speed increased. She also became an excellent speller of words she mispronounced. "And I've never been to college," she'd say, smiling, when her children asked her to spell words they were too lazy to look up in a dictionary.

Typing, however, was dead-end work. Finally frustrating. When her youngest child started high school, my mother got a full-time office job once again. (Her paycheck combined with my father's to make us—in fact—what we had already become in our imagination of ourselves—middle class.) She worked then for the (California) state government in numbered civil service positions secured by examinations. The old ambition of her youth was rekindled. During the lunch hour, she consulted bulletin boards for announcements of openings. One day she saw mention of something called an "anti-poverty agency." A typing job. A glamorous job, part of the governor's staff. "A knowledge of Spanish required." Without hesitation she applied and became nervous only when the job was suddenly hers.

"Everyone comes to work all dressed up," she reported at night. And didn't need to say more than that her co-workers wouldn't let her answer the phones. She was only a typist, after all, albeit a very fast typist. And an excellent speller. One morning there was a letter to be sent to a Washington cabinet officer. On the dictating tape, a voice referred to urban guerrillas. My mother typed (the wrong word, correctly): "gorillas." The mistake horrified the anti-poverty bureaucrats who shortly after arranged to have her returned to her previous position. She would go no further. So she willed her ambition to their children. "Get all the education you can; with an education you can do anything." (With a good education *she* could have done anything.)

When I was in high school, I admitted to my mother that I planned to become a teacher someday. That seemed to please her. But I never tried to explain that it was not the occupation of teaching I yearned for as much as it was something more elusive: I wanted to *be* like my teachers, to possess their knowledge, to assume their authority, their confidence, even to assume a teacher's persona.

In contrast to my mother, my father never verbally encouraged his children's academic success. Nor did he often praise us. My mother had to remind him to "say something" to one of his children who scored some academic success. But whereas my mother saw in education the opportunity for job advancement, my father recognized that education provided an even more startling possibility: it could enable a person to escape from a life of mere labor.

In Mexico, orphaned when he was eight, my father left school to work as an "apprentice" for an uncle. Twelve years later, he left Mexico in frustration and arrived in America. He had great expectations then of becoming an engineer. ("Work for my hands and my head.") He knew a Catholic priest who promised to get him money enough to study full time for a high school diploma. But the promises came to nothing. Instead there was a dark succession of warehouse, cannery, and factory jobs. After work he went to night school along with my mother. A year, two passed. Nothing much changed, except that fatigue worked its way into the bone; then everything changed. He didn't talk anymore of becoming an engineer. He stayed outside on the steps of the school while my mother went inside to learn typing and shorthand.

By the time I was born, my father worked at "clean" jobs. For a time he was a janitor at a fancy department store. ("Easy work; the machines do it all.") Later he became a dental technician. ("Simple.") But by then he was pessimistic about the ultimate meaning of work and the possibility of ever escaping its claims. In some of my earliest memories of him, my father already seems aged by fatigue. (He has never really grown old like my mother.) From boyhood to manhood, I have remembered him in a single image: seated, asleep on the sofa, his head thrown back in a hideous corpselike grin, the evening newspaper spread out before him. "But look at all you've accomplished," his best friend said to him once. My father said nothing. Only smiled.

It was my father who laughed when I claimed to be tired by reading and writing. It was he who teased me for having soft hands. (He seemed to sense that some great achievement of leisure was implied by my papers and books.) It was my father who became angry while watching on television some woman at the Miss America contest tell the announcer that she was going to college. ("Majoring in fine arts.") "College!" he snarled. He despised the trivialization of higher education, the inflated grades and cheapened diplomas, the half education that so often passed as mass education in my generation.

It was my father again who wondered why I didn't display my awards on the wall of my bedroom. He said he liked to go to doctors' offices and see their certificates and degrees on the wall. ("Nice.") My citations from school got left in closets at home. The gleaming figure astride one of my trophies was broken, wingless, after hitting the ground. My medals were placed in a jar of loose change. And when I lost my high school diploma, my father found it as it was about to be thrown out with the trash. Without telling me, he put it away with his own things for safekeeping.

These memories slammed together at the instant of hearing that refrain familiar to all scholarship students: "Your parents must be proud. . . ." Yes, my parents were proud. I knew it. But my parents regarded my progress with more than mere pride. They endured my early precocious behavior—but with what private anger and humiliation? As their children got older and would come home to challenge ideas both of them held, they argued before submitting to the force of logic or superior factual evidence with the disclaimer, "It's what we were taught in our

time to believe." These discussions ended abruptly, though my mother remembered them on other occasions when she complained that our "big
ideas" were going to our heads. More acute was her complaint that the
family wasn't close anymore, like some others she knew. Why weren't we
close, "more in the Mexican style"? Everyone is so private, she added.
And she mimicked the yes and no answers she got in reply to her questions. Why didn't we talk more? (My father never asked.) I never said.

I was the first in my family who asked to leave home when it came
time to go to college. I had been admitted to Stanford, one hundred miles
away. My departure would only make physically apparent the separation
that had occurred long before. But it was going too far. In the months preceding my leaving, I heard the question my mother never asked except indirectly. In the hot kitchen, tired at the end of her workday, she demanded
to know, "Why aren't the colleges here in Sacramento good enough for
you? They are for your brother and sister." In the middle of a car ride, not
turning to face me, she wondered, "Why do you need to go so far away?"
Late at night, ironing, she said with disgust, "Why do you have to put us
through this big expense? You know your scholarship will never cover it
all." But when September came there was a rush to get everything ready.
In a bedroom that last night I packed the big brown valise, and my mother
sat nearby sewing initials onto the clothes I would take. And she said no
more about my leaving.

Months later, two weeks of Christmas vacation: the first hours home
were the hardest. ("What's new?") My parents and I sat in the kitchen for
a conversation. (But, lacking the same words to develop our sentences and
to shape our interests, what was there to say? What could I tell them of the
term paper I had just finished on the "universality of Shakespeare's appeal"?) I mentioned only small, obvious things: my dormitory life; weekend trips I had taken; random events. They responded with news of their
own. (One was almost grateful for a family crisis about which there was
much to discuss.) We tried to make our conversation seem like more than
an interview.


## II

From an early age I knew that my mother and father could read and
write both Spanish and English. I had observed my father making his way
through what, I now suppose, must have been income tax forms. On other
occasions I waited apprehensively while my mother read onion-paper letters airmailed from Mexico with news of a relative's illness or death. For
both my parents, however, reading was something done out of necessity
and as quickly as possible. Never did I see either of them read an entire
book. Nor did I see them read for pleasure. Their reading consisted of
work manuals, prayer books, newspaper, recipes.

Richard Hoggart imagines how, at home,

> [the scholarship boy] sees strewn around, and reads regularly
> himself, magazines which are never mentioned at school,
> which seem not to belong to the world to which the school in-
> troduces him; at school he hears about and reads books never
> mentioned at home. When he brings those books into the house
> they do not take their place with other books which the family
> are reading, for often there are none or almost none; his books
> look, rather, like strange tools.

In our house each school year would begin with my mother's careful instruction: "Don't write in your books so we can sell them at the end of the
year." The remark was echoed in public by my teachers, but only in part:
"Boys and girls, don't write in your books. You must learn to treat them
with great care and respect."

OPEN THE DOORS OF YOUR MIND WITH BOOKS, read the red and white poster
over the nun's desk in early September. It soon was apparent to me that
reading was the classroom's central activity. Each course had its own
book. And the information gathered from a book was unquestioned. READ
TO LEARN, the sign on the wall advised in December. I privately wondered:
What was the connection between reading and learning? Did one learn
something only by reading it? Was an idea only an idea if it could be written down? In June, CONSIDER BOOKS YOUR BEST FRIENDS. Friends? Reading was,
at best, only a chore. I needed to look up whole paragraphs of words in a
dictionary. Lines of type were dizzying, the eye having to move slowly
across the page, then down, and across. . . . The sentences of the first
books I read were coolly impersonal. Toned hard. What most bothered
me, however, was the isolation reading required. To console myself for
the loneliness I'd feel when I read, I tried reading in a very soft voice.
Until: "Who is doing all that talking to his neighbor?" Shortly after, reme-
dial reading classes were arranged for me with a very old nun.

At the end of each school day, for nearly six months, I would meet
with her in the tiny room that served as the school's library but was actually only a storeroom for used textbooks and a vast collection of *National
Geographic*s. Everything about our sessions pleased me: the smallness of
the room; the noise of the janitor's broom hitting the edge of the long hallway outside the door; the green of the sun, lighting the wall; and the old
woman's face blurred white with a beard. Most of the time we took turns.
I began with my elementary text. Sentences of astonishing simplicity
seemed to me lifeless and drab: "The boys ran from the rain. . . . She
wanted to sing. . . . The kite rose in the blue." Then the old nun would
read from her favorite books, usually biographies of early American presidents. Playfully she ran through complex sentences, calling the words
alive with her voice, making it seem that the author somehow was speaking directly to me. I smiled just to listen to her. I sat there and sensed for
the very first time some possibility of fellowship between a reader and a
writer, a communication, never *intimate* like that I heard spoken words at
home convey, but one nonetheless *personal*.

One day the nun concluded a session by asking me why I was so reluctant to read by myself. I tried to explain; said something about the way written words made me feel all alone—almost, I wanted to add but didn't, as when I spoke to myself in a room just emptied of furniture. She studied my face as I spoke; she seemed to be watching more than listening. In an uneventful voice she replied that I had nothing to fear. Didn't I realize that reading would open up whole new worlds? A book could open doors for me. It could introduce me to people and show me places I never imagined existed. She gestured toward the bookshelves. (Bare-breasted African women danced, and the shiny hubcaps of automobiles on the back covers of the *Geographic* gleamed in my mind.) I listened with respect. But her words were not very influential. I was thinking then of another consequence of literacy, one I was too shy to admit but nonetheless trusted. Books were going to make me "educated." *That* confidence enabled me, several months later, to overcome my fear of the silence.

In fourth grade I embarked upon a grandiose reading program. "Give me the names of important books," I would say to startled teachers. They soon found out that I had in mind "adult books." I ignored their suggestion of anything I suspected was written for children. (Not until I was in college, as a result, did I read *Huckleberry Finn* or *Alice's Adventures in Wonderland.*) Instead, I read *The Scarlet Letter* and Franklin's *Autobiography*. And whatever I read I read for extra credit. Each time I finished a book, I reported the achievement to a teacher and basked in the praise my effort earned. Despite my best efforts, however, there seemed to be more and more books I needed to read. At the library I would literally tremble as I came upon whole shelves of books I hadn't read. So I read and I read and I read: *Great Expectations;* all the short stories of Kipling; *The Babe Ruth Story;* the entire first volume of the *Encyclopedia Britannica* (A–ANSTEY); the *Iliad; Moby Dick; Gone with the Wind; The Good Earth; Ramona; Forever Amber; The Lives of the Saints; Crime and Punishment; The Pearl.* . . . Librarians who initially frowned when I checked out the maximum ten books at a time started saving books they thought I might like. Teachers would say to the rest of the class, "I only wish the rest of you took reading as seriously as Richard obviously does."

But at home I would hear my mother wondering, "What do you see in your books?" (Was reading a hobby like her knitting? Was so much reading even healthy for a boy? Was it the sign of "brains"? Or was it just a convenient excuse for not helping about the house on Saturday mornings?) Always, "What do you see . . . ?"

What *did* I see in my books? I had the idea that they were crucial for my academic success, though I couldn't have said exactly how or why. In the sixth grade I simply concluded that what gave a book its value was some major idea or theme it contained. If that core essence could be mined and memorized, I would become learned like my teachers. I decided to record in a notebook the themes of the books that I read. After reading *Robinson Crusoe,* I wrote that its theme was "the value of learning to live by oneself." When I completed *Wuthering Heights,* I noted the danger of "letting emotions get out of control." Rereading these brief moralistic appraisals usually left me disheartened. I couldn't believe that they were really the source of reading's value. But for many more years, they constituted the only means I had of describing to myself the educational value of books.

In spite of my earnestness, I found reading a pleasurable activity. I came to enjoy the lonely good company of books. Early on weekday mornings, I'd read in my bed. I'd feel a mysterious comfort then, reading in the dawn quiet—the blue-gray silence interrupted by the occasional churning of the refrigerator motor a few rooms away or the more distant sounds of a city bus beginning its run. On weekends I'd go to the public library to read, surrounded by old men and women. Or, if the weather was fine, I would take my books to the park and read in the shade of a tree. A warm summer evening was my favorite reading time. Neighbors would leave for vacation and I would water their lawns. I would sit through the twilight on the front porches or in backyards, reading to the cool, whirling sounds of the sprinklers.

I also had favorite writers. But often those writers I enjoyed most I was least able to value. When I read William Saroyan's *The Human Comedy,* I was immediately pleased by the narrator's warmth and the charm of his story. But as quickly I became suspicious. A book so enjoyable to read couldn't be very "important." Another summer I determined to read all the novels of Dickens. Reading his fat novels, I loved the feeling I got—after the first hundred pages—of being at home in a fictional world where I knew the names of the characters and cared about what was going to happen to them. And it bothered me that I was forced away at the conclusion, when the fiction closed tight, like a fortune-teller's fist—the futures of all the major characters neatly resolved. I never knew how to take such feelings seriously, however. Nor did I suspect that these experiences could be part of a novel's meaning. Still, there were pleasures to sustain me after I'd finish my books. Carrying a volume back to the library, I would be pleased by its weight. I'd run my fingers along the edge of the pages and marvel at the breadth of my achievement. Around my room, growing stacks of paperback books reenforced my assurance.

I entered high school having read hundreds of books. My habit of reading made me a confident speaker and writer of English. Reading also enabled me to sense something of the shape, the major concerns, of Western thought. (I was able to say something about Dante and Descartes and Engels and James Baldwin in my high school term papers.) In these various ways, books brought me academic success as I hoped that they would. But I was not a good reader. Merely bookish, I lacked a point of view when I read. Rather, I read in order to acquire a point of view. I vacuumed books for epigrams, scraps of information, ideas, themes—anything to fill the hollow within me and make me feel educated. When one of my teachers suggested to his drowsy tenth-grade English class that a person could not have a "complicated idea" until he had read at least two thousand books, I heard the remark without detecting either its irony or its very complicated truth. I merely determined to compile a list of all the books I had ever read. Harsh with myself, I included only once a title I might have read several times. (How, after all, could one read a book more than once?) And I included only those books over a hundred pages in length. (Could anything shorter be a book?)

There was yet another high school list I compiled. One day I came across a newspaper article about the retirement of an English professor at a nearby state college. The article was accompanied by a list of the "hundred most important books of Western Civilization." "More than anything else in my life," the professor told the reporter with finality, "these books have made me all that I am." That was the kind of remark I couldn't ignore. I clipped out the list and kept it for the several months it took me to read all of the titles. Most books, of course, I barely understood. While reading Plato's *Republic,* for instance, I needed to keep looking at the book jacket comments to remind myself what the text was about. Nevertheless, with the special patience and superstition of a scholarship boy, I looked at every word of the text. And by the time I reached the last word, relieved, I convinced myself that I had read *The Republic.* In a ceremony of great pride, I solemnly crossed Plato off my list.

## III

The scholarship boy pleases most when he is young—the working-class child struggling for academic success. To his teachers, he offers great satisfaction; his success is their proudest achievement. Many other persons offer to help him. A businessman learns the boy's story and promises to underwrite part of the cost of his college education. A woman leaves him her entire library of several hundred books when she moves. His progress is featured in a newspaper article. Many people seem happy for him. They marvel. "How did you manage so fast?" From all sides, there is lavish praise and encouragement.

In his grammar school classroom, however, the boy already makes students around him uneasy. They scorn his desire to succeed. They scorn him for constantly wanting the teacher's attention and praise. "Kiss Ass," they call him when his hand swings up in response to every question he hears. Later, when he makes it to college, no one will mock him aloud. But he detects annoyance on the faces of some students and even some teachers who watch him. It puzzles him often. In college, then in graduate school, he behaves much as he always has. If anything is different about him it is that he dares to anticipate the successful conclusion of his studies. At last he feels that he belongs in the classroom, and this is exactly the source of the dissatisfaction he causes. To many persons around him, he appears too much the academic. There may be some things about him that recall his beginnings—his shabby clothes; his persistent poverty; or his dark skin (in those cases when it symbolizes his parents' disadvantaged condition)—but they only make clear how far he has moved from his past. He has used education to remake himself.

It bothers his fellow academics to face this. They will not say why exactly. (They sneer.) But their expectations become obvious when they are disappointed. They expect—they want—a student less changed by his schooling. If the scholarship boy, from a past so distant from the classroom, could remain in some basic way unchanged, he would be able to prove that it is possible for anyone to become educated without basically changing from the person one was.

Here is no fabulous hero, no idealized scholar-worker. The scholarship boy does not straddle, cannot reconcile, the two great opposing cultures of his life. His success is unromantic and plain. He sits in the classroom and offers those sitting beside him no calming reassurance about their own lives. He sits in the seminar room—a man with brown skin, the son of working-class Mexican immigrant parents. (Addressing the professor at the head of the table, his voice catches with nervousness.) There is no trace of his parents' in his speech. Instead he approximates the accents of teachers and classmates. Coming from *him* those sounds seem suddenly odd. Odd too is the effect produced when *he* uses academic jargon—bubbles at the tip of his tongue: "*Topos* . . . negative capability . . . vegetation imagery in Shakespearean comedy." He lifts an opinion from Coleridge, takes something else from Frye or Empson or Leavis. He even repeats exactly his professor's earlier comment. All his ideas are clearly borrowed. He seems to have no thought of his own. He chatters while his listeners smile—their look one of disdain.

When he is older and thus when so little of the person he was survives, the scholarship boy makes only too apparent his profound lack of *self-confidence*. This is the conventional assessment that even Richard Hoggart repeats:

> [The scholarship boy] tends to over-stress the importance of examinations, of the piling-up of knowledge and of received opinions. He discovers a technique of apparent learning, of the acquiring of facts rather than of the handling and use of facts. He learns how to receive a purely literate education, one using only a small part of the personality and challenging only a limited area of his being. He begins to see life as a ladder, as permanent examination with some praise and some further exhortation at each stage. He becomes an expert imbiber and doler-out; his competence will vary, but will rarely be accompanied by genuine enthusiasms. He rarely feels the reality of knowledge, of other men's thoughts and imaginings, on his own pulses. . . . He has something of the blinkered pony about him. . . .

But this is criticism more accurate than fair. The scholarship boy is a very bad student. He is the great mimic; a collector of thoughts, not a thinker;

the very last person in class who ever feels obliged to have an opinion of his own. In large part, however, the reason he is such a bad student is because he realizes more often and more acutely than most other students—than Hoggart himself—that education requires radical self-reformation. As a very young boy, regarding his parents, as he struggles with an early homework assignment, he knows this too well. That is why he lacks self-assurance. He does not forget that the classroom is responsible for remaking him. He relies on his teacher, depends on all that he hears in the classroom and reads in his books. He becomes in every obvious way the worst student, a dummy mouthing the opinions of others. But he would not be so bad—nor would he become so successful, a *scholarship* boy—if he did not accurately perceive that the best synonym for primary "education" is "imitation."

Those who would take seriously the boy's success—and his failure—would be forced to realize how great is the change any academic undergoes, how far one must move from one's past. It is easiest to ignore such considerations. So little is said about the scholarship boy in pages and pages of educational literature. Nothing is said of the silence that comes to separate the boy from his parents. Instead, one hears proposals for increasing the self-esteem of students and encouraging early intellectual independence. Paragraphs glitter with a constellation of terms like *creativity* and *originality*. (Ignored altogether is the function of imitation in a student's life.) Radical educationalists meanwhile complain that ghetto schools "oppress" students by trying to mold them, stifling native characteristics. The truer critique would be just the reverse: not that schools change ghetto students too much, but that while they might promote the occasional scholarship student, they change most students barely at all.

From the story of the scholarship boy there is no specific pedagogy to glean. There is, however, a much larger lesson. His story makes clear that education is a long, unglamorous, even demeaning process—*a nurturing never natural to the person one was before one entered a classroom.* At once different from most other students, the scholarship boy is also the archetypal "good student." He exaggerates the difficulty of being a student, but his exaggeration reveals a general predicament. Others are changed by their schooling as much as he. They too must re-form themselves. They must develop the skill of memory long before they become truly critical thinkers. And when they read Plato for the first several times, it will be with awe more than deep comprehension.

The impact of schooling on the scholarship boy is only more apparent to the boy himself and to others. Finally, although he may be laughable—a blinkered pony—the boy will not let his critics forget their own change. He ends up too much like them. When he speaks, they hear themselves echoed. In his pedantry, they trace their own. His ambitions are theirs. If his failure were singular, they might readily pity him. But he is more troubling than that. They would not scorn him if this were not so.

## *IV*

Like me, Hoggart's imagined scholarship boy spends most of his years in the classroom afraid to long for his past. Only at the very end of his schooling does the boy-man become nostalgic. In this sudden change of heart, Richard Hoggart notes:

> He longs for the membership he lost, "he pines for some Nameless Eden where he never was." The nostalgia is the stronger and the more ambiguous because he is really "in quest of his own absconded self yet scared to find it." He both wants to go back and yet thinks he has gone beyond his class, feels himself weighted with knowledge of his own and their situation, which hereafter forbids him the simpler pleasures of his father and mother. . . .

According to Hoggart, the scholarship boy grows nostalgic because he remains the uncertain scholar, bright enough to have moved from his past, yet unable to feel easy, a part of a community of academics.

This analysis, however, only partially suggests what happened to me in my last year as a graduate student. When I traveled to London to write a dissertation on English Renaissance literature, I was finally confident of membership in a "community of scholars." But the pleasure that confidence gave me faded rapidly. After only two or three months in the reading room of the British Museum, it became clear that I had joined a lonely community. Around me each day were dour faces eclipsed by large piles of books. There were the regulars, like the old couple who arrived every morning, each holding a loop of the shopping bag which contained all their notes. And there was the historian who chattered madly to herself. ("Oh dear! Oh! Now, what's this? What? Oh, my!") There were also the faces of young men and women worn by long study. And everywhere eyes turned away the moment our glance accidentally met. Some persons I sat beside day after day, yet we passed silently at the end of the day, strangers. Still, we were united by a common respect for the written word and for scholarship. We did form a union, though one in which we remained distant from one another.

More profound and unsettling was the bond I recognized with those writers whose books I consulted. Whenever I opened a text that hadn't been used for years, I realized that my special interests and skills united me to a mere handful of academics. We formed an exclusive—eccentric!—society, separated from others who would never care or be able to share our concerns. (The pages I turned were stiff like layers of dead skin.) I began to wonder: Who, beside my dissertation director and a few faculty members, would ever read what I wrote? And: Was my dissertation much more than an act of social withdrawal? These questions went unanswered in the silence of the Museum reading room. They remained to trouble me after I'd leave the library each afternoon and feel myself shy—unsteady, speaking simple sentences at the grocer's or the butcher's on my way back to my bed-sitter.

Meanwhile my file cards accumulated. A professional, I knew exactly how to search a book for pertinent information. I could quickly assess and summarize the usability of the many books I consulted. But whenever I started to write, I knew too much (and not enough) to be able to write anything but sentences that were overly cautious, timid, strained brittle under the heavy weight of footnotes and qualifications. I seemed unable to dare a passionate statement. I felt drawn by professionalism to the edge of sterility, capable of no more than pedantic, lifeless, unassailable prose.

*Then* nostalgia began.

After years spent unwilling to admit its attractions, I gestured nostalgically toward the past. I yearned for that time when I had not been so alone. I became impatient with books. I wanted experience more immediate. I feared the library's silence. I silently scorned the gray, timid faces around me. I grew to hate the growing pages of my dissertation on genre and Renaissance literature. (In my mind I heard relatives laughing as they tried to make sense of its title.) I wanted something—I couldn't say exactly what. I told myself that I wanted a more passionate life. And a life less thoughtful. And above all, I wanted to be less alone. One day I heard some Spanish academics whispering back and forth to each other, and their sounds seemed ghostly voices recalling my life. Yearning became preoccupation then. Boyhood memories beckoned, flooded my mind. (Laughing intimate voices. Bounding up the front steps of the porch. A sudden embrace inside the door.)

For weeks after, I turned to books by educational experts. I needed to learn how far I had moved from my past—to determine how fast I would be able to recover something of it once again. But I found little. Only a chapter in a book by Richard Hoggart. . . . I left the reading room and the circle of faces.

I came home. After the year in England, I spent three summer months living with my mother and father, relieved by how easy it was to be home. It no longer seemed very important to me that we had little to say. I felt easy sitting and eating and walking with them. I watched them, nevertheless, looking for evidence of those elastic, sturdy strands that bind generations in a web of inheritance. I thought as I watched my mother one night: of course a friend had been right when she told me that I gestured and laughed just like my mother. Another time I saw for myself: my father's eyes were much like my own, constantly watchful.

But after the early relief, this return, came suspicion, nagging until I realized that I had not neatly sidestepped the impact of schooling. My desire to do so was precisely the measure of how much I remained an academic. *Negatively* (for that is how this idea first occurred to me): my need to think so much and so abstractly about my parents and our relationship was in itself an indication of my long education. My father and mother did not pass their time thinking about the cultural meanings of their experience. It was I who described their daily lives with airy ideas. And yet, *positively:* the ability to consider experience so abstractly allowed me to shape into desire what would otherwise have remained indefinite, meaningless longing in the British Museum. If, because of my schooling, I had grown culturally separated from my parents, my education finally had given me ways of speaking and caring about that fact.

My best teachers in college and graduate school, years before, had tried to prepare me for this conclusion, I think, when they discussed texts of aristocratic pastoral literature. Faithfully, I wrote down all that they said. I memorized it: "The praise of the unlettered by the highly educated is one of the primary themes of 'elitist' literature." But, "the importance of the praise given the unsolitary, richly passionate and spontaneous life is that it simultaneously reflects the value of a reflective life." I heard it all. But there was no way for any of it to mean very much to me. I was a scholarship boy at the time, busily laddering my way up the rungs of education. To pass an examination, I copied down exactly what my teachers told me. It would require many more years of schooling (an inevitable miseducation) in which I came to trust the silence of reading and the habit of abstracting from immediate experience—moving away from a life of closeness and immediacy I remembered with my parents, growing older—before I turned unafraid to desire the past, and thereby achieved what had eluded me for so long—the end of education.

NOTE

[1] All quotations in this essay are from Richard Hoggart, *The Uses of Literacy* (London: Chatto and Windus, 1957), chapter 10. [Author's note]

. . . . . . . . . . .

## QUESTIONS FOR A SECOND READING

1. In *Hunger of Memory*, the book from which "The Achievement of Desire" is drawn, Rodriguez says several times that the story he tells, although it is very much his story, is also a story of our common experience—growing up, leaving home, becoming educated, entering the world. When you reread this essay, look particularly for sections or passages you might bring forward as evidence that this is, in fact, an essay which can give you a way of looking at your own life, and not just his. And look for sections that defy universal application. To what degree *is* his story the story of our common experience? Why might he (or his readers) want to insist that his story is everyone's story?

2. At the end of the essay, Rodriguez says:

> It would require many more years of schooling (an inevitable miseducation) in which I came to trust the silence of reading and the habit of abstracting from immediate experience—moving away from a life of closeness and immediacy I remembered with my parents, growing older—before I turned unafraid to desire the past, and thereby achieved what had eluded me for so long—the end of education.

What do you think, as you reread this essay, is the "end of education"? And what does that end (that goal? stopping point?) have to do with "miseducation," "the silence of reading," "the habit of abstracting from immediate experience," and "desiring the past"?


### ASSIGNMENTS FOR WRITING

1. You could look at the relationship between Richard Rodriguez and Richard Hoggart as a case study of the relation of a reader to a writer or a student to a teacher. Look closely at Rodriguez's references to Hoggart's book, *The Uses of Literacy*, and at the way Rodriguez made use of that book to name and describe his own experience as a student. What did he find in the book? How did he use it? How does he use it in his own writing?

   Write an essay in which you discuss Rodriguez's use of Hoggart's *The Uses of Literacy*. How, for example, would you compare Rodriguez's version of the "scholarship boy" with Hoggart's? (At one point, Rodriguez says that Hoggart's account is "more accurate than fair." What might he have meant by that?) And what kind of reader is the Rodriguez who is writing "The Achievement of Desire"—is he still a "scholarship boy," or is that description no longer appropriate?

   Note: You might begin your research with what may seem to be a purely technical matter, examining how Rodriguez handles quotations and works Hoggart's words into paragraphs of his own. On the basis of Rodriguez's use of quoted passages, how would you describe the relationship between Hoggart's words and Rodriguez's? Who has the greater authority? Who is the expert, and under what conditions? What "rules" might Rodriguez be said to follow or to break? Do you see any change in the course of the essay in how Rodriguez uses block quotations? in how he comments on them?

2. Rodriguez insists that his story is also everyone's story. Take an episode from your life, one that seems in some way similar to one of the episodes in "The Achievement of Desire," and cast it into a shorter version of Rodriguez's essay. Your job here is to look at your experience in Rodriguez's terms, which means thinking the way he does, noticing what he would notice, interpreting details in a similar fashion, using his key terms, seeing through his point of view; it could also mean imitating his style of writing, doing whatever it is you see him doing characteristically while he writes. Imitation, Rodriguez argues, is not necessarily a bad thing; it can, in fact, be one of the powerful ways in which a person learns.

   Note: This assignment can also be used to read against "The Achievement of Desire." Rodriguez insists on the universality of his experience leaving home and community and joining the larger public life. You could highlight the differences between your experience and his. You should begin by imitating Rodriguez's method; you do not have to arrive at his conclusions, however.

3.   What I am about to say to you has taken me more than twenty years to admit: *A primary reason for my success in the classroom was that I couldn't forget that schooling was changing me and separating me from the life I enjoyed before becoming a student.* (p. 623)

   If, because of my schooling, I had grown culturally separated from my parents, my education finally had given me ways of speaking and caring about that fact. (p. 639)

   As you reread Rodriguez's essay, what would you say are his "ways of speaking and caring"? One way to think about this question is to trace how the lessons he learned about reading, education, language, family, culture, and class shifted as he moved from elementary school through college and graduate school to his career as a teacher and a writer. What scholarly abilities did he learn that provided him with "ways of speaking and caring" valued in the academic community? Where and how do you see him using them in his essay?

   Write an essay in which you discuss how Rodriguez reads (reviews, summarizes, interprets) his family, his teachers, his schooling, himself, and his books. What differences can you say such reading makes to those ways of speaking and caring that you locate in the text?

## MAKING CONNECTIONS

1. Paulo Freire, in "The 'Banking' Concept of Education" (p. 348), discusses the political implications of the relations between teachers and students. Some forms of schooling, he says, can give students control over their lives, but most schooling teaches students only to submit to domination by others. If you look closely at the history of Rodriguez's schooling from the perspective of Freire's essay, what do you see? Write an essay describing how Freire might analyze Rodriguez's education. How would he see the process as it unfolds throughout Rodriguez's experience, as a student, from his early schooling (including the study he did on his own at home), through his college and graduate studies, to the position he takes, finally, as the writer of "The Achievement of Desire?"

2. Both Carolyn Kay Steedman, in "Exiles" (p. 645), and Rodriguez, in "The Achievement of Desire," write accounts of growing up and leaving a working class family. The texts, however, are quite different in shape and feel and, although this is harder to trace out, in what they identify as the consequences of class in a person's education and passage to adulthood. There are obvious points of difference—differences of nationality, language, gender, generation—and there are subtle differences in their use of "class" as a way of understanding an individual's ways of living, working, and thinking.

   Write an essay in which you consider the different accounts of class, culture, family, and education in "Exiles" and "The Achievement of Desire."

3. In the introduction to *Landscape for a Good Woman,* Carolyn Kay Steedman says, "This book is about lives lived out on the borderlands, lives for which the central interpretative devices of the culture don't quite work." And in "Exiles," the selection from that book included in *Ways of Reading,* she writes an account of family life within and against the standard or official narratives of "normal," sentimental, middle class family life.

   Rodriguez, in "The Achievement of Desire," is also writing against what he feels to be the standard, official, or normal narrative of childhood, education, and family life. Write an essay in which you consider these two selections as revisionary narratives—that is, as works in writing that resist and revise the expectations of readers and the expectations of the genre. Where, in particular, are these writers most visible *as writers* in their texts? Where and how do they address their readers? Where and how are they most concerned with autobiography as a genre?

# CAROLYN KAY STEEDMAN

$C$*AROLYN KAY STEEDMAN is a historian whose work examines childhood and children in Britain from the late eighteenth century to the present. Steedman is a cultural historian, which means that she is concerned not simply with stories, narrative accounts of this child or that in Britain's past, but with the idea of childhood as it has functioned in particular historical periods and social settings. She is interested in childhood as a category, a structure of possibility and expectation, determined by a culture's needs and desires, and within which real people learn to know, value, and organize their lives. She teaches in the Department of Arts Education at the University of Warwick, in England. She is the author of nine books, including* The Tidy House: Little Girls Writing *(1984);* Language, Gender and Childhood *(1986);* Landscape for a Good Woman: A Story of Two Lives *(1987), the book from which "Exiles" was drawn;* Childhood, Culture and Class in Britain: Margaret McMillan, 1860–1931 *(1990);* Past Tenses: Essays on Writing, Autobiography and History *(1992); and* Strange Dislocations: Childhood and the Idea of Human Interiority, 1780–1930 *(1995).*

*The two lives alluded to in the title of* Landscape for a Good Woman *are Steedman's and her mother's. The setting, or landscape, is Britain's class system (a system more visible in Britain than in the United States; here we tend to think in terms of race or ethnicity when we think about the defining differences between people or neighborhoods). Steedman says,*

> *This book is about lives lived out on the borderlands, lives for which the central interpretative devices of the culture don't quite work. It has a childhood at its centre—my childhood, a personal past—and it is about the disruption of that fifties childhood by the one my mother had lived out before me, and the stories she told about it. Now, the narrative of both these childhoods can be elaborated by the marginal and secret stories that other working-class girls and women from a recent historical past have to tell.*

Steedman, like her mother and her grandmother, grew up in a working class family. This is why she says her life was lived out "on the borderlands" and this is why she says her experience was not represented by the "central interpretive devices of the culture"—that is, the stories of "normal," middle class family life as represented on television, in the movies, and in children's literature. And the two stories of mother and daughter are set in relation to the available accounts of working class families, in fiction, history, and sociology. Landscape for a Good Woman *critically examines the accounts of working class family life as written into the standard histories of pre- and post-War Britain, accounts, according to Steedman, that rely too heavily on stereotype and generalization, that deny working class individuals any complex mental and imaginative life and any psychological depth or individuality.*

*The selection that follows represents the second of the three major sections of the book, called "Stories," "Exiles," and "Interpretations." "Exiles" is the most autobiographical in form of the three. Steedman refers to the two chapters in "Exiles," "The Weaver's Daughter" and "A Thin Man," as "case studies" and says*

> *The written case-study allows the writers to enter the present into the past, allows the dream, the wish or the fantasy of the past to shape current time, and treats them as evidence in their own right. In this way, the narrative form of case-study shows what went into its writing, shows the bits and pieces from which it is made up, in the way that history refuses to do, and that fiction can't. Case-study presents the ebb and flow of memory, the structure of dreams, the stories that people tell to explain themselves to others.*

*The case studies in "Exiles" allow Steedman to place the stories she was told as a child (and the stories she read, like the stories of the Little Mermaid or the Snow Queen) in tension with the point of view and the understanding she has as an adult (including the "compulsions of historical explanation"). The case studies she writes are multilayered; they do not provide a linear narrative and they do not move toward an inevitable conclusion. They enact both a desire to understand the past, to know who was who and what led to what, and the impossibility of ever being certain in such knowledge.*

# Exiles

Kay and Gerda sat looking at the picture-book of animals and birds, when just at that moment the clock in the great church-tower struck five. Kay exclaimed: "Oh dear! I feel as if something had stabbed my heart! And now I've got something into my eye!" . . . "I think it's gone!" he said; but it was not gone. It was one of the glass pieces from the mirror, the troll mirror, which you no doubt remember, in which everything great and good that was reflected in it became small and ugly, while everything bad and wicked became more distinct and prominent and every fault was at once noticed. Poor Kay had got one of the fragments right into his heart. It would soon become like a lump of ice. It did not cause him any pain, but it was there.

— HANS CHRISTIAN ANDERSEN,
"The Snow Queen"

## The Weaver's Daughter

. . . Stuff slippers and white cotton stockings,
The lasses they mostly do wear,
With a dimity corduroy petticoat,
It is whiter than snow I declare;
With a fringe or a flounce round the bottom
These lasses they will have beside,
And a sash for to go round their middle
And to tie up in bunches behind.

. . . The servant girls follow the fashions,
As well as the best in the place:
They'll dress up their heads like an owl, boys,
And will think it no shame or disgrace.
They will bind up their heads with fine ribbands,
And a large bag of hair hangs behind;
And when they do walk through the streets, boys,
No peacock can touch them for pride.

— "The Lasses' Resolution to Follow
the Fashion," *c.* 1870, in Roy Palmer,
*A Touch on the Times: Songs of Social
Change,* 1770–1914, Penguin, 1974

When I was three, before my sister was born, I had a dream. It remains quite clear across the years, the topography absolutely plain, so precise in details of dress that I can use them to place the dream in historical time. We were in a street, the street so wide and the houses so distant across the road that it might not have been a street at all; and the houses lay low with gaps between them, so that the sky filled a large part of the picture. Here,

**645**

at the front, on this side of the wide road, a woman hurried along, having crossed from the houses behind. The perspective of the dream must have shifted several times, for I saw her once as if from above, moving through a kind of square, or crossing-place, and then again from the fixed point of the dream where I stood watching her, left forefront.

She wore the New Look, a coat of beige gaberdine which fell in two swaying, graceful pleats from her waist at the back (the swaying must have come from very high heels, but I didn't notice her shoes), a hat tipped forward from hair swept up at the back. She hurried, something jerky about her movements, a nervous, agitated walk, glancing round at me as she moved across the foreground. Several times she turned and came some way back towards me, admonishing, shaking her finger.

Encouraging me to follow in this way perhaps, but moving too fast for me to believe that this was what she wanted, she entered a revolving door of dark, polished wood, mahogany and glass, and started to go round and round, looking out at me as she turned. I wish I knew what she was doing, and what she wanted me to do.

In childhood, only the surroundings show, and nothing is explained. Children do not possess a social analysis of what is happening to them, or around them, so the landscape and the pictures it presents have to remain a background, taking on meaning later, from different circumstances. That dream is the past that lies at the heart of my present: it is my interpretative device, the means by which I can tell a story. My understanding of the dream built up in layers over a long period of time. Its strange lowered vista for instance, which now reminds the adult more than anything else of George Herriman's "Krazy Kat"[1] where buildings disappear and reappear from frame to frame, seems an obvious representation of London in the late forties and early fifties: all the houses had gaps in between because of the bombs, and the sky came closer to the ground than seemed right. I understood what I had seen in the dream when I learned the words "gaberdine" and "mahogany"; and I was born in the year of the New Look, and understood by 1951 and the birth of my sister, that dresses needing twenty yards for a skirt were items as expensive as children—more expensive really, because after 1948 babies came relatively cheap, on tides of free milk and orange juice, but good cloth in any quantity was hard to find for a very long time.

Detail like this provides retrospective labeling; but it is not evidence about a period of historical time. The only *evidence* that the dream offers is the feeling of childhood—all childhoods, probably—the puzzlement of the child watching from the pavement, wondering what's going on, what they, the adults, are up to, what they want from you, and what they expect you to do. It is evidence in this way, because as an area of feeling it is brought forward again and again to shape responses to quite different events. Memory alone cannot resurrect past time, because it is memory itself that shapes it, long after historical time has passed. The dream is not a fixed event of the summer of 1950; it has passed through many stages of use and exploration, and such reinterpretation gives an understanding that the child at the time can't possess: it's only recently that I've come to see who the woman in the New Look coat actually was.

Now, later, I see the time of my childhood as a point between two worlds: an older "during the War," "before the War," "in the Depression," "then"; and the place we inhabit now. The War was so palpable a presence in the first five years of my life that I still find it hard to believe that I didn't live through it. There were bomb-sites everywhere, prefabs on waste land, most things still on points, my mother tearing up the ration book when meat came off points, over my sister's pram, outside the library in the High Street in the summer of 1951, a gesture that still fills me with the desire to do something so defiant and final; and then looking across the street at a woman wearing a full-skirted dress, and then down at the forties straight-skirted navy blue suit she was still wearing, and longing, irritatedly, for the New Look; and then at us, the two living barriers to twenty yards of cloth. Back home, she said she'd be able to get it at the side door of the mill; but not here; not with you two . . .

My mother's story was told to me early on, in bits and pieces throughout the fifties, and it wasn't delivered to entertain, like my father's much later stories were, but rather to teach me lessons. There was a child, an eleven-year-old from a farm seven miles south of Coventry, sent off to be a maid-of-all-work in a parsonage in Burnley. She had her tin trunk, and she cried, waiting on the platform with her family seeing her off, for the through train to Manchester. They'd sent her fare, the people in Burnley; "But think how she felt, such a little girl, she was only eleven, with nothing but her little tin box. Oh, she did cry." I cry now over accounts of childhoods like this, weeping furtively over the reports of nineteenth-century commissions of inquiry into child labor, abandoning myself to the luxuriance of grief in libraries, tears staining the pages where Mayhew's little watercress girl tells her story. The lesson was, of course, that I must never, ever, cry for myself, for I was a lucky little girl: my tears should be for all the strong, brave women who gave me life. This story, which embodied fierce resentment against the unfairness of things, was carried through seventy years and three generations, and all of them, all the good women, dissolved into the figure of my mother, who was, as she told us, *a good mother.* She didn't go out dancing or drinking (gin, mother's ruin, was often specified. "Your mother drank gin once," my father told me years later, with nostalgic regret). She didn't go, as one mother she'd known, in a story of maternal neglect that I remember thinking was over the top at the time, and tie a piece of string round my big toe, dangle it through the window and down the front of the house, so that the drunken mother, returning from her carousing, she could tug at it, wake the child, get the front door open and send it down the shop for a basin of pie and peas. I still put myself to sleep by thinking about *not* lying on a cold pavement covered with newspapers.

The eleven-year-old who cried on Coventry station hated being a servant. She got out as soon as she could and found work in the weaving sheds—"she was a good weaver; six looms under her by the time she was sixteen"—married, produced nine children, eight of whom emigrated to the cotton mills of Massachusetts before the First World War, managed, "never went before the Guardians."[2] It was much, much later that I learned from *One Hand Tied Behind Us* that four was the usual number of looms in Lancashire weaving towns.[3] Burnley weavers were badly organized over the question of loom supervision, and my great-grandmother had six not because she was a good weaver, but because she was exploited. In 1916, when her daughter Carrie's husband was killed at the Somme, she managed that too, looking after the three-year-old, my mother, so that Carrie could go on working at the mill.

But long before the narrative fell into place, before I could dress the eleven-year-old of my imagination in the clothing of the 1870s, I knew perfectly well what that child had done, and how she had felt. She cried, because tears are cheap; and then she stopped, and got by, because no one gives you anything in this world. What was given to her, passed on to all of us, was a powerful and terrible endurance, the self-destructive defiance of those doing the best they can with what life hands out to them.

From a cotton town, my mother had a heightened awareness of fabric and weave, and I can date events by the clothes I wore as a child, and the material they were made of. Post-War children had few clothes, because of rationing, but not only scarcity, rather names like barathea, worsted, gaberdine, twill, jersey, lawn . . . fix them in my mind. The dream of the New Look must have taken place during or after the summer of 1950, because in it I wore one of my two summer dresses, one of green, one of blue gingham, which were made that year and which lasted me, with letting down, until I went to school.

Sometime during 1950, I think before the summer, before the dresses were made, I was taken north to Burnley and into the sheds, where one afternoon my mother visited someone she used to know as a child, now working there. The woman smiled and nodded at me, through the noise that made a surrounding silence. Afterwards, my mother told me that they had to lip-read: they couldn't hear each other speak for the noise of the looms. But I didn't notice the noise. The woman wore high platform-soled black shoes that I still believe I heard click on the bright polished floor as she walked between her looms. Whenever I hear the word "tending" I always think of that confident attentiveness to the needs of the machines, the control over work that was unceasing, with half a mind and hands engaged, but the looms always demanding attention. When I worked as a primary-school teacher I sometimes retrieved that feeling with a particular clarity, walking between the tables on the hard floor, all the little looms working, but needing my constant adjustment.

The woman wore a dress that seemed very short when I recalled the picture through the next few years: broad shoulders, a straight skirt patterned with black and red flowers that hung the way it did—I know now—because it had some rayon in it. The post-War years were full of women longing for a full skirt and unable to make it. I wanted to walk like that, a short skirt, high heels, bright red lipstick, in charge of all that machinery.

This was the first encounter with the landscape of my mother's past. We came once again, on the last trip I made North before I was nineteen, during the autumn or winter of 1950 when, as I can now work out, my mother was pregnant with my sister. On this particular and first visit of the late spring, the world was still clear. On the edge of the town, it seemed like the top of the street, a little beck ran through some woods, with bluebells growing there, so that memory can tell that it was May. We paddled in the shallow water; this was the clean water that they used to use for the cotton; it came from another place, where the mills were before there was steam; you could see the gravel clear beneath. We didn't pick the flowers: we left them there for other people to enjoy. She wore her green tweed jacket; it was lucky she didn't have any stockings on otherwise she'd only have had to take them off; she laughed, she smiled: the last time.

At the back of the house, through the yard to the lane, the lavatory was perched over another stream; you could see the water running past if you looked down. In this back lane I played with another child, older than me, she was four: Maureen. She was a Catholic, my grandmother said, but I could play with her, she was a nice little girl, but they weren't like us: you could tell them by their eyes. It was the women who told you about the public world, of work and politics, the details of social distinction. My grandmother's lodger, the man who was to become her third husband when his wife died ten years later, stayed self-effacingly in the background as she explained these things. Anti-Catholicism propelled my mother's placing of herself in a public sphere. A few years later she often repeated the story of Molly, her best friend at school, the priest beckoning to the Catholic child from over the road, furtively passing a betting slip; the strain of the penny collections at church with a dozen mouths to feed at home.

As a teenage worker my mother had broken with a recently established tradition and on leaving school in 1927 didn't go into the sheds. She lied to me though when, at about the age of eight, I asked her what she'd done, and she said she'd worked in an office, done clerical work. Ten years later, on my third and last visit to Burnley and practicing the accomplishments of the oral historian, I talked to my grandmother and she, puzzled, told me that Edna had never worked in any office, had in fact been apprenticed to a dry-cleaning firm that did tailoring and mending. On that same visit, the first since I was four, I found a reference written by the local doctor for my mother who, about 1930, applied for a job as a ward-maid at the local asylum, confirming that she was clean, strong, honest and intelligent. I wept over that, of course, for a world where some people might doubt her—my—cleanliness. I didn't care much about the honesty, and I knew I was strong; but there are people everywhere waiting for you to slip up, to show signs of dirtiness and stupidity, so that they can send you back where you belong.

She didn't finish her apprenticeship—I deduce that, rather than know it—sometime, it must have been 1934, came South, worked in Woolworth's on the Edgware Road, spent the War years in Roehampton, a ward-maid again, in the hospital where they mended fighter pilots' ruined faces. Now I can feel the deliberate vagueness in her accounts of those years: "When did you meet daddy?"—"Oh, at a dance, at home." There were no photographs. Who came to London first? I wish now that I'd asked that question. He worked on the buses when he arrived, showed me a canopy in front of a hotel once, that he'd pulled down on his first solo drive. He was too old to be called up (a lost generation of men who were too young for the first War, too old for the second). There's a photograph of him standing in front of the cabbages he'd grown for victory, wearing his Home Guard uniform. But what did he *do* after his time on the buses, and during the War years? Too late now to find out.

During the post-War housing shortage my father got an office job with a property company, and the flat to go with it. I was born in March 1947, at the peak of the Bulge, more babies born that month than ever before or after, and carried through the terrible winter of 1946–7. We moved to Streatham Hill in June 1951, to an estate owned by the same company (later to be taken over by Lambeth Council), and a few years after the move my father got what he wanted, which was to be in charge of the company's boiler maintenance. On his death certificate it says "heating engineer."

In the 1950s my mother took in lodgers. Streatham Hill Theatre (now a bingo hall) was on the pre-West End circuit, and we had chorus girls staying with us for weeks at a time. I was woken up in the night sometimes, the spare bed in my room being made up for someone they'd met down the Club, the other lodger's room already occupied. I like the idea of being the daughter of a theatrical landlady, but that enterprise, in fact, provides me with my most startling and problematic memories. The girl from Aberdeen really did say "Och, no, not on the table!" as my father flattened a bluebottle with his hand, but did he *really* put down a newspaper at the same table to eat his breakfast? I remember it happening, but it's so much like the books that I feel a fraud, a bit-part player in a soft and southern version of *The Road to Wigan Pier*.

I remember incidents like these, I think, because I was about seven, the age at which children start to notice social detail and social distinction, but also more particularly because the long lesson in hatred for my father had begun, and the early stages were in the traditional mode, to be found in the opening chapters of *Sons and Lovers* and Lawrence's description of the inculcated dislike of Mr Morrell, of female loathing for coarse male habits. The newspaper on the table is problematic for me because it was problematic for my mother, a symbol of all she'd hoped to escape and all she'd landed herself in. (It was at this time, I think, that she told me that her own mother, means-tested in the late 1920s, had won the sympathy of the Relieving Officer, who ignored the presence of the saleable piano because she kept a clean house, with a cloth on the table.)

Now, thirty years later, I feel a great regret for the father of my first four years, who took me out and who probably loved me, irresponsibly ("It's alright for him; he doesn't have to look after you"), and I wish I could tell him now, even though he really was a sod, that I'm sorry for the years of rejection and dislike. But we were forced to choose, early on, which side we belonged to, and children have to come down on the side that brings the food home and gets it on the table. By 1955 I was beginning to hate him—because *he* was to blame, for the lack of money, for my mother's terrible dissatisfaction at the way things were working out.

Changes in the market place, the growth of real income and the proliferation of consumer goods that marked the mid-1950s, were used by my mother to measure out her discontent: there existed a newly expanding and richly endowed material world in which she was denied a place. The new consumer goods came into the house slowly, and we were taught to understand that our material deprivations were due entirely to my father's meanness. We had the first fridge in our section of the street (which he'd got cheap, off the back of a lorry, contacts in the trade) but were very late to acquire a television. I liked the new vacuum cleaner at first, because it meant no longer having to do the stairs with a stiff brush. But in fact it added to my Saturday work because I was expected to clean more with the new machine. Now I enjoy shocking people by telling them how goods were introduced into households under the guise of gifts for children: the fridge in the house of the children we played with over the road was given to the youngest as a birthday present—the last thing an eight-year-old wants. My mother laughed at this, scornfully: the clothes and shoes she gave us as birthday presents were conventional gifts for all post-War children, but the record player also came into the house in this way, as my eleventh birthday present. I wasn't allowed to take it with me when I left, though: it really wasn't mine at all.

What happened at school was my own business, no questions ever asked, no encouragement nor discouragement ever given. It became just the thing I did, like my mother's going out to work. Later, the material conditions for educational success were provided: a table in my room, a pattern of domestic work that allowed homework to be done. From the earliest time I was expected to be competent: to iron a blouse, scrub a floor, learn to read, pass an exam; and I was. (There was, though, as my sister was to discover later, all hell to pay if you failed.) Indifference to what happened at school was useful: learning is the one untouched area of my life. So in reconstructing the pattern of this neglect, I am surprised to find myself walking up the hill with my mother from school one afternoon. She was smiling a pleased smile, and working things out, I think it must have been 1956, the day she was told that I'd be going into the eleven-plus class and so (because everyone in the class passed the exam) would be going to grammar school. I remember the afternoon because I asked her what class we were; or rather, I asked her if we were middle class, and she was evasive. I answered my own question, said I thought we must be middle class, and reflected very precisely in that moment on my mother's black, waisted coat with the astrakhan collar, and her high-heeled black suede shoes, her lipstick. She looked so much better than the fat, spreading, South London mothers around us, that I thought we had to be middle class.

The coat and the lipstick came from her own work. "If you want something, you have to go out and work for it. Nobody gives you anything; nothing comes free in this world." About 1956 or 1957 she got an evening job in one of the espresso bars opening along the High Road, making sandwiches and frying eggs. She saved up enough money to take a manicuring course and in 1958 got her diploma, thus achieving a certified skill for the first time in her forty-five years. When I registered her death I was surprised to find myself giving "manicurist" as her trade, for the possibility of a trade was something she seemed to have left behind in the North. She always worked in good places, in the West End; the hands she did were in *Vogue* once. She came home with stories and imitations of her "ladies." She told how she "flung" a sixpenny piece back at a titled woman who'd given it her as a tip: "If you can't afford any more than that Madam, I suggest you keep it." Wonderful!—like tearing up the ration books.

She knew where we stood in relation to this world of privilege and possession, had shown me the place long before, in the bare front bedroom where the health visitor spoke haughtily to her. Many women have stood thus, at the window, looking out, their children watching their exclusion: "I remember as it were but yesterday," wrote Samuel Bamford in 1849, "after one of her visits to the dwelling of that 'fine lady'" (his mother's sister, who had gone up in the world):

> she divested herself of her wet bonnet, her soaked shoes, and changed her dripping outer garments and stood leaning with her elbow on the window sill, her hand up to her cheek, her eyes looking upon vacancy and the tears trickling over her fingers.[4]

What we learned now, in the early 1960s, through the magazines and anecdotes she brought home, was how the goods of that world of privilege might be appropriated, with the cut and fall of a skirt, a good winter coat, with leather shoes, a certain voice; but above all with clothes, the best boundary between you and a cold world.

It was at this time that her voice changed, and her Lancashire accent began to disappear. Earlier, years before, she'd entertained us in the kitchen by talking really broad, not her natural dialect but a stagey variety that always preceded a rapid shift to music-hall cockney for a rendering of "She Was Only a Bird in a Gilded Cage":

It's the same the whole world over
Ain't it a bleeding shame
It's the rich what gets the pleasure,
It's the poor what gets the blame.

We weren't, I now realize by doing the sums, badly off. My father paid the rent, all the bills, gave us our pocket money, and a fixed sum of seven pounds a week housekeeping money, quite a lot in the late 1950s,[5] went on being handed over every Friday until his death, even when estrangement was obvious, and he was living most of the time with somebody else. My mother must have made quite big money in tips, for the records of her savings, no longer a secret, show quite fabulous sums being stored away in the early 1960s. When she died there was over £40,000 in building-society accounts. Poverty hovered as a belief. It existed in stories of the thirties, in a family history. Even now when a bank statement comes in that shows I'm overdrawn or when the gas bill for the central heating seems enormous, my mind turns to quite inappropriate strategies, like boiling down the ends of soap, and lighting fires with candle ends and spills of screwed up newspaper to save buying wood. I think about these things because they were domestic economies that we practised in the 1950s. We believed we were badly off because we children were expensive items, and all these arrangements had been made for us. "If it wasn't for you two," my mother told us, "I could be off somewhere else." After going out manicuring she started spending Sunday afternoons in bed, and we couldn't stay in the house or play on the doorstep for fear of disturbing her. The house was full of her terrible tiredness and her terrible resentment; and I knew it was all my fault.

Later, in 1977, after my father's death, we found out that they were never married, that we were illegitimate. In 1934 my father left his wife and two-year-old daughter in the North, and came to London. He and my mother had been together for at least ten years when I was born, and we think now that I was her hostage to fortune, the factor that might persuade him to get a divorce and marry her. But the ploy failed.

Just before my mother's death, playing about with the photographs on the front bedroom mantelpiece, my niece discovered an old photograph under one of me at three. A woman holds a tiny baby. It's the early 1930s, a picture of the half-sister left behind. But I think I knew about her and her mother long before I looked them both in the face, or heard about their existence, knew that the half-understood adult conversations around me, the two trips to Burnley in 1951, the quarrels about "her," the litany of "she," "she," "she" from behind closed doors, made up the figure in the New Look coat, hurrying away, wearing the clothes that my mother wanted to wear, angry with me yet nervously inviting me to follow, caught finally in the revolving door. We have proper birth certificates, because my mother must have told a simple lie to the registrar, a discovery about the verisimilitude of documents that worries me a lot as a historian.

•   •   •

What kind of secret was the illegitimacy? It was a real secret, that is, the product of an agreed silence on the part of two people about a real event (or absence of event), and it was an extremely well-kept secret. Yet it revealed itself at the time. Often, before I found out about it in 1977 and saw the documents, the sense of my childhood that I carried through the years was that people knew something about me, something that was wrong with me, that I didn't know myself. The first dramatic enactment of the idea that I should not embarrass people with my presence came in 1954 when the children we played with in the street suggested that I go to Sunday school with them. It is a measure of the extreme isolation of our childhood that this event took on the status of entering society itself. Tremulous for days, I then stood reluctantly on the doorstep after Sunday dinner when they called for me, clutching the hot, acrid penny that I'd been told I'd need for the collection, saying: they might not want me to come; they won't want me. From inside the house I was told to stop making a fuss and get up the road. It was a High Anglican church. We were given a little book with space for coloured stamps showing scenes from the Gospels that you received for each attendance.

> Every stamp cries duty done
> Every blank cries shame;
> Finish what you have begun
> In the Savior's name

exhorted the book inside the front cover (a familiar message; the first social confirmation of the structures of endurance that the domestic day imparted). I stayed to win many Church of England hymnals.

It wasn't I think, the legal impropriety that I knew about, the illegitimacy; rather I felt the wider disjuncture of our existence, its lack of authorization.

In 1954 the *Pirates of Penzance* was playing at the Streatham Hill Theatre, and we had one of the baritones as a lodger instead of the usual girls. He was different from them, didn't eat in the kitchen with us, but had my mother bake him potatoes and grate carrots which he ate in the isolation of the dining-room. He converted my mother to Food Reform, and when she made a salad of grated vegetables for Christmas dinner in 1955, my father walked out and I wished he'd taken us with him.

I've talked to other people whose mothers came to naturopathy in the 1950s, and it's been explained as a way of eating posh for those who didn't know about continental food. I think it did have a lot to do with the status that being different conferred, for in spite of the austerity of our childhood, we believed that we were better than other people, the food we ate being a mark of this, because our mother told us so—so successfully that even now I have to work hard at actually seeing the deprivations. But much more than difference, our diet had to do with the need, wrenched from restricted circumstances, to be in charge of the body. Food Reform promised an end to sickness if certain procedures were followed, a promise that was not, of course, fulfilled. I spent a childhood afraid to fall ill, because being ill would mean that my mother would have to stay off work and lose money.

But more fundamental than this, I think, a precise costing of our child-hood lay behind our eating habits. Brussel sprouts, baked potatoes, grated cheese, the variation of vegetables in the summer, a tin of vegetarian steak pudding on Sundays and a piece of fruit afterwards is a monotonous but healthy diet, and I can't think of many cheaper ways to feed two children and feel you're doing your best for them at the same time. We can't ever have cost very much. She looked at us sometimes, after we'd finished eat-ing. "Good, Kay, eh?" What I see on her face now is a kind of muted satis-faction; she'd done her best, though her best was limited: not her fault. Children she'd grown up with had died in the 1930s: "They hadn't enough to eat."

She brought the food home at night, buying each day's supply when she got off the bus from work. My sister's job was to meet her at the bus-stop with the wheel basket so she didn't have to carry the food up the road. We ate a day's supply at a time, so there was never much in the house overnight except bread for breakfast and the staples that were bought on Saturday. When I started to think about these things I was in a position to interpret this way of living and eating as a variation of the spending patterns of poverty described in Booth's and Rowntree's great surveys at the turn of the century; but now I am sure that it was the cheap-ness of it that propelled the practice. We were a finely balanced invest-ment, threatening constantly to topple over into the realm of demand and expenditure. I don't think, though, that until we left home we ever cost more to feed and clothe than that seven pounds handed over each week.

Now I see the pattern of our nourishment laid down, like our useful-ness, by an old set of rules. At six I was old enough to go on errands, at seven to go further to pay the rent and the rates, go on the long dreary walk to the Co-op for the divi. By eight I was old enough to clean the house and do the weekend shopping. At eleven it was understood that I washed the breakfast things, lit the fire in the winter and scrubbed the kitchen floor before I started my homework. At fifteen, when I could legally go out to work, I got a Saturday job which paid for my clothes (ex-cept my school uniform, which was part of the deal, somehow). I think that until I drop I will clean wherever I happen to be on Saturday morn-ing. I take a furtive and secret pride in the fact that I can do all these things, that I am physically strong, can lift and carry things that defeat other women, wonder with some scorn what it must be like to learn to clean a house when adult, and not to have the ability laid down as part of the growing self. Like going to sleep by contrasting a bed with a pave-ment, I sometimes find myself thinking that if the worst comes to the worst, I can always earn a living by my hands; I can scrub, clean, cook and sew: all you have in the end is your labor.

I was a better deal than my sister, because I passed the eleven plus, went to grammar school, would get a good job, marry a man who would in her words "buy me a house and you a house. There's no virtue in poverty." In the mid-1960s the Sunday color supplements were full of pictures of student life, and she came to see a university as offering the same arena of advantage as the good job had earlier done. The dreary curtailment of our childhood was, we discovered after my mother's death, the result of the most fantastic saving: for a house, the house that was never bought. When I was about seventeen I learned that V. S. Naipaul had written *A House for Mr Biswas* in Streatham Hill, a few streets away from where we lived. There are interpretations now that ask me to see the house, both the fictional one and the one my mother longed for through the years, as the place of undifferentiated and anonymous desire, to see it standing in her dream as the objects of the fairy-tales do—princesses, golden geese, palaces—made desirable in the story simply because someone wants them.[6] But for my mother, as for Mr Biswas, the house was valuable in itself because of what it represented of the social world: a place of safety, wealth and position, a closed door, a final resting place. It was a real dream that dictated the pattern of our days.

It seems now to have been a joyless childhood. There were neighbors who fed us meat and sweets, sorry for us, tea parties we went to that we were never allowed to return. I recall the awful depression of Sunday afternoons, my mother with a migraine in the front bedroom, the house an absolute stillness. But I don't *remember* the oddness; it's a reconstruction. What I remember is what I read, and playing Annie Oakley by myself all summer long in the recreation ground, running up and down the hill in my brown gingham dress, wearing a cowboy hat and carrying a rifle. Saturday-morning pictures confirmed it all: women worked hard, earned their own living; carried guns into the bargain.

The essence of being a good child is taking on the perspective of those who are more powerful than you, and I was good in this way as my sister never was. A house up the road, Sunday afternoon 1958, plates of roast lamb offered. My sister ate, but I refused; not out of sacrifice, nor because I was resisting temptation (I firmly believed that meat would make me ill, as my mother said) but because I understood (though this is the adult's formulation rather than the ten-year-old's) that the price of the meal was condemnation of my mother's oddness, and I wasn't having that. I was a very upright child.

At eight I had my first migraine (I could not please her; I might as well join her; they stopped soon after I left home) and I started to get rapidly and relentlessly short-sighted. I literally stopped seeing for a very long time. It is through the development of symptoms like these, some of them neurotic, that I can site the disasters of our childhood, and read it from an outsider's point of view. I think I passed those years believing that we were unnoticed, *unseen;* but of course we were seen, and the evidence of witnesses was retrievable by memory much later on. In 1956 when the first migraine opened a tunnel of pain one June morning, my little sister developed acute psoriasis. My teacher was worried at my failing sight, I couldn't see the board by the spring of 1957 and read a book under my desk during arithmetic lessons. Did he send a note to my mother? Surely he must have done; what else could have shaken her conviction that glasses would be bad for me? He said to me the morning after he'd seen her, "Your mother says you're doing exercises for your eyes; make sure you do them properly." I thought he was being kind, and he was; but I preserved the voice that I might later hear the disapproval in it. I think they must have used the eleven-plus and the amount of blackboard work it involved as a lever, because I got a pair of glasses before the exam.

That afternoon she walked up the road with me, what had they told her? The next year, standing by my new teacher's desk, now in the eleven-plus class, he showed my book to what must have been a student on teaching practice. "This one," he said, "has an inferiority complex." I didn't understand, had no dictionary in which to look up the words, but preserved them by my own invented syllabary, rehearsing them, to bring out for much later scrutiny. I must in fact have known that people were watching, being witnesses, for some years later I started to play a game of inviting their comment and disapproval and then withdrawing the spectacle I had placed before their eyes, making them feel ashamed of the pity they had felt. By the time I was fifteen we'd all three of us given up, huddled with tiredness and irritation in the house where my father was only now an intermittent presence. The house was a tip; none of us did any housework any more; broken china wasn't replaced; at meal times my mother, my sister and I shared the last knife between us. Responsible now for my own washing, I scarcely did any, spent the winter changing about the layers of five petticoats I wore to keep warm, top to bottom through the cold months. One morning, asked by the games mistress why I wasn't wearing my school blouse, I said I hadn't been able to find it in the place I'd put it down the night before (not true; I hadn't a clean one), presenting thus a scene of baroque household disorganization, daring her to disapprove, hoping she would.

Ten years before this, school had taught me to read, and I found out for myself how to do it fast. By the time I was six I read all the time, rapidly and voraciously. You couldn't join the library until you were seven, and before that I read my Hans Christian Andersen from back to front when I'd read it from start to finish. Kay was my name at home, and I knew that Kay, the boy in "The Snow Queen," was me, who had a lump of ice in her heart. I knew that one day I might be asked to walk on the edge of knives, like the Little Mermaid, and was afraid that I might not be able to bear the pain. Foxe's *Book of Martyrs* was in the old library, a one-volume edition with colored illustrations for Victorian children, the text pruned to a litany of death by flame. My imagination was furnished with the passionate martyrdom of the Protestant North ". . . Every blank cries shame; Finish what you have begun, In the Savior's name."

I see now the relentless laying down of guilt, and I feel a faint surprise that I must interpret it that way. My sister, younger than me, with children of her own and perhaps thereby with a clearer measure of what we lacked, tells me to recall a mother who never played with us, whose eruptions from irritation into violence were the most terrifying of experiences; and she is there, the figure of nightmares, though I do find it difficult to think about in this way. Such reworking of past time is new, infinitely surprising; and against it I must balance what it felt like then, and the implications of the history given me in small doses; that not being hungry and having a warm bed to lie in at night, I had a good childhood, was better than other people; was a *lucky* little girl.

My mother had wanted to marry a king. That was the best of my father's stories, told in the pub in the 1960s, of how difficult it had been to live with her in 1937, during the Abdication months. Mrs Simpson was no prettier than her, no more clever than her, no better than her. It wasn't fair that a king should give up his throne for her, and not for the weaver's daughter. From a traditional Labor background, my mother rejected the politics of solidarity and communality, always voted Conservative, for the left could not embody her desire for things to be *really* fair, for a full skirt that took twenty yards of cloth, for a half-timbered cottage in the country, for the prince who did not come. For my mother, the time of my childhood was the place where the fairy-tales failed.

### A Thin Man

> Roll up, roll up, come and see the mermaid,
> See the lovely lady, half a woman, half a fish.
> In went the lads to show it wasn't swank,
> When little Tommy 'Iggins put some whisky in the tank.
> Well, she got frisky, swimmin' in the whisky,
> And when she come up for air
> She bowed to the audience, gave 'er tail a swish;
> 'Er tail it come off, and she really looked delish;
> She says, 'What d'y'want, lads, a bit o' meat or fish?'
> At the Rawtenstall Annual Fair.
> – "Rawtenstall Annual Fair," 1932, from Roy Palmer,
> *A Ballad History of England,* Batsford, 1979

By the time my father could sit down in a pub with me, slightly drunk, tell me and my friends about Real Life, crack a joke about a Pakistani that silenced a whole table once, and talk about the farm laborer's—his grandfather's—journey up from Eye in Suffolk working on the building of the Great North Western Railway, up to Rawtenstall on the Lancashire–Yorkshire border, I was doing history at Sussex, and knew more than he did about the date and timing of journeys like that. My father, old but gritty, glamorous in the eyes of the class of '68, a South London wide boy with an authentic background, described his grandfather's funeral, about 1912, when a whole other family—wife, children, grandchildren—turned up out of the blue from somewhere further down the line, where they'd been established on the navvy's journey north. (This was a circumstance paralleled at his own funeral, when the friends and relations of the woman he'd been living with for part of the week since the early 1960s stole the show from us, the pathetic huddle of the family of his middle years.)

When I look in the mirror, I see her face, but I know in fact that I look more like him. A real Lancashire face. He was a thin man. I knew his height, five foot ten, but he never seemed tall; he shrank in later years to not much above my height. The silhouette of men has changed completely since the 1950s, and it is this above all else that has altered the outlines of city streets; not the shape of the buildings nor the absence of trams and the growing sleekness of cars, but the fact that men no longer wear hats— broad-brimmed felt hats, tipped slightly over one eye. The Sandeman port man loomed on the hoardings outside Hammersmith Broadway station, the first thing I can remember, sitting up in my pram: an exaggeration and extrapolation of how they all looked, huge coat swirling, trousers flapping, the broad-brimmed rakish hat. A consistent point of my mother's propaganda against him was the shoddiness of his dress and the cheapness of his clothes, his awful ties, his refusal to spend money on his appearance, his lack of taste. But memory doesn't detail him like that; rather, a silhouette, a dapper outline.

He took me out once to a bluebell wood. My sister had just been born, we were waiting to move to Streatham Hill: spring 1951. I wore one of the two gingham dresses (I can't remember which color, I can never remember the color; they are both just the dress, the clothing of dreams). He was to take me out again, but this time in the bluebell wood was really the last time. I had a sister; we were about to move; his expulsion from the domestic scene about to begin.

It was shaded, a real wood, the sunlight outside beyond the trees, with a fern-covered slope up to the left of the path, the bluebells growing up the slope, and a clearing at the top of that. Up this small incline, and my father started to pick the bluebells from in between the ferns, making a bunch. Did he give me some to hold? I can't remember, except how else to know about their white watery roots, the pale cleanness pulled from the earth? And if he did give me some, what did I do with them in the next few minutes?

The arrival of the forest-keeper was a dramatic eruption on this scene, jarring color descending on a shady place, a hairy jacket in that strange orange tweed that park-keepers still sometimes wear, plus-fours, brown boots and a pork-pie hat. He was angry with my father, shouted at him: it wasn't allowed. Hadn't he read the notice, there'd be no bluebells left if people pulled them up by the roots. He snatched the bunch from my father's hand, scattered the flowers over the ground and among the ferns, their white roots glimmering, unprotected; and I thought: yes, he doesn't know how to pick bluebells.

My father stood, quite vulnerable in memory now. He was a thin man. I wonder if I remember the waisted and pleated flannel trousers of the early 1950s because in that confrontation he was the loser, feminized, outdone? They made him appear thinner, and because of the way the ground sloped, the forest-keeper, very solid and powerful, was made to appear taller than him. In remembering this scene I always forget, always have to deliberately call to mind the fact that my father retaliated, shouted back; and that we then retreated, made our way back down the path, the tweed man the victor, watching our leaving.

All the charity I possess lies in that moment. Any account that presents its subjects as cold, or shivering or in any way unprotected recalls the precise structure of its feeling. The child who told Henry Mayhew about her life as a seller of cresses in the winter of 1850 stands on the page clutching her shawl about her thin shoulders as the very aetiology of my pity. And there is a more difficult charity that lies somewhere beneath this structure, partly obscured by figures of the imagination like the little watercress girl: pity for something that at the age of four I knew and did not know about my father (know now, and do not know), something about the roots and their whiteness, and the way in which they had been pulled away, to wither exposed on the bank.

Summer came, and we started to live in the new house. It was June, a hot afternoon out in the garden, which was soon to become a farmyard of hen-houses and duck-ponds made out of old tin baths, but now on this hot day, a couple of weeks after we'd moved from Hammersmith, the perfect and sedate little garden made by the old couple who inhabited the house for forty years. The world went wrong that afternoon: there is evidence: a photograph. My father said "Smile, Kay," and I smiled; but it is really the day of my first dislocation. I lie on my stomach on the grass, my baby sister on a rug to my right, just in front of me. I am irritated and depressed because she has come to stay. Things have changed: on removal day I turned on the kitchen tap to fill a cup with water and couldn't turn it off, and the removal man was angry with me: the first time an adult's anger has been directed at me. I remember this now. Somewhere on the grass, beyond the photograph, is an apple that I've been given to cheer me up, but that I refuse to eat. We carry moments like this through a lifetime: things were wrong; there was a dislocation between me and the world; I am not inside myself. And he said "Smile Kay," and I smiled: the first deception, the first lie.

He had a story about how he left the North, a good story, well told. He'd had a few when he first presented it to me, and listeners from that Christmas meeting of 1967 in the pub remember its inconsistencies above anything else. The setting for the tale my father tells is the Blackpool Tower ballroom, it's the summer, and Robin Richmond is playing the organ. Which year? My calculation now says it must be 1934, but he doesn't mention dates himself. Is the famous organist introduced to add glamor to the occasion and the telling of it, even though my father affects to despise the sea-side medleys he's playing? Then suddenly Robin Richmond becomes a part of the story. My father implies that he's been carrying on with the organist's woman. Anyway, there's a woman somewhere in the story, a woman to fight over. There *is* a fight. On the dance floor or in the underground car park? It's unclear; but the story suddenly shifts to the car park anyway, and it's Robin Richmond punching him, and knocking him out; yet the music seems to go on playing.

Someone knocks my father out anyway, and he either gets into, or is pushed inside a car, on to the back seat. He has a lot to sleep off. The story cuts suddenly to South London, to Balham, and Ellis wakes up, not knowing where he is. The drivers of the car have brought him all the way from Blackpool, not realizing he's in the back. It's outside a lodging house, the car; the people are friendly. He eats bacon and eggs, "looks around a bit," decides he "likes the look of the place," borrows ten pounds, goes back North to "collect a few things," coming back down again to the city in which he was to pass the next forty years of his life. He emphasized "the few things": the phrase meant more than was apparent: one day, secrets might be revealed.

It's a good story, an allegory I think, that covers a plainer tale. Something had gone wrong, he was scared, he had to get out of town. Fifteen years after the telling, long after his death, looking at the suddenly revealed photograph on the bedroom mantelpiece, I found out what it was he'd left behind.

Underneath the Hammersmith flat, the flat we left in the early summer of 1951, was a cellar. It was part of the huge gothic building next door where he worked. It ran underneath our first-floor flat too, but to reach it you had to go down the stairs and out into the street first. Down here, my father kept his tools, and sometime during the year before we moved he started to make me a dolls' house. My mother took me down there to show me work in progress, the bare toy rafters and the little roll of tiled wallpaper for the roof. My father was surprised to see us, and in retrospect it is very odd that we should have made this descent, for later on, his not understanding the conventions of emotional life, like keeping surprises a secret—or preparing any sort of surprise, giving any sort of present—was to be one of the many items on my mother's check-list of his failures.

My mother leant back against a workbench, her hands on its edge behind her. It tipped her body forward, just a little. She leant back; she laughed, she smiled. Ellis stood under the spot of light, a plane in his hand, a smile: a charmer charmed. Years later it becomes quite clear that this was the place where my mother set in motion my father's second seduction. She'd tried with having me, and it hadn't worked. Now, a second and final attempt. By the time he took me to the bluebell wood, my sister was born, and our life was set on its sad course. The scene of seduction remained a mystery for a very long time, an area of puzzlement that failed to illuminate, like the light absorbing the darkness over the workbench. When I consciously thought about the mysteries of their relationship, I used in fact a highly literary set of devices.

My intensest reading of the fairy-tales was during the summer of my seventh year. The feeling of nostalgia and regret for how things actually are was made that June as Gerda in "The Snow Queen" looked for Kay along the river banks that were eventually to lead to the queen's frozen palace, and she came to the place where the old woman, the witch, made all the rose trees sink into the dark ground so that Gerda would stay with her, not be reminded by the flowers of Kay, for whom she is searching.

Out the back, outside the room where the child reads the book, there grew a dark red rose with an ecstatic smell. The South London back gardens pressed up against the open window like a sadness in the dusk, and I lay on my bed, and read, and imagined what it was they were doing downstairs. The wireless was playing and I saw this picture: they both sat naked under the whitewood kitchen table, their legs crossed so that you couldn't really see what lay between. Each had a knife, sharp-edged with a broad yet pointed blade, and what they did with the knife, what the grown-ups did, was cut each other, making thin surface wounds like lines drawn with a sharp red pencil, from which the blood poured. In the book the Little Robber Girl whom Gerda has encountered on her journey north

> pulled out a long knife from a crevice in the wall and drew it across the reindeer's neck; the poor animal kicked with its legs, and the Robber Girl laughed and then pulled Gerda into bed with her. "Do you take the knife to bed with you?" asked Gerda, looking somewhat scared at it. "I always sleep with a knife," said the Little Robber Girl. "One never knows what may happen."

Downstairs I thought, the thin blood falls in sheets from my mother's breasts; she was the most cut, but I knew it was she who did the cutting. I couldn't always see the knife in my father's hand.

In the same book, another girl, another woman—the Little Mermaid— longs to enter the world above the sea from which she is excluded by being what she is: "More and more she came to love human beings, more and more she wished to be among them. Their world she thought, was far larger than hers." It is love that will help her enter this world, desire for the prince whom she watches obsessively, as she swims round his ship, night after night. To enter this world of adult sexuality, to gain two legs instead of a fish's tail, she strikes a bargain with the Sea Witch: she must feel every step as if walking on the edge of knives, and her tongue must be cut out. In pain, dumb and silenced, she makes her sacrifice in vain, for the prince does not love her back; and when the day of his marriage to a mortal dawns, the

Little Mermaid must die. Her sisters of the sea offer her the chance of life: by killing the prince and having his warm blood fall on her feet, her legs will join together again, into a fish's tail. But instead she sacrifices herself, flings away the knife, and is dissolved into the foam on the waves.

The fairy-tales always tell the stories that we do not yet know. Often, a few years later, I would long for my mother to get rid of my father, expel him, kill him, make him no more, so that we could lead a proper life. And what I know with hindsight about that summer of the fairy-tales, is that a new drama was in process of enactment. The removal of my father by the birth of my sister (an old, conventional story, every eldest daughter's tale) was being formalized by my mother's warfare against him, a warfare that always stopped short of banishment; and I was to end up ten, indeed twenty years later, believing that my identification was entirely with her, that whilst hating her, I was her; and there was no escape.

The Little Mermaid was not my mother sacrificing herself for a beautiful prince: I knew her sacrifice: it was not composed of love or longing for my father, rather of a fierce resentment against the circumstances that were so indifferent to her. She turns me into the Little Mermaid a few years later, swimming round and round the ship, wondering why I was not wanted, but realizing that of course, it had to be that way: "How could he do it," she said, "leave two nice little girls like you?"

Our household and the registrar general's socio-economic categories mask a complicated reality. Social class is defined by a father's occupation, and during my childhood we must have belonged to class III (manual). A heating engineer without any training, he did get inside boilers and mend them, but more often told other men what to do. He was, in effect, a foreman. I think that for my mother, years before in the 1930s, her relationship with him had been a step up, a kind of catch for the weaver's daughter. His parents had once kept a corner sweet shop, and my mother told me when I was about eleven that they'd briefly had a pony and cart before losing it, and the business. She spoke of this vehicle, in which she'd never ridden, with a diffident pride: the little nod of pleased possession. But the pleasure had to be ambiguous now: she was already long engaged in revealing my father's meanness, vulgarity and lack of ambition. When he married in 1926 he gave his trade as traveler for a firm of mill-part manufacturers in York. There's a photograph that looks as if it were taken about this time showing a woolen mill decorated for Christmas, the girls turned towards the camera, their looms still, and standing amongst them one man, my father in a collar and tie, a visitor from the mobile world outside.

If we'd lived within my father's earning power, been uncomplicatedly his children, two meals a day round the kitchen table, parents sharing a bed (and the *car*; in all those years my mother was never driven anywhere in the firm's car) then our household would actually have represented, and represented to its children, the unambiguous position of the upper working class. But it was my mother who defined our class position, and the emotional configurations that follow on such an assessment. What is more, until we were in our thirties, my sister and I continued to believe that she bore the major burden of supporting us. As children we believed that without her we'd go hungry, and the knowledge of how little we cost came very late indeed.

He had nothing to give her in exchange for herself, not even the name that the statute books would allow him to bestow on her (and probably wouldn't have given it to her had he been able). The house was rented, the weekly seven pounds was payment for us, not a gift to her. She made us out of her own desire, her own ambition, and everything that came her way in the household was a by-product of our presence and her creation of our presence. We were an insurance, a roof over her head, a minimum income. We were her way of both having him and repudiating him. We were the cake that she both had and ate, before he left (though he never really left), and after.

In 1958 I passed the eleven-plus, and in August of that year the uniform I needed for grammar school was the subject of angry debate. He'd been approached for money for the gaberdine mac, the tunic, the shoes, and he had handed some over, but not a lot. The uniform must have been a strain on the seven pounds. The issue, this Saturday afternoon, is the blouses that I will have to wear. I'm wearing a new one anyway, one from Marks & Spencer with blue embroidery round the collar, as I approach him at my mother's persuasion and drag his attention away from the form on telly. He asks why I can't wear the one I've got on. I'm profoundly irritated, outraged at his stupidity; they don't allow it, I say: it's a *rule*.

He did know some rules, but he didn't embody them: they were framed by some distant authority outside himself. For instance: I had become very timid in the years after 1951, often frightened of falling down, of appearing a fool. I disgraced him that summer in the public eye, sitting at the top of the slide on the Common, a queue of impatient children behind me, frozen with fear, quite unable to let go of the sides and slide down. In disgrace I turned round, made my shameful way down the steps again, the children parting in front of me and my father apologizing to the adults with them. He took me home and complained to my mother: there's something wrong with her, a child of five ought not to be frightened; a child of five ought to be able to slide.

He waited for me on the doorstep one time about a year later after he'd sent me down the road for a paper, because a neighbor watching me had said I was walking funny, looked flat-footed. I had my wellingtons on the wrong feet, it turned out. He knew the social prescriptions that said we ought to be alright, have *nothing wrong* with us—to be able to read, to walk straight—and that he was judged by our performance too.

In the mid-fifties he started to live in the attic, treated the place like a hotel. The firm put a telephone in the house, about 1956, so that he could deal with emergencies about burst boilers in the middle of the night. He came home at six o'clock, collected phone messages, made a mug of tea, washed, went out to his other life. Whilst we were children he always came back, sometimes before midnight. In the attic he read the *Evening Standard,* smoked a cigarette before he went to sleep. I interpret this nightly return as an expression of the ambivalent responsibility that lay in the seven pounds handed over on Friday, as a failure either to desert us or to change the situation he'd put us in: a man serving out his time, the maintenance payments as much a matter of obligation as those imposed in a bastardy order issued by a court of law. My sister says he came back because he didn't want to commit himself anywhere. He was a man of benevolent irresponsibility.

She wouldn't feed him, after about 1958, but he was allowed tea. Every morning in a red tartan dressing-gown he made his own. She must have bought the tea (that we were never permitted to drink) out of the seven pounds. Tea was tea and milk was milk (except for a brief flirtation with goats' milk, at which all the worms turned) but she had some choice over sugar, and refused to buy white poison. There was a long time, about 1960, when he complained every morning about the grittiness and how it made the tea taste. Later, I think he bought his own packets of Tate & Lyle.

We still had lodgers in the 1960s, not the glamorous turn-over of the theatrical years, but sad, long-term men. My father met the newly arrived watch-mender on the stairs and said "Hello, I'm the other lodger," and the watch-mender believed him for days. This incident was remembered, given the status of a joke (our only family joke), an explanatory device, for my father to recall ten years later in the pub, for me and my sister to remember and laugh over after my mother's funeral. Curtailment of activity and exclusion from particular rooms of the house was a rule that my mother put into effect for all those men who handed over payment to her. The watch-mender wasn't allowed to use the bath—she said he was too dirty. This stricture didn't apply, however, to the Indian student who occupied the room before him. My mother explained that Hindus had to wash in running water and that they found us dirty. He had the charm of the exotic for her: anything foreign, over which she could show a classy tolerance, was a route away from her social situation. Later, she was to call herself a Powellite.

On Saturday afternoon the front room became briefly my father's territory. Racing on the telly, bets over the phone to the bookie, mugs of tea, whisky later on. He cleared the room after the football results and when he'd checked his coupon. This usage, I now understand, was his right within the treaty negotiated somehow with my mother. I could have read those rights in other actions, in the way, for instance, if he came home early on a weekday night and found us still in the front room, he'd switch off the lights, and fire and television, and leave us in the dark as he went upstairs to the attic; and in the permanently dismantled electric fire in my room, so that I could only ever burn one bar.

My father used to say: "She's a wonderful woman, your mother," or sometimes "She's a bloody wonderful mother, Edna is." When? When I asked him, on her instructions, for something. There was a long campaign, about 1961, to get him to buy a unit to replace the deep porcelain sink in the scullery (he didn't); pressure a few years later to get him to buy a house, and then to make a will. When I hear of passive resistance, I think of my father. All pleadings were now made through me. I would feel the justice of my mother's cause, raise the matter, usually Saturday lunch times after he got home from work, and before the racing started, plead the case, argue that she worked so hard. He never capitulated; listened; then: "She's a bloody marvelous mother, your mother." I can never read this deadly rejoinder, never, however many times I rehearse it, *hear* what it was he was saying. In interpretation it falls this way, then that; I don't know what he meant. It was a statement beyond irony (though it was ironic, in a way I couldn't and wasn't expected to understand: information withheld). He meant it in some way, revealed that he had surrendered to her interpretation of events, was playing the role assigned to him. Sometimes drink was mentioned: "She doesn't drink, your mother." I think the stories of maternal neglect brought from pre-War Lancashire expressed a reality that both of them knew about. Much later, he was genuinely shocked when, at twenty-seven, I wrote to my mother and said that I didn't want to see her for a while because she upset me so much. He said then that she'd been a good mother; but he'd forgotten the unassailable irony of fifteen years before.

There were fits and starts in their relationship, so dramatically altered at Christmas 1954. They got together again, the attic temporarily abandoned, about 1961. There were meals together; I remember weeping at Sunday dinner time into a bowl of tinned fruit, the tinned food itself a sure sign that some truce was being enacted. But it didn't last. Once, a dreadful time, the other life invading ours ("There's that woman on the phone again"; "Why tell me?" "Who else is there to tell?"), I packed all his things in the suitcases, and put them in the hall. I wanted him to go, for *something to happen,* something to change. I saw the future—work, the journey home, the quick meal, television, tiredness, my mother's life— stretching ahead for ever, like the long streets of South London houses; no end ever to be seen. But he didn't go. Nothing changed.

I still see him in the street, seven years after his death, a man of his generation, an old man at a bus-stop, his clothes hanging in folds; a way of walking. I shall never see my mother in the street in this way; she, myself, walks my dreams.

When he died I spent days foolishly hoping that there would be something for me. I desperately wanted him to give me something. The woman he'd been living with handed over two bottles of elderberry wine that they'd made together out of fruit gathered from the side of the ring road where her flat was. I drank one of them and it gave me the worst hangover of my life.

He left us without anything, never gave us a thing. In the fairy-stories the daughters love their fathers because they are mighty princes, great rulers, and because such absolute power seduces. The modern psychoanalytic myths posit the same plot, old tales are made manifest: secret longings, doors closing along the corridors of the bourgeois household. But daddy, you never knew me like this; you didn't really care, or weren't allowed to care, it comes to the same thing in the end. You shouldn't have left us there, you should have taken me with you. You left me alone; you never laid a hand on me: the iron didn't enter into the soul. You never gave me anything: the lineaments of an unused freedom.

## NOTES

[1] George Herriman's Krazy Kat cartoons, syndicated throughout the USA from 1913 onwards, are reproduced in *Krazy Kat Komix*, vols 1–4, Real Free Press, Amsterdam, 1974–75.

[2] That is, never applied to the parish authorities for financial assistance under the Poor Law.

[3] Jill Liddington and Jill Norris, *One Hand Tied Behind Us: The Rise of the Women's Suffrage Movement*, Virago, 1978.

[4] Samuel Bamford, *Early Days*, 1849, quoted in David Vincent, *Bread, Knowledge and Freedom*, Methuen, 1981, p. 92.

[5] Richard Hoggart mentions the sum of £8 a week as an extravagant amount to spend on housekeeping in 1956/7. *Uses of Literacy*, p. 43.

[6] Frederic Jameson, *The Political Unconscious*, Methuen, 1981, pp. 155–57. V. S. Naipaul, *A House for Mr. Biswas*, André Deutsch, 1961. See *New York Review of Books*, 24 November 1983, for Naipaul's description of writing the book in Streatham Hill.

• • • • • • • • • • •

### QUESTIONS FOR A SECOND READING

1. To read Steedman's prose, a reader needs to learn to pay close attention to tone and voice. As a narrator, Steedman takes different positions, speaks in different voices, lets others speak through her, sometimes in a single sentence. Below are two examples. Listen closely.

   > Now, thirty years later, I feel a great regret for the father of my first four years, who took me out and who probably loved me, irresponsibly ("It's alright for him; he doesn't have to look after you"), and I wish I could tell him now, even though he really was a sod, that I'm sorry for the years of rejection and dislike. (p. 651)

   Steedman speaks carefully and reflectively: "Now, thirty years later . . ." She speaks colloquially, from within the linguistic world of her childhood: "even though he really was a sod . . ." And her mother speaks through her, as a voice from the past: "'It's alright for him; he doesn't have to look after you.'" And all of this has an effect on how we understand what she says about sorrow and regret. The prose enacts the difficulty of making a clear, unqualified statement about her feelings or about her father.
   Here is a second example:

> My sister ate, but I refused; not out of sacrifice, nor because I was re-
> sisting temptation (I firmly believed that meat would make me ill, as
> my mother said) but because I understood (though this is the adult's
> formulation rather than the ten-year-old's) that the price of the meal
> was condemnation of my mother's oddness, and I wasn't having that.
> (p. 656)

As you reread, pay close attention to shifts of tone and voice. Are
there patterns to follow? Differences in the two "case studies"? If Steedman is preparing you as a reader, how is she teaching you to read? And
why? (Who is speaking, for example, in the last sentences of "A Thin
Man?")

Choose two or three examples of "multivocal" prose, examples you
find interesting and worth discussion. Be prepared to say something
about why you think Steedman's project would require (or produce) such
prose.

2. The case studies are preceded by epigraphs drawn from fairy tale and
folk song. (It is worth noting that Disney's version of "The Little Mermaid" is very different from the Hans Christian Andersen story that is
Steedman's source.) You should assume that Steedman thought carefully
in choosing them and in placing them in the text. As you reread, think
about how these epigraphs stand as "introductions," as tools to use or instructions for you as a reader.

3. "Exiles" presents a family history; it is also a work of social history. In it,
Steedman provides a detailed account of the material goods and ways of
life present in England before and after World War II. There are many
references that will not be immediately meaningful to you: "the New
Look," "Food Reform," "naturopathy," "Burnley Weavers," "Marks and
Spencer," "Enoch Powell." They come from a different time and place.

As you reread, focus attention on the details of historical description
and identification. Read *for* the history rather than (or as well as) reading
for the account of family and feeling; read to make these references significant and meaningful. (In most cases, you can learn what you need to
know by paying attention to context.) Working closely with the text, what
can you learn about the particulars of these times and places?

## ASSIGNMENTS FOR WRITING

1. "Exiles" is not anchored by a single argument or consistent point of view.
The sketches, or "case studies," are interesting and compelling but also
are hard to read. It is hard to know what is going on. The accounts do not
reproduce the usual narratives of family and childhood, those with ready-
made sentiments and predictable outlines. Steedman's narrative, as she
said, "shows what went into its writing, shows the bits and pieces from
which it is made up, in the way that history refuses to do, and that fiction
can't."

Steedman's prose in "Exiles" is the kind that works hard at problems
of understanding and representation; it is not a simple prose of report and
summary. One of the difficulties facing readers of her work is to provide

an account of what they take to be the author's project. What is she setting out to do in these accounts of her parents? What are the issues? What is the argument? What does she hope to find or to learn or to do? To whom is she writing? to what end?

Write an essay in which you provide an account of what you take to be Steedman's project. Your account can be provisional. You can, that is, write about what you don't understand or don't quite understand, and you can find more than one purpose or desire in the text. You should not think of your account as a book report or a summary; you don't have to make everything simple, neat, and tidy. You can assume that you are writing for readers who have read "Exiles" and who are looking for help, for a way of thinking about and talking about what Steedman is doing. (Your readers do not, however, have the book in front of them.) You will need to work from quotation and example, translating passages and providing context.

2. In "A Thin Man," Steedman talks about the summer she began reading fairy-tales, in particular *The Snow Queen* and *The Little Mermaid,* and she recalls the ways those stories assisted or shaped her understanding of herself and her mother.

> The Little Mermaid was not my mother sacrificing herself for a beautiful prince: I knew her sacrifice: it was not composed of love or longing for my father, rather of a fierce resentment against the circumstances that were so indifferent to her. She turns me into the Little Mermaid a few years later, swimming round and round the ship, wondering why I was not wanted, but realizing that of course, it had to be that way: "How could he do it," she said, "leave two nice little girls like you?" (p. 663)

*Landscape for a Good Woman* is, Steedman says, a book "about the stories we make for ourselves, and the social specificity of our understanding of those stories." Throughout "Exiles" people seem to cast each other (and themselves) as characters in stories; they write themselves into available narratives. Choose one or two examples of this in "Exiles." Where do the stories come from? What do they accomplish? Whose interests—or what ends—do they serve? What problems do they create? Write an essay in which you consider the case studies as occasions for Steedman to represent and to think through the role and use of stories in this working class family history.

Note: The assignment asks you to think about the storytelling *in* "Exiles." Once you have written this essay (perhaps in preparation for discussion, perhaps as a guide for revision), it might be useful to think about the writing of "Exiles" as itself a form of storytelling. How might "Exiles" be seen as something Steedman made for herself? What is its relationship to the "official interpretive devices of the culture"? Is this act of storytelling representative of greater wisdom, dexterity, truthfulness, authority, authenticity? Is there a lesson to learn here?

3. In the opening pages of *Landscape for a Good Woman,* Steedman says

> Personal interpretations of past time—the stories that people tell themselves in order to explain how they got to the place they currently inhabit—are often in deep and ambiguous conflict with the official interpretative devices of a culture.

This sense of conflict is important to Steedman, particularly as it is related to political conflict (for her, the position of the working class in Britain). Write an essay in which you extend her project to your own time and place, to stories you have heard people tell themselves to explain how they got to the places they currently inhabit. Where and how might they be said to be in deep and ambiguous conflict with the official interpretive devices of a culture? Where and how might this *not* be the case?

Think of your essay as having two major sections. The first should be about "Exiles," a brief summary of Steedman's argument (written for someone *not* familiar with her work) to establish the context for your project. The second section is yours, but it should make use of Steedman's key terms and phrases, if only as a point of reference.

4.  It is useful to think of Steedman's prose as an enactment of a method, a way of writing a particular kind of highly personalized, highly reflexive social history. One way to study "Exiles," to feel its effects, is to imitate it, to take it as a model. For this assignment, write a parallel case study whose goal it is to say something about a particular place and time, about experiences determined by a particular social and historical setting. Steedman sees herself as representative of working class experience. You will need to think of a group for whom you can write as a representative.

As you reread "Exiles," think particularly about the features of her prose that you will incorporate into your own. And you should do this quite formally—looking for sentences whose style you will imitate, paragraphs or larger units of organization whose form you can work with. Perhaps most importantly, you will need to take a lesson from Steedman in how to establish your own position in the text. Steedman is present throughout "Exiles" in multiple ways. She writes from more than one historical vantage point (then, later, and now); she is present in more than one characterization (as a figure in a landscape, as a writer writing about that figure); she speaks in more than one register (local and academic). It is important that you see this assignment as an exercise in method and not simply as an invitation to write on a similar topic.

## MAKING CONNECTIONS

1.  Both Carolyn Kay Steedman, in "Exiles," and Richard Rodriguez, in "The Achievement of Desire" (p. 621) write accounts of growing up and leaving a working class family. The texts, however, are quite different in shape and feel and, although this is harder to trace out, in what they identify as the consequences of class in a person's education and passage to adulthood. There are obvious points of difference—differences of nationality, language, gender, generation—and there are subtle differences in their use of "class" as a way of understanding an individual's ways of living, working, and thinking.

Write an essay in which you consider the different accounts of class, culture, family, and education in "Exiles" and "The Achievement of Desire."

2. Paul Auster, in "Portrait of an Invisible Man" (p. 50), John Edgar Wideman, in "Our Time" (p. 707), and Steedman, in "Exiles," write family history. And all three writers present this as a difficult rather than a straightforward task. The difficulty is not simply a matter of having accurate records or significant recall; the difficulty is present in (a part of) writing and the relationship of a writer to language and, through language, to the past. The problems are formal problems: where to begin, how to end, how to put stories together in a way that is meaningful, that they might add up to something.

   Write an essay in which you use one of these selections to investigate another—where, perhaps, you use Auster to think about Steedman or Steedman to think about Wideman. Given what one author is doing, how do you see the work of the other? How are these projects in dialogue or conversation? Where and how do they go in completely different directions? You should imagine that your readers are familiar with both texts, but that they have not thought of bringing them together and do not have the texts handy. You will, then, need to do the work of presentation and summary as you establish the points of comparison.

3. John Berger, in "Ways of Seeing" (p. 105), said, "If we can see the present clearly enough, we shall ask the right questions of the past." And his essay is an argument about what it takes to see the present and a demonstration of what it might mean to ask the right questions of the past. Steedman is also concerned with the relationship between past and present and with how and why we might ask questions. Berger works with paintings and images, Steedman with books and stories. Both have shared concerns to improve the present and to keep contact with the past. Why?

   Write an essay in which you consider these essays, each from the point of view of the other. You will need to establish why and in what terms each author defines a concern for present and past. And you will need to bring the two essays into conversation. How would Berger respond to (perhaps review or teach) Steedman's text? What use might Steedman make of Berger?

   Note: Berger is, in fact, a point of reference in other sections of *Landscape for a Good Woman*. One way to work on this assignment would be to get a copy of the book and to see where and how Steedman invokes Berger's work.

# JANE
# TOMPKINS

*JANE TOMPKINS (b. 1940) received her B.A. from Bryn Mawr and completed both an M.A. and a Ph.D. at Yale. She has taught at Temple University, Connecticut College, Duke University, and the University of Illinois at Chicago. Among her publications are* Sensational Designs: The Cultural Work of American Fiction, 1790–1860 *(1985) and* West of Everything: The Inner Life of Westerns *(1992). She is also editor of* Reader-Response Criticism: From Formalism to Post-Structuralism *(1980). Her most recent book,* A Life in School: What the Teacher Learned *(1997) is a first-person critical account of American higher education.*

*In* Sensational Designs *Tompkins suggests that novels and short stories ought to be studied "not because they manage to escape the limitations of their particular time and place, but because they offer powerful examples of the way a culture thinks about itself, articulating and proposing solutions for the problems that shape a particular historical moment." This perspective leads Tompkins to conclude that the study of literature ought to focus not merely on those texts we call masterpieces but also on the texts of popular or best-selling authors. By studying these popular texts, Tompkins believes we can learn more of the "work" of novels and short stories, the influence they exert over the society in which they have been produced.*

*"Indians" was first published in 1986 in the influential journal of literary*

*criticism* Critical Inquiry. *It is an unusual essay in many ways, not the least of which is how it turns, as Tompkins's work often does, to anecdote and personal example. This is a surprising essay, perhaps even more surprising to faculty than to undergraduates. It is as though Tompkins was not willing to hide the "limitation of [her] particular time and place," limitations most scholars are more than happy to hide. In fact, Tompkins's selection could be said to take the reader behind the scenes of the respectable drama of academic research, offering a powerful example of how contemporary academic culture thinks about itself, articulating and proposing solutions for the problems that shape its particular historical moment. If individual interpretations are made and not found; if, for that matter, the "truths" of history or the background to American literature are made and not found, then there is every reason to acknowledge the circumstances of their making. And this is what Tompkins does. "Indians" is both a report on Tompkins's research and a reflection on the ways knowledge is produced, defended, and revised in academic life.*

# *"Indians": Textualism, Morality, and the Problem of History*

When I was growing up in New York City, my parents used to take me to an event in Inwood Park at which Indians—real American Indians dressed in feathers and blankets—could be seen and touched by children like me. This event was always a disappointment. It was more fun to imagine that you *were* an Indian in one of the caves in Inwood Park than to shake the hand of an old man in a headdress who was not overwhelmed at the opportunity of meeting you. After staring at the Indians for a while, we would take a walk in the woods where the caves were, and once I asked my mother if the remains of a fire I had seen in one of them might have been left by the original inhabitants. After that, wandering up some stone steps cut into the side of the hill, I imagined I was a princess in a rude castle. My Indians, like my princesses, were creatures totally of the imagination, and I did not care to have any real exemplars interfering with what I already knew.

I already knew about Indians from having read about them in school. Over and over we were told the story of how Peter Minuit had bought Manhattan Island from the Indians for twenty-four dollars' worth of glass beads. And it was a story we didn't mind hearing because it gave us the rare pleasure of having someone to feel superior to, since the poor Indians had not known (as we eight-year-olds did) how valuable a piece of property Manhattan Island would become. Generally, much was made of the Indian presence in Manhattan; a poem in one of our readers began: "Where we walk to school today/Indian children used to play," and we were encouraged to write poetry on this topic ourselves. So I had a fairly rich relationship with Indians before I ever met the unprepossessing people in Inwood Park. I felt that I had a lot in common with them. They, too, liked animals (they were often named after animals); they, too, made mistakes—they liked the brightly colored trinkets of little value that the white men were always offering them; they were handsome, warlike, and brave and had led an exciting, romantic life in the forest long ago, a life such as I dreamed of leading myself. I felt lucky to be living in one of the places where they had definitely been. Never mind where they were or what they were doing now.

My story stands for the relationship most non-Indians have to the people who first populated this continent, a relationship characterized by narcissistic fantasies of freedom and adventure, of a life lived closer to nature and to spirit than the life we lead now. As Vine Deloria, Jr., has pointed out, the American Indian Movement in the early seventies couldn't get people to pay attention to what was happening to Indians who were alive in the present, so powerful was this country's infatuation with people who wore loincloths, lived in tepees, and roamed the plains and forest long ago.[1] The present essay, like these fantasies, doesn't have much to do with actual Indians, though its subject matter is the histories of European-Indian relations in seventeenth-century New England. In a sense, my encounter with Indians as an adult doing "research" replicates the childhood one, for while I started out to learn more about Indians, I ended up preoccupied with a problem of my own.

This essay enacts a particular instance of the challenge poststructuralism poses to the study of history. In simpler language, it concerns the difference that point of view makes when people are giving accounts of events, whether at first or second hand. The problem is that if all accounts of events are determined through and through by the observer's frame of reference, then one will never know, in any given case, what really happened.

I encountered this problem in concrete terms while preparing to teach a course in colonial American literature. I'd set out to learn what I could about the Puritans' relations with American Indians. All I wanted was a general idea of what happened between the English settlers and the natives in seventeenth-century New England; poststructuralism and its dilemmas were the furthest thing from my mind. I began, more or less automatically, with Perry Miller, who hardly mentions the Indians at all, then proceeded to the work of historians who had dealt exclusively with the European-Indian encounter. At first, it was a question of deciding which of these authors to believe, for it quickly became apparent that there was no unanimity on the subject. As I read on, however, I discovered that the problem was more complicated than deciding whose version of events was correct. Some of the conflicting accounts were not simply contradictory, they were completely incommensurable, in that their assumptions about what counted as a valid approach to the subject, and what the subject itself was, diverged in fundamental ways. Faced with an array of mutually irreconcilable points of view, points of view which determined what was being discussed as well as the terms of the discussion, I decided to turn to primary sources for clarification, only to discover that the primary sources reproduced the problem all over again. I found myself, in other words, in an epistemological quandary, not only unable to decide among conflicting versions of events but also unable to believe that any such decision could, in principle, be made. It was a moral quandary as well. Knowledge of what really happened when the Europeans and the Indians first met seemed particularly important, since the result of that encounter was virtual genocide. This was the kind of past "mistake" which, presumably, we studied history in order to avoid repeating. If studying history couldn't put us in touch with actual events and their causes, then what was to prevent such atrocities from happening again?

For a while, I remained at this impasse. But through analyzing the process by which I had reached it, I eventually arrived at an understanding which seemed to offer a way out. This essay records the concrete experience of meeting and solving the difficulty I have just described (as an abstract problem, I thought I had solved it long ago). My purpose is not to throw new light on antifoundationalist epistemology—the solution I reached is not a new one—but to dramatize and expose the troubles antifoundationalism gets you into when you meet it, so to speak, in the road.

My research began with Perry Miller. Early in the preface to *Errand into the Wilderness*, while explaining how he came to write his history of the New England mind, Miller writes a sentence that stopped me dead. He says that what fascinated him as a young man about his country's history was "the massive narrative of the movement of European culture into the vacant wilderness of America."[2] "Vacant?" Miller, writing in 1956, doesn't pause over the word "vacant," but to people who read his preface thirty years later, the word is shocking. In what circumstances could someone proposing to write a history of colonial New England *not* take account of the Indian presence there?

The rest of Miller's preface supplies an answer to this question, if one takes the trouble to piece together its details. Miller explains that as a young man, jealous of older compatriots who had had the luck to fight in World War I, he had gone to Africa in search of adventure. "The adventures that Africa afforded," he writes, "were tawdry enough, but it became the setting for a sudden epiphany" (p. vii). "It was given to me," he writes, "disconsolate on the edge of a jungle of central Africa, to have thrust upon me the mission of expounding what I took to be the innermost propulsion of the United States, while supervising, in that barbaric topic, the unloading of drums of case oil flowing out of the inexhaustible wilderness of America" (p. viii). Miller's picture of himself on the banks of the Congo furnishes a key to the kind of history he will write and to his mental image of a vacant wilderness; it explains why it was just there, under precisely these conditions, that he should have had his epiphany.

The fuel drums stand, in Miller's mind, for the popular misconception of what this country is about. They are "tangible symbols of [America's] appalling power," a power that everyone but Miller takes for the ultimate reality (p. ix). To Miller, "the mind of man is the basic factor in human history," and he will plead, all unaccommodated as he is among the fuel drums, for the intellect—the intellect for which his fellow historians, with their chapters on "stoves or bathtubs, or tax laws," "the Wilmot Proviso" and "the chain store," "have so little respect" (p. viii, ix). His preface seethes with a hatred of the merely physical and mechanical, and this hatred, which is really a form of moral outrage, explains not only the contempt with which he mentions the stoves and bathtubs but also the nature of his experience in Africa and its relationship to the "massive narrative" he will write.

Miller's experiences in Africa are "tawdry," his tropic is barbaric because the jungle he stands on the edge of means nothing to him, no more, indeed something less, than the case oil. It is the nothingness of Africa that precipitates his vision. It is the barbarity of the "dark continent," the obvious (but superficial) parallelism between the jungle at Matadi and America's "vacant wilderness" that releases in Miller the desire to define and vindicate his country's cultural identity. To the young Miller, colonial Africa and colonial America are—but for the history he will bring to light—mirror images of one another. And what he fails to see in the one landscape is the same thing he overlooks in the other: the human beings who people it. As Miller stood with his back to the jungle, thinking about the role of mind in human history, his failure to see that the land into which European culture had moved was not vacant but already occupied by a varied and numerous population, is of a piece with his failure, in his portrait of himself at Matadi, to notice *who* was carrying the fuel drums he was supervising the unloading of.

The point is crucial because it suggests that what is invisible to the historian in his own historical moment remains invisible when he turns his gaze to the past. It isn't that Miller didn't "see" the black men, in a literal sense, any more than it's the case that when he looked back he didn't "see" the Indians, in the sense of not realizing they were there. Rather, it's that neither the Indians nor the blacks *counted* for him, in a fundamental way. The way in which Indians can be seen but not counted is illustrated by an entry in Governor John Winthrop's journal, three hundred years before, when he recorded that there had been a great storm with high winds "yet through God's great mercy it did no hurt, but only killed one Indian with the fall of a tree."[3] The juxtaposition suggests that Miller shared with Winthrop a certain colonial point of view, a point of view from which Indians, though present, do not finally matter.

. . .

A book entitled *New England Frontier: Puritans and Indians, 1620–1675,* written by Alden Vaughan and published in 1965, promised to rectify Miller's omission. In the outpouring of work on the European-Indian encounter that began in the early sixties, this book is the first major landmark, and to a neophyte it seems definitive. Vaughan acknowledges the absence of Indian sources and emphasizes his use of materials which catch the Puritans "off guard."[4] His announced conclusion that "the New England Puritans followed a remarkably humane, considerate, and just policy in their dealings with the Indians" seems supported by the scope, documentation, and methodicalness of his project (*NEF,* p. vii). The author's fair-mindedness and equanimity seem everywhere apparent, so that when he asserts "the history of interracial relations from the arrival of the Pilgrims to the outbreak of King Philip's War is a credit to the integrity of both peoples," one is positively reassured (*NEF,* p. viii).

But these impressions do not survive an admission that comes late in the book, when, in the course of explaining why works like Helen Hunt Jackson's *Century of Dishonor* had spread misconceptions about Puritan treatment of the Indians, Vaughan finally lays his own cards on the table.

> The root of the misunderstanding [about Puritans and Indians] . . . lies[s] in a failure to recognize the nature of the two societies that met in seventeenth century New England. One was unified, visionary, disciplined, and dynamic. The other was divided, self-satisfied, undisciplined, and static. It would be unreasonable to expect that such societies could live side by side indefinitely with no penetration of the more fragmented and passive by the more consolidated and active. What resulted, then, was not—as many have held—a clash of dissimilar ways of life, but rather the expansion of one into the areas in which the other was lacking. [*NEF,* p. 323]

From our present vantage point, these remarks seem culturally biased to an incredible degree, not to mention inaccurate: Was Puritan society unified? If so, how does one account for its internal dissensions and obsessive need to cast out deviants? Is "unity" necessarily a positive culture trait? From what standpoint can one say that American Indians were neither disciplined nor visionary, when both these characteristics loom so large in the ethnographies? Is it an accident that ways of describing cultural strength and weakness coincide with gender stereotypes— active/passive, and so on? Why is one culture said to "penetrate" the other? Why is the "other" described in terms of "lack"?

Vaughan's fundamental categories of apprehension and judgment will not withstand even the most cursory inspection. For what looked like evenhandedness when he was writing *New England Frontier* does not look that way anymore. In his introduction to *New Directions in American Intellectual History,* John Higham writes that by the end of the sixties

the entire conceptual foundation on which [this sort of work]
rested [had] crumbled away.... Simultaneously, in sociology,
anthropology, and history, two working assumptions ... came
under withering attack: first, the assumption that societies tend
to be integrated, and second, that a shared culture maintains
that integration.... By the late 1960s all claims issued in
the name of an "American mind" ... were subject to drastic
skepticism.[5]

"Clearly," Higham continues, "the sociocultural upheaval of the sixties
created the occasion" for this reaction.[6] Vaughan's book, it seemed, could
only have been written before the events of the sixties had sensitized
scholars to questions of race and ethnicity. It came as no surprise, therefore, that ten years later there appeared a study of European-Indian relations which reflected the new awareness of social issues the sixties had
engendered. And it offered an entirely different picture of the European-
Indian encounter.

Francis Jennings's *The Invasion of America* (1975) rips wide open the
idea that the Puritans were humane and considerate in their dealings with
the Indians. In Jennings's account, even more massively documented than
Vaughan's, the early settlers lied to the Indians, stole from them, murdered them, scalped them, captured them, tortured them, raped them,
sold them into slavery, confiscated their land, destroyed their crops,
burned their homes, scattered their possessions, gave them alcohol, undermined their systems of belief, and infected them with diseases that
wiped out 90 percent of their numbers within the first hundred years after
contact.[7]

Jennings mounts an all-out attack on the essential decency of the Puritan leadership and their apologists in the twentieth century. The Pequot
War, which previous historians had described as an attempt on the part of
Massachusetts Bay to protect itself from the fiercest of the New England
tribes, becomes, in Jennings's painstakingly researched account, a deliberate war of extermination, waged by whites against Indians. It starts with
trumped-up charges, is carried on through a series of increasingly bloody
reprisals, and ends in the massacre of scores of Indian men, women, and
children, all so that Massachusetts Bay could gain political and economic
control of the southern Connecticut Valley. When one reads this and then
turns over the page and sees a reproduction of the Bay Colony seal, which
depicts an Indian from whose mouth issue the words "Come over and
help us," the effect is shattering.[8]

But even so powerful an argument as Jennings's did not remain un-
shaken by subsequent work. Reading on, I discovered that if the events of
the sixties had revolutionized the study of European-Indian relations, the
events of the seventies produced yet another transformation. The American Indian Movement, and in particular the founding of the Native
American Rights Fund in 1971 to finance Indian litigation, and a court decision in 1975 which gave the tribes the right to seek redress for past injus-

tices in federal court, created a climate within which historians began to focus on the Indians themselves. "Almost simultaneously," writes James Axtell, "frontier and colonial historians began to discover the necessity of considering the American natives as real determinants of history and the utility of ethnohistory as a way of ensuring parity of focus and impartiality of judgment."[9] In Miller, Indians had been simply beneath notice; in Vaughan, they belonged to an inferior culture; and in Jennings, they were the more or less innocent prey of power-hungry whites. But in the most original and provocative of the ethnohistories, Calvin Martin's *Keepers of the Game,* Indians became complicated, purposeful human beings, whose lives were spiritually motivated to a high degree.[10] Their relationship to the animals they hunted, to the natural environment, and to the whites with whom they traded became intelligible within a system of beliefs that formed the basis for an entirely new perspective on the European-Indian encounter.

Within the broader question of why European contact had such a devastating effect on the Indians, Martin's specific aim is to determine why Indians participated in the fur trade which ultimately led them to the brink of annihilation. The standard answer to this question had always been that once the Indian was introduced to European guns, copper kettles, woolen blankets, and the like, he literally couldn't keep his hands off them. In order to acquire these coveted items, he decimated the animal populations on which his survival depended. In short, the Indian's motivation in participating in the fur trade was assumed to be the same as the white European's—a desire to accumulate material goods. In direct opposition to this thesis, Martin argues that the reason why Indians ruthlessly exploited their own resources had nothing to do with supply and demand, but stemmed rather from a breakdown of the cosmic worldview that tied them to the game they killed in a spiritual relationship of parity and mutual obligation.

The hunt, according to Martin, was conceived not primarily as a physical activity but as a spiritual quest, in which the spirit of the hunter must overmaster the spirit of the game animal before the kill can take place. The animal, in effect, *allows* itself to be found and killed, once the hunter has mastered its spirit. The hunter prepared himself through rituals of fasting, sweating, or dreaming which revealed the identity of his prey and where he can find it. The physical act of killing is the least important element in the process. Once the animal is killed, eaten, and its parts used for clothing or implements, its remains must be disposed of in ritually prescribed fashion, or the game boss, the "keeper" of that species, will not permit more animals to be killed. The relationship between Indians and animals, then, is contractual; each side must hold up its end of the bargain, or no further transactions can occur.

What happened, according to Martin, was that as a result of diseases introduced into the animal population by Europeans, the game suddenly disappeared, began to act in inexplicable ways, or sickened and died in plain view, and communicated their diseases to the Indians. The Indians, consequently, believed that their compact with the animals had been broken and that the keepers of the game, the tutelary spirits of each animal species whom they had been so careful to propitiate, had betrayed them. And when missionization, wars with the Europeans, and displacement from their tribal lands had further weakened Indian society and its belief structure, the Indians, no longer restrained by religious sanctions, in effect, turned on the animals in a holy war of revenge.

Whether or not Martin's specific claim about the "holy war" was correct, his analysis made it clear to me that, given the Indians' understanding of economic, religious, and physical processes, an Indian account of what transpired when the European settlers arrived here would look nothing like our own. Their (potential, unwritten) history of the conflict could bear only a marginal resemblance to Eurocentric views. I began to think that the key to understanding European-Indian relations was to see them as an encounter between wholly disparate cultures, and that therefore either defending or attacking the colonists was beside the point since, given the cultural disparity between the two groups, conflict was inevitable and in large part a product of mutual misunderstanding.

But three years after Martin's book appeared, Shepard Krech III edited a collection of seven essays called *Indians, Animals, and the Fur Trade,* attacking Martin's entire project. Here the authors argued that we don't need an ideological or religious explanation for the fur trade. As Charles Hudson writes,

> The Southeastern Indians slaughtered deer (and were prompted to enslave and kill each other) because of their position on the outer fringes of an expanding modern world-system. . . . In the modern world-system there is a core region which establishes *economic* relations with its colonial periphery. . . . If the Indians could not produce commodities, they were on the road to cultural extinction. . . . To maximize his chances for survival, an eighteenth-century Southeastern Indian had to . . . live in the interior, out of range of European cattle, forestry, and agriculture. . . . He had to produce a commodity which was valuable enough to earn him some protection from English slavers.[11]

Though we are talking here about Southeastern Indians, rather than the subarctic and Northeastern tribes Martin studied, what really accounts for these divergent explanations of why Indians slaughtered the game are the assumptions that underlie them. Martin believes that the Indians acted on the basis of perceptions made available to them by their own cosmology; that is, he explains their behavior as the Indians themselves would have explained it (insofar as he can), using a logic and a set of values that are not Eurocentric but derived from within Amerindian culture. Hudson, on the other hand, insists that the Indians' own beliefs are irrelevant to an explanation of how they acted, which can only be understood, as far as he is concerned, in the terms of a Western materialist economic and political analysis. Martin and Hudson, in short, don't agree on what counts as an explanation, and this disagreement sheds light on the preceding accounts as well. From this standpoint, we can see that Vaughan, who thought that the Puritans were superior to the Indians, and Jennings, who thought the reverse, are both, like Hudson, using Eurocentric criteria of description and evaluation. While all three critics (Vaughan, Jennings and Hudson) acknowledge that Indians and Europeans behave differently from one another, the behavior differs, as it were, within the order of the same: all three assume, though only Hudson makes the assumption explicit, that an understanding of relations between the Europeans and the Indians must be elaborated in European terms. In Martin's analysis, however, what we have are not only two different sets of behavior but two incommensurable ways of describing and assigning meaning to events. This difference at the level of explanation calls into question the possibility of obtaining any theory-independent account of interaction between Indians and Europeans.

At this point, dismayed and confused by the wildly divergent views of colonial history the twentieth-century historians had provided, I decided to look at some primary materials. I thought, perhaps, if I looked at some firsthand accounts and at some scholars looking at those accounts, it would be possible to decide which experts were right and which were wrong by comparing their views with the evidence. Captivity narratives seemed a good place to begin, since it was logical to suppose that the records left by whites who had been captured by Indians would furnish the sort of firsthand information I wanted.

I began with two fascinating essays based on these materials written by the ethnohistorian James Axtell, "The White Indians of Colonial America" and "The Scholastic Philosophy of the Wilderness."[12] These essays suggest that it would have been a privilege to be captured by North American Indians and taken off to Canada to dwell in a wigwam for the rest of one's life. Axtell's reconstruction of the process by which Indians taught European captives to feel comfortable in the wilderness, first taking their shoes away and giving them moccasins, carrying the children on their backs, sharing the scanty food supply equally, ceremonially cleansing them of their old identities, giving them Indian clothes and jewelry, assiduously teaching them the Indian language, finally adopting them into their families, and even visiting them after many years if, as sometimes happened, they were restored to white society—all of this creates a compelling portrait of Indian culture and helps to explain the extraordinary attraction that Indian culture apparently exercised over Europeans.

But, as I had by now come to expect, this beguiling portrait of the Indians' superior humanity is called into question by other writings on Indian captivity—for example, Norman Heard's *White into Red,* whose summation of the comparative treatment of captive children east and west of the Mississippi seems to contradict some of Axtell's conclusions:

> The treatment of captive children seems to have been similar in initial stages. . . . Most children were treated brutally at the time of capture. Babies and toddlers usually were killed immediately and other small children would be dispatched during the rapid retreat to the Indian villages if they cried, failed to keep the pace, or otherwise indicated a lack of fortitude needed to become a worthy member of the tribe. Upon reaching the village, the child might face such ordeals as running the gauntlet or dancing in the center of a throng of threatening Indians. The prisoner might be so seriously injured at this time that he would no longer be acceptable for adoption.[13]

One account which Heard reprints is particularly arresting. A young girl captured by the Comanches who had not been adopted into the family but used as a slave had been peculiarly mistreated. When they wanted to wake her up the family she belonged to would take a burning brand from the fire and touch it to her nose. When she was returned to her parents, the flesh of her nose was completely burned away, exposing the bone.[14]

Since the pictures drawn by Heard and Axtell were in certain respects irreconcilable, it made sense to turn to a firsthand account to see how the Indians treated their captives in a particular instance. Mary Rowlandson's "The Soveraignty and Goodness of God," published in Boston around 1680, suggested itself because it was so widely read and had set the pattern for later narratives. Rowlandson interprets her captivity as God's punishment on her for failing to keep the Sabbath properly on several occasions. She sees everything that happens to her as a sign from God. When the Indians are kind to her, she attributes her good fortune to Divine Providence; when they are cruel, she blames her captors. But beyond the question of how Rowlandson interprets events is the question of what she saw in the first place and what she considered worth reporting. The following passage, with its abrupt shifts of focus and peculiar emphases, makes it hard to see her testimony as evidence of anything other than the Puritan point of view:

> Then my heart began to fail: and I fell weeping, which was the first time to my remembrance, that I wept before them. Although I had met with so much Affliction, and my heart was many times ready to break, yet could I not shed one tear in their sight: but rather had been all this while in a maze, and like one astonished: but not I may say as, Psal. 137.1. *By the Rivers of Babylon, there we sate down; yea, we wept when we remembered Zion.* There one of them asked me, why I wept, I could hardly tell what to say: yet I answered, they would kill me: No,

said he, none will hurt you. Then came one of them and gave me two spoon-fulls of Meal to comfort me, and another gave me half a pint of Pease; which was more worth than many Bushels at another time. Then I went to see King Philip, he bade me come in and sit down, and asked me whether I woold smoke it (a usual Complement nowadayes among Saints and Sinners) but this no way suited me. For though I had formerly used Tobacco, yet I had left it ever since I was first taken. It seems to be a Bait, the Devil layes to make men loose their precious time: I remember with shame, how formerly, when I had taken two or three pipes, I was presently ready for another, such a bewitching thing it is: But I thank God, he has now given me power over it; surely there are many who may be better imployed than to ly sucking a stinking Tobacco-pipe.[15]

Anyone who has ever tried to give up smoking has to sympathize with Rowlandson, but it is nonetheless remarkable, first, that a passage which begins with her weeping openly in front of her captors, and comparing herself to Israel in Babylon, should end with her railing against the vice of tobacco; and, second, that it has not a word to say about King Philip, the leader of the Indians who captured her and mastermind of the campaign that devastated the white population of the English colonies. The fact that Rowlandson has just been introduced to the chief of chiefs makes hardly any impression on her at all. What excites her is a moral issue which was being hotly debated in the seventeenth century: to smoke or not to smoke (Puritans frowned on it, apparently, because it wasted time and presented a fire hazard). What seem to us the peculiar emphases in Rowlandson's relation are not the result of her having *screened out* evidence she couldn't handle, but of her way of constructing the world. She saw what her seventeenth-century English Separatist background made visible. It is when one realizes that the biases of twentieth-century historians like Vaughan or Axtell cannot be corrected for simply by consulting the primary materials, since the primary materials are constructed according to *their* authors' biases, that one begins to envy Miller his vision at Matadi. Not for what he didn't see—the Indian and the black—but for his epistemological confidence.

Since captivity narratives made a poor source of evidence for the nature of European-Indian relations in early New England because they were so relentlessly pietistic, my hope was that a better source of evidence might be writings designed simply to tell Englishmen what the American natives were like. These authors could be presumed to be less severely biased, since they hadn't seen their loved ones killed by Indians or been made to endure the hardships of captivity, and because they weren't writing propaganda calculated to prove that God had delivered his chosen people from the hands of Satan's emissaries.

The problem was that these texts were written with aims no less specific than those of the captivity narrative, though the aims were of a different sort. Here is a passage from William Wood's *New England's Prospect,* published in London in 1634.

> To enter into a serious discourse concerning the natural condi-
> tions of these Indians might procure admiration from the people
> of any civilized nations, in regard of their civility and good na-
> tures. . . . These Indians are of affable, courteous and well dis-
> posed natures, ready to communicate the best of their wealth to
> the mutual good of one another; . . . so . . . perspicuous is their
> love . . . that they are as willing to part with a mite in poverty as
> treasure in plenty. . . . If it were possible to recount the courte-
> sies they have showed the English, since their first arrival in
> those parts, it would not only steady belief, that they are a loving
> people, but also win the love of those that never saw them, and
> wipe off that needless fear that is too deeply rooted in the con-
> ceits of many who think them envious and of such rancorous
> and inhumane dispositions, that they will one day make an end
> of their English inmates.[16]

However, in a pamphlet published twenty-one years earlier, Alexander Whitaker of Virginia has this to say of the natives:

> These naked slaves . . . serve the divell for feare, after a most
> base manner, sacrificing sometimes (as I have heere heard)
> their own Children to him. . . . They live naked in bodie, as if
> their shame of their sinne deserved no covering: Their names
> are as naked as their bodie: They esteem it a virtue to lie, de-
> ceive and steale as their master the divell teacheth to them.[17]

According to Robert Berkhofer in *The White Man's Indian,* these divergent reports can be explained by looking at the authors' motives. A favorable report like Wood's, intended to encourage new emigrants to America, naturally represented Indians as loving and courteous, civilized and
generous, in order to allay the fears of prospective colonists. Whitaker, on
the other hand, a minister who wishes to convince his readers that the Indians are in need of conversion, paints them as benighted agents of the
devil. Berkhofer's commentary constantly implies that white men were to
blame for having represented the Indians in the image of their own desires and needs.[18] But the evidence supplied by Rowlandson's narrative,
and by the accounts left by early reporters such as Wood and Whitaker,
suggests something rather different. Though it is probably true that in certain cases Europeans did consciously tamper with the evidence, in most
cases there is no reason to suppose that they did not record faithfully what
they saw. And what they saw was not an illusion, was not determined by
selfish motives in any narrow sense, but was there by virtue of a *way* of
seeing which they could no more consciously manipulate than they could
choose not to have been born. At this point, it seemed to me, the ethnocen-
tric bias of the firsthand observers invited an investigation of the cultural

situation they spoke from. Karen Kupperman's *Settling with the Indians* (1980) supplied just such an analysis.

Kupperman argues that Englishmen inevitably looked at Indians in exactly the same way that they looked at other Englishmen. For instance, if they looked down on Indians and saw them as people to be exploited, it was not because of racial prejudice or antique notions about savagery, it was because they looked down on ordinary English men and women and saw them as subjects for exploitation as well.[19] According to Kupperman, what concerned these writers most when they described the Indians were the insignia of social class, of rank, and of prestige. Indian faces are virtually never described in the earliest accounts, but clothes and hairstyles, tattoos and jewelry, posture and skin color are. "Early modern Englishmen believed that people can create their own identity, and that therefore one communicates to the world through signals such as dress and other forms of decoration who one is, what group or category one belongs to."[20]

Kupperman's book marks a watershed in writings on European-Indian relations, for it reverses the strategy employed by Martin two years before. Whereas Martin had performed an ethnographic analysis of Indian cosmology in order to explain, from within, the Indians' motives for engaging in the fur trade, Kupperman performs an ethnographic study of seventeenth-century England in order to explain, from within, what motivated Englishmen's behavior. The sympathy and understanding that Martin, Axtell, and others extend to the Indians are extended in Kupperman's work to the English themselves. Rather than giving an account of "what happened" between Indians and Europeans, like Martin, she reconstructs the worldview that gave the experience of one group its context. With her study, scholarship on European-Indian relations comes full circle.

It may well seem to you at this point that, given the tremendous variation among the historical accounts, I had no choice but to end in relativism. If the experience of encountering conflicting versions of the "same" events suggests anything certain it is that the attitude a historian takes up in relation to a given event, the way in which he or she judges and even describes "it"—and the "it" has to go in quotation marks because, depending on the perspective, that event either did or did not occur—this stance, these judgments and descriptions are a function of the historian's position in relation to the subject. Miller, standing on the banks of the Congo, couldn't see the black men he was supervising because of his background, his assumptions, values, experiences, goals. Jennings, intent on exposing the distortions introduced into the historical record by Vaughan and his predecessors stretching all the way back to Winthrop, couldn't see that Winthrop and his peers were not racists but only Englishmen who looked at other cultures in the way their own culture had taught them to see one another. The historian can never escape the limitations of his or her own position in history and so inevitably gives an account that is an extension of the circumstances from which it springs. But it seems to me that when one is confronted with this particular succession of stories, cultural and historical relativism is not a position that one can comfortably assume. The phenomena to which these histories testify— conquest, massacre, and genocide, on the one hand; torture, slavery, and murder on the other—cry out for judgment. When faced with claims and counterclaims of this magnitude one feels obligated to reach an under- standing of what actually did occur. The dilemma posed by the study of European-Indian relations in early America is that the highly charged na- ture of the materials demands a moral decisiveness which the succession of conflicting accounts effectively precludes. That is the dilemma I found myself in at the end of this course of reading, and which I eventually came to resolve as follows.

After a while it began to seem to me that there was something wrong with the way I formulated the problem. The statement that the materials on European-Indian relations were so highly charged that they demanded moral judgment, but that the judgment couldn't be made because all pos- sible descriptions of what happened were biased, seemed to contain an in- ternal contradiction. The statement implied that in order to make a moral judgment about something, you have to know something else first— namely, the facts of the case you're being call upon to judge. My complaint was that their perspectival nature would disqualify any facts I might en- counter and that therefore I couldn't judge. But to say as I did that the mate- rials I had read were "highly charged" and therefore demanded judgment suggests both that I was reacting to something real—to some facts—*and* that I judged them. Perhaps I wasn't so much in the lurch morally or epistemo- logically as I had thought. If you—or I—react with horror to the story of the girl captured and enslaved by Comanches who touched a firebrand to her nose every time they wanted to wake her up, it's because we read this as a story about cruelty and suffering, and not as a story about the conventions of prisoner exchange or the economics of Comanche life. The *seeing* of the story as a cause for alarm rather than a droll anecdote or a piece of curious information is evidence of values we already hold, of judgments already made, of facts already perceived as facts.

My problem presupposed that I couldn't judge because I didn't know what the facts were. All I had, or could have, was a series of different per- spectives, and so nothing that would count as an authoritative source on which moral judgments could be based. But, as I have just shown, I did judge, and that is because, as I now think, I did have some facts. I seemed to accept as facts that ninety percent of the native American population of New England died after the first hundred years of contact, that tribes in eastern Canada and the northeastern United States had a compact with the game they killed, that Comanches had subjected a captive girl to casual cru- elty, that King Philip smoked a pipe, and so on. It was only where different versions of the same event came into conflict that I doubted the text was a record of something real. And even then, there was no question about cer- tain major catastrophes. I believed that four hundred Pequots were killed near Saybrook, that Winthrop was the Governor of the Massachusetts Bay Colony when it happened, and so on. My sense that certain events, such as the Pequot War, did occur in no way reflected the indecisiveness that overtook me when I tried to choose among the various historical versions. In fact, the need I felt to make up my mind was impelled by the conviction that certain things *had* happened that shouldn't have happened. Hence it was never the case that "what happened" was completely unknowable or unavailable. It's rather that in the process of reading so many different approaches to the same phenomenon I became aware of the difference in the attitudes that informed these approaches. The awareness of the interests motivating each version cast suspicion over everything, in retrospect, and I ended by claiming that there was nothing I could know. This, I now see, was never really the case. But how did it happen?

Someone else, confronted with the same materials, could have decided that one of these historical accounts was correct. Still another person might have decided that more evidence was needed in order to decide among them. Why did I conclude that none of the accounts was accurate because they were all produced from some particular angle of vision? Presumably there was something in my background that enabled me to see the problem in this way. That something, very likely, was poststructuralist theory. I let my discovery that Vaughan was a product of the fifties, Jennings of the sixties, Rowlandson of a Puritan worldview, and so on lead me to the conclusion that all facts are theory dependent because that conclusion was already a thinkable one for me. My inability to come up with a true account was not the product of being situated nowhere; it was the product of certitude that existed *somewhere else,* namely, in contemporary literary theory. Hence, the level at which my indecision came into play was a function of particular beliefs I held. I was never in a position of epistemological indeterminacy, I was never *en abyme.* The idea that all accounts are perspectival seemed to me a superior standpoint from which to view all the versions of "what happened," and to regard with sympathetic condescension any person so old-fashioned and benighted as to believe that there really was some way of arriving at the truth. But this skeptical standpoint was just as firm as any other. The fact that it was also seriously disabling—it prevented me from coming to any conclusion about what I had read—did not render it any less definite.

At this point something is beginning to show itself that has up to now been hidden. The notion that all facts are only facts within a perspective has the effect of emptying statements of their content. Once I had Miller and Vaughan and Jennings, Martin and Hudson, Axtell and Heard, Rowlandson and Wood and Whitaker, and Kupperman; I had Europeans and Indians, ships and canoes, wigwams and log cabins, bows and arrows and muskets, wigs and tattoos, whiskey and corn, rivers and forts, treaties and battles, fire and blood—and then suddenly all I had was a metastatement about perspectives. The effect of bringing perspectivism to bear on history was to wipe out completely the subject matter of history. And it follows that bringing perspectivism to bear in this way on any subject matter would have a similar effect; everything is wiped out and you are left with nothing but a single idea—perspectivism itself.

But—and it is a crucial but—all this is true only if you believe that there is an alternative. As long as you think that there are or should be facts that exist outside of any perspective, then the notion that facts are perspectival will have this disappearing effect on whatever it touches. But if you are convinced that the alternative does not exist, that there really are no facts except as they are embedded in some particular way of seeing the world, then the argument that a set of facts derives from some particular worldview is no longer an argument against that set of facts. If all facts share this characteristic, to say that any one fact is perspectival doesn't change its factual nature in the slightest. It merely reiterates it.

This doesn't mean that you have to accept just anybody's facts. You can show that what someone else asserts to be a fact is false. But it does mean that you can't argue that someone else's facts are not facts *because they are only the product of a perspective,* since this will be true of the facts that you perceive as well. What this means then is that arguments about "what happened" have to proceed much as they did before poststructuralism broke in with all its talk about language-based reality and culturally produced knowledge. Reasons must be given, evidence adduced, authorities cited, analogies drawn. Being aware that all facts are motivated, believing that people are always operating inside some particular interpretive framework or other is a pertinent argument when what is under discussion is the way beliefs are grounded. But it doesn't give one any leverage on the facts of a particular case.[21]

What this means for the problem I've been addressing is that I must piece together the story of European-Indian relations as best I can, believing this version up to a point, that version not at all, another almost entirely, according to what seems reasonable and plausible, given everything else that I know. And this, as I've shown, is what I was already doing in the back of my mind without realizing it, because there was nothing else I *could* do. If the accounts don't fit together neatly, that is not a reason for rejecting them all in favor of a metadiscourse about epistemology; on the contrary, one encounters contradictory facts and divergent points of view in practically every phase of life, from deciding whom to marry to choosing the right brand of cat food, and one decides as best one can given the evidence available. It is only the nature of the academic situation which makes it appear that one can linger on the threshold of decision in the name of an epistemological principle. What has really happened in such a case is that the subject of debate has changed from the question of what happened in a particular instance to the question of how knowledge is arrived at. The absence of pressure to decide what happened creates the possibility for this change of venue.

The change of venue, however, is itself an action taken. In diverting attention from the original problem and placing it where Miller did, on "the mind of man," it once again ignores what happened and still is happening to American Indians. The moral problem that confronts me now is not that I can never have any facts to go on, but that the work I do is not directed toward solving the kinds of problems that studying the history of European-Indian relations has awakened me to.

## NOTES

[1] See Vine Deloria, Jr., *God is Red* (New York, 1973), pp. 39–56.

[2] Perry Miller, *Errand into the Wilderness* (Cambridge, Mass., 1964), p. vii; all further references will be included in the text.

[3] This passage from John Winthrop's *Journal* is excerpted by Perry Miller in his anthology *The American Puritans: Their Prose and Poetry* (Garden City, N.Y., 1956), p. 43. In his headnote to the selections from the *Journal*, Miller speaks of Winthrop's "characteristic objectivity" (p. 37).

[4] Alden T. Vaughan, *New England Frontier: Puritans and Indians, 1620–1675* (Boston, 1965), pp. vi–vii; all further references to this work, abbreviated *NEF*, will be included in the text.

[5] John Higham, intro. to *New Directions in American Intellectual History*, ed. Higham and Paul K. Conkin (Baltimore, 1979), p. xii.

[6] Ibid.

[7] See Francis Jennings, *The Invasion of America: Indians, Colonialism, and the Cant of Conquest* (New York, 1975), pp. 3–31. Jennings writes: "The so-called settlement of America was a *re*settlement, reoccupation of a land made waste by the diseases and demoralization introduced by the newcomers. Although the source data pertaining to populations have never been compiled, one careful scholar, Henry D. Dobyns, has provided a relatively conservative and meticulously reasoned estimate conforming to the known effects of conquest catastrophe. Dobyns has calculated a total aboriginal population for the western hemisphere within the range of 90 to 112 million, of which 10 to 12 million lived north of the Rio Grande" (p. 30).

[8] Jennings, fig. 7, p. 229; and see pp. 186–229.

[9] James Axtell, *The European and the Indian: Essays in the Ethnohistory of Colonial North America* (Oxford, 1981), p. viii.

[10] See Calvin Martin, *Keepers of the Game: Indian Animal Relationships and the Fur Trade* (Berkeley and Los Angeles, 1978).

[11] See the essay by Charles Hudson in *Indians, Animals, and the Fur Trade: A Critique of "Keepers of the Game,"* ed. Shepard Krech III (Athens, Ga., 1981), pp. 167–69.

[12] See Axtell, "The White Indians of Colonial America" and "The Scholastic Philosophy of the Wilderness," *The European and the Indian*, pp. 168–206 and 131–67.

[13] J. Norman Heard, *White into Red: A Study of the Assimilation of White Persons Captured by Indians* (Metuchen, N.J., 1973), p. 97.

[14] See ibid., p. 98.

[15] Mary Rowlandson, "The Soveraignty and Goodness of God, Together with the Faithfulness of His Promises Displayed; Being a Narrative of the Captivity and Restauration of Mrs. Mary Rowlandson (1676)," in *Held Captive by Indians: Selected Narratives, 1642–1836*, ed. Richard VanDerBeets (Knoxville, Tenn., 1973), pp. 57–58.

[16] William Wood, *New England's Prospect*, ed. Vaughan (Amherst, Mass., 1977), pp. 88–89.

[17] Alexander Whitaker, *Goode Newes from Virginia* (1613), quoted in Robert F. Berkhofer, Jr., *The White Man's Indian: Images of the American Indian from Columbus to the Present* (New York, 1978), p. 19.

[18] See, for example, Berkhofer's discussion of the passages he quotes from Whitaker (*The White Man's Indian*, pp. 19, 20).

[19] See Karen Ordahl Kupperman, *Settling with the Indians: The Meeting of English and Indian Cultures in America, 1580–1640* (Totowa, N.J., 1980), pp. 3, 4.

[20] Ibid., p. 35.

[21] The position I've been outlining is a version of neopragmatism. For an exposition, see *Against Theory: Literary Studies and the New Pragmatism*, ed. W. J. T. Mitchell (Chicago, 1985).

• • • • • • • • • • • •

## QUESTIONS FOR A SECOND READING

1. Tompkins's essay can be divided into three parts: the account of her childhood understanding of Indians; the account of her research into scholarly and first-person accounts of the relations between the Indians and the settlers in New England; and a final conclusion (beginning on p. 686). The conclusion, in many ways, is the hardest part of the essay to understand. Like the conclusion to Clifford Geertz's "Deep Play: Notes on the Balinese Cockfight" (p. 364), it assumes not only that you have followed a chain of reasoning but that you have access to the larger philosophical questions that have preoccupied the academic community. In this sense the conclusion presents special problems for a student reader. Why might one be dissatisfied with "metadiscourse"? What kind of work is Tompkins talking about, for example, when she says, "The moral problem that confronts me now is . . . that the work I do is not directed toward solving the kinds of problems that studying the history of European-Indian relations has awakened me to"?

   As you reread the essay, look to see how the first two sections might be seen as a preparation for the conclusion. And as you reread the concluding section (which you may have to do several times), try to imagine the larger, unspoken issues it poses for those who teach American literature or who are professionally involved in reading and researching the past.

2. One of the things to notice about Tompkins's essay is how neatly all the pieces fit together in her narrative. If you wanted to read against this essay, you might say that they fit together *too* neatly. The seemingly "natural" progression from book to book or step to step in this account of her research and her thinking could be said to reveal the degree to which the story was shaped or made, constructed for the occasion. Real experience is never quite so tidy.

   As you reread the essay, be aware of the narrative as something made and ask yourself, How does she do that? What is she leaving out? Where is she working hard to get her material to fit? This is partly a matter of watching how Tompkins does her work—looking at paragraphs, for instance, and seeing how they represent her material and her reading of that material. It is also a matter of looking for what is not there, for seams that indicate necessary or unconscious omissions (as though while writing this essay, too, she "did not care to have any real exemplars interfering with what I already knew").

## ASSIGNMENTS FOR WRITING

1. Tompkins's essay tells the story of a research project. It also, however, "reads" that narrative—that is, not only does Tompkins describe what she did, or what other people said, but she reflects on what her actions or the work of others might be said to represent. She writes about "point of view" or "frame of reference" and the ways they might be said to determine how people act, what they write, and what they know.

    Write an essay that tells a similar story, one of your own, using Tompkins's essay as a model. There are two ways you might do this:

    a. You could tell the story of a research project, a paper (most likely a term paper) you prepared for school. This does not have to be a pious or dutiful account. Tompkins, after all, is writing against what she takes to be the predictable or expected account of research as the disinterested pursuit of truth—in which a student would go to the library to "find" the truth about the Indians and the settlers. And she writes in a style that is not solemnly academic. Like Tompkins, you can tell what you take to be the untold story of term-paper research, you can reflect on the "problem" of such research by turning to your own account.

        Your account should begin well before your work in the library—that is, you too will want to show the "prehistory" of your project, the possible connections between school work and your life outside school. It should also tell the story of your work with other people's writing. The purpose of all this is to reflect on how knowledge is constructed and how you, as a student, have been expected to participate (and how you have, in fact, participated) in that process.

    b. You could tell the story of a discovery that did not involve reading or library research; in fact, you could tell the story of a discovery that did not involve school at all. In this sense you would be working in response to the first section of Tompkins's essay, in which what she knows about Indians is constructed from a combination of cultural models and personal desire.

2. In her essay Tompkins offers her experience as a representative case. Her story is meant to highlight a problem central to teaching, learning, and research—central, that is, to academic life. As a student, you can read this essay as a way of looking in on the work and concerns of your faculty (a group represented not only by Tompkins but by those against whom she is arguing). Write an essay directed to someone who has not read "Indians," someone who will be entering your school as a first-year student next semester. Your job is to introduce an incoming freshman to the academy, using Tompkins as your guide. You will need to present her argument and her conclusion in such a way as to make clear the consequences of what she says for someone about to begin an undergraduate education.

Remember, you are writing to an incoming student; you will want to capture that audience's attention.

## MAKING CONNECTIONS

1. As Tompkins reviews the books she gathered in her project, she presents each in terms of its point of view, the "aims" with which it was written. She sees these books, that is, not as sources of truth but as representations of Indians and settlers, representations shaped by a theory, an agenda, or the cultural-historical situation of the scholar. The differences between the sources are not matters of right and wrong, nor are they simply matters of individual style.

   In a parallel way, take two essays from *Ways of Reading* that deal with a single subject and treat them as cases of different points of view or frames of reference. "When We Dead Awaken: Writing as Re-Vision" by Adrienne Rich (p. 603) or "A Room of One's Own" by Virginia Woolf (p. 750) are particularly suggestive for a project like this. They both deal with the situation of women writers. In fact, Rich's essay makes specific reference to Woolf and her work. One sign of Rich's difference from Woolf, then, will be the way she reads Woolf.

   Write an essay in which you look at the differences between Rich's essay and Woolf's (or two others of your choice) and speculate on how those differences might reflect different times (different frames of reference) and different agendas (different points of view), even though they deal with a common topic and could easily be said to make a similar argument.

2. In "Our Time" (p. 707), John Edgar Wideman writes about the problems he has "knowing" and writing about his brother Robby. In this sense, both "Our Time" and "Indians" are about the problems of understanding, about the different relationship between "real exemplars" and what we know. Write an essay in which you compare these two selections, looking in particular at the differences in the ways each author represents this problem and its possible solutions. Although you are working from only two sources, you could imagine that your essay is a way of investigating the differences between the work of a "creative" writer and that of a scholar.

# ALICE
# WALKER

*A* LICE WALKER, *the youngest of eight children in a sharecropping family,*
*was born in 1944 in Eatonton, Georgia. She is now one of the most widely*
*read contemporary American novelists. In her work, she frequently returns to*
*scenes of family life—some violent, some peaceful. "I was curious to know," she*
*writes, "why people of families (specifically black families) are often cruel to each*
*other and how much of this cruelty is caused by outside forces. . . . Family rela-*
*tionships are sacred. No amount of outside pressure and injustice should make us*
*lose sight of that fact." In her nonfiction, Walker has helped to define a historical*
*context for the contemporary black artist, a legacy that has had to be recovered*
*from libraries and archives. The essay that follows, "In Search of Our Mothers'*
*Gardens," defines black history as a family matter. It begins by charting the vio-*
*lence done to women who "died with their real gifts stifled within them" and con-*
*cludes with Walker's recollection of her own mother, a recollection that enables*
*her to imagine generations of black women handing on a "creative spark" to those*
*who follow.*

*In addition to* In Search of Our Mothers' Gardens *(1983), Walker has*
*written novels, including* The Third Life of Grange Copeland *(1970) and* The
Color Purple *(1982), which won the Pulitzer Prize; collections of poems, includ-*
*ing* Revolutionary Petunias *(1973) and* Good Night, Willie Lee, I'll See You
in the Morning *(1979); two collections of short stories,* In Love and Trouble

*(1973) and* You Can't Keep a Good Woman Down *(1981), and a biography of* Langston Hughes. *She has also served as an editor at* Ms. *magazine. After graduating from Sarah Lawrence College in 1965, she taught at a number of colleges and universities, including Wellesley College and Yale University. She has held a Guggenheim Fellowship and a National Endowment for the Arts fellowship. She lives in San Francisco and teaches at the University of California at Berkeley.*

*While pursuing her own career as a writer, Walker has fought to win recognition for the work of Zora Neale Hurston, a black woman author and anthropologist whose best-known work is the novel* Their Eyes Were Watching God *(1937). Hurston died penniless in a Florida welfare home. Walker's recent work includes* Living by the Word *(1988), a collection of essays, letters, journal entries, lectures, and poems on the themes of race, gender, sexuality, and political freedom;* To Hell with Dying *(1988), a children's picture book;* The Temple of My Familiar *(1989), and* Possessing the Secret of Joy *(1992), both novels; and* Her Blue Body Everything We Know: Earthling Poems, 1965–1990 *(1991), a collection of poems. Walker has also co-written, with Michael Meade, the introduction to a sound recording by Sobonfu Some entitled* We Have No Word for Sex *(1994), an African oral tale. Her latest book,* Anything We Love Can Be Saved: A Writer's Activism *(1997), is a collection of essays.*

# In Search of
# Our Mothers' Gardens

> I described her own nature and temperament. Told how they needed a larger life for their expression. . . . I pointed out that in lieu of proper channels, her emotions had overflowed into paths that dissipated them. I talked, beautifully I thought, about an art that would be born, an art that would open the way for women the likes of her. I asked her to hope, and build up an inner life against the coming of that day. . . . I sang, with a strange quiver in my voice, a promise song.
>
> —"AVEY," JEAN TOOMER, *Cane*
> *The poet speaking to a prostitute who falls asleep while he's talking*

When the poet Jean Toomer walked through the South in the early twenties, he discovered a curious thing: black women whose spirituality was so intense, so deep, so *unconscious,* they were themselves unaware of the richness they held. They stumbled blindly through their lives: creatures so abused and mutilated in body, so dimmed and confused by pain, that they considered themselves unworthy even of hope. In the selfless abstractions their bodies became to the men who used them, they became more than "sexual objects," more even than mere women: they became "Saints." Instead of being perceived as whole persons, their bodies became shrines: what was thought to be their minds became temples suitable for worship. These crazy Saints stared out at the world, wildly, like lunatics—or quietly, like suicides; and the "God" that was in their gaze was as mute as a great stone.

Who were these Saints? These crazy, loony, pitiful women?

Some of them, without a doubt, were our mothers and grandmothers.

In the still heat of the post-Reconstruction South, this is how they seemed to Jean Toomer: exquisite butterflies trapped in an evil honey, toiling away their lives in an era, a century, that did not acknowledge them, except as "the *mule* of the world." They dreamed dreams that no one knew—not even themselves, in any coherent fashion—and saw visions no one could understand. They wandered or sat about the countryside crooning lullabies to ghosts, and drawing the mother of Christ in charcoal on courthouse walls.

They forced their minds to desert their bodies and their striving spirits sought to rise, like frail whirlwinds from the hard red clay. And when those frail whirlwinds fell, in scattered particles, upon the ground, no one mourned. Instead, men lit candles to celebrate the emptiness that remained, as people do who enter a beautiful but vacant space to resurrect a God.

Our mothers and grandmothers, some of them: moving to music not yet written. And they waited.

They waited for a day when the unknown thing that was in them would be made known; but guessed, somehow in their darkness, that on the day of their revelation, they would be long dead. Therefore to Toomer they walked, and even ran, in slow motion. For they were going nowhere immediate, and the future was not yet within their grasp. And men took our mothers and grandmothers, "but got no pleasure from it." So complex was their passion and their calm.

To Toomer, they lay vacant and fallow as autumn fields, with harvest time never in sight; and he saw them enter loveless marriages, without joy; and become prostitutes, without resistance; and become mothers of children, without fulfillment.

For these grandmothers and mothers of ours were not Saints, but Artists; driven to a numb and bleeding madness by the springs of creativity in them for which there was no release. They were Creators, who lived lives of spiritual waste, because they were so rich in spirituality—which is the basis of Art—that the strain of enduring their unused and unwanted talent drove them insane. Throwing away this spirituality was their pathetic attempt to lighten the soul to a weight their work-worn, sexually abused bodies could bear.

What did it mean for a black woman to be an artist in our grandmothers' time? In our great-grandmothers' day? It is a question with an answer cruel enough to stop the blood.

Did you have a genius of a great-great-grandmother who died under some ignorant and depraved white overseer's lash? Or was she required to bake biscuits for a lazy backwater tramp, when she cried out in her soul to paint watercolors of sunsets, or the rain falling on the green and peaceful pasturelands? Or was her body broken and forced to bear children (who were more often than not sold away from her)—eight, ten, fifteen, twenty children—when her one joy was the thought of modeling heroic figures of rebellion, in stone or clay?

How was the creativity of the black woman kept alive, year after year and century after century, when for most of the years black people have been in America, it was a punishable crime for a black person to read or write? And the freedom to paint, to sculpt, to expand the mind with action did not exist. Consider, if you can bear to imagine it, which might have been the result if singing, too, had been forbidden by law. Listen to the voices of Bessie Smith, Billie Holiday, Nina Simone, Roberta Flack, and Aretha Franklin, among others, and imagine those voices muzzled for life. Then you may begin to comprehend the lives of our "crazy," "Sainted" mothers and grandmothers. The agony of the lives of women who might have been poets, Novelists, Essayists, and Short-Story Writers (over a period of centuries), who died with their real gifts stifled within them.

And, if this were the end of the story, we would have cause to cry out in my paraphrase of Okot p'Bitek's great poem:

> O, my clanswomen
> Let us all cry together!
> Come,
> Let us mourn the death of our mother,
> The death of a Queen
> The ash that was produced
> By a great fire!
> O, this homestead is utterly dead
> Close the gates
> With *lacari* thorns,
> For our mother
> The creator of the Stool is lost!
> And all the young women
> Have perished in the wilderness!

But this is not the end of the story, for all the young women—our mothers and grandmothers, *ourselves*—have not perished in the wilderness. And if we ask ourselves why, and search for and find the answer, we will know beyond all efforts to erase it from our minds, just exactly who, and of what, we black American women are.

One example, perhaps the most pathetic, most misunderstood one, can provide a backdrop for our mothers' work: Phillis Wheatley, a slave in the 1700s.

Virginia Woolf, in her book *A Room of One's Own*, wrote that in order for a woman to write fiction she must have two things, certainly; a room of her own (with key and lock) and enough money to support herself.

What then are we to make of Phillis Wheatley, a slave, who owned not even herself? This sickly, frail black girl who required a servant of her own at times—her health was so precarious—and who, had she been white, would have been easily considered the intellectual superior of all the women and most of the men in the society of her day.

Virginia Woolf wrote further, speaking of course not of our Phillis, that "any woman born with a great gift in the sixteenth century [insert "eighteenth century," insert "black woman," insert "born or made a slave"] would certainly have gone crazed, shot herself, or ended her days in some lonely cottage outside the village, half witch, half wizard [insert "Saint"], feared and mocked at. For it needs little skill and psychology to be sure that a highly gifted girl who had tried to use her gift of poetry would have been so thwarted and hindered by contrary instincts [add "chains, guns, the lash, the ownership of one's body by someone else, submission to an alien religion"], that she must have lost her health and sanity to a certainty."

The key words, as they relate to Phillis, are "contrary instincts." For when we read the poetry of Phillis Wheatley—as when we read the novels of Nella Larsen or the oddly false-sounding autobiography of that freest of all black women writers, Zora Hurston—evidence of "contrary instincts" is everywhere. Her loyalties were completely divided, as was, without question, her mind.

But how could this be otherwise? Captured at seven, a slave of wealthy, doting whites who instilled in her the "savagery" of the Africa they "rescued" her from . . . one wonders if she was even able to remember her homeland as she had known it, or as it really was.

Yet, because she did try to use her gift for poetry in a world that made her a slave, she was "so thwarted and hindered by . . . contrary instincts, that she . . . lost her health. . . ." In the last years of her brief life, burdened not only with the need to express her gift but also with a penniless, friendless "freedom" and several small children for whom she was forced to do strenuous work to feed, she lost her health, certainly. Suffering from malnutrition and neglect and who knows what mental agonies, Phillis Wheatley died.

So torn by "contrary instincts" was black, kidnapped, enslaved Phillis that her description of "the Goddess"—as she poetically called the Liberty she did not have—is ironically, cruelly humorous. And, in fact, has held Phillis up to ridicule for more than a century. It is usually read prior to hanging Phillis's memory as that of a fool. She wrote:

> The Goddess comes, she moves divinely fair,
> Olive and laurel binds her *golden* hair.
> Wherever shines this native of the skies,
> Unnumber'd charms and recent graces rise. [My italics]

It is obvious that Phillis, the slave, combed the "Goddess's" hair every morning, prior, perhaps, to bringing in the milk, or fixing her mistress's lunch. She took her imagery from the one thing she saw elevated above all others.

With the benefit of hindsight we ask, "How could she?"

But at last, Phillis, we understand. No more snickering when your stiff, struggling, ambivalent lines are forced on us. We know now that you were not an idiot or a traitor; only a sickly little black girl, snatched from your home and country and made a slave; a woman who still struggled to sing the song that was your gift, although in a land of barbarians who praised you for your bewildered tongue. It is not so much what you sang, as that you kept alive, in so many of our ancestors, *the notion of song.*

Black women are called, in the folklore that so aptly identified one's status in society, "the *mule* of the world," because we have been handed the burdens that everyone else—*everyone* else—refused to carry. We have also been called "Matriarchs," "Superwomen," and "Mean and Evil Bitches." Not to mention "Castraters" and "Sapphire's Mama." When we have pleaded for understanding, our character has been distorted; when we have asked for simple caring, we have been handed empty inspirational appellations, then stuck in the farthest corner. When we have asked for love, we have been given children. In short, even our plainer gifts, our labors of fidelity and love, have been knocked down our throats. To be an artist and a black woman, even today, lowers our status in many respects, rather than raises it: and yet, artists we will be.

Therefore we must fearlessly pull out of ourselves and look at and identify with our lives the living creativity some of our great-grandmothers were not allowed to know. I stress *some* of them because it is well known that the majority of our great-grandmothers knew, even without "knowing" it, the reality of their spirituality, even if they didn't recognize it beyond what happened in the singing at church—and they never had any intention of giving it up.

How they did it—those millions of black women who were not Phillis Wheatley, or Lucy Terry or Frances Harper or Zora Hurston or Nella Larsen or Bessie Smith; or Elizabeth Catlett, or Katherine Dunham, either—brings me to the title of this essay, "In Search of Our Mothers' Gardens," which is a personal account that is yet shared, in its theme and its meaning, by all of us. I found, while thinking about the far-reaching world of the creative black woman, that often the truest answer to a question that really matters can be found very close.

In the late 1920s my mother ran away from home to marry my father. Marriage, if not running away, was expected of seventeen-year-old girls. By the time she was twenty, she had two children and was pregnant with a third. Five children later, I was born. And this is how I came to know my mother: she seemed a large, soft, loving-eyed woman who was rarely impatient in our home. Her quick, violent temper was on view only a few times a year, when she battled with the white landlord who had the misfortune to suggest to her that her children did not need to go to school.

She made all the clothes we wore, even my brothers' overalls. She made all the towels and sheets we used. She spent the summers canning vegetables and fruits. She spent the winter evenings making quilts enough to cover all our beds.

During the "working" day, she labored beside—not behind—my father in the fields. Her day began before sunup, and did not end until late at night. There was never a moment for her to sit down, undisturbed, to unravel her own private thoughts; never a time free from interruption—by work or the noisy inquiries of her many children. And yet, it is to my mother—and all our mothers who were not famous—that I went in search of the secret of what has fed that muzzled and often mutilated, but vibrant, creative spirit that the black woman has inherited, and that pops out in wild and unlikely places to this day.

But when, you will ask, did my overworked mother have time to know or care about feeding the creative spirit?

The answer is so simple that many of us have spent years discovering it. We have constantly looked high, when we should have looked high—and low.

For example: in the Smithsonian Institution in Washington, D.C., there hangs a quilt unlike any other in the world. In fanciful, inspired, and yet simple and identifiable figures, it portrays the story of the Crucifixion. It is considered rare, beyond price. Though it follows no known pattern of quilt-making, and though it is made of bits and pieces of worthless rags, it is obviously the work of a person of powerful imagination and deep spiritual feeling. Below this quilt I saw a note that says it was made by "an anonymous black woman in Alabama, a hundred years ago."

If we could locate this "anonymous" black woman from Alabama, she would turn out to be one of our grandmothers—an artist who left her mark in the only materials she could afford, and in the only medium her position in society allowed her to use.

As Virginia Woolf wrote further, in *A Room of One's Own*:

> Yet genius of a sort must have existed among women as it must have existed among the working class. [Change this to "slaves" and the "wives and daughters of sharecroppers."] Now and again an Emily Brontë or a Robert Burns [change this to "a Zora Hurston or a Richard Wright"] blazes out and proves its presence. But certainly it never got itself on to paper. When, however, one reads of a witch being ducked, of a woman possessed by devils [or "Sainthood"], of a wise woman selling herbs [our root workers], or even a very remarkable man who had a mother, then I think we are on the track of a lost novelist, a suppressed poet, or some mute and inglorious Jane Austen. . . . Indeed, I would venture to guess that Anon, who

wrote so many poems without singing them, was often a
woman. . . .

And so our mothers and grandmothers have, more often than not
anonymously, handed on the creative spark, the seed of the flower they
themselves never hoped to see: or like a sealed letter they could not
plainly read.

And so it is, certainly, with my own mother. Unlike "Ma" Rainey's
songs, which retained their creator's name even while blasting forth from
Bessie Smith's mouth, no song or poem will bear my mother's name. Yet
so many of the stories that I write, that we all write, are my mother's stories. Only recently did I fully realize this: that through years of listening to
my mother's stories of her life, I have absorbed not only the stories themselves, but something of the manner in which she spoke, something of the
urgency that involves the knowledge that her stories—like her life—must
be recorded. It is probably for this reason that so much of what I have
written is about characters whose counterparts in real life are so much
older than I am.

But the telling of these stories, which came from my mother's lips as
naturally as breathing, was not the only way my mother showed herself as
an artist. For stories, too, were subject to being distracted, to dying without conclusion. Dinners must be started, and cotton must be gathered before the big rains. The artist that was and is my mother showed itself to
me only after many years. This is what I finally noticed.

Like Mem, a character in *The Third Life of Grange Copeland,* my mother
adorned with flowers whatever shabby house we were forced to live in.
And not just your typical straggly country stand of zinnias, either. She
planted ambitious gardens—and still does—with over fifty different varieties of plants that bloom profusely from early March until late November. Before she left home for the fields, she watered her flowers, chopped
up the grass, and laid out new beds. When she returned from the fields
she might divide clumps of bulbs, dig a cold pit, uproot and replant roses,
or prune branches from her taller bushes or trees—until night came and it
was too dark to see.

Whatever she planted grew as if by magic, and her fame as a grower of
flowers spread over three counties. Because of her creativity with her
flowers, even my memories of poverty are seen through a screen of
blooms—sunflowers, petunias, roses, dahlias, forsythia, spirea, delphini-
ums, verbena . . . and on and on.

And I remember people coming to my mother's yard to be given cuttings from her flowers; I hear again the praise showered on her because
whatever rocky soil she landed on, she turned into a garden. A garden so
brilliant with colors, so original in its design, so magnificent with life and
creativity, that to this day people drive by our house in Georgia—perfect
strangers and imperfect strangers—and ask to stand or walk among my
mother's art.

I notice that it is only when my mother is working in her flowers that she is radiant, almost to the point of being invisible—except as Creator: hand and eye. She is involved in work her soul must have. Ordering the universe in the image of her personal conception of Beauty.

Her face, as she prepares the Art that is her gift, is a legacy of respect she leaves to me, for all that illuminates and cherishes life. She has handed down respect for the possibilities—and the will to grasp them.

For her, so hindered and intruded upon in so many ways, being an artist has still been a daily part of her life. This ability to hold on, even in very simple ways, is work black women have done for a very long time.

This poem is not enough, but it is something, for the woman who literally covered the holes in our walls with sunflowers.

> They were women then
> My mama's generation
> Husky of voice—Stout of
> Step
> With fists as well as
> Hands
> How they battered down
> Doors
> And ironed
> Starched white
> Shirts
> How they led
> Armies
> Headragged Generals
> Across mined
> Fields
> Booby-trapped
> Kitchens
> To discover books
> Desks
> A place for us
> How they knew what we
> *Must* know
> Without knowing a page
> Of it
> Themselves

Guided by my heritage of a love of beauty and a respect for strength—in search of my mother's garden, I found my own.

And perhaps in Africa over two hundred years ago, there was just such a mother; perhaps she painted vivid and daring decorations in oranges and yellows and greens on the walls of her hut; perhaps she sang—in a voice like Roberta Flack's—*sweetly* over the compounds of her village; perhaps she wove the most stunning mats or told the most ingenious stories of all the village storytellers. Perhaps she was herself a poet—although only her daughter's name is signed to the poems that we know.

Perhaps Phillis Wheatley's mother was also an artist.

Perhaps in more than Phillis Wheatley's biological life is her mother's signature made clear.

•   •   •   •   •   •   •   •   •   •   •   •

### QUESTIONS FOR A SECOND READING

1. In the essay, Walker develops the interesting notion of "contrary in-stincts," particularly when she discusses Phillis Wheatley. The problem for Walker (and others) is that Wheatley would idolize a fair-haired white woman as a goddess of liberty rather than turn to herself as a model, or to the black women who struggled mightily for their identities and liberty. Walker asks, "How could she?" As you reread the essay, pay attention to the sections in which Walker discusses "contrary instincts." How would you define this term? What kind of answers does this essay make possible to the question "How could she?"

2. Bessie Smith, Roberta Flack, Phillis Wheatley, Zora Neale Hurston— Walker's essay is filled with allusions to black women artists; in fact, the essay serves as a kind of book list or reader's guide; it suggests a program of reading. Jean Toomer, however, is a man, and Virginia Woolf, a white woman; the references aren't strictly to black women. As you reread this essay, pay attention to the names (go to the library and track down some you don't know; you can use the bibliographical index in a good dictio-nary or ask a reference librarian to help you look up the information). What can you make of the collection of writers, poets, singers, and artists Walker sets down as a heritage? What use does she make of them?

3. As you reread the essay, note the sections in which Walker talks about herself. How does she feel about her mother, the history of black women in America, and "contrary instincts"? How would you describe Walker's feelings and attitudes toward herself, the past, and the pressures of living in a predominantly white culture? In considering these questions, don't settle for big words like "honest," "sensitive," or "compassionate." They are accurate, to be sure, but they are imprecise and don't do justice to Walker's seriousness and individuality.

### ASSIGNMENTS FOR WRITING

1. Walker's essay poses a number of questions about the history of African American women in America, including how their "creative spirit" sur-vived in the face of oppressive working and living conditions. At one point, Walker describes her mother's life in the late 1920s, after she ran away from home to marry Walker's father. Her mother's difficult life was filled with unrelenting work, yet she managed to keep a "vibrant, creative spirit" alive. At another point, Walker writes, "Our mothers and grand-

mothers, some of them: moving to music not yet written. And they waited . . . for a day when the unknown thing that was in them would be made known; but guessed, somehow in their darkness, that on the day of their revelation, they would be long dead" (p. 695).

Walker uses Virginia Woolf's term "contrary instincts" as a way to imagine this legacy of the creative spirit in the face of oppressive conditions, revising it, making it her own to fit the situations she's discussing as she weaves it into her writing. How would you say that Walker puts this term, "contrary instincts," to use in her own project? How do you understand Walker's rewriting of *A Room of One's Own?* What does Walker's use of the term allow her to understand about the creative spirit of African American women, including Phillis Wheatley and her own mother? How might Walker's essay itself stand as a response to this tradition?

Write an essay in which you discuss Walker's project as a creative endeavor, one in which she reconceives, or rewrites, texts from the past. What would you say, in other words, that Walker creates as she writes her essay?

2.  In her essay Walker raises the question of what it meant (and what it still means) to be a black woman and an artist, and her response proceeds from examples that take her mother and herself, among others, into account. As you read her essay, observe Walker's methods of working. How does she build her arguments? Where does her evidence come from? her authority? To whom is she appealing? What do her methods allow her to see (and say) and not to see? And, finally, how might her conclusions be related to her methods?

    Write a paper in which you examine Walker's essay in terms of the methods by which it proceeds. Consider the connections among her arguments, evidence, supposed audience, and conclusions, and feel free to invent names and descriptions for what you would call her characteristic ways of working. Remember that your job is to invent a way of describing how Walker works and how her methods—her ways of gathering materials, of thinking them through, of presenting herself and her thoughts, of imagining a world of speakers and listeners—might be related to the issues she raises and the conclusions she draws.

## MAKING CONNECTIONS

1.  Throughout "Our Time" (p. 707) by John Edgar Wideman, Robby talks about his contrary instincts, his ambivalent feelings toward making it in the "square" world. How can you consider Robby in light of Walker's observations about contrary instincts and the way black women lived in the past? Write an essay in which you explore how Wideman's understanding of his brother Robby's contrary instincts is different from Walker's understanding of her mother's contrary instincts.

2.  At key points in her essay, Alice Walker refers to Virginia Woolf's *A Room of One's Own* (p. 750). Not only does she cite passages, but she revises them to bring them to bear on her experience or to make them serve her

argument. There is a similar moment in Ralph Ellison's "An Extravagance of Laughter" (p. 257), where he cites and revises W. B. Yeats's argument on masks.

Use these examples to think about the relationship between African American writers and a white European intellectual heritage. Why do these writers do what they do with these passages? Work closely with the changes they make in the texts, and think about the writers' possible intentions. (Why, for example, wouldn't they avoid such moments?) And think about differences as well as similarities—in what ways might Walker and Ellison be said to be working toward different ends or different effects?

# JOHN EDGAR

# WIDEMAN

*J*OHN EDGAR WIDEMAN *was born in 1941 in Washington, D.C., but spent most of his youth in Homewood, a neighborhood in Pittsburgh. He earned a B.A. from the University of Pennsylvania, taught at the University of Wyoming, and is currently a professor of English at the University of Massachusetts at Amherst. In addition to the nonfiction work* Brothers and Keepers *(1984), from which this selection is drawn, Wideman has published a number of critically acclaimed works of fiction, including* The Lynchers, Reuben, Philadelphia Fire: A Novel, Fever: Twelve Stories, *and a series of novels set in Homewood:* Damballah, Hiding Place, *and* Sent for You Yesterday *(which won the 1984 PEN/Faulkner Award). The latter novels have been reissued as a set, titled* The Homewood Trilogy. *His most recent books include* Fever *(1996),* The Cattle Killing *(1996), and* Hiding Place *(1998). In 1994, Wideman published another work of nonfiction,* Fatheralong: A Meditation on Fathers and Sons, Race and Society.

*In the preface to this collection, Wideman writes,*

> *The value of black life in America is judged, as life generally in this country is judged, by external, material signs of success. Urban ghettoes are dangerous, broken-down, economically marginal pockets of*

*real estate infected with drugs, poverty, violence, crime, and since black life is seen as rooted in the ghetto, black people are identified with the ugliness, danger, and deterioration surrounding them. This logic is simpleminded and devastating, its hold on the American imagination as old as slavery; in fact, it recycles the classic justification for slavery, blaming the cause and consequences of oppression on the oppressed. Instead of launching a preemptive strike at the flawed assumptions that perpetuate racist thinking, blacks and whites are doomed to battle endlessly with the symptoms of racism.*

*In these three books again bound as one I have set myself to the task of making concrete those invisible planes of existence that bear witness to the fact that black life, for all its material impoverishment, continues to thrive, to generate alternative styles, redemptive strategies, people who hope and cope. But more than attempting to prove a "humanity," which should be self-evident anyway to those not blinded by racism, my goal is to celebrate and affirm.* Where did I come from? Who am I? Where am I going?

Brothers and Keepers *is a family story; it is about Wideman and his brother Robby. John went to Oxford as a Rhodes scholar, and Robby went to prison for his role in a robbery and a murder. In the section that follows, "Our Time," Wideman tries to understand his brother, their relationship, where they came from, where they are going. In this account, you will hear the voices of Robby, John, and people from the neighborhood, but also the voice of the writer, speaking about the difficulty of writing and the dangers of explaining away Robby's life.*

Brothers and Keepers *is not the first time Wideman has written to or about his brother. The first of the Homewood series,* Damballah *(1981), is dedicated to Robby. The dedication reads:*

> *Stories are letters. Letters sent to anybody or everybody. But the best kind are meant to be read by a specific somebody. When you read that kind you know you are eavesdropping. You know a real person somewhere will read the same words you are reading and the story is that person's business and you are a ghost listening in.*
>
> *Remember. I think it was Geral I first heard call a watermelon a letter from home. After all these years I understand a little better what she meant. She was saying the melon is a letter addressed to us. A story for us from down home. Down Home being everywhere we've never been, the rural South, the old days, slavery, Africa. That juicy, striped message with red meat and seeds, which always looked like roaches to me, was blackness as cross and celebration, a history we could taste and chew. And it was meant for us. Addressed to us. We were meant to slit it open and take care of business.*
>
> *Consider all these stories as letters from home. I never liked watermelon as a kid. I think I remember you did. You weren't afraid of becoming instant nigger, of sitting barefoot and goggle-eyed and Day-Glo black and drippy-lipped on massa's fence if you took one bite of the forbidden fruit. I was too scared to enjoy watermelon. Too self-conscious. I let people rob me of a simple pleasure. Watermelon's still*

tainted for me. But I know better now. I can play with the idea even if
I can't get down and have a natural ball eating a real one.

Anyway . . . these stories are letters. Long overdue letters from
me to you. I wish they could tear down the walls. I wish they could
snatch you away from where you are.

# Our Time

*You remember what we were saying about young black men in the street-
world life. And trying to understand why the "square world" becomes completely
unattractive to them. It has to do with the fact that their world is the GHETTO
and in that world all the glamour, all the praise and attention is given to the slick
guy, the gangster especially, the ones that get over in the "life." And it's because
we can't help but feel some satisfaction seeing a brother, a black man, get over on
these people, on their system without playing by their rules. No matter how much
we have incorporated these rules as our own, we know that they were forced on us
by people who did not have our best interests at heart. So this hip guy, this gangster or player or whatever label you give these brothers that we like to shun because of the poison that they spread, we, black people, still look at them with some
sense of pride and admiration, our children openly, us adults somewhere deep inside. We know they represent rebellion—what little is left in us. Well, having
lived in the "life," it becomes very hard—almost impossible—to find any contentment in joining the status quo. Too hard to go back to being nobody in a world
that hates you. Even if I had struck it rich in the life, I would have managed to
throw it down the fast lane. Or have lost it on a revolutionary whim. Hopefully
the latter.*

*I have always burned up in my fervent passions of desire and want. My
senses at times tingle and itch with my romantic, idealistic outlook on life, which
has always made me keep my distance from reality, reality that was a constant insult to my world, to my dream of happiness and peace, to my people-for-people
kind of world, my easy-cars-for-a-nickel-or-a-dime sorta world. And these driving
passions, this sensitivity to the love and good in people, also turned on me because
I used it to play on people and their feelings. These aspirations of love and desire
turned on me when I wasn't able to live up to this sweet-self morality, so I began
to self-destruct, burning up in my sensitivity, losing direction, because nowhere
could I find this world of truth and love and harmony.*

*In the real world, the world left for me, it was unacceptable to be "good," it
was square to be smart in school, it was jive to show respect to people outside the
street world, it was cool to be cold to your woman and the people that loved you.
The things we liked we called "bad." "Man, that was a bad girl." The world of the
angry black kid growing up in the sixties was a world in which to be in was to be
out—out of touch with the square world and all of its rules on what's right and*

*wrong. The thing was to make your own rules, do your own thing, but make sure it's contrary to what society says or is.*

                                                              I SHALL ALWAYS PRAY

## I

Garth looked bad. Real bad. Ichabod Crane anyway, but now he was a skeleton. Lying there in the bed with his bones poking through his skin, it made you want to cry. Garth's barely able to talk, his smooth, medium-brown skin yellow as pee. Ichabod legs and long hands and long feet, Garth could make you laugh just walking down the street. On the set you'd see him coming a far way off. Three-quarters leg so you knew it had to be Garth the way he was split up higher in the crotch than anybody else. Wilt the Stilt with a lean bird body perched on top his high waist. Size-fifteen shoes. Hands could palm a basketball easy as holding a pool cue. Fingers long enough to wrap round a basketball, but Garth couldn't play a lick. Never could get all that lankiness together on the court. You'd look at him sometimes as he was trucking down Homewood Avenue and think that nigger ain't walking, he's trying to remember how to walk. Awkward as a pigeon on roller skates. Knobby joints out of whack, arms and legs flailing, going their separate ways, his body jerking to keep them from going too far. Moving down the street like that wouldn't work, didn't make sense if you stood back and watched, if you pretended you hadn't seen Garth get where he was going a million times before. Nothing funny now, though. White hospital sheets pulled to his chest. Garth's head always looked small as a tennis ball way up there on his shoulders. Now it's a yellow, shrunken skull.

Ever since Robby had entered the ward, he'd wanted to reach over and hide his friend's arm under the covers. For two weeks Gar had been wasting away in the bed. Bad enough knowing Gar was dying. Didn't need that pitiful stick arm reminding him how close to nothing his main man had fallen. So fast. It could happen so fast. If Robby tried to raise that arm it would come off in his hand. As gentle as he could would not be gentle enough. The arm would disintegrate, like a long ash off the end of a cigarette.

Time to leave. No sense in sitting any longer. Garth not talking, no way of telling whether he was listening either. And Robby has nothing more to say. Choked up the way he gets inside hospitals. Hospital smell and quiet, the bare halls and bare floors, the echoes, something about all that he can't name, wouldn't try to name, rises in him and chills him. Like his teeth are chattering the whole time he's inside a hospital. Like his entire body is trembling uncontrollably, only nobody can see it or hear it but him. Shaking because he can't breathe the stuffy air. Hot and cold at the same time. He's been aching to leave since he entered the ward. Aching to get up and bust through the big glass front doors. Aching to pounce on that spidery arm flung back behind Gar's head. The arm too wasted to belong to his friend. He wants to grab it and hurl it away.

Robby pulls on tight white gloves the undertaker had dealt out to him and the rest of the pallbearers. His brown skin shows through the thin material, turns the white dingy. He's remembering that last time in Garth's ward. The hospital stink. Hot, chilly air. A bare arm protruding from the sleeve of the hospital gown, more dried-up toothpick than arm, a withered twig, with Garth's fingers like a bunch of skinny brown bananas drooping from the knobby tip.

Robby had studied the metal guts of the hospital bed, the black scuff marks swirling around the chair's legs. When he'd finally risen to go, his chair scraping against the vinyl floor broke a long silence. The noise must have roused Garth's attention. He'd spoken again.

You're good, man. Don't ever forget, Rob. You're the best.

Garth's first words since the little banter back and forth when Robby had entered the ward and dragged a chair to the side of Gar's bed. A whisper scarcely audible now that Robby was standing. Garth had tried to grin. The best he could manage was a pained adjustment of the bones of his face, no more than a shadow scudding across the yellow skull, but Robby had seen the famous smile. He hesitated, stopped rushing toward the door long enough to smile back. Because that was Gar. That was the way Gar was. He always had a smile and a good word for his cut buddies. Garth's grin was money in the bank. You could count on it like you could count on a good word from him. Something in his face would tell you you were alright, better than alright, that he believed in you, that you were, as he'd just whispered, "the best." You could depend on Garth to say something to make you feel good, even though you knew he was lying. With that grin greasing the lie you had to believe it, even though you knew better. Garth was the gang's dreamer. When he talked, you could see his dreams. That's why Robby had believed it, seen the grin, the bright shadow lighting Garth's face an instant. Out of nothing, out of pain, fear, the certainty of death gripping them both, Garth's voice had manufactured the grin.

Now they had to bury Garth. A few days after the visit to the hospital the phone rang and it was Garth's mother with the news of her son's death. Not really news. Robby had known it was just a matter of time. Of waiting for the moment when somebody else's voice would pronounce the words he'd said to himself a hundred times. *He's gone. Gar's dead.* Long gone before the telephone rang. Gar was gone when they stuck him up in the hospital bed. By the time they'd figured out what ailed him and admitted him to the hospital, it was too late. The disease had turned him to a skeleton. Nothing left of Garth to treat. They hid his messy death under white sheets, perfumed it with disinfectant, pumped him full of drugs so he wouldn't disturb his neighbors.

The others had squeezed into their pallbearers' gloves. Cheap white cotton gloves so you could use them once and throw them away like the rubber ones doctors wear when they stick their fingers up your ass. Michael, Cecil, and Sowell were pallbearers, too. With Robby and two men from Garth's family they would carry the coffin from Gaines Funeral Parlor to the hearse. Garth had been the dreamer for the gang. Robby counted four black fingers in the white glove. Garth was the thumb. The hand would be clumsy, wouldn't work right without him. Garth was different. But everybody else was different, too. Mike, the ice man, supercool. Cecil indifferent, ready to do most anything or nothing and couldn't care less which it was. Sowell wasn't really part of the gang; he didn't hang with them, didn't like to take the risks that were part of the "life." Sowell kept a good job. The "life" for him was just a way to make quick money. He didn't shoot up; he thought of himself as a businessman, an investor not a partner in their schemes. They knew Sowell mostly through Garth. Perhaps things would change now. The four survivors closer after they shared the burden of Gar's coffin, after they hoisted it and slid it on steel rollers into the back of Gaines's Cadillac hearse.

Robby was grateful for the gloves. He'd never been able to touch anything dead. He'd taken a beating once from his father rather than touch the bloody mousetrap his mother had nudged to the back door with her toe and ordered him to empty. The brass handle of the coffin felt damp through the glove. He gripped tighter to stop the flow of blood or sweat, whatever it was leaking from him or seeping from the metal. Garth had melted down to nothing by the end so it couldn't be him nearly yanking off Robby's shoulder when the box shifted and its weight shot forward. Felt like a coffin full of bricks. Robby stared across at Mike but Mike was a soldier, eyes front, riveted to the yawning rear door of the hearse. Mike's eyes wouldn't admit it, but they'd almost lost the coffin. They were rookie pallbearers and maneuvering down the carpeted front steps of Gaines Funeral Parlor they'd almost let Garth fly out their hands. They needed somebody who knew what he was doing. An old, steady head to show them the way. They needed Garth. But Garth was long gone. Ashes inside the steel box.

They began drinking later that afternoon in Garth's people's house. Women and food in one room, men hitting the whiskey hard in another. It was a typical project apartment. The kind everybody had stayed in or visited one time or another. Small, shabby, featureless. Not a place to live. No matter what you did to it, how clean you kept it or what kind of furniture you loaded it with, the walls and ceilings were not meant to be home for anybody. A place you passed through. Not yours, because the people who'd been there before you left their indelible marks everywhere and you couldn't help adding your bruises and knots for the next tenants. You could rent a kitchen and bedroom and a bathroom and a living room, the project flats were laid out so you had a room for each of the things people did in houses. Problem was, every corner was cut. Living cramped is one thing and people can get cozy in the closest quarters. It's another thing to live in a place designed to be just a little less than adequate. No slack, no space to personalize, to stamp the flat with what's peculiar to your style. Like a man sitting on a toilet seat that's too small and the toilet too close to the bathtub so his knees shove against the enamel edge. He can move his bowels that way and plenty of people in the world have a lot less but he'll never enjoy sitting there, never feel the deep down comfort of belonging where he must squat.

Anyway, the whiskey started flowing in that little project apartment. Robby listened, for Garth's sake, as long as he could to old people reminiscing about funerals they'd attended, about all the friends and relatives they'd escorted to the edge of Jordan, old folks sipping good whiskey and moaning and groaning till it seemed a sin to be left behind on this side of the river after so many saints had crossed over. He listened to people express their grief, tell sad, familiar stories. As he got high he listened less closely to the words. Faces and gestures revealed more than enough. When he split with Mike and Cecil and their ladies, Sowell tagged along. By then the tacky, low-ceilinged rooms of the flat were packed. Loud talk, laughter, storytellers competing for audiences. Robby half expected the door he pushed shut behind himself to pop open again, waited for bottled-up noise to explode into the funky hallway.

Nobody thinking about cemeteries now. Nobody else needs to be buried today, so it was time to get it on. Some people had been getting close to rowdy. Some people had been getting mad. Mad at one of the guests in the apartment, mad at doctors and hospitals and whites in general who had the whole world in their hands but didn't have the slightest idea what to do with it. A short, dark man, bubble-eyed, immaculately dressed in a three-piece, wool, herringbone suit, had railed about the callousness, the ignorance of white witch doctors who, by misdiagnosing Garth's illness, had sealed his doom. His harangue had drawn a crowd. He wasn't just talking, he was testifying, and a hush had fallen over half the room as he dissected the dirty tricks of white folks. If somebody ran to the hospital and snatched a white-coated doctor and threw him into the circle surrounding the little fish-eyed man, the mourners would tear the pale-faced devil apart. Robby wished he could feed them one. Remembered Garth weak and helpless in the bed and the doctors and nurses flitting around in the halls, jiving the other patients, ignoring Gar like he wasn't there. Garth was dead because he had believed them. Dead because he had nowhere else to turn when the pain in his gut and the headaches grew worse and worse. Not that he trusted the doctors or believed they gave a flying fuck about him. He'd just run out of choices and had to put himself in their hands. They told him jaundice was his problem, and while his liver rotted away and pain cooked him dizzy Garth assured anyone who asked that it was just a matter of giving the medicine time to work. To kill the pain he blew weed as long as he had strength to hold a joint between his lips. Take a whole bunch of smoke to cool me out these days. Puffing like a chimney till he lost it and fell back and Robby scrambling to grab the joint before Garth torched hisself.

When you thought about it, Garth's dying made no sense. And the more you thought the more you dug that nothing else did neither. The world's a stone bitch. Nothing true if that's not true. The man had you coming and going. He owned everything worth owning and all you'd ever get was what he didn't want anymore, what he'd chewed and spit out and left in the gutter for niggers to fight over. Garth had pointed to the street and said, If we ever make it, it got to come from there, from the curb. We got to melt that rock till we get us some money. He grinned then, Ain't no big thing. We'll make it, brother man. We got what it takes. It's our time.

Something had crawled in Garth's belly. The man said it wasn't nothing. Sold him some aspirins and said he'd be alright in no time. The man killed Garth. Couldn't kill him no deader with a .357 magnum slug, but ain't no crime been committed. Just one those things. You know, everybody makes mistakes. And a dead nigger ain't really such a big mistake when you think about it. Matter of fact you mize well forget the whole thing. Nigger wasn't going nowhere, nohow. I mean he wasn't no brain surgeon or astronaut, no movie star or big-time athlete. Probably a dope fiend or gangster. Wind up killing some innocent person or wasting another nigger. Shucks. That doctor ought to get a medal.

Hey, man. Robby caught Mike's eye. Then Cecil and Sowell turned to him. They knew he was speaking to everybody. Late now. Ten, eleven, because it had been dark outside for hours. Quiet now. Too quiet in his pad. And too much smoke and drink since the funeral. From a bare bulb in the kitchen ceiling light seeped down the hallway and hovered dimly in the doorway of the room where they sat. Robby wondered if the others felt as bad as he did. If the cemetery clothes itched their skin. If they could smell grave dust on their shoes. He hoped they'd finish this last jug of wine and let the day be over. He needed sleep, downtime to get the terrible weight of Garth's death off his mind. He'd been grateful for the darkness. For the company of his cut buddies after the funeral. For the Sun Ra tape until it ended and plunged them into a deeper silence than any he'd ever known. Garth was gone. In a few days people would stop talking about him. He was in the ground. Stone-cold dead. Robby had held a chunk of crumbly ground in his white-gloved fingers and mashed it and dropped the dust into the hole. Now the ground had closed over Garth and what did it mean? Here one day and gone the next and that was that. They'd bury somebody else out of Gaines tomorrow. People would dress up and cry and get drunk and tell lies and next day it'd be somebody else's turn to die. Which one of the shadows in this black room would go first? What did it matter? Who cared? Who would remember their names; they were ghosts already. Dead as Garth already. Only difference was, Garth didn't have it to worry about no more. Garth didn't have to pretend he was going anywhere cause he was there. He'd made it to the place they all were headed fast as their legs could carry them. Every step was a step closer to the stone-cold ground, the pitch-black hole where they'd dropped Garth's body.

Hey, youall. We got to drink to Garth one last time.

They clinked glasses in the darkness. Robby searched for something to say. The right words wouldn't come. He knew there was something proper and precise that needed to be said. Because the exact words eluded him, because only the right words would do, he swallowed his gulp of heavy, sweet wine in silence.

He knew he'd let Garth down. If it had been one of the others dead, Michael or Cecil or Sowell or him, Garth wouldn't let it slide by like this, wouldn't let it end like so many other nights had ended, the fellows nodding off one by one, stupefied by smoke and drink, each one beginning to shop around in his mind, trying to figure whether or not he should turn in or if there was a lady somewhere who'd welcome him in her bed. No. Garth would have figured a way to make it special. They wouldn't be hiding in the bushes. They'd be knights in shining armor around a big table. They'd raise their giant, silver cups to honor the fallen comrade. Like in the olden days. Clean, brave dudes with gold rings and gold chains. They'd draw their blades. Razor-edged swords that gleam in the light with jewels sparkling in the handles. They'd make a roof over the table when they stood and raised their swords and the points touched in the sky. A silver dagger on a satin pillow in the middle of the table. Everybody roll up their sleeves and prick a vein and go round, each one touching everybody else so the blood runs together and we're brothers forever, brothers as long as blood flows in anybody's arm. We'd ride off and do unbelievable shit. The dead one always with us cause we'd do it all for him. Swear we'd never let him down.

It's our time now. We can't let Garth down. Let's drink this last one for him and promise him we'll do what he said we could. We'll be the best. We'll make it to the top for him. We'll do it for Garth.

Glasses rattled together again. Robby empties his and thinks about smashing it against a wall. He'd seen it done that way in movies but it was late at night and these crazy niggers might not know when to stop throwing things. A battlefield of broken glass for him to creep through when he gets out of bed in the morning. He doesn't toss the empty glass. Can't see a solid place anyway where it would strike clean and shatter to a million points of light.

My brother had said something about a guy named Garth during one of my visits to the prison. Just a name mentioned in passing. *Garth* or *Gar*. I'd asked Robby to spell it for me. Garth had been a friend of Robby's, about Robby's age, who died one summer of a mysterious disease. Later when Robby chose to begin the story of the robbery and killing by saying, "It all started with Gar dying," I remembered that first casual mention and remembered a conversation with my mother. My mom and I were in the kitchen of the house on Tokay Street. My recollection of details was vague at first but something about the conversation had made a lasting impression because, six years later, hearing Robby say the name *Garth* brought back my mother's words.

My mother worried about Robby all the time. Whenever I visited home, sooner or later I'd find myself alone with Mom and she'd pour out her fears about Robby's *wildness,* the deep trouble he was bound for, the web of entanglements and intrigues and bad company he was weaving around himself with a maddening disregard for the inevitable consequences.

I don't know. I just don't know how to reach him. He won't listen. He's doing wrong and he knows it but nothing I say makes any difference. He's not like the rest of youall. You'd misbehave but I could talk to you or smack you if I had to and you'd straighten up. With Robby it's like talking to a wall.

I'd listen and get angry at my brother because I registered not so much the danger he was bringing on himself, but the effect of his escapades on the woman who'd brought us both into the world. After all, Robby was no baby. If he wanted to mess up, nobody could stop him. Also Robby was my brother, meaning that his wildness was just a stage, a chaotic phase of his life that would only last till he got his head together and decided to start doing right. Doing as the rest of us did. He was my brother. He couldn't fall too far. His brushes with the law (I'd had some, too), the time he'd spent in jail, were serious but temporary setbacks. I viewed his troubles, when I thought about them at all, as a form of protracted juvenile delinquency, and fully expected Robby would learn his lesson sooner or later and return to the fold, the prodigal son, chastened, perhaps a better person for the experience. In the meantime the most serious consequence of his wildness was Mom's devastating unhappiness. She couldn't sustain the detachment, the laissez-faire optimism I had talked myself into. Because I was two thousand miles away, in Wyoming, I didn't have to deal with the day-to-day evidence of Robby's trouble. The syringe Mom found under his bed. The twenty-dollar bill missing from her purse. The times he'd cruise in higher than a kite, his pupils reduced to pinpricks, with his crew and they'd raid the refrigerator and make a loud, sloppy feast, all of them feeling so good they couldn't imagine anybody not up there on cloud nine with them enjoying the time of their lives. Cruising in, then disappearing just as abruptly, leaving their dishes and pans and mess behind. Robby covering Mom with kisses and smiles and drowning her in babytalk hootchey-coo as he staggers through the front door. Her alone in the ravaged, silent kitchen, listening as doors slam and a car squeals off on the cobblestones of Tokay, wondering where they're headed next, wishing, praying Robby will return and eat and eat and eat till he falls asleep at the table so she can carry him upstairs and tuck him in and kiss his forehead and shut the door gently on his sleep.

I wasn't around for all that. Didn't want to know how bad things were for him. Worrying about my mother was tough enough. I could identify with her grief, I could blame my brother. An awful situation, but simple too. My role, my responsibilities and loyalties were clear. The *wildness* was to blame, and it was a passing thing, so I just had to help my mother survive the worst of it, then everything would be alright. I'd steel myself for the moments alone with her when she'd tell me the worst. In the kitchen, usually, over a cup of coffee with the radio playing. When my mother was alone in the house on Tokay, either the TV or a radio or both were always on. Atop the kitchen table a small clock radio turned to WAMO, one of Pittsburgh's soul stations, would background with scratchy gospel music whatever we said in the morning in the kitchen. On a morning like that in 1975, while I drank a cup of coffee and part of me, still half-asleep, hidden, swayed to the soft beat of gospel, my mother had explained how upset Robby was over the death of his friend, Garth.

It was a terrible thing. I've known Garth's mother for years. He was a good boy. No saint for sure, but deep down a good boy. Like your brother. Not a mean bone in his body. Out there in the street doing wrong, but that's where most of them are. What else can they do, John? Sometimes I can't blame them. No jobs, no money in their pockets. How they supposed to feel like men? Garth did better than most. Whatever else he was into, he kept that little job over at Westinghouse and helped out his mother. A big, playful kid. Always smiling. I think that's why him and Robby were so tight. Neither one had good sense. Giggled and acted like fools. Garth no wider than my finger. Straight up and down. A stringbean if I ever saw one. When Robby lived here in the house with me, Garth was always around. I know how bad Robby feels. He hasn't said a word but I know. When Robby's quiet, you know something's wrong. Soon as his eyes pop open in the morning he's looking for the party. First thing in the morning he's chipper and chattering. Looking for the party. That's your brother. He had a match in Garth.

Shame the way they did that boy. He'd been down to the clinic two or three times but they sent him home. Said he had an infection and it would take care of itself. Something like that anyway. You know how they are down there. Have to be spitting blood to get attention. Then all they give you is a Band-Aid. He went back two times, but they kept telling him the same dumb thing. Anybody who knew Garth could see something awful was wrong. Circles under his eyes. Sallow look to his skin. Losing weight. And the poor thing didn't have any weight to lose. Last time I saw him I was shocked. Just about shocked out my shoes. Wasn't Garth standing in front of me. Not the boy I knew.

Well, to make a long story short, they finally took him in the hospital but it was too late. They let him walk the streets till he was dead. It was wrong. Worse than wrong how they did him, but that's how those dogs do us every day God sends here. Garth's gone, so nothing nobody can say will do any good. I feel so sorry for his mother. She lived for that boy. I called her and tried to talk but what can you say? I prayed for her and prayed for Garth and prayed for Robby. A thing like that tears people up.

It's worse if you keep it inside. And that's your brother's way. He'll let it eat him up and then go out and do something crazy.

Until she told me Garth's story I guess I hadn't realized how much my mother had begun to change. She had always seemed to me to exemplify the tolerance, the patience, the long view epitomized in her father. John French's favorite saying was, Give 'em the benefit of the doubt. She could get as ruffled, as evil as the rest of us, cry and scream or tear around the house fit to be tied. She had her grudges and quarrels. Mom could let it all hang out, yet most of the time she radiated a deep calm. She reacted strongly to things but at the same time held judgment in abeyance. Events, personalities always deserved a second, slower appraisal, an evaluation outside the sphere of everyday hassles and vexations. You gave people the benefit of the doubt. You attempted to remove your ego, acknowledge the limitations of your individual view of things. You consulted as far as you were equipped by temperament and intelligence a broader, more abiding set of relationships and connections.

You tried on the other person's point of view. You sought the other, better person in yourself who might talk you into relinquishing for a moment your selfish interest in whatever was at issue. You stopped and considered the long view, possibilities other than the one that momentarily was leading you by the nose. You gave yourself and other people the benefit of the doubt.

My mother had that capacity. I'd admired, envied, and benefited infinitely from its presence. As she related the story of Garth's death and my brother's anger and remorse, her tone was uncompromisingly bitter. No slack, no margin of doubt was being granted to the forces that destroyed Garth and still pursued her son. She had exhausted her reserves of understanding and compassion. The long view supplied the same ugly picture as the short. She had an enemy now. It was that revealed truth that had given the conversation its edge, its impact. *They* had killed Garth, and his dying had killed part of her son; so the battle lines were drawn. Irreconcilably. Absolutely. The backside of John French's motto had come into play. Giving someone the benefit of the doubt was also giving him enough rope to hang himself. If a person takes advantage of the benefit of the doubt and keeps on taking and taking, one day the rope plays out. The piper must be paid. If you've been the one giving, it becomes incumbent on you to grip your end tight and take away. You turn the other cheek, but slowly, cautiously, and keep your fist balled up at your side. If your antagonist decides to smack rather than kiss you or leave you alone, you make sure you get in the first blow. And make sure it's hard enough to knock him down.

Before she told Garth's story, my mother had already changed, but it took years for me to realize how profoundly she hated what had been done to Garth and then Robby. The gentleness of my grandfather, like his fair skin and good French hair, had been passed down to my mother. Gentleness styled the way she thought, spoke, and moved in the world. Her easy disposition and sociability masked the intensity of her feelings. Her attitude to authority of any kind, doctors, clerks, police, bill collectors, newscasters, whites in general partook of her constitutional gentleness. She wasn't docile or cowed. The power other people possessed or believed they possessed didn't frighten her; she accommodated herself, offered something they could accept as deference but that was in fact the same resigned, alert attention she paid to roaches or weather or poverty, any of the givens outside herself that she couldn't do much about. She never engaged in public tests of will, never pushed herself or her point of view on people she didn't know. Social awkwardness embarrassed her. Like most Americans she didn't like paying taxes, was suspicious of politicians, resented the disparity between big and little people in our society and the double standard that allowed big shots to get away with murder. She paid particular attention to news stories that reinforced her basic political assumption that power corrupts. On the other hand she knew the world was a vale of tears and one's strength, granted by God to deal with life's inevitable calamities, should not be squandered on small stuff.

In spite of all her temperamental and philosophic resistance to extremes, my mother would be radicalized. What the demonstrations, protest marches, and slogans of the sixties had not effected would be accomplished by Garth's death and my brother's troubles. She would become an aggressive, acid critic of the status quo in all its forms: from the President ("If it wasn't for that rat I'd have a storm door to go with the storm windows but he cut the program") on down to bank tellers ("I go there every Friday and I'm one of the few black faces she sees all day and she knows me as well as she knows that wart on her cheek but she'll still make me show my license before she'll cash my check"). A son she loved would be pursued, captured, tried, and imprisoned by the forces of law and order. Throughout the ordeal her love for him wouldn't change, couldn't change. His crime tested her love and also tested the nature, the intent of the forces arrayed against her son. She had to make a choice. On one side were the stark facts of his crime: robbery, murder, flight; her son an outlaw, a fugitive; then a prisoner. On the other side the guardians of society, the laws, courts, police, judges, and keepers who were responsible for punishing her son's transgression.

She didn't invent the two sides and initially didn't believe there couldn't be a middle ground. She extended the benefit of the doubt. Tried to situate herself somewhere in between, acknowledging the evil of her son's crime while simultaneously holding on to the fact that he existed as a human being before, after, and during the crime he'd committed. He'd done wrong but he was still Robby and she'd always be his mother. Strangely, on the dark side, the side of the crime and its terrible consequences, she would find room to exercise her love. As negative as the elements were, a life taken, the grief of the survivors, suffering, waste, guilt, remorse, the scale was human; she could apply her sense of right and wrong. Her life to that point had equipped her with values, with tools for sorting out and coping with disaster. So she would choose to make her fight there, on treacherous yet familiar ground—familiar since her son was there—and she could place herself, a woman, a mother, a grieving, bereaved human being, there beside him.

Nothing like that was possible on the other side. The legitimacy of the other side was grounded not in her experience of life, but in a set of rules seemingly framed to sidestep, ignore, or replace her sense of reality. Accepting the version of reality encoded in *their* rules would be like stepping into a cage and locking herself in. Definitions of her son, herself, of need and frailty and mercy, of blackness and redemption and justice had all been neatly formulated. No need here for her questions, her uncertainty, her fear, her love. Everything was clean and clear. No room for her sense that things like good and evil, right and wrong bleed into each other and create a dreadful margin of ambiguity no one could name but could only enter, enter at the risk of everything because everything is at stake and no one on earth knows what it means to enter or what will happen if and when the testing of the margin is over.

She could love her son, accept his guilt, accept the necessity of punishment, suffer with him, grow with him past the stage of blaming everyone but himself for his troubles, grieve with him when true penitence began to exact its toll. Though she might wish penance and absolution could be achieved in private, without the intervention of a prison sentence, she understood dues must be paid. He was her son but he was also a man who had committed a robbery in the course of which another woman's son had been killed. What would appall her and what finally turned her against the forces of law and order was the incapacity of the legal system to grant her son's humanity. "Fair" was the word she used—a John French word. She expected them to treat Robby fair. Fairness was what made her willing to give him up to punishment even though her love screamed no and her hands clung to his shoulders. Fairness was what she expected from the other side in their dealings with her and her son.

She could see their side, but they steadfastly refused to see hers. And when she realized fairness was not forthcoming, she began to hate. In the lack of reciprocity, in the failure to grant that Robby was first a man, then a man who had done wrong, the institutions and individuals who took over control of his life denied not only his humanity but the very existence of the world that had nurtured him and nurtured her—the world of touching, laughing, suffering black people that established Robby's claim to something more than a number.

Mom expects the worst now. She's peeped their hole card. She understands they have a master plan that leaves little to accident, that most of the ugliest things happening to black people are not accidental but the predictable results of the working of the plan. What she learned about authority, about law and order didn't make sense at first. It went against her instincts, what she wanted to believe, against the generosity she'd observed in her father's interactions with other Homewood people. He was fair. He'd pick up the egg rolls he loved from the back kitchen door of Mr. Wong's restaurant and not blame Wong, his old talking buddy and card-playing crony, for not serving black people in his restaurant. Wong had a family and depended on white folks to feed them, so Wong didn't have any choice and neither did John French if he wanted those incredible egg rolls. He treated everyone, high and low, the same. He said what he meant and meant what he said. John French expected no more from other people than he expected from himself. And he'd been known to mess up many a time, but that was him, that was John French, no better, no worse than any man who pulls on his britches one leg at a time. He needed a little slack, needed the benefit of that blind eye people who love, or people who want to get along with other people, must learn to cast. John French was grateful for the slack, so was quick to extend it to others. Till they crossed him.

My mother had been raised in Homewood. The old Homewood. Her relations with people in that close-knit, homogeneous community were based on trust, mutual respect, common spiritual and material concerns. Face-to-face contact, shared language and values, a large fund of communal experience rendered individual lives extremely visible in Homewood. Both a person's self-identity ("You know who you are") and accountability ("Other people know who you are") were firmly established.

If one of the Homewood people said, "That's the French girl" or, "There goes John French's daughter," a portrait with subtle shading and complex resonance was painted by the words. If the listener addressed was also a Homewood resident, the speaker's voice located the young woman passing innocently down Tioga Street in a world invisible to outsiders. A French girl was somebody who lived in Cassina Way, somebody you didn't fool with or talk nasty to. Didn't speak to at all except in certain places or on certain occasions. French girls were church girls, Homewood African Methodist Episcopal Zion Sunday-school-picnic and social-event young ladies. You wouldn't find them hanging around anywhere without escorts or chaperones. French girls had that fair, light, bright, almost white redbone complexion and fine blown hair and nice big legs but all that was to be appreciated from a distance because they were nice girls and because they had this crazy daddy who wore a big brown country hat and gambled and drank wine and once ran a man out of town, ran him away without ever laying a hand on him or making a bad-mouthed threat, just cut his eyes a certain way when he said the man's name and the word went out and the man who had cheated a drunk John French with loaded dice was gone. Just like that. And there was the time Elias Brown was cleaning his shotgun in his backyard. Brown had his double-barreled shotgun across his knees and a jug of Dago Red on the ground beside him and it was a Saturday and hot and Brown was sweating through his BVD undershirt and paying more attention to the wine than he was to the gun. Next thing you know, *Boom!* Off it goes and buckshot sprayed down Cassina Way, and it's Saturday and summer like I said, so chillens playing everywhere but God watches over fools and babies so nobody hit bad. Nobody hit at all except the little French girl, Geraldine, playing out there in the alley and she got nicked in her knee. Barely drew blood. A sliver of that buckshot musta ricocheted off the cobblestones and cut her knee. Thank Jesus she the only one hit and she ain't hit bad. Poor Elias Brown don't quite know what done happened till some the mens run over in his yard and snatch the gun and shake the wine out his head. What you doing, fool? Don't you know no better all those children running round here? Coulda killed one these babies. Elias stone drunk and don't hear nothing, see nothing till one the men say French girl. Nicked the little French girl, Geraldine. Then Elias woke up real quick. His knees, his dusty butt, everything he got starts to trembling and his eyes get big as dinner plates. Then he's gone like a turkey through the corn. Nobody seen Elias for a week. He's in Ohio at his sister's next time anybody hear anything about Elias. He's cross there in Ohio and still shaking till he git word John French ain't after him. It took three men gon over there telling the same story to get Elias back to Homewood. John French ain't mad. He *was* mad but he ain't mad now. Little girl just nicked is all and French ain't studying you, Brown.

You heard things like that in Homewood names. Rules of etiquette, thumbnail character sketches, a history of the community. A dire warning to get back could be coded into the saying of a person's name, and a further inflection of the speaker's voice could tell you to ignore the facts, forget what he's just reminded you to remember and go on. Try your luck.

Because Homewood was self-contained and possessed such a strong personality, because its people depended less on outsiders than they did on each other for so many of their most basic satisfactions, they didn't notice the net settling over their community until it was already firmly in place. Even though the strands of the net—racial discrimination, economic exploitation, white hate and fear—had existed time out of mind, what people didn't notice or chose not to notice was that the net was being drawn tighter, that ruthless people outside the community had the power to choke the life out of Homewood, and as soon as it served their interests would do just that. During the final stages, as the net closed like a fist around Homewood, my mother couldn't pretend it wasn't there. But instead of setting her free, the truth trapped her in a cage as tangible as the iron bars of Robby's cell.

Some signs were subtle, gradual. The A & P started to die. Nobody mopped filth from the floors. Nobody bothered to restock empty shelves. Fewer and fewer white faces among the shoppers. A plate-glass display window gets broken and stays broken. When they finally close the store, they paste the going-out-of-business notice over the jagged, taped crack. Other signs as blatant, as sudden as fire engines and patrol cars breaking your sleep, screaming through the dark Homewood streets. First Garth's death, then Robby's troubles brought it all home. My mother realized her personal unhappiness and grief were inseparable from what was happening *out there*. Out there had never been further away than the thousand insults and humiliations she had disciplined herself to ignore. What she had deemed petty, not worth bothering about, were strings of the net just as necessary, as effective as the most dramatic intrusions into her life. She decided to stop letting things go by. No more benefit of the doubt. Doubt had been cruelly excised. She decided to train herself to be as wary, as unforgiving as she'd once been ready to live and let live. My mother wouldn't become paranoid, not even overtly prickly or bristling. That would have been too contrary to her style, to what her blood and upbringing had instilled. The change was inside. What she thought of people. How she judged situations. Things she'd say or do startled me, set me back on my heels because I didn't recognize my mother in them. I couldn't account for the stare of pure unadulterated hatred she directed at the prison guard when he turned away from her to answer the phone before handing her the rest-room key she'd requested, the vehemence with which she had cussed Richard Nixon for paying no taxes when she, scraping by on an income of less than four thousand dollars a year, owed the IRS three hundred dollars.

Garth's death and Robby's troubles were at the center of her new vision. Like a prism, they caught the light, transformed it so she could trace the seemingly random inconveniences and impositions coloring her life to their source in a master plan.

I first heard Garth's story in the summer of 1975, the summer my wife carried our daughter Jamila in her belly, the summer before the robbery and killing. The story contained all the clues I'm trying to decipher now. Sitting in the kitchen vaguely distracted by gospel music from the little clock radio atop the table, listening as my mother expressed her sorrow, her indignation at the way Garth was treated, her fears for my brother, I was hearing a new voice. Something about the voice struck me then, but I missed what was novel and crucial. I'd lost my Homewood ear. Missed all the things unsaid that invested her words with special urgency. People in Homewood often ask: You said that to say what? The impacted quality of an utterance either buries a point too obscurely or insists on a point so strongly that the listener wants the meat of the message repeated, wants it restated clearly so it stands alone on its own two feet. If I'd been alert enough to ask that question, to dig down to the root and core of Garth's story after my mother told it, I might have understood sooner how desperate and dangerous Homewood had become. Six years later my brother was in prison, and when he began the story of his troubles with Garth's death, a circle completed itself; Robby was talking to me, but I was still on the outside, looking in.

That day six years later, I talked with Robby three hours, the maximum allotted for weekday visits with a prisoner. It was the first time in life we'd ever talked that long. Probably two and a half hours longer than the longest, unbroken, private conversation we'd ever had. And it had taken guards, locks, and bars to bring us together. The ironies of the situation, the irony of that fact, escaped neither of us.

I listened mostly, interrupting my brother's story a few times to clarify dates or names. Much of what he related was familiar. The people, the places. Even the voice, the words he chose were mine in a way. We're so alike, I kept thinking, anticipating what he would say next, how he would say it, filling in naturally, easily with my words what he left unsaid. Trouble was our minds weren't interchangeable. No more than our bodies. The guards wouldn't have allowed me to stay in my brother's place. He was the criminal. I was the visitor from outside. Different as night and day. As Robby talked I let myself forget that difference. Paid too much attention to myself listening and lost some of what he was saying. What I missed would have helped define the difference. But I missed it. It was easy to half listen. For both of us to pretend to be closer than we were. We needed the closeness. We were brothers. In the prison visiting lounge I acted toward my brother the way I'd been acting toward him all my life, heard what I wanted to hear, rejected the rest.

When Robby talked, the similarity of his Homewood and mine was a trap. I could believe I knew exactly what he was describing. I could relax into his story, walk down Dunfermline or Tioga, see my crippled grandmother sitting on the porch of the house on Finance, all the color her pale face had lost blooming in the rosebush beneath her in the yard, see Robby in the downstairs hall of the house on Marchand, rapping with his girl on the phone, which sat on a three-legged stand just inside the front door. I'd slip unaware out of his story into one of my own. I'd be following him, an obedient shadow, then a cloud would blot the sun and I'd be gone, unchained, a dark form still skulking behind him but no longer in tow.

The hardest habit to break, since it was the habit of a lifetime, would be listening to myself listen to him. That habit would destroy any chance of seeing my brother on his terms; and seeing him in his terms, learning his terms, seemed the whole point of learning his story. However numerous and comforting the similarities, we were different. The world had seized on the difference, allowed me room to thrive, while he'd been forced into a cage. Why did it work out that way? What was the nature of the difference? Why did it haunt me? Temporarily at least, to answer these questions, I had to root my fiction-writing self out of our exchanges. I had to teach myself to listen. Start fresh, clear the pipes, resist too facile an identification, tame the urge to take off with Robby's story and make it my own.

I understood all that, but could I break the habit? And even if I did learn to listen, wouldn't there be a point at which I'd have to take over the telling? Wasn't there something fundamental in my writing, in my capacity to function, that depended on flight, on escape? Wasn't another person's skin a hiding place, a place to work out anxiety, to face threats too intimidating to handle in any other fashion? Wasn't writing about people a way of exploiting them?

A stranger's gait, or eyes, or a piece of clothing can rivet my attention. Then it's like falling down to the center of the earth. Not exactly fear or panic but an uneasy, uncontrollable momentum, a sense of being swallowed, engulfed in blackness that has no dimensions, no fixed points. That boundless, incarcerating black hole is another person. The detail grabbing me functions as a door and it swings open and I'm drawn, sucked, pulled in head over heels till suddenly I'm righted again, on track again and the peculiarity, the ordinariness of the detail that usurped my attention becomes a window, a way of seeing out of another person's eyes, just as for a second it had been my way in. I'm scooting along on short, stubby legs and the legs are not anybody else's and certainly not mine, but I feel for a second what it's like to motor through the world atop these peculiar duck thighs and foreshortened calves and I know how wobbly the earth feels under those run-over-at-the-heel, split-seamed penny loafers. Then just as suddenly I'm back. I'm me again, slightly embarrassed, guilty because I've been trespassing and don't know how long I've been gone or if anybody noticed me violating somebody else's turf.

Do I write to escape, to make a fiction of my life? If I can't be trusted with the story of my own life, how could I ask my brother to trust me with his?

The business of making a book together was new for both of us. Difficult. Awkward. Another book could be constructed about a writer who goes to a prison to interview his brother but comes away with his own story. The conversations with his brother would provide a stage for dramatizing the writer's tortured relationship to other people, himself, his craft. The writer's motives, the issue of exploitation, the inevitable conflict between his role as detached observer and his responsibility as a brother would be at the center of such a book. When I stopped hearing Robby and listened to myself listening, that kind of book shouldered its way into my consciousness. I didn't like the feeling. That book compromised the intimacy I wanted to achieve with my brother. It was as obtrusive as the Wearever pen in my hand, the little yellow sheets of Yard Count paper begged from the pad of the guard in charge of overseeing the visiting lounge. The borrowed pen and paper (I was not permitted into the lounge with my own) were necessary props. I couldn't rely on memory to get my brother's story down and the keepers had refused my request to use a tape recorder, so there I was. Jimmy Olson, cub reporter, poised on the edge of my seat, pen and paper at ready, asking to be treated as a brother.

We were both rookies. Neither of us had learned very much about sharing our feelings with other family members. At home it had been assumed that each family member possessed deep, powerful feelings and that very little or nothing at all needed to be said about these feelings because we all were stuck with them and talk wouldn't change them. Your particular feelings were a private matter and family was a protective fence around everybody's privacy. Inside the perimeter of the fence each family member resided in his or her own quarters. What transpired in each dwelling was mainly the business of its inhabitant as long as nothing generated within an individual unit threatened the peace or safety of the whole. None of us knew how traditional West African families were organized or what values the circular shape of their villages embodied, but the living arrangements we had worked out among ourselves resembled the ancient African patterns. You were granted emotional privacy, independence, and space to commune with your feelings. You were encouraged to deal with as much as you could on your own, yet you never felt alone. The high wall of the family, the collective, communal reality of other souls, other huts like yours eliminated some of the dread, the isolation experienced when you turned inside and tried to make sense out of the chaos of your individual feelings. No matter how grown you thought you were or how far you believed you'd strayed, you knew you could cry *Mama* in the depths of the night and somebody would tend to you. Arms would wrap round you, a soft soothing voice lend its support. If not a flesh-and-blood mother then a mother in the form of song or story or a surrogate, Aunt Geral, Aunt Martha, drawn from the network of family numbers.

Privacy was a bridge between you and the rest of the family. But you had to learn to control the traffic. You had to keep it uncluttered, resist the temptation to cry wolf. Privacy in our family was a birthright, a union card granted with family membership. The card said you're one of us but also certified your separateness, your obligation to keep much of what defined your separateness to yourself.

An almost aesthetic consideration's involved. Okay, let's live together. Let's each build a hut and for security we'll arrange the individual dwellings in a circle and then build an outer ring to enclose the whole village. Now your hut is your own business, but let's in general agree on certain outward forms. Since we all benefit from the larger pattern, let's compromise, conform to some degree on the materials, the shape of each unit. Because symmetry and harmony please the eye. Let's adopt a style, one that won't crimp anybody's individuality, one that will buttress and enhance each member's image of what a living place should be.

So Robby and I faced each other in the prison visiting lounge as familiar strangers, linked by blood and time. But how do you begin talking about blood, about time? He's been inside his privacy and I've been inside mine, and neither of us in thirty-odd years had felt the need to exchange more than social calls. We shared the common history, values, and style developed within the tall stockade of family, and that was enough to make us care about each other, enough to insure a profound depth of mutual regard, but the feelings were undifferentiated. They'd seldom been tested specifically, concretely. His privacy and mine had been exclusive, sanctioned by family traditions. Don't get too close. Don't ask too many questions or give too many answers. Don't pry. Don't let what's inside slop out on the people around you.

The stories I'd sent to Robby were an attempt to reveal what I thought about certain matters crucial to us both. Our shared roots and destinies. I wanted him to know what I'd been thinking and how that thinking was drawing me closer to him. I was banging on the door of his privacy. I believed I'd shed some of my own.

We were ready to talk. It was easy to begin. Impossible. We were neophytes, rookies. I was a double rookie. A beginner at this kind of intimacy, a beginner at trying to record it. My double awkwardness kept getting in the way. I'd hidden the borrowed pen by dropping my hand below the level of the table where we sat. Now when in hell would be the right moment to raise it? To use it? I had to depend on my brother's instincts, his generosity. I had to listen, listen.

Luckily there was catching up to do. He asked me about my kids, about his son, Omar, about the new nieces and nephews he'd never seen. That helped. Reminded us we were brothers. We got on with it. Conditions in the prisons. Robby's state of mind. The atmosphere behind the prison walls had been particularly tense for over a year. A group of new, younger guards had instituted a get-tough policy. More strip searches, cell shakedowns, strict enforcement of penny-ante rules and regulations. Grown men treated like children by other grown men. Inmates yanked out of line and punished because a button is undone or hair uncombed. What politicians demanded in the free world was being acted out inside the prison. A crusade, a war on crime waged by a gang of gung-ho guards against men who were already certified casualties, prisoners of war. The walking wounded being beaten and shot up again because they're easy targets. Robby's closest friends, including Cecil and Mike, are in the hole. Others who were considered potential troublemakers had been transferred to harsher prisons. Robby was warned by a guard. We ain't caught you in the shit yet, but we will. We know what you're thinking and we'll catch you in it. Or put you in it. Got your buddies and we'll get you.

The previous summer, 1980, a prisoner, Leon Patterson, had been asphyxiated in his cell. He was an asthma sufferer, a convicted murderer who depended on medication to survive the most severe attacks of his illness. On a hot August afternoon when the pollution index had reached its highest count of the summer, Patterson was locked in his cell in a cell block without windows and little air. At four o'clock, two hours after he'd been confined to the range, he began to call for help. Other prisoners raised the traditional distress signal, rattling tin cups against the bars of their cells. Patterson's cries for help became screams, and his fellow inmates beat on the bars and shouted with him. Over an hour passed before any guards arrived. They carted away Patterson's limp body. He never revived and was pronounced dead at 10:45 that evening. His death epitomized the polarization in the prison. Patterson was seen as one more victim of the guards' inhumanity. A series of incidents followed in the ensuing year, hunger strikes, melees between guards and prisoners, culminating in a near massacre when the dog days of August hung once more over the prison.

One of the favorite tactics of the militant guards was grabbing a man from the line as the prisoners moved single-file through an archway dividing the recreation yard from the main cell blocks. No reason was given or needed. It was a simple show of force, a reminder of the guards' absolute power, their right to treat the inmates any way they chose, and do it with impunity. A sit-down strike in the prison auditorium followed one of the more violent attacks on an inmate. The prisoner who had resisted an arbitrary seizure and strip search was smacked in the face. He punched back and the guards jumped him, knocked him to the ground with their fists and sticks. The incident took place in plain view of over a hundred prisoners and it was the last straw. The victim had been provoked, assaulted, and surely would be punished for attempting to protect himself, for doing what any man would and should do in similar circumstances. The prisoner would suffer again. In addition to the physical beating they'd administered, the guards would attack the man's record. He'd be written up. A kangaroo court would take away his *good time*, thereby lengthening the period he'd have to wait before becoming eligible for probation or parole. Finally, on the basis of the guards' testimony he'd probably get a sixty-day sojourn in the hole. The prisoners realized it was time to take a stand. What had happened to one could happen to any of them. They rushed into the auditorium and locked themselves in. The prisoners held out till armed state troopers and prison guards in riot gear surrounded the building. Given the mood of that past year and the unmistakable threat in the new warden's voice as he repeated through a loudspeaker his refusal to meet with the prisoners and discuss their grievances, everybody inside the building knew that the authorities meant business, that the forces of law and order would love nothing better than an excuse to turn the auditorium into a shooting gallery. The strike was broken. The men filed out. A point was driven home again. Prisoners have no rights the keepers are bound to respect.

That was how the summer had gone. Summer was bad enough in the penitentiary in the best of times. Warm weather stirred the prisoners' blood. The siren call of the streets intensified. Circus time. The street blooming again after the long, cold winter. People outdoors. On their stoops. On the corners. In bright summer clothes or hardly any clothes at all. The free-world sounds and sights more real as the weather heats up. Confinement a torture. Each cell a hotbox. The keepers take advantage of every excuse to keep you out of the yard, to deprive you of the simple pleasure of a breeze, the blue sky. Why? So that the pleasant weather can be used as a tool, a boon to be withheld. So punishment has a sharper edge. By a perverse turn of the screw something good becomes something bad. Summer a bitch at best, but this past summer as the young turks among the guards ran roughshod over the prisoners, the prison had come close to blowing, to exploding like a piece of rotten fruit in the sun. And if the lid blew, my brother knew he'd be one of the first to die. During any large-scale uprising, in the first violent, chaotic seconds no board of inquiry would ever be able to reconstruct, scores would be settled. A bullet in the back of the brain would get rid of troublemakers, remove potential leaders, uncontrollable prisoners the guards hated and feared. You were supremely eligible for a bullet if the guards couldn't press your button. If they hadn't learned how to manipulate you, if you couldn't be bought or sold, if you weren't into drug and sex games, if you weren't cowed or depraved, then you were a threat.

Robby understood that he was sentenced to die. That all sentences were death sentences. If he didn't buckle under, the guards would do everything in their power to kill him. If he succumbed to the pressure to surrender dignity, self-respect, control over his own mind and body, then he'd become a beast, and what was good in him would die. The death sentence was unambiguous. The question for him became: How long could he survive in spite of the death sentence? Nothing he did would guarantee his safety. A disturbance in a cell block halfway across the prison could provide an excuse for shooting him and dumping him with the other victims. Anytime he was ordered to go with guards out of sight of other prisoners, his escorts could claim he attacked them, or attempted to escape. Since the flimsiest pretext would make murdering him acceptable, he had no means of protecting himself. Yet to maintain sanity, to minimize their opportunities to destroy him, he had to be constantly vigilant. He had to discipline himself to avoid confrontations, he had to weigh in terms of life and death every decision he made; he had to listen and obey his keepers' orders, but he also had to determine in certain threatening situations whether it was better to say no and keep himself out of a trap or take his chances that this particular summons was not the one inviting him to his doom. Of course to say no perpetuated his reputation as one who couldn't be controlled, a bad guy, a guy you never turn your back on, one of the prisoners out to get the guards. That rap made you more dangerous in the keepers' eyes and therefore increased the likelihood they'd be frightened into striking first. Saying no put you in no less jeopardy than going along with the program. Because the program was contrived to kill you. Directly or indirectly, you knew where you were headed. What you didn't know was the schedule. Tomorrow. Next week. A month. A minute. When would one of them get itchy, get beyond waiting a second longer? Would there be a plan, a contrived incident, a conspiracy they'd talk about and set up as they drank coffee in the guards' room or would it be the hair-trigger impulse of one of them who held a grudge, harbored an antipathy so elemental, so irrational that it could express itself only in a burst of pure, unrestrained violence?

If you're Robby and have the will to survive, these are the possibilities you must constantly entertain. Vigilance is the price of survival. Beneath the vigilance, however, is a gnawing awareness boiling in the pit of your stomach. You can be as vigilant as you're able, you can keep fighting the good fight to survive, and still your fate is out of your hands. If they decide to come for you in the morning, that's it. Your ass is grass and those

minutes, and hours, days and years you painfully stitched together to put
off the final reckoning won't matter at all. So the choice, difficult beyond
words, to say yes or say no is made in light of the knowledge that in the
end neither your yes nor your no matters. Your life is not in your hands.

The events, the atmosphere of the summer had brought home to
Robby the futility of resistance. Power was absurdly apportioned all on
one side. To pretend you could control your own destiny was a joke. You
learned to laugh at your puniness, as you laughed at the stink of your farts
lighting up your cell. Like you laughed at the seriousness of the masturbation ritual that romanticized, cloaked in darkness and secrecy, the simple,
hungry shaking of your penis in your fist. You had no choice, but you always had to decide to go on or stop. It had been a stuttering, stop, start,
maybe, fuck it, bitch of a summer, and now, for better or worse, we were
starting up something else. Robby backtracks his story from Garth to another beginning, the house on Copeland Street in Shadyside where we
lived when he was born.

I know that had something to do with it. Living in Shadyside with
only white people around. You remember how it was. Except for us and
them couple other families it was a all-white neighborhood. I got a thing
about black. See, black was like the forbidden fruit. Even when we went to
Freed's in Homewood, Geraldine and them never let me go no farther
than the end of the block. All them times I stayed over there I didn't go
past Mr. Conrad's house by the vacant lot or the other corner where Billy
Shields and them stayed. Started to wondering what was so different
about a black neighborhood. I was just a little kid and I was curious. I really wanted to know why they didn't want me finding out what was over
there. Be playing with the kids next door to Freed, you know, Sonny and
Gumpy and them, but all the time I'm wondering what's round the corner, what's up the street. Didn't care if it was *bad* or good or dangerous or
what, I had to find out. If it's something bad I figured they would have
told me, tried to scare me off. But nobody said nothing except, No. Don't
you go no farther than the corner. Then back home in Shadyside nothing
but white people so I couldn't ask nobody what was special about black.
Black was a mystery and in my mind I decided I'd find out what it was all
about. Didn't care if it killed me, I was going to find out.

One time, it was later, I was close to starting high school, I overheard
Mommy and Geraldine and Sissy talking in Freed's kitchen. They was
talking about us moving from Shadyside back to Homewood. The biggest
thing they was worried about was me. How would it be for me being in
Homewood and going to Westinghouse? I could tell they was scared. Specially Mom. You know how she is. She didn't want to move. Homewood
scared her. Not so much the place but how I'd act if I got out there in the
middle of it. She already knew I was wild, hard to handle. There'd be too
much mess for me to get into in Homewood. She could see trouble
coming.

And she was right. Me and trouble hooked up. See, it was a question of being somebody. Being my own person. Like youns had sports and good grades sewed up. Wasn't nothing I could do in school or sports that youns hadn't done already. People said, Here comes another Wideman. He's gon be a good student like his brothers and sister. That's the way it was spozed to be. I was another Wideman, the last one, the baby, and everybody knew how I was spozed to act. But something inside me said no. Didn't want to be like the rest of youns. Me, I had to be a rebel. Had to get out from under youns' good grades and do. Way back then I decided I wanted to be a star. I wanted to make it big. My way. I wanted the glamour. I wanted to sit high up.

Figured out school and sports wasn't the way. I got to thinking my brothers and sister was squares. Loved youall but wasn't no room left for me. Had to figure out a new territory. I had to be a rebel.

Along about junior high I discovered Garfield. I started hanging out up on Garfield Hill. You know, partying and stuff in Garfield cause that's where the niggers was. Garfield was black, and I finally found what I'd been looking for. That place they was trying to hide from me. It was heaven. You know. Hanging out with the fellows. Drinking wine and trying anything else we could get our hands on. And the ladies. Always a party on the weekends. Had me plenty sweet little soft-leg Garfield ladies. Niggers run my butt off that hill more than a couple times behind messing with somebody's piece but I'd be back next weekend. Cause I'd found heaven. Looking back now, wasn't much to Garfield. Just a rinky-dink ghetto up on a hill, but it was the street. I'd found my place.

Having a little bit of a taste behind me I couldn't wait to get to Homewood. In a way I got mad with Mommy and the rest of them. Seemed to me like they was trying to hold me back from a good time. Seemed like they just didn't want me to have no fun. That's when I decided I'd go on about my own business. Do it my way. Cause I wasn't getting no slack at home. They still expected me to be like my sister and brothers. They didn't know I thought youns was squares. Yeah. I knew I was hipper and groovier than youns ever thought of being. Streetwise, into something. Had my own territory and I was bad. I was a rebel. Wasn't following in nobody's footsteps but my own. And I was a hip cookie, you better believe it. Wasn't a hipper thing out there than your brother, Rob. I couldn't wait for them to turn me loose in Homewood.

Me being the youngest and all, the baby in the family, people always said, ain't he cute. That Robby gon be a ladykiller. Been hearing that mess since day one so ain't no surprise I started to believing it. Youns had me pegged as a lady's man so that's what I was. The girls be talking the same trash everybody else did. Ain't he cute. Be petting me and spoiling me like I'm still the baby of the family and I sure ain't gon tell them stop. Thought I was cute as the girls be telling me. Thought sure enough, I'm gon be a star. I loved to get up and show my behind. Must have been good at it too cause the teacher used to call me up in front of the class to perform. The kids'd get real quiet. That's probably why the teacher got me up. Keep the class quiet while she nods off. Cause they'd listen to me. Sure nuff pay attention.

Performing always come natural to me. Wasn't nervous or nothing. Just get up and do my thing. They liked for me to do impressions. I could mimic anybody. You remember how I'd do that silly stuff around the house. Anybody I'd see on TV or hear on a record I could mimic to a T. Bob Hope, Nixon, Smokey Robinson, Ed Sullivan. White or black. I could talk just like them or sing a song just like they did. The class yell out a famous name and I'd do the one they wanted to hear. If things had gone another way I've always believed I could have made it big in show business. If you could keep them little frisky kids in Liberty School quiet you could handle any audience. Always could sing and do impressions. You remember Mom asking me to do them for you when you came home from college.

I still be performing. Read poetry in the hole. The other fellows get real quiet and listen. Sing down in there too. Nothing else to do, so we entertain each other. They always asking me to sing or read. "Hey, Wideman. C'mon man and do something." Then it gets quiet while they waiting for me to start. Quiet and it's already dark. You in your own cell and can't see nobody else. Barely enough light to read by. The other fellows can hear you but it's just you and them walls so it feels like being alone much as it feels like you're singing or reading to somebody else.

Yeah. I read my own poems sometimes. Other times I just start in on whatever book I happen to be reading. One the books you sent me, maybe. Fellows like my poems. They say I write about the things they be thinking. Say it's like listening to their own self thinking. That's cause we all down there together. What else you gonna do but think of the people on the outside. Your woman. Your kids or folks, if you got any. Just the same old sad shit we all be thinking all the time. That's what I write and the fellows like to hear it.

Funny how things go around like that. Go round and round and keep coming back to the same place. Teacher used to get me up to pacify the class and I'm doing the same thing in prison. You said your teachers called on you to tell stories, didn't they? Yeah. It's funny how much we're alike. In spite of everything I always believed that. Inside. The feeling side. I always believed we was the most alike out of all the kids. I see stuff in your books. The kinds of things I be thinking or feeling.

Your teachers got you up, too. To tell stories. That's funny, ain't it.

I listen to my brother Robby. He unravels my voice. I sit with him in the darkness of the Behavioral Adjustment Unit. My imagination creates something like a giant seashell, enfolding, enclosing us. Its inner surface is velvet-soft and black. A curving mirror doubling the darkness. Poems are Jean Toomer's petals of dusk, petals of dawn. I want to stop. Savor the sweet, solitary pleasure, the time stolen from time in the hole. But the image I'm creating is a trick of the glass. The mirror that would swallow Robby and then chime to me: You're the fairest of them all. The voice I hear issues from a crack in the glass. I'm two or three steps ahead of my brother, making fiction out of his words. Somebody needs to snatch me by the neck and say, Stop. Stop and listen, listen to him.

The Behavioral Adjustment Unit is, as one guard put it, "a maximum-security prison within a maximum-security prison." The "Restricted Housing Unit" or "hole" or "Home Block" is a squat, two-story cement building containing thirty-five six-by-eight-foot cells. The governor of Pennsylvania closed the area in 1972 because of "inhumane conditions," but within a year the hole was reopened. For at least twenty-three hours a day the prisoners are confined to their cells. An hour of outdoor exercise is permitted only on days the guards choose to supervise it. Two meals are served three hours apart, then nothing except coffee and bread for the next twenty-one. The regulation that limits the time an inmate can serve in the BAU for a single offense is routinely sidestepped by the keepers. "Administrative custody" is a provision allowing officials to cage men in the BAU indefinitely. Hunger strikes are one means the prisoners have employed to protest the harsh conditions of the penal unit. Hearings prompted by the strikes have produced no major changes in the way the hole operates. Law, due process, the rights of the prisoners are irrelevant to the functioning of this prison within a prison. Robby was sentenced to six months in the BAU because a guard suspected he was involved in an attempted escape. The fact that a hearing, held six months later, established Robby's innocence, was small consolation since he'd already served his time in the hole.

Robby tells me about the other side of being the youngest: Okay, you're everybody's pet and that's boss, but on the other hand you sometimes feel you're the least important. Always last. Always bringing up the rear. You learn to do stuff on your own because the older kids are always busy, off doing their things, and you're too young, left behind because you don't fit, or just because they forget you're back here, at the end, bringing up the rear. But when orders are given out, you sure get your share. "John's coming home this weekend. Clean up your room." Robby remembers being forced to get a haircut on the occasion of one of my visits. Honor thy brother. Get your hair cut, your room rid up, and put on clean clothes. He'll be here with his family and I don't want the house looking like a pigpen.

I have to laugh at the image of myself as somebody to get a haircut for. Robby must have been fit to be tied.

Yeah, I was hot. I mean, you was doing well and all that, but shit, you were my brother. And it was my head. What's my head got to do with you? But you know how Mommy is. Ain't no talking to her when her mind gets set. Anything I tried to say was "talking *back*," so I just went ahead to the man and got my ears lowered.

I was trying to be a rebel but back then the most important thing still was what the grown-ups thought about me. How they felt meant everything.

Everything. Me and Tish and Dave were the ones at home then. You was gone and Gene was gone so it was the three of us fighting for attention. And we fought. Every crumb, everytime something got cut up or parceled out or it was Christmas or Easter, we so busy checking out what the other one got wasn't hardly no time to enjoy our own. Like a dogfight or cat fight all the time. And being the youngest I'm steady losing ground most the time. Seemed like to me, Tish, and Dave the ones everybody talked about. Seemed like my time would never come. That ain't the way it really was, I know. I had my share cause I was the baby and ain't he cute and lots of times I know I got away with outrageous stuff or got my way cause I could play that baby mess to the hilt. Still it seemed like Dave and Tish was the ones really mattered. Mommy and Daddy and Sis and Geral and Big Otie and Ernie always slipping some change in their pockets or taking them to the store or letting them stay over all night in Homewood. I was a jealous little rascal. Sometimes I thought everybody thought I was just a spoiled brat. I'd say damn all youall. I'd think, Go on and love those square turkeys, but one day I'll be the one coming back with a suitcase full of money and a Cadillac. Go on and love them good grades. Robby gon do it his own way.

See, in my mind I was Superfly. I'd drive up slow to the curb. My hog be half a block long and these fine foxes in the back. Everybody looking when I ease out the door clean and mean. Got a check in my pocket to give to Mom. Buy her a new house with everything in it new. Pay her back for the hard times. I could see that happening as real as I can see your face right now. Wasn't no way it wasn't gon happen. Rob was gon make it big. I'd be at the door, smiling with the check in my hand and Mommy'd be so happy she'd be crying.

Well, it's a different story ain't it. Turned out different from how I used to think it would. The worst thing I did, the thing I feel most guilty behind is stealing Mom's life. It's like I stole her youth. Can't nothing change that. I can't give back what's gone. Robbing white people didn't cause me to lose no sleep back then. Couldn't feel but so bad about that. How you gon feel sorry when society's so corrupt, when everybody got their hand out or got their hand in somebody else's pocket and ain't no rules nobody listens to if they can get away with breaking them? How you gon apply the rules? It was dog eat dog out there, so how was I spozed to feel sorry if I was doing what everybody else doing. I just got caught is all. I'm sorry about that, and damned sorry that guy Stavros got killed, but as far as what I did, as far as robbing white people, ain't no way I was gon torture myself over that one.

I tried to write Mom a letter. Not too long ago. Should say I did write the letter and put it in a envelope and sent it cause that's what I did, but I be crying so much trying to write it I don't know what wound up in that letter. I wanted Mom to know I knew what I'd done. In a way I wanted to say I was sorry for spoiling her life. After all she did for me I turned around and made her life miserable. That's the wrongest thing I've done and I wanted to say I was sorry but I kept seeing her face while I was writing the letter. I'd see her face and it would get older while I was looking.

She'd get this old woman's face all lined and wrinkled and tired about the eyes. Wasn't nothing I could do but watch. Cause I'd done it and knew I done it and all the letters in the world ain't gon change her face. I sit and think about stuff like that all the time. It's better now. I think about other things too. You know like trying to figure what's really right and wrong, but there be days the guilt don't never go away.

I'm the one made her tired, John. And that's my greatest sorrow. All the love that's in me she created. Then I went and let her down.

When you in prison you got plenty of time to think, that's for damned sure. Too much time. I've gone over and over my life. Every moment. Every little thing again and again. I lay down on my bed and watch it happening over and over. Like a movie. I get it all broke down in pieces then I break up the pieces then I take the pieces of the pieces and run them through my hands so I remember every word a person said to me or what I said to them and weigh the words till I think I know what each and every one meant. Then I try to put it back together. Try to understand where I been. Why I did what I did. You got time for that in here. Time's all you got in here.

Going over and over things sometimes you can make sense. You know. Like the chinky-chinky Chinaman sittin' on the fence. You put it together and you think, yes. That's why I did thus and so. Yeah. That's why I lost that job or lost that woman or broke that one's heart. You stop thinking in terms of something being good or being evil, you just try to say this happened because that happened because something else came first. You can spend days trying to figure out just one little thing you did. People out there in the world walk around in a daze cause they ain't got time to think. When I was out there, I wasn't no different. Had this Superfly thing and that was the whole bit. Nobody could tell me nothing.

Seems like I should start the story back in Shadyside. In the house on Copeland Street. Nothing but white kids around. Them little white kids had everything, too. That's what I thought, anyway. Nice houses, nice clothes. They could buy pop and comic books and candy when they wanted to. We wasn't that bad off, but compared to what them little white kids had I always felt like I didn't have nothing. It made me kinda quiet and shy around them. Me knowing all the time I wanted what they had. Wanted it bad. There was them white kids with everything and there was the black world Mommy and them was holding back from me. No place to turn, in a way. I guess you could say I was stuck in the middle. Couldn't have what the white kids in Shadyside had, and I wasn't allowed to look around the corner for something else. So I'd start the story with Shadyside, the house on Copeland.

Another place to start could be December 29, 1950—the date of Robby's birth. For some reason—maybe my mother and father were feuding, maybe we just happened to be visiting my grandmother's house when my mother's time came—the trip to the hospital to have Robby began from Finance Street, from the house beside the railroad tracks in

Homewood. What I remember is the bustle, people rushing around, yelling up and down the stairwell, doors slammed, drawers being opened and shut. A cold winter day so lots of coats and scarves and galoshes. My mother's face was very pale above the dark cloth coat that made her look even bigger than she was, carrying Robby the ninth month. On the way out the front door she stopped and stared back over her shoulder like she'd forgotten something. People just about shoving her out the house. Lots of bustle and noise getting her through the crowded hallway into the vestibule. Somebody opened the front door and December rattled the glass panes. Wind gusting and whistling, everybody calling out last-minute instructions, arrangements, goodbyes, blessings, prayers. My mother's white face calm, hovering a moment above it all as she turned back toward the hall, the stairs where I was planted, halfway to the top. She didn't find me, wasn't looking for me. A thought had crossed her mind and carried her far away. She didn't know why so many hands were rushing her out the door. She didn't hear the swirl of words, the icy blast of wind. Wrapped in a navy-blue coat, either Aunt Aida's or an old one of my grandmother's, which didn't have all its black buttons but stretched double over her big belly, my mother was wondering whether or not she'd turned off the water in the bathroom sink and deciding whether or not she should return up the stairs to check. Something like that crossing her mind, freeing her an instant before she got down to the business of pushing my brother into the world.

Both my grandfathers died on December 28. My grandmother died just after dawn on December 29. My sister lost a baby early in January. The end of the year has become associated with mournings, funerals; New Year's Day arrives burdened by a sense of loss, bereavement. Robby's birthday became tainted. To be born close to Christmas is bad enough in and of itself. Your birthday celebration gets upstaged by the orgy of gift giving on Christmas Day. No matter how many presents you receive on December 29, they seem a trickle after the Christmas flood. Plus there's too much excitement in too brief a period. Parents and relatives are exhausted, broke, still hung over from the Christmas rush, so there just isn't very much left to work with if your birthday comes four short days after Jesus'. Almost like not having a birthday. Or even worse, like sharing it with your brothers and sister instead of having the private oasis of your very own special day. So Robby cried a lot on his birthdays. And it certainly wasn't a happy time for my mother. Her father, John French, died the year after Robby was born, one day before Robby's birthday. Fifteen years and a day later Mom would lose her mother. The death of the baby my sister was carrying was a final, cruel blow, scaring my mother, jinxing the end of the year eternally. She dreaded the holiday season, expected it to bring dire tidings. She had attempted at one point to consecrate the sad days, employ them as a period of reflection, quietly, privately memorialize the passing of the two people who'd loved her most in the world. But the death of my father's father, then the miscarriage within this jinxed span of days burst the fragile truce my mother had effected with the year's end. She withdraws into herself, anticipates the worse as soon as Christmas decorations begin appearing. In 1975, the year of the robbery and murder, Robby was on the run when his birthday fell. My mother was sure he wouldn't survive the deadly close of the year.

Robby's birthday is smack dab in the middle of the hard time. Planted like a flag to let you know the bad time's arrived. His adult life, the manhood of my mother's last child, begins as she is orphaned, as she starts to become nobody's child.

I named Robby. Before the women hustled my mother out the door into a taxi, I jumped down the stairs, tugged on her coattail, and reminded her she'd promised it'd be Robby. No doubt in my mind she'd bring me home a baby brother. Don't ask me why I was certain. I just was. I hadn't even considered names for a girl. Robby it would be. Robert Douglas. Where the Douglas came from is another story, but the Robert came from me because I liked the sound. Robert was formal, dignified, important. Robert. And that was nearly as nice as the chance I'd have to call my little brother Rob and Robby.

He weighed seven pounds, fourteen ounces. He was born in Allegheny Hospital at 6:30 in the evening, December 29, 1950. His fingers and toes were intact and quite long. He was a plump baby. My grandfather, high on Dago Red, tramped into the maternity ward just minutes after Robby was delivered. John French was delighted with the new baby. Called him Red. A big fat little red nigger.

December always been a bad month for me. One the worst days of my life was in December. It's still one the worst days in my life even after all this other mess. Jail. Running. The whole bit. Been waiting to tell you this a long time. Ain't no reason to hold it back no longer. We into this telling-the-truth thing so mize well tell it all. I'm still shamed, but there it is. You know that TV of youall's got stolen from Mommy's. Well, I did it. Was me and Henry took youall's TV that time and set the house up to look like a robbery. We did it. Took my own brother's TV. Couldn't hardly look you in the face for a long time after we done it. Was pretty sure youall never knowed it was me, but I felt real bad round youns anyway. No way I was gon confess though. Too shamed. A junkie stealing from his own family. See. Used to bullshit myself. Say I ain't like them other guys. They stone junkies, they hooked. Do anything for a hit. But me, I'm Robby. I'm cool. I be believing that shit, too. Fooling myself. You got to bullshit yourself when you falling. Got to do it to live wit yourself. See but where it's at is you be doing any goddam thing for dope. You hooked and that's all's to it. You a stone junkie just like the rest.

Always wondered if you knew I took it.

Mom was suspicious. She knew more than we did then. About the dope. The seriousness of it. Money disappearing from her purse when nobody in the house but the two of you. Finding a syringe on the third floor. Stuff like that she hadn't talked about to us yet. So your stealing the TV was a possibility that came up. But to me it was just one of many. One of the things that could have happened along with a whole lot of other possibilities we sat around talking about. An unlikely possibility as far as I was concerned. Nobody wanted to believe it was you. Mom tried to tell us how it *could* be but in my mind you weren't the one. Haven't thought about it much since then. Except as one of those things that make me worry about Mom living in the house alone. One of those things making Homewood dangerous, tearing it down.

I'm glad I'm finally getting to tell you. I never could get it out. Didn't want you to think I'd steal from my own brother. Specially since all youall done to help me out. You and Judy and the kids. Stealing youall's TV. Don't make no sense, does it? But if we gon get the story down mize well get it all down.

It was a while ago. Do you remember the year?

Nineteen seventy-one was Greens. When we robbed Greens and got in big trouble so it had to be the year before that, 1970. That's when it had to be. Youns was home for Christmas. Mommy and them was having a big party. A reunion kinda cause all the family was together. Everybody home for the first time in a long time. Tish in from Detroit. David back from Philly. Youns in town. My birthday, too. Party spozed to celebrate my birthday too, since it came right along in there after Christmas. Maybe that's why I was feeling so bad. Knowing I had a birthday coming and knowing at the same time how fucked up I was.

Sat in a chair all day. I was hooked for the first time. Good and hooked. Didn't know how low you could feel till that day. Cold and snowing outside. And I got the stone miseries inside. Couldn't move. Weak and sick. Henry too. He was wit me in the house feeling bad as I was. We was two desperate dudes. Didn't have no money and that Jones down on us.

Mommy kept asking, What's wrong with you two? She was on my case all day. What ails you, Robby? Got to be about three o'clock. She come in the room again: You better get up and get some decent clothes on. We're leaving for Geral's soon. See cause it was the day of the big Christmas party. Geral had baked a cake for me. Everybody was together and they'd be singing Happy Birthday Robby and do. The whole bit an I'm spozed to be guest of honor and can't even move out the chair. Here I go again disappointing everybody. Everybody be at Geral's looking for me and Geral had a cake and everything. Where's Robby? He's home dying cause he can't get no dope.

Feeling real sorry for myself but I'm hating me too. Wrapped up in a blanket like some damned Indin. Shivering and wondering how the hell Ima go out in this cold and hustle up some money. Wind be howling. Snow pitching a bitch. There we is. Stuck in the house. Two pitiful junkies.

Scheming how we gon get over. Some sorry-assed dudes. But it's comical in a way too, when you look back. To get well we need to get money. And no way we gon get money less we go outside and get sicker than we already is. Mom peeking in the room, getting on my case. Get up out that chair, boy. What are you waiting for? We're leaving in two minutes.

So I says, Go on. I ain't ready. Youns go on. I'll catch up with youns at Geral's.

Mommy standing in the doorway. She can't say too much, cause youns is home and you ain't hip to what's happening. C'mon now. We can't wait any longer for you. Please get up. Geral baked a cake for you. Everybody's looking forward to seeing you.

Seem like she stands there a hour begging me to come. She ain't mad no more. She's begging. Just about ready to cry. Youall in the other room. You can hear what she's saying but you can't see her eyes and they tearing me up. Her eyes begging me to get out the chair and it's tearing me up to see her hurting so bad, but ain't nothing I can do. Jones sitting on my chest and ain't no getup in me.

Youns go head, Mommy. I'll be over in a little while. Be there to blow them candles out and cut the cake.

She knew better. Knew if I didn't come right then, chances was I wasn't coming at all. She knew but wasn't nothing she could do. Guess I knew I was lying too. Nothing in my mind cept copping that dope. Yeah, Mom. Be there to light them candles. I'm grinning but she ain't smiling back. She knows I'm in trouble, deep trouble. I can see her today standing in the doorway begging me to come with youns.

But it ain't meant to be. Me and Henry thought we come up with a idea. Henry's old man had some pistols. We was gon steal em and hock em. Take the money and score. Then we be better. Wouldn't be no big thing to hustle some money, get the guns outa hock. Sneak the pistols back in Henry's house, everything be alright. Wouldn't even exactly be stealing from his old man. Like we just borrowing the pistols till we score and take care business. Henry's old man wouldn't even know his pistols missing. Slick. Sick as we was, thinking we slick.

A hundred times. Mom musta poked her head in the room a hundred times.

What's wrong with you?

Like a drum beating in my head. What's wrong with you? But the other thing is stronger. The dope talking to me louder. It says get you some. It says you ain't never gon get better less you cop.

We waited long as we could but it didn't turn no better outside. Still snowing. Wind shaking the whole house. How we gon walk to Henry's and steal them pistols? Henry live way up on the hill. And the way up Tokay then you still got a long way to go over into the projects. Can't make it. No way we gon climb Tokay. So then what? Everybody's left for Geral's. Then I remembers the TV youns brought. A little portable Sony black-and-white, right? You and Judy sleeping in Mom's room and she has her TV already in there, so the Sony ain't unpacked. Saw it sitting with youall's suitcases over by the dresser. On top the dresser in a box. Remembered it and soon's I did I knew we had to have it. Sick as I was that TV had to go. Wouldn't really be stealing. Borrow it instead of borrowing the pistols. Pawn it. Get straight. Steal some money and buy it back. Just borrowing youall's TV.

Won't take me and Henry no time to rob something and buy back the TV. We stone thieves. Just had to get well first so we could operate. So we took youns TV and set the house up to look like a robbery.

I'm remembering the day. Wondering why it had slipped completely from my mind. I feel like a stranger. Yet as Robby talks, my memory confirms details of his recollection. I admit, yes. I was there. That's the way it was. But *where* was I? Who was I? How did I miss so much?

His confessions make me uncomfortable. Instead of concentrating on what he's revealing, I'm pushed into considering all the things I could be confessing, should be confessing but haven't and probably won't ever. I feel hypocritical. Why should I allow my brother to repose a confidence in me when it's beyond my power to reciprocate? Shouldn't I confess that first? My embarrassment, my uneasiness, the clinical, analytic coldness settling over me when I catch on to what's about to happen.

I have a lot to hide. Places inside myself where truth hurts, where incriminating secrets are hidden, places I avoid, or deny most of the time. Pulling one piece of that debris to the surface, airing it in the light of day doesn't accomplish much, doesn't clarify the rest of what's buried down there. What I feel when I delve deeply into myself is chaos. Chaos and contradiction. So how up front can I get? I'm moved by Robby's secrets. The heart I have is breaking. But what that heart is and where it is I can't say. I can't depend on it, so he shouldn't. Part of me goes out to him. Heartbreak is the sound of ice cracking. Deep. Layers and layers muffling the sound.

I listen but I can't trust myself. I have no desire to tell everything about myself so I resist his attempt to be up front with me. The chaos at my core must be in his. His confession pushes me to think of all the stuff I should lay on him. And that scares the shit out of me. I don't like to feel dirty, but that's how I feel when people try to come clean with me.

Very complicated and very simple too. The fact is I don't believe in clean. What I know best is myself and, knowing what I know about myself, clean seems impossible. A dream. One of those better selves occasionally in the driver's seat but nothing more. Nothing to be depended upon. A self no more or less in control than the countless other selves who each, for a time, seem to be running things.

Chaos is what he's addressing. What his candor, his frankness, his confession echo against. Chaos and time and circumstances and the old news, the bad news that we still walk in circles, each of us trapped in his own little world. Behind bars. Locked in our cells.

But my heart can break, does break listening to my brother's pain. I just remember differently. Different parts of the incident he's describing come back. Strange thing is my recollections return through the door he opened. My memories needed his. Maybe the fact that we recall different things is crucial. Maybe they are foreground and background, propping each other up. He holds on to this or that scrap of the past and I listen to what he's saved and it's not mine, not what I saw or heard or felt. The pressure's on me then. If his version of the past is real, then what's mine? Where does it fit? As he stitches his memories together they bridge a vast emptiness. The time lost enveloping us all. Everything. And hearing him talk, listening to him try to make something of the nothing, challenges me. My sense of the emptiness playing around his words, any words, is intensified. Words are nothing and everything. If I don't speak I have no past. Except the nothing, the emptiness. My brother's memories are not mine, so I have to break into the silence with my own version of the past. My words. My whistling in the dark. His story freeing me, because it forces me to tell my own.

I'm sorry you took so long to forgive yourself. I forgave you a long time ago, in advance for a sin I didn't even know you'd committed. You lied to me. You stole from me. I'm in prison now listening because we committed those sins against each other countless times. I want your forgiveness. Talking about debts you owe me makes me awkward, uneasy. We remember different things. They set us apart. They bring us together searching for what is lost, for the meaning of difference, of distance.

For instance, the Sony TV. It was a present from Mort, Judy's dad. When we told him about the break-in and robbery at Mom's house, he bought us another Sony. Later we discovered the stolen TV was covered by our homeowner's policy even though we'd lost it in Pittsburgh. A claim was filed and eventually we collected around a hundred bucks. Not enough to buy a new Sony but a good portion of the purchase price. Seemed a lark when the check arrived. Pennies from heaven. One hundred dollars free and clear since we already had the new TV Mort had surprised us with. About a year later one of us, Judy or I, was telling the story of the robbery and how well we came out of it. Not until that very moment when I caught a glimpse of Mort's face out of the corner of my eye did I realize what we'd done. Judy remembers urging me to send Mort that insurance check and she probably did, but I have no recollection of an argument. In my mind there had never been an issue. Why shouldn't we keep the money? But when I saw the look of surprise and hurt flash across Mort's face, I knew the insurance check should have gone directly to him. He's a generous man and probably would have refused to accept it, but we'd taken advantage of his generosity by not offering the check as soon as we received it. Clearly the money belonged to him. Unasked, he'd replaced the lost TV. I had treated him like an institution, one of those faceless corporate entities like the gas company or IRS. By then, by the time I saw the surprise in Mort's face and understood how selfishly, thoughtlessly, even corruptly I'd behaved, it was too late. Offering Mort a hundred dollars at that point would have been insulting. Anything I could think of saying sounded hopelessly lame, inept. I'd fucked up. I'd injured someone who'd been nothing but kind and generous to me. Not intentionally, consciously, but that only made the whole business worse in a way because I'd failed him instinctively. The failure was a measure of who I was. What I'd unthinkingly done revealed something about my relationship to Mort I'm sure he'd rather not have discovered. No way I could take my action back, make it up. It reflected a truth about who I was.

That memory pops right up. Compromising, ugly. Ironically, it's also about stealing from a relative. Not to buy dope, but to feed a habit just as self-destructive. The habit of taking good fortune for granted, the habit of blind self-absorption that allows us to believe the world owes us everything and we are not responsible for giving anything in return. Spoiled children. The good coming our way taken as our due. No strings attached.

Lots of other recollections were triggered as Robby spoke of that winter and the lost TV. The shock of walking into a burgled house. How it makes you feel unclean. How quickly you lose the sense of privacy and security a house, any place you call home, is supposed to provide. It's a form of rape. Forced entry, violation, brutal hands defiling what's personal, and precious. The aftershock of seeing your possessions strewn about, broken. Fear gnawing at you because what you thought was safe isn't safe at all. The worst has happened and can happen again. Your sanctuary has been destroyed. Any time you walk in your door you may be greeted by the same scene. Or worse. You may stumble upon the thieves themselves. The symbolic rape of your dwelling place enacted on your actual body. Real screams. Real blood. A knife at your throat. A stranger's weight bearing down.

Mom put it in different words but she was as shaken as I was when we walked into her house after Geral's party. Given what I know now, she must have been even more profoundly disturbed than I imagined. A double bind. Bad enough to be ripped off by anonymous thieves. How much worse if the thief is your son? For Mom the robbery was proof Robby was gone. Somebody else walking round in his skin. Mom was wounded in ways I hadn't begun to guess at. At the root of her pain were your troubles, the troubles stealing you away from her, from all of us. The troubles thick in the air as that snow you are remembering, the troubles falling on your head and mine, troubles I refused to see. . . .

Snowing and the hawk kicking my ass but I got to have it. TV's in a box under my arm and me and Henry walking down Bennett to Homewood Avenue. Need thirty dollars. Thirty dollars buy us two spoons. Looking for One-Arm Ralph, the fence. Looking for him or that big white Cadillac he drives.

Wind blowing snow all up in my face. Thought I's bout to die out there. Nobody on the avenue. Even the junkies and dealers inside today.

Wouldn't put no dog out in weather like that. So cold my teeth is chattering, talking to me. No feeling in my hands but I got to hold on to that TV. Henry took it for a little while so's I could put both my hands in my pockets. Henry lookin bad as I'm feeling. Thought I was gon puke. But it's too goddamn cold to puke.

Nobody in sight. Shit and double shit's what I'm thinking. They got to be somewhere. Twenty-four hours a day, seven days a week somebody doing business. Finally we seen One-Arm Ralph come out the Hi Hat.

This TV, man, Lemme hold thirty dollars on it.

Ralph ain't goin for it. Twenty-five the best he say he can do. Twenty-five don't do us no good. It's fifteen each for a spoon. One spoon ain't enough. We begging the dude now. We got to have it, man. Got to get well. We good for the money. Need thirty dollars for two hits. You get your money back.

Too cold to be standing around arguing. The dude go in his pocket and give us the thirty. He been knowing us. He know we good for it. I'm telling him don't sell the TV right away. Hold it till tomorrow we have his money. He say, You don't come back tonight you blow it. Ralph a hard motherfucker and don't want him changing his mind again about the thirty so I say, We'll have the money tonight. Hold the TV till tonight, you get your money.

Now all we got to do is find Goose. Goose always be hanging on the set. Ain't nobody else dealing, Goose be out there for his people. Goose an alright dude, but even Goose ain't out in the street on no day like this. I know the cat stays over the barbershop on Homewood Avenue. Across from Murphy's five-and-ten. I goes round to the side entrance, the alleyway tween Homewood and Kelly. That's how you get to his place. Goose lets me in and I cop. For some reason I turn up the alley and go toward Kelly instead of back to Homewood the way I came in. Don't know why I did it. Being slick. Being scared. Henry's waiting on the avenue for me so I go round the long way just in case somebody pinned him. I can check out the scene before I come back up the avenue. That's probably what I'm thinking. But soon's I turn the corner of Kelly, Bam. Up pops the devil.

Up against the wall, Squirrel.

It's Simon and Garfunkel, two jive undercover cops. We call them that, you dig. Lemme tell you what kind of undercover cops these niggers was. Both of em wearing Big Apple hats and jackets like people be wearing then but they both got on police shoes. Police brogans you could spot a mile away. But they think they slick. They disguised, see. Apple hats and hippy-dip jackets. Everybody knew them chumps was cops. Ride around in a big Continental. Going for bad. Everybody hated them cause everybody knew they in the dope business. They bust a junkie, take his shit and sell it. One them had a cousin. Biggest dealer on the Hill. You know where he getting half his dope. Be selling again what Simon and Garfunkel stole from junkies. Some rotten dudes. Liked to beat on people too. Wasn't bad enough they robbing people. They whipped heads too.

Soon's I turn the corner they got me. Bams me up against the wall.
They so lame they think they got Squirrel. Think I'm Squirrel and they
gon make a big bust. We got you, Squirrel. They happy, see, cause Squirrel
dealing heavy then. Thought they caught them a whole shopping bag of
dope.

Wearing my double-breasted pea coat. Used to be sharp but it's
raggedy now. Ain't worth shit in cold weather like that. Pockets got holes
and the dope dropped down in the lining so they don't find nothing the
first time they search me. Can tell they mad. Thought they into something
big and don't find shit. Looking at each other like, What the fuck's going
on here? We big-time undercover supercops. This ain't spozed to be happening to us. They roughing me up too. Pulling my clothes off and shit.
Hands all down in my pockets again. It's freezing and I'm shivering but
these fools don't give a fuck. Rip my goddamn pea coat off me. Shaking it.
Tearing it up. Find the two packs of dope inside the lining this time. Ain't
what they wanted but they pissed off now. Take what they can get now.

What's this, Squirrel? Got your ass now.

Slinging me down the alley. I'm stone sick now. Begging these cats for
mercy. Youall got me. You got your bust. Lemme snort some the dope,
man. Little bit out each bag. You still got your bust. I'm dying. Little taste
fore you lock me up.

Rotten motherfuckers ain't going for it. They see I'm sick as a dog.
They know what's happening. Cold as it is, the sweat pouring out me. It's
sweat but it's like ice. Like knives cutting me. They ain't give back my
coat. Snowing on me and I'm shaking and sweating and sick. They can see
all this. They know what's happening but ain't no mercy in these dudes.
Henry's cross the street watching them bust me. Tears in his eyes. Ain't
nothing he can do. The street's empty. Henry's bout froze too. Watching
them sling my ass in their Continental. Never forget how Henry looked
that day. All alone on the avenue. Tears froze in his eyes. Seeing him like
that was a sad thing. Last thing I saw was him standing there across
Homewood Avenue before they slammed me up in the car. Like I was in
two places. That's me standing there in the snow. That's me so sick and
cold I'm crying in the empty street and ain't a damn thing I can do about
it.

By the time they get me down to the Police Station, down to No. 5 in
East Liberty, I ain't no more good, sure nuff. Puking. Begging them punks
not to bust me. Just bout out my mind. Must have been a pitiful sight.
Then's when Henry went to Geral's house and scratched on the window
and called David out on the porch. That's when youall found out I was in
trouble and had to come down and get me. Right in the middle of the
party and everything. Henry's sick too and he been walking round Homewood in the cold didn't know what to do. But he's my man. He got to
Geral's so youall could come down and help me. Shamed to go in so he
scratched on the window to get Dave on the porch.

Party's over and youns go to Mommy's and on top everything else find the house broke in and the TV gone. All the stuff's going through my mind. I'm on the bottom now. Low as you can go. Had me in a cell and I was lying cross the cot staring at the ceiling. Bars all round. Up cross the ceiling too. Like in a cage in the zoo. Miserable as I could be. All the shit staring me in the face. You're a dope fiend. You stole your brother's TV. You're hurting Mommy again. Hurting everybody. You're sick. You're nothing. Looking up at the bars on the ceiling and wondering if I could tie my belt there. Stick my neck in it. I wanted to be dead.

Tied my belt to the ceiling. Then this guard checking on me he starts to hollering.

What you doing? Hey, Joe. This guy's trying to commit suicide.

They take my clothes. Leave me nothing but my shorts. I'm lying there shivering in my underwear and that's the end. In a cage naked like some goddamn animal. Shaking like a leaf. Thinking maybe I can beat my head against the bars or maybe jump down off the bed head first on the concrete and bust my brains open. Dead already. Nothing already. Low as I can go.

Must have passed out or gone to sleep or something, cause it gets blurry round in here. Don't remember much but they gave back my clothes and took me Downtown and there was a arraignment next morning.

Mommy told me later, one the cops advised her not to pay my bond. Said the best thing for him be to stay in jail awhile. Let him see how it is inside. Scare im. But I be steady beggin. Please, please get me out here. Youns got soft-hearted. Got the money together and paid the bond.

What would have happened if you left me to rot in there till my hearing? Damned if I know. I probably woulda went crazy, for one thing. I do know that. Know I was sick and scared and cried like a baby for Mommy and them to get me out. Don't think it really do no good letting them keep me in there. I mean the jail's a terrible place. You can get everything in jail you get in the street. No different. Cept in jail it's more dangerous cause you got a whole bunch of crazies locked up in one little space. Worse than the street. Less you got buddies in there they tear you up. Got to learn to survive quick. Cause jail be the stone jungle. Call prison the House of Knowledge cause you learns how to be a sure nuff criminal. Come in lame you leave knowing all kinds of evil shit. You learn quick or they eats you up. That's where it's at. So you leave a person in there, chances are they gets worse. Or gets wasted.

But Mom has that soft heart anyway and she ain't leaving her baby boy in no miserable jail. Right or wrong, she ain't leaving me in no place like that. Daddy been talking to Simon and Garfunkel. Daddy's hip, see. He been out there in the street all his life and he knows what's to it. Knows those guys and knows how rotten they is. Ain't no big thing they catch one pitiful little junkie holding two spoons. They wants dealers. They wants to look good Downtown. They wants to bust dealers and cop beaucoup dope so's they can steal it and get rich. Daddy makes a deal with them rats. Says if they drop the charges he'll make me set up Goose. Finger Goose and then stay off Homewood Avenue. Daddy says I'll do that so they let me go.

No way Ima squeal on Goose but I said okay, it's a deal. Soon's I was loose I warned Goose. Pretend like I'm trying to set him up so the cops get off my ass but Goose see me coming know the cops is watching. Helped him, really. Like a lookout. Them dumb motherfuckers got tired playing me. Simon got greedy. Somebody set him up. He got busted for drugs. Still see Garfunkel riding round in his Continental but they took him off the avenue. Too dangerous. Everybody hated them guys.

My lowest day. Didn't know till then I was strung out. That's the first time I was hooked. Started shooting up with Squirrel and Bugs Johnson when Squirrel be coming over to Mom's sometimes. Get up in the morning, go up to the third floor, and shoot up. They was like my teachers. Bugs goes way back. He started with Uncle Carl. Been shooting ever since. Dude's old now. Call him King of the Junkies, he been round so long. Bugs seen it all. You know junkies don't hardly be getting old. Have their day then they gone. Don't see em no more. They in jail or dead. Junkie just don't have no long life. Fast life but your average dopehead ain't round long. Bugs different. He was a pal of Uncle Carl's back in the fifties. Shot up together way back then. Now here he is wit Squirrel and me, still doing this thing. Everybody knows Bugs. He the King.

Let me shoot up wit em but they wouldn't let me go out in the street and hustle wit em. Said I was too young. Too green.

Learning from the King, see. That's how I started the heavy stuff. Me and Squirrel and Bugs first thing in the morning when I got out of bed. Mom was gone to work. They getting themselves ready to hit the street. Make that money. Just like a job. Wasn't no time before I was out there, too. On my own learning to get money for dope. Me and my little mob. We was ready. Didn't take us no time fore we was gangsters. Gon be the next Bugs Johnson. Gon make it to the top.

Don't take long. One day you the King. Next day dope got you and it's the King. You ain't nothing. You lying there naked bout to die and it don't take but a minute. You fall and you gone in a minute. That's the life. That's how it is. And I was out there. I know. Now they got me jammed up in the slammer. That's the way it is. But nobody could tell me nothing then. Hard head. You know. Got to find out for myself. Nobody could tell me nothing. Just out of high school and my life's over and I didn't even know it. Too dumb. Too hardheaded. I was gon do it my way. Youns was square. Youns didn't know nothing. Me, I was gon make mine from the curb. Hammer that rock till I was a supergangster. Be the one dealing the shit. Be the one running the junkies. That's all I knew. Street smarts. Stop being a chump. Forget that nickel-dime hoodlum bag. Be a star. Rise to the top.

You know where that got me. You heard that story. Here I sit today behind that story. Nobody to blame but my ownself. I know that now. But things was fucked up in the streets. You could fall in them streets, Brother. Low. Them streets could snatch you bald-headed and turn you around and wring you inside out. Streets was a bitch. Wake up some mornings and you think you in hell. Think you died and went straight to hell. I know cause I been there. Be days I wished I was dead. Be days worser than that.

•   •   •   •   •   •   •   •   •   •   •   •   •

## QUESTIONS FOR A SECOND READING

1. Wideman frequently interrupts this narrative to talk about the problems he is having as a writer. He says, for example, "The hardest habit to break, since it was the habit of a lifetime, would be listening to myself listen to him. That habit would destroy any chance of seeing my brother on his terms; and seeing him in his terms, learning his terms, seemed the whole point of learning his story" (p. 722). What might Wideman mean by this— listening to himself listen? As you reread "Our Time," note the sections in which Wideman speaks to you directly as a writer. What is he saying? Where and how are you surprised by what he says?

   Wideman calls attention to the problems he faces. How does he try to solve them? Are you sympathetic? Do the solutions work, so far as you are concerned?

2. Wideman says that his mother had a remarkable capacity for "[trying] on the other person's point of view." Wideman tries on another point of view himself, speaking to us in the voice of his brother Robby. As you reread this selection, note the passages spoken in Robby's voice and try to infer Robby's point of view from them. If you look at the differences between John and Robby as evidenced by the ways they use language to understand and represent the world, what do you notice?

3. Wideman talks about three ways he could start Robby's story: with Garth's death, with the house in Shadyside, and with the day of Robby's birth. What difference would it make in each case if he chose one and not the others? What's the point of presenting all three?

## ASSIGNMENTS FOR WRITING

1. At several points in the essay, Wideman discusses his position as a writer, telling Robby's story, and he describes the problems he faces in writing this piece (or in "reading" the text of his brother's life). You could read this selection, in other words, as an essay about reading and writing.

   Why do you think Wideman talks about these problems here? Why not keep quiet and hope that no one notices? Choose three or four passages in which Wideman refers directly or indirectly to his work as a writer, and write an essay defining the problems Wideman faces and explaining why you think he raises them as he does. Finally, what might this have to do with your work as a writer—or as a student in this writing class?

2. Wideman tells Robby's story in this excerpt, but he also tells the story of his neighborhood, Homewood; of his mother; and of his grandfather John French. Write an essay retelling one of these stories and explaining what it might have to do with Robby and John's.

3. "Our Time" is a family history, but it is also a meditation on the problems of writing family histories—or, more generally, the problems of writing about the "real" world. There are sections in "Our Time" where Wideman speaks directly about the problems he faces as a writer. And the unusual features in the prose stand as examples of how he tried to solve these problems—at certain points Wideman writes as an essayist, at others like a storyteller; at certain points he switches voices and/or typeface; the piece breaks up into sections, it doesn't move from introduction to conclusion. Think of these as part of Wideman's method, as his way of working on the problems of writing as practical problems, where he is trying to figure out how to do justice to his brother and his story.

As you prepare to write this assignment, read back through the selection to think about it as a way of doing one's work, as a project, as a way of writing. What are the selection's key features? What is its shape or design? How does Wideman, the writer, do what he does? And you might ask: What would it take to learn to write like this? How is this writing related to the writing taught in school? Where and how might it serve you as a student?

Once you have developed a sense of Wideman's method, write a Wideman-like piece of your own, one that has the rhythm and the moves, the shape and the design of "Our Time." As far as subject matter is concerned, let Wideman's text stand as an invitation (inviting you to write about family and neighborhood) but don't feel compelled to follow his lead. You can write about anything you want. The key is to follow the essay as an example of a *way* of writing—moving slowly, turning this way and that, combining stories and reflection, working outside of a rigid structure of thesis and proof.

## MAKING CONNECTIONS

1. Various selections in this book can be said to be "experimental" in their use of nonfiction prose. These are essays that don't do what essays are supposed to do. They break the rules. They surprise. The writers work differently than most writers. They imagine a different project (or they imagine their project differently).

Although any number of the selections in *Ways of Reading* might be read alongside "Our Time," here are some that have seemed interesting to our students: Gloria Anzaldúa, the essays from *Borderlands/La frontera* (p. 22); Paul Auster, "Portrait of an Invisible Man" (p. 50); Susan Griffin,

"Our Secret" (p. 404); Carolyn Kay Steedman, "Exiles" (p. 645); and Virginia Woolf, the excerpt from *A Room of One's Own* (p. 750).

Choose one selection to compare with Wideman's and write an essay in which you both explain and explore the projects represented by the two pieces of writing. How do they address a reader's expectations? How do they manipulate the genre? How do they reimagine the features we take for granted in the genre of the essay—sentences and paragraphs; introductions and conclusions; argument, narrative, and exposition? And what is to be gained (or what is at stake) in writing this way? (Would you, for example, argue that these forms of writing should be taught in college?) You should assume that you are writing for someone who is a sophisticated reader but who is not familiar with these particular essays. You will need, that is, to be careful in choosing and presenting examples.

2.  Both Harriet Jacobs, in "Incidents in the Life of a Slave Girl" (p. 459), and Wideman speak directly to the reader. They seem to feel that there are problems of understanding in the stories they have to tell and in their relations to their subjects and audiences. Look back over both stories and mark the passages in which the authors address you as a reader. Ask yourself why the authors might do this. What do they reveal about their work as writers at such moments? How would you describe the relationship each writer has with her or his subject matter? As a reader of each of these stories, how would you describe the relationship between the authors and yourself as the "audience"?

    After you have completed this preliminary research, write an essay in which you discuss these two acts of writing *as* acts of writing—that is, as stories in which the writers are self-conscious about their work as writers and make their audience aware of their self-consciousness. What differences or connections exist between you, the authors, and their subject matter? How do these differences or connections influence you as a reader?

# VIRGINIA
# WOOLF

*V*IRGINIA WOOLF *is generally considered one of the twentieth century's major British writers. Born in London in 1882, Woolf was the daughter of prominent figures in London artistic circles, and her parents encouraged the young girl in her intellectual pursuits. But even as a child Woolf was made aware of the different expectations her culture held for men and women. For, while the female children of the household were taught at home by their mother and a series of tutors and governesses, the boys were sent away to school. Later in her life Woolf expressed her bitterness over the inequities of this system of education, a system shared by most Victorian families.*

*Woolf began her literary career studying Greek, reading in her father's library, and meeting in her parents' home some of the leading figures of British arts and letters. After her father's death in 1904, Woolf and her sister and two brothers moved to Bloomsbury, where their home became a center for young writers and intellectuals trying to shake free from the restrictions of Victorian life and culture. Woolf began teaching in a working women's college in South London and writing reviews for the prestigious* Times Literary Supplement.

*Woolf's first review, published in 1904, when she was twenty-two, was the beginning of a distinguished career which ultimately encompassed six volumes of essays and reviews, two biographies, two book-length essays, several volumes of letters and diaries, nine novels, and two collections of short stories. In addition to being one of the cofounders (with her husband, Leonard) of the Hogarth Press, a publishing company which produced editions of the work of the poet T. S. Eliot, short story writer Katherine Mansfield, and English translations of the work of Sigmund Freud, Woolf is considered one of the finest literary critics of her time and arguably one of the most innovative novelists of the twentieth century. Her novels include* Mrs. Dalloway *(1925),* To the Lighthouse *(1927),* Orlando *(1928), and* The Waves *(1931).* Orlando *is the imaginary biography of a character who lives for four hundred years and changes from male to female in the late seventeenth century. It has been called the companion piece to* A Room of One's Own.

*The following selection is the first and last chapters of Woolf's extended essay* A Room of One's Own, *a revised version of two papers she read at the women's colleges at Oxford, Girton and Newnham. The two chapters here frame Woolf's lecture on the topic "women and fiction." Because the final chapter alludes to what has come before, it is useful to have a brief sketch of the middle chapters.*

*In these chapters Woolf surveys what men have said about women, and she looks over the history of women's writing, from Renaissance England to the early twentieth century. In Chapter 3 she imagines what might have happened if Shakespeare had had a sister. This young woman, Judith, might have been*

> *as adventurous, as imaginative, as agog to see the world as [her brother] was. But she was not sent to school. She had no chance of learning grammar and logic, let alone of reading Horace and Virgil. She picked up a book now and then. . . . But then her parents came in and told her to mend the stockings or mind the stew and not moon about with books and papers. They would have spoken sharply but kindly, for they were substantial people who knew the conditions of life for a woman and loved their daughter—indeed, more likely than not she was the apple of her father's eye.*

*Finally, the young girl is promised in marriage to a man she does not desire, and she runs away to London to try her fortune in the theater.*

> *What is true . . . , so it seemed to me, reviewing the story of Shakespeare's sister as I had made it, is that any woman born with a great gift in the sixteenth century would certainly have gone crazed, shot herself, or ended her days in some lonely cottage outside the village, half witch, half wizard, feared and mocked at. For it needs little skill in psychology to be sure that a highly gifted girl who had tried to use her gift for poetry would have been so thwarted and hindered by other people, so tortured and pulled asunder by her own contrary instincts, that she must have lost her health and sanity to a certainty. No girl could have walked to London and stood at a stage door and forced her way into the presence of actor-managers without doing herself a violence and suffering an anguish which may have been irrational—for chastity may be a fetish invented by certain societies for unknown reasons—but were none the less inevitable. . . . To have lived a free life in London in the sixteenth century would have meant for a woman who was poet and playwright a nervous stress and dilemma*

*which might well have killed her. Had she survived, whatever she had written would have been twisted and deformed, issuing from a strained and morbid imagination. And undoubtedly, I thought, looking at the shelf where there are no plays by women, her work would have gone unsigned.*

*Chapters 1 and 6 establish Woolf's project and her way of addressing her audience. They are marked by a strong and distinctive style. For one thing, Woolf delivers most of the lecture through the voice of a character ("call me Mary Beton, Mary Seton, Mary Carmichael, or by any name you please—it is not a matter of any importance"). In a letter to a friend, Dame Ethel Smyth, Woolf once said, "I didn't write* A Room *without considerable feeling . . . ; I'm not cool on the subject. And I forced myself to keep my own figure fictitious, legendary. If I had said, 'Look here, I am uneducated because my brothers used the family funds'—which is the fact—'well,' they'd have said, 'she has an axe to grind'; and no one would have taken me seriously." Although this essay is "signed," Woolf leaves open some questions about the status and the presence of its author. As you read, you will want to think about the ways this essay might be seen as an example of the problems and possibilities for a woman's writing.*

# A Room of One's Own

## Chapter One

But, you may say, we asked you to speak about women and fiction—what has that got to do with a room of one's own? I will try to explain. When you asked me to speak about women and fiction I sat down on the banks of a river and began to wonder what the words meant. They might mean simply a few remarks about Fanny Burney; a few more about Jane Austen; a tribute to the Brontës and a sketch of Haworth Parsonage under snow; some witticisms if possible about Miss Mitford; a respectful allusion to George Eliot; a reference to Mrs. Gaskell and one would have done. But at second sight the words seemed not so simple. The title women and fiction might mean, and you may have meant it to mean, women and what they are like; or it might mean women and the fiction that they write; or it might mean women and the fiction that is written about them; or it might mean that somehow all three are inextricably mixed together and you want me to consider them in that light. But when I began to consider the subject in this last way, which seemed the most interesting, I soon saw that it had one fatal drawback. I should never be able to come to a conclusion. I should never be able to fulfill what is, I understand, the first duty of a lecturer—to hand you after an hour's discourse a nugget of pure truth to wrap up between the pages of your notebooks and keep on the mantelpiece for ever. All I could do was to offer you an opinion upon one minor point—a woman must have money and a room of her own if she is to write fiction; and that, as you will see, leaves the great problem of the true nature of woman and the true nature of fiction unsolved. I have shirked the duty of coming to a conclusion upon these two questions—women and fiction remain, so far as I am concerned, unsolved problems. But in order to make some amends I am going to do what I can to show you how I arrived at this opinion about the room and the money. I am going to develop in your presence as fully and freely as I can the train of thought which led me to think this. Perhaps if I lay bare the ideas, the prejudices, that lie behind this statement you will find that they have some bearing upon women and some upon fiction. At any rate, when a subject is highly controversial—and any question about sex is that—one cannot hope to tell the truth. One can only show how one came to hold whatever opinion one does hold. One can only give one's audience the chance of drawing their own conclusions as they observe the limitations, the prejudices, the idiosyncrasies of the speaker. Fiction here is likely to contain more truth than fact. Therefore I propose, making use of all the liberties and licenses of a novelist, to tell you the story of the two days that preceded my coming here—how, bowed down by the weight of the subject which you have laid upon my shoulders, I pondered it, and made it work in and out of my daily life. I need not say that what I am about to describe has no existence; Oxbridge is an invention; so is Fernham; "I" is only a convenient term for somebody who has no real being. Lies will flow from my lips, but there may perhaps be some truth mixed up with them; it is for you to seek out this truth and decide whether any part of it is worth keeping. If not, you will of course throw the whole of it into the wastepaper basket and forget all about it.

Here then was I (call me Mary Beton, Mary Seton, Mary Carmichael, or by any name you please—it is not a matter of any importance) sitting on the banks of a river a week or two ago in fine October weather, lost in thought. That collar I have spoken of, women and fiction, the need of coming to some conclusion on a subject that raises all sorts of prejudices and passions, bowed my head to the ground. To the right and left bushes of some sort, golden and crimson, glowed with the color, even it seemed burnt with the heat, of fire. On the further bank the willows wept in perpetual lamentation, their hair about their shoulders. The river reflected whatever it chose of sky and bridge and burning tree, and when the undergraduate had oared his boat through the reflections they closed again, completely, as if he had never been. There one might have sat the clock round lost in thought. Thought—to call it by a prouder name than it deserved—had let its line down into the stream. It swayed, minute after minute, hither and thither among the reflections and the weeds, letting the water lift it and sink it, until—you know the little tug—the sudden conglomeration of an idea at the end of one's line: and then the cautious hauling of it in, and the careful laying of it out? Alas, laid on the grass how small, how insignificant this thought of mine looked; the sort of fish that a good fisherman puts back into the water so that it may grow fatter and be one day worth cooking and eating. I will not trouble you with that thought now, though if you look carefully you may find it for yourselves in the course of what I am going to say.

But however small it was, it had, nevertheless, the mysterious property of its kind—put back into the mind, it became at once very exciting, and important; and as it darted and sank, and flashed hither and thither, set up such a wash and tumult of ideas that it was impossible to sit still. It was thus that I found myself walking with extreme rapidity across a grass plot. Instantly a man's figure rose to intercept me. Nor did I at first understand that the gesticulations of a curious-looking object, in a cutaway coat and evening shirt, were aimed at me. His face expressed horror and indignation. Instinct rather than reason came to my help; he was a Beadle; I was a woman. This was the turf; there was the path. Only the Fellows and Scholars are allowed here; the gravel is the place for me. Such thoughts were the work of a moment. As I regained the path the arms of the Beadle sank, his face assumed its usual repose, and though turf is better walking than gravel, no very great harm was done. The only charge I could bring against the Fellows and Scholars of whatever the college might happen to be was that in protection of their turf, which has been rolled for three hundred years in succession, they had sent my little fish into hiding.

What idea it had been that had sent me so audaciously trespassing I could not now remember. The spirit of peace descended like a cloud from heaven, for if the spirit of peace dwells anywhere, it is in the courts and quadrangles of Oxbridge on a fine October morning. Strolling through those colleges past those ancient halls the roughness of the present seemed smoothed away; the body seemed contained in a miraculous glass cabinet through which no sound could penetrate, and the mind, freed from any contact with facts (unless one trespassed on the turf again), was at liberty to settle down upon whatever meditation was in harmony with the moment. As chance would have it, some stray memory of some old essay about revisiting Oxbridge in the long vacation brought Charles Lamb to mind—Saint Charles, said Thackeray, putting a letter of Lamb's to his forehead. Indeed, among all the dead (I give you my thoughts as they came to me), Lamb is one of the most congenial; one to whom one would have liked to say, Tell me then how you wrote your essays? For his essays are superior even to Max Beerbohm's, I thought, with all their perfection, because of that wild flash of imagination, that lightning crack of genius in the middle of them which leaves them flawed and imperfect, but starred with poetry. Lamb then came to Oxbridge perhaps a hundred years ago. Certainly he wrote an essay—the name escapes me—about the manuscript of one of Milton's poems which he saw here. It was *Lycidas* perhaps, and Lamb wrote how it shocked him to think it possible that any word in *Lycidas* could have been different from what it is. To think of Milton changing the words in that poem seemed to him a sort of sacrilege.

This led me to remember what I could of *Lycidas* and to amuse myself with guessing which word it could have been that Milton had altered, and why. It then occurred to me that the very manuscript itself which Lamb had looked at was only a few hundred yards away, so that one could follow Lamb's footsteps across the quadrangle to that famous library where the treasure is kept. Moreover, I recollected, as I put this plan into execution, it is in this famous library that the manuscript of Thackeray's *Esmond* is also preserved. The critics often say that *Esmond* is Thackeray's most perfect novel. But the affectation of the style, with its imitation of the eighteenth century, hampers one, so far as I remember; unless indeed the eigtheenth-century style was natural to Thackeray—a fact that one might prove by looking at the manuscript and seeing whether the alterations were for the benefit of the style or of the sense. But then one would have to decide what is style and what is meaning, a question which—but here I was actually at the door which leads into the library itself. I must have opened it, for instantly there issued, like a guardian angel barring the way with a flutter of black gown instead of white wings, a deprecating, silvery, kindly gentleman, who regretted in a low voice as he waved me back that ladies are only admitted to the library if accompanied by a Fellow of the College or furnished with a letter of introduction.

That a famous library has been cursed by a woman is a matter of complete indifference to a famous library. Venerable and calm, with all its treasures safe locked within its breast, it sleeps complacently and will, so far as I am concerned, so sleep forever. Never will I wake those echoes, never will I ask for that hospitality again, I vowed as I descended the steps in anger. Still an hour remained before luncheon, and what was one to do? Stroll on the meadows? sit by the river? Certainly it was a lovely autumn morning; the leaves were fluttering red to the ground; there was no great hardship in doing either. But the sound of music reached my ear. Some service or celebration was going forward. The organ complained magnificently as I passed the chapel door. Even the sorrow of Christianity sounded in that serene air more like the recollection of sorrow than sorrow itself; even the groanings of the ancient organ seemed lapped in peace. I had no wish to enter had I the right, and this time the verger might have stopped me, demanding perhaps my baptismal certificate, or a letter of introduction from the Dean. But the outside of these magnificent buildings is often as beautiful as the inside. Moreover, it was amusing enough to watch the congregation assembling, coming in and going out again, busying themselves at the door of the chapel like bees at the mouth of a hive. Many were in cap and gown; some had tufts of fur on their shoulders; others were wheeled in bath chairs; others, though not past middle age, seemed creased and crushed into shapes so singular that one was reminded of those giant crabs and crayfish who heave with difficulty across the sand of an aquarium. As I leant against the wall the University indeed seemed a sanctuary in which are preserved rare types which would soon be obsolete if left to fight for existence on the pavement of the

Strand. Old stories of old deans and old dons came back to mind, but before I had summoned up courage to whistle—it used to be said that at the sound of a whistle old Professor ——— instantly broke into a gallop—the venerable congregation had gone inside. The outside of the chapel remained. As you know, its high domes and pinnacles can be seen, like a sailing ship always voyaging never arriving, lit up at night and visible for miles, far away across the hills. Once, presumably, this quadrangle with its smooth lawns, its massive buildings, and the chapel itself was marsh too, where the grasses waved and the swine rooted. Teams of horses and oxen, I thought, must have hauled the stone in wagons from far countries, and then with infinite labor the gray blocks in whose shade I was now standing were poised in order one on top of another, and then the painters brought their glass for the windows, and the masons were busy for centuries up on that roof with putty and cement, spade and trowel. Every Saturday somebody must have poured gold and silver out of a leathern purse into their ancient fists, for they had their beer and skittles presumably of an evening. An unending stream of gold and silver, I thought, must have flowed into this court perpetually to keep the stones coming and the masons working; to level, to ditch, to dig, and to drain. But it was then the age of faith, and money was poured liberally to set these stones on a deep foundation, and when the stones were raised, still more money was poured in from the coffers of kings and queens and great nobles to ensure that hymns should be sung here and scholars taught. Lands were granted; tithes were paid. And when the age of faith was over and the age of reason had come, still the same flow of gold and silver went on; fellowships were founded; lectureships endowed; only the gold and silver flowed now, not from the coffers of the king, but from the chests of merchants and manufacturers, from the purses of men who had made, say, a fortune from industry, and returned, in their wills, a bounteous share of it to endow more chairs, more lectureships, more fellowships in the university where they had learnt their craft. Hence the libraries and laboratories; the observatories; the splendid equipment of costly and delicate instruments which now stands on glass shelves, where centuries ago the grasses waved and the swine rooted. Certainly, as I strolled round the court, the foundation of gold and silver seemed deep enough; the pavement laid solidly over the wild grasses. Men with trays on their heads went busily from staircase to staircase. Gaudy blossoms flowered in window boxes. The strains of the gramophone blared out from the rooms within. It was impossible not to reflect—the reflection whatever it may have been was cut short. The clock struck. It was time to find one's way to luncheon.

It is a curious fact that novelists have a way of making us believe that luncheon parties are invariably memorable for something very witty that was said, or for something very wise that was done. But they seldom spare a word for what was eaten. It is part of the novelist's convention not to mention soup and salmon and ducklings, as if soup and salmon and ducklings were of no importance whatsoever, as if nobody ever smoked a cigar or drank a glass of wine. Here, however, I shall take the liberty to defy that convention and to tell you that the lunch on this occasion began with soles, sunk in a deep dish, over which the college cook had spread a counterpane of the whitest cream, save that it was branded here and there with brown spots like the spots on the flanks of a doe. After that came the partridges, but if this suggests a couple of bald, brown birds on a plate you are mistaken. The partridges, many and various, came with all their retinue of sauces and salads, the sharp and the sweet, each in its order; their potatoes, thin as coins but not so hard; their sprouts, foliated as rosebuds but more succulent. And no sooner had the roast and its retinue been done with than the silent serving man, the Beadle himself perhaps in a milder manifestation, set before us, wreathed in napkins, a confection which rose all sugar from the waves. To call it pudding and so relate it to rice and tapioca would be an insult. Meanwhile the wineglasses had flushed yellow and flushed crimson; had been emptied; had been filled. And thus by degrees was lit, halfway down the spine, which is the seat of the soul, not that hard little electric light which we call brilliance, as it pops in and out upon our lips, but the more profound, subtle, and subterranean glow, which is the rich yellow flame of rational intercourse. No need to hurry. No need to sparkle. No need to be anybody but oneself. We are all going to heaven and Vandyck is of the company—in other words, how good life seemed, how sweet its rewards, how trivial this grudge or that grievance, how admirable friendship and the society of one's kind, as, lighting a good cigarette, one sunk among the cushions in the window seat.

If by good luck there had been an ashtray handy, if one had not knocked the ash out of the window in default, if things had been a little different from what they were, one would not have seen, presumably, a cat without a tail. The sight of that abrupt and truncated animal padding softly across the quadrangle changed by some fluke of the subconscious intelligence the emotional light for me. It was as if some one had let fall a shade. Perhaps the excellent hock was relinquishing its hold. Certainly, as I watched the Manx cat pause in the middle of the lawn as if it too questioned the universe, something seemed lacking, something seemed different. But what was lacking, what was different, I asked myself, listening to the talk. And to answer that question I had to think myself out of the room, back into the past, before the war indeed, and to set before my eyes the model of another luncheon party held in rooms not very far distant from these; but different. Everything was different. Meanwhile the talk went on among the guests, who were many and young, some of this sex, some of that; it went on swimmingly, it went on agreeably, freely, amusingly. And as it went on I set it against the background of that other talk, and as I matched the two together I had no doubt that one was the descendant, the legitimate heir of the other. Nothing was changed; nothing was different save only—here I listened with all my ears not entirely to what was being said, but to the murmur or current behind it. Yet, that was it—

the change was there. Before the war at a luncheon party like this people would have said precisely the same things but they would have sounded different, because in those days they were accompanied by a sort of humming noise, not articulate, but musical, exciting, which changed the value of the words themselves. Could one set that humming noise to words? Perhaps with the help of the poets one could. A book lay beside me and, opening it, I turned casually enough to Tennyson. And here I found Tennyson was singing:

> There has fallen a splendid tear
>     From the passion-flower at the gate.
> She is coming, my dove, my dear;
>     She is coming, my life, my fate;
> The red rose cries, "She is near, she is near";
>     And the white rose weeps, "She is late";
> The larkspur listens, "I hear, I hear";
>     And the lily whispers, "I wait."

Was that what men hummed at luncheon parties before the war? And the women?

> My heart is like a singing bird
>     Whose nest is in a water'd shoot;
> My heart is like an apple tree
>     Whose boughs are bent with thick-set fruit;
> My heart is like a rainbow shell
>     That paddles in a halcyon sea;
> My heart is gladder than all these
>     Because my love is come to me.

Was that what women hummed at luncheon parties before the war?

There was something so ludicrous in thinking of people humming such things even under their breath at luncheon parties before the war that I burst out laughing, and had to explain my laughter by pointing at the Manx cat, who did look a little absurd, poor beast, without a tail, in the middle of the lawn. Was he really born so, or had he lost his tail in an accident? The tailless cat, though some are said to exist in the Isle of Man, is rarer than one thinks. It is a queer animal, quaint rather than beautiful. It is strange what a difference a tail makes—you know the sort of things one says as a lunch party breaks up and people are finding their coats and hats.

This one, thanks to the hospitality of the host, had lasted far into the afternoon. The beautiful October day was fading and the leaves were falling from the trees in the avenue as I walked through it. Gate after gate seemed to close with gentle finality behind me. Innumerable beadles were fitting innumerable keys into well-oiled locks; the treasure house was being made secure for another night. After the avenue one comes out upon a road—I forget its name—which leads you, if you take the right turning, along to Fernham. But there was plenty of time. Dinner was not till half past seven. One could almost do without dinner after such a luncheon. It is strange how a scrap of poetry works in the mind and makes the legs move in time to it along the road. Those words—

> There has fallen a splendid tear
>   From the passion-flower at the gate.
> She is coming, my dove, my dear—

sang in my blood as I stepped quickly along towards Headingley. And then, switching off into the other measure, I sang, where the waters are churned up by the weir:

> My heart is like a singing bird
>   Whose nest is in a water'd shoot;
> My heart is like an apple tree . . .

What poets, I cried aloud, as one does in the dusk, what poets they were!

In a sort of jealousy, I suppose, for our own age, silly and absurd though these comparisons are, I went on to wonder if honestly one could name two living poets now as great as Tennyson and Christina Rossetti were then. Obviously it is impossible, I thought, looking into those foaming waters, to compare them. The very reason why the poetry excites one to such abandonment, such rapture, is that it celebrates some feeling that one used to have (at luncheon parties before the war perhaps), so that one responds easily, familiarly, without troubling to check the feeling, or to compare it with any that one has now. But the living poets express a feeling that is actually being made and torn out of us at the moment. One does not recognize it in the first place; often for some reason one fears it; one watches it with keenness and compares it jealously and suspiciously with the old feeling that one knew. Hence the difficulty of modern poetry; and it is because of this difficulty that one cannot remember more than two consecutive lines of any good modern poet. For this reason—that my memory failed me—the argument flagged for want of material. But why, I continued, moving on towards Headingley, have we stopped humming under our breath at luncheon parties? Why has Alfred ceased to sing

> She is coming, my dove, my dear?

Why has Christina ceased to respond

> My heart is gladder than all these
> Because my love is come to me?

Shall we lay the blame on the war? When the guns fired in August 1914, did the faces of men and women show so plain in each other's eyes that romance was killed? Certainly it was a shock (to women in particular with their illusions about education, and so on) to see the faces of our rulers in the light of the shell fire. So ugly they looked—German, English, French—so stupid. But lay the blame where one will, on whom one will, the illusion which inspired Tennyson and Christina Rossetti to sing so passionately about the coming of their loves is far rarer now than then. One has only to read, to look, to listen, to remember. But why say "blame"? Why, if it was an illusion, not praise the catastrophe, whatever it was, that destroyed illusion and put truth in its place? For truth . . . those dots mark the spot where, in search of truth, I missed the turning up to Fernham. Yes indeed, which was truth about these houses, for example, dim and festive now with their red windows in the dusk, but raw and red and squalid, with their sweets and their bootlaces, at nine o'clock in the morning? And the willows and the river and the gardens that run down to the river, vague now with the mist stealing over them, but gold and red in the sunlight—which was the truth, which was the illusion about them? I spare you the twists and turns of my cogitations, for no conclusion was found on the road to Headingley, and I ask you to suppose that I soon found my mistake about the turning and retraced my steps to Fernham.

As I have said already that it was an October day, I dare not forfeit your respect and imperil the fair name of fiction by changing the season and describing lilacs hanging over garden walls, crocuses, tulips, and other flowers of spring. Fiction must stick to facts, and the truer the facts the better the fiction—so we are told. Therefore it was still autumn and the leaves were still yellow and falling, if anything, a little faster than before, because it was now evening (seven twenty-three to be precise) and a breeze (from the southwest to be exact) had risen. But for all that there was something odd at work:

> My heart is like a singing bird
>   Whose nest is in a water'd shoot;
> My heart is like an apple tree
>   Whose boughs are bent with thick-set fruit—

perhaps the words of Christina Rossetti were partly responsible for the folly of the fancy—it was nothing of course but a fancy—that the lilac was shaking its flowers over the garden walls, and the brimstone butterflies were scudding hither and thither, and the dust of the pollen was in the air. A wind blew, from what quarter I know not, but it lifted the half-grown leaves so that there was a flash of silver gray in the air. It was the time between the lights when colors undergo their intensification and purples and golds burn in windowpanes like the beat of an excitable heart; when for some reason the beauty of the world revealed and yet soon to perish (here I pushed into the garden, for, unwisely, the door was left open and no beadles seemed about), the beauty of the world which is so soon to perish, has two edges, one of laughter, one of anguish, cutting the heart asunder. The gardens of Fernham lay before me in the spring twilight, wild and open, and in the long grass, sprinkled and carelessly flung, were daffodils and bluebells, not orderly perhaps at the best of times, and now windblown and waving as they tugged at their roots. The windows of the building, curved like ships' windows among generous waves of red brick, changed from lemon to silver under the flight of the quick spring clouds.

Somebody was in a hammock, somebody, but in this light they were phantoms only, half guessed, half seen, raced across the grass—would no one stop her?—and then on the terrace, as if popping out to breathe the air, to glance at the garden, came a bent figure, formidable yet humble, with her great forehead and her shabby dress—could it be the famous scholar, could it be J—— H—— herself? All was dim, yet intense too, as if the scarf which the dusk had flung over the garden were torn asunder by star or sword—the flash of some terrible reality leaping, as its way is, out of the heart of the spring. For youth——

Here was my soup. Dinner was being served in the great dining hall. Far from being spring it was in fact an evening in October. Everybody was assembled in the big dining room. Dinner was ready. Here was the soup. It was a plain gravy soup. There was nothing to stir the fancy in that. One could have seen through the transparent liquid any pattern that there might have been on the plate itself. But there was no pattern. The plate was plain. Next came beef with its attendant greens and potatoes—a homely trinity, suggesting the rumps of cattle in a muddy market, and sprouts curled and yellowed at the edge, and bargaining and cheapening, and women with string bags on Monday morning. There was no reason to complain of human nature's daily food, seeing that the supply was sufficient and coal miners doubtless were sitting down to less. Prunes and custard followed. And if any one complains that prunes, even when mitigated by custard, are an uncharitable vegetable (fruit they are not), stringy as a miser's heart, and exuding a fluid such as might run in miser's veins who have denied themselves wine and warmth for eighty years and yet not given to the poor, he should reflect that there are people whose charity embraces even the prune. Biscuits and cheese came next, and here the water jug was liberally passed round, for it is the nature of biscuits to be dry, and these were biscuits to the core. That was all. The meal was over. Everybody scraped their chairs back; the swing doors swung violently to and fro; soon the hall was emptied of every sign of food and made ready no doubt for breakfast next morning. Down corridors and up staircases the youth of England went banging and singing. And was it for a guest, a stranger (for I had no more right here in Fernham than in Trinity or Somerville or Girton or Newnham or Christchurch), to say, "The dinner was not good," or to say (we were now, Mary Seton and I, in her sitting room), "Could we not have dined up here alone?" for if I had said anything of the kind I should have been prying and searching into the secret economies of a house which to the stranger wears so fine a front of gaiety and courage. No, one could say nothing of the sort. Indeed, conversation for a moment flagged. The human frame being what it is, heart, body, and brain all mixed together, and not contained in separate compartments as they will be no doubt in another million years, a good dinner is of great importance to good talk. One cannot think well, love well, sleep well, if one has not dined well. The lamp in the spine does not light on beef and prunes. We are all *probably* going to heaven, and Vandyck is, we *hope*, to meet us round the next corner—that is the dubious and qualifying state of mind that beef and prunes at the end of the day's work breed between them. Happily my friend, who taught science, had a cupboard where there was a squat bottle and little glasses—(but there should have been sole and partridge to begin with)—so that we were able to draw up to the fire and repair some of the damages of the day's living. In a minute or so we were slipping freely in and out among all those objects of curiosity and interest which form in the mind in the absence of a particular person, and are naturally to be discussed on coming together again—how somebody has married, another has not; one thinks this, another that; one has improved out of all knowledge, the other most amazingly gone to the bad— with all those speculations upon human nature and the character of the amazing world we live in which spring naturally from such beginnings. While these things were being said, however, I became shamefacedly aware of a current setting in of its own accord and carrying everything forward to an end of its own. One might be talking of Spain or Portugal, of book or racehorse, but the real interest of whatever was said was none of those things, but a scene of masons on a high roof some five centuries ago. Kings and nobles brought treasure in huge sacks and poured it under the earth. This scene was forever coming alive in my mind and placing itself by another of lean cows and a muddy market and withered greens and the stringy hearts of old men—these two pictures, disjointed and disconnected and nonsensical as they were, were forever coming together and combating each other and had me entirely at their mercy. The best course, unless the whole talk was to be distorted, was to expose what was in my mind to the air, when with good luck it would fade and crumble like the head of the dead king when they opened the coffin at Windsor. Briefly, then, I told Miss Seton about the masons who had been all those years on the roof of the chapel, and about the kings and queens and nobles bearing sacks of gold and silver on their shoulders, which they shoveled into the earth; and then how the great financial magnates of our own time came and laid checks and bonds, I suppose, where the others had laid ingots and rough lumps of gold. All that lies beneath the colleges down there, I said; but this college, where we are now sitting, what lies beneath its gallant red brick and the wild unkempt grasses of the garden? What force is behind the plain china off which we dined, and (here it popped out of my mouth before I could stop it) the beef, the custard, and the prunes?

Well, said Mary Seton, about the year 1860—Oh, but you know the story, she said, bored, I suppose, by the recital. And she told me—rooms were hired. Committees met. Envelopes were addressed. Circulars were drawn up. Meetings were held; letters were read out; so-and-so has promised so much; on the contrary, Mr. —— won't give a penny. The *Saturday Review* has been very rude. How can we raise a fund to pay for offices? Shall we hold a bazaar? Can't we find a pretty girl to sit in the front row? Let us look up what John Stuart Mill said on the subject. Can anyone persuade the editor of the —— to print a letter? Can we get Lady —— to sign it?

Lady ——— is out of town. That was the way it was done, presumably, sixty years ago, and it was a prodigious effort, and a great deal of time was spent on it. And it was only after a long struggle and with the utmost difficulty that they got thirty thousand pounds together.[1] So obviously we cannot have wine and partridges and servants carrying tin dishes on their heads, she said. We cannot have sofas and separate rooms. "The amenities," she said, quoting from some book or other, "will have to wait."[2]

At the thought of all those women working year after year and finding it hard to get two thousand pounds together, and as much as they could do to get thirty thousand pounds, we burst out in scorn at the reprehensible poverty of our sex. What had our mothers been doing then that they had no wealth to leave us? powdering their noses? looking in at shop windows? flaunting in the sun at Monte Carlo? There were some photographs on the mantelpiece. Mary's mother—if that was her picture—may have been a wastrel in her spare time (she had thirteen children by a minister of the church), but if so her gay and dissipated life had left too few traces of its pleasures on her face. She was a homely body; an old lady in a plaid shawl which was fastened by a large cameo; and she sat in a basket chair, encouraging a spaniel to look at the camera, with the amused, yet strained expression of one who is sure that the dog will move directly the bulb is pressed. Now if she had gone into business; had become a manufacturer of artificial silk or a magnate on the Stock Exchange; if she had left two or three thousand pounds to Fernham, we could have been sitting at our ease tonight and the subject of our talk might have been archaeology, botany, anthropology, physics, the nature of the atom, mathematics, astronomy, relativity, geography. If only Mrs. Seton and her mother and her mother before her had learnt the great art of making money and had left their money, like their fathers and their grandfathers before them, to found fellowships and lectureships and prizes and scholarships appropriated to the use of their own sex, we might have dined very tolerably up here alone off a bird and a bottle of wine; we might have looked forward without undue confidence to a pleasant and honorable lifetime spent in the shelter of one of the liberally endowed professions. We might have been exploring or writing; mooning about the venerable places of the earth; sitting contemplative on the steps of the Parthenon, or going at ten to an office and coming home comfortably at half past four to write a little poetry. Only, if Mrs. Seton and her like had gone into business at the age of fifteen, there would have been—that was the snag in the argument—no Mary. What, I asked, did Mary think of that? There between the curtains was the October night, calm and lovely, with a star or two caught in the yellowing trees. Was she ready to resign her share of it and her memories (for they had been a happy family, though a large one) of games and quarrels up in Scotland, which she is never tired of praising for the fineness of its air and the quality of its cakes, in order that Fernham might have been endowed with fifty thousand pounds or so by a stroke of the pen? For, to endow a college would necessitate the suppression of families altogether. Making a fortune and bearing thirteen children—no human being could stand it. Consider the facts, we said. First there are nine months before the baby is born. Then the baby is born. Then there are three or four months spent in feeding the baby. After the baby is fed there are certainly five years spent in playing with the baby. You cannot, it seems, let children run about the streets. People who have seen them running wild in Russia say that the sight is not a pleasant one. People say, too, that human nature takes its shape in the years between one and five. If Mrs. Seton, I said, had been making money, what sort of memories would you have had of games and quarrels? What would you have known of Scotland, and its fine air and cakes and all the rest of it? But it is useless to ask these questions, because you would never have come into existence at all. Moreover, it is equally useless to ask what might have happened if Mrs. Seton and her mother and her mother before her had amassed great wealth and laid it under the foundations of college and library, because, in the first place, to earn money was impossible for them, and in the second, had it been possible, the law denied them the right to possess what money they earned. It is only for the last forty-eight years that Mrs. Seton has had a penny of her own. For all the centuries before that it would have been her husband's property—a thought which, perhaps, may have had its share in keeping Mrs. Seton and her mothers off the Stock Exchange. Every penny I earn, they may have said, will be taken from me and disposed of according to my husband's wisdom—perhaps to found a scholarship or to endow a fellowship in Balliol or Kings, so that to earn money, even if I could earn money, is not a matter that interests me very greatly. I had better leave it to my husband.

At any rate, whether or not the blame rested on the old lady who was looking at the spaniel, there could be no doubt that for some reason or other our mothers had mismanaged their affairs very gravely. Not a penny could be spared for "amenities"; for partridges and wine, beadles and turf, books and cigars, libraries and leisure. To raise bare walls out of the bare earth was the utmost they could do.

So we talked standing at the window and looking, as so many thousands look every night, down on the domes and towers of the famous city beneath us. It was very beautiful, very mysterious in the autumn moonlight. The old stone looked very white and venerable. One thought of all the books that were assembled down there; of the pictures of old prelates and worthies hanging in the paneled rooms; of the painted windows that would be throwing strange globes and crescents on the pavement; of the tablets and memorials and inscriptions; of the fountains and the grass; of the quiet rooms looking across the quiet quadrangles. And (pardon me the thought) I thought, too, of the admirable smoke and drink and the deep armchairs and the pleasant carpets: of the urbanity, the geniality, the dignity which are the offspring of luxury and privacy and space. Certainly our mothers had not provided us with anything comparable to all this— our mothers who found it difficult to scrape together thirty thousand pounds, our mothers who bore thirteen children to ministers of religion at St. Andrews.

So I went back to my inn, and as I walked through the dark streets I pondered this and that, as one does at the end of the day's work. I pondered why it was that Mrs. Seton had no money to leave us; and what effect poverty has on the mind; and what effect wealth has on the mind; and I thought of the queer old gentlemen I had seen that morning with tufts of fur upon their shoulders; and I remembered how if one whistled one of them ran; and I thought of the organ booming in the chapel and of the shut doors of the library; and I thought how unpleasant it is to be locked out; and I thought how it is worse perhaps to be locked in; and, thinking of the safety and prosperity of the one sex and of the poverty and insecurity of the other and of the effect of tradition and of the lack of tradition upon the mind of a writer, I thought at last that it was time to roll up the crumpled skin of the day, with its arguments and its impressions and its anger and its laughter, and cast it into the hedge. A thousand stars were flashing across the blue wastes of the sky. One seemed alone with an inscrutable society. All human beings were laid asleep—prone, horizontal, dumb. Nobody seemed stirring in the streets of Oxbridge. Even the door of the hotel sprang open at the touch of an invisible hand—not a boots was sitting up to light me to bed, it was so late.

## Chapter Six

Next day the light of the October morning was falling in dusty shafts through the uncurtained windows, and the hum of traffic rose from the street. London then was winding itself up again; the factory was astir; the machines were beginning. It was tempting, after all this reading, to look out of the window and see what London was doing on the morning of the twenty-sixth of October 1928. And what was London doing? Nobody, it seemed, was reading *Antony and Cleopatra*. London was wholly indifferent, it appeared, to Shakespeare's plays. Nobody cared a straw—and I do not blame them—for the future of fiction, the death of poetry, or the development by the average woman of a prose style completely expressive of her mind. If opinions upon any of these matters had been chalked on the pavement, nobody would have stooped to read them. The nonchalance of the hurrying feet would have rubbed them out in half an hour. Here came an errand boy; here a woman with a dog on a lead. The fascination of the London street is that no two people are ever alike; each seems bound on some private affair of his own. There were the businesslike, with their little bags; there were the drifters rattling sticks upon area railings; there were affable characters to whom the streets serve for clubroom, hailing men in carts and giving information without being asked for it. Also there were funerals to which men, thus suddenly reminded of the passing of their own bodies, lifted their hats. And then a

very distinguished gentleman came slowly down a doorstep and paused
to avoid collision with a bustling lady who had, by some means or other,
acquired a splendid fur coat and a bunch of Parma violets. They all
seemed separate, self-absorbed, on business of their own.

At this moment, as so often happens in London, there was a complete
lull and suspension of traffic. Nothing came down the street; nobody
passed. A single leaf detached itself from the plane tree at the end of the
street, and in that pause and suspension fell. Somehow it was like a signal
falling, a signal pointing to a force in things which one had overlooked. It
seemed to point to a river, which flowed past, invisibly, round the corner,
down the street, and took people and eddied them along, as the stream at
Oxbridge had taken the undergraduate in his boat and the dead leaves.
Now it was bringing from one side of the street to the other diagonally a
girl in patent leather boots, and then a young man in a maroon overcoat; it
was also bringing a taxicab; and it brought all three together at a point directly beneath my window; where the taxi stopped; and the girl and the
young man stopped; and they got into the taxi; and then the cab glided off
as if it were swept on by the current elsewhere.

The sight was ordinary enough; what was strange was the rhythmical
order with which my imagination had invested it; and the fact that the ordinary sight of two people getting into a cab had the power to communicate something of their own seeming satisfaction. The sight of two people
coming down the street and meeting at the corner seems to ease the mind
of some strain, I thought, watching the taxi turn and make off. Perhaps to
think, as I had been thinking these two days, of one sex as distinct from
the other is an effort. It interferes with the unity of the mind. Now that effort had ceased and that unity had been restored by seeing two people
come together and get into a taxicab. The mind is certainly a very mysterious organ, I reflected, drawing my head in from the window, about which
nothing whatever is known, though we depend upon it so completely.
Why do I feel that there are severances and oppositions in the mind, as
there are strains from obvious causes on the body? What does one mean
by "the unity of the mind," I pondered, for clearly the mind has so great a
power of concentrating at any point at any moment that it seems to have
no single state of being. It can separate itself from the people in the street,
for example, and think of itself as apart from them, at an upper window
looking down on them. Or it can think with other people spontaneously,
as, for instance, in a crowd waiting to hear some piece of news read out. It
can think back through its fathers or through its mothers, as I have said
that a woman writing thinks back through her mothers. Again if one is a
woman one is often surprised by a sudden splitting off of consciousness,
say in walking down Whitehall, when from being the natural inheritor of
that civilization, she becomes, on the contrary, outside of it, alien and critical. Clearly the mind is always altering its focus, and bringing the world
into different perspectives. But some of these states of mind seem, even if
adopted spontaneously, to be less comfortable than others. In order to

keep oneself continuing in them one is unconsciously holding something back, and gradually the repression becomes an effort. But there may be some state of mind in which one could continue without effort because nothing is required to be held back. And this perhaps, I thought, coming in from the window, is one of them. For certainly when I saw the couple get into the taxicab the mind felt as if, after being divided, it had come together again in a natural fusion. The obvious reason would be that it is natural for the sexes to cooperate. One has a profound, if irrational, instinct in favor of the theory that the union of man and woman makes for the greatest satisfaction, the most complete happiness. But the sight of the two people getting into the taxi and the satisfaction it gave me made me also ask whether there are two sexes in the mind corresponding to the two sexes in the body, and whether they also require to be united in order to get complete satisfaction and happiness. And I went on amateurishly to sketch a plan of the soul so that in each of us two powers preside, one male, one female; and in the man's brain, the man predominates over the woman, and in the woman's brain, the woman predominates over the man. The normal and comfortable state of being is that when the two live in harmony together, spiritually cooperating. If one is a man, still the woman part of the brain must have effect; and a woman also must have intercourse with the man in her. Coleridge perhaps meant this when he said that a great mind is androgynous. It is when this fusion takes place that the mind is fully fertilized and uses all its faculties. Perhaps a mind that is purely masculine cannot create, any more than a mind that is purely feminine, I thought. But it would be well to test what one meant by man-womanly, and conversely by woman-manly, by pausing and looking at a book or two.

Coleridge certainly did not mean, when he said that a great mind is androgynous, that it is a mind that has any special sympathy with women; a mind that takes up their cause or devotes itself to their interpretation. Perhaps the androgynous mind is less apt to make these distinctions than the single-sexed mind. He meant, perhaps, that the androgynous mind is resonant and porous; that it transmits emotion without impediment; that it is naturally creative, incandescent, and undivided. In fact one goes back to Shakespeare's mind as the type of the androgynous, of the man-womanly mind, though it would be impossible to say what Shakespeare thought of women. And if it be true that it is one of the tokens of the fully developed mind that it does not think specially or separately of sex, how much harder it is to attain that condition now than ever before. Here I came to the books by living writers, and there paused and wondered if this fact were not at the root of something that had long puzzled me. No age can ever have been as stridently sex-conscious as our own; those innumerable books by men about women in the British Museum are a proof of it. The Suffrage campaign was no doubt to blame. It must have roused in men an extraordinary desire for self-assertion; it must have made them lay emphasis upon their own sex and its characteristics which they would not have troubled to think about had they not been challenged. And when one is challenged, even by a few women in black bonnets, one retaliates, if one has never been challenged before, rather excessively. That perhaps accounts for some of the characteristics that I remember to have found here, I thought, taking down a new novel by Mr. A, who is in the prime of life and very well thought of, apparently, by the reviewers. I opened it. Indeed, it was delightful to read a man's writing again. It was so direct, so straightforward after the writing of women. It indicated such freedom of mind, such liberty of person, such a confidence in himself. One had a sense of physical well-being in the presence of this well-nourished, well-educated, free mind, which had never been thwarted, or opposed, but had had full liberty from birth to stretch itself in whatever way it liked. All this was admirable. But after reading a chapter or two a shadow seemed to lie across the page. It was a straight dark bar, a shadow shaped something like the letter "I." One began dodging this way and that to catch a glimpse of the landscape behind it. Whether that was indeed a tree or a woman walking I was not quite sure. Back one was always hailed to the letter "I." One began to be tired of "I." Not but what this "I" was a most respectable "I"; honest and logical; as hard as a nut, and polished for centuries by good teaching and good feeding. I respect and admire that "I" from the bottom of my heart. But—here I turned a page or two, looking for something or other—the worst of it is that in the shadow of the letter "I" all is shapeless as mist. Is that a tree? No, it is a woman. But . . . she has not a bone in her body, I thought, watching Phoebe, for that was her name, coming across the beach. Then Alan got up and the shadow of Alan at once obliterated Phoebe. For Alan had views and Phoebe was quenched in the flood of his views. And then Alan, I thought, has passions; and here I turned page after page very fast, feeling that the crisis was approaching, and so it was. It took place on the beach under the sun. It was done very openly. It was done very vigorously. Nothing could have been more indecent. But . . . I had said "but" too often. One cannot go on saying "but." One must finish the sentence somehow. I rebuked myself. Shall I finish it. "But— I am bored!" But why was I bored? Partly because of the dominance of the letter "I" and the aridity, which, like the giant beech tree, it casts within its shade. Nothing will grow there. And partly for some more obscure reason. There seemed to be some obstacle, some impediment of Mr. A's mind which blocked the fountain of creative energy and shored it within narrow limits. And remembering the lunch party at Oxbridge, and the cigarette ash and the Manx cat and Tennyson and Christina Rossetti all in a bunch, it seemed possible that the impediment lay there. As he no longer hums under his breath, "There has fallen a splendid tear from the passion-flower at the gate," when Phoebe crosses the beach, and she no longer replies, "My heart is like a singing bird whose nest is in a water'd shoot," when Alan approaches what can he do? Being honest as the day and logical as the sun, there is only one thing he can do. And that he does, to do him justice, over and over (I said, turning the pages) and over again. And that, I added, aware of the awful nature of the confession, seems somehow dull. Shakespeare's indecency uproots a thousand other things in one's mind, and is far from being dull. But Shakespeare does it for pleasure; Mr. A, as the nurses say, does it on purpose. He does it in protest. He is protesting against the equality of the other sex by asserting his own superiority. He is therefore impeded and inhibited and self-conscious as Shakespeare might have been if he too had known Miss Clough and Miss Davies. Doubtless Elizabethan literature would have been very different from what it is if the woman's movement had begun in the sixteenth century and not in the nineteenth.

What, then, it amounts to, if this theory of the two sides of the mind holds good, is that virility has now become self-conscious—men, that is to say, are now writing only with the male side of their brains. It is a mistake for a woman to read them, for she will inevitably look for something that she will not find. It is the power of suggestion that one most misses, I thought, taking Mr. B the critic in my hand and reading, very carefully and very dutifully, his remarks upon the art of poetry. Very able they were, acute and full of learning; but the trouble was, that his feelings no longer communicated; his mind seemed separated into different chambers; not a sound carried from one to the other. Thus, when one takes a sentence of Mr. B into the mind it falls plump to the ground—dead; but when one takes a sentence of Coleridge into the mind, it explodes and gives birth to all kinds of other ideas, and that is the only sort of writing of which one can say that it has the secret of perpetual life.

But whatever the reason may be, it is a fact that one must deplore. For it means—here I had come to rows of books by Mr. Galsworthy and Mr. Kipling—that some of the finest works of our greatest living writers fall upon deaf ears. Do what she will a woman cannot find in them that fountain of perpetual life which the critics assure her is there. It is not only that they celebrate male virtues, enforce male values, and describe the world of men; it is that the emotion with which these books are permeated is to a woman incomprehensible. It is coming, it is gathering, it is about to burst on one's head, one begins saying long before the end. That picture will fall on old Jolyon's head; he will die of the shock; the old clerk will speak over him two or three obituary words; and all the swans on the Thames will simultaneously burst out singing. But one will rush away before that happens and hide in the gooseberry bushes, for the emotion which is so deep, so subtle, so symbolical to a man moves a woman to wonder. So with Mr. Kipling's officers who turn their backs; and his Sowers who sow the Seed; and his Men who are alone with their Work; and the Flag—one blushes at all these capital letters as if one had been caught eavesdropping at some purely masculine orgy. The fact is that neither Mr. Galsworthy nor Mr. Kipling has a spark of the woman in him. Thus all their qualities seem to a woman, if one may generalize, crude and immature. They lack suggestive power. And when a book lacks suggestive power, however hard it hits the surface of the mind it cannot penetrate within.

And in that restless mood in which one takes books out and puts them back again without looking at them I began to envisage an age to come of pure, of self-assertive virility, such as the letters of professors (take Sir Walter Raleigh's letters, for instance) seem to forbode, and the rulers of Italy had already brought into being. For one can hardly fail to be impressed in Rome by the sense of unmitigated masculinity; and whatever the value of unmitigated masculinity upon the state, one may question the effect of it upon the art of poetry. At any rate, according to the newspapers, there is a certain anxiety about fiction in Italy. There has been a meeting of academicians whose object it is "to develop the Italian novel." "Men famous by birth, or in finance, industry, or the Fascist corporations" came together the other day and discussed the matter, and a telegram was sent to the Duce expressing the hope "that the Fascist era would soon give birth to a poet worthy of it." We may all join in that pious hope, but it is doubtful whether poetry can come out of an incubator. Poetry ought to have a mother as well as a father. The Fascist poem, one may fear, will be a horrid little abortion such as one sees in a glass jar in the museum of some county town. Such monsters never live long, it is said; one has never seen a prodigy of that sort cropping grass in a field. Two heads on one body do not make for the length of life.

However, the blame for all this, if one is anxious to lay blame, rests no more upon one sex than upon the other. All seducers and reformers are responsible, Lady Bessborough when she lied to Lord Granville; Miss Davies when she told the truth to Mr. Greg. All who have brought about a state of sex-consciousness are to blame, and it is they who drive me, when I want to stretch my faculties on a book, to seek it in that happy age, before Miss Davies and Miss Clough were born, when the writer used both sides of his mind equally. One must turn back to Shakespeare then, for Shakespeare was androgynous; and so was Keats and Sterne and Cowper and Lamb and Coleridge. Shelley perhaps was sexless. Milton and Ben Johnson had a dash too much of the male in them. So had Wordsworth and Tolstoi. In our time Proust was wholly androgynous, if not perhaps a little too much of a woman. But that failing is too rare for one to complain of it, since without some mixture of the kind the intellect seems to predominate and the other faculties of the mind harden and become barren. However, I consoled myself with the reflection that this is perhaps a passing phase; much of what I have said in obedience to my promise to give you the course of my thoughts will seem out of date; much of what flames in my eyes will seem dubious to you who have not yet come of age.

Even so, the very first sentence that I would write here, I said, crossing over to the writing table and taking up the page headed Women and Fiction, is that it is fatal for any one who writes to think of their sex. It is fatal to be a man or woman pure and simple; one must be woman-manly or man-womanly. It is fatal for a woman to lay the least stress on any grievance; to plead even with justice any cause; in any way to speak consciously as a woman. And fatal is no figure of speech; for anything written with that conscious bias is doomed to death. It ceases to be fertilized. Brilliant and effective, powerful and masterly, as it may appear for a day or two, it must wither at nightfall; it cannot grow in the minds of others. Some collaboration has to take place in the mind between the woman and the man before the act of creation can be accomplished. Some marriage of opposites has to be consummated. The whole of the mind must lie wide open if we are to get the sense that the writer is communicating his experience with perfect fullness. There must be freedom and there must be peace. Not a wheel must grate, not a light glimmer. The curtains must be close drawn. The writer, I thought, once his experience is over, must lie back and let his mind celebrate its nuptials in darkness. He must not look or question what is being done. Rather, he must pluck the petals from a rose or watch the swans float calmly down the river. And I saw again the current which took the boat and the undergraduate and the dead leaves; and the taxi took the man and the woman, I thought, seeing them come together across the street, and the current swept them away, I thought, hearing far off the roar of London's traffic, into that tremendous stream.

Here, then, Mary Beton ceases to speak. She has told you how she reached the conclusion—the prosaic conclusion—that it is necessary to have five hundred a year and a room with a lock on the door if you are to write fiction or poetry. She has tried to lay bare the thoughts and impressions that led her to think this. She has asked you to follow her flying into the arms of a Beadle, lunching here, dining there, drawing pictures in the British Museum, taking books from the shelf, looking out of the window. While she has been doing all these things, you no doubt have been observing her failings and foibles and deciding what effect they have had on her opinions. You have been contradicting her and making whatever additions and deductions seem good to you. That is all as it should be, for in a question like this truth is only to be had by laying together many varieties of error. And I will end now in my own person by anticipating two criticisms, so obvious that you can hardly fail to make them.

No opinion has been expressed, you may say, upon the comparative merits of the sexes even as writers. That was done purposely, because, even if the time had come for such a valuation—and it is far more important at the moment to know how much money women had and how many rooms than to theorize about their capacities—even if the time had come I do not believe that gifts, whether of mind or character, can be weighed like sugar and butter, not even in Cambridge, where they are so adept at putting people into classes and fixing caps on their heads and letters after their names. I do not believe that even the Table of Precedency which you will find in Whitaker's *Almanac* represents a final order of values, or that there is any sound reason to suppose that a Commander of the Bath will ultimately walk in to dinner behind a Master in Lunacy. All this pitting of sex against sex, of quality against quality; all this claiming of superiority and imputing of inferiority, belong to the private-school stage of human existence where there are "sides," and it is necessary for one side to beat another side, and of the utmost importance to walk up to a platform and receive from the hands of the Headmaster himself a highly ornamental pot. As people mature they cease to believe in sides or in Headmasters or in highly ornamental pots. At any rate, where books are concerned, it is notoriously difficult to fix labels of merit in such a way that they do not come off. Are not reviews of current literature a perpetual illustration of the difficulty of judgment? "This great book," "this worthless book," the same book is called by both names. Praise and blame alike mean nothing. No, delightful as the pastime of measuring may be, it is the most futile of all occupations, and to submit to the decrees of the measurers the most servile of attitudes. So long as you write what you wish to write, that is all that matters; and whether it matters for ages or only for hours, nobody can say. But to sacrifice a hair of the head of your vision, a shade of its color, in deference to some Headmaster with a silver pot in his hand or to some professor with a measuring rod up his sleeve, is the most abject treachery, and the sacrifice of wealth and chastity which used to be said to be the greatest of human disasters, a mere flea bite in comparison.

Next I think that you may object that in all this I have made too much of the importance of material things. Even allowing a generous margin for symbolism, that five hundred a year stands for the power to contemplate, that a lock on the door means the power to think for oneself, still you may say that the mind should rise above such things; and that great poets have often been poor men. Let me then quote to you the words of your own Professor of Literature, who knows better than I do what goes to the making of a poet. Sir Arthur Quiller-Couch writes:[3]

> What are the great poetical names of the last hundred years or so? Coleridge, Wordsworth, Byron, Shelley, Landor, Keats, Tennyson, Browning, Arnold, Morris, Rossetti, Swinburne— we may stop there. Of these, all but Keats, Browning, Rossetti were University men; and of these three, Keats, who died young, cut off in his prime, was the only one not fairly well to do. It may seem a brutal thing to say, and it is a sad thing to say: but, as a matter of hard fact, the theory that poetical genius bloweth where it listeth, and equally in poor and rich, holds little truth. As a matter of hard fact, nine out of those twelve were University men: which means that somehow or other they procured the means to get the best education England can give. As a matter of hard fact, of the remaining three you know that Browning was well to do, and I challenge you that, if he had not been well to do, he would no more have attained to write *Saul* or *The Ring and the Book* than Ruskin would have attained to writing *Modern Painters* if his father had not dealt prosperously in business. Rossetti had a small private income; and, moreover, he painted. There remains but Keats; whom Atropos slew young, as she slew John Clare in a madhouse, and James Thomson by the laudanum he took to drug disappointment. These are dreadful facts, but let us face them. It is—however dishonoring to us as a nation—certain that, by some fault

in our commonwealth, the poor poet had not in these days, nor
has had for two hundred years, a dog's chance. Believe me—
and I have spent a great part of ten years in watching some
three hundred and twenty elementary schools—we may prate
of democracy, but actually, a poor child in England has little
more hope than had the son of an Athenian slave to be emancipated into that intellectual freedom of which great writings are
born.

Nobody could put the point more plainly. "The poor poet has not in
these days, nor has had for two hundred years, a dog's chance . . . a poor
child in England has little more hope than had the son of an Athenian
slave to be emancipated into that intellectual freedom of which great writings are born." That is it. Intellectual freedom depends upon material
things. Poetry depends upon intellectual freedom. And women have always been poor, not for two hundred years merely, but from the beginning of time. Women have had less intellectual freedom than the sons of
Athenian slaves. Women, then, have not had a dog's chance of writing poetry. That is why I have laid so much stress on money and a room of one's
own. However, thanks to the toils of those obscure women in the past, of
whom I wish we knew more, thanks, curiously enough, to two wars, the
Crimean which let Florence Nightingale out of her drawing room, and the
European War which opened the doors to the average woman some sixty
years later, these evils are in the way to be bettered. Otherwise you would
not be here tonight, and your chance of earning five hundred pounds a
year, precarious as I am afraid that it still is, would be minute in the
extreme.

Still, you may object, why do you attach so much importance to this
writing of books by women when, according to you, it requires so much
effort, leads perhaps to the murder of one's aunts, will make one almost
certainly late for luncheon, and may bring one into very grave disputes
with certain very good fellows? My motives, let me admit, are partly selfish. Like most uneducated Englishwomen, I like reading—I like reading
books in the bulk. Lately my diet has become a trifle monotonous; history
is too much about wars; biography too much about great men; poetry has
shown, I think, a tendency to sterility, and fiction—but I have sufficiently
exposed my disabilities as a critic of modern fiction and will say no more
about it. Therefore I would ask you to write all kinds of books, hesitating
at no subject however trivial or however vast. By hook or by crook, I hope
that you will possess yourselves of money enough to travel and to idle, to
contemplate the future or the past of the world, to dream over books and
loiter at street corners and let the line of thought dip deep into the stream.
For I am by no means confining you to fiction. If you would please me—
and there are thousands like me—you would write books of travel and
adventure, and research and scholarship, and history and biography, and
criticism and philosophy and science. By so doing you will certainly profit
the art of fiction. For books have a way of influencing each other. Fiction

will be much better for standing cheek by jowl with poetry and philosophy. Moreover, if you consider any great figure of the past, like Sappho, like the Lady Murasaki, like Emily Brontë, you will find that she is an inheritor as well as an originator, and has come into existence because women have come to have the habit of writing naturally; so that even as a prelude to poetry such activity on your part would be invaluable.

But when I look back through these notes and criticize my own train of thought as I made them, I find that my motives were not altogether selfish. There runs through these comments and discursions the conviction—or is it the instinct?—that good books are desirable and that good writers, even if they show every variety of human depravity, are still good human beings. Thus when I ask you to write more books I am urging you to do what will be for your good and for the good of the world at large. How to justify this instinct or belief I do not know, for philosophic words, if one has not been educated at a university, are apt to play one false. What is meant by "reality"? It would seem to be something very erratic, very undependable—now to be found in a dusty road, now in a scrap of newspaper in the street, now in a daffodil in the sun. It lights up a group in a room and stamps some casual saying. It overwhelms one walking home beneath the stars and makes the silent world more real than the world of speech—and then there it is again in an omnibus in the uproar of Piccadilly. Sometimes, too, it seems to dwell in shapes too far away for us to discern what their nature is. But whatever it touches, it fixes and makes permanent. That is what remains over when the skin of the day has been cast into the hedge; that is what is left of past time and of our loves and hates. Now the writer, as I think, has the chance to live more than other people in the presence of this reality. It is his business to find it and collect it and communicate it to the rest of us. So at least I infer from reading *Lear* or *Emma* or *La recherche du temps perdu.* For the reading of these books seems to perform a curious couching operation on the senses; one sees more intensely afterwards; the world seems bared of its covering and given an intenser life. Those are the enviable people who live at enmity with unreality; and those are the pitiable who are knocked on the head by the thing done without knowing or caring. So that when I ask you to earn money and have a room of your own, I am asking you to live in the presence of reality, an invigorating life, it would appear, whether one can impart it or not.

Here I would stop, but the pressure of convention decrees that every speech must end with a peroration. And a peroration addressed to women should have something, you will agree, particularly exalting and ennobling about it. I should implore you to remember your responsibilities, to be higher, more spiritual; I should remind you how much depends upon you, and what an influence you can exert upon the future. But those exhortations can safely, I think, be left to the other sex, who will put them, and indeed have put them, with far greater eloquence than I can compass. When I rummage in my own mind I find no noble sentiments about being companions and equals and influencing the world to higher ends. I find myself saying briefly and prosaically that it is much more important to be oneself than anything else. Do not dream of influencing other people, I would say, if I knew how to make it sound exalted. Think of things in themselves.

And again I am reminded by dipping into newspapers and novels and biographies that when a woman speaks to women she should have something very unpleasant up her sleeve. Women are hard on women. Women dislike women. Women—but are you not sick to death of the word? I can assure you that I am. Let us agree, then, that a paper read by a woman to women should end with something particularly disagreeable.

But how does it go? What can I think of? The truth is, I often like women. I like their unconventionality. I like their subtlety. I like their anonymity. I like—but I must not run on in this way. That cupboard there,—you say it holds clean table napkins only; but what if Sir Archibald Bodkin were concealed among them? Let me then adopt a sterner tone. Have I, in the preceding words, conveyed to you sufficiently the warnings and reprobation of mankind? I have told you the very low opinion in which you were held by Mr. Oscar Browning. I have indicated what Napoleon once thought of you and what Mussolini thinks now. Then, in case any of you aspire to fiction, I have copied out for your benefit the advice of the critic about courageously acknowledging the limitations of your sex. I have referred to Professor X and given prominence to his statement that women are intellectually, morally, and physically inferior to men. I have handed on all that has come my way without going in search of it, and here is a final warning—from Mr. John Langdon Davies.[4] Mr. John Langdon Davies warns women "that when children cease to be altogether desirable, women cease to be altogether necessary." I hope you will make a note of it.

How can I further encourage you to go about the business of life? Young women, I would say, and please attend, for the peroration is beginning, you are, in my opinion, disgracefully ignorant. You have never made a discovery of any sort of importance. You have never shaken an empire or led an army into battle. The plays of Shakespeare are not by you, and you have never introduced a barbarous race to the blessings of civilization. What is your excuse? It is all very well for you to say, pointing to the streets and squares and forests of the globe swarming with black and white and coffee-colored inhabitants, all busily engaged in traffic and enterprise and lovemaking, we have had other work on our hands. Without our doing, those seas would be unsailed and those fertile lands a desert. We have borne and bred and washed and taught, perhaps to the age of six or seven years, the one thousand six hundred and twenty-three million human beings who are, according to statistics, at present in existence, and that, allowing that some had help, takes time.

There is truth in what you say—I will not deny it. But at the same time may I remind you that there have been at least two colleges for women in existence in England since the year 1866; that after the year of 1880 a married woman was allowed by law to possess her own property; and that in 1919—which is a whole nine years ago—she was given a vote? May I also remind you that the most of the professions have been open to you for close on ten years now? When you reflect upon these immense privileges and the length of time during which they have been enjoyed, and the fact that there must be at this moment some two thousand women capable of earning over five hundred a year in one way or another, you will agree that the excuse of lack of opportunity, training, encouragement, leisure, and money no longer holds good. Moreover, the economists are telling us that Mrs. Seton has had too many children. You must, of course, go on bearing children, but, so they say, in twos and threes, not in tens and twelves.

Thus, with some time on your hands and with some book learning in your brains—you have had enough of the other kind, and are sent to college partly, I suspect, to be uneducated—surely you should embark upon another stage of your very long, very laborious, and highly obscure career. A thousand pens are ready to suggest what you should do and what effect you will have. My own suggestion is a little fantastic, I admit; I prefer, therefore, to put it in the form of fiction.

I told you in the course of this paper that Shakespeare had a sister; but do not look for her in Sir Sidney Lee's life of the poet. She died young—alas, she never wrote a word. She lies buried where the omnibuses now stop, opposite the Elephant and Castle. Now my belief is that this poet who never wrote a word and was buried at the crossroads still lives. She lives in you and in me, and in many other women who are not here tonight, for they are washing up the dishes and putting the children to bed. But she lives; for great poets do not die; they are continuing presences; they need only the opportunity to walk among us in the flesh. This opportunity, as I think, it is now coming within your power to give her. For my belief is that if we live another century or so—I am talking of the common life which is the real life and not of the little separate lives which we live as individuals—and have five hundred a year each of us and rooms of our own; if we have the habit of freedom and the courage to write exactly what we think; if we escape a little from the common sitting room and see human beings not always in their relation to each other but in relation to reality; and the sky, too, and the trees or whatever it may be in themselves; if we look past Milton's bogey, for no human being should shut out the view; if we face the fact, for it is a fact, that there is no arm to cling to, but that we go alone and that our relation is to the world of reality and not only to the world of men and women, then the opportunity will come and the dead poet who was Shakespeare's sister will put on the body which she has so often laid down. Drawing her life from the lives of the unknown who were her forerunners, as her brother did before her, she will be born. As for her coming without that preparation, without that effort on our part, without that determination that when she is born again she shall find it possible to live and write her poetry, that we cannot expect, for that would be impossible. But I maintain that she would come if we worked for her, and that so to work, even in poverty and obscurity, is worth while.

NOTES

[1] "We are told that we ought to ask for £30,000 at least. . . . It is not a large sum, considering that there is to be but one college of this sort for Great Britain, Ireland, and the Colonies, and considering how easy it is to raise immense sums for boys' schools. But considering how few people really wish women to be educated, it is a good deal."—Lady Stephen, *Life of Miss Emily Davies.*

[2] Every penny which could be scraped together was set aside for building, and the amenities had to be postponed.—R. Strachey, *The Cause.*

[3] *The Art of Writing,* by Sir Arthur Quiller-Couch.

[4] *A Short History of Women,* by John Langdon Davies.

• • • • • • • • • • • •

## QUESTIONS FOR A SECOND READING

1. One of the difficulties in reading "A Room of One's Own" is getting a feel for the tone of voice on the page—or, more properly, the tones of voice. Not only are there different voices speaking to you, but they speak as though they *were* speaking—that is, they rely on inflection and context to give you a sense of how a sentence is to be taken. How, for example, are you to read a line like this one near the conclusion of the final chapter: "Young women, I would say, and please attend, for the peroration is beginning, you are, in my opinion, disgracefully ignorant"? Who is speaking here? Or in whose voice is the speaker speaking? and to whom? That is, what kind of listener is imagined here? As you reread the essay, think about how its lines might be delivered and pay attention to shifts in tone of voice. You will need to do this not only to pick up the fine grain of the argument but also to see the argument about women's writing that is being *enacted* in this prose.

2. There are many unusual gestures and surprises in Woolf's prose. And these could be thought of as part of her argument about women's writing—that is, it is possible to see the writing in the essay as an enactment of her argument about the place of a woman writer in the context of a genre representing the voices and habits of men. The opening word of the book, for example, is "but," itself a bit of a surprise. "But, you may say, we asked you to speak about women and fiction—what has that got to do with a room of one's own?" From the very beginning, the text stands contrary to conventional expectations about style, subject, and presentation.

    As you reread the chapters, mark sections or places that break what you take to be the conventions of the essay, particularly the essay as it could be said to be a masculine genre. And as you mark them, think about what these moments might be said to represent. If they are resisting or revising the genre, why? to what end? with what possible intention?

3. As you read these two chapters you have the sense that you have been taken into someone else's thoughts as they are being developed. A sentence is broken, for example, when the speaker misses a turn in the road. Behind this fiction of spontaneous utterance, however, is a writer at work, not walking down the street but sitting somewhere and writing, constructing this moment that you will experience at some other time and place. *This* writer is hard to find, however, behind the "I" of the speaker and the "I" of Mary Seton. At one point, in fact, Woolf says that the "I" in these sentences "is only a convenient term for somebody who has no real being."

As you reread these chapters, mark sections you could use to talk about their strategies of presentation and how these strategies are consistent (or inconsistent) with the argument the text makes about women's writing.

### ASSIGNMENTS FOR WRITING

1. The title page of the original edition of *A Room of One's Own* said, "This essay is based upon two papers read to the Arts Society at Newnham and the Odtaa at Girton in October 1928. The papers were too long to be read in full, and have since been altered and expanded." As either an essay or the text of a public lecture, *A Room of One's Own* is full of surprises. It doesn't sound like the usual lecture; it doesn't do what essays usually do. At many places and in many ways it takes liberties with the conventions of the genre, with the essay's or the lecture's characteristic ways of addressing the audience, gathering information, and presenting an argument.

As you reread these chapters and prepare to write about them, make note of the ways Woolf (the writer writing the text) constructs a space for speaker and audience, a kind of imaginary place where a woman can do her work, find a way of speaking, think as she might like to think, and prepare others to listen. Look for interesting and potentially significant ways she defies or transforms what you take to be the conventions of the essay. (See the second "Question for a Second Reading.") You might especially want to look at those places where Woolf seems to be saying, "I know what I should be doing here, but I won't. I'll do this instead."

Choose four such moments and write an essay in which you discuss Woolf's chapters as a performance, a demonstration of a way of writing that pushes against the usual ways of manipulating words. While there is certainly an argument *in* Woolf's essay, your paper will be about the argument represented *by* the essay, an argument enacted in a way of writing. What is Woolf doing? How might you explain what she is doing and why? In what ways might her essay be seen as an example of someone working on the problems of writing? of a woman's writing? And what might this have to do with you, a student in a writing class?

2. In the opening of her essay, Woolf says that the "I" of her text "is only a convenient term for somebody who has no real being." And at the be-

ginning of the last chapter (in reference to a new novel by "Mr. A"), she says,

> But after reading a chapter or two a shadow seemed to lie across the page. It was a straight dark bar, a shadow shaped something like the letter "I." One began dodging this way and that to catch a glimpse of the landscape behind it. Whether that was indeed a tree or a woman walking I was not quite sure. Back one was always hailed to the letter "I." One began to be tired of "I." (p. 766)

It's hard to know what to make of this, as an argument about either the position of women or writing. Read back through Woolf's essay, noting sections you could use to investigate the ways an "I" is or is not present in this text and to investigate the argument that text makes about a writer's (or speaker's) presence. (See the third "Question for a Second Reading.")

Write an essay in which you examine the ways Woolf, a writer, is and is not present in this piece of writing. Where and how does she hide? And why? Whom do you find in her place? How might this difficulty over the presence of the writer be said to be a part of Woolf's argument about women and writing? And what might this have to do with you and the writing you are doing, either in this class or in school generally?

### MAKING CONNECTIONS

1. In a section of the book not included here, Woolf talks about sentences. She says that one of the problems women writers face is that the sentences available to them are men's sentences, unsuitable for a woman's use: "The weight, the pace, the stride of a man's mind are too unlike her own for her to lift anything substantial from him successfully." Moreover, she says, "a book is not made of sentences laid end to end, but of sentences built, if an image helps, into arcades or domes. And this shape too has been made by men out of their own needs for their own uses."

   Sentences, and sentences built into shapes—let's take Woolf's line of thought seriously and inquire into the characteristic shapes of some writing that seems "manly" or "womanly." You will need to begin by gathering interesting specimens—sentences, paragraphs, whatever "shapes" seem significant and manageable. Begin with Woolf's essay and turn to two others in this book—one that seems more manly than womanly and one that seems more womanly than manly. You will need to gather sentences, paragraphs, or passages from these essays as well. (Keep in mind that these types of prose are not necessarily determined by the sex of the writer.) Write an essay in which you present and discuss these pieces of writing as representative ways of gathering material, of thinking it through, of presenting oneself and one's thoughts, of imagining a world of speakers and listeners.

2. In "When We Dead Awaken: Writing as Re-Vision" (p. 603), Adrienne Rich says the following of Woolf's prose:

   > In rereading Virginia Woolf's *A Room of One's Own* (1929) for the first time in some years, I was astonished at the sense of effort, of pains taken, of dogged tentativeness, in the tone of that essay. And I

recognized that tone. I had heard it often enough, in myself and in other women. It is the tone of a woman almost in touch with her anger, who is determined not to appear angry, who is *willing* herself to be calm, detached, and even charming in a roomful of men where things have been said which are attacks on her very integrity. Virginia Woolf is addressing an audience of women, but she is acutely conscious—as she always was—of being overheard by men: by Morgan and Lytton and Maynard Keynes and for that matter by her father, Leslie Stephen. She drew the language out into an exacerbated thread in her determination to have her own sensibility yet protect it from those masculine presences. Only at rare moments in that essay do you hear the passion in her voice; she was trying to sound as cool as Jane Austen, as Olympian as Shakespeare, because that is the way the men of the culture thought a writer should sound. (p. 606)

Let's assume that this is a way of reading *A Room of One's Own*, but not the last word. It can be seen as opening a space for a response, for a conversation. Write an essay in which you offer a response to Rich, one rooted in your own experience reading (or rereading) these chapters.

Before you begin writing, you should reread the chapters, paying particular attention to tone and voice, looking for passages you can use in forming a response to Rich. You should also reread Rich's essay, not only for what she says about Woolf but for the examples she offers of tone and voice, of a woman writing, conscious, as Rich is too, of the context provided by the men of the culture. You can offer your reading not only of Woolf's prose but of Rich's prose as well.

# Assignment
# Sequences

# WORKING WITH
# ASSIGNMENT
# SEQUENCES

*THE ASSIGNMENT SEQUENCES* that follow are different from the single writing assignments at the end of each essay. The single writing assignments are designed to give you a way back into the works you have read. They define the way you, the reader, can work on an essay by writing about it—testing its assumptions, probing its examples, applying its way of thinking to a new setting or to new material. A single assignment might ask you to read what Paulo Freire has to say about education and then, as a writer, to use Freire's terms and methods to analyze a moment from your own schooling. The single assignments are designed to demonstrate how a student might work on an essay, particularly an essay that is long or complex, and they are designed to show how pieces that might seem daunting are open, manageable, and managed best by writing.

The assignment sequences have a similar function, but with one important difference. Instead of writing one paper, or working on one or two selections from the book, you will be writing several essays and reading several selections. Your work will be sequential as well as cumulative. The work you do on Freire, for example, will give you a way of beginning with Mary Louise Pratt, or Adrienne Rich. It will give you an angle of vision. You won't be a newcomer to such discussions. Your previous reading will make the new essay rich with association. Passages or examples will jump

781

out, as if magnetized, and demand your attention. And by reading these essays in context, you will see each writer as a single voice in a larger discussion. Neither Freire, nor Pratt, nor Rich, after all, has had the last word on the subject of education. It is not as though, by working on one of the essays, you have wrapped the subject up, ready to be put on the shelf.

The sequences are designed, then, so that you will be working not only on essays but on a subject, like education (or history, or culture, or the autobiography), a subject that can be examined, probed, and understood through the various frames provided by your reading. Each essay becomes a way of seeing a problem or a subject; it becomes a tool for thinking, an example of how a mind might work, a way of using language to make a subject rich and alive. In the assignment sequences, your reading is not random. Each sequence provides a set of readings that can be pulled together into a single project.

The sequences allow you to participate in an extended academic project, one with several texts and several weeks' worth of writing. You are not just adding one essay to another (Freire + Pratt = ?) but trying out an approach to a subject by revising it, looking at new examples, hearing what someone else has to say, and beginning again to take a position of your own. Projects like these take time. It is not at all uncommon for professional writers to devote weeks or even months to a single essay, and the essay they write marks not the end of their thinking on the subject, but only one stage. Similarly, when readers are working on a project, the pieces they read accumulate on their desks and in their minds and become part of an extended conversation with several speakers, each voice offering a point of view on a subject, a new set of examples, or a new way of talking that resonates with echoes from earlier reading.

A student may read many books, take several courses, write many papers; ideally each experience becomes part of something larger, an education. The work of understanding, in other words, requires time and repeated effort. The power that comes from understanding cannot be acquired quickly—by reading one essay or working for a few hours. A student, finally, is a person who choreographs such experiences, not someone who passes one test only to move on to another. And the assignment sequences are designed to reproduce, although in a condensed period of time, the rhythm and texture of academic life. They invite you to try on its characteristic ways of seeing, thinking, and writing. The work you do in one week will not be lost when it has bearing on the work you do in the next. If an essay by Virginia Woolf has value for you, it is not because you proved to a teacher that you read it, but because you have put it to work and made it a part of your vocabulary as a student.

## Working with a Sequence

Here is what you can expect as you work with a sequence. You begin by working with a single story or essay. You will need to read each piece twice, the second time with the "Questions for a Second Reading" and the assignment sequence in mind. Before rereading the selection, in other words, you should read through the assignments to get a sense of where you will be headed. And you should read the questions at the end of each selection. (You can use those questions to help frame questions of your own.) The purpose of all these questions, in a sense, is to prepare the text to speak—to bring it to life and insist that it respond to your attention, answer your questions. If you think of the authors as people you can talk to, if you think of their pages as occasions for dialogue (as places where you get to ask questions and insist on responses)—if you prepare your return to those pages in these ways, you are opening up the essays or stories (not closing them down or finishing them off) and creating a scene where you get to step forward as a performer.

While each sequence moves from selection to selection in *Ways of Reading*, the most significant movement in the sequence is defined by the essays you write. Your essays provide the other major text for the course. In fact, when we teach these sequences, we seldom have any discussion of the assigned readings before our students have had a chance to write. When we talk as a group about Rich's "When We Dead Awaken: Writing as Re-Vision," for example, we begin by reproducing one or two student essays, handing them out to the class, and using them as the basis for discussion. We want to start, in other words, by looking at ways of reading Rich's essay—not at her essay alone.

The essays you write for each assignment in a sequence might be thought of as work-in-progress. Your instructor will tell you the degree to which each essay should be finished—that is, the degree to which it should be revised and copyedited and worked into a finished performance. In our classes, most writing assignments go through at least one revision. After we have had a chance to see a draft (or after a draft has been seen by others in the class), and after we have had some discussion of sample student essays we ask students to read the assigned essay or story one more time and to rework their essays to bring their work one step further—not necessarily to finish the essays (as though there would be nothing else to say) but to finish up this stage in their work and to feel their achievement in a way a writer simply cannot the first time through. Each assignment, then, really functions as two assignments in the schedule for the course. As a consequence, we don't "cover" as many essays in a semester as students might in another class. But coverage is not our goal. In a sense, we are teaching our students how to read slowly and closely, to return to a text rather than set it aside, to take the time to reread and rewrite and to reflect on what these activities entail. Some of these sequences, then, contain more readings or more writing assignments than you can address in a quarter or semester. Different courses work at different paces. It is important, however, to preserve time for rereading and rewriting. The sequences were written with the assumption that they would be revised to meet the needs of teachers, students, and programs. As you look at your syllabus, you may find, then, that reading or writing assignments have been changed, added, or dropped.

You will be writing papers that can be thought of as single essays. But you will also be working on a project, something bigger than its individual parts. From the perspective of the project, each piece you write is part of a larger body of work that evolves over the term. You might think of each sequence as a revision exercise, where the revision looks forward to what comes next as well as backward to what you have done. This form of revision asks you to do more than complete a single paper; it invites you to resee a subject or reimagine what you might say about it from a new point of view. You should feel free, then, to draw on your earlier essays when you work on one of the later assignments. There is every reason for you to reuse ideas, phrases, sentences, even paragraphs as your work builds from one week to the next. The advantage of work-in-progress is that you are not starting over completely every time you sit down to write. You've been over this territory before. You've developed some expertise in your subject. There is a body of work behind you.

Most of the sequences bring together several essays from the text and ask you to imagine them as an extended conversation, one with several speakers. The assignments are designed to give you a voice in the conversation as well, to allow you to speak in turn and to take your place in the company of other writers. This is the final purpose of the assignment sequence: after several weeks' work on the essays and on the subject that draws them together, you will begin to establish your own point of view. You will develop a position from which you can speak with authority, drawing strength from the work you have done as well as from your familiarity with the people who surround you.

This book brings together some of the most powerful voices of our culture. They speak in a manner that asks for response. The assignments at the end of each selection and, with a wider range of reference, the assignment sequences here at the end of the book demonstrate that there is no reason for a student, in such company, to remain silent.

○—○—○—○—○—○—○—○—○—○—○—○—○—○—○

# The Aims of Education

Paulo Freire
Adrienne Rich
Mary Louise Pratt
Susan Griffin

*Y*OU HAVE BEEN in school for several years, long enough for your experiences in the classroom to seem natural, inevitable. The purpose of this sequence is to invite you to step outside a world you may have begun to take for granted, to look at the ways you have been taught and at the unspoken assumptions behind your education. The eight assignments that follow bring together four essays that discuss how people (and particularly students) become trapped inside habits of thought. These habits of thought (they are sometimes referred to as "structures" of thought; Adrienne Rich calls them the "assumptions in which we are drenched") become invisible (or seem natural) because of the ways our schools work or because of the ways we have traditionally learned to use language when we speak, read, or write.

The essays brought together in this sequence provide powerful critiques of the usual accounts of education. The first two (by Paulo Freire and Adrienne Rich) argue that there are, or should be, ways of using language that can enable a person to break free from limited or limiting ways of thinking. The next, by Mary Louise Pratt, examines the classroom as an imagined community and discusses the nature of a student's participation in that community. The last reading in this sequence, the selection from Susan Griffin's *A Chorus of Stones,* is presented as an example of an alternative intellectual or academic project, one driven by a desire to know and understand the past but written outside the usual conventions of history or the social sciences. The writing assignments that accompany the readings provide an opportunity for you to test the arguments in the individual essays by weighing them against scenes and episodes from your own schooling. Some ask you to work within a specific argument (Rich's account of patriarchy, for example), and some ask you to experiment with the conventions of academic prose. (In some classes, students may be asked to work with a selection of these assignments.) The final assignment provides an occasion for you to draw material from all the essays you have written for this sequence into a final and more comprehensive statement on schools and schooling.

•  •  •  •  •  •  •  •  •  •  •  •

ASSIGNMENT 1

## Applying Freire to Your Own Experience as a Student [Freire]

> The teacher talks about reality as if it were motionless, static, compartmentalized, and predictable. Or else he expounds on a topic completely alien to the existential experience of the students. His task is to "fill" the students with the contents of his narration—contents which are detached from reality, disconnected from the totality that engendered them and could give them significance. Words are emptied of their concreteness and become a hollow, alienated, and alienating verbosity. (p. 348)
>
> —PAULO FREIRE
> *The "Banking" Concept of Education*

Surely, anyone who has made it through twelve years of formal education can think of a class, or an occasion outside of class, to serve as a quick example of what Freire calls the "banking" concept of education, where students are turned into "containers" to be "filled" by their teachers. If Freire is to be useful to you, however, he must do more than call up quick examples. He should allow you to say more than that a teacher once treated you like a container (or that a teacher once gave you your freedom).

Write an essay that focuses on a rich and illustrative incident from your own educational experience and read it (that is, interpret it) as Freire would. You will need to provide careful detail: things that were said and done, perhaps the exact wording of an assignment, a textbook, or a teacher's comments. And you will need to turn to the language of Freire's argument, to take key phrases and passages from his argument and see how they might be used to investigate your case.

To do this you will need to read your account as not simply the story of you and your teacher, since Freire is not writing about individual personalities (an innocent student and a mean teacher, a rude teacher, or a thoughtless teacher) but about the roles we are cast in, whether we choose to be or not, by our culture and its institutions. The key question, then, is not who you were or who your teacher was but what roles you played and how those roles can lead you to better understand the larger narrative or drama of Education (an organized attempt to "regulate the way the world 'enters into' the students").

Note: Freire would not want you to work passively or mechanically, as though you were merely following orders. He would want you to make your own mark on the work he has begun. Use your example, in other words, as a way of testing and examining what Freire says, particularly those passages that you find difficult or obscure.

. . . . . . . . . . .

ASSIGNMENT 2

## *Studying Rich as a Case in Point*
## [Freire, Rich]

The truth is, however, that the oppressed are not "marginals," are not men living "outside" society. They have always been "inside"—inside the structure which made them "beings for others." The solution is not to "integrate" them into the structure of oppression, but to transform that structure so that they can become "beings for themselves." Such transformation, of course, would undermine the oppressors' purposes. . . . (pp. 350–51)
— PAULO FREIRE
*The "Banking" Concept of Education*

For a poem to coalesce, for a character or an action to take shape, there has to be an imaginative transformation of reality which is in no way passive. . . . Moreover, if the imagination is to transcend and transform experience it has to question, to challenge, to conceive of alternatives, perhaps to the very life you are living at that moment. You have to be free to play

> around with the notion that day might be night, love might be
> hate; nothing can be too sacred for the imagination to turn into
> its opposite or to call experimentally by another name. For
> writing is renaming. (p. 610)
>
> —ADRIENNE RICH
> *When We Dead Awaken: Writing as Re-Vision*

Both Freire and Rich talk repeatedly about transformations—about transforming structures, transforming the world, transforming the way language is used, transforming the relations between people. In fact, the changes in Rich's poetry might be seen as evidence of her transforming the structures from within which she worked. And, when Freire takes a situation we think of as "natural" (teachers talking and students sitting silent) and names it "banking education," he makes it possible for students and their teachers to question, challenge, conceive of alternatives, and transform experience. Each, in other words, can be framed as an example in the language of the other—Freire in Rich's terms, Rich in Freire's. For both, this act of transformation is something that takes place within and through the use of language.

Rich's essay could be read as a statement about the aims of education, particularly if the changes in her work are taken as evidence of something the poet learned to do. Rich talks about teachers, about people who helped her to reimagine her situation as a woman and a poet, and about the work she had to do on her own.

For this assignment, take three of the poems Rich offers as examples of change in her writing—"Aunt Jennifer's Tigers," the section from "Snapshots of a Daughter-in-Law," and "Planetarium"—and use them as a way of talking about revision. What, to your mind, are the key differences between these poems? What might the movement they mark be said to represent? And what do these poems, as examples, have to do with the argument about writing, culture, and gender in the rest of the essay?

As you prepare to write, you might also ask some questions in Freire's name. For example: What problems did Rich pose for herself? How might this be taken as an example of a problem-posing education? In what ways might Rich be said to have been having a "dialogue" with her own work? Who was the teacher (or the teachers) here and what did the poet learn to do?

You are not alone as you read these poems, in other words. In fact, Rich provides her own commentary on the three poems, noting what for her are key changes and what they represent. You will want to acknowledge what Rich has to say, to be sure, but you should not be bound by it. You, too, are a person with a point of view on this issue. Rich (with Freire) provides a powerful language for talking about change, but you want to be sure to carve out space where you have the opportunity to speak as well.

. . . . . . . . . . . .

ASSIGNMENT 3

# *Tradition and the Writing of the Past* [Rich]

> We need to know the writing of the past, and know it differently than we have ever known it; not to pass on a tradition but to break its hold over us. (p. 605)
> — ADRIENNE RICH
> *When We Dead Awaken: Writing as Re-Vision*

"We need to know the writing of the past," Rich says. The "we" of that sentence can be read as an invitation to you. Look back over your own writing (perhaps the drafts and revisions you have written for this course), and think back over comments teachers have made, textbooks you have seen; think about what student writers do and what they are told to do, about the secrets students keep and the secrets teachers keep. You can assume, as Rich does, that there are ways of speaking about writing that are part of the culture of schooling and that they are designed to preserve certain ways of writing and thinking and to discourage others. Write an essay in which you reflect on the writing of the past and its presence in your own work as a writer.

One might argue, in other words, that there are ways of writing that are part of schooling. There are traditions here, too. As you look at the evidence of the "past" in your own work, what are its significant features: What might you name this tradition (or these traditions)? What are the "official" names? What do these names tell us? What do they hide? What difference might it make to name tradition in terms of gender and call it "patriarchal"?

How would you illustrate the hold this tradition has on your work or the work of students generally? What might you have to do to begin to "know it differently," "to break its hold," or to revise? And, finally, why would someone want (or not want) to make such a break?

• • • • • • • • • • • •

ASSIGNMENT 4

# *The Contact Zone* [Pratt]

> The idea of the contact zone is intended in part to contrast with
> ideas of community that underlie much of the thinking about
> language, communication, and culture that gets done in the
> academy. (p. 590)
>
> —MARY LOUISE PRATT
> *Arts of the Contact Zone*

Citing Benedict Anderson and what he calls "imagined communities,"
Pratt argues that our idea of community is "strongly utopian, embodying
values like equality, fraternity, liberty, which the societies often profess
but systematically fail to realize." Against this utopian vision of community, Pratt argues that we need to develop ways of understanding (even
noticing) social and intellectual spaces that are not homogeneous, unified;
we need to develop ways of understanding and valuing difference. And,
for Pratt, the argument extends to schooling. "What is the place," she asks,

> of unsolicited oppositional discourse, parody, resistance, cri-
> tique in the imagined classroom community? Are teachers sup-
> posed to feel that their teaching has been most successful when
> they have eliminated such things and unified the social world,
> probably in their own image? Who wins when we do that?
> Who loses? (p. 593)

Such questions, she says, "may be hypothetical, because in the United
States in the 1990s, many teachers find themselves less and less able to do
that even if they want to."

"In the United States in the 1990s." "The imagined classroom." From
your experience, what scenes might be used to represent schooling in the
1990s? How are they usually imagined (idealized, represented, interpreted, valued)? What are the implications of Pratt's argument?

Write an essay in which you use Pratt's terms to examine a representative scene from your own experience with schools and schooling. What
examples, stories, or images best represent your experience? How might
they be interpreted as examples of community? as examples of "contact
zones"? As you prepare your essay, you will want to set the scene as carefully as you can, so that someone who was not there can see it fully. Think
about how someone who has not read Pratt might interpret the scene.
And think through the various ways *you* might interpret your example.
And you should also think about your position in an argument about

school as a "contact zone." What do you (or people like you) stand to gain or lose when you adopt Pratt's point of view?

•   •   •   •   •   •   •   •   •   •   •

ASSIGNMENT **5**

# The Pedagogical Arts of the Contact Zone [Pratt]

> Meanwhile, our job in the Americas course remains to figure out how to make that crossroads the best site for learning that it can be. We are looking for the pedagogical arts of the contact zone. These will include, we are sure, exercises in storytelling and in identifying with the ideas, interests, histories, and attitudes of others; experiments in transculturation and collaborative work and in the arts of critique, parody, and comparison (including unseemly comparisons between elite and vernacular cultural forms); the redemption of the oral; ways for people to engage with suppressed aspects of history (including their own histories), ways to move *into and out of* rhetorics of authenticity; ground rules for communication across lines of difference and hierarchy that go beyond politeness but maintain mutual respect; a systematic approach to the all-important concept of *cultural mediation.* (p. 595)
>
>        —MARY LOUISE PRATT
>        *Arts of the Contact Zone*

    Pratt writes generally about culture and history, but also about reading and writing and teaching and learning, about the "literate" and "pedagogical" arts of this place she calls the "contact zone." Think about the class you are in—its position in the curriculum, in the institution. Think about its official goals (and its unofficial goals). Think about the positions represented by the students, the teacher. Think about how to think about the class, in Pratt's terms, as a "contact zone."

    And think about the unusual exercises represented by her list: "storytelling," "experiments in transculturation," "critique," "parody," "unseemly comparisons," moving into and out of "rhetorics of authenticity"—these are some of them. Take one of these suggested exercises, explain what you take it to mean, and then go on to discuss how it might be put into practice in a writing class. What would students do? to what end? How would their work be evaluated? What place would the exercise have in the larger sequence of assignments over the term, quarter, or semester? In your terms, and from your point of view, what might you learn from such an exercise?

Or you could think of the question this way: What comments would a teacher make on one of the papers you have written so far in order that its revision might stand as one of these exercises? How would the revision be different from what you are used to doing?

Write an essay in which you present and discuss an exercise designed to serve the writing class as a "contact zone."

•  •  •  •  •  •  •  •  •  •  •  •

ASSIGNMENT 6

# *Writing against the Grain* [Griffin]

As you reread "Our Secret," think of Griffin's prose as experimental, as deliberate and crafted. She is trying to do something that she can't do in the "usual" essay form. She wants to make a different kind of argument and engage her reader in a different manner. And so she mixes personal and academic writing. She assembles fragments and juxtaposes seemingly unrelated material in surprising and suggestive relationships. She breaks the "plane" of the page with italicized inter-sections. She organizes her material, that is, but not in the usual mode of thesis-example-conclusion. The arrangement is not nearly so linear. At one point, when she seems to be prepared to argue that German child-rearing practices produced the Holocaust, she quickly says:

> Of course there cannot be one answer to such a monumental riddle, nor does any event in history have a single cause. Rather a field exists, like a field of gravity that is created by the movements of many bodies. Each life is influenced and it in turn becomes an influence. Whatever is a cause is also an effect. Childhood experience is just one element in the determining field. (p. 409)

Her prose serves to create a "field," one where many bodies are set in relationship.

It is useful, then, to think about Griffin's prose as the enactment of a method, as a way of doing a certain kind of intellectual work. One way to study this, to feel its effects, is to imitate it, to take it as a model. For this assignment, write a Griffin-like essay, one similar in its methods or organization and argument. You will need to think about the stories you might tell, about the stories and texts you might gather (stories and texts not your own). As you write, you will want to think carefully about arrangement and about commentary (about where, that is, you will speak to your reader *as* the writer of the piece). You should not feel bound to Griffin's subject matter, but you should feel that you are working in her spirit.

• • • • • • • • • • • •

ASSIGNMENT 7

## The Task of Attention [Griffin]

I am looking now at the etching called *Poverty*, made in 1897. Near the center, calling my attention, a woman holds her head in her hands. (p. 413)

—SUSAN GRIFFIN
*Our Secret*

This is one of the many moments where Griffin speaks to us as though in the midst of her work. The point of this assignment is to think about that work—what it is, how she does it, and what it might have to do with schools and schooling. She is, after all, doing much of the traditional work of scholars—going to the archive, studying old materials, traveling and interviewing subjects, learning and writing history.

And yet this is not the kind of prose you would expect to find in a textbook for a history course. Even if the project is not what we usually think of as a "research" project, Griffin is a careful researcher. Griffin knows what she is doing. Having experimented with a Griffin-like essay, go back now to look again (this time with a writer's eye) at both the features of Griffin's prose and the way she characterizes her work as a scholar, gathering and studying her materials.

Write an essay in which you present an account of *how* Griffin does her work. You should use her words and examples from the text, but you should also feel that it is your job to explain what you present and to comment on it from the point of view of a student. As you reread, look to those sections where Griffin seems to be speaking to her readers about her work—about how she reads and how she writes, about how she gathers her materials and how she studies them. What is she doing? What is at stake in adopting such methods? How might they be taught? Where in the curriculum might (should?) such lessons be featured?

• • • • • • • • • • •

ASSIGNMENT **8**

## *Putting Things Together*
## [Freire, Rich, Pratt, Griffin]

This is the final assignment of this sequence, and it is the occasion for you to step back and take stock of all that you have done. Perhaps the best way for you to do this is by making a statement of your own about the role of reading and writing in an undergraduate education. You might, for example, write a document for students who will be entering your school for the first time, telling them what they should expect or what they should know about reading and writing if they want to make the most of their education. Or this might be an essay written for an alumni magazine or a paper for a faculty committee charged with reviewing undergraduate education. Or you might want to think of this essay as primarily autobiographical, as that chapter of your autobiography where you think through your experiences with schooling.

You should feel free to draw as much as you can from the papers you have already written, making your points through examples you have already examined, perhaps using your own work with these assignments as an example of what students might be expected to do.

# The Arts of the Contact Zone

Mary Louise Pratt
Gloria Anzaldúa
Harriet Jacobs
W. E. B. Du Bois

*T*HIS SEQUENCE allows you to work closely with the argument of Mary Louise Pratt's "Arts of the Contact Zone," not so much through summary (repeating the argument) as through extension (working under its influence, applying its terms and protocols). In particular, you are asked to try your hand at those ways of reading and writing Pratt defines as part of the "literate arts of the contact zone," ways of reading and writing that have not historically been taught or valued in American schools.

Pratt is one of the country's most influential cultural critics. In "Arts of the Contact Zone," she makes the argument that our usual ways of reading and writing assume identification—that is, we learn to read and write the texts that express our own position and point of view. As a result, texts that reproduce different ways of thinking, texts that allude to different cultural systems, seem flawed, wrong, or inscrutable. As a counterposition, Pratt asks us to imagine scenes of reading, writing, teaching, and learning as "contact zones," places of contact between people who can't or don't or won't necessarily identify with one another.

In the first assignment, you are asked to search for or produce a document to exemplify the arts of the contact zone, working in library archives, searching the streets, or writing an "autoethnography." This is a big job, and probably new to most students; it is a project you will want to come back to and revise. The next assignments ask you to look at three selections in *Ways of Reading* that exemplify or present movements of cultural contact: Gloria Anzaldúa's *Borderlands/La frontera*, a text that announces itself as the product of a mixed, *mestiza* cultural position; Harriet Jacobs's "Incidents in the Life of a Slave Girl," a slave narrative (or "autoethnography"); and W. E. B. Du Bois's reading of black education in the American South. The final assignment asks you to think back over both Pratt's argument and your work to make a more general statement about the arts of the contact zone.

• • • • • • • • • • • •

ASSIGNMENT 1

# The Literate Arts of the
# Contact Zone [Pratt]

Here, briefly, are two descriptions of the writing one might find or expect in the "contact zone":

> Autoethnography, transculturation, critique, collaboration, bilingualism, mediation, parody, denunciation, imaginary dialogue, vernacular expression—these are some of the literate arts of the contact zone. Miscomprehension, incomprehension, dead letters, unread masterpieces, absolute heterogeneity of meaning—these are some of the perils of writing in the contact zone. They all live among us today in the transnationalized metropolis of the United States and are becoming more widely visible, more pressing, and, like Guaman Poma's text, more decipherable to those who once would have ignored them in defense of a stable, centered sense of knowledge and reality. (p. 590)

> We are looking for the pedagogical arts of the contact zone. These will include, we are sure, exercises in storytelling and in identifying with the ideas, interests, histories, and attitudes of others; experiments in transculturation and collaborative work and in the arts of critique, parody, and comparison (including unseemly comparisons between elite and vernacular cultural forms); the redemption of the oral; ways for people to engage with suppressed aspects of history (including their own histories), ways to move *into and out of* rhetorics of authenticity; ground rules for communication across lines of difference and hierarchy that go beyond politeness but maintain mutual respect; a systematic approach to the all-important concept of *cultural mediation.* (p. 595)

Here are two ways of working on Pratt's idea of the "contact zone." Choose one.

1. One way of working with Pratt's essay, of extending its project, would be to conduct your own local inventory of writing from the contact zone. You might do this on your own or in teams, with others from your class. You will want to gather several similar documents, your "archive," before you make a final selection. Think about how to make that choice. What makes one document stand out as representative? Here are two ways you might organize your search:

   a. You could look for historical documents. A local historical society might have documents written by Native Americans ("Indians") to the white settlers. There may be documents written by slaves to masters or to northern whites explaining their experience. There may be documents written by women (suffragettes, for example) trying to negotiate for public positions or rights. There may be documents from any of a number of racial or ethnic groups—Hispanic, Jewish, Irish, Italian, Polish, Swedish—trying to explain their positions to the mainstream culture. There may, perhaps at union halls, be documents written by workers to owners. Your own sense of the heritage of your area should direct your search.

   b. Or you could look at contemporary documents in the print that is around you, texts that you might otherwise overlook. Pratt refers to one of the characteristic genres of the Hispanic community, the *"testimonio."* You could look for songs, testimonies, manifestos, statements by groups on campus, stories, autobiographies, interviews, letters to the editor. You could look at the writing of any marginalized group, particularly writing intended, at least in part, to represent the experience of outsiders to the dominant culture (or to be in dialogue with that culture or to respond to that culture). These documents, if we follow Pratt's example, would encompass the work of young children or students, including college students.

   Once you have completed your inventory, choose a document you would like to work with and write an essay that presents it carefully and in detail (perhaps in even greater detail than Pratt's presentation of the *New Chronicle*). You will, in other words, need to set the scene, summarize, explain, and work block quotations into your essay. You might imagine that you are presenting this to someone who would not have seen it and would not know how to read it, at least not as an example of the literate arts of the contact zone.

2. Another way of extending the project of Pratt's essay would be to write your own autoethnography. It should not be too hard to locate a setting or context in which you are the "other"—the one who speaks from outside rather than inside the dominant discourse. Pratt says that the

position of the outsider is marked not only by differences of language and ways of thinking and speaking but also by differences in power, authority, status. In a sense, she argues, the only way those in power can understand you is in *their* terms. These are terms you will need to use to tell your story, but your goal is to describe your position in ways that "engage with representations others have made of [you]" without giving in or giving up or disappearing in their already formed sense of who you are.

This is an interesting challenge. One of the things that will make the writing difficult is that the autoethnographic or transcultural text calls upon skills not usually valued in American classrooms: bilingualism, parody, denunciation, imaginary dialogue, vernacular expression, storytelling, unseemly comparisons of high and low cultural forms—these are some of the terms Pratt offers. These do not fit easily with the traditional genres of the writing class (essay, term paper, summary, report) or its traditional values (unity, consistency, sincerity, clarity, correctness, decorum).

You will probably need to take this essay (or whatever it should be called) through several drafts. (In fact, you might revise this essay after you have completed assignments 2 and 3.) It might be best to begin as Pratt's student, using her description as a preliminary guide. Once you get a sense of your own project, you may find that you have terms or examples to add to her list of the literate arts of the contact zone.

•   •   •   •   •   •   •   •   •   •   •

ASSIGNMENT 2

## *Borderlands* [Pratt, Anzaldúa]

In "Arts of the Contact Zone," Pratt talks about the "autoethnographic" text, "a text in which people undertake to describe themselves in ways that engage with representations others have made of them," and about "transculturation," the "processes whereby members of subordinated or marginal groups select and invent from the materials transmitted by a dominant or metropolitan culture."

Write an essay in which you present a reading of *Borderlands/La frontera* as an example of an autoethnographic and/or transcultural text. You should imagine that you are writing to someone who is not familiar with either Pratt's argument or Anzaldúa's thinking. Part of your work, then, is to present Anzaldúa's text to readers who don't have it in front of them.

You have the example of Pratt's reading of Guaman Poma's *New Chronicle and Good Government.* And you have her discussion of the "literate arts of the contact zone." Think about how Anzaldúa's text might be similarly read, and about how her text does and doesn't fit Pratt's description. Your goal should be to add an example to Pratt's discussion and to qualify it, to alter or reframe what she has said now that you have had a chance to look at an additional example.

· · · · · · · · · · · ·

ASSIGNMENT 3

# *Autoethnography* [Pratt, Jacobs]

Here is Mary Louise Pratt on the "autoethnographic" text:

> Guaman Poma's *New Chronicle* is an instance of what I have proposed to call an *autoethnographic* text, by which I mean a text in which people undertake to describe themselves in ways that engage with representations others have made of them. Thus if ethnographic texts are those in which European metropolitan subjects represent to themselves their others (usually their conquered others), autoethnographic texts are representations that the so-defined others construct *in response to* or in dialogue with those texts. [T]hey involve a selective collaboration with and appropriation of idioms of the metropolis or the conqueror. These are merged or infiltrated to varying degrees with indigenous idioms to create self-representations intended to intervene in metropolitan modes of understanding. Autoethnographic works are often addressed to both metropolitan audiences and the speaker's own community. Their reception is thus highly indeterminate. Such texts often constitute a marginalized group's point of entry into the dominant circuits of print culture. It is interesting to think, for example, of American slave autobiography in its autoethnographic dimensions, which in some respects distinguish it from Euramerican autobiographical tradition. (pp. 585–86)

Reread Harriet Jacobs's "Incidents in the Life of a Slave Girl" after reading Pratt's essay. Using the example of Pratt's work with the *New Chronicle,* write an essay presenting a reading of Jacobs's text as an autoethnographic and/or transcultural text. You should think about not only how it might be read from this point of view but also how, without this perspective, it might (in Pratt's terms) be misread or unread. Imagine that you are working to put Pratt's ideas to the test but also to see what you can say on your own about "Incidents" as a text, as something written and read.

•   •   •   •   •   •   •   •   •   •   •   •   •

ASSIGNMENT 4

## Writing from Within [Pratt, Du Bois]

Here, from "Arts of the Contact Zone," is Mary Louise Pratt on the "autoethnographic" text:

> Guaman Poman's New Chronicle is an instance of what I have proposed to call an autoethnographic text, by which I mean a text in which people undertake to describe themselves in ways that engage with representations others have made of them. Thus if ethnographic texts are those in which European metropolitan subjects represent to themselves their others (usually their conquered others), autoethnographic texts are representations that the so-defined others construct in response to or in dialogue with those texts. [T]hey involve a selective collaboration with and appropriation of idioms of the metropolis or the conqueror. These are merged or infiltrated to varying degrees with indigenous idioms to create self-representations intended to intervene in metropolitan modes of understanding. . . . Such texts often constitute a marginalized group's point of entry into the dominant circuits of print culture. (pp. 585–86)

The chapters from W. E. B. Du Bois's The Souls of Black Folk present an interesting opportunity to think about Pratt's concept of the "autoethnographic text." While the book is written to represent African American life, thought, and culture (the "souls of black folk") to a white, metropolitan audience, Du Bois's relationship to his subject is not a simple one. As a writer writing about southern black culture, he is urban, highly educated, and a northerner by birth. The first of the three chapters, "Of the Meaning of Progress," could be read as ethnography—that is, as a documentary account written by an outsider. In the remaining two chapters, Du Bois writes from the inside, as a black educator representing to others the circumstances and urgencies in the university education of African American men.

Using the example of Pratt's work with the New Chronicle, write an essay in which you present a reading of two of Du Bois's chapters ("Of the Meaning of Progress" and one of the others) as examples of the "arts of the contact zone." You should look, in particular, at the differences in style, form, and address in the two chapters.

What do these examples allow you to add to Pratt's discussion of the autoethnographic and/or transcultural text? Where do you see Du Bois working to insure that he can be heard (and read) by white readers? Where do you see him working to preserve his own integrity and the integrity of his subjects—where, that is, do you see him establishing his authority? In what ways is he not simply giving in to the prejudices and expectations of his readers?

• • • • • • • • • • •

ASSIGNMENT 5

# On Culture
## [Pratt, Anzaldúa, Jacobs, Du Bois]

In some ways, the slipperiest of the key words in Pratt's essay "Arts of the Contact Zone" is "culture." At one point Pratt says,

> If one thinks of cultures, or literatures, as discrete, coherently structured, monolingual edifices, Guaman Poma's text, and indeed any autoethnographic work, appears anomalous or chaotic—as it apparently did to the European scholars Pietschmann spoke to in 1912. If one does not think of cultures this way, then Guaman Poma's text is simply heterogeneous; as the Andean region was itself and remains today. Such a text is heterogeneous on the reception end as well as the production end: it will read very differently by people in different positions in the contact zone. (p. 589)

If one thinks of cultures as "coherent structures, monolingual edifices" the text appears one way; if one thinks otherwise the text is "simply heterogeneous." What might it mean to make this shift in the way one thinks of culture? Can you do it—that is, can you read the *New Chronicle* (or its excerpts) from both points of view? Better yet—what about your own culture and its key texts? Can you, for example, think of a group that you participate in as a "community"? Where and how does it represent itself to others? Where and how does it do this in writing? What are its "literate arts"?

The assignments in this sequence are an exercise in reading texts as heterogeneous, as contact zones. As a way of reflecting back over your work in this sequence, write an essay in which you explain the work you have been doing to someone not in the course, someone who is interested in reading, writing, and learning, but who has not read Pratt, Anzaldúa, Jacobs, or Du Bois.

## SEQUENCE THREE

# Autobiographical Explorations

Ralph Ellison

Richard Rodriguez

Carolyn Kay Steedman

Jane Tompkins

*AUTOBIOGRAPHICAL WRITING* has been a regular feature of writing courses since the nineteenth century, when writing courses were introduced to the undergraduate curriculum. There are a variety of reasons for the prevalence of autobiography, not the least of which is the pleasure students take in thinking about and writing about their lives and their world. There is also a long tradition of published autobiographical writing, particularly in the United States. The title of this sequence puts a particular spin on that tradition, since it points to a more specialized use of autobiography, phrased here as "exploration." What is suggested by the title is a use of writing (and the example of one's experience, including intellectual experience) to investigate, question, explore, inquire. Often the genre is not used for these purposes at all. Autobiographical writing is often used for purposes of display or self-promotion, or to further (rather than question) an argument (about success, about how to live a good or proper or fulfilling life).

There are two threads to this sequence. The first is to invite you to experiment with the genre of "autobiographical exploration." The second is to foreground the relationship between your work and the work of others, to think about how and why and where you are prepared to write autobiographically (prepared not only by the lessons you've learned in school but by the culture and the way it invites you to tell—and live—the story of your life). And, if you are working inside a conventional field, a predictable way of writing, the sequence asks where and how you might make your mark or assert your position—your identity as a person (a character in a life story) and as a writer (someone working with the conventions of life-writing).

The first four assignments ask you to write from within the example of other writers, writers engaged in "revisionary" projects: Ralph Ellison, Richard Rodriguez, Carolyn Kay Steedman, and Jane Tompkins. One of the difficulties, for a student, of an extended project like this is finding a way of writing differently. An autobiographical project *without* the readings (where, in a sense, you were writing on your own) might well produce each week only more of the same, the same story written in the same style. Our goal is to make you aware of the options available to you as a writer as you think about, write, and represent your life. You should think of these assignments as asking not for mere or mechanical imitation, but as invitations to think about areas of your life as these authors have and to imagine the problems and potential of life-writing through the example of their prose, its style and methods.

The last assignment in the sequence is a retrospective assignment. Here you are asked to think back over what you have done and to write a "Preface" to your work, a short essay to prepare other readers to understand what you have been working on and best appreciate the problems and achievements of your work. We will be asking you to think of yourself as an author, to read what you have written and to write about your texts, as, perhaps, you have sometimes been asked to write *about* the works of other authors.

This sequence is accompanied by a minisequence titled "Autobiographical Explorations (II)." This alternative sequence provides similar assignments but with different readings. They can be substituted for assignments in the first "Autobiographical Explorations" sequence or added to those assignments.

·  ·  ·  ·  ·  ·  ·  ·  ·  ·  ·  ·

ASSIGNMENT 1

# *Autobiographical Exploration* [Ellison]

Early in his essay, Ellison refers to "An Extravagance of Laughter" as an "autobiographical exploration." He is writing from his past and from memory, but he is also engaged, as a writer, in a process of exploration. For Ellison, this essay represents a *way* of writing, a method, one that combines autobiography with a desire to analyze and to explore (to think about experience, not just recount it) and, at least in Ellison's case, to also think broadly about ideas and issues (about W. B. Yeats and masks, about humor, about race relations in the North and South in the 1930s).

As you prepare to write this assignment, read through the essay again thinking about it as a way of doing one's work, as a project, as a way of writing. What are its key features? What is its shape or design? How does Ellison, the writer, do what he does? And, you might ask: What would it take to learn to write like this? How is this writing related to the writing taught in school? Where and how might it serve you as a student? (The third "Questions for a Second Reading" following the essay is designed to prompt this kind of reflection.)

Once you have developed a sense of Ellison's method, write an autobiographical exploration of your own, one that has the rhythm and the moves, the shape and the design of "An Extravagance of Laughter." As far as subject matter is concerned, let Ellison's text stand as an invitation (inviting you to write about race or difference or region or travel or difficult moments), but don't feel compelled to follow his lead. You can write about anything you want (but you would be wise, we've learned, to stay away from childhood experiences and to stick with more adult experiences). The key is to follow the essay as an example of a *way* of writing— moving slowly, turning this way and that, combining stories and reflection, working outside of more predictable forms—either straightforward chronological narrative (first this, then that) or a rigid structure of thesis and proof.

•   •   •   •   •   •   •   •   •   •   •

ASSIGNMENT 2

# *Desire, Reading, and the Past*
## [Rodriguez]

In "The Achievement of Desire," Richard Rodriguez tells stories of home but also stories of reading, of moments when things he read allowed him a way of reconsidering or revising ("framing," he calls it) the stories he would tell himself about himself. It is a very particular account of neighborhood, family, ethnicity, and schooling.

At the same time, Rodriguez insists that his story is also everyone's story—that his experience is universal. Take an episode from your life, one that seems in some ways similar to one of the episodes in "The Achievement of Desire," and cast it into a shorter version of Rodriguez's essay. Try to make use of your reading in ways similar to his. Think about what you have read lately in school, perhaps in this anthology.

In general, however, your job in this assignment is to look at your experience in Rodriguez's terms, which means thinking the way he does, noticing what he would notice, interpreting details in a similar fashion, using his key terms, seeing through his point of view; it could mean imitating his style of writing, doing whatever it is you see him doing characteristically when he writes. Imitation, Rodriguez argues, is not necessarily a bad thing; it can, he argues, be one of the powerful ways a person learns. Let this assignment serve as an exercise.

•   •   •   •   •   •   •   •   •   •   •   •

ASSIGNMENT 3

# *Doubleness* [Steedman]

It is useful to think of Steedman's prose as an enactment of a method, a way of writing a particular kind of highly personalized, highly reflexive social history. One way to study "Exiles," to feel its effects, is to imitate it, to take it as a model. For this assignment, write a parallel "case study" whose goal is to say something about a particular place and time, about experiences determined by a particular social and historical setting. Steedman sees herself as representative of working class experience. You will need to think of the group for whom you can write as a representative.

As you reread "Exiles," think particularly about the features of her prose that you will incorporate into your own. Do this quite formally, looking for sentences whose style you will imitate and paragraphs or larger units of organization whose form you can work with. Perhaps most importantly, you will need to take a lesson from Steedman in how to establish your own position in the text. Steedman is present in "Exiles" in multiple ways. She writes from more than one historical vantage point (then, later, and now); she is present in more than one characterization (as a figure in a landscape, as a writer writing about that figure); she speaks in more than one register (local and academic). It is important that you see this assignment as an exercise in method and not simply as an invitation to write on a similar topic.

. . . . . . . . . . . .

ASSIGNMENT 4

## *Personal Experience as Intellectual Experience*
## [Tompkins]

Jane Tompkins's essay "Indians" tells the story of a research project, one undertaken as a professor prepares to teach a course, but with reference to its own prehistory, way back to the author's childhood in New York City. Tompkins provides an example of how personal experience is not simply action in the world but also (and often) intellectual experience, a narrative defined by books read, courses taken, changes of mind, new understandings.

Using Tompkins's essay as a model, write a personal essay that tells a similar story, one drawing on your own experiences. You could tell the story of a research project, a paper (most likely a term paper) you prepared for school. This does not have to be a pious or dutiful account. Tompkins, after all, is writing *against* what she takes to be the predictable or expected account of research as the disinterested pursuit of truth—in which a student would go to the library to "find" the truth about the Indians and the settlers. And she writes in a style that is not solemnly academic. Like Tompkins, you can tell what you take to be the untold story of term-paper research, you can reflect on the problem of such research as a story of learning. Or you could tell the story of any important experience you have had as a student or, out of school, as a person who observes, reads, and thinks. Your goal should be to think of your story *as* a story, with characters and scenes (and, perhaps, dialogue), with action, suspense, and surprises.

. . . . . . . . . . . .

ASSIGNMENT 5

## *The "I" of the Personal Essay*
## [Ellison, Rodriguez, Steedman, Tompkins]

The assignments in this sequence have been designed to prompt autobiographical writing. They have been invitations for you to tell your story and to think about the ways stories represent a person and a life. They have also, of course, been exercises in imitation, in writing "like" Ellison,

Rodriguez, Steedman, and Tompkins, in casting your story in their terms. These exercises highlight the ways in which your story is never just your own but also written through our culture's sense of what it means to be a person, to live, grow, change, learn, experience. No writer simply gets to invent childhood. Childhood, like adulthood, is a category already determined by hundreds of thousands of representations of life—in books, in songs, on TV, in paintings, in the stories we tell ourselves about ourselves. As you have written these four personal narratives, you have, of course, been "telling the truth," just as you have also, of course, been creating a character, setting scenes, providing certain representations that provide a version of (but that don't begin to sum up) your life.

Read back over the four essays you have written (and perhaps revised). As you read, look for examples of where you feel you were doing your best work, where you are proud of the writing and interested in what it allows you to see or to think (where the "investigations" seem most worthwhile).

And think about what is *not* contained in these essays. What experiences are missing? What point of view? What ways of speaking or thinking or writing? If you were to go back to assemble these pieces into a longer essay, what would you keep and what would you add or change? What are the problems facing a writer, like you, trying to write a life, to take experience and represent it in sentences?

With these questions in mind, reread the four essays you have written and write a "Preface," a short piece introducing a reader to what you have written (to your work—and perhaps work you may do on these essays in the future).

**SEQUENCE FOUR**

# Autobiographical Explorations (II)

Adrienne Rich

Paul Auster

John Edgar Wideman

*T*HIS SEQUENCE provides an alternative set of readings for Sequence Three. All of these can be used to represent personal narrative as a writing problem, as something risky, even dangerous, as something to work on and to work on carefully, not as something simple or easy or to be taken for granted.

• • • • • • • • • •

ASSIGNMENT **1**

## *A Moment of Hesitation* [Rich]

> I have hesitated to do what I am going to do now, which is to use myself as an illustration. For one thing, it's a lot easier and less dangerous to talk about other[s]. (p. 606)

> Until we can understand the assumptions in which we are
> drenched we cannot know ourselves. (p. 604)
> — ADRIENNE RICH
> *When We Dead Awaken: Writing as Re-Vision*

Write an essay in which you, like Rich (and perhaps with similar hesitation), use your experience as an illustration, as a way of investigating
not just your situation but the situations of people like you. Tell a story
from your recent past and use it to talk about the ways you might be said
to have been shaped or named or positioned by an established and powerful culture. You could imagine that this assignment is a way for you to use
(and put to the test) some of Rich's key terms, words like "re-vision," "renaming," "structure," and "patriarchy."

• • • • • • • • • • • •

ASSIGNMENT **2**

# *The Anecdote as a Form of Knowledge* [Auster]

At one point in "Portrait of an Invisible Man," Auster says:

> The rampant, totally mystifying force of contradiction. I under-
> stand now that each fact is nullified by the next fact, that each
> thought engenders an equal and opposite thought. Impossible
> to say anything without reservation: he was good, or he was
> bad; he was this, or he was that. All of them are true. At times I
> have the feeling that I am writing about three or four different
> men, each one distinct, each one a contradiction of all the oth-
> ers. Fragments. Or the anecdote as a form of knowledge.
>     Yes. (p. 94)

What might it mean to claim the anecdote as a form of knowledge? Write
an essay in which you take "Portrait of an Invisible Man" as an experiment in thinking through anecdotes and fragments. Auster uses familiar
metaphors for human understanding—wandering, entering the darkness.
He makes lists, gathers materials, interprets, moves toward closure (or
some sense of an ending). He worries that "when the moment arrives for
me to say the one truly important thing (assuming it exists), I will not be
able to say it." Yet he does write into and past those moments, and it could
be said that he's building arguments, coming to understand many things,
among them, of course, would be his father, himself, his family, their past,
but also memory, thinking, writing, history.
    Write an essay in which you discuss the forms of knowledge

represented in "Portrait of an Invisible Man." Discuss (and document) the
forms of knowledge, where they lead, what they can do (and can't do),
and what, with them, one has in the end.

•  •  •  •  •  •  •  •  •  •  •  •

ASSIGNMENT 3

## Anecdotal Investigations [Auster]

Reread "Portrait of an Invisible Man" with an eye toward those features that make Auster's prose distinctive, unusual, experimental. There
are, for example, the line breaks marking off sections (or fragments); the
use of photos and other documentary material, including newspapers and
passages from his reading; and the mix of narrative, report, and reflection.
As you reread, think of these features in relation to what he says about his
project, about the problems of writing about a person and about the past.

Once you have studied this piece of writing *as* a piece of writing, write
an Auster-like piece of your own, one that has the design, the ambitions,
and the rhythms of "Portrait." You might be tempted to shape your project around a subject similar to his and write family history. This would be
fine, but don't feel that you have to. Whatever you write about should interest and compel you and contain examples (materials) you won't (or
can't) easily explain. This assignment does not, in other words, ask you to
begin with an idea or an outline; it is not an exercise in topic sentence, example, and conclusion; it does not ask for an essay with the structure of
thesis and proofs.

•  •  •  •  •  •  •  •  •  •  •  •

ASSIGNMENT 4

## Old Habits [Wideman]

Wideman frequently interrupts the narrative in "Our Time" to talk
about the problems he is having as a writer. He says, for example, "The
hardest habit to break, since it was the habit of a lifetime, would be listening to myself listen to him. That habit would destroy any chance of seeing
my brother on his terms; and seeing him in his terms, learning his terms,
seemed the whole point of learning his story" (p. 722).

Wideman gives you the sense of a writer who is aware from the inside, while writing, of the problems inherent in the personal narrative. This genre always shades and deflects; it is always partial and biased; in its very attempts to be complete, to understand totally, it reduces its subject in ways that are unacceptable. And so you can see Wideman's efforts to overcome these problems—he writes in Robby's voice; he starts his story three different times, first with Garth, later with the neighborhood, hoping that a variety of perspectives will overcome the limits inherent in each; he stops and speaks to us not as the storyteller but as the writer, thinking about what he is doing and not doing.

Let Wideman's essay provide a kind of writing lesson. It highlights problems; it suggests alternatives. Using Wideman, then, as your writing teacher, write a family history of your own. Yours will most likely be shorter than Wideman's, but let its writing be the occasion for you also to work on a personal narrative as a writing problem, an interesting problem that forces a writer to think about the limits of representation and point of view (about who gets to speak and in whose terms, about who sums things up and what is left out in this accounting).

SEQUENCE FIVE

# Close Reading/Close Writing

Carolyn Kay Steedman

Ralph Ellison

W. E. B. Du Bois

Paul Auster

Ralph Waldo Emerson

*T*HIS SEQUENCE is a set of exercises designed to encourage close attention to detail. Skilled readers need to know how to read closely for
meaning and effect—to see detail and not just the gist of the text or the
"big picture." (The exercises will help you to be a better reader of Steedman, Ellison, Du Bois, Auster, and Emerson.) Skilled writers need to know
how to attend to subtleties in phrasing and punctuation that assist in the
organization of complex, multivocal sentences.

Each exercise provides (or asks you to select) a sample sentence or
paragraph from the text, one that is characteristic or exemplary of the author's style. It asks you to imitate that sentence or paragraph (that is, to
write in parallel). And it asks you to describe sentences, not through textbook terms (subject, predicate, direct object), but in terms of what the sentence *does*. The prose statement calls attention to writing as *action*, as a way
of doing something with words.

The examples below can be extended to any of the selections in *Ways of
Reading.* They serve both to prepare readers to read closely and as writing
exercises.

• • • • • • • • • • • •

ASSIGNMENT **1**

## *Tone, Voice, Doubling* [Steedman]

To read Steedman's prose, a reader needs to learn to pay close attention to tone and voice. As a narrator, Steedman takes different positions, speaks in different voices, lets others speak through her, sometimes in a single sentence. Below are two examples. Listen closely.

> Now, thirty years later, I feel a great regret for the father of my first four years, who took me out and who probably loved me, irresponsibly ("It's alright for him; he doesn't have to look after you"), and I wish I could tell him now, even though he really was a sod, that I'm sorry for the years of rejection and dislike. (p. 651)

Steedman speaks carefully and reflectively: "Now, thirty years later. . . ." She speaks colloquially, from within the linguistic world of her childhood, "even though he really was a sod." And her mother speaks through her, as a voice from the past: "It's alright for him; he doesn't have to look after you." And all of this has an effect on how we understand what she says about sorrow and regret. The prose enacts the difficulty of making a clear, unqualified statement about her feelings or about her father.

Here is a second example:

> My sister ate, but I refused; not out of sacrifice, nor because I was resisting temptation (I firmly believed that meat would make me ill, as my mother said) but because I understood (though this is the adult's formulation rather than the ten-year-old's) that the price of the meal was condemnation of my mother's oddness, and I wasn't having that. (p. 656)

Write two sentences with exactly the same number of words, the same phrasing and the same punctuation as the two above. (We'll call these parallel sentences.) You can provide the subject matter. The words, of course, should be different. When you are done, write a one-sentence description of what Steedman is *doing* in those sentences.

When you are done, go back to "Exiles," choose two or three examples that seem characteristic of Steedman's prose, examples you find interesting and worth discussion. Be prepared to say something about why you think Steedman's project would require (or produce) such writing.

•   •   •   •   •   •   •   •   •   •   •   •

A S S I G N M E N T   **2**

## *Extending, Postponing, Highlighting* [Ellison]

Here are the opening sentences of "An Extravagance of Laughter":

> In December 1983 the good news that Erskine Caldwell had
> reached his eightieth birthday reminded me that although I
> have had the pleasure of seeing him on and off for some
> twenty years, I have never been able to offer him an apology
> for an offense of which I was guilty back in the 1930s. Perhaps I
> failed because my offense took the form of laughter—or, to be
> more precise, of a particular quality and an *extravagance* of
> laughter; which, since it came at the expense of Caldwell's
> most famous work of comedy, may explain both my confusion
> and my reluctance. And since the work in question was *de-
> signed* and intended to evoke laughter, any account of why I
> should term my particular laughter "offensive" will require a
> bit of autobiographical exploration which may well enable me
> both to understand my failure to apologize and to clarify the
> role which that troublesome moment of laughter was to play in
> my emotional and intellectual development. (p. 257)

Write a parallel sentence, one with the same phrasing and punctuation
(including the italics and scare quotes) as Ellison's. You can provide the
subject matter. You can use fewer words, if you need to, but try to retain
words like "perhaps" and phrases like "to be more precise."

When you are done, write a sentence that describes what Ellison is
*doing* in these sentences—not what he *says* but what these kinds of sentences allow him to *do*.

•   •   •   •   •   •   •   •   •   •   •   •

A S S I G N M E N T   **3**

## *Figurative Language* [Du Bois]

Throughout these three chapters, Du Bois's writing is rich in figurative
language and rich in allusion, in references to a history of writing, reading, and thinking. Du Bois's prose is not straightforward and simple. It is
carefully worked and highly elaborated. Here, from the beginning of "Of
the Training of Black Men," is an example:

From the shimmering swirl of waters where many, many thoughts ago the slave-ship first saw the square tower of Jamestown, have flowed down to our day three streams of thinking: one swollen from the larger world here and overseas, saying, the multiplying of human wants in culture-lands calls for the world-wide cooperation of men in satisfying them. Hence arises a new human unity, pulling the ends of earth nearer, and all men, black, yellow, and white. The larger humanity strives to feel in this contact of living Nations and sleeping hordes a thrill of new life in the world, crying, "If the contact of Life and Sleep be Death, shame on such Life." To be sure, behind this thought lurks the afterthought of force and dominion,—the making of brown men to delve when the temptation of beads and red calico cloys.

The second thought streaming from the death-ship and the curving river is . . . (p. 238)

Reread the selections from *The Souls of Black Folk* and choose three passages where the language calls attention to itself, passages that show evidence of a writer trying to *do* something unusual or out of the ordinary, create certain effects, or present certain challenges.

Review these passages carefully and be prepared to talk about what Du Bois is doing and why he is doing it. For the purposes of this exercise, assume that Du Bois is doing something other than decorating his sentences or making the writing "pretty." Assume that he is trying to think things through, and this writing is a necessary part of that thinking. Or assume that he is trying to make certain demands on himself, his subject matter, and his reader, and this language is evidence of these demands. Or assume that he is trying to establish an identity for himself, as a writer; what is that identity? Or assume that he is trying to teach a reader how to read; what is this way of reading? What, then, is Du Bois doing in the sentences you have chosen?

Finally, write a passage of your own to parallel one of those you have selected. And write a sentence describing what this kind of writing allows you to do. What, for example, are the pleasures and possibilities, the risks or liabilities of writing this way?

•   •   •   •   •   •   •   •   •   •   •   •

A S S I G N M E N T   **4**

## *White Space* [Auster]

The most distinctive formal feature in "Portrait of an Invisible Man" is the line breaks (the white space or gaps between sections). Auster uses both paragraph breaks and line breaks to punctuate or organize his prose. As you reread, see if you can find the pattern or logic to this.

When you are done, write a brief paragraph describing what you take to be Auster's logic in determining when to mark paragraph boundaries and when to mark section boundaries. Describe what these two ways of breaking the page allow him to do as a writer.

Finally, write a page of prose that makes use of both paragraph and line breaks, in the manner of Auster. Write a brief account of what it is you find you can *do*, as a writer, with this use of white space that you wouldn't be able to do otherwise.

Note: you could create a similar exercise with Susan Griffin's "Our Secret."

•   •   •   •   •   •   •   •   •   •   •   •

A S S I G N M E N T   **5**

## *Order, Sequence, Closure* [Emerson]

Emerson's prose is difficult to read, and the difficulty is not simply the difficulty of long sentences or big words. Emerson's writing is difficult because it is unusual. His sentences and paragraphs don't do what we are trained to think sentences and paragraphs are supposed to do. As readers, we are not trained to read him.

As you reread, see if you can derive a "theory" to account for Emerson's prose. Write a one-page essay in which you provide a description of what Emerson is doing and what he can achieve by writing as he does. What are his characteristic sentences? How are they constructed? How are they voiced? How would you outline or describe a characteristic paragraph? If you take a section, say the section he marks as section II, how is it organized? How does he get from paragraph to paragraph and from beginning to end? And how is this system different from the system you were taught in school—as both a reader and a writer? Finally, as an exercise, write an Emersonian paragraph.

• • • • • • • • • • •

ASSIGNMENT 6

# Classroom Lesson

Most composition courses require a handbook of rules and models for writers. And most writers keep a handbook as a ready, desk reference. Here is a sample from *A Writer's Reference,* Third Edition (1995), by Diana Hacker.

# E1

## Parallelism

If two or more ideas are parallel, they should be expressed in parallel grammatical form. Single words should be balanced with single words, phrases with phrases, clauses with clauses.

A kiss can be a comma, a question mark, or an exclamation point.
—Mistinguett

This novel is not to be tossed lightly aside, but to be hurled with great force.
—Dorothy Parker

In matters of principle, stand like a rock; in matters of taste, swim with the current.
—Thomas Jefferson

**E3-b** Place phrases and clauses so that readers can see at a glance what they modify.

Although phrases and clauses can appear at some distance from the words they modify, make sure that your meaning is clear. When phrases or clauses are oddly placed, absurd misreadings can result.

MISPLACED       The king returned to the clinic where he underwent
                heart surgery in 1992 in a limousine sent by the
                White House.

REVISED         Traveling in a limousine sent by the White House,
                the king returned to the clinic where he underwent
                heart surgery in 1992.

The king did not undergo heart surgery in a limousine. The revision
corrects this false impression.


Given the work you have done with these exercises, prepare a response to the handbook as a writer's guide. You could write a brief review, perhaps directed at college students who will be using a handbook;
you could write your own alternative or parodic handbook entries. Your
goal is to bring together what you have done in the form of advice for
writers that can stand next to the advice provided by the handbook.

o–o–o–o–o–o–o–o–o–o–o–o–o–o–o

# SEQUENCE SIX

# Doing Documentary Work

Robert Coles

W. J. T. Mitchell

Walker Percy

W. E. B. Du Bois

*D*OCUMENTARY WORK has traditionally combined words and images in  an attempt to capture and bring forward areas of the world or areas of human experience that would otherwise remain hidden from view. The impulse is thought to be generous and politically progressive— that is, those doing documentary work have assumed that by providing accounts of, for example, the conditions of poverty, this knowledge would lead those with money and power to act to ameliorate those conditions. This sequence is designed to both introduce you to a key text in the history of documentary work, James Agee and Walker Evans's *Let Us Now Praise Famous Men,* as it is featured in two recent books, Robert Coles's *Doing Documentary Work* and W. J. T. Mitchell's *Picture Theory,* to raise questions about the past and present of the documentary tradition. Coles and Mitchell situate Agee and Evans's project in the history of documentary and the theoretical issues surrounding current debates about the use of words and images to represent the "real" world. The first of three assignments asks you to work with their arguments. Assignments 4 and 5 turn to issues of representation (the ability of writing to capture the "real") as represented by the work of a novelist, essayist, and philosopher, Walker Percy, and an early twentieth-century sociologist, W. E. B. Du Bois. The final assignment asks you to work with Du Bois's text to think about the use and status of writing in representing the "real" before and after the age of photojournalism.

•  •  •  •  •  •  •  •  •  •  •  •  •

ASSIGNMENT 1

## *Images* [Coles]

In "The Tradition: Fact and Fiction," Robert Coles offers three interesting examples of artists cropping or choosing photographic images of working class life (the couple in the car, the father and daughter on the porch, the girl picking cotton). Go back to those images and the discussions around them. Be sure that you can represent the argument Coles is making about Lange or Evans and the choices they made in producing or selecting a final image. Then, take time to think about alternative arguments. (Coles provides one example in his father's response to "Ditched, Stalled, and Stranded.") How might you argue for one of the discarded images? Against the close-up view?

Write an essay in which you begin with Coles's account of the images, summarizing what he says for someone who has not read the essay (or who read it a while ago and won't take time to pick it up again). You will need to represent the photographs, their history, and the points that Coles is making. Then, you will need to engage and extend the discussion. Coles, for example, seems to take for granted that the decisions the artists made were good decisions. Were they? What is at stake in choosing one photograph over another or in cropping the image to remove context and to focus in on the individual face? What was at stake for Coles?

And where and how might you enter this discussion? There should, in other words, be sections of your essay where you are speaking for Coles (and for Evans and Lange); there should also, however, be extended sections where you speak, thinking about the examples and engaging the issues raised by others.

•   •   •   •   •   •   •   •   •   •   •   •

ASSIGNMENT 2

## *Image and Text* [Mitchell]

To introduce the four case studies in "The Photographic Essay: Four Case Studies," Mitchell says, "I want to examine four photo-essays that, in various ways, foreground the dialectic of exchange and resistance between photography and language." For this assignment, work closely with the four case studies to bring forward what remains implied in Mitchell's text, the *differences* in the four cases. What *are* the "various ways" they foreground the dialectic of exchange and resistance between photography and language? What position does Mitchell seem to take on the value or achievement of each of the four books? What seems to you to be the important or significant or interesting differences? Mitchell's essay is designed to prepare you to be a reader of the photographic essay. From the examples Mitchell gives, what sorts of books would you be hoping to find?

You should imagine that you are writing for someone who has not read "The Photographic Essay." You will need, then, to be sure to represent and summarize the text. The point of the summary, however, is to define a position from which you can begin to do your work. And, to repeat what was said above, your work is to bring forward what Mitchell does not foreground—his sense of the differences between the four cases and the implication or value of those differences. And, in relation to what you see in Mitchell, your job is to articulate your own position on the range, importance, and possibility of the genre of the photo-essay.

•   •   •   •   •   •   •   •   •   •   •   •

ASSIGNMENT 3

## *Let Us Now Praise Famous Men* [Coles, Mitchell]

Both Coles and Mitchell write about the genre of the photo-essay and, in particular, about *Let Us Now Praise Famous Men,* the "classic" text by James Agee and Walker Evans. Write an essay in which you elaborate the differences in their approaches to and accounts of this text. You can imagine that you are writing for a reader who has read none of the texts at hand, so you will need to be careful in summary (perhaps reproducing some of the illustrations). What does each notice or choose to notice in the text? How are these decisions related to the larger projects of the two authors? to their underlying commitments and concerns? And, finally, where are you on the differences between the two? Would you align yourself with one or the other writer? From their example is there a position you would define as your own or as an alternative?

Note: Your work with this project would be greatly enhanced by your reviewing the full text of *Let Us Now Praise Famous Men*. With the text, you can establish a more complete sense of context, including what both writers miss or leave out. You can think about the agenda or desires that led to their selection of exemplary material.

• • • • • • • • • • • •

ASSIGNMENT 4

# *The Loss of the Creature*
## [Coles, Mitchell, Percy]

Walker Percy's essay "The Loss of the Creature" can be read as an interesting counterpoint to the documentary projects considered by Mitchell and Coles. Percy has his own ways of being skeptical about the possibilities of capturing the "real." The individuals who populate his essay—tourists and ethnographers, students and scholars—are all shown, finally, to be limited in their ability to see and know the worlds around them.

And, as a writer and scholar, Percy's relationship to the real world is neither ethnographic nor archival. When he needs an example, he makes one up. He does not, in other words, interview tourists at the Grand Canyon or observe their behavior or document them by photograph. He does not seek out diaries or letters or written accounts of people's experience at the canyon. In relation to his subject, he occupies a very different position than does James Agee or Walker Evans or Robert Coles or W. J. T. Mitchell.

For this assignment, bring Percy into the discussion you have begun in the previous assignments. Perhaps the best way to do this is to consider the first three essays you have written as drafts, selecting and combining and, in the revision, bringing in Walker Percy as both a speaker and as an example. What, for example, does Percy have to add? What does he clarify for you? What does he cast into relief? Where do you place him in relation to Coles and Mitchell?

•  •  •  •  •  •  •  •  •  •  •

A S S I G N M E N T  **5**

# *The Written Record* [Du Bois]

In "The Forethought," the introduction to *The Souls of Black Folk,* Du Bois writes

> Herein lie buried many things which if read with patience may show the strange meaning of being black here in the dawning of the Twentieth Century. This meaning is not without interest to you, Gentle Reader; for the problem of the Twentieth Century is the problem of the color-line.

This can be read as a sign of Du Bois's concern that his book will be misread and misunderstood. In "The Forethought," he makes one more attempt to prepare a reader for his book and the project it represents. What might it mean to read this book with "patience"? Who is his "gentle reader" (and is that phrase offered with faith or with irony)?

The first of the three chapters, "Of the Meaning of Progress," stands as a written documentary record of a small, rural, black community as Du Bois saw it in the summers of 1886 and 1887. As a sociologist and a historian, Du Bois presented his readers, black as well as white, with detailed accounts of areas of black experience that would otherwise have remained invisible, unrepresented, and unknown. It is worth recalling that the book that preceded *The Souls of Black Folk, The Philadelphia Negro,* was a study commissioned by the University of Pennsylvania and based on interview, observation, and questionnaire. And from 1897 on, Du Bois was planning, proposing, and supervising a series of sociological studies of black American life. "Of the Meaning of Progress" can be read as a report on black life in a rural community. How is the report organized? What does it choose to see or to ignore? If you read closely, how does Du Bois, *the writer,* establish his relationship to the scenes and people described? How does he represent his relationship to his audience? Where and how does his writing either embody or resist the problem of the color-line?

• • • • • • • • • • • •

ASSIGNMENT 6

## *Words and Images*
## [Du Bois, Coles, Mitchell]

For this assignment, go back to the essay you wrote on Du Bois in assignment 5 and revise it. The first goal of revision should be to work on your reading of Du Bois and to work on what you have written, particularly in light of the responses you have received from your instructor and students in your class.

You should also, however, move to reconsider the arguments of Coles and Mitchell. They are writing about a genre, the photographic essay, not available to Du Bois, who was writing at a time when the photographic image was not so ready or prevalent. Can you find a way of using the terms and concerns articulated by Coles and/or Mitchell to describe what Du Bois is doing in his prose? What is lost and what is gained by the absence of visual images in Du Bois's text? With your sense of his text in mind, what is lost and what is gained by the presence of visual images in contemporary documentary representations? (That is, how might the reading of a text like "Of the Meaning of Progress" give one a different awareness of the ways we have come to rely on pictures to present documentary evidence?)

○–○–○–○–○–○–○–○–○–○–○–○–○–○–○

# Experimental Readings and Writings

Susan Griffin

Carolyn Kay Steedman

Paul Auster

Gloria Anzaldúa

*T*HIS SEQUENCE offers you opportunities to work with selections that are striking both for what they have to say and for the ways they use writing. In each case the writer is experimenting, pushing against or stepping outside of conventional ways of writing and thinking. The sequence is an opportunity to learn about these experimental ways of writing from the inside, as a practitioner, as someone who learns from doing the very thing that he or she is studying. You will be asked to try out the kinds of writing you've read in the course. For example, the first assignment asks you to step into Susan Griffin's shoes, to mix personal and academic writing, and in doing so, you are challenged to do a kind of intellectual work on subject matter to which you feel strong (though maybe contrary and paradoxical) ties.

The second assignment challenges you to work on a set of issues in a manner similar to Carolyn Kay Steedman's in her essay "Exiles." The third assignment asks you to study Griffin's and Steedman's essays as examples of methods, as ways of doing intellectual work.

In assignment 4, you're asked to think about memoir and anecdote as ways of thinking (through Paul Auster's essay, "Portait of an Invisible Man"). Assignment 5 then moves you to the most unconventional text in the series, chapters from Gloria Anzaldúa's mixed-language book, *Borderlands/La frontera*. She describes her writing as "a crazy dance," "an assemblage, a montage, a beaded work." And here, again, you are asked to work from inside of this unconventional project, with its unconventional style. The sixth and final assignment asks you to step back and study the experimental work you have completed. It is also an occasion for you to think through the relationship of experimental writing and the writing you learn in school. You are invited to comment on what might be gained or lost from doing this kind of experimental work.

•  •  •  •  •  •  •  •  •  •  •  •

ASSIGNMENT 1

# A Mix of Personal and Academic Writing [Griffin]

To tell a story, or to hear a story told, is not a simple transmission of information. Something else in the telling is given too, so that, once hearing, what one has heard becomes a part of oneself. (p. 431)

I have come to believe that every life bears in some way on every other. The motion of cause and effect is like the motion of a wave in water, continuous, within and not without the matrix of being, so that all consequences, whether we know them or not, are intimately embedded in our experience. (p. 425)

— SUSAN GRIFFIN
*Our Secret*

It is useful to think of Griffin's prose as experimental. She is trying to do something that she can't do in the "usual" essay form. She wants to make a different kind of argument or engage her reader in a different manner. And so she mixes personal and academic writing. She assembles fragments and puts seemingly unrelated material into surprising and suggestive relationships. She breaks the "plane" of the page with italicized inter-sections. She organizes her material, that is, but not in the usual mode of thesis-example-conclusion. Nor does she only represent people's stories, including her own. The arrangement is not nearly so linear. At one point, when she seems to be prepared to argue that German child-rearing practices produced the Holocaust, she quickly says:

Of course there cannot be one answer to such a monumental riddle, nor does any event in history have a single cause.

> Rather a field exists, like a field of gravity that is created by the movements of many bodies. Each life is influenced and it in turn becomes an influence. Whatever is a cause is also an effect. Childhood experience is just one element in the determining field. (p. 409)

Her prose serves to create a "field," one where many bodies are set in relationship.

It is useful, then, to think about Griffin's prose as the enactment of a method, as a way of doing a certain kind of intellectual work, a work to which she has strong personal and emotional ties. One way to study this, to feel its effects, is to imitate it, to take it as a model. For this assignment, write a Griffin-like essay, one similar to "Our Secret" in its methods of organization and argument. You will need to think about the stories you might tell, about the stories and texts you might gather (stories and texts not your own), stories to which you are drawn by an emotional and intellectual curiosity. As you write, you will want to think carefully about arrangement and about commentary (about where, that is, you will speak to your reader *as* the writer of the piece). You should not feel bound to Griffin's subject matter, but you should feel that you are working in her spirit with subjects that matter to you.

· · · · · · · · · · ·

ASSIGNMENT 2

## *Investigating Memory* [Steedman]

It is useful to think of Steedman's prose as an enactment of a method, a way of writing a particular kind of highly personalized, highly reflexive social history. One way to study "Exiles," to feel its effects, is to imitate it, to take it as a model. For this assignment, write a parallel "case study" whose goal is to say something about a particular place and time, about experiences determined by a particular social and historical setting. Steedman sees herself as representative of "working class" experience. You will need to think of the group for whom you can write as a representative.

As you reread "Exiles," think particularly about the features of her prose that you will incorporate into your own. And you should do this quite formally, looking for sentences whose style you will imitate and paragraphs or larger units of organization whose form you can work with. Perhaps most important, you will need to take a lesson from Steedman in how to establish your own position in the text. Steedman is present in "Exiles" in multiple ways. She writes from more than one historical vantage

point (then, later, and now); she is present in more than one characterization (as a figure in a landscape, as a writer writing about that figure); she
speaks in more than one register (local and academic). It is important that
you see this assignment as an exercise in method and not simply as an invitation to write on a similar topic.

•   •   •   •   •   •   •   •   •   •   •

ASSIGNMENT 3

## *Writing the Past* [Griffin, Steedman]

Carolyn Kay Steedman and Susan Griffin are both trained as historians. Both write as historians. Both are committed to studying and understanding the past. The prose of "Exiles" and "Our Secret," however,
demonstrate that for both writers, the writing of history is a difficult
rather than a straightforward task. The difficulty is not simply a matter of
having accurate records or significant recall; the difficulty is present in (a
part of) writing and the relationship of a writer to language and, through
language, to the past, and the problems are formal problems: where to
begin, how to end, how to put stories together in a way that is meaningful,
that they might add up to something.

Write an essay in which you use one of these selections to investigate
another—where, perhaps, you use Griffin to think about Steedman or
Steedman to think about Griffin. Given what one author is doing, how do
you see the work of the other? How are these projects in dialogue or conversation? Where and how do they go in completely different directions?
What, as examples, do they have to say to a student of writing about the
"rules" most often taken for granted in a writing class—rules governing
sentences and paragraphs; introductions, bodies and conclusions; narrative, argument, and exposition? You should imagine that your readers are
familiar with both texts but have not thought of bringing them together
and do not have the texts handy. You will, then, need to do the work of
presentation and summary as you establish the points of comparison.

•  •  •  •  •  •  •  •  •  •  •  •  •

ASSIGNMENT 4

## *Fragments* [Auster]

Reread "Portrait of an Invisible Man" with an eye toward those features that make Auster's prose distinctive, unusual, experimental. There are, for example, the line breaks marking off sections (or fragments); the use of photos and other documentary material, including newspapers and passages from his reading; and the mix of narrative, report, and reflection. As you reread, think of these features in relation to what he says about his project, about the problems of writing about a person, and about the past.

Once you have studied this piece of writing *as* a piece of writing, write an Auster-like piece of your own, one that has the design and the ambitions and the rhythms of "Portrait." You might be tempted to shape your project around a subject similar to his and write family history. This would be fine, but don't feel that you have to. Write about something that interests and compels you that has examples (materials) you won't (or can't) easily explain. This assignment does not, in other words, ask you to begin with an idea or an outline; it is not an exercise in topic sentence, example, and conclusion; it does not ask for an essay with the structure of thesis and proofs.

•  •  •  •  •  •  •  •  •  •  •

ASSIGNMENT 5

## *A Crazy Dance* [Anzaldúa]

In looking at this book that I'm almost finished writing, I see a mosaic pattern (Aztec-like) emerging, a weaving pattern, thin here, thick there. . . . This almost finished product seems an assemblage, a montage, a beaded work with several leitmotifs and with a central core, now appearing, now disappearing in a crazy dance. The whole thing has had a mind of its own, escaping me and insisting on putting together the pieces of its own puzzle with minimal direction from my will. It is a rebellious, willful entity, a precocious girl-child forced to grow up too quickly, rough, unyielding, with pieces of feather sticking out here and there, fur, twigs, clay. My child, but not for much longer. This female being is angry, sad, joyful, is Coatlicue, dove, horse, serpent, cactus. Though it is a flawed thing—

clumsy, complex, groping blind thing, for me it is alive, infused
with spirit. I talk to it; it talks to me.

—GLORIA ANZALDÚA
*Borderlands / La frontera*

Gloria Anzaldúa has described her text in *Borderland/La frontera* as a
kind of crazy dance; it is, she says, a text with a mind of its own, "putting
together the pieces of its own puzzle with minimal direction from my
will." Hers is a prose full of variety and seeming contradictions; it is a
writing that could be said to represent the cultural "crossroads" which is
her experience/sensibility.

As an experiment whose goal is the development of an alternate (in
Anzaldúa's terms, a mixed or *mestiza*) understanding, write an autobiographical text whose shape and motives could be described in her terms: a
mosaic, woven, with numerous overlays; a montage, a beaded work, a
crazy dance, drawing upon the various ways of thinking, speaking, understanding that might be said to be part of your own mixed cultural position, your mixed sensibility.

To prepare for this essay, think about the different positions you could
be said to occupy, the different voices that are part of your background or
present, the competing ways of thinking that make up your points of
view. Imagine that your goal is to present your world and your experience
to those who are not necessarily prepared to be sympathetic or to understand. And, following Anzaldúa, you should work to construct a mixed
text, not a single unified one. This will be hard, since you will be writing
what might be called a "forbidden" text, one you have not been prepared
to write.

●　●　●　●　●　●　●　●　●　●　●

ASSIGNMENT 6

# *Writing and Schooling*
## [Griffin, Steedman, Auster, Anzaldúa]

You have written five assignments so far, and all of them, with perhaps the exception of the third—the one in which you were asked to write
about Griffin's and Steedman's methods—could be described as experimental. (It might be worth asking: Did you write a conventional essay for
the third? Did you have a choice?)

The selections you took as your models, writing by Griffin, Steedman,
Auster, and Anzaldúa, certainly did not follow the usual guidelines for

school writing. They broke some rules. They pushed the limits. They didn't do what essays or poems are supposed to do, at least by certain standards. They were frustrated by the limits of the usual ways of doing things with words. In a sense, they saw "good" writing as a problem, a problem they could work on as writers. Most likely, the same things could be said about your writing in this sequence. You did things that stood outside of (or that stood against) the forms of writing most often taught in school.

Read over your work. What were you able to do that you wouldn't, or couldn't, have done if you had written in a more conventional style? Be as precise as you can. How and where does this writing differ from the writing you have been taught in school? Again, be as precise as you can—go to old papers, textbooks, or syllabi to look for examples of "good writing" and the standard advice to young writers. Given what you have seen, where and how might more experimental writing be used in the schools (or in schooling)? What role might it play in courses that are not writing courses? What role might it play in a young writer's education?

Write an essay in which you use the example of your work in this sequence to think about writing and the teaching of writing in our schools.

○—○—○—○—○—○—○—○—○—○—○—○—○

# Experts and Expertise

W. J. T. Mitchell

Adrienne Rich

Clifford Geertz

John Edgar Wideman

Walker Percy

*THE FIRST FOUR ASSIGNMENTS* in this sequence give you the chance to think about familiar settings or experiences through the work of writers who have had a significant effect on contemporary culture: W. J. T. Mitchell, Adrienne Rich, Clifford Geertz, and John Edgar Wideman.

In "The Photographic Essay: Four Case Studies," W. J. T. Mitchell asks his readers to think about the power of words and images through the example of the photographic essay as they can be seen to represent a "dialectic of exchange and resistance between photography and language." In "When We Dead Awaken: Writing as Re-Vision," Adrienne Rich examines the history and possibility of women's writing. Clifford Geertz, in "Deep Play: Notes on the Balinese Cockfight," provides an extended account and interpretation of the cock fight as a feature of Balinese culture. And John Edgar Wideman, in "Our Time," uses a family story to investigate the conditions of life in a black, urban neighborhood.

In each case, you will be given the opportunity to work alongside these thinkers as an apprentice, carrying out work they have begun. The final assignment in the sequence will ask you to look back on what you have done, to take stock, and with Walker Percy's account of the oppressive nature of expertise in mind, to draw some conclusions about the potential and consequences of this kind of intellectual apprenticeship.

• • • • • • • • • • •

ASSIGNMENT **1**

## *Words and Images* [Mitchell]

These four books provide the central examples for Mitchell's study: *Let Us Now Praise Famous Men,* James Agee and Walker Evans; *Camera Lucida,* Roland Barthes; *The Colonial Harem,* Malek Alloula; and *After the Last Sky,* Edward Said and Jean Mohr. Jacob Riis's *How the Other Half Lives* also provides an important illustration in the second section of the essay. Go to the library to study one of these texts. Or, find an example of a "photographic essay" that you could put alongside Mitchell's examples.

For this assignment, take up Mitchell's project by extending his work in "The Photographic Essay" and considering new or additional examples. You should assume that you are writing for a reader who is familiar with Mitchell's essay. (This reader, however, will not have the book open on his or her desk.) Your work is to put Mitchell to the test—to extend, test, and perhaps challenge or qualify his account of the genre. As with his project, the basic questions are these: What relationship between photography and writing do [these examples] articulate? What tropes of differentiation govern the division of labor between photographer and writer, image and text, the viewer and the reader?

• • • • • • • • • • •

ASSIGNMENT **2**

## *Looking Back* [Rich]

Re-vision—the act of looking back, of seeing with fresh eyes, of entering an old text from a new critical direction—is for women more than a chapter in cultural history: it is an act of survival. Until we can understand the assumptions in which we are drenched we cannot know ourselves. (p. 604)

I have hesitated to do what I am going to do now, which is to use myself as an illustration. For one thing, it's a lot easier and less dangerous to talk about other[s]. (p. 606)
— ADRIENNE RICH
*When We Dead Awaken: Writing as Re-Vision*

In "When We Dead Awaken," Rich is writing not to tell her story but to tell a collective story, the story of women or women writers, a story in which she figures only as a representative example. In fact, the focus on individual experience might be said to run against the argument she has to make about the shaping forces of culture and history, in whose context knowing oneself means knowing the assumptions in which one is "drenched."

Yet Rich tells her story—offering poems, anecdotes, details from her life. Write an essay in which you too (and perhaps with similar hesitation) use your own experience as an illustration, as a way of investigating not just your situation but the situation of people like you. (Think about what materials you might have to offer in place of her poems.) Tell a story of your own and use it to talk about the ways you might be said to have been shaped or named or positioned by an established and powerful culture. You should imagine that this assignment is a way for you to use (and put to the test) some of Rich's key terms, words like "re-vision," "renaming," "structure," and "patriarchy."

• • • • • • • • • • •

A S S I G N M E N T  **3**

# Seeing Your World through
# Geertz's Eyes [Geertz]

> The culture of a people is an ensemble of texts, themselves en-
> sembles, which the anthropologist strains to read over the
> shoulders of those to whom they properly belong. (p. 391)
> — CLIFFORD GEERTZ
> *Deep Play: Notes on the Balinese Cockfight*

Geertz talks about "reading" a culture while peering over the shoul-ders of those to whom it properly belongs. In "Deep Play," he "reads" the cockfight over the shoulders of the Balinese. But the cockfight is not a single event to be described in isolation. It is itself a "text," one that must be understood in context. Or, as Geertz says, the cockfight is a "Balinese reading of Balinese experience; a story they tell themselves about themselves."

The job of the anthropologist, Geertz says, is "formulating sociological principles, not . . . promoting or appreciating cockfights." And the ques-tion for the anthropologist is this: "What does one learn about such prin-ciples from examining culture as an assemblage of texts?" Societies, he says, "like lives, contain their own interpretations. One has only to learn how to gain access to them."

Anthropologists are experts at gaining access to cultures and at performing this kind of complex reading. One of the interesting things about being a student is that you get to (or you have to) act like an expert even though, properly speaking, you are not. Write an essay in which you prepare a Geertzian "reading" of some part of our culture you know well (sorority rush, window shopping in a shopping mall, slam dancing, studying in the library, decorating a dorm room, tailgate parties at the football game, whatever). Ideally, you should go out and observe the behavior you are studying, looking at the players and taking notes with your project in mind. You should imagine that you are working in Geertz's spirit, imitating his method and style and carrying out work that he has begun.

• • • • • • • • • • • •

ASSIGNMENT 4

## *Wideman as a Case in Point*
## [Wideman]

> The hardest habit to break, since it was the habit of a lifetime, would be listening to myself listen to him. That habit would destroy any chance of seeing my brother on his terms; and seeing him in his terms, learning his terms, seemed the whole point of learning his story. However numerous and comforting the similarities, we were different. The world had seized on the difference, allowed me room to thrive, while he'd been forced into a cage. (p. 722)
>
> — JOHN EDGAR WIDEMAN
> *Our Time*

At several points in this selection, Wideman discusses his position as a writer, researching and telling Robby's story, and he describes the problems he faces in writing this piece (and in "reading" the text of his brother's life). You could read this excerpt, in other words, as an essay on reading and writing.

Why do you think Wideman brings himself and these problems into the text? Why not keep quiet and hope no one notices? Choose three or four passages where Wideman refers directly or indirectly to the work he is doing as he writes this piece, and write an essay describing this work and why you think Wideman refers to it as he does. If he confronts problems, what are they and how does he go about solving them? If Wideman is an expert, how might you describe his expertise? And what might his example say to you as you think about your work as a student? as a writer?

• • • • • • • • • • • •

ASSIGNMENT 5

## *On Experts and Expertise*
## [Mitchell, Rich, Geertz, Wideman, Percy]

The whole horizon of being is staked out by "them," the experts. The highest satisfaction of the sightseer (not merely the tourist but any layman seer of sights) is that his sight should be certified as genuine. The worst of this impoverishment is that there is no sense of impoverishment. (p. 571)

I refer to the general situation in which sovereignty is surrendered to a class of privileged knowers, whether these be theorists or artists. A reader may surrender sovereignty over that which has been written about, just as a consumer may surrender sovereignty over a thing which has been theorized about. The consumer is content to receive an experience just as it has been presented to him by theorists and planners. The reader may also be content to judge life by whether it has or has not been formulated by those who know and write about life. (p. 571)

— WALKER PERCY
*The Loss of the Creature*

In the last four assignments you were asked to try on other writers' ways of seeing the world. You looked at what you had read or done, and at scenes from your own life, casting your experience in the terms of others.

Percy, in "The Loss of the Creature," offers what might be taken as a critique of such activity. "A reader," he says, "may surrender sovereignty over that which has been written about, just as a consumer may surrender sovereignty over a thing which has been theorized about." Mitchell, Rich, Geertz, and Wideman have all been presented to you as, in a sense, "privileged knowers." You have been asked to model your own work on their examples.

It seems safe to say that, at least so far as Percy is concerned, surrendering sovereignty is not a good thing to do. If Percy were to read over your work in these assignments, how do you think he would describe what you have done? If he were to take your work as an example in his essay, where might he place it? And how would his reading of your work fit with your sense of what you have done? Would Percy's assessment be accurate, or is there something he would be missing, something he would fail to see?

Write an essay in which you describe and comment on your work in this sequence, looking at it both from Percy's point of view and from your own, but viewing that work as an example of an educational practice, a way of reading (and writing) that may or may not have benefits for the reader.

Note: You will need to review carefully those earlier papers and mark sections that you feel might serve as interesting examples in your discussion. You want to base your conclusions on the best evidence you can. When you begin writing, it might be useful to refer to the writer of those earlier papers as a "he" or a "she" who played certain roles and performed his or her work in certain characteristic ways. You can save the first person, the "I," for the person who is writing this assignment and looking back on those texts.

# History and Ethnography: Reading the Lives of Others

Clifford Geertz

Patricia Nelson Limerick

John Edgar Wideman

Mary Louise Pratt

*WRITING REMAINS* one of the most powerful tools we have for preserving and understanding the past and the present. This is simple to say. What good writing is, and what writing is good for—these questions are constantly debated by writers and academics. There are big philosophical questions here (what is the borderline between the truth and fiction, between what is there and what is a product of imagination or point of view?). There are practical questions (how do you learn to write history or ethnography? how do you revise it to make it better?). And both the philosophical questions and the practical questions have bearing on the work a student performs in the undergraduate curriculum, where students are constantly called upon to read and write textual accounts of human experience. This sequence is designed to give you a chance to do the work firsthand, to write a history or ethnography, and to think about and revise that work through the work of critics and theorists.

The first two assignments ask you to prepare first drafts of an ethnography and a history, written in response to the examples of Clifford Geertz (an anthropologist) and Patricia Nelson Limerick (a historian). The third assignment asks you to read "Our Time," by John Edgar Wideman. Wideman, in professional terms, is neither an anthropologist nor a historian. He is, rather, a fiction writer who has turned his hand to nonfiction, to write about African American culture and his family. With Wideman as a lever for thinking about issues of representation, you are asked to turn to all three essays to prepare a guide for writers, and, in the fourth assignment, you are asked to revise one of your earlier essays. The next assignment takes an additional theoretical step, looking (through Mary Louise Pratt's essay "Arts of the Contact Zone") at problems of representation as they are rooted more generally in culture, history, and ideology (and not just in the work of an individual writer and his or her text). The last assignment is an opportunity for a further revision, one that includes a section of reflection on the work you have done.

• • • • • • • • • • •

ASSIGNMENT 1

## *Ethnography* [Geertz]

> As in more familiar exercises in close reading, one can start anywhere in a culture's repertoire of forms and end up anywhere else. One can stay, as I have here, within a single, more or less bounded form and circle steadily within it. One can move between forms in search of broader unities or informing contrasts. One can even compare forms from different cultures to define their character in reciprocal relief. But whatever the level at which one operates, and however intricately, the guiding principle is the same: societies, like lives, contain their own interpretations. One has only to learn how to gain access to them. (pp. 391–92)
>
> — CLIFFORD GEERTZ
> *Deep Play: Notes on the Balinese Cockfight*

Geertz says that "the culture of a people is an ensemble of texts, themselves ensembles, which the anthropologist strains to read over the shoulders of those to whom they properly belong." Anthropologists are expert at "reading" in this way; they are trained to do it.

One of the interesting things about being a student is that you get to (or you have to) act like an expert even though you are not "officially" credentialed. Write an essay in which you prepare a Geertzian "reading" of the activities of some subgroup or some part of our culture you know well. Ideally, you should go out and observe the behavior you are studying ("straining to read over the shoulders" of those to whom this "text" properly belongs), examining it and taking notes with your project in mind. You should imagine that you are working in Geertz's spirit, imitating his method and style and carrying out work that he has begun. (It might be wise, however, to focus more locally than he does. He writes about a national culture—the Balinese cockfight as a key to Bali. You should probably not set out to write about "America" but about something more local. And you should write about some group of which you are not already a part, a group which you can imagine as "foreign," different, other.)

• • • • • • • • • • •

ASSIGNMENT 2

## *History* [Limerick]

> One skill essential to the writing of Western American history is a capacity to deal with multiple points of view. It is as if one were a lawyer at a trial designed on the principle of the Mad Hatter's tea party—as soon as one begins to understand and empathize with the plaintiff's case, it is time to move over and empathize with the defendant. Seldom are there only two parties or only two points of view. (pp. 504–05)
>
> — PATRICIA NELSON LIMERICK
> *Empire of Innocence*

One way to work on Limerick's selection is to take the challenge and write history—to write the kind of history, that is, that takes into account the problems she defines: the problems of myth, point of view, fixed ideas. You are not a professional historian, you are probably not using this book in a history course, and you probably don't have the time to produce a carefully researched history, one that covers all the bases, but you can think of this as an exercise in history writing, a minihistory, a place to start. Here are two possible starting points:

1. Go to your college library or, perhaps, the local historical society and find two or three first-person accounts of a single place, person, or event in your community. (This does not have to be a history of the American West.) Try to work with original documents. The more varied the accounts, the better. Then, working with these texts as your primary sources, write a history, one that you can offer as a response to Limerick's selection.
2. While you can find materials in a library, you can also work with records that are closer to home. Imagine, for example, that you are going to write a family or a neighborhood history. You have your

own memories and experiences to work from, but for this to be a history (and not a "personal essay"), you will need to turn to other sources as well: interviews, old photos, newspaper clippings, letters, diaries—whatever you can find. After gathering your materials, write a family or neighborhood history, one that you can offer as a response to Limerick's work.

Choose one of the two projects. When you are done, write a short one-page memo to Limerick. What can you tell her about the experience of a novice historian that she might find useful or interesting?

•  •  •  •  •  •  •  •  •  •  •  •

A S S I G N M E N T  **3**

# A Writer's Guide
# [Wideman, Geertz, Limerick]

While John Edgar Wideman is not writing history or ethnography in "Our Time," at least not in the strict sense of the terms, he is writing about others and about the past—he is trying to recover, represent, and understand the story of his brother Robby, his family, and their neighborhood. He is trying to recover all those factors that might be said to have led to or produced his brother's present situation.

It is interesting to read "Our Time," Geertz's "Deep Play," and Limerick's "Empire of Innocence" as alternate ways of thinking about the problems of history and ethnography. As you reread these selections, mark passages you might use to illustrate the styles, methods, and/or concerns of each writer. You should reread the essays as a group, as part of a single project investigating the problems of writing about other people and about the past. Each essay could be read as both a reflection on writing and a practical guide for those who follow. What do they say about method? What tips do they offer, directly or through their examples? What cautions?

Write an essay in which you present, as though for a textbook or manual, a "Practical Guide for the Writer of History and Ethnography," drawn from the work of Wideman, Geertz, and Limerick.

• • • • • • • • • • • •

ASSIGNMENT 4

## *Revision*
## [Geertz, Limerick, Wideman]

Go back to the first two essays you wrote for this sequence, the ethnography and the history, and choose one to revise. As always with revision, you should select the best essay, the one you care about the most. Your goal in revising this paper should be to take it on to its next step, not necessarily to fix it or clean it up or finish it, but to see how you can open up and add to what you have begun. As you prepare, you should consider the guidelines you wrote in assignment 3.

• • • • • • • • • • • •

ASSIGNMENT 5

## *Reading Others* [Pratt]

Pratt, in "Arts of the Contact Zone," makes the case for the difficulties of reading, as well as writing, the "other":

> Autoethnography, transculturation, critique, collaboration, bilingualism, mediation, parody, denunciation, imaginary dialogue, vernacular expression—these are some of the literate arts of the contact zone. Miscomprehension, incomprehension, dead letters, unread masterpieces, absolute heterogeneity of meaning—these are some of the perils of writing in the contact zone. They all live among us today in the transnationalized metropolis of the United States and are becoming more widely visible, more pressing, and, like Guaman Poma's text, more decipherable to those who once would have ignored them in defense of a stable, centered sense of knowledge and reality. (p. 590)
>
> We are looking for the pedagogical arts of the contact zone. These will include, we are sure, exercises in storytelling and in identifying with the ideas, interests, histories, and attitudes of others; experiments in transculturation, and collaborative work and in the arts of critique, parody, and comparison (including

> unseemly comparisons between elite and vernacular cultural
> forms); the redemption of the oral; ways for people to engage
> with suppressed aspects of history (including their own histo-
> ries), ways to move *into and out of* rhetorics of authenticity;
> ground rules for communication across lines of difference and
> hierarchy that go beyond politeness but maintain mutual re-
> spect; a systematic approach to the all-important concept of *cul-*
> *tural mediation.* (p. 595)

One way of working with Pratt's essay, of extending its project, would be
to conduct your own local inventory of writing from the contact zone. You
might do this on your own or in teams, with others from your class. Here
are two ways you might organize your search:

1.  You could look for historical documents. A local historical society
    might have documents written by Native Americans ("Indians") to
    the white settlers. There may be documents written by slaves to mas-
    ters or to northern whites. There may be documents written by
    women to men (written by the suffragettes, for example) negotiating
    public positions or rights. There may be documents from any of a
    number of racial or ethnic groups—Hispanic, Jewish, Irish, Italian,
    Polish, Swedish—trying to explain their positions to the mainstream
    culture. There may, perhaps at union halls, be documents written by
    workers to owners. Your own sense of the heritage of your area
    should direct your search.
2.  Or you could look at contemporary documents in the print that is
    around you, texts that you might otherwise overlook. Pratt refers to
    one of the characteristic genres of the Hispanic community, the "*testi-*
    *monio.*" You could look for songs, testimonies, manifestos, statements
    by groups on campus, stories, autobiographies, interviews, letters to
    the editor. You could look at the writing of any marginalized group,
    particularly writing intended, at least in part, to represent the experi-
    ence of outsiders to the dominant culture (or to be in dialogue with
    that culture or to respond to that culture). These documents, if we fol-
    low Pratt's example, would include the work of young children or
    students, including college students.

Once you have completed your inventory, choose a document you
would like to work with and present it carefully and in detail (perhaps in
even greater detail than Pratt's presentation of the *New Chronicle*). You
might imagine that you are presenting this to someone who would not
have seen it and would not know how to read it, at least not as an example
of the literate arts of the contact zone.

. . . . . . . . . . . .

ASSIGNMENT 6

## Revision (Again)
## [Geertz, Limerick, Wideman, Pratt]

Pratt has provided a way to think about the problems of writing about the past or present as they are rooted in culture, history, and ideology (and not simply in the work of an individual writer on his or her text). You can't escape your position in the scene of contact, she argues—there is, in other words, no place outside of history or culture that is pure or free, offering a clear view of the past or others. This does not mean, however, that there is nothing to do. Behind Pratt's essay is a clear concern for improving the "literate arts" of the contact zone, for improving reading or writing.

Go back to the revision you prepared in assignment 4 and take it through one more revision. For the purposes of this sequence, it is a final draft, although few writers ever assume that their work is "finished." For this draft, your goal should be to bring your work to some provisional close. You want to make it as elegant and eloquent (and nicely produced) as you can. You also want to make it as thoughtful and responsible as it can be—that is, you want to show, in your practice, that you are conscious of the problems inherent in writing ethnography or history.

For this draft, whether you are writing an ethnography or a history, you should also add a short final reflective section (like Geertz's "Saying Something of Something"), in which you think about your work in the essay, reflecting not so much on what you have learned as on what you have done. This is a space where you can step out of your role as historian or ethnographer to think about the writing and your work as a writer.

○—○—○—○—○—○—○—○—○—○—○—○—○—○—○

SEQUENCE TEN

# On Difficulty

Virginia Woolf
Michel Foucault
John Edgar Wideman
Ralph Waldo Emerson

*T*HE FIVE ASSIGNMENTS in this sequence invite you to consider the nature of difficult texts and how the problems they pose might be said to belong simultaneously to language, to readers, and to writers. The sequence presents four difficult essays. The assumption the sequence makes is that they are difficult for all readers, not just students, and that the difficulty is necessary, strategic, not a mistake or evidence of a writer's failure.

The first assignment asks you to look closely at Virginia Woolf's "A Room of One's Own" in order to discuss the position in which she puts you, the reader, as she makes her argument. The second asks you to look at Michel Foucault's "Panopticism," particularly as it could be said to present an argument that is at once eloquent yet hard to understand. The third and fourth assignments ask you to look at texts with unusual modes of development (John Edgar Wideman's "Our Time" and Ralph Waldo Emerson's "The American Scholar"). Both of these texts argue that just as writers need to write differently at times, so do readers need to learn to read differently. The assignments ask you to consider how and why. And the last assignment is a retrospective. It asks you to read back over your work and pull together what you've learned into a "theory of difficulty."

•  •  •  •  •  •  •  •  •  •  •  •

## I Will Try to Explain [Woolf]

The first chapter of *A Room of One's Own* begins: "But, you may say, we asked you to speak about women and fiction—what has that got to do with a room of one's own? I will try to explain." There are many unusual gestures and turns in Woolf's prose. And these could be thought of as part of her argument about women's writing—that is, it is possible to see the writing in the essay as an enactment of her argument about the place of a woman writer in the context of a genre representing the voices and habits of men. The opening word of the book, for example, is "but," itself a bit of a surprise. And the explanation that follows moves in several directions, but never straight to the finish. From the very beginning, the text stands contrary to conventional expectations about style, subject, and presentation.

As you reread these chapters and prepare to write about them, make note of the ways Woolf (the writer writing the text) constructs a space for speaker and audience, a kind of imaginary place where a woman can do her work, find a way of speaking, think as she might like to think, and prepare others to listen. Look for interesting and potentially significant ways she defies or transforms what you take to be the conventions of the essay. You might especially want to take a look at those places where Woolf seems to be saying, "I know what I should be doing here, but I won't. I'll do this instead."

Choose four such moments and write an essay in which you discuss Woolf's chapters as a performance, a demonstration of a way of writing that pushes against the usual ways of manipulating words. While there is certainly an argument *in* Woolf's essay, your paper will be about the argument represented *by* the essay, an argument enacted in a way of writing. What is Woolf doing? How might you explain her motives? the effects of her prose? What does she assume of her readers? In what ways might her essay be seen as an example of someone working on the problems of writing? of a woman's writing? And what might this have to do with you, a student in a writing class?

•   •   •   •   •   •   •   •   •   •   •

ASSIGNMENT **2**

## *Foucault's Fabrication* [Foucault]

About three quarters of the way into "Panopticism," Foucault says,

> Our society is one not of spectacle, but of surveillance; under
> the surface of images, one invests bodies in depth; behind the
> great abstraction of exchange, there continues the meticulous,
> concrete training of useful forces; the circuits of communication
> are the supports of an accumulation and a centralization of
> knowledge; the play of signs defines the anchorages of power;
> it is not that the beautiful totality of the individual is ampu-
> tated, repressed, altered by our social order, it is rather that the
> individual is carefully fabricated in it, according to a whole
> technique of forces and bodies. (pp. 333–34)

This prose is eloquent and insists on its importance to our moment and
our society; it is also very hard to read or to paraphrase. Who is doing
what to whom? How do we think about the individual being carefully
fabricated in the social order?

Take this selection as a problem to solve. What is it about? What are its
key arguments, its examples and conclusions? Write an essay that summarizes "Panopticism." Imagine that you are writing for readers who have
read the chapter (although they won't have the pages in front of them)
and who are at sea as to its argument. You will need to take time to present and discuss examples from the text. Your job is to help your readers
figure out what it says. You get the chance to take the lead and be the
teacher. In addition, you should feel free to acknowledge that you don't
understand certain sections even as you write about them.

So how do you write about something you don't completely understand? Here's a suggestion. When you have completed your summary,
read it over and treat it as a draft. Ask questions like these: What have I left
out? What was I tempted to ignore or finesse? Go back to those sections of
the chapter that you ignored and bring them into your essay. Revise by
adding discussions of some of the very sections you don't understand. You
can write about what you think Foucault might be saying—you can, that
is, be cautious and tentative; you can admit that the text is what it is, hard
to read. You don't have to master this text. You do, however, need to see
what you can make of it.

•   •   •   •   •   •   •   •   •   •   •   •

ASSIGNMENT 3

# A Story of Reading [Wideman]

At several points in "Our Time," Wideman interrupts the narrative to discuss his position as a writer telling Robby's story. He describes the problems he faces in writing this piece (or in "reading" the text of his brother's life). You could read this selection, in other words, as an essay about reading and writing. It is Wideman's account of his work.

And, as a narrative, "Our Time" is made up of sections, fragments, different voices. It is left to the reader, in a sense, to put the pieces together and complete the story. There is work for a reader to do, in other words, and one way to account for that work is to call it "practice" or "training." Wideman wants to force a reader's attention by offering a text that makes unusual demands, a text that teaches a reader to read differently. If you think of your experience with the text, of how you negotiated its terrain, what is the story of reading you might tell? In what way do your difficulties parallel Wideman's—at least those he tells us about when he stops to talk about the problems he faces as a writer?

Write an essay in which you tell the story of what it was like to read "Our Time" and compare your experience working with this text with Wideman's account of his own.

A story of reading—this is not a usual school exercise. Usually you are asked what texts mean, not what it was like to read them. As you prepare for this assignment, think back as closely as you can to your experience the first time through. And you will want to reread, looking for how and where Wideman seems to be deliberately working on his reader, defying expectation and directing response. You want to tell a story that is rich in detail, precise in accounting for moments in the text. You want to bring forward the features that can make your story a good story to read—suspense, action, context, drama. Since this is your story, you are one of the characters. You will want to refer to yourself as you were at the moment of reading while also reserving a space for you to speak from your present position, as a person thinking about what it was like to read the text, and as a person thinking about Wideman and about reading. You are telling a story, but you will need to break the narrative (as Wideman breaks his) to account in more general terms for the demands Wideman makes on readers. What habits does he assume a reader will bring to this text? How and why does he want to break them?

• • • • • • • • • • • •

ASSIGNMENT **4**

# *Reading Emerson* [Emerson]

There is no question but that Emerson's text is difficult to read, and the difficulty is not simply a matter of big or unusual words. The text just doesn't *do* what we expect it to do. Some of its elusiveness can be attributed to the time during which it was written—expectations were different then—but this should not keep you from making the most of your responses as a reader. For one thing, it's not completely true; not everyone in the mid-nineteenth century in the United States wrote like Emerson. He was considered to have a distinctive style. For another, it assumes that a nonspecialist cannot or should not read works from the past. One way of imagining your connection to Emerson is to imagine that your encounter with this text is somehow typical, that Emerson is your contemporary.

Take a section of the essay that you find characteristically difficult. (Section II is an interesting one to work with.) Reread it, paying close attention to the experience of reading. Where are you surprised? Where are you confused? How might this be part of a strategy, part of Emerson's design? What is Emerson doing? What is he teaching you to do? This should be an exercise in close reading. You want to pay attention to how sentence leads to sentence, paragraph leads to paragraph, and to notice the ways examples or statements are offered, used, and taken away.

Write an essay in which you describe in close detail the story of what it was like to read this section of "The American Scholar." Tell a story of reading, one where you and Emerson are the main characters—complicated characters, not stick figures (the Naive Student and the Inscrutable Genius). When you are done, see what connections you can make with Emerson's argument—with what he says about the proper relationship between readers and writers. Does he practice what he preaches?

• • • • • • • • • • • •

ASSIGNMENT 5

# A Theory of Difficulty
## [Woolf, Foucault, Wideman, Emerson]

Now that you have worked with these four texts, you are in a good position to review what you have written about each of them in order to say something more general about difficulty—difficulty in writing, difficulty in reading.

Write an essay in which you present a theory of difficulty, a kind of guide, something that might be useful to students who are regularly asked to confront difficult assignments. You will want to work from your previous essays—pulling out sections, revising, reworking examples for this new essay. Don't let your earlier work go unacknowledged. But, at the same time, feel free to move out from these readings to other materials, examples, or situations.

SEQUENCE ELEVEN

# Reading Culture

John Berger
Susan Bordo
Michel Foucault
W. J. T. Mitchell

*I*N THIS SEQUENCE, you will be reading and writing about culture. Not Culture, something you get if you go to the museum or a concert on Sunday, but culture—the images, words, and sounds that pervade our lives and organize and represent our common experience. This sequence invites your reflection on the ways culture "works" in and through the lives of individual consumers.

The difficulty of this sequence lies in the way it asks you to imagine that you are not a sovereign individual, making your own choices and charting the course of your life. This is conceptually difficult, but it can also be distasteful, since we learn at an early age to put great stock in imagining our own freedom. Most of the readings that follow ask you to imagine that you are the product of your culture; that your ideas, feelings, and actions, your ways of thinking and being, are constructed for you by a large, organized, pervasive force (sometimes called history, sometimes called culture, sometimes called ideology). You don't feel this to be the case, but that is part of the power of culture, or so the argument goes. These forces hide themselves. They lead you to believe that their constructions are naturally, inevitably there, that things are the way they are because that is just "the way things are." The assignments in this sequence ask you to read against your common sense. You will be expected to try on the role of the critic—to see how and where it might be useful to recognize complex motives in ordinary expressions.

The authors in this sequence all write as though, through great effort, they could step outside culture to see and criticize its workings. The assignments in this sequence will ask you both to reflect on this type of criticism and to participate in it. The first assignment is an exercise in the kind of historical reading represented by the work of John Berger, a reading designed to take a painting from the context of The Museum or High Culture and to put it back (Berger would say) into the context of history and of the images that dominate daily life. The second and third assignments draw on Susan Bordo's essay, "Hunger as Ideology." Like Berger, Bordo investigates the relationship of images to our sense of the past and our understanding of the present. The fourth assignment turns to Foucault to bring the terms and examples of *Discipline and Punish* into the discussion of ideology, power, and contemporary culture. The fifth turns to W. J. T. Mitchell's study of the photographic essay, a study that allows him a different angle from which to consider the power of words and images. The final assignment is a retrospective and asks you to revise and reconsider the work you have done in this sequence.

•　•　•　•　•　•　•　•　•　•　•　•

ASSIGNMENT 1

## *Looking at Pictures* [Berger]

> Original paintings are silent and still in a sense that information never is. Even a reproduction hung on the wall is not comparable in this respect for in the original the silence and stillness permeate the actual material, the paint, in which one follows the traces of the painter's immediate gestures. This has the effect of closing the distance in time between the painting of the picture and one's own act of looking at it. . . . What we make of that painted moment when it is before our eyes depends upon what we expect of art, and that in turn depends today upon how we have already experienced the meaning of paintings through reproductions. (p. 125)
>
> — JOHN BERGER
> *Ways of Seeing*

While Berger describes original paintings as silent in this passage, it is clear that these paintings begin to speak if one approaches them properly, if one learns to ask "the right questions of the past." Berger demonstrates one route of approach, for example, in his reading of the Hals paintings, where he asks questions about the people and objects and their relationship to the painter and the viewer. What the paintings might be made to say, however, depends upon the viewer's expectations, his or her sense of the questions that seem appropriate or possible. Berger argues that, because of the way art is currently displayed, discussed, and reproduced, the viewer expects only to be mystified.

For this assignment, imagine that you are working against the silence and mystification Berger describes. Go to a museum—or, if that is not possible, to a large-format book of reproductions in the library (or, if that is not possible, to the reproductions in "Ways of Seeing")—and select a painting that seems silent and still, yet invites conversation. Your job is to figure out what sorts of questions to ask, to interrogate the painting, to get it to speak, to engage with the past in some form of dialogue. Write an essay in which you record this process and what you have learned from it. Somewhere in your essay, perhaps at the end, turn back to Berger's chapter to talk about how this process has or hasn't confirmed what you take to be Berger's expectations.

Note: If possible, include with your essay a reproduction of the painting you select. (Check the postcards at the museum gift shop.) In any event, you want to make sure that you describe the painting in sufficient detail for your readers to follow what you say.

•   •   •   •   •   •   •   •   •   •   •   •

ASSIGNMENT 2

# The Ideology of Hunger [Bordo]

Bordo extends an invitation to her students to "bring in examples that appear to violate traditional gender-dualities and the ideological messages contained in them." These, she said, will "display a complicated and bewitching tangle of new possibilities and old patterns of representation."

Write an essay in which you take up Bordo's invitation. On your own, or with a group, collect a set of advertisements (or images from other sources) that represent food and eating, women and men. Find examples and counterexamples to what she takes to be the traditional gender-dualities and the ideological messages contained in them. To present your project to others, you'll need to write descriptions of the ads, as Bordo does, so that your readers will be able to read them (to see them and understand them) as you do. You'll need to place your examples in relation to Bordo's argument about the "old dualities and ideologies" and to what she says about images that "stabilize" and "destabilize." You will need, in other words, to put her terms to work on your examples. Your goal should be to not only reproduce Bordo's project but to extend it, to refine it, to put it to the test. You should find yourself moving toward a statement of your own about the ideology of hunger in present-day America. And you should imagine that you are writing for a reader unfamiliar with Bordo's essay and its key terms.

•  •  •  •  •  •  •  •  •  •  •

A S S I G N M E N T   3

## Ideology and Agency [Bordo, Berger]

In "Hunger as Ideology," Bordo refers to John Berger and his work in *Ways of Seeing*. Both Berger and Bordo are concerned with how we see and read images; both are concerned to correct the ways images are used and read; both trace the ways images serve the interests of money and power; both are writing to get the attention of the public and teach readers how and why they should pay a different kind of attention to the images around them.

For this assignment, use Bordo's work in "Hunger as Ideology" to re-consider Berger's "Ways of Seeing." Write an essay in which you consider the two essays as examples of an ongoing project. As each considers the uses of images, who is doing what to whom? to what end? by what means?

Berger's essay precedes Bordo's by about a quarter of a century. If you look closely at one or two of their examples, and if you look at the larger concerns in their arguments, are they saying the same thing? doing the same work? If so, why? Why is such work still necessary? If not, how do their projects differ? And how might you account for those differences?

•  •  •  •  •  •  •  •  •  •  •

A S S I G N M E N T   4

## On Agency [Foucault]

[The Panopticon] is an important mechanism, for it automa-tizes and disindividualizes power. Power has its principle not so much in a person as in a certain concerted distribution of bodies, surfaces, lights, gazes; in an arrangement whose inter-nal mechanisms produce the relation in which individuals are caught up. The ceremonies, the rituals, the marks by which the sovereign's surplus power was manifested are useless. There is a machinery that assures dissymmetry, disequilibrium, difference. Consequently, it does not matter who exercises power. Any individual, taken almost at random, can operate the machine: in the absence of the director, his family, his friends, his visitors, even his servants. Similarly, it does not matter what motive animates him: the curiosity of the indiscreet, the malice of a child, the thirst for knowledge of a philosopher who wishes to visit this museum of human nature, or the perversity of those who take pleasure in spying and punishing. The more numerous those anonymous and temporary observers are, the greater the risk for the inmate of being surprised and the greater his anxious awareness of being observed. The Panopticon is a marvelous machine which, whatever use one may wish to put it to, produces homogeneous effects of power. (pp. 321–22)

— MICHEL FOUCAULT
*Panopticism*

Foucault's work has changed our ways of thinking about "who is doing what to whom." Write an essay in which you explain Foucault's understanding of the Panopticon as a mechanism of power. You will need to paraphrase Foucault's argument, translate his terms, and, where appropriate, cite and deploy his terms. Present Foucault's account as you understand it, and be willing to talk about what you don't understand—or don't quite understand.

As part of your essay, and in order to examine his argument and his terms, use Foucault as a way of thinking about Bordo and Berger. How might Foucault treat the material they select for their examples? (As you write, it would be strategically useful to limit yourself to one example from each.) How does each of the three writers account for *agency* in their descriptions of the workings of power? What do you make of the differences in their accounts of power and knowledge? What do they imply about how one might live in or understand the world? What might they have to do with the ways you, or people like you, live in and understand the world?

•   •   •   •   •   •   •   •   •   •   •   •   •

ASSIGNMENT 5

# Reading Images [Mitchell]

In the introduction to *Picture Theory*, W. J. T. Mitchell says,

> What we need is a critique of visual culture that is alert to the
> power of images for good and evil and that is capable of dis-
> criminating the variety and historical specificity of their uses.

One way to think about the "variety and historical specificity" of the use
of images is to look at the examples Mitchell provides in this chapter, examples of writers using images as the subjects of their writing, but also the
example of his own use and "reading" of those images.

At times, Mitchell is quick to include us in his ways of reading. In response to the Walker Evans photograph of Annie Mae Gudger, he says:

> There is something deeply disturbing, even disagreeable, about
> this (unavoidable) aestheticizing response to what after all is a
> real person in desperately impoverished circumstances. Why
> should we have a right to look on this woman and find her fa-
> tigue, pain, and anxiety beautiful? (p. 534)

His readers are written into the "we" of such sentences. At times he highlights the "reading" represented by the writer of the photo-essay, as he
does, for example, in his account of Roland Barthes use of Nadar's "The
Artist's Mother (or Wife)." And at times he singles himself out as an individual case, as, for example, when he says of the postcard image of the
"Arabian Woman with the Yachmak":

> Can an American observer, in particular, see these pho-
> tographs as anything more than quaint, archaic pornography,
> hauntingly beautiful relics of a lost colonial era, "collector's
> items" for a coffee-table book? I don't have a simple answer to
> this question, but my first impulse is to register a feeling of
> *impotence* in the face of these women, whose beauty is now
> mixed with danger, whose nakedness now becomes a veil that
> has always excluded me from the labyrinth of their world.
> (pp. 547–48)

Write an essay in which you present a close reading of Mitchell's text,
looking specifically at the ways it figures (or represents) readers reading.
What variety of readings does he chart? Where and how are they histori-
cally specific? What lessons are there to be learned from these examples?
What does Mitchell seem to be saying about appropriate ways of reading?
Where would you position him in relation to Berger and Bordo?

. . . . . . . . . . . .

ASSIGNMENT 6

## *Visual Culture*
## [Berger, Bordo, Foucault, Mitchell]

Three of the writers you have been reading—Berger, Bordo and Mitchell—are concerned about the use and status of images, concerned with what happens to them (and to us) when they are packaged, deployed, reproduced, turned into text. For all of these writers, the use of images is a sign of the health of the individual and the health of the culture.

Write an essay in which you revise and bring together the essays you have written for this sequence. You can treat them as individual statements, revising each, ordering them, writing an introduction, conclusion, and necessary transitions. Or you can revise more radically and combine what you have into some other form.

Your goal should be to bring the writers into conversation with each other, to use one selection to weigh, evaluate, and understand another. And your goal should be to find a way, yourself, to enter the conversation—to find a space, a voice, a set of examples and concerns. Where and how do these issues touch you and people like you (some group for whom you feel authorized to speak)? Where do you feel a similar urgency? Where and how would you qualify or challenge the position of these other writers? Where and how would you join them?

# The Uses of Reading

Ralph Waldo Emerson and Edward T. Channing
Alice Walker
David Bartholomae and Anthony Petrosky

*T*HE PURPOSE of this sequence is to provide context for Emerson's "The American Scholar." The first assignment asks you to think about the practical and institutional implications of Emerson's argument. It was offered, after all, to students and teachers and hoped to have bearing on what went on in classes like the class you are taking, classes required on almost every campus in the United States. The second assignment asks for a close reading of the essay. It asks you to think about the prose itself as a lesson in reading. The third assignment provides a long excerpt from one of Edward T. Channing's *Lectures Read to the Seniors in Harvard College,* lectures well known to Emerson. The fourth assignment asks you to consider Alice Walker's sense of an African American literary heritage. The final assignment returns attention to attitudes toward reading in contemporary American education, with *Ways of Reading* offered as an example.

. . . . . . . . . . .

A S S I G N M E N T  **1**

## *The Mind of the Past* [Emerson]

Let's imagine Emerson himself as a teacher who wants to have his students read "The American Scholar" (perhaps along with some other selections from this anthology). What kind of assignment might he give? What, that is, would he ask you to *do* with the reading? (You might use the assignments in *Ways of Reading* as a point of reference. Are they Emersonian?) Write an essay that considers both how, in practice, a modern teacher might encourage an Emersonian use of books and what, so far as you are concerned, a modern student might get from such an exercise.

. . . . . . . . . . .

A S S I G N M E N T  **2**

## *Figuring Readers* [Emerson]

There is no question but that Emerson's text is difficult to read, and the difficulty is not simply a matter of big or unusual words. The text just doesn't *do* what we expect it to do. Some of its elusiveness can be attributed to the time during which it was written—expectations were different then—but this should not keep you from making the most of your responses as a reader. For one thing, it's not completely true; not everyone in the mid-nineteenth century in the United States wrote like Emerson. He was considered to have a distinctive style. For another, it assumes that a nonspecialist cannot or should not read works from the past. One way of imagining your connection to Emerson is to imagine that your encounter with this text is somehow typical—that Emerson is your contemporary.

Take a section of the essay that you find characteristically difficult. (Section II is an interesting one to work with.) Reread it, paying close attention to the experience of reading. Where are you surprised? Where are you confused? How might this be part of a strategy, part of Emerson's design? What is Emerson doing? What is he teaching you to do? This should be an exercise in close reading. You want to pay attention to how sentence leads to sentence, paragraph leads to paragraph, and to notice the ways examples or statements are offered, used, and taken away.

Write an essay in which you describe in close detail the story of what it was like to read this section of "The American Scholar." Tell a story of reading, one where you and Emerson are the main characters—complicated characters, not stick figures (the Naive Student and the Inscrutable Genius). When you are done, see what connections you can make with Emerson's argument—with what he says about the proper relationship between readers and writers. Does he practice what he preaches?

• • • • • • • • • • • •

ASSIGNMENT 3

## What Good Use Can I Make of Reading?
## [Channing, Emerson]

The following is an excerpt from one of Edward T. Channing's *Lectures Read to the Seniors in Harvard College* (1856). The lecture was titled "A Writer's Preparation." The excerpt responds to the question, "What good use can I make of reading as part of my preparation?" Channing was the Boylston Professor of Rhetoric and Oratory at Harvard from 1819 to 1851. Emerson was a student at Harvard from 1817 to 1821.

Let's imagine that Emerson attended Channing's lecture. He was certainly in a position to be influenced by Channing's argument. The question is not whether Emerson had Channing's lecture in mind when he wrote "The American Scholar." Channing, of course, was not the only one to be thinking about and writing about the use of books. At the same time, however, every writer in New England in the mid-nineteenth century could be said to have had Channing in their minds. He was an important figure and held an influential position. He was certainly a force in the minds of those students who were in Emerson's audience, if only because of his presence on campus.

How might one use Channing's lecture to contextualize and to think about Emerson's argument? As you reread "The American Scholar," both its style and its argument, how would you characterize Emerson's lecture in relation to the one printed below by Channing? Emerson is speaking to the next generation of students, students who (perhaps) have heard or will have heard Channing's lecture. Reading these two texts together, how might you reconstruct and understand what Emerson was saying in his lecture about the influence of "the mind of the Past,—in whatever form, whether of literature, of art, of institutions, that mind is inscribed"? If Channing was in the audience, what was Emerson saying to him? to his students?

## Lectures Read to the Seniors in Harvard College

At school and college I suppose books are looked upon, partly, as requiring of [the student] a certain amount of hard work, for some mysterious good that they are to yield by and by. As connected with his exercises in composition, they are consulted upon particular subjects for facts, thoughts and illustrations to be applied directly to a present task; and probably some favorite author is remembered for fascinating peculiarities of style which, with the natural love of imitation in early life, the student is pleased to exhibit on his own page. There is no cause for wonder that such a use is made of resources so near at hand, by one who is now for the first time called on to perform exercises so grave and so alarming to his self-diffidence. The research, moreover, may be useful beyond its serving a present emergency. The bad effects of the practice it is not easy to prevent, because it is not easy so to define and press them that they will be felt or even apprehended by the young. The indirect benefit of reading and by far the highest,—I mean its exercising the mind, forming the judgment and taste, and breathing a spirit, far better than that of emulation, the spirit of independence and self-reliance,—this indirect effect of good books, though never wholly lost upon the young, is yet scarcely valued as it should be till we reach a time of life, when we are disposed to examine a little both the influences which have shaped our minds, and those which, unhappily, failed to make a decided impression.

Many are the complaints which are brought against books. If they were confined to our ill selection, or to hurtful habits of reading, they might, though very seasonable, attract little notice. But books are said to make us indolent and self-indulgent; to create a love of plodding accumulation or a morbid taste for bibliographical curiosities; a vain self-complacency in the amount of our reading, such as is never produced by other modes of acquisition; and a general disposition to stop at what we read, to acquiesce in opinions, and take pride in calling men masters. I cannot undertake to refute in detail what I think to be wrong in these accusations, or to state with proper qualifications what is unquestionably true in them, and wisely intended for counsel and warning. A brief notice of the last complaint is all that I propose to myself, and merely for the purpose of considering the supposed unfavorable influence of reading on originality. I put out of view all who can properly be called plagiarists, and have little more respect for those who reject, as far as they may, all foreign aid.

The only question is, do books make us less independent, less ourselves, than any other source of knowledge or exhilaration? Some contend that this is the ordinary effect of high cultivation and abundant reading; that there will always be less of character in literature where colleges, libraries, teachers and learned associations abound; and they see the want increasing with the multiplication and lower prices of books. If we doubt this influence and support ourselves by citing eminent examples to the contrary, they treat those as exceptions or explain away their authority, and still maintain that the fewer direct helps you give the writer, the better. At first thought, originality would seem to be too strong a quality to be hurtfully affected by circumstances of any kind. Let us try to see what it is, that we may better understand its perils.

The word *original,* is commonly used to denote the character of a mind which, from its constitution and natural action,—not from weak and random eccentricity, but from sound, inherent activity,—takes its own view of things and makes its own use of them. Originality supposes that we draw from original sources; but not in the same sense that the voyager or naturalist draws absolutely new facts from exploring oceans or the kingdoms of nature. It is not of the least moment whether a subject be just brought to the notice of men, or be the oldest and commonest; nor yet from what quarter or in what way it comes; for, if an original mind acts at all, it must act up to its character; it must reflect itself upon whatever it studies.* So that we are justified in saying that what it draws from its subject owes, in one sense, its existence to this mind, and bears its stamp.

It belongs to its nature to spread itself over everything that comes in its way, if there be any possibility of sympathy; not, however, for the purpose of saying something new and strange, but because it loves and seeks exercise. Hence it is always likely to be well filled; not simply that it has ample collections, but because of its power to give new forms to things and convert them to its special use. It is rich, not by hoarding borrowed treasures but by turning everything into gold. So cheerful, healthy and active does this quality seem to be, that we are almost constrained to think that it must manifest itself most strongly and generously when it is exposed to a variety of objects and interests.

Some, however, believe that isolation is peculiarly favorable to originality. No doubt a hermit may be original in the absence both of men and of books; but not because of his solitude or his privations. His condition would look very unpromising to most men. Imagine him forever by himself, musing upon himself, revolving a few favorite opinions, and buried in speculations all of one character. This, certainly, is the most perfect seclusion. But his habits seem more likely to produce harsh and narrow peculiarity than expansive and animated individuality. He will probably soon have much of the oddness, of the constant reference to self and repetition of self which we commonly observe in solitary men. He may learn to exaggerate trifles because they are his, and remain stationary in the contemplation of his darling conceits. There is good reason to think that the mind may be made as feeble in its whole character by turning perpetually upon itself and refusing help or impulse from abroad, as by immersing itself in books and resting in the thoughts and reports of other men. There are madmen and sluggards in cells as well as in libraries. So that, on the

---

* 'Originality never works more fruitfully than in a soil rich and deep with the foliage of ages.' —*Westminster Review,* January, 1854.

whole, it does not belong to us to say that a man's condition, tastes, pursuits, his great learning or his meagre learning, have anything to do with the manifestation of original qualities. This seems to lie wholly with himself.

A book then may be as strictly an original source as anything else. As giving us information only, it is sometimes as new and animating as the ocean to an inland man. Besides, what nobler or more original study can we have than that of a man in his writings,—a contemplative being,—and often more fully disclosed to us there, than he could be in a life of action; and brought near to us for our minute inspection and full sympathy.

But there is a vague notion that a book differs from all other literary sources in one important point, so far as the present question is concerned; and the distinction is, that what we read has already been revolved by a human mind. The germ or element of thought, once common property, is no longer in its simple state. It is appropriated by being modified, colored, combined with other substances and capable of peculiar application after being subjected to this hidden transmutation. A charm is now thrown round it, a consecration that must be violated. A seal, not to be mistaken, is set upon it, and you cannot use the thought unless by taking it avowedly just as you find it. And the same, of course, would be as true of what we hear as of what we read.

This theory of property and inviolability is pleasing and not without foundation. But what a strange idea must the objector have of the use we may lawfully make of another man's thoughts. We may never have occasion to borrow them; but is this the only or even the best service to which we can honestly put them? Do we wrong the owner because we are warmed into admiration, strengthened, purified, made happy by his words, and better prepared for our peculiar work? "Does he suffer loss because our lamp is lighted at his?"

But there are more direct and equally honorable modes of using what others have written. We frequently hear it said, in no malicious sense, that a man makes what he reads his own. It did not pass into his memory to remain there in its original shape, like an historical date or the buried talent. It exercised his mind and received a character from it. He does not seek for it in his memory as a laid-up treasure; it is not copied as a brilliant passage from his common-place book; but it springs up in connection with his own thoughts, and becomes so intimately a part of them that he does not suspect that he is indebted for it to another. The first proprietor, should he recognize it, would have no other feeling than of delight to see his property in such good hands and turned to so good account. This, to be sure, is not the highest use we can make of another man's mind, but it will serve to answer a somewhat over-refined objection.

That a student is exposed to perils from his constant association with great writers is not disputed. I refer not to the grossest of these perils,— such as the temptation to take the thoughts or copy the style of another,—

nor yet to the subtle enchantment which draws one unconsciously into imitation of his special favorite or of the popular idol of the day. There is danger from terror as well as from love. A man may be discouraged by contemplating excellence. His sense of this excellence is of itself proof of no small capacity and resource on his own part, and, if left to its natural and free action, would swell into generous, sustaining admiration and reverence. But it may also create self-distrust; and this may degenerate, if not into envy, yet, into despair or peevish uneasiness at the idea that he cannot reach another's elevation. Why, rather, does there not spring up the glowing thought,—I, too, have a height before me, which none other may reach? Of course it cannot be his ambition to do precisely what another has done. He would be content to do as well in a different direction. But who is to pass upon the question of comparative merit? There is no common measure of excellence any more than of minds. And, in this indefinite state of the case, (the best possible for us all,) each must do his own work according to his power and natural tendencies.

Goethe told Eckermann that if he had been an Englishman he should have been over-powered by Shakspeare.* He must have tried to avoid him and choose a new course for himself. A monstrous delusion, probably, even in his own case, and certainly one which does not appear to have led Shakspeare's countrymen astray. To shun greatness in another, for whatever cause, is as spiritless as servile waiting upon it. The mere instituting of comparisons between ourselves and others is a proof, or, at any rate, the beginning of weakness. It not only blinds us to our own secret forces, but prevents our seeing anything truly. We gradually lose the power of discerning what is good and beautiful in the very writers who have gained this fatal possession of our admiration. They disown us, and we perceive it not. At last, we are led to believe that readers will adopt our rule of estimation, and judge us, not for ourselves, but according as we stand in relation to men of established name.

To one who is thus perplexed and dispirited, the simple truth is the best direction: You will never be judged by competent readers with any such reference, or with any reference that does not concern yourself alone. You will not be condemned for being as bad as another, or worse,—or praised for being as good as another, or better. All will depend upon the never-deceiving evidence that what you do is your own,—that it proceeds from your own resources or your own barrenness.

　　　　　　　　　　　　　　　　— EDWARD T. CHANNING
　　　　　　　　　　　　　　　*Lectures Read to the Seniors in*
　　　　　　　　　　　　　　　*Harvard College* (1856)

---

* If I remember right, he was speaking of the advantage there is in nations' having different languages.

• • • • • • • • • • •

ASSIGNMENT 4

## *Contrary Instincts* [Walker]

In "In Search of Our Mothers' Gardens," Alice Walker uses the term "contrary instincts" when she discusses Phillis Wheatley. The problem for Walker (and others) is that Wheatley would idolize a fair-haired white woman as a goddess of liberty rather than turn to herself as a model or to the black women who struggled mightily for their identities and their liberty.

Walker's essay is filled with allusions to black women artists: Bessie Smith, Roberta Flack, Phillis Wheatley, Zora Neale Hurston; in fact, the essay serves as a kind of book list or reader's guide; it suggests a program of reading. (The references aren't strictly to black women. Jean Toomer was a man and Virginia Woolf was white.)

As you reread this essay, pay attention to the names. (Go to the library and track down some you don't know and take a look at some of their work; skimming is fine.) Write an essay in which you reflect on the use Walker invites of the minds of the past (including books and writers). Would you say that she is working in the tradition of Emerson and "The American Scholar"? If not, how would you characterize her position in relation to his?

• • • • • • • • • • •

ASSIGNMENT 5

## *Ways of Reading*
## [Bartholomae and Petrosky]

Reread the "Introduction" to *Ways of Reading*. It, too, takes a position on the proper use of books. Given the work that you have done in this sequence, you are prepared to read it not as a simple statement of "how things are" but as a position taken in a tradition of concern over the role of reading in the preparation of Americans. Write an essay in which you consider the introduction in relation to Emerson, Channing, Walker, and the ways they articulate the proper uses of reading. Where would you place this book (or its goals as stated in the "Introduction") in relation to an Emersonian tradition? And what about you—do you see your own interests and concerns, the values you hold (or those held by people you admire), the abilities you might need or hope to gain—do you see these represented in what you have read?

# SEQUENCE THIRTEEN

# Ways of Seeing

### John Berger
### W. J. T. Mitchell

*T*HIS SEQUENCE works closely with John Berger's "Ways of Seeing" and his argument about the relationship between a spectator (one who sees and "reads" a painting) and knowledge, in his case a knowledge of history. The opening assignment asks for a summary account of Berger's argument. Assignment 2 then asks you to put Berger to the test by extending his project and producing a "reading" of a painting of your own choice. The third assignment turns again to Berger, this time to his use of paintings by Rembrandt and Caravaggio. You are asked in assignment 4 to turn to W. J. T. Mitchell's argument about words and images as a way of providing context to Berger (and an additional set of terms and concerns). The final assignment is a revision of your reading of a painting, this time with additional commentary to theorize and contextualize the work that you have done.

•  •  •  •  •  •  •  •  •  •  •  •  •

ASSIGNMENT 1

# *Ways of Seeing* [Berger]

We are not saying that there is nothing left to experience before
original works of art except a sense of awe because they have
survived. The way original works of art are usually approached—through museum catalogues, guides, hired cassettes, etc.—is not the only way they might be approached.
When the art of the past ceases to be viewed nostalgically, the
works will cease to be holy relics—although they will never re-
become what they were before the age of reproduction. We are
not saying original works of art are now useless. (pp. 124–25)

– JOHN BERGER
*Ways of Seeing*

Berger argues that there are barriers to vision, problems in the ways
we see or don't see original works of art, problems that can be located in
and overcome by strategies of approach. For Berger, what we lose if we
fail to see properly is history: "If we 'saw' the art of the past, we would situate ourselves in history. When we are prevented from seeing it, we are
being deprived of the history which belongs to us" (p. 108). It is not hard
to figure out who, according to Berger, prevents us from seeing the art of
the past. He says it is the ruling class. It *is* difficult, however, to figure out
what he believes gets in the way and what all this has to do with history.

For this assignment, write an essay explaining what, as you read
Berger, gets in the way when we look at paintings, and what it is that we
might do to overcome the barriers to vision (and to history). Imagine that
you are writing for someone interested in art, perhaps preparing to go to a
museum, but someone who has not read Berger's essay. You will, that is,
need to be careful in summary and paraphrase.

. . . . . . . . . . . .

A S S I G N M E N T  **2**

# A Painting in Writing [Berger]

> Original paintings are silent and still in a sense that informa-
> tion never is. Even a reproduction hung on a wall is not compa-
> rable in this respect for in the original the silence and stillness
> permeate the actual material, the paint, in which one follows
> the traces of the painter's immediate gestures. This has the ef-
> fect of closing the distance in the time between the painting of
> the picture and one's own act of looking at it. . . . What we
> make of that painted moment when it is before our eyes de-
> pends upon what we expect of art, and that in turn depends
> today upon how we have already experienced the meaning of
> paintings through reproductions. (p. 125)
>
> — JOHN BERGER
> *Ways of Seeing*

While Berger describes original paintings as silent in this passage, it is
clear that these paintings begin to speak if one approaches them properly,
if one learns to ask "the right questions of the past." Berger demonstrates
one route of approach, for example, in his reading of the Hals paintings,
where he asks questions about the people and objects and their relationships to the painter and the viewer. What the paintings might be made to
say, however, depends upon the viewer's expectations, his or her sense of
the questions that seem appropriate or possible. Berger argues that, because of the way art is currently displayed, discussed, and reproduced,
the viewer expects only to be mystified.

For this paper, imagine that you are working against the silence and
mystification Berger describes. Go to a museum—or, if that is not possible,
to a large-format book of reproductions in the library (or, if that is not possible, to the reproductions in this essay)—and select a painting that seems
silent and still, yet invites conversation. Your job is to figure out what
sorts of questions to ask, to interrogate the painting, to get it to speak, to
engage with the past in some form of dialogue. Write an essay in which
you record this process and what you have learned from it. Somewhere in
your paper, perhaps at the end, turn back to Berger's essay and speak to it
about how this process has or hasn't confirmed what you take to be
Berger's expectations.

Note: If possible, include with your essay a reproduction of the painting you select. (Check the postcards at the museum gift shop.) In any

event, you want to make sure that you describe the painting in sufficient detail for your readers to follow what you say.

. . . . . . . . . . .

ASSIGNMENT 3

## *Berger Writing* [Berger]

> If the new language of images were used differently, it would, through its use, confer a new kind of power. Within it we could begin to define our experiences more precisely in areas where words are inadequate. . . . Not only personal experience, but also the essential historical experience of our relation to the past: that is to say the experience of seeking to give meaning to our lives, of trying to understand the history of which we can become the active agents. (p. 127)
>
> — JOHN BERGER
> *Ways of Seeing*

As a writer, Berger is someone who uses images (including some of the great paintings of the Western tradition) "to define . . . experience more precisely in areas where words are inadequate."

In a wonderful book, *And Our Faces, My Heart, Brief as Photos,* a book that is both a meditation on time and space and a long love letter (if you can imagine such a combination), Berger writes about paintings to say what he wants to say to his lover. We have included two examples, descriptions of Rembrandt's *Woman in Bed* and Caravaggio's *The Calling of St. Matthew.*

Read these as examples, as lessons in how and why to look at, to value, to think with, to write about paintings. Then use these (or one of them) as a way of thinking about the concluding section of "Ways of Seeing" (pp. 125–27). You can assume that your readers have read Berger's essay but have difficulty grasping what he is saying in that final section, particularly since it is a section that seems to call for action, asking the reader to do something. Of what use might Berger's example be in trying to understand what we might do with and because of paintings? How is his writing different from yours? Would you attribute these differences to training and education? What else?

•  •  •  •  •  •  •  •  •  •  •  •

ASSIGNMENT **4**

## *Picture Theory* [Berger, Mitchell]

In "Ways of Seeing," John Berger says "original paintings are silent and still in a sense that information never is." Both Berger and W. J. T. Mitchell, in "The Photographic Essay: Four Case Studies" are interested in the use of images, what happens to them when they are packaged, deployed, reproduced, turned into text. For both, the use of images is a sign of the health of the individual and the health of the culture.

Write an essay in which you use Mitchell's essay to weigh, evaluate, and understand Berger, both the Berger of "Ways of Seeing" and the Berger who speaks for Rembrandt's *Woman in Bed* and Caravaggio's *The Calling of St. Matthew*. You will need, of course, to take time to summarize what Mitchell says and to establish his position on the relationship of words and images. And you will need to think (as Mitchell might think) about the difference between photographs and paintings and what is at stake in providing a written account of a painted image.

Once you have established his point of view, turn to Berger, particularly the example he provides of someone who places words next to images. Perhaps the questions to ask would be these: What relationship between painting and writing do [these examples] articulate? What tropes of differentiation govern the division of labor between photographer [or painter] and writer, image and text, the viewer and the reader?

•  •  •  •  •  •  •  •  •  •  •  •

ASSIGNMENT **5**

## *Revision* [Mitchell, Berger]

For this assignment, go back to the essay you wrote for assignment 2, your representation of a painting, and revise it. You should imagine that your work is both the work of reconsideration (rethinking, looking again, changing what you have written) and addition (filling in the gaps, considering other positions and points of view, moving in new directions, completing what you have begun). As you do this work, you can draw on the comments you have received from your instructor and (perhaps) from other students in your class.

As you work on addition, please also add a section of commentary in which you bring Mitchell and Berger, their terms and arguments, to bear on what you have written. You can imagine that as part of your essay; or you can imagine it as a separate piece, as an introduction, afterword, or coda.

# Working with the Past

Richard Rodriguez and Richard Hoggart
Carolyn Kay Steedman
Harriet Jacobs
Alice Walker

*T*HIS SEQUENCE takes a close and extended look at the relations between a writer and the past, including that part of the past which is
represented by other books and by tradition and convention. The point of
the sequence is to examine instances where authors directly or indirectly
work under the influence of others. Much of the usual talk about "creativity" and "originality" hides the ways in which all texts allude to others,
the ways all draw upon (and sometimes, revise) the work of the past. By
erasing the past, readers give undue attention to an author's "genius" or
independence, losing sight of the larger cultural and historical field within
which (and sometimes against which) a writer works. (And, while this
connection is not highlighted in the sequence, it is possible for you to see
your own work with *Ways of Reading* mirrored in the work of these other
writers. As you write in response to their work, they write in response to
others'.)

The first assignment gives precise, material definition to the past, representing it in an extended passage from Richard Hoggart's *The Uses of Literacy*. Hoggart is a British cultural critic, the son of working class parents,
who writes in the section included here about "the scholarship boy"—that
is, the working class boy in a more elite educational environment. Richard
Rodriguez, in "The Achievement of Desire," alludes to and quotes from

this section of Hoggart's book. The assignment asks you to look at the larger text from which Rodriguez drew to ask questions about what he missed, what he left out, and how he read.

The next two assignments consider the "prior text" as something written more deeply, broadly, and generally into the culture and its memory. Carolyn Kay Steedman writes, for example, about the ways in which her experience wouldn't conform to the "central" or "official" stories of childhood and family, the stories, she said, "people tell themslevs in order to explain how they got to the place they currently inhabit." The final three assignments work with Harriet Jacobs's autobiographical narrative, "Incidents in the Life of a Slave Girl," and Alice Walker's "In Search of Our Mothers' Gardens." Readers are often tempted to read the Jacobs narrative as, in a sense, coming from nowhere, since the stereotypical figure of the slave is of someone who cannot read and write. It is hard for readers to place Jacobs in relation to either slave culture or the culture of American literacy. These assignments ask you to imagine both Jacobs's representation of her own past through the collection of "incidents" that make up her narrative and her relationship to other texts, represented by the assumptions she makes about her readers and the way they will read. With Walker, we return to a more direct discussion of tradition and legacy, this time with particular reference to the legacy of African American women's writing. This sequence is accompanied by a minisequence, "Working with the Past (II)" (p. 888). This alternative sequence provides similar assignments but with different readings. They can be substituted for assignments in the opening sequence.

• • • • • • • • • • •

ASSIGNMENT 1

## *The Scholarship Boy* [Rodriguez, Hoggart]

At the end of this assignment, you will find an extended section from Richard Hoggart's *The Uses of Literacy*. This is the book Rodriguez found in the British Museum, the book he used, he says, to "frame the meaning of my academic success." The section here is the one that surrounds the passages Rodriguez cites in "The Achievement of Desire." Read the Hoggart excerpt and think about these questions: How might you compare Rodriguez's version of the "scholarship boy" with Hoggart's? How might you explain the importance of Hoggart's book to Rodriguez? What kind of reader is the Rodriguez who is writing "The Achievement of Desire"—is he still a "scholarship boy" or is that description no longer appropriate?

You could look at the relationship between Rodriguez and Hoggart as a case study in the possible relations between a writer and a prior text or between a student and a teacher. Read the two together, taking notes to assist such a comparative reading. As you read Rodriguez's discussion of Hoggart's book, pay attention to both the terms and passages Rodriguez selects and those he ignores, and pay attention to what Rodriguez *does* with what he selects. Look closely at how Rodriguez reads and presents Hoggart's text.

As you read Hoggart's account of the scholarship boy, try to read from outside Rodriguez's point of view. How else might these passages be read? In what ways might Hoggart be said to be saying what Rodriguez says he is saying? In what ways might he be said to be saying something else, something Rodriguez misses or ignores? In what ways might Hoggart be said to be making a different argument, telling a different story? What position or point of view or set of beliefs would authorize this other reading, the reading from outside Rodriguez's point of view? And, if you can establish this "alternative" reading, what does that tell you about the position or point of view or set of beliefs that authorize Rodriguez's use of the text?

As you prepare to write about Rodriguez's use of Hoggart, think about how you will describe his performance. What, for example, might you attribute to strategy, to Rodriguez's intent? What might you attribute to blindness (a failure to see or notice something in the text)? What might you attribute to the unconscious (a fear of the text, a form of repression, a desire to transform the text into something else)? These are conventional ways of telling the story of reading. What use are they to your project? Can you imagine others?

Write an essay in which you discuss Rodriguez as an example of a reader and writer working with a prior text. Your goal should be to understand Rodriguez and "The Achievement of Desire" better but also to think about the implications of his "case" for readers and writers in the undergraduate curriculum.


## A Scholarship Boy

> For my part I am very sorry for him. It is an uneasy lot at best, to be what we call highly taught and yet not to enjoy: to be present at this great spectacle of life and never to be liberated from a small hungry shivering self.
>
> — GEORGE ELIOT


This is a difficult chapter to write, though one that should be written. As in other chapters, I shall be isolating a group of related trends: but the consequent dangers of over-emphasis are here especially acute. The three immediately preceding chapters have discussed attitudes which could from one point of view appear to represent a kind of poise. But the people most affected by the attitudes now to be examined—the "anxious and the uprooted"—are to be recognised primarily by their lack of poise, by their uncertainty. About the self-indulgences which seem to satisfy many in their class they tend to be unhappily superior: they are much affected by the cynicism which affects almost everyone, but this is likely to increase their lack of purpose rather than tempt them to "cash in" or to react into further indulgence.

In part they have a sense of loss which affects some in all groups. With them the sense of loss is increased precisely because they are emotionally uprooted from their class, often under the stimulus of a stronger critical intelligence or imagination, qualities which can lead them into an unusual self-consciousness before their own situation (and make it easy for a sympathiser to dramatise their *"Angst"*). Involved with this may be a physical uprooting from their class through the medium of the scholarship system. A great many seem to me to be affected in this way, though only a very small proportion badly; at one boundary the group includes psychotics; at the other, people leading apparently normal lives but never without an underlying sense of some unease.

It will be convenient to speak first of the nature of the uprooting which some scholarship boys experience. I have in mind those who, for a number of years, perhaps for a very long time, have a sense of no longer really belonging to any group. We all know that many do find a poise in their new situations. There are "declassed" experts and specialists who go into their own spheres after the long scholarship climb has led them to a Ph.D. There are brilliant individuals who become fine administrators and officials, and find themselves thoroughly at home. There are some, not necessarily so gifted, who reach a kind of poise which is yet not a passivity nor even a failure in awareness, who are at ease in their new group without any ostentatious adoption of the protective colouring of that group, and who have an easy relationship with their working-class relatives, based not on a form of patronage but on a just respect. Almost every working-class boy who goes through the process of further education by scholarships finds himself chafing against his environment during adolescence. He is at the friction-point of two cultures; the test of his real education lies in his ability, by about the age of twenty-five, to smile at his father with his whole face and to respect his flighty young sister and his slower brother. I shall be concerned with those for whom the uprooting is particularly troublesome, not because I underestimate the gains which this kind of selection gives, nor because I wish to stress the more depressing features in contemporary life, but because the difficulties of some people illuminate much in the wider discussion of cultural change. Like transplanted stock, they react to a widespread drought earlier than those who have been left in their original soil.

I am sometimes inclined to think that the problem of self-adjustment is, in general, especially difficult for those working-class boys who are only moderately endowed, who have talent sufficient to separate them from the majority of their working-class contemporaries, but not to go much farther. I am not implying a correlation between intelligence and lack of unease; intellectual people have their own troubles: but this kind of anxiety often seems most to afflict those in the working-classes who have been pulled one stage away from their original culture and yet have not the intellectual equipment which would then cause them to move on to join the "declassed" professionals and experts. In one sense, it is true, no one is ever "declassed"; and it is interesting to see how this occasionally obtrudes (particularly today, when ex-working-class boys move in all the managing areas of society)—in the touch of insecurity, which often appears as an undue concern to establish "presence" in an otherwise quite professional professor, in the intermittent rough homeliness of an important executive and committee-man, in the tendency to vertigo which betrays a lurking sense of uncertainty in a successful journalist.

But I am chiefly concerned with those who are self-conscious and yet not self-aware in any full sense, who are as a result uncertain, dissatisfied, and gnawed by self-doubt. Sometimes they lack will, though they have intelligence, and "it takes will to cross this waste." More often perhaps, though they have as much will as the majority, they have not sufficient to resolve the complex tensions which their uprooting, the peculiar problems of their particular domestic settings, and the uncertainties common to the time create.

As childhood gives way to adolescence and that to manhood, this kind of boy tends to be progressively cut off from the ordinary life of his group. He is marked out early: and here I am thinking not so much of his teachers in the "elementary" school as of fellow-members of his family. " 'E's got brains," or " 'E's bright," he hears constantly; and in part the tone is one of pride and admiration. He is in a way cut off by his parents as much as by his talent which urges him to break away from his group. Yet on their side this is not altogether from admiration: " 'E's got brains," yes, and he is expected to follow the trail that opens. But there can also be a limiting quality in the tone with which the phrase is used; character counts more. Still, he has brains—a mark of pride and almost a brand; he is heading for a different world, a different sort of job.

He has to be more and more alone, if he is going to "get on." He will have, probably unconsciously, to oppose the ethos of the hearth, the intense gregariousness of the working-class family group. Since everything centres upon the living-room, there is unlikely to be a room of his own; the bedrooms are cold and inhospitable, and to warm them or the front room, if there is one, would not only be expensive, but would require an imaginative leap—out of the tradition—which most families are not capable of making. There is a corner of the living-room table. On the other side Mother is ironing, the wireless is on, someone is singing a snatch of song, or Father says intermittently whatever comes into his head. The boy has to cut himself off mentally, so as to do his homework, as well as he can. In summer, matters can be easier; bedrooms are warm enough to work in: but only a few boys, in my experience, take advantage of this. For the boy is himself (until he reaches, say, the upper forms) very much of *both* the worlds of home and school. He is enormously obedient to the dictates of the world of school, but emotionally still strongly wants to continue as part of the family circle.

So the first big step is taken in the progress towards membership of a different sort of group or to isolation, when such a boy has to resist the central domestic quality of working-class life. This is true, perhaps particularly true, if he belongs to a happy home, because the happy homes are often the more gregarious. Quite early the stress on solitariness, the encouragement towards strong self-concern, is felt; and this can make it more difficult for him to belong to another group later.

At his "elementary" school, from as early as the age of eight, he is likely to be in some degree set apart, though this may not happen if his school is in an area which each year provides a couple of dozen boys from "the scholarship form" for the grammar-schools. But probably he is in an area predominantly working-class and his school takes up only a few scholarships a year. The situation is altering as the number of scholarships increases, but in any case human adjustments do not come as abruptly as administrative changes.

He is similarly likely to be separated from the boys' groups outside the home, is no longer a full member of the gang which clusters round the lamp-posts in the evenings; there is homework to be done. But these are the male groups among which others in his generation grew up, and his detachment from them is emotionally linked with one more aspect of his home situation—that he now tends to be closer to the women of the house than to the men. This is true, even if his father is not the kind who dismisses books and reading as "a woman's game." The boy spends a large part of his time at the physical centre of the home, where the woman's spirit rules, quietly getting on with his work whilst his mother gets on with her jobs—the father not yet back from work or out for a drink with his mates. The man and the boy's brothers are outside, in the world of men; the boy sits in the women's world. Perhaps this partly explains why many authors from the working-classes, when they write about their childhood, give the women in it so tender and central a place. There is bound to be occasional friction, of course—when they wonder whether the boy is "getting above himself," or when he feels a strong reluctance to break off and do one of the odd jobs a boy is expected to do. But predominantly the atmosphere is likely to be intimate, gentle, and attractive. With one ear he hears the women discussing their worries and ailments and hopes, and he tells them at intervals about his school and the work and what the master said. He usually receives boundless uncomprehending sympathy: he knows they do not understand, but still he tells them; he would like to link the two environments.

This description simplifies and overstresses the break; in each individual case there will be many qualifications. But in presenting the isolation in its most emphatic form the description epitomises what is very frequently found. For such a boy is between two worlds, the worlds of school and home; and they meet at few points. Once at the grammar-school, he quickly learns to make use of a pair of different accents, perhaps even two different apparent characters and differing standards of value. Think of his reading-material, for example: at home he sees strewn around and reads regularly himself, magazines which are never mentioned at school, which seem not to belong to the world to which the school introduces him; at school he hears about and reads books never mentioned at home. When he brings those books into the house they do not take their place with other books which the family are reading, for often there are none or almost none; his books look, rather, like strange tools.

He will perhaps, especially today, escape the worst immediate difficulties of his new environment, the stigma of cheaper clothes, of not being able to afford to go on school-holiday trips, of parents who turn up for the grammar-school play looking shamefully working-class. But as a grammar-school boy, he is likely to be anxious to do well, to be accepted or even to catch the eye as he caught the eye, because of his brains, at the "elementary" school. For brains are the currency by which he has bought his way, and increasingly brains seem to be the currency that tells. He tends to make his schoolmasters over-important, since they are the cashiers in the new world of brain-currency. In his home-world his father is still his father; in the other world of school his father can have little place: he tends to make a father-figure of his form-master.

Consequently, even though his family may push him very little, he will probably push himself harder than he should. He begins to see life, for as far as he can envisage it, as a series of hurdle-jumps, the hurdles of scholarships which are won by learning how to amass and manipulate the new currency. He tends to over-stress the importance of examinations, of the piling-up of knowledge and of received opinions. He discovers a technique of apparent learning, of acquiring of facts rather than of the handling and use of facts. He learns how to receive a purely literate education, one using only a small part of the personality and challenging only a limited area of his being. He begins to see life as a ladder, as a permanent examination with some praise and some further exhortation at each stage. He becomes an expert imbiber and doler-out; his competence will vary, but will rarely be accompanied by genuine enthusiasms. He rarely feels the reality of knowledge, of other men's thoughts and imaginings, on his own pulses; he rarely discovers an author for himself and on his own. In this half of his life he can respond only if there is a direct connection with the system of training. He has something of the blinkered pony about him; sometimes he is trained by those who have been through the same regimen, who are hardly unblinkered themselves, and who praise him in the degree to which he takes comfortably to their blinkers. Though there is a powerful, unidealistic, unwarmed realism about his attitude at bottom, that is his chief form of initiative; of other forms—the freely-ranging mind, the bold flying of mental kites, the courage to reject some "lines" even though they are officially as important as all the rest—of these he probably has little, and his training does not often encourage them. This is not a new problem; Herbert Spencer spoke of it fifty years ago: but it still exists: "The established systems of education, whatever their matter may be, are fundamentally vicious in their manner. They encourage *submissive receptivity* instead of *independent activity.*"

There is too little stress on action, on personal will and decision; too much goes on in the head, with the rather-better-than-normal intellectual machine which has brought him to his grammar-school. And because so often the "good" boy, the boy who does well, is the one who with his conscientious passivity meets the main demand of his new environment, he gradually loses spontaneity so as to acquire examination-passing reliability. He can snap his fingers at no one and nothing; he seems set to make an adequate, reliable, and unjoyous kind of clerk. He has been too long "afraid of all that has to be obeyed." Hazlitt, writing at the beginning of the nineteenth century, made a wider and more impassioned judgment on trends in his society; but it has some relevance here and now:

> Men do not become what by nature they are meant to be, but what society makes them. The generous feelings, and high propensities of the soul are, as it were, shrunk up, seared, violently wrenched, and amputated, to fit us for our intercourse with the world, something in the manner that beggars maim and mutilate their children, to make them fit for their future situation in life.

Such a scholarship boy has lost some of the resilience and some of the vitality of his cousins who are still knocking about the streets. In an earlier generation, as one of the quicker-witted persons born into the working-classes, he would in all probability have had those wits developed in the jungle of the slums, where wit had to ally itself to energy and initiative. He plays little on the streets; he does not run round delivering newspapers: his sexual growth is perhaps delayed. He loses something of the gamin's resilience and carelessness, of his readiness to take a chance, of his perkiness and boldness, and he does not acquire the unconscious confidence of many a public-school-trained child of the middle-classes. He has been trained like a circus-horse, for scholarship winning.

As a result, when he comes to the end of the series of set-pieces, when he is at last put out to raise his eyes to a world of tangible and unaccommodating things, of elusive and disconcerting human beings, he finds himself with little inner momentum. The driving-belt hangs loosely, disconnected from the only machine it has so far served, the examination-passing machine. He finds difficulty in choosing a direction in the world where there is no longer a master to please, a toffee-apple at the end of each stage, a certificate, a place in the upper half of the assessable world.

He is unhappy in a society which presents largely a picture of disorder, which is huge and sprawling, not limited, ordered, and centrally-heated; in which the toffee-apples are not accurately given to those who work hardest nor even to the most intelligent: but in which disturbing imponderables like "character," "pure luck," "ability to mix" and "boldness" have a way of tipping the scales.

His condition is made worse because the whole trend of his previous training has made him care too much for marked and ticketed success. This world, too, cares much for recognisable success, but does not distribute it along the lines on which he has been trained to win it. He would be happier if he cared less, if he could blow the gaff for himself on the world's success values. But they too closely resemble the values of school; to reject them he would have first to escape the inner prison in which the school's tabulated rules for success have immured him.

He does not wish to accept the world's criterion—get on at any price (though he has an acute sense of the importance of money). But he has been equipped for hurdle-jumping; so he merely dreams of getting-on, but somehow not in the world's way. He has neither the comforts of simply accepting the big world's values, nor the recompense of feeling firmly critical towards them.

He has moved away from his "lower" origins, and may move farther. If so, he is likely to be nagged underneath by a sense of how far he has come, by the fear and shame of a possible falling-back. And this increases his inability to leave himself alone. Sometimes the kind of job he gets only increases this slightly dizzy sense of still being on the ladder; unhappy on it, but also proud and, in the nature of his condition, usually incapable of jumping-off, of pulling-out of that particular race:

> Pale, shabby, tightly strung, he had advanced from post to post in his insurance office with the bearing of a man about to be discharged. . . . Brains had only meant that he must work harder in the elementary school than those born free of them. At night he could still hear the malicious chorus telling him that he was a favourite of the master. . . . Brains, like a fierce heat, had turned the world to a desert round him, and across the sands in the occasional mirage he saw the stupid crowds, playing, laughing, and without thought enjoying the tenderness, the compassion, the companionship of love.

That is over-dramatised, not applicable to all or even to most—but in some way affecting many. It affects also that larger group, to which I now turn, of those who in some ways ask questions of themselves about their society, who are because of this, even though they may never have been to grammar-schools, "between two worlds, one dead, the other powerless to be born." They are the "private faces in public places" among the working-classes; they are Koestler's "thoughtful corporals"; they are among those, though not the whole of those, who take up many kinds of self-improvement. They may be performing any kind of work, from manual labour to teaching; but my own experience suggests that they are to be found frequently among minor clerks and similarly black-coated workers, and among elementary school-teachers, especially in the big cities. Often their earnestness for improvement shows itself as an urge to act like some people in the middle-classes; but this is not a political betrayal: it is much nearer to a mistaken idealism.

This kind of person, and we have seen that this is his first great loss, belongs now to no class, usually not even to what is called, loosely enough, the "classless intelligentsia." He cannot face squarely his own working-class, for that, since the intuitive links have gone, would require a greater command in facing himself than he is capable of. Sometimes he is ashamed of his origins; he has learned to "turn up his nose," to be a bit superior about much in working-class manners. He is often not at ease about his own physical appearance which speaks too clearly of his birth; he feels uncertain or angry inside when he realises that that, and a hundred habits of speech and manners, can "give him away" daily. He tends to visit his own sense of inadequacy upon the group which fathered him; and he provides himself with a mantle of defensive attitudes. Thus he may exhibit an unconvincing pride in his own gaucheness at practical things—"brain-workers" are never "good with their hands." Underneath he knows that his compensatory claim to possess finer weapons, to be able to handle "book-knowledge," is insecurely based. He tries to read all the good books, but they do not give him that power of speech and command over experience which he seeks. He is as gauche there as with the craftsman's tools.

He cannot go back; with one part of himself he does not want to go back to a homeliness which was often narrow: with another part he longs for the membership he has lost, "he pines for some Nameless Eden where he never was." The nostalgia is the stronger and the more ambiguous because he is really "in quest of his own absconded self yet scared to find it." He both wants to go back and yet thinks he has gone beyond his class, feels himself weighted with knowledge of his own and their situation, which hereafter forbids him the simpler pleasures of his father and mother. And this is only one of his temptations to self-dramatisation.

If he tries to be "pally" with working-class people, to show that he is one of them, they "smell it a mile off." They are less at ease with him than with some in other classes. With them they can establish and are prepared to honour, seriously or as a kind of rather ironical game, a formal relationship; they "know where they are with them." But they can immediately detect the uncertainty in his attitudes, that he belongs neither to them nor to one of the groups with which they are used to performing a hierarchical play of relations; the odd man out is still the odd man out.

He has left his class, at least in spirit, by being in certain ways unusual; and he is still unusual in another class, too tense and overwound. Sometimes the working-classes and the middle-classes can laugh together. He rarely laughs; he smiles constrainedly with the corner of his mouth. He is usually ill at ease with the middle-classes because with one side of himself he does not want them to accept him; he mistrusts or even a little despises them. He is divided here as in so many other ways. With one part of himself he admires much he finds in them: a play of intelligence, a breadth of outlook, a kind of style. He would like to be a citizen of that well-polished, prosperous, cool, book-lined, and magazine-discussing world of the successful intelligent middle-class which he glimpses through doorways or feels awkward among on short visits, aware of his grubby finger-nails. With another part of himself he develops an asperity towards that world: he turns up his nose at its self-satisfactions, its earnest social concern, its intelligent coffee-parties, its suave sons at Oxford, and its Mrs. Miniverish or Mrs. Ramseyish cultural pretensions. He is rather over-ready to notice anything which can be regarded as pretentious or fanciful, anything which allows him to say that these people do not know what life is really like. He wavers between scorn and longing.

— RICHARD HOGGART
*The Uses of Literacy* (1957)

•   •   •   •   •   •   •   •   •   •   •

ASSIGNMENT 2

## *Life Stories* [Steedman]

In "A Thin Man," Steedman talks about the summer she began reading fairy tales, in particular "The Snow Queen" and "The Little Mermaid." She recalls the ways those stories assisted or shaped her understanding of herself and her mother. This section ends:

> The Little Mermaid was not my mother sacrificing herself for a beautiful prince: I knew her sacrifice: it was not composed of love or longing for my father, rather of a fierce resentment against the circumstances that were so indifferent to her. She turns me into the Little Mermaid a few years later, swimming round and round the ship, wondering why I was not wanted, but realizing that of course, it had to be that way: "How could he do it," she said, "leave two nice little girls like you?" (p. 663)

*Landscape for a Good Woman* is, Steedman says, a book "about the stories we make for ourselves, and the social specificity of our understanding of those stories." Throughout "Exiles" people seem to cast each other (and themselves) as characters in stories; they write themselves into available narratives. Choose one or two examples of this in "Exiles." Where do the stories come from? What do they accomplish? Whose interests—or what ends—do they serve? What problems do they create? Write an essay in which you consider the case studies as occasions for Steedman to represent and to think through the role and use of stories in this working class family history.

Note: The assignment asks you to think about the storytelling *in* "Exiles." Once you have written this essay (perhaps in preparation for discussion, perhaps as a guide for revision), it might be useful to think about the writing of "Exiles" as itself a form of storytelling. How might "Exiles" be seen as something Steedman made for herself? What is its relationship to the "official interpretive devices of the culture"? Is this act of storytelling representative of greater wisdom, dexterity, truthfulness, authority, authenticity? Is there a lesson to learn here?

•   •   •   •   •   •   •   •   •   •   •   •

ASSIGNMENT 3

# The Scholarship Girl
## [Rodriguez, Steedman]

Both Carolyn Kay Steedman, in "Exiles," and Richard Rodriguez, in "The Achievement of Desire" write accounts of growing up and leaving a working class family. The texts, however, are quite different in shape, feel, and (though harder to trace out) in what they identify as the consequences of class in a person's education and passage to adulthood. There are obvious points of difference—differences of nationality, language, gender, generation—and there are subtle differences in their use of "class" as a way of understanding an individual's ways of living, working, and thinking.

Write an essay in which you consider the different accounts of class, culture, family, and education in "Exiles" and "The Achievement of Desire." How do they differently represent the problems of living with, understanding, and representing the past? How do the writers understand and represent the relationship between their story and the "official interpretative devices of the culture"?

. . . . . . . . . . .

A S S I G N M E N T   **4**

## *A Life Story* [Jacobs]

> By creating a narrator who presents her private sexual history as a subject of public political concern, Jacobs moves her book out of the world of conventional nineteenth-century polite discourse. In and through her creation of Linda Brent, who yokes her success story as a heroic slave mother to her confession as a woman who mourns that she is not a storybook heroine, Jacobs articulates her struggle to assert her womanhood and projects a new kind of female hero.
> — JEAN FAGIN YELLIN
> "Introduction," *Incidents in the Life of a Slave Girl*

In an essay titled "The Voice of the Southern Slave," literary critic Houston Baker says,

> The voice of the unwritten self, once it is subjected to the linguistic codes, literary conventions, and audience expectations of a literate population, is perhaps never again the authentic voice of black American slavery. It is, rather, the voice of a self transformed by an autobiographical act into a sharer in the general public discourse about slavery.

This voice shares not only in the general public discourse about slavery but also in the general public discourse representing family, growing up, love, marriage, virtue, childbirth. It shares in the discourse of "normal" life—that is, life outside of slavery. For a slave, the self and its relations to others had a different public construction. A slave was property. A mother didn't have the right to her children, a woman to her body. While some may say that this was true generally of women in the nineteenth century (and the twentieth), slavery enacted and enforced the most extreme social reservations about a woman's rights and selfhood.

The passage from Baker's essay allows us to highlight the gap between a life and a narrative, between a person (Harriet Jacobs) and a person rendered on the page (Linda Brent), between the experience of slavery and the conventional ways of telling the story of life, between experience and the ways experience is shaped by a writer, readers, and a culture.

Write an essay in which you examine Jacobs's work as a writer. Consider the ways she works on her reader (a figure she both imagines and constructs) and also the ways she works on her material (a set of experiences but also a language and the story and conventional ways of representing a young woman's life). Where *is* Jacobs in this text? What is her work? What can you say about the sources of her work, the models or conventions it draws upon, deploys, or transforms? The narrative was written in retrospect when Jacobs was older and free, as a series of incidents. You can read the text as a writer's reconstruction of the past. What can you say about the ways Jacobs, as a writer, works with the past?

• • • • • • • • • • • •

ASSIGNMENT 5

## *Working with the Past* [Walker]

In her essay "In Search of Our Mothers' Gardens," Walker views the "creative spirit" of African American women as a legacy passed down from generation to generation, in spite of societal barriers: "Our mothers and grandmothers, some of them: moving to music not yet written. And they waited . . . for a day when the unknown thing that was in them would be made known; but guessed, somehow in their darkness, that on the day of their revelation they would be long dead" (p. 695).

Walker (much like Rodriguez, who "borrows" from Hoggart) uses Virginia Woolf's term "contrary instincts" to explain this legacy. And her essay is filled with passages from other texts. How does she use these? Why? What is the relationship of the "creative spirit" to the work of the past, at least as that relationship is both argued and represented in Walker's prose?

Write an essay in which you discuss Walker's project as a "creative" endeavor. What work does she do when she borrows the term "contrary instincts" from Woolf? What about the other allusions to the past, to texts written and unwritten? How might you characterize this work? Taking Walker's position as an African American artist of today into consideration, how might this essay be read as part of the tradition of creativity she charts? How might it be read as part of a tradition? How might it be read as an example of "creativity"? Or, to pose the question in different terms, what might you say Walker "creates" as she writes this essay?

. . . . . . . . . . . .

ASSIGNMENT 6

## *Legacies* [Walker, Jacobs]

Walker's reading of the history of African American women focuses on the "creative spirit" of these women in the face of oppression. Of her mother, Walker writes:

> Her face, as she prepares the Art that is her gift, is a legacy of respect she leaves to me, for all that illuminates and cherishes life. She has handed down respect for the possibilities—and the will to grasp them. (p. 701)

And to the poet Phillis Wheatley, she writes,

> But at last, Phillis, we understand. No more snickering when your stiff, struggling, ambivalent lines are forced on us. We know now that you were not an idiot or a traitor; only a sickly little black girl, snatched from your home and country and made a slave; a woman who still struggled to sing the song that was your gift, although in a land of barbarians who praised you for your bewildered tongue. It is not so much what you sang, as that you kept alive, in so many of our ancestors, *the notion of song.* (p. 698)

Although Walker chooses to focus on artists other than Harriet Jacobs in her essay, one could imagine ways in which Jacobs's example is appropriate to Walker's discussion of African American women's creativity.

Write an essay in which you extend Walker's project by considering how and where Jacobs's work as a writer would or would not serve Walker's argument. You can draw on the essays you wrote for assignments 4 and 5 for this essay, but you should treat them as material for a revision. You should reread Jacobs, and you should reread your essay with a mind to sections that you can rework. What legacy might Jacobs be said to create? What kind of example might she provide? How would it serve or alter Walker's argument? Why might Jacobs be overlooked?

o—o—o—o—o—o—o—o—o—o—o—o—o—o—o—o—o—o

# SEQUENCE FIFTEEN

# Working with the Past (II)

Virginia Woolf

Alice Walker

Ralph Ellison

Susan Griffin

*T*HIS SEQUENCE provides a variation on sequence ten. For a full description of the rationale behind the sequence, see the introduction to sequence ten, page 845.

This sequence begins with our selection from *A Room of One's Own,* chapters that can be seen as a rewriting of a tradition of essayist literature. After examining Woolf's revision of the texts of the past, you are asked to look at Walker's rewriting of Woolf and to think about what this contemporary African American writer has changed and what she has preserved in turning to a text written by a British woman in the early twentieth century. The next assignment looks at a similar moment in Ralph Ellison's "An Extravagance of Laughter." Like Walker, he rewrites the words of a key figure in British literature, W. B. Yeats. And, more generally, his essay, like Susan Griffin's (which follows) can be read as both a meditation on history and a reworking of the conventions of the prose essay. A final assignment asks you to reflect on the work you have done with these materials.

•   •   •   •   •   •   •   •   •   •   •

ASSIGNMENT **1**

## *Reading the Past* [Woolf]

The title page of the original edition of *A Room of One's Own* said, "This essay is based upon two papers read to the Arts Society of Newnham and the Odtaa at Girton in October 1928. The papers were too long to be read in full, and have since been altered and expanded." As either an essay or the text of a public lecture, *A Room of One's Own* is full of surprises. It doesn't sound like the usual lecture; it doesn't do what essays usually do. At many places and in many ways it takes liberties with the conventions of the genre, with the essay's or the lecture's characteristic ways of addressing the audience, gathering information, and presenting an argument.

As you reread these chapters and prepare to write about them, make note of the ways Woolf (the writer writing the text) constructs a space for speaker and audience, a kind of imaginary place where a woman can do her work, find a way of speaking, think as she might like to think, and prepare others to listen. Look for interesting and potentially significant ways she defies or transforms what you take to be the conventions of the essay. You might especially want to take a look at those places where Woolf seems to be saying, "I know what I should be doing here, but I won't. I'll do this instead."

Choose four such moments and write an essay in which you discuss Woolf's chapters as a performance, a demonstration of a way of writing that pushes against the usual ways of manipulating words. While there is certainly an argument *in* Woolf's essay, your paper will be about the argument represented *by* the essay, an argument enacted in a way of writing. What is Woolf doing? How might you explain what she is doing and why? In what ways might her essay be seen as an example of someone working with the writing of the past? with the figure of the woman writer? with the textual spaces available to women? What does she preserve? What does she revise? How might you define her attitude to the past?

• • • • • • • • • • •

ASSIGNMENT 2

## Rewriting "A Room of One's Own" [Walker]

On page 696, Walker invokes and then rewrites a passage from Woolf's *A Room of One's Own*. The passage she cites comes from chapter 3, not included in our selections from Woolf's text, in which Woolf imagines what might have happened if Shakespeare had had a sister. (See the headnote to our selections from *A Room of One's Own*, p. 748, for a discussion of this chapter and the context of the passage Walker cites.)

Read closely to see how, where, and why Walker invokes and then rewrites Woolf. Write an essay in which you describe and explain the translation or transformation Walker makes. What does she change? Why? What, from this, can we infer about Walker's attitude toward Woolf? her way of reading Woolf? her sense of the uses of the past? And how might you connect what Walker does as a writer with the argument of her essay, an argument about legacy? Does Walker honor Woolf? And why choose Woolf, a British woman, white, the daughter of privilege? How might you explain the role Woolf plays in Walker's text?

• • • • • • • • • • •

ASSIGNMENT 3

## Rewriting Yeats [Ellison]

In the middle of "An Extravagance of Laughter," Ellison cites W. B. Yeats, the Irish poet, on "masks" in a passage that concludes with the (perhaps surprising) assertion that "active virtue . . . is the wearing of a mask." And then, to make Yeats's words work for him, Ellison has to imagine a revision of the passage, adapting it as a concept that can be used to think about African American experience. As you reread, let the opening of the essay lead you to that passage. Then, when you get there, take a moment to work out the Ellison revision of Yeats: What does it say once the substitutions are made? And, from that, how do you read the rest of the essay, an essay that could be said to rework the standard accounts of the civil rights movement and to revise the conventions of the essay? Write an essay in which you represent Ellison's use of the past in "An Extravagance of Laughter." If the essay recounts (and offers) a lesson in thinking about change and thinking about the past, what is it? How might it speak to you or to your generation?

•  •  •  •  •  •  •  •  •  •  •  •

ASSIGNMENT **4**

# *Writing History* [Griffin]

At several points in her essay, Griffin argues that we—all of us, especially all of us who read her essay—are part of a complex web of connections. She asks, for example,

> Who are we? The question is not simple. What we call the self is part of a larger matrix of relationship and society. Had we been born to a different family, in a different time, to a different world, we would not be the same. All the lives that surround us are in us. (p. 441)

Later she asks, "Is there any one of us who can count ourselves outside the circle circumscribed by our common past?" (p. 449). At another point she speaks of a "field,"

> like a field of gravity that is created by the movements of many bodies. Each life is influenced and it in turn becomes an influence. Whatever is a cause is also an effect. Childhood experience is just one element in the determining field. (p. 409)

One way of thinking about this concept of the self (and of interrelatedness), at least to think about it under Griffin's guidance, is to work on the connections implied and asserted in her text. In her essay, Griffin writes *about* the past—how we can know it, what its relation is to the present, why we should care. In the way she writes, however, she is also making an argument about how we can know and understand the past—in, for example, the way she represents key figures, like Himmler, or minor figures, like Leo.

As you reread the selection, look for powerful and surprising juxtapositions, for fragments that stand together in interesting and suggestive ways. Think about the arguments represented by the blank space between those sections. (And look for Griffin's written statements about "relatedness.") Look for connections that seem important to the text (and to you) and representative of Griffin's thinking (and yours).

Write an essay in which you use these examples to think through your

understanding of Griffin's claims for this "larger matrix," the "determining field," or our "common past."

•   •   •   •   •   •   •   •   •   •   •   •

## On Reading the Past
## [Woolf, Walker, Ellison, Griffin]

You have written about Virginia Woolf, and her use of the tradition of
the essay (the roles it allows the writer, its ways of thinking and presenting examples, its methods of address), and you have written about Alice
Walker and her use of Woolf. You've also written about Susan Griffin and
Ralph Ellison. All these writers, it is safe to say, write with a desire to clear
a space for other writers, to make it possible for writers (like you) to do
what they have not been prepared to do, to do what they may have believed to be impossible or forbidden.

In your own education, both directly and indirectly, you have been
given lessons in how and why to read the texts of the past. You have been
instructed in the "proper" ways to use books, or any prior text, in papers
that you write—most likely in the form of term papers but perhaps in
other forms as well. Think about the ways you have been prepared to
work with the past. Consider a variety of examples, including your best
moments in school, when you felt you had done something powerful or
important or interesting or exciting or useful. Write an essay in which,
through these examples from your education, and through the examples
provided by your reading, you discuss the ways your education (and
American schooling generally) prepares and/or fails to prepare its students to use and understand the works of the past.

# Writing History

Patricia Nelson Limerick
Jane Tompkins

*T*HIS SHORT SEQUENCE has two goals: to present two views of the
"problem of history" (the problem of representing and understanding the past) and to use these accounts as an introduction to academic life
(or to the forms of theorizing particular to that branch of the academy preoccupied by the problems of understanding the past). The first two assignments ask you to translate articles by Patricia Nelson Limerick and Jane
Tompkins for an audience of beginning undergraduates. Your goal is to
teach your audience something about the essays but also to use the essays
as an introduction to the ways academics think and work. The final assignment asks you to write a short history (a local, family, or neighborhood history) and to think about your work in the context of problems of
method presented by Limerick and Tompkins. You are working as a
novice; they are working as professionals. The questions the sequence
ends with are these: what would Limerick and Tompkins have to say to
you about your work? What do you have to say to them about theirs?

• • • • • • • • • • • •

ASSIGNMENT 1

## *The Legacy of Conquest* [Limerick]

"Empire of Innocence" is a chapter from Patricia Limerick's book, *The Legacy of Conquest*. It both presents episodes from the history of the American West and thinks out loud about history as something written (about the problems of history as reading and writing problems). In it, Limerick offers criticism and advice, an account of the problems of Western history and how they might be addressed (concerns about "point of view" and about "myth," for example). As you reread, look for passages that define both the problems and the possible solutions for those who read and write about the past.

Write an essay in which you present Limerick's account of the problems of history to a novice, someone new to Limerick and new to the academy. You should assume that your reader has not read the selection in this textbook—you will, that is, need to set the scene, to summarize, paraphrase, quote, and explain. Your goal is to give your reader not only a sense of what Limerick says but an idea of why it might be important to a student in the early stages of a college or university career.

• • • • • • • • • • • •

ASSIGNMENT 2

## *"Indians"* [Tompkins]

In "Indians," Tompkins offers her experience researching and writing about Native Americans in colonial America as a representative case. Her story is meant to highlight a problem central to teaching, learning, and research—central, that is, to academic life. As a student, you can read this essay as a way of looking in on the work and concerns of your faculty (a group represented not only by Tompkins but by those against whom she is arguing). Write an essay directed to someone who has not read "Indians," someone who will be entering your school as a first-year student next semester. Your job is to introduce an incoming freshman to the academy, using Tompkins as your guide. (Since you've already written about Limerick, and since you can assume that the same readers will read both essays, you can bring Limerick in as a point of reference or comparison.)

You will need to present Tompkins's argument and her conclusion in such a way as to make clear the consequences of what she says for someone about to begin an undergraduate education.

.   .   .   .   .   .   .   .   .   .   .   .

A S S I G N M E N T  3

# *Writing History* [Limerick, Tompkins]

One way to work on these selections is to take the challenge and write history—to write the kind of history, that is, that takes into account the problems defined by Limerick and Tompkins: the problems of myth, point of view, fixed ideas, facts and perspective, morality. You are not a professional historian, you are probably not using this book in a history course, and you probably don't have the time to produce a carefully researched history, one that covers all the bases, but you can think of this as an exercise in history writing, a minihistory, a place to start. Here are two options:

1. Go to your college library or, perhaps, the local historical society and find two or three first-person accounts of a single place, person, or event in your community. Try to work with original documents. The more varied the accounts, the better. Then, working with these texts as your primary sources, write a history, one that you can offer as a response to Limerick and Tompkins.
2. While you can find materials in a library, you can also work with records that are closer to home. Imagine, for example, that you are going to write a family or a neighborhood history. You have your own memories and experiences to work from, but for this to be a history (and not a "personal essay"), you will need to turn to other sources as well: interviews, old photos, newspaper clippings, letters, diaries—whatever you can find. After gathering your materials, write a family or neighborhood history, one that you can offer as a response to Limerick and Tompkins.

Choose one of the two projects. When you are done, write a quick one-page memo to the experts, Limerick and Tompkins. What can you tell them about the experience of a novice historian that they might find useful or interesting?

## SEQUENCE SEVENTEEN

# Writing Projects

Paul Auster
Carolyn Kay Steedman
John Edgar Wideman

*T*HE PURPOSE of this sequence is to invite you to work closely with pieces of writing that call attention to themselves as writing, that make visible writing as a problem, a fundamental problem of representation and understanding. The five assignments that follow bring together works of nonfiction that question their ability to represent the "real." The opening assignments direct your work with those readings; the final assignments ask you to imagine a writing project informed by what you have read.

. . . . . . . . . . .

ASSIGNMENT 1

## *A Portrait* [Auster]

By writing "Portrait of an Invisible Man," Auster memorializes his father. As you follow the accounts of the father, you learn also about the other major character in this text, the son. The "Paul Auster" in the text is also a literary invention, a "character." And yet the writing is neither sentimental nor celebratory; it is surprisingly unsympathetic. Neither father nor son plays the roles we expect them to play. The text does not offer the usual narrative of reconciliation; the writer does not take ready positions of admiration or tribute. The writing does not represent or evoke emotional response. One might call it "calculated," although Auster keeps saying that he has no (or can find no) plan. The prose refuses to turn to cliché and it refuses to come to clear conclusion. (What is the point of the account of the murder, for example?)

For most readers, "Portrait of an Invisible Man" is difficult, even troubling. It is useful to begin with the assumption that Auster causes this trouble on purpose. And, having done it, he brings it to publication. He obviously thinks that what he has done was worth doing, worth doing not only for himself (and, perhaps, for his father), but also for all of us (as we think, perhaps, about fathers or families, memory or the past). As you read back through this piece, what *was* Auster doing? And why? How might you explain or justify this piece of writing?

Write an essay, perhaps cast as a review, in which you explain what you think Auster is doing in this piece and why someone might read it with interest. (You can think of a review as an account of the selection for those who have not yet read it.) Don't feel that you have to be positive in your assessment; if you are negative, you do need, however, to take the work seriously and not simply dismiss it as unpleasant, mean-spirited, or self-aggrandizing.

• • • • • • • • • • •

## A Case Study [Steedman]

In the opening pages of *Landscape for a Good Woman,* Steedman says:

> Personal interpretations of past time—the stories that people
> tell themselves in order to explain how they got to the place
> they currently inhabit—are often in deep and ambiguous con-
> flict with the official interpretative devices of a culture.

This sense of conflict is important to Steedman, particularly as it is related
to political conflict (for her, the position of the working class in Britain).
Write an essay in which you extend her project to your own time and
place, to stories you have heard people tell themselves to explain how
they got to the place they currently inhabit. Where and how might they be
said to be in deep and ambiguous conflict with the official interpretive devices of a culture? Where and how might this *not* be the case?

Think of your essay as having two major sections. The first should be
about "Exiles," a brief summary of Steedman's project in the two case
studies. (This should be written for someone *not* familiar with her work.
Its purpose is to establish the context for your project.) The second section
is yours, but it should make use of Steedman's key terms and phrases, if
only as a point of reference.

• • • • • • • • • • •

## Fact and Fiction [Wideman]

> The hardest habit to break, since it was the habit of a lifetime,
> would be listening to myself listen to him. That habit would
> destroy any chance of seeing my brother on his terms; and see-
> ing him in his terms, learning his terms, seemed the whole
> point of learning his story. However numerous and comforting
> the similarities, we were different. The world had seized on the
> difference, allowed me room to thrive, while he'd been forced
> into a cage. Why did it work out that way? What was the na-
> ture of the difference? Why did it haunt me? Temporarily at
> least, to answer these questions, I had to root my fiction-writing
> self out of our exchanges. I had to teach myself to listen. Start

fresh, clear the pipes, resist too facile an identification, tame the urge to take off with Robby's story and make it my own. (p. 722)

I couldn't rely on memory to get my brother's story down and the keepers had refused my request to use a tape recorder, so there I was. Jimmy Olsen, cub reporter, poised on the edge of my seat, pen and paper at ready, asking to be treated as a brother. (p. 723)

— JOHN EDGAR WIDEMAN
*Our Time*

At several points in "Our Time," Wideman discusses his position as a fiction writer writing nonfiction, and the difficulties he faces in writing about his brother and his family and their past (or in "reading" the text of his brother's life). At one point he says, "I had to root my fiction-writing self out of our exchanges. I had to teach myself to listen. Start fresh, clear the pipes, resist too facile an identification, tame the urge to take off with Robby's story and make it my own" (p. 722). What might Wideman mean by this—rooting out his "fiction-writing self"? resisting "too facile an identification"? making Robby's story his own? You have here the example of a fiction writer thinking through many of the questions that have been yours in this sequence.

As you reread "Our Time," note and mark the sections where Wideman speaks directly about his work as a writer. And note those sections where indirectly, in practice, through methods and devices, he seems to be working out the problems of writing on the borderline between fiction and fact. Which sections seem to best represent the "real"? Which sections seem contrived, fictional? What convinces you that the "real" scenes are real? What convinces Wideman?

Choose three or four passages from "Our Time" you can discuss in detail and write an essay in which you take Wideman the writer and "Our Time" as a case study of the relationships between writing, fiction, and fact.

•   •   •   •   •   •   •   •   •   •   •   •

## A Project
## [Auster, Steedman, Wideman]

Now it is time for you to try your hand at this. Write a piece of your own that tries to capture the "real" but that, at the same time, makes visible your awareness of the difficulty of such a project. You can, if you choose, take Auster, Steedman, or Wideman as your immediate model. (Check the "Writing Assignments" at the end of each selection, which will suggest ways to do this.) As you review what they have written, think particularly about the features of the prose that you will incorporate into your own. You should do this quite formally—looking for sentences whose style you will imitate and paragraphs or larger units of organization whose form you can work with, examples of the use of dialogue, image, and setting. Perhaps most important, you will need to take a lesson in how to establish your own position in the text—not simply as a character, part of the story, but as a writer.

Whether you work from a single model or some position you can take from all three, it is important that you see this assignment as an exercise in method and not simply as an invitation to write a family history. (You need not, in fact, feel that a family history is required. You can write on any piece of the "real" that you choose.)

•   •   •   •   •   •   •   •   •   •   •   •

## Commentary
## [Auster, Steedman, Wideman]

This is the final assignment in the sequence. It is the occasion for you to reflect on the work you have done. Write an essay in which you comment on your project in assignment 4, perhaps on its reception by others in your class, and through it to your work as a writer in relation to the work of Auster, Steedman, and/or Wideman.

You could think of this essay as a kind of extended introduction or afterword to what you have written. Or you could think of it as a plan for revision. You could think of it as the occasion to write about the relationship of this kind of writing to the world you imagine outside this classroom—the world of work, the rest of the curriculum, the community, the circle of family, lovers, and friends. However you imagine this assignment, you should be sure to allude to at least one of the readings in this sequence.

(continued from p. iv)

permission of Éditions de Minuit. Pieter Breughel the Elder, "The Procession to Calvary." Erich Lessing/Art Resource, New York. Reprinted by permission of Kunst Historisches Museum, Vienna. Frans Hals, "Regents of the Old Men's Alms House" and "Regentesses of the Old Men's Alms House." Reprinted by permission of Frans Halsmuseum. Vincent van Gogh, "Wheatfield with Crows." Vincent van Gogh Foundation/Van Gogh Museum, Amsterdam. Reprinted by permission of Stedelijk Museum. Jan Vermeer, "Woman Pouring Milk." Reprinted with the permission of Rijksmuseum-Stichting. Caravaggio, "The Calling of St. Matthew." Scala/Art Resource, New York. Rembrandt, "Woman in Bed." Reprinted with permission of the National Gallery of Scotland.

Susan Bordo, "Hunger as Ideology." From *Unbearable Weight: Feminism, Western Culture, and the Body*, by Susan Bordo. Copyright © 1993 The Regents of the University of California. Used by permission.

Robert Coles, "The Tradition: Fact and Fiction." From *Doing Documentary Work* by Robert Coles. Copyright © 1997 by Robert Coles. Used by permission of Oxford University Press, Inc. Lange and Evans photographs courtesy of the Library of Congress.

Ralph Ellison, "An Extravagance of Laughter." From *Going to the Territory* by Ralph Ellison. Copyright © 1986 by Ralph Ellison. Reprinted by permission of Random House, Inc.

Michel Foucault, "Panopticism." From *Discipline and Punish* (New York: Pantheon Books, 1977). Originally published in French as *Surveiler et Punir* by Éditions Gallimard, Paris. Copyright © 1975 by Éditions Gallimard. Translation copyright © 1977 by Alan Sheridan. Reprinted by permission of Georges Borchardt, Inc. *L'art d'écrire* engraved by Prévost, from *L'Encyclopédie*, 1763. Reprinted by permission of L'institut National de Recherche Pédagogique, Musée National de l'Education. Jeremy Bentham, *Plan of the Panopticon* from *The Works of Jeremy Bentham*, edited by Bowring, 1843. Reprinted by permission of Oxford University Press.

Paulo Freire, "The 'Banking' Concept of Education." From *Pedagogy of the Oppressed*, by Paulo Freire. Copyright © 1970, 1993 by Paulo Freire. Reprinted by permission of The Continuum Publishing Company.

Clifford Geertz, "Deep Play: Notes on the Balinese Cockfight." Reprinted by permission of *Daedalus*, Journal of the American Academy of Arts and Sciences, from the issue titled "Myth, Symbol, and Culture," Winter 1972, vol. 101, no. 1

Susan Griffin, "Our Secret." From *A Chorus of Stones*, by Susan Griffin. Copyright © 1992 by Susan Griffin. Used by permission of Doubleday, a division of Bantam Doubleday Dell Publishing Group, Inc.

Patricia Nelson Limerick, "Empire of Innocence." From *The Legacy of Conquest: The Unbroken Past of the American West*, by Patricia Nelson Limerick. Copyright © 1987 by Patricia Nelson Limerick. Reprinted by permission of W. W. Norton & Company, Inc.

W. J. T. Mitchell, "The Photographic Essay: Four Case Studies." From *Picture Theory*, by W. J. T. Mitchell. Reprinted by permission of The University of Chicago Press. Jacob Riis, "Lodgers in Bayard St. Tenement," from *How the Other Half Lives* (1890). Photo reproduced courtesy of the Museum of the City of New York. Robert Frank, Parade—Hoboken, New Jersey (1955–1956), from *The Americans* (1958). Copyright © Robert Frank. Courtesy PaceWildensteinMacGill, New York. Walker Evans, photographs from *Let Us Now Praise Famous Men* (1939) by James Agee and Walker Evans. Photographs courtesy of the Library of Congress. Walker Evans, "Annie Mae Gudger." Copyright © Walker Evans Archive, The Metropolitan Museum of Art. Margaret Bourke-White, HAMILTON, ALABAMA, "We managed to get along," from *You Have Seen Their Faces*, by Erskine Caldwell and Margaret Bourke-White. Courtesy of the Estate of Margaret Bourke-White. Daniel Boudinet, "Polaroid, 1979," from Roland Barthes, *Camera Lucida* (1981). Photo Daniel Boudinet © Ministère de la Culture, France. Nadar, "The Artist's Mother (or Wife)," in Roland Barthes, *Camera Lucida* (1981). Caisse Nationale des Monuments Historiques et des Sites, Paris. "Scenes and Types: Arabian Woman with the Yachmak," from *The Colonial Harem* (1986), by Malek Alloula, translated by Myrna and Wlad Godzich (French edition, 1981; English edition, Minneapolis: University of Minnesota Press, 1986). Jean Mohr, "Mayor of Jerusalem," page spread from *After the Last Sky*, by Edward W. Said. Photographs by Jean Mohr. Copyright © 1986 by Edward W. Said. Reprinted by permission of Pantheon Books, a division of Random House, Inc. Jean Mohr, "Amman, 1984. Mrs. Farraj," from *After the Last Sky*, by Edward W. Said. Photographs by Jean Mohr. Copyright © 1986 by Edward W. Said. Reprinted by permission of Pantheon Books, a division of Random House, Inc. Jean Mohr, "Elderly Palestinian Villager, Ramallah, 1984," from *After the Last Sky*, by Edward Said. Photographs by Jean Mohr. Copyright © 1986 by Edward W. Said. Reprinted by permission of Pantheon Books, a division of Random House, Inc.

Walker Percy, "The Loss of the Creature." From *The Message in the Bottle*, by Walker Percy. Copyright © 1975 by Walker Percy. Reprinted by permission of Farrar, Straus & Giroux, Inc.

Mary Louise Pratt, "Arts of the Contact Zone." From *Profession 91*. Copyright © 1991. Reprinted by permission of the Modern Language Association of America.

Adrienne Rich, "When We Dead Awaken: Writing as Re-Vision." From *On Lies, Secrets, and Silence: Selected Prose 1966–1978*, by Adrienne Rich. Copyright © 1979 by W. W. Norton & Company, Inc. Reprinted by permission of the author and W. W. Norton & Company, Inc. "Aunt Jennifer's Tigers," copyright © 1993, 1951 by Adrienne Rich. "The Loser," copyright © 1993, 1967, 1963 by Adrienne Rich. Copyright © 1969 by W. W. Norton & Company, Inc. "Planetarium," copyright ©